Correlation Table:
National Educational Technology Standards for Teachers (NETS•T)
Addressed by Each Scenario-based Exercise in
Educational Technology in Action

Scenario, Page #	I		II					III				IV			V				VI				
	A	B	A	B	C	D	E	A	B	C	D	A	B	C	A	B	C	D	A	B	C	D	E
Ch.2, S1 – p. E-9		X	X		X											X					X		
Ch.2, S2 – p. E-9		X	X		X											X							
Ch.3, S1 – p. E-15	X							X		X				X		X					X		
Ch.3, S2 – p. E-16								X	X	X	X			X		X							
Ch.4, S1 – p. E-21	X		X			X	X	X			X			X		X					X		
Ch.4, S2 – p. E-22			X			X	X	X	X	X	X			X		X				X			X
Ch.5, S1 – p. E-27		X				X	X									X						X	
Ch.5, S2 – p. E-28			X			X	X							X		X			X				
Ch.6, S1 – p. E-33			X	X		X	X			X				X		X							
Ch.6, S2 – p. E-34				X				X						X		X							
Ch.7, S1 – p. E-41	X		X		X			X	X	X	X			X		X							
Ch.7, S2 – p. E-42			X	X	X		X	X	X	X	X	X	X	X		X			X				
Ch.8, S1 – p. E-47										X	X			X		X	X	X					X
Ch.8, S2 – p. E-48		X	X		X			X		X	X			X		X							
Ch.9, S1 – p. E-53		X	X		X	X	X	X		X	X	X	X	X		X							
Ch.9, S2 – p. E-54		X		X		X	X							X		X		X	X			X	
Ch.10, S1 – p. E-59			X		X		X		X		X					X							
Ch.10, S2 – p. E-60			X			X	X	X	X	X	X			X		X		X					
Ch.11, S1 – p. E-67			X		X	X	X	X	X	X	X			X		X		X					
Ch.11, S2 – p. E-68			X			X	X	X	X		X			X		X							
Ch.12, S1 – p. E-73		X	X			X	X	X		X	X					X							
Ch.12, S2 – p. E-74		X	X		X	X	X	X		X	X				X	X		X					
Ch.13, S1 – p. E-79				X		X	X	X		X	X			X		X							
Ch.13, S2 – p. E-80			X	X	X	X	X	X	X		X					X		X	X			X	
Ch.14, S1 – p. E-85		X						X		X	X			X		X							X
Ch.14, S2 – p. E-86			X	X	X	X	X	X		X	X			X		X							
Ch.15, S1 – p. E-91		X	X		X	X	X	X	X	X	X			X		X							X
Ch.15, S2 – p. E-92				X		X	X	X	X		X			X		X		X					
Ch.16, S1 – p. E-97			X			X	X	X	X		X	X	X	X		X				X			X
Ch.16, S2 – p. E-98		X	X		X	X	X		X		X					X				X			X

The National Educational Technology Standards for Teachers (NETS•T)

I. TECHNOLOGY OPERATIONS AND CONCEPTS – *Teachers demonstrate a sound understanding of technology operations and concepts. Teachers:*

A. demonstrate introductory knowledge, skills, and understanding of concepts related to technology (as described in the ISTE National Education Technology Standards for Students).

B. demonstrate continual growth in technology knowledge and skills to stay abreast of current and emerging technologies.

II. PLANNING AND DESIGNING LEARNING ENVIRONMENTS AND EXPERIENCES – *Teachers plan and design effective learning environments and experiences supported by technology. Teachers:*

A. design developmentally appropriate learning opportunities that apply technology-enhanced instructional strategies to support the diverse needs of learners.

B. apply current research on teaching and learning with technology when planning learning environments and experiences.

C. identify and locate technology resources and evaluate them for accuracy and suitability.

D. plan for the management of technology resources within the context of learning activities.

E. plan strategies to manage student learning in a technology-enhanced environment.

III. TEACHING, LEARNING, AND THE CURRICULUM – *Teachers implement curriculum plans, that include methods and strategies for applying technology to maximize student learning. Teachers:*

A. facilitate technology-enhanced experiences that address content standards and student technology standards.

B. use technology to support learner-centered strategies that address the diverse needs of students.

C. apply technology to develop students' higher order skills and creativity.

D. manage student learning activities in a technology-enhanced environment.

IV. ASSESSMENT AND EVALUATION – *Teachers apply technology to facilitate a variety of effective assessment and evaluation strategies. Teachers:*

A. apply technology in assessing student learning of subject matter using a variety of assessment techniques.

B. use technology resources to collect and analyze data, interpret results, and communicate findings to improve instructional practice and maximize student learning.

C. apply multiple methods of evaluation to determine students' appropriate use of technology resources for learning, communication, and productivity.

V. PRODUCTIVITY AND PROFESSIONAL PRACTICE – *Teachers use technology to enhance their productivity and professional practice. Teachers:*

A. use technology resources to engage in ongoing professional development and lifelong learning.

B. continually evaluate and reflect on professional practice to make informed decisions regarding the use of technology in support of student learning.

C. apply technology to increase productivity.

D. use technology to communicate and collaborate with peers, parents, and the larger community in order to nurture student learning.

VI. SOCIAL, ETHICAL, LEGAL, AND HUMAN ISSUES – *Teachers understand the social, ethical, legal, and human issues surrounding the use of technology in PK-12 schools and apply those principles in practice. Teachers:*

A. model and teach legal and ethical practice related to technology use.

B. apply technology resources to enable and empower learners with diverse backgrounds, characteristics, and abilities.

C. identify and use technology resources that affirm diversity.

D. promote safe and healthy use of technology resources.

E. facilitate equitable access to technology resources for all students.

Educational Technology in Action

Problem-Based Exercises for Technology Integration

M. D. Roblyer
University of Maryland University College

Upper Saddle River, New Jersey
Columbus, Ohio

Dedication

For Bill and Paige –
The high-touch part of my high-tech life

Vice President and Executive Publisher: Jeffery W. Johnston
Editor: Debra A. Stollenwerk
Development Editor: Kimberly J. Lundy
Editorial Assistant: Mary Morrill
Production Editor: JoEllen Gohr
Production Manager: Pamela D. Bennett
Design Coordinator: Diane C. Lorenzo
Cover Designer: Ali Mohrman
Director of Marketing: Ann Castel Davis
Marketing Manager: Darcy Betts Prybella
Marketing Services Manager: Tyra Poole

NOTE: Every effort has been made to provide accurate and current Internet information in this book. However, the Internet and information posted on it are constantly changing; it is inevitable that some of the Internet addresses listed in this textbook will change.

Pearson Education Ltd.
Pearson Education Singapore Pte. Ltd.
Pearson Education Canada, Ltd.
Pearson Education—Japan
Pearson Education Australia Pty. Limited
Pearson Education North Asia Ltd.
Pearson Educación de Mexico, S.A. de C.V.
Pearson Education Malaysia Pte. Ltd.

10 9 8 7 6 5 4 3 2 1
ISBN: 0-13-117392-8

Table of Contents

Preface

Why This Booklet Was Developed

Like teaching itself, integrating technology into educational practice is challenging work, full of exciting opportunities and complex problems. *Educational Technology in Action* brings these challenges to life by providing a series of hypothetical technology integration exercises based on actual situations and events.

These real-world problems give educators opportunities to reflect on and apply concepts they have read about in *Integrating Educational Technology into Teaching* (Roblyer, 2003). Participating in this simulated problem-solving helps prepare readers for the real world of technology in schools.

Contents of the Booklet

This booklet features the Technology Integration Planning (TIP) Model introduced in Chapter 2 of *Integrating Educational Technology into Teaching*. Based on a systematic instructional design process, the TIP Model addresses problems and planning needs unique to using technology resources in teaching and learning. This information is presented in three parts, and two features are included to help readers understand and apply it:

- **Part I** – Chapter 1 gives an overview of the purpose of the TIP Model and each of its five phases. Chapters 2-6 focus on each phase in turn, along with exercises to provide insight into and practice on the underlying concepts.
- **Part II** – Chapters 7-10 introduce and provide practice in technology integration strategies for each of several technologies: instructional software, software tools, multimedia/hypermedia, and Internet/distance learning materials.
- **Part III** – Chapters 11-16 describe and provide exercises on technology integration strategies for six content areas: language arts/foreign languages, mathematics/science, social studies, art/music, physical education/health, and special education.
- **End-of-Part Review Exercises** – These are in the booklet at the end of each part and duplicated online at: **http://www.prenhall.com/roblyer**. Students will click on the *Educational Technology in Action* module and use the links in it to answer the questions.
- **Tutorials CD** – Instructional exercises in the booklet often refer to students creating or using Microsoft *Word* and Microsoft *Excel* documents, web pages, and *PowerPoint* presentations. The CD included with this booklet has sample step-by-step tutorials that give readers hands-on practice in using *Word, Excel, Netscape Composer*, and *PowerPoint* to design products for four of the curriculum lessons described in the exercises. (**NOTE:** The *Adobe Acrobat Reader*® required to view the tutorials is on the CD.)

Chapter Organization

Each chapter has the following components:

- **Introduction** – This section gives an overview of the chapter and a summary of the information required to solve the problems in the chapter.
- **Scenarios to Read and Analyze** – Each chapter has two scenarios in which decisions were made about technology-based policies, resources, applications, and planning steps. Each is followed by questions that ask readers to reflect on the decisions and analyze their impact.
- **Problems to Analyze and Solve** – Each chapter has five problems that ask readers to apply what they know about technology integration by imagining they are educators who must make decisions about technology integration. In each case, they tell what they think is appropriate to do.

NOTE: Readers may notice that most scenarios and problem exercises focus on middle and high school levels. Although the question of whether or not to emphasize technology uses at lower levels remains controversial, this booklet reflects the position that a greater number of demonstrably effective uses of technology are at middle and high school levels.

Correlation with Educational Technology Standards

The scenarios in Chapters 2-16 are designed to address ISTE's National Educational Technology Standards for Teachers (NETS-T). A listing of the NETS-T and the correlation chart are listed at the front of this book.

Other Instructor Resources Available with This Booklet

Educational Technology in Action is one of a set of ancillary resources that expand on topics introduced in *Integrating Educational Technology into Teaching* (Roblyer, 2003). Its problem-based format can support introductory instructional technology courses, methods and issues courses, administrative methods courses, and workshops on technology integration. Readers may also find it helpful to use some or all of the following support materials packaged with the *Integrating Educational Technology into Teaching* textbook:

The Companion Website (CW) at http://www.prenhall.com/roblyer – A set of materials that includes a Syllabus Manager™ for the instructor, and, to support each chapter: a self-test of multiple-choice items, *PowerPoint* slides that outline chapter topics, a message board area and chat room on which students may post comments and exchange ideas with others in response to *Questions for Thought and Discussion* (Activity 3 at end of each textbook chapter), and a place to add to students' electronic portfolios.

Integrating Technology Across the Curriculum CD-ROM (ISBN: 0-13-042319-X) – A searchable database with over 550 technology integration ideas, stored by grade level, technology used, content area, and topic. Each entry is labeled according to ISTE National Educational Technology Standards (NETS) for Students it addresses. Each chapter has a suggested exercise with the CD.

Starting Out on the Internet: A Learning Journey for Teachers (ISBN: 0-13-110970-7) – Reviews basic Internet concepts for teachers and has interactive activities students do on the CW.

The Computerized Test Bank (CTB) – A variety of test-item formats (multiple choice, true-false, short answer, essay) for each chapter.

Educational Technology in Action: Problem-based Exercises for Technology Integration – This booklet includes:

- **Scenarios to Guide Whole-class Discussion** – Focus on issues and steps specific to a phase of technology integration or integration strategies for a type of technology resource or a content area. Everyone reads the scenario and the instructor uses the questions that follow it to initiate and structure class discussion.

- **Problems for Small-Group Work** – Can be used to check individual knowledge, but are most useful when assigned to small groups of students to discuss and analyze. The questions after each problem help focus the discussion on important concepts.

- **Tutorial CD** – Students get individual hands-on practice in creating the products discussed in some of the exercises.

How to Use This Booklet With Other Instructor Resources

For instructors teaching with the *Integrating Educational Technology into Education* (*IETT*) textbook, the following sequence is recommended to make use of these resources:

Step 1: Students read the chapter and take CW Self-Test

The CW self-test is a great way for students to review information in each chapter to make sure they have read and remembered important concepts.

Step 2: Introduce the chapter topics with CW *PowerPoint* Slides

The instructor can use the slides on the CW to introduce the topics in class or ask the students to review them before class. This sets the stage for the hands-on work in the class.

Step 3: Use *Educational Technology in Action* in combination with *IETT*'s end-of-chapter individual and collaborative activities for in-class and homework learning activities

To guide meaningful learning, instructors can use this booklet in conjunction with the Collaborative Activities in *IETT*'s end-of-chapter exercises. Instructors can do some of the exercises in class and assign additional ones for homework. Use these two resources in the following way:

- Use exercises in Part I of this booklet *in place of* the Collaborative Activities for *IETT*'s Chapter 2 (page 48).

- Use exercises in Part II of this booklet *to supplement* Collaborative Activities in *IETT*'s Chapters 4-9. Instructors may choose some or all of the exercises.

- Have each student choose *one* of *IETT*'s Chapters 10-15 for further study. They do the chapter exercises in this booklet associated with the *IETT* chapter they choose.

- Have students do the products in the Tutorials CD as individual homework exercises to give them hands-on practice in creating technology products.

Step 4: Students do CD-ROM and CW Exercises outside class

For after-class homework, the book includes end-of-chapter exercises students do with the *Integrating Technology Across the Curriculum* CD, and Questions for Thought and Discussion they do on the CW Message Board.

Step 5: Assign CTB and Portfolio activities as final assessments

Two kinds of activities can be useful for final course assessments: the Computerized Test Bank (CTB) and the Portfolio activities. Instructors may choose to have students do these at the end of Parts (e.g., once a month or so), or at the end of each chapter, if time allows.

Acknowledgments

As American entrepreneur Henry Kaiser said, "Problems are only opportunities in work clothes." Preparing this booklet of problems about technology integration presented two kinds of opportunities. As a professional in the field of educational technology, I was challenged to scrutinize even more carefully the issues and decisions each teacher must confront when considering when and how to use technology in a classroom. For those who use this booklet as part of their teacher preparation program, it offers compelling and convincing insights made possible by reading the stories of others – always a powerful way to learn.

Yet let us not downplay the "work clothes" aspect of these opportunities. Writing this "little booklet" was like creating a small, populated world, complete with descriptions of personalities and their environments. Suffice it to say, it took longer than six days. In its pages, teachers will recognize even more clearly the work involved in using technologies. Learning new ways of enhancing one's teaching is one thing; finding time to do it is quite another! Yet these all are opportunities that cannot be ignored. Choosing to respond to them is a *sine qua non* of excellence.

For giving me the opportunity to write this book, I am again indebted to my friend, mentor, and editor, Debbie Stollenwerk, and to other Merrill professionals who made it take shape and become a useful instructional product: JoEllen Gohr, Kim Lundy, Mary Morrill, and Dan Parker.

As always, I am grateful for the continuing support of my family, Bill and Paige Wiencke, and of friends such as Sherry Alter and Paul Belt, Marilyn and Herb Comet, Pat Gagné, Barbara Hansen, Megan Hurley, FJ and Maxine King, Sharon and Jon Marshall, Sharon Milner, Mary Ann Myers, Gwen McAlpine and Paul Zimmer, and Myrtle Parks. I welcome the opportunity to thank them once again for the continuing gifts of their love and friendship.

M. D. Roblyer

Part I:
Introducing the Technology Integration Planning (TIP) Model

Chapter 1
Overview of the TIP Model

Background on the TIP Model

The Technology Integration Planning (TIP) Model introduced in the textbook *Integrating Educational Technology into Teaching* (Roblyer, 2003) gives teachers a systematic way to address challenges involved in integrating technology into teaching. In each of the model's five phases, teachers perform a set of planning and implementation steps that help assure their technology use will be efficient and successful in meeting needs they identify. This section gives an overview of the five phases, describes the focus of each phase, and lists and explains issues teachers address at each stage.

Phase 1: Determine relative advantage

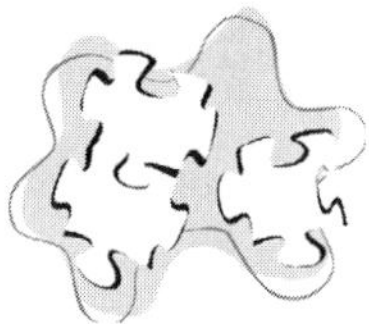

Phase 2: Decide on objectives and assessments

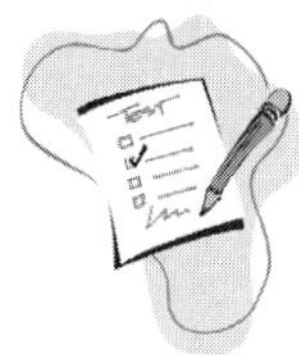

Phase 3: Design integration strategies

Phase 4: Prepare the instructional environment

Phase 5: Evaluate and revise integration strategies

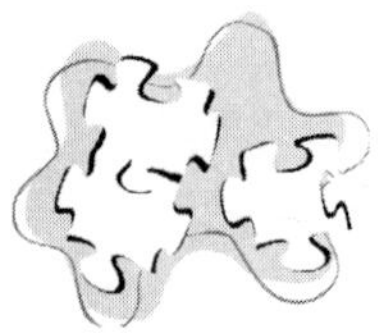

Phase 1: Determine relative advantage

Focus: *Why should I use a technology-based method?* Teachers look at their current teaching problems and identify technology-based methods that may offer good solutions.

In his best-selling book on how and why innovations get adopted, Everett Rogers (*Diffusion of Innovation*, 1995) says that people resist changing how they do things, even if new ways are better. However, people are more likely to change if they see clearly the benefits of a new method over an old one. He calls this seeing a "relative advantage." The following make it easier to see relative advantage:

1. **Compatibility** – Methods consistent with their cultural values and beliefs and others adopted in the past. For example, teachers see using technology as compatible with their views of what it means to be a good teacher.

2. **Complexity** – Easy enough for them to learn and to carry out on a frequent basis. Teachers who use technology-based methods feel that they are both feasible to learn and not too time-consuming to do routinely.

3. **Trialability** – Being able to try it out a little before making a final decision.

4. **Observability** – Seeing others they respect or emulate using the new method successfully. For many teachers, observability is a kind of trialability, since they "try out" the method vicariously through other teachers or trainers.

At this Phase, teachers review their curriculum and teaching methods and identify instructional problems for which technology might offer a good solution. Trialability and observability help them review a technology-based method and determine if it is compatible with their values and easy enough for them to learn and implement. Then they make a decision on its relative advantage for them.

Summary of Issues to address in Phase 1:

- Are there any topics or curriculum objectives I have difficulty teaching?
- Do any of these instructional problem areas have technology-based solutions?
- What is the relative advantage of the technology-based solutions?
- Is the relative advantage sufficient to justify the effort involved?

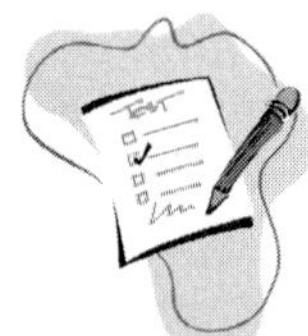

Phase 2: Decide on objectives and assessments

Focus: *How will I know students have learned?* Teachers decide skills they want students to learn from the lesson(s) and design ways to assess how well students have learned and how effectively the activity has been carried out.

To be sure a technology successfully addressed the problems they identified in Phase 1, teachers state expectations in the form of observable, measurable outcomes, then design materials to measure outcomes. For many skills, teachers use traditional assessments (e.g., multiple choice, short answer, true-false, matching, essay). For more complex skills such as web site production work or cooperative group work, teachers may either design or acquire the following kinds of materials:

- **Performance checklists** – Lists of tasks students have to accomplish for credit. Performance checklists list tasks and points awarded for accomplishing them. For example, students get a point for carrying out each step an experiment.
- **Criterion checklists** – Lists of criteria students must meet in their work and products. If students must not only do tasks but also must do them to a certain level of quality, the criteria are listed with the point spread possible. For example, students must locate 10 web sites that meet stated criteria for 1-3 points each.
- **Rubrics** – A set of descriptions of levels of performance (e.g., low, medium, high) on each of several aspects of the product or activity (e.g., content quality). Look at the following web site to see example rubrics and use a template to help design them: **http://rubistar.4teachers.org/index.shtml**

Sometimes, teachers gather data through observations to see if desired behaviors are increasing. If they want to see if students are enjoying the new methods or have better attitudes toward the subject, they also may have a non-instructional outcome such as "Higher motivation to do group production work" and state an objective to define it. They usually design self-report instruments to measure these outcomes.

Summary of Issues to address in Phase 2:

- What kinds of performances do I expect from students to show they learned?
- What is the best way for me to assess students' learning progress and products: e. g., written tests (multiple choice, true-false, matching, short answer, essays), performance or criterion checklists, rubrics?
- Do the desired instruments exist or do I have to develop them?
- What other methods could gauge success (e.g., observations, attitude instruments)?

Phase 3: Design integration strategies

Focus: *What teaching strategies and activities will work best?* Teachers decide on instructional strategies and how to carry them out.

When teachers create an instructional design for technology integration, they consider the characteristics of their topic and the needs of their students and decide on an instructional course of action that addresses both within the constraints of their classroom environment. This means making decisions about:

- **Instructional approaches** – Teachers may teach topics in a traditional, directed manner: present new concepts, have students practice, test student knowledge. Inquiry-based (constructivist) approaches, on the other hand, require students to discover at least some concepts that were once just told to them. Decisions about which instructional approaches to use drives all other ones on curriculum, grouping, and sequence.
- **Curriculum approaches** – Some content areas once taught as separate topics (single subject approach) are now taught in combination (interdisciplinary approach). Some teachers feel that this better reflects real life, where a problem may call for applying skills in several content areas.
- **Grouping** – In some situations, individual students must learn and demonstrate mastery of skills. In others, teachers have the option to place students in pairs or small groups.
- **Sequence** – As teachers design the sequence of steps in the integration activity, they consider ways to encourage equity of technology use, as well as to make sure students have prerequisite technology skills that allow them to learn effectively from the resources.

Summary of Issues to address in Phase 3:

- Should activities be directed, constructivist, or a combination of these?
- Will the instruction be single subject or interdisciplinary?
- Should activities be individual, paired, small group, large group, whole class?
- What strategies should I use to encourage females and minority students to be integrally involved with the technologies?
- What sequence of activities should I teach?
- Have I built in demonstrations of the skills students will need to use both equipment and the specific software?
- Have I allowed students enough time to get used to materials before beginning a graded activity?

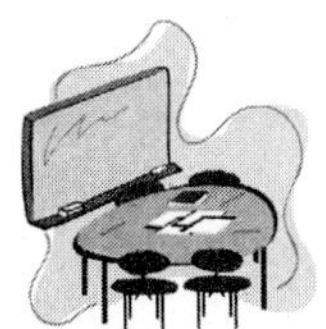

Phase 4: Prepare the environment

Focus: *Are essential conditions in place to support teaching and learning?* Teachers organize the teaching environment so technology plans can be carried out effectively.

Since research on effective technology uses shows that teachers can integrate technology successfully *only* if they have adequate hardware, software, and technical support available to them, the International Association for Technology in Education (ISTE NETS for Students, 2000) lists a set of *essential conditions* that are necessary to unleash the potential power of technology tools and methods. The school and district must provide many of these essential conditions, but for each technology integration strategy, the teacher considers which conditions are in place and to what degree. This helps shape the kind of integration possible for the situation. For example, if 30 computers would be ideal, but only five are available, the teacher adapts the plan accordingly.

Summary of Issues to address in Phase 4:

- How many computers and copies of software will be needed to carry out the activities?
- How many computers and copies of software are available?
- Over what time period and for how long will technology resources be needed?
- Do I need to schedule time in a lab or media center?
- If demonstrations and learning stations are to be used, will projection devices or large-screen monitors be needed?
- What other equipment, software, media, and resources will be needed (e.g., printers, software)?
- Have I checked out the legality of the uses I want to make?
- Have I provided for students' privacy and safety?
- Have I made all necessary access provisions for students with physical disabilities?
- Have I become familiar with troubleshooting procedures specific to the piece of hardware or software package being used? (Equipment and software manuals often list such procedures.)
- Have I built in time to test run an equipment setup before students arrive?
- Have I built in time to back up important files? Have I trained students to back up theirs?
- Do I have the original program disks/discs handy to reinstall them if necessary?
- Do I have a backup plan if I cannot use the resources as I had planned?

Phase 5: Evaluate and revise

Focus: *What worked well? What could be improved?* Teachers review outcome data and information on technology-integrated methods and determine what should be changed to make them work better next time.

In addition to collecting formal data on instructional and other outcomes, teachers sometimes interview students and observers to ask what they think could be improved. Some teachers keep daily notes or logs on implementation problems and issues. As they review all the information, teachers can use the following *Technology Impact Checklist* (Roblyer, 2003) to help them reflect on whether the problems they identified in Phase 1 have, indeed, been addressed successfully:

How Do You Know When You've Integrated Technology Well?

-An outside observer sees the technology activity as a seamless part of the lesson.
-The reason for using the technology is obvious to you, the students, and others.
-The students are focusing on learning, not on the technology.
-You can describe how technology is helping a particular student.
-You would have difficulty accomplishing lesson objectives if the technology weren't there.
-You can explain easily and concisely what the technology is supposed to contribute.
-All students are participating with the technology and benefiting from it.

How Do You Know When You HAVEN'T Integrated Technology Well?

-You consistently see the technology as more trouble than it's worth.
-You have trouble justifying cost and preparation time in terms of benefits to your students.
-Students spend more time trying to make the technology work than on learning the topic.
-The problem you were trying to address is still there.

Summary of Issues to address in Phase 5:

- Have I identified an instructional problem to solve?
- Have I identified types of evidence that will indicate to me whether or not the new strategy is solving or might help solve the problem?
- Have I solicited feedback from students about how to improve activities?
- Have I used instruments to collect data on the impact of the activity?
- Have I reviewed results and determined if the strategy has solved the problem or could solve the problem with changes?
- Have I considered alternative ways to set up equipment so activities go more smoothly?
- What do I need to change to achieve better impact?

Chapter 2

Problem-based Exercises on Phase 1 of the TIP Model: *Determining the Relative Advantage*

Introduction to Phase 1 Concepts

Every teacher has topics – and sometimes whole subject areas – that they find especially challenging to teach. Some concepts are so abstract or foreign to students that they struggle to understand them; some topics students find so boring, tedious, or irrelevant that they have trouble attending to them. Some learning requires time-consuming tasks that students resist doing. Good teachers spend much time trying to meet these challenges and make concepts more engaging or easier to grasp, or make tasks more efficient to accomplish.

Recognizing relative advantage. Technology-based strategies offer many unique benefits to teachers as they look for instructional solutions to these problems. However, time and effort to plan and carry out technology-based methods and sometimes involves additional expense. Teachers have to consider the benefits of using such a method compared to their current ones and decide if the benefits are worth the additional effort and cost.

As described in Chapter 1 of this booklet, Everett Rogers (*Diffusion of Innovations*, 1995) refers to this decision as seeing the "relative advantage" for using a new method *Integrating Educational Technology into Teaching* (2003) lists several kinds of learning problems and technology solutions with potential for high relative advantage to teachers (pp. 43-44). However, these lists are merely general guidelines. Being able to recognize specific instances of these problems in a classroom context and knowing how to match them with an appropriate technology solution takes both practice and an in-depth knowledge of the characteristics of each technology.

This booklet provides some of the practice you will need, but to make this practice most helpful, first read in *Integrating Educational Technology into Teaching* about the features and applications of each technology before doing the practice problems in chapters 7-10 of this booklet. Also, before doing practice problems in chapters 11-16, read about problems and technology solutions specific to each content area.

Phase 1 questions. The first phase in integrating technology requires answering two questions about technology's relative advantage in a given situation. These questions are listed on the next page with suggestions for answering them in actual classroom situations.

1. **What is the problem I am addressing?** To make sure a technology application is a good solution, begin with a clear statement of a teaching and learning problem. This is sometimes difficult to do. It is a natural human tendency to jump to a quick solution rather than recognize the real problem. Also, everyone may not see a problem the same way. Use the following guidelines to answer the question of "what is the problem?"

   - **Do not focus on technologies** – Remember that knowing how to use a technology appropriately is part of a *solution*, and is not in itself a *problem* to solve. Therefore, avoid problem statements like "Students do not know how to use spreadsheets efficiently" or "Teachers are not having their students use the Internet." Not having the skills to use a technology (e.g., a spreadsheet or the Internet) is an instructional problem, but not the kind of teaching/learning problem to consider here. It is sometimes true that teachers are given a technology and told to implement it. In these situations, they must decide if there is a real teaching or learning problem the new resource can help meet. However, if teachers have a technology available and choose not to use it, it may mean they can see no relative advantage to using it; non-use of a technology is not in itself a problem to address with the TIP Model.

   - **Look for evidence** – Look for observable indications there really is a problem. Examples of evidence are: students consistently achieve lower grades on a skill area, a formal or informal survey shows that teachers have trouble getting students to attend to learning tasks, or teachers observe that students are refusing to turn in required assignments in a certain area.

2. **Do technology-based methods offer a solution with sufficient relative advantage?** Analyze the benefits of the technology-based method in light of the effort and cost to implement it and make a final decision. Use the following guidelines to answer the question of "Is technology a good solution?"

   - **Estimate the impact** – Consider the benefits others have gained from using a technology as a solution. Is it likely you will realize similar benefits?

   - **Consider the required effort and expense** – How much time and work will it take to implement the technology solution? Is it likely to be worth it?

The problem-based exercises in this chapter give you hands-on practice in applying Phase 2 of the TIP Model concepts you read in Chapter 1. Through scenario-based problem situations, you see how teachers go about answering these key questions by using trialability and observability to determine the complexity, compatibility, and relative advantage of technology-based solutions.

Scenarios to Read and Analyze – Read each scenario and answer the questions after it using information you read in Chapter 1 about the TIP Model:

Scenario 1, Phase 1 – Mia and Lars, teachers from two different high schools, were discussing strategies for including multicultural activities in the social studies curriculum.

"I'm thinking of trying something new this year," said Mia. "Our principal gives us travel money to go to a conference or workshop each year, so this year I went to a workshop at the Highmarkes School District. They described an online project with partner schools in countries all over the world. One teacher told about her partners in Israel and Spain. She said students exchange information with designated partners and answer assigned questions to research each other's backgrounds and locales. Then they work in groups on travel brochures or booklets to e-mail each other. They even take digital photos of each other and scan pictures from school yearbooks. It sounded like a great way for my kids to learn about other cultures while they learn geography and civics."

"Wow," said Lars. "It's great your principal does that; our principal doesn't. But that project sounds like a lot of trouble. Would you have to do it all yourself?"

"Our library-media center has a technology resource guy that helps us when we run into technical problems," said Mia. "And, you know, most of us at my school have Internet connections in our classrooms now."

"We're still waiting for that in my school," said Lars. "My classes usually look in books for information on assigned countries and do a research paper or poster. However, they do bring in foods from their own cultures. Last year, we had a smorgasbord with five or six different authentic cuisines. What great egg rolls!"

Mia nodded, "Yes, I've done that, too, and they do seem to enjoy it. I don't think it makes much of an impression, though, as far as appreciating other cultures. I still hear a lot of racial epithets used in the halls, and jokes about students' color or race-specific characteristics – real and imagined."

Lars shook his head, "Well, I don't think there's much we can do about that."

"Maybe not," sighed Mia, "but it's sure harder to demean people from other cultures when you've really worked with them and gotten to know them. I thought I'd give this way a try. The teacher from Highmarkes said she'd help me get started. I thought I'd go over and visit her class to see how she organizes it."

"Well," said Lars. "I'd be interested to hear if you think it's worth the trouble."

S1.1 What relative advantages does Mia see for the technology-based approach – i.e., in what ways does she seem to think it might be better than her previous one?

S1.2 How did trialability and observability help Mia see the relative advantage?

S1.3 Why do you think Lars doesn't see the relative advantage?

S1.4 What do you think might help persuade Lars of the relative advantage?

Scenario 2, Phase 1 – Leroy was a veteran middle school science teacher in a large, suburban school district. Despite the many awards he had won for his teaching, he was becoming increasingly dissatisfied with the way students were learning science in his school. He felt that, despite his efforts to make his class hands-on and project-based, his students tended to see science as facts and procedures unrelated to real-life problems. Other teachers in the school taught science in an even more traditional way than he did, with limited group projects and hands-on experiments. He felt most students left middle school without learning the usefulness of scientific inquiry.

One day, he attended a science conference where he heard a university professor and a science teacher presenting software they had designed and used with middle school students. The software began with a video problem scenario presented as it if were a real live newscast. The video said that an alien spaceship was orbiting earth and broadcasting a plea for help. Aliens on board were from several planets in a galaxy whose sun had exploded. They escaped but now needed new habitats that would meet the needs of their various species. They asked earth for help in matching them with planets and moons each might find habitable. (*See end of chapter note.)

The conference presenters went on to tell about the rich, inquiry-based environment the software provided and the teacher support materials that came with it. There were built-in information banks about planets and their moons, probes they could design and "send out" to collect data, daily lesson plans, suggestions for grouping – even practice test items and rubrics for judging products. They said the software had drawn students into activities that helped them learn scientific inquiry approaches, rather than isolated facts and steps.

The whole idea of integrating this kind of activity into science instruction fired Leroy's imagination. He decided to have his students do this for his solar system unit instead of building models of planets. If it worked well, he would try getting other teachers to adopt it and would look for other project-based software simulations they could use. When he got back to town, he invited Arvella, district science coordinator, to his school to see the demo he had gotten at the conference.

"Whew! This looks complicated, Leroy!" said Arvella. Are you sure the kids can do this? Don't you think it might frustrate them – all these probes and stuff?"

"I don't think so," said Leroy. "I'll bet they get it faster than the teachers do."

"Hmm," said Arvella, "if it works, we could build it into district curriculum."

S2.1 What kind of relative advantage does Leroy see for this software – i.e., how will it address the problems he has identified?

S2.2 Why does Leroy feel it would meet his needs better than model building?

S2.3 Why did Arvella view the activity differently than Leroy?

S2.4 Assuming it works well, would requiring it in the curriculum be a good way of showing other teachers the relative advantage of using this software?

Phase 1 Problems to Analyze and Solve

P.1. You are a high school mathematics teacher. At a faculty meeting, your principal announced that the district had purchased a site license for an SAT preparation program. He said that any teacher could obtain a copy of the software for use in the classroom by attending a Saturday training program that the district will hold.

P1.1 What kinds of benefits to your students and to you would motivate you to consider using the software, and how could you find out about them?
P.1.2 What experiences could provide the trialability and observability to help you decide if using this software had relative advantage for you, and how would you go about obtaining these experiences?
P.1.3 What could the district and/or principal do to help you decide?

P.2. You are a third grade teacher and are talking with another third grade teacher in her classroom. She shows you how she uses spreadsheets to demonstrate math concepts such as graphing data from a table of numbers. She says has been using spreadsheet software to keep her home budgets and she realized how visual it made math concepts, so she started using it with some of her math lessons. You have never used spreadsheets, but you are interested in the approach she is using.

P2.1 What problem does the spreadsheet activity seem to be addressing?
P2.2 What kinds of questions would you ask her to help you decide if this activity would have relative advantage for you and your students?
P2.3 Why might this activity have more immediate relative advantage for her than for you?

P.3. Scores on the state's test of writing skills are unusually low for your district's eighth graders, and a university English education professor has been hired as a consultant to help improve them. At a one-day staff development workshop, the professor describes how having students write e-mails to students at other sites can motivate them to write more and want to improve their writing style and mechanics. After the workshops, several teachers complain among themselves that the method is worthless and that the day had been a waste of their time.

P3.1 What did the professor assume about the causes of students' writing problems?
P3.2 What are some reasons this may not have been the best way to demonstrate the relative advantage of this approach?
P3.3 What might be a better way to explore whether or not this method had relative advantage over the way teachers currently teach writing?

P.4. The superintendent of the Wellmade School District felt that every student should be "connected to the Information Superhighway," so he decided to install Internet connections in every school classroom in the district. The hardware and installations were funded through a federal grant and local business sponsors. Two years later, it became apparent that only about 25% of the teachers were using the Internet with students, and most uses were "casual surfing."

P4.1 Why do you think the teachers did not see the relative advantage of this technology?
P4.2 If you were made responsible for integrating this technology into instructional activities, how would you translate the superintendent's rationale into problems and solutions the teachers could understand?
P4.3 How would you use trialability and observability to help teachers see the relative advantage of this innovation?

P.5. The principal of a high school visited a school district where all teachers used handheld computers to assess students as they worked on small group projects. Teachers were able to take notes as they walked around the classroom; then they downloaded the notes to their own classroom computer workstations, where it could be graded and printed out. The teachers seemed to feel this resource was a time-saver and helped them do instructional activities they couldn't do before. Your principal comes to you, the lead science teacher in the school, and asks you if you think you and other teachers would like to have handheld computers.

P5.1 What information would you need to make a decision about the relative advantage of this resource?
P5.2 How could the principal help you obtain the information you need?
P5.3 What would you need to know about the complexity and compatibility of this technology before you could answer the principal's question?

* **NOTE:** Scenario 2 is based upon an actual award-winning software package called *Alien Rescue*, designed as a collaborative project of the University of Texas at Austin, the University of Louisiana at Lafayette, and Texas A&M University. Anyone interested in learning more about this software may contact Dr. Susan Pedersen at: spedersen@coe.tamu.edu.

Chapter 3

Problem-based Exercises on Phase 2 of the TIP Model: *Deciding on Objectives and Assessments*

Introduction to Phase 2 Concepts

Writing objectives is a good way of setting clear expectations for what technology-based methods will accomplish. Usually, teachers expect a new method will improve *student behaviors*, e.g., better achievement, more on-task behaviors, improved attitudes. Sometimes, however, changes in *teacher behaviors* are important, e.g., saving time on a task. In either case, objectives should focus on *outcomes* that are observable (e.g., demonstrating, writing, completing), rather than internal ones that cannot be seen or measured (e.g., being aware, knowing, understanding, or appreciating).

After stating objectives, teachers create ways to assess how well outcomes have been accomplished. Sometimes, they can use existing tests and rubrics. For others, they have to create instruments or methods to measure the behaviors.

Example outcomes, objectives, and assessments. Here are a few examples of outcomes, objectives to state them in a measurable form, and assessment methods matched to them:

- **Higher achievement outcome:** Overall average performance on an end-of-chapter test will improve by 20%. (Assess achievement with a test.)

- **Cooperative work outcome:** All students will score at least 15 out of 20 on the cooperative group skill rubric. (Use an existing rubric to grade skills.)

- **Attitude outcome:** Students will indicate satisfaction with the simulation lesson by an overall average score of 20 of 25 points. (Create an attitude survey to assess satisfaction.)

- **Improved motivation:** Teachers will observe better on-task behavior in at least 75% of the students. (Create and use an observation sheet.)

Phase 2 questions. This phase in integrating technology requires answering two questions about outcomes and assessment strategies. These questions are listed on the next page with suggestions for answering them in actual classroom situations:

1. **What outcomes do I expect from using the new methods?** Think about problems you are trying to solve and what would be acceptable indications that the technology solution has succeeded in resolving them. Use the following guidelines:

- **Focus on results, not processes** – Think about the *end results* you want to achieve, rather than the *processes* to help you get there. Avoid statements like "Students will learn cooperative group skills" which tells a process students use to achieve the outcome (improved cooperative group skills). Instead, state what you want students to be able to do as a result of the multimedia project, for example "90% of students will score 4 out of 5 on a cooperative groups skills rubric."
- **Make statements observable and measurable** – Avoid vague statements that cannot be measured like "Students will understand how to work cooperatively."

2. **What are the best ways of assessing these outcomes?** The choice of assessment depends on the nature of the outcome. See the following guidelines:

- **Use written tests to assess skill achievement outcomes** – Written cognitive tests (e.g., short answer, multiple choice, true-false, matching) and essay exams remain the most common classroom assessment strategy for many formal knowledge skills.
- **Use evaluation criteria checklists to assess complex tasks or products** – When students must create complex products such as multimedia presentations, reports, or web pages, teachers may give students a set of criteria that specify requirements each product must meet. Points are awarded for meeting each criterion.
- **Use rubrics to assess complex tasks or products** – Rubrics fulfill the same role as evaluation criteria checklists and are sometimes used in addition to them. Their added value is giving students descriptions of various levels of quality. Teachers usually associate a letter grade with each level of quality (Level 5 = A, Level 4 = B, etc.).
- **Use surveys or semantic differentials to assess attitude outcomes** – When the outcome is improved attitudes, teachers either design a list of survey questions for students to answer or have students react to a question (e.g., "How do you feel about math?") by checking a line between each of several sets of bipolar adjectives to indicate their level of feeling (e.g., "Warm _ _ _ _ _ Cold? Happy _ _ _ _ _ Sad?")
- **Use observation instruments to measure frequency of behaviors** – For example, if teachers wanted to see an increase in students' use of scientific language, they could create a chart to keep track of this use on a daily basis.

Problem-based exercises in this chapter give you hands-on practice in applying Phase 2 of the TIP Model concepts. Through scenario-based problem situations, you see how teachers go about deciding on appropriate outcomes, stating objectives, and matching good assessment strategies to them.

Scenarios to Read and Analyze – The following scenarios are continuations of the ones begun in Chapter 2. Answer the questions using information you have read about Phase 2 of the TIP Model in the Introduction to this chapter and in Chapter 1:

Scenario 1, Phase 2 – Mia was so impressed with the online project at Highmarkes School District, she decided to try it out in her own classroom. She reflected on the problems she saw with her current methods of addressing multicultural awareness and what she wanted her students to learn about other cultures that they didn't seem to be learning now. She decided on the following outcomes: better attitudes toward people of other cultures, increased learning about similarities and differences among cultures, skills in using the Internet and e-mail for communication, and positive attitudes toward instruction. She created these objectives to measure the outcomes:

- **Attitudes toward cultures:** At least 75% of students will demonstrate an improved attitude toward the culture being studied by achieving a higher score on an attitude measure after the Internet activity than before.
- **Knowledge of cultures:** Each student group will score at least 90% on a rubric on a brochure or booklet that reflects knowledge of the characteristics (both unique and common to our own) of the language, geography, people, governments and other information about the culture being studied.
- **Internet skills:** At least 90% of students will demonstrate they can independently do 95% of listed skills on e-mail, browsers, and search engine use.

For the last outcome, she wasn't sure what to require and decided to ask her colleague Lars if he knew of any good measures. For other outcomes, she designed:

- **Semantic differential:** She knew a good way to measure attitudes was with set of adjectives with lines between them: EX: cruel _ _ _ _ _ kind). Before and after the project, students answer a question like "How do you feel about people from ____?" by marking a line between the adjectives to indicate how they feel.
- **Knowledge of cultures:** After listing all the characteristics she wanted to see reflected in their products, she created a rubric to assess them.
- **Internet skills:** She listed the skills and created a checklist handout of them.

S1.1 Add bipolar adjectives and create a sheet for a semantic differential instrument that Mia might use to assess attitudes toward other cultures.
S1.2 What are some features you think should be assessed in the product rubric?
S1.3 If you were Lars, how would you advise Mia to state the fourth outcome?
S1.4 What instrument or method would you advise her to select or create to assess how well the fourth outcome had been accomplished?

Scenario 2, Phase 2 – Leroy decided to use in his science classroom the inquiry-based software he had learned about at the conference. As he thought about what he wanted to achieve with this new method, he made mental comparisons of how students currently viewed learning science and how he wanted them to look at it. He decided that, in addition to passing his usual test on solar system information, he wanted students to achieve the following outcomes: demonstration of problem solving approach to assigned problems, ability to create new problems to solve and design methods to solve them, increased transfer of the language of scientific inquiry to tasks outside the aliens unit, and increased enjoyment of using scientific inquiry methods. He developed the following objectives to measure the outcomes:

- **Problem solving approaches:** All students working in small groups will create well-designed problem statements, solutions steps, and workable solutions for at least 1 of 3 problems assigned.
- **New problem creation:** At least 75% of groups will be able to generate at least one new problem to explore related to the alien simulation software.
- **Scientific inquiry language use transfer:** At least 80% of students will be heard using the language of scientific inquiry outside the unit.

He wasn't sure how to deal with the "science enjoyment" outcome and decided to ask district science coordinator Arvella how she would state and assess this outcome. For the other assessments, he decided on the following:

- **Problem solving criterion checklist:** He decided to use the software Teacher Manual's checklist of steps students should complete and criteria they should meet for each step.
- **Problem creation rubric:** He designed a rubric based on a list of features that well-designed problems should reflect.
- **Scientific language observation instrument:** He designed an observation instrument with students' names and a daily checklist. Each day he would check off names of students he or others had observed using the terms or phrases that indicated use of inquiry approaches.

S2.1 Leroy wonders if he has set the criteria for success too low in the first outcome objective. What features of the situation might help him decide on good criteria?
S2.2 What features might you include in a rubric to assess well-designed problems?
S2.3 If you were Arvella, how would you tell Leroy to state an "enjoyment" outcome?
S2.4 What kind of instrument or method would you advise Leroy to select or create to assess the "science enjoyment" outcome?

Phase 2 Problems to Analyze and Solve

P1. You are a middle school language arts teacher. You would like to have your students begin word-processing their written stories and compositions instead of writing them by hand or typing them. Right now, they write as little as possible, and getting them to make corrections is always like pulling teeth. You hope word processing will increase the amount they write and make them more likely to revise their work based on your feedback at least once for each written product.

P1.1 How would you state an outcome objective about increasing the amount students write?
P1.2 How would you state an outcome objective about getting students to make corrections?
P1.3 What would be a good way to assess these two outcomes?

P2. You are a guidance counselor who would like junior level students to use new software the state has provided to help them prepare for the state graduation test. You feel that using this software even an hour a week will raise students' scores as much as 20% across the junior class.

P2.1 How would you state the objective for this performance outcome?
P2.2 Would you consider any increase less than 20% as an adequate indication of the software's usefulness for juniors? How could you reflect this in the objective statement?
P2.3 What would you use to assess how well this objective was accomplished?

P.3 You are a high school French teacher who wants students to have a "language immersion" learning experience, yet you and your students cannot afford to travel to a French-speaking locale. You decide to try a "virtual immersion experience" by having your students visit French language web sites and locate information to prepare a product in French (e.g., a brochure about a vacation spot in a French-speaking location, a restaurant menu with French descriptions and prices). You feel this activity will improve translation test scores and encourage students to use the French language in classroom conversation.

P3.1 How would you state an objective for an "improved translation test scores" outcome?
P3.2 How would you state an objective for the "increased French conversation" outcome?
P3.3 What would be a way to measure accomplishment of the second objective?

P4. As a school district science coordinator, you would like the high school biology teachers to begin using a dissection simulation program in lieu of actual dissections of pigs, which has always been done in the past. You feel this will save both time and money for materials. Some biology teachers are reluctant to make this change; they say that students cannot learn as much about anatomy and dissection techniques from a simulation as they can from the "real thing." However, they agree to a test of the software in a couple classes.

P4.1 What would be the expectations of the simulation method in terms of general outcomes?

P4.2 If you were one of the biology teachers, how would you state objectives matched to these outcomes?

P4.3 What instruments or information would you use to assess the "saving time and money" objective?

P5. You are a special education resource teacher for a school district. You attended a workshop about having students use presentation software (e.g., *PowerPoint*) for "book reports" and other summaries of works they have read. The workshop presenters say that students at all ability levels can use the software and find it more motivating to do such reports than regular written ones. Since you have heard complaints from teachers of gifted students and students with learning disabilities about how difficult it is to motivate students to do these reports, you would like to try this technique with both student groups. However, you are concerned that the students with disabilities might find the software frustrating.

P5.1 How would you state an outcome objective related to student motivation toward doing book reports?

P5.2 How would you state a different outcome objective related to use of the software by students with learning disabilities?

P5.3 What methods and materials would you use to assess these objectives?

Chapter 4

Problem-based Exercises on Phase 3 of the TIP Model: *Designing Integration Strategies*

Introduction to Phase 3 Concepts

Teachers make many design decisions as they integrate technologies into teaching, but the most important decision is whether the methods students will use to learn should be primarily directed (a teacher or expert source presents information for students to absorb) or primarily inquiry-based or constructivist (students do hands-on activities to generate their own learning). This decision usually drives all others about grouping, lesson sequence, and types of learning activities.

Deciding on teaching/learning methods. Use the following guidelines to help determine whether methods should be directed, inquiry-based, or a combination of both:

Choose directed methods when:	Choose inquiry-based methods when:
• It will be clear to students how they apply skills to real-world situations. • Students are highly motivated to learn the content. • Students are inexperienced in the topic and are not likely to have any knowledge base or prerequisite skills. • Students need to learn skills as quickly and efficiently as possible. • Content is concrete and unambiguous and lends itself to direct teaching.	• Students usually have problems seeing applications to real-world problems. • Students usually are unmotivated to learn content in traditional ways. • Students have had previous experience with the topic and already have acquired some skills in the content. • There is adequate time for hands-on learning and assessment. • Content is abstract and difficult for learners to grasp without hands-on work.

Phase 3 questions. This phase in integrating technology requires answering three questions about instructional strategies, technology materials, and implementation strategies. These questions are listed on the next page with suggestions for answering them in actual classroom situations:

1. **What kinds of instructional methods are needed in light of content objectives and student characteristics?** After using the guidelines listed on the previous page to decide whether the methods should be primarily directed or constructivist, also consider the following:

   - **Content approach** – Should the approach be single-subject or interdisciplinary? Sometimes school or district requirements dictate this decision, and sometimes teachers combine subjects into a single unit of instruction as a way to cover concepts and topics that they may not otherwise have time to teach. Most often, however, interdisciplinary approaches are used to model how real-life activities require using a combination of skills from several content areas.
   - **Grouping approach** – Should the students work as individuals, pairs, in small groups, or as a whole class? These decisions are made in light of how many computers or software copies are available, as well as the following guidelines:

     - **Whole class:** For demonstrations or to guide whole-class discussion prior to student work
     - **Individual:** When students have to demonstrate individual mastery of skills at the end of the lesson or project
     - **Pairs:** For peer tutoring; higher ability students work with those of lesser ability
     - **Small group:** To model real-world work skills by giving students experience in cooperative group work

2. **How can technology best support these methods?** Think about how you will carry out the technology-based solution you identified in Phase 2.

3. **How can I prepare students adequately to use technologies?** When designing a sequence of activities that incorporates technology tools, be sure to leave enough time for demonstrating tools to students and allowing them to become comfortable using them before they do a graded product.

After you have considered all these aspects, create a sequence of steps and a timeline for carrying out the lesson or project.

Problem-based exercises in this chapter give you hands-on practice in applying Phase 3 of the TIP Model concepts you read about in Chapter 1. Actual classroom application requires in-depth knowledge about capabilities of technology resources and their uses in content areas. However, exercises in this chapter focus on fundamental instructional decisions that are common to all content areas and that are required for effective integration of any technologies.

Scenarios to Read and Analyze – The following scenarios are continuations of the ones begun in Chapter 2. Answer the questions using information you have read about Phase 3 of the TIP Model in the Introduction to this chapter and in Chapter 1:

Scenario 1, Phase 3 – Mia knew that the changes she wanted to bring about in students' attitudes toward other cultures could not be done by telling them information and testing them on it. They would need to draw their own conclusions by working and communicating with people from other cultures. However, she felt many of the technical skills for Internet and e-mail use could be taught in a fairly directed way, since students would be motivated to use the most efficient methods to communicate with others and to obtain information for their products. Practice with these skills throughout the project would give them the level of mastery they needed.

She decided that students should work in groups of four with designated tasks for each person in the group. The project web site had some good suggestions on how to assign tasks and organize group work. It also had the following suggested sequence of activities for introducing and carrying out the project.

- **Step 1:** Sign up on project web site; obtain partner school assignments.
- **Step 2:** Teachers in partner schools contact each other and exchange notes on organizing instruction.
- **Step 3:** Teachers organize classroom resources for work on project.
- **Step 4:** Introduce project to students: display project information from project web site and discuss previous products done by other sites.
- **Step 5:** Assign students to groups; discuss task assignments with all members.
- **Step 6:** Teach beginning e-mail and Internet skills, if necessary.
- **Step 7:** Students do initial e-mail contacts/chats and introduce each other.
- **Step 8:** Teacher works with groups to identify information for final product.
- **Step 9:** Students do Internet searches to locate required information; take digital photos and scan required images; exchange information with partner sites.
- **Step 10:** Students do production work; exchange final products with partners.
- **Step 11:** Do debriefing and assessments of student work.

S1.1 Are Mia's activities inquiry-based (constructivist), directed, or a combination of both? Explain.

S1.2 What items would you need to cover with your "partner teacher" to coordinate instructional activities for the project?

S1.3 What teacher-directed methods could you use to introduce e-mail/browser/search engine skills efficiently?

S1.4 What could you include on the list of "required information for final product" to assure students learned geography, history, and biology/botany about the area?

Scenario 2, Phase 3 – Leroy realized that his students would learn inquiry-based methods only by seeing them in action and practicing them over time. His methods would have to be designed to facilitate, rather than direct, student learning and to encourage them to think on their own. He felt this project would be a good way for students to begin learning these complex skills, but he also knew the unit would take them more time than usual as they became used to new ways of thinking about science and about learning itself.

He also realized that students had to be prepared to answer conceptual and factual questions about the solar system on the state's required exams, so he would have to provide some diagnostic testing over these concepts and facts and, if necessary, some remedial practice. Luckily, the software Teacher Manual (TM) provided test items like this to cover background information, and he could supplement them with some of his own.

With these things in mind, he reviewed the software's Teacher Manual for how to keep the activity on track and created the following sequence of project activities:

- **Day 1:** Assign students to groups and assign one student from each group to log on computers with other members watching. Show them how to run the opening video. Allow them to explore the software environment on their own.
- **Day 2:** Have class review the problem by asking the probing questions listed in the TM. Allow groups to explore software further to answer any questions they don't remember answers to from first day.
- **Days 3-5:** Hold discussions about how they will collaborate and use inquiry approach to solve the problems. They develop their own inquiry problem statements. Demonstrate software features they will need. Students practice using them and define lists of alien needs.
- **Days 6-10:** Students use software features to explore planets and moons and develop hypotheses about best matches for each alien species.
- **Days 11-13:** Groups present their findings on best places for each species. Groups write up final selections in required format.
- **Days 14-16:** Final reflections, assessments, remedial practice, where necessary.

S2.1 Where might Leroy incorporate writing assignments to make this project more interdisciplinary?

S2.2 What strategies would you suggest Leroy build in to make sure girls are as involved as boys in the project?

S2.3 If some students demonstrated that they needed review of solar systems concepts, can you think of a fun, creative way they could do this on Days 15-16?

S2.4 At what point would you suggest Leroy introduce the idea of generating new problems to explore using the software resources?

Phase 3 Problems to Analyze and Solve

P1. Harriet is a high school AP composition teacher. She wants her students to do more spelling and grammar proofreading of their own written work and make required revisions on these items before turning papers in to her for grading. She feels word processing features will help them learn this habit, so she introduces the software to them in class. They have never used word processing before, but she feels AP students can learn word processing on their own. After a demonstration of word processing features on Monday, she tells them to go to the computer lab the next two class periods, do a word-processed paper, and turn it in to her at the end of the class period Wednesday. When she grades the papers, she realizes they are far worse than usual. Not only are ideas not as well-developed, spelling and grammar are worse. She decides the whole idea was a failure.

P1.1 What reasons related to Harriet's teaching sequence might explain this failure?
P1.2 Why do you think ideas in student papers were not as well-developed as usual?
P1.3 What are two things you suggest she do differently if she tries this again?

P2. You are a geometry teacher for gifted ninth grade students. They do well on end-of-chapter tests, but you want them to develop more insight on the practical applications of geometry in daily life. The book you are using has Internet enrichment activities that call for students to work together in small groups to identify such applications. You decide to do these enrichment activities in one class period at the end of the unit to try it out.

P2.1 Do your methods for integrating the enrichment activities need to be primarily directed or inquiry-based?
P2.2 What would you have to do when you introduce these Internet-based enrichment activities to make sure they were successful?
P2.3 Do you think one class period for the activities will be okay? Why or why not?

P3. Juan is an elementary teacher who has his young students use a software package that encourages thinking about problem solving. It calls for them to build simulated products that match an example product on the screen. After having them work in small groups to build several products, he asks them to reflect on and explain their methods for solving the problems.

P3.1 Are Juan's methods directed, inquiry-based, or a combination? Explain.
P3.2 What could he do to make sure boys don't dominate the "building activities?"
P3.3 What must Juan do before students use the software for the first time?

P4. Luella is a language arts teacher who uses a software package with vocabulary practice items to improve students' performance on a college entrance exam. Before she has them use the software, she describes test-taking tips and strategies and then shows them how to use the software. Since she feels students can help each other with difficult words, she has them work in groups of three to practice the software. They take turns practicing for about 15 minutes at the end of each class period for the last two weeks of the grading period.

P4.1 Are Luella's methods primarily directed or inquiry-based?
P4.2 Do you think this group-based strategy is a good one for the activity? Why or why not?
P4.3 Do you think 15 minutes of group practice at the end of each class period will be enough to increase students' performance? Why or why not?

P5. You are a middle school science teacher who wants to get his students more used to solving problems that require collecting and analyzing data. You decide to have them use new Microcomputer-based Labs (MBL's) the school has bought. The MBL's are handheld computers with sensors connected to them to measure light, temperature, voltage, movement, and speed. You plan an experiment where they collect temperature of various items under inside and outside conditions. Then they download the data to a computer in the classroom and chart the data to detect trends. You have 32 students, but there are only 8 MBL's. You plan to have them work in groups and you assign various roles for each student in the group.

P5.1 Are the methods you will use directed, inquiry-based, or a combination? Explain.
P5.2 What could you do to make sure boys don't dominate the actual data collection use of the available MBL's?
P5.3 What will you have to do before students use the MBL's to collect data "in the field" for the first time?

Chapter 5

Problem-based Exercises on Phase 4 of the TIP Model: *Preparing the Instructional Environment*

Introduction to Phase 4 Concepts

If teachers could obtain all the teaching resources they needed whenever they wanted them, they would make all Phase 4 planning decisions after they had decided on best instructional strategies in Phase 3. In practice, teachers make many Phase 3 and 4 decisions at the same time. Most teachers usually decide how they will teach something in light of what they have available to teach it.

Essential conditions for effective technology uses. In Phase 4, teachers make sure their instructional environment meets all of the following essential conditions required for successful technology integration:

- **Adequate hardware, software, and media** – Enough computers are available and there are sufficient legal copies of instructional resources.

- **Time to use resources** – Hardware and enough legal copies of software have been obtained or scheduled for the time needed.

- **Special needs of students** – Provisions have been made for access by students with disabilities and for all students' privacy and safety.

- **Planning for technology use** – Teachers are familiar enough with the hardware and software to use it efficiently and do necessary troubleshooting; they have allowed time for testing and backup of files; they have a backup plan in the event technology resources fail to work as planned.

Phase 4 questions. This phase in integrating technology requires answering three questions about preparing an instructional environment that will support technology integration. These questions are listed on the next page with suggestions for answering them in actual classroom situations:

1. **What equipment, software, media, and materials will I need to carry out the instructional strategies?** As you create ways to stretch scarce resources, be sure that your strategies are ethical and in keeping with the reasons you chose a technology-based solution in the first place. Some guidelines:

- **Computers:** If enough computers aren't available to support the individual format you wanted, consider organizing the integration plan around student pairs or small groups. Also consider having computer and non-computer learning stations that individuals or groups cycle through, completing various activities at each one. However, if students must master skills on an individual basis, consider scheduling time in a computer lab when all students in the class can use resources at once.
- **Copies of software and media:** Unless a software or media package specifically allows it, making copies of published software or media is illegal, even if copies are used on a temporary basis. Inquire about education-priced lab packs and site licenses.
- **Access to peripherals:** In addition to computers, remember to plan for adequate access to printers, printer paper, and any other needed peripherals (e.g., probes, handhelds).
- **Handouts and other materials:** Prepare and copy any necessary support materials. Unless learning to use the software without guidance is a goal of the project, consider creating summary sheets to remind students how to do basic operations.

2. **How should resources be arranged to support instruction and learning?**

- **Access by students with disabilities:** For students with visual or hearing deficits, consider software or adaptive devices created especially to address these disabilities.
- **Privacy and safety issues:** Students should never use the Internet without adult supervision and should never do unplanned chat sessions. If possible, firewall software should be used to prevent accidental access to inappropriate sites.

3. **What planning is required to make sure technology resources work well?**

- **Troubleshooting:** Computers, like all machines, will occasionally break down. Learn simple diagnostic procedures so you can correct some problems without assistance.
- **Test-runs and backup plans:** Leave sufficient time to learn and practice using resources before students use them, but also try out the resources again just before class begins. Have a backup plan in case something goes wrong at the last minute.

The problem-based exercises in this chapter give you hands-on practice in applying Phase 4 of the TIP Model concepts you read in Chapter 1. Through scenario-based problem situations, you see how teachers go about arranging classroom and other resources to support technology-based methods.

Scenarios to Read and Analyze – The following scenarios are continuations of the ones begun in Chapter 2. Answer the questions using information you have read about Phase 4 of the TIP Model in the Introduction to this chapter and in Chapter 1:

Scenario 1, Phase 4 – As soon as she realized her students would be able to participate in the Internet project, Mia began to get organized. First, she made a timeline of project activities, so she would know when her students needed to use computers. She made sure to build in enough time to demonstrate the project site and get students used to using the browser and search engine. Then she began the following planning and preparation activities:

- **Handouts for students** – To make sure groups knew the tasks each member should do, she created handouts of timelines and what should be accomplished at each stage of the project. She also made a checklist of information students were to collect and made copies so students could check off what they had done as they went. She got a list of technical skills and tips on using search engines and browser from the project web site. To keep track of who was using these skills adequately, she created a matrix checklist of the skills with all students' names on it. She wanted everyone to know how she would grade work, so she made copies of the assessment instruments (rubric and technical skills checklist) and gave them to the students.

- **Computer schedule** – She had a classroom workstation consisting of five networked computers, each with Internet connection, so she set up a schedule for small groups to use the computers. She knew that some students would need to scan pictures, download image files from the digital camera, and process them for sending to their partner schools, so she scheduled some additional time in the computer lab for this work. She thought that students could also do other work in the library/media center after school, if they needed still more time.

S1.1 Later, Mia remembered an additional planning step: how students would do production work on their products. What planning would she have to do to make this possible?

S1.2 If Mia wanted to do a demonstration and display of the project web site to the whole class at one time, what resource would she have to arrange for to do this?

S1.3 Mia was concerned that students didn't reveal too much personal information about themselves to their partner schools. What guidelines should she give them about information exchanges to protect their privacy and security?

S1.4 If the network or Internet access were interrupted for a day, what could Mia have them do to make good use of their time during this delay?

Scenario 2, Phase 4 – After reading the software Teacher Manual (TM) and reflecting on the presentation he had heard at the conference, Leroy decided to take the TM's advice and resist the tendency to over-direct students. He knew he had to keep to a timeline in order to complete the project on schedule, but he also realized that the software designers were warning that too much structure would work against the purpose and design of the software. Keeping this in mind, he began his planning:

- **Software skills** – The software was quite rich with features, tools, and resources, which Leroy found fascinating. However, he realized the software was so complex, he couldn't be expert on everything in it. In fact, he knew that some of his students would probably become more expert than he in a very short time! However, he wanted to become as familiar with it as possible so he could answer students' initial questions, so he went through it carefully and took notes.

- **Handouts** – The TM gave a chart to help students keep track of each species' needs. Leroy prepared a group task sheet and inserted this and other helpful notes.

- **Lesson planning** – Leroy was such a veteran in his content area, he usually didn't work from a lesson plan. However, this project was so new and different from his usual methods, he felt he needed to make daily notes. He left space for items he would add as his class progressed, so he would be even more prepared next time.

- **Software copies** – He knew the software was available to teachers only from the university who developed it. It was free, but he had to sign an agreement that only his class would be using it. He completed the paperwork and obtained the software. He made sure each copy worked on the equipment they had available.

- **Computer scheduling** – The trickiest part would be scheduling time on computers in the computer lab, since he had only one computer in his room. He arranged with the lab coordinator to have the lab on the days he needed it. He also spoke with the principal, who agreed to give him an extra computer for his room.

S2.1 One of the tasks students did to collect information was to design and send out space probes, which the TM said was a fairly complex activity. Why didn't Leroy create a directions sheet for them on how to do such a complex task?

S2.2 Why didn't Leroy feel he needed to know more than his students about all facets of the software?

S2.3 What should Leroy tell students who might want a copy of the software?

S2.4 Later, Leroy remembered he needed to do something to prepare for assessment at the end of the unit. Look back at Phase 3. What will he need to prepare?

Phase 4 Problems to Analyze and Solve

P.1. Bill wants to use a commercial math software package to help his students practice solving real-life problems that require setting up algebra equations. He has a five-station license for the package. Students are at many levels with algebra skills; some are quite good at this kind of problem; others need a lot of time to figure out each one. He has 30 students in his class; however, he has only a three-computer workstation in his room.

P1.1 Another math teacher advises him to make enough copies for the computer lab and have his students use it there. Is this a good idea? Why or why not?
P1.2 Yet another math teacher advises him to have a three-team competition, where each team of 10 students does a "relay race" and tries to get the most problems correct in a class period. Is this a good idea? Why or why not?
P1.3 Can you think of any other creative approaches Bill might use to have all his students use the software there in his classroom, rather than the lab?

P.2. Aubrey plans to use a science simulation software package to have his students gain experience with setting and testing complex hypotheses. He saw the software demonstrated at a workshop and ordered a copy. He plans to demonstrate it on his classroom computer and have the class work on the problems as a whole group. His class begins on September 10, and the software is due to arrive September 7.

P2.1 Do you see any problem with how Aubrey plans to use the software in his classroom?
P2.2 Can you think of another way to use it that might be more effective?
P2.3 What essential planning steps is Aubrey probably neglecting in this time frame?

P.3. One of Leroy's (in Scenario 2) colleagues sees the science software and is very intrigued. He would like to use the software in his own classroom. He plans to use only one copy of the software on his classroom computer and says he will have students view the demo and solve the problems as a whole class.

P3.1 In light of what you read in Scenario 2, would it be okay for Leroy to give him one copy? Why or why not?
P3.2 If you were Leroy, what would be the best way you could help your colleague?
P3.3 In light of what you read about the software designer's intent, do you think his colleague has a good plan for using the software? Why or why not?

P.4. Sally is a language arts teacher who wants her students to word-process the poems they are writing for her poetry unit. She has three computers in her classroom. However, the principal wants to control use of paper in the school, so Sally has no classroom printer. She plans to have her students do a written draft of the poems at home, then come in and enter them into the computers. Then Sally will transfer the poems to disk, take them to the computer lab and print them out, and bring the copies back for students to work on further.

P4.1 Is Sally's plan a feasible one? Why or why not?
P4.2 Can you think of another way to plan for printing when she has no printer in the room?
P4.3 Do you think it is a good idea to have students do written drafts first before they do them on word processing? Why or why not?

P.5. Esmerelda is having her students do a social studies project where they do "virtual interviews" of experts on various periods in U.S. history. She schedules time in the computer lab and has them locate experts by searching Internet sites. She gives them an initial list of sites, but encourages them to branch out from there, looking for additional sites on their own. There is no lab manager and she has to go back to the classroom for periods of time as they work, but she knows they are competent Internet users and can be trusted not to leave the lab without permission. For their contacts with experts, she has them prepare a standard e-mail with the school name; their names, ages, addresses, and personal e-mail address, if they have one; and a description of what they would like to know.

P5.1 Assuming she is correct that students will not leave the lab with permission, is Esmeralda's plan for having students use the Internet a good one? Why or why not?
P5.2 Do you see any problems with the e-mail she is having them send?
P5.3 How would you change her plan to improve it?

Chapter 6

Problem-based Exercises on Phase 5 of the TIP Model: *Evaluating and Revising Integration Strategies*

Introduction to Phase 5 Concepts

As teachers complete a technology-based project with students, they begin reviewing evidence on how successful the strategies and plans were in solving the problem they identified. They use this information to decide what should be changed in objectives, strategies, and implementation tasks to assure even more success next time.

Evaluation issues. In Phase 5, teachers look at the following kinds of issues:

- **Were objectives achieved?** This is the primary criterion of success for the activity. Teachers review achievement, attitude, and observation data they have collected and decide if the technology-based method solved the problem(s) they had in mind. These data help them determine what should be changed to make the activity work better.

- **What do students say?** Some of the best suggestions on needed improvements come from students. Informal discussions with them yield a unique "consumer" focus on the activity.

- **Could improving instructional strategies improve results?** Technologies in themselves usually improve little; it is the way teachers use them that is critical. Look at the design of both the technology use and the learning activities surrounding it.

- **Could improving the environment improve results?** Sometimes a small change such as better scheduling or access to a printer can make a big difference in the success of the project.

- **Have I integrated technology well?** Use the Technology Impact Checklist (see Chapter 1, page 6 of this booklet) to determine if the activity has been "worth it."

Phase 5 questions. This phase in integrating technology requires answering two summary questions about evaluating and revising technology integration strategies. These questions are listed on the next page with suggestions for answering them in actual classroom situations:

1. **How well has the technology integration strategy worked?** To answer this question, review the collected data and use the checklist on page 6 of this booklet.

- **Achievement data:** If the problem was low student achievement, do data show students are achieving better than they were before? If the goal was improved motivation or attitudes, are they achieving at least as well as they did before? Is higher achievement consistent across the class, or did some students seem to profit more than others?

- **Attitude data:** If the problem was low motivation or students refusing to do required work, are there indications this behavior has improved? Has it improved for everyone or just for certain students?

- **Student comments:** Be sure to ask both lower-achieving and higher-achieving students for their opinions. Even if achievement and motivation seem to be improved, what do students say about how the activity went? Would they like to do similar activities again?

2. **What could be improved to make it work better?** Remember that the first time you do a technology-based activity, you can expect it will take longer and you will encounter more errors than in subsequent uses. The following areas are most often cited as needing improvement:

- **Scheduling:** If students request any change, it is usually for more time. This may or may not be feasible, but you can review the schedule to determine if additional time can be built in for learning software and/or for production work.

- **Technical skills:** It usually takes longer than expected for students to learn the new technology tools. How can this learning be expedited or supported better?

- **Efficiency:** The teacher complaint is usually that the activity took longer than expected to plan and carry out. Review the schedule to see if there is there any way this can be expedited.

The problem-based exercises in this chapter give you hands-on practice in applying Phase 5 of the TIP Model concepts you read in Chapter 1. Through scenario-based problem situations, you see how teachers go about evaluating and revising their technology integration strategy to maximize success and impact.

Scenarios to Read and Analyze – The following scenarios are continuations of the ones begun in Chapter 2. Answer the questions using information you have read about Phase 5 of the TIP Model in the Introduction to this chapter and in Chapter 1:

Scenario 1, Phase 5 – Mia and Lars were discussing her Internet-based multicultural project. "What do you think, Mia, was it worth all the work?" said Lars.

"Lars, just look at these pre-post data on the semantic differential," Mia said, clearly pleased with the results. "Nearly every student showed a major improvement in how they felt about people from the countries we were studying. It's hard to believe how much the e-mails and products affected how they look at other cultures. You've seen some of their products. I can't remember my students being so excited about something they've produced. Some booklets are more polished-looking than others, but they all show such insights and have such a wealth of information. Even I learned something from them. The web searches they did made a big difference."

Lars was impressed by the products, but still doubtful. "Yes, I can see these represent some real effort, and I'll admit I'm surprised by the quality, but how about what YOU had to do? Didn't it take a long time to get them up to speed on the technical skills? I remember you had some problems there?"

"Yes," admitted Mia, "It was touch-and-go there for awhile in the second week. When I talked to students about it, they told me what confused them and gave me some ideas on how I could do it better next time. You know my students; they aren't shy about telling me how I SHOULD have done it!

"One thing that became clear quickly," Mia continued, "was that production work is so time-consuming. I'm going to have to change the schedule somehow. I also have to make sure they know the deadlines are firm. They'd search and take digital photos forever, if I let them, and never get to do their products. We spent so much time on that, we didn't really have time to discuss their findings on comparisons of cultures."

"Well, I admit this captures my interest," said Lars. "But I can't help but wonder if their results would have been as good with just the e-mail exchanges and no time-consuming production work."

"Hmm, good question," said Mia.

S1.1 Although all Mia's groups did well on content overall, rubric scores revealed that most groups scored lower on one area: comparisons of cultural similarities and differences. What step could Mia add that may improve this outcome next time?

S1.2 Can you suggest a way of collecting data next time to answer Lars' question?

S1.3 If you found that only five of the seven groups were doing well on their final products, what might be one way to find out more about why this was happening?

S1.4 One teacher who observed the project told Mia it might be good to have the school district media/materials production office do the final work on the products for the students. Does this seem like a good idea? Why or why not?

Scenario 2, Phase 5 – Leroy was telling Arvella how his "aliens project" went. "I think I've created a monster," said Leroy, smiling, "but in a good way. My students are rabid to do more projects like this one. It became like a culture, with experts on various planets and even probe design specialists. And have you heard about the 'Alien Rescue Club' they've started?"

"Yes," said Arvella, grinning, "I've certainly heard about this project from other teachers. But what everyone wants to know is: did it improve their science skills?"

"I would have expected that this much excitement about a science activity had to have an impact on their inquiry skills, and I wasn't wrong," said Leroy. "They seemed to do better with each probe they designed and each set of data they got to analyze. Perhaps best of all, they started talking like scientists. Since the end of the project, nearly all of the students are using what I call 'inquiry-speak' when they do other work. I've even had some girls asking about careers in space exploration. I sent them to look at the NASA sites and the Space Camp sites on the Internet.

"Their problem solving checklists reflected good progress, too," Leroy continued. "Scores on the first ones they did were a little low, but the last ones were really fine in all groups. I only had two real problems. One was when some group members had to leave for special school events. That left a 'hole' in the group, and we had to improvise. Several students had to miss the last two days of the project for the band trip. The other problem was with getting access to computers. It would really have helped to have more computers right there in the room. I wish I had a five-computer workstation and printer like Amelia, the English teacher. That would make a big difference."

"How about their scores on the solar system test?" asked Arvella. "Were they better or worse, would you say?"

"That varied a lot," Leroy acknowledged. "I'm still trying to figure out why some students did so much better than others. Still, their attitudes toward science seem way up, and they are more on task than I've ever seen them. I think it was worth the 'controlled chaos' it created! Sometimes I felt like they were in charge of the classroom, and I was just a helpful assistant. It was a new feeling."

"Interesting," mused Arvella. "Maybe you should be 'just' a helpful assistant to them. Maybe that's the way it should be. What do you think?"

S2.1 Why do you think some of the students didn't do as well on the solar system test? Was there anything happening that could have affected their learning?

S2.2 Can you think of a way to improve results on the test for next time?

S2.3 How would you respond to Arvella's query? Is it okay for a teacher to be "just an assistant" in the classroom?

Phase 5 Problems to Analyze and Solve

P.1. Frank had his students do a one-week project using census data from the U. S. Census Bureau's GIS web site to answer questions about characteristics of their local area and do comparisons of growth patterns in various parts of the city. He wanted them to get a more active, hands-on role in exploring how population relates to civic issues. He had assigned four groups of eight students each, with each student in charge of a different part of the product. When he analyzed data from the project, he was encouraged with their progress over the concepts. He found that three of the four groups met criteria on their product. However, he overheard one of his students say they never wanted to do a project like this again.

P1.1 Would you say Frank's project was a success? Why or why not?
P1.2 How could he find out more about what the students did and didn't like about the project?
P1.3 Can you suggest any changes to the time frame and grouping strategies that may help him achieve better results?

P.2. From another language arts teacher, Verna heard about using *Inspiration*™ software to have students do concept maps before writing compositions. She always had trouble getting her lower-achieving sixth graders to create outlines before they started writing, and she thought doing concept maps might help. She showed them how to use the software and let them experiment with copying an example she had created. Then they did one of their own to prepare for a writing assignment. When she looked at what they had produced, most seemed to have thought through the ideas and were ready to do a well-structured composition. When she asked three of her better students how they liked the software, they expressed great delight with it and told her they wanted to use it again.

P2.1 Would you say Verna's technology use was a success? Why or why not?
P2.2 What performance data should she look at carefully to help her decide how successful it had been in addressing the problem?
P2.3 Is the interview data she gathered sufficient to get an accurate reading on how students liked the activity? Why or why not? What else might she do?

P.3. Geraldo wanted his students to do a project with multimedia software that would foster "habits of mind" such as solving problems and group cooperation in science learning, as well as improve their communication and writing skills. In week 1, he divided them into groups of three and had them use the Internet to locate a biome and answer questions about its characteristics. In week 2, he introduced a new multimedia software package to them and had them prepare presentations of their findings. By week 3 they were doing compositions to analyze and compare their findings across groups using a set of guidelines Geraldo gave them. However, they took a lot longer with their multimedia projects, and had only two days to complete their written compositions. Composition grades were very poor, and only three of the seven groups met criteria on the multimedia rubrics.

P3.1 Do Geraldo's findings indicate he should abandon this project or modify it? Explain.
P3.2 Why do you think they did so poorly on the multimedia projects?
P3.3 What change in his planning might improve the composition results?

P.4. Wilfred was a special education resource teacher who wanted to give students with dysgraphia (non-writing behavior) an alternative way to do homework and class assignments. He showed a couple of the students how to use a small portable "computer companion" with a keyboard and word processing program. They did their work wherever they were and downloaded it to a computer later and printed it out. Students quickly learned how to do the activity and were delighted with their new ability. For the first time, they turned in all assignments on time. However, on a brief survey he gave to the special education teachers, four of the five teachers indicated they would not use it for their own students with dysgraphia.

P4.1 Would you say findings indicate the project was a success? Why or why not?
P4.2 What should he do to find out why teachers responded in this way?
P4.3 What other data or information could he gather about the quality of students' written assignments that could help him decide how to improve the strategy?

P.5. Ivana had her tenth-grade health students use a nutrition simulation program to track their eating habits and weight gains/losses over the term. They worked in small groups to discuss, compare, and contrast data and write summary recommendations for each person on how to improve eating habits and weight. Data on the test and rubric showed that students' grasp of the subject was higher than ever before. However, data from the attitude survey showed that most girls disliked the work they did.

P5.1 Would you say findings indicate the project was a success? Why or why not?
P5.2 Why do you think the female students may have disliked this project?
P5.3 What could be changed to make the activity more successful?

PART I REVIEW EXERCISES
Introducing the Technology Integration Planning Model

Do **Exercises 1-5** on the Companion Website at: http://www.prenhall.com/roblyer. Click on the link for *Educational Technology in Action* Review Exercises, and use the links in each of the following sections to answer the review questions. Do **Exercise 6** by loading the Tutorials CD and using the files in the Part I Review Exercises Folder.

Exercise 1. Determining Relative Advantage

Teachers choose technology-based methods over other methods when they see the "relative advantage," i.e., the new method offers enough benefits to convince them to use it instead of the old one. Relative advantage is a perception or belief shaped by teachers' experience and by information they receive. One way teachers learn that a technology-based method has relative advantage is through reading research results. The Center for Applied Research in Educational Technology (CARET), a project of the International Society for Technology in Education (ISTE), summarizes "best evidence" research results on the impact of technology in education. Look at the results for the Student Learning area.

I.1 What are five questions CARET says teachers can ask to determine if technology-based methods have impact on student learning?

I.2 Describe two studies at the CARET web site that offer convincing evidence that a technology-based method has more impact on student learning than another method.

Exercise 2. Deciding on Objectives and Assessments

How should teachers decide on specific outcome objectives they want students to achieve? Most teachers look to more general outcome statements provided by state and/or district curriculum standards to help them derive specific student outcomes. Another source of curriculum outcomes is *Standards for Success*, a document created by the Association of American Universities (AAUU) to list competencies students should have before they enter college. When teachers need tools to assess curriculum outcomes, Kathy Schrock's Guide for Educators offers a variety of instruments teachers can use or modify.

I.3 Review the *Standards for Success* document and click on Standards for one of the content areas. Create an outcome statement based on one of these standards that you feel technology could help students achieve.

I.4 To assess the outcome, select an assessment instrument from Kathy Schrock's Guide for Educators web site. Modify it to match the outcome, if necessary.

Exercise 3. Designing Integration Strategies

Many excellent models of directed, constructivist, and combination strategies are available at the Blue Web 'N web site, a collection of links to outstanding online lessons.

I.5 Most "Web-based Tutorials" at the Blue Web 'N site use a directed approach. Select a tutorial under one of the content areas and state outcomes it is designed to achieve.
I.6 Most of the "Activities" at the Blue Web 'N site are based on constructivist approaches. Select one for a content area and state outcomes it is designed to achieve.

Exercise 4. Preparing the Instructional Environment

As teachers set up their classrooms for integrating technology, they must be aware of laws and regulations related to software and media. The Software and Information Industry Association (SIIA) has several summaries that can help answers teachers' questions about whether or not a planned use of software or media is legal under current rules. Also, teachers must be aware of district and/or school Internet usage policies (Acceptable Internet Use Policy or AUP) described in Warlick's article on the Education World site.

I.7 Read the SIIA's "*Is it OK for Schools to Copy Software?*" and answer this question: A science teacher has purchased a single copy of a simulation software package for the math/science department. She and the math teacher want to use it for an interdisciplinary project. She makes him a copy so that both will have it in their classrooms. Why is this permitted or not permitted under copyright law?
I.8 According to Warlick's article, what four things must every AUP contain? Why?

Exercise 5. Evaluating and Revising Instructional Strategies

Teachers can collect information in addition to achievement data to evaluate the impact of a technology-based integration strategy. Look at ideas for getting student feedback on this page at the Indiana University web site. Learn about attitude instruments or interviews you can design to assess the success of your integration strategy. Look at the Fermiab Education Office for an example classroom observation instrument and rubric.

I.9 Look at the *Technology Impact Checklist* on page 6 of this booklet. Create a Likert scale for this checklist with points for each "degree of agreement." Decide on a total score that would convince you that your technology-based strategy was successful.
I.10 Create 3-5 questions for a structured interview with your students to determine what aspects of your strategy need to be revised in order to improve them.

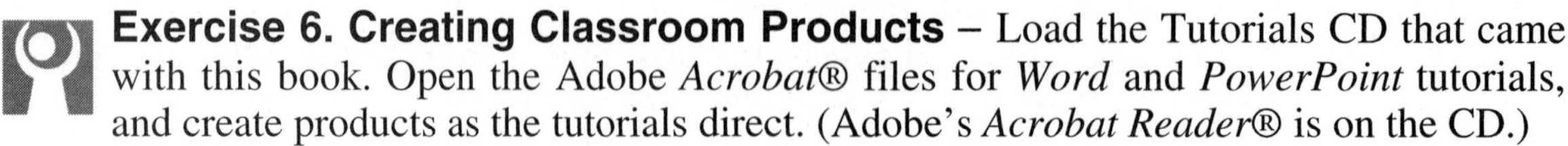

Exercise 6. Creating Classroom Products – Load the Tutorials CD that came with this book. Open the Adobe *Acrobat*® files for *Word* and *PowerPoint* tutorials, and create products as the tutorials direct. (Adobe's *Acrobat Reader*® is on the CD.)

Part II:
Using the TIP Model to Integrate Technology Resources

Chapter 7

Problem-based Exercises on Using the TIP Model for Instructional Software Integration

Introduction to Instructional Software Integration

Instructional software materials are programs created for the sole purpose of assisting teaching and learning in one of two ways: (1) delivering instruction using directed methods or (2) supporting learning using inquiry-based methods. Few software packages can be classified as a single category (e.g., a "tutorial package"). Each contains one or more of the following five software functions that help deliver or support instruction:

- **Drill and practice** – Presents items, prompts responses, gives feedback when students need multiple opportunities to work problems or practice for the purpose of committing information to memory. (Supports directed methods only)
- **Tutorial** – Acts like a human tutor by providing all information, guidance, and practice a student needs in order to learn a topic. (Supports directed methods only)
- **Simulation** – Models real or imaginary systems (e.g., genetic experiments, the government for a new fictional country) in order to help students learn the principles underlying the systems. (Supports directed or constructivist methods)
- **Instructional game** – Provides a drill or simulation with game-based rules and challenges. (Supports directed or constructivist methods)
- **Problem solving** – Either (1) teaches directly (through explanation and/or practice) the general approaches and steps involved in solving problems, or (2) helps students learn to solve problems in a given content area. (Supports directed or constructivist methods)

The following chart gives a brief summary of the instructional benefits and classroom applications of each of these five basic instructional software functions.

Instructional Software	Sample Instructional Benefits	Sample Classroom Uses
Drill and practice	• Gives immediate feedback on correctness of answers • Increases motivation for students to practice • Saves teacher time on grading student work	• Supplement or replace assigned worksheets and homework • Prepare students for tests

Instructional Software	Sample Instructional Benefits	Sample Classroom Uses
Tutorial	• Supplements or replaces teacher presentations • Presents instruction in more visual, self-paced, motivating way than teacher-delivered presentations	• Provides self-paced review of a topic after students have received classroom instruction • Supplies alternative way of learning when usual strategies do not work • Supplies instruction on topics for which teachers are not available
Simulation	• Compresses time or slows down processes so they can be studied • Makes demonstrations interactive • Allows safe experimentation • Allows simulated experiences that are not possible in real life • Saves money on consumable resources • Allows experiments to be repeated with variations • Makes situations controllable so they can be studied	• Replaces or supplements lab experiments, role playing, and field trips • Introduces new topics • Fosters exploration and process learning • Provides format that encourages cooperative group work
Instructional games	• Provides highly motivating format for practice	• Replaces worksheets and exercises • Provides format that encourages cooperative group work • Rewards good work
Problem solving	• Directed benefits: Focuses attention on required problem solving skills • Constructivist: Allows self-discovery of principles	• Allows concentrated practice of key problem solving skills • Fosters exploration and process learning • Provides format that encourages cooperative group work

Problem-based exercises in this chapter give you hands-on practice in matching software functions to instructional needs and integrating software into instructional environments. Through scenario-based problem situations, you can see how teachers go about selecting and using instructional software.

Scenarios to Read and Analyze – The following scenarios are examples of integrating instructional software. After reading Chapter 4 in *Integrating Educational Technology into Teaching* (2003), answer the questions about using the TIP Model to integrate these strategies effectively:

Scenario 1, Software – Based on a lesson idea in: "Breeding Mice the Easy Way" by Randy Bell, Emily Yam, and Lynn Bell. *Learning and Leading with Technology,* 2003, Vol. 30, Number 7, pp. 22-27.

Elton, a high school biology teacher, was talking with Qing, a colleague from another school. "Do you ever get frustrated when you teach your kids Mengelian genetics principles?" asked Elton. "It's such exciting stuff to me, yet I can't get them interested. I guess there's just such a disconnect between the actual breeding results that display principles and how I can show it to them. Most of them just don't get it."

"Actually, I have been using something pretty exciting," said Qing. "There is a software I heard about at a workshop last fall and had a chance to play with after the demo. It has an excellent tutorial sequence in the introduction and a simulation that lets students do hands-on experiments to explore dominant and recessive traits. It's called *Mouse Genetics*, and it's available online at http://www.explorescience.com".

"Really?" said Elton. "How do you use it in your classroom?"

"I start off with a whole-class discussion, asking them how they think dog and cat breeders get the physical features they want. Then we go through the tutorial with a big-screen monitor on my classroom computer; the kids really get involved because the presentation is so interactive and visual. I just have to keep my better students from shouting out all the answers. Then I break them into groups and pose a simple question about offspring they expect in a certain situation. They go into the "Virtual Mouse House" and do the simulation to answer the question. It takes off from there. They get good experience creating explanations for unexpected results, and that leads naturally into deriving Mendel's Laws. For a final project, I have each group do a *PowerPoint* presentation of a law with examples. It's pretty neat."

"I'll say!" said Elton enthusiastically. "Can I use your handouts, do you think?"

S1.1 What problem did these biology teachers have and in what ways did the software provide a good solution? What is the relative advantage of the new method?

S1.2 Is the method Qing describes directed, inquiry-based, or a combination? Explain.

S1.3 How can Qing structure the demo activity to keep his better students from dominating it and keep the other students from participating? How would it change the activity if Elton has only one computer in his class?

S1.4 What outcomes would Elton and Qing want to assess? What measures could they use to assess them?

Scenario 2, Software –Based on a lesson idea in: "Do you think you might be wrong? Confirmation bias in problem solving" by J. Johnson. *Arithmetic Teacher*, 1987, Vol. 34, No. 9, pp. 13-16.

"Middle school students think they know everything, don't they?" Farley, the eighth-grade math teacher remarked to his colleague Vidalia. "I think that could be one of culprits responsible for their high error rate on math word problems in some of the standardized tests. They jump to conclusions and don't bother to test them out once they think they've got the answer. I wish I could get them to stop that behavior."

"I agree completely," said Vidalia, "and I have a software package that I use to help them see that very problem and use a systematic approach to getting correct answers. It's called *King's Rule*®, and it lets them generate and test hypotheses in math. It has a 'Hidden Rules Game' my students just love; I think it changes how they look at solving problems."

"Wow!" Farley exclaimed. "How does it work?"

"Let's say the software presents the number sequence 16-18-20. I ask the students to give me the rule and another example of it. Invariably, my class smart-aleck will say 'Oh, that's stupid. It's just counting by two's!' I say 'Okay, let's put in an example, and they say something like '4-6-8.' It's correct, of course, but it's not the right answer. I say, 'Does anyone else have another idea?' They know something's up and, with a little coaching, I get them to try something like 4-8-12, and it says it's correct. That flabbergasts them; it also draws them in. They start proposing alternatives like 'ascending numbers,' so I ask 'How would you eliminate that rule?'"

"After the demo," continued Vidalia, "They are rabid to use the software. But first I give them a set of rules THEY have to abide by as they work in small groups: (1) First, list all rules that could apply. (2) Test each one by coming up with a way to eliminate it. (3) State the rule on a paper handout I give them. I tell them they have to start with the 'Easy' level and proceed to harder ones, and also that they have to give everyone a turn and leave out no one in the group."

"Wow, this is great!" said Farley. "Do you have a way of testing how well they can do this and whether this ability actually transfers to word problems?"

"The software has a built-in quiz they can take, said Vidalia nodding, "Then I give them a paper quiz. I haven't really checked for transfer yet. Any suggestions?"

S2.1 What problems did the teachers have? How did software provide good solutions? What software functions are used? (NOTE: Names aren't always accurate!)

S2.2 How could Farley find out if students' skills transferred to other math problems?

S2.3 If the teachers needed more than one copy of the software for the small-group work, what would they need to do to provide this?

S2.4 When Farley tried the activity, he found that 24 of his 30 students could pass the quiz. What could he do to find out why some students still had problems?

Instructional Software Integration Problems to Analyze and Solve

P.1. Andie uses a program called *Spelling Bee* to give her students practice before a spelling test or the language arts part of a standardized test. She knows the secret to her students' doing well in spelling is getting them to spend time on thinking about the words; she finds she can get them to spend more time with helpful practicing than she would with any paper-pencil exercise or other format. The software presents words via audio prompt and lets students enter correct spellings. They get points for every correct answer. If they play alone and attain a score they are shooting for, they win the spelling bee. They can also compete against each other in pairs.

P1.1 What software function is Andie using? What did it offer that made it a good match for the problem?
P1.2 If Andie wanted to have students practice in pairs to compete against each other, how would she have to do this to make sure some students wouldn't become too frustrated by losing all the time?
P1.3 Since the software gives audio prompts and feedback, what would Andie have to do if she wanted to use this effectively in a classroom of 30 students?

P.2. Sydney's students were not interested in learning about the U. S. Constitution. She wants to show them it is a document that affects their lives every day and in many situations they or people they know might encounter. Rather than just telling them about it, she found a software package that lets them practice applying it. They role-play various people faced with creating articles of confederation that would let them deal effectively with issues such as: threats to their borders, needs for currency, trade disputes, internal disagreements about key issues, and separate rights for states vs. central power. As they work in groups on various problems, they come to understand why laws are necessary and how they affect our lives. As a final activity, each group presents an article of confederation and illustrates how it works in practice.

P2.1 What software function is Sydney using? What did it offer that made it a good match for the problem?
P2.2 What outcomes would you want to assess after this activity? How would you state these outcomes?
P2.3 How would you measure students' progress on these outcomes?

P.3. In her Spanish I class, Sharon is having her students write an e-mail newsletter describing in Spanish their school and events in their community to students in a Puerto Rico classroom. She finds that her students' Spanish vocabulary is very limited, and she wants to give them practice in using Spanish equivalents for many English words. She locates a software package that provides vocabulary practice by presenting words in English or Spanish to which they must supply equivalents in the opposite language. If they supply the correct word, the program pronounces both words. The Teacher Manual gives a list of all the words.

P3.1 What kind of software function does this software provide and why does Sharon think the students need it?
P3.2 Would it be best for students to use this package individually, in small groups, or as a whole class?
P3.3 How would you assess whether this program was helping students learn enough vocabulary?

P.4. Carson finds that students in his honors algebra class can solve algebra equations, but they can't identify situations in everyday life that require them to set up and solve a simple equation. He finds a software package that has "virtual stores" in which students must solve various problems in order to "buy" items. They must use algebra equations to solve these problems. Carson has his students work in small groups to practice solving the problems and stating strategies they used.

P4.1 What kind of software function does this software provide and why does Carson think the students need it?
P4.2 What outcomes should Carson expect and how should he state them?
P4.3 What would be the best ways to assess these outcomes?

P.5. Wanda's science class is an academically diverse group, with some students learning concepts very quickly and others needing much more time to review and work on them. She has found a software series that provides a complete teaching sequence (instruction, practice items, testing) on each topic in the middle school physical sciences. Some students use it for review of topics they find particularly difficult. Others use it to "catch up" when they have been absent. However, the faster students also use it to jump ahead and learn advanced topics on their own.

P5.1 What kind of software function does this software provide and what problem does Wanda have that it addresses?
P5.2 Would one copy of the software meet Wanda's needs? Why or why not?
P5.3 How could Wanda find out if most students like using the software?

Chapter 8

Problem-based Exercises on Using the TIP Model for Software Tool Integration

Introduction to Software Tool Integration

Software tools are programs created for the purpose of helping people accomplish various tasks. For example, word processing software helps people produce and format typed text, and graphics software tools help them produce and format images. Most software tools were originally designed for use in the workplace, rather than the school. Though most were not created specifically for education, they have become useful resources for teachers and students because each supplies one or more of these benefits:

- **Makes work more efficient** – Most software tools make it easier and faster to create written or digital products and to revise and update them once they are created. Using these tools can motivate students to do activities they would not otherwise attempt.
- **Improves appearance of products** – By using software tools, teachers and students no longer need to rely on expensive professionals to produce polished-looking products such as newsletters or certificates. Users of software tools are limited only by their own creativity and design skills.
- **Improves information accuracy** – Some software tools make it easier to do calculations and keep more accurate records. They also make it easier to spot and correct content errors.
- **Supports interaction and sharing** – Since software tools can do the manual labor involved in creating products and can support research and information-gathering, they make it easier for groups to work together on projects. Also, putting products in a digital format makes it easier to share them on a disk or via e-mail.

The following chart gives a brief summary of the instructional software tools and sample classroom applications of each. Read more about these tools and their uses in Chapters 5-6 of *Integrating Educational Technology into Teaching* (Roblyer, 2003).

Sample Software Tools	Sample Classroom Uses
Word processing	Teacher letters, flyers, and other documents; student writing processes; dynamic group products; language exercises
Spreadsheets	Demonstrations of math principles; student tables and charts; support for math problem solving; asking "what if?" questions; data storage and analysis; projecting grades

Databases	Teacher resource inventories; personalized letters; ready access to student information; support for teaching research and study skills, organization skills, posing and testing hypotheses, searching for information during research
Desktop publishing software	Working individually or in small groups, students create their own letterhead, brochures, flyers/posters, newsletters, books
Test generators/test item banks	Teachers can create test item banks and generate various versions of tests from them. Can administer tests online.
Worksheet /puzzle generators	Teachers produce exercises for student skill practice
IEP generators	Teachers create Individual Educational Plans (IEP's) for special education students
Certificate makers	Teachers and students create awards and recognitions
Form makers	Teachers create forms to gather data from students, others
Gradebooks	Teachers keep track of and calculate students grades
Statistical packages	Teachers and students analyze data from experiments and research projects
CMI and testing tools	Teachers keep track of student and class progress on required curriculum objectives; use data to support decision-making
Image processing tools	Teachers and students use to illustrate documents, web pages
Charting/graphing tools	Students use to create charts and graphs to illustrate and study data summaries
Clip art, video, and sound collections	Teachers and students insert these into documents and media they create
Video development tools	Teachers can create video demonstrations; students create videos to illustrate principles they have learned
Outliners	Help students organize their ideas to prepare for writing
Concept mapping software	Students use these to help organize their ideas visually in preparation for writing and to show how sub-concepts that make up a topic area are related to each other
Scheduling software	Helps teachers organize their time and plan activities
Electronic encyclopedias, atlases, and dictionaries	Help students research topics they have been assigned
CAD systems	Helps students create visual models of houses and other structures as they study design concepts
Music editors	Help students create and revise their own musical pieces
MBLs/CBLs	Help students collect and analyze data from experiments
GPS and GIS systems	Help students study geographical information and concepts

Problem-based exercises in this chapter give you hands-on practice in matching software functions to instructional needs and integrating software into instructional environments. Through scenario-based problem situations, you can see how teachers go about selecting and using software tools.

Scenarios to Read and Analyze – The following scenarios are examples of integrating software tools into curriculum lessons. After reading Chapters 5-6 in *Integrating Educational Technology into Teaching* (Roblyer, 2003), answer the questions about using the TIP Model to integrate these strategies effectively:

Scenario 1, Software Tools – Based on a lesson idea in: "Desktop Poetry Project" by Emily Scharf and Judith Cramer. *Learning and Leading with Technology,* 2002, Vol. 29, N0. 6, pp. 28-31, 50-51.

Mort and Chloe, two middle school language arts teachers, were talking in the teachers lounge. "You know what a pain it is to put together the annual eighth-grade literary magazine," said Chloe. "We spend all those hours and hours of typing and editing, then have to format it for the print shop to work with? Well, I think I've found a way to cut all the trouble in half and let ALL the students participate in the publication instead of just a selected few."

"This I've got to hear," said Mort. "I'm the one who usually gets the job of telling students they weren't selected for the magazine. It would be so much better if they all knew their work would appear. I think it would really motivate them to do their best in class."

"Yes, that's what I have been thinking," agreed Chloe. "If my plan works, I think it would keep every student's interest in the language arts class they take the semester before they graduate; you know, the one where they have to study all the poetry forms?"

"Okay, now I'm really interested," laughed Mort. "What is this strategy? Magic?"

Chloe smiled. "Sort of. I guess you could call it 'desktop publishing magic.' Our technology resource teacher, Fiona, and I came up with the idea of students creating an eighth-grade student poetry anthology. Every student would study the poetry forms and present their favorite ones in class, as they usually do. But then they begin work on their anthology contributions. If they all do their poems in Microsoft *Word*®, we can put the files on our school server, which would make them easy to download and work on. Then the students can help create style sheets in Adobe *PageMaker*® for each section of the anthology. By selecting typefaces and creating page designs, it will help them learn more about how poems often communicate meaning by the ways they appear on the page."

"This sounds so neat!" exclaimed Mort. "Count me in!"

"There's plenty to do," said Chloe, reaching for a pen. "Can I put you down for creating assessment strategies to evaluate and grade students' work?"

S1.1 What problems did these teachers have and in what ways did the software project provide a good solution? What is the relative advantage of doing the anthology?
S1.2 Is this project directed, inquiry-based, or a combination? Explain.
S1.3 How would you recommend arranging the desktop publishing software so that all 70 eighth-grade students could help with the design tasks??
S1.4 What outcomes need to be assessed? How would you recommend they be assessed?

Scenario 2, Software Tools – Based on a lesson idea in: "Geography is Everywhere: Connecting Schools and Communities with GIS" by Marsha Alibrandi. *Learning and Leading with Technology,* 2002, Vol. 29, No. 7, pp. 32-37.

"Why so glum, Keisha?" said Ernie, sitting down beside the social studies teacher in the lunchroom.

"I'm not really glum, Ernie," said Keisha. "I guess I'm just thinking about how I can do a project I want to do. You've heard about Global Information Systems, a.k.a, GIS, haven't you? In the workshop I went to last summer, they said GIS tools are going to become as essential to studying geography and local issues as word processing is to learning to write. I'd always like my students to learn the most up-to-date tools so I try to teach them to use what the professionals use in their workplaces. I know of some local GIS sources, but I'm trying to figure out a meaningful project they can do with GIS data."

"Maybe I can suggest something," said Ernie. "You know my class does the environmental studies project every fall in the Little River area. They collect water samples and do tests to analyze sources of degradation and contaminants. Then they try to determine the sources of these withdrawals and contaminants. It would be great to have GIS information to help students with these analyses."

"Wow, this could be so powerful!" said Keisha thoughtfully. "Maybe our classes could work together in the fall. I could teach my Current Social Issues class how to use the systems, and then they could help your students create a database of their findings linked to GIS data from the town planning office. I know they would help me out with this."

"How about if I could get our local school partner Allied Industries to donate some handheld Global Positioning Systems for my students to use as they collect data? Wouldn't that help identify the locations for our database?"

"Sure, that would be great!" said Keisha, nodding. "The two would work together well, and it would make it clearer to all the students how GIS data are used in the GPS's they see in their cars. This sounds like a winner to me!"

"It also sounds like a lot of work for us," said Ernie, grinning. "Most of my good ideas seem to mean more work for me. I guess we need to get started, huh?"

S2.1 What instructional problems did Keisha see that she wanted to address in a new project? In what ways were GIS's such a good solution to the problem(s)?

S2.2 What work was Ernie referring to that they would have to do? In which phase(s) of the TIP Model would this work occur?

S2.3 If you were purchasing the handheld GPS's for 35 students to use, how many would you request that the school's company partner donate?

S2.4 What outcomes would need to be assessed in each class (Current Issues and Environmental Science) and how would you recommend they be assessed?

Software Tool Integration Problems to Analyze and Solve

P.1. Gilbert wanted to demonstrate various principles of probability to his junior high advanced math students and then let them test hypotheses on data sets to show the principles in action. However, the exercises he had them do required a series of calculations on a set of numbers. It took the students a long time to do these calculations with a calculator because they had to keep re-entering the numbers and made a lot of entry errors. All the time spent on entering figures and correcting errors made it difficult for them to focus on the hypothesis testing.

P1.1 What software tool would you recommend Gilbert use to address this problem?
P1.2 What would be the relative advantage of using this software tool?
P1.3 Would it be better to have the students work individually or in groups to do the exercises? How would you arrange the computer systems to carry out this strategy?

P.2. Chinita was teaching her students higher-level study skills. She wanted to show them how they could outline a complicated article by drawing a diagram to illustrate the ideas in it and how they relate to each other. She found this visual display worked very well for her, and she wanted her students to learn it, too. However, she found the approach didn't work very well because students who were just learning this technique tended to make a lot of mistakes drawing the boxes and connecting lines, and then they didn't want to do the work of erasing and revising them.

P2.1 What software tool would you recommend Chinita use to address this problem?
P2.2 What would be the relative advantage of using this software tool?
P2.3 Would this kind of activity be best done on an individual basis, in pairs, or in groups? Explain why.

P.3. Whenever Jackie had her students do a research project for her social studies class, she would send them to the library/media center to look up the information in reference books. Since several students usually wanted to use the same text, there was a lot of wasted time; it was difficult to keep students focused on the information-gathering. Jackie had heard about a software tool that several students could use easily at the time same and had pictures and videos, as well as text descriptions, so students got more out of the information they did find.

P3.1 What software tool does Jackie have in mind to address this problem?
P3.2 What would be the relative advantage of using this software tool?
P3.3 How would it be possible for a class of 30 students to use this tool at the same time?

P.4. Hortense's Consumer Math classes have over 40 students each. She likes to give them weekly quizzes to make sure everyone is keeping up on the skills and spot students who may need additional help. However, the class is so large and students sit so close together, she also feels she needs several different versions of each test to prevent "sharing answers." She has heard about a software tool that she can use to create a pool of items and that lets her generate different versions of the same test from the items.

P4.1 What software tool would you recommend Hortense use to address this problem?
P4.2 What would be the relative advantage of using this software tool?
P4.3 If she wanted the versions to be very different from each other, what would she have to do to make this tool work well for her purposes?

P.5. Charlene wants to make her middle school classes hands-on, with students doing experiments by collecting and analyzing their own data. However, taking accurate readings of variables such as temperature is very difficult for her students to do. Also, the students find the repetitious recording and calculating very boring, and it is difficult to keep them focused on the experiment. She has heard about a software tool that can collect temperature readings quickly and feed the data automatically into a computer for analysis. She thinks that using this tool will be much more motivating to her students than doing all the operations by hand.

P5.1 What software tool would you recommend Charlene use to address this problem?
P5.2 What would be the relative advantage of using this software tool?
P5.3 If Charlene has 36 students in a class and only 5 such tools, how could she arrange the tool so that all students could learn to use it?

Chapter 9

Problem-based Exercises on Using the TIP Model for Multimedia/Hypermedia Integration

Introduction to Multimedia and Hypermedia Integration

Newspapers, radio, and television are media that allow various forms of communication in our society. Education, too, has its media to allow teachers and students to communicate information in various ways. Increasing use of multimedia/hypermedia tools in education reflects our growing cultural reliance on interactive modes of communication. Although books and other static text materials remain important information sources, students expect to experience pictures, video, animation, and sound in the classroom, just as they do outside it.

Many changes have taken place in the world of multimedia in recent years. Materials such as Microsoft *PowerPoint*® that were once just a sequence of text-and-image slides have gradually added sound, video, and other features. Also, many of today's most popular products developed with presentation or video software are now displayed on the Internet. It is for these reasons that the words "multimedia" (i.e., many media) and "hypermedia" (i.e., interconnected media) have come to be used interchangeably. (See multimedia tools to develop and display web pages for the Internet described in the next chapter.) The following are some of the benefits multimedia/hypermedia materials bring to education:

- **Variety of channels for communicating information** – Supplementing text-based information with pictures, video, and sound captures students' attention; using multiple channels makes it more likely they will understand and remember concepts.
- **Interactive qualities** – Multimedia materials that require student input and offer immediate feedback help keep them involved in the learning activity.
- **Flexibility for demonstrating learning** – In line with Gardner's Multiple Intelligences Theory, multimedia allow students more than one way to show what they have learned.
- **Support for practicing creativity, critical thinking, and information organization** – When students create their own multimedia products, they have opportunities to think creatively and critically about how best to communicate and organize information.
- **Support for cooperative group work** – Multimedia production also gives students a motivating format for learning skills required for working cooperatively in groups.

The following chart gives a brief summary of the types of multimedia/hypermedia sample classroom applications of each. Read more about these materials and their uses in Chapter 7 of *Integrating Educational Technology into Teaching* (Roblyer, 2003).

Types of Multimedia/Hypermedia	Sample Classroom Uses of Multimedia/Hypermedia
Commercial multimedia/hypermedia packages: Interactive instructional software	Use for the same classroom applications as instructional software (See Chapter 7 in this book.)
Interactive storybooks	Use to supplement or replace children's traditional book reading to promote reading comprehension and encourage critical thinking about story structure
Reference materials (electronic encyclopedias, atlases, dictionaries)	Support student research and information-gathering for individual and group reports and projects
Interactive videodisc systems	Although interactive CD and DVD formats have superceded videodisc ones, many schools still use videodiscs for demonstrations to introduce topics, illustrate concepts, and make learning more visual, especially in history and science topics.
Multimedia/hypermedia authoring systems: Presentation software (e.g., Microsoft *PowerPoint®*)	Use for teacher presentations and demonstrations; and student book reports, project reports, presentations, and personal portfolios
Video production/editing (e.g., *iMovie®, Adobe Premiere®*)	Use to teach visual communication methods and for student project presentations, newscasts, dramatizations, and video clips for a web page
Hypermedia software (e.g., *HyperStudio®,* and *Macromedia Director®*)	Use for teacher presentations and demonstrations; and student book reports, project reports, presentations, and personal portfolios

Problem-based exercises in this chapter give you hands-on practice in integrating multimedia/hypermedia uses into instructional environments. Through scenario-based problem situations, you can see how teachers go about using multimedia/hypermedia tools of various kinds to support and enhance learning.

Scenarios to Read and Analyze – The following scenarios are examples of integrating multimedia/hypermedia tools into curriculum lessons. After reading Chapter 7 in *Integrating Educational Technology into Teaching* (Roblyer, 2003), answer the questions about using the TIP Model to integrate these strategies effectively:

Scenario 1, Multimedia/Hypermedia – Based on a lesson idea in: "Reading and Writing the Digital Way: Using Digital Books to Teach Math" by Trena L. Wilkerson. *Learning and Leading with Technology,* 2001, Vol. 29, Number 3, pp. 42-45, 60-61.

Lavinia, the math resource teacher for the Premier Elementary School, was listening to Edwardo and Wilma, two of the school's second-grade teachers.

"You know," said Edwardo, "I'm really tired of seeing so many of my students mentally 'drop out' of my math lessons at such a young age. Math concepts are so relevant to their lives, not to mention their success in school; but as hard as I try, I can't get some of them in touch with the whole idea of thinking mathematically. They just don't get it."

"I feel the same way," agreed Wilma. "My students like manipulatives and games, but there is only so much you can do with them. I keep thinking we need to make our math strategies more exciting and engaging. Kids spend hours on those computer games, but we can't get them to focus for 30 minutes on math ideas."

"You know," said Lavinia, "I saw something at the math magnet school last week that might be the answer you're looking for. They use *PowerPoint®* and *HyperStudio®* to create what they called 'digital books' to illustrate math principles like whole-number operations, number sets, patterns, and geometric shapes. It didn't take teachers long to create them, and they seemed to have great fun at it. During class, they projected each book on a big screen so students could go up and touch things as the class discussed it; they even had an audio feature to read it aloud if students wanted to use it after the demonstration.

"After the lesson," continued Lavinia, "students got to create their own digital book pages to show what they learned, so it became an assessment activity. The teachers had a template set up, so it was easy for their students to insert clip art and draw lines to represent math ideas. The teachers say they have never seen kids so excited about doing math!"

"This sounds so neat," exclaimed Edwardo. "Can I visit the school and see how they do it?" "Me, too," said Wilma. "When do we start?"

S1.1 What problems did the teachers have for which Lavinia felt a digital book strategy provided a good solution? What is the relative advantage of doing such an activity?

S1.2 Is this project directed, inquiry-based, or a combination? Explain.

S1.3 What equipment and software would you need to obtain to carry out such lessons and how many of each would you need?

S1.4 How would you assess whether or not students' attitudes about math had changed as a result of this strategy?

Scenario 2, Multimedia/Hypermedia – Based on a lesson idea in: "Digital Video Goes to School" by Helen Hoffenberg and Marianne Handler. *Learning and Leading with Technology,* 2001, Vol. 29, No. 2, pp. 10-15.

The high school's faculty meeting was just breaking up and teachers were gathering their belongings and walking out, talking and laughing on their way down the hall. "Hey, Latifah," said Phil, the history teacher, walking up to the school principal, "Do you have a minute? I have this idea I want to run by you."

"Uh-oh," laughed Latifah, "Another of your ideas! What's your brainstorm, Phil?"

"Well," said Phil, "You know how excited students get about doing the video news and weather announcements each morning? The Technology Class members are the only ones who get to do them, but they have such a great time taping and interviewing and creating funny scripts. Sometimes I hear students in my classes talking about the morning videos, so they really seem to capture their attention. I've been thinking I want to give more students opportunities to do video production projects. I was talking to a friend of mine at Topnotch High School, and she says they have their students do video projects in nearly every content area. They find it helps keep students more involved in the content and gives them practice in organizing ideas, talking to people – even in reading and writing. The teachers put some of the videos on their school Web server so they can show them to friends and parents."

"It does sound interesting," said Latifah. "Is this something you that would work just for your history classes, Phil, or would other teachers here be interested in doing it?"

"Actually," said Phil, "I've already talked to several other teachers and we've brainstormed what I think are some good ideas. Luther in Physical Education and Stella in Physics had this idea for working together to have students create video demonstrations of physics principles in sports. I'd love to get my students interviewing local history experts and creating historical videos. Tim in Biology thought we might combine my project with his unit on local ecologies. Phyllis in Technology Education said she'd teach us how to use digital video cameras and storyboard the scripts for the final products. What do you think?"

Latifah smiled. "I think you're about to ask me for some money," she said. "Yes?"

"Actually," said Phil, "All we would need is a couple more digital cameras, and I've found an incredible price on this web site that gives discounts for educators. A real steal!"

S2.1 What instructional problems did Phil see that he wanted to address with video-based projects? What did he feel was the relative advantage of this strategy?

S2.2 What other planning tasks would be necessary for teachers to carry out in preparation for projects like this (e.g., students' skills involved in interviewing, taping).

S2.3 Pick any of the projects Phil describes and list some of the outcomes that would need to be assessed. What would be good ways to assess them?

S2.4 Can you think of any privacy and legal issues that teachers would have to address so students could take video of local people and places?

Multimedia/Hypermedia Integration Problems to Analyze and Solve

P.1. Joaquin is looking for a more motivating alternative to traditional written book reports. His fifth-grade students don't especially like reading books or writing book reports. Joaquin was talking to a colleague who uses *HyperStudio®* multimedia software to make doing book reports more appealing to students.

P1.1 Describe how you think using *HyperStudio®* multimedia software would make it more likely Joaquin's students would enjoy doing book reports.
P1.2 What would be the relative advantage of using this software tool?
P1.3 Would it be better to have the students work individually or in groups to do the exercises? How would you arrange the computer systems to carry out this strategy?

P.2. Clint and Sandy, two junior high school social studies teachers, plan a school-wide project to document the history of the local area by focusing on the families whose personal histories are intertwined with the history of the region. They plan to have students interview many individual family members and research local sources of historical information. Then they want the students to organize all the information into a book about the history of the local region.

P2.1 What multimedia tools could Clint and Sandy use to enhance and support this project?
P2.2 What would be the relative advantage of using such multimedia tools?
P2.3 This kind of project would require a lot of work to research and organize information and to produce the final product. Suggest some ways this work could be divided up and accomplished among classes to model for students how to organize work tasks in a large, complex project.

P.3. Eli is a fourth-grade teacher who has several students in his class who speak English as a second language. He works on increasing the comprehension skills for each of his students and encourages them to read books and stories to practice their skills. His students who speak English as their second language have trouble reading independently, and Eli does not have the time to read to each of them individually. He would like a way they can have books read aloud to them in an enjoyable way and also answer comprehension questions about what they have heard and read.

P3.1 What software tool could help Eli address this problem?
P3.2 What would be the relative advantages of using this software tool with his students who speak English as a second language?
P3.3 How would it be possible for these students to use this tool in class but not disturb or distract other students?

P.4. Elinor is a high school curriculum coordinator who wants the students to prepare an electronic portfolio they can take with them to display the quality of their work and what they have accomplished throughout their courses. She would like this to include film footage of them giving class presentations, as well as digital samples of their work. The completed portfolio for graduating seniors would be placed on a CD they could take with them.

P4.1 What software tool would you recommend Elinor use to address this problem?
P4.2 What would be the relative advantage of using this software tool?
P4.3 If she wanted teachers to assist with this activity, what would she have to make sure was done before the portfolio concept was introduced to students?

P.5. Belinda's eighth-grade language arts students have a spelling test every Friday, and spelling counts for 10% of their overall semester grade. There is no time during the regular class period during the week to allow students to practice, and it is obvious from their grades that many students do not study the words outside class. Belinda thought of a way to use Microsoft *PowerPoint*® software to make sure her students see all the spelling words and hear them pronounced every time they come in the classroom and every time they leave.

P5.1 How do you think Belinda uses *PowerPoint*® software to address this problem?
P5.2 What would be the relative advantage of using *PowerPoint*® software for this purpose?
P5.3 Which of *PowerPoint*®'s multimedia benefits is Belinda using for this activity?

Chapter 10

Problem-based Exercises on Using the TIP Model for Integrating the Internet and Other Distance Resources into the Curriculum

Introduction to Integrating the Internet and Other Distance Resources

The Internet and its related resources (e.g., e-mail, instant messaging, listservs) have become such fixtures of modern life that it is difficult to remember when we didn't rely on them. It makes sense that resources that permeate so many activities in our society should also be integrated into students' learning experiences. The following are some of the most important benefits the Internet and its related materials bring to education:

- **Easy and rapid communication** – Through e-mail and web pages, students, teachers, and parents can more easily exchange and keep each other updated on important information.
- **Access to expert resources and information not locally available** – Each local community has information resources (e.g., libraries), expert resources (e.g., professionals such as police and doctors), and information-rich locations (e.g., local factories, museums) that students can use as experts sources when they study various topics. The Internet expands these expert resources to include people, sites, and locations all over the world.
- **Access to up-to-date information** – News, weather, and other web sites provide students with up-to-the-minute information and data sources for use in projects and lessons.
- **Easy sharing of information and work products** – The capability to exchange notes, e-mail files, and view information on web pages supports students as they work on projects with each other and with teachers.
- **Support for cooperative group work** – Web research and web site production gives students motivating formats to learn skills required for working cooperatively in groups.
- **Support for learning information and visual literacy skills** – Evaluating and designing web pages is a useful, motivational way to teach skills students will need to be savvy consumers and developers of visual and text information.

The following chart gives a brief summary of some the types of Internet and distance learning resources and sample teaching and learning applications of each. Read more about these materials and their integration strategies in Chapter 8 of *Integrating Educational Technology into Teaching* (Roblyer, 2003).

Types of Internet Resources	Sample Classroom Applications of Internet Resources
Web browsers	Virtual field trip projects; self-instructional tutorials; support for classroom communications among students, teachers, and parents; webquest projects to solve problems or locate information; social action projects; web-based scavenger hunts
Search engines	Online research on assigned topics and projects, locating contact information for experts
E-mail and listservs	Keypal projects, telementoring activities
Chatrooms and instant messaging	Support for project work among students and teachers working together on projects at a distance
Web page development resources	Students' development of web pages and sites to display work products

Problem-based exercises in this chapter give you hands-on practice in integrating the Internet and other distance resources into instructional environments. Through scenario-based problem situations, you can see how teachers go about selecting and using these tools to support teaching and learning.

Scenarios to Read and Analyze – The following scenarios are examples of integrating the Internet and other distance resources into curriculum lessons. After reading Chapter 8 in *Integrating Educational Technology into Teaching* (Roblyer, 2003), answer the questions about using the TIP Model to integrate these strategies effectively:

Scenario 1, Internet – Based on a lesson idea in: "Virtual Art" by Glen Bull and Gina Bull. *Learning and Leading with Technology,* 2001, Vol. 29, No. 3, pp. 54-58.

Gertrude, local sculptor and artist and mother of two elementary school children, was talking with her daughter's teacher, Cecily.

"I despair, Cecily, I just really despair of getting our kids exposed to high-quality art in this backwater," said Gertrude, waving her hands dismissively in the general direction of the small, rural town where they lived. "Of course, I take my girls to the city whenever I can, and there is always my illustrated art book collection. But, really, my dear, no art museums close enough for our children to visit? It's an educational tragedy!"

Cecily smiled. "Yes, I agree it does present a challenge. We want all our students to be artistically literate, as well as read-and-writing literate, don't we? I think you'll be interested in one of the projects I'm doing this year. Next month we're taking a virtual field trip to major art exhibits around the world. I've already identified some of the web sites. Most of the major art institutes and museums have extensive web collections, you know.

"Look at this site the Chicago Art Institute just put up to show its collection of Iraqi art objects from 2500 B.C.," she continued, walking over to her classroom computer. "We can't get to Chicago, of course, and the exhibit will be there only a short time anyway, but the web site will be up for the rest of the year or longer." She clicked on the bookmarked web site and displayed some of the objects. Gertrude's eyes grew wider with each page she saw.

"This is remarkable!" Gertrude exclaimed. "I wanted to see this exhibit myself, but I just can't get away this time of year."

"Yes," said Cecily, "This is one of about a dozen museum sites we'll see. In a way, it's better than going to them in person; we can see more items faster this way. The kids will have a list of items to find and questions to answer about the paintings, sculptures, and other objects they see. Then they'll do their own art based on ideas they get from the museums. Finally, we'll make a web site collection of their work and put it on the school server."

"My dear, this is sensational!" cried Gertrude. "Perhaps there is hope for our children's art education after all! I hope you'll let me help with this."

S1.1 What problems did Cecily and Gertrude see that the Internet project could help with? What are the relative advantages of doing a virtual field trip as opposed to a real one?
S1.2 Is this project directed, inquiry-based, or a combination? Explain.
S1.3 What materials would Cecily have to prepare before she began this project?
S1.4 How might Cecily introduce this project to the students? How might Gertrude help?

Scenario 2, Internet – Based on a lesson idea found on the following page of the Poway (San Diego) High School web site: http://www.powayusd.com/PUSDPHS/--dbase/--dmoore/warquest/index.html

Elmo and Ricardo, two high school history teachers, were sitting in the library media center, planning their courses for the coming year.

"You know, Elmo, last year while the war was going on, it was a hot topic," said Ricardo, looking over the curriculum guide. "It seemed to spark the kids' interest in all kinds of related topics. Everyone wanted to know more about that region of the world and how our government works during a crisis; my students seemed even more interested in studying about past wars. But for kids this year, the whole thing will be old news again. This year, as we study the wars in which America has participated this past century, I'd like to try something new – something that would make a connection to their lives and bring home to them what wars mean to them personally."

"I know what you mean," said Elmo, nodding. "I saw a webquest the other day that I have been thinking we should try this year."

"What's a webquest?" asked Ricardo, looking up from his curriculum guide.

"Let me show you," said Elmo, going over to one of the center's computers. Ricardo followed him and sat down next to him as Elmo typed in the site URL.

"Webquests are online projects in which students solve a problem or create a product based on their research. In this webquest, each student takes a perspective on war from a list: nurse, statesman, poet, statistician, conscientious objector, war hero. We show them these questions: (1) Under what conditions would you serve your country to fight a war? (2) What types of conflict are worth a fight (war)? (3) What would you be willing to fight for? (4) When is war worth the costs of war? The best part is that the project web site helps schools like us pair up their students with students of their own age who live in a country that has experienced war. The partners communicate by e-mail and exchange information to answer the questions. The last activity is a joint letter they write to a person in government who has decision-making powers (i.e., President, congressperson, or a leader of another country), giving a summary of their findings about the costs of wars."

"This could be very powerful," said Ricardo, leaning back in his chair and putting his hands behind his head. "We could even have debates between groups of students. If we did videos of them, we could put those on the site, as well."

S2.1 What instructional problems did Elmo see that he felt a webquest could address?

S2.2 What would be the relative advantage of using a webquest format for this topic??

S2.3 What kinds of Phase IV planning tasks can you think of that would need to be done in preparation for this project?

S2.4 What outcomes would need to be assessed in this webquest, and how would you recommend they be assessed?

Problems to Analyze and Solve

P.1. Each year, Gill has his fifth-grade students identify an issue of current popular concern, e.g., local pollution problems, homeless or migrant people, quality of education for students with English as a second language. Gill has them use the Internet to research what other communities and groups are saying and doing about this problem. Then the students develop a position statement with a proposed solution and post it on the school's Internet. They request that feedback on their site be e-mailed to the teacher.

P1.1 What relative advantage does Gill see for using the Internet for this project as opposed to other resources?
P1.2 According to the textbook, what is the name for this kind of problem-based learning?
P1.3 Why do they have people e-mail feedback to the teacher rather than the students?

P.2. Larry is trying to get his English students to think about possible careers in journalism or other areas that require writing. He has his students contact one or more of the people he knows in these areas who have agreed to be interviewed online. They answer students' questions about how they entered the field, what they do on a daily basis, and what they do and don't like about their work. When they complete the interview, they write a summary and present it to the class.

P2.1 What relative advantage does Larry see for using the Internet for this project as opposed to other resources?
P2.2 According to the textbook, what is the name for this kind of online activity?
P2.3 Why doesn't Larry let the students research and find their own people to be their online information sources?

P.3. Each year, Prida has her ninth-grade students do a project in which they interview ninth-graders at other schools and create a newsletter documenting their current shared views and concerns and stories they feel are noteworthy. The newsletter is posted on the school's web page. When the newsletter is done, Prida contacts the teachers of the cooperating ninth-grade classrooms and gives them the URL for the newsletter. The teachers ask their students to create and e-mail Prida "Letters to the Editor" giving their comments and opinions about the newsletter stories.

P3.1 What relative advantages does Prida see for using the Internet for this project as opposed to other resources?
P3.2 What relative advantages do the other teachers see for having their students use the Internet and e-mail as opposed to other resources?
P3.3 What outcomes might Prida assess for this project and how would she assess them?

P.4. To introduce his unit on the American presidents, Lonnie has his students do a web-based scavenger hunt. He gives them a list of questions about Presidents and a list of web sites with annotations about the kinds of information they supply about the Presidents and other historical figures. He also has them document the search method they used to locate each of their answers. Then he asks them to write a brief description of other noteworthy facts/data they found in the course of the hunt. He awards several kinds of "prizes" for the hunt: most correct answers at end of allotted time, most efficient/organized search techniques, and best "other information" found.

P4.1 What relative advantages does Lonnie see for using the Internet for this project as opposed to other resources?
P4.2 Why do you think Lonnie recognizes three different aspects about the hunt?
P4.3 Do you think Lonnie should have his students work individually, in pairs, or in small groups to do this kind of activity? Explain why.

P.5. Each semester, Carla and Wally, science teachers in two different schools, give their students an ecological problem to solve related to conditions in their local area. After each class has collected data from online sources provided by Carla and Wally, they each have to analyze the data, figure out the cause of the problem, and create a proposed solution. They use the project web site to display their collected data and solutions. Local scientists and interested citizens are asked to judge the solutions and write an analysis of the feasibility of each. Then the students discuss their solutions and how they might improve them, based on the judges' input.

P5.1 What relative advantages do Carla and Wally see for using the Internet for this project as opposed to other resources?
P5.2 According to the textbook, what is the name for this kind of problem-based learning?
P5.3 Why would Carla and Wally have judges assess the answers, rather than evaluating the solutions themselves?

PART II REVIEW EXERCISES
Using the TIP Model to Integrate Technology Resources

Do **Exercises 1-4** on the Companion Website at: http://www.prenhall.com/roblyer. Click on the link for *Educational Technology in Action* Review Exercises, and use the links in each of the following sections to answer the review questions. Do **Exercise 5** by loading the Tutorials CD and using the file in the Part II Review Exercises Folder.

Exercise 1. Integrating Instructional Software

As you read in Chapter 4 of *Integrating Educational Technology into Teaching*, teachers choose and integrate instructional software (courseware) packages according to the functions they fulfill: drill and practice, tutorial, simulation, instructional game, and problem solving. The following are some good sources for high-quality software: Broderbund, Pearson Education Technologies, PLATO, Riverdeep Interactive Learning, Sunburst Communications, and Tom Snyder. Sources for Integrated Learning Systems (ILSs), which may include any of these software functions, include: Compass Learning, Pearson Interactive Technologies, and ScienceMedia eLearning Solutions.

II.1 The names and categories that companies give their packages do not always match the actual functions of the software. Using the companies listed above as sources of instructional software, select an example software title that fulfills each of the five functions. Describe how each might be used in a classroom lesson.

II.2 Most ILS's are now completely online, but some have other delivery options. Look at the ILS products offered by each company above; describe how each delivers its ILS.

Exercise 2. Integrating Software Tools

The International Society for Technology in Education (ISTE) has a variety of lesson plans for using various software tools, including those described in Chapter 5. Some of the software tools described in Chapter 6 of *Integrating Educational Technology into Teaching* are online. Also, see the puzzle-maker, lesson plan designer, test maker, and worksheet generator at the DiscoverySchool.com site.

II.3 Go to the ISTE site and do a search for each of the tools described in Chapter 5 (word processing or word-processing, spreadsheet, database). Select one lesson for each tool and describe how it integrates the tool into a classroom lesson.

II.4 Select one of the online software tools at the DiscoverySchool.com site and create a product that could be helpful in a classroom lesson.

Exercise 3. Integrating Multimedia/Hypermedia

When teachers use multimedia software for classroom projects or presentations, they often select *HyperStudio®* or *Microsoft PowerPoint®*. Macromedia's *Director® or Authorware®* are higher-end software packages for those who want to do more complex, full-featured designs. For video development software, teachers usually select *iMovie® or FinalCut Pro®* from Apple, Inc. or Windows Movie Maker® from Microsoft Higher-end programs include Adobe *Premiere®* and Pinnacle Edition® by Pinnacle Systems.

II.5 Imagine that you are a classroom teacher and want to have your students develop their own multimedia presentations. You want to write a proposal to a local company to fund the purchase of software for your classroom use. Since you have five Windows XP computers in your classroom, you want to purchase five copies of multimedia software. Check out the deals offered at the *HyperStudio®* and *Microsoft PowerPoint®*, then compare these prices with those at online "warehouse" stores such as PC Connection or Computer Discount Warehouse. Create a spreadsheet to compare the prices. Enter the company names in the spreadsheet as row names, and have two columns for the prices: Single Copy Price and License/Lab Pack Price.

II.6 Do this same activity for video development software.

Exercise 4. Integrating the Internet and Other Distance Resources

To prepare for Internet projects in which students create their own web pages, teachers need several materials. Among these are: web-page development software and assessment instruments to evaluate students' products. Netscape Composer® is free web page development software that is very simple for teachers and students to learn. More full-featured software includes Microsoft's FrontPage® and Macromedia's Dreamweaver®. For assessment tools, check out the rubrics on Kathy Schrock's Guide for Educators.

II.7 If you do not already have it on your computer, download the Netscape™ browser and create a simple web page. (For directions, see Chapter 11 in the booklet *Starting Out on the Internet* that comes with your textbook.) Compare its features with those of another software such as Microsoft's FrontPage® and Macromedia's Dreamweaver®.

II.8 Open your browser and go to the URL for Kathy Schrock's Guide for Educators http://school.discovery.com/schrockguide/assess.html). Bookmark it. Review each of the five rubrics for evaluating student's web page products. From the *Integrating Technology Across the CD* disc that came with your textbook, locate five lesson plans that call for students to create web page products. Tell which of the rubrics would be appropriate for assessing each product or if a new rubric would have to be developed.

Exercise 5. Creating Classroom Products – Load the Tutorials CD that came with this book. Open the Adobe *Acrobat®* file for the *Netscape Composer®* tutorial, and create the product as the tutorial directs. (Adobe *Acrobat Reader®* is on the CD.)

Part III:
Using the TIP Model in the Content Areas

Chapter 11

Problem-based Exercises on Using the TIP Model to Integrate Technology into English/Language Arts and Foreign Language Education

Introduction to Technology in English and Language Arts Education

Literacy skills are so critical to success in school that there is a sense of urgency about students acquiring them soon enough and at a high enough level to be able to apply them to other learning tasks. However, teachers often find it difficult to motivate students to spend the necessary time on these skills. Technology integration strategies and resources that can help meet these challenges are described in detail in Chapter 10 of *Integrating Educational Technology into Teaching* (Roblyer, 2003) and are summarized briefly here:

- **Motivating students to write** – Students are notoriously reluctant writers, yet practicing writing is the only way they can learn to do it well. Strategies to encourage and support writing include: using story starter software; connecting students via e-mail or the Internet with other students at a distance; and publishing their individual or group writing products in desktop-published, multimedia, or web page format.
- **Making outlining easier and/or more visual** – Students can use outlining software to create planning outlines that are easier to revise than those developed in handwritten or typed form. Students who need a more visual connection between abstract ideas and written outlines find it helpful to do "visual outlines" with concept-mapping software.
- **Engaging students in editing and revising written products** – Word processing software has revolutionized writing instruction in the same way it has transformed office communications. Depending on how teachers use word processing in the context of their writing programs, students will write and revise more than they would in other formats. Word processing also has unique features (e.g., spelling and grammar checkers) that encourage students to improve mechanical aspects of their writing.
- **Motivating students to practice reading for comprehension and vocabulary development** – Since practice is also key to increasing reading comprehension and vocabulary, software packages may be used to make this practice faster and more fun. Interactive storybooks also help engage students in practicing these skills.
- **Making practice of reading, language skills, spelling, and grammar skills easier** – Word processing-based practice exercises or software-based practice exercises supply interaction and fast feedback to make it more likely students will practice these skills.
- **Engaging students in reading literature** – Finally, teachers use Internet sites and multimedia products to make literature come alive and engage student interest.

Introduction to Technology in Foreign Language Education

Foreign language instruction shares many of the same challenges as instruction for English as a first language, e.g., finding ways to engage students in reading and writing and motivating them to practice the language skills involved. The primary obstacle unique to second language learning is that teachers want students to speak, read, and/or write in a language other than English while immersed in an English-speaking culture. As with reading, writing, and literature skills in English, technology integration strategies and resources that can help meet the unique needs of foreign language learning are described in detail in Chapter 10 of *Integrating Educational Technology into Teaching* (Roblyer, 2003); they are summarized briefly here:

- **Motivating students to practice using the language** – Most current software designed to help students learn a foreign language is in a multimedia format. This allows students to hear the language spoken and even see videos of people speaking it in context. These packages have the same benefits as practice exercises for English: they supply interaction and fast feedback in an individualized, self-paced environment to motivate students to spend more time on the skills.
- **Virtual immersion into the culture of the language** – The greatest disadvantage for most students learning a foreign language is that they cannot travel to the locations where the language is in daily common use around them. They learn the language disconnected from the culture in which it is used, which makes the experience more abstract and, thus, more difficult to learn. Virtual field trips on the Internet and multimedia software provide a simulated immersion in the culture of the language.
- **Allowing connections and collaboration with other students for practice** – Working with other students who are using the language is another kind of immersion experience. Collaboration on webquests and designing web pages and multimedia products give students meaningful opportunities to use the language they are learning. E-mail projects can link students with native speakers of a language to help encourage practice and motivate students to do their best work communicating with the new language.

See English/language arts standards at: http://www.ncte.org/standards/
See standards for foreign language learning at: http://www.actfl.org/
(Click on Special projects.)

Problem-based exercises in this chapter give you hands-on practice in integrating technologies into English/language arts and foreign language instruction. Through scenario-based problem situations, you can see how teachers go about selecting and using these tools to support teaching and learning.

Scenarios to Read and Analyze – The following scenarios are examples of integrating technology-based strategies into curriculum lessons for English and foreign languages. After reading Chapter 10 in *Integrating Educational Technology into Teaching* (Roblyer, 2003), answer the questions about using the TIP Model to integrate these strategies:

Scenario 1, English instruction – Based on a lesson idea on the following page of the Tramline Field Trips web site: http://www.field-guides.com/lit/shake/

Dietrich, a history teacher at Bonhoffer High School, was at his classroom computer, his body shaking and tears streaming down his face, as his colleague Sabine, an English teacher, came by for their meeting. She did a doubletake as she looked in the door, then rushed in. "Dietrich, are you hurt?" she asked anxiously. Then she realized he was laughing.

"It's okay, Sabine," said Dietrich, wiping his eyes. "I was just looking at this Shakespeare site you told me we could use for our co-teaching project. This one page lets students create their own taunts in Elizabethan language. Look at the one I just did: 'Thou spleeny tardy-gaited pignut!' Isn't that great? I've been sitting here creating taunts."

"You scared me to death," said Sabine, smiling. "Yes, this is one of the reasons I thought it would be perfect. Did you see the page on this site about the bubonic plague and the one on Elizabethan dress? We could do several activities that combine my unit on sonnets with your European history unit. I thought we could use this 'taunts' activity and the other language pages to get them interested in the similarities and differences between the English spoken in Shakespeare's time and our own. Then we can move on to discussions of the events that helped shape Shakespeare's perspectives."

"Yes," Dietrich agreed, "This would really help set the stage, so to speak. I thought we might have them do a historical background scavenger hunt with some of the other history sites I've used for this period. Then we could have them do a *PowerPoint®* presentation of events that shaped the times in which Shakespeare lived."

Sabine said, "I'm hoping our students will find this and the other activities as interesting as you did. I have such trouble drawing comparisons between the 1600's and our own times, and helping them understand the language differences when they read Romeo and Juliet is so difficult. I hate to water it down just so they can understand the story." She pointed to a page on the site. "I thought I could use this sonnet page just before they write their own sonnets," she said. "It's so interactive, it really helps them get started."

"Yes" said Dietrich, "this will be one unit they'll tell their friends about."

S1.1 What problems did Sabine and Dietrich see that the Shakespeare site could help with? What are the relative advantages of the activities they are proposing?
S1.2 What would be some of the outcomes that they would want to assess?
S1.3 What kinds of assessment tools would they need to design to assess the outcomes?
S1.4 How might they handle two classes working together for this interdisciplinary unit?

Scenario 2, Foreign language learning – Based on a lesson idea found in: "Cyber Traveling Through the Loire Valley" by Jane Chenuau. *Learning and Leading with Technology,* 2000, Vol. 28, Number 2, pp. 22-27.

Madeleine the foreign languages resource teacher for the Paramount School District was having lunch with Claire, the Paramount Middle School's sixth-grade French teacher.

"So what are you planning this school year, Claire?" asked Madeleine as she scanned the café's menu. "I'll bet you didn't ask me here just to sample the crêpes du jour."

Claire smiled. "Yes, even though they are wonderful here. Madeleine, I'm so excited about my new project, I had to tell you about it. You know how I'm always trying to find ways to have my students translate things from English-to-French and back again? It's always a challenge to get them motivated enough to look up and learn new words they need to describe events and places in any depth. I always feel if I can find an activity they find compelling, they'll spend so much more time using the language and new vocabulary. I thought I'd begin with virtual field trips to the chateaux in the Loire Valley. Remember the trip I took there last summer? This is the next best thing to bringing them along with me."

Claire took a page from her book bag and showed it to Madeleine. "See this list of tasks? After I have them 'visit' the chateaux and learn about their histories, the students will work in pairs or trios to complete these tasks to design and draw their own chateaux. They place each one – virtually – somewhere in the Loire Valley. Then they use the French version of *AppleWorks*® to describe it and its history. We can scan their drawings to use on the web pages they will create. It's a cultural immersion activity, but for a clear purpose."

"I see what you have in mind," said Madeleine. "Each group's page can be put on the school's virtual showcase site. They'll love having their names on them! But will anyone besides you and they and few others be able to read all these pages written in French?"

"This is the best part," said Claire, pointing to the last task on the sheet. "They have a link on their page to the English translation which, of course, they have to do, too. So they have to do both kinds of translations. Then I link their pages to an introduction site, where I explain the project. Their names will be the links to each one. This project will cover three of the 'Five C's' in the Foreign Language Standards: Communications, Cultures, and Connections. However, I'll need more copies of the French *AppleWorks*® software so they can work either in my room or the lab. That will help them get everything done efficiently."

"We'd better talk about this over dessert," laughed Claire, signaling for the waiter. "Maybe some nice Napoleons will give us some ideas on how to conquer this problem."

S2.1 What instructional problems did Claire have that she felt this project could address?
S2.2 What is the relative advantage of this project compared to non-technology ones?
S2.3 What kind of assessment instrument was Claire showing Madeleine? How would you state the outcome(s) she is trying to assess with it?
S2.4 What other outcomes would need to be assessed and how could Claire assess them?

English/Language Arts/Foreign Language Integration Problems to Analyze and Solve

P.1. Mabel has noticed that her students do not prepare an outline to plan what they will write for a composition assignment. She has taught them how to do outlines, but they seem unwilling or unable to do them. They have a great deal of trouble organizing information in writing, and she thinks it might be better for them to create a diagram that shows in pictures how concepts are related. She has heard about a software tool that can help them do this activity easier and faster.

P1.1 What technology resource would help Mabel address this problem?
P1.2 What would be the relative advantage of using this resource as opposed to others?
P1.3 Would it be better to have the students work individually or in groups to do the activity? Explain why.

P.2. Gerald has his class work in small groups to create a short story. As a whole class, they discuss the plot and characters; then each group writes a part of the story. They exchange sections and critique each other's parts. Then they do a final version. After the draft is complete, they post the story on the school's web server along with stories posted from past classes.

P2.1 What would be the relative advantages for Gerald's students to use word processing for their drafts instead of doing typed or handwritten drafts?
P2.2 What would be the relative advantages of posting the story on the Internet when it is completed?
P2.3 What outcomes would Gerald probably want to assess in addition to quality of writing in the final product? Suggest a way to carry out this assessment.

P.3. Nate notices that some of his students make a lot of homonym/homophone errors in their writing. He decides to have them practice correct usage with a software package designed especially for this purpose. The software shows one sentence at a time with a word missing, and gives two possible word choices. Students pick one of the words, and the software tells them immediately if it is correct or not and why. Nate allows them to practice for no more than 10 minutes. As they end their session, the software tells them a total score and which words they still need to practice.

P3.1 What are the relative advantages to Nate himself to use drill and practice software to address this problem? What are the relative advantages to Nate's students?
P3.2 Why does Nate allow them to practice for no more than 10 minutes?
P3.3 Would it be better for Nate's students to do the practice individually, in pairs, or in small groups? Explain why.

P.4. Sheila is helping her AP Spanish students prepare for the exam. Sheila knows that there will be a lot of vocabulary on the exam many of the students may not have encountered. She decided to offer them the opportunity to practice vocabulary using a Spanish drill-and-practice program she has available. However, she has only one copy.

P4.1 How would you recommend Sheila have her students use this one copy of the software?
P4.2 What would be the relative advantage of using this software?
P4.3 What data could Sheila gather to get some indication the program was helping her students be better prepared for the exam?

P.5. Jules would like to motivate his students to spend more time on their German translations. They will do practice exercises he creates for them only under duress. He hears about a web site that will link up individual students to an e-pal in a German school so they can communicate in both German and English.

P5.1 What would be the relative advantages for Jules to use this strategy with his students?
P5.2 How would you advise Jules to structure this project to make it most meaningful for both students in this country and in Germany?
P5.3 Would you advise Jules to encourage student to communicate with the German students from their home computers, if they have them? Why or why not?

Chapter 12

Problem-based Exercises on Using the TIP Model to Integrate Technology into Science and Mathematics Education

Introduction to Technology in Science and Mathematics Education

Mathematics and science share so much content and have such similar teaching challenges that it is logical they also share so many of the same technology integration strategies. No only do many science subjects require mathematics skills, but both science and math also have many abstract and/or complex concepts that students often find difficult to understand and/or master. Technology-based strategies can help teachers meet these and other challenges involved in teaching mathematics and science topics. These strategies and resources to carry them out are described in detail in Chapter 11 of *Integrating Educational Technology into Teaching* (Roblyer, 2003) and are summarized briefly here:

- **Helping students visualize abstract or complex concepts** – Mathematics is, by its nature, an abstract area. It is a language of symbols designed to help people communicate in a standard way about topics such as numerical relationships, measurement, and probability. Science, too, has many phenomena that cannot be observed directly but must be represented symbolically. Strategies that help make these abstract concepts more concrete for students just learning them include: software- and web-based simulations and manipulatives (e.g., *Geometer's Sketchpad*®), video-based scenarios to represent problems, and spreadsheet demos.
- **Supporting low-level calculations in high-level learning** – Although students are expected to learn basic math skills, many higher-level concepts in mathematics and science require many time-consuming basic calculations; doing them by hand is not only inefficient, it can interfere with learning. For these kinds of learning tasks, students use Calculators and calculator-based labs (CBL's), spreadsheets, and statistical analysis programs to do low-level calculations so they can concentrate on high-level concepts.
- **Facilitating data collection and analysis during experiments** – Experiments and hypothesis-testing often require time-consuming data collection and subsequent analysis of the collected data. Students can use handheld probeware (Microcomputer-based Labs or MBL's) to make data collection more efficient; handheld Calculator-based labs (CBL's) and statistical analysis programs help with the analyses. These are not only time-saving tools, but they are also the tools of modern science, so it is important that students see them in action and have opportunities to use them to solve problems.

- **Providing supportive inquiry environments** – Recent science standards emphasize the importance of inquiry skills, or being able to use a systematic, logical approach to identifying a problem and gathering information required to solve it. Environments that can support the learning of inquiry skills are so complex that they are difficult to create and manage. Web-based formats make these environments easier for teachers to set up and monitor, and their built-in feedback and support mechanisms make them easier for students to use as they learn inquiry skills.

- **Allowing communication and collaboration opportunities** – Electronic communications (e.g., e-mail and web pages) are becoming essential tools for scientists, so it makes sense that students would use them as they learn science skills. Students also find them useful for obtaining help from their teachers and other expert sources. Faster, easier communications makes it more feasible to have students working together on problems, which is both more motivating to students and a better reflection of problem solving in the workplace.

- **Helping students practice required skills** – Although de-emphasized in modern mathematics and science standards, students still have to memorize and call to mind quickly several kinds of facts and simple rules in both areas. Drill-and-practice and game software provide a fast, efficient way for students to practice and get immediate feedback on correctness. This strategy is especially important as students prepare for important timed tests. If the need is urgent, teachers can create their own drills using multimedia software or a test item bank.

See science standards at: http://www.nap.edu/books/0309053269/html/index

See mathematics standards at: http://standards.nctm.org/

Problem-based exercises in this chapter give you hands-on practice in integrating technologies into science and mathematics instruction. Through scenario-based problem situations, you can see how teachers go about selecting and using these tools to support teaching and learning.

Scenarios to Read and Analyze – The following scenarios are examples of integrating various technology-based strategies into curriculum lessons for science and mathematics. After reading Chapter 11 in *Integrating Educational Technology into Teaching* (Roblyer, 2003), answer the questions about using the TIP Model to integrate these strategies:

Scenario 1, Mathematics instruction – Based on a lesson idea found in: "Teaching Fractions using a Simulated Sharing Activity" by Joe Garofalo & Brian Sharp. *Learning and Leading with Technology,* 2003, Vol. 30, No. 7, pp. 36-41.

Elementary teachers Li and Alfred were talking after school in the teacher's lounge. "You look tired, Li," said Alfred. "Tough day?"

"Teaching fractions wears me out," sighed Li. "And I haven't even started it yet! I've been thinking for months about how I can do it better. It's not just keeping them interested in mathematics, although you know how hard *that* is! It's also that I just don't think they understand why they are learning things like division and fractions, you know?"

"I know exactly what you mean," said Alfred, sitting down at the table with a cup of coffee. "You want them to think mathematically and start seeing the connections. All they seem to want to do is get the problems out of the way as quickly as possible. I've tried various materials and strategies. Manipulatives seem to keep them interested longer, but I still don't think they get the significance of the concepts. Elle over at Topflight Elementary tried giving her students cookies and having them divide them up among various numbers of kids. What a disaster! They were intensely interested in the cookies, though."

Li sat up straight and looked at Alfred. "Cookies!" she exclaimed.

"Yes, that's right, she used cookies," said Alfred, sipping his coffee.

"No, it just reminded me of an online project someone at the district curriculum conference mentioned. It had kids sharing 'virtual cookies' with friends. They did the division with animations on a computer screen, but then they talked about *why* they chose the methods they used to divide them. I'll bet they could repeat each sharing session several times, if they wanted to. Why didn't I see this before? This could work! Sharing food is something they really identify with, and the online format makes it so much more feasible."

"It would be even better if the screen showed the fraction symbols as they did the division," said Alfred thoughtfully. "Do you know if it allows that?"

"I believe it does," said Li, "But I'm going to a computer right now and find out."

"Wait for me!" said Alfred. "I want to see how it compares with my own methods."

S1.1 What problems did Li see that the online format could help with?
S1.2 What are the relative advantages of doing this activity in a computer-based format?
S1.3 Would this activity be done best in an individual or small-group format? Explain.
S1.4 How could Alfred help Li compare the effectiveness of this strategy with others she had used? What outcome(s) could they use as criteria to compare results?

Scenario 2, Science and mathematics instruction – Based on a lesson idea found on the following page of the web site for NSF- and NASA-sponsored Project SkyMath at: http://www.unidata.ucar.edu/staff/blynds/Skymath.html#mod

Ingrid, the science teacher at Fastpace Junior High was sitting at her classroom computer when Claude, the math teacher dropped by to borrow a book.

"Hey, Ingrid, do you have that curriculum ideas text from the workshop?" he asked.

"Come on in, Claude," said Ingrid. "You might find this web site more interesting!"

"Find something good?" asked Claude, sitting down beside her.

"You know how we've been looking for a project that helps teach inquiry skills in a hands-on way and also helps students see how mathematics and science work together in the real world? Well, I think I just found it," said Ingrid, pointing to the screen.

"See," she continued, "it says here that the module has students learning mathematical principles by focusing on a single central concept from weather: temperature. It calls for students to work in small groups collecting and analyzing weather data. Then the site has them exchange data and messages electronically with students in other locations. They work together to identify and solve problems that have many possible solutions. Isn't this great?"

"How do they collect the data?" asked Claude. "Do they take actual readings or do they just look at data available on the Internet?"

"It looks like they do both," said Ingrid. "They learn how state, national, and world weather agencies collect data. Then they pose local weather-related questions, decide on a common set of data to answer them, and design a process for collecting the data."

"Sounds good for you," said Claude. "But how exactly does this relate to math skills?"

"Think about what they have to do with the weather data," said Ingrid. "For example, observing minimum and maximum temperatures, calculating average temperatures, and stating a 'typical temperature' in terms of a mode, median, and mean for a given data set. It also has them use weather data to identify and describe mathematically significant patterns in data sets and make predictions based on probabilities."

"Wow!" said Claude, "We could have them use a spreadsheet to graph pairs of Fahrenheit and Celsius temperatures and talk about slope and intercepts. Then we'd have them use slope of the line to develop the rule for converting Fahrenheit and Celsius scales. I can see how this could clarify some fairly abstract math concepts so well."

"All this and students working with classes in other locations. Wouldn't they love that?" said Ingrid. "Now if we can just arrange for your students to work with mine."

S2.1 What instructional problems did Ingrid see that this project could address?
S2.2 What would be the relative advantage of using technologies for such a project?
S2.3 What kinds of Phase IV planning tasks can you think of that would need to be done in preparation for this project?
S2.4 What electronic resources could help Ingrid's students work with Claude's?

Science and Mathematics Integration Problems to Analyze and Solve

P.1. Ariel, the AP mathematics teacher, wanted to have her students do simple correlations with two data sets to demonstrate the mathematical principles involved. However, it took students too long to do these calculations by hand and there were too many data entry errors using a calculator.

P1.1 What technology-based strategy could Ariel use to address this problem?
P1.2 What would be the relative advantage of using this strategy?
P1.3 Would it be better to carry out this strategy as a whole class or with students working individually or in groups? Explain how you would do it.

P.2. Boris was trying to show his teenage students in the business education program how they could figure out quickly how much car they could buy with the money they had. He wanted to show them the relationship between the down payment, interest rate, and length of the loan and how this all affected monthly payments and the total they would spend on the car at the end of the loan period. However, he wanted them to be able to do the calculations quickly, so they could focus on the underlying math concepts.

P2.1 What technology-based strategy could Boris use to address this problem?
P2.2 What would be the relative advantage of using this strategy?
P2.3 Describe the steps you might use to carry out a simple lesson using this strategy.

P.3. Ahmed wanted his students to take readings at a local stream to do an experiment on acid and alkaline substances in water. He wanted to use the handheld probeware devices when they went on the field trip. With these devices, they could collect the data, bring the readings back in a data file, and download the file to the computer for analysis. However, he had 27 students and only 15 handhelds.

P3.1 What grouping strategy could Ahmed use to make the available devices work well with this many students?
P3.2 Explain how you would advise Ahmed have his students carry out the strategy.
P3.3 What would be the relative advantage of using this strategy as opposed to manual methods of collecting the readings?

P.4. Lydia was the school counselor in charge of helping students prepare for the test her school district had developed to select those students eligible for the special math/science magnet program, which offered all expenses paid to those who were selected. She knew a lot about the kinds of items that would be on the test, and she knew some of the students needed to practice some of the skills.

P4.1 What technology-based strategy would you recommend Lydia use to address this problem?
P4.2 What would be the relative advantage of using this strategy, as opposed to a paper-pencil format?
P4.3 Should students practice individually, in pairs, or in small groups? Explain.

P.5. Guido's ninth-grade students had a lot of problems understanding many geometry concepts. They seemed to understand them better when he drew the figures and angles for them as he explained the concepts, but this was not feasible for every problem. It took too long, and he couldn't draw well enough to show everything clearly.

P5.1 What technology-based strategy would you recommend Guido use to address this problem?
P5.2 What would be the relative advantage of using this strategy?
P5.3 If Guido has 32 students in his class and only one computer, what would you recommend he do to carry out this strategy most effectively?

Chapter 13

Problem-based Exercises on Using the TIP Model to Integrate Technology into Social Studies Education

Introduction to Technology in Social Studies Education

Social studies is not one topic but many: civics, economics, geography, history, and political science, among others. The teacher's challenge is to show students that by studying these topics, they are really learning about themselves and their place in our society and our world community, that they are part of what President Bush in his 2001 Inaugural Address called "a long story – a story we continue, but whose end we will not see." Technology-based strategies can help teachers meet these challenges in teaching social studies topics. These strategies and resources to carry them out are described in detail in Chapter 12 of *Integrating Educational Technology into Teaching* (Roblyer, 2003) and are summarized briefly here:

- **Demonstrating more graphically the connections between students' lives and other times and cultures** – Recent events have shown how important it is for students to see more clearly the way in which our past shapes our present and that, although our culture is important, we are part of a world community of cultures. Strategies that help students make these connections include software- and web-based simulations, virtual field trips, and online projects with distant students.
- **Making geographic and mapping concepts more visual** – Students often find it difficult see the connection between the symbol systems we call maps and the real world around them. Software- and web-based mapping utilities can help students design and read maps more easily, and GIS and GPS systems help facilitate use of geographic and other data to research and explore connections among geography, population, weather, and other factors that contribute to our environment.
- **Engaging students in learning about history** – History is typically one the most difficult subjects to teach because the past is often so dry and unreal – and, therefore, uninteresting – to students. Technology-based strategies that can help make history come alive for students include: virtual field trips, software- and web-based simulations, and online and multimedia research and development projects.
- **Allowing communication and collaboration opportunities** – As with many other topics, students are often more motivated to learn about social studies topics when they collaborate with other students on research and development projects. E-mail and the Internet allow faster, easier communications to make this joint work more feasible.

- **Helping students visualize abstract or complex economics concepts** – Economics requires mathematic problem solving and presents many of the same learning problems as other mathematics topics. Using software- and web-based simulations lets students interact with systems in which economics principles are being used and can help make many abstract concepts more concrete. Also, students can do Internet-based research to obtain up-to-the-minute status information on financial conditions and see demonstrations that help clarify production and distribution principles.
- **Facilitating student practice in required skills** – As with mathematics and science topics, modern instruction in social studies does not emphasize memorization. However, there are still many facts students need to learn and memorize (e.g., states and capitals, countries in various continents). Drill and practice and instructional game software provide fast, efficient ways for students to practice and get immediate feedback on correctness as they learn these facts.

See social studies standards at: http://www.ncss.org/standards/

Problem-based exercises in this chapter give you hands-on practice in integrating technologies into social studies instruction. Through scenario-based problem situations, you can see how teachers go about selecting and using these tools to support teaching and learning.

Scenarios to Read and Analyze – The following scenarios are examples of integrating various technology-based strategies into curriculum lessons for social studies. After reading Chapter 12 in *Integrating Educational Technology into Teaching* (Roblyer, 2003), answer the questions about using the TIP Model to integrate these strategies:

Scenario 1, Social studies instruction – Based on a lesson idea found in: "At the Source" by Terry Hongell and Patty Taverna. *Learning and Leading with Technology,* 2003, Vol. 30, No. 6, pp. 46-49.

Nick, an elementary school teacher, was sitting in the school computer lab when Margaret, the school principal, came in. "There you are, Nick," said Margaret. "I've been looking all over for you. I wanted to see if we could place another student in your class."

Nick sighed. "Sure, Margaret, why not? If I can find a way to interest the ones I've got, one more should be no problem."

"You sound a little perplexed, Nickie," said Margaret. "Anything I can do?"

"Maybe you can listen to me talk through this. Did you ever try to create one project that met a bunch of different criteria?" asked Nick. Margaret nodded and sat down. "Well," continued Nick, "I want to get my fourth graders interested in studying local history, but I want it to be something they can all identify with. I'd like them to do some research on it, but not just copying down stuff from an encyclopedia. I want them to do it in a way that gets them thinking about *how* to do research, and how they should synthesize information after they find it. I want them to work in groups, so they can learn how to collaborate and cooperate; even at their age, I think it's so important they have opportunities to do this. Finally, I want them to create something that we can display; you know, something tangible that reflects their work and what they learned – something they can show their parents."

"You never do anything simple, do you, Todd?" laughed Margaret. "Get any ideas yet?"

"Maybe I have," said Nick. "We could study a local hero from our own town: Colonel Cresap. Everything around here, including the school, is named after him, and I know there would be a lot on the Internet about him. The kids could work in groups, each one using web sites to research an aspect of his life. I could create a little booklet for each group to keep track of its work and to put in text and images we could add to a project web site."

"You could ask his great-great-granddaughter, Doreeda Cresap Downs to come and speak to the class. I'll bet she'd have some great photos you could scan," said Margaret.

"That's right," said Nick. "We could video her and put it on the site. We could even include a visual timeline with the images. Give me 50 more students; I'll handle 'em all!"

S1.1 What problems did Nick see that the online project could help with?
S1.2 What are the relative advantages of doing this activity in this format?
S1.3 What should Nick include in his booklet to help students synthesize information?
S1.4 What outcomes should Nick assess and what methods could he used to assess them?

Scenario 2, Social studies instruction – Based on a lesson idea from the Tramline Field Trips web site: http://www.tramline.com/tours/cross/world/_tourlaunch1.htm

Virginia, a high school history teacher, walked into the Band Room just as Carter, the school's band director, was finishing a summer workshop with a group of flute students. "Hi, Carter, everything humming along here?" she said brightly.

"You and your music puns," said Carter, gathering up sheet music. "You're probably here about the benefit concert, but I can't talk now. I'm meeting with parents about the proposed band trip. We've been asked to march in a parade in London, you know."

"Yes," said Virginia, "Actually, that's why I wanted to talk to you. Some of the other teachers and I have come up with a way to merge the trip with our social studies curriculum and, at the same time, give students who can't go on the trip a chance to participate in it."

"How would that work?" asked Carter. "I feel bad about so many students not being able to afford to travel that far. It would be wonderful if everyone could go."

"In a way, they can," said Virginia. "The trip won't be until December. What we'd like to do this coming semester is plan a different activity that relates to the trip for each of several classes. There is an Internet site called 'Windows on the World' that we could use to guide the activities. It has everything you should know about international travel. There is a section on passports and other legal aspects of preparing to travel abroad, one on changing currency, another on time zones and, of course, there are several U. S. State Department sites that give travel warnings and describe how an embassy works in a foreign country. We could use the *CIA World Factbook* site to research information about England and France – I know you all will want to take the Chunnel over to Paris before you come home. The site even has an interactive World Map and, of course, we can use *Mapquest®* to prepare an itinerary and follow you as you go. LuAnn would like her science class to track the weather as you travel to various locations and use the Travel Health section of the Centers for Disease Control site. We could prepare our own web site to display our findings.

"But best of all," she continued, "I think we can give a few students digital cameras and handheld computers to take with them. They can take images and video and keep a journal to send back the same day to us as we follow your trip. We could put it all on our band trip web site and update it daily as you guys travel. It will be like the whole school is going with you. What do you think?"

"Ginny, I think you've come up with an award-winning arrangement!" said Carter.

"Carter! A music pun!" laughed Virginia. "On that note, I guess I'll go start planning."

S2.1 What problems did Virginia see that this project could address?
S2.2 What would be the relative advantage of using these technologies for the activities?
S2.3 What kinds of Phase IV planning tasks can you think of that would need to be done in preparation for this project?
S2.4 What would Virginia have to do before placing these images on the school web site?

Social Studies Integration Problems to Analyze and Solve

P.1. Dale wanted to show his sociology students how they could test hypotheses about correlations among social factors such as population centers and crime statistics. He had heard of a technology tool that would allow students to do this with maps, so they could see at a glance if their hypotheses were correct.

P1.1 What technology-based strategy could Dale use to address this need?
P1.2 What would be the relative advantage of using this strategy?
P1.3 What would you suggest Dale have his students produce to show the results of their work? How might he assess this product?

P.2. Francesca's students would be studying the Early American period in our country's history in the Spring semester, and she wanted to make the class more engaging than it had been in the past. She wished she could have her students visit places like Williamsburg, Philadelphia, and Monticello, but they did not live near any of these sites.

P2.1 What technology-based strategy could Francesca use to address this problem?
P2.2 What would be the relative advantage of using this strategy?
P2.3 What could Francesca's students produce to show what they had learned? How might she assess this product?

P.3. Alison's social studies students were about to study the U. S. Constitution. She not only wanted to show them what was included in our Constitution, but she also wanted them to see all the factors that must be considered when any new country creates a charter to guide its development and reflect its national principles. She had heard about software that allowed students to do this in a role-playing way.

P3.1 What technology-based tool could Alison use to address this need?
P3.2 What would be the relative advantage of using this strategy instead of holding a class discussion on this topic?
P3.3 Should students work individually, in pairs, in small groups, or as a whole class on this activity? Explain.

P.4. Fern wanted to have her students study about their local area, so she arranged to have them work via e-mail with a class of students in another state. They exchanged background information about each other's locations and asked questions about weather conditions, favorite spots to visit, and other items of interest to both. Finally, they each worked on a travel brochure that included a local map and summarized the information they had gathered. They ended the project by e-mailing each other a copy of the brochure.

P4.1 What problems did Fern address with this technology-based strategy?
P4.2 What would be the relative advantage of using this strategy, as opposed to having students do a brochure without contacting other students?
P4.3 What outcomes should be assessed in such a project, and how might they be assessed?

P.5. Levar's students were studying how the stock market both reflects our country's economy and helps shape it. He asked them to track five stocks over the course of two months and chart their progress. At the same time, they tracked events in the country and the world that may affect stock market performance for the stocks they picked. They ended the project by describing the events that corresponded with major dips and peaks and how they think these events affected the stocks.

P5.1 What problems is Levar addressing with this technology-based strategy?
P5.2 If Levar had the students work in small groups on this activity, explain how this strategy might best be carried out in the classroom.
P5.3 What would be a good way for Levar to have students present their findings? Explain why this presentation strategy would be effective.

Chapter 14

Problem-based Exercises on Using the TIP Model to Integrate Technology into Art and Music Education

Introduction to Technology in Music Education

Although it strikes some people as incongruous that machines could transform an area that emphasizes personal creativity, computers and other electronic devices have done just that in the music curriculum. Technology has been thoroughly integrated throughout the spectrum of music instruction, from composition to skills practice. Technology's role in music education is unique in that it supports so many teaching techniques that would not otherwise be feasible in a typical classroom. Technology-based strategies to support the teaching of music are described in detail in Chapter 13 of *Integrating Educational Technology into Teaching* (Roblyer, 2003) and summarized briefly here:

- **Allowing easier creation and editing of individual and group music composition** – Students come to understand music best when they create it. Without technology, writing and editing notation for student-created musical pieces would be a laborious and tedious process. Musical instrument digital interface (MIDI) keyboards, in combination with sequencers and music editors, make it easier for students to play their own musical pieces, see the musical notations that result from them, change the music notations quickly and easily, and combine their work with that of other students.
- **Making possible monitored practice** – With systems that connect a teacher station to keyboards and students with headphones, it is also easy for teachers to monitor and assist individuals as whole classrooms of students play at the same time.
- **Supporting individual performance practice** – Sequencing programs also make it possible for teachers to supply an entire orchestra, minus the tracks of one or more instruments, so students can practice a given piece by themselves and *en ensemble*.
- **Providing easy access to musical selections** – In music appreciation, Internet sites and multimedia collections make it easier for teachers and students to access quickly and easily information about composers' backgrounds and hear samples of their works.
- **Facilitating student practice in required skills** – Practice is a way of life for musicians, and technology can make it more likely that students will spend the time they need on practice. In addition to the support technology provides for performance practice described above, drill-and-practice and instructional game software provide a fast, efficient, motivational way for students to do skills practice such as identifying keys in which music is written and names of notes on a scale.

Introduction to Technology in Art Education

- **Fostering creativity through production and manipulation of images** – With digital equipment and image manipulation software, students can build their creative skills as they develop and store their original images or change existing ones.
- **Making possible novel graphic design techniques** – Many graphic techniques (e.g., tweening, morphing) can be done only with computer software. Software tools let students explore graphic design in unique ways.
- **Allowing easy sharing of creative works** – By digitizing creative works and placing them on disk or web sites, students can more easily share their work with others and allow teachers to review them and offer critiques.
- **Providing easy access to images of artworks** – Technology can support art appreciation in the same ways it does music appreciation. Internet sites and multimedia collections make it easier for teachers and students to access quickly and easily information about artists' backgrounds and view samples of their works. Virtual field trips and scavenger hunts are ways to motivate students to look at the available sites.

See music standards at: http://www.menc.org/publication/books/standards.htm

See art education standards at: http://www.ed.gov/pubs/ArtsStandards.html

Problem-based exercises in this chapter give you hands-on practice in integrating technologies into music and art instruction. Through scenario-based problem situations, you can see how teachers go about selecting and using these tools to support teaching and learning.

Scenarios to Read and Analyze – The following scenarios are examples of integrating various technology-based strategies into curriculum lessons for music and art. After reading Chapter 13 in *Integrating Educational Technology into Teaching* (Roblyer, 2003), answer the questions about using the TIP Model to integrate these strategies:

Scenario 1, Music – Based on an idea in: "Music Technology in an Inner City Intermediate School" by Shelley Jacobson, 1993. *The Computing Teacher*, Vol. 20, No. 8, pp. 33-34.

Willa, music director for the elementary school, was talking with Henry, the school district music coordinator, after a professional development workshop. "I know it will take some doing. I plan to have two fund-raising activities this year alone, both with the help of some of the more music-minded parents, but I think it will be worth it. By next year, I plan to have an entire MIDI network in the music room."

Henry frowned, "Is that the best use of your resources, Willa?" he asked. "Think how many instruments and how much sheet music you could buy with what it will take to set it all up. Remember you'll need to get music editing software, and keyboards, as well."

"Yes, that's all in my plan," said Willa, patting her notebook. "In my visits to some of the larger districts up north, I've seen some wonderful things happening when teachers use these resources. They told me that students who had never had an interest in music caught the bug when they were able to create their own songs; and when kids saw the notation come up when they played a tune on a keyboard, you could just see the light snap on in their heads! They got so excited about embellishing their tunes and, of course, it was so easy with the music stored in the system. They could just bring it up again anytime."

"But will it be worth all the money and time it will take you to set it up?" Henry asked incredulously. "Think of the maintenance! What will happen when something breaks?"

"Henry, I'll be able to teach 30 kids at one time in one room – all playing a different version of 'Heart and Soul!'" said Willa, laughing. "With sequencers, we'll even be able to let more advanced students play in ensemble pieces with different parts. I'm so excited!"

"Well, it will make it easier for our kids to practice their basic music skills," said Henry. "I've seen the merits of the practice software you bought last year. But the costs ..."

"Wish me luck, Henry!" said Willa, walking quickly toward towards the group of administrators in the front of the room. "I'm going to catch the superintendent before she leaves. She has a daughter in fourth grade; maybe we can get a little help with funding."

S1.1 What problems did Willa see that the MIDI network could help with?

S1.2 What are the relative advantages of having it, as opposed to the music resources Henry described?

S1.3 What data should Willa collect to show Henry the technology resources are making a difference in students' learning and are worth the investment of time and funds?

S1.4 What planning tasks should Willa do to address some of the items Henry brought up?

Scenario 2, Art – Based on a lesson idea in: "From All Sides Now: Weaving Technology and Multiple Intelligences into Science and Art" by Carol Lach, Ellen Little, and Deborah Nazzaro. *Learning and Leading with Technology,* 2003, Vol. 30, No. 6, pp. 32-35, 59.

Chauncey, a fourth-grade teacher, and Etienne, art resource teacher, were on a field trip with students to a local museum of natural history. "This is a great opportunity for the kids," said Chauncey, as he looked over a display of shells. "Thanks for agreeing to help out."

"Hey, no problem," said Etienne good-naturedly. "I've been wanting to talk to you anyway about an idea I've had for a project that combines art and science."

"Really?" said Chauncey. "Sounds kind of neat. What do you have in mind?"

"Well," said Etienne. "It occurred to me when I observed your class last year that you are teaching a lot of concepts about how things are structured in nature, you know, repetitive patterns found in shells, flowers, and so on. I liked the way you described how nature works in patterns, that it's predictable."

"Thanks," said Chauncey. "I'm not sure how many of the kids really get it, though. Sometimes I can just see their little eyes glaze over when we talk about permutations."

"I know what you mean," said Etienne. "But how about if we made it a little more interactive and had them do something to make the concept a little more concrete for them? We could give them a collection of some objects like leaves and plants we have gathered. For some objects, we could give them digital pictures. We also give them a group of patterns and structures and ask them to look for them in the objects. I envision them working in small groups – maybe divide up the collection among the groups, you know? Then when they have matched up the patterns with the objects, we have them create a tree or flower or shell of their own on the computer by drawing and repeating the pattern they found and moving the copies around. They could even paint the patterns different colors on-screen. Then we could print out the products and display them. I've seen projects like this done, and the kids sometimes come up with some really beautiful pieces.

"I don't think this lesson would take very long to do," continued Etienne. "Maybe an hour or so for each of two days. Would that fit in with your science periods?"

"I think it would be great," said Chauncey, looking at Etienne with astonishment. "What a creative idea, Etienne! I guess that's why you're the artist, huh?"

"Ha! It's much more challenging to get the kids to be artists!" said Etienne, smiling. "Or better yet, getting them to see the art in science and vice versa. Maybe this will help."

S2.1 What problems did Etienne feel this project could address?

S2.2 What would be the relative advantage of using image software for the activities?

S2.3 What would be some additional ways to display students' work in addition to printing it out and posting it?

S2.4 What data should Etienne and Chauncey collect to see the impact of this lesson on students' learning and attitudes?

Art and Music Integration Problems to Analyze and Solve

P.1. Orson, a music performance teacher, has been talking to his friend and colleague Liam, who is a music teacher in Dublin, Ireland. Orson and Liam would like to have their students work together on creating new musical pieces based on a series of Irish folk tunes that Liam has collected in the rural areas near the city. Liam would send recordings of the tunes, and the students would play them and work on variations based on them. However, the teachers and students need a way to make both the music production tasks and communicating their products faster and easier.

P1.1 What technology-based strategies could Orson and Liam use to address these needs?
P1.2 What would be the relative advantages of using these strategies?
P1.3 What would be a good way to display their products, once they were created?

P.2. Danielle, the school's music teacher, is doing an interdisciplinary project with Merrill, the history teacher. They plan to have Merrill's students research backgrounds of the musical composers of the Romantic period, listen to some of their works, and locate information on events of the times that helped shape their perspectives and, consequently, the music they created.

P2.1 What technology-based strategy could Danielle and Merrill use to carry out such a project?
P2.2 What would be the relative advantage of using this strategy?
P2.3 If they wanted to have Merrill's students work in small groups, how would they implement this in Merrill's class?

P.3. Students in Hadley's music appreciation class were preparing for their end-of-semester recitals. There were a variety of musical pieces, and Hadley would be accompanying each student during the recital. He wanted students to be able to practice individually with accompaniment, but he did not have time to accompany each of them as they practiced.

P3.1 What technology-based tool could Hadley use to address this need?
P3.2 What would be the relative advantage of using this strategy instead of allowing them to practice without accompaniment?
P3.3 If Hadley has 30 music students and only 8 stations, what strategy could he use to allow each student to practice individually?

P.4. Lucien wanted to teach his art students some visual literacy skills he had been reading about. He had heard that these skills were becoming increasingly important for students as consumers of news information and potential buyers of products. He wanted to show them how easy it was to create fictional images that looked real or alter real images to create false impressions.

P4.1 What technology-based strategy could Lucien use to address this need?
P4.2 Why could this skill probably not be taught in a non-technology way?
P4.3 How could Lucien arrange this activity so students could work on it in groups?

P.5. Samantha was an art resource teacher in a small, rural school district. She wanted her students to have opportunities to look at and appreciate various works of art and learn something about the artists. However, they were far from any art museum, and there was no money for field trips even if there was one close by.

P5.1 What technology-based strategy could Samantha use to address this need?
P5.2 What planning would Samantha have to do before she introduced this activity to students?
P5.3 What could Samantha do to help structure this activity to keep students on task?

Chapter 15

Problem-based Exercises on Using the TIP Model to Integrate Technology into Health Education and Physical Education

Introduction to Technology in Health Education

The more we find out through research and experience about what it takes for people to lead longer, healthier lives, the more important it becomes to help them learn and begin to apply this information to their own lives at an early age. However, health-related issues are interrelated with students' attitudes and beliefs and are frequently difficult to influence through school instruction. The visual, interactive nature of video and multimedia technologies can play a uniquely powerful role in raising students' awareness of important health information and changing their perspectives on health and fitness. Technology-based strategies to support the teaching of health concepts are described in detail in Chapter 14 of *Integrating Educational Technology into Teaching* (Roblyer, 2003) and summarized briefly here:

- **Clarifying human physical functions** – For many young people, the body is a mysterious and unknown territory. Their lack of knowledge about how it works can result in assumptions that could prove dangerous. Software- and web-based simulations allow students to explore this territory in a very visual way, making unseen, internal processes observable and easier to understand.
- **Helping students visualize and monitor characteristics of healthy lifestyles** – Students need models of healthy behavior to help them see the behaviors they need to adopt. Video-based demonstrations and simulations can provide these models, and web-supported projects give students opportunities to practice and tools to help monitor desirable behaviors.
- **Assisting with presentations of controversial issues** – Modern society is filled with controversial issues students need to know about and shape their own opinions on. Many teachers have difficulty talking to students about these issues, and students can be uncomfortable listening to adults discuss them. Video presentations and software- and web-based simulations offer safe, private environments for learning sensitive topics.
- **Helping students obtain accurate, reliable information about health issues** – As students learn about health issues and start to ask their own questions about healthy and unhealthy behaviors, they need objective, reliable sources of information. Carefully selected Internet sites can be an invaluable source of knowledge and insights on diseases, treatments, prescription and over-the-counter drugs, and human problems such as addiction and domestic violence.

Introduction to Technology in Physical Education

- **Demonstrating and providing feedback on physical performance** – In sports and other areas of physical performance, students need models of what they are aiming for, as well as errors to avoid. Videos and software- and web-based simulations can provide models that can be viewed whenever and as many times as students need to see them.
- **Helping students monitor fitness and performance indicators** – As students begin to set goals for personal fitness, they need quick and easy ways to monitor their progress toward their goals. Handheld computers and electronic monitoring devices (e.g., heart monitors) can help supply this vital information; software such as spreadsheets and specially-designed software can help them store their information so they can compare their performances across time.
- **Supporting interdisciplinary approaches** – As both health and physical education become optional, rather than required, courses in school curriculum, it becomes increasingly important to integrate activities that emphasize health and fitness concepts into instruction for other disciplines. Group-based Internet and multimedia projects help provide a way to accomplish this.

See health standards at:
http://www.aacps.org/AACPS/BOE/INSTR/CURR/health/nhestandard.htm

See physical education standards at:
http://www.aahperd.org/naspe/template.cfm?template=programs-ncate.html#standards

Problem-based exercises in this chapter give you hands-on practice in integrating technologies into health and physical education. Through scenario-based problem situations, you can see how teachers go about selecting and using these tools to support teaching and learning.

Scenarios to Read and Analyze – The following scenarios are examples of integrating technology-based strategies into curriculum lessons for health and physical education. After reading Chapter 14 in *Integrating Educational Technology into Teaching* (Roblyer, 2003), answer the questions about using the TIP Model to integrate these strategies:

Scenario 1, Health – Based on the "Nutrition Track" lesson from the *Microsoft Productivity in the Classroom* collection. ©1997 by the Microsoft Corporation.

Ophelia, the science resource teacher for the school district, was talking with Fred, a science teacher from the middle school. "I wonder if I could interest you in trying a curriculum project I heard about at the regional conference last week?" asked Ophelia.

"Sure," said Fred. "I've enjoyed working with that human body simulation program you told me about last year. The kids get a kick out of seeing those processes work and naming the parts of their body in each system."

"I think they'll like this, too," said Ophelia. "You know how I'm always looking for ways to show students 'healthy ideas' they can apply to their own lives. I saw one on nutrition that I think would be great."

"It better have fireworks in it," said Fred, laughing. "Their mothers harangue them so much about eating right, they don't want to hear it anymore."

"This is a good one, I think," said Ophelia. "It's very hands-on, which I know is a criterion for all your science projects, and it makes the idea of a healthy diet a more visual concept for them. I think it will get them engaged in monitoring their own diets."

"Let's hear it," said Fred. "I'm engaged in it already."

"Good!" said Ophelia. "You begin by looking on the U.S. Department of Agriculture's web site. They have the Food Pyramid there and a recommendation for what you should eat on a daily basis to maintain a healthy diet. Then you give them a page to track what they eat for five days. They can calculate their average results and create pie charts showing the average number of servings for each food group in their diets. This lets them see clearly how their diet compares, on average, to the USDA's recommended diet."

"That's a lot of calculating," said Fred. "And they have a hard time drawing pie charts."

"You use a spreadsheet to keep the data," said Ophelia. "It draws them automatically."

"This sounds great," said Fred. "After all the weight I gained over the holiday, maybe I should track what I eat along with them. I could use a better approach to my own nutrition."

- S1.1 What problems did Ophelia see that this project could help address?
- S1.2 What are the relative advantages of using technologies to support this approach, as opposed to having students do the data-keeping and summary charts by hand?
- S1.3 Describe an efficient arrangement for students to enter their data and do calculations.
- S1.4 How could Ophelia get an indication of whether or not this project changed student attitudes about their eating habits and maintaining better nutrition?

Scenario 2, Physical education – Based on a lesson idea from the Kids 'n Fitness web site at: http://exchange.co-nect.net/Teleprojects/project/?pid=16&cid=3

Roberto and Marina, physical education teachers from the same school, were talking after a basketball game. "That was fun," said Roberto. "It's good to see so many of the students here. However, sometimes I think watching a game is as close as many of them will get to real physical fitness."

"Yes," sighed Marina, "Now that physical education courses are no longer required at our schools in this district, it's getting more difficult for them to stay in shape; the results are noticeable. Everyone expects kids will do an after-school sport, but it doesn't always happen that way. I think even the principal has lost sight of how the lack of physical exercise affects students and, ultimately, can have an impact on their work in school."

"That's right," agreed Roberto. "That's why I wanted to talk to you about an online project I found out about the other day at a meeting."

"A computer project?" said Marina, "That's all we need is for them to spend even more time indoors on electronic gadgets."

Roberto laughed, "No they don't sit at a computer to do this activity, but I'll bet they will want to check the project site once in awhile to see our school results."

Marina looked at Roberto doubtfully. "Let me explain," said Roberto. "There is a web site where schools around the country submit how much they've exercised in various kinds of activities. Teachers can sign up their classes to submit their results and compete with other schools. I've talked to Wilber, the math teacher, and he's agreed to let me introduce the project in his classes. We show students a series of exercise activities they can do, and Wilber has agreed to create a spreadsheet to keep track of the exercises they submit. He'll award points to students each week they turn in an exercise summary. At the end of each week, he'll use the spreadsheet data to build a graph of their performance and post it outside his class in the hall. Then he'll submit their data to the web site, and they can see how they compare. We thought we'd tell the principal about the project, too, so he'll have our results read on the morning announcements. I'll be he'll encourage the kids to exercise so we can compare favorably with other schools! What do you think?"

"I think it's inspired!" exclaimed Marina. "Who would have thought computers can motivate students to exercise more?"

S2.1 What problems did Roberto feel students have that he felt this project could address?
S2.2 What would be the relative advantage of using image software for the activities?
S2.3 What would be a good way to arrange for students to be involved with putting the data into the spreadsheet and checking the web site?
S2.4 What data should Roberto collect to see the impact of this project on students' exercise patterns after the project ends?

Health and Physical Education Integration Problems to Analyze and Solve

P.1. Felicia wanted all her physical education students to keep a "fitness portfolio." She wants them to enter weekly entries on what they have accomplished on their own fitness plans and on assigned exercises and activities, their entries on a fitness journal, and video clips of their performances. She wants them to be able to update it and share it easily with other students and their parents and friends.

P1.1 What technology-based strategies could Felicia use to address these needs?
P1.2 What would be the relative advantages of using these strategies?
P1.3 Why does Felicia want students be able to share the portfolio easily with parents and friends?

P.2. Whenever his tennis students are practicing various new skills he has just introduced, Larue takes videos of their performances with his digital camera. Later that day, he and the students look at their performances together and analyze how they could improve their techniques.

P2.1 What problem(s) does this technology-based strategy address?
P2.2 What is the relative advantage of using this strategy?
P2.3 What are two reasons Larue may want to use a digital video camera as opposed to a regular video camera to record students' performances?

P.3. Estelle wants her students to be prepared for drug-related situations they may encounter outside school. She knows that it does no good to talk to them about what they should do in these situations. She has found a software package that includes a set of short videos, each with a different drug-related scenario. At the end of each scenario, students have an opportunity to choose from a list of responses and see what might happen after each choice.

P3.1 What problem(s) does this technology-based strategy address?
P3.2 What is the relative advantage of using this strategy?
P3.3 Should students work individually, in pairs, in small groups, or as a whole class on this activity? Explain.

P.4. Corey knows that his 10th- and 11th-grade students have and will have a lot of questions about issues related to drugs, sex, and domestic violence. They will be graduating soon, and he wants to make sure they know some of the places they can go for accurate, reliable information from health agencies and other authoritative sources. He decides to have them do an in-class scavenger hunt to locate answers to various questions by looking at some of the key sites.

P4.1 What problem(s) does Corey's technology-based strategy address?
P4.2 What is the relative advantage of using this strategy as opposed to just giving them a list of the web sites?
P4.3 Should students work individually, in pairs, in small groups, or as a whole class on this activity? Explain.

P.5. Elise is a physical education teacher who wants each of her students to set fitness goals for themselves. She has students decide how many exercises of each kind they will do each week and what their target heart rate should be. She has them keep track of how well they have met their goals. However, keeping this information in the notebook she has set up for each class is becoming cumbersome and difficult to update. In addition, she cannot easily calculate averages across the class or how much a student has fallen short of or exceeded a goal.

P5.1 What technology-based strategy could Elise use to address this need?
P5.2 What would be a good way to organize the ongoing task of entering and updating student information? Should Elise do it or should the students? Explain.
P5.3 What could Samantha do to help structure this activity to keep students on task?

Chapter 16

Problem-based Exercises on Using the TIP Model to Integrate Technology into Special Education

Introduction to Technology in Special Education

Special education, like social studies, is not one area, but many. However, it is unique among the disciplines, since it is delineated by student characteristics, rather than by content. Students in special education range from those with unusually high talents to those with severe mental and physical disabilities. Technology resources have been used successfully in all these areas, but have had especially dramatic results with students who have deficits. Technology-based strategies to support instruction for all special education areas are described in detail in Chapter 15 of *Integrating Educational Technology into Teaching* (Roblyer, 2003) and summarized briefly here:

- **Compensating for students' physical deficits to allow full participation** – Devices and software are available to allow students who could not do so otherwise to receive information or complete class assignments. For students who cannot use regular keyboards for computer input, there are alternate keyboards and/or word completion or word selection software. Students who cannot speak intelligibly can do so by using "talking" (speech synthesized) word processing software or software that lets them select words from a computer screen and produce speech-synthesized responses. Students with visual deficits can use text enlargement software, software that reads to them, and/or machines that produce their work from Braille input. Students with hearing deficits can use software that presents information in text form or through close-captioned video.
- **Allowing collaboration in mainstreamed classes** – Many of the technology resources that help support small-group work (e.g., multimedia and web page development projects) also require tasks at many different levels of difficulty. This kind of learning environment allows students to work together despite varying ability levels.
- **Allowing multiple ways to demonstrate learning** – Online research and multimedia/web page development projects allow gifted students opportunities to use their various talents. Those who are good at writing or structuring information can work cooperatively with those who excel at music or graphic design; each can make a valuable contribution to the product; each learns valuable skills in working with others.
- **Supporting students' organization and study skills** – Students with mental and physical disabilities often have difficulty processing and organizing new information. Interactive study tools and personal organizers help motivate students to work on these important skills.

- **Skills practice** – Although not recommended as the sole or even primary use of technology for students with mental disabilities, drill-and-practice and instructional game software frequently can provide the private, high-feedback environment that can encourage these students to learn basic skills.

See standards for special education teachers at:
http://www.nbpts.org/standards/stdsoverviews.cfm
(Look under "Exceptional Needs")

Problem-based exercises in this chapter give you hands-on practice in integrating technologies into special education. Through scenario-based problem situations, you can see how teachers go about selecting and using these tools to support teaching and learning.

Scenarios to Read and Analyze – The following scenarios are examples of integrating various technology-based strategies into curriculum lessons for special education. After reading Chapter 15 in *Integrating Educational Technology into Teaching* (Roblyer, 2003), answer the questions about using the TIP Model to integrate these strategies:

Scenario 1, Special needs – Based on an idea in "Multimedia and Students with Learning Disabilities: The Road to Success" by Michael Speziale and Lynne LaFrance, 1992. *The Computing Teacher*, Vol. 20, No. 3, pp. 31-34.

Rob, the vocational English teacher, was designing a web page on his classroom computer when Jessica, the mother of one of his students, dropped by.

"Hey, Rob, see any good sites?" said Jessica, looking over his shoulder.

"Hi, Jessica!" said Rob. "Yes, as a matter of fact, I just had a great idea for a curriculum project, and I'm designing a web site to support it. I hope it'll be a good one."

"Is this another activity Eric can do?" asked Jessica. "You seem to have a way of making him feel like he is an important part of your class; he loves coming here."

"I'm glad to hear that," said Rob amiably. "Yes, this is another one I'm hoping Eric will find very interesting. He is probably one of my young teenagers hoping to get a driver's license, right? Well, I thought I would have my class create an online study guide of the state driver's manual. It will give them lots of practice in reading and writing, and they'll learn a lot about structuring information for others to read."

"Doing this online guide, it sounds difficult," said Jessica. "With all Eric's reading disabilities, will he be able to do the work?"

"Yes, I've thought about that," said Rob. "You know several of my students have reading difficulties; two of them have already failed the written portion of the driver's exam and are really discouraged. I'm going to pair each of them with a student who reads comparatively well. Then we'll divide up the driver's manual and have each pair work on a section. They'll summarize the rules and use pictures to clarify them. I thought we'd scan in images from the manual, and they can create others as they feel they need to have them. Then, we'll put each section on a web page, and I'll create the main page to link with all the sections. I thought we'd finish by having each pair create a little quiz over the material in their section and add that to the site. Then we could have the students try to answer the questions in class. Of course, they can use this guide to study whenever they need to."

"I think this will be another one Eric will love." said Jessica. "Wait until I tell him!"

S1.1 What problems did Rob see that this project could help address?

S1.2 What are the relative advantages of using online technologies to support this approach, as opposed to having students prepare a guide in paper format?

S1.3 How could Rob arrange to have all the student pairs working at the same time?

S1.4 On what kinds of outcomes should students be assessed?

Scenario 2, Special needs – Based on an idea in "Practical Ideas: Literature, Computers, and Students with Special Needs" by Diane Schipper. *The Computing Teacher*, Vol. 19, No. 2, pp. 33-37.

Irving, a language arts teacher in the middle school, helped his student Mali begin her work at the computer. As she began to use the Braille-enhanced keyboard to type her story, the speech synthesizer read her words aloud. Irving showed Mali how she could turn off the voice whenever she wanted to, then turn it back on to read passages she had written.

As the system continued reading the passages aloud, teachers who were walking by peered in the door to see what Irving was doing. Nadine, the Spanish teacher, could not contain her curiosity and walked in. "Irving, what is this? A reading robot?" she asked.

"Nope, just a talking word processor, Nadine" said Irving. "Mali here has problems seeing the screen, and this helps her keep track of what she is writing, doesn't it, Mali?"

The girl nodded and smiled. "Yes, this is great!" she said. "Now I'll be able to write so much faster and get more done. When I hear it read to me, I can spot what I am doing wrong so quickly."

"I'm also thinking of using this software with David, my student with speech difficulties," said Irving. "This will let him type his communications to us, and we can understand what he says better. I'm thinking it may also help him with his written language development. You know, he has problems with his writing, as well as speaking."

"You don't think he will be put off by the speech-synthesized voice, do you?" asked Nadine.

"I don't think so," said Irving. "Mali likes it, and the other kids seem intrigued by it."

"I wonder if it could help my students with reading disabilities," said Nadine. "Perhaps if I pair them with students who are better readers and they work together on a written product, the speech synthesis could give the poorer readers auditory feedback on what they write. What do you think, Irving?" she asked.

"I think it's worth a try," said Irving. "We should do whatever we can to help these guys use language better – even if it means using 'reading robots,' right?"

S2.1 What problems did Irving have that using this system could address?
S2.2 What would be the relative advantage of using this system with Mali? With David?
S2.3 When other students are present, what could Irving do prevent them from being disturbed by the talking computer as Mali uses it?
S2.4 What would be a good way to find out if David dislikes the speech-synthesized voice and if he and/or Nadine's students produce more and/or better-written work as a result of the software and synthesizer?

Special Education Integration Problems to Analyze and Solve

P.1. Cordelia had a student with cerebral palsy who could not control her hands enough to write or use a computer keyboard. Cordelia believed her student was bright; she contributed some valuable things verbally and seemed interested in everything they did. However, she was unable to complete most class assignments.

P1.1 What technology-based strategies could Cordelia use to address these needs?
P1.2 What would be the relative advantages of using these strategies?
P1.3 Should Cordelia have her student with cerebral palsy work alone or with other students? Explain.

P.2. Arturo was a science teacher who had been assigned to teach a group of gifted students. The principal had asked Arturo to create learning activities that would challenge and motivate these students to learn science and mathematics and offer a way they each could demonstrate individual learning using particular kinds of intelligence.

P2.1 What technology-based strategy could Arturo use to carry out such a project?
P2.2 What would be the relative advantage of using this strategy?
P2.3 Describe how Arturo might manage this kind of activity in a classroom.

P.3. Bart was a fifth-grade teacher who had three low-achieving students with very low mathematics test scores. It was clear they each lacked basic skills in math facts and operations. Bart had no time to work with each of these students individually, but he knew they needed practice in the skills they lacked. They also needed motivation to practice the skills, since each had failed so frequently in previous classes.

P3.1 What technology-based strategy could Bart use to address this need?
P3.2 What would be the relative advantage of using this strategy?
P3.3 Should these students work individually, in pairs, or as a small group on this activity? Explain.

P.4. Theodore was a seventh-grade social studies teacher who had two students with learning disabilities. Neither student could read or write very well. However, both had talents. One was an avid photographer, and the other liked to draw and paint. Theodore wanted to create an activity that allowed them to participate fully in classroom projects and have their talents recognized. He felt this recognition would help motivate them to spend time on other learning activities.

P4.1 What technology-based strategy could Theodore use to address this need?
P4.2 What would be the relative advantage of using this strategy?
P4.3 How could Theodore determine whether or not these two students felt more positive about other class work as a result of participation in this activity?

P.5. Zeke was a fifth-grade teacher. He had a nonverbal student whose vocal cords had become injured in a traffic accident. The student was very intelligent, but he was depressed and discouraged because he could not communicate with his teachers or his classmates. Zeke had overheard some of the children referring to this student as "The Dummy." Zeke wanted to find a way to allow this student to communicate in class to show the other students he was not a "dummy" and allow him to participate more fully in learning activities.

P5.1 What technology-based tool could Zeke use to address this need?
P5.2 What would be the relative advantage of using this tool?
P5.3 Give an example of a learning activity in a content area (e.g., language arts, science, social studies) that would make use of this tool.

PART III REVIEW EXERCISES
Using the TIP Model in the Content Areas

Do **Exercises 1-6** on the Companion Website at: http://www.prenhall.com/roblyer. Click on the link for *Educational Technology in Action* Review Exercises, and use the links in each of the following sections to answer the review questions. Do **Exercise 7** by loading the Tutorials CD and using the file in the Part III Review Exercises Folder.

Exercise 1. Integrating Technology into Language Instruction

Technology-based strategies can help achieve standards for English/Language Arts and Foreign Languages. In the *Integrating Technology Across the Curriculum* disc that came with your textbook, do a search on lesson ideas in each area; read some of the examples.

III.1 Review the six integration strategies for English/language arts listed in Chapter 11, page 65 of this booklet. Create a lesson idea based on one of the six strategies. Tell which of the English/Language Arts Standards your lesson could help meet.

III.2 Review the three integration strategies for foreign languages in Chapter 11, page 66 of this booklet. Create a lesson idea based on one of these strategies. Tell which standards under the five "C's" for Foreign Languages this lesson could help meet.

Exercise 2. Integrating Technology into Math and Science Instruction

Technology-based strategies can help achieve the standards for mathematics and science. In the *Integrating Technology Across the Curriculum* disc that came with your textbook, do a search on lesson ideas in each area; read some of the examples.

III.3 Review the three technology integration strategies for mathematics listed in Chapter 12, page 71 of this booklet. Create a lesson idea based on one of these strategies. Tell which of the mathematics standards this lesson could help meet.

III.4 Review the three technology integration strategies for science listed in Chapter 12, page 72 of this booklet. Create a lesson idea based on one of these strategies. Tell which of the science standards this lesson could help meet.

Exercise 3. Integrating Technology into Social Studies Instruction

Technology-based strategies can help achieve the standards for social studies. In the *Integrating Technology Across the Curriculum* disc that came with your textbook, do a search on lesson ideas for this area; read some of the examples.

III.5 Review the six technology integration strategies for social studies listed in Chapter 13, page 77-78 of this booklet. Create a lesson idea based on one of these strategies. Tell which of the social studies standards this lesson could help meet.

Exercise 4. Integrating Technology into Music and Art Instruction

Technology-based strategies can help achieve the standards for music and art. In the *Integrating Technology Across the Curriculum* disc that came with your textbook, do a search on lesson ideas in each area; read some of the examples.

III.6 Review the five technology integration strategies for music listed in Chapter 14, page 83 of this booklet. Create a lesson idea based on one of these strategies. Tell which of the music standards this lesson could help meet.

III.7 Review the four technology integration strategies for art listed in Chapter 14, page 84 of this booklet. Create a lesson idea based on one of these strategies. Tell which of the art standards this lesson could help meet.

Exercise 5. Integrating Technology into Health and Physical Education

Technology-based strategies can help achieve the standards for physical education and health. In the *Integrating Technology Across the Curriculum* disc that came with your textbook, do a search on lesson ideas in each area; read some of the examples.

III.8 Review the four technology integration strategies for physical education listed in Chapter 15, page 89 of this booklet. Create a lesson idea based on one of these strategies. Tell which physical education standards this lesson could help meet.

III.9 Review the three technology integration strategies for health listed in Chapter 15, page 90 of this booklet. Create a lesson idea based on one of these strategies. Tell which of the health standards this lesson could help meet.

Exercise 6. Integrating Technology into Special Education

In the *Integrating Technology Across the Curriculum* disc that came with your textbook, do a search on lesson ideas for special education; read some of the examples.

III.10 Review the five technology integration strategies for special education listed in Chapter 16, page 95-96 of this booklet. Create a lesson idea for students with disabilities based on one of these strategies.

III.10 Create a lesson idea for gifted students based on one of these strategies

Exercise 7. Creating Classroom Products – Load the Tutorials CD that came with this book. Open the Adobe *Acrobat®* file for the Microsoft *Excel* tutorial, and create the product as the tutorial directs. (Adobe's *Acrobat Reader®* is on the CD.)

Integrating Educational Technology into Teaching

THIRD EDITION

M. D. Roblyer

University of Maryland University College

Merrill
Prentice Hall

Columbus, Ohio
Upper Saddle River, New Jersey

Library of Congress Cataloging in Publication Data
Roblyer, M. D.
Integrating educational technology into teaching / by M. D. Roblyer.—3rd ed.
p. cm.
Includes bibliographical references and indexes.
ISBN 0-13-042319-X
1. Educational technology—United States. 2. Computer-assisted instruction—United States. 3. Curriculum planning—United States. I. Title.

LB1028.3 .R595 2003
371.33—dc21

2002024641

Vice President and Publisher: Jeffery W. Johnston
Editor: Debra A. Stollenwerk
Editorial Assistant: Mary D. Morrill
Development Editor: Heather Doyle Fraser
Production Editors: Kimberly J. Lundy and JoEllen Gohr
Design Coordinator: Diane C. Lorenzo
Photo Coordinator: Valerie Schultz
Cover Designer: Linda Sorrells-Smith
Cover Art: Linda Bronson
Production Manager: Pamela D. Bennett
Director of Marketing: Ann Castel Davis
Marketing Manager: Krista Groshong
Marketing Coordinator: Tyra Cooper

This book was set in Times by Carlisle Communications, Ltd. It was printed and bound by Courier Kendallville, Inc. The cover was printed by Phoenix Color Corp.

Chapter Opening Photo Credits: Valerie Schultz/Merrill, p. 4; Kathy Kirtland/Merrill, p. 27; Anthony Magnacca/Merrill, pp. 51, 86, 143, 235, 253, 271, 302, 315; A. Ramey/PhotoEdit, p. 116; Bill Wiencke, p. 163, Charles Gupton/Corbis, p. 189; Bill Wiencke and Carrollton Elementary School, p. 220; Patrick O'Lear/PhotoEdit, p. 287.

Pearson Education Ltd.
Pearson Education Australia Pty. Limited
Pearson Education Singapore Pte. Ltd.
Pearson Education North Asia Ltd.
Pearson Education Canada, Ltd.
Pearson Educación de Mexico, S.A. de C.V.
Pearson Education—Japan
Pearson Education Malaysia Pte. Ltd.
Pearson Education, *Upper Saddle River, New Jersey*

10 9 8 7 6 5 4 3 2 1
ISBN 0-13-042319-X

To Bill and Paige Wiencke whose love is, as Arthur Clarke said of advanced technology, indistinguishable from magic

ABOUT THE AUTHOR

M. D. Roblyer has been a technology-using teacher and a contributor to the field of educational technology for nearly 30 years. She began her exploration of technology's benefits for teaching in 1971 as a graduate student at one of the country's first successful instructional computer training sites, Pennsylvania State University, where she helped write tutorial literacy lessons in Coursewriter II on an IBM 1500 dedicated instructional mainframe. While obtaining a Ph.D. in instructional systems at Florida State University, she worked on several major courseware development and training projects with Control Data Corporation's PLATO system. After working as instructional technology coordinator for the Florida Educational Computing Project (the predecessor of what is now the state's Office of Educational Technology), she became a private consultant, working for companies such as Random House and the Apple Computer Company. In 1981–1982, she designed one of the early microcomputer software series, *Grammar Problems for Practice,* in conjunction with the Milliken Publishing Company.

She has written extensively and served as contributing editor for educational technology publications such as *Educational Technology* and *Learning and Leading with Technology.* Her book with Castine and King, *Assessing the Impact of Computer-based Instruction: A Review of Research* (Haworth, 1988), is widely considered the most comprehensive review and meta-analysis ever written on the effects of computer technology on learning. Her recent research has focused on identifying ways to help make distance learning courses and programs more effective learning experiences for students in high school and postsecondary education.

Currently, she is Adjunct Professor of Educational Technology, teaching online for the University of Maryland University College's web-based graduate programs from her home in Carrollton, Georgia. She is married to William R. Wiencke and is the mother of a daughter, Paige.

PREFACE

. . . scientific knowledge will doubtless continue to improve our ability to get the things we value, (but) nothing in science can ever tell us what to value. . .we have to write the script ourselves.

Steven Weinberg, in *The Future of Science and the Universe,* 2001

In his book *Telecosm,* a paean to the golden future that he predicts technology soon will make possible, George Gilder speaks of new technology that "makes men into bandwidth angels," capable of electronically enhanced flight "beyond the fuzzy electrons and frozen pathways of the microcosm to a boundless realm. . . ." Gilder is the acolyte for those who see unlimited access to technology as equivalent to heaven. But David Denby, writing in *The New Yorker* about the Evernet (the next incarnation of the Internet), sees the potential for something less celestial. "Are we truly standing on the edge of greater freedom and personal control?" he wonders. "Or are we unwittingly putting ourselves in thrall to a system that will dazzle us with choices yet dislocate us, pull us apart, even consume us?"

Weinberg seems to see clearly that both futures are possible and neither is inevitable. The difference, he says, depends on "the script," that is, a recognition and articulation of what we value about ourselves, our society, our civilization. These are the guideposts, he says, that will show us how to use well the products of our scientific knowledge. So inspired and guided, we can create a future in which technology is our ally rather than our undoing, our salvation rather than our damnation.

What are the values that should underlie our use of technology in education? The following are suggested as essential elements:

- **Good teaching comes first.** Recent innovations in bandwidth-enabled distance resources gave renewed hope to those who predicted, as did their predecessors in the 1960s, that technology would eliminate the personality of teachers from the instructional equation. Our experience with web-based learning in the past 5 years, however, has shown that interaction with teachers, flawed and variable as it may be, is more important than ever before. This textbook proposes that technology is, above all, a channel for helping teachers communicate better with students. It can make good teaching even better, but it cannot make bad teaching good. Consequently, technology-using teachers never can be a force for improved education unless they are first and foremost informed, knowledgeable shapers of their craft. Before integrating technology into their teaching, educators must know a great deal, for example, why there are different views on appropriate teaching strategies, how societal factors and learning theories have shaped these views, and how each strategy can address differing needs.
- **Technology is us.** Rather than seeing technology as some foreign invader come to confuse and complicate the simple life of the past, we can recognize that technology is very much *our own response* to overcoming obstacles that stand in the way of a better, more productive way of life. As Walt Kelly's "profound 'possum" Pogo said, "We has met the enemy, and he is us." *Technology is us*—our tools, our methods, and our own creative attempts to solve problems in our environment. There will be turmoil as we go through periods of transition, adapting to the new environment we ourselves have created. But technology is, by definition, intended to be part of our path to a better life, rather than an obstacle in its way.
- **We control how technology is used in education.** As a follow-up to our recognition that "technology is us," we must recognize the truth of Peter Drucker's statement: "The best way to predict the future is to create it." Both individual teachers and teaching organizations must see themselves as enlightened shapers of our future. Each teacher must take a position as a "script writer," helping to articulate the vision for what the future of education should look like; each should acquire skills to help work toward realizing that vision.

The purpose of this book is to show how we are challenged to shape the future of educational technology. How we respond to this challenge is guided by how we see it helping us accomplish our own informed vision of what teaching and learning should be. Our approach to accomplishing this purpose rests on three premises:

- **Integration methods should be based in both learning theory and teaching practice.** There is no shortage of innovative ideas in the field of instructional technology; new and interesting methods come forward about as often as new and improved gadgets. Those who would build on the knowledge of the past should know why they do what they do, as well as how to do it. Thus, we have linked various technology-based integration strategies to well-researched theories of learning, and we have illustrated them with examples of successful practices based on these theories.
- **Integration should match specific teaching and learning needs.** Technology has the power to improve teaching and learning, but it can also make a teacher's life more complicated. Therefore, each resource should be examined for its unique qualities and its potential benefits for teachers and students. Teachers should not use a tool simply because it is new and available—each integration strategy should be matched to a recognized need. We do not oppose experimentation, but we do advocate informed use.
- **Old integration strategies are not necessarily bad; new strategies are not necessarily good.** As technology products change and evolve at lightning speed, there is a decided tendency toward throwing out older teaching methods with the older machines. Sometimes this is a good idea; sometimes it would be a shame. Each of the integration strategies recommended in this book is based on methods with proven usefulness to teachers and students. Some of the strategies are based on directed methods that have been used for some time; other strategies are based on the newer, constructivist learning models. Each is recommended on the basis of its usefulness rather than its age.

This edition differs in some structural ways from the first two, but its goal remains the same: *to help teachers see their role in shaping the future of technology in education.* This book can help them perceive that writing a script for the future requires some faith in ourselves, a belief that we can fly into the future with wings of our own making.

Who Will Find This Book Helpful?

This book is designed to help teach both theoretical and practical characteristics of technology integration strategies. It is useful in several different types of education settings:

- **As primary instructional material.** It benefits instructional technology courses for preservice teachers and workshops and graduate courses for inservice teachers.
- **As supplemental instructional material.** It supports research and content-area methods courses.
- **As a reference.** It provides topical information in K–12 school libraries/media centers and university college of education libraries and media centers.

New to This Edition

This edition has added new information and reorganized some information from the first and second editions to help make sense of both new and emerging concepts. Readers will note the following changes and improvements:

- **A technology integration model for teachers.** Chapter 2 offers a more detailed, step-by-step approach to guide teachers in integrating technology, linked to rubrics and checklists (in the Appendix) to assess the impact of their integration.
- **Additional learning theory and assessment information.** Chapter 3 has additional *InSight* boxes: one summarizing John Dewey's contributions and another describing how to structure and use electronic portfolios. This edition also includes a variety of rubrics and checklists for assessing technology's impact on teaching and learning. These have been placed in the Appendix for easy reference.
- **A focus on relative advantages of technology tools.** In light of teachers' key role as potential adopters of innovation, it is important to clarify even further the unique benefits offered by each educational technology resource. In this edition, these advantages are identified in terms of what diffusion of innovations expert Everett Rogers called their "relative advantage" to teachers and students.
- **Revised and updated multimedia/hypermedia chapter.** Chapter 7, Integrating Multimedia and Hypermedia into Teaching and Learning, has been revised to reflect recent innovations in and integration strategies for authoring, presentation, and video editing software.
- **Expanded coverage of the Internet.** In recognition of the growing importance of the Internet in communications and distance learning, Chapter 8 provides expanded coverage of distance learning with an even greater emphasis on web-based learning.
- **Expert authors for content area chapters.** In this edition, Chapters 10 through 15 have been written by content-area experts who detail appropriate, up-to-date integration strategies for each of the subject areas.
- **Additional technology integration ideas and Internet links on a CD-ROM database.** This textbook is

packaged with a CD-ROM containing a searchable database of technology integration lesson ideas for many content areas. Spanning a variety of content areas and grade levels, these teacher-tested lessons are keyed to national content standards and ISTE technology standards. For this edition, 250 new ideas have been added, and most have links to Internet sites containing additional information. Users can modify existing lesson ideas or add new ones. Look for the CD-ROM icon throughout the text. A User Manual is printed after the index and is also contained on the CD-ROM.

- **Enhanced Companion Website.** A website with additional support materials that is integrated with the text is available at http://www.prenhall.com/roblyer. Look for the Companion Website icon at the end of each chapter. **For more specific information about the features of this website, please read the Discover the Companion Website section following the preface.**

Educational Technology in Action

This new section of the 2004 Update of *Integrating Educational Technology into Teaching,* based on the Technology Integration Planning (TIP) Model in Chapter 2, gives students opportunities to solve real-world problems and to practice applying concepts they have read about in the text. Participating in this simulated problem solving helps prepare teachers for the real world of technology in schools.

The scenarios, problems, and exercises in this section are aligned to all but one chapter of the text. All scenarios in Chapters 2–16 are designed to address ISTE's National Educational Technology Standards for Teachers (NETS*T). Students can complete the exercises online at **http://www.prenhall.com/roblyer** by clicking on the *Educational Technology in Action* module and using the links there to answer the questions.

Also accompanying this section of the text is a **tutorials CD** designed to give students hands-on practice in using Microsoft Word, Excel, Netscape Composer, and PowerPoint to design products for four of the curriculum lessons described in the exercises.

Organization of the Text

This text is organized into four sections—one of background and three of resources and applications.

Part I: Introduction and Background on Integrating Technology in Education.
Einstein is said to have observed that "Everything should be made as simple as possible, but not more so." Using technology as a force for change becomes simpler when one understands the foundations on which integration strategies are based—but that is no small task in itself. This section provides a "big picture" background on technology's role in education, reviews a variety of planning issues to be addressed prior to and during integration, provides a technology integration model for teachers, and describes learning theories and teaching/learning models related to technology integration.

Part II: Using Software and Media Tutors and Tools: Principles and Strategies.
To paraphrase a popular jingle, "Software—it ain't just CAI anymore." This section describes more than 40 types of instructional software products ranging from drill and practice to integrated learning systems, from word processing to groupware. Multimedia and hypermedia are covered in this section, because they fit so well under the rubric of tools. Each software and media product description covers unique qualities, potential benefits, and sample integration strategies.

Part III: Linking to Learn: Principles and Strategies.
This section represents the most significant revision from the first edition. In light of the growing importance of connecting people and resources for a technology-permeated future, two chapters are devoted to the types and uses of distance technologies. As with Part II, example lesson plans or activities are given for each recommended integration strategy. Chapter 9 provides a "link to the future," courtesy of William R. Wiencke, in describing technologies that are changing the way members of our society live, work, and communicate.

Part IV: Integrating Technology Across the Curriculum.
The six chapters in this part describe and give updated examples of technology integration strategies and resources for several different content areas: language arts and foreign languages, math and science, social sciences, the arts, physical education and health education, and special education. Although these chapters separate the areas into topics, the chapters themselves recognize and incorporate the current trends toward thematic, interdisciplinary instruction. Many of the examples cross discipline boundaries and serve to illustrate how the concepts of several content areas can be merged into a single lesson or learning activity—and how technology can support the process.

Special Features

Each chapter has the following features to help both the instructor and the student.

- **A list of descriptive topics and objectives.** This list appears at the beginning of each chapter.
- **Illustrative screens.** Figures show screen displays from software and media resources whenever possible.

- **Summary tables of important information.** These aid comprehension, recall, and analysis.
- **Sample, teacher-designed technology integration ideas.** All from published sources, these materials match integration strategies. ISTE National Educational Technology Standards for Students are identified for each one, and links are given to additional information on the Prentice Hall Companion Website and on the integration idea CD-ROM, *Integrating Technology Across the Curriculum.*
- **Exercises.** Improved end-of-chapter questions, many of them linked to the Companion Website and CD-ROM, call for students to analyze and apply what they have read to problems in education and in applying technology. The portfolio development and classroom collaboration exercises are linked to ISTE National Educational Technology Standards for Teachers.
- **A list of sample resources.** References for further reading end each chapter.

Supplements to Accompany This Text

Instructors have access to the following resources:

- **A booklet to help support students' introduction to Internet use.** Packaged with each copy of the text, the booklet *Starting Out on the Internet: A Learning Journey for Teachers* is a valuable resource as students begin exploring the Internet.
- **An interactive CD-ROM.** This CD-ROM is packaged with the book and contains a searchable database of over 500 technology integration lesson ideas for many content areas.
- **A comprehensive Instructor's Manual.** The manual contains content overviews, teaching strategies and activities, and additional resources (including a list of web sites).
- **A computerized Test Bank.** Available for either Windows or Macintosh, the Test Bank includes a variety of question formats, such as true/false, multiple choice, short answer, and essay.

Acknowledgments

As has been the case with the last two editions, keeping up with technology is like running to catch a speeding bus—it certainly does leave you breathless. Educational technology not only is changing rapidly, but it is also expanding quickly and in unpredictable directions. It is an ever more challenging task to capture and communicate its scope and essence. However, several people helped me meet this challenge.

The following reviewers provided insightful and practical critiques and advice, all of which helped to clarify the prose and sharpen the focus: Leslie Hall, University of New Mexico; Cindy Kovalik, The University of Akron; John Savery, DePaul University; Cary Sheffield, California University of Pennsylvania; and Rosemary Skeele, Seton Hall University.

As usual, the enormous professional and personal support given by the Merrill editorial staff is impossible to measure. The firm vision and competent direction of my editor and friend Debbie Stollenwerk not only helped me conceptualize and carry out the work on this edition, but also gave me the encouragement I needed to see it through to completion. With skill and professionalism, the support, editorial, and production team members (Heather Doyle Fraser, Mary Morrill, Penny Burleson, Kim Lundy, and JoEllen Gohr) made my ideas and words both attractive as well as useful.

As before, I would like to thank my family and friends for taking second place for so many weekends and holidays while I dedicated the time and work required for this latest revision. I would like to recognize the enduring love and patience of my family, Bill and Paige Wiencke and Becky Kelley; the tenacious loyalty of friends like Sherry Alter and Paul Belt, Marilyn and Herb Comet, Barbara Hansen, Sharon and Jon Marshall, Gwen McAlpine and Paul Zimmer, Sharon Milner, and Mary Ann Myers; and the support offered by new colleague Megan Hurley at the University of Maryland University College. Also, I would like to continue to remember and acknowledge the enduring contributions of those who are with us now only in memory: S. L. Roblyer and Catherine Pryor Roblyer, and Raymond and Marjorie Wiencke.

And, as always, I recognize the contributions of all the educators who have worked so long and so hard to make it possible for us to "write the right script" for the education system of the future.

M. D. Roblyer

Discover the Companion Website Accompanying This Book

The Prentice Hall Companion Website: A Virtual Learning Environment

Technology is a constantly growing and changing aspect of our field that is creating a need for content and resources. To address this emerging need, Prentice Hall has developed an online learning environment for students and professors alike—Companion Websites—to support our textbooks.

In creating a Companion Website, our goal is to build on and enhance what the textbook already offers. For this reason, the content for each user-friendly website is organized by topic and provides the professor and student with a variety of meaningful resources.

For the Professor

Every Companion Website integrates **Syllabus Manager™**, an online syllabus creation and management utility.

- **Syllabus Manager™** provides you, the instructor, with an easy, step-by-step process to create and revise syllabi, with direct links into Companion Website and other online content without having to learn HTML.
- Students can access your syllabus during any study session. All they need to know is the web address for the Companion Website and the password you've assigned to your syllabus.
- After you have created a syllabus using **Syllabus Manager™**, students may enter the syllabus for their course section from any point in the Companion Website.
- Clicking on a date, the student is shown the list of activities for the assignment. The activities for each assignment are linked directly to actual content, saving time for students.
- Adding assignments consists of clicking on the desired due date, then filling in the details of the assignment—name of the assignment, instructions, and whether it is a one-time or repeating assignment.
- In addition, links to other activities can be created easily. If the activity is online, a URL can be entered in the space provided, and it will be linked automatically in the final syllabus.
- Your completed syllabus is hosted on our servers, allowing convenient updates from any computer on the Internet. Changes you make to your syllabus are immediately available to your students at their next logon.

For the Student

Each chapter of the Companion Website contains the following features for students:

- **Portfolio and Collaborative Activities.** These activities help students build their own electronic professional portfolio and are linked to the **ISTE National Educational Technology Standards for Teachers.** They also are featured at the end of each chapter of the text.
- **Integration Activities.** These activities link the book content and the resources on the CD-ROM database that accompanies the book. They are also featured at the end of each chapter of the text.
- **Related Sites.** This section contains web sites specific to chapter content and assists students in using the Web to do additional research on chapter topics and key issues.
- **Chapter Objectives.** Objectives alert the reader to what will be covered in the chapter.
- **Multiple Choice Self-Quizzes.** The interactive, multiple choice self-quizzes enable students to test themselves on their knowledge of the concepts introduced in the text.

Students can submit their quiz online and receive immediate feedback on their level of understanding of chapter topics through Results Reporter. This feature gives a graph representation of how the user scored in addition to a percentage score correct, how many questions answered correctly/incorrectly, and the number of questions left unanswered.

- **Resources.** This section gives students and professors alike access to additional content information and online resources regarding educational technology.
- **Message Board.** A true message board environment where students and professors can initiate new message "threads" as they see fit.
- **Chat.** Real-time chat with anyone who is using the text anywhere in the country. Ideal for distance learning, Q & A sessions, and scheduled interaction with instructors, discussion groups, study groups, class projects, etc.
- ***Microsoft PowerPoint*® transparencies.**

To take advantage of these available resources, please visit the Companion Website that accompanies *Integrating Educational Technology into Teaching,* Third Edition, at

http://www.prenhall.com/roblyer

Brief Contents

CONTENTS

CHAPTER 6

CHAPTER 7

PART III

LINKING TO LEARN: PRINCIPLES AND STRATEGIES 187

CHAPTER 8

CHAPTER 9

PART IV

INTEGRATING TECHNOLOGY ACROSS THE CURRICULUM 233

CHAPTER 10

CHAPTER 11

CHAPTER 12

CHAPTER 13

NOTE: Every effort has been made to provide accurate and current Internet information in this book. However, the Internet and information posted on it are constantly changing, so it is inevitable that some of the Internet addresses listed in this textbook will change.

PART I

Introduction and Background on Integrating Technology in Education

The chapters in this part will help teachers learn:

1. How technology in education has evolved from its beginnings to its present-day resources and applications and where it might be going in the future
2. Issues and concerns that become important when implementing technology resources in schools and classrooms
3. How learning theories influence the development of technology integration strategies

Introduction: We Want to Be Ready

About 20 years ago, when microcomputers were beginning to appear somewhat regularly in K–12 classrooms, the author visited two teachers at a middle school to see how they were using some recent purchases: two Apple II computers and instructional software, primarily simple mathematics games and drills. As the teachers demonstrated the programs and their classroom applications, they coped with a variety of technical problems.

Some of the software was designed for an earlier version of the Apple operating system, and each disk required a format adjustment every time it was used. Other programs would stall when students entered something the programmers had not anticipated; users either would have to adjust the code or restart the programs. In addition, the computers needed a small device to allow text to appear in both upper- and lowercase on the screen, but this worked with only some programs. In spite of these and other problems, the teachers were excited about their computer resources and spoke with enthusiasm about their hopes, plans, and expectations.

"You guys are obviously doing a great job with your computers," the visitor said, "and I don't mean to seem negative about them. But this sure seems like an awful lot of trouble for what you get out of it. What motivates you to keep investing all the time you do?" The teachers' answer was both instructive and prophetic: "We know the time is coming when computers will be in all classrooms. Software will be better and equipment will be easier to use. When this time comes, we want to be among those prepared to use computers in teaching. We want to be ready."

As we look today at what technology is doing—and what it promises to do—in classrooms across the country, we see that those middle school teachers were right: What is happening now is worth the preparation. Computers and other technology resources have improved in capabilities and user-friendliness to educators. Some of the most innovative and promising practices in education today involve technology, and the promise of even more exciting capabilities foreshadow even greater benefits for teachers.

This book presents some of the most powerful and capable educational technology resources available today. It also demonstrates how teachers can take advantage of this power and capability. Despite these advances, "being ready" still requires an investment of teacher time. This introductory section discusses the knowledge and skills teachers need to prepare themselves to apply technology, especially computer technology, effectively in classrooms.

What Do Teachers Need to Be Ready for Technology?

In a field with a wide range of powerful and complex tools, experts cannot help but disagree about what teachers need to know and where they should begin. Not long ago, many experts believed that teachers who wanted to become "computer literate" must learn to write programs in computer languages such as FORTRAN and BASIC. Few people today believe that teachers need this level of technical skill; however, textbooks continue to provide a wide variety of information for beginning technology users. The background information in this section is based on the following steps that beginning technology users need to take:

Develop a Philosophy and Vision

Teachers must observe where current resources and types of applications fit in the history and current scope of the field. Then they must begin developing personal perspectives on the current and future role of technology in education and a vision for how it can help in their own classrooms.

Purchase Products

Teachers must become informed, knowledgeable consumers of computer products and select wisely among available alternatives.

Identify and Solve Problems

To discriminate between problems they can correct and those that will require outside help, teachers must be able to troubleshoot computer systems they use.

Speak the Language

Sufficient understanding of the terms and concepts related to technology allows users to exchange information with other teachers and experts and to ask and answer questions to expand their knowledge.

See Where Technology Fits in Education

Perhaps the most important—and the most difficult—challenge is for teachers to identify specific teaching and learning problems that technology can help address or how it can create important educational opportunities that did not exist without it. As part of this process, teachers decide what they need to make these changes occur. This process of determining where and how technology fits is known among users of educational technology as *integration.*

Required Background for Teachers

In Part I, three chapters provide the information and skills that will help teachers accomplish their goals.

Chapter 1: Educational Technology in Context: The Big Picture

Computer technology has nearly a 50-year history in education; other kinds of technology have been in use for much longer. Classroom technology resources have changed dramatically over time, but a broad perspective of the field helps illuminate many of today's concepts, terms, and activities. Chapter 1 describes the history of computer resources and related applications of educational technology in order to show how they have evolved—and are still evolving—into the tools described later in this book. The chapter also provides a general overview of technology resources in education today and where computer technology fits into this picture.

Chapter 2: Planning and Implementation for Effective Technology Integration

Educators must resolve many complex issues to apply technology solutions to educational problems. They must address many concerns before and during implementation to ensure that technology has the desired effects on students and schools. These concerns range from funding to selection and placement of technology resources. Although planning at community and school levels also is important, Chapter 2 acts as a planning guide primarily for the teacher.

The chapter discusses each of the issues involved and recommends useful and practical steps educators can take to deal with preparation and implementation issues.

Chapter 3: Learning Theories and Integration Models

The last chapter in Part I provides an important link between learning and technology. It emphasizes the need to reach beyond the "nuts and bolts" of how technology resources work. Successful integration requires a connection between how people learn and how teachers employ technology to assist and enhance this learning. Chapter 3 begins with an overview of learning theories and related research findings and introduces two different perspectives on how to integrate technology into teaching and learning activities. These two perspectives are known as *directed models* and *constructivist models.* Finally, Chapter 3 identifies technology integration strategies based on each of these models.

1 CHAPTER

Educational Technology in Context: The Big Picture

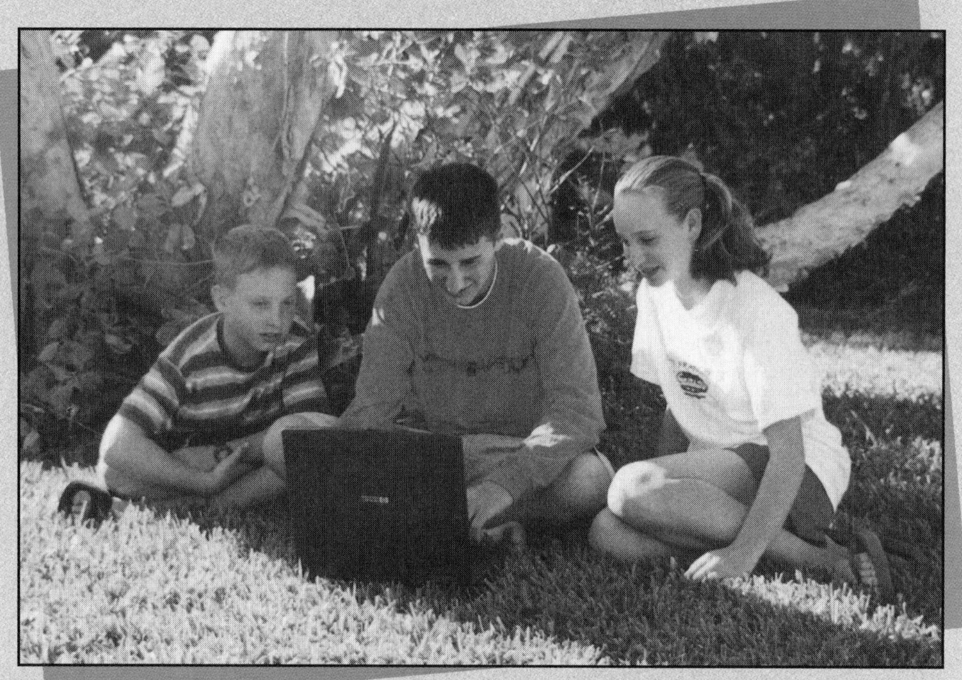

Science is a process, not an edifice, and sheds old concepts as it grows.

Timothy Ferris in *Coming of Age in the Milky Way* (1988)

The more we know of our heritage, the more we earn the right to lead the field forward in our own time.

Don Ely in Paul Saettler's *The Evolution of American Educational Technology* (1990)

This chapter covers the following topics:

- Various definitions of key educational technology terms and how they originated
- A brief history of computer technology in education and what we have learned from it
- Justification for technology purchases by relating them to potential improvements in teaching and learning
- An overview of current technology systems and applications in education and the major issues and concerns that guide their uses
- Issues that shape technology's current and future role in restructuring education.

Objectives

1. Given an evolving definition of the term *educational technology*, give four different aspects of that definition and identify professional associations and events that represent each view.
2. Identify periods in the history of educational computing and describe what we have learned from past applications and decisions.
3. Identify reasons to help justify a school or district's purchase and use of technology.
4. Identify the general categories of educational technology hardware resources: stand-alone computer, network, centralized processor, and related device/system.
5. Identify the general categories of educational technology software resources: instructional software, software tool, multimedia, distance learning, or a virtual reality environment.
6. Explain the impact of each of the following societal issues on current uses of technology in education: cultural diversity, educational equity, ethical practices, and the increasing role of technology in modern life.

When a classroom teacher browses the Internet for new teaching materials or has students design a multimedia presentation, that teacher is using some of the latest and best of what is commonly called *technology in education* or *educational technology.* But educational technology is not new at all, and it is by no means limited to the use of equipment, let alone electronic equipment. Modern tools and techniques are simply the latest developments in a field that some believe is as old as education itself.

In his excellent, comprehensive historical description, *The Evolution of American Educational Technology* (1990), Paul Saettler begins by pointing out that "Educational technology . . . can be traced back to the time when tribal priests systematized bodies of knowledge, and early cultures invented pictographs or sign writing to record and transmit information. . . . It is clear that educational technology is essentially the product of a great historical stream consisting of trial and error, long practice and imitation, and sporadic manifestations of unusual individual creativity and persuasion" (p. 4).

This chapter explores the link between the early applications of educational technology and those of today and tomorrow. This exploration includes some historical and technical background. Some readers will grow impatient when they encounter these paragraphs of description and explanation. This impatience is understandable in a field where the real excitement for teachers and students lies in hands-on exploration of the newest gadgets and techniques. We encourage you to read this information for three reasons:

- **Looking back before going ahead.** This information shows where the field is headed by demonstrating where it began. It points out the current status in the evolution of the technology of education along with changes in goals and methods over time. It provides a foundation on which to build more successful and useful structures to respond to the challenges of modern education.
- **Learning from past mistakes.** This background also helps those just embarking on their first applications of educational technology to make the best use of their learning time by avoiding mistakes that others have made and by choosing directions that experience has shown to be promising.
- **Developing a "big picture."** Finally, this background helps new learners to develop mental pictures of the field, what Ausubel (1968) might call *cognitive frameworks* through which to view all applications—past, present, and future.

What Is "Educational Technology"?

Origins and Definitions of Key Terms

Teachers will see references to the terms *educational technology* and *instructional technology* in many professional journals. Perhaps no other topics are the focus of so much new development in so many content areas, yet no single, acceptable definition for these terms dominates the field. Paul Saettler, a recognized authority on the history of instructional and educational technology, notes uncertainty even about the origins of the terms. The earliest reference he can confirm for the term *educational technology* was in an interview with W. W. Charters in 1948; the earliest known reference he finds for the term *instructional technology* was in a 1963 foreword by James Finn for a technology development project sponsored by the National Education Association.

For many educators, any mention of technology in education immediately brings to mind the use of some device or a set of equipment, particularly computer equipment. Muffoletto (1994) says that "Technology is commonly thought of in terms of gadgets, instruments, machines, and devices . . . most (educators) will defer to technology as computers" (p. 25). Only about 15 years ago, a history of technology in education since 1920 placed the emphasis on radio and television, with computers as an afterthought (Cuban, 1986). If such a description were written now, the Internet might be a central focus. Twenty years from now the focus might be intelligent computer-assisted instruction or virtual reality or whatever they are called then.

In one sense, all these views are correct, since definitions of state-of-the-art instruction usually mention the most recently developed tools. But Saettler (1990) urges those seeking precision to remember that "the historical function of educational technology is a *process* rather than a product. No matter how sophisticated the media of instruction may become, a distinction must always be made between the process of developing a technology of education and the use of certain products or media within a particular technology of instruction" (p. 4). Therefore, in the view of most writers, researchers, and practitioners in the field, useful definitions of educational technology must focus on the process of applying tools for educational purposes as well as the tools and materials used. As Muffoletto (1994) puts it, "Technology . . . is not a collection of machines and devices, but a way of acting" (p. 25). Based on this background, the authors assign educational technology the following "evolving" definition:

> Educational technology is a combination of the processes and tools involved in addressing educational needs and problems, with an emphasis on applying the most current tools: computers and their related technologies.

Four Perspectives on Educational Technology: Media, Instructional Systems, Vocational Training, and Computers

If educational technology is viewed as both processes and tools, it is important to begin by examining four different historical perspectives on these processes and tools, all of which have helped shape current practices in the field. These influences come to us from four groups whose origins and views are summarized in Figure 1.1.

Technology in education as media and audiovisual communications. The earliest view of educational technology is one that continues today: technology as media. According to Saettler (1990), this view grew out of the *audiovisual movement:* ways of delivering information used as alternatives to lectures and books. Beginning in the 1930s, some higher education instructors proposed that media such as slides and films delivered information in more concrete, and therefore more effective, ways. This perspective later developed into *audiovisual communications,* the "branch of educational theory and practice concerned primarily with the design and use of messages which control the learning process" (Saettler, 1990, p. 9). However, the view of technology as media continued to dominate areas of education and the communications industry. Saettler reports that as late as 1986, the National Task Force on Educational Technology used a definition that equated educational technology with media, treating computers simply as another medium.

The Association for Educational Communications and Technology (AECT) tends to represent this view of technology as media and communications systems. Originally a department of the National Education Association (NEA) that focused on audiovisual instruction, the AECT was until recently concerned primarily with devices that carry messages and the applications of these devices in instructional situations. After a reorganization in 1988, it broadened its mission to include other concerns such as instructional uses of telecommunications and computer/information systems. Several of its divisions, however, still focus on the concerns of media educators and many of its state affiliates still refer to themselves as media associations.

Technology in education as instructional systems. The instructional design or instructional systems movement took shape in the 1960s and 1970s, adding another dimension to the media-and-communications view of technology in education. Systems approaches to solving educational problems originated in military and industrial training but later emerged in university research and development projects. K–12 school practices began to reflect systems approaches when university personnel began advocating them in their work with schools. These approaches were based on the belief that both human *and* nonhuman resources (teachers and media, respectively) could be parts of a system for addressing an instructional need. From this viewpoint, educational technology was seen not just as a medium for communicating instructional information, but as a systematic approach to designing, developing, and delivering instruction matched to carefully identified needs (Heinich, Molenda, Russell, & Smaldino, 2000). Resources for delivering instruction were identified only after detailed analysis of learning tasks and objectives and the kinds of instructional strategies required to teach them.

From the 1960s through the 1980s, applications of systems approaches to instruction were influenced and shaped by learning theories from educational psychology. Behaviorist theories held sway initially and cognitive theories gained influence later. Views of instructional systems in the 1990s also were influenced by popular learning theories; however, these theories criticized systems approaches as too rigid to foster some kinds of learning, particularly

Figure 1.1 Four Perspectives That Shaped Educational Technology

Four Historical Perspectives	Origins	Current Organization
Media and AV communications	Higher education instructors, 1930s	AECT
Instructional systems	Military/industrial trainers; later, university R&D, 1960s–1970s	ISPI
Vocational training (technology education)	Industry trainers, vocational educators, 1980s	ITEA
Computer systems (educational computing)	Programmers, systems analysts; later, university R&D, 1960s	ISTE

higher order ones. Thus, the current view of educational technology as instructional systems seems to be changing once again. (See Chapter 3 for more information on two approaches to educational technology as instructional systems and how each influences methods of integration.)

Just as the AECT had its origins in the media systems view of educational technology, the International Society for Performance Improvement (ISPI) grew out of the view of educational technology as a systems approach to instruction. Originally named the National Society for Programmed Instruction, the ISPI is still concerned primarily with creating and validating instructional systems in order to improve productivity and competence in the workplace.

Technology in education as vocational training tools. Another popular view of technology in education has developed from the perspective of technology as tools used in business and industry. Generally referred to as *technology education,* this view originated with industry trainers and vocational educators in the 1980s and reflects their need for technology to enhance training in specific job skills. This perspective is based on two premises. First, it holds that one important function of school learning is to prepare students for the world of work. Therefore, students need to learn about and use technology that they will encounter after graduation. For example, technology educators believe that all students should learn word processing to help them to perform in many jobs or professions. Second, technology educators believe that vocational training can be a practical means of teaching all content areas such as math, science, and language. Technology education also includes other topics such as robotics, manufacturing systems, and computer-assisted design (CAD) systems.

The organization that espouses this view is the International Technology Education Association (ITEA), formerly the American Industrial Arts Association. The ITEA has helped shape a major paradigm shift in vocational training in K–12 schools. Most schools currently are changing from industrial arts curricula centered in wood shops to technology education courses taught in labs equipped with high-technology stations such as CAD stations and robotics systems.

Technology in education as computers and computer-based systems. The advent of computers in the 1950s created yet another view of educational technology. Business, industry, and military trainers, as well as educators in K–12 and higher education, recognized the instructional potential of computers. Many of these trainers and educators predicted that computer technology would quickly transform education and become the most important component of educational technology. Although instructional applications of computers did not produce the anticipated overnight success, they inspired the development of another branch of educational technology. From the time that computers came into classrooms in the 1960s until about 1990, this perspective was known as *educational computing* and encompassed both instructional and support applications of computers.

Educational computing applications originally were influenced by technical personnel such as programmers and systems analysts. By the 1970s, however, many of the same educators involved with media, audiovisual communications, and instructional systems were directing the course of research and development in educational computing. By the 1990s, these educators began to see computers as part of a combination of technology resources, including media, instructional systems, and computer-based support systems. At that point, educational computing became known as *educational technology.*

The organization that represents this view of technology in education is the International Society for Technology in Education (ISTE), the product of a merger between two computer-oriented groups: the International Council for Computers in Education (ICCE) and the International Association for Computers in Education (IACE). IACE was known for most of its existence from 1960 until 1986 as the Association for Educational Data Systems (AEDS). A major ISTE publication, *The Computing Teacher,* reflected the original computer orientation of the organization. In 1995, it was renamed *Learning and Leading with Technology.* Currently, ISTE is an influential force leading the movement for technology skill standards for teachers and students.

This Textbook's Emphasis on Technology in Education

Each of these perspectives on technology in education has made significant contributions to the current body of knowledge about processes and tools to address educational needs. But, as Saettler (1990) points out, no single paradigm that attempts to describe educational technology can characterize satisfactorily what is happening with technology in education today and what will happen in the future. Furthermore, all of the organizations described here seem engaged in a struggle to claim the high-profile term *educational technology.* Each seems determined to assign a definition based on the perspective and concerns of its members; each wants to be identified with and help shape the future of educational technology. However, these often-conflicting views of the role of technology in education confuse newcomers to the field and make it difficult for them to learn the role of technology; the resources and issues differ depending on whose descriptions teachers hear and which publications they read. This textbook attempts to address the disparate views on this topic in the following ways:

- **Processes.** For the processes, or instructional procedures for applying tools, we look to two different areas. First, we look at learning theories based on the sciences of human behavior. Some of these theories are systems oriented; others are based on various views of how best to foster learning. Second, this textbook acknowledges that many of the applications of technology focus on preparing students for future jobs by helping them acquire skills in using current tools as well as skills in "learning to learn" for tools of the future that are not yet invented—or even imagined.

- **Tools.** Although this textbook looks at technology tools as an overlapping combination of media, instructional systems, and computer-based support systems, it emphasizes a subset of all these resources, focusing primarily on computers and their roles in instructional systems.

There are three reasons for this focus:

1. Computers as media are more complex and more capable than other media such as films or overheads and require more technical knowledge to operate.
2. Computer systems are currently moving toward subsuming many other media within their own resources. For example, CD-ROMs and DVDs now store images that once were shown on filmstrips, slides, and videotape. Presentation software can generate overhead transparencies.
3. The complexity of computer-based systems traditionally has made it more complicated for educators to integrate various forms of software and computer-driven media into other classroom activities. Educators can see much more easily—some would say even intuitively—how to integrate less technical media such as films or overheads.

Thus, "integrating educational technology" refers to the process of determining which *electronic tools* and which methods for implementing them are appropriate for given classroom situations and problems.

Looking Back: How Has the Past Influenced Today's Educational Technology?

In no small part, developments in computer technology have shaped the history of educational technology. Because we have learned much from our past experience that can and should help any future work in this area, this section describes some of this history and what we have learned from it.

A Brief History of Educational Computing Activities and Resources

Many of today's technology-oriented teachers have been using computer systems only since microcomputers came into common use, but a thriving educational computing culture predated microcomputers by 20 years. When integrated circuits made computers both smaller and more accessible to teachers and students, microcomputers became a major turning point in the history of the field. This history is told primarily in two periods: before and after the introduction of microcomputers (Niemiec & Walberg, 1989; Roblyer, 1992). (See Figure 1.2.) Although they used earlier technologies, each of these activities had an impact on current computer and Internet uses in education.

What Have We Learned from the Past?

A history of educational technology is interesting, but useless unless we apply the information to future decisions and actions. What have we learned from some 50 years of applying technology to educational problems that can improve our strategies now? Educators are encouraged to draw their own conclusions from these and other descriptions they might read. However, the following points also are important:

- **No technology is a panacea for education.** Educators and parents tend to look to technology for answers to education's most difficult problems, but great expectations for products like Logo and integrated learning systems (ILSs) have taught us that even the most current, capable technology resources offer no quick, easy, or universal solutions. Computer-based materials and strategies are usually tools in a larger system and must be integrated carefully with other resources and with teacher activities. A recent book by Cuban (2001) proposes that technology was "oversold" from the beginning and is not having the system-changing impact many thought it would. Trend (2001) proposes that overuse of distance learning can create more problems than it solves. If we begin with more realistic expectations in mind, we have more potential for success and impact on teaching and learning. Planning must always begin with this question: What specific needs do my students and I have that (any given) resources can help meet?
- **Computer literacy/technological literacy offers a limited integration rationale.** Many parents and educators want technology tools in the classroom primarily because they feel technical skills will give students the *technological literacy* to prepare them for the workplace. But an employability rationale provides limited guidelines for how and where to integrate technology. The capabilities of technology resources and methods must be matched to content area skills that display an obvious need for improvement in our current system of education, for example, reading, writing, and mathematics skills; research and information gathering; and problem solving and analysis.
- **Stand-alone computers and networked computers have benefits and limitations.** In education, the pendulum swung from networked systems to stand-alone systems, then back to networks (the Internet). Yet no single delivery system or configuration has proven ideal for all situations. Networks make it more feasible to standardize materials across classrooms, schools, or

Figure 1.2 A Brief History of Computers in Education

The Pre-Microcomputer Era

1950—First instructional use of a computer. A computer-driven flight simulator is used to train pilots at MIT.

1959—First use with schoolchildren. An IBM 650 computer helps to teach binary arithmetic to New York City elementary school students.

1960–1970—University time-sharing systems. In 22 universities around the country, faculty and students use mainframe systems to teach programming and to develop programs and utilities to share them among themselves. The first meeting of these groups in Iowa City in 1979 was the National Education Computing Conference (NECC), now the largest educational technology conference in the country.

Early 1970s—Intense interest in CAI (*computer-assisted instruction*) development and research. Large-scale, federally funded projects use mainframe and minicomputer systems in schools, colleges, and universities.

First computing system dedicated to instruction: IBM 1500 system. At its height, the IBM 1500 is used by 25 universities and school districts. Stanford University uses a high-level language called *Coursewriter* to prepare lessons called *courseware* or *instructional software*. Also is the first multimedia learning station with a cathode-ray tube (CRT) screen, earphones, a microphone, an audiotape player, and a slide projector. IBM discontinued support for the IBM 1500 in 1975.

First minicomputer for instruction: Digital Equipment Corporation's PDP-1. Patrick Suppes, Stanford University professor and founder of Computer Curriculum Corporation (CCC), leads extensive research and development efforts with this system and the IBM 1500. These efforts earn him the honorary title "Grandfather of Computer-Assisted Instruction."

Late 1970s—Computer Curriculum Corporation (CCC) and the Control Data Corporation (CDC). These two companies dominate the educational computing field.

Programmed Logic for Automatic Teaching Operations (PLATO) developed. In conjunction with CDC, Don Bitzer at the University of Illinois develops PLATO, a terminal with a plasma screen (argon/neon gas contained between two glass plates with wire grids running through them), a specially designed keyboard, and an authoring system similar to *Coursewriter* called *Tutor*, used to develop tutorial lessons and complete courses rather than just drill-and-practice lessons.

William Norris, CDC president, announces that PLATO will revolutionize classroom practice (Norris, 1977), channeling significant funding and personnel into development of PLATO between 1965 and 1980.

Time-Shared Interactive Computer-Controlled Information Television (TICCIT). Victor Bunderson and Dexter Fletcher at Brigham Young University add a color television to a computer learning station.

Computer-managed instruction (CMI) systems emerge. Systems based on skill mastery models are developed by the American Institutes for Research (Program for Learning in Accordance with Needs, or PLAN) and the University of Pittsburgh (Individually Prescribed Instruction or IPI).

Administrative computing systems emerge. Educational organizations computerize administrative activities (e.g., student and staff records, attendance, report cards). Because mainframe computer systems are both expensive and technically complex, school district offices, rather than schools or individual teachers, control both instructional and administrative computer hardware and applications, and data-processing specialists administer most of the systems.

Interest in CAI declines. Lack of local control is unpopular with teachers, who neither understand the computer systems that deliver the instruction nor have much say in the curriculum developed for them. By the late 1970s, it becomes clear that computers cannot revolutionize classrooms in the same way that they were changing business offices in post–World War II America.

The Microcomputer Era

1977—First microcomputers enter schools. Focus shifts from mainframes to desktop systems, transforming the computer's role in education. Classroom teachers, rather than large companies or school district offices, begin to determine computer uses. Some administrative applications begin to migrate to school-based computers, much to the dismay of personnel in district data-processing centers. Microcomputers make school-based management more feasible.

Early 1980s—Software publishing movement begins. New software market for education emerges driven primarily by teachers. Nonprofit Minnesota Educational Computing Consortium (MECC), with funding from the National Science Foundation, becomes the largest single provider of courseware. Other major software publishing companies and cottage industries emerge.

Courseware evaluation movement begins. Since lessons on microcomputers are not of uniform quality or usefulness, courseware evaluations are provided by the Northwest Regional Educational Laboratory's *MicroSIFT* project, the Educational Products Information Exchange (EPIE), professional organizations, magazines, and journals. Other organizations compile and summarize reviews. Many of these activities cease as school districts develop committees to select courseware.

Teacher-driven courseware authoring movement begins. As teachers clamor for more input into the design of courseware, *authoring systems* emerge as the predecessors of modern tools such as *HyperStudio*. Some authoring systems are high-level languages (PILOT and SuperPILOT); others are menu-based systems (GENIS, PASS). Interest fades as teachers realize how much time, expertise, and work have to be invested to develop courseware more useful than what they could buy.

Computer literacy movement begins. Educational computing pioneer Dr. Arthur Luehrmann (Roblyer, 1992) coins the term *computer literacy* to mean programming skills and skills with tools such as word processing. Andrew Molnar (1978) writes that students who were not "computer literate" would be left behind academically, further widening the gap between the advantaged and disadvantaged. By 1985, computer literacy skills begin to appear in required curricula around the country, but by around 1990, they are dropped because computer literacy cannot be defined by any specific set of skills.

Logo and the problem-solving movement emerges. From 1980 until about 1987, Logo and Logo-based products (*Logowriter, LegoLogo*), activities, and research dominate the field. Seymour Papert, MIT mathematics professor and student of developmental theorist Jean Piaget (see Chapter 3) (Cuban, 1986), promotes Logo as a programming language for young children in his popular book *Mindstorms*. Logo challenges traditional instructional methods and computer uses that had supported them (drill and practice, tutorial uses) and assumes the characteristics of a craze: Logo clubs, user groups, and T-shirts fill the schools. Although research showed that Logo could be useful in some contexts, by 1985 interest wanes. Though still in use, Logo's main contribution becomes a new outlook on how technology could be used to restructure educational methods.

1980s–1990s—Integrated learning systems (ILSs) emerge. Schools realize that networked systems are more cost effective than standalone microcomputers to provide computer-managed instruction and practice. In 1991, curriculum trends move toward less structured and teacher-directed methods, and companies begin to market other networked systems sometimes called *multimedia learning systems, integrated technology systems,* or *open learning systems* (Hill, 1993, p. 29). Systems networked with a central server mark a significant movement away from single computer systems under the control of individual teachers and back toward more centralized control of instructional computing resources.

The Internet Era

1994—The birth of the World Wide Web. Although a text-based version of the Internet had been used by university educators since the 1980s (see Chapter 8), the program *Mosaic* makes it possible to see information as a combination of pictures and text; popular interest is sparked in a way no one had predicted. Teachers recognize the power of the Internet: ready access to people and information, the ability to send and receive multimedia displays, and an increasingly realistic simulation of "being there." The *Information Superhighway* becomes an expressway for education.

1998—ISTE creates computer standards. The International Society for Technology in Education sponsors National Educational Technology Standards (NETS) for students, teachers and, later, administrators.

2000 and beyond—Multimedia uses of the web emerge. Distance learning becomes increasingly common at all levels of education. Web-based videoconferencing and other forms of communication become more common.

districts; allow easier tracking of student usage and progress; and facilitate collaboration among teachers and students. Stand-alone computers offer more individual and/or local control and are more flexible to schedule and access. Each type of system will continue to be needed.

- **Teachers usually do not develop technology materials or curriculum.** Teaching is one of the most time- and labor-intensive jobs in our society. With so many demands on their time, most teachers cannot be expected to develop software or create most technology integration strategies. In the past, publishers, school or district developers, or personnel in funded projects have provided this assistance; this seems unlikely to change in the future.
- **Technically possible does not equal desirable, feasible, or inevitable.** A popular saying is that today's technology is yesterday's science fiction. But science fiction also shows us that technology brings undesirable—as well as desirable—changes. For example, distance technologies have allowed people to attend professional conferences online, rather than by traveling to another location; however, people continue to want to travel and meet face to face. As we write this book, procedures for human cloning are within reach, and genetic engineering is increasingly feasible. In education, we can simulate face-to-face communication to an increasingly realistic degree. All of these new technological horizons make it evident that it is time to analyze carefully the implications of each implementation decision. Better technology demands that we become critical consumers of its power and capability. We are responsible for deciding just which science fiction becomes reality.
- **Things change faster than teachers can keep up.** History in this field has shown that resources and accepted methods of applying them will change, sometimes quickly and dramatically. This places a special burden on already overworked teachers to continue learning new resources and changing their teaching methods. Gone are the days—if, indeed, they ever existed—when a teacher could rely on the same handouts, homework, or lecture notes from year to year. Educators may not be able to predict the future of educational technology, but they know that it will be different from the present; that is, they must anticipate and accept the inevitability of change and the need for a continual investment of their time.
- **Older technologies can be useful.** Technology in education is an area especially prone to what Roblyer (1990) called the "glitz factor." With so little emphasis on finding out what actually works, any "technological guru" who gives a glib rationale for new methods can lead a new movement in education. When dramatic improvements fail to appear, educators move on to the next fad. This approach fails to solve real problems and it draws attention away from the effort to find legitimate solutions. Worse, teachers sometimes throw out methods that had potential if only they had realistic expectations. The past has shown that teachers must be careful, analytical consumers of technological innovation, looking to what has worked in the past to guide their decisions and measure their expectations. Educational practice tends to move in cycles, and "new" methods often are old methods in new dressing. In short, teachers must be as informed and analytical as they want their students to become.
- **Teachers always will be important.** With each new technological development that appears on the horizon, the old question seems to resurface: Will computers replace teachers? The developers of the first instructional computer systems in the 1960s foresaw them replacing many teacher positions; some advocates of today's distance learning methods envision a similar impact on future education. Yet the answer to the old question is the same and is likely to remain so: Good teachers are more essential than ever. One reason for this was described in *MegaTrends:* ". . . whenever new technology is introduced into society, there must be a counterbalancing human response . . . the more high tech (it is), the more high touch (is needed)" (Naisbitt, 1984, p. 35). We need more teachers who understand the role technology plays in society and in education, who are prepared to take advantage of its power, and who recognize its limitations. In an increasingly technological society, we need more teachers who are both technology savvy and child centered.

Why Use Technology? Developing a Sound Rationale

The history of educational technology also teaches us the importance of the "why?" question. Many educators, parents, and students believe the reasons for using technology seem so obvious that everyone should recognize them. Their commonsense rationale is based on two major beliefs: (1) Technology is everywhere and therefore, should be in education—what Miller (2001) calls the "societal inevitability" rationale, and (2) research has shown how and where computer-based methods are effective. Both of these commonly held beliefs have some validity and both provide rationales for using technology—at least as far as they go. But we also need answers to some practical questions:

1. Should technology take over most or all of a teacher's role? If not, how should it fit in with what teachers already do?
2. Should schools rely on computers at all levels, for all students, or for all topics? If not, which levels, students, or topics are best suited to computer-based methods?
3. Does some reliable information suggest specific benefits of using technology in certain ways?

To justify the expensive and time-consuming task of integrating technology into education, teachers must identify specific contributions that technology can and should make to an improved education system. Funding agencies, for example, can reasonably ask why a school should choose a technology-based resource or method over another path to reach its desired goals. As Soloman (1995) said, "It's the vision thing . . . we first have to ask 'What do we need technology for?' We must create our vision, define technology's role in our schools, then plan for its use" (p. 66). The rationale we choose for using technology will guide our goals and help identify the skills and resources needed to accomplish these goals.

Problems with research-based justifications for educational technology. Many educators look to educational research for evidence of technology's present and potential benefits. But though technology (especially computers) has been in use in education since the 1950s, research results have not made a strong case for its impact on teaching and learning. In general, the number and quality of studies on educational impact have been disappointing (Roblyer, Castine, & King, 1988). But researchers such as Clark (1983, 1985, 1991, 1994) have openly criticized "computer-based effectiveness" research such as meta-analyses to summarize results across studies comparing computer-based and traditional methods. After considerable research in this area, Clark concluded that most such studies suffered from confounding variables. The studies attempted to show a greater impact on achievement of one method over the other without controlling for other factors such as instructional methods, curriculum contents, or novelty. These differences could either increase or decrease achievement. Clark (1985) exhorted educators to "avoid rationalizing computer purchases by referencing the achievement gains" (p. 259) in such studies. Kozma (1991, 1994) responded to these challenges by proposing that research should look at technology not as a medium to deliver information but in the context of "the learner actively collaborating with the medium to construct knowledge" (p. 179).

A study funded by the Milken Foundation and reported in *Education Week* (Archer, 1998) found that higher achievement scores on the National Assessment of Educational Progress (NAEP) were linked with certain kinds of technology uses at certain grade levels (p. 12):

- Eighth graders whose teachers used computers for simulations and applications performed better than eighth graders whose teachers did not.
- Fourth graders whose teachers used computers for "math/learning games" performed better than fourth graders whose teachers did not.
- In both grades, students whose teachers had had professional development did better than those whose teachers had no training. Schools with these teachers also were higher in indicators of good "school climate" (e.g., better attendance rates).

The Milken study confirmed what many educators had been saying for years: Simply having students use computers does not raise achievement. The impact comes from the kinds of uses, they feel, particularly with those requiring higher level thinking.

These results, while encouraging, still could be subject to the confounding variables described by Clark. In addition to these general findings, several promising lines of research and several aspects of technology use (shown in Figure 1.3) can help supply a rationale for continuing or expanding the use of technology in education.

Justifying technology use: The case for motivation. Motivating students to learn, to enjoy learning, and to want to learn more has assumed greater importance in recent years as we recognize strong correlations between dropping out of school and undesirable outcomes such as criminal activity. The drive to keep students in school is an urgent national priority. Technology has an important role to play in achieving this goal. Kozma and Croninger (1992) described several ways in which technology might help to address the cognitive, motivational, and social needs of at-risk students; Bialo and Sivin (1989) listed several software packages that were either designed or adapted to appeal to these kinds of

Figure 1.3 Elements of a Rationale for Using Technology in Education

1. **Motivation**
   - Gaining learner attention
   - Engaging the learner through production work
   - Increasing perceptions of control
2. **Unique instructional capabilities**
   - Linking learners to information and education sources
   - Helping learners visualize problems and solutions
   - Tracking learner progress
   - Linking learners to learning tools
3. **Support for new instructional approaches**
   - Cooperative learning
   - Shared intelligence
   - Problem solving and higher level skills
4. **Increased teacher productivity**
   - Freeing time to work with students by helping with production and record-keeping tasks
   - Providing more accurate information more quickly
   - Allowing teachers to produce better looking, more "student-friendly" materials more quickly
5. **Required skills for an information age**
   - Technology literacy
   - Information literacy
   - Visual literacy

students. Technology-based methods have successfully promoted several kinds of motivational strategies that may be used individually or in combination:

- **Gaining learner attention.** Renowned learning theorist Robert Gagné (1965) proposed that gaining the learner's attention is a critical first event in providing optimal conditions for instruction. Although other aspects of instruction must direct this attention toward meaningful learning, the visual and interactive features of many technology resources seem to help focus students' attention and encourage them to spend more time on learning tasks (Pask-McCartney, 1989; Summers, 1990–1991). Substantial empirical evidence indicates that teachers frequently capitalize on the novelty and television-like attraction of computers and multimedia to achieve the essential instructional goal of capturing and holding students' attention.
- **Engaging the learner through production work.** To make learning more meaningful to students, teachers often try to engage them in creating their own technology-based products. This strategy has been used effectively with word processing (Franklin, 1991; Tibbs, 1989), hypermedia (LaRoue, 1990; Volker, 1992), computer-generated art (Buchholz, 1991), and telecommunications (Marcus, 1995; Taylor, 1989). Students seem to like the activities because they promote creativity, self-expression, and feelings of self-efficacy and result in professional-looking products they can view with pride.
- **Increasing perceptions of control.** Many students are motivated by feeling they are in control of their own learning (Arnone & Grabowski, 1991; Relan, 1992). Learner control seems to have special implications for at-risk students and others who have experienced academic failure. When students perceive themselves as in control of their learning, the result has been called *intrinsic motivation,* or being motivated by the awareness that they are learning. This finding, reported from the earliest uses of computer-based materials, continues to be one of the most potentially powerful reasons for using technology resources as motivational aids. However, when learning paths become complex (with hypertext environments and interactive videodisc applications), students with weak learning skills seem to profit most when teachers supply structure to the activities (Kozma, 1991, 1994; McNeil & Wilson, 1991).

Justifying technology use: Unique instructional capabilities. Another powerful case for using technology resources is that some technological media can facilitate unique learning environments or contribute unique features to make traditional learning environments more powerful and effective.

- **Linking learners to information sources.** As Miller (2001) notes, technology expands learning environments for students by letting them access primary source materials, obtain information, and have experiences with people and places that they could not otherwise have.
- **Linking learners to education sources.** Through distance learning, learners of all ages have access to education and training educational opportunities they would not have otherwise. Physical distance from the instructor no longer is an obstacle to completing a course or a degree.
- **Helping learners visualize problems and solutions.** Kozma (1991) reports that interactive visual media (videodisc applications) seem to have unique instructional capabilities for topics that involve social situations or problem solving. He notes that these media provide powerful visual means of "representing social situations and tasks such as interpersonal problem solving, foreign language learning, or moral decision making" (p. 200). The growing number of visual products designed for these kinds of topics (the *AIDS* videodisc from ABC News, Computer Curriculum Corporation's *SuccessMaker*) indicates that designers and educators are recognizing and exploiting these unique and powerful qualities.
- **Tracking learner progress.** Integrated learning systems and subsequent products based on them have capitalized on the computer's unique ability to capture, analyze, and present data on students' performances during learning. A teacher attempting to demonstrate a set of skills to a large group of students needs accurate, up-to-date, easy-to-analyze information on what each student is and is not learning. A well-designed computer-based system for data collection (sometimes called a *computer-managed instruction* or *CMI* system; see Chapter 6) can most effectively provide this essential information. Small, palm-top computers allow teachers and researchers to keep moment-to-moment records of their observations of students; we anticipate affordable expert systems that can provide instruction, analyze students' errors and learning styles, and provide feedback tailored to unique learning needs (McArthur & Stasz, 1990).
- **Linking learners to learning tools.** The ability to link learners at distant sites with each other and with widely varied online resources long has been recognized for its unique potential to support instruction and enhance learning (Marcus, 1995). These capabilities include getting access to information not available through local sources, developing research and study skills that will benefit students in all future learning, and providing multicultural activities without leaving the classroom. Some unique affective benefits have also been observed, including increased multicultural awareness as students of different cultures interact online (Roblyer, 1991) and enhanced communication skills when students correspond with each other (Cohen & Riel, 1989).

Justifying technology use: Support for new instructional approaches. The educational system is struggling to revamp its instructional goals and methods in preparation for the complex demands of life in the technology-driven 21st century (SCANS Report, 1992). Educators are beginning to look at technology resources to help make these new directions at once feasible and motivational to students. Several new instructional initiatives can benefit from applications of technology:

- **Cooperative learning.** Because the traditional American cultural emphasis on individualism is seen as insufficient for the complex problem solving that lies ahead, there is increased emphasis on small-group instruction that involves cooperative learning. Many technology-based activities lend themselves to cooperative, small-group work: development of hypermedia products and special-purpose databases and research projects using online and offline databases and videodiscs and multimedia.
- **Shared intelligence.** An emerging definition for intelligence is termed *shared intelligence* or *distributed intelligence.* According to some theorists, the capabilities afforded by new technologies make the concept of intelligence as something that resides in each person's head too restrictive. "Intellectual partnership with computers suggests the possibility that resources enable and shape activity and do not reside in one or another agent but are genuinely distributed between persons, situations, and tools" (Polin, 1992, p. 7). Therefore, some educators hypothesize that the most important role for technology might be to change the goals of education as well as the measures of educational success.
- **Problem solving and higher order skills.** Basic communications and mathematics skills remain essential, but so is the need to solve problems and think critically about complex issues. In addition, curriculum is beginning to reflect the belief that students need not master basic skills before going on to higher level skills. The engaging qualities of technology resources such as multimedia and the Internet allow teachers to set complex, long-term goals that call for basic skills, thus motivating students to learn the lower level skills they need at the same time they acquire higher level ones.

Justifying technology use: Increased teacher productivity. An important but often overlooked reason for using technology resources is to help teachers cope with their growing paperwork load. Teachers and organizations have recognized that if they spend less time on record keeping and preparation they can spend more time analyzing student needs and having direct contact with students. Teachers can become more productive through training in technology-based methods and quick access to accurate information that may help them meet individual needs. Many technology resources can help teachers increase their productivity: word processing, spreadsheet, database, gradebook, graphics, desktop publishing, instructional management, and test generator programs along with online communications between teachers (e-mail) and other online services.

Justifying technology use: Required skills for an Information Age. A final and most compelling reason for integrating technology into teaching and learning is the need for students to learn skills that will prepare them to become lifelong learners in an information society. Since the emergence of the Internet, many of the processes used to locate and communicate information now involve some form of technology. Three kinds of competencies are becoming widely recognized as basic skills for citizens of an Information Age (Moursund, 1995).

- **Technology literacy.** Soloman (1995) says that "Technology for students is about economic competitiveness" (p. 67). The ISTE, the group that recently collaborated with the National Council for the Accreditation of Teacher Education (NCATE) to develop educational technology standards for preservice programs, also developed the National Educational Technology (NET) Standards (International Society for Technology in Education [ISTE], 2000) for K–12 students. Standards for all students are shown in Figure 1.4; standards specific to each grade level and to certain content areas also are available at the ISTE web site (http:://www.iste.org). Both sets of standards recognize that technology skills are becoming required job skills. Many states are also establishing their own required technology skills for K–12 students. This trend makes it essential that teachers both model and teach the use of technology-based methods to their students.
- **Information literacy.** Although information literacy skills may be simply a subset of the technology literacy skills described previously, some educators think they are so important they should receive special emphasis (Roblyer, 1998a; Truett, 1996). Johnson and Eisenberg (1996) call them the "Big Six" skills: task definition, information-seeking strategies, location and access, use of information, synthesis, and evaluation. Although they predate the World Wide Web, the information explosion fostered by the Internet has made the Big Six skills more important to learning and more involved with technology. However, Roblyer (1998a) notes that students seem to find the first three skills—the ones requiring use of technology procedures—more enjoyable and easier to do. It is the application and analysis tasks that present the most difficulty. However, all of these skills appear likely to be essential ones.
- **Visual literacy.** Like information literacy, visual literacy may be thought of as a subset of technology literacy. However, because our society relies more heavily on images and visual communication strategies, educators are beginning to emphasize the special need for better visual literacy skills (Christopherson, 1997; Roblyer, 1998b). Christopherson says that a visually

Figure 1.4 ISTE's National Educational Technology Standards (NETS) for Students

1. **Basic operations and concepts**
   - Students demonstrate a sound understanding of the nature and operation of technology systems.
   - Students are proficient in the use of technology.
2. **Social, ethical, and human issues**
   - Students understand the ethical, cultural, and societal issues related to technology.
   - Students practice responsible use of technology systems, information, and software.
   - Students develop positive attitudes toward technology uses that support lifelong learning, collaboration, personal pursuits, and productivity.
3. **Technology productivity tools**
   - Students use technology tools to enhance learning, increase productivity, and promote creativity.
   - Students use productivity tools to collaborate in constructing technology-enhanced models, prepare publications, and produce other creative works.
4. **Technology communications tools**
   - Students use telecommunications to collaborate, publish, and interact with peers, experts, and other audiences.
   - Students use a variety of media and formats to communicate information and ideas effectively to multiple audiences.
5. **Technology research tools**
   - Students use technology to locate, evaluate, and collect information from a variety of sources.
   - Students use technology tools to process data and report results.
   - Students evaluate and select new information resources and technological innovations based on the appropriateness for specific tasks.
6. **Technology problem-solving and decision-making tools**
   - Students use technology resources for solving problems and making informed decisions.
   - Students employ technology in the development of strategies for solving problems in the real world.

Source: Reprinted with permission from *National Educational Technology Standards for Students—Connecting Curriculum and Technology,* copyright © 2000, ISTE (International Society for Technology in Education), 800.336.5191 (U.S. & Canada) or 541.302.3777 (Int'l), iste@iste.org, www.iste.org. All rights reserved. Permission does not constitute an endorsement by ISTE. For more information about the NETS Project, contact Lajeane Thomas, Director, NETS Project, 318.257.3923, lthomas@latech.edu.

literate person can interpret, understand, and appreciate the meaning of visual messages; communicate more effectively through applying the basic principles and concepts of visual design; produce visual messages using the computer and other technology; and use visual thinking to conceptualize solutions to problems (p. 173). Roblyer (1998b) reports on research that correlates visual literacy skills to higher scores on intelligence tests and to later success in more technical vocational areas such as engineering. Christopherson observes that "students with visual communication skills are more marketable" (p. 174) but that these skills soon will be required rather than merely desirable. These reports create a powerful reason for teachers to integrate technology at early levels into students' communication methods.

Looking Around, Looking Ahead: What Factors Shape the Current and Future Climate for Technology in Education?

As we have seen from our historical overview, educational technology is defined by the resources available at a given time and the ways in which educators apply them to solve educational problems. We have also seen that educational technology is set in a larger context of societal influences that shape its use and determine, to a large extent, the impact it will have. As the history of educational technology demonstrates, the field is most often driven by a combination of educational trends and priorities, economic factors, and the marketing efforts of individuals and companies. This section gives an overview of current technology resources, how they are used, and societal factors and issues that shape their impact.

Current Educational Technology Systems and Their Applications

To some extent, education's integration of technology-based methods reflects currently available equipment and materials and how they are used in other areas of society. However, as recent federal and other reports emphasize (National Center for Education Statistics, 1999a, 1999b; President's Committee, 1997; Wired Digital, 2001), many available devices and technology materials are in limited use in schools; they may be too expensive, schools may lack the infrastructure to support them, or teachers may be unfamiliar with and untrained in their use. Yet it is essential that educators realize the potential—as well as the current reality—of technology in education. Technology resources currently used in education and how they relate to each other are depicted in Figure 1.5 as a metaphorical educational

Figure 1.5 The Educational Technology "Tree of Knowledge"

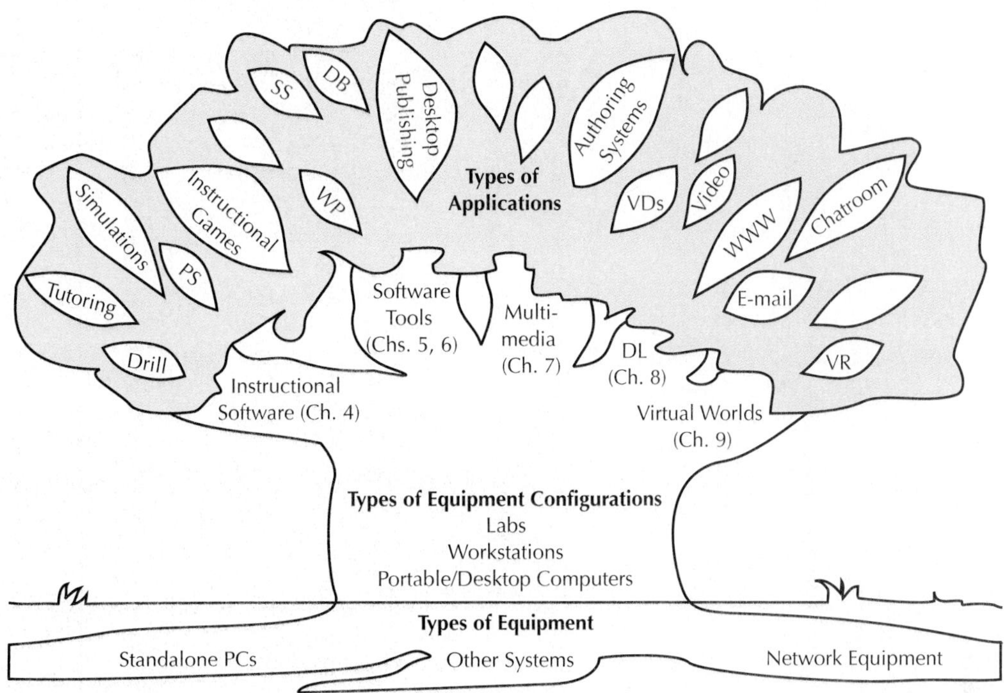

technology "Tree of Knowledge," with the types of resources as branches and the applications under each as leaves.

Equipment types. Basic equipment types include standalone microcomputers, networks, and computer-related devices and systems such as virtual reality and input/output (I/O) devices.

Equipment configurations. The various types of equipment may be configured as single units, workstations (a classroom learning station consisting of two or three microcomputers with a scanner and printer), labs, and movable media-type carts. The benefits of each configuration are discussed in more detail in Chapter 2. (See Figure 1.6 for more details on equipment and equipment configurations common to education.)

Software and materials. These are discussed in more detail later in this text: instructional software (Chapter 4), tool software (Chapters 5 and 6), multimedia/hypermedia (Chapter 7), distance applications (Chapter 8), and emerging resources (Chapter 9).

Types of applications. Computer applications in education can be categorized as:

- **Instructional.** Students use them to learn information or skills through demonstrations, examples, explanation, or problem solving.
- **Productivity.** Both teachers and students use them to support planning, materials development, and record keeping.
- **Administrative.** Administrators at school, state, and district levels use these to support record keeping and exchanges of information among various agencies.

Today's Big Issues in Education and Technology: Societal, Cultural/Equity, Educational, and Technical

One of the things that makes teaching so challenging is that it goes on in an environment that mirrors—and sometimes magnifies—some of society's most profound and problematic issues. Adding computers to this mix makes the situation even more complex. Yet to integrate technology successfully into their teaching, educators must recognize and be prepared to work in this environment with all of its subtleties and complexities. Some of today's important issues and their implications for technological trends in education are described here and summarized in Figure 1.7. (Chapter 2 gives recommendations for addressing these issues in ways that help ensure technology integration will have the maximum positive impact on teaching and learning.)

Societal issues. Economic, political, and social trends have a great impact on whether or not innovations take hold, or have limited acceptance, or are ignored completely. Some national reports such as *Fool's Gold* by the Alliance for Childhood (Cordes & Miller, 2001) are openly critical of the influence of technology on children. Others, like the summary by Shields and Berman (2000) in a recent issue of *The Future of Children,* are less negative but still cite an urgent need for guidelines to shape future technology use. At this time, these trends are generating strong pro- and anti-technology views:

Figure 1.6 Current Equipment and Equipment Configurations Used in Education

Equipment Categories	Types of Equipment	Examples	TYPICAL CONFIGURATIONS				Typical Uses
			Single Units	Workstations	Labs	Carts	
Stand-alone microcomputers	Portable units						
	Laptop computers	Macintosh iMac IBM Thinkpad	X	X	X		Instruction, productivity
	Handheld palm computers	Palm OS	X				Instruction, productivity
	Desktop microcomputers	IBM Pentium IV, Macintosh	X	X	X	X	Instruction, productivity, multimedia development
Networks	Local area networks (LANs)	Computers networked in a school			X		ILSs, multimedia development, Internet access, and administrative tasks
	Metropolitan area networks (MANs)	A city-wide network of connected computers					Connections among school computers in schools throughout a city
	Wide area networks (WANs)	Interconnected LANs or MANs					Connections among computers and networks for information exchange, e-mail, distance learning management, and delivery
Related devices and systems	Videodisc players: E-Books	Pioneer Laserdisc	X			X	Instruction, multimedia development
	Virtual reality systems	NASA training systems	X				Instruction, R&D projects; simulated activities (flight simulators)
	Graphing calculators	TI graphing calculator	X		X		
	Input devices	Scanners, video cameras, etc.					Used with various computer systems
	Output devices	Printers, plotters, projection panels, etc.					Used with various computer systems

Figure 1.7 Current Trends and Issues Shaping the Use of Technology in Education

Types of Issues Having Impact on Technology in Education	Topics Under Each Issue	Current Issues Having Impact on Technology in Education	Implications for Technology in Education
Societal	Economic trends	Education costs increasing	Distance learning (DL) emphasis to make education more cost effective
	Political trends	Politicians call for lower cost, more effective education	More reliance on DL and other technologies to increase consistency of quality, stretch scarce resources
	Social trends	Recognition of need for technology literacy	Computers becoming a required student purchase
		Increased communications results in less privacy	Possible suspicion of technology-delivered education
		Growing popular distrust of technology	Possible suspicion of technology-delivered education
		Increased societal dependence on Internet also increases risk of online predators, plagiarism	Educators must assume more responsibility for monitoring students online
Cultural/Equity	Economic/ Ethnic	Lower income schools equals less access to computers	Low-income students must have equal access to technology
		More minority students in lower income schools	Minority students must have equal access to technology
	Multicultural	"Computer culture" is pervasive in society	Students must use computers regardless of cultural bias
	Gender	Technology remains a male-dominated area	Females' use of computers in education must increase
	Special needs	Special devices and methods can allow students with special needs equal access to technology but are expensive to obtain and implement	Students with disabilities must receive equal access to technology regardless of high costs to educational system
Educational	Directed versus constructivist views	Directed uses of technology (drill, tutorial) are proven effective but often considered passé	Demonstrated effective technology uses may be discarded
		Constructivist uses are emphasized but little evidence exists on their effectiveness	More research needed on newer technology uses
	Single-subject versus interdisciplinary	Past emphasis on teaching subjects in isolation	Continued emphasis on use of single skill software
		Current trend toward integrated curriculum or merging several subjects into one activity	Increasing use of multimedia and other technologies that support more complex, interdisciplinary activities
Technical	Rapid change	Technology changes too quickly for teachers to keep up	The latest technologies are in limited use in education
		Educators cannot afford most current technology	Schools usually have out-of-date equipment, materials
	Complexity	Teacher training is not keeping up with technology developments	Majority of teachers have insufficient training in technology materials and uses
		Schools lack the infrastructure to keep up with new technologies	Schools cannot take advantage of newest, most powerful technological developments

- **Pro-technology movements in society.** The increasing costs of education and dissatisfaction with current education systems have made us look closely at what technology can do to make teaching and learning more cost effective. Distance learning, for example, often is seen as a way to decrease the costs of delivering a quality education, while educational institutions see it as an opportunity for increased enrollment. Distance learning as a delivery system has become much more popular than, say, computer software used on stand-alone computers or even networked systems. Also, many institutions feel that computers play such an important part in learning that they should be required student purchases, a trend that is being analyzed regarding its implications for lower income students who may have trouble affording their purchase and upkeep. But it is evident that technology, both as a tool and an instructional delivery system, is enjoying unprecedented widespread support at all levels of education. This support has been particularly evident in the increased federal funding earmarked for technology.
- **Anti-technology movements in society.** Despite technology's growing popularity in education, some people feel the costs of technology outweigh its benefits. Critics point out that ordinary activities like driving a car are complicated by the pervasive presence of computers because they become susceptible to computer error as well as mechanical error. Increased communications made possible by e-mail, cellular phones, and fax machines mean a person can never be alone or out of the reach of authority—a situation many feel runs counter to the freedom and independence that symbolize the American lifestyle. Some feel that increased technology fuels a trend toward moral decay and see "cyberspace as an electronic red-light district" (Young, 1998)—an environment that nurtures cyberporn and cyberpunk. A Luddite-tinged backlash against the onslaught of technology in society has emerged (Healy, 1998; Quittner, 1995; Stoll, 1995, 1999), and a parallel backlash exists in education. Some like Oppenheimer (1997) believe that the costs of technology have resulted in school districts cutting programs—music, art, physical education—that enrich children's lives. How much counter-technology views will influence support for technology in education is unknown at this time, but educators must be aware that they exist and that they can exert a powerful influence on the level of local support that technology integration could receive.
- **The need for socialization.** Even technology proponents like Rifkin (2000) say that parents are worried about the effect on their children of gaining too much of their world knowledge and experience from virtual, rather than real, worlds. Parents feel that character education requires "direct and intimate participation with others in real time and space" (p. 254). Schools should supply both kinds of experiences, they say, if our students are to be "equipped for their social obligations to the larger community as well as for the commercial opportunities that lie in cyberspace" (p. 254). Recognizing the impact of overuse of computers on children's socialization, the American Academy of Pediatricians has called for limiting children's use of media to 1 to 2 hours per day (McNabb, 2001).
- **Dangers of online use for children.** In addition to the potential for overuse of technology, recent studies have confirmed some actual dangers to children on the Internet. Mitchell, Finkelhor, and Wolak (2001) found that about 19% of all youths between the ages of 10 and 17 who regularly use the Internet encounter sexual predators. These alarming findings have sparked much debate over how to protect children as they embark on activities essential to helping them become informed citizens of the Information Age.
- **The new plagiarism.** One negative consequence of quick access to information on the Internet is that cheating has never been so easy. Not only have Internet sites sprung up from which students can obtain completed papers, it is also easy for students to "cut and paste" parts of other materials they find online without citing their source (Gardiner, 2001). Still other sites have emerged to help teachers catch the cheaters (http://Turnitin.com, http://Plagiarism.org). Controversy swirls around how best to deal with this problem (Howard, 2001; Young, 2001).

Cultural and equity issues. Four factors that reflect the complex racial and cultural fabric of our society continue to have a great impact on technology use. As Molnar pointed out in his landmark 1978 article "The Next Great Crisis in American Education: Computer Literacy," the power of technology is a two-edged sword, especially for education. While it presents obvious potential for changing education and empowering teachers and students, technology also may further divide members of our society along socioeconomic, ethnic, and cultural lines and widen the gender gap. Teachers will lead the struggle to make sure technology use promotes, rather than conflicts with, the goals of a democratic society. Factors that must be considered include economic bias, multicultural issues, gender bias, and accommodations for students' special needs.

Economic and ethnic inequity. Some evidence supports Molnar's 1978 prediction that students with initial educational advantages will get more access to technology resources than those who could use the extra help. Demographic studies by Becker (1985, 1986a, 1986b) confirmed the predictable correlation between school districts' socioeconomic levels and their levels of microcomputer resources. Many educators observe that students from wealthier families are far more likely to have computers and other technology resources at home than those from poorer families. All of these conditions are well documented (Goslee, 1998; National Telecommunications and

Information Administration [NTIA], 1998; Neuman, 1991; Sanders & Stone, 1986).

Evidence of the educational and/or economic crises that Molnar predicted has been more difficult to obtain. Widespread recognition of the need for computer literacy as conceived in 1982 never really emerged. However, it seems logical that students who have more access to computers also will have better, more efficient learning tools at their disposal; this access seems likely to become increasingly important as technological learning tools increase in power. Use of technology tools may also logically correlate to students' ability to enter mathematics, science, and technical areas such as engineering. It seems certain that poorer students could be hampered in their learning (and therefore earning) potential due to their unequal access to technology tools.

The same problems with differences in technology access between economic subgroups also may apply to ethnic groups. Engler (1992) reported that the number of course prerequisites for computer programming studies (usually in mathematics classes) often increases as the percentage of minority enrollment increases. Although this may be an unintended inequity, minority students clearly do not have the same access to these courses as do their white peers. According to a study reported by Miller, in 1998 the technology gap may be narrowing for Hispanic students, but remains wide between whites and African-Americans. Another study by Hoffman and Novak (1998) confirms that African-Americans are less likely than whites to have a computer at home (44% versus 29%), although more likely to have access to one at work.

Data show clearly that minorities continue to be underrepresented in the fields of mathematics, science, and engineering (Leslie, McClure, & Oaxaca, 1998). Though less access to technology in K–12 schools may not have caused this problem, it clearly has the potential to make it worse and prolong its effects.

Multicultural inequity. Roblyer, Dozier-Henry, and Burnette (1996) describe several current uses of technology related to multicultural education, including telecommunications activities to promote communications among people of different cultures; applications that address the special language, visual, and experience needs of ESL and ESOL students; and multimedia applications with examples that enhance understanding of cultures. But they also describe several culture-related problems surrounding technology use. For example, "The reverence with which technology is held in the U.S. may be in direct contradiction to the perceptions of cultures that are heavily relationship oriented" (Roblyer et al., 1996, p. 9). These authors also acknowledge the existence of a growing counter–computer culture in the United States that is based on social, psychological, and even religious grounds.

They also observe an overreliance on technology to achieve the goals of multicultural education. They find that while technology can be helpful (making students aware of cultures other than their own, creating an interest in interacting with people of other cultures, and teaching about common attributes of all cultures despite their many differences), the next steps are more difficult because they require accepting, learning from, and appreciating people of other cultures. Schools must build on the relatively superficial activities of tele-pals and learning about various foods and holidays in other cultures. Technology may have a limited role in a deeper and more meaningful study.

Recent findings by Hoffman and Novak (1998) raise the issue of whether cultural factors help determine desire or willingness to use computers. Their studies found that even adjusting for income, whites were far more likely to have computers at home than African-Americans. Also, white students without computers at home were far more likely to have used the Web in other locations than were African-American students. As Hoffman and Novak said, these findings are in urgent need of further explication.

Gender inequity. Research has documented thoroughly the fact that girls tend to use computers less than boys (Bohlin, 1993; Margolis & Fisher, 2002; Sanders, 1993; Warren-Sams, 1997). This unequal proportion extends to vocational areas where computers are more frequently used: mathematics, science, and technical areas such as engineering and computer science (Engler, 1992; Fear-Fenn & Kapostacy, 1992; Fredman, 1990; Holmes, 1991; Leslie, McClure, & Oaxaca, 1998; Nelson & Watson, 1991; Sanders & Stone, 1986; Stumpf & Stanley, 1997). A variety of reasons have been proposed for this disparity. Children may be reacting to stereotypes on television and in publications where men appear as primary users of computers. Depictions of women using computers tend to involve clerical tasks. The association of technology with machines, mathematics, and science—all stereotypically male areas—makes girls think of computers as masculine.

Gender bias may spring up in software that features competitive activities preferred more by males than females and an emphasis on violent video games that appeal more to boys. Finally, many blame subtle and overt classroom practices for making girls think that computers are not intended for them. These range from a lack of female teacher role models to teachers' assumptions that girls are simply not as interested in computer work. Whatever combination of factors is involved, females clearly are being excluded in large numbers from using the power of technology and jobs that require technology skills.

Equity for students with special needs. Neuman (1991) warns that technology and equity are not "inevitable partners." She lists factors that can inhibit equitable access to technology for rural students and for those with handicaps or those who are differently abled. (The special problems of rural schools in supplying their students with adequate technology resources are discussed in Chapter 2.) Thurston (1990) and Holland (1995) observe that rural schools have more severe equity problems of all types (economic, gender, and ethnic equity) than their urban counterparts.

A variety of adaptive devices have been designed to allow students with handicaps to take advantage of the power of technology and to enhance personal freedom. However, Neuman (1991) and Engler (1992) report potential inequities in funding for these devices, and computer resources often are housed in locations that are not wheelchair accessible. A more subtle kind of technology inequity has been observed with students who have handicaps, a learning disability, or lower abilities (Engler, 1992; Fredman, 1990). Frequently, these students' uses of computers have been limited to low-level ones such as remedial drill-and-practice applications. The more powerful, higher level applications such as hypermedia production work often are directed toward higher ability students. This finding is especially disconcerting because many of these subgroups are also at-risk students who might profit from the motivation stimulated by higher level uses.

Educational issues. Trends in the educational system are intertwined with trends in technology and society. Two kinds of issues currently of great interest to educators have special implications for the ways technology will be used in teaching and learning.

- **The directed versus constructivist debate.** Chapter 3 describes two different ways of viewing teaching and learning and the implications of this dichotomy for technology applications. Roblyer (1996) refers to these contrasting views as the directed versus constructivist debate. Directed methods are more traditional, teacher-delivered ones, and technology uses matched to them have a longer, more established tradition of addressing certain kinds of educational problems. However, educators who promote constructivist teaching and learning strategies are critical of directed methods, calling them outmoded and unsuccessful in addressing education's most pressing problems. Proponents of directed methods feel that constructivist methods are unscientific and impractical. This debate is unfortunate, since the authors of this text feel strongly that each kind of strategy—and the technology uses matched to them—can be useful. Educators who take a position in favor of one strategy only may ignore many potentially useful applications.
- **Interdisciplinary versus single-subject instruction.** The debate over interdisciplinary studies versus single-subject emphasis is not new in education. Plato thought that interdisciplinary instruction would allow a student to gain a broad understanding of complex ideas. Aristotle believed that pure knowledge of a discipline is necessary to gain true understanding. The debate over breadth versus depth continues today. The traditional structure of the curriculum is usually divided into discrete subject areas, teaching each in isolation. Curriculum designers saw this as the most efficient way to ensure that instruction is given in specific skills for a variety of content areas. To a great extent, the integration of technology into the curriculum has followed a similar pattern. Software companies and developers have geared their products to traditional subject areas; this method of integrating technology persists widely today.

  In recent years, however, curriculum development has reflected a tendency to link several disciplines in the context of a single unit or lesson. This trend toward interdisciplinary instruction may, in fact, reflect a much larger societal trend as people recognize that systems work much better when there are connections between components. Teachers who become more comfortable with technology in their classrooms seem to take more flexible, even experimental, approaches to teaching. This trend, coupled with a concerted effort by many software companies to offer products that model subject-area integration, portends an integrated environment for technology in curriculum.
- **The role of distance learning.** Although distance learning has been around since the 1940s in various forms, the Internet has generated unprecedented interest in learning environments in which the student and the instruction are not in the same physical space. Distance learning courses have become *de rigueur* in most higher education institutions, and are becoming increasingly common at the K–12 levels (Roblyer, 2002). However, not all students succeed in these settings, and dropout rates for distance courses usually are higher than for traditional ones. Educators face a growing challenge to shape the role and impact of the distance learning movement. At its best, distance learning provides unique and valuable access to educational opportunities for learners of all ages and backgrounds. At worst, it may create, as Durden (2001) charges, a sharp division between wealthy students, who can afford the benefits of a face-to-face education, and poor, foreign-born, and nonwhite students who can afford only a distance one. Durden feels that distance education provides mainly workplace training, while face-to-face education allows students the liberal arts education that increases their access to power and success.

Technical issues. As Chapter 9 documents, technology changes so quickly that many businesses and industries whose survival depends on anticipating technological change employ whole teams of people to keep up to date on various changes, anticipated changes, and the implications of these changes for their product or service (Remnick, 1997). The "business of education" also will be affected by changing technology, but educational organizations are much less equipped to anticipate and cope with change. Teachers have little time for training in new applications or methods for integrating them—even if they could afford them. In addition, schools currently lack the infrastructure to allow access to new applications (President's Commit-

Figure 1.8 ISTE's National Educational Technology Standards (NETS) for Teachers

I. TECHNOLOGY OPERATIONS AND CONCEPTS

Teachers demonstrate a sound understanding of technology operations and concepts. Teachers:

A. Demonstrate introductory knowledge, skills, and understanding of concepts related to technology (as described in the ISTE *National Education Technology Standards for Students*).

B. Demonstrate continual growth in technology knowledge and skills to stay abreast of current and emerging technologies.

II. PLANNING AND DESIGNING LEARNING ENVIRONMENTS AND EXPERIENCES

Teachers plan and design effective learning environments and experiences supported by technology. Teachers:

A. Design developmentally appropriate learning opportunities that apply technology-enhanced instructional strategies to support the diverse needs of learners.

B. Apply current research on teaching and learning with technology when planning learning environments and experiences.

C. Identify and locate technology resources and evaluate them for accuracy and suitability.

D. Plan for the management of technology resources within the context of learning activities.

E. Plan strategies to manage student learning in a technology-enhanced environment.

III. TEACHING, LEARNING, AND THE CURRICULUM

Teachers implement curriculum plans that include methods and strategies for applying technology to maximize student learning. Teachers:

A. Facilitate technology-enhanced experiences that address content standards and student technology standards.

B. Use technology to support learner-centered strategies that address the diverse needs of students.

C. Apply technology to develop students' higher order skills and creativity.

D. Manage student learning activities in a technology-enhanced environment.

IV. ASSESSMENT AND EVALUATION

Teachers apply technology to facilitate a variety of effective assessment and evaluation strategies. Teachers:

A. Apply technology in assessing student learning of subject matter using a variety of assessment techniques.

B. Use technology resources to collect and analyze data, interpret results, and communicate findings to improve instructional practice and maximize student learning.

C. Apply multiple methods of evaluation to determine students' appropriate use of technology resources for learning, communication, and productivity.

V. PRODUCTIVITY AND PROFESSIONAL PRACTICE

Teachers use technology to enhance their productivity and professional practice. Teachers:

A. Use technology resources to engage in ongoing professional development and lifelong learning.

B. Continually evaluate and reflect on professional practice to make informed decisions regarding the use of technology in support of student learning.

C. Apply technology to increase productivity.

D. Use technology to communicate and collaborate with peers, parents, and the larger community in order to nurture student learning.

VI. SOCIAL, ETHICAL, LEGAL, AND HUMAN ISSUES

Teachers understand the social, ethical, legal, and human issues surrounding the use of technology in PK–12 schools and apply those principles in practice. Teachers:

A. Model and teach legal and ethical practice related to technology use.

B. Apply technology resources to enable and empower learners with diverse backgrounds, characteristics, and abilities.

C. Identify and use technology resources that affirm diversity.

D. Promote safe and healthy use of technology resources.

E. Facilitate equitable access to technology resources for all students.

Also see ISTE NETS for Administrators at http://www.iste.org

Source: Reprinted with permission from *National Educational Technology Standards for Teachers,* copyright © 2000, ISTE (International Society for Technology in Education), 800.336.5191 (U.S. & Canada) or 541.302.3777 (International). iste@iste.org, www.iste.org. All rights reserved. Permission does not constitute an endorsement by ISTE. For more information about the NETS Project, contact Lajeane Thomas, Director, NETS Project, 318.257.3923, lthomas@latech.edu.

tee, 1997). In addition, technology use in recent years has increased in technical complexity; a prime example is the increasing dependence on networks. School and district computer networks are becoming recognized as a way of connecting people with each other and with resources and as a means of increasing the power and usefulness of stand-alone machines. Although a powerful solution, networks are so technically complex that most educators find it difficult to comprehend enough about them to make good decisions on their many options and uses.

The answer seems to lie in adopting two strategies. First, all technology-using educators should understand network basics such as the types of networks available, their most common uses, and the most common components and connection methods. Second, those tasked with maintaining an existing network either must assign or become a network administrator or an expert in the functions of that particular system.

New Challenges and the Skills to Deal with Them

Clearly, 21st-century educators will have to deal with issues that their predecessors could not even have imagined and must have skills and knowledge not previously recognized. The National Council for the Accreditation of Teacher Education, the agency responsible for accrediting colleges of education, has joined with ISTE in not only establishing standards for teaching about technology in education, but also saying that schools of education should increase their emphasis on the use of technology in teacher training (NCATE, 1997). Thus, the ISTE National Educational Technology Standards (NETS) for Teachers, shown in Figure 1.8, have become the benchmark for technology infusion in teacher education programs. NETS for Teachers are specified for each chapter, technology integration idea, and end-of-chapter activities in this text.

Exercises

Record and apply what you have learned.

Chapter 1 Self-Test

To review terms and concepts in this chapter, take the Chapter 1 self-test. Select Chapter 1 from the front page of the Companion Website (located at http://www.prenhall.com/roblyer), then choose the *Multiple Choice* module.

Portfolio Activities

ISTE The following activities address ISTE National Educational Technology Standards for Teachers (NETS-T) and will help you add to your professional portfolio. To complete these activities online and save or submit the materials electronically, select Chapter 1 from the front page of the Companion Website (http://www.prenhall.com/roblyer), then choose the *Portfolio* module.

1. ***Overview of the Field (NETS-T Standard: I-B)*** Demonstrate your knowledge about the various kinds of equipment, software, and media used in educational technology and understand how these relate to each other by preparing your own overview of the field like the one shown in Figure 1.5. Instead of a "tree metaphor," select your own way of showing the resources (chart, concept map, or picture of an educational technology building).
2. ***Professional Skills (NETS-T Standard: I-B)*** Using word processing or other software, prepare your own checklist of the ISTE competencies given in this chapter. As you acquire each competency throughout this course and other experiences, indicate on your checklist where and how you learned this skill.

Questions for Thought and Discussion

These questions may be used for small-group or class discussion or may be subjects for individual or group activities. To take part in these discussions online, select Chapter 1 from the front page of the Companion Website (http://www.prenhall.com/roblyer), then choose the *Message Board* module.

1. In his book *High Tech Heretic,* Clifford Stoll (1999) says that "You certainly can get an excellent education without a computer" (p. 32), and "When every student . . . is pressed to become a computer maven, and only the incompetent are allowed to become plumbers, neither our programs nor our pipes will hold water" (p. 123). What information from Chapter 1 might help you respond to his statements?
2. Saettler (1990) said that "Computer information systems are not just objective recording devices. They also reflect concepts, hopes, beliefs, attitudes" (p. 539). What concepts, hopes, beliefs, and attitudes do our past and current uses of technology reflect?
3. Richard Clark's now-famous comment about the impact of computers on learning was that the best current evidence is that media are mere vehicles that deliver instruction but do not influence student achievement any more than the truck that delivers our groceries causes changes in our nutrition (Clark, 1983, p. 445). Why do you think this statement has had such a dramatic impact on the field of educational technology?
4. In his article on "cybercheating," Gardiner (2001) says, ". . . I understand that the temptation of exchanging hours of research and writing for a few minutes of searching seems like a good deal as the deadline looms. . . . I wondered how I could ever overcome the power of the Internet and the lure of cheating" (p. 174). Can you suggest arguments you might make to students to persuade them that cybercheating, while easy and quick, is not in their best interests?

Collaborative Activities

ISTE

The following activities address ISTE National Educational Standards for Teachers (NETS-T) and can be done in small groups. Each group should present the findings to the class in a format they know how to use (word-processed report, presentation software, multimedia product). Completed group products can be copied and shared with the entire class and/or included in each person's personal portfolio.

1. ***Educational Technology Defined*** Prepare an overview of the four areas of emphasis in educational technology: media, systems, vocational training, and computers. For each emphasis, explain what the emphasis is, why it is an important aspect, what people and groups are involved, and what impact it has on how education uses technology.
2. ***History of Computers in Education: People and Projects (NETS-T Standard: VI-A)*** Prepare a report on one of the following topics:
   - Five People Who Changed Education with Technology (choose your own top 5)
   - Five Things We Learned from the Mainframe/Minicomputer Era of Educational Technology
   - Five Ways Microcomputers Changed the Face of Education
   - Five Important Lessons We (Should Have) Learned from Past Uses of Technology in Education
3. ***Technology in Education: Issues and Concerns*** Prepare and carry out a debate for the class on one of the following topics:
   - Do Schools Need More Computers or More Teachers? ***(NETS-T Standard: V-B)***
   - Is Technology Further Widening the Gap Between Rich and Poor? ***(NETS-T Standards: VI-C, E)***
   - When School Budgets for Technology Are Limited, Should Technology Resources Be Focused on Basic Skills or on Higher Level Thinking? ***(NETS-T Standards: VI-B, C)***

Integrating Technology Across the Curriculum Activities

The *Integrating Technology Across the Curriculum* CD-ROM is a set of technology integration ideas and links to online lessons, arranged as a searchable database. The CD comes packaged with this textbook. Complete the following exercise to give you an introduction to the resources available on this CD:

Look at Figure 1.5, the educational technology "tree of knowledge." The "branches" are the types of technology (e.g., Chapter 4, instructional software; Chapters 5 and 6, software tools; Chapter 7, multimedia), and the applications (e.g., drill, tutorial, simulations, word processing) are the "leaves" on these branches. Make a chart of sample technology integration ideas under each technology type and application for your content area. Create a chart like the one below. Use the "branch" (i.e., chapter) names as the row headings and the applications and integration idea names under each as the column headings. (**HOW TO BEGIN:** On the Main Page, click on Find an Idea, and select the Find by Criteria option. Scroll down to select the Content Area you want. When you get the listing of lessons for your Content Area, click on the first one in the list. Go to the descriptors for the lesson to see which chapter it falls under. Page from entry to entry by clicking the Next Lesson button.)

Sample Integration Ideas for English/Language Arts

Types of Resources	Name of Resource	Name of Lesson Idea
Ch. 4 Instructional Software		
Ch. 5 Prod. Software Tools	Word Processing	Connecting Writing to Reading
Ch. 6 Other Software Tools		
Ch. 7 Multimedia	Authoring software	Multimedia Memoirs

References

Archer, J. (1998). The link to higher scores. *Education Week, 18*(5), 10–21.

Arnone, M., & Grabowski, B. (1991). Effects of variations in learner control on children's curiosity and learning from interactive video. Proceedings of Selected Research Presentations at the Annual Convention of the AECT (ERIC Document Reproduction No. ED 334 972).

Ausubel, D. (1968). *Educational psychology: A cognitive view.* New York: Holt, Rinehart & Winston.

Becker, H. (1985). *The second national survey of instructional uses of school computers: A preliminary report* (ERIC Document Reproduction Service No. ED 274 307).

Becker, H. (1986a). *Instructional uses of school computers.* Reports from the 1985 National Survey. Issue No. 1 (ERIC Document Reproduction Service No. ED 274 319).

Becker, H. (1986b). *Instructional uses of school computers.* Reports from the 1985 National Survey. Issue No. 3 (ERIC Document Reproduction Service No. ED 279 303).

Bialo, E., & Sivin, J. (1989). Computers and at-risk youth: Software and hardware that can help. *Classroom Computer Learning, 9*(5), 48–55.

Bohlin, R. (1993). Computers and gender difference: Achieving equity. *Computers in the Schools, 9*(2–3), 155–166.

Buchholz, W. (1991). A learning activity for at-risk ninth through twelfth grade students in creating a computer-generated children's storybook design. Master's thesis, New York Institute of Technology (ERIC Document Reproduction No. ED 345 695).

Christopherson, J. (1997). The growing need for visual literacy at the university. Proceedings of the International Visual Literacy Association 1996 Annual Meeting, Cheyenne, WY (ERIC Document Reproduction No. 408 963).

Clark, R. (1983). Reconsidering research on learning from media. *Review of Educational Research, 53*(4), 445–459.

Clark, R. (1985). Evidence for confounding in computer-based instruction studies: Analyzing the meta-analyses. *Educational Communications and Technology Journal, 33*(4), 249–262.

Clark, R. (1991). When researchers swim upstream: Reflections on an unpopular argument about learning from media. *Educational Technology, 31*(2), 34–40.

Clark, R. E. (1994). Media will never influence learning. *Educational Technology Research and Development, 42*(2), 21–29.

Cohen, M., & Riel, M. (1989). The effect of distant audiences on children's writing. *American Educational Research Journal, 26*(2), 143–159.

Cordes, C., & Miller, E. (2000). *Fool's gold: A critical look at computers in childhood.* College Park, MD: Alliance for Childhood.

Cuban, L. (1986). *Teachers and machines: The classroom use of technology since the 1920s.* New York: Teachers College Press.

Cuban, L. (2001). *Oversold and underused.* Boston: Harvard University Press.

Durden, W. (2001, October 19). Liberal arts for all, not just the rich. *Chronicle of Higher Education.* Available online: http://chronicle.com.

Engler, P. (1992). Equity issues and computers. In G. Bitter (Ed.), *Macmillan encyclopedia of computers.* New York: Macmillan.

Fear-Fenn, M., & Kapostacy, K. (1992). Math + science + technology = Vocational preparation for girls: A difficult equation to balance. Columbus, OH: Ohio State University, Center for Sex Equity (ERIC Document Reproduction No. 341 863).

Franklin, S. (1991). Breathing life into reluctant writers: The Seattle Public Schools laptop project *Writing Notebook, 8*(4), 40–42.

Fredman, A. (1990). *Yes, I can. Action projects to resolve equity issues in educational computing.* Eugene, OR: International Society for Technology in Education.

Gagné, R. (1965). *The conditions of learning.* New York: Holt, Rinehart & Winston.

Gardiner, S. (2001). Cybercheating: A new twist on an old problem. *Phi Delta Kappan, 83*(2), 172–176.

Goslee, S. (1998, June). *Losing ground bit by bit: Low-income communities in the information age.* Washington, DC: The Benton Foundation and the National Urban League. Available online: http://www.benton.org/Library/Low-Income/home.html.

Healy, J. (1998). *Failure to connect: How computers affect our children's minds—for better or worse.* New York: Simon & Schuster.

Heinich, R., Molenda, M., Russell, J., & Smaldino, S. (2000). *Instructional media and technologies for learning.* Upper Saddle River, NJ: Merrill/Prentice Hall.

Hill, M. (1993). Chapter 1 revisited: Technology's second chance. *Electronic Learning, 12*(1), 27–32.

Hoffman, D., & Novak, T. (1998, April 17). Bridging the racial divide on the Internet. *Science, 280*(5362), 390–391.

Holland, H. (1995). Needles in a haystack. *Electronic Learning, 14*(7), 26–28.

Holmes, N. (1991). The road less traveled by girls. *School Administrator, 48*(10, 11, 14), 16–20.

Howard, R. (2001, November 16). Forget about policing plagiarism—just teach. *Chronicle of Higher Education.* Available online: http://chronicle.com.

International Society for Technology in Education. (2000). *National educational technology standards for students.* Eugene, OR: Author.

Johnson, D., & Eisenberg, M. (1996). Computer literacy and information literacy: A natural combination. *Emergency Librarian, 23*(5), 12–16.

Kozma, R. (1991). Learning with media. *Review of Educational Research, 61*(2), 179–211.

Kozma, R. (1994). Will media influence learning? Reframing the debate. *Educational Technology Research and Development, 42*(2), 5–17.

Kozma, R., & Croninger, R. (1992). Technology and the fate of at-risk students. *Education and Urban Society, 24*(4), 440–453.

LaRoue, A. (1990). The M.A.P. shop: Integrating computers into the curriculum for at-risk students. *Florida Educational Computing Quarterly, 2*(4), 9–21.

Leslie, L., McClure, G., & Oaxaca, R. (1998). Women and minorities in science and engineering. A life sequence analysis. *Journal of Higher Education, 69*(3), 239–276.

Marcus, S. (1995). E-meliorating student writing. *Electronic Learning, 14*(4), 18–19.

Margolis, J., & Fisher, A. (2002). *Unlocking the clubhouse: Women in computing.* Cambridge, MA: The MIT Press.

McArthur, D., & Stasz, C. (1990). An intelligent tutor for basic algebra (ERIC Document Reproduction No. ED 334 069).

McNabb, M. (2001). In search of appropriate usage guidelines. *Learning and Leading with Technology, 29*(2), 50–54.

McNeil, B., & Wilson, K. (1991). Meta-analysis of interactive video instruction: A 10-year review of achievement effects. *Journal of Computer-Based Instruction, 18*(1), 1–6.

Miller, L. (1998, April 30). Hispanic "tech-gap" less gaping. *USA Today,* p. 1D.

Miller, S. E. (2001). Technology: What's it good for? *Learning and Leading with Technology, 28*(6), 42–45.

Mitchell, K., Finkelhor, D., & Wolak, J. (2001). Risk factors for and impact of online sexual solicitation of youth. *Journal of the American Medical Association, 285*(23), 3011–3014.

Molnar, A. (1978). The next great crisis in American education: Computer literacy. *AEDS Journal, 12*(1), 11–20.

Moursund, D. (1995). The basics do change. *Learning and Leading with Technology, 23*(1), 6–7.

Muffoletto, R. (1994).Technology and restructuring education: Constructing a context. *Educational Technology, 34*(2), 24–28.

Naisbitt, J. (1984). *MegaTrends.* New York: Warner Books.

National Center for Education Statistics. (1999a). *Status of education reform in public elementary and secondary schools.* Washington, DC: U.S. Department of Education.

National Center for Education Statistics. (1999b). *Teacher quality: A report on the preparation and qualifications of public school teachers.* Washington, DC: U.S. Department of Education.

National Council for Accreditation of Teacher Education. (1997). *Technology and the new professional teacher. Preparing for the 21st century classroom.* Washington, DC: Author.

National Telecommunications and Information Administration, U.S. Commerce Department. (1998, July). *Falling through the net II: New data on the digital divide.* Washington, DC: Author. Available online: http://www.ntia.doc.gov/ntiahome/net2.

Nelson, C., & Watson, J. (1991). The computer gender gap: Children's attitudes, performance, and socialization. *Journal of Educational Technology Systems, 19*(4), 345–353.

Neuman, D. (1991). Beyond the chip: A model for fostering equity. *School Library Media Quarterly, 18*(3),158–164.

Niemiec, R., & Walberg, R. (1989). From teaching machines to microcomputers: Some milestones in the history of computer-based instruction. *Journal of Research on Computing in Education, 21*(3), 263–276.

Norris, W. (1977). Via technology to a new era in education. *Phi Delta Kappan, 58*(6), 451–459.

Oppenheimer, T. (1997). The computer delusion. *The Atlantic Monthly, 280*(1), 45–62.

Pask-McCartney, C. (1989). A discussion about motivation. Proceedings of Selected Research Presentations at the Annual Convention of the AECT. (ERIC Document Reproduction No. ED 308 816)

Polin, L. (1992). Looking for love in all the wrong places? *The Computing Teacher, 20*(2), 6–7.

President's Committee of Advisors on Science and Technology. (1997, March). *Report to the president on the use of technology to strengthen K–12 education.* Washington, DC: Executive Office of the President of the United States.

Quittner, J. (1995). Back to the real world. *Time, 145*(16), 56–57.

Relan, A. (1992). Motivational strategies in computer-based instruction: Some lessons from theories and models of motivation. Proceedings of Selected Research Presentations at the Annual Convention of the AECT. (ERIC Document Reproduction No. ED 348 017)

Remnick, D. (1997, October 20 and 27). The next magic kingdom: Future perfect. *The New Yorker,* 210–224.

Rifkin, J. (2000). *The age of access.* New York: Tarcher/Putnam.

Roblyer, M., Castine, W., & King, F. J. (1988). *Assessing the impact of computer-based instruction: A review of recent research.* New York: Haworth Press.

Roblyer, M. (1990). The glitz factor. *Educational Technology, 30*(10), 34–36.

Roblyer, M. (1991). Electronic hands across the ocean: The Florida–England connection. *The Computing Teacher, 19*(5), 16–19.

Roblyer, M. (1992). Computers in education. In G. Bitter (Ed.), *Macmillan encyclopedia of computers.* New York: Macmillan.

Roblyer, M., Dozier-Henry, O., & Burnette, A. (1996). Technology and multicultural education: The "uneasy alliance." *Educational Technology, 35*(3), 5–12.

Roblyer, M. D. (1996). The constructivist/objectivist debate: Implications for instructional technology research. *Learning and Leading with Technology, 24*(2), 12–17.

Roblyer, M. D. (1998a). The other half of knowledge: Information literacy skills. *Learning and Leading with Technology, 25*(6), 54–55.

Roblyer, M. D. (1998b). Visual literacy: Views on a new rationale for teaching with technology. *Learning and Leading with Technology, 26*(2), 51–54.

Roblyer, M. D. (2002). Virtual high schools in the U.S.—Current views, future visions. In J. Bradley (Ed.), *The open classroom. Distance learning in schools.* London: Kogan Page Publishing Company.

Saettler, P. (1990). *The evolution of American educational technology.* Englewood, CO: Libraries Unlimited.

Sanders, J. (1993). Closing the gender gap. *Executive Educator, 15*(9), 32–33.

Sanders, J., & Stone A. (1986). *The neuter computer. Computers for girls and boys.* New York: Neal Schuman Publishers.

SCANS (Secretary's Commission on Achieving Necessary Skills) Report. (1992). Washington, DC: U.S. Department of Labor.

Shields, M., & Berman, R. (2000). Children and computer technology: Analysis and recommendations. *The Future of Children, 10*(2). Available online: http://www.futureofchildren.org/cct/index.htm.

Soloman, G. (1995). Planning for technology. *Learning and Leading with Technology, 23*(1), 66–67.

Stoll, C. (1995). *Silicon snake oil: Second thoughts on the information highway.* New York: Doubleday.

Stoll, C. (1999). *High-tech heretic: Why computers don't belong in the classroom and other reflections by a computer contrarian.* New York: Doubleday.

Stumpf, H., & Stanley, J. (1997). The gender gap in advanced placement computer science. *College Board Review, 181,* 22–27.

Summers, J. (1990–1991). Effect of interactivity upon student achievement, completion intervals, and affective perceptions. *Journal of Educational Technology Systems, 19*(1), 53–57.

Taylor, D. (1989). Communications technology for literacy work with isolated learners. *Journal of Reading, 32*(7), 634–639.

Thurston, L. (1990). Girls, computers, and amber waves of grain: Computer equity programming for rural teachers. Paper presented at the Annual Conference of the National Women's Studies Association (ERIC Document Reproduction Service No. ED 319 660).

Tibbs, P. (1989). Video creation for junior high language arts. *Journal of Reading, 32*(6), 558–559.

Trend, D. (2001). *Welcome to cyberschool.* Lanham, MD: Rowman and Littlefield.

Truett, C. (1996). Information literacy: When computers aren't enough. *Learning and Leading with Technology, 23*(5), 65–67.

Volker, R. (1992). Applications of constructivist theory to the use of hypermedia. Proceedings of Selected Research Presentations at the Annual Convention of the AECT. (ERIC Document Reproduction No. ED 348 037).

Warren-Sams, B. (1997, June). *Closing the equity gap in technology access and use.* Portland, OR: Northwest Regional Educational Laboratory.

Wired Digital Inc. (2001, April 2). Are teachers using the net? Available online: http://www.wired.com/news/culture/0,1284,42658,00.html.

Young, J. (1998, March 23). "Techno-realists" hope to enrich debate over policy issues in cyberspace. *Chronicle of Higher Education.* Available online: http://chronicle.com.

Young, J. (2001, July 6). The cat-and-mouse game of plagiarism detection. *Chronicle of Higher Education.* Available online: http://chronicle.com.

CHAPTER 2

Planning and Implementation for Effective Technology Integration

"Let the ideas speak for themselves," more than one scientist told me, "and never mind the people involved." Alas, it isn't quite that simple.

Paula McCorduck, from *Machines Who Think* (1979)

This chapter covers the following topics:

- Procedures for developing school/district technology plans
- Strategies and tips for locating outside funding sources for technology purchases and uses
- Characteristics of effective technology teacher staff development and training for technology
- Recommendations for optimizing school district and school purchases of hardware and software
- School and district responsibilities for supporting ethical and legal technology use
- A technology integration planning model that includes procedures and issues teachers can address when planning, designing, and implementing effective technology integration strategies

Objectives

1. Identify school and district resources, policies, and procedures teachers should have in place to provide necessary support for effective classroom integration of technology.
2. For each of several classroom situations where technology is being used or planned for use, describe an ethical and legal response a teacher might have to the situation.
3. Use the five-phase technology integration planning model to develop a sample classroom technology integration strategy.
4. Develop an action research plan to evaluate the impact of a given technology integration strategy.

The Need for Two Levels of Planning: What the School and District Can Do Versus What Teachers Can Do

The literature on educational technology is full of glowing promises of dramatic and meaningful improvements to classroom activities and outcomes. But the mere presence of technology is not an automatic guarantee for improved education. Despite its potential power, educational technology has had some well-documented, high-profile failures (Ferrell, 1986; Morehouse, Hoaglund, & Schmidt, 1987; The revolution that fizzled, 1991), and the most recent research shows that *how* technology is integrated is more important than *how much* it is used (Archer, 1998).

Success with any technology is rarely serendipitous. Certain factors profoundly affect whether or not technology helps education take a leap forward or a pratfall. Furthermore, technology has its high-profile critics (Baines, 1997; Oppenheimer, 1997; Stoll, 1995, 1999), and justifying the high costs of technology in education is becoming increasingly important. Planning is the key to addressing these concerns. This chapter describes planning that should be done both by school and district personnel and by teachers to increase the likelihood that technology will have the desired impact on teaching and learning. There is, of course, overlap among these roles, depending on the size of the schools and districts involved. Figure 2.1 provides a checklist of planning and support tasks to be done by district, school, and classroom personnel.

The first section in this chapter looks at school and district responsibilities. For technology to work in classrooms, most teachers depend on their school and district to provide several kinds of support. Teachers do not have time for these tasks, and some decisions about the selection and use of technology resources are more cost effective if made at the upper levels of an education system, such as by state resource coordinators or school district administrators. This maximizes the usefulness of activities such as documenting a plan for how schools will use technology, obtain funding, and train teachers; locating funding; obtaining equipment and software bids; and hiring experts and consultants with specialized expertise.

Even though state agencies and school districts may make many planning and preparation decisions that affect the schools, the current trend is for each school to develop and maintain its own technology. Jankowski (1996) gives planning guidelines specific to school-level technology plans, and the Southern Technology Council (1997) gives many good examples of planning at this level. Some of the issues particularly important for school-level technology planning and implementation include methods of optimizing resources and setting up and maintaining facilities.

The teacher's primary responsibility is developing and implementing effective technology integration plans. The second section in this chapter reviews and gives examples of a technology integration planning model for teachers. This model represents the decisions and tasks teachers address when planning for effective technology integration.

Technology Integration Planning Tasks at District and School Levels

Developing District and School Technology Plans

Most reports (Apple Computer Company, 1991; Brody, 1995; Bruder, 1993; Dyrli & Kinnaman, 1994; See, 1992; Wall, 1994) recommend assigning planning tasks to a technology planning committee made up of both educators and technology experts as well as representatives from all groups in the school or district. Such committees are most effective when appointed by top-level administrators who give them authority to implement what they recommend. Kwajewski (1997) adds one more concern: Educational leaders must view technology as a "core value" if it is to work effectively in the school system.

Setting appropriate goals and developing sound plans for reaching them are such commonsense prerequisites for success in any endeavor that it could be assumed that any technology project would follow a well-conceived plan. Sadly, this is not always the case. Surveys indicate that schools and districts often purchase technology resources without first adopting technology usage plans (Dyrli & Kinnaman, 1994a). Technology experts and technology-oriented educators generally agree that developing and maintaining a school-level or a district-level plan increases significantly the likelihood of receiving the full benefits of technology's potential for improving teaching, learning, and productivity. A technology plan helps a school or district save money, achieve specific goals, and build in community support for the plans.

Several good sources document the steps that a planning committee should follow to develop a sound technology plan. The following summary of planning steps and guidelines is based on recommendations from Dyrli and Kinnaman (1994a), Wall (1994), and Brody (1995). Kimball and

Figure 2.1 Checklist of Technology Integration Planning and Support Tasks for School District, School, and Teaching Personnel

Tasks for School District Personnel

___ 1. Identify and appoint members of a committee to develop a technology plan.

___ 2. Develop a technology plan that includes:
- A vision for how technology will improve and restructure the system
- A well-documented rationale for using technology resources
- Description of the current status of technology
- List of goals that describes a guiding framework for using technology
- Description of activities to accomplish goals, including teacher training
- Identify effective measures to address: equitable access and use; ethical behavior of all staff, educators, and students
- An evaluation plan for measuring progress toward goals
- A budget that specifies annual amounts for technology.

___ 3. Identify and apply to funding sources, including state and local sources and grant agencies.

___ 4. Develop and publicize district position statements on ethical and legal use of technology resources.

___ 5. Hold staff development and training in technology skills.

Tasks for School District and/or School Personnel

___ 1. Put measures into place to optimize classroom and shared hardware and software resources.

___ 2. Select, purchase, and place hardware and software resources to meet identified needs.

___ 3. Set up and publicize procedures for using computers in classrooms and labs.

___ 4. Set up procedures for maintaining and repairing equipment.

___ 5. Set up procedures to keep equipment and materials secure from vandalism and theft.

___ 6. Set up measures to prevent spread of viruses.

Tasks for Teachers

___ 1. Match curriculum needs with technology resources.

___ 2. Plan activities that integrate technology into learning activities using available resources.

___ 3. Prepare an optimal classroom environment to support technology use.

___ 4. Prepare and test equipment and technology materials prior to use by students.

___ 5. Prepare students to use technology effectively and ethically.

___ 6. Try out and revise technology-based activities.

Sibley (1997–1998) provide a comprehensive rubric for assessing the quality of technology plans. (See Figure A.1 in the Appendix.) Finally, Mississippi State University's National Center for Technology Planning provides a comprehensive planning guide and also state, district, and school examples of good technology plans at its web site (http:// www.nctp.com/ guidebook.cfm).

Coordinate school and district planning. Some decisions are best made at the district level and some are best left for each school to consider, but plans at each level should be coordinated with each other. It is helpful if each school has a technology liaison/coordinator to act as the school's representative in a district-wide planning committee.

Involve teachers and other personnel at all levels. To obtain widespread support for a plan, the planning team should include parents, community leaders, school and district administrators, and teachers. Involving teachers is especially important. Any technology plan must show where and how technology resources will fit into instructional plans for all grade levels and content areas. Just as curriculum plans require input from teachers, technology plans depend on direct guidance from those who will implement them.

Budget yearly amounts for technology purchases. Technology changes too rapidly for schools to expect one-time purchases of equipment or software to suffice. A technology plan should allow for yearly upgrades and additions to keep resources current and useful.

Make funding incremental. Few schools' yearly budgets allow for the purchase of all needed resources or teacher training. A plan should identify a specific amount to spend each year and a priority list of activities to fund over the life of the plan.

Emphasize teacher training. Knowledgeable people are as important to a technology plan as up-to-date technology resources. Successful technology programs hinge on well-trained, motivated teachers. A technology plan should acknowledge and address this need with appropriate training activities.

Apply technology to needs and integrate curriculum. Effective planning focuses on the correct questions. For example, planners should ask "What are our current unmet needs and how can technology address them?" Too many planners skip this question and jump to "How can we use this equipment and software?" It is difficult to identify needs since the emergence of new technology has a way of changing them. Many educators did not realize they needed faster communications until the fax machine, e-mail, and cellular telephones became available. Curriculum integration should also focus on unmet needs. Technology should become an integral part of new methods to make education more efficient, exciting, and successful. Planners should ask "What are we teaching now that we can teach better with technology?" and "What can we teach with technology that we could not teach before but that should be taught?"

Keep current and build in flexibility. Both technology and users' opinions about how to implement technology change daily. Leading-edge technology solutions can become out of date soon after their development as more capable resources emerge and new research and information clarify what works best. To keep up with these changes, educators must constantly read and attend conferences, workshops, and meetings. Each school's and district's technology plan should address how it will obtain and use technology resources over a 3- to 5-year period. But any technology plan should be designed to incorporate new information and changing priorities through yearly reviews and revisions (See, 1992).

Finding Funding for Technology Resources

Experts agree that adequate funding can determine the success or failure of even the best technology plans. The summary of guidelines on funding provided by Insight 2.1 is based on recommendations from Ritchie and Boyle (1998) and Soloman (2001).

School and District Staff Development and Training for Technology

Despite general agreement on the necessity of technology skills teachers need, Sheingold (1991) pinpoints a fundamental stumbling block that will complicate teacher integration of technology for some time to come: "Teachers will have to confront squarely the difficult problem of creating a school environment that is fundamentally different from the one they themselves experienced" (p. 23). Using technology does not stop with computer-based grades or assigning students to use word processing to produce traditional book reports. Instead, technology confronts teachers with both new possibilities and imperatives for radical changes in teaching behaviors.

Recent national studies continue to confirm that only 20% to 25% of all teachers feel comfortable using technology in their classrooms (U.S. Department of Energy [DOE], 1999). At least some of this problem is due to teachers receiving inadequate training and staff development in the appropriate applications of technology to instructional problems and needs. Recognizing this training must begin at preservice levels, in 1999 the federal Department of Education began an initiative called *Preparing Tomorrow's Teachers to Use Technology* (see http://www.pt3.org). The purpose of this initiative was to infuse technology into teacher training programs across the country. Hundreds of programs have taken advantage of this opportunity, and evidence is growing that teachers are entering schools better trained in technology uses.

Bray (1999) says that effective training requires an eight-step approach: create a team, set goals and a vision, identify needs, define where you are now, develop a list of learning opportunities, design and implement an action plan, design and support individual learning plans (ILPs), and evaluate and address the plan's effectiveness (p. 15). She also supplies a list of stages teachers may go through as they learn how to use technology in the classroom. These range from informational (they want to know more about technology but their current uses are limited to simple tools such as grading programs) to refocusing (they invent new ways of using technology with their students).

Roblyer and Erlanger (1998) summarize findings from the literature on what makes teacher training programs most effective in helping teachers get to higher stages of awareness about technology:

- **Hands-on, integration emphasis.** Technology integration skills cannot be learned by sitting passively in a classroom, listening to an instructor, or watching demonstrations. Participants must have an opportunity to navigate through a program and complete a set of steps to create a new product. The focus must be on how to use the technology resources in classrooms, rather than just technical skills.
- **Training over time.** Many schools are discovering that traditional models of staff development, particularly "one-shot" inservice training for the entire faculty, are ineffective for teaching skills and for helping teachers develop methods to use computers as instructional tools (Benson, 1997). Technology inservice training must be ongoing.
- **Modeling, mentoring, and coaching.** Instructors who model the use of technology in their own teaching long have been acknowledged as the most effective teacher trainers (Handler, 1992; Wetzel, 1993). Research also indicates that one-to-one mentoring and coaching programs are effective for new teachers (Benson, 1997). Linking teachers to each other and to staff developers has also been shown to be effective (Office of Technology Assessment [OTA], 1995; Ringstaff & Yocam, 1995). Most teachers seem to learn computer skills through colleague interaction and information sharing (Oliver, 1994).
- **Post-training access.** Teachers not only need adequate access to technology to accomplish training, they also need access *after* training to practice and use what they have learned (Standish, 1996).

Purchasing Software and Hardware

Although teachers depend on their schools and district offices to take leadership in providing necessary resources,

InSight 2.1

Finding Funding for Technology

Funding Sources

The five categories of grants are federal, state, corporate, private, and community. Literally hundreds of sources can be found under each of these categories, and they are constantly changing. Usually, districts are more interested in the first four, because these sources usually have budgets for funding larger projects. Schools and teachers usually have smaller projects and seek funding from local community sources such as companies, individuals, and groups.

- For federal funding sources, consult http://www.ed.gov.
- For sources specific to your state, look for links from your state Department of Education web site.
- For other sources, note that most large companies have a foundation that funds education and community projects. Look up company web sites and look for a link to this information. Also, consult issues of professional education magazines and most issues of *Learning and Leading with Technology* and *Technology and Learning Magazine* for columns on funding sources and deadlines.

Writing Successful Proposals

There are only a few basic rules for writing a winning proposal, but they are often ignored. Educators who do follow these rules have an excellent chance of obtaining at least some level of outside funding for their projects.

1. **Read and follow the guidelines.** This is the most important and most often neglected step. No matter how great your idea, if your idea doesn't address directly the primary goals of the agency, your proposal won't make it past the secretary's desk. For example, some agencies cannot fund equipment; some focus only on funding equipment. Some agencies accept only proposals from K–12 groups; some accept only those from higher education. There must be a close match between your proposed activity and the funding priorities reflected in the agency's guidelines.
2. **Organize the proposal.** Most funding agencies want to see the following components: a concise executive overview (one to two pages maximum), a statement of needs the proposal addresses, statements of specific goals and objectives, a narrative summary (as brief as possible), a budget spreadsheet that identifies costs in categories, and a budget narrative that explains the costs.
3. **Write in clear and compelling language.** Does your prose sing to others as well as it sings to you? The only way to know is to ask as many people as possible to read it and suggest changes before you submit the proposal. It can be an ego-shattering process, but there is no substitute for honest reviews.

Online Grant Writing Guides

Soloman (2001) recommends that novices to the proposal-writing enterprise look at one or more of the following "short courses" on how to write effective proposals. Most of those have links to sources, as well as basics on how to write proposals.

- **About.com's Advice for Secondary School Educators:** http://www.7-12educators.about.com/education/7-12educators/cs/grantwriting/
- **Eisenhower National Clearinghouse Guidelines and Opportunities:** http://www.enc.org/professional/funding/
- **Grant Writing for Educators:** http://capecod.net/~dkeefe/Grantwriting_for_Educators.htm
- **Guide for Proposal Writing Created at Michigan State University:** http://www.LearnerAssociates.net/proposal
- **Guidelines for Beginners—An Educator's Guide:** http://www.uml.edu/College/Education/Faculty/lebaron/GRANTBEGIN
- **National Science Foundation Proposal Writing Guide:** http://www.her.nsf.gov/HER/DUE/documents/general/9783/proposal.htm
- **Proposal Writing Short Course:** http://www.fdncenter.org/grants/grantwriting.html
- **TERC Grant Writing Guide:** http://www.ra.terc.edu/publications/TERC/pubs/TERCGrantManual/TOC
- **West Ed's Proposal Writing Tips:** http://www.wested.org/tie/granttips.html

Characteristics of Successful Applicants

Ritchie and Boyle (1998) say that schools and projects that obtain funding have several characteristics in common. They have ideas for how to make things better; keep in constant touch with funding opportunities; have things already written up so they are able to respond quickly when opportunities arise; have one or more good writers handy; are passionate about their work; are relentless and experienced; and can follow directions well. This is as true about individual teachers seeking funding as it is about schools and other education organizations.

Building on Success

To continue receiving outside funding, educators who have a funded project must do two things on a continuing basis:

1. **Carry out what you proposed.** To be funded again, you have to show you did good things with what you already received.
2. **Publicize your successes.** This is no time to keep one's light under a bushel. Ask school and district public relations personnel to help spread the word about your good work. Create publications and web sites to document accomplishments. Ask the local newspaper or TV and radio stations to come for a show-and-tell session. Give talks and presentations to local groups, and never miss an opportunity to get your project on the agendas of school meetings.

Generate New Funding Opportunities

An invited proposal usually is a successful proposal, and sometimes invitations to submit proposals come from unexpected sources. One teacher had created a small, funded social studies project using the Internet to help students contact military veterans. She was surprised when her state senator read about it in the local newspaper and invited her to submit a $50,000 proposal to take a year's sabbatical and teach others how to get involved in her project. View funded projects as seeds for new opportunities, rather than one-time activities.

Sources: Ritchie, D., & Boyle, K. (1998). Finding the bucks for technology. *Learning and Leading with Technology, 26*(2), 46–50; and Soloman, G. (2001). Deconstructing a grant. *Technology & Learning, 21*(11), 44–52.

teacher input in this process is critically important. When schools and districts make hardware and software purchases, they are making curricular decisions. Therefore, it seems important for them to begin by asking teachers, "What do you need to integrate technology the way you want?" Then they can consider the factors shown in Figure 2.2.

Schools never will have the budgets for technology that they need to support instruction. Like any good steward, they must make best use of the funds they have. Strategies for optimizing the budget allocation for technology include (California's Education Council, 1998; Jordan, 1996; Ohlrich, 1996) the following:

- Require competitive bids for large items or frequently used supplies.
- Upgrade current software whenever possible.
- Recycle whenever possible.
- Use older equipment to meet lower profile, noninstructional needs.
- Use donated equipment.
- Share resources among groups whenever feasible.
- Assemble systems from the working parts of each broken computer.
- Use parent volunteers to locate funds for new equipment.
- Hold fund-raising events.

The problem of hardware incompatibility. Incompatibility problems add to the expense of technology investments. Educators must guard against two kinds of incapability: differences among brands and those between older and the upgraded versions of a single brand. Both can pose obstacles to educators with limited funds. As computer companies become more sensitive to the needs of their customers, they are attempting to maintain some degree of compatibility when they upgrade their products.

Some larger school districts and schools minimize compatibility problems by simultaneously purchasing and upgrading most or all of their technology resources. These larger entities frequently use their purchasing power to get computer and software companies to help them find solutions to incompatibilities between versions and brands. This preferred strategy requires a great deal of top-down management authority, careful planning, and arduous negotiations with computer companies.

However, most schools either cannot or do not operate this way. They always encounter incompatibility problems because they never have the funds they need to replace older equipment and software with up-to-date versions. The most common school technology inventory consists of a variety of resources acquired at different times for different purposes. Such a school should try to make the most effective possible use of the resources it has while allocating

Figure 2.2 Factors to Consider in Software and Hardware Selection

Software Factors

1. **Quality.** Use software reviews and recommendations, pilot test the software before buying it, review support documentation on program operation.
2. **Number (and type) of copies.** Use companies' flexible pricing structures: "lab packs" or price discounts for buying multiple copies, site licenses, or networked versions.
3. **Source of best prices.** Use dealers who offer lower prices than the publisher.
4. **Match with curriculum and students.** Choose wisely between two packages that seem to do the same thing (match software carefully to the student levels and curriculum-specific needs).

Hardware Factors

1. **Type of hardware platforms.** Consider software compatibility; when considering Macintosh or PC machines, consider ease of use for target population; pricing for comparable features; who will support equipment; and intended use.
2. **How many computers?**

   Number of computers to buy is based on how equipment will be configured and used (classroom computers or workstations versus centralized learning lab or media center).

   Number of computers per lab depends on how many people to serve and how often.
3. **Individual computer characteristics.** Consider size of random access memory or RAM; size of the hard drive, number, speed, and kind of peripherals (CD-ROMs, DVDs, modems); and computer processor speed.
4. **Other kinds of equipment**

   Modems

   Video cameras

   CD-ROM and DVD drives

   Large-screen projection devices

   Printers (inkjet and laser printers, speed of each)

   Calculator-based labs (CBLs), microcomputer-based labs (MBLs)

a part of its yearly budget for upgrades and new technology. Several strategies help educators to make the best use of available resources while dealing with incompatible brands and versions: group similar resources, use older equipment for simpler purposes, and upgrade or sell older equipment.

In all of these strategies, schools do not attempt to make different brands compatible or older equipment compatible with newer acquisitions. They simply isolate incompatible systems from each other by having each perform different functions. It is essential that educators recognize that a state-of-the-art microcomputer does not exist. Technical developments are happening so rapidly that microcomputer buyers should follow practices similar to those for car purchases. Look for the features you need and those that will probably stay around a while, and be aware that a computer is out of date when you "drive it off the lot."

School and District Responsibilities for Ethical and Legal Technology Use

In many ways, technology users represent the society in a microcosm. The culture, language, and problems of the larger society also emerge among technology users, and their activities reflect many of the rules of conduct and values of society in general. Top-level state, district, and school planning should be prepared for the problems that will arise when people try to work outside those values and rules. Carpenter (1996) gives an excellent summary of these ethical issues. Planning should address three major kinds of ethical and legal issues: copyright infringement, illegal access, and online ethics.

Recognizing and preventing copyright infringement. Software packages are much like books: Companies put up development money to produce them and then sell copies in the hope of recouping their initial investments and earning profits. Like book publishers, software companies protect their products against illegal copying under U.S. copyright law. When microcomputer software became an industry, the problem of illegal copying of disks, called *software piracy,* became widespread. Illegal copying has also become common among individuals, especially in education where teachers usually need multiple copies but cannot afford per-copy prices. Many school personnel either are not aware of laws protecting software copyrights, do not feel it is important enough to observe these laws, or have not understood clearly when copying is illegal. Even when teachers clearly grasp these issues, their students may make illegal copies; both schools and districts and their personnel can be held legally responsible unless they have developed and publicized policies against software piracy and taken measures to enforce them (Becker, 1992; Simpson, 2001).

Simpson (2001) gives an excellent summary of the laws related to software copying, recommendations on publicizing software policies, and example copyright statements that schools and districts can use. The Software and Information Industry Association (SIIA) has also developed summary guidelines for software copying and media communication that are available on request. (For more information, see their web site: http://www.spa.org.) Simpson emphasizes that software companies are serious about enforcing software copyright laws and will prosecute offenders. Administrative organizations must protect themselves against copyright infringement suits by stating and publicizing a policy regarding software copying, by requiring teacher and staff training on the topic, and by requiring hard drive and network programs that discourage users from making illegal copies. Districts and schools should also consider options for providing adequate numbers of copies for their users (e.g., by purchasing site licenses, lab packs, or networkable versions).

Recognizing and preventing illegal access. When computer users gain illegal access to private information, the problem is known either as *computer crime* or *hacking.* Individuals gain illegal access to computerized records for illicit purposes such as transferring bank funds into their own accounts or gathering confidential information from which they can profit. Computer crime also includes software piracy and acts of mischief such as sending out viruses and destroying information.

Hackers are people who are so captivated by the power and intricacies of computer systems that they adopt computer activities as a hobby. Hacking is not illegal but becomes a crime when it turns toward exploring ways to invade privately held information. It is a serious problem in education, since students just learning about the computer can easily cross the line between harmless exploration and illegal access. Schools and districts that maintain computer files on students and staff must take steps to restrict illegal access.

Dealing with online ethics issues. The increased usage of the Internet in education presents several kinds of problems for schools and districts. There have been many demonstrations of just how easy it is to inadvertently run across web sites containing shocking images or solicitations, and a recent national survey reported that 19% of all young people using the Internet had been approached by predators. The situation is so alarming that the U.S. Congress passed the Children's Internet Protection Act to encourage schools to take measures that will keep children away from Internet materials that could be harmful to them (McNabb, 2001). Some states or districts address this problem by placing *firewall software* on their networks. Firewall software prevents access to specific web site addresses or to web sites that contain certain keywords or phrases. Other districts or schools choose to use commercially available filtering software such as the 10 packages reviewed by Munro (1998). Unfortunately, firewalls and filtering software have been found to create a new set of problems for schools by preventing their users from connecting to many legitimate educational sites. Technical support personnel often are frustrated by the time it takes to figure out why a firewall is preventing access to a legitimate site and how to work around it.

School and District Responsibilities for Ensuring Equity of Technology Use

The American Association of University Women (AAUW) has produced some of the best (and most controversial) research on inequities in education for girls and minority groups. It is well documented that females are poorly represented in technical professions in sciences and engineering. Most experts believe that the basis for this inequity begins at early levels of education. Both the research and strategies for addressing inequities are documented in a series of reports (see the AAUW web site at http://www.aauw.org). One of these reports (*Tech-Savvy: Educating Girls in the New Computer Age,* 2000) deals specifically with current inadequacies in how girls are taught to use technology and what schools must do to address this problem. Another recent book also offers detailed suggestions on this topic (Margolis & Fisher, 2002).

Engler (1992) and Warren-Sams (1997) recommend strategies that can help state and district leaders and policy makers ensure more equitable access to technology for all students. Warren-Sams' booklet, *Closing the Equity Gap in Technology Access and Use,* describes three major areas in which inequities can arise: access, types of use, and curriculum. She suggests dozens of solutions to put into place at administrative, district, and school levels. Engler's practical recommendations include the following:

- **Accountability measures.** Monitor and document disproportionate participation by ethnic groups in order to increase awareness of the problem.
- **Incentives and priority funding.** Tie state grant funds and entitlements to districts' efforts to address the needs of underrepresented students.
- **Innovative programs.** Develop and support new initiatives aimed at improving student access to technology.
- **Enrichment programs.** Supply funding for computer contests, summer camps with technology themes, and similar activities directed at offering special opportunities to disadvantaged students.
- **Recognition.** State-level and district-level awards and publications could feature successful equity-related technology programs.

Business and community partnerships. Place business-sponsored magnet schools and other programs in neighborhoods where students have usually had lower access to technology resources.

- **Staff development.** Educate teachers, parents, and school personnel to increase their expectations and support of girls, minorities, and other groups.
- **Student recruitment.** Set entrance requirements for special and gifted programs to include alternatives to test scores (e.g., portfolios) to encompass a wider variety of student groups and actively seek participation of these students.

Another responsibility that usually falls to school and district agencies is selecting software that is free of cultural bias and culture-related problems. Miller-Lachman (1994) provides a checklist of criteria for selecting software free of such biases and problems:

- What is the purpose of presenting other cultures? (p. 26) (Is it integral to the program or an irrelevant add-on?)
- Do people of color and their cultures receive as much attention as people of European descent? (p. 27)
- How accurate is the presentation of various nationalities? (p. 27) (For example, portraying ancient Egyptians as having pink-colored skin would not be accurate.)
- Are the language and terms appropriate? (p. 27) (For example, referring to people from any culture as savages is pejorative.)
- Do the illustrations or sounds distort or ridicule members of other cultures? (p. 28)
- Does the program present a true picture of the culture's diversity and complexity? (p. 28)
- Who are the characters and what roles do they play? (p. 28) (Are the "good guys" always white, but the villains always include persons of color?)
- From whose perspective is the story presented? (p. 29) Is the viewpoint of the software always that of the settlers and never the Native Americans?
- Should some simulations not be played? What kinds of actions are the players asked to undertake so that they may succeed? For example, should students engage in treachery and theft in order to capture an Aztec treasure? (p. 29)

A major strategy recommended by Engler (1992), Salehi (1990), and others is networking with others to identify resources, either through statewide systems or local projects. Communicating electronically can allow minority students and teachers to exchange information with others of similar or different ethnic backgrounds in the United States and other countries. This opportunity can create a powerful motivation to learn about and use higher level technology skills while building multicultural awareness.

Finally, schools and district decision makers must recognize obstacles to technology access for students with physical disabilities and understand how to bring about access. They, much more than teachers, are tasked with ensuring compliance with federal laws regarding access to appropriate technologies for students with mental and physical disabilities. See Chapter 15 for further details on this topic.

Setting Up and Maintaining Physical Facilities

Schools have developed several common arrangements for technology equipment. Figure 2.3 details the benefits and limitations of each. These choices are influenced by the kinds of instruction that a school needs and wants to emphasize (Milone, 1989). Labs, for example, are usually considered more useful for providing group instruction and are more common at secondary levels; individual workstations

Figure 2.3 Types of Technology Facilities and Their Use

	Benefits/Possibilities	Limitations/Problems	Common Uses
Laboratories	Centralized resources are easier to maintain and keep secure; software can be networked and shared.	Need permanent staff to supervise and maintain resources. Students must leave their classrooms.	See below
Special-purpose labs	Permanent setups of group resources specific to the needs of certain content areas or types of students.	Usually exclude other groups. Isolate resources.	Programming courses; word processing classes of students in mathematics, science, etc.; teacher work labs; vocational courses (CAD, robotics); Chapter I students; multimedia production courses and activities
General-use computer labs open to all school groups	Accommodate varied uses by different groups.	Difficult to schedule specific uses. Usually available to only one class at a time.	Student productivity tasks (preparation of reports, assignments); class demonstrations; follow-up work
Library/media center labs	Same as general-use labs, but permanent staff are already present. Ready access to all materials to promote integration of computer and noncomputer resources.	Same as general-use labs Staff will need special training. Classes cannot do production or group work that may bother other users of the library/media center.	Same as general-use labs
Mobile workstations	Stretch resources by sharing them among many users.	Moving equipment increases breakage and other maintenance problems. Sometimes difficult to get through doors or up stairs.	Demonstrations, short-term uses
Mobile PCs (laptops, handhelds)	On-demand access.	Portability increases security problems	Individual student or teacher production and data gathering tasks; teachers' assessment tasks
Classroom workstations	Easily accessible to teachers and students.	No immediate assistance available to teachers. Only a few students can use at one time.	Tutoring and drills; demonstrations; production tasks for cooperative learning groups; e-mail between other teachers
Stand-alone classroom computers	Easily accessible to teachers and students.	Same as classroom workstations.	Tutoring and drills; whole-class demonstrations; pairs/small work groups

seem better suited to small-group, classroom work, and they appear more often in lower grades.

Ideally, a school would use what Fraundorf (1997) describes as a "distributed approach," that is, a combination of labs and classroom computers. Each classroom should have a workstation capable of performing the full gamut of technology-based instructional and productivity activities from word processing to multimedia applications. This station should act as a learning area to support either individual or small-group work. In addition to classroom resources, every school with an enrollment of 1,000 students or more should also have at least one general-purpose lab with at least 15 to 20 stations to serve the productivity needs of students and teachers. Generally, larger schools have more special-purpose labs.

Designing technology resources for the classroom. Although every school may not be able to attain these ideal conditions immediately, each school should identify the facilities it wants in its technology plan and set up a priority list that will help it work toward achieving them.

Designing a microcomputer lab. Bunson (1988) gives a rather complete list of concerns to address when setting up a microcomputer lab in a media center. These include *environmental factors* (equipment and traffic flow; furniture; power outlets, uninterrupted power sources, and backup power; antistatic mats and sprays; and proper temperature, lighting, and acoustics) and *administration* (copyright enforcement; equipment distribution, control, and access;

staff responsibilities and training; budgeting for hardware, software, personnel, supplies, and maintenance).

Manczuk (1994) addresses other concerns such as equity and access issues to ensure that special populations (e.g., users with physical handicaps) can benefit from the center; automated systems to maintain and locate resources easily; security measures and safety features; and "scaled down" workstations for smaller students (Wilson, 1991).

Maintenance requirements. Despite all their power and capabilities, computers and related technologies are simply machines. They are subject to the same mundane and frustrating problems as any equipment; that is, they can break down, malfunction, or become damaged or stolen. As microcomputers came into schools in greater numbers in the 1980s, these problems became increasingly important—and expensive to fix. Schools found that the initial cost of equipment was only a fraction of the funds required to keep it available and useful to teachers. They have found no easy answers to maintenance and security issues, and these subjects represent an important aspect of planning for technology use. This section describes some ongoing maintenance and security concerns that will continue to powerfully affect teachers' ability to integrate technology.

Lab rules. Most labs adopt rules intended to extend the lives of the resources they buy and to ensure that the labs fulfill the purposes for which they were designed. Teachers will find that most of these same rules should apply to classroom workstations. Lab rules and regulations should be posted prominently and should apply to everyone who uses the lab, from the principal to the teacher aides:

- No eating, drinking, or smoking should be allowed near equipment.
- Lab resources should be reserved for instructional purposes only.
- Only authorized lab personnel should check out lab resources.
- Group work should be encouraged, but lab users should show respect for others by maintaining appropriate noise levels.
- Schedules for use should be strictly observed.
- Problems with equipment should be reported promptly to designated personnel.

Maintenance needs and options. Each teacher who uses technology needs training in simple troubleshooting procedures such as making sure a printer is plugged in and online or what to do if a computer says a disk is "unreadable." Educators should not be expected to address more complicated diagnostic and maintenance problems. Nothing is more frustrating than depending on a piece of equipment to complete an important student project only to discover it is broken or malfunctioning. Cuban, Kirkpatrick, and Peck (2001) cite equipment problems as a major obstacle to effective technology integration. A technology plan must make some prior provision to expediently replace and repair equipment designated for classroom use.

Schools can minimize technology repair problems if users follow good usage rules and conduct preventive maintenance procedures. Even under the best circumstances, however, computers and other equipment will break or suffer damage. A school with more resources can expect to need a larger repair budget.

Schools and districts have tried to deal with these problems in many ways. Whole businesses have sprung up to provide maintenance for microcomputers. Educational organizations usually choose one of the following maintenance options: maintenance contracts with outside suppliers; in-house maintenance office, built-in maintenance with each equipment purchase; and a repair and maintenance budget. Each of these methods has its problems and limitations and debate continues over which method or combination of methods is most cost effective depending on an organization's size and its number of computers and peripherals.

Securing resources. Microcomputers and peripherals such as disk drives and printers can be very portable. Security is a separate, but equally important, equipment maintenance issue. Loss of equipment from vandalism and theft is a common problem in schools. Again, several options are available to deal with this problem: monitoring and alarm systems, security cabinets, and lock-down systems. As with maintenance strategies, each method of protecting equipment from loss is less than perfect and each involves considerable expense. Everyone should start with the assumption that unprotected equipment *will* be stolen. Although security can be a significant technology-related expense, it is usually cheaper than replacing stolen or vandalized equipment.

Viruses: Causes, prevention, and cures. Computer viruses are programs written specifically to cause damage or do mischief to other programs or information (Hansen & Koltes, 1992). Like real viruses, these programs can be passed to other programs with which they come in contact. For instance, they can be passed by connecting one computer to another via telecommunications or by inserting a disk containing the virus into a computer. Some viruses are carried into a computer system on *Trojan horses,* or attractive programs ostensibly designed for another purpose but which also carry instructions that get around protection codes (Lee, 1992). Some viruses are *worms,* or programs designed specifically to run simultaneously with other programs; others are *logic bombs* that carry out destructive activities at certain dates or times. Many different strains of viruses plague computer systems and more are being generated all the time. Hansen and Koltes (1992) hypothesize that most viruses are written out of curiosity or as intellectual challenges. Less often, they seem to have been produced as destructive forms of political or personal protest or revenge. However, Mungo and Clough (1992) warn that this latter kind of activity may be increasing.

The impact of a virus can take many forms. Some viruses eat through data stored in a computer. Others replicate copies of themselves in computer memory and destroy files. Still others print mischievous messages or cause unusual screen displays. No matter what their purposes, viruses have the general effect of tying up computer resources, frustrating users, and wasting valuable time. Even after a virus has been detected and removed from hard drives, it can return if users do not diligently examine their floppy disks as they insert them into the cleaned computer.

Randall (1998) warns that passing viruses via the Internet is becoming commonplace. Since computer viruses are currently as widespread and as communicable as the common cold and they often can interfere with planned activities, teachers and schools must take precautions against contracting these electronic diseases. Dormady (1991) recommends a four-point program to minimize the impact of viruses: establish good practices (scan systems and disks regularly, back up important data or files); enforce safety policies (no unauthorized programs); use virus management programs and "cookie managers" (Randall, 1998); and educate users on how to prevent, detect, and remove viruses.

A Technology Integration Planning Model for Teachers

Although the school and district can and must provide resources and support, the work of technology integration into the curriculum must be done by individual teachers or teachers working in teams. Even if the educational community and/or school has done its best to plan for and support technology implementation, most schools around the country do not have the funds to provide an adequate level of equipment, materials, or technical support for teachers as they integrate technology. Despite this limitation, each teacher or teaching team is responsible for creating an environment in which technology can effectively enhance learning. IDE's *Technology Infusion Toolkit 2000* is a multimedia planning guide to acquaint teachers with all the elements of a technology-infused classroom. (See Figure 2.4 for a sample.)

This section describes a five-part technology integration planning model for teachers. This model assumes that teachers have considerable knowledge about current technology applications in their content area, as well as skills in using various technology resources. Armed with such knowledge and skills, teachers can use this model to analyze instructional situations to make sure technology is used appropriately and effectively. To aid in learning this model, it is presented here as a five-phase sequence. However, these decisions are rarely sequential. Rather, they are dealt with as integrated concerns to solve a problem: how to use technology to improve teaching and learning. See Figure 2.5 for a checklist of these concerns and Figure 2.6 for a classroom example of how a teacher might work through these steps.

Phase 1: Determining the "Relative Advantage"—Why Use Technology?

Technology as innovation: What is "relative advantage?" Perhaps one of the reasons technology isn't working as well or as efficiently in education as many had hoped by now is that too frequently technology is chosen for insufficient reasons: because the school has it on hand; the teacher next door is using it; the principal likes it; or it is part of the school culture. None of these reasons is necessarily a bad motivation, but if technology is to improve, teachers must recognize the difference between a technology solution that makes a difference and one that is an inessential add-on, between one that improves the quality of the teaching/learning experience, and one that is simply innovative.

In his best-selling 1995 book *Diffusion of Innovation,* Everett Rogers makes the point that people find change very stressful and difficult and, thus, they do not necessarily change the way they do things—that is, adopt innovative methods—because it is good for them to change. However, they are most likely to accept change if the innovation has desirable levels of each of five kinds of characteristics:

- **Relative advantage.** They must be persuaded that the new way of doing things has clear benefits over current methods.
- **Compatibility.** They must feel the new method is compatible with their values and beliefs, with previous innovations they accepted, and with their current needs.
- **Complexity.** They must perceive the new method as being easy enough for them to learn and to implement.
- **Trialibility.** It helps people change if they can do it gradually; if they can try it out a little before having to adopt it completely.
- **Observability.** It also helps if they are able to see others adopting and using the new method. Watching someone else who has adopted the innovation is a form of trialibility.

Rogers' research showed that the most important of these characteristics is the degree of perceived *relative advantage.* The other four characteristics are really just ways of helping people arrive at whether or not the innovative method has sufficient advantages over the old method to make it worth their while to change. As the example in Figure 2.6 shows, Ms. Zimmer saw the technology (software simulations) as having benefits over the way she had been teaching. However, the *trialibility* and *observability* of the methods gave her the opportunity to come to this conclusion and to realize that simulations had a low enough complexity level to be feasible. These opportunities also helped her realize that software uses had *compatibility* with her role as a teacher, and had low enough *complexity* to make it feasible for teachers and students to use them.

What kinds of teaching/learning problems have technology-based solutions? As a first step, therefore, teachers

Figure 2.4 Sample Screens from IDE's *Technology Infusion Toolkit 2000*

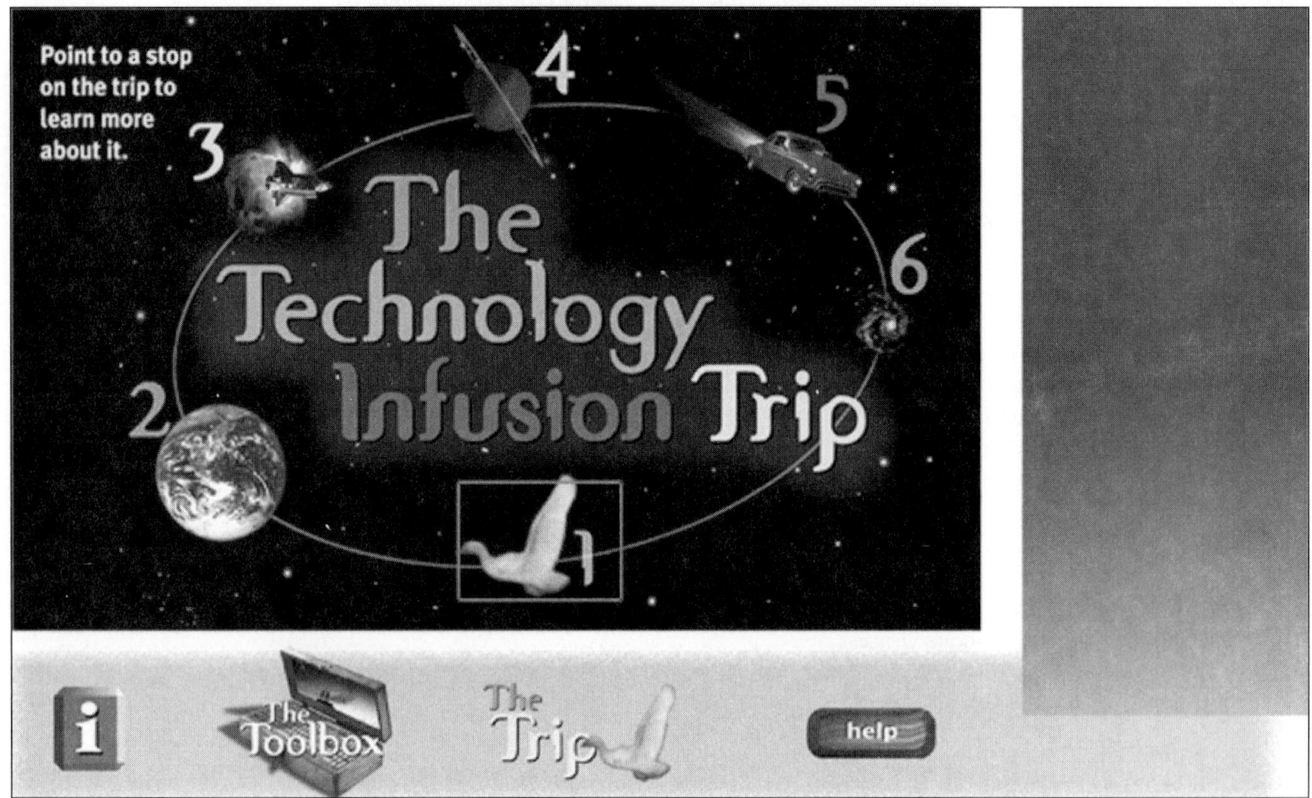

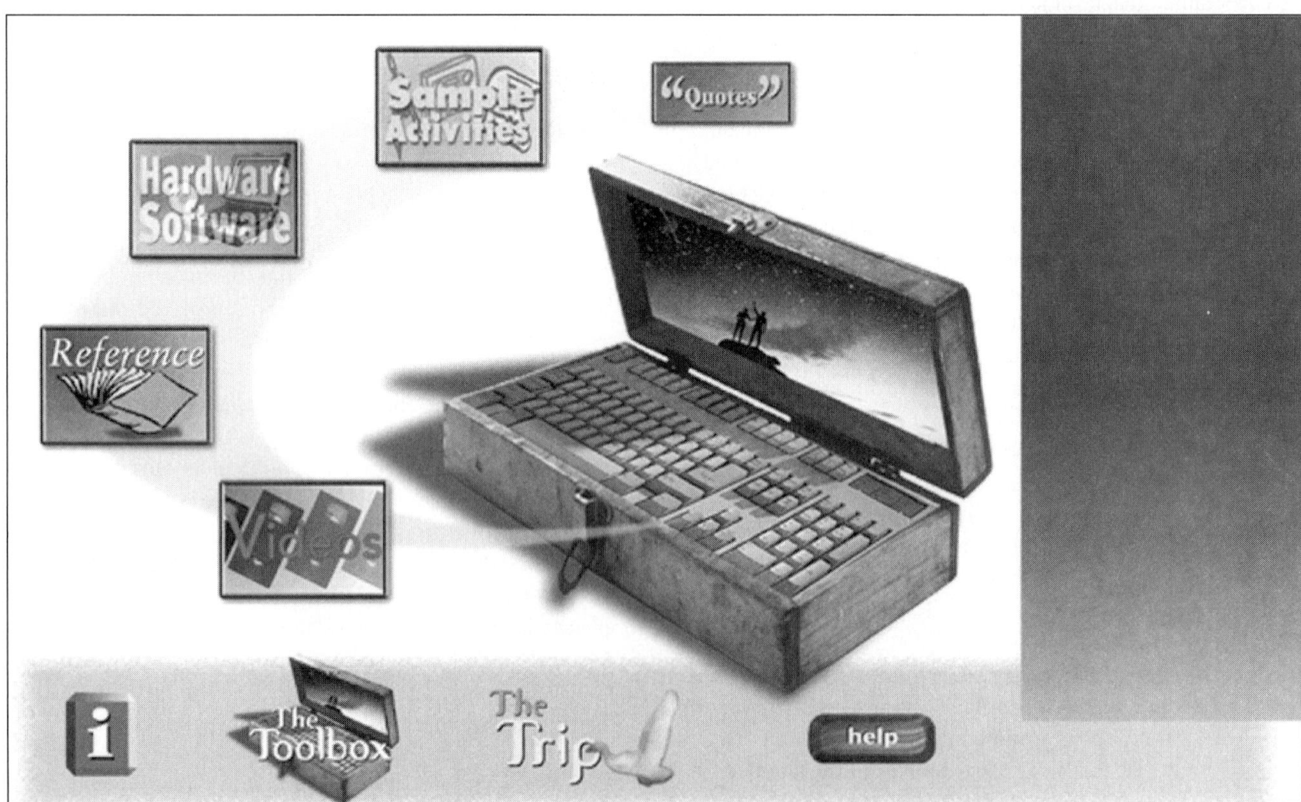

Source: Courtesy of IDE Corporation.

Figure 2.5 Checklists for Applying the Technology Integration Planning Model

Phase 1: Determining the "Relative Advantage"—Why Use Technology?

_____ Are there any topics or curriculum objectives I have difficulty teaching?

_____ Do any of these instructional problem areas have technology-based solutions?

_____ What is the relative advantage of the technology-based solutions?

_____ Is the relative advantage sufficient to justify the effort involved in adopting these solutions?

Phase 2: Planning Assessments — What Are Appropriate Assessment Strategies?

_____ What kinds of performances do I expect from students to show they have learned the topic?

_____ What is the best way for me to assess students' learning progress and products: e. g., written tests (multiple choice, true-false, matching, short answer, essays), performance checklists, rubrics?

_____ Do the desired instruments exist or do I have to develop them?

Phase 3: Planning Instruction — What Are Appropriate Integration Strategies?

_____ Will the instruction be single subject or interdisciplinary?

_____ Should the instructional activities be individual, paired, small group, large group, whole class, or a combination of these?

_____ Should activities be directed, constructivist, or a combination of these?

_____ What strategies should I use to encourage females and minority students to be integrally involved with the technologies?

_____ What sequence of activities should I teach?

_____ Have I allowed students enough time to get used to materials before beginning a graded activity?

_____ Have I built in demonstrations of the skills students will need to use both the equipment and the specific software?

Phase 4: Logistics — How Do I Prepare the Classroom Environment and Instructional Materials?

_____ How many computers and copies of software will be needed to carry out the activities?

_____ How many computers and copies of software are available?

_____ Over what time period and for how long will technology resources be needed?

_____ Do I need to schedule time in a lab or media center?

_____ If demonstrations and learning stations are to be used, will projection devices or large-screen monitors be needed?

_____ What other equipment, software, media, and resources will be needed (e.g., printers, printer paper, software/probeware, videodiscs/CDs)?

_____ Have I checked out the legality of the uses I want to make?

_____ Have I provided for students' privacy and safety?

_____ Have I made all necessary access provisions for students with physical disabilities?

_____ Have I become familiar with troubleshooting procedures specific to the piece of hardware or software package being used (equipment and software manuals often list such procedures)?

_____ Have I built in time to test run an equipment setup before students arrive?

_____ Have I built in time to back up important files? Have I trained students to back up theirs?

_____ Do I have the original program disks/discs handy to reinstall them if necessary?

_____ Do I have a backup plan if I cannot use the resources as I had planned?

Phase 5: Evaluating and Revising Integration Strategies — How Do I Know It's Working?

_____ Have I identified an instructional problem to solve?

_____ Have I identified types of evidence that will indicate to me whether or not the new strategy is solving or might help solve the problem?

_____ Have I solicited feedback from students about how to improve activities?

_____ Have I used instruments to collect data on the impact of the activity?

_____ Have I reviewed the data and comments and determined if the strategy has solved the problem or could solve the problem with changes?

_____ Have I considered alternative ways to set up equipment to make the activities go more smoothly?

_____ What do I need to change to achieve better impact?

Figure 2.6 Technology Integration Planning Model: The Neuwave Example

Phase 1: Determining the "Relative Advantage"—Why Use Technology?

The district: For the last few years since the arrival of the new superintendent, the Neuwave School District had been promoting the use of computers for teacher instruction and productivity. After receiving extensive training and demonstrations in each school over the course of a year, all teachers were required to use a computerized grade-keeping software. During the next year, they were trained in e-mail use and began to receive all administrative notices via the district-wide e-mail system. After some initial complaints and tense days for the technical support staff, these innovations became an accepted part of daily life in the schools.

Compatibility – Teachers see technology innovations as compatible with school and classroom culture.

Trialibility– Teachers get a chance to try out the technology innovation before adopting it.

The district began a free workshop series for teachers on how to use various technology resources in the classroom. They offered small incentives (e.g., free software for home or school use) to those willing to attend training and integrate these new methods in their curriculum. Every teacher in the district had attended at least one of these workshops, and their curriculum plans gradually began to reflect the integration of many different technologies: e-mail and the Internet, productivity tools, instructional software, and multimedia and video production.

Observability – Teachers see others using technology innovations successfully in their own classrooms.

The school: During teacher planning days, teachers were invited to present and attend show-and-tell sessions in their classrooms to learn about each others' innovative teaching methods. The principals encouraged teachers to participate in these sessions and displayed products developed by the teachers on bulletin boards and walls around the school.

The classroom: Ms. Zimmer, a middle school math teacher, attended a district-sponsored workshop on simulation software packages and tried out several packages herself. Also, she attended show-and-tell sessions presented by two teachers in her school on their projects with simulations. She could see from these demonstrations that the packages were very rich and complex environments, but she was confident that she could learn them as easily and her students could use them as successfully as others had.

Complexity– Teachers see the technology innovation as not too difficult for them or their students to use.

She had been using books, worksheets, and paper maps to help her students learn decimal and metric distance measurement. However, she could see from their end-of-unit test scores that when it came to applying measurement concepts to real-life problems, many of them could not make the connection. She began to realize that a simulation had the features that might help her with this problem.

Relative advantage– Teachers see the benefits of a technology innovation over current methods.

She had considered various ways of setting up practice problems that were both realistic and interesting to the students. She concluded that a software simulation that required measurement skills and that showed results visually would be a more efficient way to allow practice with real-world problems than would other methods such as map making or taking imaginary trips. She also knew her students would find it motivational; they would be more likely to spend time on it. Also, she saw this was something that could be learned either individually or in small groups. After reviewing simulations available in the School Library Media Center, Ms. Zimmer decided to use a program called *Microsoft Flight Simulator*, which has students take simulated flying trips while following a map and keeping track of instrument readings such as speed and altitude.

Source: From Microsoft® *Flight Simulator* software. Screen shot reprinted by permission of Microsoft Corporation.

Figure 2.6 *(continued)*

Phase 2: Planning Assessments—What Are Appropriate Assessment Strategies? She made two checklists: one for all the measurement skills she wanted students to practice, and one for group participation. She decided to give verbal feedback to groups on the accuracy of their maps.

Phase 3: Planning Instruction—What Are Appropriate Integration Strategies?
Ms. Zimmer decided to include the simulation activity just before her unit on metric measurement skills. She designed the following activity sequence with *Flight Simulator*:

- Day 1: Preparation and software practice. To make sure students can use the software to do the assignment she had in mind, do a whole-class software demonstration with one of the preprogrammed demonstration flights that came with the software. Hand out a worksheet she prepares made up of questions and problems, along with each of several screen shots from the software. Ask the students to review the screen shots and answer the questions for homework.

- Day 2: Teacher-led work. Ask students to work in small groups to take a "flight" during which they watch the screen, read the instruments, and keep track of the readings in a logbook. Have them discuss speed and altitude during the "flight" and answer a set of teacher-prepared questions such as: "Would it take longer to get there if the speed were 60 miles per hour or 60 kilometers per hour?" and "If the speed is 60 mph, how many kilometers per hour is that?"

- Day 3: Student-directed work. Again working in small groups, have students draw a map showing the desired flight path between two locations. Supply them with some elements to make the task doable: a part of the map they are to develop, a compass rose, and a point of departure. ("You are here.") They use a logbook to draw the airplane's path, then take the "flight." They show the missing areas of the map, indicate distances between buildings and estimate altitudes. Groups share printouts of their results, and each group gets verbal feedback on the accuracy of their maps; each student gets individual feedback on the checklist skills.

Phase 4: Logistics—How Do I Prepare the Classroom Environment and Instructional Materials?
Ms. Zimmer had four computers in her own classroom. She contacted the Library Media Center and confirmed they had a site license for *Microsoft Flight Simulator* and it was legal for her to use it on all four computers at once. She designed a sequence for Days 2 and 3 by which half the students in the class would work on maps while the other half did "flight time." Then they would reverse activities. Then, she scheduled a computer projection system from the Library Media Center to use for her whole-class demonstration. Finally, she developed the worksheet with the questions, problems, and screen shots to give to the students, and she obtained some airline travel posters to put on the classroom walls to "set the scene" for the activity.

Phase 5: Evaluating and Revising Integration Strategies—How Do I Know It's Working?
Ms. Zimmer tried out the lesson and used the following "self-assessment" to review how it worked for her:

- Did everyone seem to understand how to use the software after the initial activities?
- Did all students (boys and girls) become engaged in the tasks?
- Were the maps and "flights" as accurate as hoped?
- Did most students score well on the map checklist?

Also, she administered a brief student survey to see how students responded to this simulated exercise in real-world distance measurement. The students seemed enthusiastic about the activity, and many asked if they could do more simulations like this. Some students observed that they would have liked more "flight" practice time with sample maps before doing their own maps. Ms. Zimmer decided it might be a better use of class time to reserve time in a computer lab so all groups could work with a computer at the same time.

Ms. Zimmer was happy to find that girls' comments seemed as positive as those from boys, and both performed equally well on the final mapping activities. She also found that the subsequent metric measurement unit went much more smoothly than it ever had before, and scores on the final unit test were more uniformly high than in previous years. She decided that the student performance on the tasks was sufficient to justify continuing this strategy. She signed up to present her project and her findings to other teachers in the Neuwave School District.

must find the answer to this question: What is the *relative advantage* of a technology-based method over other methods? The answer to this question may come about in several ways, but it usually begins with a teaching/learning problem teachers recognize they are having difficulty addressing with traditional methods. Figure 2.7 shows examples of teaching/learning problems for which technology may provide a solution with good relative advantage. Some of these are described as addressing learning problems, and some look at logistical problems such as making it easier and faster to do tasks. But ultimately, all of these are problems that can impact student learning.

Teachers may begin by looking at technology integration on a limited, single-problem basis. Later, as they gain experience in infusing technology, they may start to see how they can combine these technologies to modify and enhance their entire classroom learning environment (see Figure 2.9 later in this section). Chapter 3 discusses the cognitive rationales underlying these technology integration strategies, as discussed next.

Matching needs with technology-based strategies. To make connections such as these in specific content areas, teachers must be well acquainted with current technology resources and know how each can enhance teaching and learning. Then they begin to recognize places in their curriculum where the use of technology can create a relative advantage. Lesson activities/examples are given throughout Chapters 4 through 15.

Phase 2: Planning Assessments—What Are Appropriate Assessment Strategies?

When teachers design instruction systematically, as they do when they use an instructional systems design model (see Chapter 3), they plan assessment strategies *before* they design instructional strategies. This design sequence has the effect of making the students' after-instruction performance the focal point of the activity; what the teacher does is not as important as what the student does.

What are appropriate assessment strategies? It depends on the kind of skill being learned and the kind of student performance the teacher wants to measure. Traditional assessment methods such as written tests (multiple choice, true–false, matching, short answer, essays) are still very appropriate for many kinds of skills, especially for lower level ones, and for assessing individual performance. But many educators have come to believe that assessments for higher levels should require more "authentic" performances, that is, actions that reflect the skill in a more accurate, real-world context.

To document these higher level performances, students frequently are asked to prepare portfolio entries such as multimedia products and web pages. Rubrics and checklists frequently are used to assess the quality of these products. (See Appendix for examples.)

Rubrics. Jonassen, Peck, and Wilson (1999) say that a rubric is "a tool used for assessing complex performance" (p. 221) in a way that gives input and feedback to help improve the performance. A rubric consists of a set of elements that describe the performance together with a scale (e.g., 1–5 points) based on levels of performance for each element. Teachers can develop their own rubrics by identifying several aspects that they hope to see reflected in a high-quality product or performance. For example, in a multimedia product, they might look for aspects such as originality, screen design, and accuracy of content. Then they design several descriptive ratings ranging from low quality to high quality. Then they can use rubrics to rate a product or performance on the quality they see reflected in each of the elements they identified as necessary. Jonassen et al. (1999) describe characteristics of rubrics that can serve as authentic assessments (pp. 223–224), including the following:

- All important elements of the behavior are represented as strands to be assessed.
- Elements are unidimensional (i.e., discrete, not overlapping behaviors).
- Rating scales for each aspect of behavior are distinct, comprehensive, and descriptive.
- The instrument communicates clearly to students and parents.
- The instrument yields rich information that can help improve a student's level of performance, rather than just serving as a basis for grading.

Checklists. These are simply lists of behaviors and criteria that the teacher considers important. For example, in a software simulation activity, the teacher may look for evidence that students worked well with assigned group members, explored each required area, printed out the required items, explained their findings in a document, and gave a clear presentation of their findings to the class. Then the teacher checks off each item as reflected or not reflected in the students' work. Teachers also may choose to award a range of points on each activity on the checklist, depending on how well students did on the activity.

In addition to developing their own rubrics and checklist, teachers may choose to use several general rubrics and checklists others have developed to assess technology-based products and performances (see Figures A.10, A.13, and A.2 in the Appendix):

- Rubric for middle school web pages (Chenau, 2000)
- Rubric for WebQuests (Bernie Dodge web site)
- Rubric for cooperative group work (Dixon & Ruetten, 1999; Truett, 2001)

Figure 2.7 Teaching/Learning Problems and Technology Solutions with Potential for High Relative Advantage

Learning Problems	Technology Solutions with Potential for High Relative Advantage
Problem: The topic is difficult for students because concepts are new and foreign to their experience.	**Technologies:** Simulation software; video-based problem solving **Relative Advantage:** Visual examples make it easier to grasp the nature of systems, problems, and applications.
Problem: The topic is difficult for students to learn because the concepts involved are abstract and complex (e.g., physics, biology, mathematics).	**Technologies:** Simulation software; spreadsheet examples; graphing calculator uses; math tools (e.g., Geometer's *Sketchpad*) **Relative Advantage:** More visual, graphic displays make abstract concepts more concrete; makes it easier to manipulate and see relationships between variables involved in system.
Problem: Learning objectives are high level, but time-consuming manual skills (e.g., handwriting, calculations, data collection) interfere with acquiring higher level skills.	**Technologies:** Tool software (e.g., word processing, spreadsheets, probeware) **Relative Advantage:** Takes low-level labor out of doing complex tasks; allows students to focus on higher level skills.
Problem: Students need skill practice, but find it uninteresting and/or tedious on paper.	**Technologies:** Drill-and-practice software or instructional game software functions **Relative Advantage:** Combination of on-screen displays, interaction, and immediate feedback can combine to create motivating practice.
Problem: Students find the subject matter uninteresting or irrelevant to their lives.	**Technologies:** Video-based problem solving, multimedia, and Internet resources **Relative Advantage:** In appropriate instructional designs, the visual nature of these resources can make it easier for teachers to illustrate relevance.
Problem: Students fail to transfer skills they have learned to situations in which they can use them.	**Technologies:** Simulation and problem-solving software functions, video scenarios, development of electronic products **Relative Advantage:** When used in project-based instruction, these resources can help make links to real-world problems clearer, more visual.
Problem: Students lack product design skills; they do not like preparing and presenting written reports and presentations.	**Technologies:** Desktop publishing, multimedia software, web page production **Relative Advantage:** Students often find it motivating to prepare products that look professional and polished looking.
Problem: Students need to learn to work collaboratively and present products as a group. The teacher needs a format that will motivate students to work in this way.	**Technologies:** Multimedia software production, web page production **Relative Advantage:** Provides format in which group work makes sense; students can contribute to group products without being in the same physical space; allows students to make different contributions to the products based on their strengths.
Problem: Students need practice in skills that will make them technologically competitive as students and as workers (technology literacy, information literacy, and visual literacy).	**Technologies:** All software tools and all communications and presentation technologies **Relative Advantage:** Illustrates, simulates, and gives practice in skills and tools students will need in work situations.

Figure 2.7 ***(continued)***

Logistical Problems	Technology Solutions with Potential for High Relative Advantage
Problem: There is not enough time for extensive, teacher-corrected practice; doing so would leave limited time for teachers to provide help to individual students.	**Technologies:** Drill-and-practice software functions, handheld computer systems with assessment software **Relative Advantage:** Student feedback is immediate; teacher is freed for other tasks.
Problem: Students are capable of advanced instruction but teachers are not available to teach them.	**Technologies:** Tutorial software functions; self-instructional multimedia modules; distance learning courses **Relative Advantage:** If well-designed, can provide a structured, effective learning environment for capable students.
Problem: Teachers need to make time spent on labor-intensive tasks (e.g., handwriting, calculations, data collection) more efficient for them and their students.	**Technologies:** Tool software (e.g., word processing, spreadsheets, probeware) **Relative Advantage:** Takes labor out of doing tasks and making changes to information; better use of time spent on tasks.
Problem: The school has insufficient consumable materials for many learning activities (e.g., science labs, workbooks).	**Technologies:** Simulation software, CD-ROM-based texts **Relative Advantage:** On-computer reading material and activities are more cost effective because they are not consumed.
Problem: To do required research, students need information and expertise not available locally.	**Technologies:** Internet and e-mail projects; multimedia encyclopedias and atlases **Relative Advantage:** Information sources are easier and quicker to access.
Problem: It is time consuming to make corrections to written products (e.g., compositions, book reports) and displays (e.g., projects).	**Technologies:** Word processing and multimedia software, web pages **Relative Advantage:** It is easier to make changes and add updates on the screen than to typed or hand-produced materials.

Phase 3: Planning Instruction—What Are Appropriate Integration Strategies?

Teachers must address several interrelated concerns during their systematic instructional planning process. These concerns include how to handle curriculum topics, instructional grouping decisions, provisions for equity, and sequencing plans.

Single-subject vs. interdisciplinary instruction. Many subjects that for years were taught as separate courses or topics are now taught in combination. Two primary reasons are given for considering an interdisciplinary curriculum approach. First, many educators feel that teaching skills from various areas together better reflects real-life situations, because skills are rarely used in isolation from each other outside school. It also aids transfer, they feel, if students see practical applications for skills they learn in school. Second, some schools no longer have the resources to require certain courses or cannot spend as much time on them as they once did (e.g., health, physical education, music, art, foreign languages). Including these less emphasized topics in units and projects for required courses (e.g., math, sciences, language arts) allows less emphasized topics to be covered more adequately.

Individual vs. group strategies. Should learning activities be individual, paired, small group, large group, whole class, or a combination of these? If mastery learning is the goal, most teachers feel individualization is the curriculum strategy of choice. Students have to demonstrate they can do the skill by themselves and, ideally, should learn at their own pace until they reach a mastery level. However, the ability to work in groups and solve problems cooperatively with others is becoming more valued as a characteristic of successful employees. Teachers may look for opportunities where it makes sense to put students in pairs or groups to work together. Whole-class instruction usually is best for demonstrations, especially when followed by group work.

Directed, constructivist, or combined strategies. Chapter 3 discusses two different instructional approaches, both of which technology can support. Directed approaches are traditional teaching methods: instruction followed by individual practice and testing. Constructivist approaches usually are much less structured and revolve more around participation in group work and learning by doing. Teacher plans must adopt one of these approaches, or a combination of them. To select appropriate methods, teachers review the kinds of performances they are looking for at the end of the instruction, then decide on the best ways of fostering them.

Planning for equity. School districts and schools must arrange support to ensure equitable access and use of resources for minorities, females, and students with mental and physical handicaps. But it falls to teachers to design and implement curriculum to involve these underserved groups. Young (2000) and Margolis and Fisher (2002) confirm that girls begin at early levels of education to perceive computer technology as a male domain. Teachers have the task of changing this perception.

Fiore (1999), Ettenheim, Furger, Siegman, and McLester (2000), Margolis and Fisher (2002), and the report by the American Association of University Women (2000) offer dozens of tips to get girls more involved with technology. However, many of these suggestions are appropriate for involving *any* students who have the mistaken impression that technology is not meant for them. Fiore notes that girls appear to be reluctant to work with technology because they often are outnumbered by boys, feel less confident in their technical skills, and are uncomfortable with the idea of being identified with a nontraditional role. Teacher-designed technology integration strategies should build in as many of the following characteristics as possible to counteract these problems:

- **Be careful of competition.** Students usually like competition. But more reticent students may prefer competition in groups, rather than with individuals.
- **Emphasize creativity, not just remediation.** Because disadvantaged students are more likely to have deficiencies in basic skills, teachers tend to limit technology integration strategies for these students to remedial uses. As a result, students tend to think of technology as something done *to* them, rather than something that *empowers* them. All students should have opportunities for activities that promote higher level thinking and problem solving.
- **Design activities around software and web sites likely to have widespread appeal.** For example, boys are more likely than girls to enjoy action-oriented software games. But some software and web sites are popular with all students. Some resources target the interests of girls (e.g., http://www.planetgirl.com) or of certain cultures. Teachers can make a special effort to use some of these "targeted" resources from time to time.
- **Provide for equal opportunities.** Design strategies that ensure each student has a turn. Have sign-up sheets and "girls first" days to make sure the strategy works. If boys and girls are placed in groups or pairs, make sure roles are defined so that no one is left out.
- **Promote female and minority products.** Look for and include web sites made by females and minority students. Try to invite females and minority experts to speak or be involved with students via e-mail.
- **Create experts.** During the course of assignments, plan for each student to become a "classroom expert" in some aspect of the technologies being used.

Learning sequence. Integrating technology often means coordinating resources both inside and outside a classroom. Therefore, teachers will find it useful to sketch out a daily or weekly sequence of anticipated activities. Although most teachers do not want or need detailed daily lesson plans, a general plan of action helps teachers determine which instructional activities will require technology resources and which days these resources will be required. During this phase, teachers should build in time for teaching of technical skills students will need in order to use both the equipment and the specific software for the lesson, as well as time for them to get used to materials before beginning a graded activity.

Phase 4: Logistics—How Do I Prepare the Classroom Environment and Instructional Materials?

In an ideal school and classroom environment, teachers would identify needed resources *after* deciding on a learning sequence. However, in reality, they usually decide on what activities they can do in light of resources they know will be available. Most required planning revolves around working within the constraints of the number of available computers and copies of software.

Teaching configurations: One computer, workstations, or labs. The teacher must decide if the technology-based activities they want to do can be accomplished with resources available in the classroom, or if they must take students to a computer lab. Many classrooms are networked to a central server, allowing access to the Internet and other networked resources. However, the classroom may not contain as many computers as are needed for an activity. Teachers can choose from three configurations:

- **One-computer classrooms.** Although not an optimal situation, one-computer classrooms are commonplace, and a great deal has been written on how to make best use of this limited resource. Collis (1988) wrote the definitive book on planning and activities for one-computer classrooms. More recently, Kahn's book (1998) and articles by Dillon (1996) and Tan (1998) offer suggestions for one-computer activities, including demonstrations, posing problems that cooperative groups work on later, and letting students watch the collection and analysis of scientific data. These activities work better if the teacher has a projection system or large monitor attached to the computer so everyone in the class can see the screen display clearly. Some software packages are designed specifically to promote problem solving and cooperative work in a one-computer classroom.

- **Classroom workstations.** Some classrooms are equipped with two to four computers that share peripherals such as a scanner and printer. This configuration often is referred to as a teacher workstation. Teachers can use this configuration by setting up "learning stations." Each computer in the workstation is set up for a different phase in the development of a product or with different research tasks (e.g., one with Internet, one with encyclopedia, one with word processing and graphics).
- **Computer labs.** If the whole class needs to be working on computers at the same time, a teacher may decide to take large groups or an entire class to a nearby lab or media center. Whole-class work in a lab usually becomes necessary at some point for large projects such as developing multimedia presentations. Since labs can be the most popular places in the school, teachers usually have to schedule lab time well in advance for special projects.

Addressing copyright and other legal/ethical issues. An increasing number of schools have networks, since they allow teachers classroom access to the Internet and centralized access to software. Schools with no such central access often must purchase multiple copies of software and media to stay within copyright law. Some educators find it difficult to understand why they cannot make multiple copies of one legal copy, or why they are not permitted to make temporary copies and destroy them after a learning activity is completed. However, without specific permission from the publisher, making such copies is illegal. Sometimes, this means that teachers have to develop alternate plans, for example, having small groups use software rather than whole class using it at once. Rather than looking on the necessity of obtaining legal copies as an imposition, teachers may want to consider it an opportunity to model ethical behavior. Students always learn from what teachers do, as well as what they say to do. No matter what the topic being taught, teachers can set high expectations for their students' ethical behavior, communicate them clearly and consistently, and model such behaviors themselves on a daily basis.

Ensuring students' safety and privacy. As discussed earlier, the Internet can be dangerous territory for unwary and unmonitored young people. Teachers are the first line of defense in keeping students away from dangerous web sites and from contact with online predators. Several strategies are recommended. Always review web sites before giving URLs to students. Never allow students long periods of unmonitored Internet use. (Some experts recommend prohibiting student use of open chat rooms in schools, since it is difficult to know participants' true identities.) Make students aware of the potential dangers and the rules that are in place to protect them.

Ensuring equity for students with disabilities. Access is the key issue for students with physical handicaps. These students usually depend on teachers for their learning about technological devices and software that help make learning opportunities more equal to those of students without disabilities. For example, students with visual impairments may need versions of software with enlarged type. Students with physical disabilities may need special input devices. (See Chapter 15 for more information on this topic.)

Ensuring smooth classroom operations. Anything that has as much power and versatility as a computer system also has the ability to have an amazing number of things go wrong. Teachers can turn potential catastrophes into learning experiences by becoming well acquainted with the technologies they plan to use and involving students in on-the-spot troubleshooting. Doing test runs and making backup media for important files are always good ideas and, in case the worst happens (e.g., power failure), be sure to have a backup plan for the day.

Phase 5: Evaluating and Revising Integration Strategies—How Do I Know It's Working?

Trying something new when things may not work out as expected is a great opportunity for teachers to model risk-taking behaviors to students. But making improvements in teaching over time requires teachers to adopt a systematic approach to observing what worked, what didn't, and how it can be improved. The name for this approach is *action research,* and teachers may find there is no better use for it than in the context of technology-based activities.

Strategies for action research. According to Gay and Airasian (2000), action research is "a process in which . . . teachers collect evidence and make decisions about their own knowledge, performance, beliefs, and effects in order to understand and improve them" (p. 593). Every time a teacher adopts an innovative approach such as using a new technology resource, that teacher is testing a hypothesis: The innovation will help students learn better. But do they, in fact, learn better? Is the innovation being used to best advantage? Gay and Airasian say that there is only one way to answer these questions with any degree of certainty: Teachers must carry out continuing studies of their own methods and make improvements based on their findings.

Gay and Airasian (2000) stress that teacher reflection is an important part of action research, but that the most useful kinds of reflections are those based on "formal, tangible evidence that can be used to independently corroborate or validate [teachers'] own views of practice" (p. 595). In other words, teachers gather data and use them as objective evidence of what's working, what's not, and why. This confirmation process seems especially important when teachers choose technology-based methods, which are often more time consuming and expensive than other methods.

Action research is a four-step process: (1) identifying the problem, (2) gathering data, (3) summarizing and interpreting results, and (4) determining what changes (if any) need to be made. The teacher carries out all of these steps, so the research methods should be those with which teachers are most familiar and can carry out efficiently.

Assessments for action research: Surveys and impact rubrics. What kinds of data should a teacher collect? Depending on the problem being researched, Gay and Airasian (2000) recommend that teachers use one or more of the following data collection approaches (p. 597):

- **Teacher self-reflection tools:** checklists, ratings, or questionnaires
- **Media recording and analysis:** audio or videotaping of sample performances
- **Student feedback tools:** teacher-made questionnaires, surveys, and journals
- **Student performance data:** test results, essays, class projects
- **External or peer evaluation:** a colleague observes and provides feedback on a teacher's practices
- **Journaling:** teachers' written reflections on classroom events.

In addition to instruments they develop themselves for specific topics, teachers may want to use two additional assessments to help collect data on the impact of their technology-based activities. Figure A.3 in the Appendix, based on one provided by Milone (1998), helps teachers assess the value and impact of a specific activity.

The most effective kind of technology integration takes time and the insight that come with experience. The technology classroom impact rubric in Figure A.4 in the Appendix is based on one developed by Sun (2000) and can help teachers determine the level of technology integration at which they currently are working and give them an idea of higher levels of classroom infusion and impact to which they can aspire as they become more proficient with technology integration. As this rubric indicates, levels of technology integration can be assessed according to four different aspects: how often technology is used (frequency), who initiates the use (source of direction), the relationship of the technology use to other instructional activities (nature of integration), and the purpose of the technology uses.

Turning findings into instructional improvements. The most important part of action research is the final step: deciding what the data show and modifying instructional activities based on the findings. Teachers will find that some activities require only minor procedural adjustments, as Ms. Zimmer did in Phase 5 of the example given earlier in Figure 2.6. Or a teacher may decide to drop an activity as being too time consuming for the amount of impact it has. However, if the activity works well, they may decide to expand on it to achieve higher levels of integration as indicated in the technology classroom impact rubric.

Exercises

Record and apply what you have learned.

Chapter 2 Self-Test

To review terms and concepts in this chapter, take the Chapter 2 self-test. Select Chapter 2 from the front page of the Companion Website (located at http://www.prenhall.com/roblyer), then choose the *Multiple Choice* module.

Portfolio Activities

ISTE The following activities address ISTE National Educational Technology Standards for Teachers (NETS-T) and will help you add to your professional portfolio. To complete these activities online and save or submit the materials electronically, select Chapter 2 from the front page of the Companion Website (http://www.prenhall.com/roblyer), then choose the *Portfolio* module.

1. ***Technology Planning and Support (NETS-T Standard: I-B)*** Using the checklist in Figure 2.1, create a checklist a teacher might use to determine items that are available at school and district levels to support classroom use of technology. For example: Is there a technology plan in place? Was it developed by a planning committee? Does the technology plan have all necessary components? (You may produce a word-processed text outline or a chart or diagram on the computer.)
2. ***Integration Strategy (NETS-T Standards: III-A, B, C, D)*** Assume you are a classroom teacher at a level and type of school of your choice. You have one computer in your classroom, and the school has one computer lab that all teachers share. You have an idea for using a computer resource. Using Phases 1 through 4 of the technology integration planning model checklist (Figure 2.5), describe how you would go about deciding how to integrate the technology into a classroom activity.
3. ***Evaluation Strategy (NETS-T Standards: IV-A, V-B)*** For the technology use you described above, use Phase 5 of the technology integration planning model checklist (Figure 2.5) to outline an action research plan that will help you determine whether or not your technology use is having the impact you hoped. Be sure to include a description of the data to be collected and collection methods and instruments you would need, as well as the procedures for using them to assess the impact of the technology-based strategy.

Questions for Thought and Discussion

These questions may be used for small-group or class discussion or may be subjects for individual or group activities. To take part in these discussions online, select Chapter 2 from the front page of the Companion Website (http://www.prenhall.com/roblyer), then choose the *Message Board* module.

1. Sheingold (1991) said that teachers will have to confront squarely the difficult problem of creating a school environment that is fundamentally different from the one they themselves experienced (p. 23). In what ways is the current K–12 environment different from the one you experienced? Do you feel this presents an obstacle to effective use of technology in your teaching? What are some strategies you feel might help teachers overcome this obstacle?
2. NCATE's document *Technology and the New Professional Teacher* (1997) said that, in addition to technology skills, teachers need an attitude that is fearless in the use of technology, encourages them to take risks, and inspires them to be lifelong learners (p. 4). What current factors and activities can help teachers develop such an attitude? What factors make it difficult for them to acquire it?

Collaborative Activities

ISTE

The following activities address ISTE National Educational Technology Standards for Teachers (NETS-T) and can be done in small groups. Each group should present the findings to the class in a format they know how to use (word-processed report, presentation software, multimedia product). Completed group products can be copied and shared with the entire class and/or included in each person's personal portfolio.

Set 1. ***Each group chooses one*** Each group chooses or is assigned one of the following situations. Each group should develop an appropriate response, describe it for the class, and cite information and concepts from the chapter that make them feel their answer is appropriate.

Problem 1 (NETS-T Standards: V-B, D) You are a technology-using teacher at a high school. You have just learned that a school board member has recommended that the school district hire an outside consultant to develop a district-wide technology plan and present it to the board for approval and implementation. How would you respond to this recommendation?

Problem 2 (NETS-T Standard: VI-A) You are a teacher in a middle school and want to use an expensive science software package for one of your instructional activities. You have access to a 15-computer lab, but you find out the school owns only one legal copy of the software. One of the other science teachers confides that he simply places the software on the hard drives of each computer and, when students are finished using it, he erases it from the hard drives. Would you recommend doing this? Why or why not?

Problem 3 (NETS-T Standards: VI-C, E) You are talking with another teacher about your plans for having your students develop multimedia reports of their research on famous scientists. The teacher says that he has found girls do not like these kinds of activities and usually aren't as good at them as boys. Therefore, he has stopped having females do any activities with technology materials in his class. Does this sound like a good approach to this problem? Why or why not? Can you recommend an improved one?

Problem 4 (NETS-T Standard: VI-D) One of the teachers in your school told you about a project in which his students were doing research on the Internet. One of the students said he had "met" someone in a chat room who was an astronaut in the NASA program. The teacher encouraged several other students who were interested in space careers to contact the same person in the chat room and do a group presentation of their findings. Does this sound like a good strategy to you? Why or why not?

Problem 5 (NETS-T Standards: VI-A, C) In a school faculty meeting, some of the teachers say they need better ways to assess the technology skills students are learning. They propose that a committee of teachers get together to create a test bank of multiple-choice items that could be placed on scan sheets and used across all classes. How would you respond?

Set 2. **All groups** Develop an idea for a technology-based activity that would require your school to purchase resources such as multimedia hardware and software or more computers with Internet access. Develop a brief proposal to a principal, district, or funding agency that outlines the costs of these resources and gives a convincing justification for the purchases by explaining the unique benefits you expect from the activity.

Integrating Technology Across the Curriculum Activities

The *Integrating Technology Across the Curriculum* CD-ROM is a set of technology integration ideas and links to online lessons, arranged as a searchable database. The CD comes packaged with this textbook. Complete the following exercise using this CD:

One of the descriptors for the integration ideas is *relative advantage,* a concept described in this chapter. Make a chart of some examples of relative advantage that technology holds for your content area. Create a chart like the one you did in Chapter 1. This time, label the chart like the one below. List the types of relative advantage on the left and locate an integration idea that reflects each kind.

Types of Relative Advantage	Name of Lesson Plan
Makes abstract topics more visual, concrete	

References

American Association of University Women. (2000). *Tech-savvy: Educating girls in the new computer age.* Washington, DC: Author.

Apple Computer Company. (1991). *Apple technology in support of learning: Creating and managing an academic computer lab.* Sunnyvale, CA: Author.

Archer, J. (1998). The link to higher scores. *Education Week, 18*(5), 10–21.

Baines, L. (1997). Future schlock: Using fabricated data and politically correct platitudes in the name of education reform. *Phi Delta Kappan, 78*(7), 492–498.

Becker, G. (1992). *Copyright: A guide to information and resources.* Lake Mary, FL: Gary H. Becker Consultants.

Benson, D. (1997). Technology training: Meeting teacher's changing needs. *Principal, 76*(3), 17–19.

Bray, B. (1999). Eight steps to success: Technology staff development that works. *Learning and Leading with Technology, 27*(3), 14–20.

Brody, P. (1995). *Technology planning and management handbook.* Englewood Cliffs, NJ: Educational Technology.

Bruder, I. (1993). Technology in the USA: An educational perspective. *Electronic Learning, 13*(2), 20–28.

Bunson, S. (1988). Design and management of an IMC micro center. *Educational Technology, 28*(8), 29–36.

California's Education Council for Technology in Learning. (1998). Donated computers in K–12 education. *Learning and Leading with Technology, 25*(5), 52–56.

Carpenter, C. (1996). Online ethics: What's a teacher to do? *Learning and Leading with Technology, 23*(6), 40–41, 60.

Chenau, J. (2000). Cyber traveling through the Loire Valley. *Learning and Leading with Technology, 28*(2), 22–27.

Collis, B. (1988). *Computers, curriculum, and whole-class instruction.* Belmont, CA: Wadsworth Publishing Co.

Cuban, L., Kirkpatrick, H., & Peck, C. (2001). High access and low use of technologies in high school classrooms: Explaining an apparent paradox. *American Educational Research Journal, 38*(4), 813–834.

Dillon, R. (1996). Team problem solving activities. *Learning and Leading with Technology, 24*(1), 21.

Dixon, J., & Ruetten, M. (1999). A slice of data. *Learning and Leading with Technology, 27*(2), 22–27.

Dormady, D. (1991). Computer viruses: Suggestions on detection and prevention. *Florida Technology in Education Quarterly, 3*(4), 93–98.

Dyrli, O., & Kinnaman, D. (1994a). District wide technology planning: The key to long-term success. *Technology and Learning, 14*(7), 50–54.

Engler, P. (1992). Equity issues and computers. In G. Bitter (Ed.), *Macmillan encyclopedia of computers.* New York: Macmillan.

Ettenheim, S., Furger, R., Siegman, L., & McLester, S. (2000). Tips for getting girls involved. *Technology & Learning, 20*(8), 34–36.

Ferrell, B. (1986). Evaluating the impact of CAI on mathematics learning: Computer immersion project. *Journal of Educational Computing Research, 2*(3), 327–336.

Fiore, C. (1999). Awakening the tech bug in girls. *Learning and Leading with Technology, 26*(5), 10–17.

Fraundorf, M. (1997). Distributed computers and labs: The best of both worlds. *Learning and Leading with Technology, 24*(7), 50–53.

Gay, L., & Airasian, P. (2000). *Educational research: Contemporary analysis and applications* (6th ed.). Upper Saddle River, NJ: Merrill/Prentice Hall.

Handler, M. (1992). Preparing new teachers to use technology: Perceptions and suggestions for teacher educators. *Computers in Education, 20*(2), 147–156.

Hansen, B., & Koltes, S. (1992). Viruses. In G. Bitter (Ed.), *Macmillan encyclopedia of computers.* New York: Macmillan.

Jankowski, L. (1996). Guidelines for school technology development plans. *Learning and Leading with Technology, 23*(5), 38–40.

Jonassen, D., Peck, K., & Wilson, B. (1999). *Learning with technology: A constructivist perspective.* Upper Saddle River, NJ: Merrill/Prentice Hall.

Jordan, A. (1996). Back from the dead: Rescuing computers from the morgue. *Learning and Leading with Technology, 24*(2), 61–62.

Kahn, J. (1998). *Ideas and strategies for the one-computer classroom.* Eugene, OR: International Society for Technology in Education.

Kimball, C., and Sibley, P. (1997–1998). Am I on the mark? Technology planning for the e-rate. *Learning and Leading with Technology, 25*(4), 52–57.

Kwajewski, K. (1997). Technology as a core value. *Learning and Leading with Technology, 24*(5), 54–56.

Lee, J. (1992). Hacking. In G. Bitter (Ed.), *Macmillan encyclopedia of computers.* New York: Macmillan.

Manczuk, S. (1994). Planning for technology: A newcomer's guide. *Journal of Youth Services in Libraries, 7*(2), 199–206.

Margolis, J., & Fisher, A. (2002). *Unlocking the clubhouse: Women in computing.* Cambridge, MA: The MIT Press.

McCullen, C. (1999). Taking aim: Tips for evaluating students in a digital age. *Technology & Learning, 19*(7), 48–50.

McNabb, M. (2001). In search of appropriate usage guidelines. *Learning and Leading with Technology, 29*(2), 50–54.

Milone, M. (1989). Classroom or lab: How to decide which is best. *Classroom Computer Learning, 10*(1), 34–43.

Milone, M. (1998). Technology integration master class. *Technology and Learning, 19*(1), 6–10.

Miller-Lachman, L. (1994). Bytes and bias: Eliminating cultural stereotypes from educational software. *School Library Journal, 40*(11), 26–30.

Morehouse, D., Hoaglund, M., & Schmidt, R. (1987). *Technology demonstration project final report.* Menomonie, WI: Quality Evaluation & Development.

Mungo, P., & Clough, B. (1992). *Approaching zero: The incredible underworld of hackers, phreakers, virus writers, and keyboard criminals.* New York: Random House.

Munro, K. (1998, March 24). Monitor a child's access. *PC Magazine,* 185–194.

NCATE. (1997). *Technology and the new professional teacher.* Washington, DC: Author.

Office of Technology Assessment. (1995). *Teachers and technology: Making the connection* (OTA-EHR-616). Washington, DC: U.S. Government Printing Office.

Ohlrich, K. (1996). Parent volunteers: An asset to your technology plan. *Learning and Leading with Technology, 24*(2), 51–52.

Oliver, H. (1994). Book review. Education and informatics worldwide: The state of the art and beyond. *Journal of Research on Computing in Education, 26*(2), 285–290.

Oppenheimer, T. (1997). The computer delusion. *The Atlantic Monthly, 280*(1), 45–62.

Randall, N. (1998, March 24). Defend against invaders. *PC Magazine,* 177–182.

Ringstaff, C., & Yocam, K. (1995). *Creating an alternative context for teacher development: The ACOT teacher development centers* (ACOT Report, H#18). Cupertino, CA: Apple Computer Co.

Ritchie, D., & Boyle, K. (1998). Finding the bucks for technology. *Learning and Leading with Technology, 26*(2), 46–50.

Roblyer, M. D., & Erlanger, W. (1998). Preparing Internet-ready teachers: Which methods work best? *Learning and Leading with Technology, 26*(4), 59–61.

Rogers, E. (1995). *Diffusion of innovations.* New York: The Free Press.

Salehi, S. (1990). *Promoting equity through educational technology networks.* Baltimore, MD: Maryland State Department of Education (ERIC Document Reproduction Service No. ED 322 897).

See, J. (1992). Ten criteria for effective technology plans. *The Computing Teacher, 19*(8), 34–35.

Sheingold, K. (1991). Restructuring for learning with technology: The potential for synergy. *Phi Delta Kappan, 73*(1), 17–27.

Simpson, C. M. (2001). *Copyright for schools: A practical guide (2nd ed.).* Worthington, OH: Linworth Publishing, Inc.

Soloman, G. (2001). Deconstructing a grant. *Technology & Learning, 21*(11), 44–52.

Southern Technology Council. (1997). *Making technology happen.* Research Triangle Park, NC: Author.

Standish, D. (1996). Ignite technology: Making the difference with staff development. *Educational Media and Technology Yearbook, 21,* 126–135.

Stoll, C. (1995). *Silicon snake oil: Second thoughts on the information highway.* New York: Doubleday.

Stoll, C. (1999). *High-tech heretic: Why computers don't belong in the classroom and other reflections by a computer contrarian.* New York: Doubleday.

Sun, J. (2000). How do we know it's working? *Learning and Leading with Technology, 27*(7), 32–35, 41, 49

Tan, S. B. (1998). Making one-computer teaching fun. *Learning and Leading with Technology, 25*(5), 6–10.

The revolution that fizzled. (1991, May 20). *Time,* 48.

Truett, C. (2001). Sherlock Holmes on the Internet: Language arts teams up with the computing librarian. *Learning and Leading with Technology, 29*(2), 36–41.

U.S. Department of Energy. (1999). Teacher quality: A report on the preparation and qualifications of public school teachers (Report NCES 1999–080). Washington, DC: National Center for Education Statistics.

Wall, T. (1994). A technology planning primer. *American School Board Journal, 81*(3), 45–47.

Warren-Sams, B. (1997, June). *Closing the equity gap in technology access and use.* Portland, OR: Northwest Regional Educational Laboratory.

Wetzel, K. (1993). Teacher educators use of computers in teaching. *Journal of Technology and Teacher Education, 1*(4), 335–352.

Wilson, J. (1991). Computer laboratory workstation dimensions: Scaling down for elementary school children. *Computers in the Schools, 8*(4), 41–48.

Young, B. (2000). Gender differences in student attitudes towards computers. *Journal of Research on Computing in Education, 33*(2), 204–213.

CHAPTER 3

Learning Theories and Integration Models

Our major concern is to find a reasonable answer to the question: What is learning?

Robert M. Gagné, from *The Conditions of Learning*

Anyone who makes a responsible and systematic study of the human animal eventually feels the awe that moved Shakespeare to write "What a piece of work is a man!"

George B. Leonard, from *Education and Ecstasy*

This chapter covers the following topics:

- Background on behavioral and cognitive learning theories
- How these learning theories contributed to current models of instruction
- Technology integration strategies based on each model of instruction
- An example of how these approaches are combined in a curriculum unit

Objectives

1. Describe concepts associated with behaviorist theories and information processing and other cognitive learning theories.
2. Identify teaching/learning problems that directed and constructivist models were designed to address.
3. Identify teaching practices associated with directed and constructivist approaches.
4. Identify technology integration strategies associated with directed and constructivist approaches.
5. Identify a lesson that integrates technology using directed and constructivist approaches.

Introduction

Debate surrounds the question of what is the most appropriate instructional role for technology, particularly computer technology. Prior to about 1980, the answer would have been easy. According to respected writers of the time (Taylor, 1980), the issue divided people into three groups: those who advocated using computers primarily as tools (for word processing and numerical calculations), those who viewed them mainly as teaching aids or tutors (for drills, tutorials, and simulations), and those who believed the most powerful use was programming (the tutee use). But these groups generally would have agreed that each of these approaches had its place, and there were popular classroom strategies for each use. These were simpler times, both for educational technology and for education itself, although few would have believed it then.

Changes Brought About by Technology

In subsequent years, two trends have affected profoundly the course of educational technology: (1) an increase in the number and types of technology resources available, and (2) dramatic shifts in beliefs about the fundamental goals and strategies of education itself. These two trends have not developed in isolation; their roots are intertwined in the larger social and economic conditions that define and shape our modern world. In the past, educational goals reflected society's emphasis on the need for basic skills—such as reading, writing, and arithmetic—and an agreed-on body of information considered essential for everyone. Students were deemed educated if they could read at a certain comprehension level; apply grammar, usage, and punctuation rules in written work; solve arithmetic problems that required addition, subtraction, multiplication, and division; and state certain series of historical facts.

As technology has become more capable and more pervasive, everyday life has become more complex. When students in the class of 2015 graduate, many will take jobs that did not exist when they entered school and will use technologies not yet invented in the first few years of the twenty-first century. More information is considered important to learn than ever before, and the base of essential information grows constantly. Many educators now believe that the world is changing too quickly to define education in terms of specific information or skills; they believe education should focus on more general capabilities such as "learning to learn" skills that will help future citizens cope with inevitable technological change. Educators believe that knowing what questions to ask and how to ask them will be as important as, or more important than, giving the "right answers." In sum, technology has both increased the number of decisions that people must make and forced them to become more skilled decision makers.

Current Educational Goals and Methods: Two Views

As education changes to reflect new social and educational needs, teaching strategies also change; consequently, strategies change for integrating technology into teaching and learning. Today, educators' definition of the appropriate role of technology depends on their perceptions of the goals of education itself and appropriate instructional methods to help students attain those goals.

Most educators seem to agree that changes are needed in education. But learning theorists disagree on which strategies will best achieve today's educational goals. This controversy has served as a catalyst for two different views on teaching and learning. One view, which we will call *directed instruction,* is grounded primarily in behaviorist learning theory and the information-processing branch of the cognitive learning theories. The other view, which we will refer to as *constructivist,* evolved from other branches of thinking in cognitive learning theory. A few technology applications such as drill and practice and tutorials are associated only with directed instruction; most others (problem solving, multimedia production, web-based learning) can enhance either directed instruction or constructivist learning, depending on how they are used.

The author of this book sees meaningful roles for both directed instruction and constructivist strategies and the technology applications associated with them; both can help schools meet the many and varied requirements of learning. That belief guides the purposes of this chapter.

An Overview of Directed and Constructivist Instructional Methods

A Comparison of Terminologies and Models

Differences in terminologies. People with radically different views on an issue frequently use different terms to describe essentially the same things. Sfard (1998) says that differences in the language used to describe learning spring from two different metaphors used for learning: the acquisition metaphor and the participation metaphor. She notes that ". . . the acquisition metaphor is likely to be more prominent in older writings, [and] more recent studies are often dominated by the participation metaphor" (p. 5). These differences in language signal fundamental differences in thinking about how learning takes place and how we can foster it. Figure 3.1 introduces these differences.

How did these differences come about? It is important to recognize that both directed instruction and constructivist approaches attempt to identify what Gagné (1985) called the *conditions of learning* or the "sets of circumstances that obtain when learning occurs" (p. 2). Both approaches are based on the work of respected learning theorists and psychologists who have studied both the behavior of human beings as learning organisms and the behavior of students in schools and classrooms. The two approaches diverge when they define *learning* and describe the conditions required to make learning happen and the kinds of problems that interfere most with learning. They disagree because they attend to different philosophies and learning theories, and they take different perspectives on improving current educational practice. Yet many believe that both kinds of strategies may prove useful to teachers for addressing commonly recognized instructional and educational problems.

Differences in philosophical foundations. The differences begin with underlying epistemologies: beliefs about the origins, nature, and limits of human knowledge. Constructivists and objectivists (those who espouse directed methods) come from separate and different epistemological "planets," although both nurture many different tribes or cultures (Molenda, 1991; Phillips, 1995). Philosophical differences can be summarized in the following way:

- **Objectivists.** Knowledge has a separate, real existence of its own outside the human mind. Learning happens when this knowledge is transmitted to people and they store it in their minds.
- **Constructivists.** Humans construct all knowledge in their minds by participating in certain experiences; learning happens when one constructs both mechanisms for learning and his or her own unique version of the knowledge, colored by background, experiences, and aptitudes (Sfard, 1998; Willis, 1995).

Two issues of *Educational Technology* (May and September 1991) do a good job of explaining these philosophical differences and the instructional approaches that sprang from them.

Differences in procedures and processes. Not surprisingly, differences in language and philosophies between constructivists and objectivists signal dramatic differences in the curriculum and teaching and learning methods that each considers appropriate and effective. Sometimes, these differences of opinion have generated strident debate in the literature (Baines & Stanley, 2000). Some of the ways in which these differences are reflected in the classroom are summarized in Figure 3.2.

Figure 3.1 Differences in Terminology Among Objectivists and Constructivists

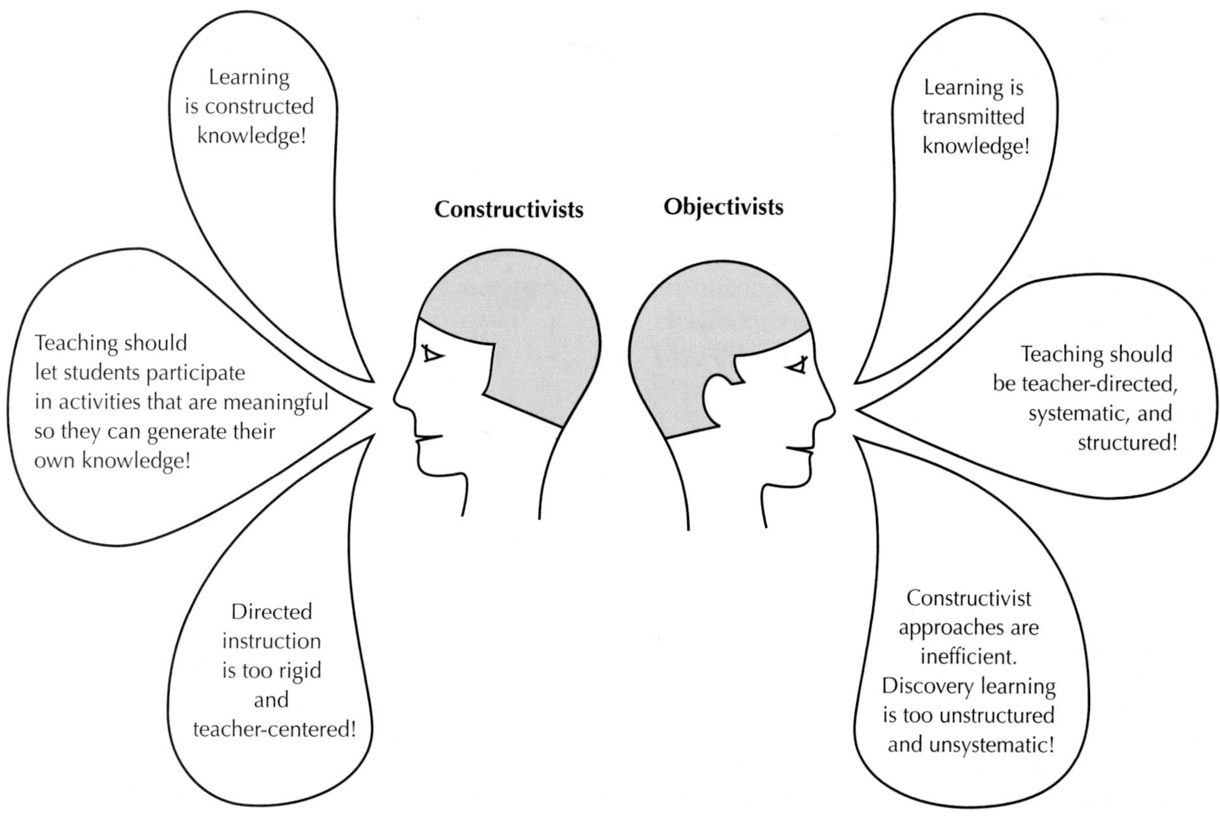

Figure 3.2 Methodological Differences Between Directed and Constructivist Models

	Directed	Constructivist
Teacher roles	Transmitter of knowledge; expert source; director of skill/concept development through structured experiences	Guide and facilitator as students generate their own knowledge; collaborative resource and assistant as students explore topics
Student roles	Receive information; demonstrate competence; all students learn same material	Collaborate with others; develop competence; students may learn different material
Curriculum characteristics	Based on skill and knowledge hierarchies; skills taught one after the other in set sequence	Based on projects that foster both higher level and lower level skills concurrently
Learning goals	Stated in terms of mastery learning and behavioral competence in a scope and sequence	Stated in terms of growth from where student began and increased ability to work independently and with others
Types of activities	Lecture, demonstration, discussions, student practice, seatwork, testing	Group projects, hands-on exploration, product development
Assessment strategies	Written tests and development of products matched to objectives; all tests and products match set criteria; same measures for all students	Performance tests and products such as portfolios; quality measured by rubrics and checklists; measures may differ among students

Merging the two approaches. As Molenda (1991) observed, an *either–or* stance seems to gain us little. Rather, both sides need to find a way to merge the two approaches in a way that will benefit learners and teachers. A link between the two planets must be forged so that students may travel freely from one to the other, depending on the characteristics of the topics at hand and individual learning needs. Sfard (1998) agrees that "one metaphor is not enough" (p. 10) to explain how all learning takes place or to address all problems inherent in learning.

Bereiter (1990) initially supported directed instruction methods and later shifted toward constructivist principles. He suggests that much of what educators want students to achieve is sufficiently complex that none of the existing learning theories can account for how it is actually learned, let alone the conditions that should be arranged to facilitate learning. He points out the futility of theory and research that attempts to (1) identify relevant social, environmental, or individual influences on learning such as prior experiences, types of reinforcement, and learning styles; and (2) quantify their comparative contribution to what he calls difficult learning, that is, higher order thinking and problem solving.

Bereiter (1990) also observes that each of these contributing factors tends to interact with the others, thus changing their relative importance. He quotes Cronbach's vivid metaphor: "Once we attend to interactions [between these relevant factors], we enter a hall of mirrors that extends to infinity" (p. 606). Practicing teachers could encounter endless variations of explanations about how people learn or fail to learn. Escaping from this hall of mirrors will require, Bereiter maintains, a more all-inclusive learning theory than those currently available. In light of Bereiter's observations, the debate between directed and constructivist proponents seems likely to inspire different methods primarily because they focus on different kinds of problems (or different aspects of the same problems) confronting teachers and students in today's schools. Like the blind men trying to describe the elephant, each focuses on a different part of the problem, and each is correct in limited observations.

Instructional Needs and Problems Addressed by Directed Instruction Strategies

Although they are based primarily on early theories of learning, directed instruction methods target some very real problems that originated many years ago but are still with us.

America emerged from World War II with an intense awareness of the importance of education. More students were staying in school than ever before, and schools were serving ever-increasing numbers of students with widely varying capabilities. More students than ever before aspired to college studies, which they viewed as a key to realizing "the American dream." Despite this dramatic increase in the numbers of students and the pressure it placed on school resources, schools still had to certify that students had earned high school diplomas and were ready for entrance into higher education. At the same time, teachers had to meet the individual pacing and remedial needs of each student while ensuring that all students were learning required skills. Individualization became both the goal and the terror of teachers in the 1960s.

By the 1970s, *systems approaches* were widely proposed as a way for teachers and others to design self-instructional packages for students to separate directed instruction from the need for the teacher to deliver it. Self-instruction was more efficient than trying to serve the pacing and content needs of each student. It also ensured that instruction was replicable, that is, quality was uniform from presentation to presentation. However, systems approaches also were seen as a way to design more effective teacher-delivered presentations.

In the 1970s and 1980s, many educators recognized how technology resources such as computer software could help them overcome some of the logistic obstacles to individualized instruction. Some courseware helped students get needed practice; other courseware guided their learning of difficult concepts through step-by-step, self-paced teaching sequences; still other courseware let students change the variables in given situations (population growth, stock market purchases) and see the effects of their decisions. All of these activities allowed teachers time to work with students who needed personal help. Teachers were encouraged to design more systematic instruction and to insert computer-based materials as needed to carry out the sequences they designed.

In the 2000s and for the foreseeable future, teachers still face the problems of having too many students, too many required skills to teach, and not enough time to deal with individual learning differences. The teacher accountability and standards movements that emerged in the late 1990s and early 2000s have made this situation even more evident. Systematically designed, self-instructional materials often have been used to teach many important skills. They have proven especially useful for students who need a structured learning environment. Depending on other important factors, various kinds of drills, tutorials, and other older kinds of packages have effectively supplemented and, more rarely, replaced teacher-led directed instruction. Studies comparing teacher-led versus computer-based instruction in certain skill areas and with certain kinds of students have frequently found that students can learn faster via computer-based learning systems. Of course, this is not always the case; the key requirements seem to include students' motivation to learn, a well-designed overall instruction routine, and an integral role for the technology resource in the plan.

Instructional Needs and Problems Addressed by Constructivist Strategies

In the late 1970s and 1980s, criticism of the educational system accelerated and a critical perspective of curriculum gained prominence. Many educators began to echo critics from years before that education pursued inappropriate, outdated goals; they felt that education should go beyond programs to learn isolated skills and memorize facts. They called for more emphasis on the abilities to solve problems, find information, and think critically about information. In other words, critics called for more emphasis on learning *how* to learn instead of learning specific content.

They also decried the large number of required skills and traditional learning activities that seemed abstract and unrelated to any practical skills. Students could see little relevance between skills they learned in school and those they used in their daily lives. Individualized learning drew criticism because students did not develop the ability to work well together in groups, an important workplace competency for the 1990s and beyond. These were not new criticisms, but the increase in the school dropout rate and poor national performance compared to other countries' gave the issues the status of a national crisis. The United States was "a nation at risk" (National Commission on Excellence in Education, 1983), and some changes had to be made.

New ideas from cognitive science propose the importance of *anchoring instruction* in activities that students find meaningful and authentic in the context of their own experiences. Proponents of these theories say that students who learn skills in isolation from such real-life problem solving will not remember to apply this prerequisite information when required. They also believe that passive learners, students who view learning as something that happens *to* them rather than something they generate, are more likely to be poorly motivated to learn. To answer all of these needs, constructivists propose arranging instruction around problems that students find compelling and that require them to acquire and use skills and knowledge to formulate solutions. Constructivists call for more emphasis on engaging students in the process of learning than on finding a single correct answer.

Many newer technology applications such as multimedia development and web-based learning seem to provide ideal conditions for nurturing constructivist curriculum goals. They provide vivid visual support, which helps students develop better mental models of problems to be solved. These visual media help make up for student deficiencies in such prerequisites as reading skills; they help to involve and motivate students by using graphics and other devices students find interesting and attractive. Visual media also let students work together in cooperative groups to construct products. In short, they meet all of the requirements for fulfilling the constructivist prescription for improving learning environments and refocusing curriculum.

How Learning Theories Shape Teaching Practices and Technology Uses

Clearly, the instructional problems identified by objectivists and constructivists are common to most schools or classrooms, regardless of level or type of students or content. Recent research by the University of California at Irvine and the University of Minnesota (Becker, 2000) indicates that constructivist beliefs and practices are more evident among elementary school teachers and less so at high school levels, especially in areas such as math, science, and social studies. Teachers will always use some directed instruction as the most efficient means of teaching students required skills; teachers will always need motivating, cooperative learning activities to ensure that students want to learn and that they can transfer what they learn to problems they encounter. Tinker (1998) warns that "It is a fallacy to think that technology will make traditional content outdated. . . . The corollary to this thinking that traditional content is less important than learning to learn . . . is a dangerous doctrine" (p. 2). Proficient technology-oriented teachers must learn to combine directed instruction and constructivist approaches. To implement each of these strategies, teachers select technology resources and integration methods that are best suited to their specific needs.

Together, the two ostensibly different views of reality may merge to form a new and powerful approach to solving some of the major problems of the educational system, each contributing an essential element of the new instructional formula. Some practitioners believe that constructivism will eventually dominate overall educational goals and objectives such as learning to apply scientific methods, while systematic approaches will ensure that specific prerequisite skills are learned. Tennyson (1990) has suggested, for example, that about 30% of learning time be spent on what he terms *acquiring knowledge*—verbal information and procedural knowledge. The remaining 70% should be spent on the *employment of knowledge* (contextual skills, cognitive strategies, and creative processes).

During the first decade of the 2000s, teachers will test Tennyson's and others' proposals for merging systematic and constructivist methods in classrooms across the country; educators will confront the task of identifying the best mix of approaches for each content area. The decade will also bring challenges to traditional views on curriculum organization such as interdisciplinary courses versus single-subject ones as well as how schools can best help students to learn (direct teaching or transmission of knowledge versus providing resources and guiding learning). As they prepare to meet this challenge, teachers need to know how these methods came about, how each addresses classroom needs, and how each suggests that they integrate technology resources. Subsequent sections of this chapter will give more specific information on the origins and uses of each of the two approaches described here. Figure 3.3 gives characteristic features of directed instruction and constructivist models.

Figure 3.3 Summary of Characteristics of Two Teaching/Learning Models

Directed Instructional Models Tend to:

1. Focus on teaching sequences of skills that begin with lower level skills and build to higher level skills.
2. Clearly state skill objectives with test items matched to them.
3. Stress more individualized work than group work.
4. Emphasize traditional teaching and assessment methods: lectures, skill worksheets, activities, and tests with specific expected responses.

Constructivist Learning Models Tend to:

1. Focus on learning through posing problems, exploring possible answers, and developing products and presentations.
2. Pursue global goals that specify general abilities such as problem-solving and research skills.
3. Stress more group work than individualized work.
4. Emphasize alternative learning and assessment methods: exploration of open-ended questions and scenarios, doing research and developing products; assessment by student portfolios, performance checklists, and tests with open-ended questions; and descriptive narratives written by teachers.

Theoretical Foundations of Directed Instruction

Learning Theories Associated with Directed Instruction

Two different theories of learning contributed to the development of directed instruction:

- **Behavioral theories.** Behavioral theorists concentrated on immediately observable, thus, behavioral, changes in performance (tests) as indicators of learning.
- **Information-processing theories.** These theories developed from a branch of cognitive psychology that focused on the memory and storage processes that make learning possible. They viewed the process of learning in human beings as similar to that of how a computer processes information. Theorists in this area explored how a person receives information and stores it in memory, the structure of memory that allows learning something new to relate to and build on something learned previously, and how a learner retrieves information from short- and long-term memory and applies it to new situations.

The early work of giants in behavioral psychology such as B. F. Skinner and Edward Thorndike was followed by the work of information-processing theorists such as Richard Atkinson and David Ausubel. Robert Gagné was a leader in building on both of these behavioral and cognitive theories to recommend approaches to instruction. Gagné also played a key role in an area of development referred to as *instructional systems design* or the systematic design of instruction. Others associated with research and development underlying these systems approaches include Leslie Briggs, Robert Glaser, Lee Cronbach, David Merrill, Charles Reigeluth, Michael Scriven, and Robert Tennyson.

The Contributions of Behavioral Theories

Considered the grandfather of behaviorism, B. F. Skinner generated much of the experimental data that serves as the basis of behavioral learning theory. (See InSight 3.1.) Skinner and others viewed the teacher's job as modifying the behavior of students by setting up situations to reinforce students when they exhibited desired responses, teaching them to exhibit the same response in all such situations. These behavioral principles underlie two well-known trends in education: behavior modification techniques in classroom management and programmed instruction. Although current use of programmed instruction is limited, its principles form much of the basis of effective drill and practice and tutorial courseware.

The Contributions of Information-Processing Theories

Many educational psychologists found the emphasis on observable outcomes of learning unsatisfying. They did not agree with behaviorists' views that stimulus–response learning alone could form the basis for building higher level skills. As they focused on capabilities such as rule learning and problem solving, they became more concerned with the internal processes that went on during learning. With this knowledge, they hoped to arrange appropriate instructional conditions to promote learning of these kinds of skills. (See InSight 3.2.)

InSight 3.1

Skinner's Behaviorist Theories of Learning: Building on the S–R Connection

Before B. F. Skinner, theories of learning were dominated by *classical conditioning* concepts proposed by Russian physiologist Ivan Pavlov, who said that behavior is largely controlled by involuntary physical responses to outside stimuli (e.g., dogs salivating at the sight of a can of dog food). Skinner's *operant conditioning* theory said that people can have mental control over their responses (e.g., a child reasons he will get praise if he behaves well in school). Eggen and Kauchak (2001) said that Skinner believed "behavior is more controlled by the *consequences of actions* than by events *preceding the actions.* A consequence is an outcome (stimulus) after the behavior (that can) influence future behaviors" (p. 220). Skinner's work made him "the most influential psychologist of the 20th century" (Eggen & Kauchak, 2001, p. 220).

Skinner reasoned that the internal processes (those inside the mind) involved in learning could not be seen directly. (Scientific work had not advanced sufficiently at that time to observe brain activity.) Therefore, he concentrated on cause-and-effect relationships that could be established by observation. He found that human behavior could be shaped by "contingencies of reinforcement" or situations in which *reinforcement* for a learner is made contingent on a desired response. He identified three kinds of situations that can shape behavior:

- **Positive reinforcement.** A situation is set up so that an *increase* in a desired behavior will result from a stimulus. For example, to earn praise or good grades (positive reinforcement), a learner studies hard for a test more often (desired behavior).
- **Negative reinforcement.** A situation is set up so that an *increase* in a desired behavior will result from avoiding or removing a stimulus. For example, a student dislikes going to detention (negative reinforcement), so to avoid detention again, the student is quiet in class more often (desired behavior).
- **Punishment.** A situation is set up so that a *decrease* in a desired behavior will result from undesirable consequences, such as when a student is given a failing grade (punishment) when she cheats on a test (undesirable behavior), so she is less likely to cheat in the future.

Implications for education. Skinner's influential book, *The Technology of Learning* (1968), gave a detailed theory of how classroom instruction should reflect these behaviorist principles, and many of his classroom management and instructional techniques still are widely used today. To Skinner, teaching was a process of arranging contingencies of reinforcement effectively to bring about learning. He believed that even such high-level capabilities as critical thinking and creativity could be taught in this way; it was simply a matter of establishing chains of behavior through principles of reinforcement. Skinner felt that programmed instruction was the most efficient means available for learning skills. Educational psychologists such as Benjamin Bloom also used Skinner's principles to develop methods that became known as *mastery learning.*

Implications for technology integration. Most original drill-and-practice software was based on Skinner's reinforcement principles, for example, when students knew they would get praise or an entertaining graphic if they gave correct answers. Tutorial software usually is based on the idea of programmed instruction. Because the idea behind drill software is to increase the frequency of correct answering in response to stimuli, these packages often are used to help students memorize important basic information, while tutorial software gives students an efficient path through concepts they want to learn.

Sources: Gagné, R. (1985). *The conditions of learning* (4th ed.). New York: Holt, Rinehart and Winston; Skinner, B. F. (1938). *The behavior of organisms.* New York: Appleton; Skinner, B. F. (1968). *The technology of teaching.* New York: Appleton; and Eggen, P., & Kauchak, D. (2001). *Educational psychology: Windows on classrooms (5th ed.).* Upper Saddle River, NJ: Merrill/Prentice Hall. Photo from Corbis-Bettman.

INSIGHT 3.2

The Information-Processing Theorists: The Mind as Computer

Behaviorists like Skinner focused only on external, directly observable indicators of human learning. Many people found this explanation insufficient to guide instruction. During the 1950s and 1960s, a group of researchers known as the cognitive-learning theorists began to hypothesize a model that would help people "visualize what is impossible to observe directly" (Eggen & Kauchak, 2001, p. 258). Though some constructivists disassociate themselves with them, the information-processing theorists were among the first and most influential of the cognitive-learning theorists. They hypothesized processes inside the brain that allow human beings to learn and remember.

Although no single, cohesive information-processing theory of learning summarizes the field, the work of the information-processing theorists is based on a model of memory and storage originally proposed by Atkinson and Shiffrin (1968). According to them, the brain contains certain structures that process information much like a computer. This model of the mind as computer hypothesizes that the human brain has three kinds of memory or "stores" (see model from Ormrod, 2000, p. 225):

- **Sensory registers.** The part of memory that receives all the information a person senses
- **Short-term memory (STM).** Also known as working memory, the part of memory where new information is held temporarily until it is either lost or placed into long-term memory
- **Long-term memory (LTM).** The part of memory that has an unlimited capacity and can hold information indefinitely.

According to this model, learning occurs in the following way. First, information is sensed through receptors: eyes, ears, nose, mouth, and/or hands. This information is held in the sensory registers for a very short time (perhaps a second), after which it either enters STM or is lost. Many information-processing theorists believe that information can be sensed but lost before it gets to STM if the person is not paying attention to it. Anything people pay attention to goes into working memory, where it can stay for about 5 to 20 seconds (Ormrod, 2000). After this time, if information is not processed or practiced in a way that causes it to transfer to LTM, then it, too, is lost. Information-processing theorists believe that for new information to be transferred to LTM, it must be linked in some way to prior knowledge already in LTM. Once information does enter LTM, it is there essentially permanently, although some psychologists believe that even information stored in LTM can be lost if not used regularly (Ormrod, 2000).

Implications for education. Information-processing views of learning have become the basis for many common classroom practices. For example, teachers ask interesting questions and display eye-catching materials to increase the likelihood that students will pay attention to a new topic. While presenting information, they give instructions that point out important points and characteristics in the new material and suggest methods of "encoding" or remembering them by linking them to information students already know. Teachers also give students practice exercises to help ensure the transfer of information from short- to long-term memory.

Educational psychologists such as Gagné (see InSight 3.3) and Ausubel provided many instructional guidelines designed to enhance the processes of attention, encoding, and storage. Gagné proposed that teachers use a hierarchical "bottom-up approach," making sure that students learn lower order skills first and build on them. Ausubel, by contrast, recommended a "top-down" approach; he proposed that teachers provide "advance organizers" or overviews of the way information will be presented to help students develop mental frameworks on which to "hang" new information (Gage & Berliner, 1988).

Implications for technology integration. Information-processing theories have also guided the development of artificial intelligence (AI) applications, an attempt to develop computer software that can simulate the thinking and learning behaviors of humans. Much of the drill and practice software available is designed to help students encode and store newly learned information into long-term memory.

A Model of the Human Memory System

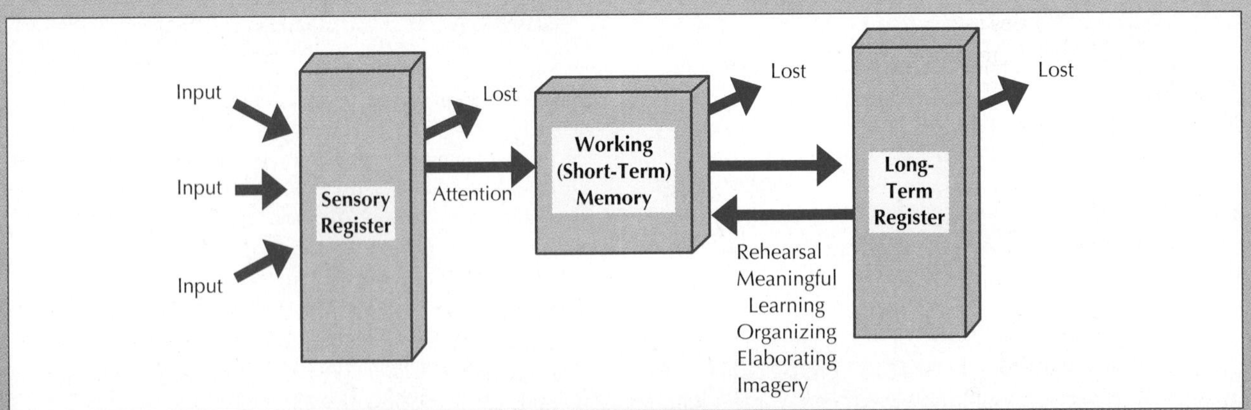

Source: From *Educational psychology: Developing learners* (3rd ed.), by J. Ormrod, p. 225, copyright © 2000 Prentice Hall, Upper Saddle River, NJ.

Sources: Atkinson, R., & Shiffrin, R. (1968). Human memory: A proposed system and its control processes. In K. Spence & J. Spence (Eds.), *The psychology of learning and motivation* (Vol. 2). New York: Academic Press; Eggen, P., & Kauchak, D. (2001). *Educational psychology: Windows on classrooms (5th ed.).* Upper Saddle River, NJ: Merrill/Prentice Hall; Gage, N., & Berliner, D. (1988) *Educational psychology* (4th ed.). Boston: Houghton Mifflin; Gagné, R. (1985). *The conditions of learning* (4th ed.). New York: Holt, Rinehart and Winston; Klatzky, R. (1980). *Human memory: Structures and processes* (2nd ed.). San Francisco: Freeman; and Ormrod, J. (2001). *Educational psychology: Developing learners (3rd ed.).* Upper Saddle River, NJ: Merrill/Prentice Hall.

Characteristics of Directed Instruction

Teaching methods based primarily on behaviorist and information-processing learning theories usually are associated with more traditional, teacher-directed forms of instruction. Robert Gagné (see InSight 3.3) is considered a leader in developing instructional guidelines for directed instruction that combine the behavioral and information-processing learning theories. He asserted that teachers must accomplish at least three tasks to link these learning theories with teaching practices:

1. **Ensure prerequisite skills are acquired.** Teachers must make sure that students have all the prerequisite skills they need to learn a new skill. This may involve identifying component skills and the order in which they should be taught. Gagné referred to this group of skills as a *learning hierarchy.*
2. **Supply instructional conditions.** Teachers must arrange for appropriate instructional conditions to support the internal processes involved in learning; that is, they must supply sequences of carefully structured presentations and activities that help students understand (process), remember (encode and store), and transfer (retrieve) information and skills.
3. **Determine the type of learning.** Finally, teachers must vary these conditions for several different kinds of learning. (The kinds of learning, along with brief descriptions of related instructional conditions, are shown in InSight 3.3.)

Behaviorist and information-processing theories have not only helped establish key concepts such as types of learning and instructional conditions required to bring about each type; they also laid the groundwork for more efficient methods of creating directed instruction. These methods, known as systematic instructional design or systems approaches (see InSight 3.4), incorporated information from learning theories into step-by-step procedures for preparing instructional materials. Systematic methods came about largely in response to logistical problems in meeting large numbers of individual needs. They were adopted more often by military and industrial trainers, however, than by K–12 classroom teachers (Saettler, 1990; Wager, 1992).

Systems approaches contribute to courseware development primarily through the design of self-contained tutorial packages. However, when teachers plan their own directed instruction with technology, thinking about instruction as a system may help them develop guidelines to evaluate their own teaching effectiveness and the usefulness of their computer-based resources. For example, they may pose and answer the following kinds of questions about the components of their instructional systems to evaluate and improve their plans and materials:

- **Instructional goals and objectives.** Am I teaching what I intended to teach? Do the goals and objectives of the courseware materials match my own?
- **Instructional analysis (task analysis).** Do my students have all of the lower level skills they need to learn successfully what I want to teach them? Does the courseware require prerequisite skills my students lack?
- **Tests and measures.** Do the tests I will use measure what I will teach (e.g., the objectives)? Do the items included in the courseware materials match my own measures?
- **Instructional strategies.** Are my instructional activities carefully structured to provide appropriate conditions (instructional events) for the kind of learning involved (supplying examples and explanation as well as gaining attention)? What part do chosen courseware resources play in the activities and why?
- **Evaluating and revising instruction.** Have I successfully presented the instruction I envisioned? How could I improve it to make it more effective? Has the courseware successfully played the part I envisioned for it? Do I need better strategies for using it? Do I need better courseware?

Directed Methods: Problems Raised Versus Problems Addressed

The learning theories and instructional design approaches associated with directed instruction have profoundly affected American curriculum and classroom practices during the past five decades. Some would say that at least part of the impact has been negative. Programmed instruction, an early method based on behavioral principles and systematic methods, usually was successful, but students found it boring. During the 1970s, the behavioral emphasis on observable outcomes was translated into performance objectives and individual skill testing in K–12 schools—requirements often unpopular among teachers. In many cases, schools did not follow systematic design with systematic methods; for example, many school districts required specific performance objectives for all curricula but never linked them to any instructional materials or tests. In other cases, widespread "teaching to the tests" made curriculum dry and apparently disconnected from any application outside the classroom. Constructivism is, in part, a backlash against the perceived regimentation arising from this emphasis.

Criticisms of directed methods. The greatest current criticisms of directed methods focus on their irrelevance to the needs of today's students. Critics of directed instruction cite several problems:

- **Students cannot do problem solving.** Many parents and educators feel that traditional methods have too narrow a focus. They feel these methods break topics into discrete skills and teach them in isolation from how they are applied. They blame this limitation for poor national test scores on more global skills of problem solving and reasoning (Cognition and Technology

INSIGHT 3.3

Gagné's Principles: Providing Tools for Teachers

Gagné built on the work of behavioral and information-processing theorists by translating principles from their learning theories into practical instructional strategies that teachers could employ with directed instruction. He is best known for three of his contributions in this area: the events of instruction, the types of learning, and learning hierarchies.

Events of instruction. Gagné used the information-processing model of internal processes to derive a set of guidelines that teachers could follow to arrange optimal "conditions of learning." His set of nine "Events of Instruction" was perhaps the best known of these guidelines (Gagné, Briggs, & Wager, 1992):

1. Gaining attention
2. Informing the learner of the objective
3. Stimulating recall of prerequisite learning
4. Presenting new material
5. Providing learning guidance
6. Eliciting performance
7. Providing feedback about correctness
8. Assessing performance
9. Enhancing retention and recall.

Types of learning. Gagné identified several types of learning as behaviors students demonstrate after acquiring knowledge. These differ according to the conditions necessary to foster them. He showed how the Events of Instruction would be carried out slightly differently from one type of learning to another (Gagné et al., 1992):

1. Intellectual skills
   - Problem solving
   - Higher order rules
   - Defined concepts
   - Concrete concepts
   - Discriminations
2. Cognitive strategies
3. Verbal information
4. Motor skills
5. Attitudes.

Learning hierarchies. The development of "intellectual skills," Gagné believed, requires learning that amounts to a building process. Lower level skills provide a necessary foundation for higher level ones. For example, to learn to work long division problems, students first would have to learn all the prerequisite math skills, beginning with number recognition, number facts, simple addition and subtraction, multiplication, and simple division. Therefore, to teach a skill, a teacher must first identify its prerequisite skills and make sure the student possesses them. He called this list of building block skills a *learning hierarchy.*

Implications for education. Gagné's Events of Instruction and learning hierarchies have been widely used to develop systematic instructional design principles. (See InSight 3.4.) Although his work has had more impact on designing instruction for business, industry, and the military than for K–12 schools, many school curriculum development projects still use a learning hierarchy approach to sequencing skills.

Implications for technology integration. Gagné, Wager, and Rojas (1981) showed how Gagné's Events of Instruction could be used to plan lessons using each kind of instructional software (drill, tutorial, simulation). They said that only a tutorial could "stand by itself" and accomplish all of the necessary events of instruction; the other kinds of software required teacher-led activities to accomplish events before and after software use.

Sources: Gagné, R. (1985). *The conditions of learning* (4th ed.). New York: Holt, Rinehart and Winston; Gagné, R., Briggs, L., & Wager, W. (1992). *Principles of instructional design.* Orlando, FL: Harcourt, Brace, Jovanovich; and Gagné, R., Wager, W., & Rojas, A. (1981). Planning and authoring computer-assisted instruction lessons. *Educational Technology, 21*(9), 17–26. Photo courtesy of Robert Gagné.

Group at Vanderbilt [CTGV], 1991b). The CTGV report says that "The thinking activities that are of concern include the ability to write persuasive essays, engage in informal reasoning, explain how data relate to theory in scientific investigations, and formulate and solve moderately complex problems that require mathematical reasoning" (p. 34).

- **Students cannot apply skills.** Directed instruction also is blamed for resulting in what Whitehead called "inert knowledge" (Brown, Collins, & Duguid, 1989). That is, students can do skills when asked to do them, but they cannot recognize situations where the skills apply in real life. Knowledge is "inert" because students do not spontaneously transfer it to where it is useful.
- **Students find learning unmotivating and irrelevant.** Some critics of directed methods feel that teaching skills as separate, discrete units tends to isolate students from each other and from the authentic situations students find motivating and relevant. This makes learning repetitive and predictable—what the CTGV calls an industrial assembly line approach to transmitting knowledge. The CTGV repeatedly cited Corey's (1944) article, *Poor Scholar's Soliloquy,* in which a student of obvious intelligence and capability describes how he performs poorly in school because he cannot relate to the tasks his teachers assign. The CTGV said that this 55+-year-old article highlighted an old, ongoing problem: "Many students seem to learn effectively in the context of authentic, real-life activities yet have great difficulty learning in the decontextualized, arbitrary-task atmosphere of schools" (p. 9). They also felt that students' lack of interest in school tasks leads directly to higher dropout rates.

INSIGHT 3.4

Systems Approaches and the Design of Instruction: Managing the Complexity of Teaching

Although there are many versions of the systematic design process, Bradens (1996) describes the steps of this model in the accompanying diagram. His article also gives a comprehensive discussion of the ongoing controversies surrounding the terms *instructional design* and *systems approaches.*

Saettler (1990) says that the development of "scientifically based instructional systems" (p. 343) precedes this century, but he also points out that modern instructional design models and methods have their roots in the collaborative work of Robert Gagné and Leslie Briggs. These notable educational psychologists developed a way to transfer "laboratory-based learning principles" gleaned from military and industrial training to create an efficient way of developing curriculum and instruction for schools.

Gagné specialized in the use of instructional task analysis (see steps 4 and 5 in Bradens's model) to identify required subskills and conditions of learning for them. Briggs's expertise was in systematic methods of designing training programs to save companies time and money in training their personnel. When they combined the two areas of expertise, the result was a set of step-by-step processes known as a systems approach to instructional design, or systematic instructional design, which came into common use in the 1970s and 1980s.

One component of a systematic instructional design process was the use of learning hierarchies to develop curriculum maps (Gagné, Briggs, & Wager, 1992, p. 24). According to Saettler (1990), "the 1960s produced most of the major components of the instructional design process" (p. 345). Names associated with this era include Robert Mager (instructional objectives), Glaser (criterion-referenced testing), and Cronbach and Scriven (formative and summative evaluation). Other major contributors to modern instructional design models include David Merrill (component display theory) and Charles Reigeluth (elaboration theory).

Implications for education. Systems approaches to designing instruction have had great influence on training programs for business, industry, and the military, and somewhat less influence on K–12 education. However, performance objectives and sequences for instructional activities still are widely used. Most lesson planning models call for performance objectives (sometimes called behavioral objectives) to be stated in terms of measurable, observable learner behaviors.

Implications for technology integration. Most directed models for using technology resources are based on systems approaches, that is, teachers set objectives for a lesson, then develop a sequence of activities. A software package or an Internet activity is selected to carry out part of the instructional sequence. For example, the teacher may introduce a principle of genetics, then allow students to experiment with a simulation package to "breed" cats in order to see the principle in action.

Bradens's 1996 Instructional Design Model

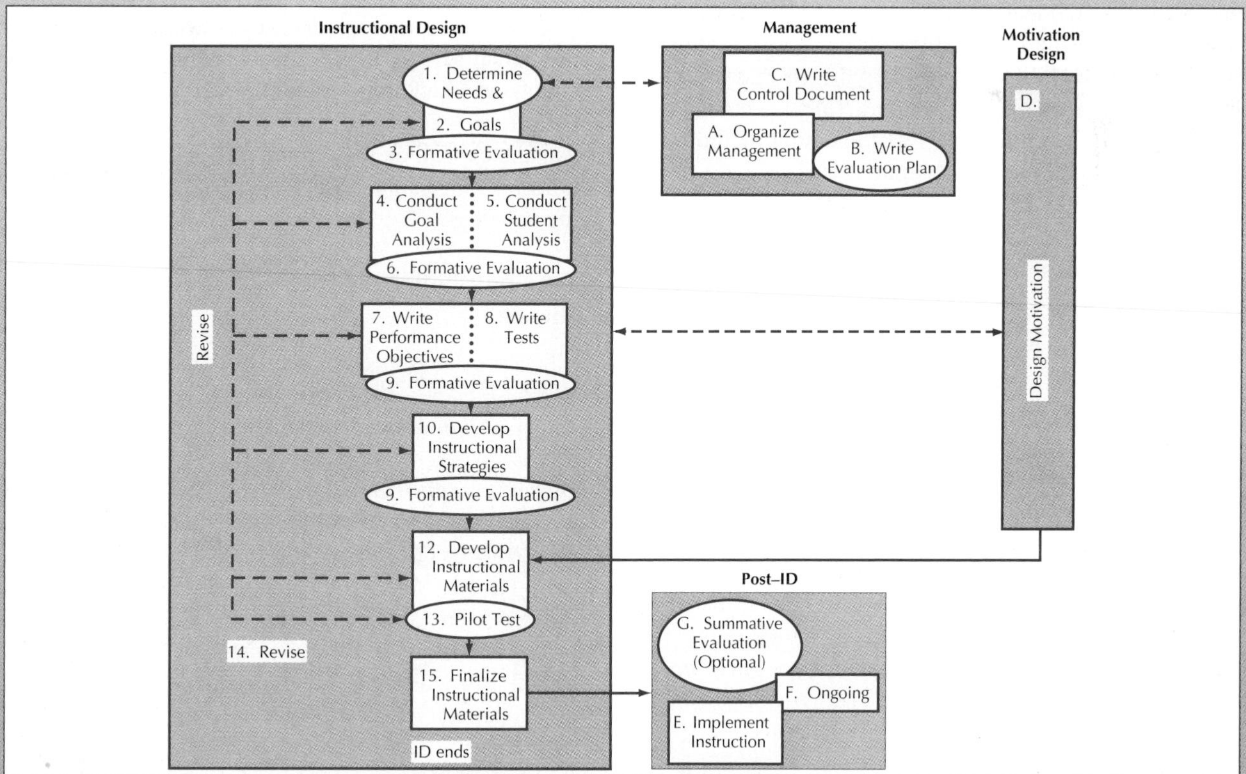

Source: Bradens, R. (1996). The case for linear instructional design and development: A commentary on models, challenges, and myths. *Educational Technology, 36*(2), 5–23.

Sources: Gagné, R., Briggs, L., & Wager, W. (1992). *Principles of instructional design.* Orlando, FL: Harcourt, Brace, Jovanovich; and Saettler; P. (1990). *The evolution of American educational psychology.* Englewood, CO: Libraries Unlimited.

- **Students cannot work cooperatively.** Observers of economic trends in this country and throughout the world seem to feel that national economic survival depends, in large part, on how well workers work together to solve problems of mutual concern. Cooperative group work has rarely been emphasized in American schools, especially at secondary levels. Directed instruction seems geared toward individual learning, so it has been accused of isolating learners from each other and neglecting much-needed social skills.

Current uses of directed methods. In modern classrooms, teachers do not use programmed instruction to teach skills, nor do they design many individual lessons with specific objectives and tests for each one. Teachers use lesson plans primarily to communicate clearly to supervisors or substitutes what will happen in the classroom, but lesson plans usually are not considered strict sequences to be followed exactly. Methods other than or in addition to objective test items are used to determine what students have learned.

But teachers still must arrange conditions of learning, and they are still largely responsible for answering the question, "What behaviors will I look for in my students to show me they have learned what I expected them to learn?" Teachers may find these traditional methods the best choice when they identify students who need more structured learning than others, or that certain prerequisite skills can best be learned through directed instruction. Although behaviorism may be viewed as an archaic and outmoded theory (Bradens, 1996), a considerable body of research indicates that teaching methods based on it work well for certain situations. Carnine, Silbert, and Kameenui (1997) and Stein, Silbert, and Carnine (1997) document its effectiveness in teaching reading and mathematics skills. A special issue of *Educational Technology* (October 1993) gives additional examples:

- Fluency practice in precision teaching of basic reading and math skills to young learners (Spence & Hively, 1993)
- Performance management contingencies to improve the study habits and achievement of college students (Mallott, 1993)
- Structured, teacher-directed techniques to teach problem-solving and higher order thinking skills to at-risk students (Carnine, 1993)
- Proposed application of behavioral techniques to teach the required behaviors leading to creativity (Epstein, 1993).

Directed or "scripted" programs such as DISTAR, which were developed many years ago based on behavioral principles, continue to be highly effective in many schools (Raspberry, 1998).

Theoretical Foundations of Constructivism

Molenda (1991) has said that "constructivism comes in different strengths . . . from weak to moderate to extreme" (p. 47). Phillips (1995) referred to constructivism as made up of many "sects, each of which harbors some distrust of its rivals" (p. 5). The differences among those who think of themselves as constructivists makes it difficult to settle on a single definition for constructivism. However, these differences may be explained by examining the variations in learning theories that underlie constructivist approaches.

Learning Theories Associated with Constructivism

Constructivist strategies are based on principles of learning derived from branches of cognitive science. This area focused specifically on students' motivation to learn and ability to use what they learn outside the school culture. Constructivist strategies try to respond to perceived deficiencies in behaviorist and information-processing theories and the teaching methods based on them. In addition, constructivists try to inspire students to see the relevance of what they learn and to prevent what the CTGV (1990) calls *inert knowledge,* or student failure to transfer what is already known to the learning of other skills that require prior knowledge.

These theories are based on the ideas of revered educational philosophers, psychologists, and practitioners such as John Dewey, Lev Vygotsky, Jerome Bruner, Jean Piaget, and Howard Gardner. Later work by Seymour Papert, John Seely Brown, the Cognition and Technology Group at Vanderbilt, Rand Spiro, D. N. Perkins, Ann Brown, Joe Campione, Carl Bereiter, and Marlene Scardamalia expand on these principles and develop specifications for translating these theories of cognition into teaching practices.

The Contributions of Early Cognitive Learning Theories

Educators credit theorists such as John Dewey, Lev Vygotsky, Jean Piaget, and Jerome Bruner with some of the fundamental premises of constructivist thinking.

Dewey's social constructivism. John Dewey is well known for laying the theoretical groundwork for many characteristics of today's educational system. (See InSight 3.5.) He was responsible for furthering the progressive movement in American education, principles that are now being reexamined for possible applications in today's school restructuring efforts. Several of Dewey's ideas support constructivist models of teaching and learning. Among these ideas is the need to center student instruction around relevant, meaningful activities. Prawat (1993) recalled Dewey's label of "worse than useless" (p. 6) any instruction that did not center around problems already within the child's experience.

INSIGHT 3.5

John Dewey: Educational Reform as Social Activism

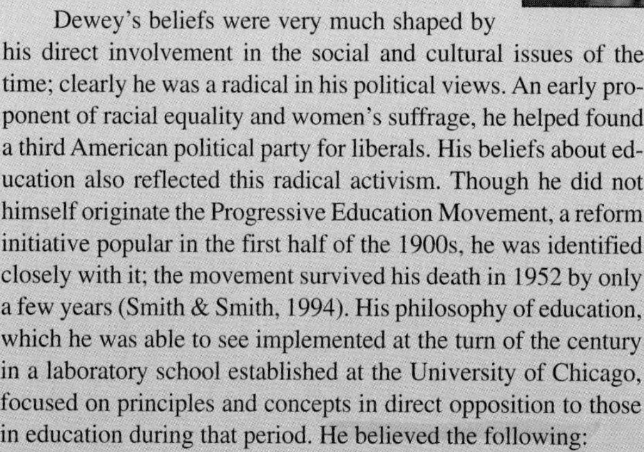

John Dewey is considered a philosopher rather than a learning theorist, an educational writer rather than an educational researcher. He was born in 1859 and most of his contributions to education predated those of the other famous individuals described here. Yet no one voice in education has had more pervasive and continuing influence on educational practice. In many ways, he can be thought of as the Grandfather of Constructivism, but he also advocated a merging of "absolutism" and "experimentalism" in much the same way as this chapter calls for using a combination of directed and constructivist methods.

Dewey's beliefs were very much shaped by his direct involvement in the social and cultural issues of the time; clearly he was a radical in his political views. An early proponent of racial equality and women's suffrage, he helped found a third American political party for liberals. His beliefs about education also reflected this radical activism. Though he did not himself originate the Progressive Education Movement, a reform initiative popular in the first half of the 1900s, he was identified closely with it; the movement survived his death in 1952 by only a few years (Smith & Smith, 1994). His philosophy of education, which he was able to see implemented at the turn of the century in a laboratory school established at the University of Chicago, focused on principles and concepts in direct opposition to those in education during that period. He believed the following:

- **Curriculum should arise from students' interests.** Dewey deplored standardization. He felt curriculum should be flexible and tailored to the needs of each student, a "pedocentric" strategy rather than the "scholiocentric" one of the time. He advocated letting each child's experiences determine individual learning activities.
- **Curriculum topics should be integrated, rather than isolated from each other.** He felt that isolating topics from one another prevented learners from grasping the whole of knowledge and caused skills and facts to be viewed as unrelated bits of information.
- **Education is growth, rather than an end in itself.** He did not share the common view of the time that education is preparation for work. He found that this view served to separate society into social classes and promote elitism. Rather, he looked on education as a way of helping individuals understand their culture and develop their relationship to and unique roles in society.
- **Education occurs through its connection with life, rather than through participation in curriculum.** He felt that social consciousness was the ultimate aim of all education. To be useful, all learning had to be in the context of social experience. However, he found that school skills such as reading and mathematics were becoming ends in themselves, disconnected from any meaningful social context.
- **Learning should be hands-on and experience based, rather than abstract.** He objected to commonly used teaching methods that used a "one-way channel of communication—from teacher to student through direct drill and memorization . . ." (Smith & Smith, 1994). He believed that meaningful learning resulted from students working cooperatively on tasks that were directly related to their interests.

Dewey's writings (e.g., *The School and Society,* 1899; *The Child and the Curriculum,* 1902; *How We Think,* 1910; *Schools of Tomorrow,* 1915; *Democracy and Education,* 1916; *Experience and Education,* 1938) spanned an era of monumental change in America's cultural identity and helped reform the country's education system to reflect those changing times.

Implications for education. Although it is difficult to say whether or not Dewey's philosophies directly caused some of the trends in current educational practice, today's interdisciplinary curriculum and hands-on, experience-based learning are very much in tune with Dewey's lifelong message. However, it also is likely he would deplore the current standards movement and the use of testing programs to determine school promotion and readiness for graduation.

Implications for technology integration. As Bruce (2000) noted, Dewey would likely have approved of technologies like the Internet being used to help students communicate with each other and learn more about their society. Dewey's emphasis on the need for cooperative learning would mesh well with technologies used for developing group projects and presentations. However, as Dewey himself recognized, the central problem with all these resources is combining them into a curriculum that encourages intellectual challenge.

Sources: Bruce, B. (2000). Dewey and technology. *The Journal of Adolescent and Adult Literacy, 42*(3), 222–226; Campbell, J. (1995). *Understanding John Dewey.* Chicago: Open Court; Fishman, S., & McCarthy, L. (1998). *John Dewey.* New York: Teachers College Press; Perrone, V. (1991). *A letter to teachers.* San Francisco: Jossey-Bass Publishers; and Smith, L. G., & Smith, J. K. (1994). *Lives in education* (2nd ed.). New York: St. Martin's Press. Photo from Library of Congress.

Vygotsky's scaffolding. The work of renowned human development theorist Lev Vygotsky (see InSight 3.6) also contributed key support for constructivist approaches. His twin concepts of *scaffolding* and the *zone of proximal development* are important for constructivists. Prawat (1993) observed that "Vygotsky emphasized the importance of social relations in all forms of complex mental activity" (p. 10); likewise, constructivists feel that teachers can most effectively provide scaffolding or help in acquiring new knowledge through collaboration with others.

Piaget's stages of development. The internationally famous developmental psychologist Piaget (see InSight 3.7) is generally regarded as a major contributor of theoretical

InSight 3.6

The Contributions of Lev Vygotsky: Building a Scaffold to Learning

For many years, the writings of Russian philosopher and educational psychologist Lev Semenovich Vygotsky had more influence on the development of educational theory and practice in America than in his own country. Davydov (1995) notes that Vygotsky's landmark book, *Pedagogical Psychology,* though written in 1926, was not published in Russia until 1991. Davydov attributes this lack of attention to the nature of the Russian government up until the time of *perestroika.* ". . . Vygotsky's general ideas could not be used for such a long time in the education system of a totalitarian society—they simply contradict all of its principles" (p. 13). What were these educational concepts that were so threatening to a communistic state but found such a warm reception in a democracy?

Vygotsky felt that cognitive development was directly related to and based on social development (Gage & Berliner, 1988; Ormrod, 2000). What children learn and how they think are derived directly from the culture around them: ". . . children begin learning from the world around them, their social world, which is the source of all their concepts, ideas, facts, skills, and attitudes. . . .[O]ur personal psychological processes begin as social processes, patterned by our culture" (Gage & Berliner, 1988, p. 124). An adult perceives things much differently than a child does, but this difference decreases as children gradually translate their social views into personal, psychological ones. Vygotsky's theories, with their emphasis on individual differences, personal creativity, and the influence of culture on learning, were discordant with the aims of the USSR, a government designed to "subjugate the education of young people to the interests of a militarized state that needed citizens only as devoted cogs" (Davydov, 1995, p. 12).

Vygotsky referred to the difference between these two levels of cognitive functioning (adult/expert and child/novice) as the *zone of proximal development.* He felt that teachers could provide good instruction by finding out where each child was in his or her development and building on the child's experiences. He called this building process "scaffolding." Ormrod (2001) said that teachers promote students' cognitive development by presenting some classroom tasks that "they can complete only with assistance, that is, within each student's zone of proximal development" (p. 59). Gage and Berliner (1988) feel that problems occur when the teacher leaves too much for the child to do independently, thus slowing the child's intellectual growth. "In the zone of proximal development, social knowledge—knowledge acquired through social interaction—becomes individual knowledge and individual knowledge grows and becomes more complex" (Gage & Berliner, 1988, p. 126).

Implications for education. Davydov (1995) found six basic implications for education in Vygotsky's ideas (p. 13):

1. Education is intended to develop children's personalities.
2. The human personality is linked to its creative potential, and education should be designed to discover and develop this potential to its fullest in each individual.
3. Teaching and learning assume that students master their inner values through some personal activity.
4. Teachers direct and guide the individual activities of the students, but they do not force their will on them or dictate to them.
5. The most valuable methods for student learning are those that correspond to their individual developmental stages and needs; therefore, these methods cannot be uniform across students.
6. These ideas had heavy influence on constructivist thought; Vygotsky's works were very much in tune with constructivist concepts of instruction based on each child's personal experiences and learning through collaborative, social activities.

Implications for technology integration. Many constructivist models of technology use the concepts of scaffolding and developing each individual's potential. Many of the more visual tools, from Logo to virtual reality, are used under the assumption that they can help bring the student up from their level of understanding to a higher level by showing graphic examples and by giving them real-life experiences relevant to their individual needs.

Sources: Davydov, V. (1995). The influence of L. S. Vygotsky on education theory, research, and practice. *Educational Researcher, 24*(3), 12–21; Gage N., & Berliner, D. (1988). *Educational psychology* (4th ed.). Boston: Houghton Mifflin; and Ormrod, J. (2000). *Educational psychology: Developing learners* (3rd ed.). Upper Saddle River, NJ: Merrill/Prentice Hall.

principles for constructivist thinking. While some educators feel that Piaget's ideas have been applied inappropriately, some of his basic premises seem related to constructivist approaches.

Bruner's relevance principle. Some of the principles associated with educational theorist Jerome Bruner (see InSight 3.8) seem to coincide with those of Vygotsky and Piaget, providing further theoretical support for constructivist theory. Like Piaget, Bruner believed children go through various stages of intellectual development. But unlike Piaget, Bruner supported intervention. He was primarily concerned with making education more relevant to student need at each stage, and he believed that teachers could accomplish this by encouraging active participation in the learning process. Active participation, he felt, was best achieved by providing discovery learning environments that would let children explore alternatives and recognize relationships between ideas (Bruner, 1973).

InSight 3.7

Jean Piaget's Theories: Cognitive Development in Children

As Flavell (1985) observed, "Piaget's contributions to our knowledge of cognitive development have been nothing short of stupendous" (p. 4). His examination of how thinking and reasoning abilities develop in the human mind began with observations of his own children and developed into a career that spanned some 60 years. He referred to himself as a "genetic epistemologist," or a scientist who studies how knowledge begins and develops in individuals. Both believers in and critics of Piagetian principles agree that his work was complex, profound, sometimes misunderstood, and usually oversimplified. However, at least two features of this work are widely recognized as underlying all of Piaget's theories: his stages of cognitive development and his processes of cognitive functioning.

Piaget believed that all children go through four stages of cognitive development. While the ages at which they experience these stages vary somewhat, he felt that each developed higher reasoning abilities in the same sequence:

- **Sensorimotor stage (from birth to about 2 years).** Characteristics of children: They explore the world around them through their senses and through motor activity. In the earliest stage, they cannot differentiate between themselves and their environments (if they cannot see something, it does not exist). Also, they begin to have some perception of cause and effect; develop the ability to follow something with their eyes.
- **Preoperational stage (from about age 2 to about age 7).** Characteristics of children: They develop greater abilities to communicate through speech and to engage in symbolic activities such as drawing objects and playing by pretending and imagining; develop numerical abilities such as the skill of assigning a number to each object in a group as it is counted; increase their level of self-control and are able to delay gratification, but are still fairly egocentric; and are unable to do what Piaget called conservation tasks (tasks that call for recognizing that a substance remains the same even though its appearance changes, e.g., shape is not related to quantity).
- **Concrete operational stage (from about age 7 to about age 11).** Characteristics of children: They increase in abstract reasoning ability and ability to generalize from concrete experiences; and can do conservation tasks.
- **Formal operations stage (from about age 12 to about age 15).** Characteristics of children: They can form and test hypotheses, organize information, and reason scientifically; and can show results of abstract thinking in the form of symbolic materials (e.g., writing, drama).

Piaget believed a child's development from one stage to another was a gradual process of interacting with the environment. Children develop as they confront new and unfamiliar features of their environment that do not fit with their current views of the world. When this happens, he said, a "disequilibrium" occurs that the child seeks to resolve through one of two processes of adaptation. The child either fits the new experiences into his or her existing view of the world (a process called *assimilation*) or changes that schema or view of the world to incorporate the new experiences (a process called *accommodation*). Though recent research has raised questions about the ages at which children's abilities develop, and it is widely believed that age does not determine development alone, Ormrod (2000) summarizes Piaget's basic assumptions about children's cognitive development in the following way:

- Children are active and motivated learners.
- Children's knowledge of the world becomes more integrated and organized over time.
- Children learn through the processes of assimilation and accommodation.
- Cognitive development depends on interaction with one's physical and social environment.
- The processes of equilibration (resolving disequilibrium) help to develop increasingly complex levels of thought.
- Cognitive development can occur only after certain genetically controlled neurological changes occur.
- Cognitive development occurs in four qualitatively different stages.

Implications for education. Educators do not always agree on the implications of Piaget's theories for classroom instruction. One frequently expressed instructional principle based on Piaget's stages is the need for concrete examples and experiences when teaching abstract concepts to young children who may not yet have reached a formal operations stage. Piaget himself repeatedly expressed a lack of interest in how his work applied to school-based education, calling it "the American question." He pointed out that much learning occurs without any formal instruction, as a result of the child interacting with the environment. However, constructivist educators tend to claim Piaget as the philosophical mentor who guides their work.

Implications for technology integration. Many technology-using teachers feel that using visual resources such as Logo and simulations can help raise children's developmental levels more quickly than they would have occurred through maturation; thus children who use these resources can learn higher level concepts than they normally would not have been able to understand until they were older. However, research evidence to support their belief still is being gathered. Other educators feel that young children should experience things in the "real world" before seeing them represented in the more abstract ways they are shown in software, for example, computer simulations.

Sources: Flavell, J. (1985). *Cognitive development* (2nd ed.). Englewood Cliffs, NJ: Prentice Hall; and Ormrod, J. (2000). *Educational psychology: Developing learners* (3rd ed.). Upper Saddle River, NJ: Merrill/Prentice Hall. Photo from Corbis-Bettman.

INSIGHT 3.8

The Contributions of Jerome Bruner: Learning as Discovery

Like Piaget, Jerome Bruner was interested in children's stages of cognitive development. Bruner described development in three stages (Gage & Berliner, 1988):

- **Enactive stage (from birth to about age 3).** Children perceive the environment solely through actions that they initiate. They describe and explain objects solely in terms of what a child can do with them. The child cannot tell how a bicycle works, but can show what to do with it. Showing and modeling have more learning value than telling for children at this stage.
- **Iconic stage (from about age 3 to about age 8).** Children can remember and use information through imagery (mental pictures or icons). Visual memory increases and children can imagine or think about actions without actually experiencing them. Decisions are still made on the basis of perceptions, rather than language.
- **Symbolic stage (from about age 8).** Children begin to use symbols (words or drawn pictures) to represent people, activities, and things. They have the ability to think and talk about things in abstract terms. They can also use and understand what Gagné would call "defined concepts." For example, they can discuss the concept of toys and identify various kinds of toys, rather than defining them only in terms of toys they have seen or handled. They can better understand mathematical principles and use symbolic idioms such as "Don't cry over spilt milk."

Bruner also identified six indicators or "benchmarks" that revealed cognitive growth or development (Gage & Berliner, 1988, pp. 121–122; Owen, Froman, & Moscow, 1981, p. 49). He said they:

1. Respond to situations in varied ways, rather than always in the same way.
2. Internalize events into a "storage system" that corresponds to the environment.
3. Have increased capacity for language.
4. Can interact systematically with a tutor (parent, teacher, or other role model).
5. Use language as an instrument for ordering the environment.
6. Have increasing capacity to deal with multiple demands.

Implications for education. Unlike Piaget, Bruner was very concerned about arrangements for school instruction that acknowledged and built on the stages of cognitive development. The idea of discovery learning is largely attributed to him. Discovery learning is "an approach to instruction through which students interact with their environment—by exploring and manipulating objects, wrestling with questions and controversies, or performing experiments" (Ormrod, 2000, p. 442). Bruner felt that students were more likely to understand and remember concepts they had discovered in the course of their own exploration. However, research findings have yielded mixed results for discovery learning, and the relatively unstructured methods recommended by Bruner have not found widespread support (Eggen & Kauchak, 2001; Ormrod, 2000). Teachers have found that discovery learning is most successful when students have prerequisite knowledge and undergo some structured experiences.

Implications for technology integration. Many of the more "radical constructivist" uses of technology employ a discovery learning approach suggested by Bruner. For example, rather than telling students how logic circuits work, a teacher might allow students to use a simulation that lets them discover the rules themselves. Most school uses of technology, however, use what Eggen and Kauchak (2001) call a guided discovery learning approach. For example, a teacher may introduce a problem scenario such as those in the *Adventures of Jasper Woodbury* videodiscs, then help students develop their approaches to solving the problem.

Sources: Eggen, P., & Kauchak, D. (2001). *Educational psychology: Windows on classrooms* (5th ed.). Upper Saddle River, NJ: Merrill/Prentice Hall; Gage, N., & Berliner, D. (1988). *Educational psychology* (4th ed.). Boston: Houghton Mifflin; Goetze, E., Alexander, P., & Ash, M. (1992). *Educational psychology: A classroom perspective.* New York: Merrill/Macmillan; Bruner, J. (1966). *Toward a theory of instruction.* Boston: Little, Brown; Ormrod, J. (2000). *Educational psychology: Developing learners* (3rd ed.). Upper Saddle River, NJ: Merrill/Prentice Hall; and Owen, S., Froman, R., & Moscow, H. (1981). *Educational psychology.* Boston: Little, Brown. Photo courtesy of Jerome Bruner.

Theoretical foundations of constructivism. From these theorists, constructivists derived the premise that educational experiences should foster a child's progress through stages of development. Constructivists tend to perceive much of today's education as too structured and geared to activities that are inappropriate for children's current developmental levels. These experiences, they say, can actually slow students' progress by inhibiting their innate desire to make sense of the world at each stage of their cognitive development. Like Bruner, most constructivists call for instructional intervention, that is, for teachers to provide learning activities designed not only to match but to accelerate movement through these stages. They also feel that education should provide children with more opportunities for cognitive growth through exploration, unstructured learning, and problem solving.

The Contributions of Later Work Based on Cognitive Principles

Several lines of research and development based on principles from cognitive science have profoundly affected educational practice, particularly instructional applications of technology. This section discusses some major contributors to this research.

InSight 3.9

Seymour Papert: Turtles and Beyond

One of Piaget's most famous American pupils, Seymour Papert, has influenced profoundly the field of educational technology. Papert began his career as a mathematician. After studying with Jean Piaget in Geneva from 1959 to 1964, Papert became impressed with Piaget's way of "looking at children as active builders of their own intellectual structures" (Papert, 1980, p. 19). Papert subsequently joined the Artificial Intelligence Laboratory at the Massachusetts Institute of Technology and began experimenting with Logo, a new programming language, and its use with young children. One of his colleagues was also working with children, teaching them to control a robot in the shape of a turtle. The MIT team decided to combine the two concepts, integrating an on-screen "turtle" into the Logo language. This addition provided the vital link that Papert felt would allow children to move more easily from the concrete operations of earlier stages of Piaget's hypothesis to more abstract (formal) ones. In 1980, Papert published his theories in a book entitled *Mindstorms: Children, Computers, and Powerful Ideas.* This book challenged then-current instructional goals and methods for both mathematics and educational technology, and it became the first widely recognized constructivist statement of educational practice with technology resources.

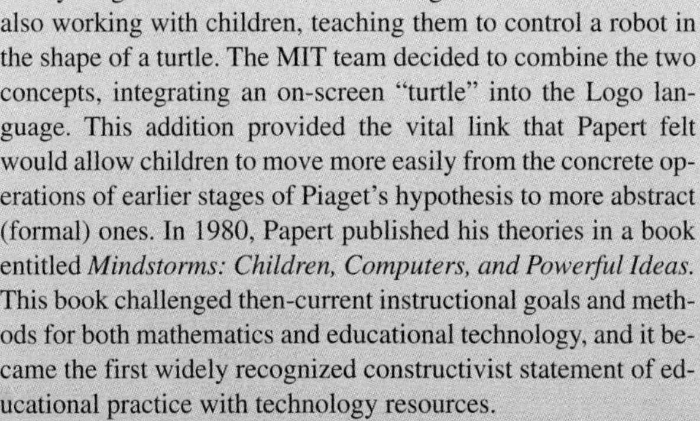

Implications for education and technology integration. As Papert himself observed, "I make a slightly unorthodox interpretation of [Piaget's] theoretical position and a very unorthodox interpretation of the implications of his theory for education" (Papert, 1980, p. 217). Piaget himself was not concerned with instructional methods or curriculum matters, and he had no interest in trying to accelerate the stages of cognitive development. Papert, on the other hand, felt that children could advance in their intellectual abilities more quickly with the right kind of environment and assistance. He described the requirements of such an environment in his 1980 book:

- **Discovery learning and "powerful ideas."** Although he never used the term *discovery learning,* Papert felt that children should be allowed to "teach themselves" with Logo. Reflecting the Piagetian concept of disequilibrium, he explained that "in a Logo environment, new ideas are often acquired as a means of satisfying a personal need to do something one could not do before" (Papert, 1980, p. 74). He felt that children need great flexibility to develop their own "powerful ideas" or insights about new concepts.
- **Logo and the microworlds concept.** Papert perceived Logo as a resource with ideal properties for encouraging learning. Because Logo is graphics oriented, it allows children to see cause-and-effect relationships between the logic of programming commands and the pictures that result. This logical, cause-and-effect quality of Logo activities makes possible "microworlds," or self-contained environments where all actions are orderly and rule governed. He called these microworlds "incubators for knowledge" where children could pose and test out hypotheses.

When research studies on educational applications of Logo failed to yield the improvements expected by educators, many of Papert's concepts became even more controversial. Papert criticized these research efforts as "technocentric," saying that they focused more on Logo itself than on the methods used with it. However, Logo as an "instructional method" dropped out of common use in the early 1990s.

Although Logo is not in common use today, Papert's constructivist emphasis has had a distinct influence on the use of newer technology resources. Until Papert's work, the quality of software and media were judged almost solely on how well they reflected systematic design principles. After Logo, technology resources began to be evaluated according to how they could be used as "microworlds" and "incubators for knowledge" in which learners could generate their own knowledge.

Source: Papert, S. (1980). *Mindstorms: Children, computers, and powerful ideas.* New York: Basic Books. Photo courtesy of Scholastic, Inc.

Papert's microworlds. Seymour Papert, a mathematician and pupil of Piaget (see InSight 3.9), was one of the first vocal critics of using technology in the context of traditional instructional methods. In his 1980 book *Mindstorms,* he became one of the first to raise national consciousness about the potential role of technology in creating alternatives to what he perceived as inadequate and harmful educational methods. Bass (1985) observed that "In many ways, the development of Logo has paralleled the recent development of Piagetian theory" (p. 107). However, even Bass admitted that while the focus of Piaget's colleagues may have changed, Piaget himself was never "particularly concerned with what he called 'the American question' of how to influence [children's] development through planned learning environments" (p. 113).

John Seely Brown and cognitive apprenticeships. Brown and his colleagues at the Institute for Research on Learning focused on the work of cognitive psychologists who built on Vygotsky's hypotheses (Brown et al., 1989). Brown et al. were especially concerned with the relationship between this work and a problem they observed throughout much school learning. They refer to this problem as *inert knowledge,* a term introduced in 1929 by Whitehead. Brown et al. found that many school practices reduce the likelihood that children will transfer learned skills to later problem solving that requires those skills. The researchers observe that "it is common for students to acquire algorithms, routines, and decontextualized definitions that they cannot use and that, therefore, lie inert" (p. 33). They say this is because skills often are taught in abstract ways and in isolation from actual, authentic application. For example, students often learn multiplication facts and procedures, but fail to recognize applications of these skills to real-life problems or to word problems that require multiplication. Students often feel that activities like multiplication are something done in a school culture with no real utility or application outside school.

What students learn, Brown et al. (1989) argue, should not be separated from *how* they learn it. Students must come to understand how to transfer knowledge, they say, by learning it at the same time as they apply it in meaningful ways. This can best be accomplished by providing *cognitive apprenticeships,* activities that call for authentic problem solving, that is, problem solving in settings that are familiar and useful to the student. Such tasks require students to use knowledge in content areas as tools, much as an apprentice tailor would use a sewing machine and scissors. For example, the researchers suggest teaching multiplication in the context of coin problems "because in the community of fourth grade students, there is usually a strong, implicit, shared understanding of coins" (p. 38). Through these kinds of activities, multiplication becomes useful and real beyond the school culture. They refer to this kind of teaching and learning as *situated cognition,* and like Vygotsky, they feel it can best be accomplished through collaborative (group) learning.

Vanderbilt's cognition and technology group and anchored instruction. A group of researchers at Vanderbilt's Learning and Technology Center built on the concepts of situated cognition and collaborative learning introduced by Brown et al. (1989) as well as Vygotsky's concept of scaffolding. (See InSight 3.10.) They recommended anchoring instruction in situations where students not only create answers to problems, but also generate many aspects of the problem statements. The researchers referred to this active involvement in problem solving as *generative learning* and pointed out that video-based technologies have unique qualities to support these kinds of problem-solving environments.

Cognitive flexibility theory and radical constructivism. Rand Spiro and a group of researchers that included Feltovich, Jacobson, Coulson, Anderson, and Jehng developed a constructivist theory in reaction to a perceived failure of many current instructional approaches—including some constructivist ones. Spiro et al. say that current classroom methods are more suited to learning in well-structured knowledge domains, while much of what students should learn lies in "ill-structured domains." For example, ". . . basic arithmetic is well-structured, while the process of applying arithmetic in solving word problems drawn from real situations is more ill-structured" (Spiro, Feltovich, Jacobson, & Coulson, 1991, p. 26). For learning in these ill-structured domains, Spiro et al. say, students need a different way of thinking about learning. "The interpretation of constructivism that has dominated much of cognition and educational psychology for the past 20 years or so has frequently stressed the retrieval of organized packets of knowledge, or schemas, from memory. . . . We argue that . . . ill-structured knowledge domains often render [these] schemas inadequate" (p. 28).

Spiro et al. (1991) say that the new constructivism of their cognitive flexibility theory is "doubly constructive." That is, it calls for students to generate not only solutions to new problems, but also the prior knowledge needed to solve the problems. This kind of constructivism demands even less direct teaching and even more exploration on the part of students than those of Brown et al. (1989) and CTGV. Perkins (1991) calls this the difference between "BIG (beyond the information given) instruction" and "WIG (without the information given) instruction" (p. 20). Because they call for an even greater departure from directed instruction methods than other constructivists, those who hold views similar to those of Spiro et al. are sometimes referred to as *radical constructivists.*

Gardner's theory of multiple intelligences. Gardner's theory (see InSight 3.11) that many kinds of intelligence exist is not strictly constructivist. But it does coincide with the constructivist emphasis on group work, both as a function of distributed intelligence and as a necessary social skill. According to Gardner, since students may vary greatly in strength and aptitude, each can make a unique and valuable contribution to a group product. Many teachers find Gardner's theory intuitively appealing; it reinforces their own observations and experiences with students. Perhaps more important, however, it helps justify having different goals and criteria for success for each student, rather than a one-size-fits-all set for everyone.

Characteristics of Constructivism

Constructivism challenges the traditional goals of education and proposes restructured, innovative teaching approaches. Constructivist goals focus on students' ability to solve real-life, practical problems, and its methods call for students to construct knowledge themselves rather than simply receiving it from knowledgeable teachers. As Figure 3.3 indicates, students typically work in cooperative groups rather than individually. They tend to focus on projects that require solutions to problems rather than on instructional sequences that require learning certain content skills. In contrast to directed instruction, where the teacher sets the goals and delivers most of the instruction, the job of the teacher in constructivist models is to arrange for required resources and act as a guide to students while they set their own goals and "teach themselves."

InSight 3.10

The Cognition and Technology Group at Vanderbilt: Tying Technology to Constructivism

A research team located at the Learning Technology Center at Vanderbilt University has helped establish some practical guidelines for integrating technology based on constructivist principles. This team, known as the Cognition and Technology Group at Vanderbilt (CTGV), proposed an instructional approach based on concepts introduced by Vygotsky, Whitehead, and Brown et al. (1989). It has also developed several technology products modeling this approach that have achieved widespread use in American education. Several related concepts provide the theoretical foundation for the CTGV team's approach:

- **Preventing inert knowledge.** The CTGV hypothesized that teaching without a direct relationship to children's personal experience often resulted in their acquiring what Whitehead referred to as *inert knowledge.* That is, students never actually applied the knowledge they had learned because they could not see its relationship to problems they encountered. Inert knowledge is "knowledge that can usually be recalled when people are explicitly asked to do so, but is not used spontaneously in problem solving even though it is relevant" (CTGV, 1990, p. 2).
- **The nature of situated cognition and the need for anchored instruction.** Brown et al. (1989) suggested that teachers could prevent the problem of inert knowledge by situating learning in the context of what they called authentic experiences and practical apprenticeships—activities that learners considered important because they emulated the behavior of experts (adults) in the area. In this way, students see the link between school learning and real-life activities. The CTGV felt that teachers can meet the criteria for situated cognition by anchoring instruction in highly visual problem-solving environments. "Anchored instruction provides a way to recreate some of the advantages of apprenticeship training in formal educational settings involving groups of students" (CTGV, 1990, p. 2).
- **Building knowledge through generative activities.** Like Vygotsky, the CTGV believes that learning is most meaningful to students when it builds (scaffolds) on experiences they have already had. Students are also more likely to remember knowledge that they build or "generate" themselves, rather than that which they simply receive passively (CTGV, 1991b).

Implications for education and technology integration. The CTGV proposed that the best way of providing instruction that would meet all the required criteria was to present it as videodisc-based scenarios posing interesting but difficult problems for students to solve. The first of these technology-based products, the *Jasper Woodbury Problem Solving Series,* focused on mathematics problems. Another, *The Young Children's Literacy Series,* addressed reading and language skills (CTGV, 1993). Both of these products were designed to build on children's existing knowledge in a way that would emphasize knowledge transfer to real-life situations.

Sources: Brown, J. S., Collins, A., & Duguid, P. (1989). Situated cognition and the culture of learning. *Educational Researcher, 18*(1), 32–41; Cognition and Technology Group at Vanderbilt (1990). Anchored instruction and its relationship to situated cognition. *Educational Researcher, 19*(6), 2–10; Cognition and Technology Group at Vanderbilt (1991b). Technology and the design of generative learning environments. *Educational Technology, 31*(5), 34–40; and Cognition and Technology Group at Vanderbilt (1993). The Jasper experiment: An exploration of issues in learning and instructional design. *Educational Technology Research and Development, 40*(1), 65–80. Photo courtesy of Billie Kingsley, Vanderbilt University, photographer David Crenshaw.

For example, rather than teaching an isolated objective such as identifying animals by phylum and genus, teachers may arrange for students to carry out cooperative projects that investigate the behavior of animals in the local environment. The ability to classify animals into phylum and genus becomes one of several by-products of the students' observations.

Sometimes instructional activities based on constructivist models are more time consuming, since they may call for teachers to organize and facilitate group work and to evaluate it in authentic ways. By comparison, paper-and-pencil tests are both quicker to develop and easier to administer. Many commercially available instructional materials based on constructivist models are recent designs. Since these materials may have been in use only briefly, teachers often have limited information available on how to smooth classroom implementation or what problems to anticipate. This is especially true with activities involving newer technologies such as interactive video and multimedia. The knowledge base on these kinds of classroom activities is growing, but teachers still are adapting classroom strategies and coping with the logistics of setting up and using such equipment and media.

It also is important to recognize potential contradictions in theorists' views on how teachers should carry out constructivist approaches. As Spiro et al. (1991) observe, there are many variations on what is meant by constructivist (p. 22). For example, Papert (1987) feels that learning activities should be fairly unstructured and open-ended, frequently with no goal in mind other than discovery of powerful ideas. Spiro et al. also call for varied opportunities for exploration when learning in ill-structured knowledge domains, but they seem to advocate at least some acquisition of specific skills and information. The guidelines set forth by CTGV are still more goal-oriented and call for students to generate solutions to specific problems. Teachers must analyze the needs of their students and decide which constructivist strategies seem most appropriate for meeting these needs.

The work of researchers and theorists such as Papert, Brown et al., CTGV, and Perkins have contributed especially important guidelines on how to develop instructional activities according to constructivist models. Since these guidelines do not always agree, teachers cannot usually follow all of them within the same instructional activity. But each of the principles discussed next is still considered characteristic of constructivist purposes and designs.

Problem-oriented activities. Most constructivist models focus on students solving problems, either in a specific content area such as mathematics or using an interdisciplinary approach. For example, such a problem might require a combination of mathematics, science, and language arts skills. Jungck (1991) says that constructivist methods frequently combine problem posing, problem solving, and persuasion of peers (p. 155). Problems may be posed in terms of specific goals (e.g., how to develop an information package to help persuade classmates to stop littering the beach), as "what if" questions (e.g., what would life be like on earth if we had half the gravity we now have?), or as open-ended questions (e.g., in light of what you know about the characters and the times in which they lived, what is the best ending for this story?). These kinds of problems are *usually* more complex than those associated with directed instruction, and they require students to devote more time and more diverse skills to solve them.

Visual formats and mental models. CTGV is especially concerned that instructional activities help students build good "mental models" of problems to be solved. They feel that teachers can promote this work most effectively by posing problems in visual, as opposed to written, formats. These researchers say that "Visual formats allow students to develop their own pattern recognition skills, and they are dynamic, rich, and spatial" (1990, p. 3). This degree of visual support is felt to be particularly important for low-achieving, at-risk students who may have reading difficulties and for students with little expertise in the area in which the problems are posed.

Rich, complex environments. Many constructivist approaches seem to call for what Perkins (1991) terms "richer learning environments" (p. 19) in contrast to the minimalist classroom environment that usually relies primarily on the teacher, a textbook, and prepared materials. Perkins observes that many constructivist models are facilitated by combinations of five kinds of resources: information banks such as textbooks and electronic encyclopedias to access required information; symbol pads such as notebooks and laptop computers to support learners' short-term memories; construction kits, including Legos, Tinkertoys, and Logo to let learners manipulate and build; phenomenaria (e.g., a terrarium or computer simulation) to allow exploration; and task managers like teachers and electronic tutors to provide assistance and feedback as students complete tasks.

Cooperative or collaborative (group) learning. Most constructivist approaches heavily emphasize work in groups rather than as individuals to solve problems. This arrangement achieves several aims that advocates of constructivism and directed instruction alike consider important. CTGV (1991a) observes that gathering students in cooperative groups seems to be the best way to facilitate generative learning. Perkins (1991) points out that cooperative learning illustrates distributive intelligence at work. In a distributive definition of intelligence, accomplishment is not a function simply of individual capabilities but the product of individuals and tools, each of which contributes to achieving desired goals. Finally, cooperative learning seems an ideal environment for students to learn how to share responsibility and work together toward common goals, skills they will find useful in a variety of settings outside school.

Learning through exploration. All constructivist approaches call for some flexibility in achieving desired goals. Most stress exploration rather than merely getting the right answer and a high degree of what advocates of directed instruction call *discovery learning*. Constructivists differ among themselves, however, about how much assistance and guidance a teacher should offer. Only a few constructivists feel that students should have complete freedom and unlimited time to discover the knowledge they need. Perkins (1991) says, "Education given over entirely to WIG (without any given) instruction would prove grossly inefficient and ineffective, failing to pass on in straightforward ways the achievements of the past" (p. 20).

Authentic (performance-based) assessment methods. When the goals and methods of education change in the ways described here, teachers also need new methods of evaluating student progress. Thus, constructivist learning environments exhibit more qualitative assessment strategies rather than quantitative ones. Some popular assessment methods center on student portfolios with examples of students' work and products they have developed (Bateson, 1994; Young, 1995); narratives written by teachers to describe each student's work habits and areas of strength and weakness; and performance-based assessments in combination with checklists of criteria for judging student performance (Linn, 1994).

INSIGHT 3.11

Gardner's Theory of Multiple Intelligences

Of all the learning and developmental theories embraced by constructivists, Howard Gardner's is the only one that attempts to define the role of intelligence in learning. His work is based on Guilford's pioneering work on the structure of intellect (Eggen & Kauchak, 2001) and Sternberg's view of intelligence as influenced by culture (Ormrod, 2000). Gardner's theory (1983) is that at least eight different and relatively independent types of intelligence exist (see table below).

Implications for education. If Gardner's theory is correct, then IQ tests (which tend to stress linguistic and logical-mathematical abilities) may not be the best way to judge a given student's ability to learn, and traditional academic tasks may not be the best reflection of ability. Ormrod (2000) points out that "to the extent that intelligence is culture-dependent, intelligent behavior is likely to take different forms in children from different ethnic backgrounds" (p. 156). Teachers, then, should try to determine which type or types of intelligence each student has and direct the student to learning activities that capitalize on these innate abilities. Gardner and Hatch (1989) give suggestions for how best to do this. Also, teachers may consider learning activities based on distributed intelligence, where each student makes a different, but valued contribution to creating a product or solving a problem.

Implications for technology integration. Gardner's theory meshes well with the trend toward using technology to support group work. When educators assign students to groups to develop a multimedia product, they can assign students roles based on their type of intelligence. For example, those with high interpersonal intelligence may be the project coordinators, those with high logical-mathematical ability may be responsible for structure and links, and those with spatial ability may be responsible for graphics and aesthetics.

Types of Intelligence	Description	Reflected in Activities
Linguistic	Uses language effectively	Writer, journalist, poet
	Is sensitive to the uses of language	
	Writes clearly and persuasively	
Musical	Understands musical structure and composition; communicates by writing or playing music	Composer, pianist, conductor
Logical-mathematical	Reasons logically in math terms	Scientist, mathematician, doctor
	Recognizes patterns in phenomena	
	Formulates and tests hypotheses and solves problems in math and science	
Spatial	Perceives the world in visual terms	Artist, sculptor, graphic artist
	Notices and remembers visual details	
	Can recreate things after seeing them	
Bodily-kinesthetic	Uses the body skillfully	Dancer, athlete, watchmaker
	Manipulates things well with hands	
	Uses tools skillfully	
Intrapersonal	Is an introspective thinker	Self-aware/self-motivated person
	Is aware of one's own motives	
	Has heightened metacognitive abilities	
Interpersonal	Notices moods and changes in others	Psychologist, therapist, salesperson
	Can identify motives in others' behavior	
	Relates well with others	
Naturalist	Can discriminate among living things	Botanist, biologist

Sources: Eggen, P., & Kauchak, D. (2001). *Educational psychology: Windows on classrooms (5th ed.)*. Upper Saddle River, NJ: Merrill/Prentice Hall; Gardner, H. (1983). *Frames of mind.* New York: Basic Books; Gardner, H., & Hatch, T. (1989). Multiple intelligences go to school: Educational implications of the theory of multiple intelligences. *Educational Researcher, 18*(8), 4–10; Ormrod, J. (2000). *Educational psychology: Developing learners (3rd ed.)*. Upper Saddle River, NJ: Merrill/Prentice Hall. Photo courtesy of C. Jerry Bauer, 1994.

Constructivist Methods: Problems Raised Versus Problems Addressed

Criticisms of constructivist methods. Despite the current popularity of constructivism, its principles and practices have stimulated a variety of criticisms. Two issues of *Educational Technology* magazine (May and September 1991) provided a forum for describing and debating the merits of constructivist learning strategies. Discussion focused on the following issues:

- **It is difficult for teachers to certify individual's skill learning.** Reigeluth (1991) pointed out that, although constructivists deplore formal tests or objective measurements, schools must sometimes certify that students have learned key skills. "It is not sufficient to know that a doctor was on a team of medical students that performed the operation successfully; you want to know if the doctor can do it without the team" (p. 35). As calls for teacher accountability and adherence to standards in American education grow ever louder, the problem of certifying learning is becoming a pivotal issue.
- **Prerequisite skills may be lacking.** Constructivist strategies often call for students to approach and solve complex problems. But both Tobias (1991) and Molenda (1991) point out that, regardless of their motivation, many students may lack the prerequisite abilities that would allow them to handle this kind of problem solving.
- **Students may not choose the most effective instruction.** Constructivist tasks often require students to learn how to teach themselves, that is, to choose methods by which they will learn and solve problems. But Tobias (1991) quotes a study by Clark (1982) that indicates that students often learn the least from instructional methods they prefer most. Critics of constructivism say that students often need "the sage on the stage" to guide them.
- **Not all topics suit constructivist methods.** Many educators feel that constructivist methods serve some purposes more effectively than others. For example, constructivist activities frequently seek to teach the problem-solving methods used by experts in a content area (thinking like a historian), rather than asking students to learn any specific content or skills such as historical facts. Molenda (1991) points out that constructivists may be surprised to learn that this is not what many parents and educators have in mind. "Parents and school people [are] . . . much more interested in communicating our cultural heritage to the next generation. Facts are viewed as powerful ends in themselves" (p. 45). Tobias (1991) notes that constructivists often favor depth of coverage on one topic over breadth of coverage on many topics: "Students taught the first term of American history from a constructivist perspective may have a very profound understanding of the injustices imposed by taxation without representation. . . . however, would they learn anything about the War of 1812, Shay's Rebellion, the Whiskey Rebellion, or the Monroe Doctrine?" (p. 42).
- **Skills may not transfer to practical situations.** Constructivists feel that problem solving taught in authentic situations in school will transfer more easily to problems that students must solve in real life. Yet Tobias (1991) found little evidence from related research to indicate that such transfer will occur. Baines and Stanley (2000) question whether or not students learn as much from constructivist methods as from directed ones.

Current constructivist trends. Despite these criticisms, interest in constructivist methods is on the rise, and research is increasing to measure the impact of learning based on student problem solving and product development (CTGV, 1995). It is possible that the coming years will witness some dramatic shifts in curriculum goals and methods that largely follow constructivist principles. An increasing number of schools and districts already are emphasizing alternative assessments such as portfolios and group projects, either in addition to or in place of traditional testing.

In recent years, the movement in education to integrate technology into teaching has become closely identified with the restructuring movement. Many educators believe they cannot make curriculum reflect constructivist characteristics *without* technology. Constructivists offer this combination of problem-oriented activities, cooperative group work, tasks related to students' interests and backgrounds, and highly visual formats provided by technology resources as components of a powerful antidote to some of the country's most pervasive and recalcitrant social and educational problems.

Technology Integration Strategies: Directed, Constructivist, and Combined Approaches

Subsequent chapters in this book describe and give examples of integration strategies for various types of courseware materials and technology media. However, all of these strategies implement a group of general integration principles. Some draw on the unique characteristics of a technology resource to meet certain kinds of learning needs. Others take advantage of a resource's ability to substitute for materials lacking in schools or classrooms. Teachers may use many or all of the following strategies at the same time. However, it is important to recognize that each of the integration strategies described here addresses specific instructional needs identified by educational theorists and practitioners. Strategies are not employed because technology is the wave of the future or because students should occasionally use computers because it is good for them. The authors advocate making a conscious effort to match technology resources to problems that educators cannot address in other, easier ways.

Integration Strategies Based on Directed Models

Integration to remedy identified weaknesses. One premise of constructivist theorists is that students are motivated to learn prerequisite skills if they see their relevance when the need arises in the context of group or individual projects. However, experienced teachers know that even the most motivated students do not always learn skills as expected. These failures occur for a variety of reasons, many of which are related to learners' internal capabilities and not all of which are thoroughly understood. Curriculum is currently moving toward allowing students to acquire skills on more flexible schedules. But when the absence of prerequisite skills presents a barrier to higher level learning or to passing tests, directed instruction usually is the most efficient way of providing them. For example, if a student does not learn to read when it is developmentally appropriate, research has shown great success in identifying and remedying specific weaknesses among the component skills (Torgeson, 1986; Torgeson, Waters, Cohen, & Torgeson, 1988). Materials such as drills and tutorials have proven to be valuable resources that help teachers provide this kind of individualized instruction. Well-designed resources like these not only can give students effective instruction but also are frequently more motivating and less threatening than teacher-delivered instruction to students who find learning difficult.

Integration to promote fluency or automaticity of prerequisite skills. Some kinds of prerequisite skills benefit students more if they can apply the skills without conscious effort. Gagné (1982) and Bloom (1986) referred to this as *automaticity of skills,* and Hasselbring and Goin (1993) call it *fluency* or *proficiency.* Students need rapid recall and performance of a wide range of skills throughout the curriculum, including simple math facts, grammar and usage rules, and spelling. Some students acquire automaticity through repeated use of the skills in practical situations. Others acquire this automatic recall more efficiently through isolated practice. Drill and practice, instructional game and, sometimes, simulation courseware all provide ideal means of practice tailored to individual skill needs and learning pace.

Integration to make systematic learning efficient for highly motivated students. Current educational methods are sometimes criticized for failure to interest and motivate students because activities and skills are irrelevant to students' needs, experiences, and interests. However, some students' motivation to learn springs from internal rather than external sources. These internally motivated students do not need explicit connections between specific skills and practical problems. Such students may be motivated by desire to please authority figures, by long-range goals (e.g., attending college), or simply by knowing they are achieving at high levels. In addition, interest in a subject kindled originally by a cooperative class project may spur students to learn everything they can about the field. Self-motivated students pursue skills they believe are related to their topics or provide foundations for later concepts. For such learners, the most desirable method of learning is the most efficient one. Directed instruction for these students can frequently be supported by well-designed self-instructional tutorials and simulations—assuming the teacher can locate high-quality materials on the desired topics.

Assessment Strategies for Directed Models

It should not be surprising that more traditional assessment methods are frequently used with directed (i.e., more traditional) integration strategies. Usually, this is because directed strategies are also mastery learning strategies, and teachers require clear, easily observable evidence that students have adequately mastered the skills.

- **Measures of achievement in directed environments.** Typical assessments for directed models are written objective tests (multiple choice, true/false, matching, short answer) and essays. Essays often are used to assess higher level performances such as writing a composition.
- **Grading strategies for directed products.** For directed learning, measures are graded according to preset criteria for what constitutes acceptable performance. Very often, a software package includes tests and built-in criteria for passing them. Essays usually are graded with a criteria checklist or writing rubric.

Integration Strategies Based on Constructivist Models

Integration to foster creativity. Although creative work is not usually considered a primary goal of education, many educators and parents consider it highly desirable. Some argue that students can be educated without being creative, but few schools want to graduate students who cannot think or act creatively. Resources such as Logo, problem-solving courseware, and computer graphics tools require neither consumable supplies nor any particular artistic or literary skill. They also allow students to revise creative works easily and as many times as desired. These qualities have provided uniquely fertile, nonthreatening environments for fostering development of students' creativity.

Integration to facilitate self-analysis and metacognition. If students are conscious of the procedures they use to go about solving problems, perhaps they can more easily improve on their strategies and become more effective problem solvers. Consequently, teachers often try to get students to analyze their procedures to increase their efficiency. Resources such as Logo, problem-solving courseware, and multimedia applications often are considered ideal environments for constructivist activities that get students to think about how they think.

Integration to increase transfer of knowledge to problem solving. The CTGV team points out unique capabilities of certain technology resources to address the problem of inert knowledge. They observe that this problem often occurs when students learn skills in isolation from problem applications. When students later encounter problems that require the skills, they do not realize how the skills could be relevant. Problem-solving materials in highly visual videodisc-based formats allow students to build rich mental models of problems to be solved (CTGV, 1991a). Students need not depend on reading skills, which may be deficient, to build these mental models. Thus, supporters hypothesize that teaching skills in these highly visual, problem solving environments helps to ensure that knowledge will transfer to higher order skills. These technology-based methods are especially desirable for teachers who work with students in areas such as mathematics and science where inert knowledge is frequently a problem.

Integration to foster group cooperation. One skill area currently identified as an important focus for schools' efforts to restructure curriculum (U.S. Department of Labor, 1992) is the ability to work cooperatively in a group to solve problems and develop products. Although schools certainly can teach cooperative work without technology resources, a growing body of evidence documents students' appreciation of cooperative work as both more motivating and easier to accomplish when it uses technology. For example, descriptions of students who develop their own multimedia products and presentations are more common in current literature on teaching cooperative skills to at-risk students.

Integration to allow for multiple and distributed intelligence. Integration strategies with group cooperative activities also give teachers a way to allow students of widely varying abilities to make valuable contributions on their own terms. Since each student is seen as an important member of the group in these activities, the activities themselves are viewed as problems for group—rather than individual—solution. This strategy has implications for enhancing students' self-esteem and for increasing their willingness to spend more time on learning tasks. It also helps students see that they can help each other accomplish tasks and can learn from each other as well as from the teacher or from media.

Assessment Strategies for Constructivist Models

Constructivists tend to eschew traditional assessment strategies as being too limiting to measure real progress in complex learning and too removed from real-life tasks to be authentic. However, teachers recognize that even the most innovative activities require a reliable and valid means of measuring student progress. Assessment and grading strategies commonly used in constructivist environments are given here.

- **Measures of achievement in constructivist environments.** The most common assessment strategies are project assignments (e.g., web pages, multimedia products, desktop published publications), self-report instruments (e.g., student-prepared journals or other descriptions), and portfolio entries. Electronic portfolios often are used as products in themselves or to act as organizing devices for products over time. (See InSight 3.12.)
- **Grading strategies for constructivist products.** Rubrics and performance checklists are frequently used to grade these products. Usually, teachers design their own rubrics and checklists to match the specific performances in their curricula. However, some generic measures (e.g., the Multimedia Project Rubric in Figure A.8 in the Appendix) are becoming more commonly used.

Enabling Integration Strategies: Useful with Either Model

Some integration strategies are more general in purpose and can address the needs of either model. These "enabling" strategies seem to be appearing with increasing frequency in combination with other directed or constructivist strategies described in this chapter. They seem to support the other strategies and make them more feasible and practical.

Integration to generate motivation to learn. Teachers who work with at-risk students often point to the need to capture students' interest and enthusiasm as a key to success and frequently as their most difficult challenge. Some educators assert that today's television-oriented students are increasingly likely to demand more motivational qualities in their instruction than students in previous generations. Constructivists argue that instruction must address students' affective needs as well as their cognitive ones, hypothesizing that students will learn more if what they are learning is interesting and relevant to their needs. They recommend the highly visual and interactive qualities of Internet and multimedia resources as the basis of these strategies. However, proponents of directed methods make similar claims about highly structured, self-instructional learning environments. They say that some students find it very motivating to learn at their own pace, in a private environment, because they receive immediate feedback on their progress. It seems evident that appropriate integration strategies to address motivation problems depend on the needs of the student; either constructivist or directed integration strategies can be used to increase motivation to learn.

Integration to optimize scarce personnel and material resources. Anyone associated with public schools will readily admit that current resources and personnel are not optimal. For example, real problems result from schools having too many students and not enough teachers. Many

INSIGHT 3.12

Portfolios for Student Assessment: How They Work

Why Student Portfolios?

Portfolios are a collection of a student's work products over time, arranged so that they and others can see how their skills have developed and progressed. Portfolios must also include criteria for selecting and judging content. The portfolio concept originated in higher education with colleges of arts, music, and architecture. Work in these areas could not be measured well through traditional tests. Instead of final exams, these students had to have a professional portfolio when they graduated to demonstrate their level of accomplishment in their field. For today's technology-integrated curriculum, which often calls for multimedia work products, many teachers are turning to student portfolios as the assessment strategy of choice. See Barrett (2000) for more advice on portfolio development, and Hanfland (1999) for tips on portfolio development for young children.

What Electronic Formats Are Available?

Although older students could decide on their own portfolio format, teachers usually provide the portfolio structure and tell students how to fill in the content. Teachers can choose from several kinds of resources for these structures. See Barrett (2000) for an in-depth review of the advantages and disadvantages of each:

- **"Ready-made" software packages.** These include the *Learner Profile* (Sunburst) or the *Grady Profile* (Auerbach). Teachers can use these instead of creating their own structure. These systems usually are built on database software, with fields to attach files of written and visual products.
- **PDF documents.** To store and display documents (with or without graphics), teachers can use *Adobe Acrobat* software to create electronic versions of pages. These are essentially "pictures of pages" and are easy to store and share with others.
- **Multimedia authoring software.** Early multimedia structures were in *HyperCard* or *HyperStudio,* but some teachers now structure portfolios with more advanced packages such as *Macromedia Director* or *Authorware.* These packages allow more advanced and sophisticated video and audio presentations. Portfolios also can be structured around multimedia presentation software such as *PowerPoint,* which offers primarily a linear, slideshow-type format but is comparatively easy to develop and display.
- **Databases.** Relational database software such as *FileMaker Pro* and *Microsoft Access* is helpful to teachers who must keep track of many students' work. They offer teachers the advantage of cataloguing work and creating profiles of achievement across groups of students.
- **Web pages.** Portfolios also may be posted on the Internet, where they can be more easily shared with others. Like multimedia packages, these portfolios can offer sophisticated video and audio presentations.
- **Video.** Although analog video offered only a low-cost, linear format, digital video offers much more flexible, interactive formats to display portfolio elements.

How Should a Teacher Use a Portfolio?

Five steps are involved in portfolio development and use:

1. **Deciding on format and structure.** Teachers must decide which electronic format is most appropriate to their needs and those of their students. Except in the case of predesigned packages, the teacher produces a model structure.
2. **Introducing the requirements.** Because students must design their products to fit in the portfolio structure, teachers must introduce the requirements early in the instructional process (e.g., at the beginning of a unit or a school year). An example or model of what the teacher expects in a completed portfolio usually serves this purpose.
3. **Monitoring the collection.** In addition to defining the portfolio structure, teachers also have to set up a classroom management system to make sure students add their products in a timely way.
4. **Assessing progress.** The teacher does frequent assessments of progress and, if desired, has students do presentations of their work.
5. **Providing feedback.** The final step is informing the student of progress and recommending ways to improve the products. Steps 3 through 5 occur on an ongoing basis throughout the development of the portfolio.

The American Association for Higher Education has developed a book on how to create electronic portfolios (*Electronic Portfolios: Emerging Practices in Student, Faculty, and Institutional Learning,* AAHE, 2002) and a searchable database of sample e-portfolios. For more information, see http://aahe.ital.utexas.edu/electronicportfolios/index.html.

Sources: Barrett, H. C. (2000). Create your own electronic portfolio. *Learning and Leading with Technology, 27*(7), 14–21; and Hanfland, P. (1999). Electronic portfolios. *Learning and Leading with Technology, 26*(6), 54–57.

of the courseware materials described in later chapters can help make up for the lack of required resources in the school or classroom—from consumable supplies to qualified teachers. For example, drill-and-practice programs can replace worksheets, a good tutorial program can offer instruction in topics for which teachers are in short supply, and a simulation can let students repeat experiments without depleting chemical supplies or other materials.

Integration to remove logistical hurdles. Some technology tools offer no instructional sequence or tasks but help students complete learning tasks more efficiently. These tools support directed instruction by removing or reducing logistical hurdles to learning. For example, word processing programs do not teach students how to write but let students write and rewrite more quickly, without the labor of handwriting. Computer-assisted design (CAD) software does not teach students how to design a house but allows them to try out designs and features to see what they look like before building models or structures. A CD-ROM may contain only a set of pictures of sea life but can let a teacher illustrate concepts about sea creatures more quickly and easily than with books. The Part II chapters in this textbook discuss tools that make learning more efficient and less laborious for students.

Integration to develop information literacy and visual literacy. A rationale underlying many of the most popular directed and constructivist integration strategies is the need to give students practice in using modern methods of communicating information. For example, when students use presentation software instead of cardboard charts to give a report, they gain experience for college classrooms and business offices where computer-based presentations are the norm. When they develop multimedia book reports, instead of a paper ones, they use more visually complex methods that are commonplace in our media-permeated culture. Using technology to communicate visually represents Information Age skills students will need both for higher education and in the workplace.

Combining Integration Strategies in Curriculum Planning

This chapter and subsequent chapters describe an established, well-documented knowledge base on how to integrate technology resources effectively into both directed instruction and constructivist activities. This chapter proposes that directed and constructivist models each address specific classroom needs and problems and that both will continue to be useful.

But the author of this text goes one step further in this description; they propose that neither model in itself can meet the needs of all students in a classroom. Teachers must merge directed and constructivist activities to form a new and more useful school curriculum. Even Gagné, a leader in promoting systematic, directed methods, proposed that effective, useful instruction sometimes calls for *integration of objectives* in the context of a complex, motivational learning activity that he refers to as an *enterprise* (Gagné & Merrill, 1990). His description of the nature of this enterprise sounds much like the kinds of activities often proposed by constructivists. In fact, one of his three kinds of enterprises calls for a *discovering schema.*

At this time, however, teachers find few practical guidelines for combining directed and constructivist approaches and integration strategies into a single curriculum. The concept of combining them at all is currently in an exploratory stage. Although teachers across the country are probably combining approaches in classroom activities, formal descriptions of effective applications are rare and lack detail. The guidelines and examples given here to indicate how this curriculum development might occur are derived from teachers' writings, discussions, and examples from the literature.

Recommended Guidelines for Designing Technology-Integrated Curriculum

The technology integration planning model described in Chapter 2 can be helpful in planning effective technology-integrated instructional activities. The following guidelines can be helpful as teachers work through this planning.

Match instructional needs with integration strategies. The two models described here each have appropriate uses to meet certain kinds of instructional needs. Figure 3.4 gives a summary of these needs and the strategies that can address them. Note the overlap here between the learning needs described in Chapter 2 (see Figure 2.7) and the instructional needs in Figure 3.4. However, the following points reflect concerns teachers have when structuring an appropriate model.

Match the assessment to the activity. It is especially important to measure students' accomplishments in a way that suits the kinds of learning activities they have done. For example, a teacher should not guide students through a problem-solving activity based on video scenarios, and then give a multiple-choice test on how to solve mathematics word problems. Students know they must earn grades of some kind. As with all classroom learning, they should understand from the start the criteria by which the teacher will measure performance.

Allow enough time. Curriculum that includes constructivist activities requires a long-term view of skills development. Ideally, students experience a combination of teacher-directed and self-directed work throughout their time in school. Curriculum planned for short, discrete lessons leaves little of the flexibility that both teachers and students need to accomplish curriculum goals. Also, when strategies are new to teacher and students, learning activities often take more time than the familiar routines of directed instruction would require. Teachers who are beginning to introduce technology-integrated activities may find that it takes a while to learn the management techniques they need to guide and facilitate learning. Students also need enough time to complete their tasks and follow up on newly discovered interests.

Be flexible. Although planning is essential to successful technology integration, plans should be flexible. If the teacher notices in the middle of a mathematics problem-solving project that students lack prerequisite skills, the lesson may have to stop to allow some direct teaching before it can proceed.

Figure 3.4 Integration Strategies Matched to Teaching/Learning Models

	Types of Instructional Needs	Directed Strategies	Constructivist Strategies
1	Providing for skill remediation	X	
2	Providing for skill mastery and fluency	X	
3	Providing systematic self-instruction	X	
4	Fostering creativity		X
5	Fostering metacognition		X
6	Increasing transfer of knowledge to problem solving		X
7	Fostering group cooperation and problem solving		X
8	Allowing for multiple and distributed intelligences		X
9	Increasing motivation to learn	X	X
10	Optimizing learning resources	X	X
11	Removing logistical hurdles to learning	X	X
12	Fostering information literacy and visual literacy communication skills	X	X

Don't be afraid to experiment. Despite the demands on teachers to prepare their students well, they should have the same opportunity for exploration and risk-taking that they give to students. Teachers will not develop new and more effective methods without making some mistakes along the way. Combining directed and constructivist curriculum requires a delicate balance of informal and formal situations, problem solving and drill and practice, and generated and memorized knowledge. It is a difficult balance to strike, but it is worth the effort.

Examples of Technology-Integrated Units

Directed Integration Strategy: Building Science Vocabulary with Electronic Encyclopedias

This integration is designed to satisfy instructional needs 1, 11, and 12 from Figure 3.4 and is based on ideas from Harriss (1992).

- **Rationale.** Ms. Harriss is a science teacher who finds that a big challenge in teaching her middle school students is helping them expand their science vocabularies. She also finds it difficult to develop students' independent use of reference tools that could help them with later learning in all classes. She finds they will look up words and other information only when she tells them to and only when they need information about a specific item. Even then, they rarely use their findings as study guides. She decides to address all of these needs with an ongoing class assignment to give students practice in using electronic encyclopedias and in word processing study notes.
- **Preparing for encyclopedia use.** Before the first assignment, Ms. Harriss uses one computer and a projection system to show the whole class how to use the encyclopedia and dictionary/glossary feature to look up unfamiliar words. Then she demonstrates how to copy a definition, paste it into a word processing page, and save it into a file on the classroom computer hard drive. As she demonstrates these procedures, she and the students write a set of step-by-step directions on how to use the encyclopedia to look up definitions. After the demonstration is over, she prints these directions, posts them beside the computer station, and places additional copies in a folder where students can get them if they are going elsewhere to use a computer.
- **Research activities.** At the beginning of each new unit (e.g., planets in the solar system), Ms. Harriss reminds the students that part of their assignment for the unit is to look up five new words in the encyclopedia dictionary/glossary, learn the definitions, and paste them into their word processing study file. (She also provides other assignments for them to use the encyclopedia to do small-group research on topics in the unit and report on their results.)
- **Assessment strategies.** At the end of each unit, Ms. Harriss compiles all students' unknown words for the unit on one page of the file and the definitions on another page in the file. She gives each student a copy of

the file and asks them to make sure they can match up the words and definitions. She also makes a *PowerPoint* presentation of the words used in context, one word to a frame, and sets the presentation to display each word automatically for about 10 seconds each, so students see them as they enter the classroom and while they are doing other classwork. During the week that students review for the end-of-unit test, she reminds them to look over their completed words list. She tests their vocabulary knowledge in the written component of the unit exam.

Primarily Constructivist Integration: A Presidential Elections Web Quest

This integration is designed to satisfy instructional needs 6, 7, and 12 from Figure 3.4 and is based on ideas from DeVincentis and King (2000).

- **Rationale.** Mr. King finds that his students have little interest in learning about the processes involved in American elections. Though quick to take positions based on what they have heard from their parents and friends, they are slow to discuss and compare their views with those who differ in their beliefs. Also, they find the details of elections complicated and frustrating. Mr. King knows that these students soon will be voters themselves, and he would like to develop their understanding of how a U.S. election works and the issues and problems involved. He also wants them to learn how to work together better with others to explore issues and develop common positions.
- **Introducing the web quest.** Mr. King uses a web quest format for the activity. He demonstrates the web site and shows students how they can look up assignments and links to materials on it at any time. The site has several parts, which Mr. King reviews with the students:
  - A description of their challenge: to answer questions about current processes in each area of elections and recommend changes where these processes could be improved
  - A list of items to include in their final presentation
  - Web sites they can go to for information on each area
  - A grading rubric for their *PowerPoint* presentations.
- **Learning activities.** The students form small groups of three to four students each with each group assigned to explore web sites and answer questions about a specific area of the elections process: primary caucuses, party conventions and nominations, nominee campaigning, advertising practices, voting processes, the electoral college, and the inauguration. The whole class meets to discuss questions they would like to see answered about each of these processes. The group is to select three to five questions requested by class members and locate information to answer them. They also must give a basic description of how the process works and any problems they see that they feel need to be addressed.
- **Product development, display, and assessment.** Each group presents its findings, displays the *PowerPoint* presentations to the class, and discusses the answers to the students' questions. Mr. King grades the group presentations with the rubric he gave them previously.

Combined Directed and Constructivist Integration: Improving French Language Skills

This integration is designed to satisfy instructional needs 2, 4, 5, 6, 7, and 12 in Figure 3.4.

- **Rationale.** Ms. Gaston, a high school French teacher, has a group of students who have had a previous course in French but are at varying levels of proficiency. Some have problems because they have a relatively small French vocabulary; some have a good grasp of vocabulary but have minor grammatical and structure problems; and some are fairly proficient with the language. The teacher designed a strategy to involve all the students in an activity that will give them practical application of their skills while letting each work from where they are to build proficiency with the language.
- **Introducing the unit.** The teacher explains to students that, through her involvement in an online Internet listserv, she has established contact with a teacher of English in Paris. They will do a joint project in which the students will do a "language exchange" activity resulting in a product. The project will revolve around exploring each other's language as a reflection of their culture. The teacher explains that they will do one such project each semester. This semester, the American group gets to choose the product. The next semester, the French group decides on the product.
- **Learning activities.** She asks the students to think about how our use of language shows things about where we live, what we consider important, and how we think as a culture. She asks them to consider these aspects and suggest products that might help demonstrate similarities and differences between themselves and their French counterparts. After much discussion, they decide to create a dictionary of expressions for various emotions (surprise, anger, affection, disgust) and publish their findings on the school web site. The American group will supply an introduction in French; the Paris class will supply one in English. The teacher forms groups and assigns roles that represent an area of expertise these students have with the language. She explains they each will be graded on his or her contribution to the final product:
  - *Vocabulary group.* These are the students who need work on their French vocabulary. She assigns these

students to brush up on their basic vocabulary with a drill-and-practice program she has tailored to meet their needs and placed in the language lab. If the class needs any vocabulary words, this group is in charge of locating them and spelling them correctly. Also, they will prepare a glossary of major vocabulary words used in the booklet.

- *Grammar and usage group.* Students who need some help with syntax and usage work with a *HyperStudio* tutorial the teacher has prepared. The tutorial reviews the most common language syntax problems for beginners in French. For the class project, this group will oversee the development of the booklet's introduction and description statements.
- *E-mail group.* Students with the highest level of proficiency with the language are assigned to exchange background information, favorite activities, and so on, with their counterparts by writing a series of e-mail messages.

For the first two weeks, the groups spend the first 10 to 15 minutes of each class meeting doing their assigned tasks. Then the groups meet for the remainder of the period to work on the production tasks. The whole class then reviews the products of the e-mail group by viewing them on a large computer monitor. Each group lends its expertise in editing the final messages for vocabulary and syntax before the messages are sent.

- **Product development, display, and assessment.** The following 3 weeks are spent working together to structure the booklet and exchange information with the French students. The final 2 weeks are spent on production tasks. Students prepare their summary and post it on the school's web site. Also, they make a printout and the teacher works with them to prepare a bulletin board to display their work. The teacher grades their work using a cooperative group rubric and a checklist developed for the project.

Exercises

Record and apply what you have learned.

Chapter 3 Self-Test

To review terms and concepts in this chapter, take the Chapter 3 self-test. Select Chapter 3 from the front page of the Companion Website (located at http://www.prenhall.com/roblyer), then choose the *Multiple Choice* module.

Portfolio Activities

ISTE The following activities address ISTE National Educational Technology Standards for Teachers (NETS-T) and will help you add to your professional portfolio. To complete these activities online and save or submit the materials electronically, select Chapter 3 from the front page of the Companion Website (http://www.prenhall.com/roblyer), then choose the *Portfolio* module.

1. ***Overview of Learning Theories (NETS-T Standard: II-B)*** Prepare a chart that summarizes the learning theorists and theories that support directed model and constructivist models. Use the following headings in the format shown in the chart below (a first entry is already given in the chart as an example).
2. ***Contrasts Between Directed and Constructivist Models (NETS-T Standards: II-B, V-A)*** Create a diagram, chart, or caricature (for an example, see Figure 3.1) that shows the differences between the two models described in this chapter. Contrast them according to language they use, teaching/learning problems they address, and/or the methods they use.

Question for Thought and Discussion

These questions may be used for small-group or class discussion or may be subjects for individual or group activities. To take part in these discussions online, select Chapter 3 from the front page of the Companion Website (http://www.prenhall.com/roblyer), then choose the *Message Board* module.

1. Seymour Papert (1987) criticized traditional experimental research methods because they are ". . . based on a concept of changing a single factor in a complex situation while keeping everything else the same . . . [which is] radically incompatible with the enterprise of rebuilding an education system in which nothing will be the same" (p. 22). What aspects of the current education system do you think need to be changed? How do constructivist methods propose to change them? If we do not use experimental research, what methods should we use to determine our changes have improved the education system?

	Name of Theorist(s)	Name of Theory	Three Major Terms Used in the Theory	Applications/ Related Names
Directed Model	B. F. Skinner	Behaviorism	Learning contingencies Reinforcement Observable behaviors	Mastery learning (Benjamin Bloom) Programmed instruction
Constructivist Model				

Collaborative Activities

The following activities address ISTE National Educational Technology Standards for Teachers (NETS-T) and can be done in small groups. Each group should present the findings to the class in a format they know how to use (word-processed report, presentation software, multimedia product). *Each summary should have a graphic representation with it.* Completed group products may be copied and shared with the entire class and/or included in each person's personal portfolio.

1. ***The Directed/Constructivist Debate (NETS-T Standards: II-B, V-B)*** Prepare a debate on the benefits of using directed versus constructivist models for teaching and learning. Each small group should gather evidence to support arguments on *one* of the following aspects of *one* of the models: real, practice problems they address; the soundness of their underlying theories; and the usefulness in preparing students for future education and work. The group members working on the directed models comprise the panel arguing for directed strategies, while the members working on constructivist models comprise the opposite panel. Present the debate in class, with the instructor acting as moderator.
2. ***Directed and Constructivist Examples (NETS-T Standards: II-B, V-B)*** Use Internet resources and software company catalogs to locate an example of a directed learning activity such as remediation of skill weaknesses with drills and tutorials and a constructivist activity such as group projects with multimedia or web page development. Develop a presentation that describes each one and shows why it is a good reflection of the directed or constructivist model.
3. ***Example Integration Strategies (NETS-T Standards: II-B, V-B)*** Each group chooses or is assigned one of the types of technology integration strategies described earlier in this chapter. Each group locates or develops a classroom example that reflects this strategy and presents it to the class *without telling the class the strategy.* The class members identify the strategy being used.

Integrating Technology Across the Curriculum Activities

The *Integrating Technology Across the Curriculum* CD-ROM is a set of technology integration ideas and links to online lessons, arranged as a searchable database. The CD comes packaged with this textbook. Complete the following exercise using this CD:

Look at Figure 3.4 in this chapter, Integration Strategies Matched to Teaching/Learning Models. Select 10 of the technology integration ideas from the CD and make a list of their titles. For each one, identify which type of integration strategy is being used and describe why you think the integration idea is an example of the strategy.

References

Atkinson, R., & Shiffrin, R. (1968). Human memory: A proposed system and its control processes. In K. Spence & J. Spence (Eds.), *The psychology of learning and motivation* (Vol. 2). New York: Academic Press.

Baines, L., & Stanley, G. (2000). We want to see the teacher. *Phi Delta Kappan, 82*(4), 327–330.

Bass, J. (1985). The roots of Logo's educational theory: An analysis. *Computers in the Schools, 2*(2–3), 107–116.

Bateson, D. (1994). Psychometric and philosophic problems in "authentic" assessment: Performance tasks and portfolios. *Alberta Journal of Educational Research, 40*(2), 233–245.

Becker, H. J. (2000, April). Constructivist-compatible beliefs and practices among U.S. teachers. *Teaching, Learning and Computing Newsletter,* University of California at Irvine.

Bereiter, C. (1990). Aspects of an educational learning theory. *Review of Educational Research, 60*(4), 603–624.

Bloom, B. (1986). Automaticity. *Educational Leadership, 43*(5), 70–77.

Bradens, R. (1996). The case for linear instructional design and development: A commentary on models, challenges, and myths. *Educational Technology, 36*(2), 5–23.

Brown, J. S., Collins, A., & Duguid, P. (1989). Situated cognition and the culture of learning. *Educational Researcher, 18*(1), 32–41.

Bruner, J. (1973). *The relevance of education.* New York: W. W. Norton & Company.

Carnine, D. (1993). Effective teaching for higher cognitive functioning. *Educational Technology, 33*(10), 29–33.

Carnine, D., Silbert, J., & Kameenui, E. (1997). *Direct instruction reading* (3rd ed.). Upper Saddle River, NJ: Merrill/Prentice Hall.

Clark, R. E. (1982). Antagonism between achievement and enjoyment in ATI studies. *Educational Psychologist, 17*(2), 92–101.

Cognition and Technology Group at Vanderbilt (1990). Anchored instruction and its relationship to situated cognition. *Educational Researcher, 19*(6), 2–10.

Cognition and Technology Group at Vanderbilt (1991a, May). Integrated media: Toward a theoretical framework for utilizing their potential. *Proceedings of the Multimedia Technology Seminar,* Washington, DC.

Cognition and Technology Group at Vanderbilt (1991b). Technology and the design of generative learning environments. *Educational Technology, 31*(5), 34–40.

Cognition and Technology Group at Vanderbilt (1993). The Jasper experiment: An exploration of issues in learning and instructional design. *Educational Technology Research and Development, 40*(1), 65–80.

Cognition and Technology Group at Vanderbilt (1995). Looking at technology in context: A framework for understanding technology and education research. In D. C. Berliner (Ed.), *The handbook of educational psychology.* New York: Macmillan.

Corey, S. M. (1944). Poor scholar's soliloquy. *Childhood Education, 33,* 219–220.

DeVicentis, C., & King, P. A. (2000). Election 2000 and beyond. *Learning and Leading with Technology, 28*(2), 36–38.

Educational Technology (May 1991), *31*(5); and (September 1991), *31*(9). Special issues on constructivist versus directed approaches.

Educational Technology (October 1993), *32*(10). Special issue on current uses of behavioral theories.

Eggen, P., & Kauchak, D. (2001). *Educational psychology: Windows on classrooms (5th ed.).* Upper Saddle River, NJ: Merrill/Prentice Hall.

Epstein, R. (1993). Generativity theory and education. *Educational Technology, 33*(10), 40–45.

Gagné, R. (1982). Developments in learning psychology: Implications for instructional design. *Educational Technology, 22*(6), 11–15.

Gagné, R. (1985). *The conditions of learning.* New York: Holt, Rinehart & Winston.

Gagné, R., Briggs, L., & Wager, W. (1992). *Principles of instructional design.* Orlando, FL: Harcourt, Brace, Jovanovich.

Gagné, R., & Merrill, R. (1990). Integrative goals for instructional design. *Educational Technology Research and Development, 38*(1), 23–30.

Gagné, R., Wager, W., & Rojas, A. (1981). Planning and authoring computer-assisted instruction lessons. *Educational Technology, 21*(9), 17–26.

Gardner, H. (1983). *Frames of mind.* New York: Basic Books.

Gardner, H., & Hatch, T. (1989). Multiple intelligences go to school: Educational implications of the theory of multiple intelligences. *Educational Researcher, 18*(8), 4–10.

Harriss, S. (1992). Let's build our science vocabularies. *The Florida Technology in Education Quarterly, 4*(2), 71–72.

Hasselbring, T., & Goin, L. (1993). Integrated technology and media. In E. Polloway & J. Patton (Eds.), *Strategies for teaching learners with special needs.* New York: Merrill Publishing Co.

Jungck, J. (1991). Constructivism, computer exploratoriums, and collaborative learning: Construction scientific knowledge. *Teaching Education, 3*(2), 151–170.

Linn, R. (1994). Performance assessment: Policy promises and technical measurement standards. *Educational Researcher, 23*(9), 4–14.

Mallott, R. (1993). The three-contingency model of performance management and support in higher education. *Educational Technology, 33*(10), 21–28.

Molenda, M. (1991). A philosophical critique on the claims of "constructivism." *Educational Technology, 31*(9), 44–48.

National Commission on Excellence in Education. (1983). *A nation at risk.* Washington, DC: U.S. Department of Education.

Ormrod, J. (2001). *Educational psychology: Developing learners (3rd ed.).* Upper Saddle River, NJ: Merrill/Prentice Hall.

Papert, S. (1980). *Mindstorms: Children, computers, and powerful ideas.* New York: Basic Books.

Papert, S. (1987). Computer criticism vs. technocentric thinking. *Educational Researcher, 16*(1), 22–30.

Perkins, D. (1991). Technology meets constructivism: Do they make a marriage? *Educational Technology, 31*(5), 18–23.

Phillips, D. C. (1995). The good, the bad, and the ugly: The many faces of constructivism. *Educational Researcher, 24*(7), 5–12.

Prawat, R. (1993). The value of ideas: Problems versus possibilities in learning. *Educational Researcher, 22*(6), 5–16.

Raspberry, W. (1998, March 30). Sounds bad, but it works. *Washington Post,* p. A25.

Reigeluth, C. (1991). Reflections on the implications of constructivism for educational technology. *Educational Technology, 33*(10), 34–37.

Saettler, P. (1990). *The evolution of American educational technology.* Englewood, CO: Libraries Unlimited.

Sfard, A. (1998). One–two metaphors for learning and the dangers of choosing just one. *Educational Researcher, 27*(2), 4–13.

Skinner, B. F. (1938). *The behavior of organisms.* New York: Appleton.

Skinner, B. F. (1968). *The technology of teaching.* New York: Appleton.

Spence, I., & Hively, W. (1993). What makes Chris practice? *Educational Technology, 35*(6), 5–23.

Spiro, R., Feltovich, P., Jacobson, M., & Coulson, R. (1991). Knowledge representation, content specification, and the development of skill in situation-specific knowledge assembly: Some constructivist issues as they relate to cognitive flexibility theory and hypertext. *Educational Technology, 31*(9), 22–25.

Stein, M., Silbert, J., & Carnine, D. (1997). *Designing effective mathematics instruction: Direct instruction mathematics* (3rd ed.). Upper Saddle River, NJ: Merrill/Prentice Hall.

Taylor, R. (1980). *The computer in the school: Tutor, tool, tutee.* New York: Teachers College Press.

Tennyson, R. (1990). Integrated instructional design theory: Advancements from cognitive science and instructional technology. *Educational Technology, 30*(7), 9–15.

Tinker, R. (1998, Winter). Teaching and learning in the knowledge society. *The Concord Consortium Newsletter,* 1–2, 14.

Tobias, S. (1991). An eclectic examination of some issues in the constructivist–ISD controversy. *Educational Technology, 31*(9), 41–43.

Torgeson, J. (1986). Using computers to help learning disabled children practice reading: A research-based perspective. *Learning Disabilities Focus, 1*(2), 72–81.

Torgeson, J., Waters, M., Cohen, A., & Torgeson, J. (1988). Improving sight word recognition skills in learning disabled children: An evaluation of three computer program variations. *Learning Disabilities Quarterly, 11,* 125–133.

U.S. Department of Labor (1992). SCANS (The Secretary's Commission on Achieving Necessary Skills) report. Washington, DC: U.S. Government Printing Office.

Wager, W. (1992). Instructional systems fundamentals: Pressures to change. *Educational Technology, 33*(2), 8–12.

Willis, J. (1995). A recursive, reflective model based on constructivist-interpretivist theory. *Educational Technology, 33*(10), 15–20.

Young, M. (1995). Assessment of situated learning using computer environments. *Journal of Science Education and Technology, 4*(1), 89–96.

PART II

Integrating Software and Media Tutors and Tools: Principles and Strategies

The chapters in this part will help teachers learn:

1. To identify the various teaching and learning functions that instructional software can fulfill
2. The unique capabilities of each of the resources known as software tools
3. The capabilities and educational applications of multimedia and hypermedia systems
4. To match specific kinds of instructional software and software tools to classroom needs
5. To design lesson integration strategies for instructional software, technology tools, and multimedia/hypermedia.

Introduction

As Part I illustrated, the field of educational technology is characterized by controversy and change, and the dynamic nature of computer technology has only reinforced this characteristic. Lack of consensus about the terminology of instructional technology reflects this changing and evolving nature. As with the terms used to describe directed and constructivist methods (see Part I overview), no agreement has ever emerged about the terms for various educational computing resources or how to categorize them.

Until microcomputers entered schools, classroom computing resources usually were classified under three general headings: computer-assisted instruction (CAI), computer-managed instruction (CMI), and other. CAI usually referred mainly to drill-and-practice, tutorial, and simulation software; CMI encompassed testing, record-keeping, and reporting software. During the 1980s, other authors began using many more inclusive terms to refer to instructional uses of computers such as computer-based instruction (CBI), computer-based learning (CBL), and computer-assisted learning.

In 1980, Taylor proposed a classification system for instructional technology that grouped computer resources according to their functions. This classification system consisted of three terms: tutor, tool, and tutee. The tutor functions included those in which the "computer [was] programmed by experts in both programming and in a subject matter . . . and the student [was] then tutored by the computer" (p. 3). In its tool functions, the computer "had some useful capability programmed into it such as statistical analysis . . . or word processing" (p. 3). Tutee functions helped the student learn about logic processes or how computers worked by "teaching" (programming) computers to perform various activities in languages like BASIC or Logo.

Although many technology-oriented educators still observe these categories by broadening the definitions of *tutor* and *tools* (and dropping the *tutee* designation), the field has produced no neat classification system for technology resources. There simply are too many different resources and applications, and experts have found no feasible way to agree on terminology. The authors of this textbook recommend that *teachers prepare themselves for this lack of consensus on terms and labels so they can recognize the functions of technology products under any name or in any medium.* After teachers recognize the functions each resource fulfills, they will be ready to match functions to their own instructional and productivity needs.

The chapters in Part II deal with technology resources that involve a computer program (software). Some resources such as probeware, a music editor, or a graphing calculator combine software with hardware, such as a probe or a music synthesizer, in order to accomplish their functions. The resources in Part II are addressed in four chapters: instructional software or courseware, productivity software, software tools, and multimedia/hypermedia. Each of these chapters describes resources and suggests integration strategies for them based on directed and constructivist models.

Chapter 4: Integrating Instructional Software into Teaching and Learning

This text usually substitutes the term *courseware* for *instructional software.* Most people think of instructional software as performing a tutor function, which is common to directed instruction models. However, some courseware also can function as a tool in integration strategies that are based on constructivist models. Software described in this chapter fulfills the following instructional roles:

- Tutorial
- Drill and practice
- Simulation
- Instructional games
- Problem solving.

Chapter 4 also covers networked delivery systems that provide these software functions and keep track of students' usage of them. In directed models, these systems usually are termed *integrated learning systems (ILSs).* Educators who implement constructivist models also may use the term ILSs, but they intend different uses of these software tools.

Chapter 5: Integrating Word Processing, Spreadsheet, and Database Software Tools into Teaching and Learning

Chapter 6: Integrating Other Software Tools into Teaching and Learning

Since computers came into common use outside of the business office, software tools have emerged to fill a variety of functions. We call these packages *tool software* because they each make unique contributions to tasks that people need to do. They support students with many repetitive and/or mechanical operations involved in learning, for example:

- Handwriting, when the focus of instruction is writing a story or a composition
- Arithmetic calculations, when the purpose of the lesson is solving algebra problems
- Organizing information, when the purpose of the lesson is showing how to classify animals according to common features
- Presenting information clearly and attractively, when the purpose of the presentation is showing the results of a research project.

Software tools contribute to teaching in the same way that power tools contribute to designing and building a house as compared to using hand tools. Tools make it easier to carry out the mechanics of building the house, but they can also profoundly affect the complexity of the designs that builders may attempt. Similarly, technology tools not only make learning faster and easier, they also make possible more complex, higher level methods than would be achievable without such tools.

Two different chapters focus on tool software. Chapter 5 describes and gives integration strategies for three of the most commonly discussed computer programs under the category of classroom technology tools: word processing, spreadsheet, and database software. The popularity of these tools probably results from two facts. They were among the first tools to be developed and used in education, especially with microcomputers; thus, the literature documents more uses and classroom integration strategies for them than for most of the tools developed later. Also, these three functions are commonly found as components of so-called *integrated software packages* or *software suites*. (These are different from the integrated learning systems or ILSs discussed in Chapter 4.) As parts of a single integrated software package, the products of these tools may be used separately or "copied and pasted" from one to the other. For example, a teacher may prepare an illustration of a budget on a spreadsheet program, copy it, and paste it into a word-processed handout that describes the contents of budgets and how to prepare them. Although word processing, spreadsheet, and database programs usually are discussed and taught together as a group, each has a distinct set of characteristics and range of applications in education.

Even though these three tools have come to be known as "productivity software," Chapter 5 describes and illustrates both productivity and instructional applications for them. Both types of applications are necessary classroom activities, but each fulfills a different purpose to support and enhance teachers' activities:

Productivity Uses

These activities may have little to do with actual teaching (e.g., explaining or illustrating new concepts, or making information clearer or learning activities more enjoyable), but they do help teachers use their time more efficiently so that their subsequent interaction with students can be more meaningful. For example, teachers may record and calculate grades and track club budgets on a spreadsheet; they can then redirect the time they save on this activity to allow more contact with their students. Teachers may keep track of classroom instructional resources suitable for various instructional levels and purposes in a database, which can help them select materials targeted to the needs of each of their students. Productivity applications earn their name because they help make teachers more productive in accomplishing their professional tasks in the same way that technology tools can make office staff more productive for the companies in which they work.

Instructional Uses

Many of the same tools that improve teacher productivity also enhance instruction. For example, a spreadsheet helps students keep track of data during an experiment or predict the effects on sums or averages of changing numbers in a column or row. Students can be taught to develop their own databases to help them learn how to organize and search for information. These tools are called *instructional applications* because they serve valuable purposes in direct learning activities, even though they may not deliver information in the same way a tutorial, drill, or simulation program does.

Chapter 6 describes the features and applications of many more software tools that support teaching and learning tasks. These include resources to save teacher time, products to enhance and support production and presentation tasks, tools for managing data, and other support tools specific to the needs of certain disciplines. Some of these tools, like desktop publishing software and presentation software, are becoming as popular as the "basic three" described in Chapter 5. Others, like MBL or probeware, are targeted to limited, albeit important, instructional functions. This chapter divides software support tools into six general categories or functions:

- **Materials generators** help teachers produce instructional materials.
- **Data collection and analysis tools** help teachers collect and organize numerical information that indicates student progress.
- **Graphics tools** allow production of images and illustration of documents.
- **Planning and organizing tools** help teachers and students conceptualize their work before they begin.
- **Research and reference tools** are electronic versions of encyclopedias, atlases, and dictionaries and are usually stored on CD-ROM.
- **Tools to support specific content areas** assist with activities associated with certain content areas.

Chapter 7: Integrating Multimedia and Hypermedia into Teaching and Learning

The final chapter in Part II focuses on some of the most exciting technology resources in education today. Multimedia and hypermedia applications can be done with a variety of different hardware and software combinations ranging from simple uses of presentation software to sophisticated multimedia authoring systems. Perhaps more than any other technology resources, these applications help teachers and students reflect and draw from the diversity of images and motion that characterize the world around us. To do this, they use resources that range from predrawn, still pictures to full-motion video. This chapter describes each of the configurations that can be used in classrooms, including commercial multimedia software and interactive videodisc systems, and three kinds of authoring software: presentation software, digital video editing systems, and multimedia/hypermedia authoring systems.

4 CHAPTER

Integrating Instructional Software into Teaching and Learning

The fact that individuals bind themselves with strong emotional ties to machines ought not to be surprising. The instruments [we] use become . . . extensions of [our] bodies.

Joseph Weizenbaum in
Computer Power and Human Reason (1976, p. 9)

This chapter covers the following topics:

- Definitions, issues, integration strategies, and technology integration ideas based on a directed instructional model for:
  - Drill-and-practice functions
  - Tutorial functions
- Definitions, issues, integration strategies, and technology integration ideas based on both directed and constructivist models for:
  - Simulation functions
  - Instructional game functions
  - Problem-solving functions
- Characteristics and uses of integrated learning systems (ILSs)
- Criteria and methods for evaluating and selecting software

Objectives

1. For each description of a classroom need for instructional materials, identify one or more types of instructional software functions that could meet the need.
2. Plan lesson activities that integrate instructional software using a directed learning strategy.
3. Plan lesson activities that integrate instructional software using a constructivist learning strategy.

Introduction

What Is Instructional Software?

The *Neuwave* example described in Chapter 2 (Figure 2.6) illustrates an example of what Weizenbaum (1976) called using computers as "extensions of [our] bodies." Such uses have a long history in education. From the time people began to recognize the potential power of a computer to do tasks quickly and systematically, they also began exploring and experimenting with its capability to emulate and improve on the functions of a human teacher. If computer programs could be written to do essentially anything, why could not computers be programmed to teach? Many educators and developers pursued this goal of the computer as teacher during the 1960s and 1970s. Some, like William Norris (1977) who developed Control Data's PLATO teaching systems, believed that computer-based education was the only logical alternative to education's "outdated, labor-intensive ways" (p. 451). Norris believed that education could become more productive if computers were to take over much of the traditional role of teachers.

Today, after about 30 years of development and experimentation, there is less talk of computers replacing teachers, but programs like the one described in the Figure 2.6 example still exist that perform various teaching functions. While these programs are not alternatives to human teachers, as envisioned by Norris, they can enhance teaching and learning in many ways. This chapter shows how programs like the one in the Figure 2.6 lesson empowers teachers, rather than replaces them.

Products written in computer languages (e.g., Basic, Assembler, C++ , Java) and which are designed and developed to perform tasks are called *applications software* or *programs.* Instructional software (or courseware) is applications software that is designed specifically to deliver or assist with student instruction on a topic. Although software such as word processing and spreadsheet programs also can enhance instructional activities, this textbook differentiates between such tools and instructional software. Software tools serve a variety of purposes other than teaching; instructional software packages are programs developed for the *sole purpose* of delivering instruction or supporting learning activities.

Problems in Identifying and Classifying Software Functions

Computer-assisted instruction (CAI) originated in the early days of educational technology as a name for instructional software, and the term is still in common use. However, some kinds of instructional software are designed with more constructivist purposes in mind and do not actually deliver instruction per se; therefore many people consider the term CAI outdated and misleading. Teachers may hear instructional software referred to as *computer-based instruction (CBI), computer-based learning (CBL),* or *computer-assisted learning* along with more generic terms such as *software learning tools.*

Names for the types of instructional software functions also vary, but they are usually identified as drill and practice, tutorial, simulation, instructional game, and problem solving. Although these terms originated because each type had clearly different characteristics and uses, much of today's software defies easy classification for three reasons:

1. **Developers use terms interchangeably.** There seems to be no consensus among developers for what terms to use to describe various types of programs. Some developers refer to a drill program that gives extensive feedback as a *tutorial.* Others refer to *simulations* or *problem-solving* functions as *games.*
2. **Packages contain more than one activity.** Many software packages contain several different activities, each of which serves a different purpose. For example, a program like *Millie's Math House* has a number of straight drill activities along with some problem-solving and game activities.
3. **Software is becoming multimedia.** Tergan (1998) notes that since more software is incorporating hypermedia and multimedia environments (including Internet links), it makes it more difficult to analyze learner–system interactions, isolate instructional roles in a software package, and identify the type of software functions involved.

In light of these issues, educators who use software for instruction will find it useful to analyze all of the activities in a package and classify each one according to its instructional functions. For example, one may not be able to refer to an entire package as a tutorial or a drill, but it is possible and desirable to identify a particular activity according to whether it provides skill practice or opportunities for solving problems. As this chapter will show, each software function serves different purposes during learning and, consequently, has its own appropriate integration strategies.

Insights on Software Classifications and Integration Strategies

Gagné, Wager, and Rojas (1981) suggested a way to look at courseware that can help educators analyze a given product as to its instructional function(s) and design appropriate integration strategies that make use of these functions. Gagné et al. observed that drills, tutorials, and simulations each accomplish a different combination of the Events of Instruction (see them in Chapter 3, InSight 3.3 on Gagné's principles). The nine events are a set of guidelines identified by Gagné that can help teachers arrange optimal "conditions for learning" for various types of knowledge and skills. By determining which of the events a courseware package fulfills, educators can determine the teaching role it serves and where it might fit in the instructional process. The five common courseware types accomplish the following functions:

- **Drills (or drill and practice)** allow learners to work problems or answer questions and get feedback on correctness (accomplishes events 6 and 7).
- **Tutorials** act like human tutors by providing all the information and instructional activities a learner needs to master a topic: information summaries, explanation, practice routines, feedback, and assessment. (Gagné et al. say that a tutorial should accomplish all nine events. However, depending on how it is implemented, it can accomplish at least events 3 through 8).
- **Simulations** model real or imagined systems to show how those systems or similar ones work (accomplishes events 6 and 7, and usually also accomplishes events 2, 4, and 5).
- **Instructional games** are designed to increase motivation by adding game rules to learning activities; usually either drills or simulations (usually accomplishes events 1, 6, and 7).
- **Problem-solving programs** teach directly, through explanation and/or practice, the steps involved in solving problems or help learners acquire problem-solving skills by giving them opportunities to solve problems (can accomplish events 3 through 7 and event 9).

When a teacher evaluates a courseware package for possible use, a recommended strategy is to analyze and identify which Events of Instruction each activity accomplishes, classify it as to type(s), and then design one or more integration strategies that make effective use of its functions. For example, the software and integration example described in Figure 2.6 accomplishes events 5, 6, and 7.

Programming Languages as Instructional Software

This chapter focuses on classroom uses of instructional software, while Chapters 5 and 6 address productivity and instructional uses of the resources known as software tools. However, programming languages may be considered a hybrid software, merging the capabilities of both instructional software and tools. Programming languages were created to develop computer programs that make computers do various tasks. For example, word processing programs are written in programming languages as are drills, tutorials, and other forms of instructional software. However, teachers also use programming languages as a tool to teach as well as to develop programs. (See Technology Integration Idea 4.1.)

One of the most widely known of the programming languages used for instruction is Logo. The work of Seymour Papert (see Chapter 3) and his colleagues at the Massachusetts Institute of Technology made Logo "widely used throughout the world as an introductory programming language and mathematical learning environment for students in elementary and secondary schools" (p. 615). Papert hoped that it would become "a context which is to learning mathematics what living in France is to learning French" (p. 6).

Although not as popular as it was in the 1980s, Logo and its derivative materials such as *Microworlds* software

TECHNOLOGY INTEGRATION IDEA 4.1

Using Programming Languages

TITLE: Problem Solving à la vos Savant

CONTENT AREA/TOPIC: Logic and organizational skills

GRADE LEVEL: Middle to high school

NETS FOR STUDENTS: Standards 1, 6

DESCRIPTION: For high school students, beginning programming is a good way to gain practice in organizational skills that are fundamental to problem solving. This activity is based on a problem from Marilyn vos Savant's *Parade Magazine* column "Ask Marilyn." The column posed this question: "Suppose you are on a game show and you're given a choice of three doors. Behind one is a car; behind the others, goats. You pick a door—say No. 1—and the host, who knows what's behind the other doors, opens another door—say No. 3—which has a goat. He then says to you, 'Do you want to pick door 2?' Is it to your advantage to switch your choice?" (p. 12). Marilyn vos Savant said the odds of winning the car increase from 1-in-3 to 2-in-3 by switching doors. Ask students if they agree. Then show them how to create a program to test their solution.

Source: Wagner, P. (1992). Gamer 1, 2, 3: The vas (sic) Savant challenge. *The Computing Teacher, 19*(5), 12–14.

still are used for many instructional purposes. Logo often is used to introduce young children to problem solving through programming and to explore concepts in content areas such as mathematics, science, and language arts (Galas, 1998; Gonsalves & Lopez, 1998; Weinstein, 1999). Logo also led the way for other programming resources to be used in the same instructional ways. Ploger and Vedova (1999) describe a "programming system" called *Boxer,* which combines a programming language with text processing and graphics capabilities to help students learn number sense concepts.

Drill and Practice Activities

Drill and Practice: Definition and Characteristics

Drill and practice activities provide exercises in which students work example items, usually one at a time, and receive feedback on their correctness. Programs vary considerably in the kind of feedback they provide in response to student input. They range from a simple display like "OK" or "No, try again" to elaborate animated displays or verbal explanations. Some programs simply present the next item if the student answers correctly.

Types of drill and practice are sometimes distinguished by the sophistication with which the program tailors the practice session to student needs (Merrill & Salisbury, 1984). The most basic drill and practice function often is described as a *flashcard activity.* A student sees a set number of questions or problems on the screen and answers one at a time. Examples of instructional software that reflect this type of function are shown in Figures 4.1 and 4.2.

A more sophisticated form of drill and practice moves students on to advanced questions after they get a number of questions correct at some predetermined mastery level; it may also send them back to lower levels if they answer a certain number wrong. Some programs automatically review questions that students get wrong before going on to other levels. Movement between levels often is transparent to students since the program may do it automatically without any indication of what it is doing. Sometimes, however, the program may congratulate students on good progress before proceeding to the next level, or it may allow them to choose their next activities.

Figure 4.1 Drill and Practice in the Word Concepts *small, medium,* and *large* from *Edmark's Millie's Math House*

Student selects shoes from the shelf that fit each foot.

Source: Used by permission of Edmark Corporation.

Figure 4.2 Drill and Practice in Spelling Words from Encore Education Software's *Elementary Advantage*

After reviewing a list of various spelling words and definitions, the computer pronounces a word as its definition appears on the screen. The student types in the word, and the computer tells whether the spelling is correct.

Source: Used by permission of Encore Education Software.

In addition to meeting general criteria for good instructional courseware (see listing and discussion of courseware criteria in Figure 4.12 later in this chapter), well-designed drill and practice programs should also meet other criteria:

Control over the presentation rate. Unless the questions are part of a timed review, students should have as much time as they wish to answer and examine the feedback before proceeding to later questions. If the program provides no specific feedback for correct answers, it usually is acceptable to present later questions without any further entries from students.

Appropriate feedback for correct answers. Although some courseware designers stress the importance of positive feedback for correct answers, not all programs provide it. If students' answers are timed, or if their session time is limited, they may find it more motivating simply to move quickly to later questions. Positive feedback should not be so elaborate and time consuming that it detracts from the lesson's purpose. No matter how attractive the display, students tend to tire of it after a while and it ceases to motivate them.

Better reinforcement for correct answers. Some programs inadvertently motivate students to get wrong answers. This happens when a program gives more exciting or interesting feedback for wrong answers than for correct ones. The most famous example of this design error occurred in an early version of a popular microcomputer-based math drill series. Each correct answer got a smiling face, but two or more wrong answers produced a full-screen, animated crying face that students found very amusing. Consequently, many students tried to answer incorrectly to see it. The company corrected this flaw, but this classic error still exists today in other programs.

Issues Related to Drill and Practice

Drill and practice courseware activities were among the earliest and most well-recognized instructional uses of computers and are still used extensively in schools. These activities have frequently been shown to allow the effective rehearsal students need to transfer newly learned information into long-term memory (Merrill & Salisbury, 1984; Salisbury, 1990). However, drill and practice is also the most maligned of the courseware activities, sometimes informally referred to among its critics as "drill and kill." This derision results, in part, from perceived overuse. Many authors have criticized teachers for presenting drills for overly long periods or for teaching functions that drills are ill suited to accomplish. For example, teachers may expose students to drill and practice courseware as a way of introducing new concepts rather than just practicing and reinforcing familiar ones.

But probably the most common reason for the virulent criticism of drill and practice courseware is its identification as an easily targeted icon for what many people consider an outmoded approach to teaching. Critics claim that introducing isolated skills and directing students to practice them directly contradicts the trend toward restructured curriculum in which students learn and use skills in an integrated way within the context of their own projects that specifically require the skills.

Although curriculum increasingly emphasizes problem solving and higher order skills, teachers still give students on-paper practice (e.g., worksheets or exercises) for many skills to help them learn and remember correct procedures. Many teachers feel that such practice gives students more rapid recall and use of basic skills as prerequisites to advanced concepts. They like students to have what Gagné (1982) and Bloom (1986) call *automaticity* or *automatic recall* of these lower order skills to help them master higher order ones faster and more easily. Kahn (1998–1999) cites drill and practice as a worthwhile software substitute for paper worksheets. The usefulness of drill programs in providing this kind of practice has been well documented, but the programs seem especially popular among teachers of students with learning disabilities (Hasselbring, 1988; Higgins & Boone, 1993; Okolo, 1992). The following are examples of skills for which students could use a drill program to gain necessary proficiency:

- Automatic recall of arithmetic facts is required for most higher level mathematics ranging from long division to algebra.
- Keyboard proficiency is a prerequisite for assignments that require extensive typing.
- Graded compositions require rapid recall and application of correct sentence structure, spelling, and principles of grammar and usage.
- Many schools still require students to memorize facts such as states and capitals and names of planets.
- College entrance exams and other standardized tests require quick recall of many facts

Despite the increasing emphasis on problem solving and higher order skills, it is likely that some form of drill and practice courseware probably will be useful in many classrooms for some time to come. Such programs address needs for these and other required skills. Rather than ignoring drill and practice software as outmoded, teachers should seek to select and use these kinds of programs for uses they can best accomplish.

How to Use Drill and Practice in Teaching

Benefits of drill functions. Drill and practice programs may be used whenever teachers feel the need for on-paper exercises such as worksheets. Drill courseware provides several acknowledged benefits as compared to paper exercises:

- **Immediate feedback.** When students practice skills on paper, they frequently do not know until much later whether or not they did their work correctly. To quote a common saying, "Practice does not make perfect; practice makes permanent." As they complete work incorrectly, students may actually be memorizing the wrong skills. Drill and practice courseware informs them immediately whether or not their responses are accurate, so they can make quick corrections. This helps both "debugging" (identifying errors in their procedures) and retention (helps to place the skills in long-term memory for ready access later).
- **Motivation.** Many students refuse to do the practice they need on paper, either because they failed so much that the whole idea is abhorrent, or they have poor handwriting skills, or simply dislike writing. In these cases, computer-based practice may motivate students to do the practice they need. Computers don't get impatient or give disgusted looks when a student gives a wrong answer.
- **Saving teacher time.** Since teachers do not have to present or grade drill and practice, students can do this activity essentially on their own while the teacher addresses other student needs.

Classroom applications of drill functions. On some occasions, even the most creative and innovative teacher may take advantage of the benefits of drill and practice courseware to have students practice using isolated skills.

■ **To supplement or replace worksheets and homework exercises.** Whenever students have difficulty with higher order tasks ranging from reading and writing to mathematics, teachers may have to stop and identify specific prerequisite skills that these students lack and provide the instruction and practice they need to go forward. In these cases, learning may require a rehearsal activity to make sure information is stored in long-term memory so students can retrieve it easily. Drills' motivation, immediate feedback, and self-pacing can make it more productive for students to practice required skills on the computer rather than on paper.

■ **In preparation for tests.** Despite the new emphasis on student portfolios and other authentic assessment measures, students can expect to take several kinds of objective examinations in their education careers. When they need to prepare to demonstrate mastery of specific skills in important examinations (e.g., for end-of-year grades or for college entrance), drill and practice courseware can help them focus on their deficiencies and correct them. An example integration strategy for drill functions is shown in Technology Integration Idea 4.2.

Guidelines for using drill and practice. Observe the following guidelines when designing integration strategies for drill and practice functions:

■ **Set time limits.** Teachers should limit the time devoted to drill assignments to 10 to 15 minutes per day. This ensures that students will not become bored and that the drill and practice strategy will retain its effectiveness. Also, teachers should be sure students have been introduced previously to the concepts underlying the drills; drill courseware should serve mainly to debug and to help students retain their grasp of familiar concepts.

■ **Assign individually.** Because self-pacing and personalized feedback are among the most powerful benefits of drills, these activities usually work best for individual computer use. However, some teachers with limited technology resources have found other, ingenious ways to capitalize on the motivational and immediate feedback capabilities of drills. If all students in a class benefit from practice in a skill using a drill program, the teacher may divide them into small groups to compete with each other for the best group scores. The class could even be divided into two groups for a "relay race" competition over which group can complete the assignment the fastest with the most correct answers.

■ **Use learning stations.** If not all students need the kind of practice that a drill provides, the teacher may make courseware one of several learning stations to serve students with identified weaknesses in one or more key skills. The key to using drill and practice appropriately is to match its inherent capabilities with the identified learning needs of individual students.

Tutorial Activities

Tutorials: Definition and Characteristics

Tutorial courseware uses the computer to deliver an entire instructional sequence similar to a teacher's classroom instruction on the topics. This instruction usually is expected to be complete enough to stand alone; the student should be able to learn the topic without any help or other materials from outside the courseware. Unlike other courseware activities, tutorials are true teaching courseware. Gagné et al. (1981) stated that good tutorial courseware should address all instructional events. (See the discussion of Gagné's Events of Instruction in Chapter 3.) Gagné et al. show how a tutorial may vary its strategies to accomplish events for different kinds of learning ranging from verbal information to complex applications of rules and problem solving.

TECHNOLOGY INTEGRATION IDEA 4.2

Integration of Drill and Practice Courseware

TITLE: Traffic Officer

CONTENT AREA/TOPIC: Language arts—letter cases

GRADE LEVEL: Elementary

NETS FOR STUDENTS: Standard 3

DESCRIPTION: Each student is given either an upper- or lowercase letter card. Students identify letters as a full group. One child is chosen as the traffic officer. Two areas are designated as parking lots, one for uppercase letters and one for lowercase letters. The traffic officer directs the other students' "cars" to the correct parking lot according to letter case. Students will be guided through this activity by the teacher. After letters are sorted ("cars are parked"), the class counts the number of letters in each group. The teacher introduces the class to the parking lot activity on the *Muppet Word Book* disk. At centers or workshops, individual students or small groups of students practice classifying letter cases with the *Muppet Word Book* parking lot activity and the traffic officer game. Students complete the traffic officer worksheet as an assessment activity.

Source: Cobb, L., Dunn, A., and Henry, G. (1991). Name games. *The Florida Technology in Education Quarterly, 3*(2), 63–66.

People may confuse drill activities with tutorial ones for two reasons. First, drill courseware may provide elaborate feedback that reviewers may mistake for tutorial explanations required by Gagné's events 4 and 5. Even courseware developers may claim that a package is a tutorial when it is, in fact, a drill activity with detailed feedback. Second, a good tutorial should include one or more practice sequences to address events 6 and 7, so reviewers easily become confused about the primary purpose of the package.

Tutorials often are categorized as linear and branching tutorials (Alessi & Trollip, 2001). A simple, linear tutorial gives the same instructional sequence of explanation, practice, and feedback to all learners regardless of differences in their performance. A more sophisticated, branching tutorial directs learners along alternate paths depending on how they respond to questions and whether or not they show mastery of certain parts of the material. Even branching tutorials can range in complexity by the amount of branching they allow and how fully they diagnose the kinds of instruction a student needs.

Some tutorials also have computer-management capabilities; teachers may "tell" such a program at what level to start for a student and get reports on each student's progress through the instruction. Although a tutorial program does not need these components, data collection and management features often make it more useful to teachers.

As the description of Events of Instruction implies, tutorials are most often geared toward learners who can read fairly well, usually older students or adults. Since tutorial instruction is expected to stand alone, it is difficult to explain or give appropriate guidance on-screen to a nonreader. However, some tutorials aimed at younger learners have found clever ways to explain and demonstrate concepts with graphics, succinct phrases or sentences, or audio directions coupled with screen devices.

Figure 4.3 Tutorial on Study Skills from *SkillsBank Study Skills*

In this "finding definitions" study skill, the student sees a sequence of screens with explanations on how to locate and use dictionary definitions. After reading this description and seeing correct examples, the student is given practice items.

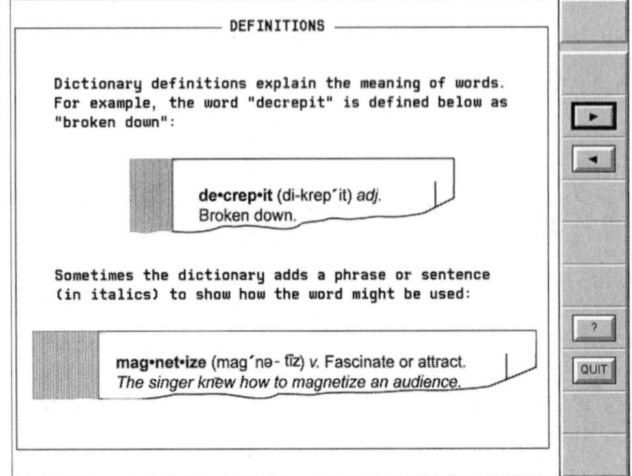

Source: *SkillsBank Study Skills* © 1996 SkillsBank Corporation. Used by permission.

Figure 4.4 Tutorial on States of Matter from Intellectum Plus's *PhysicaElementa: States of Matter*

The student sees a sequence of screens with explanations, descriptions, and animated examples of solids, liquids, gases, and how they can change states. After reading this description, students can view animated demonstrations of these principles.

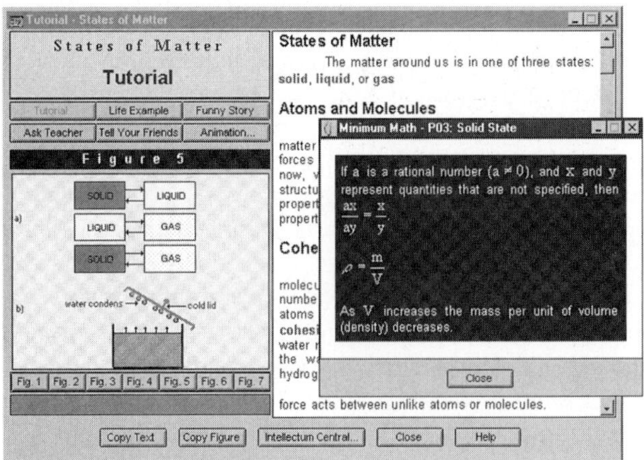

Source: Used by permission of Intellectum Plus.

Some of the best tutorial courseware activities are in packages that accompany newly purchased computers or applications software, for example, *Introduction to Microsoft Works.* While tutorials are found more frequently on mainframe or file server systems than on microcomputers, some good tutorials are available on stand-alone systems. Examples of these tutorials are given in Figures 4.3 and 4.4.

Being a good teacher is a difficult assignment for any human, let alone a computer. However, courseware must accomplish this task to fulfill tutorial functions. In addition to meeting general criteria for good instructional courseware, well-designed tutorial programs should also meet several additional standards:

- **Extensive interactivity.** The most frequent criticism of tutorials is that they are "page-turners," that is, they ask students to do very little other than read. Good tutorials, like good teachers, should require students to give frequent and thoughtful responses to questions and problems and they should supply appropriate practice and feedback to guide students' learning.
- **Thorough user control.** *User control* refers to several aspects of the program. First, students should always be able to control the rate at which text appears on the screen. The program should not go on to the next information or activity screen until the user presses a key or gives some other indication of having completed the necessary reading. Next, the program should offer students the flexibility to review explanations, examples, or sequences of

instruction or move ahead to other instruction. The program should also provide frequent opportunities for students to exit as desired.

- **Appropriate and comprehensive teaching sequence.** The program's structure should provide a suggested or required sequence of instruction that builds on concepts and covers the content adequately. It should provide sufficient explanation and examples in both original and remedial sequences. In sum, it should compare favorably to an expert teacher's presentation sequence for the topic.
- **Adequate answer-judging and feedback capabilities.** Whenever possible, programs should allow students to answer in natural language and should accept all correct answers and possible variations of correct answers. They should also give appropriate corrective feedback when needed, supplying this feedback after only one or two tries rather than frustrating students by making them keep trying indefinitely to answer something they may not know.

Although some authors insist that graphics form part of tutorial instruction (Baek & Layne, 1988), others emphasize judicious use of graphics to avoid interfering with the purpose of the instruction (Eiser, 1988). Eiser is among those who recommend evaluation and record keeping on student performance as part of any tutorial.

Issues Related to Tutorials

Tutorials attract the same criticism as drill and practice for teacher-directed methods; that is, they deliver traditional instruction in skills rather than letting students create learning experiences through generative learning and development projects. Also, since good tutorials are difficult to design and program, critics charge that tutorials represent trivial or even counterproductive uses of the computer. A number of tutorials fail to meet criteria for good programs of this kind, thus contributing to this perception.

Tutorials are difficult to find, even for those who want to use them. Software publishers describe fewer packages as tutorials than any other kind of microcomputer courseware. Part of the reason for this comes from the difficulty and expense of designing and developing them. A well-designed tutorial sequence emerges from extensive research into how to teach the topic well, and its requirements for programming and graphics can become fairly involved. Designers must know what learning tasks the topic requires, what sequence students should follow, how best to explain and demonstrate essential concepts, common errors that students are likely to display, and how to provide instruction and feedback to correct those errors. Tutorials can be large, so they often work slowly on microcomputers. Larger tutorials must be delivered via integrated learning systems or other networked systems, making them expensive.

These problems become still more difficult because teachers frequently disagree about what they should teach for a given topic, how to teach it most effectively, and in what order to present learning tasks. A teacher may choose not to purchase a tutorial with a sound instructional sequence because it does not cover the topic the way he or she presents it. Not surprisingly, courseware companies tend to avoid programs that are problematic both to develop and market.

How to Use Tutorials in Teaching

Benefits of tutorial functions. It is unfortunate that microcomputer tutorials are so rare; a well-designed tutorial on a nontrivial topic can be a valuable instructional tool. Since a tutorial can include drill and practice routines, helpful features include the same ones as for drills (immediate feedback to learners and time savings) plus the additional benefit of self-contained, self-paced substitutes for teacher presentations.

Classroom applications of tutorial functions. Self-instructional tutorials should in no way threaten teachers, since few conceivable situations make a computer preferable to an expert teacher. However, the tutorial's unique capability of presenting an entire interactive instructional sequence can assist in several classroom situations:

- **Self-paced reviews of instruction.** On many occasions, students need repeated instruction on a topic after the teacher's initial presentation. Some students may be slower to understand concepts and need additional time on them. Others seem to learn better in a self-paced mode without the pressure to move at the same pace as the rest of the class. Still others may need review before a test. Teachers can help these students by providing tutorials at learning stations to review previously presented material while the teacher works with other students.
- **Alternative learning strategies.** Tutorials also provide alternative means of presenting material to support various learning strategies. Some students, typically advanced ones, prefer to structure their own learning activities and proceed on their own. A good tutorial allows students to glean much background material prior to meeting with a teacher or others to do assessment and/or further work assignments.
- **Instruction when teachers are unavailable.** Some students have problems when they surge ahead of their class rather than falling behind it. The teacher cannot leave the rest of the class to provide the instruction that such an advanced student needs. Many schools, especially those in rural areas, may not offer certain courses because they cannot justify the expense of hiring a teacher for comparatively few students who will need physics, German, trigonometry, or other lower demand courses. Well-designed tutorial courses, especially in combination with other methods such as distance learning, can help meet these students' needs.

Guidelines for using tutorials. Like drill and practice functions, tutorial functions are designed primarily to serve individuals. Depending on which of the above strategies it promotes, a tutorial may form a classroom learning station or may be available for checkout at any time in a library/media center. Many successful uses of tutorials have been documented over the years (Arnett, 2000; CAI in Music, 1994; Cann & Seale, 1999; Graham, 1994, 1998; Kraemer, 1990; Murray et al., 1988; Steinberg & Oberem, 2000), but microcomputer tutorials that fulfill the functions listed still are found but rarely in classroom use. Although they have considerable value and are popular in military and industrial training, schools and colleges have never fully tapped their potential as teaching resources. The expense of developing them and difficulty of marketing them may be to blame for this situation. However, recent trends toward combining tutorial courseware with video media and distance education may bring tutorial functions into more common use (see Technology Integration Idea 4.3).

Simulation Activities

Simulations: Definition and Characteristics

A simulation is a computerized model of a real or imagined system designed to teach how a system works. Unlike tutorial and drill and practice activities in which the structure is built into the package, learners usually must create their own sequence for using simulations. The person using the courseware usually chooses tasks and the order in which to do them. Alessi and Trollip (2001) identify two main types of simulations: those that teach about something and those that teach how to do something. They further divide the "about" simulations into physical and iterative types and they divide the "how to" simulations into procedural and situational types.

Physical simulations. Users manipulate objects or phenomena represented on the screen. For example, students see selections of chemicals with instructions to combine them to see the result or they may see how various electrical circuits operate. (See Figure 4.5.)

Iterative simulations. These speed up or slow down processes that usually either take so long or happen so quickly that students could not ordinarily see the events unfold. For example, courseware may show the effects of changes in demographic variables on population growth or the effects of environmental factors on ecosystems. Alessi and Trollip (2001) refer to this type as "iterative" because the student can run it over and over again with different values, observing the results each time. Biological simulations like those on genetics are popular, since they help students experiment with natural laws like the laws of genetics by pairing animals with given characteristics and showing the resulting offspring.

Procedural simulations. These activities teach the appropriate sequences of steps to perform certain procedures. They include diagnostic programs, in which students try to identify the sources of medical or mechanical problems, and flight simulators, in which students simulate piloting an airplane or other vehicle (e.g., *Microsoft Flight Simulator* shown in Chapter 2).

Situational simulations. These programs give students hypothetical problem situations and ask them to react. Some simulations allow for various successful strategies such as letting students play the stock market or operate businesses. Others have most desirable and least desirable options such as choices when encountering a potentially volatile classroom situation. (See Figure 4.6.)

TECHNOLOGY INTEGRATION IDEA 4.3

Integration of Tutorial Courseware

TITLE: Interactive Algebra

CONTENT AREA/TOPIC: Mathematics/algebra

GRADE LEVEL: Middle to high school

NETS FOR STUDENTS: Standards 3, 4

DESCRIPTION: Students can use this software as a review after the material has been introduced in class to help ensure that they understand the concepts and are prepared for taking end-of-year exams. Teachers introduce each of the algebra concepts in the usual way. However, instead of assigning worksheets or other practice to make sure students understand and remember concepts, the teacher assigns each student to go through the software tutorial sequence on the topic. Then the teacher holds a cooperative roundtable review. This review is especially important for more complex concepts such as "What do the slope and *x-y* coordinates in a linear equation mean?" As students state one thing they remember about the topic, the teacher or one of the students enters the contribution into a computer connected to a projection system for all to see. Students continue adding information, asking questions, and giving comments about the topic, until the teacher feels that they have an adequate comprehension of the concepts.

Source: Based on ideas from the American Education Corporation's *Advanced Learning System Teacher Resource Guide* (1998).

Figure 4.5 Simulation on Electricity from Edmark's *Virtual Labs: Electricity*

This program provides images of batteries, switches, resistors, and elements necessary to create and test electrical circuits. The student selects elements, places them on a simulated board, and tests them. The program illustrates how they work when properly assembled.

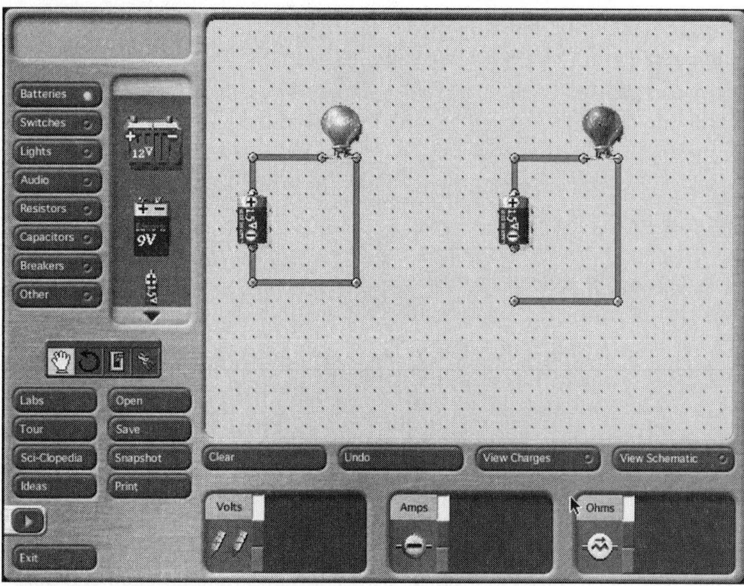

Source: Used by permission of Edmark Corporation.

These types only clarify the various forms a simulation might take. *Teachers need not classify a given simulation into one of these categories.* They need to know only that all simulations show students what happens in given situations when they choose certain actions. Simulations usually emphasize learning about the system itself, rather than learning general problem-solving strategies. For example, a program called *The Factory* has students build products by selecting machines and placing them in the correct sequence. Since the program emphasizes solving problems in correct sequence rather than manufacturing in factories, it should probably be called a problem-solving activity rather than a

Figure 4.6 Simulation from MAXIS/Electronic Arts' *SimCity 2000*™

This popular simulation lets users build their own cities, create a budget for them, populate them, and run them, including responding to intermittent disasters.

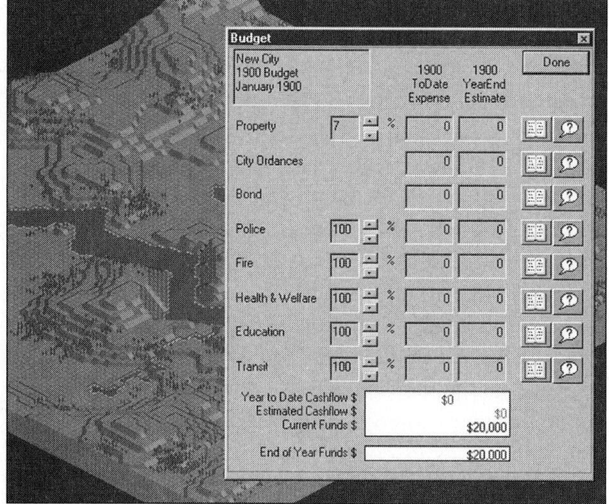

Source: Images courtesy of Electronic Arts™.

simulation. Programs such as *SimCity* (MAXIS/Electronic Arts), which let students design their own cities, provide more accurate examples of building simulations (Adams, 1998).

Since simulations promote such widely varied purposes, it is difficult to provide specific criteria for selecting high-quality ones. By one frequently cited criterion, *fidelity,* a more realistic and accurate representation of a system makes a better simulation (Reigeluth & Schwartz, 1989). However, even this is not a criterion for judging all simulations (Alessi, 1988). Reigeluth and Schwartz describe some design concerns for simulations based on instructional theory. They list important simulation components including a scenario, a model, and an instructional overlay that lets learners interact with the program. Since the screen often presents no set sequence of steps, simulations—more than most courseware—need good accompanying documentation. A set of clear directions helps the teacher learn how to use the program and show the students how to use it rapidly and easily.

Issues Related to Simulations

Most educators acknowledge the instructional usefulness of simulations; however, some are concerned about the accuracy of the programs' models. For example, when students see simplified versions of these systems in a controlled situation, they may get inaccurate or imprecise perspectives on the systems' complexity. Students may feel they know all about how to react to situations because they have experienced simulated versions of them. Many educators feel especially strongly that situational simulations must be followed at some point by real experiences. Many teachers of very young children feel that learners at early stages of their cognitive development should experience things first with their five senses rather than on computer screens.

Some simulations are viewed as complicated ways to teach very simple concepts that could just as easily be demonstrated on paper, with manipulatives, or with real objects. For example, students usually are delighted with the simulation of the food chain called *Odell Lake,* a program that lets students see what animals prey on what other animals in a hypothetical lake. However, some wonder whether or not such a computer simulation is necessary or even desirable to teach this concept. Hasselbring and Goin (1993) point out that students can often master the activities of a simulation without actually developing effective problem-solving skills; on the contrary, such applications actually can encourage counterproductive behaviors. For example, some simulations initially provide little information with which to solve problems, and students are reduced to "trial-and-error guessing rather than systematic analysis of available information" (p. 156). Teachers must carefully structure integration strategies so that students will not use simulations in inappropriate ways.

Simulations are considered among the most potentially powerful computer courseware resources; however, as with most courseware, their usefulness depends largely on the program's purpose and how well it fits in with the purpose of the lesson and student needs. Teachers are responsible for recognizing the unique instructional value of each simulation and using it to best advantage.

How to Use Simulations in Teaching

Benefits of simulation functions. Simulations have long been recognized for their unique teaching capabilities. Depending on the topic, a simulation can provide one or more of the following benefits (Alessi & Trollip, 2001):

- **Compress time.** This feature is important whenever students study the growth or development of living things (e.g., pairing animals to observe the characteristics of their offspring) or other processes that take a long time (e.g., the movement of a glacier). A simulation can make something happen in seconds that normally takes days, months, or longer. Consequently, feedback is faster than in real life and students can cover more variations of the activity in a shorter time.
- **Slow down processes.** Conversely, a simulation can also model processes normally invisible to the human eye because they happen so quickly. For example, physical education students can study the slowed-down movement of muscles and limbs as a simulated athlete throws a ball or swings a golf club.
- **Get students involved.** Simulations can capture students' attention by placing them in charge of things and asking that most motivating of questions: "What would *you* do?" The results of their choices can be immediate and graphic. It also allows users to interact with the program instead of just seeing its output.
- **Make experimentation safe.** Whenever learning involves physical danger, simulations are the strategy of choice. This is true any time students are learning to drive vehicles, handle volatile substances, or react to potentially dangerous situations. They can experiment with strategies in simulated environments that might result in personal injury to themselves or others in real life.
- **Make the impossible possible.** This is the most powerful feature of a simulation. Very often, teachers simply cannot give students access to the resources or the situations that simulations can. Simulations can show students what it would be like to walk on the moon or to react to emergencies in a nuclear power plant. They can see cells mutating or hold countrywide elections. They can even design new societies or planets and see the results of their choices.
- **Save money and other resources.** Many school systems are finding dissections of animals on a computer screen much less expensive than on real frogs or cats and just as instructional. (It also is easier on the animals!) Depending on the subject, a simulated experiment may be just as effective as a learning experience but at a fraction of the cost.

■ **Repeat with variations.** Unlike real life, simulations let students repeat events as many times as they wish and with unlimited variations. They can pair any number of cats or make endless airplane landings in a variety of conditions to compare the results of each set of choices.

■ **Make situations controllable.** Real-life situations often are confusing, especially to those seeing them for the first time. When many things happen at once, students have difficulty focusing on the operation of individual components. Who could understand the operation of a stock market by looking at the real thing without some introduction? Simulations can isolate parts of activities and control the background noise. This makes it easier for students to see what is happening later when all the parts come together in the actual activity.

Classroom applications of simulation functions. Real systems are usually preferable to simulations, but a simulation can suffice when a teacher considers the real situation too time consuming, dangerous, expensive, or unrealistic for a classroom presentation. Simulations should be considered in the following situations, keeping in mind that the real activity is preferable:

■ **In place of or as supplements to lab experiments.** When adequate lab materials are not available, teachers should try to locate computer simulations of the required experiments. Many teachers find that simulations offer effective supplements to real labs, either to prepare students for making good use of the actual labs, or as follow-ups with variations on the original experiments without using up consumable materials. Some simulations actually allow users to perform experiments that they could not otherwise manage or that would be too dangerous for students (see Technology Integration Idea 4.4).

■ **In place of or as supplements to role playing.** When students take on the roles of characters in situations, computer simulations can spark students' imaginations and interests in the activities. However, many students either refuse to role play in front of a class or get too enthusiastic and disrupt the classroom. Computerized simulation can take the personal embarrassment and logistical problems out of the learning experience and make classroom role playing more controllable.

■ **In place of or as supplements to field trips.** Seeing an activity in the real setting can be a valuable experience, especially for young children. Sometimes, however, desired locations are not within reach of the school and a simulated experience of all or part of the process is the next best thing. As with labs, simulations provide good introductions or follow-ups to field trips.

■ **Introducing a new topic.** Courseware that allows students to explore the elements of an environment in a hands-on manner frequently provides students' first in-depth contact with a topic. This seems to accomplish several purposes. First, it is a nonthreatening way to introduce new terms and unfamiliar settings. Students know that they are not being graded, so they feel less pressure than usual to learn everything right away. A simulation can become simply a get-acquainted look at a topic. Simulations can also build students' initial interest in a topic. Highly graphic, hands-on activities draw them into the topic and whet their appetite to learn more. Finally, some software helps students see how certain prerequisite skills relate to the topic; this may motivate students more strongly to learn the skills than if the skills were introduced in isolation from the problems to which they apply. An example of this is *Decisions! Decisions!* software by Tom Snyder on social studies topics such as the U.S. Constitution and elections.

■ **Fostering exploration and process learning.** Teachers often use content-free simulation/problem-solving software as motivation for students to explore their own cognitive processes. Since this kind of courseware

---

TECHNOLOGY INTEGRATION IDEA 4.4

Directed Integration of Simulation Courseware

TITLE: Earthquake!

CONTENT AREA/TOPIC: Earth science concepts

GRADE LEVEL: Elementary

NETS FOR STUDENTS: Standards 3, 5, 6

DESCRIPTION: Students learn to work cooperatively with a group to perform an experiment to explain the movement of an earthquake. The teacher begins with a basic review of an earthquake and its causes and discusses tectonic plates and the role they play in the earth's crust. Students build a simulated building, start up the software, and set up the seismoscope according to directions in the instruction manual. They simulate earthquakes by shaking the table as the software collects data. Students review data gathered and discuss how they show that an earthquake has occurred.

Source: Smith, K. (1992). Earthquake! *The Florida Technology in Education Quarterly, 4*(2), 68–70.

requires students to learn no specific content, it is easier to get them to concentrate on problem-solving steps and strategies. However, with content-free products, it is even more important than usual that teachers draw comparisons between skills from the courseware activities and those in the content areas to which they want to transfer the experience. For example, *The Incredible Laboratory* (Sunburst) presents an implicit emphasis on science process skills that the teacher may want to point out. These kinds of activities may be introduced at any time, but it seems more fruitful to use them just prior to content area activities that will require the same processes.

■ **Encouraging cooperation and group work.** Sometimes a simulated demonstration can capture students' attention quickly and effectively and interest them in working together on a product. For example, a simulation on immigration or colonization might be the "grabber" a teacher needs to launch a group project in a social studies unit (see Technology Integration Idea 4.5).

Guidelines for using simulation functions. Simulations offer more versatile implementation than tutorials or drills. They usually work equally effectively with a whole class, small groups, or individuals. A teacher may choose to introduce a lesson to the class by displaying a simulation or to divide the class into small groups and let each solve problems. Because they instigate discussion and cooperative work so well, simulations usually are considered more appropriate for pairs and small groups than for individuals. However, individual use certainly is not precluded.

The market offers many simulations, but it often is difficult to locate one on a desired topic. The field of science seems to include more simulations than any other area (Andaloro, 1991; Mintz, 1993; Richards, 1992; Ronen, 1992; Simmons & Lunetta, 1993; Smith, 1992), but use of simulations is also popular in social sciences topics (Adams, 1998; Allen, 1993; Clinton, 1991; Estes, 1994). However, more simulations currently are in development and feature videodisc and online supplements to combine the control, safety, and interactive features of computer simulations with the visual impact of pictures of real-life devices and processes.

Instructional Games

Instructional Games: Definition and Characteristics

Instructional games are courseware whose function is to increase motivation by adding game rules to learning activities. Even though teachers often use them in the same way as drill and practice or simulation courseware, games usually are listed as a separate courseware activity because their instructional connotation to students is slightly different. When students know they will play a game, they expect a fun and entertaining activity because of the challenge of the competition and the potential for winning (Randel, Morris, Wetzel, & Whitehill, 1992). Naturally, classroom instruction should not consist entirely of these kinds of activities, no matter how instructional or motivational they are. Teachers intersperse games with other activities to hold attention or to give rewards for accomplishing other activities.

As with simulations, the categories described here merely illustrate the various forms an instructional game may take. Teachers should not feel that they have to classify specific games into categories. But it is important to recognize the common characteristics that set instructional games apart from other types of courseware: game rules,

TECHNOLOGY INTEGRATION IDEA 4.5

Constructivist Integration of Simulation Courseware

TITLE: Community Planning Projects with *SimCity*

CONTENT AREA/TOPIC: Social studies—citizenship/group cooperation in social projects

GRADE LEVEL: 7

NETS FOR STUDENTS: 3, 5, 6

DESCRIPTION: This lesson helps raise students' awareness of responsibility to become informed citizens, shows how they can participate in local decision making, and gives practice in working cooperatively with a group to carry out a social project. The software allows the development of a comprehensive plan for the township. Have a representative from the county planning and zoning office talk with the students about factors of concern to community development. The teacher then introduces students to the *SimCity* software. They form teams of four to five students each and start their own community planning projects with *SimCity*. Each group meets every week to discuss and develop its plan. As a group, they decide how to select and place features such as roads, homes, and utilities. After recording their decisions on paper, they enter them into the program and observe the results. They discuss feedback that the program gives them on areas such as taxes, crime rates, and public opinion. After their plans are complete, each group presents its plan to the teacher and explains and defends their choices.

Source: Jacobson, P. (1992). Save the cities! *SimCity* in grades 2–5. *The Computing Teacher, 20*(2), 14–15.

elements of competition or challenge, and amusing or entertaining formats. These elements generate a set of mental and emotional expectations in students that make game-based instructional activities different from nongame ones.

Since instructional games often amount to drills or simulations overlaid with game rules (see Figure 4.7), the same criteria, such as better reinforcement for correct answers than for incorrect ones, should apply to most games. When Malone (1980) examined the evidence on what makes things fun to learn, he found that the most popular games included elements of adventure and uncertainty and levels of complexity matched to learners' abilities. However, teachers should examine instructional games carefully for their value as both educational and motivational tools. Teachers should also assess the amount of physical dexterity that games require of students and make sure that students will not be frustrated instead of motivated by the activities. Games that call for violence or combat need careful screening, not only to avoid parent criticism, but also because girls often perceive the attraction of these activities differently than boys and because such games sometimes depict females as targets of violence.

Figure 4.7 Instructional Game from Sunburst Communications' *How the West Was One + Three × Four*

The program provides practice in math order of operations. The student tries to move a vehicle along steps on a trail by answering math problems that combine numbers using math order of operations.

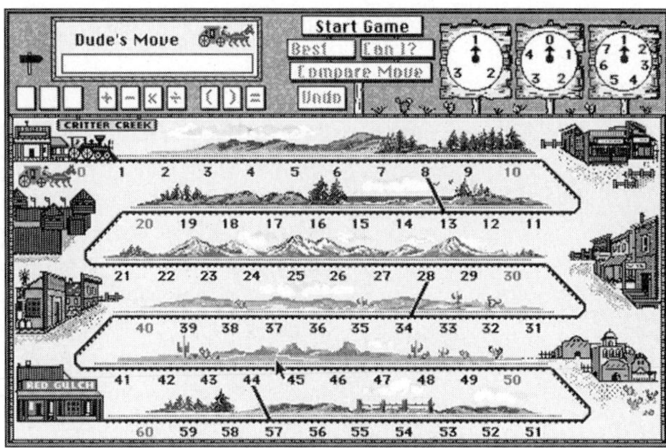

Source: Used by permission of Sunburst Communications.

Issues Related to Instructional Games

A classroom without elements of games and fun would be a dry, barren landscape for students to traverse. In their review of the effectiveness of games for educational purposes, Randel et al. (1992) found "[the fact] that games are more interesting than traditional instruction is both a basic for using them as well as a consistent finding" (p. 270). They also observed that retention over time favors the use of simulations/games. Yet many educators believe that games, especially computer-based ones, are overused and misused (McGinley, 1991). Other teachers believe games convince students that they are escaping from learning, and that they draw attention away from the intrinsic value and motivation of learning. Critics also feel that winning the game becomes a student's primary focus and the instructional purpose is lost in the pursuit of this goal. Observers disagree about whether getting lost in the game is a benefit or a problem.

Some teachers believe that any time they can sneak learning in under the guise of a game, it is altogether a good thing (McGinley, 1991). Other teachers believe that students can become confused about which part of the activity is the game and which part is the skill; they may then have difficulty transferring their skill to later nongame situations. For example, the teacher's manual for Sunburst's *How the West Was One + Three × Four* reminds teachers that some students can confuse the math operations rules with the game rules and that teachers must help them recognize the need to focus on math rules and use them outside the game. Recent studies seem to indicate that instructional games can be useful in fostering higher order skills, but that their usefulness hinges on how teachers employ them (Henderson, Klemes, & Eshet, 2000; Rieber, Smith, & Noah, 1998).

Although students obviously find many computer games exciting and stimulating, educational value sometimes is difficult to pinpoint. Teachers must try to balance the motivation that instructional games bring to learning against the classroom time they take away from nongame strategies. For example, students may become immersed in the challenge of the *Carmen Sandiego* series, but more efficient ways to teach geography may be just as motivating. Successful uses of games have been reported in many content areas (Flowers, 1993; Muckerheide, Mogill, & Mogill, 1999; Trotter, 1991).

How to Use Instructional Games in Teaching

Several kinds of instructional opportunities invite teachers to take advantage of the motivational qualities of games:

- **In place of worksheets and exercises.** This role resembles that of drill and practice (see Technology Integration Idea 4.6).
- **To foster cooperation and group work.** Like simulations, many instructional games serve as the basis for or introductions to group work. A game's interactive and motivational qualities help interest students in the topic and present opportunities for competition among groups.
- **As a reward.** Perhaps the most common use of games is to reward good work. This is a valid role for instructional courseware, but teachers should avoid overuse of it. Otherwise, the game can lose its motivational value and become an "electronic babysitter." Some schools actually bar games from classrooms for fear that they will overemphasize the need for students to be entertained.

TECHNOLOGY INTEGRATION IDEA 4.6

Integration of Instructional Game Courseware: Practicing Math Rules of Operation

TITLE: Please! Please! Remember My Dear Aunt Sally!

CONTENT AREA/TOPIC: Mathematics—order of mathematics operations

GRADE LEVEL: Middle school

NETS FOR STUDENTS: Standards 1, 3

DESCRIPTION: Before beginning instruction, use worksheets to ensure that all students know basic math operations and symbols (+, −, ×, ÷); reteach if necessary. Demonstrate the game to the students and let them play it as a group activity. Make sure the students know that the order of operations is a mathematical rule that always applies and not a game rule applicable only to this program. Explain the mnemonic "Please, Please Remember My Dear Aunt Sally" and the meaning of the order of operations. Worksheets help students practice and remember these rules; the teacher checks and assists with their work. When all students seem able to work the problems, demonstrate *HTWWO* and review the rules. Students practice one game as a group. Make arrangements for students to practice their skills on the game in the classroom or computer lab for a large group activity. Students help each other play the game against the computer. Give special recognition to students who win the most games in a period.

Source: Culpeper, G., Myers, E., and Roblyer, M. D. (1991). Please, please remember my dear Aunt Sally! *The Florida Technology in Education Quarterly, 3*(2), 87–88.

Problem-Solving Courseware

Problem-Solving Courseware: Definition and Characteristics

Teachers may find the topic of problem solving both alluring and perplexing. No goal in education seems more important today than making students good problem solvers, yet no area is as ill defined and difficult to understand. Even scientists have difficulty defining problem solving. Funkhouser and Dennis (1992) quoted an earlier author as saying that "Problem solving [means] the behaviors that researchers who say they are studying problem solving, study" (p. 338). Sherman (1987–1988) was somewhat more specific, claiming that all problem solving involves three components: recognition of a goal (an opportunity for solving a problem), a process (a sequence of physical activities or operations), and mental activity (cognitive operations to pursue a solution). Sherman said that problem solving is a relatively sophisticated mental ability that is difficult to learn and that it is highly idiosyncratic. That is, problem-solving ability depends on "knowledge, prior experience, and motivation, and many other attributes" (p. 8).

This definition of problem solving covers a wide variety of desired component behaviors. The literature mentions such varied subskills for problem solving as metacognition, observing, recalling information, sequencing, analyzing, finding and organizing information, inferring, predicting outcomes, making analogies, and formulating ideas. Since even the definition of problem solving inspires ongoing controversy in education, it is not surprising that opinions differ dramatically about the proper role of courseware and other technology products in helping to foster this important capability. The positions lean toward two general ways in which teachers can view problem solving. Which of these views a teacher uses will determine the strategy for teaching problem solving and the application of related technology resources.

Two views on fostering problem solving. Some teachers view problem solving as a high-level skill that can be taught directly, at least in part, by specific instruction and practice in its component strategies and subskills. Others suggest placing students in problem-solving environments and, with some coaching and guidance, letting them develop their own heuristics for attacking and solving problems. Although the purposes of the two views overlap somewhat, one is directed more toward supplying prerequisite skills for specific kinds of problem solving. The other view aims more toward motivating students to attack problems and to recognize solving problems as an integral part of everyday life. Blosser (1988) confirms this dichotomy, saying that "Problem solving includes . . . an attitude or predisposition toward inquiry as well as the actual processes by which individuals . . . gain knowledge." Students need to combine these two elements; teachers must make ongoing adjustments to the amount of time they spend on each kind of approach in each of several content areas.

Two types of problem-solving courseware for directed instruction. Two distinct types of courseware purport to teach problem-solving skills. One is specific to teaching content area skills, primarily in mathematics. (For example, *The Geometric Supposer* by Sunburst encourages students to learn strategies for solving geometry problems by drawing and manipulating geometric figures.) The other type of problem-solving software focuses on general, content-free skills such as recalling facts, breaking a problem into a sequence of steps, or predicting outcomes. For example, Sunburst's *Memory Castle* is designed to help students remember instructions and follow directions.

Most courseware is specifically designed to focus on one of these two approaches; however, some authors point out that programs can help teach problem solving without being specifically designed to do so (Gore, 1987–1988). Courseware implements numerous approaches to teach each of these kinds of skills. Some use challenge strategies (*The King's Rule* by Sunburst); others use puzzle games (*Safari Search* by Sunburst), adventure games (*Carmen Sandiego* by The Learning Company; *My Make Believe Castle* by Logo Computer Systems), or simulation approaches (*The Factory* by Sunburst). Still others are what might be called problem-solving "environments." These more complex, multifaceted packages offer a variety of tools to allow students to create solutions to problems presented by video scenario (*Alien Rescue,* University of Texas). See Figures 4.8 through 4.11 for examples.

Issues Related to Problem-Solving Courseware

Names versus skills. As mentioned earlier, courseware packages use many terms to describe problem solving and

Figure 4.8 Problem Solving of Sequence Skills from Sunburst Communications' *The Factory*

By selecting a sequence of machines to create a given product, students learn that problems must be analyzed and solved in a certain order to achieve desired results.

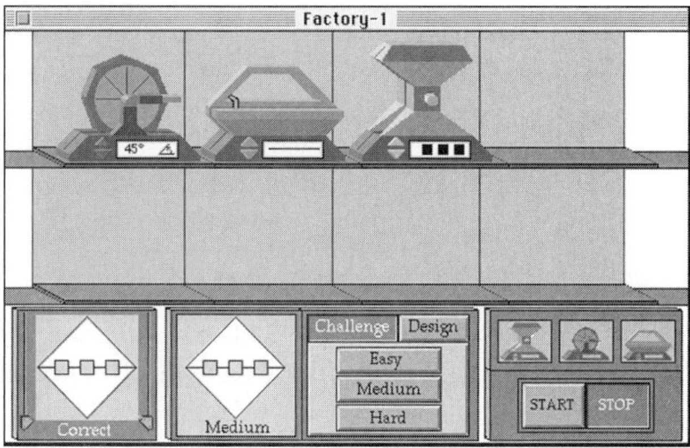

Source: Used by permission of Sunburst Communications.

Figure 4.9 Problem Solving of Confirmation Bias from Sunburst Communications' *The King's Rule*

Students are given a number pattern (e.g., 5, 10, 15, 20) and must determine the rule that results in the pattern by entering other number sequences that also follow the rule. This program helps address the problem of "confirmation bias" that results when students fail to gather sufficient evidence before giving an answer.

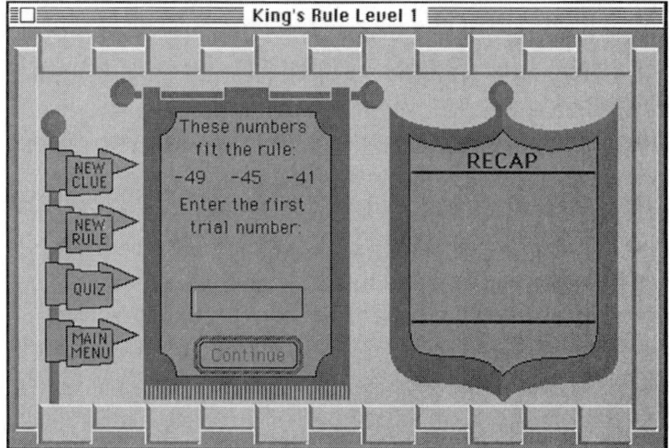

Source: Used by permission of Sunburst Communications.

Figure 4.10 Problem Solving with Geometry from *The Geometer's Sketchpad*

This program is a dynamic construction and exploration tool. Students construct an object and explore its mathematical properties by dragging the object with the mouse. They first visualize and analyze a problem, and then make conjectures before attempting a proof.

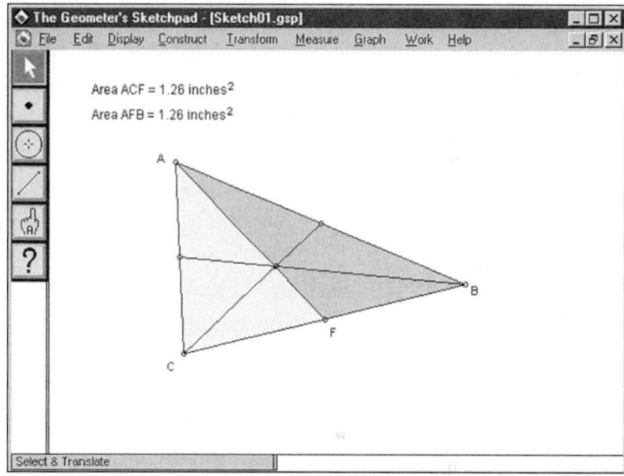

Source: *The Geometer's Sketchpad*®, Key Curriculum Press, 1150 65th Street, Emeryville, CA 94608, 1-800-995-MATH.

Figure 4.11 Problem-Solving Environment from *Alien Rescue*

This program shows a video challenging students to find homes for each of several displaced aliens circling Earth in a spaceship. The software offers a variety of tools to let students research planets and moons in our galaxy.

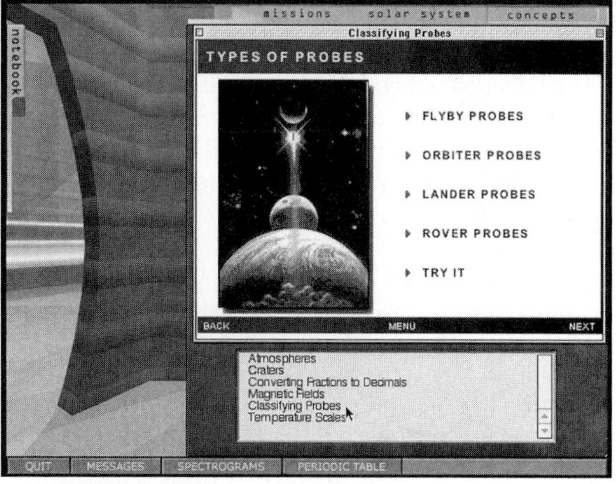

Source: Used by permission of The Alien Rescue Team 2001–2002.

their exact meanings are not always clear. Terms that appear in courseware catalogs as synonyms for problem solving include thinking skills, critical thinking, higher level thinking, higher order cognitive outcomes, reasoning, use of logic, and decision making. In light of this diversity of language, teachers can identify the skills that a courseware package addresses by looking at its activities. For example, a courseware package may claim to teach inference skills. One would have to see how it defines *inference* by examining the tasks it presents, which may range from determining the next number in a sequence to using visual clues to predict a pattern.

Courseware claims versus effectiveness. It would be difficult to find a courseware catalog that did not claim that its products foster problem solving. However, few publishers of courseware packages that purport to teach specific problem-solving skills have data to support their claims. When students play a game that requires skills related to problem solving, they do not necessarily learn these skills. They may enjoy the game thoroughly and even be successful at it without learning any of the intended skills. Teachers may have to do their own field testing to confirm that courseware is achieving the results they want.

Possible harmful effects of directed instruction. Some researchers believe that direct attempts to teach problem-solving strategies actually can be counterproductive for some students. Mayes (1992) reports on studies that found "teaching-sequenced planning to solve problems to high ability learners could interfere with their own effective processing" (p. 243). In a review of research on problem solving in science, Blosser (1988) also found indications that problem-solving instruction may not have the desired results if the instructional strategy does not suit certain kinds of students. For example, students with high math anxiety and low visual preference or proportional reasoning abilities will profit from instruction in problem solving only if it employs visual approaches.

The problem of transfer. Although some educators feel that general problem-solving skills such as inference and pattern recognition will transfer to content-area skills, scant evidence supports this view. In the 1970s and 1980s, for example, many schools taught programming in mathematics classes under the hypothesis that the planning and sequencing skills required for programming would transfer to problem-solving skills in math. Research results never supported this hypothesis. In general, research tends to show that skill in one kind of problem solving will transfer primarily to similar kinds of problems that use the same solution strategies. Researchers have identified nothing like "general thinking skills," except in relation to intelligence (IQ) variables.

How to Use Problem-Solving Courseware in Teaching

Benefits, applications, and guidelines for using directed strategies with problem-solving courseware. Integration of courseware into direct teaching of problem-solving skills places even more responsibility than usual on teachers. Usually, teachers want to teach clearly defined skills. To teach problem solving, they must decide which particular kind of problem-solving ability students need to acquire and how best to foster it. For example, Stokes (1999) recommends that students use a teacher-designed reflection sheet and keep a log of problem-solving strategies and outcomes. With clearly identified skills and a definite teaching strategy, problem-solving courseware has unique abilities to help focus students' attention on required activities. This kind of courseware can get students to apply and practice desired behaviors specific to a content area or more general abilities in problem solving. These six steps can help teachers to integrate courseware for these purposes:

1. Identify problem-solving skills or general capabilities to build or foster skills in:
   a. solving one or more kinds of content-area problems (building algebra equations);
   b. using a scientific approach to problem solving (identifying the problem, posing hypotheses, planning a systematic approach); and
   c. components of problem solving such as following a sequence of steps or recalling facts.
2. Decide on an activity or a series of activities that would help teach the desired skills (see Technology Integration Idea 4.7).
3. Examine courseware to locate materials that closely match the desired abilities, remembering to not judge capabilities on the basis of vendor claims alone.
4. Determine where the courseware fits into the teaching sequence (for example, to introduce the skill and gain attention or as a practice activity after demonstrating problem solving or both).
5. Demonstrate the courseware and the steps to follow in solving problems.
6. Build in transfer activities and make students aware of the skills they are using in the courseware.

Benefits, applications, and guidelines for using constructivist strategies with problem-solving courseware. Like many technology resources, some software with problem-solving functions can be employed in directed ways, but are designed for implementation using more constructivist models. These models give students no direct training in or introduction to solving problems; rather they place students in highly motivational problem-solving environ-

TECHNOLOGY INTEGRATION IDEA 4.7

Problem-Solving Courseware Activity: Addressing Confirmation Bias When Determining Number Rules in Mathematics

TITLE: Are You Sure Your Answer Is Correct?

CONTENT AREA/TOPIC: Mathematics—testing hypotheses in problem-solving strategies

GRADE LEVEL: Middle school

NETS FOR STUDENTS: Standards 3, 6

DESCRIPTION: This activity draws students' attention to the problem of confirmation bias in problem solving. Students play the Hidden Rule Game, in which the program generates three numbers and students have to give their own sets of three numbers that follow the same rule. The program tells them whether or not their sets follow the rule. As students consider the numbers, the teacher must ask questions to help them generate evidence to support their positions. For example, suppose the numbers are 16, 18, 20. Students must be encouraged to gather confirming evidence and submit their rules carefully. They may jump to the conclusion that the rule is "Jumps of two," when it may be "all even numbers" or "ascending numbers."

Source: Johnson, J. (1987). Do you think you might be wrong? Confirmation bias in problem solving. *Arithmetic Teacher, 34*(9), 13–16.

ments and encourage them to work in groups to solve problems. Bearden and Martin (1998) describe such a strategy using a problem-solving software combined with a listserv for students to share their results. (Also see Martin and Bearden, 1998.)

Constructivists believe this kind of experience helps students in three ways. First, they expect that students will be more likely to acquire and practice content-area, research, and study skills for problems they find interesting and motivating. For example, to succeed in the *Carmen Sandiego* software series, students must acquire both some geography knowledge and some ability to use reference materials that accompany the package. Also, they must combine this learning with deductive skills to attack and solve detective-type problems (Robinson & Schonborn, 1991).

Second, constructivists claim that this kind of activity helps keep knowledge and skills from becoming inert because it gives students opportunities to see how information applies to actual problems. They learn the knowledge and its application at the same time. Finally, students gain opportunities to discover concepts themselves, which they frequently find more motivating than being told or, as constructivists might say, *programmed* with the information (McCoy, 1990).

Guidelines for using problem-solving software. Seven steps help teachers integrate problem-solving courseware according to constructivist models:

1. Allow students sufficient time to explore and interact with the software, but provide some structure in the form of directions, goals, a work schedule, and organized times for sharing and discussing results.
2. Vary amount of direction and assistance, depending on each student's needs.
3. Promote a reflective learning environment; let students talk about their work and the methods they use.
4. Stress thinking processes rather than correct answers.
5. Point out the relationship of courseware skills and activities to other kinds of problem solving.
6. Let students work together in pairs or small groups.
7. For assessments, use alternatives to traditional paper-and-pencil tests.

Problem-solving and simulation activities work so similarly in constructivist models that it usually is difficult to differentiate between them. Integration strategies for either usually are the same.

Integrated Learning Systems

Integrated Learning Systems: Definition and Characteristics

Integrated learning systems (ILSs) are the most powerful—and the most expensive—of available courseware products, primarily because they are more than just courseware and because they require more than one computer to run them. From the time they were introduced in the early 1970s until recently, ILSs were computer networks: a combination of instruction and management systems that ran on terminals or microcomputers connected to a larger computer. However, a new way of providing ILS-type capability is offering the curriculum online via the Internet, rather than through a local network.

Regardless of the delivery system, an ILS is characterized by a "one-stop shopping" approach to providing courseware, what Brush (1998) refers to as a "turnkey implementation process for integrating computer-based education into a curriculum" (p. 7). Each ILS offers a variety of instructional techniques in one place, usually as a package complete with technical maintenance and teacher training. They present strengths like prepared curricula and ease of use so that school personnel need not know a great deal about technology to use them. Consequently, they usually simplify integration decisions by defining schoolwide curriculum rather than individual lessons.

In addition to providing a combination of drill and practice, tutorial, simulation, problem-solving, and tool courseware, an ILS is capable of maintaining detailed records on individual student assignments and performance data and supplying printouts of this information to teachers. Bailey and Lumley (1991, p. 21) include the following as characteristics of an ILS:

- Instructional objectives specified, with each lesson tied to those objectives
- Lessons integrated into the standard curriculum
- Courseware that spans several grade levels in comprehensive fashion
- Management systems that collect and record results of student performance.

ILS courseware and management software are housed on a central computer or *server,* which students may access via a local network or the Internet. As each student signs onto a microcomputer connected to the server or Internet, the file server sends (or downloads) student assignments and courseware to the station and proceeds to keep records on what the students do during time spent on the system. The teacher makes initial assignments for work on the system, monitors student progress by reviewing ILS printouts, and provides additional instruction or support where needed.

The first ILSs on the market in the 1970s were primarily drill and practice delivery systems designed to improve student performance on the isolated skills measured by standardized tests. These self-contained, mainframe-based systems predated the microcomputer era, and they did not run any software besides their own. Usually housed in labs, they were designed for use in pull-out programs to supplement teachers' classroom activities, that is, students were pulled out of classrooms daily or weekly and sent to ILS labs for remedial or reinforcement work. However, these systems have evolved into multipurpose products that can run software and courseware other than their own; they can now provide a variety of instructional support from enrichment to complete curriculum. As with other media such as videodiscs, school districts view ILSs as alternatives to traditional classroom materials such as textbooks. Brush reported that as of 1998, estimates were that between 11% and 25% of all U.S. schools owned ILSs.

The courseware component of an ILS. Instructional activities available on an ILS range from simple drill and practice to extensive tutorials. Many ILSs are moving toward complete tutorial systems intended to replace teachers in delivering entire instructional sequences. An ILS usually includes instruction on the entire scope and sequence of skills in a given content area; for example, it may cover all discrete mathematics skills typically presented in grades 1 through 6.

The management system component of an ILS. The capability that differentiates ILSs from other networked systems is the emphasis on individualized instruction tied to records of student progress. A typical ILS gives teachers progress reports across groups of students as well as the following kinds of information on individual performance:

- Lessons and tests completed
- Questions missed on each lesson by numbers and percentages
- Numbers of correct and incorrect tries
- Time spent on each lesson and test
- Pretest and post-test data.

Issues Related to ILSs

The costs of ILSs. The primary criticism of ILSs centers on their expense compared to their impact on improving learning. Bentley (1991) warned that "The search for less expensive alternatives to the ILS is only logical considering how difficult it would be to find options that are *more* expensive" (p. 25). ILS proponents, on the other hand, feel that the students who experience the most success with ILSs are those whose needs are typically most difficult to meet (Bender, 1991; Bracy, 1992; Shore & Johnson, 1992). ILS proponents say there is value in any system that can help potential dropouts stay in school or help remedy the deficiencies of students with learning disabilities. They point to studies and personal testimony from teachers over the years that attest to the motivational qualities of allowing students to work at their own pace and experience success each time they work on the system.

Research on ILS impact. When Becker (1992) reported his summary of some 30 studies of ILS effectiveness, he found widely varied results with various implementation methods and systems. Students generally tend to do somewhat better with ILSs than with other methods, and results were sometimes substantially superior to non-ILS methods. But Becker found no predictable pattern for successful and unsuccessful ILSs. He concluded that data were not sufficient either to support or oppose the purchase of an ILS in a given school or district.

A subsequent large-scale study of ILS use in Indiana reported by Estep, McInerney, and Vockell (1999–2000) found no differences on statewide achievement test scores between schools who did and did not use an ILS. An extensive study of ILS use in New York City schools reported varying results (Miller, 1997). However, Brush, Armstrong, and Barbrow (1999) found that two different resources offered in the same ILS had different impacts on achievement. Individualized software designed to provide foundations instruction had less impact than software that could be selected by teachers to supplement their own instruction. In summary, it seems to be as Van Dusen and Worthen (1995) observed: The impact of ILS varies greatly with implementation methods.

Concerns about the role of ILSs. In a follow-up to his literature review on ILS uses, Becker (1994) criticized uses of ILSs that encourage "mindless adherence to the principle of individualized instruction" (p. 78). Brush (1998) agreed with Becker, finding that ". . . lack of teacher involvement (in ILS use) has led to improper coordination between classroom-based and computer-based instructional activities . . . and lack of teacher understanding regarding effective strategies and procedures for using ILSs" (p. 7).

An early concern expressed by many educators (White, 1992) that the cost of ILSs combined with the comprehensive nature of their curricula might cause schools to view them as replacements for teachers has not yet proven to be a real problem. However, the fear expressed by Maddux and Willis (1993) remains: that ILSs can have the effect of shaping or driving a school's curriculum rather than responding to it.

Despite the amount of curriculum they cover and the number of activities they include, the success of ILSs hinges primarily on how they are viewed and implemented. When used only as a teacher replacement to provide individual student instruction, they seem less effective. When viewed as a supplement to other teacher methods and carefully integrated into a total teaching program, they seem more likely to have the desired impact on raising achievement.

One way to ensure appropriate and cost-effective uses of ILS products may be through a careful, well-planned purchasing process that involves both teachers and administrators. One such process was developed by the California Department of Education (Armstrong, 1999). This five-stage process (planning, pre-evaluation, evaluation, selection, and implementation/post-evaluation) is designed to "establish selection procedures that ensure that . . . curricular goals remain at the heart of the selection process" (p. 3). Guidelines to potential ILS purchasers based on those offered by Smith and Sclafani (1989), Chrisman (1992), and Vaille and Hall (1998) are summarized here:

- Clearly identify the problem the ILS is supposed to solve and understand the instructional theory on which the system is based.
- Determine whether the ILS is a closed system (one that provides 80% or more of the instruction for a given course) or an open system (one linked to the school's resources).
- Find out if the system's scope and sequence are matched to that of the school.
- Determine the target population for which the system was designed and whether or not it closely matches the characteristics of students with whom the ILS will be used.
- Consider the adequacy of the reporting and management system for the school's needs.
- Consider how much of its resources the school must spend on hardware and software.
- Project the educational benefits to the school from the system and compare them with the costs.
- Request that vendors inform the school on ILS updates.
- Carefully evaluate the grade-level courseware, management system, customization, and online tools and be sure they match the school's expectations.
- Set up reasonable terms of procurement and calculate the personnel and fiscal impact of the ILS.

How to Use ILSs in Teaching

Since an ILS creates a combination of the materials already described previously in this chapter, its potential benefits are similar. The highly interactive, self-pacing features of an ILS can help to motivate students who need highly structured environments; these activities free up the teacher's time for students who need personal assistance. Also, teachers can personalize instructional activities for each student by reviewing the extensive information on student and class progress provided by the ILS management system.

Successful uses of ILSs have been reported for two different kinds of teaching approaches: directed and constructivist.

Directed applications for ILSs. In a directed teaching approach, an ILS system can be used for remediation and as a mainstream delivery system.

- **For remediation.** Although ILSs are expensive alternatives to other kinds of delivery systems, White (1992) observes that "they will probably play an increasing role in the large urban systems that have faced achievement test scores that seem intractable to the usual classroom solutions" (p. 36). However, schools still must determine how ILS functions coordinate and complement those of the classroom teacher. Most ILS uses serve target populations that have typically presented the most difficult problems for traditional classroom activities: Chapter I groups, ESOL students, special education students, and at-risk students. Schools have tried and usually failed to reach these students with other methods.

■ **As a mainstream delivery system.** Rather than using an ILS only as a backup system to address educational problems, a school may let an ILS do the initial job of teaching whole courses for all students in a grade level. In light of the expense of ILSs, these uses are more rare. However, some alternative projects, like the Edison Project (Walsh, 1999), predict that the costs of using technology in this way will amount to substantially less over time than teacher salaries. Using ILSs to increase student-to-teacher ratios has stimulated ongoing debate and study.

In either of these uses, teachers still have important roles to play. As Blickman (1992) puts it, "ILSs allow teachers a comfortable transition from the role of deliverer of instruction to manager of instruction . . . [T]eachers are still actively engaged in the teaching process but as 'guides' or facilitators as opposed to distributors of information" (p. 46). American educators generally assume that ILSs should not be seen as "teacher proof" but rather "teacher enhancing." Teachers must still assign initial levels of work, follow up on student activities on the system, and give additional personal instruction when needed.

Constructivist applications for ILSs. Just as an integrated learning system combines several kinds of courseware to create a skill-based, directed learning environment, a network can also combine several kinds of technology resources to support the goals of constructivist learning approaches. When networks provide technology resources of constructivist design and use, the resulting products are sometimes labeled with terms other than ILS to differentiate them from what some educators consider more traditional uses of technology. For example, they may be called *integrated technology systems (ITSs), integrated learning environments, multimedia learning systems,* or *open learning systems* (Armstrong, 1999; Hill, 1993, p. 29).

ILS products useful for constructivist purposes provide varieties of unstructured tools on the same networked system as directed ones. Typically, there will be some kind of information bank (electronic encyclopedias), symbol pads (word processing and/or desktop publishing software), construction kits (Logo or other graphic languages or tools), and phenomenaria (computer simulations and/or problem-solving resources). They also usually have data-collection systems to track student usage of the system (Mageau, 1990). Thus, this kind of networked product can provide what Perkins (1991) called a "rich environment."

Evaluating and Selecting Instructional Software

In the 1980s, microcomputer courseware began to flood the educational market from such diverse sources as state projects, major publishing houses, and even cottage industries. This torrent made educators increasingly aware that simply putting instructional routines on the computer did not ensure that they would take advantage of its potential power as an instructional tool. Indeed, some of the products were so bad that they could be worse than no instruction at all.

It was during this era that courseware quality became a major issue in education and courseware evaluation evolved into a popular and highly publicized practice. Many professional magazines created sections to report the results of product evaluations; indeed, whole magazines like *Courseware Review* were developed to publish such evaluations. The Northwest Regional Lab's Microsoft Project and the Educational Products Information Exchange (EPIE) were just two of the many organizations that sprang up for the sole purpose of reviewing and recommending good instructional courseware.

As the field of educational technology matured and educators refined their attitudes toward computer use, the mystique of courseware faded and assumed more of the mundane aspects of purchasing any good instructional material. During the 1980s, teachers primarily evaluated and selected their own courseware. Now, state- and school district-level personnel increasingly control these purchases. Thus, the evaluation procedures and criteria have changed considerably from the early days of microcomputers. Regardless of who chooses the products, teachers should recognize that just because courseware addresses certain topics or skills, it does not mean that it will meet their needs.

The Need for Evaluation

Courseware quality is less troublesome now than it was in the early days of microcomputers when technical soundness frequently caused problems. For example, courseware programming did not anticipate all possible answers a student might give and did not account for all possible paths through a sequence of instruction. Consequently, programs frequently would "break" or stop when these unusual situations occurred. Early courseware also strongly emphasized entertainment value, giving less attention to educational value.

Courseware producers have obviously learned much from their early errors and problems, and overall quality has improved considerably. But educators still have good reasons for spending some time reviewing and/or evaluating courseware before selecting it for classroom use. Computerized instruction is not necessarily effective instruction, and eye-catching screen displays should not be the primary criteria for selecting materials.

Teachers should review courseware even after prescreening by committees or experts. Very often, state- or district-level committees are responsible only for selecting courseware that does not have gross problems and reaches the desired general level in a general content or topic area. Each teacher must then determine which specific curriculum needs and specific grade levels the package addresses and whether or not courseware functions fit with planned teaching strategies. It cannot be emphasized enough that courseware must match clearly identified instructional needs. It should *not* be used simply because it is available at a discount or supplied free by the state or district.

Courseware Evaluation Procedures: A Recommended Sequence

Evaluation procedures and criteria vary dramatically depending on whether a teacher is selecting courseware for a single classroom or is part of a district-level committee screening materials for use by many schools. One major difference is that committees generally must justify decisions to purchase one package over another by using weighted criteria checklists and assigning total point scores to individual packages. Small groups or individual teachers use much less formal procedures and criteria.

This section is designed primarily for individual teachers or small organizations like individual schools that (1) do not have large organizations purchasing courseware for them, (2) wish to supplement resources purchased for them by others, or (3) want to review preselected courseware to determine its usefulness for their immediate needs. These procedures are intended to help teachers anticipate and deal with problems related to courseware quality and to assist them in matching courseware to their classroom needs. The following sequence is recommended when selecting courseware for classroom use:

1. **Begin with an identified need.** Know what topics and skills you want to address and how you think you will use technology. This will require some knowledge of what kinds of instructional support technology has to offer.

2. **Locate titles.** As mentioned earlier in this section, teachers should probably not base their courseware purchasing decisions on descriptive reviews. Recommendations from colleagues and professional magazines and journals should serve primarily as leads. Some good sources for leads are:

- The Association for Supervision and Curriculum Development's (ASCD) summary of "Only the Best" software produced from their review of 25 annual software evaluations from organizations in the United States and Canada (ASCD, 1999)
- ISTE's *2001 Educational Software Preview Guide* (Johnson, 2001) with hundreds of reviewed and recommended titles
- The California Instructional Technology Clearinghouse, a searchable database with hundreds of software reviews, is available at http://clearinghouse.k12.ca.us
- The Educational Software Selector (TESS), a searchable database produced by the Consumers Union and containing more than 19,000 software product descriptions, is available at http://www.epie.com.

Once teachers discover a package they find interesting, they should use one or both of the next two general procedures to determine its usefulness.

3. **Complete hands-on reviews.** There is no substitute for running the courseware. Teachers should avoid reviewing demo packages (abbreviated versions of actual courseware), which can be misleading substitutes for the real thing. A typical hands-on review consists of two or three passes through a program: once to assess the package's capabilities and what it covers, and again to make incorrect responses and press keys that aren't supposed to be pressed in order to determine the program's ability to handle typical student use. Depending on its capabilities, the teacher may choose to go through the program one more time to review the usefulness and/or quality of particular demonstrations or presentations. Evaluation checklists such as the one given later in this chapter (see Figure 4.12) are usually helpful to guide teachers in a hands-on review. Tergan (1998) says that, given the number of packages teachers have to choose from and the time it takes to review each one, checklists can be a useful tool if the evaluator knows what to look for. He advocates that teachers either develop their own checklist or adopt one that seems thorough and well designed. Though many checklists are based on rating software and assigning points to various aspects, teachers usually are much less concerned with a total score than with making sure they have looked at all relevant characteristics.

4. **Collect student reviews.** Experienced teachers usually can tell from their own hands-on reviews when instructional materials are appropriate for their students. Even so, they are sometimes surprised at student reactions to courseware. Students sometimes encounter unexpected problems, or they may not seem to get out of the activity what the teacher expected they would. If at all possible, it is beneficial to field test courseware by observing students using it, getting their reactions, and, if possible, collecting data on their achievement. Gill, Dick, Reiser, and Zahner (1992) describe a detailed method for evaluating software that involves collecting data on student use.

Courseware Evaluation Procedures: Recommended Criteria

The set of recommended evaluation criteria in Figure 4.12 represents a synthesis from many sources (Comer & Geissler, 1998; Hoffman & Lyons, 1997; Roblyer, 1983). Teachers may find it helpful to use the essential criteria checklist shown in Figure 4.13 for the first pass, then use the more comprehensive list for a second pass. In addition to these essential criteria, teachers also may want to review the optional criteria described in Figure 4.14. These criteria may make the difference when teachers locate two or more packages that meet the essential criteria.

Figure 4.12 Explanation of Essential Criteria for Evaluating Instructional Courseware

Many sets of courseware criteria are available, but they tend to vary widely depending on the educational philosophy of the evaluator and the courseware functions being reviewed. Courseware criteria may be divided into two types: those that confirm *essential characteristics* are present and criteria that review *optional or situational characteristics* and are sometimes applicable and sometimes not, depending on the user's needs. The following is a comprehensive list of *essential criteria* based on Roblyer (1983), Hoffman and Lyons (1997), Lockard and Abrams (2001), and Vaille and Hall (1998). (See the essential criteria checklist in Figure 4.13. In addition to the following essential characteristics, this checklist contains a recommended format for such checklists, as well as essential criteria specific to several types of course functions.)

I. Essential Instructional Design and Pedagogy Characteristics: Does It Teach?

- **Appropriate teaching strategy, based on best known methods.** This covers a wide range of needs related to teaching methodology, e.g., providing enough examples for concept development, presenting ideas in a logical order, and including various components required for learning. For example, most educators would consider a mathematics package to be pedagogically flawed if it is intended for very young children and has no graphics. Learners at early stages of development are known to need concrete examples rather than text only.
- **Presentation on screen contains nothing that misleads or confuses students.** One particularly blatant error of this type was in a courseware package intended to teach young children about how the human body works. It depicted the human heart as a square box. Another, a math program, displayed a number of objects based on what the student answered, but never bothered to change the number of objects if it was a wrong answer. Thus, the student could be seeing the corrected numeral but the wrong number of objects.
- **Comments to students not abusive or insulting.** Programs must be sensitive to student's feelings, even if comments are intended humorously. One program based on a well-known cartoon cat with an acerbic personality belittled the student's name, saying "What kind of name is that for a worthy opponent?" It also commented on the student's "lack of mental ability" when a wrong answer was supplied. Although this was in keeping with the cat's persona, it was still inappropriate.
- **Readability at an appropriate level for students who will use it.** Although this may apply to any use of language in any program, it is particularly applicable to tutorials, which may require many explanations. For example, one tutorial for math skills at about the second-grade level had a great many explanations to read at about a fourth-grade level. This would probably not be an appropriate expectation for students who were having trouble with this level of math.
- **Graphics fulfill important purpose and are not distracting to learners.** Pictures and animation are considered motivational to students, but this is not always true. For example, animated feedback may be charming the first 10 times the students see it, but may achieve just the opposite effect after that. Also, some courseware attracts students' attention by flashing text or objects on the screen. This can be distracting when one is trying to focus on other screen text. Early courseware used a device called "scrolling" which had text moving up the screen as the student tried to read it, but this was quickly identified as a distracting mechanism and is rarely seen now.

II. Essential Content Characteristics: Is Content Accurate, Current, and Appropriate?

- **No grammar, spelling, or punctuation errors on the screen.** Even though a program may be on a nonlanguage topic, it should reflect correct spelling, grammar, and word uses, since students learn more than just the *intended* skills from instructional materials. One early courseware release on punctuation skills misspelled the word "punctuation" three different ways in the program!
- **All content accurate and up to date.** Many people are surprised to find accuracy errors with courseware material; they seem to trust content presented on a computer, as if the computer would correct the text itself if it becomes out of date! Content inaccuracies have been observed in a number of packages. For example, one program referred to blood as a "red substance," which, of course, is not always true. Instructional materials in social studies should be carefully screened for inaccurate reflections of country names, which are changing rapidly. Examples should be free of slang or other content that dates material and makes it less than useful to current students.
- **No racial or gender stereotypes; not geared toward only one sex or to certain races.** Look for diversity in the names and examples used. Are they all for "Dick and Jane" and are they always in the suburbs? Also review examples for gender stereotypes. Are all doctors men? Are all homemakers women? One famous simulation package required that students sign on only as males!
- **Social characteristics.** Does courseware exhibit a sensitive treatment of moral and/or social issues? For example, do games and simulations avoid unnecessary violence?
- **Match to instructional needs.** Does courseware match district or state curriculum objectives teachers are required to teach?

Figure 4.12 *(continued)*

III. Essential User Interface Characteristics: Is It "User Friendly" and Easy to Navigate?

- **User has appropriate control of movement within the program.** Depending on the purpose of the program, students normally should be able to go from screen to screen and read each screen at their own desired rate. They should also have obvious exit options available at any time.
- **User can turn off sound, if desired.** Since courseware may be used in classrooms, the teacher should have the ability to make the courseware quiet so it will not disturb others.
- **Interface is intuitive.** Screens and usage are consistent, allowing students to be able to use the software without extensive assistance.

IV. Essential Technical Soundness Characteristics: Does It Work Correctly?

- **Program loads consistently, without error.** A common problem in early courseware, problems of this kind now are seen rarely.
- **Program does not break, no matter what the student enters.** Again, this was a more common problem in early courseware. Programs should be designed to expect any possible answer, not just the correct or most obvious ones. When unexpected answers are entered, they should give an appropriate response to get the student back on track.
- **Program works on desired platform.** If one needs a Macintosh OS-based program, a program written exclusively for Windows is of little use (and vice versa). Also, the program should work on the version of the operating system one needs (e.g., Windows NT vs. Windows 2000).
- **Program does what the screen says it should do.** If the screen indicates the student should be able to exit or go to another part of the program, this capability should be allowed as stated.
- **Online links work correctly.** A feature in many new courseware packages is the capability of linking students to Internet web sites for additional demonstrations or interactions with others. If links are given, they should work as designated. If links are to nonworking sites, the user should have the option to eliminate or correct them.
- **Videos and animations work correctly.** If a screen is to display a moving graphic object (e.g., video or animation), it should work as indicated. Sometimes, a graphic requires so much memory it works too slowly to be practical for the classroom.

Selecting Software for Constructivist Versus Directed Uses

Although descriptions of instructional software in the literature are changing, many references to courseware evaluation criteria and evaluation methods focus on products to be used with directed instruction. While many criteria are appropriate for software designed for both kinds of uses, additional details often are lacking on what to look for in software that will be used with constructivist methods. Constructivist activities tend to emphasize multimedia and distance learning products rather than drill or tutorial software. For example, Litchfield (1992) lists criteria for "inquiry-based science software and interactive multimedia programs." Checklists by Hoffman and Lyons (1995) and Vaille and Hall (1998) are among those that include criteria for more open-ended products. Further criteria and methods for evaluating multimedia and online multimedia products will be discussed in Chapters 7 and 8.

Figure 4.13 Essential Criteria Checklist for Evaluating Instructional Courseware

The following is an example checklist based on essential qualities that can be used to discriminate between acceptable and unacceptable courseware material. If courseware does not meet these criteria, it probably should not be considered for purchase. For each item, indicate Y for yes if it meets the criterion, or N for no if it does not.

Title ______________________ Publisher ______________________

Content Area ______________________ Hardware Required: ______________________

Courseware functions:

______	Drill and practice	______	Instructional game
______	Tutorial	______	Problem solving
______	Simulation	______	Other:

I. Instructional Design and Pedagogical Soundness

______ Teaching strategy is matched to student needs/levels and is based on accepted methods
______ Presentation on screen contains nothing that misleads or confuses students
______ Readability and difficulty are at an appropriate level for students who will use it
______ Comments to students are not abusive or insulting
______ Graphics fulfill important purpose (motivation, information) and are not distracting to learners

Criteria specific to drill-and-practice functions:

______ High degree of control over presentation rate (unless the method is timed review)
______ Appropriate feedback for correct answers (none, if timed; not elaborate or time consuming)
______ Feedback is more reinforcing for correct than for incorrect responses

Criteria specific to tutorial functions:

______ High degree of interactivity (not just reading information)
______ High degree of user control (forward and backward movement, branching upon request)
______ Comprehensive teaching sequence so instruction is self-contained and stand-alone
______ Adequate answer-judging capabilities for student-constructed answers to questions

Criteria specific to simulation functions:

______ Appropriate degree of fidelity (accurate depiction of system being modeled)
______ Good documentation available on how program works

Criteria specific to instructional game functions:

______ Low quotient of violence or combat-type activities
______ Amount of physical dexterity required appropriate to students who will use it

II. Content

______ No grammar, spelling, or punctuation errors on the screen
______ All content accurate and up to date
______ No racial or gender stereotypes; not geared toward only one sex or to certain races
______ Exhibits a sensitive treatment of moral and/or social issues (e.g., perspectives on war or capital punishment)
______ Content matches required curriculum objectives

III. User Flexibility

______ User normally has some control of movement within the program (e.g., can go from screen to screen at desired rate; can read text at desired rate; can exit program when desired)
______ Can turn off sound, if desired
______ Interface is easy to use (e.g., similar format from screen to screen for forward and back movement in program)

IV. Technical Soundness

______ Program loads consistently, without error
______ Program does not break, no matter what the student enters
______ Program does what the screen says it should do
______ Program works on desired platform
______ If included, online links work as indicated
______ If included, animations and videos work as indicated

Decision:

______ Is recommended for purchase and use
______ Is not recommended

Figure 4.14 Optional Criteria for Evaluating Instructional Courseware

Teachers reviewing courseware may consider a great many other criteria depending on their needs, the program's purpose, and the intended audience. These are detailed in Roblyer (1983), Hoffman and Lyons (1997), Lockard and Abrams (2001), and Vaille and Hall (1998). Many of these criteria, which are listed below, are subjective in nature or dependent on teacher needs; it is up to the teacher to decide whether or not the courseware meets them and/or whether or not they are important enough to affect selection decisions.

Optional Instructional Design Criteria

- **Stated objectives.** Does the courseware state its objectives and are stated objectives likely to be attained through courseware activities?
- **Prerequisite skills.** Are skills specified that students will need in order to use the courseware activities and are students likely to be able to acquire the skills?
- **Interest quotient.** Are examples and strategies likely to interest students at the targeted level?
- **Presentation logic.** Do instructional units follow a logical sequence based on skill hierarchies?
- **Tests.** Do tests match stated skills and are they good measures of the skills?
- **Significance.** Are stated skills "educationally significant" (e.g., in the curriculum)?
- **Use of medium.** Does courseware make good use of computer capabilities?
- **Field testing.** Is there evidence the courseware has been used with students and revised based on this feedback before its release?

Optional Interface/Navigation Criteria

- **Student ease of use.** Is the program easy to use for the intended students? Does it require physical dexterity to answer items the students may not have even though they know the correct answers? Is a lot of typing required?
- **Required keys.** Are the keys required to input answers easy to remember (e.g., pressing back arrow for going back)?
- **Input devices.** Are alternate input devices allowed to make courseware more usable for special populations?
- **Directions.** Are there on-screen directions on how to use it?
- **Shortcuts.** Lengthy introductory screens may be bypassed, if desired.
- **Support materials.** Are there print support materials to support on-screen activities?
- **Optional assistance.** Is a "HELP" feature available if the student runs into difficulty?
- **Optional directions.** Can students skip directions, if they desire, and go straight to the activities?
- **Creativity.** Do materials foster creativity rather than just rote learning?
- **Summary feedback.** Are students given an on-screen summary of performance when they finish working?

Optional Teacher Use Criteria

- **Teacher ease of use.** Can teachers figure out, with minimum effort, how to work the program?
- **Management.** Does courseware contain adequate record-keeping and management capabilities?
- **Teacher manuals.** Are clear, nontechnical teacher manuals available with the courseware? Are manuals well produced and do they include a good table of contents and index?
- **Ease of integration.** Are courseware materials designed to integrate easily into other activities the teacher is doing?
- **Teacher assistance.** Does courseware improve the teacher's ability to teach the subject?
- **Adaptability.** Can teachers modify and adapt the courseware for their needs by changing content (e.g., spelling words) or format (e.g., animated versus written feedback)?

Optional Presentation Criteria

- **Graphics features.** Are graphics, animation, and color used for instructional purposes rather than flashiness?
- **Colors.** Are colors required or is software still useful on noncolor monitors?
- **Screen layout.** Are screens so "busy" or cluttered that they interfere with reading?
- **Audio and speech capabilities.** Is audio and speech of adequate quality so students can understand it easily?
- **Video and animation.** Do moving graphics display clearly, quickly, and without jerkiness? Are they in a high enough resolution to be useful?
- **Required peripherals.** Does the program require peripherals the schools are likely to have (e.g., light pens, speech synthesizers)?
- **Screen printing.** Can key screens from the courseware (e.g., summary performances) be printed?

Figure 4.14 ***(continued)***

Optional Technical Criteria

- **Response judging.** Does the response judging allow for ALL possible correct answers and disallow ALL possible incorrect ones?
- **Timing.** Does the program present itself quickly so displays and responses are accomplished without noticeable delays?
- **Portability.** Can teachers transfer the courseware from one machine to another?
- **Compatibility.** Does courseware run on more than one platform?
- **Components.** Are all required drivers and plug-ins identified and either provided or easily downloadable online?
- **Technical manuals.** Do teacher or user manuals contain technical documentation on program operation and any technical features or options? Does the manual tell how to install and uninstall the program?

Optional Publisher Support

- **Cost effectiveness.** Is the price of the package appropriate in light of what it accomplishes?
- **Available versions.** Is the program available in desired versions (e.g., network or site license)? Does the company provide for free or discounted upgrades later?
- **Preview allowed.** Will the company allow free previews? Will they refund the purchase price or supply a replacement if user is not satisfied, or if software is lost, stolen, or damaged?
- **Backup.** Is a backup disk provided or can user make one?
- **Training.** For more complicated course packages, is on-site or web-based training provided to buyers, and is there a newsletter or other way to communicate applications and updates?
- **Packaging.** Is it made to stand up to normal school and classroom wear? Are disks labeled clearly as to program part and platform?
- **Ongoing support.** Does the company answers questions and provide help for problems via local representatives, a toll-free telephone line, or a web site?

Exercises

Record and apply what you have learned.

Chapter 4 Self-Test

To review terms and concepts in this chapter, take the Chapter 4 self-test. Select Chapter 4 from the front page of the Companion Website (located at http://www.prenhall.com/roblyer), then choose the *Multiple Choice* module.

Portfolio Activities

ISTE The following activities address ISTE National Educational Technology Standards for Teachers (NETS-T) and will help you add to your professional portfolio. To complete these activities online and save or submit the materials electronically, select Chapter 4 from the front page of the Companion Website (http://www.prenhall.com/roblyer), then choose the *Portfolio* module.

1. ***Instructional Software Examples (NETS-T Standards: I-B, II-C)*** From instructional software packages, select at least one that represents each function described in this chapter. Using word processing or multimedia software, prepare a description of the software that focuses on which function(s) it fulfills.
2. ***Instructional Software in a Content Area (NETS-T Standards: I-B, II-C, V-B)*** On the Internet, do a search for software examples in your content area or grade level. Prepare a list of the sites with good examples of each type of software function.

Questions for Thought and Discussion

These questions may be used for small-group or class discussion or may be subjects for individual or group activities. To take part in these discussions online, select Chapter 4 from the front page of the Companion Website (http://www.prenhall.com/roblyer), then choose the *Message Board* module.

1. The tendency to refer to drill and practice software by the derogatory term "drill and kill" is growing. Is this because the number of situations is diminishing in which drill and practice software would be the strategy of choice or because people fail to recognize appropriate situations for using it?
2. Some schools, like those with a college preparatory focus, do not allow the use of instructional games of any kind. Is there a compelling case to be made for allowing the use of instructional game software to achieve specific educational goals? That is, can games do something in an instructional situation that no other strategy is able to do? If so, what?

Collaborative Activities

ISTE

The following activities address ISTE National Educational Technology Standards for Teachers (NETS-T) and can be done in small groups. Each group should present the findings to the class in a format they know how to use (word-processed report, presentation software, multimedia product). Completed group products can be copied and shared with the entire class and/or included in each person's personal portfolio.

1. ***Courseware Evaluation (NETS-T Standards: I-B, II-C)*** Class members obtain one or more example instructional software packages, either from the instructor or from their own schools. Working in small groups, each selects one of the categories of software criteria (e.g., instructional design, content, user interface) from the courseware criteria checklists in Figures 4.17 and 4.18. Using the criteria under the category, the groups evaluate the courseware package. Each group also identifies the functions they believe are represented in the package. Each group prepares a description and demonstration to illustrate the software characteristics they observe. They present these to the class.
2. ***Matching Curriculum Needs with Instructional Software (NETS-T Standards: II-A, B, C)*** Instructor and students agree on a set of specific state or national (e.g., NCTE, NCTM, NSTA) curriculum standards and/or skills on which each small group will work. Each group identifies one or more instructional software packages that could help teachers address each skill. They present their findings to the class.
3. ***Lesson Integration Strategies for Instructional Software (NETS-T Standards: II-A through E; II-C, D; III-B; IV-A, B)*** Using the five-step integration sequence described in the lesson in Chapter 2, Figure 2.6, example, small groups prepare an integration sequence for an instructional software package to be used in a real or fictional classroom. (Students should pay special attention to the "justification" description in Step 1: What's the Relative Advantage—Why Use Instructional Software?) They present their findings to the class.

Integrating Technology Across the Curriculum Activities

The *Integrating Technology Across the Curriculum* CD-ROM is a set of technology integration ideas and links to online lessons, arranged as a searchable database. The CD comes packaged with this textbook. Complete the following exercise using this CD:

Simulations are considered some of the most powerful and versatile of the instructional software functions. Most simulations are used in science and social studies content areas, but the ways they are integrated differ greatly between the two content areas. Locate three to five integration ideas for science and a like number for the social studies area; compare and contrast the integration strategies used in the two lessons. Prepare a two-paragraph description summarizing the differences in integration strategies between science simulations and social studies simulations, and identify what you can conclude about the instructional needs simulations can meet in each content area.

References

Adams, C. (1998). Teaching and learning with SimCity 2000. *Journal of Geography, 97*(2), 47–55.

Alessi, S. (1988). Fidelity in the design of computer simulations. *Journal of Computer-Based Instruction, 15*(2), 40–47.

Alessi, S., & Trollip, S. (2001). *Multimedia for learning: Methods and development.* Needham Heights, MA: Allyn and Bacon.

Allen, D. (1993). Exploring the earth through software. Teaching with technology. *Teaching PreK–8, 24*(2), 22–26.

Andaloro, G. (1991). Modeling in physics teaching: The role of computer simulation. *International Journal of Science Education, 13*(3), 243–254.

Armstrong, S. (1999). *A framework for evaluating integrated learning systems/multimedia instructional systems.* Modesto, CA: California Instructional Technology Clearinghouse.

Arnett, P. (2000). Mastering reading and writing with technology. *Media & Methods, 37*(1), 12–14.

Association for Supervision and Curriculum Development (ASCD). (1999). *Only the best: The annual guide to the highest rated educational software and multimedia.* Alexandria, VA: Author (ERIC Reproduction No. ED 437 897).

Baek, Y., & Layne, B. (1988). Color, graphics, and animation in a computer-assisted learning tutorial lesson. *Journal of Computer-Based Instruction, 15*(4), 31–35.

Bailey, G., & Lumley, D. (1991). Supervising teachers who use integrated learning systems. *Educational Technology, 31*(7), 21–24.

Bearden, D., & Martin, K. (1998). My make believe castle: An epic adventure in problem solving. *Learning and Leading with Technology, 25*(5), 21–25.

Becker, H. (1992). Computer-based integrated learning systems in the elementary and middle grades: A critical review and synthesis of evaluation reports. *Journal of Educational Computing Research, 8*(1), 1–41.

Becker, H. (1994). Mindless or mindful use of integrated learning systems. *International Journal of Educational Research, 21*(1), 65–79.

Bender, P. (1991). The effectiveness of integrated computer learning systems in the elementary school. *Contemporary Education, 63*(1), 19–23.

Bentley, E. (1991). Integrated learning systems: The problems with the solution. *Contemporary Education, 63*(1), 24–27.

Blickman, D. (1992). The teacher's role in integrated learning systems. *Educational Technology, 32*(9), 46–48.

Bloom, B. (1986). Automaticity. *Educational Leadership, 43*(5), 70–77.

Blosser, P. (1988). Teaching problem solving—Secondary school science (ERIC Document Reproduction No. ED 309 049).

Bracy, G. (1992). The bright future of integrated learning systems. *Educational Technology, 32*(9), 60–62.

Brush, T. (1998). Embedding cooperative learning into the design of integrated learning systems: Rationale and guidelines. *Educational Technology Research and Development, 46*(3), 5–18.

Brush, T., Armstrong, J., & Barbrow, D. (1999). Design and delivery of integrated learning systems: Their impact on student achievement and attitudes. *Journal of Educational Computing Research, 21*(4), 475–486.

CAI in music. (1994). *Teaching Music, 1*(6), 34–35.

Cann, A., & Seale, J. (1999). Using computer tutorials to encourage reflection. *Journal of Biological Education, 33*(3), 130–132.

Chrisman, G. (1992). Seven steps to ILS procurement. *Media and Methods, 28*(4), 14–15.

Clinton, J. (1991). Decisions, decisions. *The Florida Technology in Education Quarterly, 3*(2), 93–96.

Comer, R., & Geissler, C. (1998). *A methodology for software evaluation.* Paper presented at the 1998 meeting of the Society for Information Technology and Teacher Education, Washington, DC, March 10–14 (ERIC Document Reproduction No. ED 421 140).

Eiser, L. (1988). What makes a good tutorial? *Classroom Computer Learning, 8*(4), 44–47.

Estep, S., McInerney, W., & Vockell, E. (1999–2000). An investigation of the relationship between integrated learning systems and academic achievement. *Journal of Educational Technology Systems, 28*(1), 5–19.

Estes, C. (1994). The real-world connection. *Simulation and Gaming, 25*(4), 456–463.

Flowers, R. (1993). New teaching tools for new teaching practices. *Instructor, 102*(5), 42–45.

Funkhouser, C., & Dennis, J. (1992). The effects of problem-solving software on problem-solving ability. *Journal of Research on Computing in Education, 24*(3), 338–347.

Gagné, R. (1982). Developments in learning psychology: Implications for instructional design. *Educational Technology, 22*(6), 11–15.

Gagné, R., & Merrill, M. D. (1990). Integrative goals for instructional design. *Educational Technology Research and Development, 38*(1), 23–30.

Gagné, R., Wager, W., & Rojas, A. (1981). Planning and authoring computer-assisted instruction lessons. *Educational Technology, 21*(9), 17–26.

Galas, P. (1998). From presentation to programming. *Learning and Leading with Technology, 25*(4), 18–21.

Gill, B., Dick, W., Reiser, R., & Zahner, J. (1992). A new model for evaluating instructional software. *Educational Technology, 32*(3), 39–48.

Gonsalves, D., & Lopez, J. (1998). Catch your students with microworlds games. *Learning and Leading with Technology, 26*(3), 19–21.

Gore, K. (1987–1988). Problem solving software to implement curriculum goals. *Computers in the Schools, 4*(3–4), 7–16.

Graham, R. (1994). A computer tutorial for psychology of learning courses. *Teaching of Psychology, 21*(2), 116–166.

Graham, R. (1998). A computer tutorial on the principles of stimulus generalization. *Teaching of Psychology, 25*(2), 149–151.

Hasselbring, T. (1988). Developing math automaticity in learning handicapped children. *Focus on Exceptional Children, 20*(6), 1–7.

Hasselbring, T., & Goin, L. (1993). Integrating technology and media. In E. Polloway & J. Patton (Eds.), *Strategies for teaching learners with special needs* (5th ed.). New York: Merrill.

Henderson, L., Klemes, J., & Eshet, Y. (2000). Just playing a game? Educational simulation software and cognitive outcomes. *Journal of Educational Computing Research, 22*(1), 105–129.

Higgins, K., & Boone, R. (1993). Technology as a tutor, tools, and agent for reading. *Journal of Special Education Technology, 12*(1), 28–37.

Hill, M. (1993). Chapter I revisited: Technology's second chance. *Electronic Learning, 13*(1), 27–32.

Hoffman, J. L., & Lyons, D. L. (1997). Evaluating instructional software. *Learning and Leading with Technology, 25*(2), 52–56.

Johnson, J. (1987). Do you think you might be wrong? Confirmation bias in problems solving. *Arithmetic Teacher, 34*(9), 13–16.

Johnson, J. M. (2001). *2001 educational software preview guide.* Eugene, OR: ISTE.

Kahn, J. (1998–1999). The same but different: The computer as an alternate medium. *Learning and Leading with Technology, 26*(4), 15–18.

Kraemer, K. (1990). SEEN: Tutorials for critical reading. *Writing Notebook, 7*(3), 31–32.

Litchfield, B. (1992). Science: Evaluation of inquiry-based science software and interactive multimedia programs. *The Computing Teacher, 19*(6), 41–43.

Lockard, J., & Abrams, P., (2001). *Computers for twenty-first century educators* (5th ed.). New York: Longman.

Maddux, C., & Willis, J. (1993, Spring/Summer). Integrated learning systems: What decision-makers need to know. *ED TECH Review,* 3–11.

Mageau, T. (1990). ILS: Its new role in schools. *Electronic Learning, 10*(1), 22–24.

Malone, T. (1980). *What makes things fun to learn? A study of intrinsically motivating computer games.* Palo Alto, CA: Xerox Palo Alto Research Center.

Martin, K., & Bearden, D. (1998). Listserv learning. *Learning and Leading with Technology, 26*(3), 39–41.

Mayes, R. (1992). The effects of using software tools on mathematics problem solving in secondary school. *School Science and Mathematics, 92*(5), 243–248.

McCoy, L. (1990). Does the Supposer improve problem solving in geometry? (ERIC Document Reproduction No. ED 320 775).

McGinley, R. (1991). Start them off with games! *The Computing Teacher, 19*(3), 49.

Merrill, D., & Salisbury, D. (1984). Research on drill and practice strategies. *Journal of Computer-Based Instruction, 11*(1), 19–21.

Miller, H. L. (1997). The New York City Public Schools Integrated Learning Systems Project. *International Journal of Educational Research, 27*(2), 91–183.

Mintz, R. (1993). Computerized simulation as an inquiry tool. *School Science and Mathematics, 93*(2), 76–80.

Muckerheide, P., Mogill, A., & Mogill, H. (1999). In search of a fair game. *Mathematics and Computer Education, 33*(2), 142–150.

Murray, T., et al. (1988). An analogy-based computer tutorial for remediating physics misconceptions (ERIC Document Reproduction No. ED 299 172).

Norris, W. (1977). Via technology to a new era in education. *Phi Delta Kappan, 58*(6), 451–459.

Okolo, C. (1992). The effect of computer-assisted instruction format and initial attitude on the arithmetic facts proficiency and continuing motivation of students with learning disabilities. *Exceptionality: A Research Journal, 3*(4), 195–211.

Papert, S. (1980). *Mindstorms: Children, computers, and powerful ideas.* New York: Basic Books.

Perkins, D. (1991). Technology meets constructivism: Do they make a marriage? *Educational Technology, 31*(5), 18–23.

Ploger, D., & Vedova, T. (1999). Programming dynamic charts in the elementary classroom. *Learning and Leading with Technology, 26(5)*, 38–41.

Randel, J., Morris, B., Wetzel, C., & Whitehill, B. (1992). The effectiveness of games for educational purposes: A review of recent research. *Simulation and Gaming, 23*(3), 261–276.

Reigeluth, C., & Schwartz, E. (1989). An instructional theory for the design of computer-based simulations. *Journal of Computer-Based Instruction, 16*(1), 1–10.

Richards, J. (1992). Computer simulations in the science classroom. *Journal of Science Education and Technology, 1*(1), 67–80.

Rieber, L., Smith, L., & Noah, D. (1998). The value of serious play. *Educational Technology, 38*(6), 29–37.

Robinson, M., & Schonborn, A. (1991) Three instructional approaches to *Carmen Sandiego* software series. *Social Education, 55*(6), 353–354.

Roblyer, M. (1983). How to evaluate software reviews. *Executive Educator, 5*(9), 34–39.

Ronen, M. (1992). Integrating computer simulations into high school physics teaching. *Journal of Computers in Mathematics and Science Teaching, 11*(3–4), 319–329.

Salisbury, D. (1990). Cognitive psychology and its implications for designing drill and practice programs for computers. *Journal of Computer-Based Instruction, 17*(1), 23–30.

Sherman, T. (1987–1988). A brief review of developments in problem solving. *Computers in the Schools, 4*(3–4), 171–178.

Shore, A., & Johnson, M. (1992). Integrated learning systems: A vision for the future. *Educational Technology, 32*(9), 36–39.

Simmons, P., & Lunetta, V. (1993). Problem-solving behaviors during a genetics computer simulation. *Journal of Research in Science Teaching, 30*(2), 153–173.

Smith, K. (1992). Earthquake! *The Florida Technology in Education Quarterly, 4*(2), 68–70.

Smith, R. A., & Sclafani, S. (1989). Integrated teaching systems: Guidelines for evaluation. *The Computing Teacher, 17*(3), 36–38.

Steinburg, R., & Oberem, G. (2000). Research-based instructional software in modern physics. *Journal of Computers in Mathematics and Science Teaching, 19*(2), 115–136.

Stokes, J. (1999). Problem solving software, equity, and allocation of roles. *Learning and Leading with Technology, 26*(5), 6–9, 30.

Taylor, R. (1980). *The computer in the school: Tutor, tool, and tutee.* New York: Teachers College Press.

Tergan, S. (1998). Checklists for the evaluation of education software: Critical review and prospects. *Innovations in Education and Training, 35*(1), 9–20.

Trotter, A. (1991). In the school game, your options abound. *Executive Educator, 13*(6), 23.

Vaille, J., & Hall, J. (1998). Guidelines for the evaluation of instructional technology resources. Eugene, OR: ISTE.

Van Dusen, L., & Worthen, B. (1995). Can integrated instructional technology transform the classroom? *Educational Leadership, 53*(2), 28–33.

Walsh, J. (1999). Edison Project, now Edison Schools Inc., plans to go public. *Education Week, 19*(1), 6.

Weinstein, P. (1999). Computer programming revisited. *Technology & Learning, 19*(8), 38–42.

Weizenbaum, J. (1976). *Computer power and human reason.* San Francisco: W. H. Freeman & Co.

White, M. (1992). Are ILSs good for education? *Educational Technology, 32*(9), 49–50.

5 CHAPTER

Integrating Word Processing, Spreadsheet, and Database Software Tools into Teaching and Learning

Hence, could a machine be invented which would instantaneously arrange on paper each idea as it occurs to us, without any exertion on our part, how extremely useful would it be considered.

Henry David Thoreau,
as quoted by David Humphreys
in *Computers in English and the Language Arts* (1989)

This chapter covers the following topics:

- Definitions and characteristics of word processing software, spreadsheets, and databases
- Unique relative advantages or benefits of these software tools over other tools for various classroom activities
- Example classroom uses for each tool

Objectives

1. Use correct terminology to identify features and capabilities of word processing, spreadsheet, and database software tool programs.
2. Describe specific kinds of teaching and learning tasks for both teachers and students that each kind of tool can support.
3. Identify applications for software tools that educators would find valuable to make their work more efficient and productive.
4. Develop lesson activities that integrate the functions and capabilities of the software tools.

Introduction to Software Tools

Why Use Software Tools?

In education and, indeed, in most other areas of our information society, three of the most widely used software support tools are word processing, spreadsheet, and database programs. (Presentation software, covered in Chapter 7 under multimedia applications, is also becoming very popular.) As Thoreau envisioned, word processing and the other software tools have become not only "extremely useful," but an indispensable part of our daily work. Teachers choose them for the qualities and benefits they bring to the classroom and the potential they offer not only to make more productive use of our time, but also to shape and guide the kinds of activities we are able to undertake. Depending on the capabilities of the tool and the needs of the situation, these programs can offer several benefits:

- **Improved productivity.** Getting organized, producing instructional materials, and accomplishing paperwork tasks all go much faster when software tools are used. Using a technology tool to do these tasks can free up valuable time that can be rechanneled toward working with students or designing learning activities.
- **Improved appearance.** Software tools help teachers and students produce polished-looking materials that resemble the work of professional designers. The quality of classroom products is limited only by the talents and skills of the teachers and students using the tools. Students appreciate receiving attractive-looking materials and find it rewarding and challenging to produce handsome products of their own.
- **Improved accuracy.** Software tools make it easier to keep precise, accurate records of events and student accomplishments. More accurate information can support better instructional decisions about curriculum and student activities.
- **More support for interaction.** Software tools have capabilities that promote interaction among students or allow input from several people at once. These qualities can encourage many creative, cooperative group-learning activities.

Software Suites Versus Integrated Packages

In the late 1980s, software companies began to sell combinations of several software tools in one package; this trend has increased in recent years. Since they usually are cheaper than buying each tool separately, these packages are becoming increasingly popular in education and business. Keizer (1997) differentiates between *integrated packages,* which usually include word processing, spreadsheet, database, and graphics tools, and *software suites,* which usually contain one or more additional programs and may come in a variety of versions or combinations tailored to meet certain kinds of needs. For example, *ClarisWorks* and *Microsoft Works* are integrated packages containing productivity software tools, while the most popular suite, *Microsoft Office,* has several separate applications. While any of these packages may be useful, depending on the needs of the classroom and the types of software included, the current trend is toward using *Microsoft Office,* since it includes *Microsoft Word* and *Microsoft PowerPoint,* two of the most popular applications.

Using Word Processing Software in Teaching and Learning

Introduction to Word Processing

Word processing defined. Word processing is, simply put, typing on a computer. The term *word processor* can refer either to a computerized machine set up primarily to do word processing (an electronic typewriter) or to a general-purpose computer that can use word processing software. This chapter describes how to use microcomputers with word processing software, since this is the kind of word processing resource that educators usually use in classrooms.

Word processing can support nearly any kind of task or teaching activity that was previously done by hand or with a typewriter and offers more capability and versatility than either of these methods. Since a word processing document is prepared on-screen before being printed onto paper, the writer can correct errors, insert or delete words or sentences, and even move lines or paragraphs around before printing the document. The writer can easily change the words or appearance because the document is stored in the computer's memory and, hopefully, on a disk or a hard drive. Once stored or saved, documents can be changed or reprinted later. Subsequent sections of this chapter describe and illustrate word processing capabilities and benefits for both teacher productivity and for teaching and learning tasks.

Types of word processing software. Although most word processing software packages have very similar capabilities, some are especially designed for writing instruction. The latter word processors provide a variety of prewriting and language analysis features. This type of software frequently includes other materials such as prepared activity files that have been developed to help teachers use word processing software for various writing exercises. The newest development in word processing software is software designed for use with handheld computers. These have the complete word processing functions of a full-size program and can transfer files to or from a computer or the Internet.

General word processing features and capabilities. Word processing represents a significant improvement over typing on a typewriter. Although word processing capabilities and procedures vary from program to program, most programs have several features in common that cannot be duplicated by other resources:

- **Storing documents for later use.** The most powerful advantage of word processing over typewriters is the ability to handle documents more than once without reentering the same text. Once created on the screen, a document can be stored on disk, reloaded into the computer's memory later, and either modified or printed out again.
- **Erasing and inserting text.** Changes to typed documents require physical erasing or simply starting over; word processing allows a writer to insert additional letters, spaces, lines, or paragraphs easily into a document.
- **Search and replace.** If an error is repeated throughout a document, a word processing program can easily correct the error by searching the document for all occurrences and changing them as specified.
- **Moving or copying text.** Sometimes a writer decides that a paragraph would sound better or seem more logical in a different location, or perhaps the writer wants to repeat a given line several times throughout a document. Word processing allows users to cut and paste or copy and paste; that is, specify a block of text and either move it or repeat it in the places specified.
- **Word wraparound.** Typists usually must place "carriage returns" (a legacy term from the typewriter era) at the ends of lines. Word processing software does this automatically with a feature called *word wraparound.* Most word processors also allow users to do automatic hyphenation of words at line breaks.
- **Changing of style and appearance easily.** Word processing allows a writer to employ a variety of fonts, typestyles, margins, line spacings, and indentations in a single document.
- **Justification.** A unique feature of a word processing program is the ability to justify both right and left margins in a document, sometimes referred to as *full justification.* However, users also can easily specify that a given line or block of text be centered or right or left justified.
- **Automatic headers, footers, and pagination.** Word processors can automatically place text at the top (header) or bottom (footer) of each page in a document with or without page numbering (pagination). Headers and footers often are used for titles and page numbering.
- **Inserting text prepared on other word processors.** Each word processing program has software commands to apply formatting; these commands are specific to the package. Therefore, one program may not be able to read a document prepared in another. However, many word processors can store documents as text or ASCII (American Standard Code for Information Interchange) files or as Rich Text Format (RTF) files. These formats remove all or most formatting commands, so another word processor can read a file stored in one of these ways. Also, most word processors have filters or program functions that will accept and translate files originally prepared and stored on other word processors.
- **Checking and correcting spelling.** Spell checking is a word processing capability that compares words in a document to those stored in its dictionary files. The program identifies words in the document that it cannot find in the dictionary and suggests possible corrections.
- **Suggesting words.** In addition to a spell-checking dictionary, a program may include access to a thesaurus. A user can request a synonym or an alternate suffix for a given word.
- **Reviewing style and grammar.** Some word processing software can check text features such as sentence length, frequency of word use, and subject–verb agreement. This function may also suggest changes or corrections to the text.
- **Allowing insertion of graphics.** Most programs allow users to insert pictures stored as graphics files within their documents; most also have draw features that allow users to create and place their own pictures within their documents.
- **Merging text with data files.** Word processing programs are beginning to include a feature called "data merge," which allows the user to store data fields such as names and addresses to enter automatically into documents such as letters. When the program prints the letter or other document, it automatically inserts information from the data fields as directed. Thus, a teacher could write one parent letter and merge it with a student data bank to print a personalized letter for each parent. This feature effectively uses a database capability within the word processing program. However, it is no longer necessary to use a separate database program in order to do a data merge.
- **Tables.** Most new word processing software allows users to set up tables to support organizing information into rows and columns without using tabs.
- **Templates.** Word processing packages also come with a variety of templates that may be used to develop documents more quickly. For example, preformatted templates are usually provided for resumes, newsletters, and brochures. These can be very useful both for

Figure 5.1 Sample Word Processing Newsletter Template from *Appleworks*

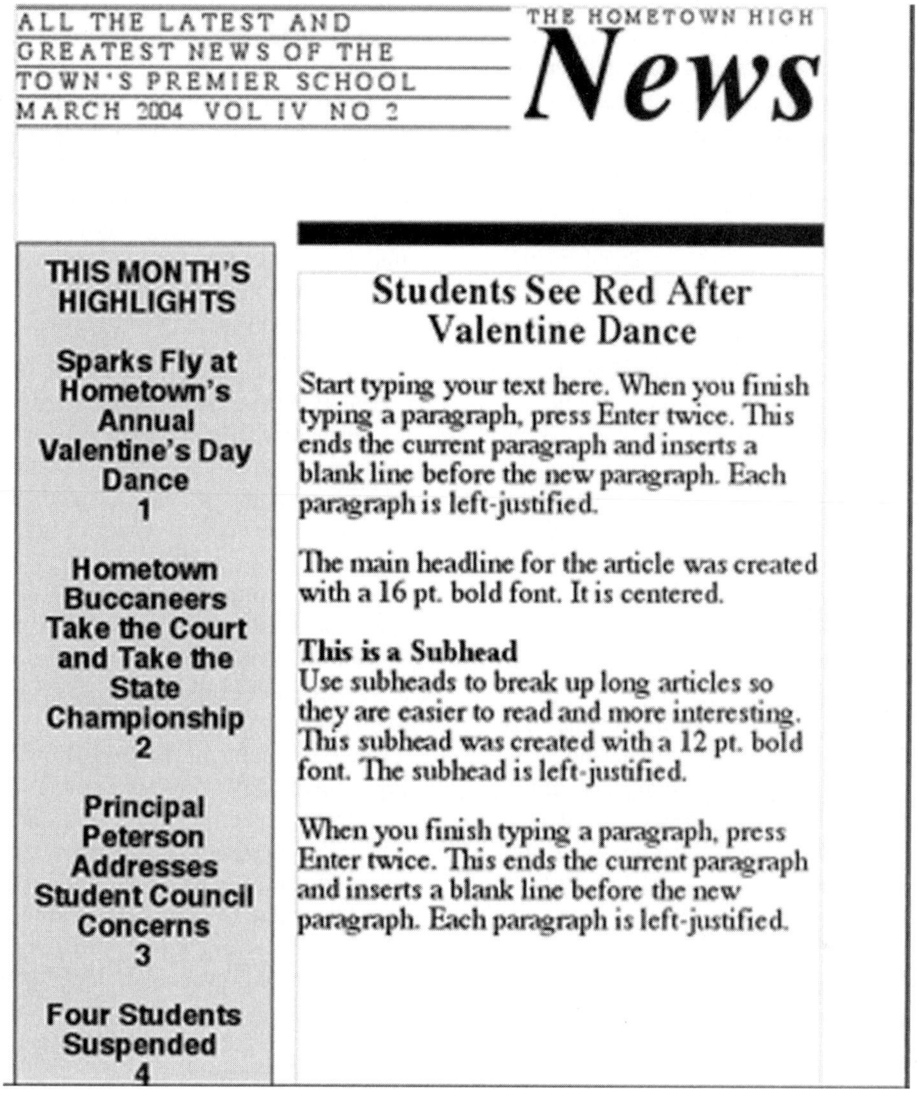

ALL THE LATEST AND
GREATEST NEWS OF THE
TOWN'S PREMIER SCHOOL
MARCH 2004 VOL IV NO 2

THE HOMETOWN HIGH
News

THIS MONTH'S HIGHLIGHTS

Sparks Fly at Hometown's Annual Valentine's Day Dance
1

Hometown Buccaneers Take the Court and Take the State Championship
2

Principal Peterson Addresses Student Council Concerns
3

Four Students Suspended
4

Students See Red After Valentine Dance

Start typing your text here. When you finish typing a paragraph, press Enter twice. This ends the current paragraph and inserts a blank line before the new paragraph. Each paragraph is left-justified.

The main headline for the article was created with a 16 pt. bold font. It is centered.

This is a Subhead
Use subheads to break up long articles so they are easier to read and more interesting. This subhead was created with a 12 pt. bold font. The subhead is left-justified.

When you finish typing a paragraph, press Enter twice. This ends the current paragraph and inserts a blank line before the new paragraph. Each paragraph is left-justified.

Source: Courtesy of Apple Computer, Inc.

novice users and busy teachers. Figure 5.1 shows an example newsletter template packaged with *Appleworks.*

- **Voice recognition.** One of the newest word processing features available in some software packages is the ability to receive text via dictated words, rather than as typed entries. This feature is made possible by combining word processing software with voice recognition software.

The Impact of Word Processing in Education

Relative advantage of word processing. Perhaps no other technology resource has had as great an impact on education as word processing. Not only does it offer a great degree of versatility and flexibility, but it also is "model-free" instructional software, that is, it reflects no particular instructional approach. A teacher can use it to support any kind of directed instruction or constructivist activity. Since its value as an aid to teaching and learning is universally acknowledged, word processing has become the most commonly used software in education. It offers many general relative advantages (unique benefits over and above other methods) to teachers and students:

- **Time savings.** Word processing helps teachers use preparation time more efficiently by letting them modify materials instead of creating new ones. Writers can also make corrections to word processing documents more quickly than they could achieve on a typewriter or by hand.
- **Better appearances.** Materials from word processing software look more polished and professional than handwritten or typed materials. It is not surprising that

students seem to like the improved appearance that word processing gives to their work (Harris, 1985).

- **Sharing methods.** Word processing allows materials to be shared easily among writers. Teachers can exchange lesson plans, worksheets, or other materials on disk and modify them to fit their needs. Students can also share ideas and products among themselves.

Issues related to word processing in education. Educators seem to agree that word processing is a valuable application, but some aspects of its use in education are controversial:

- **When to introduce word processing.** The development of word processing software designed for young children has allowed schools to introduce word processing to students as young as 4 or 5 years old. Although some educators feel that word processing will free students from the physical constraints of handwriting and enable them to advance more quickly in their written expression skills, others wonder about the impact of this early use on students. It may affect their willingness to spend time developing handwriting abilities and other activities requiring fine-motor skills.
- **The necessity of keyboarding skills.** Another ongoing discussion in education asks whether students need to learn keyboarding, or typing on the computer, either prior to or in conjunction with word processing activities. Some educators feel that students will never become really productive on the computer until they learn 10-finger keyboarding. Others feel that the extensive time spent on keyboarding instruction and practice could be better spent on more important skills.
- **Effects on handwriting.** While no researchers have conducted formal studies of the impact of frequent word processing use on handwriting legibility, computer users commonly complain that their handwriting isn't what it used to be, ostensibly because of infrequent opportunities to use their handwriting skills.
- **Impact on assessment.** Some organizations have students answer essay-type test questions with word processing, rather than by handwriting or even typing them. This practice introduces several issues. Roblyer (1997) reviewed research that found students' word-processed compositions tend to receive *lower* grades than handwritten ones. This surprising finding indicates that educational organizations that allow students to choose either handwriting or word processing must be careful to establish guidelines and special training to ensure that raters do not inadvertently discriminate against students who choose word processing.

Teachers and administrators are still deciding how best to deal with these issues. Since word processing is becoming an increasingly pervasive presence in both home and classroom writing activities, more information should soon become available to help educators make informed decisions about how best to employ its capabilities.

Relative advantage of word processing: Findings from research. Research on the benefits of word processing in education yields contradictory findings. Results of studies of the effects of word processing on quality and quantity of writing are mixed (Bangert-Drowns, 1993). Three different reviews of research (Bangert-Drowns, 1993; Hawisher, 1989; Snyder, 1993) found that these differences in findings may reflect differences in researchers' choices of types of word processing systems, prior experience and writing ability of students, and types of writing instruction to evaluate. Generally, word processing seems to improve writing and attitudes toward writing only if it is used in the context of good writing instruction and if students have enough time to learn word processing procedures before the study begins. Figure 5.2 summarizes some of the findings of the three research reviews.

Generally, studies seem to conclude that students who use word processing in the context of writing instruction programs tend to write more, revise more (at least on a sur-

Figure 5.2 Findings from Reviews of Word Processing in Education

	Hawisher (26 studies) (1989)	Snyder (57 studies) (1993)	Bangert-Drowns (32 studies) (1993)
Better quality of writing	No conclusion	No conclusion	Positive results
Greater quantity of writing	Positive results	Positive results	Positive results
More surface (mechanical) revisions	No conclusion	Positive results	No conclusion
More substantive (meaning) revisions	No conclusion	No improvement	No conclusion
Fewer mechanical errors	Positive results	Positive results	Not reviewed
Better attitude toward writing	Positive results	Positive results	No improvement
Better attitude toward word processing	No conclusion	Positive results	Not reviewed

face level), make fewer errors, and have better attitudes toward their writing than students who do not use word processing. Teachers who use word processing with their students should not expect writing quality to improve automatically. Improvements of that kind depend largely on factors such as the type of writing instruction. A review by Reed (1996) found that the type of word processor students use may have an impact. Younger, less able writers may profit from word processing software with more prompts, while this kind of word processor may actually inhibit the writing of older, more able writers who prefer learner-controlled word processing. But the *potential* value of word processing has been established, making it one of the most validated uses of technology in education.

Word Processing in the Classroom

When to use word processing: Teacher productivity. Word processing can help teachers prepare classroom materials they previously typed or wrote out by hand. These include handouts or other instructional materials, lesson plans and notes, reports, forms, letters to parents or students, flyers, and newsletters. Word processing benefits these tasks by saving preparation time, especially if the teacher prepares the same documents each school year. For example, a teacher may send the same letter to parents every year simply by changing the dates and adding new information. Teachers may want to keep files of templates or model documents that they can easily update and reuse with minimal effort. Here are some suggestions for additions to this file of reusable documents:

- Beginning of the year welcome letter
- Permission letters for field trips and other events
- Request for fee payments letter
- Fund-raising letter
- List of class rules
- Flyers and other announcements
- Periodic student progress letters to parents
- Frequently used worksheets and exercises
- Student information sheets and handouts
- Annual reports for the school
- Lesson plans and notes
- Newsletters and letterhead stationeries.

When to use word processing: Teaching and learning activities. Students can also use word processing for almost any written work, regardless of subject area, that they would otherwise write by hand. Research shows that word processing alone cannot improve the quality of student writing, but can help them make corrections more efficiently; this can motivate them to write more and take more interest in improving their written work. Some current word processing applications include the following:

- **Writing processes.** Students can use word processing to write, edit, and illustrate stories; to produce reports in content areas; to keep notes and logs on classroom activities; and for any written assignments. (See Technology Integration Ideas 5.1 through 5.3.)

TECHNOLOGY INTEGRATION IDEA 5.1

TITLE: Writing Through Webbing for Elementary Students

CONTENT AREA/TOPIC: Writing skills

GRADE LEVEL: 1

NETS FOR STUDENTS: Standards 1, 3, 4

DESCRIPTION: This lesson addresses the problem very young students have with beginning writing. They have a lot to say, but often it is difficult for them to get started. Teachers use word processing in a five-step process to help students learn writing skills:

Think → Draw → Tell → Write → Share

Three activities introduce students to this five-step process and encourage them to use it to start writing:

1. Preparing to write. At the beginning of the school year, the teacher takes photos of the students in the class and inserts them in their written documents. Students are encouraged to think about what they will write by describing themselves to the class in terms of their favorite food, sports, TV shows, and pets.
2. Planning through webbing. Using an integrated software package such as *Appleworks,* students enter the information about themselves into a "webbing" template and place a picture of themselves in it.
3. Writing activities. Using information in the web, students begin composing a summary about themselves, and teachers enter the information into a word processing file as the students dictate it.

Source: Etchinson, C. (1995). A powerful web to weave—Developing writing skills for elementary students. *Learning and Leading with Technology, 23*(3), 14–15.

TECHNOLOGY INTEGRATION IDEA 5.2

TITLE: Process Writing and Word Processing

CONTENT AREA/TOPIC: Writing process skills

GRADE LEVEL: High school juniors and seniors

NETS FOR STUDENTS: Standards 1, 3, 4

DESCRIPTION: Students use word processing for all aspects of the writing process in a one-semester elective writing course. A networked lab is used for the writing activities. Students write several small assignments and one 500- to 700-word essay in each of four units. In the final unit, they write longer (25-page) research papers that combine text and graphics. In addition to writing and revising their work, students maintain writing logs in which they record what they accomplish each day. They also complete lessons on the basic skills of analytical and persuasive writing. Students' writing is reviewed daily by the teacher and writing groups. They review completed drafts with a teacher and decide on appropriate revisions. When a draft is revised and completed, the teacher evaluates it based on the criteria and makes notes on any areas that need improvement.

Source: VerMulm, L. (1993). The Christa McAuliffe Writing Center: Process writing with a networked Mac lab. *The Computing Teacher, 20*(7), 48–53.

TECHNOLOGY INTEGRATION IDEA 5.3

TITLE: Cartoon Commentaries on the Computer

CONTENT AREA/TOPIC: Writing persuasive essays

GRADE LEVEL: Middle school

NETS FOR STUDENTS: Standards 1, 3, 4

DESCRIPTION: This activity uses cartoons and comic strips to focus on two different skill areas that often present problems to middle school students and their teachers: writing persuasive essays or position papers and analyzing current affairs. Two computers are set up—one with drawing software and one with word processing software. The class is divided into small groups of three to four students each and the teacher distributes newspapers to the groups. The students go through the papers, selecting at least two comic strips and/or editorial cartoons. They "write the story" or idea of the comic using either a dialog, narrative, or essay form. Each group reports to the class on its analysis. The teacher asks the groups to add another paragraph to their write-ups to express their own opinions about the comic's purposes. To initiate their responses, the teacher asks questions such as these: Do you support the purpose and point of view of the person doing the cartoon? Why or why not? What mix of images and text does the person use to make his point? Is this mix effective? Again, these write-ups are shared with the class and used as the basis for discussions.

Source: Reissman, R. (1994). Computer cartoon commentaries. *The Computing Teacher, 21*(5), 23–25.

■ **Dynamic group products.** Teachers can assign group poems or letters with various students, adding and changing lines or producing elements of the whole document in a word processing program. (See Technology Integration Ideas 5.4 through 5.6.)

■ **Individual language, writing, and reading exercises.** Special word processing exercises allow individual students to work on-screen combining sentences, adding or correcting punctuation, or writing sentences for spelling words. Word processing may also make possible a variety of reading/language-related activities ranging from decoding to writing poetry and enjoying literature. Viau (1998) points out that adding colors to text can be the basis for activities to enhance critical thinking during writing instruction. (See Technology Integration Ideas 5.7 through 5.11.) Note that some of these integration ideas are not on the accompanying CD-ROM.

■ **Encouraging writing across the curriculum.** A recent trend in education is to encourage writing skills in courses and activities other than those designed to teach English and language arts. This practice of writing-through-the-curriculum is in keeping with the new emphasis on integrated, interdisciplinary, and thematic curricula. Word processing can encourage these integrated activities. (See Technology Integration Ideas 5.12 through 5.14.)

TECHNOLOGY INTEGRATION IDEA 5.4

TITLE: A Class Literary Paper

CONTENT AREA/TOPIC: Writing descriptive essays

GRADE LEVEL: Middle school

NETS FOR STUDENTS: Standards 1, 3, 4

DESCRIPTION: The teacher uses word processing to let students develop a literary paper as a group in order to model the process. A computer is attached to a large monitor so all students can see. The class creates a class essay on William Faulkner's "A Rose for Emily," which they are reading and discussing. They first brainstorm a list of ideas and the class selects "Emily" as their theme. They look through the story, searching for images or words illustrating Emily's connection with the Old South, and fill the monitor with their ideas. By the end of the class, students develop a thesis, an outline, and a substantial amount of content for the essay. More importantly, they have a clearer grasp of the process for writing such a paper.

Source: Wresch, W. (1991). Collaborative writing projects for the information age. *The Computing Teacher, 18*(2), 19–21.

TECHNOLOGY INTEGRATION IDEA 5.5

TITLE: A Class Poem

CONTENT AREA/TOPIC: Writing poetry

GRADE LEVEL: 8

NETS FOR STUDENTS: Standards 1, 3, 4

DESCRIPTION: A connection between reading and writing is built by having students write a class poem modeled after Walt Whitman's "Song of Myself." After students read the original poem, the teacher sets up six stations in the computer lab. Each is labeled with a beginning line from the poem:

I hear . . . I understand . . . I saw . . . I want . . . Injustices . . . and Who are you?

Students move from computer to computer adding one idea to each category. For example, at the "Who are you?" station, students are encouraged to add words, phrases, or ideas that describe a typical eighth-grade student. The resulting lists are then saved, printed, and made available to all students for use in writing their own poems. When the individual poems are completed, students have the option of combining their efforts into a class poem. Groups of students decide which parts of individual poems should be included and in what order. The final poem is printed, used as a choral reading, and displayed on bulletin boards.

Source: Wresch, W. (1991). Collaborative writing projects for the information age. *The Computing Teacher, 18*(2), 19–21.

TECHNOLOGY INTEGRATION IDEA 5.6

TITLE: A Class Novel

CONTENT AREA/TOPIC: Writing novels

GRADE LEVEL: High school

NETS FOR STUDENTS: Standards 1, 3, 4

DESCRIPTION: The class explores the genre of science fiction by creating its own science fiction novel on the word processor. They begin by imagining possible sites for the novel. After creating a fictional planet and city, they decide to focus on one period in the planet's history. They then develop character outlines, with each student contributing one character for the novel. The teacher encourages students to let the characters reflect their own personalities and interests. Each student is asked to imagine an incident in the planet's history and describe it in a 3- to 5-page story; word processing is used for all phases of this process. Students also use graphics programs to illustrate their stories and provide detail for the imaginary planet and its events.

Source: Wresch, W. (1991). Collaborative writing projects for the information age. *The Computing Teacher, 18*(2), 19–21.

TECHNOLOGY INTEGRATION IDEA 5.7

TITLE: Investigating Sentence Variety

CONTENT AREA/TOPIC: Writing sentences

GRADE LEVEL: 5 and up

NETS FOR STUDENTS: Standards 1, 3, 4

DESCRIPTION: This exercise helps students focus on making sentences vary in length and structure. The word processor is used to set off sentences in paragraphs so they can be more easily read and reviewed. Students select an essay they have already written and revised. They load the file into the computer, select their longest single paragraph, and set it off from the others by inserting blank lines before and after it. They search for periods in the paragraph and replace them with a period and a Return or Enter. Sentences are isolated from each other in a list. Students determine whether or not all sentences have the same structure and/or length. If so, they edit them by combining some (especially those that have overlapping meanings), omitting those that do not communicate meaning clearly, adding new sentence beginnings, and rearranging word order within sentences to vary rhythm and structure.

Source: Elder, J., Schwartz, J., Bowen, B., & Goswami, D. (1989). *Word processing in a community of writers* (pp. 117–132). New York: Garland.

TECHNOLOGY INTEGRATION IDEA 5.8

TITLE: Creating Coherence Between Sentences

CONTENT AREA/TOPIC: Writing paragraphs by combining sentences

GRADE LEVEL: 5 and up

NETS FOR STUDENTS: Standards 1, 3, 4

DESCRIPTION: This exercise gets students to focus on the relationships between sentences. The word processor is used to scramble sentences and then put them back together in order to examine how they fit together to communicate meaning. Students begin the exercise in the same way as in TII 5.7, Investigating Sentence Variety. They isolate the sentences in a list. Then they use cut-and-paste functions to scramble the sentences in random order in the list. They look for clues that signal where they go together, that is, which words "link back" or "forecast ahead." In the best test of coherence, each student should have a partner who uses the cut-and-paste function to rearrange the sentences in their intended order. If the person cannot put them in the desired order, the links between the sentences may not be explicit enough. If this is the case, students will have to make the connections clearer.

Source: Elder, J., Schwartz, J., Bowen, B., & Goswami, D. (1989). *Word processing in a community of writers* (pp. 117–132). New York: Garland.

TECHNOLOGY INTEGRATION IDEA 5.9

TITLE: Appreciating Punctuation

CONTENT AREA/TOPIC: Punctuation

GRADE LEVEL: 5 and up

NETS FOR STUDENTS: Standards 1, 3, 4

DESCRIPTION: This exercise encourages students to look at the important role of punctuation in writing. The word processor is used first to remove punctuation and capitalization and then to restore them. Students load or type a paragraph onto the screen, removing all punctuation marks and all capital letters as well as all extra spaces at the ends of sentences. The teacher points out how difficult it is to read without these "clues" to meaning. Students trade computers and try to restore all the punctuation marks, capital letters, and spaces in their partners' paragraphs. They save their files to different names, load the original versions at the same time, and compare their versions with the originals. If the versions differ, students examine whether or not other punctuation or capitalization is necessary for meaning and change it as needed.

Source: Elder, J., Schwartz, J., Bowen, B., & Goswami, D. (1989). *Word processing in a community of writers* (pp. 117–132). New York: Garland.

TECHNOLOGY INTEGRATION IDEA 5.10

TITLE: Writing Poetry to Develop Literacy

CONTENT AREA/TOPIC: Poetry writing

GRADE LEVEL: All ages

NETS FOR STUDENTS: Standards 1, 3, 4

DESCRIPTION: Students use the word processor to write several styles of poems that focus on sounds. These poetry exercises become a way of practicing and improving fluency in decoding skills. The students are introduced to a variety of forms of "experimental poetry," which is "an attempt to express writers' frustration with the limitations of language to describe the rapid changes in culture. . . . The writers tried to obliterate meaning by replacing traditional rules for writing poetry with randomness" (Nelson, 1994, p. 39). The results are forms of poetry that emphasize sound as opposed to meaning. Writing these poems gives students motivational opportunities to practice decoding without relying on context while they exercise their own creativity. In each of these forms, students use the unique capabilities of the word processor to facilitate the development of their poems: dada, sound poems, optophonetic poems, oulipo, snowballing, iceograms, iterative poetry, and transformations.

Source: Nelson, M. H. (1994). Processing poetry to develop literacy. *The Computing Teacher, 22*(3), 39–41.

TECHNOLOGY INTEGRATION IDEA 5.11

TITLE: Using Color in Composition

CONTENT AREA/TOPIC: Examining the purpose of various types of text

GRADE LEVEL: Middle to high school

NETS FOR STUDENTS: Standards 1, 3, 4

DESCRIPTION: Students use the word processor's font color option to highlight various functions in compositions and advertisements in different colors. Examples: topic sentences, emotion-evoking content, factual content, and descriptive words and phrases. In compositions, they follow up these activities by analyzing how the text elements contribute to the paragraph meaning, and try to add text in a way that continues the purpose of the text. In advertisements, they analyze how the words and phrases work to shape the reader's perceptions.

Source: Viau, E. (1998). Color me a writer: Teaching students to think critically. *Learning and Leading with Technology, 25*(5), 17–20.

TECHNOLOGY INTEGRATION IDEA 5.12

TITLE: Word Processing in Early Foreign Language Learning

CONTENT AREA/TOPIC: French word usage, agreements, and verb conjugations

GRADE LEVEL: 7–8

NETS FOR STUDENTS: Standards 1, 3, 4

DESCRIPTION: Word processing is used to help young foreign language students get more interested in writing and pay more attention to detail in word usage, agreements, and verb conjugations. Although the activities described here focus on use with middle school students, similar ones could be adapted for upper elementary and high school or adult levels. Beginning language students need the practice of writing simple compositions in the language they are studying. Yet students who have limited vocabulary and grammar mastery frequently find this writing task difficult and tedious. Word processing lets them make corrections more quickly; combining writing with graphics makes the activity more exciting and helps students convey complex thoughts they are not yet able to express. Using fancy fonts with authentic punctuation and characters is helpful. Suggested writing projects that incorporate these resources for French language learning include autobiographies, menus, developing comic strips, and family albums.

Source: Lewis, P. (1997). Using productivity software for beginning language learning. *Learning and Leading with Technology, 24*(8), 14–17.

TECHNOLOGY INTEGRATION IDEA 5.13

TITLE: Using Technology to Study Biospheres

CONTENT AREA/TOPIC: Ecology

GRADE LEVEL: Junior high

NETS FOR STUDENTS: Standards 1, 3, 4, 5

DESCRIPTION: In addition to word processing software, students use a variety of technology tools to learn about the design and uses of biospheres. Biospheres offer a rich environment in which students can collaborate with others as they practice their research and inquiry skills. Students form small-group cooperative teams. They can use newspapers, magazines, books, and electronic encyclopedias to gather information on biospheres and begin to learn about biosphere design. They record their facts and design aspects in a word processor file. They use online resources such as Internet searches to locate experts in biosphere design and e-mail questions to them. Teams collect visuals of biosphere designs. Each team exchanges visuals with one other team and critiques the scientific accuracy of the designs. After the teams complete their critiques, they review all the various team critiques. Then the teams begin using the scanned images to create and present their own final biosphere designs.

Source: Reissman, R. (1992). A biosphere research expedition. *The Computing Teacher, 20*(1), 32–33.

TECHNOLOGY INTEGRATION IDEA 5.14

TITLE: Exploring Political Parties

CONTENT AREA/TOPIC: Civics

GRADE LEVEL: Middle school

NETS FOR STUDENTS: Standards 1, 3, 4, 5

DESCRIPTION: Students use word processing and graphics software to develop research skills as they explore what it means to be a Democrat, Republican, or Independent. The words "Democrat," "Republican," "Independent," "Third Party," and "None of the Above" are typed on a computer with a large monitor so the whole class can see. The class is divided into Party Probe teams of three to four students, each with two side-by-side computers. One computer has a word processing program on the screen; the other has a graphics program. The teacher asks the students to take 10 minutes to come up with as many visual and verbal associations as they can for each party. To assist them, she distributes some cartoons and newspaper articles on political events. One member of the team is appointed the sketch artist for the visual images, and another is the recorder for the verbal associations. As they discuss these results, the students check off associations that are on more than one list. They talk about where they found their information and where they could get more information.

Source: Reissman, R. (1994). Party probe: A technology-supported introduction to political parties research. *The Computing Teacher, 21*(7), 21–22.

Using Spreadsheet Software in Teaching and Learning

Introduction to Spreadsheet Software

Spreadsheet defined. Electronic spreadsheet programs organize and manipulate numerical data. The term *spreadsheet* comes from the pre-computer word for an accountant's ledger: a book for keeping records of numerical information such as budgets and cash flow. Unlike the term *word processing,* which refers only to the computer software or program, the term spreadsheet can refer either to the program itself or to the product it produces. Spreadsheet products are sometimes also called *worksheets.* Information in a spreadsheet is stored in rows and columns. Each row–column position is called a *cell,* which may contain numerical values, words or character data, and formulas or calculation commands.

A spreadsheet helps users manage numbers in the same way that word processing helps manage words. Bozeman (1992) described spreadsheets as a way to "word process numbers" (p. 908). Spreadsheets were the earliest application software available for microcomputers. Some people credit them with starting the microcomputer revolution, since the availability of the first spreadsheet software, *Visicalc,* motivated many people to buy a microcomputer.

Teachers today typically use electronic spreadsheets for work that involves keeping track of and calculating numerical data such as budgets and grades. Spreadsheets

Teaching Students to Use Word Processing

Recommended Activity Sequence

To take advantage of the power of word processing in their classroom, teachers may have to teach their students word processing basics and help them build their skills over time. A sequence for developing these skills and a set of curriculum-based exercises is available in a separate text by Mills and Roblyer (2003).

Common Mistakes and Misconceptions

Beginning users of word processing experience some common problems. Teachers may want to review them before beginning the exercises. If students encounter problems, they may want to review this list again:

- **Forgetting to move the cursor before typing.** The computer does not automatically place text as desired. The user must indicate a spot for new text using the mouse or command keys to place the cursor at the desired location. Beginners often have their eyes on the place they want to insert a letter or word but forget to move the cursor there first. They are surprised when their typing appears somewhere other than where they had intended.
- **Forgetting to highlight before changing a format.** The same kind of problem occurs when beginners want to change the appearance of text (centering a title or inserting an automatic paragraph indent). The computer will not change the correct part of the text unless the user highlights the text *first* and *then* selects the option. If the selected option doesn't work, be sure to indicate which part of the text the format should change.
- **Losing part of the document.** Unless a computer system has a large (19-inch) screen, an entire document may not fit on one screen. As the user types, the top of the document scrolls up the screen and out of view. Beginners sometimes become distressed because they cannot see all they have typed and think it may be lost. They should use the scroll box or scroll arrows to bring the missing part of the document into view on the screen.
- **Forgetting automatic wraparound at the ends of lines.** Beginners sometimes use the typewriter convention of hitting the Return key at the end of each line. This will make large spaces appear in the text when the document prints out on paper. Remember to press Return or Enter *only* at the ends of paragraphs.
- **Problems with naming and saving files.** Word processing is frequently the first application that beginning computer users learn. Thus, this may provide their first experience with the concepts of storing and replacing documents in computer memory. The most common error is forgetting to save a document before closing it. Novice users may think they need to save only once and are surprised to open a document later and find that some of what has been typed is missing. Always remember to save a document before closing it.
- **Incorrect spacing at the top or bottom of the document.** Beginners are sometimes surprised when their printed documents have different top and bottom margins than what they saw on a screen. This can be caused by two problems:
  1. **Setting paper in the printer.** The printer is a separate machine from the computer. When it receives a command to print from the computer, it will begin printing wherever the paper is positioned, even if the paper is already positioned halfway up the page. If unexpectedly large or small spaces fall at the top of a document, students must check to see if the paper is positioned in the printer at the top of the sheet.
  2. **Extra blank lines in the document.** Even though blank lines do not always appear on the word processing screen, the computer knows they are there and allows space for them on the printed page. Beginners do not always realize that when they press Return or Enter, they insert a blank line that is as real to the program as text lines. If the paper is set at the top of the page and unexpected blank spaces still appear at the end of a printed document, see if blank lines appear in the document itself. If so, delete them by highlighting them and pressing the Delete key.
- **Problems with search and replace.** This handy feature is easy to misuse and can result in unexpected changes to the document. Seasoned users joke about the accountant who wanted to change the wording in all his letters from TO CUSTOMERS to BY CUSTOMERS. He instructed the word processor to automatically search and replace all text from "TO" to "BY." The computer changed everything to BY CUSBYMERS. Before changing all instances of some text, be sure you can predict the result accurately.

process calculations faster, more accurately, and with more visual feedback than other tools such as calculators. For example, if a worksheet is set up to add a column of expense items, the cell showing the sum will change automatically in response to any change to one of the expense items. If a worksheet is set up to calculate a student's grade average, the cell showing the cumulative average will be updated if the points change for any of the grades. These capabilities allow both teachers and students to play with numbers and see the results. This section of the chapter helps teachers to define both the capabilities and the classroom applications of spreadsheets. It will describe capabilities and benefits of spreadsheets for teacher productivity and teaching and learning.

Types of spreadsheet programs and products. Like word processing software, a spreadsheet program can form an application of its own or be part of an integrated package such as *Microsoft Works* that also contains word processing and database software. When spreadsheet capabilities were combined with database capabilities, the result became a powerful, multipurpose product such as *Excel* or *Quattro-Pro*. Teachers usually select a program like *Excel* to present business education concepts to high school students or to handle more complex record-keeping tasks than simple grade keeping.

Teachers also use spreadsheet derivatives. Gradebooks or grade-keeping packages are special-purpose spreadsheets designed exclusively to store and calculate grades. Some software publishers also sell spreadsheet templates, predesigned worksheets for special instructional purposes such as demonstrating concepts of budgeting.

General spreadsheet features and capabilities. Spreadsheet packages offer significant improvements over calculating values by hand or with a calculator. Like word processing documents, spreadsheets can easily be edited and stored for later use. Although spreadsheet capabilities and procedures vary from program to program, most programs have the following features in common:

- **Calculations and comparisons.** Spreadsheets calculate and manipulate stored numbers in a variety of ways through formulas. In addition to the addition, subtraction, multiplication, and division specified in formulas, spreadsheets also manipulate data in many more complex ways through function commands. These include mathematical functions such as logarithms and roots, statistical functions such as sums and averages, trigonometric functions such as sines and tangents, logical functions such as Boolean comparisons, and financial functions such as periodic payments and rates. Most spreadsheets also offer special-purpose functions such as lookup tables. These are sets of numbers that are automatically compared with those in the spreadsheet and assigned a value if they match. For example, a teacher might have a lookup table to assign letter grades based on students' final numerical grades. Formulas also allow users to weight given grades.
- **Automatic recalculation.** This is the most powerful advantage that spreadsheets offer. When any number changes, the program updates all calculations related to that number.
- **Copying cells.** Once a user enters a formula or other information into a cell, it can be copied automatically to other cells. This can save time, for example, when placing a long formula at the end of each of 20 rows; the user can simply copy the information from the first row to other rows.
- **Line up information in columns.** Spreadsheets store data by row–column positions, a format that makes information easy to read and digest at a glance.
- **Create graphs that correspond to data.** A spreadsheet program displays entered and calculated data in a chart or graph such as a pie chart or bar graph. Figure 5.3 shows an example spreadsheet and a bar chart derived from its data.
- **Use worksheets prepared on other programs.** Spreadsheet programs have software commands, invisible to the user, that perform formatting features such as centering text in columns. Since these program commands vary from package to package, one spreadsheet program cannot usually read and manipulate a worksheet prepared on another program. However, many spreadsheet programs allow a document to be saved as a text, ASCII, or SYLK file. When stored in this way, a whole worksheet or specific parts can be brought in (imported) and used in another spreadsheet program.

The Impact of Spreadsheets in Education

Relative advantages of spreadsheets. Spreadsheet programs are in widespread use in classrooms at all levels of education. Teachers use them primarily with mathematical topics but sometimes for other purposes. They offer teachers and students several kinds of unique benefits:

- **Time savings.** Spreadsheets save valuable time by allowing teachers and students to complete essential calculations quickly. They save time not only by making initial calculations faster and more accurate, but their automatic recalculation features also make it easy to update products such as grades and budgets. Entries also can be changed, added, or deleted easily, with formulas that automatically recalculate final grades.
- **Creating charts.** Although spreadsheet programs are intended for numerical data, their capability to store information in columns makes them ideal tools for designing informational charts such as schedules and attendance lists that may contain few numbers and no calculations at all.
- **Answering "what if?" questions.** Spreadsheets help people visualize the impact of changes in numbers. Since values are automatically recalculated when changes are made in a worksheet, a user can play with numbers and immediately see the result. This capability makes it feasible to pose "what if?" questions and answer them quickly and easily.
- **Motivation.** Many teachers feel that spreadsheets make working with numbers more fun. Collis (1988) described spreadsheets as "sufficiently enjoyable and interesting in themselves that students can sometimes be experiencing the pleasure of exploring math at the same time as they are doing math" (p. 264). Students sometimes perceive mathematical concepts as dry and boring; spreadsheets can make these concepts so graphic that students express real delight with seeing how they work.

Issues related to spreadsheets. One of the few disagreements related to spreadsheets in education is whether to use them to keep grades or to rely instead on grade-keeping packages (gradebooks) designed especially for this purpose. Spreadsheets usually offer more flexibility in designing formats and allowing special-purpose calculation functions, while gradebooks are simpler to use and require

Figure 5.3 Charts and Graphs Prepared with Spreadsheets

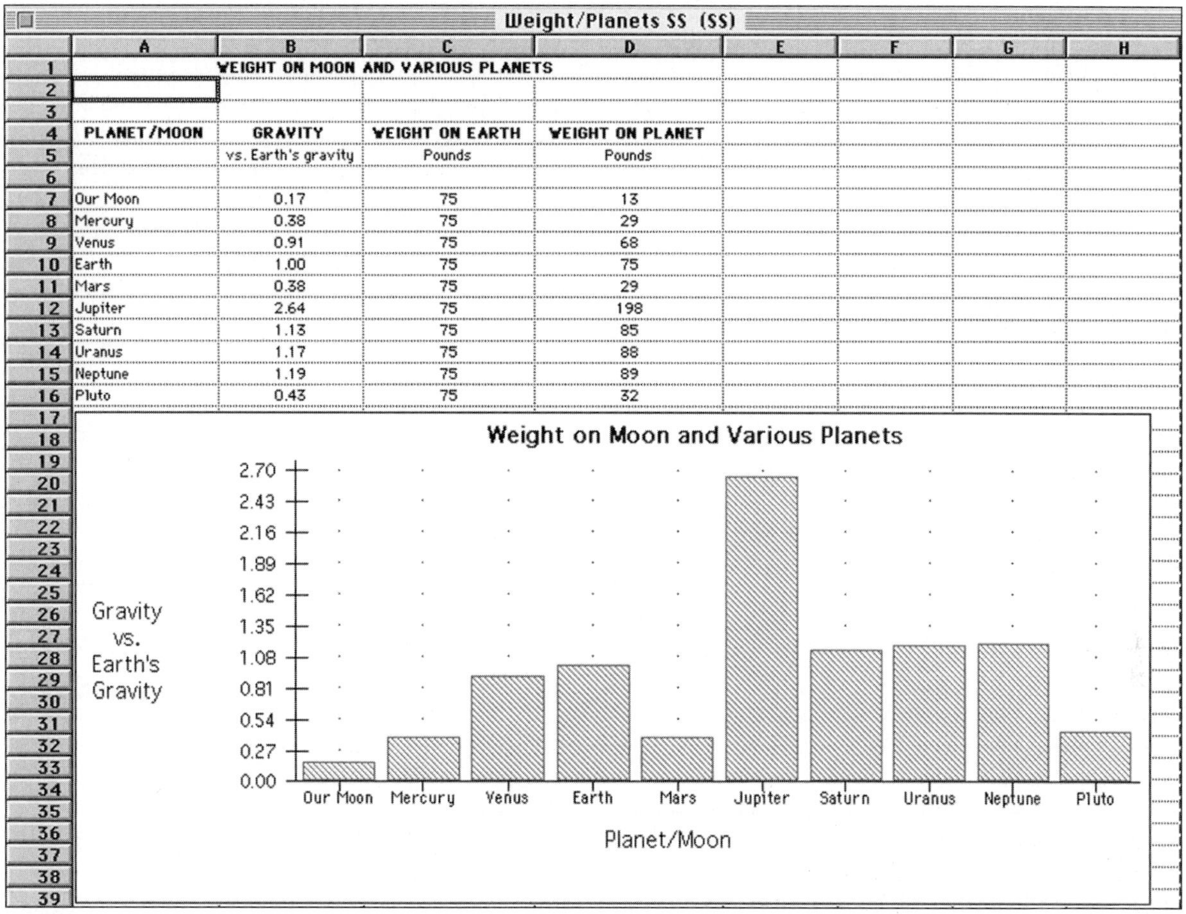

Weight/Planets SS (SS)

WEIGHT ON MOON AND VARIOUS PLANETS

PLANET/MOON	GRAVITY vs. Earth's gravity	WEIGHT ON EARTH Pounds	WEIGHT ON PLANET Pounds
Our Moon	0.17	75	13
Mercury	0.38	75	29
Venus	0.91	75	68
Earth	1.00	75	75
Mars	0.38	75	29
Jupiter	2.64	75	198
Saturn	1.13	75	85
Uranus	1.17	75	88
Neptune	1.19	75	89
Pluto	0.43	75	32

little setup other than entering students' names and assignment grades. Teachers appear to be about evenly divided on which is better; the choice comes down to personal preference.

Because spreadsheet use creates no researchable issues of the kind word processing does, there are no research results to report in this area. Studies show, however, that spreadsheets can be useful tools for teaching topics ranging from problem solving (Sutherland, 1993) to statistical analysis methods (Klass, 1988). The literature contains numerous testimonials by teachers who have used spreadsheets successfully in teaching topics ranging from mathematics to social studies.

Spreadsheets in the Classroom

Applications of spreadsheets: Teacher productivity. Teachers can use spreadsheets to help them prepare classroom materials and complete calculations that they would otherwise have to do by hand or with a calculator. An example spreadsheet a teacher might use for keeping grades is shown in Figure 5.4. They help with many activities and products in education, including these:

- Grade keeping to keep records and to prepare grade charts for posting
- Club and/or classroom budgets
- Computerized checkbooks for clubs or other organizations
- Attendance charts
- Performance assessment checklists.

Applications of spreadsheets: Teaching and learning activities. The literature reflects an increasing variety of applications for spreadsheets. Although their teaching role focuses primarily on mathematics lessons, spreadsheets have also effectively supported instruction in science, social studies, and even language arts. Lewis (2001) offers 40 different lessons to help teach various curriculum topics in grades K–8. Teachers can use spreadsheets in many ways to enhance learning:

- **Demonstrations.** Whenever concepts involve numbers and concrete representation can clarify the ideas, spreadsheets contribute to effective teaching demonstrations. Spreadsheets offer an efficient way of demonstrating numerical concepts such as multiplication and percentages and numerical applications such as the concept of electoral votes versus popular votes. A worksheet can make a picture out of abstract concepts and provide a graphic illustration of what the teacher is trying to communicate. (See Technology Integration Idea 5.15.)

Figure 5.4 Example Gradebook Using Spreadsheets

	A	B	C	D	E	F	G	H	I	J	K	L	M	N	O	P
1	Fall 2004 Grades	- PERIOD 4 Social Studies														
2																
3			Individual Assignments						Prod.	Prod.		Test	Test		Final	FINAL
4			1	2	3	4	5		1	2		#1	#2		Avg.	GRADE
5			8%	8%	8%	8%	8%		20%	20%		10%	10%			
6																
7	Adams, Alma		89	92	84	96	80		88	95		54	70		84.28	B
8	Betts, Lee		95	84	81	77	90		91	95		90	100		90.36	A
9	Bradley, Brindell															
10	Brush, Jason		86	95	96	90	90		91	95		87	45		86.96	A
11	Dirk, Dwan		80	97	90	83	90		97	100		75	100		92.10	A
12	Gretsky, Gerald		72	75	90	97	90		77	76		81	50		77.62	C
13	Howard, Kay		84	89	79	97	100		91	90		78	80		87.92	B
14	Johnson, Betty		89	98	96	96	90		94	90		94	100		93.72	A
15	Jones, Natalie															
16	Lane, Michael		83	85	72	50	76		91	95		76	80		82.08	B
17	McBur, Yolanda		96	100	96	96	77		91	90		81	100		91.50	A
18	McClellan, Will		45	100	92	95	100		97	100		99	100		93.86	A
19	Morrison, Addie		97	93	92	96	90		88	95		93	100		93.34	A
20	Moultrie, Fred		98	91	88	89	100		91	90		56	80		87.08	B
21	Sanders, Lillie		97	90	88	85	100		94	90		83	100		91.90	A
22	Shepherd, April															
23	Williams, Peter		93	65	92	82	56		80	70		71	100		78.14	C
24																
25																

TECHNOLOGY INTEGRATION IDEA 5.15

TITLE: Using Spreadsheets to Demonstrate Concepts—How the Electoral Vote Works

CONTENT AREA/TOPIC: Civics

GRADE LEVEL: 5

NETS FOR STUDENTS: Standards 1, 3, 4, 5

DESCRIPTION: A spreadsheet is used to display data from a U.S. presidential election to show how popular votes and electoral votes differ and how it is possible for a person to win the popular vote and still lose the election. After the class holds a mock election and assigns electoral votes to each class in the school based on enrollment numbers, a spreadsheet is set up to match the list of classes and their popular and electoral votes. Data on election results are entered after the election is held and the spreadsheet is displayed on a large monitor so the whole class can see the results as they are entered. They are able to see that if very few of the popular votes in key areas are changed, the results of the election would be reversed. The class discusses these results as well as the possibility that a candidate could win the popular vote and lose the electoral vote.

Source: Goldberg, K. (1991). Bringing mathematics to the social studies classroom: Spreadsheets and the electoral process. *The Computing Teacher, 18*(1), 35–38.

■ **Student products.** Students can use spreadsheets to create neat timelines, charts, and graphs as well as products that require them to store and calculate numbers. (See Technology Integration Idea 5.16.)

■ **Support for problem solving.** Spreadsheets take over the task of doing arithmetic functions so students can focus on higher level concepts (Black, 1999; Hauger, 2000; Ploger, Rooney, & Klingler, 1996). By answering "what if?" questions, spreadsheets help teachers encourage logical thinking, develop organizational skills, and promote problem solving. (See Technology Integration Ideas 5.17 through 5.21.)

■ **Storing and analyzing data.** Whenever students must keep track of data from classroom experiments, spreadsheets help organize these data and perform required descriptive statistical analyses. (See Technology Integration Idea 5.22.)

■ **Projecting grades.** Students can be taught to use spreadsheets to keep track of their own grades. They can do their own "what if?" questions to see what scores they need to make on their assignments to project desired class grades. This simple activity can play an important role in encouraging them to take responsibility for setting goals and achieving them.

TECHNOLOGY INTEGRATION IDEA 5.16

TITLE: Using Spreadsheets for Student Products—Generating a Class Profile

CONTENT AREA/TOPIC: Creating data charts and graphs

GRADE LEVEL: Middle to high school

NETS FOR STUDENTS: Standards 1, 3, 4, 5

DESCRIPTION: Students use a spreadsheet to generate charts and graphs of data they have gathered. The teacher introduces graphing concepts by having students interpret some commercially produced charts and graphs. Then they assign charts to do without benefit of spreadsheet software. (This gives concrete experience that teaches both the benefit of using a spreadsheet to produce these items and the procedures for generating them.) Then the teacher demonstrates how to use spreadsheet software to create charts and graphs. Students generate and conduct a brief class survey on a topic of interest. They use the spreadsheet to collect the data and display it in chart or graph form. The products are displayed on a bulletin board as "A Profile of the Class." If additional surveys of other classes are done, the results can be posted on a bulletin board and compared across classes.

Source: Beaver, J. (1992). Using computer power to improve your teaching—Part II: Spreadsheets and graphing. *The Computing Teacher, 19*(6), 22–24.

TECHNOLOGY INTEGRATION IDEA 5.17

TITLE: Using Spreadsheets to Teach Problem Solving—Understanding Probability

CONTENT AREA/TOPIC: Probability and statistics

GRADE LEVEL: Middle and junior high school

NETS FOR STUDENTS: Standards 1, 3, 4, 5, 6

DESCRIPTION: Students use spreadsheets to do calculations as they learn a four-step sequence for problem solving. The teacher prepares students to learn the problem-solving approach by reviewing the contradiction strategy. This procedure attacks a problem by identifying clues to aid in the solution and then answering questions about which solutions are possible and not possible. When students are comfortable with this approach, the teacher introduces spreadsheet use in the context of two types of problems: coin problems and ratio problems. In a coin problem, students know a certain number of coins and a total sum and must determine how many of each coin could give the sum. In the ratio problem, students must find three 3-digit numbers that use all of the digits 1 through 9 only once; the ratio of the first number to the second number must be 1:2 and the ratio of the first number to the third number must be 1:3 (a 1:2:3 ratio). For each kind of problem, the teacher presents a prepared spreadsheet to support the necessary calculations. Then, the four-step problem-solving procedure is introduced: Understand the problem, devise a plan, carry out the plan, and look back. The class works through these problems in small groups and then discusses procedures and solutions together.

Source: Sgroi, R. (1992). Systematizing trial and error using spreadsheets. *Arithmetic Teacher, 39*(7), 8–12.

TECHNOLOGY INTEGRATION IDEA 5.18

TITLE: Using Spreadsheets to Teach Problem Solving—The Pizza Problem

CONTENT AREA/TOPIC: Hypothesis testing in mathematics

GRADE LEVEL: Elementary school

NETS FOR STUDENTS: Standards 1, 3, 4, 5, 6

DESCRIPTION: Students use a spreadsheet to help do numerical calculations involved in problem solving. Spreadsheets can help with the calculations involved in solving problems and can support the conceptual development related to these activities. With the first problem, students visit a pizza parlor that serves three different size pizzas (small, medium, and large) and divides them into four, six, and eight portions. Students discuss whether individual portions are equal across all three sizes. They talk about whether it is more cost effective to buy two small pizzas of four portions each, or one large pizza with eight portions. They make initial estimates and then measure the pizzas. After discussion of the best methods to use and after making some initial calculations, they form initial hypotheses, look at the kinds of calculations necessary to solve the problems, and enter the data and formulas into the spreadsheet. After determining the solution to their problem, they change the pricing parameters to answer "what if?" questions. Then they change the radii of the pizzas until the cost for all sizes is equal.

Source: Paul, J. (1995). Pizza and spaghetti. *The Computing Teacher, 22*(7), 65–67.

TECHNOLOGY INTEGRATION IDEA 5.19

TITLE: Using Spreadsheets to Teach Problem Solving—Scale Modeling

CONTENT AREA/TOPIC: Scales in mathematics

GRADE LEVEL: 5–12

NETS FOR STUDENTS: Standards 1, 3, 4, 5, 6

DESCRIPTION: From this kind of activity, students learn that a scale is a relationship between a linear measurement on a model and the corresponding measurement on the actual object. They can use spreadsheets to create and use scales in order to build models or to study the features of real systems. For example, they can create a spreadsheet of the planets in the solar system, entering the diameter of each planet and the sun. They can decide on a scale and enter a formula to determine the diameter in that scale. Building a model from this scale would help students study the relative sizes of these bodies.

Source: Albrecht, B., & Davis, P. (2000). Measurement and modeling. *Learning and Leading with Technology, 28*(2), 32–35, 39–41.

TECHNOLOGY INTEGRATION IDEA 5.20

TITLE: Using Spreadsheets to Teach Problem Solving—Solve a Pattern, Find a Formula

CONTENT AREA/TOPIC: Math word problems

GRADE LEVEL: 6–12

NETS FOR STUDENTS: Standards 1, 3, 4, 5, 6

DESCRIPTION: Many mathematics word problems involving patterns can be solved by building a table. For example, to figure out how many bricks there would be in a pyramid if the bottom row is 50 bricks and the pyramid is 50 bricks high, students can build a table manually to solve this kind of problem, but they still would have to calculate the sum of the first 50 integers. By entering a formula in the spreadsheet and copying down, the calculations are done automatically, taking the labor out of the problem solving. They develop the formula by looking at the numbers involved in the first couple of rows in the table and figuring out the pattern.

Source: Feicht, L. (2000). Finding the formula: Using a spreadsheet to solve a pattern. *Learning and Leading with Technology, 27*(6), 36–41.

TECHNOLOGY INTEGRATION IDEA 5.21

TITLE: Using Spreadsheets to Teach Problem Solving—The Twelve Days of Christmas Conundrum

CONTENT AREA/TOPIC: Math word problems

GRADE LEVEL: 4

NETS FOR STUDENTS: Standards 1, 3, 4, 5, 6

DESCRIPTION: To do this "holiday problem solving," students create a spreadsheet to figure out how many items would be involved in the "12 Days of Christmas" song. They build the spreadsheet by entering the number of days, then the number of items for that day. Then they copy across for the remaining days, and enter a formula to sum the number of partridges, turtle doves, etc. Finally, they enter a formula to sum the number of items for each day and the total overall. This strategy can be the basis of other similar problems.

Source: Baugh, I. (1999–2000). The twelve days of Christmas. *Learning and Leading with Technology, 27*(4), 18–21.

Using Database Software in Teaching and Learning

Introduction to Database Software

Database defined. Databases are computer programs that allow users to store, organize, and manipulate information, including both text and numerical data. Database software can perform some calculations but its real power lies in allowing the user to locate information through keyword searches. Unlike word processing software, which can be compared to a typewriter, or a spreadsheet, which can be compared to a calculator, a database program has no electronic counterpart. It is most often compared to a file cabinet or a Rolodex card file. Like these pre-computer devices,

TECHNOLOGY INTEGRATION IDEA 5.22

TITLE: Using Spreadsheets to Store and Analyze—M&M Counts

CONTENT AREA/TOPIC: Mathematics hypothesis testing

GRADE LEVEL: 3

NETS FOR STUDENTS: Standards 1, 3, 4, 5, 6

DESCRIPTION: Students use a spreadsheet to record the results of their M&M counts and do various activities with estimation and prediction. The teacher must prepare for this activity by developing a paper M&M Record Form for each student and a spreadsheet for use by the whole class. Each student pair receives a bag of M&Ms and a form. They count and separate by color the M&Ms in their bag. Given what they know about the contents of their own bags, students use estimation and prediction to project what they will find by color and number for the whole class. Each student pair fills out its M&M Record Form. The pairs take turns entering their data into the spreadsheet. When all data are in the spreadsheet, the students reevaluate their predictions. The teacher shares the spreadsheet sums and averages using an overhead projector and LCD panel and the class compares predictions with the actual totals and averages. The teacher ends by summarizing the prediction and estimation processes the class has used.

Source: Based on a lesson from *Microsoft Productivity in the Classroom*. Copyright 1997 by the Microsoft Corporation.

Teaching Students to Use Spreadsheets

Recommended Activity Sequence

To take advantage of the power of spreadsheet software in their classroom, teachers may have to teach their students spreadsheet basics and help them build their skills over time. A sequence for developing these skills and a set of curriculum-based exercises is available in a separate text by Mills and Roblyer (2003).

Common Mistakes and Misconceptions

Many beginning spreadsheet users encounter some common problems. If you are having problems, look over this list to see if you can find a solution:

- **Forgetting to highlight cells to be formatted.** The computer cannot format a cell in the spreadsheet until the user highlights the affected cells *first* and *then* selects the option. If a chosen formatting option doesn't work for the cells you are trying to format, be sure you first indicate the part of the worksheet where the format should apply.
- **Difficulties in developing formulas.** Perhaps the most common problems in spreadsheet use have to do with creating formulas. This results from failing to complete the first step in the procedure for creating formulas: placing the cursor in the correct cell. The next most common problem results from pressing the Right Arrow key (instead of the Return or Enter key) to leave the cell while creating a formula. Rather than moving the pointer, this action adds something to the formula. Many students become confused when they see a formula grow as they struggle to leave the cell. Another common problem with formulas is accidentally including the formula cell itself in the formula's calculation. This is sometimes called a *circular reference error.* Even if an error message does not appear, this error usually is spotted quickly because the formula results in much larger numbers than expected.

the purpose of a database is to store important information in a way that makes it easy to locate later. This capability becomes increasingly important as society's store of essential information continues to grow in volume and complexity.

People often use the term *database* to refer both to the computer program and the product it creates; however, database products are also sometimes called *files.* While a spreadsheet stores an item of data in a cell, a database stores one item of data in a location usually called a *field.* Although each field represents one item of information in a database, perhaps the more important unit of information is a record, since it relates directly to the designated purpose of the database file. For example, in a database of student records, each record corresponds to a student and it consists of several fields of information about the student such as name, address, age, and parents' names. In a database of information on a school's inventory of instructional resources, each record represents one resource and consists of several fields describing aspects such as title, publisher, date published, and location.

Database software packages vary considerably in the format and appearance of information. Figure 5.5 shows an example database file on genetic traits observed in students (Revenaugh, 1997). Designed to help teach about heredity and how genetics determines human characteristics, the database holds a record for each student in the class and each item about a student (such as age, eye color, and height) appears in a field.

Figure 5.5 Example Database for Instruction: Genetic Characteristics

Source: "Microsoft Access" from *Productivity Tools in the Classroom* by Microsoft Corporation. © Microsoft Corp.

The importance of databases. Teachers face a challenge in trying to do justice to the usefulness of database software in a classroom or curriculum. Unlike word processing or spreadsheet programs, instruction using databases may require a fairly dramatic shift in the way a teacher thinks and teaches. Some cite the database program's potential for facilitating new, constructivist teaching strategies as the source of its reputation as an indispensable classroom tool. Heine (1994) said, "A database is one of the computer tools that students should be able to use by the end of elementary school" (p. 39). Teachers have long recognized the unique capabilities of database software to support instruction in problem solving, research skills, and information management. Teachers also have found databases useful for teaching higher level concepts such as classification and keyword searching to young students (Hollis, 1990; Jankowski, 1993–1994). Students as young as 6 or 7 can begin to learn how to classify and group people or animals according to characteristics and how to locate entries that match a certain description.

However, the productivity uses of databases for teachers have not proven as popular as those with tools such as word processing. Most teachers need not create their own management system to keep inventories of classroom materials or records on student performance, relying instead on systems in the main office for such vital information. Teachers use prepared databases much more widely than ever before; however, they do not usually create them.

Types of database programs and products. Database programs can be categorized in several ways. The first classification separates packages according to purpose. As with word processing and spreadsheet programs, a database program can be an application on its own such as *FileMaker Pro* or part of an integrated package such as *Microsoft Works* or *AppleWorks* that also contains software for word processing, spreadsheets, graphics production, and/or telecommunications. There are also prepared database files that give access to existing collections of information. Prepared databases usually are designed to support learning of curriculum topics or make research tasks more efficient. Sometimes these collections are available on media such as CD-ROM, computer disk, or online via telecommunications.

Another way to categorize database products is according to their schemes for storing and organizing information. A flat file database program produces a single file consisting of records, each with several fields. Another kind of database program, a *relational database,* links or relates separate files through a common field called a *key field.* For example, a student database containing personal background data may be linked to another student database with course and grade histories. These files are linked through a common field such as student name or Social Security number. The database program can draw reports from either file through the key field.

A final way to categorize database products is according to their levels of capability. More capable systems are also more complex to use, but some complex systems provide database management systems (DBMSs) that give users helpful interfaces to the databases. This interface is a language. A structured query language (SQL) is an actual programming language which makes it easier to select items from the database for reports of various kinds. Most, but not all, relational database systems also have DBMSs.

General database features and capabilities. Database programs offer several kinds of capabilities for handling information that could not be used for information stored in a noncomputer format such as on paper in file folders in a file cabinet. Although capabilities and procedures vary from program to program, most programs have the following features:

- **Allowing changes to information.** To make changes to paper documents, one must locate documents from each of the file folders that contain copies of the information. One must then retype or otherwise alter the sheets of paper. Computer users can access information stored in a database from a number of locations (either via disk or at a terminal), no matter where it is physically stored. Changing data usually means simply calling up the file and editing information on-screen in one or more fields or giving a command to search and update all the information that meets certain criteria.
- **Sorting information alphabetically or numerically.** The computer's ability to put data in order is handy when information is stored in a database. The program can sort or order records according to data in any one of the fields. For example, student records could be printed out alphabetically according to the Last Name field, or the same information could sort student information from youngest to oldest by the Age field.
- **Searching for information.** All database programs allow users to search for and compare information according to keywords. For example, a teacher might want to lo-

cate the records of all teenaged students in a certain grade. If the information were stored in file folders, the teacher would have to go through each one, look up the person's birthday, and check to see if it fell before a certain date. With a database, the teacher could simply give a command to display all records whose Age field contained a number higher than 12 or whose Birthdate field contained a year lower than a certain year.

■ **Automatically retrieving reports or information summaries.** Storing information in databases makes it easier to prepare summaries across all data elements. For example, a teacher may want to group students for work outside class on group projects; the database could indicate when each student could meet outside class time. The teacher could search for all students who had free periods at the same time and assign these students to work together.

■ **Merging with word processing documents.** A user can insert information stored in a database automatically in several letters or other word processing documents simply by preparing one document and putting field names in it instead of actual names or other information. The information stored in those fields for each record is automatically inserted as each copy of the document is printed out. This process is called *merging* the database with the word processing document.

The Impact of Databases in Education

Relative advantages of databases. Database programs and products are in widespread use in classrooms at all levels of education. They offer teachers and students the following kinds of unique benefits:

■ **Reducing data redundancy.** In education, as in business and industry, many organizations need access to the same kinds of information on the same people or resources. In pre-computer days, each organization had to maintain its own stores of information that were often identical to those of other organizations. For example, each school office and school district office might have duplicate files on teachers and students. Nowadays, since databases can be accessed from multiple locations, an organization needs to keep only one actual copy of these kinds of information. This cuts down on both the expense and the physical space needed to store the information.

■ **Saving time locating and/or updating information.** People need to locate information and keep it accurate—time is money. It takes time to find the information and keep it updated for everyone who needs it. Since a database stores information in a central computer instead of in several different file folders in various offices, users can find information more quickly and they can more easily make changes whenever updates are needed. For example, if a student's address or legal guardian changes, updating the information in a database is both quicker and easier than locating and changing it in many file folders.

■ **Allowing comparisons of information through searches across files.** Electronic databases also offer an important capability of locating information that meets several criteria at once. For example, a teacher may want to locate all of the resources in video format at a certain grade level that focus on a certain topic. A database search would make locating these materials an easy task compared to a search of library shelves. For a large collection of information, this kind of search is possible *only* if information is stored in a database.

Issues related to databases. Databases are permanent and pervasive parts of life in the information age. They allow users to locate bits of important data in a landscape crowded with information; they support decisions with confirmed facts rather than assumptions; and they put the power of knowledge at our fingertips. Yet this power is not without its dangers, and knowing how to find information is not the same as knowing what one can or should do with it.

Simplifying access versus safeguarding privacy. Each of our names is listed, along with much of our personal information, on literally dozens of databases. This cataloging begins when we are born—even before we are named—when we appear on the hospital's patient database. Our doctors and schools—even our places of worship—have our names and other notes about us in their databases. Whenever we apply for credit cards, driver's licenses, or jobs, we enter still more databases. These information entities reside on computers that can communicate and exchange notes, so information in one database can be shared with many information systems. Education, like other systems in our society, has come to depend on ready access to these information sources.

However, easy access to information about people long has been recognized as a threat to personal privacy. If information is easy to access, it may also be easy for unauthorized people to obtain and possibly misuse or for organizations to use it in ways that violate basic human rights. In the Privacy Act of 1974, Congress formally recognized the problems presented by government access to information on private citizens. This law requires that federal agencies identify publicly the records they maintain on U.S. citizens. It also limits the kinds of information that can be kept and requires that people be told what information the government keeps on them.

As teachers begin to keep student information in classroom databases and use information from school and district databases, they must recognize their responsibility to safeguard this private information and protect it from unauthorized access. Sometimes this means keeping disks in secure places; sometimes it means making sure passwords remain secret. It may also mean deleting information if parents or students request that it be deleted. It always means being sensitive to who is looking at screens or printouts containing personal student information.

Instructional uses of databases. The literature reflects extensive applications of databases for instructional purposes. There are several reasons for this early popularity. First, databases are, like word processing and spreadsheets, a completely philosophy-free technology resource. They can be used in teacher-directed ways or to support student-directed projects. Second, databases are a relatively inexpensive type of software, with a wide range of capabilities; thus, they can be used effectively in ways ranging from very simple to very complex. Hunter (1983) and Collis (1988) were among the first to document the uses of microcomputer databases for instructional purposes. Their books contain many varied lesson plans and demonstrate that databases could underlie teaching and learning activities for many content areas and grade levels. Early database applications were frequently offered to teachers as good ways to teach problem-solving skills (Watson, 1993). However, some 10 years of use and research on the instructional applications of databases has shown that simply having students use them does not ensure learning of desired research and problem-solving skills.

Collis (1990) summarized six different studies on instructional uses of databases. She found that students can use databases to acquire useful skills in searching for and using information, but they need guidance to ask relevant questions and analyze results. If allowed to proceed on their own, students may regard a simple printed list of results as a sufficient measure of success. Studies by Maor (1991) in science and Ehman, Glenn, Johnson, and White (1992) in social studies yielded essentially the same results. Databases offer the most effective and meaningful help when they are embedded in a structured problem-solving process and when the activity includes class and small-group discussion of search results.

Using Databases in the Classroom

When to use databases: Teacher productivity. Most teachers can and do use databases to search for information about students and classroom resources. Today's classroom databases, unlike those from a decade ago, are produced and provided by the school or district, rather than created by the teacher. Teachers rely on these databases to make their work more efficient and productive in several ways:

- **Inventorying and locating instructional resources.** Teachers can look up titles and descriptions of instructional resources in a database system to help them identify materials that meet certain instructional needs. If a school has a large collection of resources used by all of the teachers, the school's library/media center probably catalogs this collection on a database designed for this purpose.
- **Using information on students to plan instruction and enhance motivation.** Student records information allows teachers to meet individual student needs in several ways. For example, a teacher might find information on student reading levels or learning problems. Information kept on each child's sports and other extracurricular activities could influence designs of motivating lessons and selection of materials that would attract attention. Personal touches for each student are easier to accomplish when all the information is on a database. A teacher might begin each week with a birthday search of the student database to give special congratulations or a banner for each student's birthday.
- **Using information on students to respond to questions or perform required tasks.** Teachers often are asked to supply personal information on students or deal with situations relating to their personal needs, yet it is difficult to remember everything on dozens of students. For example, some students require special medication; the teacher is responsible for reminding them to take it. A teacher might need to decide quickly whether a particular adult is authorized to take a child from the school. The school may provide a database with these kinds of information so the teacher can look them up quickly.
- **Sending personalized letters to parents and others.** The capability to merge database information with a word processing document is convenient whenever the teacher wants to send personalized notes to parents or to the students themselves. The teacher can create only one letter or note; the database program takes care of the personalizing.

When to use databases: Teaching and learning activities. When database software became available for microcomputers in the 1980s, instructional activities that made use of these tools quickly became popular. Thus, the literature reflects an increasing variety of applications for databases. The heaviest uses seem to be in social studies, but effective applications have been designed for topics in content areas from language arts to science. Here are some ways teachers use databases to enhance learning:

- **Teaching research and study skills.** Skills in locating and organizing information to answer questions and learn new concepts have always been as fundamental as reading and writing skills. Students need good research and study skills not only for school assignments, but also to help them learn on their own outside school. As the volume of information in our society increases, the need to learn how to locate important information quickly also grows. Before computers, families strived to buy reference tools such as a good dictionary and a set of encyclopedias so that children could do research for their school reports and other assignments. Today, these and other sources are stored on electronic media and students need to know how to do computer searches of these references. (See Technology Integration Ideas 5.23 and 5.24.) In one sense, electronic formats make it easier to access information; thus, they support student learning and make it easier to acquire study skills. However, because of the unique capabilities offered by databases, looking up information in electronic formats is a far different activity than doing research in books. To take advantage of the new information resources available to them, students must learn new skills such as using keywords and Boolean logic (looking for references with the keywords Macintosh AND Apple but NOT fruit). They must also learn skills in operating computer equipment and

TECHNOLOGY INTEGRATION IDEA 5.23

TITLE: Teaching Research and Study Skills—A Database Journal for Mathematics

CONTENT AREA/TOPIC: Math study skills

GRADE LEVEL: 4

NETS FOR STUDENTS: Standards 1, 3, 4, 5, 6

DESCRIPTION: In this activity, students keep a mathematics journal to enhance their learning and help them remember and apply what they learn. They use a database to help them record and manage information on what happened in class each day, what they learned, and how to apply it in real life. For example, students frequently feel they have not learned much in a mathematics class. To give them a more concrete picture of mathematics skills they have acquired, ask them to review what they have learned about a specific topic under the "Today I Learned" field. Although they may feel they have not learned a lot, their own notes will show them what they have accomplished. Have them sort the "Feeling" field to identify and tell the teacher the topics they enjoyed most and least. Have them determine how the topic they are about to learn relates to what they've already learned. Have them use one or more keywords to search the "Summary" field. For example, if they are about to begin a unit on measurement, have them do a search on the word "measure" and see what turns up.

Source: Gettys, D. (1994). Journaling with a database. *The Computing Teacher, 22*(2), 37–40.

TECHNOLOGY INTEGRATION IDEA 5.24

TITLE: Teaching Research and Study Skills—Surveying Activities

CONTENT AREA/TOPIC: Analyzing data from a survey

GRADE LEVEL: All grades

NETS FOR STUDENTS: Standards 1, 3, 4, 5, 6

DESCRIPTION: Curriculum blending or curriculum overlapping is the practice of having students at all ability levels—including those with physical or learning disabilities—work on the same activities, but grading them differently. The authors propose that having students do surveys and analyze the data are ideal activities for this purpose. The teacher selects a topic for the survey. The topic in this article was "favorite fruits." Older students may gather more types of data (e.g., on characteristics of people surveyed), whereas younger students may collect fewer types of data. For students with physical disabilities, you may set up a station to support asking the questions and recoding the responses. Select a location and time of day at which students will do the surveying. (Be sure to get approval from the administration.) Have students rehearse a questioning sequence in advance, so it will move quickly when they actually begin the survey. Many different kinds of analysis activities can be done, depending on students' ages and abilities.

Source: Judd-Wall, J. (1996). Curriculum blending: Computerized surveying activities for everyone. *Learning and Leading with Technology, 23*(8), 61–64.

using procedures and commands required by database software. Many database activities are designed to introduce these kinds of searches along with information for a report or a group project.

■ **Teaching organization skills.** Students need to understand concepts related to handling information. To solve problems, they must locate the right information and organize it in such a way that they can draw relationships between isolated elements. One way to teach these skills is to have students develop and use their own databases; many examples of this kind of activity have been reported. Even very young students can learn about organizing information by creating databases of information about themselves, including birth dates, heights, weights, eye colors, pets, and parents' names. They can then do simple searches of their databases to summarize information about the members of their class. These kinds of activities help students understand what information is and how to use it. In later grades, students can design and create databases related to areas of study. For example, a class might create a database of descriptive information on candidates running for office in their state or in a national election. (See Technology Integration Ideas 5.25 and 5.26.)

■ **Understanding the power of information "pictures."** Students need to understand the persuasive power of information organized into databases. Sometimes a database can generate an information "picture" that may not be visible in any other way. Although these pictures may or may not be completely accurate, many decisions are based on them. For example, the U.S. government uses information databases on those who have been convicted of past income tax

Technology Integration Idea 5.25

TITLE: Teaching Organization Skills—A Database Yearbook

CONTENT AREA/TOPIC: Organizing information for research

GRADE LEVEL: 2

NETS FOR STUDENTS: Standards 1, 3, 4, 5, 6

DESCRIPTION: The second-grade teachers introduce the yearbook project to students by talking about the district's curricular theme ("Beginnings") and about the things students would like to know about each other. Each class brainstorms the 10 most important kinds of information about themselves. Then all the second-grade teachers consolidate the areas into the final 10 to be included in the database. The computer teacher creates a database template and models for the teachers how to collect the information with their classes by using butcher paper on the wall. Once the classes collect the information, students work in pairs to enter it into the database in their own classrooms. When the database is completed, teachers help the students use it to answer questions about themselves, for example, "How many kids like pizza?" and "What is the class's favorite color?" Teachers then create the yearbooks by printing out the database records for their classes and adding a picture for each student, a graphic cover, and an introduction. Many kinds of learning activities can be designed based on this information.

Source: Hollis, R. (1990). Database yearbooks in the second grade. *The Computing Teacher, 17*(6), 14–15.

Technology Integration Idea 5.26

TITLE: Teaching Organization Skills—A Personal Music Database

CONTENT AREA/TOPIC: Organizing information for research

GRADE LEVEL: Middle school

NETS FOR STUDENTS: Standards 1, 3, 4, 5, 6

DESCRIPTION: Students learn how to organize and manage data by creating a database that catalogs their music collection of CDs and tapes. They sort, analyze, and print selected database records in answer to questions about their favorite music recordings and performing artists. After discussions of the advantages (inexpensive) and disadvantages (easy to lose) of conventional paper-based memory boosters, explain to students that they will build a database to catalog either their home music collection of audio CDs, records, and cassette tapes or the collection available in the school music room/library. Tell students that they will learn how to manage information by creating numbered records that they arrange, retrieve, sort, and print. Information is entered about each recording artist, record, track, track title, and track length by tabbing from one field to another to move through the list. Once they have database information in *MS Word,* students can report on the results. Who's their favorite artist? What's their favorite music category? What's their favorite musical instrument? Would any of their other data collections benefit from database management?

Source: Based on a lesson from *Microsoft Productivity in the Classroom.* Copyright 1997 by the Microsoft Corporation.

offenses to generate descriptive profiles of people who may be likely to try to defraud the government in the future. Students can learn to use database information to generate these types of pictures. (See Technology Integration Idea 5.27.)

■ **Posing and testing hypotheses.** Many problem-solving activities involve asking questions and locating information to answer them. Therefore, using databases is an ideal way to teach and provide practice with this kind of problem solving. Students can either research prepared databases full of information related to a content area, or they may create their own databases, which is not as common nowadays. Either way, these activities encourage them to look for information that will support or refute a position. In lower grades, the teacher may pose the question and assign students to search databases to answer it. Later, the activity may call for students to both pose and answer appropriate questions. For example, the teacher may ask students to address popular beliefs concerning artistic or gifted people. The students formulate questions, form debate teams, and design searches of databases on famous people to support their positions. (See Technology Integration Ideas 5.28 and 5.29.)

■ **Searching for information during research.** Much of the world's information is stored in databases, and these "information banks" are becoming more available to students and other nontechnical people for everyday use. As they develop their skills in locating and analyzing information during research, students need practice in using standard searching procedures to locate information in databases. (See Technology Integration Idea 5.30.)

TECHNOLOGY INTEGRATION IDEA 5.27

TITLE: Creating Information Pictures—Getting a Clearer Focus on History

CONTENT AREA/TOPIC: U.S. history

GRADE LEVEL: High school

NETS FOR STUDENTS: Standards 1, 3, 4, 5, 6

DESCRIPTION: Students use a database of 1835 census information on Cherokee citizens of the United States to gain a more accurate historical perspective on the Cherokee lifestyle and culture than is available from traditional written sources. This activity is designed to impress social studies students with the power of database information for finding a truer picture of people or events than they can get in sources such as public papers, letters, and diaries. For example, much information about the lives of long-dead people can be gleaned from information such as tax rules, census reports, and church and business records—information that is difficult to manage without a database. The example in this lesson is a study of the Cherokee nation in the 1800s. The documents of the time paint a picture of a savage and uncultivated people. But as they begin their review of the database of 1835 census information on the Cherokee nation, students begin to see a more complex picture evident in data from the time. They write a summary of their findings and whether or not their beliefs about the events of the time have changed as a result.

Source: Thomas, R. (1991). A focus on history. *The Computing Teacher, 18*(6), 30–33.

TECHNOLOGY INTEGRATION IDEA 5.28

TITLE: Posing and Testing Hypotheses—Investigating Graveyard Data with Spreadsheets

CONTENT AREA/TOPIC: Social studies

GRADE LEVEL: Middle school

NETS FOR STUDENTS: Standards 1, 3, 4, 5, 6

DESCRIPTION: Students visit local graveyards, gather headstone data, enter them into a database, and answer questions about life span through database queries. Students work together in pairs, first dividing up the rows to work on so that all will be covered and none duplicated. They use a data collection sheet to gather surnames, first names, dates of death, ages at death, and other details they thought relevant. They use math skills to calculate the age at death from the headstone data on birth date and date of death. After they collect all the data, the class is divided into three groups, and each group enters the data in 2-hour sessions. Students scroll through the data to get a feel for what is covered and how it looks in summary form. They sort data alphabetically by surname to see what families were represented. Teachers ask students to form some questions to ask about the data and what it showed. Possible questions: Do women live longer than men? Did people live longer in the 20th century than they did in the 19th century? They sort data by date of death and by age to count occurrences in specific age or year categories. They work in pairs to make tables and graphs to represent their findings.

Source: Paul, J., and Kaiser, C. (1996). Do women live longer than men? Investigating graveyard data with computers. *Learning and Leading with Technology, 23*(8), 13–15.

TECHNOLOGY INTEGRATION IDEA 5.29

TITLE: Posing and Testing Hypotheses—A Rock Database Project

CONTENT AREA/TOPIC: Geology

GRADE LEVEL: 3–8

NETS FOR STUDENTS: Standards 1, 3, 4, 5, 6

DESCRIPTION: A unit of study on rocks forms the basis for learning science inquiry skills. A database of information on rocks helps organize the information for use in supporting these problem-solving activities. The National Geographic filmstrip "Rocks and Minerals" supplies background information on the unit. This stimulates students' natural interest in rocks and minerals and they spontaneously begin to collect rock samples to sort, observe, and classify. The teacher introduces the three main types of rocks and the rock formation cycle. Laserdisc pictures supplement reference book pictures. Students each select one mineral to research. They enter the information they find into a database. The teacher and student then develop questions and use the database to answer them. Typical questions are "Which crystal structures are the most common?" and "What makes certain minerals valuable?" A printed set of questions can be used later as a consolidating exercise. They use an MECC simulation, "Murphy's Minerals," to follow up this technique of testing and identifying minerals according to characteristics.

Source: Hartson, T. (1993). Rocks, mineral, databases, and simulations. *The Computing Teacher, 21*(1), 48–50.

TECHNOLOGY INTEGRATION IDEA 5.30

TITLE: Using Online Databases for Research—Hunting for Celestial Bodies

CONTENT AREA/TOPIC: Astronomy

GRADE LEVEL: 6 and up

NETS FOR STUDENTS: Standards 1, 3, 4, 5, 6

DESCRIPTION: Throughout the history of astronomy, ordinary people have discovered new comets and asteroids. Now databases of existing celestial bodies are available to help people determine if they have identified a previously unnamed object in the sky. Teachers can have their students choose an area of the night sky, download from the Internet two or more images taken on different evenings, and compare them to see if they have different objects in them. Then they can use a database such as *Starry Night* (a planetarium program available from Sienna Software) to see if the "new" objects are already identified. If they are not, students can contact astronomers to find out if they have discovered a new nova, asteroid, or comet.

Source: Erickson, D. (1999). Hunting for asteroids, comets, and novas. *Learning and Leading with Technology, 26*(6), 22–24.

Teaching Students to Use Databases

Common Mistakes and Misconceptions

Teaching students how to develop their own databases (i.e., select fields and enter data) is not as common an activity as it used to be. In many schools, it is limited primarily to technology education and business skills classes. However, some teachers may teach database development as a way of teaching organization skills, as described above. For teachers who do teach database development, the following problems may occur:

- **Confusing spreadsheet and database features.** Depending on the software package, a spreadsheet or worksheet may look similar to a database listing. Sometimes learners get confused about what they see on the screen and which of their activities call for which kind of software. Some spreadsheet software has many database-like capabilities in the same package. But other packages have separate software components for spreadsheet and database functions and they produce separate outputs for each one. When a spreadsheet is a separate package or component, it normally can be identified by its characteristic row numbers and column letters. Use a spreadsheet for anything that calls for extensive calculations; to organize information so it can be searched, you need database capabilities. A spreadsheet can produce a simple chart with nicely formatted straight rows and columns more easily than a database.
- **Difficulties with keyword searches.** The most useful feature of databases also presents the most difficulties for new users. A keyword search automatically reviews the whole database and selects only those records that contain certain words, phrases, or numbers. A user can combine several different keywords using the principles of Boolean logic. New users make the most mistakes with database searches when they do not understand how this logic works. When constructing a search, it is sometimes helpful to create a diagram or picture that shows graphically the expected results.

Exercises

Record and apply what you have learned.

Chapter 5 Self-Test

To review terms and concepts in this chapter, take the Chapter 5 self-test. Select Chapter 5 from the front page of the Companion Website (located at http://www.prenhall.com/roblyer), then choose the *Multiple Choice* module.

Portfolio Activities

ISTE The following activities address ISTE National Educational Technology Standards for Teachers (NETS-T) and will help you add to your professional portfolio. To complete these activities online and save or submit the materials electronically, select Chapter 5 from the front page of the Companion Website (http://www.prenhall.com/roblyer), then choose the *Portfolio* module.

1. ***Software Tools List (NETS-T Standards: I-B, II-C, D, E)*** Describe how you plan to use each of the software tools described in this chapter to support instruction in your classroom.
2. ***Tool Templates (NETS-T Standard: V-C)*** Choose an appropriate software tool and develop a template you can use from year to year for each of the following purposes:
   - Classroom letterhead
   - Grade sheets and/or attendance lists
   - Records (names, addresses, birth dates) for students in your classes.

Questions for Thought and Discussion

These questions may be used for small-group or class discussion or may be subjects for individual or group activities. To take part in these discussions online, select Chapter 5 from the front page of the Companion Website (http://www.prenhall.com/roblyer), then choose the *Message Board* module.

1. Word processing is a software valued by many teachers but is criticized by some who feel it is ruining our handwriting and making us overreliant on technology to do our writing. How would you respond to these critics?
2. The increasing use of databases in our society, combined with pervasive use of the Internet, is making it very easy to get access to personal information about anyone. What implications arise regarding the safety and privacy of students in our schools? What is the teacher's role in these privacy and security issues?

Collaborative Activities

ISTE

The following activities address ISTE National Educational Technology Standards for Teachers (NETS-T) and can be done in small groups. Each group should present the findings to the class in a format they know how to use (word-processed report, presentation software, multimedia product). Completed group products can be copied and shared with the entire class and/or included in each person's personal portfolio.

1. ***Software Tools Lesson Plans (NETS-T Standards: I-B; II-D, E; IV-C; V-C)*** Each small group selects one of the following tools and integration strategies and develops a lesson plan based on it:
   - **Word processing development.** Develop a classroom lesson activity that integrates word processing functions into instruction in one or more of these ways. For each lesson, create an example product either you or students might create for the activity:
     - Writing processes
     - Dynamic group products
     - Language and writing exercises.
   - **Spreadsheet development.** Develop a classroom lesson activity that integrates spreadsheet functions into instruction in one or more of the following ways. For each lesson, create an example product either you or students might create for the activity:
     - Presenting demonstrations
     - Developing student products
     - Supporting problem solving
     - Storing and analyzing data
     - Projecting grades.
   - **Database development.** Develop a classroom lesson activity that integrates database functions into instruction in one or more of the following ways. For each lesson, create an example product either you or students might create for the activity:
     - Teaching research and study skills
     - Teaching information organization skills
     - Creating information pictures
     - Posing and testing hypotheses.

   Each lesson activity will be evaluated according to the following criteria. It should:
     - Have a realistic time frame, so students can learn to use the software before applying it.
     - Use the unique capabilities of the software to support instructional activities.
     - Save instructional time, support the logistics involved in the lesson, and/or make possible instructional activities that would be impossible otherwise.

Integrating Technology Across the Curriculum Activities

The *Integrating Technology Across the Curriculum* CD-ROM is a set of technology integration ideas and links to online lessons, arranged as a searchable database. The CD comes packaged with this textbook. Complete the following exercises using this CD:

1. Word processing is a software tool that teachers can use to encourage writing across the curriculum. Locate lesson ideas that demonstrate some of the ways word processing can foster writing skills in content areas such as mathematics, science, and social studies. Review the lessons and make a chart like the ones you did for Chapters 1 and 2, but this time, make it look like the one at right:

Sample Integration Ideas for Word Processing Across the Curriculum

Content Areas	Name of Lesson Idea Using Word Processing
Mathematics	
Science	
Social studies	
Art/music	

2. Of the three tools commonly seen in integrated software packages (word processing, spreadsheets, databases), which is the most popular instructional tool for each content area? Hypothesize an answer to this question, then check your hypothesis against the number of plans you find on the CD for each content area. Make a chart similar to the one at right to display your results. After you determine the most common software for each area, tell why you think it is so popular.

Content Areas	Word Processing	Spreadsheet	Databases
Mathematics			
Science			
Social studies			
Art/music			

References

Bangert-Drowns, R. (1993). The word processor as an instructional tool: A meta-analysis of word processing in writing instruction. *Review of Educational Research, 63*(1), 69–93.

Black, T. R. (1999). Simulations on spreadsheets for complex concepts: Teaching statistical power as an example. *Journal of Mathematics, Education, and Science Technology, 30*(4), 473–481.

Bozeman, W. (1992). Spreadsheets. In G. Bitter (Ed.), *Macmillan encyclopedia of computers.* New York: Macmillan.

Collis, B. (1988). *Computer, curriculum, and whole-class instruction.* Belmont, CA: Wadsworth.

Collis, B. (1990). *The best of research windows: Trends and issues in educational computing.* Eugene, OR: International Society for Technology in Education (ERIC Document Reproduction No. ED 323 993).

Ehman, L., Glenn, A., Johnson, V., & White, C. (1992). Using computer databases in student problem solving: A study of eight social studies teachers' classrooms. *Theory and Research in Social Education, 20*(2), 179–206.

Harris, J. (1985). Student writers and word processing. *College Composition and Communication, 36*(3), 323–330.

Hauger, G. (2000). Instantaneous rate of change: A numerical approach. *Journal of Mathematics, Education, and Science Technology, 31*(6), 891–897.

Hawisher, G. (1986, April). The effects of word processing on the revision strategies of college students. Paper presented at the Annual Meeting of the American Educational Research Association, San Francisco, CA (ERIC Document Reproduction Service No. ED 268 546).

Hawisher, G. (1989). Research and recommendations for computers and compositions. In G. Hawisher & C. Selfe (Eds.), *Critical perspectives on computers and composition instruction.* New York: Teachers College Press.

Heine, E. (1994). The world at their fingertips. *The Florida Technology in Education Quarterly, 7*(1), 38–42.

Hollis, R. (1990). Database yearbooks in the second grade. *The Computing Teacher, 17*(6), 14–15.

Humphries, D. (1989). A computer training program for teachers. In C. Selfe, D. Rodrigues, & W. Oates (Eds.), *Computers in English and the language arts.* Urbana, IL: National Council of Teachers of English.

Hunter, B. (1983). *My students use computers.* Alexandria, VA: Human Resources Research Organization.

Jankowski, L. (1993–1994). Getting started with databases. *The Computing Teacher, 21*(4), 8–9.

Keizer, G. (1997). Which software works? *FamilyPC, 4*(5), 117–121.

Klass, P. (1988, April). Using microcomputer spreadsheet programs to teach statistical concepts (ERIC Document Reproduction Service No. ED 293 726).

Lewis, P. (2001). *Spreadsheet magic: Forty lessons using spreadsheets to teach curriculum in K–8 classrooms.* Eugene, OR: ISTE.

Maor, D. (1991, April). Development of student inquiry skills: A constructivist approach in a computerized classroom environment. Paper presented at the Annual Meeting of the National Association for Research in Science Teaching, Lake Geneva, WI, April 7–10, 1991 (ERIC Document Reproduction No. ED 326 261).

Mills, S., & Roblyer, M. D. (2003). *Technology tools for teachers: A Microsoft Office Tutorial.* Columbus, OH: Merrill/Prentice Hall.

Nelson, M. H. (1994). Processing poetry to develop literacy. *The Computing Teacher, 22*(3), 39–41.

Ploger, D., Rooney, M., & Klingler, L. (1996). Applying spreadsheets and draw programs in the classroom. *Tech Trends, 41*(3), 26–29.

Reed, W. M. (1996). Assessing the importance of computer-based writing. *Journal of Research on Computing in Education, 28*(4), 418–437.

Revenaugh, M. (1997). *Productivity in the classroom.* Redmond, WA: Microsoft Corporation (http://www.microsoft.com/education/k12/resource/lessons.htm).

Roblyer, M. D. (1997). Technology and the oops! effect: Finding a bias against word processing. *Learning and Leading with Technology, 24*(7), 14–16.

Snyder, I. (1993). Writing with word processors: A research overview. *Educational Research, 35*(1), 49–68.

Sutherland, R. (1993). A spreadsheet approach to solving algebra problems. *Journal of Mathematical Behavior, 12*(4), 353–383.

Viau, E. (1998). Color me a writer: Teaching students to think critically. *Learning and Leading with Technology, 25*(5), 17–20.

Watson, J. (1993). *Teaching thinking skills with databases* (Macintosh version). Eugene, OR: ISTE.

CHAPTER 6

Integrating Other Software Tools into Teaching and Learning

[T]he notion that computers are neutral and just another technological tool may seem quite a reasonable one. . . . But . . . think of the influence the automobile and television have had on our culture. The evidence is accumulating that computers are having a decided impact on the way our schools and society organize, communicate, and make decisions.

Joe Nathan, from *Micro-Myths,* 1985

This chapter covers the following topics:

- Definition and characteristics of a variety of software tools
- Unique advantages of each tool for various classroom activities
- Example classroom uses for each tool

Objectives

1. Use correct terminology to identify features and capabilities of several software tools.
2. Describe specific kinds of teaching and learning tasks for both teachers and students that each kind of tool can support.
3. Identify applications for software tools that educators would find valuable in making their work more efficient and productive.
4. Develop lesson activities that integrate the functions and capabilities of each of several software tools.

Introduction to Other Software Support Tools

Why Use Software Support Tools?

In Chapter 5, we discussed three of the most widely used software support tools: word processing, spreadsheet, and database programs. These have come to be viewed as the "basic three." However, a wide variety of other computer-based products exist that can support teachers and students in a multitude of teaching and learning tasks. These tools vary greatly in their purposes, the kinds of benefits they offer, and their utility for teachers. Some, such as electronic gradebooks and CMI tools, are designed to organize and analyze information; they are fast earning an image as indispensable aids for teachers struggling to cope with increasing amounts of data related to student performance and achievement. Other tools, such as certificate makers and clip art packages, serve merely to improve the appearance of instructional products and make it easier for teachers and students to produce attractive, professional-looking materials that inspire pride.

The tools described in this chapter range in importance from nearly essential to nice to have, and in function from presenting instruction to supporting background tasks that make a classroom run smoothly. However, each one has unique and powerful features. As Nathan (1985) emphasized, these tools, if used wisely and creatively, have the potential not only to support classroom activities, but also to transform the very nature of the way people learn and work.

Each tool described in this chapter requires additional classroom resources and time to learn and to implement. Teachers should choose them for the qualities and benefits they bring to the classroom, rather than simply because they are available on the market. Depending on the capabilities of a particular tool and the needs of the situation, a technology support tool can offer the same kinds of benefits described for the tools in Chapter 5: improved productivity, appearance, and accuracy, and more support for interaction.

Types of Software Support Tools

This chapter divides software support tools into six general categories or functions:

- **Materials generators** help teachers produce instructional materials.
- **Data collection and analysis tools** help teachers collect and organize numerical information that indicates student progress.
- **Graphics tools** allow production of images and illustration of documents.
- **Planning and organizing tools** help teachers and students conceptualize and communicate their ideas.
- **Research and reference tools** provide electronic versions of encyclopedias, atlases, and dictionaries, usually stored on CD-ROM.
- **Tools to support specific content areas** assist with activities associated with certain content areas.

Software Support Tools Covered in Other Chapters: Web Tools and Multimedia Authoring

The purpose of this chapter is to provide a comprehensive overview of software tools used in education, but two categories of tools are addressed in other parts of this textbook. Software tools used with distance learning and the Internet, either to develop materials for use on the Internet or to allow people to use the Internet, are covered in Chapter 8. Authoring software and other software tools (e.g., including presentation software such as *PowerPoint*) associated with developing multimedia and hypermedia products are described in Chapter 7.

Using Materials Generators

Desktop Publishing Software

Definitions: Desktop publishing versus desktop publishing software. It is perhaps ironic that one of the most useful and widely used of the technology tools is one that communicates information in a traditional medium: the printed page. By allowing teachers and students to design elaborate printed products, however, desktop publishing tools give them the important advantage of complete control over a potentially powerful form of communication. This control over the form and appearance of the printed page defines the activity of desktop publishing. According to Norvelle (1992), the term *desktop publishing* was coined in 1984 by Paul Brainerd, founder of the Aldus Corporation, to focus on the role of personal computers and laser printers in making the individual-as-publisher a viable concept.

Like word processing software, desktop publishing software allows manipulation of text; the capabilities and classroom applications of these two products overlap. Both kinds of tools allow users to mix text and graphics on each page. However, the key element in desktop publishing is more control over the design and production of a document. Teachers will find that they can use any available word processing software package to create most of the desktop publishing products they want to do (e.g., classroom brochures and newsletters). The more advanced layout features offered by desktop publishing software (e.g., font sizing, text kerning, layering of text and graphics boxes) are needed only if the teacher is showing students how to design and lay out large, complex documents such as newspapers and books.

From a technical standpoint, the primary difference between word processing software and desktop publishing tools is that the latter are designed to display documents as separate pages; the user clicks on icons for each page and only one page (or facing pages) display. Word processing "flows" pages in a continuous stream; the user scrolls down to view pages in the document. Because pages are viewed as separate units, desktop publishing allows more flexibility over the placement and formats of both text and graphics on individual pages. Word processing is designed to flow text from page to page as it is typed in. Text boxes can be done in word processing software, but they are harder to manage.

In the hands of experienced users, classroom products created with desktop publishing software can be as eye-catching and professional-looking as those produced by the most prestigious ad agency in New York, Chicago, or San Francisco. Just as the quality of a word-processed article depends on the skill of the writer, the quality of a newsletter or brochure from a desktop publishing system depends on the creativity and expertise of the designer. Thus, desktop publishing software focuses on designing communications through a combination of written words and page appearance, while word processing communicates the message primarily through words (McCain, 1993; Williams, 1994).

Elements of desktop publishing. Desktop publishing software gives power to users by allowing them to control three elements: page setup, text format, and graphics. They can create text boxes of any size and place them anywhere on the page. Users can manipulate text format by changing type font, size, style, and color. As noted earlier, software offers *fonts* in an ever-increasing array from plain, typewriter-looking Courier to fancy *Park Avenue*. Font size, measured in points (1 point equals about 1/72 inch), ranges from very small to as large as will fit on a page. (The type size for text in most books is about 10 points.) *Type style* refers to appearance changes such as **boldface,** *italics,* outlining, and underlining. Desktop publishing software also allows users to choose colors of type. For example, many documents use the special effect of white type on black backgrounds. Graphics of any kind can be designed using drawing tools provided by the software or the user can import existing pictures and diagrams into the document.

Types of desktop publishing software. Teachers can choose from a wide range of desktop publishing software for classroom use. Several packages, such as Microsoft's *Publish It!,* are designed especially for education or for simple newsletter production. For more sophisticated work, teachers may select one of the higher end packages used in professional design offices like *Quark XPress* or *PageMaker.* Naturally, these more capable packages take more time to learn. Schools usually choose these for more complicated design tasks that require advanced page design features such as creating complex, layered graphics and rotating graphic and text elements on the page.

Making the most of desktop publishing software: Skills and resources. Like other technology tools, desktop publishing is most effective if the user knows something about the activity before applying the tool. Designing effective print communications is an entire field of expertise in itself with its own degree programs. Graduates frequently are in high demand in business and industry. As Knupfer and McIsaac (1989) observe, many aspects of page design can influence reading speed and comprehension. They describe four different categories of variables that have been researched: graphic design, instructional text design, instructional graphics, and computer screen design. While the last category focuses on reading from a computer screen, Knupfer and McIsaac note that some of its features apply to both electronic and print-based research (p. 129), including factors such as text density and uppercase versus lowercase type.

However, even with this in mind, teachers and students need not be professional designers to create useful desktop publishing products, and their skills will improve with practice. According to Parker (1989) and Rose (1988), desktop publishing products have greater impact and communicate more clearly if they reflect some fairly simple design criteria. Beginners may want to keep the following suggestions in mind:

- **Select and use typefaces (fonts) carefully.** Unusual typefaces can help direct the eye toward text, but too many different fonts on a page are distracting and some fancy fonts can be difficult to read. A *serif font,* a font with small curves or "hands and feet" that extend from the ends of the letters, is easier to read in paragraphs; use it for text in the main body of the document. Use *sans serif type,* a font without extensions, for titles and headlines. Make type large enough to assist the reader. For example, younger readers usually need large point sizes.
- **Use visual cueing.** When specific information on the page is important, attract readers toward it by cueing them in one of several ways. Desktop publishing allows users to employ cueing devices like frames or boxes around text, bullets or arrows to designate important points, shading the part of the page behind the text, and changing the text in some way such as to **boldface** or *italic* type. Captions for pictures, diagrams, and headings also help to guide the reader's attention.

■ **Use white space well.** There is a saying in advertising that "white space sells." Don't be afraid to leave areas in a document with nothing in them at all; this will help focus attention on areas that do contain information.

■ **Create and use graphics carefully.** Use pictures and designs to focus attention and convey information, but remember that too many elaborate pictures or graphic designs can be distracting.

■ **Avoid common text format errors.** Parker (1989) describes 10 desktop design pitfalls to avoid. These include irregularly shaped text blocks, angled type, excessive underlining, widows and orphans (leftover single words and phrases at the tops or bottoms of pages), unequal spacing, excessive hyphenation, exaggerated tabs and indentations, grammatical errors, cramped logos and addresses, and too many typefaces.

To take full advantage of desktop publishing software, a system needs the right hardware and additional software. Remember some helpful resource hints:

■ **Recommended hardware.** With any design elements, desktop publishing products always are more professional looking if printed on a laser printer or a good-quality deskjet printer rather than on a dot matrix printer. Optical scanners and digital cameras also are useful for importing pictures and other graphics into a document.

■ **Recommended software tools.** Predesigned graphic tools can be very useful. One such tool is clip art packages, which contain computer files of drawings and logos. These are available on disk or CD-ROM and can be combined with each other or with original drawings to produce a desired picture. Whenever a document will be reused with modifications, it is helpful to save it in a file of templates or predesigned products. Some online compilations of free clip art include the following:

http://www.free-graphics.com/

http://www.clip-art.com/

http://dgl.microsoft.com/

When using clip art, users should be careful to address applicable copyright stipulations.

Example classroom applications. Desktop publishing software can be used for many of the same classroom activities and products as word processing software. Desktop publishing is the tool of choice, however, to produce elaborate, graphic-oriented documents. Teachers can use desktop publishing software to help them produce notices and documents for parents, students, or faculty members. Desktop publishing also can support some highly motivating classroom projects. Hermann (1988), McCarthy (1988), Newman (1988), Willinsky and Bradley (1990), and Reissman (2000) have reported instructional benefits of these uses for both students and teachers. These include increases in children's self-esteem when they publish their own work, heightened interest in and motivation to write for audiences outside the classroom, and improved quality of instruction through teacher collaboration. Here is a list of common classroom applications and ideas for implementing them:

■ **Letterhead.** Teachers can design their own individual stationery and encourage students to do the same for themselves or for the class. Students can design letterheads for their clubs or even for the school.

■ **Flyers and posters.** Whenever teachers or students must design announcements, desktop publishing can turn the chore into an instructional adventure. A simple notice of an upcoming event can become an opportunity to learn about designing attractive and interesting communications. Teachers can smuggle in instruction in grammar and spelling.

■ **Brochures.** For more extensive information than a simple flyer can convey or for information to be presented in a series, student projects can revolve around creating brochures. Popular examples of such classroom projects include travel brochures that report on student exploration during field trips, descriptions of the local region, and creative descriptions of organizations or activities.

■ **Newsletters and magazines.** The literature has reported many examples of classroom projects built around student-designed newsletters or magazines. Sometimes this activity represents the culmination of a large project such as a series of science experiments or a social studies research unit; sometimes it simply is a way for every student to contribute writing for a class project. All of these projects are highly motivational to students, and they attract "good press" for the teacher and the school.

■ **Books and booklets.** Even very young students are thrilled to produce and display their own personal books, which sometimes represent work produced over the course of a school year. Sometimes the books show creative works resulting from a competition; frequently, examples of students' best work are collected for a particular topic or time period. Students can sell their publications as a fund-raising activity, but this kind of project reaps other benefits for students of all abilities. Teachers of low-achieving students report that getting published has a positive impact on students' self confidence and self-esteem (McCarthy, 1988). (See Technology Integration Ideas 6.1 and 6.2.)

Test Generators and Test Question Banks

Software tools help teachers with what many consider one of the most onerous and time-consuming instructional tasks: producing on-paper tests. The teacher creates and enters the questions and the program prepares the test. The teacher either may print the required number of copies on the printer or print only one copy and make the required copies on a copy machine. These tools have several advantages, even over word processing programs (Gullickson & Farland, 1991). For one, they produce tests in a standard layout; the teacher need not worry about arranging the spacing and format of the page. For another, such a pro-

TECHNOLOGY INTEGRATION IDEA 6.1

TITLE: Desktop Published Gifts

CONTENT AREA/TOPIC: Language arts

GRADE LEVEL: 5–9

NETS FOR STUDENTS: Standards 1, 3, 4, 5, 6

DESCRIPTION: This activity provides opportunities for students to develop problem-solving and production skills, as well as citizenship and collaboration abilities. Students can use several kinds of software tools to create "priceless gifts" for friends, family, and others. They begin by brainstorming a list of potential recipients. These can include professionals that help them throughout the year, for example, doctors, dentists, teachers, and scout troop leaders. The teacher illustrates some gifts created by previous classes: personalized stationery with individuals' names or "World's Greatest Mom" on it; business cards; coupon books with special services or favors the student could do for recipients; magnets or key rings with photos; scrapbooks with a series of pictures telling about a special event. Students work in small design teams to decide on their gifts. After gifts are completed, students present them to the class in a Priceless Gifts Showcase.

Source: Reissman, R. (2000). Priceless gifts. *Learning and Leading with Technology, 28*(2), 28–31.

TECHNOLOGY INTEGRATION IDEA 6.2

TITLE: In the News

CONTENT AREA/TOPIC: Language arts—newspaper production

GRADE LEVEL: Middle school

NETS FOR STUDENTS: Standards 1, 3, 4, 5, 6

DESCRIPTION: These activities show students the components of the news publication and how to produce the text and graphics layout for a publication. Discuss the project with students and show them examples of the kind of publication they will produce. Focus on the parts of a news story by having them preview a local TV broadcast looking for specific facts in each news story (who, what, when, where, why). Go on field trips to the local newspaper and TV and radio stations to talk to the professionals at these locations. Invite guest speakers from the local area such as newspaper reporters and TV and radio news reporters to speak to students. Discuss the terminology of the newspaper (which students should have been hearing about in their field trips and from speakers). Do a hands-on exploration of example newspapers, identifying the parts of each one. Teach students how to use the desktop publishing program to produce each part of one of the example layouts. Then have students move on to designing their own newspaper. They form small groups, with each group working on a section of the publication, writing their own stories, laying them out, and editing the final product. Students who have artistic talent produce the graphics, emulating the examples they have seen in other newspapers.

Source: Skinner, C., Culpepper, G., Wiggam, M., Myers, E., & Wright, J. (1991). In the news. *The Florida Technology in Education Quarterly, 3*(2), 73–74.

gram can automatically produce various forms or versions of the same test on request. Changes, deletions, and updates to questions are also easy to accomplish, again without concern for page format. The features of test generators vary, but the following capabilities are common:

■ **Test creation procedures.** The software prompts teachers to create tests item by item in formats such as multiple choice, fill in the blank, true/false, matching, and—less often—short answer and essay.

■ **Random generation of questions.** Test items are selected randomly from an item pool to create different versions. This is especially helpful when a teacher wants to prevent "wandering eye syndrome" as students take a test.

■ **Selection of questions based on criteria.** Programs usually allow teachers to specify criteria for generating a test. For example, items can be requested in a specific content area, matched to certain objectives, or in a certain format such as short-answer items only.

■ **Answer keys.** Most programs automatically provide an answer key at the time the test is generated. This is helpful with grading, especially if different versions of the test must be graded.

■ **On-screen testing and grading.** Most test generators offer only on-paper versions of tests, but, as Figure 6.1 illustrates, some allow students to take the test on-screen after it is prepared. These programs usually also provide automatic test grading and performance summary statistics for each question. Many test generators allow use of

Figure 6.1 Screen from *ExamView* Test Generator

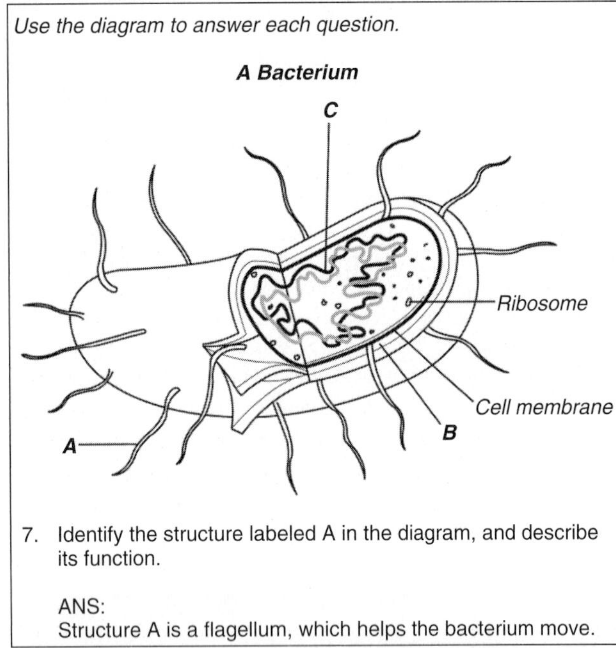

Use the diagram to answer each question.
A Bacterium
C
Ribosome
Cell membrane
A
B
7. Identify the structure labeled A in the diagram, and describe its function.
ANS:
Structure A is a flagellum, which helps the bacterium move.

Source: Used by permission of FSCreations, Inc.

existing question pools, or test question banks, and some offer these banks for purchase in various content areas. Some programs also import question banks prepared on word processors.

Worksheet and Puzzle Generators

Teachers also use software to produce worksheets, which are very similar in many ways to test generators. *Worksheet generators* help teachers produce exercises for practice rather than tests. Like the test generator, the worksheet generator software prompts the teacher to enter questions of various kinds, but it usually offers no options for completing exercises on-screen or grading them. The most common worksheet generators deal with lower level skills such as math facts, but other programs are available to generate activities such as Cloze exercises. In many cases, test generator software and worksheet generator software are similar enough to be used interchangeably and some packages are intended for both purposes. *Puzzle generators* automatically format and create crossword and word search puzzles. The teacher enters the words and/or definitions and the software formats the puzzle. Children often are fascinated by word search puzzles, but these materials may have little instructional value other than for reviewing spelling of new words. Crossword puzzles, on the other hand, can be used as exercises to review words and definitions or even low-level concepts. (See Figure 6.2.)

Two good online sources of worksheet and puzzle generation templates are available at:

http://www.online.tomsnyder.com (subscription basis)

http://www.puzzlemaker.com (free)

Figure 6.2 Screen from *Puzzlemaker* Web Site (http://www.puzzlemaker.com or http://DiscoverySchool.com)

Choose a puzzle from the list below to create your own custom puzzle.

Mazed Things™
by Isaac M. Thayer

You. ll find the **NEW** Woolly Mammoth maze and many more unique hand-drawn mazes in this section.

Computer Generated Mazes
Choose from a variety of shapes, set the size, and let the computer generate a unique maze ready for you to paste into your newsletter.

Word Search
Type in a list of words and the computer will hide them in a grid of letters. Choose the size, set a few options and you are finished.

Word Search with a Hidden Message
After all of the words are found the letters that are not used reveal a hidden message!

Criss-Cross Puzzle
Your list of words will be linked together, numbered and formatted, ready for you to print and hand out.

Number Blocks
Creates a block of numbers that will challenge arithmetic and algebra skills. Each row, column and diagonal add up to a total but some numbers are missing.

Math Square
Math formulas are linked together to form a square.

Double Puzzle
Enter a set of words or phrases to be scrambled. Then enter a final phrase that the solver will be able to put together from the letters in the clue words. The final phrase can be scrambled or numbered.

Source: Used by permission of Network Solutions Developers, Inc.

IEP Generators

The current restructuring movements in education have placed increasing emphasis on school and teacher accountability. With this comes an increase in paperwork on student progress. Teachers of special students, however, still seem to have the most paperwork requirements. Federal legislation such as PL 94–142 and the Americans with Disabilities Act requires that schools prepare an individual educational plan, or IEP, for each special student. These IEPs serve as blueprints for each special student's instructional activities and teachers must provide documentation that such a plan is on file and that it governs classroom activities. Software is available to assist teachers in preparing IEPs (Lewis, 1993). Like test and worksheet generators, IEP generators provide on-screen prompts that remind users of the required components in the plan. When a teacher finishes entering all the necessary information, the program prints out the IEP in a standard format. Some IEP generation programs also accept data updates on each student's progress, thus helping teachers with required record keeping as well as IEP preparation.

Certificate Makers

Recognizing achievement is a powerful means of motivation. Teachers have found certificates to be a useful form of this type of recognition. Certificates congratulate students for accomplishments and the students can take them home and share them with parents and friends. Certificate makers simply provide computerized help with creating such products. Most certificate makers include templates for various typical achievements. The teacher selects one appropriate for the kind of recognition desired (completing an activity or first-place winner) and enters the personalizing information for each student. This software helps teachers produce certificates quickly and easily, so they can award them frequently.

Form Makers

Like desktop publishing, form design is a special area of expertise that software can facilitate. Teachers must frequently create forms to collect information from students, parents, or faculty. Sometimes these forms are as simple as permission for students to participate in a class event, but they can become much more complicated. For example, a teacher may need forms to collect personal information from students for student records or to enter information on software packages as they are evaluated. Formatting even the simplest form can be time consuming on a word processor. Form maker software structures the process and makes the design simple to accomplish. Most such packages have some graphic abilities, allowing users to add lines and boxes for desired information. As teachers create these forms, they can store them as templates for later use, perhaps with revisions. (Also see how to create forms online in Chapter 8.)

Groupware Products

Groupware is one of the newest technology tools. The term itself has been in the educational technology lexicon only since around 1991. It refers to software products designed to promote cooperative learning among groups of students by helping them document their work as they progress. Groupware usually resembles a special-purpose word processor that allows students to enter the results of work sessions and their contributions to the development of a product. Some packages allow links via modem, so students in more than one location can work on a cooperative project. Pearlman (1994) says that these products "stimulate group activity in a one-computer or sometimes no-computer classroom" (p. 1). Cowan (1992) describes three groupware products and gives some suggestions for using them effectively with students:

- Set and communicate ahead of time well-structured rules and procedures for using the groupware. These guidelines keep the students on task and prevent collaborative activities from becoming chaotic. Teachers should participate in and monitor sessions to enforce these rules.
- Make sure that all students have opportunities to express themselves so that one or two students do not control the process of entering information.
- Groupware takes teacher time and computer resources to use. Identify ahead of time places in the curriculum that seem likely to profit from groupware as opposed to word processing software. Use groupware to improve communication and collaboration skills.

(To support student collaboration, also see the discussion on concept mapping software later in this chapter.)

Using Data Collection and Analysis Tools

Gradebooks

Although some teachers prefer to keep their grades on flexible spreadsheet software, many prefer special software designed exclusively for this purpose. A gradebook (electronic grade-keeping) program allows a teacher to enter student names, test/assignment names, data from tests, and weighting information for specific test scores. The program then analyzes the data and prints reports based on this information. Some gradebooks even offer limited-purpose word processing capabilities to enter notes about tests. The software automatically generates averages and weighted averages for each student and averages across all students on a given test. Gradebooks require less teacher setup time than spreadsheets, but also allow less flexibility on format options. Wager (1992) describes the process and criteria one group of teachers used to select a gradebook for use throughout the school. These important criteria were included:

- Capacity to track many tests/assignments
- Flexibility in report formats such as sorting by name and individual and group reports
- Wide range of peripheral support (use with various printers, networks)
- Ease of setup and use
- Use on multiple platforms.

Stanton (1994) also reviewed gradebook packages according to a list of criteria. He noted some new capabilities to look for in an electronic gradebook, including generating graphs, making seating charts, and tracking attendance.

Statistical Packages

As Gay (1993) once joked, many teachers believe that the field of statistics should be renamed *sadistics.* Yet several kinds of instructional situations may interest teachers in statistical analyses. Brumbaugh and Poirot (1993), among others, maintain that teachers should take advantage of opportunities to do research in their classrooms. If teachers do choose to do classroom research, they must follow data collection with data analysis. Depending on the type of research, several typical analyses yield helpful information, including descriptive statistics such as means and standard deviations to inferential statistics such as *t*-tests and analyses of variance.

Software can also help with qualitative data collection and analysis. Teachers may perform statistical analysis of student performance on tests. Question analysis procedures help them analyze test questions they intend to use more than once. By changing and improving questions, teachers can make their tests more accurate and reliable. Finally, teachers may have to teach beginning statistics to their own students, for example, in a business education course.

Statistical software packages perform the calculations involved in any of these kinds of procedures. Naturally, a teacher must have considerable knowledge of the proper applications of various statistical procedures; the software merely handles the arithmetic. But this alone can save considerable time. Webster (1992) reviewed several statistical software packages for use in business education courses and found that the packages varied considerably in their usefulness for this purpose.

Data Management (CMI) and Testing Tools

Definitions: CMI versus data management. The term *computer-managed instruction,* or *CMI,* is left over from when nearly all education technology software could be classified as CMI or CAI (see Chapter 1). As early as 1978, Baker admitted that a precise description of CMI did not exist because of "definitions that are as diverse as the number of existing systems" (p. 11). Baker gave examples of several such systems that were popular at the time, noting widely varying characteristics. Among these systems were the Teaching Information Processing System (TIPS), the Sherman School System, and the Program for Learning in Accordance with Needs (PLAN). At that time, there was a burgeoning interest in mastery learning in which teachers specified a sequence of objectives for students to learn and prescribed instruction to help the students master each objective. Clearly, the teacher had to keep track of each student's performance on each objective—a mammoth record-keeping task. CMI systems running on large, mainframe computers were designed to support teachers in these efforts.

Today's teachers emphasize mastery learning less than keeping students on task and monitoring their progress to make sure their work is challenging, not frustrating. Some educators feel the term *CMI* has always been a misnomer for a record-keeping routine within an instructional system rather than a type of instructional delivery. However, software tools still are available—now on microcomputers and networks—that store and analyze data on student progress during instruction and provide summary progress reports. The purpose for collecting the data may be different, but the record-keeping task is still considerable. Although some people still call this software CMI, others refer to it simply as *data management software.*

Types and functions of data management tools. Roblyer (1992) identified three different kinds of computerized data management tools: components of computer-based learning systems, computerized testing systems, and test scoring and data analysis systems.

Components of computer-based learning systems. These tools allow teachers to enter names and other student information. When each student types in his or her name, the system presents a sequence of activities tailored to that student's needs. The system also collects data as students go through the instruction. Reports show the teacher what students have accomplished and point out areas where they may still need assistance and off-computer work. Although some stand-alone microcomputer-based packages have these tools built into the software, these systems are more commonly seen as components of networked integrated learning systems (ILSs). These systems have the power and capacity to handle large amounts of data on student performance.

Computerized testing systems. With these tools, students receive actual instruction elsewhere, usually by noncomputer media. Computers facilitate on-screen testing and record keeping after instruction. Sometimes known as *computer-assisted testing,* these tools generate test forms and process performance data. They differ from test generators, which allow on-screen testing but do not give detailed reports on results for individuals and groups. Some of the major standardized tests such as the SAT and GRE are now given on computerized testing systems. These systems offer many benefits, including immediate knowledge of results. Tests can also be shorter, since the systems assess each person's ability level with fewer questions. This is because the software continuously analyzes performance and presents more or less difficult questions based on the student's performance, a capability known as *computer adaptive testing (CAT)* (Strommen, 1994). CAT is used more and more frequently for testing in professional courses like those in nursing education. The capabilities of computerized testing systems let educators go beyond the limits of multiple-choice tests and make possible alternative assessments. These systems also simplify test scheduling, since everyone need not take tests at the same time.

Probably one of the best known and widely used of the CAT systems is a product called *Accelerated Reader* or *AR* (Lopez, 2000; Poock, 1998). The purpose of the AR system is to motivate students to increase the amount of reading they do for enjoyment. It keeps track of the number of books they read and tests them on comprehension. Teachers can get individual or aggregate data on books read at each readability level. This gives them a better idea of how students are progressing in their reading abilities, and if they are spending enough time reading at desired levels. Though they caution that further study is needed to draw reliable conclusions, Topping and Paul (1999) found that schools using AR for longer periods of time show higher rates of reading, which may correlate with higher tested reading levels.

Test scoring and data analysis systems. These types of data management tools accept test data input either through the keyboard or by optically scanning bubble sheets. Tests are automatically scored and reports on the results are generated. Both devices and sheets are available from companies such as National Computer Systems or Scantron.

All of these data management systems serve two primary purposes. First, they provide clerical support for all of the calculation and paperwork tasks required to track student progress. Second, they help teachers to match instruction to the needs of each student. Each type of system provides various kinds of reports about student progress. ILS management systems usually provide the most extensive reporting. They include a wealth of feedback ranging from the number of test questions answered correctly and incorrectly on a student's test to summary data on the performance of whole classes in a topic area.

Figure 6.3 Screen from *PrintShop* Product

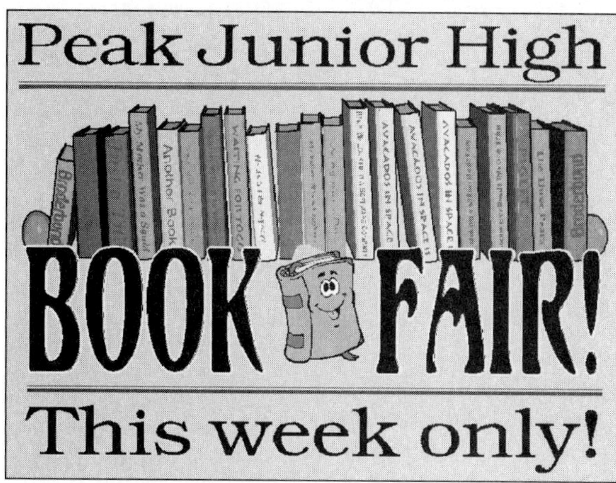

Source: Reproduced using *PrintShop*®; © 2002 Brøderbund Software, Inc. All rights reserved. Used by permission.

Using Graphics Tools

Print Graphics Packages

These software tools have a limited purpose, but one that many teachers find indispensable. Print graphics packages essentially are simple word processors designed especially for quick and easy production of one-page signs, banners, and greeting cards. One graphics program, *Print Shop Deluxe* (Brøderbund), has become one of the best-selling software packages in education. Teachers can find hundreds of uses for the products of print graphics software ranging from door signs to decorations for special events. Some schools have even held contests to design the most creative signs or banners using this program. The graphics and other options in the program are selected from menus, making the programs so easy to use that anyone can sit down and create a product in a matter of minutes. One example print product is shown in Figure 6.3.

Draw/Paint and Image Processing Programs

To produce more complex hardcopy graphics, draw/paint (or image processing) programs are the technology tool of choice. These tools usually are used to create designs and pictures that are then imported into desktop publishing systems or desktop presentation tools, as described in the following section. Just as print graphics programs are known for their simplicity and limited options, draw/paint programs are known for their sophistication and wide-ranging capabilities. Many of these packages such as *Aldus Freehand* or *Adobe PhotoShop* require considerable time to learn and implement. But some, like *Kid Pix Deluxe Studio,* are designed specifically for children to use without formal training. Catchings and MacGregor (1998) are among those who believe that draw/paint programs allow many students to develop their visual–verbal literacy and creativity. O'Bannon, Krolak, Harkelroad, and Dick (1999) show how students can practice this creativity by designing banners and images for school web pages. Technology Integration Ideas 6.3 through 6.6 illustrate some of the many instructional uses for draw/paint/image processing programs.

TECHNOLOGY INTEGRATION IDEA 6.3

TITLE: Map Skills with *Kid Pix*

CONTENT AREA/TOPIC: Geography—map skills

GRADE LEVEL: 3

NETS FOR STUDENTS: Standards 1, 3, 4, 5, 6

DESCRIPTION: Students use the *Kid Pix* drawing program to design a map as an introduction to a unit on basic geography skills. This activity starts out a 4-week unit with a whole-class demonstration of *Kid Pix* on the computer projection system. Students are given handouts describing the requirements of the project they will do and giving an example product. The map they produce should include a compass rose with an arrow and an N for North, a map title, a date, and seven map symbols of their choice. After a session for hands-on exploration of *Kid Pix,* they are given time to design and produce their own maps.

Source: Day, D. (1994). Active mapping. *The Computing Teacher, 21*(5), 27–28.

TECHNOLOGY INTEGRATION IDEA 6.4

TITLE: Exploring Tessellations with Computer Art

CONTENT AREA/TOPIC: Geometry

GRADE LEVEL: High school

NETS FOR STUDENTS: Standards 1, 3, 4, 5, 6

DESCRIPTION: This lesson combines art and mathematics by focusing on how to draw *tessellations*—the complete covering of a plane by one or more figures in a repeating pattern, with no overlapping of the figures. The author points out that this kind of lesson can be carried out in various ways. For instance, math and art teachers could exchange classes for 2 weeks or both teachers could integrate math and art into their instruction. Begin by helping students see that tessellations are one of the "building blocks of nature and the visual arts" (Wigre, 1993–1994, p. 15) by showing them presentations of various artists' work. Introduce drawing/painting software features and basic vocabulary such as tesselations, transformations, rotations, and reflections. Ask students to use a shape (e.g., equilateral triangles, squares, rectangles, or hexagons) to create a tiled design. Show them how to create the tessellation by combining polygons and by using transformations of each shape. After they cover the page with their design, students can use shading or colors to get a more finished look.

Source: Wigre, R. (1993–94). Reflections on tessellations. *The Computing Teacher, 21*(4), 15–16.

TECHNOLOGY INTEGRATION IDEA 6.5

TITLE: Drawing in the Art Curriculum

CONTENT AREA/TOPIC: Art throughout the curriculum

GRADE LEVEL: High school

NETS FOR STUDENTS: Standards 1, 3, 4, 5, 6

DESCRIPTION: Students use drawing programs in an introductory art course to pave the way for integrating art into other curriculum areas. They are first introduced to draw/paint programs in an introductory art course taught in the ninth grade. Students use visual communication skills they learn through the draw/paint programs to develop products and assignments for many other courses. For example, they may use computer images to present reports in history or science. The computer art course begins with 2 weeks of introduction to an array of computer art and graphics in which students write and talk about what they see. They refer back to visual concepts taught in the introductory art class. During this time, students also become familiar with looking up visual images in the library and using them as resources. They spend the rest of the course learning basic drawing features such as tiling (creating a design and covering a page with it) and use of clip art, as well as more advanced skills that combine a variety of drawing features. They also learn use of other equipment, such as the camcorder to design presentations. The art teacher works closely with teachers in other disciplines to develop assignments that make use of these drawing/presentation skills.

Source: Baugh, I. (1993). "Draw" them into learning. *The Computing Teacher, 21*(3), 18–20.

Charting/Graphing Software

Charting and graphing software tools automatically draw and print desired charts or graphs from data entered by users. The skills involved in reading, interpreting, and producing graphs and charts are useful both to students in school and adults in the workplace. However, those with limited artistic ability face special challenges in learning and using these skills. Fortunately, charting and graphing software takes the mechanical drudgery out of producing these useful "data pictures." If students do not have to labor over rulers and pencils as they try to plot coordinates and set points, they can concentrate on the more important aspects of the graphics: the meaning of the data and what they represent. As Duren (1990–1991) observed, this kind of activity supports students in their efforts at visualizing mathematical concepts and engaging in inquiry tasks. Graphing activities in science, social studies, and geography also profit from applications of these kinds of software tools. Moersch (1995) lists and gives example instructional applications for 10 kinds of software-produced graphs: bar, pie, stacked bar, *X/Y*, scatter, box, stem and leaf, best fit, and normal curve. (See Technology Integration Ideas 6.7 and 6.8.)

TECHNOLOGY INTEGRATION IDEA 6.6

TITLE: Bringing the Planets Closer to Home

CONTENT AREA/TOPIC: Math (measurement) and astronomy

GRADE LEVEL: 5–12

NETS FOR STUDENTS: Standards 1, 3, 4, 5, 6

DESCRIPTION: This activity is designed to make the connection between science and mathematics more hands-on and meaningful for students by having them analyze real data in the form of images. They begin by downloading NASA photos from the Internet (e.g., images of the Solar System at http://spaceart.com/solar) and converting them to an uncompressed TIF format using an image processing program such as *Adobe PhotoShop.* Their task is learning how to measure the images. First, they use the software to calibrate the images (determine the scale) by comparing the size of the image to a known measure such as the diameter of Mars. Then they multiply the measured distance by the scale to determine the size of other features they have downloaded. In this way, the students can measure and compare features that change, such as the Martian and Earth polar ice caps. These measurements can be the basis of many projects to study space phenomena.

Source: Slater, T., & Beaudrie, B. (2000). Far out measurements: Bringing the planets closer to home using image processing techniques. *Learning and Leading with Technology, 27*(5), 36–41.

TECHNOLOGY INTEGRATION IDEA 6.7

TITLE: A Project with Teeth

CONTENT AREA/TOPIC: Art throughout the curriculum

GRADE LEVEL: K–3

NETS FOR STUDENTS: Standards 1, 3, 4, 5, 6

DESCRIPTION: Teachers use e-mail to connect their K–3 students with "keypals" around the world in order to exchange information on how many teeth children lose during the year. This activity is used as a springboard for learning geography (locations of the keypals), literature and culture (tooth fairy traditions and other stories from their regions), art (creating pictures or murals illustrating tooth fairy traditions), creative writing (e-mail messages to participants, poems and rhymes on teeth), and mathematics (graphing data on lost teeth). After they have at least three months of data on lost teeth, students learn how to use a graphing program to compile the data and prepare line or bar graphs. Each student or small group may choose a part of the data to graph; then they compose a letter explaining the results to their keypals. As a cumulative or final whole-class activity, students may use a calculator to add up all the teeth data for each month from all the schools and then enter all the data into one common spreadsheet. Results may be shared among the participants through e-mail.

Source: Boehm, D. (1997). I lost my tooth! *Learning and Leading with Technology, 24*(7), 17–19.

TECHNOLOGY INTEGRATION IDEA 6.8

TITLE: Data Analysis for Young Children

CONTENT AREA/TOPIC: Mathematics—graphing concepts

GRADE LEVEL: 2–4

NETS FOR STUDENTS: Standards 1, 3, 4, 5, 6

DESCRIPTION: This project uses hand-drawn and computer-generated graphs to help students understand how to make visual representations of data. In this activity, students look at types of clothing fasteners they use (zippers, laces, etc.) They gather in small groups to count the number of fasteners and make pictorial representations of the number of each type of fastener represented in their group. Although these representations are different in each group and do not necessarily follow the usual conventions of graphing, they serve as a basis for translating the data into computer-generated graphs. The teacher helps students enter the numbers from their pictures into the graphing software and generate pie charts and line graphs. With these more traditional graphs, the students are able to interpret the meaning of graph parts such as the x and y axes and proportions of pie "slices." Discussing these concepts also gives students practice in using "mathematical talk" to express their ideas.

Source: Grant, C. (2000). Beyond just doing it: Making discerning decisions about using graphing tools. *Learning and Leading with Technology, 27*(5), 14–17, 49.

Clip Art Packages, Video Collections, and Sound Collections

Clip art packages are collections of still pictures drawn by artists and graphics designers and placed in a book or on a disk for use by others. When teachers prepare presentations with desktop publishing or presentation tools, they need not use draw/paint programs to draw original pictures. A wealth of pictures is available in the form of clip art. Most word processing and desktop publishing systems can import clip art stored on disk into a document. Draw/paint programs can also import clip art for use in designing other pictures and graphic images. Clip art from a book may be optically scanned into a computer file and stored on a disk for use with these programs. When more realistic depictions are desired, actual pictures stored on video media such as CD-ROM and videodisc may be imported in the same way.

Clip art packages and video collections are invaluable tools to help both teachers and students illustrate and decorate their written products. Teachers find that such pictures help make flyers, books, and even letters and notices look more polished and professional. Some teachers feel that students are more motivated to write their own stories and reports when they can also illustrate them.

For teachers and students who want to develop their own multimedia presentations, collections of sound effects and movie clips are also becoming more common. A system may need special hardware such as sound cards or synthesizers or software such as *Quicktime,* movie-making software, in order to incorporate these elements.

Digitizing Systems and Video Development Systems

Several other kinds of tools help users prepare graphics for both print and on-screen presentations. Digitizing programs are software tools that handle pictures scanned into the computer and stored as picture files. Users can edit these pictures as needed or include them as they are. With digital cameras, teachers can take pictures as they would with any camera, storing the images on disk instead of on film. They can then import the photos into video presentations or desktop publishing products. The number of products that assist with graphics production is increasing and new capabilities to develop and import images are constantly being developed. Teachers and students can even use movie-making software in their graphics productions. (Also see more on this topic in Chapter 7.)

Using Planning and Organizing Tools

Outlining Tools and Other Writing Aids

Several kinds of technology tools are available to help students learn writing skills or to assist accomplished writers in setting their thoughts in order prior to writing. Outlining tools are designed to prompt writers as they develop outlines to structure documents they plan to write. For example, the software may automatically indent and/or supply the appropriate number or letter for each line in the outline. Outliners are offered either within word processing packages or as separate software packages for use before word processing.

Other writing aids include software designed to get students started on writing reports or stories: a *story starter.* This kind of program provides a first line and invites students to supply subsequent lines. Other tools give students topic ideas and supply information about each topic they can use in a writing assignment. Sometimes a software package combines outlining tools and other writing aids. (See Technology Integration Idea 6.9.)

Brainstorming and Concept Mapping Tools

These might also be called *conceptualizing tools,* because they help people think through and explore ideas or topics. Tools such as *Idea Fisher* (http://www.ideafisher.com) and *Semnet* (http://www.semnet.com) help learners represent knowledge

TECHNOLOGY INTEGRATION IDEA 6.9

TITLE: Learning from Fairy Tales and Folktales

CONTENT AREA/TOPIC: Literature and writing

GRADE LEVEL: 3–6

NETS FOR STUDENTS: Standards 1, 3, 4, 5, 6

DESCRIPTION: Using a combination of *Story Weaver* and *Kid Pix Deluxe Studio,* students explore the emotional intelligence of characters depicted in fairy tales and folktales. The teacher gives students a handout of Goleman's five dimensions of emotional intelligence (Goleman, 1995), and makes sure they are familiar with procedures in using the software. Students read a folktale or fairy tale selected by the teacher, and they discuss the characters' levels of emotional intelligence (or lack of it). Some students who may have trouble expressing themselves in language use the *Kid Pix* software to illustrate how the characters behaved. The teacher challenges students to use *Story Weaver* to retell the folktale having the characters behave in more emotionally intelligent ways. After small groups do this activity, the class discusses the characters in the new stories in terms of Goleman's levels.

Source: Reissman, R., & Gil, E. (2000). Technology takes on fairy tales and folktales. *Learning and Leading with Technology, 27*(5), 18–21.

domains by providing semantic connections with given words. For example, if a user were to click on the word *whale,* the program might display several words associated with whales such as *ocean* and *sea life* as well as some less obvious connections such as *endangered species.* Programs such as these can also ask probing questions to provoke thoughts about each topic selected. *Inspiration* (http://www.inspiration.com) assists brainstorming by helping people develop concept maps. Concept maps are visual outlines of ideas that can offer useful alternatives to the strictly verbal representations provided by content outlines. (See Figure 6.4.) Dabbagh (2001), Anderson-Inman and Zeitz (1993), and Kahn (1997) discuss the learning theory behind using these powerful instructional tools and give good examples of classroom applications. (See Technology Integration Idea 6.10.)

Lesson Planning Tools

Most teachers do not rely heavily on written lesson plans to guide their teaching activities. However, many occasions demand some form of documentation to show what teachers are teaching and how they are teaching it. Tools that help teachers develop and document their descriptions of lessons are sometimes called *lesson makers* or *lesson planners.* Most of these programs simply provide on-screen prompts for specific lesson components such as objectives, materials, and activity descriptions. They also print out lessons in standard formats, similar to the way test generators format printouts of tests.

Schedule/Calendar Makers and Time Management Tools

Several kinds of tools have been designed to help teachers organize their time and plan their activities. Schedule makers help formulate plans for daily, weekly, or monthly sequences of appointments and events. Calendar makers are similar planning tools that actually print graphic calendars of chosen months or years with the planned events printed under each day. Other time management tools are available to help remind users of events and responsibilities. The teacher enters activities and the dates on which they will occur. Then, when he or she turns on the computer each day, the software displays on the screen a list of things to do. Some integrated packages combine all of these tools.

Figure 6.4 Screen from *Inspiration* Concept Mapping Software

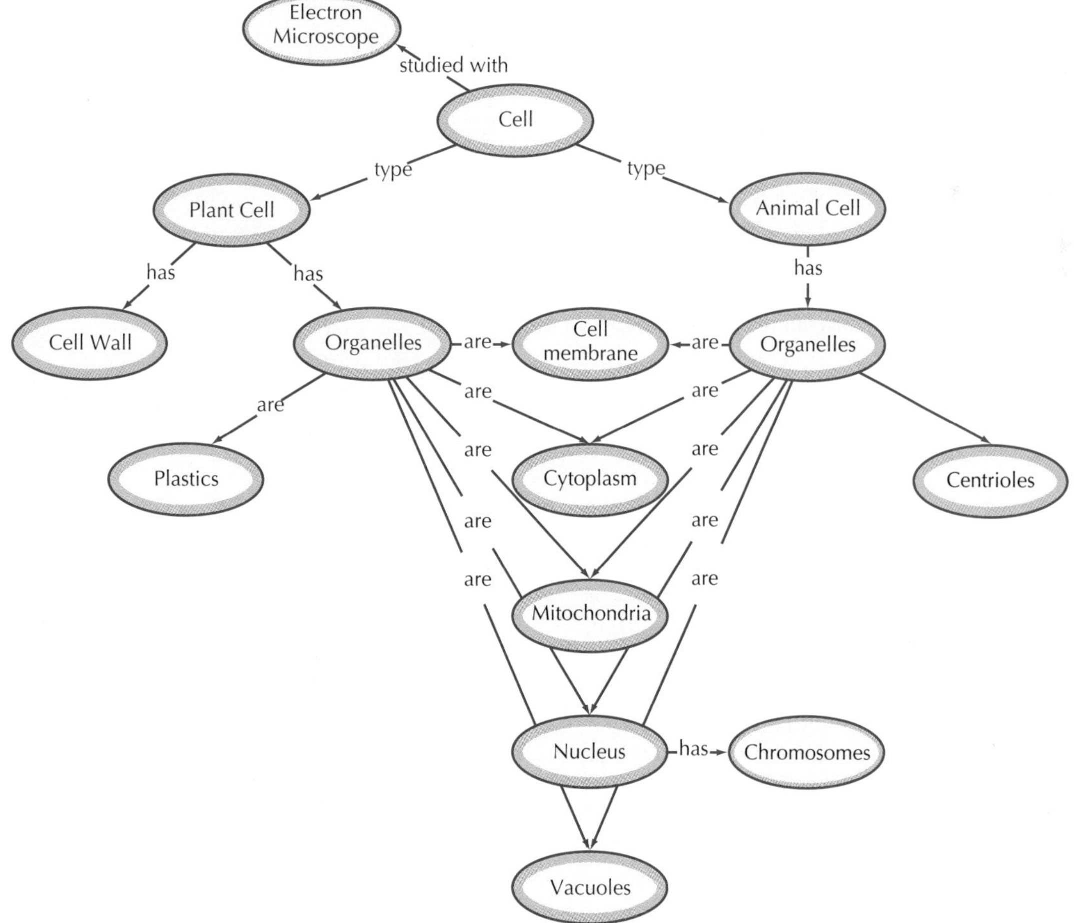

Source: Anderson-Inman, L., & Zeitz, L. (1993). Computer-based concept mapping: Active studying for active learners. *The Computing Teacher, 21*(1), 6–8, 10–11.

TECHNOLOGY INTEGRATION IDEA 6.10

TITLE: Concept Mapping in Biology

CONTENT AREA/TOPIC: Biology

GRADE LEVEL: 11

NETS FOR STUDENTS: Standards 1, 3, 4, 5, 6

DESCRIPTION: This activity introduces concept mapping as a way to represent a specific knowledge domain in graphic form. Concept mapping software eases the logistics of constructing and modifying the maps. Student-created *concept maps* (also called *semantic maps* or *webs*) can help learners construct knowledge by providing a vehicle for integrating new information with that learned previously. Because the learner plays an active role in creating and modifying the concept map, this study strategy promotes active learning and student involvement. Prior to reading an assigned chapter on cells, students are asked to create a concept map for a set of 11 new terms. They create a concept map showing how they feel these terms are related. Using *Inspiration* concept mapping software, each term is placed in a node and the lines linking the nodes are labeled. After reading the chapter on "Cell Structure," students revise their maps. After a classroom discussion of the topic, students are given another opportunity to revise their maps. On the last day of the unit, the teacher suggests augmenting the concept maps once again in preparation for the test.

Source: Anderson-Inman, L., & Zeitz, L. (1993). Computer-based concept mapping: Active studying for active learners. *The Computing Teacher, 21*(1), 6–8, 10–11.

Using Research and Reference Tools

Electronic Encyclopedias

For many years, American families kept sets of encyclopedias to support their children's education. Young people used these books for research on school projects and parents used them to take advantage of "teachable moments" when their children required more than quick answers. Now most major encyclopedias come on CD-ROM with some kind of database structure. CD-ROM encyclopedias have several advantages over books. Users can search to locate one specific item or all references on a given topic. They usually offer multimedia formats that include sound and/or film clips as well as hypertext links to related information on any topic. (See Figure 6.5.) Chapters 7 and 8 present more information on and examples of disc-based encyclopedia applications.

Figure 6.5 Screen from *World Book* Encyclopedia CD-ROM

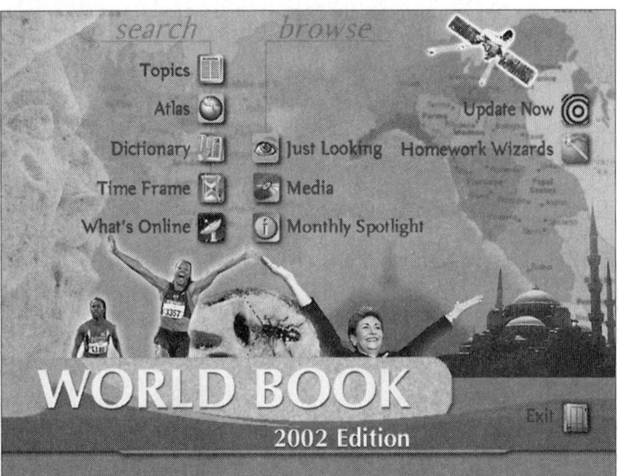

Source: Courtesy of World Book, Inc.

Atlases

Like encyclopedias, atlases are popular educational reference tools for families as well as schools. They summarize geographic and demographic information ranging from population statistics to national products. CD-ROM versions of these atlases are especially helpful since they are so interactive. Students can see information on a specific country or city or gather information on all countries or cities that meet certain criteria. Some atlases even play national songs on request!

Dictionaries (Word Atlases)

Sometimes called *word atlases,* CD-ROM dictionaries specify pronunciation, definition, and example uses for each word entry. They also offer many search and multimedia features similar to those of encyclopedias and atlases. Many CD-ROM dictionaries can play an audio clip of the pronunciation of any desired word, a capability of special help to young users and others who cannot read diacritical marks.

Using Tools to Support Specific Content Areas

CAD and 3-D Modeling/Animation Systems

A *computer-assisted design (CAD)* system is a special kind of graphics production tool that allows users to prepare sophisticated, precise drawings of objects such as houses and cars. Like presentation tools, CAD systems began to appear in classrooms after their introduction in business and industry. This kind of software is usually employed in vocational-technical classrooms to teach architecture and engineering skills. However, some teachers use CAD software to teach drawing concepts in art and related topics. More advanced graphics students may use 3-D modeling and animation software systems to do fancy visual effects such as morphing. (See Figure 6.6 for a sample of CAD software.)

Music Editors and Synthesizers

Music editor software provides blank musical bars on which the user enters the musical key, time, and individual notes that constitute a piece of sheet music. This software is designed to help people develop musical compositions on-screen, usually in conjunction with hardware such as a musical instrument digital interface (MIDI) keyboard and music synthesizer. This hardware allows the user to either hear the music after it is written or create music on the keyboard and automatically produce a written score. Steinhaus (1986–1987) explained that music editors offer powerful assistance in the processes of precomposing, composing, revising, and even performing. Forest (1993) offers examples of these activities in a school setting as well as a list of good music-related software and media. Ohler's (1998) thorough review of MIDI technology and its current applications for teaching music reminds us that technology tools can help students "flex the musical muscle that [Howard] Gardner reminds us has always been there" (p. 10). (See Chapter 13 for more classroom uses of these tools.)

Reading Tools

Both reading teachers and teachers of other topics occasionally need to determine the approximate reading level of specific documents. A teacher may want to select a story or book for use in a lesson or to confirm that works are correctly labeled as appropriate for certain grade levels. Several methods are available for calculating the reading level of a written work; all of them are time consuming and tedious to do by hand. Readability analysis software automates calculations of word count, average word length, number of sentences, or other measures of reading difficulty.

Another software tool related to reading instruction, Cloze software, provides passages with words missing in a given pattern, for example, every fifth word or every tenth word. Students read the sentences and try to fill in the words. Cloze passages have been found to be good measures of reading comprehension. Some teachers also like to use them as exercises to improve reading comprehension.

Many books for children as well as adults are available in interactive CD-ROM versions (Truett, 1993). Some of these allow children to hear narrations in English or Spanish. Others, like the Living Books series (*Just Grandma and Me*), let children explore the screen, activating animations and sounds when they click in various locations. These books are designed to provide an interesting, interactive way to read and increase reading fluency.

Microcomputer-Based Labs (MBLs) or Probeware

A technology tool that has proven particularly useful in math and science classrooms is the microcomputer-based labs (MBL), sometimes referred to as *probeware.* When these probes or sensors are connected to a graphing calculator as opposed to a computer (as described in the following section), they also are called calculator-based labs (CBLs). MBL packages consist of software accompanied by special hardware sensors designed to measure light, temperature, voltage, and/or speed (see Figure 6.7). The sensors are connected to the microcomputer and the software processes the data collected by the probes. Bitter, Camuse, and Durbin (1993) said that microcomputer probeware actually can replace several items of lab equipment such as oscilloscopes and voltmeters because MBLs outperform this traditional equipment. Ladelson (1994) points out that probeware achieves a dual purpose of gathering empirical data and revealing the relationship between science and math. Stanton (1992) describes a variety of MBLs, covering their capabilities and prices along with grade levels and science subjects they can help teach. Walsh (2001) refers to these devices as stand-alone microprocessor-based data acquisition devices or SAMDADS. He reviews 13 different data-gathering devices and describes their uses in various classroom experiments in mathematics and science. (See Figure 6.7 and Technology Integration Ideas 6.11 and 6.12.)

Figure 6.6 Sample Screen from CAD Software

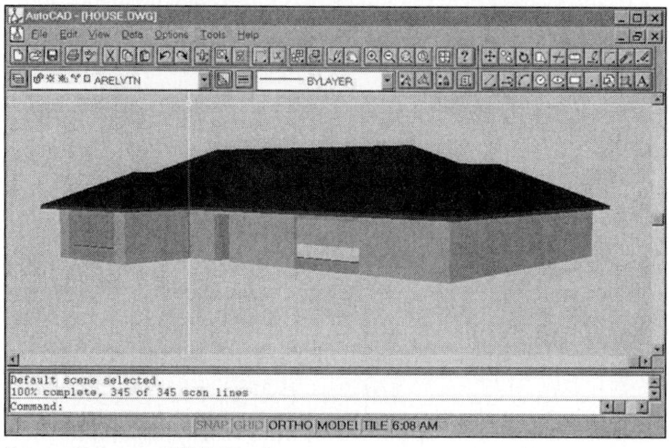

Source: Courtesy of Bill Wiencke.

Figure 6.7 Example of MBL/Probeware

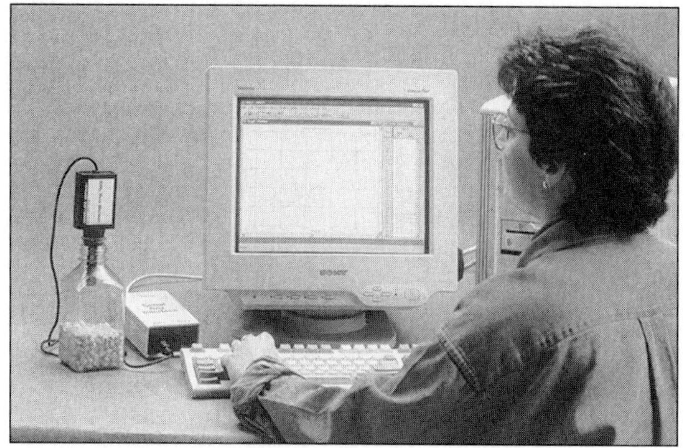

Source: Courtesy of Vernier Software.

TECHNOLOGY INTEGRATION IDEA 6.11

TITLE: Exploring the Relationship Between Science and Mathematics

CONTENT AREA/TOPIC: Concept of slope

GRADE LEVEL: High school

NETS FOR STUDENTS: Standards 1, 3, 4, 5, 6

DESCRIPTION: Students use the line equation in software that is intended for calibrating the probes in MBL probeware to explore mathematical concepts underlying the general linear equation $y = mx + b$ (where m = slope and b = the y intercept). This process establishes a relationship between the input to the computer from the probe and the value that the measurement represents. For example, if the MBL is measuring voltage, the probe is calibrated by connecting it to a AA battery previously confirmed by a multimeter to output 1.5 volts. The computer registers 215 counts for 1.5 volts. The beginning point of 0 counts and the ending point of 215 defines a line. This line is used to calibrate the probe. After the probe is calibrated, an equation is developed for the line (0, 0 and 215, 1.5). Students sketch the graph of the line defined by these points using either paper or graphing software. They predict values for counts given specific voltages using their graph by locating the value on the x axis and finding the corresponding y value for counts. They use the general linear equation $y = mx + b$ to discuss the slope of the line as the rise (vertical distance between the two points) divided by the run (horizontal distance between the points). The teacher has the students calculate the slope for their lines. They enter the value for the slope into the general linear equation and do the final equation for the example calibration. Once the equation has been determined, students calculate counts for specific voltages. When the probe is ready to be used, students bring in samples to be tested.

Source: Ladelson, L. (1994). Calibrating probeware: Making a line. *The Computing Teacher, 21*(6), 46–47.

TECHNOLOGY INTEGRATION IDEA 6.12

TITLE: The Magnetic Field in a Slinky®

CONTENT AREA/TOPIC: Physics—magnetic fields

GRADE LEVEL: High school

NETS FOR STUDENTS: Standards 1, 3, 4, 5, 6

DESCRIPTION: Students use the Vernier magnetic field sensor to determine the relationship between (1) the magnetic field and the current in a solenoid and (2) the magnetic field and the number of turns per meter in a solenoid. They connect the Vernier magnetic field sensor to the universal lab interface on a computer and set the switch on the sensor to high. Stretch the Slinky® until it is about 1 meter in length. Set up the equipment, prepare the computer for data collection, and have students begin the testing to answer the following questions: Which direction in the Slinky gives the largest magnetic field reading? How does the magnetic field inside the solenoid seem to vary along its length? To determine the relationship between magnetic field and the current in a solenoid, hold the switch closed and place the magnetic field sensor between the coils of the Slinky near the center. Rotate the sensor to find the direction that gives the largest magnetic field reading. Check the magnetic field intensity in various locations of the Slinky, as well as just outside it. Collect the data on these observations and analyze the data to answer the question. Next, gather data to determine how the relationship between a magnetic field in a solenoid is related to the spacing of the turns. Change the length of the Slinky to 0.5, 1.5, and 2.0 meters to change the number of turns per meter. Adjust the power supply to "1.5 A" when the switch is closed and collect data on each length to address the question.

Source: Contributed by Vernier Software.

Graphing Calculator

For many years, calculators have played a widespread—and often controversial—role in mathematics education. Currently, even more capable, software-programmed devices called graphing calculators (see Figure 6.8) are becoming prominent in both mathematics and higher level science curriculum. Albrecht and Firedrake (1997) describe uses in physics instruction for these devices in conjunction with the Internet and what they call "data-grabbing devices" (probeware, MBLs, or CBLs). Borenstein (1997) reviews uses of graphing calculators to make possible

Figure 6.8 TI Graphing Calculator

Source: Courtesy of Texas Instruments.

various experiments and concept demonstrations in algebra. Plymate (1998) and Manouchehri and Pagnucco (1999–2000) describe the use of graphing calculators to explore linear properties of real-world data sets and make concepts like slope more visual and understandable. (See Technology Integration Idea 6.13.)

Geographic Information Systems and Global Positioning Systems

Both of these powerful tools are useful in teaching in geography, as described in Chapter 12. A geographic information system (GIS) is a computer system that is able to store in a database a variety of information about geographic locations. After it has stored all data that describe a given location, the GIS can then display the data in map form. According to Parmenter and Burns (2001), the three primary uses of GISs are (1) to record and maintain large amounts of geographic information, (2) to produce up-to-date, customized maps, and (3) to allow analysis and comparison of information on different locations. The Global Positioning System (GPS) is a worldwide radio-navigation system made possible by a bank of 24 satellites and their ground stations. Using satellites as reference points, a GPS unit can calculate positions of anything on earth accurate to a matter of feet or inches. A GPS receiver connected to mapping software is what most people think of as a GPS. These small devices can be useful in a car, home, or even a portable laptop.

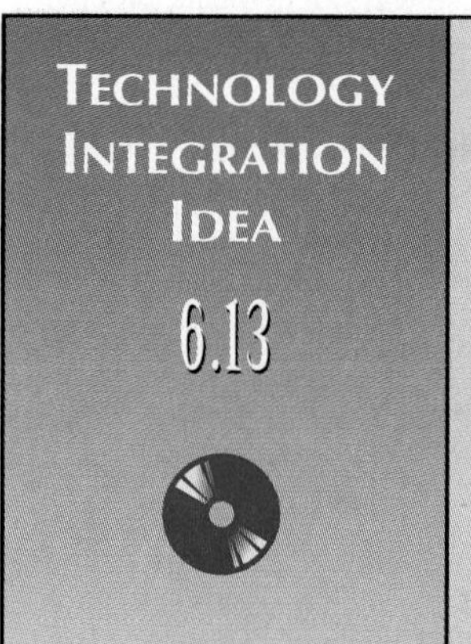

TITLE: Graphing the Ellipse

CONTENT AREA/TOPIC: Math—geometry

GRADE LEVEL: 10–12

NETS FOR STUDENTS: Standards 1, 3, 4, 5, 6

DESCRIPTION: In this activity, the students use a TI graphing calculator to add interest to the study of ellipses. The teacher begins by demonstrating occurrences of ellipses in the real world: orbits of planets and comets, arches of stone bridges (semi-ellipses), elliptical gears, various art works. Then they are challenged to use the calculators to create their own ellipses. As they add points to construct their ellipses, the teacher discusses mathematical properties needed to build them. After they understand these properties, they can use the TI software to define a macro to create the actual figures so they will be able to focus more time on exploring proofs and on investigation and problem-solving activities with the calculators.

Source: Davis, J., & Hofstetter, E. (1998). A graphing investigation of the ellipse. *Learning and Leading with Technology, 26*(2), 32–36.

Exercises

Record and apply what you have learned.

Chapter 6 Self-Test

To review terms and concepts in this chapter, take the Chapter 6 self-test. Select Chapter 6 from the front page of the Companion Website (located at http://www.prenhall.com/roblyer), then choose the *Multiple Choice* module.

Portfolio Activities

ISTE The following activities address ISTE National Educational Technology Standards for Teachers (NETS-T) and will help you add to your professional portfolio. To complete these activities online and save or submit the materials electronically, select Chapter 6 from the front page of the Companion Website (http://www.prenhall.com/roblyer), then choose the *Portfolio* module.

1. ***Software Tools List (NETS-T Standards: I-B; II-C, D, E)*** Describe how you plan to use each of the software tools described in this chapter to support instruction in your classroom.
2. ***Tool Templates (NETS-T Standard: V-C)*** Choose an appropriate software tool and develop a template you can use from year to year for each of the following purposes:

- Classroom letterhead
- Records (names, addresses, birthdates) for students in your classes
- Grade keeping
- Event announcement flyer
- Test item form and item bank for your subject area.

Questions for Thought and Discussion

These questions may be used for small-group or class discussion or may be subjects for individual or group activities. To take part in these discussions online, select Chapter 6 from the front page of the Companion Website (http://www.prenhall.com/roblyer), then choose the *Message Board* module.

1. The use of CMI systems has decreased in recent years as more group-based, constructivist methods were emphasized. How might CMI systems be of use now to support the current emphasis on standards-based education?
2. Some educators object to the use of tools such as test generators and worksheet generators, saying that they encourage teachers to use technology to maintain current methods, rather than using technology in ways that reform and improve methods. What case can you make for keeping software tools like these in classrooms?

ISTE

Collaborative Activities

The following activities address ISTE National Educational Technology Standards for Teachers (NETS-T) and can be done in small groups. Each group should present the findings to the class in a format they know how to use (word-processed report, presentation software, multimedia product). Completed group products may be copied and shared with the entire class and/or included in each person's personal portfolio.

1. ***Create a Newsletter (NETS-T Standards: V-C, D)*** Use desktop publishing software to create a newsletter for the school, classroom, or student organization. Each small group can create a section or page of the newsletter such as Notes from the Faculty, Principal Page, Music Events, and so on.
2. ***Flyer Competition (NETS-T Standards: V-C, D)*** The class works in pairs to develop a flyer or web page announcing a school event or advocating a position on a topic of current interest to the school or community. Each pair uses draw/paint software in conjunction with available clip art and scanned photos. After all flyers are printed, ask faculty members and/or parents to be judges to select the ones with the greatest impact. Post the winner and runners-up on a school bulletin board. Discuss what qualities made the winners the best.
3. ***Create a Test (NETS-T Standards: IV-A; V-C, D)*** Make a list of all the tools described in this chapter. Form small groups; each selects one or two tools. They develop five descriptions of applications teachers might do with each one. Place these descriptions in a test generator and create several versions of a review in which students must match tools appropriate for the applications. Student groups can work on these for homework.
4. ***Software Tools Lesson Plans (NETS-T Standards: II-A; III-C, D)*** Each small group selects one of the following tools and integration strategies and develops a lesson plan based on it:
   - **Desktop publishing.** Develop a classroom lesson activity that integrates desktop publishing functions into instruction in one or more of these ways: letterhead, brochures, newsletter or newspaper production, or book or booklet production.
   - **Worksheet or puzzle generation.** Develop a classroom lesson activity that uses this tool to help students practice a vocabulary, spelling, or mathematics skill.
   - **Draw/paint/image processing.** Develop a classroom lesson activity that uses this tool to promote writing or develop a geography skill such as map reading.
   - **Charting/graphing software.** Develop a classroom lesson activity that uses this tool to develop and explore a mathematics concept.
   - **Probeware (MBL) or graphing calculator (CBL).** Develop a classroom lesson activity that uses this tool to develop or explore a science concept.

Integrating Technology Across the Curriculum Activities

The *Integrating Technology Across the Curriculum* CD-ROM is a set of technology integration ideas and links to online lessons, arranged as a searchable database. The CD comes packaged with this textbook. Complete the following exercise using this CD:

Graphics software tools play a key role in many kinds of technology integration strategies. Review how various graphics tools are used by selecting 10 different lessons that make use of graphics and reviewing them. Create a chart like the one shown at right. Use the third column to write a one-sentence description of how the graphic tool enhances teaching or learning for the lesson.

Annotated Integration Ideas for Using Graphics Tools

Types of Graphics Tools	Name of Integration Idea	Brief Description of Role
Draw/paint/image processing	Creating a Database Yearbook	Adding pictures of students to yearbook
Charting/graphing		
Video development		

References

Albrecht, B., & Firedrake, G. (1997). New adventures in hands-on and far-out physics. *Learning and Leading with Technology, 25*(2), 34–37.

Anderson-Inman, L., & Zeitz, L. (1993). Computer-based concept mapping: Active studying for active learners. *The Computing Teacher, 21*(1), 6–8, 10–11.

Baker, F. (1978). *Computer-managed instruction: Theory and practice.* Englewood Cliffs, NJ: Educational Technology Publications.

Bitter, G., Camuse, R., & Durbin, V. (1993). *Using a microcomputer in the classroom* (3rd ed.). Boston: Allyn & Bacon.

Borenstein, M. (1997). Mathematics in the real world. *Learning and Leading with Technology, 24*(7), 30–39.

Brumbaugh, K., & Poirot, J. (1993). The teacher as researcher: Presenting your case. *The Computing Teacher, 20*(6), 19–21.

Catchings, M., & MacGregor, K. (1998). Stoking creative fires: Young authors use software for writing and illustrating. *Learning and Leading with Technology, 25*(6), 20–23.

Cowan, H. (1992). The art of group communication. *Electronic Learning, 11*(8), 38–39.

Dabbagh, N. (2001). Concept mapping as a mindtool for critical thinking. *Journal of Computing in Teacher Education, 17*(2), 16–23.

Duren, P. (1990–1991). Enhancing inquiry skills with graphing software. *The Computing Teacher, 20*(3), 23–25.

Forest, J. (1993). Music and the arts: Keys to a next-century school. *The Computing Teacher, 21*(3), 24–26.

Gay, L. R. (1993). *Educational research: Competencies for analysis and application* (4th ed.). Upper Saddle River, NJ: Merrill/Prentice Hall.

Goleman, D. (1995). *Emotional intelligence.* New York: Bantam Books.

Gullickson, A., & Farland, D. (1991). Using micros for test development. *Tech Trends, 35*(2), 22–26.

Hermann, A. (1988). Desktop publishing in high school: Empowering students as readers and writers (ERIC Document Reproduction No. ED 300 837).

Kahn, J. (1997). Well begun is half done: Teaching students to use concept-mapping software. *Learning and Leading with Technology, 24*(5), 39–40.

Knupfer, N., & McIsaac, M. (1989). Desktop publishing software: The effects of computerized formats on reading speed and comprehension. *Journal of Research on Computing in Education, 22*(2), 127–136.

Ladelson, L. (1994). Calibrating probeware: Making a line. *The Computing Teacher, 21*(6), 46–47.

Lewis, R. (1993). *Special education technology.* Pacific-Grove, CA: Brooks-Cole.

Lopez, S. (2000). Cat in the hat and all that. *Time Magazine, 156*(17), 6.

Manouchehri, A., & Pagnucco, L. (1999–2000). Julio's run: Studying graphs and functions. *Learning and Leading with Technology, 27*(4), 42–45.

McCain, T. (1993). *Designing for communication: The key to successful desktop publishing.* Eugene, OR: ISTE.

McCarthy, R. (1988). Stop the presses: An update on desktop publishing. *Electronic Learning, 7*(6), 24–30.

Moersch, C. (1995). Choose the right graph. *The Computing Teacher, 22*(5), 31–35.

Nathan, J. (1985). *Micro-myths: Exploring the limits of learning with computers.* Minneapolis, MN: Winston Press.

Newman, J. (1988). Online: Classroom publishing. *Language Arts, 65*(7), 727–732.

Norvelle, R. (1992). Desktop publishing. In G. Bitter (Ed.), *Macmillan encyclopedia of computers.* New York: Macmillan.

O'Bannon, B., Krolak, B., Harkelroad, M., & Dick, D. (1999). Awesome graphics: Using *PhotoShop* for web graphics. *Learning and Leading with Technology, 26*(5), 54–57.

Ohler, J. (1998). The promise of MIDI technology: A reflection on musical intelligence. *Learning and Leading with Technology, 25*(6), 6–15.

Parker, R. C. (1989). Ten common desktop design pitfalls. *Currents, 15*(1), 24–26.

Parmenter, B., & Burns, M. (2001). GIS in the classroom: Challeges, opportunities and alternatives. *Learning and Leading with Technology, 28*(7), 10–16.

Pearlman, B. (1994). Designing groupware. *ISTE Update, 6*(5), 1–2.

Plymate, L. (1998). Is it linear? *Learning and Leading with Technology, 26*(1), 16–22.

Poock, M. (1998). The Accelerated Reader: An analysis of the software's strengths and weaknesses and how it can be used to best potential. *School Library Media Activities Monthly, 14*(9), 32–35.

Reissman, R. (2000). Priceless gifts. *Learning and Leading with Technology, 28*(2), 28–31.

Reissman, R., & Gil, E. (2000). Technology takes on fairy tales and folktales. *Learning and Leading with Technology, 27*(5), 18–21.

Roblyer, M. (1992). Computers in education. In G. Bitter (Ed.), *Macmillan encyclopedia of computers.* New York: Macmillan.

Rose, S. (1988). A desktop publishing primer. *The Computing Teacher, 15*(9), 13–15.

Stanton, D. (1992). Microcomputer-based labs. *Electronic Learning Special Edition (Buyers Guide), 12*(1), 16–17.

Stanton, D. (1994). Gradebooks, the next generation. *Electronic Learning, 14*(1), 54–58.

Steinhaus, K. (1986–1987). Putting the music composition tool to work. *The Computing Teacher, 14*(4), 16–18.

Strommen, E. (1994). Can technology change the test? *Electronic Learning, 14*(1), 44–53.

Topping, K., and Paul, T. (1999). Computer-assisted assessment of practice at reading: A large scale survey using Accelerated Reader data. *Reading & Writing Quarterly, 15*(3), 213–232.

Truett, C. (1993). CD-ROM storybooks bring children's literature to life. *The Computing Teacher, 21*(1), 20–21.

Wager, W. (1992). Evaluating grade management software. *The Florida Technology in Education Quarterly, 4*(3), 59–66.

Walsh, T. (2001). SAMDADs for your classroom. *Learning and Leading with Technology, 28*(6), 32–35, 60.

Webster, E. (1992). Evaluation of computer software for teaching statistics. *Journal of Computers in Mathematics and Science Teaching, 11*(3/4), 377–391.

Wigre, R. (1993–1994). Reflections on tesselations. *The Computing Teacher, 21*(4), 15–16.

Williams, R. (1994). *The non-designer's design book: Design and typographic principles for the visual novice.* Berkeley, CA: Peachpit Press, 1994.

Willinsky, J., & Bradley, S. (1990). Desktop publishing in remedial language arts settings: Let them eat cake. *Journal of Teaching Writing, 9*(2), 223–238.

CHAPTER 7

Integrating Multimedia and Hypermedia into Teaching and Learning

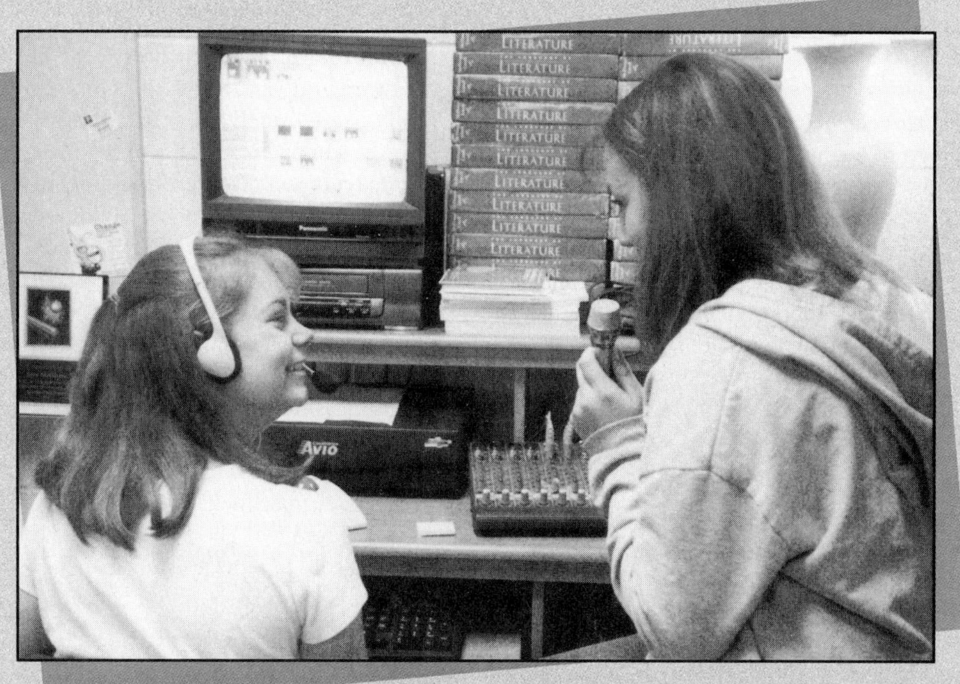

Multimedia learning is not something new. It is woven into the fabric of our childhood. . .

Tom Boyle in *Design for Multimedia Learning* (1997)

Technology is the campfire around which we will tell our stories.

Laurie Anderson

This chapter covers the following topics:

- Definitions and characteristics of multimedia and hypermedia systems
- Unique advantages and instructional uses of five types of multimedia/hypermedia resources: commercial CD-ROM and DVD multimedia software packages, commercial interactive videodiscs, presentation software, digital video systems, and various multimedia/hypermedia authoring systems
- Procedures for developing multimedia/hypermedia products using various authoring systems
- Educational applications of multimedia/hypermedia authoring systems

Objectives

1. Define multimedia and hypermedia from historic and current perspectives.
2. Design classroom lesson activities appropriate for each kind of multimedia/hypermedia product.
3. Evaluate the quality and capabilities of a commercial hypermedia product.
4. Use an authoring system to develop a product that meets visual, navigation, and instructional criteria for effective hypermedia-based instruction.
5. Design lesson activities appropriate for student development of hypermedia products.

Introduction to Multimedia and Hypermedia

We live in a multimedia world, surrounded by complex images, movement, and sound. So perhaps it is not surprising that part of our human evolution has focused on making our technology reflect the color and clamor of our surroundings. In educational technology, multimedia has been a steadily growing presence for some time. As discussed in Chapter 1, computer-based multimedia learning stations have been used since 1966, and noncomputer multimedia methods have been around even longer. This chapter looks at current classroom uses of electronic multimedia and its companion concept, hypermedia.

Multimedia and Hypermedia: How Do They Differ?

Like other educational technology concepts, definitions for multimedia and hypermedia defy consensus (Moore, Myers, & Burton, 1994; Tolhurst, 1995); people find the two concepts either too close to distinguish between or too slippery to get words around. Tolhurst quoted one source as saying, "By its very nature, [multimedia] is invertebrate. You poke it and it slithers away" (p. 21). Definitions used in this chapter come to us from two paths that were separate initially but have converged over time.

Multimedia simply means "multiple media" or "a combination of media." The media can be still pictures, sound, motion video, animation, and/or text items combined in a product whose purpose is to communicate information.

Hypermedia refers to "linked media" that have their roots in a concept developed by Vannevar Bush (1986) in his landmark article "As We May Think." In 1945, Bush proposed a "memex" machine that would let people quickly access items of information whose meanings were connected but which were stored in different places. In the 1960s, Ted Nelson coined the term *hypertext* to describe a proposed database system called Xanadu based on Bush's idea (Boyle, 1997). In this system, items of information from all over the world were to be logically connected with hypertext links. For example, one could select "apple" and get information on all related concepts such as trees, fruit—even the Garden of Eden. The technology at that time was inadequate to produce Xanadu, but the idea was the forerunner of today's hypermedia systems in which information stored in various media are connected (often via the Internet), thus the term *hypermedia.*

In current technologies such as Internet browsers (see Chapter 8) and authoring systems, most multimedia products also are hypermedia systems. That is, the media elements are linked with buttons to click on or menus from which to select. Clicking on or selecting one item sends the user to other, related items. This chapter gives many examples of hypermedia products; all also are multimedia. The combination of media such as video and audio with text makes them multimedia; the ability to get from one media/information element to another makes them hypermedia.

Types of Multimedia and Hypermedia Systems

Multimedia and hypermedia systems come in a variety of hardware, software, and media configurations and, until recently, were usually classified according to their primary storage equipment: interactive videodiscs (IVDs), CD-ROMs (compact disc–read-only memory), digital versatile discs (DVDs), and other technologies, including CD-I (compact disc–interactive), DVI (digital video interactive), and photo CDs (photographic compact discs). However, dramatic changes in the capabilities of presentation software and Internet multimedia formats, as well as the decline in use of videodisc systems, have changed the focus of this classification system. The medium on which multimedia is presented has become less important than its purpose and the type of capability it offers.

This chapter focuses on five kinds of multimedia/hypermedia formats. The first two are developed by companies and sold to educators and other consumers; the other three are authoring tools that educators and others can use to develop their own products.

- **Commercial multimedia/hypermedia software packages.** These are pre-packaged products developed by software publishing companies and offer a variety of media, including animation, video, audio, and links to the Internet. The trend is for most software packages to include all these features.
- **Commercial interactive videodisc packages.** Until the emergence of CD-ROM and DVD storage media, interactive videodiscs were the storage medium of choice for full-motion video in combination with text and still pictures. Because of the large number of IVD curriculum discs and videodiscs players that remain in schools, this technology is still in use.
- **Authoring tools: presentation software.** This authoring software used to be linear and primarily a combination of text, still pictures, and limited audio and animation. But it has grown in capability and now offers branching capabilities and the ability to include many of the same features as published products (e.g., embedded audio and video clips).

- **Authoring tools: video production and editing systems.** Digitized videos used to be difficult to produce and edit and were used primarily to capture short video clips for use in multimedia/hypermedia authored products. New video editing systems have changed this. Now anyone, even nontechnical consumers, can produce professional-looking movies with a variety of special effects like fading and titles.
- **Authoring tools: multimedia/hypermedia authoring systems.** These systems, too, have come a long way since the first versions. They are increasingly capable, allowing users to include many of the features they see in professional products with substantially greater ease.

Hypermedia systems published as web page documents also represent a powerful technology of the future. Hypermedia systems used in distance communications and online learning are described in Chapter 8.

Current and Future Impact of Multimedia and Hypermedia on Education

The current widespread educational uses of multimedia and hypermedia systems augur an even heavier reliance on these products in classrooms of the future. Educators recognize and use these systems when they see the powerful capabilities they offer to enhance classroom learning:

- **Motivation.** Hypermedia programs offer such varied options that most people seem to enjoy using them. Students who usually struggle to complete a project or term paper often will tackle a hypermedia project enthusiastically. McCarthy (1989) is among those who believes the most important characteristic of hypermedia is its ability to encourage students to be proactive learners.
- **Flexibility.** Hypermedia programs can draw on such diverse tools that they truly offer something for students who excel in any of what Gardner calls "intelligences" (see Chapter 3). For example, a student who may not be good at written expression but has visual aptitude can document learning with sound or pictures.
- **Development of creative and critical thinking skills.** The tremendous access to hypertext and hypermedia tools opens up a multitude of creative avenues for both students and teachers. Marchionini (1988) refers to hypermedia as a fluid environment that constantly requires the learner to make decisions and evaluate progress. He asserts that this process forces students to apply higher order thinking skills. Turner and Dipinto (1992) report that the hypermedia environment encourages students to think in terms of metaphors, to be introspective, and to give free rein to their imaginations.
- **Improved writing and process skills.** Turner and Dipinto (1992) also find that exposure to hypermedia authoring tools helps students by giving them a new and different perspective on how to organize and present information and a new insight into writing. Instead of viewing their writing as one long stream of text, students now see it as chunks of information to be linked.

Our society's heavy reliance on hypertext/hypermedia to communicate information seems likely to expand in the future. The accelerating number of World Wide Web pages on the Internet is evidence that linking data with hypertext and hypermedia is an effective way to present and add value to large bodies of information. Millions of people have published hypermedia documents on the Information Superhighway in the hope of attracting viewers, readers, and listeners.

Hypermedia tools also may permit sophisticated evaluations of learning. In the process of using hypermedia, people are said to "leave a track" (Simonson & Thompson, 1994), which may help teachers analyze how students approach learning tasks. Future hypermedia systems might apply pattern-recognition techniques from the field of artificial intelligence to help schools assess student mastery of higher order cognitive skills (Dede, 1994). Bagui (1998) says multimedia "may have unique capabilities to facilitate learning because of the parallels between multimedia and the natural way people learn" (p. 4), that is, through visual information and imagery.

Research on the Impact of Multimedia and Hypermedia Systems

While some reviewers have tried to capture the unique contributions of these systems on achievement (Adams, 1992; McNeil & Nelson, 1991), Lookatch (1997) echoes Clark's warning (see Chapter 1) that instructional strategies—not media—will make the difference in achievement. In summarizing research reviews of findings that could guide future educational uses of multimedia/hypermedia, Roblyer (1999) found that multimedia's benefits seem to center on its ability to offer students multiple channels through which to process information. However, researchers are cautious about recommending multimedia to support specific kinds of learning.

Swan and Meskill (1996) examined how effectively current hypermedia products support the teaching and acquisition of critical thinking skills in reading and language. They reviewed hypermedia products as to how well they made possible response-based approaches to teaching and learning literature, that is, instructional activities that "place student-generated questions at the center of learning . . . (and encourage) a problem-finding as well as a problem solving approach to critical thinking" (p. 168). They evaluated 45 hypermedia literature programs using criteria in three areas: technical items, response-based concerns, and classroom issues. The majority of the 45 products used a CD-ROM format, but 10 used a combination of CD-ROM and videodisc, and four used computer software. They found that most products were technically sound and linked well with classroom topics, but few were designed to promote the response-based methods that promote critical thinking. "Programs designed for elementary students . . . equated literature education with reading instruction; programs designed for high school . . . generally adopted a traditional text-centered approach" (p. 187). These findings indicate that teachers who want to use multimedia/hypermedia products specifically to promote higher level skills must select products judiciously and warily.

In another review of the impact of hypermedia on learner comprehension and learner control, Dillon and Gabbard (1998) echo the caution voiced by Swan and Meskill. They conclude that:

- Hypermedia's primary advantages accrue to students doing rapid searches through lengthy or multiple information resources. For other purposes, hypermedia and nonhypermedia resources seem equally useful.
- Increased learner control is more useful to higher ability students; lower ability students experience the greatest difficulty with hypermedia.
- Learner style helps determine whether or not certain hypermedia features are effective in various learning situations. Passive learners may profit more from the cueing offered by hypermedia, while more capable learners who are more willing to explore may be more capable of exploiting other hypermedia features.

Research on the Design of Multimedia and Hypermedia Systems

Stemler (1997) reviewed findings on various multimedia/hypermedia characteristics that could have an impact on the potential effectiveness of these systems: screen design, learner control and navigation, use of feedback, student interactivity, and video and audio elements. Her findings are too extensive to give adequate treatment here, but educators who are committed to high-quality multimedia development should review the full text of her article.

- **Instructional design.** Stemler recommends that developers analyze each element in a multimedia product to determine which of Gagné's nine Events of Instruction (see Chapter 3) it aims to achieve and how well it achieves it.
- **Screen design.** Well-designed screens focus learners' attention, develop and maintain interest, promote processing of information, promote engagement between learner and content, help students find and organize information, and support easy navigation through lessons (p. 343).
- **Interaction and feedback.** Keep feedback on the same screen with the question and student response and provide immediate feedback. Verify correct answers and give hints and another try for incorrect answers. Tailor feedback to the response and provide encouraging feedback, but do not make it more entertaining for students to provide wrong answers rather than correct ones. If possible, let students print out the feedback (p. 345).
- **Navigation.** Support navigation with orientation cues, clearly defined procedures, clearly labeled back-and-forth buttons, and help segments (pp. 346–347).
- **Learner control.** In general, give older and more capable students more control over the sequence; younger, less experienced students should have less control (p. 348).
- **Color.** Use color sparingly and employ it primarily for cueing and highlighting certain elements to bring them to the learner's attention. Use a consistent color scheme throughout to promote ease of use (pp. 350–351).
- **Graphics.** Use graphics as well as text to present information to serve students who prefer one kind of presentation over the other. Use graphics sparingly for other purposes (to entertain or amuse) (p. 351).
- **Animation.** Use animation sparingly and only to present dynamic processes or to highlight key information (p. 352).
- **Audio.** Use audio for short presentations of program content, but do not let it compete with video presentation. Do not require long readings on each screen. Separate material into chunks on each of several screens (p. 353).
- **Video.** Use video sequences for broader, abstract material (that with emotional impact) and for advance organizers rather than for presenting detailed information (p. 354).

Mayer and Moreno (1998) reported yet another study focusing on multimedia design issues. They found that learners using multimedia materials showed greater comprehension and retention of learned materials when pictures were accompanied by spoken words, rather than written words. They observed that this "split attention" effect was consistent with a model of working memory that had separate visual and auditory channels. Therefore, learners did not process image and text information when it was presented through the same channel (visual). More studies of this kind are urgently needed to guide design strategies for hypermedia products.

Emerging Developments in Storage Media for Multimedia Systems: Compact Disc–Read-Only Memory (CD-ROM) and Digital Versatile Disc (DVD)

In recent years, CD-ROMs and DVDs have replaced computer disks and videodiscs as the most popular storage media for motion video, as well as text, sound, and graphics of all kinds. Consumers now receive most software packages on CD rather than computer disk, and DVDs have replaced videotapes as the storage medium for movies. CD-ROM and DVD technologies all share a single core technology: Laser beams heat light-sensitive material on a disc so that a chemical reaction causes the area to either remain opaque or reflect light, thus revealing encoded information. In contrast, magnetic storage units, such as hard disks and tape devices, store data as magnetic pulses, which are read or altered by the disk drive. Generally accepted style in the industry has adopted the spelling *disk* for magnetic storage systems and *disc* for optical devices.

CD-ROMs. As music media, CD-ROMs have become as commonplace in the lives of young people as phonograph records were to their parents and grandparents. But CD-ROMs have additional capabilities undreamed of in the days of record albums and turntables. Commonly called *compact discs* or *CDs,* CD-ROMs are made of the same material as videodiscs but are smaller in size, just 4.72 inches (12 cm) in diameter. In appearance, CD-ROMs look identical to audio CDs. The main practical differences between an audio CD and a CD-ROM are what they can store and how they are used. Both store data in digital form. But audio CDs store sound, whereas CD-ROMs store text, audio, video, animation, and graphics information. CD-ROMs are known for their huge storage capacity, up to 650 MB of data, which equates to the equivalent of 250,000 pages of text, or five hundred 500-page novels. Computer systems get access to CD-ROMs through either internal or external CD-ROM players.

CD-ROM technology has adapted to allow users to store data on them as well as use them for prestored applications. Because CD-ROMs hold so much more information than disks, they are becoming valuable additions to schools' collections of storage devices, and readable/writable CD-ROM drives are becoming commonplace.

DVDs. These media look like CD-ROMs but have much greater storage capacity: currently from 4.7 GB (single sided, single layered) to 14 GB (double sided, double layered). Like CD-ROMs, DVDs began with a read-only format but are rapidly taking the place of computer disks, hard drives, and even videodiscs and CD-ROMs. They are able to store high-quality video as well as audio and text data, thus making them valuable to multimedia developers in education and elsewhere. Also, they are replacing videotape as storage media for commercially produced movies and films.

As storage media continue to evolve in capability and decrease in price, they will have a significant impact on the kinds of multimedia/hypermedia that teachers can develop. DVD technology is projected to become an important storage medium in the future, taking the place of current CD-ROMs and even hard drives. This will allow educators to include more multimedia elements, especially video sequences, which currently take up more room than may be available.

Issues Related to Multimedia and Hypermedia Use in Education

Educators have voiced several concerns recently about our media-driven culture and its role in education. A few of these are described here.

The critical importance of media literacy. As Mergendollar (1997) warns, technologies such as multimedia are an equivocal blessing. They help us communicate information more expeditiously but do not help us analyze whether or not information is accurate, relevant, or current. The more information we have, the more important it becomes to learn critical analysis, visual literacy, and information literacy skills.

Limitations of hypermedia. Although multimedia/hypermedia systems truly represent the communication method of choice both now and in the future, education's use of these resources is hampered by several problems:

- **Hardware intensity.** To take full advantage of the benefits of hypermedia technology, students need ample online development time. This presents a problem in most classroom settings due to insufficient numbers of computers. The problem is exacerbated when available computers are not configured for hypermedia authoring. For example, they may lack the capacity to digitize sound or to input video.
- **Lack of training.** Although hypermedia programs are becoming easier to use, they still require extensive training. Unfortunately, training is not a top priority in most school districts. One survey showed that staff development makes up only about 8% of technology budgets (Siegel, 1995). The toughest challenge instructional personnel face is not learning to use a particular program, but learning to integrate it within the curriculum. To help alleviate this problem, hypermedia training needs to go beyond just learning how to make an authoring program work. Training must also give serious consideration to effective curriculum integration. In addition, to ensure quality products, hypermedia training should extend to the areas of media, design, and the arts.
- **Projection needs.** Teachers often want to project students' hypermedia projects onto large screens so that others can see the results. For this, the teacher must hook up an LCD panel or a video projector to the computer. This requires an additional piece of hardware, so every classroom may not have a projection setup. A compromise solution may be to use a converter that can project the computer signal onto a large television/monitor.
- **Integration problems.** Integration of hypermedia technology into the curriculum presents some major problems. To ensure quality projects, students need sufficient time to focus, build, and reflect. The conventional school schedule, often broken into 50-minute blocks, does not lend itself to serious project development. If hypermedia authoring is to have a major impact on learning, educators will need to look at ways of infusing more flexibility into students' daily schedules. One step in the right direction might be more integration of subject matter into interdisciplinary projects.
- **Memory and storage problems.** A hypermedia project can fill a tremendous amount of storage space on a

computer's hard drive; digitized video and sound files are the major culprits. Until the compression techniques promised by DVD improve and become more cost effective, this problem will persist. Another component of this problem is the difficulty of transferring a file from one computer to another, because even very small hypermedia files will exceed the capacity of a single data disk. There are some ways of getting around these problems. Students can store files on external hard drives or zip disks. These add another cost element, but the prices are dropping rapidly.

Commercial Multimedia/Hypermedia Software Packages

Background on Commercial Multimedia/Hypermedia Software Packages

As noted in Chapter 4, instructional software is becoming increasingly multimedia and hypermedia in nature. Software tools have also seen an increasing emphasis on this format. The increased storage capability and availability of CD and DVD media has made it easier to store complex programs with motion graphics, movies, audio, and links to the Internet. Software used to be produced primarily by writing code in a computer language. Today's software is frequently produced with an authoring system such as *Macromedia Director.* The number of titles in the CD-ROM and DVD market has increased at a phenomenal rate during the past few years and will continue to grow. The *Multimedia Compendium* from Emerging Technologies (http://www.emergingtechnology.com) is a frequently updated catalog of current offerings. (See Figure 7.1.) Currently, several popular categories of multimedia/hypermedia-based products are used in classrooms.

Instructional Software

A single CD-ROM can store the equivalent of eight hundred 3.5-inch computer disks. This makes CD-ROM a wonderful technology for distributing more memory-intensive instructional software. Some companies have taken advantage of this added capacity by enhancing successful programs with multimedia features and Internet links, for example, Sunburst's *Multimedia: The Human Body.* (See Figure 7.2.)

Interactive Storybooks

These on-screen stories have become extremely popular with primary teachers and students (Glasgow, 1996, 1996–1997, 1997; Kahn, 1997). On the audio tracks, narrators read pages as the words are highlighted on screen. If a student needs to hear a word again, just clicking on it with the mouse pointer will activate the audio. Some electronic storybooks have a straightforward approach, allowing students to read them at their own pace. Other books are structured to be more interactive and open ended, some allowing students to choose the story path and ending they want each time the story is read. A recent study by Doty, Popplewell, and Byers (2001) found that students' ability to answer comprehension questions was higher when they read stories in an electronic storybook format than when they read a traditional book format.

Figure 7.1 The Multimedia Compendium

Source: Used with permission from Emerging Technology Consultants, Inc.

Reference Materials

Many reference materials are available on CD and DVD at very reasonable costs. To add still more value, these resources are accompanied by search engine software that makes searching for information both easy and efficient. Some materials have Internet links to still more material. Below are just a few of the categories and example titles.

Encyclopedias. Most of the major encyclopedias are no longer published exclusively in book format; they are available on CD and DVD. Some like Microsoft's *Encarta* were designed solely for the electronic format and are available only on disc or the Internet. However, others such as the *World Book Encyclopedia* now have a version on disc after many years in book format. (see Figure 7.3.) Many, like *World Book,* also have Internet versions or supplements.

Almanacs. Popular information collections such as *The Time Almanac* are increasingly shifting to electronic format. Some, such as the *CIA World Factbook,* are on the Internet.

Atlases. Map utilities such as the *Picture Atlas of the World* allow teachers and students to do a variety of interactive activities such as determining distances and routes from one location to another.

Collections of Development Resources

Many collections of resources used to develop multimedia are now shipped on CD-ROM. These include collections of

Figure 7.2 Screen from Sunburst's *Multimedia: The Human Body*

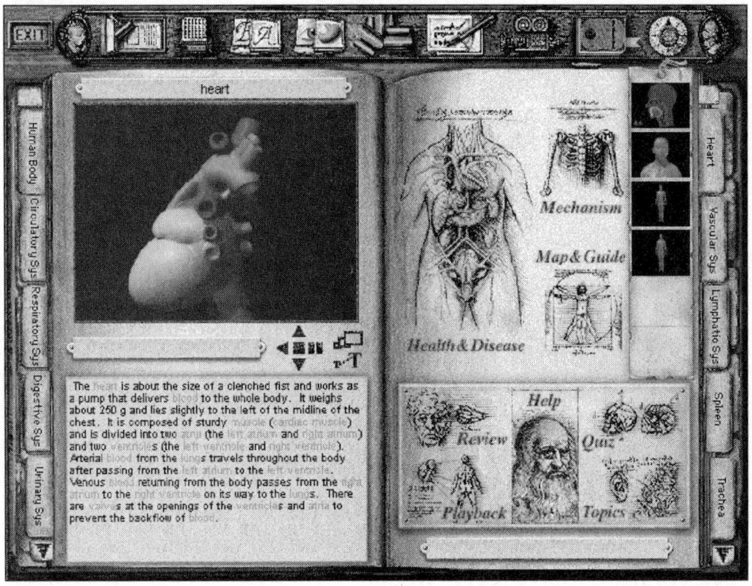

Source: © 1999, NHK Enterprises 21, Inc., licensed by NEC Interchannel, Ltd. Published by Sunburst Technology Corporation.

Figure 7.3 Screens from *World Book Encyclopedia*

The Just Looking feature enables *World Book CD-ROM* users to browse through the entire encyclopedia or just one part of it. Users can choose a random selection or an alphabetical list.

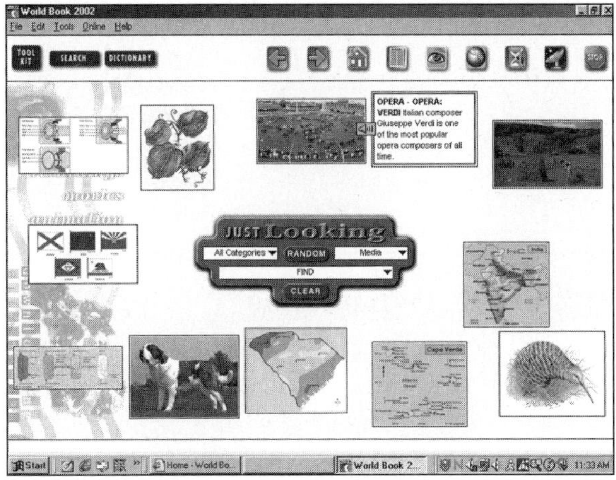

Source: Used with permission from World Book Encyclopedia.

clip art, sound effects, photographs, video clips, fonts, and document templates. Also, some major technology conferences, like the National Educational Computing Conference (NECC), distribute to each registrant proceedings, presenter handouts, vendor samples, and shareware on CD-ROM.

Integration Strategies for Commercial Multimedia/Hypermedia Products

Because products in this category vary so widely, instructional uses for them are also varied and rich. Integration strategies for instructional software are discussed in detail in Chapter 4, and strategies for software tools are described in Chapter 5. Technology Integration Ideas 7.1 and 7.2 illustrate ways some of the commercial multimedia/hypermedia resources are being used in classrooms.

Commercial Interactive Videodisc Systems

Background on IVD Systems

Videodiscs are optical storage media for random-access storage of high-quality audio and analog information. Laser videodiscs can store text, audio, video, and graphics data in analog format. *Interactive videodisc (IVD)* technology was first released in the 1970s and now has applications in both the education and business worlds. A videodisc resembles an audio CD disc, except it usually is larger in diameter. Most videodiscs are 12 inches in diameter and hold 54,000 still frames or the equivalent of 675 carousel slide trays. They represent a durable medium for storing and displaying visual information. Videodiscs are read by a laser beam, and the mechanism allows random access to any part of the disc. The random access feature is important because it avoids the need to fast forward or rewind to find a particular image as is necessary with a videotape.

IVD past, present, and future. Optical disc technology was first introduced by the Dutch firm NV Philips in 1972, leading to the release of a commercial product in 1976. Videodiscs were initially marketed as media to show movies at home. Soon after they got started in the consumer market, however, relatively low-cost VCR technology became available and emerged as the medium of choice for

TECHNOLOGY INTEGRATION IDEA 7.1

Hypermedia Projects with Multimedia/Hypermedia Reference Software Tools

TITLE: Tracking Down Trivia—A World Scavenger Hunt

CONTENT AREA/TOPIC: Research and study skills

GRADE LEVEL: 4–6

NETS FOR STUDENTS: Standards 1, 3, 4, 5

DESCRIPTION: This activity is designed to improve student skills in using CD-ROM-based encyclopedias for research. Pass out copies of a list of questions like the following to the class. Have students work in pairs on a "scavenger hunt" for information. Using an atlas and/or encyclopedia as resources, have them look up the answers to the questions. If appropriate, inject an element of competition in the activity by offering incentives to all those who answer the most questions correctly during class.

1. What is the capital city of Sweden?
2. What was E. B. White's first name?
3. Who won the Nobel Prize for Peace in 1985?
4. When did the Japanese bomb Pearl Harbor?
5. How did John Paul Jones die?
6. What is the state flower of Utah?
7. What does *illiterate* mean?
8. What gases make up the atmosphere of Jupiter?
9. What movie won the Academy Award for best picture in 1985?
10. What is a synonym for the word *supercilious*?
11. What is the chemical formula for sulfuric acid?
12. If Babe Ruth had lived 20 years longer, how old would he have been when he died?

Source: Contributed by Jack Edwards.

TECHNOLOGY INTEGRATION IDEA 7.2

Hypermedia Projects with Multimedia/Hypermedia Reference Software Tools

TITLE: Research Detectives

CONTENT AREA/TOPIC: History

GRADE LEVEL: 7–12

NETS FOR STUDENTS: Standards 1, 3, 4, 5

DESCRIPTION: This activity can help develop students' skills at locating and analyzing historical information. Distribute to small groups of students copies of a scenario involving a "theft problem" they must solve. Provide access to a CD-ROM player and a variety of CD-ROM reference tools. Microsoft's *Bookshelf* is excellent for this activity since it contains an encyclopedia, dictionary, almanac, atlas, and other resources—all on one CD-ROM. The scenario should include a list of suspects whose descriptions include high-level vocabulary and ambiguous facts that require students to use the reference resources to read up on the history cited, locate discrepancies in the suspects' stories, and analyze them to determine which suspect must be lying. Another way to do this type of project is to have students write their own scenarios, which could then be published and shared with other classes to develop their research and analytical skills.

Source: Contributed by Jack Edwards.

consumers. A videodisc player connects to a television set or computer monitor in much the same way as a VCR does. Both generally are configured to use either RF or RCA connectors. Remote controls and bar-code readers are not difficult to use but do require some training and practice. To take full advantage of the interactivity in IVD technology, the teacher must handle the mechanics of its operation smoothly.

Once a dominant form of multimedia products, videodiscs are not now generally considered cutting-edge technology. However, due to the installed base of videodisc players, they remain popular tools among many educators. According to Anne Winchester, president of Laser Learning Technologies, videodiscs are being replaced by curriculum products on CD-ROM and DVD. Titles listed in the *Multimedia Compendium* for the latter outnumber those for IVD by two to one.

Levels of interactivity. The level of interactivity of a videodisc program refers to the amount of control the program gives the user and what kinds of software and hardware the user needs to achieve control. Videodisc programs come in Level I and Level III formats. Level I, the most popular format, requires only a videodisc player and a bar-code reader to use the curriculum videodiscs designed for it. Level III requires a computer connected to a videodisc player with special cables.

The explosion of CD-ROM technology has been predicted to eclipse videodiscs, and these predictions will doubtless come true eventually. However, teachers still find Level I IVD technology an easy-to-use and effective tool. This format seems to be gradually moving to DVD players with bar-code readers. On the other hand, the future of Level III IVD seems short lived because of its awkward hardware configuration; schools will likely prefer the simpler interactive multimedia platform. Videodiscs that once were used as Level III resources may change roles to that of presentation tools and Level I uses.

Advantages of IVD Technology

IVD supports a variety of applications for teachers and students. The control options, as well as the unlimited creative potential of repurposing videodiscs by selecting bar codes from them, allow this tool to integrate effectively into most curricula. Advantages of IVD include the following:

- **Dual audio tracks.** Developers often use the second track to play program audio in a second language (usually Spanish) or to include a simpler or more detailed version of the presentation. The teacher can then let some students listen to one track through headphones while the rest of the class listens to the other track through the monitor.
- **Ease of use.** Most teachers and students feel comfortable enough to begin using Level I IVD technology with only a few hours of training. However, they may become fully comfortable only after many hours of use. Some schools allow teachers to check out videodisc players for practice at home as a means of encouraging them to use the equipment in their classrooms.
- **Quality.** High-resolution video images and audio clips stored on videodiscs provide much higher quality than videocassette tapes. Videodiscs also beat the quality of digitized video displayed directly on computer monitors.
- **Durability.** Since videodiscs are read with a laser beam, they suffer no real wear and tear with normal use. Discs are coated with plastic that generally protects them from small scratches or fingerprints. They are certain to last longer than videotapes or films.

Disadvantages of IVD Technology

- **Cost.** The cost of some videodisc programs can be quite high (e.g., $300 to $500 or more). This presents a big problem when a school's media purchasers see these programs simply as videos. Someone who can pay $49.95 for a videotape may balk at the cost of a videodisc. Schools should evaluate these higher end videodisc programs as curriculum packages, rather than just discs.
- **Read only.** The videodisc is a read-only technology, which means that users cannot record information. This is an obvious disadvantage compared to the VCR or writable CDs.
- **Hardware-intensive systems for Level III.** A Level III setup includes a videodisc player, monitor, computer, and cables. Teachers often find it burdensome to gather all of this equipment in one place. Some schools have opted to create portable multimedia stations that can easily be transported from one classroom to another. Level III interactivity also presents a cumbersome interface for the user who must pay attention to two monitors—the computer screen and the television screen.
- **Maintenance costs.** Videodisc players can be expensive to repair, and users should handle them with care. However, the industrial players sold to schools are designed to be more durable than home players.
- **Limited video capacity.** Although videodiscs provide tremendous storage capacity for still frames, when played as continuous video, the format offers only 30 minutes per side. A complete movie can fill three, four, or even five separate discs.

Classroom Uses of IVD Systems

Using bar codes. Users can scan bar codes to access chapters, individual frames, or segments of video on discs. The bar codes look like UPC codes on commercial-use products. The bar-code reader that interprets the patterns of stripes resembles the technology in many stores. Bar codes are considered the easiest way to access information from videodisc. They simplify control of the technology so the teacher can concentrate on interacting with the students without worrying about entering frame or chapter numbers with a remote control device. Vendors have taken advantage of these capabilities and now include bar codes with most Level I programs. A good example of the power of bar codes emerged when Optical Data Corporation upgraded its *Windows on Science* program. By indexing discs with bar codes, the company turned a potentially cumbersome program into one that teachers find both exciting and easy to use.

A number of software packages for Macintosh, Windows, and DOS systems (*Bar'n'Coder 3.0, Barcode Maker, Lesson Maker*) enable users to create bar codes for videodiscs. Most of these programs work similarly. The user enters the frame or time-code numbers to display and then types in a descriptor for the bar code. At the user's command to make the bar code, the program either prints it out or exports it to a word processing document.

Once the bar code is generated, it can be used in many ways. A teacher might create bar codes that access data on a videodisc dealing with geography and then glue the bar codes on appropriate parts of maps. This becomes an exploration center for students. Another instructor might use the computer to paste the bar code into a word processing file and then scan it during a teacher-directed activity. Barcode software can also make bar codes for an audio CD. Videodisc players sold since 1992 support the LB2 standard. They can play audio CDs under control of bar codes that match the standard. The "address" for the audio CD shows up on the TV monitor hooked up to the videodisc player. Users can enter this information into the bar-code program as they do for a videodisc frame to get to a specific part of the audio CD.

Interactive curriculum. Perhaps the most ambitious use of videodisc technology has been the development of entire curriculum packages around Level I technology. Examples include Optical Data Corporation's *Windows on Science* program, now in wide use, with *Windows on Math* and *Windows on Social Studies.* Some states now allow school districts to adopt these programs in lieu of textbooks. D. C. Heath's *Interactions* program uses video technology to bring interactive examples of math applications in real-world settings.

Problem solving. Discs such as Videodiscovery's *Science Sleuths* (see Figure 7.4) and *Math Sleuths* provide students with mysteries to solve. The videodisc programs offer clues in the form of interviews, textual and numeric data, photographs, and diagrams. The teacher plays an active role in guiding students via questioning techniques and just-in-time teaching.

Simulations. Optical Data's *Adventures of Jasper Woodbury* teaches middle school math with a series of simulated scenarios. Students solve real-world applied math problems by retrieving data embedded in the stories. Barcode technology comes in handy, since it enables students to review segments from the story as needed. It is designed so that the teacher can stop the action and teach certain math techniques just when needed to solve techniques problems.

Figure 7.4 Videodiscovery's videodisc *Science Sleuths*

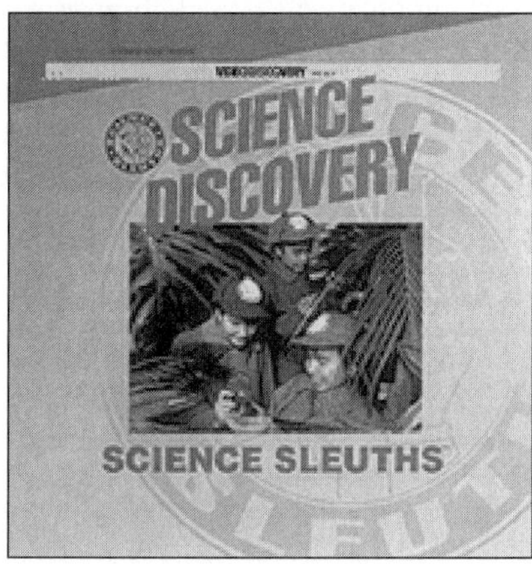

Source: Used with permission from Videodiscovery.

Visual databases. Visual databases are collections of individual pictures and short video segments. *BioSci II* was one of the earliest examples of this type of program. These databases are perhaps most useful in the areas of science and art and provide a wealth of resources for both teacher presentations and student projects.

Movies and documentaries. Schools can choose from thousands of movies, documentaries, and other general-use videodiscs at reasonable prices. These resources can yield tremendous educational benefits. Through the search feature controlled by the remote control, a teacher can access any frame or segment of a disc almost instantly. The random-access capability of the technology holds great promise for encouraging sound pedagogical uses of video as opposed to playing movies straight through.

Student presentations. Videodiscs allow students to create their own illustrated presentations on topics they have researched or books they have read (Thorpe, 1993). This is a kind of repurposing, in which students present selected frames to support and enhance their reports.

Integration Strategies for IVD Systems

Technology Integration Ideas 7.3 and 7.4 illustrate some of the many current uses for IVD multimedia/hypermedia resources.

TECHNOLOGY INTEGRATION IDEA 7.3

Hypermedia Projects with Commercial IVD Systems

TITLE: A Capital Idea—Problem Solving with *Jasper Woodbury*

CONTENT AREA/TOPIC: Mathematics in problem solving

GRADE LEVEL: Middle school

NETS FOR STUDENTS: Standards 1, 3, 4, 5, 6

DESCRIPTION: The activity described here is based on one of the *Jasper Woodbury* videodisc scenarios, "A Capital Idea." The problem the students must solve is to replace money the city can no longer provide to support class trips. The students are challenged to propose a citywide recycling plan to raise the funds and present the plan to the mayor. The emphasis in this activity is on group work and cooperation. Before beginning the work, the teacher divides the students into small groups and tells them they should develop collaborative skills within their team of listening, sharing ideas, and encouraging participation. They discuss what these skills look like in action and that working together is important to solving the problem. Then they begin the seven-stage activity: Focus (watch the video), gather information to solve the problem, organize the information and determine what is missing, analyze information for relationships, review the video for further information, synthesize information and form a problem solution, and prepare presentations that provide a problem solution.

Source: Brown, J. M., and Verhey, R. (1997). A capital idea: Project-based mathematics learning. *Learning and Leading with Technology,* 25(3), 31–37.

TECHNOLOGY INTEGRATION IDEA 7.4

Hypermedia Projects with Commercial IVD Systems

TITLE: The Salt Quest—A Persuasive Presentation

CONTENT AREA/TOPIC: The Environment

GRADE LEVEL: 5–12

NETS FOR STUDENTS: Standards 1, 3, 4, 5, 6

DESCRIPTION: Pass out a copy of the following scenario to the students. Ask them to read it.

> Military commands all over the world are in a state of high alert. A fleet of alien spacecraft has been lurking just outside earth's atmosphere for the past two days. An organization called "What's Up"—a think tank composed of highly educated men and women who for years have been convinced that extraterrestrial life exists—was asked to contact the aliens to see what they wanted. The spacecraft are from a planet called Nacl, which is in another solar system. The inhabitants of Nacl require tremendous amounts of salt to exist. They are getting close to depleting their own supplies and have been on a long search for new supplies. They have noticed that the earth's oceans are full of salt, so they thought that they would help themselves to this huge supply. You are a committee of "What's Up" members that must persuade the Naclites that it would not be a good idea to mine the salt from the oceans. The Naclites are reasonable beings who, it is thought, will move on to other places if they realize that mining the oceans would kill off millions of beautiful creatures. "What's Up" is charged with putting together a presentation that will convince the Naclites that the sea life on earth is too magnificent to be sacrificed just to satisfy their need for salt. The members decide that the presentation must have visuals, and Level I interactive video would be the best media to use.

Source: Contributed by Jack Edwards.

Three Kinds of Multimedia/Hypermedia Authoring Resources

Background on Multimedia/Hypermedia Authoring Systems

One of the most amazing things about how multimedia systems have evolved is that people with fairly nontechnical skill levels now can develop their own complex, professional-looking hypermedia products. Perhaps most importantly for schools, hypermedia authoring may play a major role in preparing students for the information-intensive and visually oriented world of the future. In tomorrow's digital world, powerful personal computers and ubiquitous electronic networking will allow people to incorporate a variety of media into their communications. Indeed, hypermedia publishing may eventually supersede paper publishing in importance and impact. Three kinds of multimedia/hypermedia authoring tools for use by both teachers and students are described in this chapter:

- Presentation software
- Video production and editing systems
- Hypermedia authoring software.

Although these systems vary in capability and authoring procedures, all allow people to summarize and display information and knowledge using a combination of text, video, animation, music, graphics, and sound effects. The array of skills and resources that students and teachers will need in order to use any of these three categories of authoring tools are described here. In addition, integration strategies common to all of these authoring formats are discussed.

Hypermedia Authoring Resources

Over time, hypermedia programs have become increasingly more powerful and user friendly, and are adding features and capabilities with every new version released. Authors now can draw on a wide variety of resources to put a full range of sound and motion in their hypermedia products. The newest feature available in hypermedia authoring is the ability to insert Internet links into products. Users can click on these links and go immediately from software screen to Internet site. This section describes some of the other common resources available in hypermedia authoring.

Audio resources. Hypermedia authoring programs offer users a number of ways to incorporate audio clips.

- **CD audio.** Cards include segments of audio CDs in CD-ROM drives or videodisc players. CDs provide digitized music, speech, or sound effects.
- **Videodiscs.** Rather than playing both the video and audio tracks of a videodisc, authors may choose to leave the video and access the audio track alone.
- **Recorded sounds.** Hypermedia programs usually allow authors to record sound into their programs. This can include voice, such as when an author records his or her reading of a poem or directions to students.
- **Prerecorded sounds.** Many hypermedia authoring programs come with built-in selections of sound effects. Authors can also add sounds from packaged collections sometimes called "clip sounds," which are stored on disk or CD-ROMs.

Video resources. Motion video clips can add a whole new dimension to a program and provide authors with many new communication possibilities. As with audio, authors have several options for incorporating video displays into a product:

- **Digitized videos.** By using a video digitizer, a hypermedia author can import video images from external sources such as a VCR, a videodisc, or a camcorder. Programs such as *Quicktime* allow authors to create and edit their own short videoclips (movies) and place them on cards. Teachers and students need to observe copyright laws when importing video in this manner. Digitized video also consumes a great deal of hard drive storage space, thus limiting the amount of video that can realistically be incorporated into a program. An external hard drive offers one solution to this problem; removable cartridge systems are very effective in this role, although the costs for the individual cartridges can be quite high. In the future, more efficient video compression routines promise greater latitude for hypermedia authors.
- **Videodiscs.** Most hypermedia programs enable authors to access either individual slides or segments of video from videodiscs. This can prove a big advantage due to the high quality of audio and video recordings from videodiscs.
- **Prerecorded videos on CD-ROMs.** Authors can buy collections of short videoclips on CD-ROM to incorporate into hypermedia programs. No copyrights inhibit use of these images, giving authors much more leeway in their presentations.

Photographs. A picture is worth a thousand words in hypermedia, as much as elsewhere. Photographs provide a powerful resource for authors in all subject areas.

- **Scanned photos.** Authors can digitize traditional photographs using scanners and then incorporate these images into hypermedia stacks.
- **Captured from video sources.** By using a video digitizer, an author can freeze images from a VCR, camcorder, or videodisc player and then import them.
- **Digital cameras.** These cameras take digitized, color pictures that can be added to hypermedia cards. Pictures can be downloaded directly from the camera to the computer's hard drive.
- **Imported from CD-ROMs.** Collections of photographs on CD-ROMs are marketed expressly for inclusion in hypermedia programs.

Graphic images. Graphics or drawings offer another tool for authors to communicate their ideas. Often an illustration will demonstrate a point that is difficult to get across with words. This aspect of hypermedia authoring is particularly appealing to artistically inclined users.

- **Created by authors.** Virtually all hypermedia programs offer basic collections of tools that let users draw or paint graphics. These tools enable users with even limited artistic talents to create credible designs and drawings.
- **Imported from clip art collections.** A vast array of clip art collections are available for purchase. These premade graphics cover a wide assortment of subject areas.
- **Scanned images.** As another alternative for accessing graphics, an image can be scanned from either a book of clip art or a drawing done in conventional art media such as pencils or paintbrushes. Since computer access often is limited, some teachers prefer students to draw their pictures by hand and then digitize them using scanners.

Animation. Animation is a highly effective tool for illustrating a concept; a student might create an animation of a seed germinating as part of a project on plants. The sources of these displays are familiar.

- **Imported from CD-ROMs.** Collections of animation are also available on CD-ROM. Like other media, these premade collections allow authors to rapidly add effective and professional animations to a project.
- **Created using animation tools.** Hypermedia programs have improved dramatically in their animation capabilities. A novice animator can now easily generate sophisticated and effective animations.

Text. In spite of the attention paid to other components of hypermedia, text still remains one of the most powerful ways of communicating ideas.

- **Writing as project develops.** All hypermedia programs offer standard word processing features that enable users to write text. In addition, text may also be added as a graphic item. This feature lets the user easily drag text around the screen and is handy for adding labels to pictures.
- **Importing from word processing files.** Most programs also let authors import text created separately in word processors. This can be a boon for an author who has saved a great deal of writing in a large collection of word processing files.

Hardware Requirements for Hypermedia Authoring

Although hypermedia authoring can be accomplished with a fairly minimal computer system, more complex products require additional hardware and software capabilities. Depending on the complexity of the product, some or all of the following hardware resources are needed.

Computer with keyboard and monitor. Hypermedia development can be done on any platform as long as the system has a hard drive and sufficient random-access memory (RAM). The minimum requirements to utilize programs like *HyperStudio* or *Macromedia Director* are much more affordable for the average classroom than they used to be.

Digital camera. Cameras like the Apple QuickTake or Sony Mavica let users take digital photographs and store them as digital files. The images can then be incorporated into hypermedia projects. Students of all ages enjoy using their own digital photographs in projects.

Scanner. If no digital camera is available, scanners can be used to digitize photos so they can be saved to a disk. Scanners also can capture still images from magazines or books.

Video digitizer. Video digitizers, also known as *digitizing boards,* capture full-motion video from video cameras, VCRs, videodisc players, or live TV. The video segments are then stored as computer files and can be edited using software like *Adobe Premier.* Both teachers and students should recognize copyright restrictions when digitizing and editing video.

Camcorders and other video input. Video cameras or camcorders, VCRs, videodiscs, or CD-ROMs are among the possible sources for motion video sequences to include in a production.

Audio card. To incorporate sound, an audio capture, playback card, and audio source such as a microphone are needed. Many computer systems sold in recent years have built-in audio cards.

CD-ROM or DVD drive. CD-ROMs and/or DVDs are essential elements in multimedia technology, and, because of their huge storage capacity, they are the only technology for storing large quantities of digitized video or audio. Hypermedia authors also can buy large collections of digitized video, audio, and still image resources on these media.

Audio speakers. To monitor quality and simply to hear the audio parts of a program, speakers are mandatory for hypermedia development. Many newer computers are shipped with either external or internal speakers.

Videodisc players. Videodiscs provide excellent resources for hypermedia authors. High-quality video or audio input can easily be accessed from any videodisc. With thousands of videodisc titles on the market and existing videodisc players in many schools, this technology will prove to be a valuable resource for years to come.

Hypermedia Authoring Procedures

Whether teachers are developing their own skills or those of their students, the hypermedia authoring process involves two distinct phases. Initially, authors need to learn the mechanics of the programs and develop their understanding of the concept of hypermedia. No one can develop a quality product without first being reasonably comfortable with the tools. However, at the next level, hypermedia authors must develop insights on the complexities of the various media and knowledge of visual and navigation design. This is a long-term process that will emerge through a great deal of experience. A number of strategies can aid the classroom teacher in helping students use their time efficiently and focus on developing quality products. Consider the following steps when students engage in hypermedia development:

1. **Review others' products.** An effective way of developing authoring skills for beginners is to look at what others have done. This is particularly true with scripting. Evaluating the scripts of existing programs can give insight into how to write scripts for new projects. Through the Internet or commercial online services, teachers can download stacks. This opens up a world of low-cost or free hypermedia resources for both teachers and students. It is also helpful to examine some effective uses of media; Ken Burns's series on the Civil War, for example, demonstrates the power of images and sound when melded together in the context of a story.
2. **Do research first.** Most hypermedia development projects require research to locate materials and data, analyze their findings, and summarize them in a format for use in the hypermedia product. It is important to allow adequate time for this research phase, for it is the heart of the learning activity.
3. **Storyboard.** Storyboarding helps students make better use of valuable computer time. On index cards or sticky notes, students can lay out what they want on each individual frame. But planning is the most difficult thing for students; they want to get right to the "fun stuff." Most students prefer to develop only on the computer. Teachers must insist that on-paper planning be done first. It may help to explain that professional media creators practice storyboarding and that even famous movie directors such as Alfred Hitchcock and Steven Spielberg storyboarded entire movies before doing a single camera shot because it saves time in the long run.
4. **Develop individual frames.** Before adding links or graphics, students should develop each frame, including text fields.
5. **Insert graphics.** Add clip art, photos, animations, movies, and other media onto each card as needed to carry out the design.
6. **Add links and/or scripts.** Only after all the cards have been developed and decorated should links be added. Most authoring software allows a storyboard format to see most or all of the cards at one time. This and the card or sticky-note storyboards help students keep links organized among cards.
7. **Test and revise the product.** After it is drafted, students should test their products, preferably with the help of others who have not been involved in its development. The aim is to revise their products and meet criteria outlined in a later section of this chapter, Evaluating Hypermedia Products. Rembelinsky (1997–1998) offers a development sequence designed specifically for creating multimedia summaries of project-based research. She recommends students do steps in each of the following general headings: written summary, historical background, creative narrative, scanned images, video, and self-evaluation.

Authoring Skills to Develop Over Time

The beauty of hypermedia authoring is that students can create products with skills that range from basic to extraordinarily complex and sophisticated. Students may begin with "the basics" and teachers can help them move on to advanced techniques in several areas.

Media literacy. Given the complexities and proliferation of different media, an understanding of media basics will become a fundamental skill for the information age. Since most people will have tremendous capabilities to adapt and alter existing media in the near future, a critically important part of instruction in hypermedia authoring will focus on how to be critical and ethical producers and consumers of media (Roblyer, 1998).

Using music and art. Visual arts and music play major roles in the effectiveness of hypermedia products. As students gain more knowledge in the theory and aesthetics of music and art, they will use these resources more productively in the authoring process.

Design principles. Many principles of desktop publishing also apply to hypermedia designs. When students first see the array of graphics and sound options available, they typically overindulge and use so many colors, graphics, and sounds that content is overshadowed. Some of the design principles that can help guide more judicious use of these options are described later in this chapter in the Evaluating Hypermedia Products section.

Creativity and novel thinking. When assessing student projects, look for and encourage creative uses of the potential of hypermedia. Too many student projects resemble glorified paper-based projects; they do not take advantage of the true power of this medium. Classroom activities that encourage creative and critical thinking in all subject areas help develop skills and a mind-set that naturally enhances the authoring process.

Considering audience. Whenever possible, teachers should try to give students an opportunity to display their projects. Students will be much more motivated if they believe their work is valued. Research on writing has shown that students will invest more effort in the writing process when they know others will read their writing. Turner and Dipinto (1992) and others have observed that this sense of audience carries over to hypermedia authoring. However, teachers sometimes find that components of a student project make sense only to the author. Younger students in particular should be reminded constantly that they need to think of their projects from the user's point of view. Encourage them to test their projects on other students, family, or friends.

Authoring Tools Type 1: Presentation Software Systems

Presentation software packages such as Microsoft's *PowerPoint* help users create on-screen descriptions, demonstrations, and summaries of information. Presentation tools are one example of a technology that migrated from business and industry to education. These tools were first adopted by business executives and salespeople who used them to give reports at meetings and presentations to clients. Their capabilities to demonstrate, illustrate, and clarify information became evident and presentation tools began to make their way into K–12 and university classrooms.

The programs allow a user to choose from an array of text, graphics, animation, audio, and video options. Presentation tools began exclusively as "electronic slide shows," but have evolved into *multimedia authoring tools,* which allow users to incorporate motion sequences from CD-ROM and other video media into their presentations.

The effectiveness of a presentation tool depends largely on the communications skills of the presenter. For large classes and other groups, presentation software products usually are used in conjunction with computer projection systems. These may be devices such as LCD panels that fit on top of overhead projectors or systems that operate as stand-alone devices. All of these devices enlarge the image produced by the software by projecting it from a computer screen onto a wall screen.

While presentation software makes it possible for students and teachers to communicate in the "grammar of multimedia," new users make some common "grammatical mistakes." Ten of the most common errors made by users of presentation software are described in InSight 7.1.

Characteristics of presentation software. These packages were originally designed to display in a linear sequence and, even though they now offer branching by allowing authors to include clickable buttons or "hot spots," many materials produced with presentation software retain this linear characteristic. Presentation software also allows authors to include graphics of all kinds, audio and video clips, and Internet links.

Presentation software packages. By far the most commonly used presentation software is Microsoft's *PowerPoint.* (See Figure 7.5.) However, other packages such as *KidPix* and presentation options within integrated productivity packages such as *AppleWorks* also offer similar "slide show" capabilities.

Authoring Tools Type 2: Video Production and Editing Systems

Once the exclusive domain of Hollywood, movies and video sequences are now a growing presence in school activities. Students and teachers are using computer-based video production and editing systems for a variety of purposes ranging from presenting the daily school news to teaching sophisticated video production skills.

INSIGHT 7.1

The Top Ten Mistakes Made by Users of Presentation Software

All of the following are qualities that can interfere with readability and/or communicating content during a *PowerPoint*-type presentation.

1. **Type too small.** Use at least a 32-point font; use larger type if the audience is large and a long distance away from the presenter.
2. **Text and background don't contrast.** The audience cannot see text too similar in hue to the background. Use text with high contrast to background (e.g., dark blue on white, black on yellow).
3. **Too much text on one frame.** The purpose of text is to focus attention on main points, not present large amounts of information. Ideas should be summarized in brief phrases.
4. **Too many different items on one frame.** Displaying too many items on one frame can interfere with reading, especially if some items are in motion. Frame designs should be simple, clear, and free of distractions.
5. **Too many fancy fonts.** Many fonts are unreadable when projected on a screen. Use a plain sans serif font for titles, a plain serif font for other text.
6. **Gratuitous graphics.** Graphics interfere with communication when used solely for decoration. They should always help communicate the content.
7. **Gratuitous sounds.** Sounds interfere with communication when used solely for effect. They should always help communicate the content.
8. **No graphics, just text.** Well-chosen graphics can help communicate messages. Text alone does not make best use of the capabilities of presentation software.
9. **Presenting in a bright room.** Frames can fade away if the room is too bright. Cover windows and turn off lights during a presentation.
10. **Reading text to audience.** Do not read what the audience can read for themselves. Use text to guide main points of discussion.

Figure 7.5 Sample *PowerPoint* Screen

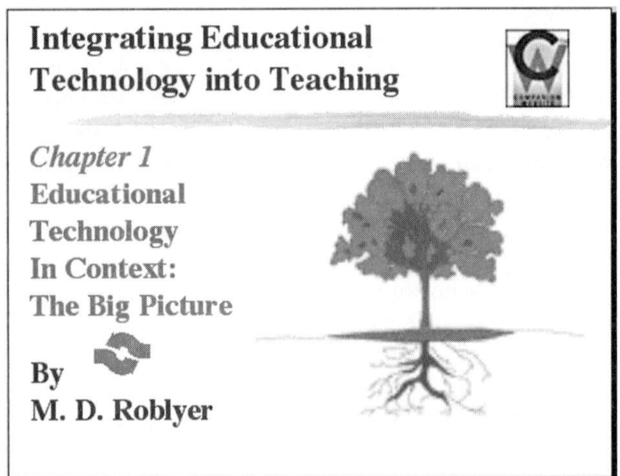

Integrating Educational
Technology into Teaching
Chapter 1
Educational
Technology
In Context:
The Big Picture
By
M. D. Roblyer

Characteristics of Video Systems. Video editing systems are to motion images what word processing is to text. The next decade likely will see an explosion in video editing and production to rival the rapid increase in word processing of documents. As Howard (2001) observed, video software can be very time consuming for anyone who wants to do high-quality videos, and especially so for novice users. However, schools across the country are beginning to use these systems to produce school news programs and to develop digitized video for use in authoring hypermedia products (Hoffenburg & Handler, 2001).

The main purpose of these software systems is to take video into a computer from a source such as a camcorder and change it into digital format (AVI or MPEG files), which allows it to be edited and combined with special effects such as titles, screen fades, and voice-over audio. It also allows the resulting digitized video clips to be inserted in a multimedia package or uploaded to the Internet. An example of a movie frame in a video editing screen is shown in Figure 7.6. At the bottom of the figure are two tracks, audio and video. By sliding markers on these tracks, students can cut, copy, and/or paste sections of a video and/or combine them with special effects such as fades or background music.

Current Video Editing Software Packages. When Apple Computer included a free copy of its video production software *iMovie* with some of its computer systems, it heralded the beginning of widespread interest in video editing among educators and other consumers. In addition to *iMovie,* popular editing software also includes the following:

- *Adobe Premiere* (Adobe)
- *Avid Xpress* (AVID Technology)
- *EditStudio* (Pure Motion)
- *Final Cut Pro* (Apple, Inc.)
- *Cute Video* (Litora, Inc.).

Joss (2001) also recommends several other hardware and software options for video production.

Authoring Tools Type 3: Hypermedia Software

Characteristics of Hypermedia Authoring Software. In the late 1980s, early hypermedia authoring programs included *HyperCard* for Macintosh, *LinkWay* for MS-DOS machines, and *TutorTech* for Apple II. These programs represented a major jump forward in technology, but because authors had to make major time commitments to learn and use the software, their use was limited. Things began to change when Roger Wagner's *HyperStudio* was released. This program used the same basic "card and stack" metaphor as *HyperCard* but eliminated much of the need for extensive scripting or for programming commands. In recent years, a number of programs have become available that emulate *HyperStudio*'s easy-to-use format. As computer power increases and becomes more affordable, even more sophisticated and easy-to-use programs than the ones described here have become available. However, teachers also can choose simpler products such as Brøderbund's *Kid Pix* or the slideshow option in *AppleWorks.*

A trend in multimedia software is toward increasingly higher end, more capable software such as *Macromedia Authorware.* Also, many multimedia packages (e.g., *Macromedia Director Shockwave Studio*) are moving toward including web page authoring and 3D production. Use of these latter packages in education is limited, but they are seeing increasing integration into high school technology education programs.

Current Hypermedia Authoring Software. Most classroom-based multimedia/hypermedia authoring is done with software such as the following:

- ***HyperStudio* (Roger Wagner, Inc.).** One of the most innovative products on the market for Mac and *Windows* computers, this product has developed a large following among teachers. It remains the most used multimedia authoring system in education.
- ***MicroWorlds Project Builder* (LCSI).** The unique emphasis on Logo gives users experience at simple programming. Separate packages are also sold as *Math Project Builder* and *Language Arts Project Builder.*
- ***Multimedia Toolbook* (Asymetrix).** This *Windows* program features video editing software, support for many file formats, and a Media Packager that gathers and compresses multimedia elements for a given product.
- ***Digital Chisel* (Pierian Spring Software).** A powerful product for Macintosh, this program supports full text-to-speech capability and includes question templates for developing tests.
- ***Macromedia Authorware.*** This authoring package has features ranging from animations to streaming video.
- ***Macromedia Director.*** This very capable and complex full-featured system is for developing multimedia products and includes video.
- ***Mpower* (Tom Snyder).** This is one of the newer authoring packages and emphasizes ease of use and ready-to-use materials for inexperienced developers.

Figure 7.6 Movie Screen from *iMovie* Video Editing Program

Integration Strategies for Hypermedia Authoring

Multimedia and hypermedia development projects are taking the place of many traditional activities to accomplish the same purposes. Some common classroom applications of multimedia and hypermedia are described here.

- **Electronic portfolios.** Student portfolios have become more common for assessment purposes, and multimedia/hypermedia have assumed a central role in portfolio development. Many teachers also are required to develop portfolios to document their teaching methods in preparation for promotion or additional certification. Portfolios are being done on all three of the multimedia/hypermedia formats described here (presentation software, video systems, and multimedia/hypermedia authoring software), although web-based portfolios also are becoming increasingly popular. (See InSight 3.12 in Chapter 3.) Many authoring programs such as *HyperStudio* include player files that run program files without the application itself. This is particularly useful when a student wants to take a project home and run it on the family computer or take it to a college or job interview.
- **Multimedia slideshows.** Although slideshow projects frequently call for presentations that are linear in format, they can be useful to help younger students develop beginning multimedia creation skills, since the focus is on the basic skills of writing text and screen design. Monahan and Susong (1996) describe how students developed simple slideshows to display their findings on wildlife. Harrison (1998–1999) describes other instructional uses of presentation software across the curriculum, and Brown (1998) describes effective uses of presentation software in a one-computer classroom.
- **Slideshow reviews and drills.** Many teachers report a simple, but highly effective use of *PowerPoint* and other presentation software. They set up a computer in the classroom to display automatically advancing frames of spelling words, vocabulary words, math facts, and information such as daily announcements. According to teachers who have used these strategies, students seem to attend to and retain much of what they see on these slideshows.
- **Tutorials.** Both teachers and students can create multimedia instructional sequences that step the user through the components of a subject. Figure 7.7 shows two cards from a *HyperStudio* tutorial on the instruments in an orchestra. In this product, the user may click on an instrument to hear it play and to read more about it.
- **Book reports.** Instead of presenting book reports verbally or as written summaries, it is becoming increasingly common for students to report on their reading through multimedia slideshows or as hypermedia products. Teachers often design a standard format or template, and students fill in the required information and add their own illustrations.
- **Research presentations.** Scholten and Whitmer (1996), Bennett and Diener (1997), and Stuhlmann (1997) point out that hypermedia presentations not only let students present their findings attractively and with impact, but the act of producing and sharing what

Figure 7.7 ***HyperStudio*** **Stack: The Sections of the Orchestra by Jolaine Sims**

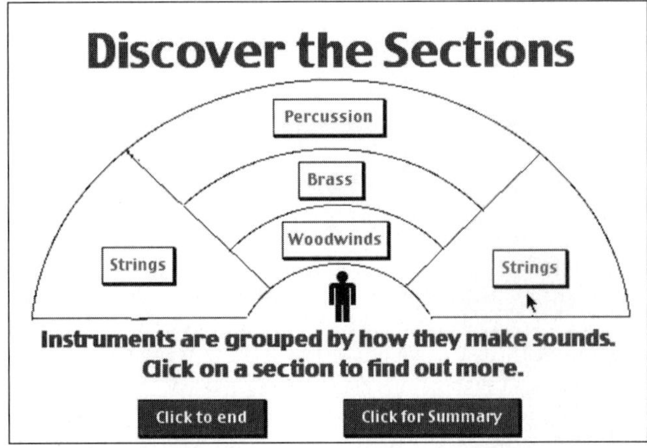

Source: Used with permission from Jolaine Sims.

they have learned also helps students learn even more about the topics and enhance their research, study, and communication skills.

- **Created tours.** Hypermedia products are an effective way to document field trips because they let others take virtual "trips" to the locations.
- **Interactive storybooks.** Fredrickson (1997) describes a use that builds on the book report purpose. Students document existing stories or write their own so they can be read interactively by others. Those reading these hypermedia stories can click on various places on the screen to hear or see parts of a story. This format also lets students go beyond one basic sequence and create their own branches and endings to stories.
- **School yearbooks.** Although still a relative novelty, more and more schools are developing their yearbooks as hypermedia products (Kwajewski, 1997).
- **School news reports and announcements.** Many middle and secondary schools are beginning to use video cameras and video editing software to produce a daily news show. These productions "star" the students themselves, and students also do the camera and editing work. News shows offer valuable opportunities to help students develop their on-camera presentation skills, as well as their technical production skills.

Procedures for Implementing Hypermedia Authoring

Like most technology resources, the impact of multimedia systems will depend heavily on how well teachers integrate them into classroom activities. Blissett and Atkins (1993) suggest that the following points are important for teachers to keep in mind when integrating interactive multimedia into the classroom:

- Provide guidance and further explanation on the nature of the task when a group gets stuck or, worse, misunderstands what to do.
- Check that the software package provides advance organizers for its conceptual content.
- Individualize the learning experience by assessing learning as it occurs and then intervening to link and relate or extend and consolidate concepts to meet the needs of particular pupils or groups.
- Ask open-ended questions that require pupils to verbalize their thought processes and review their understanding of the conceptual subject matter.
- Challenge and provoke thinking, leading to more abstract and conceptual discussions.
- Help the group to review its problem-solving strategies and direct them toward more powerful ones.
- Before assigning hypermedia projects, do training in group-work skills.

As Blissett and Adkins point out, teachers must prepare students well for hypermedia authoring activities by teaching them the technical skills they need and by setting well-defined parameters for the project. This is especially true for younger students and for all students doing such projects for the first time. Technology Integration Ideas 7.5 through 7.9 illustrate some of the many current uses for multimedia/hypermedia authoring resources ranging from *PowerPoint* to *Macromedia Director.*

Evaluating Hypermedia Products

Evaluating Commercial Hypermedia Products

To derive criteria to use in evaluating multimedia software, Gibbs, Graves, and Bernas (2000) used Delphi surveys of a panel of instructional technology experts. Perhaps not surprisingly, the list of criteria (see Figure A.7 in the Appendix) emphasizes the instructional and pedagogical aspects of the products rather than their multimedia characteristics. The result is a list similar to that found in Chapter 4 for instructional software.

TECHNOLOGY INTEGRATION IDEA 7.5

Hypermedia Projects with Electronic Encyclopedias and *PowerPoint*

TITLE: Selling a Space Mission

CONTENT AREA/TOPIC: History/science

GRADE LEVEL: Middle school

NETS FOR STUDENTS: Standards 1, 3, 4, 5

DESCRIPTION: This activity asks students to design, write, edit, and publish a brochure and prepare a *PowerPoint* presentation to "sell" a space research project. Students pair up into space mission planning teams. Each team conceptualizes a mission that would accomplish both scientific and social goals that the public could enthusiastically support, with the right encouragement. Then students "sell" their space mission. The teacher uses the Microsoft *Encarta* encyclopedia or another such resource, along with an overhead projection device or large monitor, to take a journey through the history of space exploration, from the *Sputnik* days of the 1960s through the *Apollo* moon mission, the *Challenger* disaster, and to the recent remote-robot exploration of Mars. When students design their brochure, they can paste in pictures from the encyclopedia to illustrate their slides.

Source: Based on a lesson from *Microsoft Productivity in the Classroom.* Copyright 1997 by the Microsoft Corporation.

TECHNOLOGY INTEGRATION IDEA 7.6

Hypermedia Authoring Software—*KidPix* Slideshows with Video

TITLE: Using *QuickTime* movies and *Kid Pix* in an Animal Alphabet Project

CONTENT AREA/TOPIC: Prereading skills

GRADE LEVEL: K–1

NETS FOR STUDENTS: Standards 1, 3, 4, 5

DESCRIPTION: Students combine digital photos, *QuickTime* videos, and text in *KidPix* to prepare multimedia presentations on the alphabet. During the year, students learn the letters of the alphabet by matching letters to animal names, and then learn the American sign language hand sign for the sounds. They make clay models of their animals, and the teacher makes digital photos of the animal models. With the teacher's help, students open their pictures in *KidPix* and stamp the initial letter of the animal around the picture. Finally, teachers videotape students naming the letters, their initial sounds, and the related sign language hand signs for that letter. The videos are made into *QuickTime* videos and inserted into the *KidPix* frames to complete the product: a *KidPix* slide show.

Source: Kampman, M. (1998–1999). Fat crayon multimedia digital toolbox. *Learning and Leading with Technology, 26*(4), 36–39, 48.

TECHNOLOGY INTEGRATION IDEA 7.7

Hypermedia Authoring Software—*QuickTime* Video

TITLE: Using *QuickTime* Movies in a Monarch Butterfly Project

CONTENT AREA/TOPIC: Science/biology

GRADE LEVEL: Elementary

NETS FOR STUDENTS: Standards 1, 3, 4, 5

DESCRIPTION. After visiting several Internet sites to learn more about Monarch butterflies, children videotape the development of the butterfly as it goes through the four stages of metamorphosis. The resulting movies are placed on a web page to share with other classes.

Source: Stuhlmann, J. (1997). Butterflies: Using multimedia to capture a unique science project. *Learning and Leading with Technology, 25*(3), 22–27.

TECHNOLOGY INTEGRATION IDEA 7.8

Hypermedia Authoring Software—*HyperStudio* Stacks

TITLE: A Student Autobiography

CONTENT AREA/TOPIC: Writing/language arts

GRADE LEVEL: 5–8

NETS FOR STUDENTS: Standards 1, 3, 4, 5

DESCRIPTION: This activity begins with students researching their family backgrounds. This activity should employ a questionnaire that students help generate. They take home the questionnaire and get help from relatives with filling out details of their lives. The teacher may suggest or require that the projects contain some or all of the following information:

- Events that happened the year they were born; these may be drawn from newspapers, almanacs, magazines, or parents' recollections
- Their interests and hobbies
- Information about the town where they were born
- Family tree diagrams
- Top 10 lists, including books, foods, movies, songs, people, and sports teams
- Scanned-in photos.

Students use an authoring software like *HyperStudio* to develop their products. The project culminates with an open house for relatives to view the autobiographies.

Source: Contributed by Jack Edwards.

TECHNOLOGY INTEGRATION IDEA 7.9

Hypermedia Authoring with High-End Authoring Systems

TITLE: Quilting Our History

CONTENT AREA/TOPIC: U.S. history and multimedia design

GRADE LEVEL: High school

NETS FOR STUDENTS: Standards 1, 3, 4, 5

DESCRIPTION: Students develop high-end multimedia design skills as they create a CD-ROM "quilt" that describes local history.

This schoolwide project required a great deal of planning and collaboration among teachers in several content areas, but the basic goal was to document the history of the local area and the families whose personal histories were intertwined with the history of the region. After all the content area teachers worked together to decide on the project design and how it would be carried out, students formed teams to accomplish the production tasks: researching information about the history of the local region and the families, geometric design of quilted squares to represent various families, gathering video documentation, and multimedia design. This project used a high-end multimedia software (*Macromedia Director*) along with Adobe *PhotoShop* and 3D and audio packages. The technology education classes carried out the actual multimedia design and production.

Source: van Buren, C., & Aufdenspring, D. (1998). Quilting our history: An integrated schoolwide project. *Learning and Leading with Technology, 27*(5), 22–27.

Evaluating Student-Developed Hypermedia

Dipinto and Turner (1995) suggest that student self-assessment of hypermedia projects may be the most important component of the assessment process, saying that perhaps it enables students to construct a microworld where assessment becomes a feedback mechanism, leading to further exploration and collaboration (p. 11). Several authors have developed criteria and rubrics for assessing the quality of students' hypermedia products. Litchfield (1995), Brunner (1996), and Clark (1996) describe qualities to look for in effective products. These are summarized in Appendix Figure A.8.

Exercises

Record and apply what you have learned.

Self-Test

To review terms and concepts in this chapter, take the Chapter 7 self-test. Select Chapter 7 from the front page of the Companion Website (http://www.prenhall.com/roblyer), then choose the *Multiple Choice* module.

Portfolio Activities

ISTE The following activities address ISTE National Educational Technology Standards for Teachers (NETS-T) and will help you add to your professional portfolio. To complete these activities online and save or submit the materials electronically, select Chapter 7 from the front page of the Companion Website (http://www.prenhall.com/roblyer), then choose the *Portfolio* module.

1. ***Defining Multimedia and Hypermedia (NETS-T Standards: I-B, V-A)*** Use a presentation software to develop a chart, diagram, or other graphic presentation that compares and contrasts multimedia and hypermedia. List or describe the defining qualities they share and those that make them different from each other.
2. ***Hypermedia Professional Self-Description (NETS-T Standard: V-A)*** Use a hypermedia authoring program (any of the three types) to develop a presentation that introduces your professional background, skills, and plans for the future. Use storyboards or sticky notes to storyboard the design and layout for your presentation. Review your product and make sure it meets the criteria given in this chapter.

Questions for Thought and Discussion

These questions may be used for small group or class discussion or may be subjects for individual or group activities. To take part in these discussions online, select Chapter 7 from the front page of the Companion Website (http://www.prenhall.com/roblyer), then choose the *Message Board* module.

1. Mergendollar (1997) said that multimedia environments are an "equivocal blessing" because they give us a bounty of information without indicators of its quality, accuracy, or usefulness. What are the possible consequences to education of our increasing wealth of unevaluated multimedia information?
2. Boyle (1997) said that, "Multimedia learning is not something new. It is woven into the fabric of our childhood" (p. ix). What do you think Boyle meant by that, and what implications might his observation have for enhancing children's learning experiences?

Collaborative Activities

ISTE

The following activities address ISTE National Educational Technology Standards for Teachers (NETS-T) and may be developed in small group work. Completed group products may be copied and shared with the entire class and/or included in each person's personal portfolio. Remember that most hypermedia authoring systems provide a free player that can play these student-produced products.

1. ***Create a Level I Presentation (NETS-T Standards: I-B; II-C, D; IV-A; V-A)*** Use a videodisc to design and present a persuasive presentation. The topic will depend on the disc; examples include:

   Drug and tobacco use: Teenagers should not start smoking.

   Solar system/space travel: The U.S. government should expand its space program.

   American history: The United States should/should not have dropped the bomb on Hiroshima.
2. ***Develop a Hypermedia Teaching System (NETS-T Standards: I-B; II-C, D; IV-A; V-A)*** The class divides into small groups to create a hypermedia instructional product to teach others about hypermedia authoring. Each group takes a topic and the class puts the products together at the end. For example, groups may select one of the following topics:
   - What topics lend themselves to hypermedia? Ideas and examples
   - An overview of the components of a hypermedia product
   - A review of development steps
   - A review of effective screen design procedures
   - How to add graphic images, movies, animation, and videoclips
   - Criteria and strategies to use when assessing hypermedia products.
3. ***Multimedia/Hypermedia Lesson Plans (NETS-T Standards: II-A, B; III-B, C; V-A)*** Using the integration ideas in this chapter as models and idea sources, develop a classroom integration lesson plan to teach content area skills using one of the following resources:
   - CD-ROM or DVD encyclopedia, almanac, or atlas reference materials
   - Level I videodisc curriculum package
   - Presentation software such as *PowerPoint*
   - Video production and editing software
   - Hypermedia authoring system such as *HyperStudio.*

 Integrating Technology Across the Curriculum Activities

The *Integrating Technology Across the Curriculum* CD-ROM is a set of technology integration ideas and links to online lessons, arranged as a searchable database. The CD comes packaged with this textbook. Complete the following exercise using this CD.

What role can multimedia/hypermedia play in your own content area? Select a content area and locate a technology integration idea for each of the five types of multimedia/hypermedia. Make a chart listing the types and the integration ideas.

Sample Integration Ideas for Hypermedia in Social Studies

Types of Hypermedia Tools	Name of Integration Idea
Commercial software package	
Commercial IVD	
Authoring: presentation	
Authoring: video	
Authoring: hypermedia	

References

Adams, G. L. (1992). Why interactive? *Multimedia & Videodisc Monitor, 10*(2), 20–25, 29.

Bagui, S. (1998). Reasons for increased learning using multimedia. *Journal of Educational Multimedia and Hypermedia, 7*(1), 3–18.

Bennett, N., & Diener, K. (1997). Habits of mind: Using multimedia to enhance learning skills. *Learning and Leading with Technology, 24*(6), 18–21.

Blissett, G., & Atkins, M. (1993). Are they thinking? Are they learning? A study of the use of interactive video. *Computers and Education, 21*(1–2), 31–39.

Boyle, T. (1997). *Design for multimedia learning.* London: Prentice Hall.

Brown, C. A. (1998). Presentation software and the single computer. *Learning and Leading with Technology, 26*(2), 18–21.

Brunner, C. (1996). Judging student multimedia. *Electronic Learning, 15*(6), 14–15.

Bush, V. (1986). As we may think. In S. Lambert & S. Ropiequet (Eds.), *CD-ROM: The new papyrus.* Redmond, WA: Microsoft Press. [Reprinted from *The Atlantic Monthly,* 1945, *176*(1), 101–108.]

Clark, J. (1996). Bells and whistles . . . but where are the references: Setting standards for hypermedia projects. *Learning and Leading with Technology, 23*(5), 22–24.

Dede, C. (1994). *Making the most of multimedia. Multimedia and learning: A school leader's guide,* Alexandria, VA: NSBA.

Dillon, A., & Gabbard, R. (1998). Hypermedia as an educational technology: A review of the quantitative research literature on learner comprehension, control, and style. *Review of Educational Research, 68*(3), 322–349.

Dipinto, V., & Turner, S. (1995). Zapping the hypermedia zoo: Assessing the students' hypermedia projects. *The Computing Teacher, 22*(7), 8–11.

Doty, D., Popplewell, S., & Byers, G. (2001). Interactive CD-ROM storybooks and young readers' reading comprehension. *Journal of Research on Computing in Education, 33*(4), 374–384.

Frederickson, S. (1997). Interactive multimedia storybooks. *Learning and Leading with Technology, 25*(1), 6–10.

Gibbs, W., Graves, P., & Bernas, R. (2000). Identifying important criteria for multimedia instructional courseware evaluation. *Journal of Computing in Higher Education, 12*(1), 84–106.

Glasgow, J. (1996). Part I: It's my turn! Motivating young readers. *Learning and Leading with Technology, 24*(3), 20–23.

Glasgow, J. (1996–1997). Part II: It's my turn! Motivating young readers using CD-ROM storybooks. *Learning and Leading with Technology, 24*(4), 18–22.

Glasgow, J. (1997). Keep up the good work! Using multimedia to build reading fluency and enjoyment. *Learning and Leading with Technology, 24*(5), 22–25.

Harrison, A. (1998–1999). Power up! Stimulating your students with PowerPoint. *Learning and Leading with Technology, 26*(4), 6–9.

Hoffenburg, H., & Handler, M. (2001). Digital video goes to school. *Learning and Leading with Technology, 29*(2), 10–15.

Howard, B. (2001, May 8). Lights! Camera! Learning curve! *PC Magazine.* Available online: *http://www.pcmag.com/article/0,2997,s%253D1497%2526a%253D2007,00.asp.*

Joss, M. (2001). Now playing in schools: Digital video. *Technology & Learning, 22*(3), 17–19.

Kahn, J. (1997). Scaffolding in the classroom: Using CD-ROM storybooks at a computer reading center. *Learning and Leading with Technology, 25*(2), 17–19.

Kwajewski, K. (1997). Memories in living color: Multimedia yearbooks. *Learning and Leading with Technology, 25*(2), 20–21.

Litchfield, B. (1995). Helping your students plan computer projects. *The Computing Teacher, 22*(7), 37–43.

Lookatch, R. (1997). Multimedia improves learning: Apples, oranges, and the Type I error. *Contemporary Education, 68*(2), 110–113.

Marchionini, M. (1988). Hypermedia and learning: Freedom and chaos. *Educational Technology, 28*(11), 8–12.

Mayer, R., & Moreno, R. (1998). A split attention effect in multimedia learning: Evidence for dual processing systems in working memory. *Journal of Educational Psychology, 90*(2), 312–320.

McCarthy, R. (1989). Multimedia: What the excitement's all about. *Electronic Learning, 8*(8), 26–31.

McNeil, B., & Nelson, K. (1991). Meta-analysis of interactive video instruction: A 10-year review of achievement effects. *Journal of Computer-Based Instruction, 18*(1), 106.

Mergendollar, J. (1997). What research says about technology and learning. *Principal, 76*(3), 12–14.

Monahan, S., & Susong, D. (1996). Author slide show and Texas wildlife. *Learning and Leading with Technology, 24*(2), 6–16.

Moore, M., Myers, R., & Burton, J. (1994). What multimedia might do . . . and what we know about what it does. In *Multimedia and learning: A school leader's guide.* Alexandria, VA: NSBA.

Rembelinsky, I. (1997–1998). Us and them: Multimedia explorations of prejudice and intolerance in American history. *Learning and Leading with Technology, 25*(4), 42–47.

Roblyer, M. D. (1998). Visual literacy: Seeing a new rationale for teaching with technology. *Learning and Leading with Technology, 26*(2), 51–54.

Roblyer, M. D. (1999). Our multimedia future: Recent research on multimedia's impact on education. *Learning and Leading with Technology, 26*(6), 51–53.

Scholten, B., & Whitmer, J. (1996). Hypermedia projects: Metastacks increase content focus. *Learning and Leading with Technology, 24*(3), 59–62.

Siegel, J. (1995). The state of teacher training. *Electronic Learning, 14*(8), 43–53.

Simonson, M. R., & Thompson, A. (1994). *Educational computing foundations.* New York: Merrill.

Stemler, L. (1997). Educational characteristics of multimedia: A literature review. *Journal of Educational Multimedia and Hypermedia, 6*(3–4), 339–359.

Stuhlmann, J. (1997). Butterflies! Using multimedia to capture a unique science project. *Learning and Leading with Technology, 25*(3), 22–27.

Sullivan, J. (1995). Exciting ways to use videodiscs. *Media and Methods, 31*(3), S8–S10.

Swan, K., & Meskill, C. (1996). Using hypermedia in response-based literature classrooms: A critical review of commercial applications. *Journal of Research on Computing in Education, 29*(2), 167–192.

Thorpe, B. (1993). Kids can create videodisc reports. *The Computing Teacher, 20*(2), 22–23.

Tolhurst, D. (1995). Hypertext, hypermedia, multimedia defined? *Educational Technology, 35*(2), 21–26.

Turner, S. V., & Dipinto, V. M. (1992). Students as hypermedia authors: Themes emerging from a qualitative study. *Journal of Research on Computing in Education, 25*(2), 187–199.

PART III

LINKING TO LEARN: PRINCIPLES AND STRATEGIES

The chapters in this part will help teachers learn:

1. To identify the capabilities of available distance learning resources and recognize the teaching and learning functions they can fulfill
2. To identify the role that Internet resources and strategies can play in teaching and learning
3. To identify trends in emerging technologies likely to have profound influences on educational practices in the future
4. To develop integration strategies for each of these current and future technologies that match their capabilities to classroom needs

Introduction: Reaching Out to a World of Resources

Our entry into the millennium marks nearly a half-century of computer use in society. Computers have been used in education since the beginning of their existence. But thanks to microcomputers, the last 20 years have seen an explosion of computer technology-related activity in schools and classrooms. The emergence of a graphically oriented Internet in 1994 suddenly and dramatically shifted the spotlight from stand-alone microcomputers to the importance of linking with others: other computers, other people, and other "worlds." Other developments combine with these distance resources to shape the future of educational technology. The chapters in this section focus on the resources that link us with each other as well as with our future as a civilization.

Chapter 8: Integrating the Internet and Other Distance Resources into the Curriculum

Distance learning, a means of providing courses and workshops for training and education, continues to increase in popularity and the range of applications grows steadily. This chapter reviews a variety of distance learning resources and methods to link learners with each other and with needed resources at distant sites. The Information Superhighway has become a pervasive metaphor for technology in modern culture, but educators are just beginning to develop integration strategies for the Internet. This chapter also focuses on current and anticipated uses of the Internet, both in schools and in the context of other learning communities.

Chapter 9: A Link to the Future: Emerging Developments in Technology Integration

Technologies such as virtual reality make us feel that the future has landed on our doorstep. This chapter describes technologies whose practical applications are just emerging, but whose potential power promises to shape the future of education and society. These include developments in networking, visualization, human-to-computer interfaces, and various types of computer-related equipment.

CHAPTER 8

Integrating the Internet and Other Distance Resources into the Curriculum

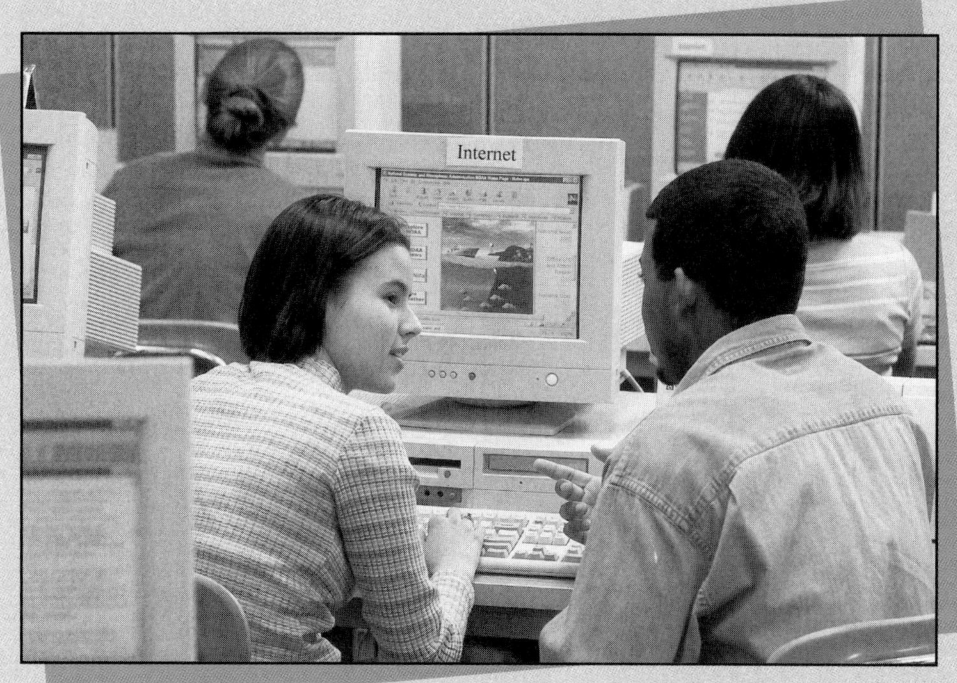

It is obvious that both teaching and learning . . . will be influenced in varying ways by "the death of distance."

Michael G. Moore, in an editorial for *The American Journal of Distance Education,* 1995

But the Net, I guarantee you, really is fire. I think it's more important than the invention of moveable type.

Brad Ferren, as quoted by David Remnick in "Future Perfect," *The New Yorker* (October 1997)

This chapter covers the following topics:

- Background on distance learning, including definitions, directions, research, and current issues
- Definitions and descriptions of various resources available to support distance learning, including five categories of Internet resources
- Description of how to design and assess teaching and learning activities that use Internet and World Wide Web technologies
- Description of how to design and assess web-based courses and programs

Objectives

1. Define distance learning, distance education, and telecommunications.
2. Describe how each of the current major issues in distance learning helps shape its impact and future directions.
3. Identify each of several distance learning resources according to its technical capabilities and its place in the hierarchy of distance learning options.
4. Describe current educational benefits and applications of various types of distance learning systems.
5. Describe the purpose of each of the following Internet resources and identify how it would meet a specific written or visual communications need: web browsers, search engines, gophers, e-mail, listservs, bulletin boards, chat rooms, FTP, images and animation, regular and streaming video/audio, electronic whiteboards, MUDs and MOOs, videoconferencing, web authoring tools, push technologies, site capturing, intranets, Internet TV, and avatars.
6. Select an appropriate web authoring tool to meet a specific need.
7. Develop plans for integrating and assessing web-based activities according to a directed or a constructivist model.
8. Explore online programs and identify examples of design and implementation procedures they have put into place to ensure their online courses and programs are effective.

Introduction: Reaching Out to a World of Resources

Technology has changed no aspect of society more quickly and dramatically than its communications capabilities. Children today regard revolutionary technologies such as fax machines, cellular phones, and the Internet as normal, everyday parts of the electronic landscape in which they live. Even in the rapid environment of technological evolution, these remarkable changes in communications have come about with incredible speed; some resources have developed from possible to pervasive in only a few years. These changes are by no means completed or even slowing down. The primary reason for this breathtaking revolution in communications is society's recognition of the importance of ready access to people and resources. If knowledge is power, as Francis Bacon said, then communication is freedom—freedom for people to reach information they need in order to acquire knowledge that can empower them. This heady freedom permeates the atmosphere of an information society.

Rapid developments in communication technologies have brought about what Moore (1995), quoting an issue of *The Economist*, called "the death of distance" which happens "when the cost of communications comes down to next to nothing, as seems likely in the first decade of the next century" (p. 1). But the death of distance seems to have given new life to education. Distance learning (DL) has not only changed how quickly educators and students can exchange and access information, it has altered the educational equation in fundamental ways. Thanks to distance technologies such as broadcast systems and the Internet, learning has escaped the physical boundaries of the classroom and the school, and students and teachers have become part of a virtual classroom they share with counterparts around the world. Our society is just beginning to understand and take advantage of the potential of this new classroom.

The Internet burst on the scene in our society and in education only a few years ago, but quickly set fire to the interest and imagination of even the least technical teachers, students, and parents. Now most computer-based distance learning applications involve some Internet resource or activity, and many rely exclusively on Internet materials. Because the Internet figures so prominently in many distance learning activities, this chapter includes a large section on this rapidly growing and evolving force in education.

What Is Distance Learning? Some Definitions

The changing definition of distance learning is a clue to the kind of impact it has had on the definition of education itself. Most past definitions of distance learning had the following key components:

- Instructor and learner separated by time and/or geographic distance
- Electronic, print resources, voice communications, and combinations of them are used to bridge the gap.

Some authorities feel the definition of distance learning is changing too quickly to have a formal definition. However, in 1998, the United States Distance Learning Association (USDLA at http://www.usdla.org/04_research_info.htm) went on record to define distance learning as follows:

> . . . the acquisition of knowledge and skills through mediated information and instruction. Distance learning encompasses all technologies and supports the pursuit of lifelong learning for all.

This definition leaves open the door to more constructivist views of learning, including the possibility that, though learning is taking place, there may not be an instructor at all and no formal or organized instruction may be offered. The USDLA definition says simply that learning may take place where learners are connected with information resources, with each other, with instructors, or with any combinations of these resources.

But the 1998 USDLA definition should not be considered the final word—or even the only one. Proponents of directed and constructivist methods (see Chapter 3) may disagree as to how this or other definitions should be interpreted. Furthermore, future definitions may serve to omit any learning activities that rely exclusively on nonelectronic forms of communications such as print. Other changes in definitions include distance learning versus distance education and telecommunications.

Distance learning versus distance education. Many authors used to differentiate between *distance education* and *distance learning,* referring to the former as the role of the instructor and the latter as the role of the learner. Now, they typically are used interchangeably.

Telecommunications. Although the most precise definition of telecommunications is communication at a distance, it is evolving into a general term for any electronic technologies (broadcast/terrestrial, computer based, or combinations of the two) used for linking people for communications purposes. Some education articles still use telecommunications, distance education, and distance learning interchangeably; but most educators now refer to distance learning/distance education as a learning process and telecommunications as the communications mechanism for making this process possible. Harris (1994) uses the term *telecomputing* coined by Kearsley, Hunter, and Furlong (1992) to describe activities in which classroom computers link groups with each other and with educational resources. However, this term is in limited use by others.

Distance Learning Directions: Past, Present, and Future

As the changes in definitions show, the past decade has brought about dramatic changes in the goals and purposes of distance learning, many of which have come about as a result of technological developments. Over the years, the rationale for distance learning activities has changed and expanded, as have the mechanisms for accomplishing them.

Past rationales and methods. The rationale for distance learning first was based on access for students and cost savings for organizations. Correspondence courses were very popular among rural and military students who needed credits for certification or graduation but who could not travel to and/or reside at educational institutions. Later, when print materials were supplemented with videotapes and instructional television (ITV), businesses found they could train workers more cheaply than having an instructor at every site. Postsecondary institutions discovered they could increase the number of students a professor could teach in one course by having the instructor broadcast lectures to students in a number of sites. Whole institutions grew up around this distance learning rationale, and many large businesses and universities used this method to some extent.

Current rationales and methods. Today's distance learning has evolved a broader and more diverse rationale for its existence, but increased student access and costs of education and training still are very much at the heart of it. Distance learning activities today are driven by a twofold focus: to increase student access to information and people, and to compete for the "education dollar" of those needing certification and degrees. With the help of what seems to be every business, school, and college in the world, the Internet has become a way to obtain any information anytime and from any location. Many institutions are working toward developing courses and degree programs students can complete without ever entering a formal classroom or seeing a live instructor. Also, although many correspondence courses in print and/or video formats still are in use, they rapidly are being replaced by electronic means. Organizations that stay with the "old" formats or that do not provide students with distance learning alternatives and options may be threatened with extinction (Sherritt, 1996).

Future rationales and methods. In the future, distance learning seems likely to focus on a new rationale: making learning environments increasingly life-like. Ready access to information resources and alternatives to traditional learning strategies will be taken for granted and print/video correspondence courses will be a distant memory. The emphasis will be on developing better quality systems to simulate "being there" and being face to face with the teacher/trainer and the other students. Distance learning will become interactive video-and-audio and virtual reality systems that allow people to exchange information as if they were in the same location. If this rationale becomes reality, distance may, indeed, be dead.

Current Issues in Distance Learning

With the increased popularity of distance learning and the Internet have also come increased concerns about their impact on education and society. When communications became more global and accessible, many in education hoped it would mean better access to high quality education for all students, regardless of location and economic status. These hopes have not been universally realized, and even increased Internet access has presented unexpected problems.

The Digital Divide. In 1978, Andrew Molnar wrote an article called "The Next Great Crisis in American Education: Computer Literacy." In it, he warned that in the Information Age to come, unequal access by students to the benefits of computer skills could further divide rich and poor. This article has proven prophetic as the Internet has increased our society-wide dependence on computer-based communications. The term *Digital Divide* was coined by Lloyd Morrisett, former president of the Markle Foundation (Hoffman & Novak, 1999) to mean a discrepancy in access to technology resources between socioeconomic groups. Upon reviewing the reports from governmental and private sources that documented the nature of this division, Roblyer (2000) found that the single greatest factor determining access is economic status, although race and gender may also play a role, depending on the type of technology. The Digital Divide is a greater problem in homes than in schools, because our society is placing a growing emphasis on making sure schools have computers and Internet access. However, even where computers are available in schools, there may also be unequal access to certain kinds of activities. For example, children in Title I programs may have access to computers, but may use them mainly for remedial work rather than for e-mail and other personal empowerment activities.

Pitfalls of Internet use. As it has become a society-wide tool, the Internet also has spawned its share of society-wide debates and problems. In many ways, it is a reflection of the best and worst qualities of our society. Books by Virginia Shea (1994) and Donald Rose (1994) discuss many of these problems. Teachers must be prepared to deal with ethical, behavioral, and privacy issues as they use the Internet and offer its use to children. People are spending increasing amounts of time communicating with each other and obtaining information online, and some problems with human behavior (and misbehavior) have already begun to emerge. These include objectionable materials, predators, viruses, copyright violations, and plagiarism. (Also see discussion of these issues in Chapter 1.)

Objectionable materials and predators. The contents of messages and web sites are difficult to monitor in resources like the Internet and may contain language or information not appropriate for the public or for minors (Carpenter, 1996; Elmer-Dewitt, 1995). Yet the Internet is designed to make information easily obtainable, and, unfortunately, such materials can be accessed all too easily by accident. Educational organizations should have mechanisms and safeguards in place to keep users from getting to these materials either accidentally or intentionally. Munro (1998) gives a comprehensive listing of filtering utilities that set up firewalls or codes to block access to sites based on keywords and/or site names.

Students should be told that the same rules about strangers in the real world apply in cyberspace and for the same reasons. Some people get on the Internet to seek out and take advantage of vulnerable young people. A recent survey (Mitchell, Finkelhor, & Wolak, 2001) found that one out of five youths between the ages of 10 and 17 who use the Internet regularly are exposed to unwanted sexual solicitations. Students should be told never to provide their complete names, addresses, or telephone numbers to any stranger they "meet" on the Internet, and they should report to teachers any people who try to get them to do so. Schools should never put full names of students on web pages. The Children's Internet Protection Act, signed into law December 21, 2000, is designed to ensure that libraries receiving federal e-rate funds take measures to keep children away from Internet materials that could be harmful to them (McNabb, 2001).

Viruses and hacking. Discussed in Chapters 1 and 2 as ethical issues related to general computer use, special problems pertain to an online environment. If host servers or individual computers do not have security software or firewalls to guard against viruses, logic bombs, worms, and Trojan horses, hackers can send them to unsuspecting users as they download seemingly harmless files or utilities from the Internet. However, many schools are finding that firewalls also can have the undesirable side effect of preventing students and teachers from accessing some harmless, useful sites. Occasionally, firewalls also can prevent those outside a network from reaching users of the network. School systems find firewalls an essential, but problematic, component of being part of the web community.

Copyright violations and plagiarism. Much of the information on web sites is for public access and use, but much of it also is copyrighted. Teachers and students should look for copyright statements on the site, and, if there is any doubt, contact the author before copying and using images or verbatim material. Plagiarism also is becoming a major problem for educators from middle school to college levels. The growing wealth of written products available on the Internet makes it all too easy for students to locate material and cite it without crediting the author or even to turn in whole papers as their own. Sites are springing up to help teachers combat this illegal behavior (e.g., http://plagiarism.org).

"Netiquette" behavior. The etiquette guidelines that govern behavior when communicating on the Internet have become known as *netiquette.* Netiquette covers not only rules on behavior during discussions, but also guidelines that reflect the unique electronic nature of the medium. Netiquette usually is enforced by fellow users who are quick to point out infractions to netiquette rules. The following summary of e-mail rules is based on published sources such as Shea's online book *Netiquette* at http://www.albion.com/netiquette/book/index.html:

- **Identify yourself.** Begin messages with a salutation and end them with your name. Most mail programs let you include a signature (a footer with your identifying information) at the end of a message, but a signature twice the size of the message itself is considered bad form.
- **Include a subject line.** Give a descriptive phrase in the subject line of the message header that tells the topic of the message (not just "Hi, there!").
- **Avoid sarcasm.** People who don't know you may misinterpret its meaning.
- **Respect others' privacy.** Do not quote or forward personal e-mail without the original author's permission.
- **Acknowledge and return messages promptly.**
- **Copy with caution.** Don't copy everyone you know on each message.

- **No "junk mail" (spam).** Don't contribute to worthless information on the Internet by sending or responding to mass postings of chain letters, rumors, etc. (The slang term for electronic junk mail is *spam.*)
- **Be concise.** Keep your messages concise—about one screen, as a rule of thumb.
- **Use appropriate language.** Avoid coarse, rough, or rude language, and observe good grammar and spelling.
- **Use appropriate emoticons and other language signals.** The use of "smiley's" or punctuation such as : –) to convey happy and : – (for sad has grown into a complete language of its own. For example, the emoticon : ' – (means the user is crying. Other signals for language include abbreviations such as "BTW" for "by the way" and "LOL" for "laughing out loud." Lists of these emoticons and abbreviations are available on many informal Internet sites.
- **Use intensifiers appropriately.** Words in capital letters convey emphasis, but whole sentences typed this way are considered yelling or "flaming." Flaming, like spamming, is considered rude behavior. Asterisks surrounding words indicate italics used for emphasis (*at last*), and words in brackets such as <grin> show one's state of mind.

Privacy issues. As Ross and Bailey (1996) note, "Student privacy in public education is a credo enforced by the Family Rights and Privacy Act" (p. 51). In their web products, teachers should be careful not to identify students with last names, addresses, and other personal information. Another privacy issue surrounds the use of "cookies," or small text files placed on a hard drive by a web server contacted on the Internet. The purpose of cookies is to provide the server with information that can help personalize web activity to your needs. For example, the cookie sends a password automatically for a secure site to which you subscribe. But cookies also may track behavior on the Internet in ways that violate privacy. Though browsers come with some built-in defenses against cookies, Randall (1998) recommends programs called "cookie managers" to control the information given to these cookies.

Development and socialization issues. Spending too much time on computers is considered by many to be harmful to children's development of relationships and social skills. The American Academy of Pediatricians, recognizing these potentially harmful effects of overexposure to mass media (including the Internet) call for limiting children's use of media to 1 to 2 hours per day (McNabb, 2001). Also, because anyone can put anything on a web page, some information children are exposed to is inaccurate or misleading. Students have been known to accept as fact anything they read on the Internet. It is becoming increasingly important that students learn to analyze Web information critically before accepting it as a valid position.

Teacher involvement and training. For any educational innovation to succeed, it must attract early involvement of classroom teachers. Teacher concerns about implementing (or being replaced by) new technologies must be determined and addressed. The most successful strategies involve teachers in early planning stages and then consistently seeking meaningful teacher input and participation. Educators need to learn how to operate and integrate the new technology tools, to implement radically different curricular approaches and associated classroom management strategies, and to become facilitators of learning. Professional development in technology applications has never kept pace with the purchase and distribution of equipment (Hawkins & Macmillan, 1993).

Positive and negative impact on education reform. Many educators predict that distance learning will reform teaching methods and increase access to quality education; however, support for distance learning is not unanimous. Even ardent advocates point out pitfalls. Van Dusen (1997) is optimistic that the distance learning movement will alter traditional, "professor-centered" methods and bring about more constructivist ones, but he emphasizes that this shift will not happen without intensive professional development. Also, he feels there is a danger that the quality of undergraduate education could suffer unless universities renew their commitment to core values. Meanwhile a backlash to distance learning-based reform methods is growing. One statement of protest drafted at the University of Washington said that while distance learning programs present ". . . a mouth-watering bonanza to . . . corporate sponsors, what they bode for education is nothing short of disastrous" (Monaghan, 1998). Recently, some critics have painted a pessimistic picture for education as a result of increased reliance on distance learning (Trend, 2001).

Current Research in Distance Learning

Despite some criticism, distance learning activities currently enjoy a wellspring of support unprecedented in the history of educational technology. Although due in large part to the popularity of the Internet, this trend is not just a fad; years of research have confirmed the effectiveness of some forms of distance learning, and studies on other strategies seem to be on the increase. Furthermore, educators at all levels are predicting that distance learning has the potential to revolutionize education in the next century (Bybee, 1996; Roblyer, 1998). This section captures some current research and activity that indicate how distance learning is helping shape the future of teaching and learning.

In the past, the most popular kind of research compared a distance learning method with a traditional one. However, several other kinds of questions also are proving useful in shaping the impact of distance learning:

- Are certain types of distance learning resources or delivery systems more effective than others?

- What are characteristics of effective distance learning courses?
- What are characteristics of students who choose distance learning?
- What are characteristics of students who are effective distance learners?
- What are characteristics of effective distance instructors?
- What cost factors enter into preparing and implementing distance education programs, and how do we determine cost effectiveness?

Effectiveness of distance learning for course delivery. Some distance learning methods are among the most well studied in education. For example, course delivery with instructional television has long been considered equivalent to face-to-face instruction in its impact on achievement and on attitudes of students (Russell, 1992). In addition, hundreds of studies conducted from 1954 through 1996 consistently found no significant difference between instruction delivered through traditional classroom methods and instruction delivered over one or more distance technologies (Russell, 1997). Although few current studies have compared the effectiveness on different types of students of instruction delivered via distance learning, evaluation from the federally funded Star Schools Program indicates that distance learning students enrolled in high school courses function slightly better than comparable students in traditional classes (Withrow, 1992). Also, in a meta-analysis of video-based distance courses or "telecourses," Machtmes and Asher (2000) found that courses with two-way interaction between instructor and students were more effective than traditional courses. There is no reason to believe that courses done on other delivery systems such as the Internet or videoconferencing will achieve different results, since the determining variable probably is always course quality rather than delivery system. Some studies attempted to capture benefits that are unique to distance learning formats, such as increased awareness and appreciation of cultural diversity (Fabos & Young, 1999; Roblyer, 1992), but true research studies in this area are rare.

Effectiveness of specific distance learning resources and strategies. Similarly, although substantially less research has been done on the impact of specific distance learning products, such as e-mail or videoconferencing, past research in other educational technology areas makes it likely that the technologies themselves will be less important than how they are used (see Clark's studies described in Chapter 2). Fabos and Young (1999) reviewed the research on "telecommunication exchange projects," which they defined as ". . . Internet-based communication projects that promote e-mail writing and reading as a primary objective" (p. 220). In addition to concluding that well-designed, useful research in this area is hard to find, they found that ". . . many of (the) expected benefits are inconclusive, overly optimistic, and even contradictory" (p. 249). Anecdotal evidence continues to mount that there are benefits to including such activities in the curriculum but, clearly, more and better research is needed to explicate these commonly held beliefs.

Course characteristics that affect success. Because specific course features have great impact on both student achievement and attitudes, substantial research has been directed toward identifying factors that make for an effective distance learning course. Though some studies focus on course factors that correlate directly to dropout rates in distance learning courses (Bernard & Amundsen, 1989; Gibson & Graf, 1992), many researchers agree with Wilkes and Burnham (1991) that course success should be measured by more than just endurance and achievement, since "highly motivated learners may be willing to endure almost (anything) to achieve a passing grade" (p. 43). Therefore, the majority of studies in this area focus on attitudes of students who complete distance learning courses. Cheng, Lehman, and Armstrong (1991), Biner (1993), and Hardy and Boaz (1997) agree that the handful of factors described here are the major contributors to course satisfaction. These include the following:

- **Degree of interaction.** Though some studies find that the convenience distance learning offers means more to students than teacher interaction (Klesius, Homan, & Thompson, 1997), the single greatest determinant of satisfaction across studies is the amount of interaction between instructor and students (Fulford & Zhang, 1993; Furst-Bowie, 1997; Smith, 1996; Thompson, 1990; Westbrook, 1997; Zirken & Sumler, 1995). McHenry and Bozik (1997) found that lack of "classroom community" among distance learners can decrease interaction and affect course satisfaction. But as is typical of distance learning and traditional classes alike, smaller class size can determine student perception of interactivity and, therefore, satisfaction with distance learning instruction. Riddle (1990) suggests that meeting students face to face for the first class meeting helps establish a rapport that can lead to better interaction throughout the course. However, Smith's (1996) study found that about 30% of the nearly 400 respondents would never choose distance learning because they felt it could never provide the degree of interaction found in a face-to-face course. Roblyer and Ekhaml (2000) created an interaction rubric to help define what interaction means in practical terms and to help instructors reflect on how they can make their courses more interactive. Roblyer and Wiencke (2002) offer an updated version. (See the Appendix.)
- **Support during course.** Many studies show that students value and profit from support during their course experiences, from registration through course activities and evaluation (Gibson & Graf, 1992; Hardy & Boaz, 1997). McHenry and Bozik (1997) find that lack of library

resources and slow transfer of paperwork are among the support problems that affect course satisfaction.

■ **Technical problems.** Consistent evidence exists that technical problems can doom the best planned course (Cheng, Lehman, & Armstrong, 1991; Thomerson & Smith, 1996). Successful courses are those that minimize technical problems.

Characteristics of people who choose distance learning. Moore and Kearsley (1996) and Hardy and Boaz (1997) find that, in the past, most distance learners have been working adults between 25 and 50 years old, married, and employed full time while taking courses; about two-thirds have been female. However, Wallace (1996) and Guernsey (1998) report that these demographics are changing as distance learning becomes more mainstream than alternative education, and that typical distance learners are becoming more like traditional students: younger and full time. Guernsey found that 500 of the 608 students taking distance learning courses at the University of Colorado also are taking regular, face-to-face courses there. Roblyer (1999) found that students who choose DL formats (at least, those choosing primarily Internet-based ones) do so because they have a higher need and desire for control over their learning environments, while students who choose traditional, face-to-face formats have a higher need and desire for interaction with instructors and other class members. It is not clear what impact it would have on students and on programs if the choice to learn from their preferred mode were taken away. Roblyer and Guarino (1999) also found that students choosing distance courses report a different set of learning needs than those choosing a traditional format.

Student characteristics that affect success with distance learning. Some researchers have tried to identify certain student capabilities or other factors that could predict whether or not a student might drop out, be less satisfied with, or do less with than others in an online activity. Hypothesized characteristics include self-motivation and ability to structure one's own learning (Gibson & Graf, 1992; Hardy & Boaz, 1997), previous experience with technology (Richards & Ridley, 1997), good attitude toward course subject matter (Coussement, 1995), and locus of control (Dille & Mezack, 1991). Recent studies confirm that higher internal locus of control and spending more time online can predict whether or not students will be successful in online learning environments (Wang & Newlin, 2000; Osborn, 2001). Also, Lim (2001) found that students' computer self-efficacy (i.e., belief in their ability to use computers effectively) could predict their degree of satisfaction in online courses. Finally, Roblyer and Marshall (2002) found that a set of four characteristics (achievement beliefs, responsibility, self-organization ability, and technology skill/access) predict reliably whether or not virtual high school students will succeed in online courses.

Characteristics of effective distance learning instructors. Cyrs (1997) emphasizes that distance learning instructors need different skills than instructors for traditional courses. His review of research reveals several areas of unique competence, all of which require experience with distance learning environments: course planning and organization that capitalize on distance learning strengths and minimize constraints; verbal and nonverbal presentation skills specific to distance learning situations; collaborative work with others to produce effective courses; ability to use questioning strategies; and ability to involve and coordinate student activities among several sites. Moskal, Martin, and Foshee (1997) refer to these skills in general as instructional design skills specific to distance learning. Dillon, Hengst, and Zoller (1991) find that these skills do not come naturally even among instructors who are effective in nondistance learning settings; and Gross (1997) and Wolcott (1996) find that few faculty are willing to learn these new skills because they are not rewarded for doing so. In their review of studies in this area, Roblyer and McKenzie (2000) found that many of the same factors that make for a successful online instructor are the same as those for any successful instructor: good communication and classroom organization skills.

Research on cost effectiveness of distance learning. The University of Idaho's Engineering Outreach home page (http://www.uidaho.edu/evo) posted a list taken from Threlkeld and Brzoska (1994) on several categories of cost factors involved with offering a distance learning course:

- **Technology.** Hardware and software
- **Transmission.** Ongoing expenses of leasing transmission access (e.g., T-1 lines, satellite)
- **Maintenance.** Repairing and updating equipment
- **Infrastructure.** Foundational network and telecommunications infrastructure located at originating and receiving sites
- **Production.** Technical and personnel support to develop/adapt teaching materials
- **Support.** Expenses needed to keep the system working successfully, for example, administrative costs, registration, advising/counseling, local support costs, facilities, and overhead costs
- **Personnel.** Instructors and support staff.

Although studies show that the initial costs of starting distance learning programs are high, research also suggests that as programs become more efficient and used over more courses, program costs should decrease (Ludlow, 1994). A recent study by Osiakwan and Wright (2001) found that, while both the variable and fixed costs of a distance training course were higher than that of a classroom course, the distance course still was more profitable because the institution can charge more for the course and it can be offered more frequently.

Resources Available to Support Audio and Video Telelearning

Although the Internet was the catalyst for an unprecedented interest in distance learning, it is by no means the only delivery system for distance learning. Indeed, distance learning can be done without any electronic assistance at all. As Simonson, Smaldino, Albright, and Zvacek (2000) note, distance learning was done by correspondence study via postal mail (a.k.a. snail mail) since the 19th century. Changes in our technological capabilities have brought about gradual changes to our methods of delivering instruction at a distance. The first major change to correspondence courses came when presentations were placed on videotape and mailed along with print materials. Later, improvements in the quality and availability of broadcast technologies made it possible to send audio and video information, either live or taped.

Distance delivery systems can be classified in any of several ways. One classification system suggested by Simonson et al. (2000) is based on Dale's cone of experience, a system designed by Edgar Dale to categorize media according to their degree of realism. Dale said media range from concrete (e.g., hands-on or multisensory experience) to abstract (verbal symbols such as text descriptions), and that younger or less experienced students require more concrete experiences before they can understand abstract ones. Thus, distance delivery systems can be classified according to the degree to which they approximate reality. (See Figure 8.1.) However, distance delivery systems also may be classified by the methods and technologies used to deliver them. (See Figure 8.2.)

Sometimes several of the technologies shown in Figure 8.2 are used in combination to achieve the desired level of realism in Figure 8.1. Currently, the most popular arrangement for distance learning (other than through the Internet) is video courses or "telecourses" (Carnavale & Young, 2001; Carr, 2001). Telecourses are more common at higher education than they are in K–12 levels, but some K–12 curriculum materials are delivered in this way (e.g., integrated science units broadcast from the University of Alabama to schools). However, videoconferencing also is becoming increasingly popular in K–12 classrooms (McCullen, 2001).

Resources Available to Support Web-Based Learning

Background on the Internet

The Internet has made such a difference in our society that it is difficult to remember when we did not depend on it for communications, instruction, and even entertainment. There is so much to learn about the uses of the Internet in education that many educators find it difficult to know where to begin. An ancillary booklet designed to meet the special needs of beginners accompanies this book. It is entitled *Starting Out on the Internet: A Learning Journey for Teachers,* and the description of Internet resources in this chapter refers readers to various parts of this booklet. Readers are encouraged to do the exercises for each of the 11 chapters in conjunction with the Companion Website.

Figure 8.1 Delivery Systems for Distance Education Classified by Degree of Realism

Most abstract, least realism	Correspondence courses with written materials (no real-time interaction with instructor; interaction with instructor only via written communications)
↓	Taped or broadcast audio mailed or downloaded to students (no real-time interaction with instructor)
	One-way, real-time audio from instructor to students (radio)
	Two-way, real-time audio between students and instructor
	Taped or broadcast video mailed or downloaded to students (no real-time interaction with instructor)
	Live video from instructor to students (accompanied by real-time audio interaction between instructor and students)
	Two-way, real-time video between instructor and students (accompanied by real-time audio interaction between instructor and students)
	Two-way, real-time audio and video between instructor and students
Most realism, least abstract	Two-way, real-time audio and video between instructor and students with supplementary multimedia presentations

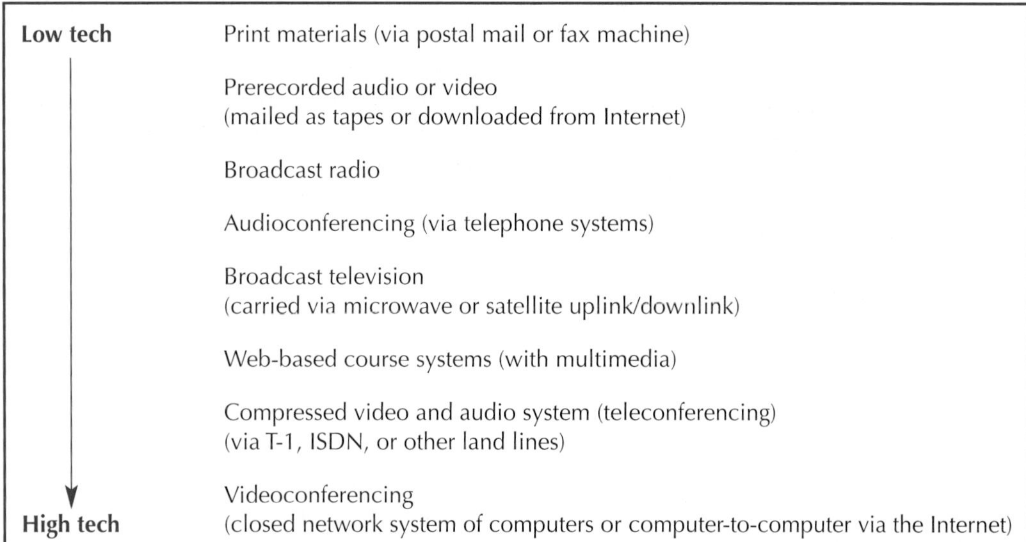

Low tech
Print materials (via postal mail or fax machine)
Prerecorded audio or video
(mailed as tapes or downloaded from Internet)
Broadcast radio
Audioconferencing (via telephone systems)
Broadcast television
(carried via microwave or satellite uplink/downlink)
Web-based course systems (with multimedia)
Compressed video and audio system (teleconferencing)
(via T-1, ISDN, or other land lines)
Videoconferencing
High tech
(closed network system of computers or computer-to-computer via the Internet)

Figure 8.2 Delivery Systems for Distance Education Classified by Technologies Used

Today's educational uses of the Internet bear little resemblance to its original purpose. Yet learning something about its original design can help educators understand how the Internet works today. The U.S. Department of Defense (DOD) developed the first version of the Internet during the 1970s to allow quick communication among researchers working on DOD projects in about 30 locations. The DOD also saw it as a way to continue communications among these important defense sites in the event of a worldwide catastrophe such as a nuclear attack. Because these projects were funded by the DOD's Advanced Research Projects Agency (ARPA), the network was originally called ARPAnet.

In the 1980s, just as desktop computers were becoming common, the National Science Foundation (NSF) funded a high-speed connection among university centers based on the ARPAnet structure. By connecting their individual networks, universities could communicate and exchange information in the same way DOD's projects had. However, these new connections had an additional, unexpected benefit. A person accessing a university network from home or school could also get access to any site connected to that network. This connection began to be called a *gateway* to all networks, and what we now call the Internet was born.

Networks connect computers to allow users to share resources and exchange information easily. The Internet has been called the ultimate network or "the mother of all networks" because it is a network of networks. It is a way for people in network sites all over the world to communicate with each other as though they were on the same local-area network. The name means literally "between or among networks." Though most people think of the Internet as synonymous with the World Wide Web (WWW), the latter really is a subset of the Internet system. The WWW is an Internet *service* that links sites around the world through hypertext documents. By bringing up a hypertext or web page document in a program called a *web browser,* one can click on text or graphics linked to other pages in other sites. In this way, one "travels" around the Internet from site to site.

Our use of the Internet depends on common procedures or *Internet protocols* that allow computers to communicate with each other, despite differences in programs or operating systems. Three important protocols are Internet protocol (IP) addresses, e-mail addresses, and uniform resource locators (URLs).

IP addresses. Each computer connected to the Internet must have a number designation called an IP address. Internet Service providers (ISPs) each have a set of these IP addresses to give out to their users. (See the Preface of the *Starting Out...* booklet.) ISPs connect to the Internet through large, high-powered computer systems (servers), most of which use the Unix operating system.

InterNIC (Internet Network Information Center), a collaborative project between AT&T and Network Solutions, Inc. (NSI) and supported by the National Science Foundation, serves as a registry for Internet addresses, ensuring that no two IP numbers are identical. Think of it as a database similar to that maintained by the Social Security Administration, which ensures that no two people have identical Social Security numbers. In 1998, the U.S. Congress allocated funds to improve this system and to help large universities who act as ISPs for educators pay for high-speed Internet connections (Biemiller & Young, 1998, May 15).

E-mail addresses and web site addresses are derived from IP addresses. Although they could be done completely with numbers based on their IP numbers, a system of names was created to make them easier for people to use and remember. The following sections explain how e-mail addresses and web site addresses are created.

E-mail addresses. An Internet address is the combination of an individual's account name or *user id* and the ISP or *host name*. For example, look at the components of the following Internet e-mail address:

mroblyer@polaris.umuc.edu

- The name *mroblyer* is the user id assigned by the ISP.
- The @ symbol sets off the *host name,* in this case, *polaris* (a server for the main organization, UMUC). The periods are essential parts of the address as well because they separate key elements of the host name. Usually the institution or company that serves as the ISP follows the server name.
- The *edu* identifies the type of company or institution, in this case, an educational organization. Other common types are *org* (organization), *com* (company), and *gov* (government). Users in countries outside the United States append two-character codes to indicate their origins. For instance, *uk* identifies England and *au* is Australia.

Uniform resource locators (URLs). Every web page or web site also has an address called a uniform resource locator (URL). (See Chapter 1 in the *Starting Out...* booklet.) A URL starts with the prefix HTTP, which stands for HyperText Transfer Protocol. A URL entered into a browser sends an HTTP command to the web server directing it to transmit the requested web page. The standard format for a URL is *http://www.prenhall.com/roblyer*. URLs and e-mail addresses look similar because both have the host name and the domain name in them.

Why has the Internet become so popular? Educators, like just about everyone in the civilized world, either seem to be on the Internet or trying to get on it. The National Center for Education Statistics (NCES) reported that the percentage of public schools connected to the Internet went from 35% in 1994 to 98% in 2000 (NCES, 2001). Of these schools, 77% had Internet connections in classrooms. Connection to the Internet has become a symbol of technology's power to shape our lives. A major benefit of the Internet is the ubiquitous, comprehensive nature of its information and services. Once connected, educators and students can use the Internet to exchange messages and files among themselves and with others anywhere in the world. Also, they can use it to locate information virtually from any place in the world. A person or site with the desired information need only be connected to the Internet and willing to provide an online listing of available resources. But the Internet's popularity does not spring merely from its wealth of information, but from three other characteristics that give widespread appeal to technical and nontechnical people alike. It is widely available, easy to use, and highly visual and graphic.

How do schools get connected? Two different types of gateways to the Internet are available: a direct connection or an account with a service provider or other organization with a direct connection.

- **Direct connection.** Larger schools and other organizations usually have direct connections to the Internet and allow any of their members to use these connections, usually free of charge. For example, if a school has an Internet connection, anyone working there may acquire an account that becomes, in effect, an Internet address. The connection with the Internet is so transparent to these users that they frequently have the illusion that their connections are free; however, they actually are paid for by the organization.

- **A service provider account.** A variety of Internet service providers (ISPs) has sprung up to sell accounts to those who do not have free access in some other way. Perhaps the best known are international companies such as America Online, but hundreds of regional and local companies also sell Internet access. Users of these accounts usually pay by the amount of time they spend connected. Service providers typically give users various software tools in addition to user IDs that act as addresses for sending and receiving information. Larger schools and higher education institutions usually provide their faculty and students with a direct Internet connection through their own network. Schools with no network usually have modem connections in classrooms and offices.

Web Browsing and Searching Resources

Using the Internet in its earliest form required familiarity with the commands used in a technical system called Unix. Today, very little needs to be known about Unix to use the Internet effectively. Several user-friendly programs called *clients* have been designed to carry out various user activities such as browsing and searching. These programs are called clients because they work through the host computers or servers on which they reside; in a sense the server "works for" them. The most popular clients are browsers, search engines, and gophers. (See Chapters 2 and 3 in the *Starting Out . . .* booklet.)

Web browsers. Web browsers allow users to move freely and effortlessly from one site to another through a text-based linking system known as *hypertext.* Browsers make using the Internet an easy point-and-click process because they let users access all available resources on the WWW to search for information. The first browser, *Mosaic,* appeared on the market in 1993 and began to attract attention to the Internet. But the two browsers that appeared subsequently, *Netscape Communicator* and *Internet Explorer,* now are the most commonly used browsers.

When a browser is first installed on a computer, it must be set up with options such as which web site will appear automatically as the *home page* when the user connects to the Internet. The most common choices for teachers to designate as a browser home page are:

- A teacher's personal home page or school home page
- The *Netscape Communicator* site or *Internet Explorer* site
- A news service such as a local newspaper's home page
- A "push technology" site that sends customized news to users' desktops on topics they specify are of most interest to them.

Browsing is considered a wandering, unstructured tour through whatever path of Internet links the user follows.

However, if teachers want a more structured search for information specific to a certain topic, they usually use a search engine.

Search engines. These programs have come to be the heart of the Internet. Starting with only a few such asYahoo! (short for "Yet Another Hierarchical Officious Oracle"), which was developed by David Filo and Jerry Yang at Stanford University, search engines have grown into a thriving enterprise. There are so many search engines, in fact, and they change so quickly that sites such as the following have been created to organize them. These sites have links to all the major search engines and give advice and instruction on how to use them for various searches:

- **Search Engine Watch** (http://www.searchenginewatch.com)
- **Search Engines: Indexes, Directories, and Libraries** (http://www.netstrider.com/search)

Gophers and digital resource centers. Gopher was a storage and search system developed at the University of Minnesota and named after the school's mascot. Developed before the advent of more graphic browsers, a server with Gopher shows its contents as a hierarchically structured menu of files. Two Gopher programs, *Veronica* and *Jughead,* allow people to search the Internet for resources stored in Gopher systems. Most Gopher databases are being converted to web sites, which can be more easily accessed with Internet search engines. Bull, Bull, and Dawson (1999) refer to sites that compile large numbers of resources and make them available to educators at large as "digital resource centers." They point out that these centers provide help to connect the work of universities and K–12 schools by providing common, shared information resources.

Communicating in Writing on the Internet

Computer-based written forms of communication are becoming as common as telephone calls.

E-mail. *Electronic mail (e-mail)* is the most common way to exchange personal, written messages between individuals or small groups. It is possible to send e-mail via an internal network, rather than the Internet, but most people with e-mail accounts also send e-mail outside their systems via the Internet. Abilock (1996) discusses how powerful e-mail can be for communications among teachers, students, and resource experts.

Listservs. *Listservs* are discussion groups on the Internet that feature ongoing "conversations" via e-mail between groups of people who share common interests. When e-mail is addressed to a listserv mailing list, it is automatically duplicated and sent to everyone on the list.

Bulletin boards (BBs). BBs, like listservs, are electronic message centers but are used for posting messages of interest to group members who visit the BB, rather than for e-mailed notices that all members receive at once. Bulletin board members must go to the BB location to review and leave messages.

Chat rooms. *Chat rooms* are Internet locations that allow "live," real-time communications between two or more users. As users in a chat room type in their comments, what they type is seen by everyone in the "room." Chat rooms are considered more interactive than any of the other written communications options. The chats held in them and in bulletin boards are sometimes known as "threaded discussions."

Instant messaging (IM). The newest type of Internet communication is made possible by a service that allows users to create a private chat room that only its members may enter. The service alerts a user when someone from the IM list wants to "talk." The person notified can then initiate a chat session. Popular with business professionals and teenagers alike, IM is just coming into use in schools.

Communicating Visually on the Internet

Although written communications retain their importance, visual communications are an emerging standard. Our society relies increasingly on images to communicate information, which means that both students and teachers must become adept at developing and using visual forms of communication in distance learning.

Images and animations. Some of the graphics tools referred to in Chapter 6 are used to develop Internet resources. Clip art, photos, and animations are standard fare on most web pages. Clip art and clip photo packages are banks of prepared images that may be inserted into web pages; a scanner can also be used to prepare an image from an original photograph or picture for use on a page. Animations are motion sequences made up of individual pictures put together to form the illusion of continuous motion. Prepared animation packages also are available.

Regular and streaming video/audio. Students and teachers need tools that allow development of audio and development and viewing of full-motion video. The programs that play the prepared audio and video are known as *plug-ins* and generally are available for downloading free from the Internet. (See Chapters 7 and 8 in the *Starting Out. . .* booklet.) Currently, there are two kinds of full-motion video on the Internet: downloaded movies and streaming (compressed) video.

- **Downloaded movies.** One kind of full-motion video is designed to play in a window on the computer screen after it is downloaded from the Internet to a computer. Programs such as Apple's *QuickTime* are used to create these movies, which usually are shot with a camcorder and stored in a Moving Picture Experts Group (MPEG) or MP3 format. To see them, one needs an MPEG player plug-in.

■ **Streaming video.** This term applies to movies that have been compressed and transmitted in the form of real-time video via the Internet. Just as an MPEG player is needed to view digitized movies, a streaming video player such as *RealVideo* is needed to see streamed video. A streamed video file begins loading from a remote web site when the user clicks on it but does not wait until the video is downloaded; it starts almost immediately after the download begins. This is especially useful for large videos that take a long time to download. However, video quality is dependent on the quality and speed of the line connecting the computer to the Internet. Knee, Musgrove, and Musgrove (2000) describe methods of producing streamed video for classroom use. For more information on streaming video, see http://www.streamingvideos.com

Desktop videoconferencing. The increasing availability of telephone switching technologies allows completely interactive communication among desktop computers. Today, computers adapted for complete two-way interaction are becoming common in schools and classrooms across the country. A typical desktop videoconferencing system has equipment—video camera, microphone, and speakers—at each workstation or learning station that allows the learner to be seen and heard by the teacher or learner at the remote site. Signals are transmitted using modems and telephone lines. Teachers can use presentation technologies such as LCD projection panels connected to the computers to expand the number of persons who may observe the on-screen video. Learners may communicate directly with teachers, peers, and experts who use compatible systems.

Current applications of desktop videoconferencing are limited by several factors. First, the cost of transmitting video data over telephone lines is high because of the large amount of bandwidth those signals require. Second, current video transmissions must deal with analog signals, making them difficult to manipulate. However, videoconferencing is on the increase, especially as equipment and line costs become cheaper and resources get easier to use (Jerram, 1995; McCullen, 2001; Walsh & Reese, 1995).

Electronic whiteboards. These are display devices typically used in distance learning classrooms to support demonstrations. Connected to the computer, they allow users at different sites to see what the instructor writes or draws and make it possible for demonstrations to be stored as computer files after they are produced. If each site has a whiteboard, users at all sites can contribute to the display. Electronic whiteboards are based on three different technologies: electromagnetic, pressure sensitive, and laser tracking. The first whiteboards were used as "reproducible chalkboards," from which instructors could print out demonstrations from class and give students copies. Currently, the most powerful use of this technology is as a large screen on which Internet pages are projected. Instructors and students need not sit at the computer to control movement through Internet sites, but can touch the whiteboard to "click" on icons and select from menus.

MUDs and MOOs. Two of the tools recommended by Odasz (1999–2000) to support online collaboration are multiuser dungeons (or dimensions or domains), that is, MUDs, and MUDs object-oriented (MOOs). These whimsical-sounding resources are programs that allow many users at different sites to interact at the same time. The environment is graphical but, unlike virtual reality, interaction is still through typed text. Odasz says that sample applications include "interactive fiction" or having students role-play characters from literature. An example MUD may be seen at http://angalon.tamu.edu/

Avatars. The future of the Internet will be increasingly visual, and one feature contributing to this is the use of *avatar* spaces. The widespread use of avatars on the Internet was proposed in Neal Stephenson's 1992 science fiction novel *Snow Crash.* Avatars are 3-D figures that serve as moving icons to represent people in virtual reality environments. These figures can be made to look much like the person they represent or may be complete fantasy figures, selected by a user to project a certain aura or point of view. Avatar spaces already are used in some Internet chat rooms and e-mail systems. Their uses in education are limited but have great potential for fostering visual literacy, motivating students to develop writing and other communication skills, and helping teach skills that involve visual design.

File Transfer Options

The Internet is useful for transferring large written documents, graphic files, and programs from one computer to another. Documents, images, and movies can be sent to a computer and displayed with the appropriate software. Many plug-ins and other useful programs are available free when downloaded from the Internet. These programs usually are sent in compressed (stuffed) format and the user must decompress (unstuff) them before they may be used. Many of the new Internet e-mail programs automatically compress and decompress these files before and after downloading if a utility program such as *Stuffit* (Aladdin Software) is stored on the computer's hard drive. Although transferring files is rapidly getting easier, a few technical issues remain concerning compatibility of files prepared in one program and sent to another. Bull, Bull, and Sigmon (1997b) describe some common problems with compatibility of transferred files and suggest some practical ways to deal with them. Many of these incompatibility problems can be overcome by sending files as PDF (portable document format) documents. Adler (2000) described some ways PDFs are useful to teachers.

One easy way to send files is merely to attach them to e-mail messages. Browsers and e-mail programs have built-in options for selecting files to send as attachments. Usually, it's as easy as selecting the attachment option from a menu while preparing an e-mail message.

An acronym for File Transfer Protocol, FTP is a common procedure for sending files on the Internet. The FTP servers that house full-text documents also have built-in search engines to allow searches for them. FTP software (e.g., CuteFTP) is needed to send or receive FTP files.

Resources to Optimize Web Power

Anyone who "surfs" the Internet regularly knows that it can be time consuming. The sheer amount of information to peruse can be confusing and factors such as traffic and line speed can slow progress. Methods are continually being developed to cope with these problems and to help people use the Internet's power more efficiently.

Push technologies. Information sent out electronically—whether requested or not—is known as *push technology.* E-mail and broadcast television are examples of push technologies. The World Wide Web (WWW), on the other hand, usually is considered a "pull technology" because a web page must be requested before it is sent. However, one push technology that helps teachers keep up with the latest news from the WWW on their topics of interest is a news service like *Infogate* (formerly *PointCast*). This free service is obtained by going to the company's web site (http://www.infogate.com), downloading the required software, and specifying what topics should be monitored. Every time a user logs onto the WWW, a summary of the news for those topics automatically appears.

Bookmarking. Once a good Internet site is found, a quick way to get back to it later is to "bookmark" the URL (address). (See Chapter 4 in the *Starting Out. . .* booklet.) Each browser has a pull-down bookmark menu; the first item on it is to add a bookmark. Selecting this option when at the URL adds a bookmark for that URL to the bookmark list. To get to the URL later, the bookmarked name is selected from the menu list; the browser then automatically goes there. Harris (1998a) says that well-prepared bookmark files are great resources for teachers and should be shared with others who have similar interests.

Site capturing. On a high-traffic day, the Internet can be as slow as a highway traffic jam. Slow-moving screens can play havoc with teachers and students trying to carry out classroom activities. An alternative is to use a product such as ForeFront's *Web Whacker,* software that downloads pages or sites to a computer's hard drive where they later can be run through a browser without benefit of Internet connection. The popularity of this software created the term "site whacking."

Intranets. Another way to speed up access to the Internet is through an internal network called an *intranet.* This network, like the Internet, is based on TCP/IP protocols, but belongs only to an organization and can be accessed only by the organization's members. An intranet's web sites look and act just like any other web sites, but the network has a firewall that will not allow unauthorized access. A school might maintain its own intranet of selected sites while allowing access to the larger Internet for less used sites (D'Ignazio, 1996). More information about creating and maintaining intranets is available from online magazines such as *Intranet Journal* (http://www.intranetjournal.com).

Internet-TV products. Products and technologies that let users connect to the Internet through their TVs are referred to collectively as Internet-TV products. Most such products, for example, WebTV, consist of a small box that connects to a telephone line and television. The box makes a connection to the Internet via telephone service, downloads web pages, and converts the downloaded web pages to a format that can be displayed on a TV. Internet-TV products also come with a remote control device that permits navigation through the WWW. These products may become very useful in schools, especially when they can access the Internet directly through the cable TV lines, rather than telephone lines. Other such Internet-based products may be on the horizon as companies look for ways to meet the growing demand for fast Internet access.

Web Page and Web Site Programming Resources

Developing personal, professional, school, and project web pages and web sites has become an excellent way for both teachers and students to learn the power of the Internet, to participate in cooperative projects, and to display the project results. Only a few years ago, Web pages could not be developed without programming and scripting tools. Now, thanks to web page development software, it is possible to develop whole sites without writing a line of code or script. However, even if one uses a web authoring program, it is good to know enough about each of the major languages to make minor adjustments or additions to developed pages. In addition to the tools described here, which are used primarily in web development and use, several general-purpose programming languages are in common use by more developers. These include C++, Visual Basic, and Practical Extraction and Report Language (PERL), a popular text-processing language used for writing CGI scripts.

Hypertext Markup Language (HTML). HTML is the Internet standard for how web pages are formatted and displayed. Many books and online sources are available to help people learn and use HTML effectively. An example of HTML and the beginning of the page it generates is shown in Figure 8.3. (Note that the example displays only the beginning of the complete code.) Beginners can find a variety of HTML tutorials, tips, and tools on the Internet. Although HTML is the language microcomputer users will hear most about, other languages are also used such as Standard Generalized Markup Language (SGML), a system for organizing and tagging elements of a document (Seamon, 1999), and Dynamic HTML (DHTML), which

Figure 8.3 Example of HTML Used to Create Web Page

M. D. Roblyer

Electronic Portfolio

Books | Articles | Video | PowerPoint

```
<html>
<head>
   <meta http-equip="Content-Type" content="text/html; charset=iso-8859-1">
   <meta name="GENERATOR" content="Mozilla/4.78 (Macintosh; U; PPC)
[Netscape]">
   <title>NEWinfoforFigure_8_3.htm</title>
</head>
<body>
<center><font face="Park Avenue"><font size=+4>M. D.
Roblyer</font></font></center>
<hr WIDTH="100%">
<center><font size=+3>Electronic Portfolio</font><font size=+3></font>
<p><font size=+3><u>Books</u> | <u>Articles</u> | <u>Video</u> I
<u>PowerPoint</u></font></center>
```

allows the same URL to display a different page depending on conditions such as the time of day or the previous pages read (Bull, Bull, & Lewis, 1998).

Java. Originally called OAK, Java is a high-level programming language developed by Sun Microsystems. An object-oriented language similar to C++, it was developed originally for more general use but has become popular for its ability to do interactive graphic and animation activities on Web pages. Many already-developed Java applications called *Java applets* are available for downloading from a Web server and can be run on any computer that has a Java-compatible Web browser. Bull, Bull, and Bull (2000) say that Java applets make possible many web page features such as animations and special effects, graphics and buttons, interactive displays, and web forms and databases. Applets also are the programs that make possible chat rooms. Bull et al. cite several web sites teachers can go to in order to obtain ready-to-use applets (http://java.sun.com/applets). The example applet in Figure 8.4 shows a counter that keeps track of the number of times the page is accessed.

Virtual Reality Modeling Language (VRML). Although not commonly used by web page developers at this time, VRML develops and displays 3-D objects on web pages. These objects give the illusion of being "real" much more than videos or animations and can create *virtual worlds.* VRML has great potential for making web pages even more interactive and life-like (Skipton, 1997). Skipton notes that most VRML packages let developers create basic shapes

Figure 8.4 Sample Java Application and Code

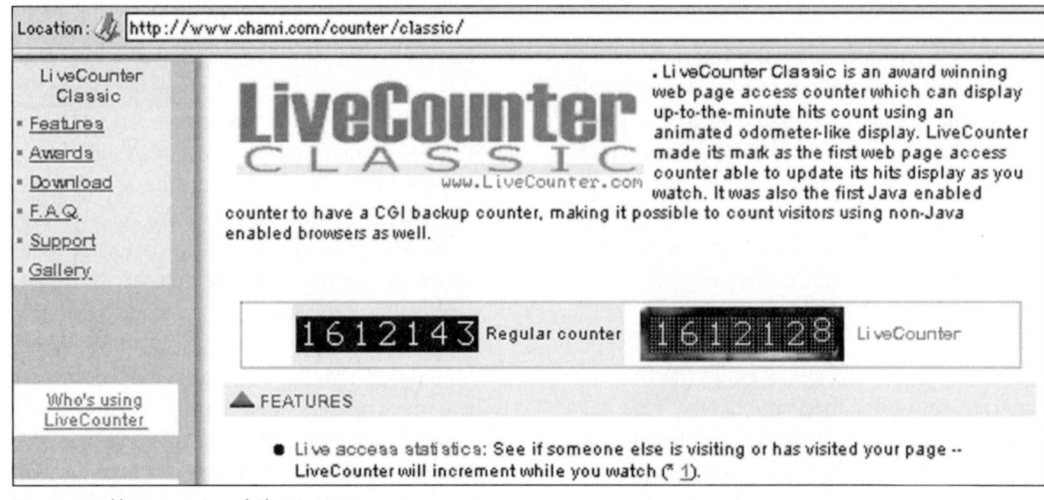

Source: Used by permission of Chami.com.

(primitives) like cubes, spheres, and cylinders and include polygon-based modeling tools for creating more complex objects. Some offer further modeling features—freeform or cutouts—that enable users to extrude or cut out shapes to create more complicated models. Skipton adds that, in combination with other programs, VRML can create "a multi-user avatar space" like that in the science fiction novel *Snow Crash* (Stephenson, 1992). See Chapter 9 for further explanation of this capability.

Common Gateway Interface (CGI). CGI is not a language, but a specification for how data will be collected. Developers can use PERL or another language to write CGI programs that create "dynamic documents." That is, web page users can insert their comments or answers into active web pages as they run on a server. Many web pages contain forms that use a CGI program to process the form's data once submitted. All information entered at these sites is gathered and processed by a CGI server, which prepares a summary of the information using a database software such as *FileMaker Pro* (FileMaker, Inc.). Repp (1999) described some uses of CGI scripts for education. These include sites for handing in student assignments, dynamic calendars that can be updated regularly, and online surveys and other research instruments for gathering and storing data. Figure 8.5 shows a CGI script to gather information across students.

Web Page and Web Site Development Tools and Procedures

Various alternatives exist for educators and students who want to develop web pages but do not want to write their own codes and/or scripts. Web development packages are authoring systems that create web pages using a point-click-and-drag strategy, very much like developing a word-processed document with images. As words are typed and graphics are inserted, the authoring program automatically generates the HTML required for the pages to be placed on the WWW. It is no longer necessary for teachers to learn HTML because software to create the code is so easy to acquire and use. (See Chapter 11 in the *Starting Out. . .* booklet.)

Figure 8.5 Example CGI Application for Collecting Data from Students

Add a Checklist question

This is a "Checklist" question. Respondents can check more than one response. Each response will be stored in the Survey Center.

Here is an example:

What is your favorite subject in school?

Name: Enter your name here

Email: Enter your address here

☐ English
☐ Science
☐ Social Studies
☐ Math

Submit

Source: Used by permission of Tom Snyder Communications.

Web development programs. Web page development capabilities are available in stand-alone software packages specially designed for this purpose (Microsoft *FrontPage*), as part of word processing software (*Microsoft Word*), or as a free software option on a browser (*Netscape Composer*) or search engine site. Two levels of web development software packages are available for teachers who want to develop their own web pages and web sites:

- **Single-page software.** For simple pages and sites, many teachers opt for a word processor or a free product such as *Netscape Composer.* With these options, teachers develop single pages (much like desktop publishing) and then combine them into a web site by inserting links.
- **Site development software.** Larger, more complex web sites and those with more sophisticated multimedia features require more advanced development software. These software packages also provide a site management capability, so teachers can keep track of the structure of the site as they develop its pages. Some software such as Adobe *GoLive!* and NetObjects *Fusion MX* are single packages that include advanced features and site management. Others, such as Macromedia *Dreamweaver Fireworks Studio* or Macromedia *Flash 5 Freehand 10 Studio* are two or more separate packages that work well together to accomplish various functions. These are considered software suites or "studios."

Web site development procedures. Because it is so easy to create web pages, nearly anyone can do it. Consequently, as Cafolla and Knee (1996) observed, "many Web pages are poorly designed because they are so easy to create" (p. 8). They give recommendations for creating web sites that are easy to navigate, attractive, and useful to others (1996, 1996–1997, 1997). Bailey and Blythe (1998) also give tips for planning, organizing, and structuring web site information. A suggested sequence follows of steps for developing a web site. (Also see Chapters 5 and 11 in the *Starting Out. . .* booklet.)

Step 1: Plan and storyboard. Without a doubt, planning and design are the most difficult—and most important—first steps in developing a web page or web course. Most people want to get to the fun of development; they do not want to spend time mapping out the structure and contents of the site. Yet planning is critical to a well-designed web site. Some people use storyboard frames or cognitive mapping software to sketch out their designs. Others use 3-inch × 5-inch sticky notes placed on large pieces of posterboard. Mapping software or sticky notes offer more flexibility to move things around. Bailey and Blythe (1998) offer procedures for how to design web page content and structure systematically. These steps include outlining (either in linear or the more flexible "mindmapped" form), diagramming, and storyboarding.

Step 2: Develop pages with text. The next step is creating blank pages and inserting the text elements such as a title, paragraphs of description, and any text labels that will serve later as links (e.g., "Go back home"). From a structural standpoint, three general designs are used for pages: basic, basic with anchors on same page, and frame pages.

Step 3: Insert images and sounds. Pictures, animations, and movies come next. Images and animations must be in GIF or JPEG format; movies and sounds must be in MPEG format. (See Chapter 6 for a description of various formats for saving graphic images.) If movies or audio are to be streamed, the page should inform the user and provide a way to obtain the plug-in needed to see or hear the item.

Step 4: Insert links and frames. After all pages are designed, set "hot spots" or links from text and images to other locations.

Step 5: Insert interactive elements. Bull, Bull, and Sigmon (1997a) describe how a web page can be made "interactive" by inserting applets, CGI scripts, and mail-to's to gather comments from users.

Step 6: Test in a browser. Many development programs have a built-in preview system, but McClelland (1997) and others recommend testing the site with an actual browser to observe how it will work when it is published on the web.

Step 7: Publish the site. For others to see created web pages, developers must send or place them on a server. This is called publishing the site. If the user can sit down at the keyboard of the computer acting as the server, the files may be moved over from a disk to the hard drive. For servers that are not nearby, the user may upload the pages to the server as FTP files.

Step 8: Gather evaluation comments, revise, and maintain the site. The best web sites are those that are updated regularly based on user comments and the continuing insights of the developers. This may be done through CGI programs built into the page or simply through inviting e-mailed comments.

More useful tips for web page developers are listed below (McClelland, 1997):

- **Observe naming conventions.** Extensions such as *.html* and *.gif* must be used on the web. Aside from the period before these suffixes, avoid punctuation in the file names, which can cause confusion as the server tries to read the files.
- **Have graphics in GIF or JPEG format.** Although some development packages convert images automatically from PICT and TIFF formats, the program may place them in an unexpected place on the hard drive, creating problems later. Therefore, McClelland recommends they be in correct format *before* they are inserted.
- **Have a GIF spacer handy.** A GIF spacer is an empty GIF file that is just a few pixels wide and tall and is created in a program such as *Adobe PhotoShop* with a white transparent background. "It comes in handy for paragraph spacing, indents, and alignment tweaks" (McClelland, 1997, p. 107).

Web Page Criteria

The set of web page evaluation criteria shown in Figure 8.6 and in the Appendix (Figure A.11) has been synthesized and compiled from those recommended by Gray (1997), Everhart (1997), and McClelland (1997). Also see the collection of web page rubrics and other assessment tools at Kathy Schrock's Guide for Educators on the Discovery web site: **http://school.discovery.com/schrockguide/assess.html#web.** Among these tools are a rubric for assessing the quality of student web pages based on work by Al Rogers, Global SchoolNet Foundation, and CyberFair Contest (see Appendix): **http://www.ux1.eiu.edu/~cfmgb/web.htm.**

Web Course Development Tools

More complex and capable than web authoring programs, web course development systems are housed on a central server and designed to allow educators at any location to develop and present whole web courses from them. Some systems such as *WebCT* and *Blackboard* were designed like franchises to allow educational institutions anywhere to use them for a fee. Other companies not only developed their own system, but also offer the courses themselves. However, some institutions like the University of Maryland University College have created their own online course systems (Web Tycho). In addition to web page development tools, all of these systems include resources such as bulletin board or conferencing systems, online chat spaces, student progress tracking, grade maintenance and distribution, course calendar, student home pages, and search engines that look for course content.

Integration Strategies for Distance Lessons: Web-Based Activities

Education is exploding with web-based instruction in many forms. This section gives a rationale for why teachers may want to consider joining the "Internet revolution" by integrating web-based instruction into their classrooms. This section also gives examples of web-based lessons and projects, and describes ways of assessing students' performance in these activities. Potential pitfalls of Internet use for students have been described elsewhere in this chapter and this book. Readers may want to consult Chapter 6 in the *Starting Out. . .* booklet for a brief overview of these potential problems and how to prevent them.

Figure 8.6 Criteria for Evaluating Web Sites

Check each of the following criteria *before* and *after* designing a page.

Content

__ All information is accurate; plan to update the page periodically. The "last time updated" date is given.
__ Information is complete but not excessive or redundant.
__ Information is well organized and clearly labeled.
__ Information is interesting, informative, and worthwhile.
__ Information is not redundant to many other sources; there is a reason to put it on the Web.
__ All text has correct spelling, grammar, and punctuation.
__ Level of content and vocabulary are appropriate for intended audience.
__ Content is free from stereotyping, coarse or vulgar language, or matter that could be offensive to typical users.
__ Author(s) of the page are clearly identified.
__ The page gives an e-mail address or other way to contact authors.

Visual and Audio Design

__ The site has a consistent look.
__ Graphics, animations, videos, and sounds make an important contribution; each serves a purpose.
__ Pages have only one or two fonts.
__ Each page uses a limited number of colors, especially for text.
__ Colors have been selected to be compatible with the Netscape 216 color palette.
__ Type colors/styles and text-to-background contrast have been selected for good readability.
__ Each graphic is designed to fit 640 × 480 pixel screens, allowing for scroll bars/toolbars.
__ Each page is limited to 2–3 screens; the most important information is at the top.
__ The pages are simply and attractively designed; they make a user want to read the information.

Navigation

__ Pages load quickly.
__ Pages have simple, consistent navigation scheme to let users get to desired places quickly and easily.
__ The first page indicates clearly how the site is organized and how to get to items of interest.
__ Links (text and icons) are easy to identify. Graphics and sounds are clearly identified.
__ Icons clearly represent the information they link to.
__ Each supporting page has a link back to the home page.

Miscellaneous (for larger sites and pages)

__ Requests for private information are secured.
__ Page information is kept short enough so that it can be printed quickly.
__ The user can choose to load alternate versions of the page such as text only or smaller images.
__ The site has its own search engine for locating items within the pages.
__ Branching is organized so that all content is no more than three clicks away from the home page.

Use the following tips to make your sites and pages easier to design and use:

__ Organize the site on paper ahead of time before putting it on the computer.
__ To speed loading, limit graphics to no more than 50K and reuse images whenever possible.
__ Use GIFs for line art or graphics with limited colors and sharp edges; use JPEGs for photos with many colors and smooth gradients. Avoid PICT and other formats that must be converted by users.
__ Test out your page with a real browser.
__ Use a GIF spacer (1 × 1 transparent GIF) to space paragraphs, indents, or alignments on pages.

Source: Based on criteria by Gray (1997), Everhart (1997), and McClelland (1997).

Background on Web-Based Activities

As recent research and commentary has indicated, web-based activities are time consuming to develop and implement and difficult to design in ways that have substantial, positive impact on students' learning (Coulter, Feldman, & Konold, 2000; Fabos & Young, 1999; Harris, 2000). As Coulter et al. say, "The Internet is no silver bullet for improving education" (p. 43). They encourage teachers considering web-based activities to ask themselves several questions before making the commitment to doing an online project. They are, in effect, asking teachers to document the relative advantage of online activities in comparison with other strategies they might use to accomplish the same purposes.

Answering the following questions, based on those outlined by Coulter et al. (2000) can form the basis of an integration plan for doing web-based activities:

1. **What is the curriculum-related purpose of the activity?** Using the Internet should not be thought of as an end in itself. The activity should accomplish some objective or purpose in required school curriculum.
2. **Does the Internet enhance the activity?** The rule of thumb is that if the activity could be done without the Internet, it probably should be! Harris (1998b) suggests that "teleresearch" activities should fulfill at least one of the following purposes:
   - **a.** To practice information-seeking skills (in a given content area)
   - **b.** To become informed about a topic of inquiry or answer a question
   - **c.** To review multiple perspectives on an issue
   - **d.** To generate data needed to explore a topic
   - **e.** To solve authentic problems
   - **f.** To publish synthesized and/or critiqued information.
3. **How will students use online resources (as opposed to just locating them)?** The object of the activity should be for students to do something with what they locate on the Internet. Once they locate information, they should be asked to determine its meaning, compile and synthesize various sources, or critique its usefulness.
4. **Do my students have the necessary skills in data analysis and information synthesis?** To make sure the project doesn't become an "information locating" exercise, it should call for additional, higher level tasks after they find the information. However, teachers must be sure their students have the prerequisite skills to do these higher level tasks.
5. **Do I have the necessary time and support for the activity I have in mind?** Harris points out that two problems frequently are cited in the failure of online activities. First, online projects can take longer than other learning strategies, and teachers do not allow sufficient time. Harris recommends doubling the original time estimate. Second, any number of technical problems can and do occur during an online project. Teachers must make sure they have technical support to resolve these problems in an efficient way so as not to slow down the momentum of the project.

Types and Examples of Web-Based Lessons and Projects

Some of the most exciting distance learning applications call for students to use technology as a means of collaboration so they can address significant problems or issues or to communicate with people in other cultures throughout the world. Judi Harris refers to these as "telecomputing activities" or "telecollaborations" (Harris, 1998b) and describes three general types of models:

1. **Interpersonal exchanges.** Students communicating via technology with other students or with teachers/experts
2. **Information collection and analysis.** Using information collections that provide data and information on request
3. **Problem solving.** Student-oriented and cooperative problem-solving projects

Harris (1997–1998, 1998b) lists 18 different strategies that fall under these three models and which she calls "wetware," or activity structures that guide teachers' actions in the project from planning through product development. Detailed descriptions of these structures may be found in her book. Some forms these models can take and some examples of each are given here.

Electronic penpals or "keypals." The simplest instructional activity in which distance technologies play a role is linking each student with a partner or penpal in a distant location to whom the student writes letters or diary-type entries. (See Technology Integration Idea 6.7 in Chapter 6.) Writing to communicate something to real people—rather than writing for teacher evaluations—encourages students to write more and with better grammar, spelling, and usage. This makes electronic correspondence an ideal activity for English or writing classes. Networking in this way also tends to eliminate social bias regarding gender, race, age, and physical appearance. Without social and cultural cues to color interactions, two people who may never have communicated with one another in person are able to build positive electronic relationships. Though not a substitute for face-to-face activities in multicultural education, electronic exchanges are an important way to begin building awareness of and appreciation for other cultures. One good resource for locating classroom keypals is http://epals.com

Individual and cooperative group research projects. Students can research a topic online working either by themselves or in groups, gathering information from electronic and paper-based sources. These research activities usually culminate in a presentation to the class and subsequent discussion of the findings. For example, students may be asked to tap various online databases for articles and reports on contributions by the space program to people's lives and modern culture. They may supplement this information with online conversations with experts they locate on the Internet. When the research is completed, the class report might include actual examples of these contributions as well as summaries delivered via multimedia or presentation software. (See Technology Integration Idea 8.1.)

Electronic mentoring (telementoring). Dyrli (1994) refers to subject matter experts who volunteer to work closely with students online as "electronic mentors" (p. 34). One source of aid in these activities—the Electronic Emissary Project at the University of Texas—links classes across the country with mentors on topics ranging from Greek literature to life support in space (p. 35). The Center for Children and Technology (CCT, 1996) describes three kinds of telementoring activities it set up to encourage young women to enter science, engineering, and other technology professions. However, they are useful strategies for all student mentoring activities and include guidance, discussion forums, and peer lounges.

- **One-to-one guidance.** Young people have private, individual "discussions" via e-mail links with professionals who give advice and guidance related to a particular field. (See Technology Integration Idea 8.2.) CCT says that before these discussions begin, mentors and students participate in separate online sessions to prepare for establishing these relationships. Mentors and students, for example, are asked to craft introductory biographies and set goals for their relationships (p. 3). Sources for telementors include Hewlett-Packard's program (http://www.telementor.org/) and the Electronic Emissary Project (http://emissary.ots.utexas.edu/emissary/index.html).
- **Discussion forums.** Students and mentors are linked in a mailing list that supports large-group discussions on topics of mutual interest. These are particularly useful in providing students with information and encouragement related to career pursuits.
- **Peer lounges.** These are smaller mailing lists set up to share information and ideas for dealing with problems and issues during large projects. A "lounge" is set up for mentors, one for students, and one for teachers. Mentors use the lounges to talk among themselves about mentoring techniques and how to deal with common problems or issues. Students use the lounge to discuss their projects and classroom issues. Teachers use the lounge to discuss their programs with other teachers. Each is considered a type of peer mentoring.

Electronic (or virtual) field trips. An electronic field trip in its simplest form fills classroom screens with visual images of a place considered to offer some educational value and to which students would not routinely be able to travel. Virtual trips are designed to explore unique locations around the world, and, by involving learners at those sites, to share the experience with other learners at remote locations. Trips may use only video programs or may include prepared curriculum guides, suggested preparation and follow-up activities, and discussion questions to help correlate experiences with specific curriculum objectives. Learners can interact with peers via telephone, computer, broadcast transmission, fax, and mail. Some typical examples of electronic field trips include a visit to the Great Wall of China, a walking tour of Washington, D.C., an exploration of an archaeological dig, and a trip to a state capitol during a legislative session. Through electronic field trips, many students imagine

TECHNOLOGY INTEGRATION IDEA 8.1

Research Projects:

TITLE: What's So Funny?

CONTENT AREA/TOPIC: Writing and cultural awareness

GRADE LEVEL: 10–11

NETS FOR STUDENTS: Standards 1, 3, 4, 5, 6

DESCRIPTION: Students use e-mail communications to explore the concept of humor from personal, cultural, and intercultural perspectives. Within individual classes, students begin to search for things they find humorous and discuss why they find particular situations, jokes, or people funny. In class and online with other schools/classes involved in the project, students then begin to look for cultural features of humor, discussing and sharing insights using e-mail as well as print materials prepared by the students. As the activity progresses, classes are encouraged to create products to send to other schools: original plays, interviews, original drawings, or jokes. Several final activities are suggested, but not planned in advance, giving students and teachers the opportunity to select their own culminating student, class, intraschool, or interschool activities. This activity helps deepen student understanding of humor and cultural differences in humor as well as to provide specific practice with computer interaction and collaborative project development. (Sharing information that is interesting to students is also an excellent international telecommunications activity.)

Source: Harris, J. (1994). Information collection activities. *The Computing Teacher, 21*(6), 32–33.

TECHNOLOGY INTEGRATION IDEA 8.2

Telementoring

TITLE: Partners Online

CONTENT AREA/TOPIC: Science

GRADE LEVEL: K–12

NETS FOR STUDENTS: Standards 1, 3, 4

DESCRIPTION: NASA has a site (http://quest.arc.nasa.gov) that students can go to pose questions to NASA experts about current space activities. NASA scientists participate in interactive chat sessions about topics ranging from the brain's functioning in microgravity to the Mars mission and space shuttle flights. The schedule of NASA experts chat sessions is available at the web site.

Source: Goldsworthy, R. (1999–2000). Collaborative classrooms. *Learning and Leading with Technology, 27*(4), 6–9, 17.

themselves leaving their neighborhoods and cities; they experience in some fashion the excitement and wonder of new places and faces—and they learn from the experience. (See Technology Integration Idea 8.3.)

Group development of products. Teachers have developed many variations on group development of products. For example, students may use e-mail to solicit and offer feedback on an evolving literary project, sometimes involving advice from professional authors. Or students may work independently toward an agreed-on goal, each student or group adding a portion of the final product. This is sometimes called *chain writing* (also described in Chapter 5 under word processing). For example, two different Missouri schools linked electronically to write and videotape a play. At one school, students developed a list of characters and a general plot outline and wrote Scenes 1 and 2. Students at the other school selected the topic for the play; developed the personalities, physical characteristics, and backgrounds of the characters; and wrote Scenes 3 and 4. Together the students developed the final story line and produced the play, exchanging the videotaped portions that they produced independently. (See Technology Integration Idea 8.4.)

Problem-based learning. Sage (2000) described problem-based learning or PBL as "learning organized around the investigation and resolution of an authentic, ill-structured problem" (p. 10). This kind of problem solving can take many forms, four of which are described here.

- **Collaborative problem solving.** This model involves several students or student groups working together to solve a problem. (See Technology Integration Idea 8.5.) These kinds of lessons were dubbed "WebQuests" by Bernie Dodge and Tom March at San Diego University and became a model for teachers across the country to use in creating their own lessons. All of these lessons give students a scenario and a task to do in response to it; usually they have a problem to solve or a project to complete.

TECHNOLOGY INTEGRATION IDEA 8.3

Virtual Field Trips

TITLE: Three Days in Munich

CONTENT AREA/TOPIC: Foreign languages

GRADE LEVEL: 6–8

NETS FOR STUDENTS: Standards 1, 3, 4, 5

DESCRIPTION: This activity lets students supplement and enhance their learning of a foreign language by planning a three-day "visit" to a foreign city on the Internet. The project in this article focuses on a German language activity, but the approach could be used with any foreign language learning. Teachers prepare for the lesson by browsing the city site themselves. In this lesson, the site used was the Young People's Guide to Munchen. On a map of Germany, the teacher points out the city of interest (e.g., Munich), passes around pictures of the city, and discusses basic characteristics such as the population and industries. Students form small groups of three to four. Each group member plans a portion of the trip: lodging, food, activities, and transportation. Each completes a teacher-designed worksheet of required information about the "trip."

Source: Bogard, E., Feyten, C., Green, J., and Taylor, G. (1997). Webspinning: Using the web to teach languages. *Learning and Leading with Technology, 24*(5), 26–28.

TECHNOLOGY INTEGRATION IDEA 8.4

Group Development of Products

TITLE: Fairy Tale Cyber Collection

CONTENT AREA/TOPIC: Writing and literature

GRADE LEVEL: K–2

NETS FOR STUDENTS: Standards 1, 3, 4

DESCRIPTION: Very young students get an opportunity to post their products on the WWW and compare them with those of other classes. Each teacher participating in the project selects a fairy tale and reads it aloud to the class. Students work together to retell the story in their own words, either writing or dictating it, depending on their skill level. Then they illustrate the story with their artwork. When the stories are developed and illustrated, they are posted on the web for all classes to read and enjoy. Teachers may choose to use these stories as the basis for many alphabet and spelling skills.

Source: Harris, J. (1997). Online to learn or in line with standards. *Learning and Leading with Technology, 28*(3), 10–15.

TECHNOLOGY INTEGRATION IDEA 8.5

Problem Solving

TITLE: The American Dream

CONTENT AREA/TOPIC: Social Studies

GRADE LEVEL: 4–10

NETS FOR STUDENTS: Standards 1, 3, 4

DESCRIPTION: In this WebQuest activity, students are asked to investigate and answer questions about the American dream. This activity makes use of the "American Memory Collection" at http://memory.loc.gov. Teachers begin by discussing the concept of the American dream. Then students write about their own visions of what the dream means to them personally and for the country. The teacher introduces the American Memory Collection and reviews research techniques for using it. Students assume roles within small groups to create a product that documents their vision for the American dream.

Source: Donlan, L. (1999). Come dream with us: America dreams. *Learning and Leading with Technology, 24*(5), 26–28.

- **Parallel problem solving.** In this strategy, students in a number of different locations can work on similar problems. They solve the problem independently and then compare their methods and results or build a database or other product with information gathered during the activity. Students in one school collaborating on a joint air quality project were surprised when they discovered through comparisons that their classroom air quality failed to meet minimum public health standards.
- **Real-time data analysis.** These activities allow students access to data from real phenomena such as weather or solar activity. Using these data, students are able to answer questions and solve problems posed for them. (See Technology Integration Idea 8.6.)
- **Simulated activities.** Two kinds of simulated activities can be done on the Internet. The first kind is a simulated activity that teachers can create. (See Technology Integration Idea 8.7.) An example of this is the Simulated Space Shuttle Program, in which different schools prepare for various missions that will take place during a specified launch period. The second kind of simulation is the web equivalent of simulation software. Hartley (2000) describes sites with a variety of virtual "labs" in which students can learn chemistry, physics, and math principles. Locations with such simulated labs include these: University of Oregon (http://jersey.uoregon.edu) and IrYdium (http://ir.chem.cmu.edu).

Social action projects. In this type of project, students are responsible for learning about and addressing important global social, economic, political, or environmental conditions. For example, students collaborating on a peace project write congressional representatives to voice concerns and present their viewpoints. The emphasis in this kind of project is collaboration to offer solutions to an issue of practical community (global or local) concern. (See Technology Integration Idea 8.8.)

TECHNOLOGY INTEGRATION IDEA 8.6

Real-Time Data Analysis

TITLE: Real-Time Earth and Space Science Data in the Classroom

CONTENT AREA/TOPIC: Earth and space science

GRADE LEVEL: 6–12

NETS FOR STUDENTS: Standards 1, 3, 4, 5, 6

DESCRIPTION: This lesson makes use of real-time physical data available on a continuous basis on the Internet, as well as image processing software to download and manipulate the data. For a period of time, students download daily data on phenomena such as weather (http://sel.noaa.gov/today.html) or solar conditions (http://umbra.nascom.nasa.gov/images/latest.html). Depending on what question they are addressing, they use one of four procedures to analyze these images: trend analysis, animation, enhancement, or measurement. Then they generate reports on what they have learned and share them with the class or other classes online.

Source: Slater, T. (1998). The data they are a'changin': Using realtime earth and space science data in the classroom. *Learning and Leading with Technology, 26*(2), 28–31, 36.

TECHNOLOGY INTEGRATION IDEA 8.7

Simulated Activities

TITLE: World Tour

CONTENT AREA/TOPIC: Interdisciplinary

GRADE LEVEL: 7–9

NETS FOR STUDENTS: Standards 1, 3, 4, 5, 6

DESCRIPTION: In this 2- to 3-week project, students create an imaginary band and take it on a world tour of eight cities in three different continents. After naming their band and designing a logo for it, they write letters to an agent describing their music, experience, and plans. They plan their itinerary by researching cities on the web and writing about their findings. In a foreign language class, they create a flyer describing their band using the language they are learning. In science, they research weather conditions in the cities. In math, they calculate airfare and other travel expenses and create a spreadsheet of their profits.

Source: Sosenke, F. (2000). World tour. *Learning and Leading with Technology, 27*(5), 32–35.

TECHNOLOGY INTEGRATION IDEA 8.8

Social Action Projects

TITLE: A Trashy Project

CONTENT AREA/TOPIC: Ecology

GRADE LEVEL: 5–7

NETS FOR STUDENTS: Standards 1, 2, 3, 4, 5, 6

DESCRIPTION: Students gather and compare data regarding the collection and dispersion of trash to see if one region conserves better than others and to assess grade level and day of the week differences. They collect information on the number of ounces of paper trash collected each day in their classroom. In addition to collecting data on the trash, students record the number in attendance each day to analyze the relative proportion of trash to the number of students. The data collected are then electronically transmitted to a central classroom where the information is pooled for distribution. The students hypothesize what the data might show and discuss local and collective data.

Source: Kelly, M., & Wiebe, J. (1994). Telecommunications, data gathering, and problem solving. *The Computing Teacher, 21*(7), 23–25.

Many other examples based on these categories of integration strategies are given in publications and web sites such as the ones listed here (also see Section 10 in the *Starting Out . . .* booklet):

- **Blue Web 'n Library** (http://www.kn.pacbell.com/wired/bluewebn/)
- **KIDPROJ** (http://www.kidlink.org/KIDPROJ/index.html)
- **The WebQuest Page** (http://edweb.sdsu.edu/webquest/webquest.html)
- **Discovery.com** (http://school.discovery.com/lessonplans/programs)
- **ThinkQuest** (http://www.thinkquest.org)

Web Site Support for Classroom Projects

Harris (1997) gives an excellent description with examples of ways to use web sites to support some types of distance learning activities. The following section summarizes Harris's work and shows that web sites can serve any of several functions or combination of functions.

Project overview, announcement, and application. Sites can introduce the goals and purposes of a project and invite people to participate. A global project, Canadian Kids from Kantata, gives a description designed to "encourage communication among indigenous peoples and later immigrants" (Harris, 1997, p. 17). The page gives a history, an explanation of how the groups involved are organized, a list of organizations and people who support the project, and links to complete an application to become a participant. The British Chatback Project's "Memories from 1945" gives information on how to subscribe to an e-mail discussion list or listserv.

Tutorial instruction. A site gives participants actual instruction and information on how to do project activities. For example, the I*EARN Learning Circle global classroom project gave a "linked set of hypertextually rich Web pages that provide step-by-step instruction for project participation" (Harris, 1997, p. 18).

Information repository and exchange. Students use web sites to add information to a collection that will be shared with others. KIDLINK's Multicultural Calendar database was a collection of descriptions written by students of holidays and festivals around the world. Students used the site to enter summaries and can search the resulting database by month, holiday, country, and author.

Project-related communication. Students working with others at distant sites share a web site to support their co-operative work. For example, a Colorado meteorologist posted a picture on a shared web site of a device students could build to help them complete an experiment in radiative processes (Harris, 1997, p. 19). These co-development web sites can be even more helpful if they build in streaming video or videoconferencing.

Project support. Web sites serve as links to resources to support project activities and make gathering information for project work more efficient.

Example project activities. "Chronology sites" exhibit an ongoing description of past, current, and planned project activities. In the GlobaLearn project, visitors to the site view artifacts found by explorers as they travel to various countries, "reporting" their findings on the web site.

Displays of student work. Students use sites to show off the products of their learning activities. Many Internet web sites show examples of students' poems, stories, pictures, and multimedia products.

Project-development centers. Finally, Web sites sometimes are set up for the specific purpose of inviting new distance learning projects. Some current ones are:

- Global SchoolNet Foundation (http://www.gsh.org)
- KIDPROJ (http://www.kidlink.org/KIDPROJ/index.html)

Directed Versus Constructivist Approaches to Integrating the Internet

The web-based activities described here can be implemented with a directed and systematic approach or with a more constructivist strategy. With directed distance learning projects, teachers tell students the purpose and objectives of the project and structure the learning activities. With constructivist projects, students develop their own goals and activities and the learning activities are more open ended. Steps in the two types of strategies are described here.

Developing directed lesson integration strategies. Many educators prefer a highly structured approach to Internet projects. Systematic planning helps ensure more efficient use of Internet resources and Royer (1997) gives a sequence for carrying out directed types of collaborative development activities. The steps she recommends are described here.

1. **Plan and prepare.** The teacher defines a project by specifying the purpose, objectives, unit activities, specifications, timeline, number of participants allowed, and logistical considerations.
2. **Post the project information.** Advertise the project on the Internet and invite participants. Include a registration form so that people can respond in a standard way with needed information. Respond to everyone who replies and, if the project is full, be sure to inform people quickly that they will not be part of this activity. As people register, post a listing of everyone registered and how many spaces are left.
3. **Carry out activities.** The teacher is responsible for ensuring that participants build motivation, keep on track, and complete products on time. Begin by having students introduce themselves and describe their backgrounds

and current activities. They may build web pages to accomplish this. Break the project into small components and set weekly or biweekly deadlines. Host a chat room, listserv, or e-mail exchange where people can discuss the project.

4. **Publish the product(s).** After the products are completed, send copies to everyone, both on paper and on the web. Send certificates of completion to each participating school.
5. **Evaluate the project.** The teacher should do a personal evaluation—documenting what went well and what didn't—and send questionnaires asking for comments to help make the next project better.

Developing constructivist lesson integration strategies. Constructivist models call for less structure set up by the teacher and more conceptual work done by students. Educators who try to get students to think critically about the world around them prefer this approach; they feel this kind of activity helps foster higher level skills in problem solving and analyzing information. Lamb, Smith, and Johnson (1997) describe steps to follow in a more open-ended, constructivist approach. They call their model for community-based learning on the web the "8 W's":

1. **Watching.** Have students begin by observing their environment in order to develop a purpose for their project. Ask them questions that lead them to think about social issues around them. Students keep journals to answer these questions and share their answers later with classmates. Then they begin to narrow the focus of their topic.
2. **Wondering.** Through brainstorming, discussing, and reflecting on their questions and ideas, students explore topics and focus on specific issues or concerns. For example, if the general topic is homeless people, the teacher poses questions to narrow the topic, such as "Where are homeless people in our town? What do they look like?"
3. **Webbing.** Students use a variety of electronic resources such as Internet sites as well as print resources to locate information and connect ideas.
4. **Wiggling.** In this phase, students look for clues, ideas, and perspectives by evaluating the quality of the information they have found. Students consider whether each information source is authoritative, objective, reliable, and relevant.
5. **Weaving.** This phase requires a high level of critical thinking as students begin to put together their ideas. They compare information from different sources, select information that seems most useful, organize the information into a solution, and decide on a way to express the results (a picture or chart).
6. **Wrapping.** Students "wrap" or package the information and solutions in a format (video, web site, or multimedia package) that will appeal to their intended audience.
7. **Waving.** In this phase, students publicize their involvement in the project and decide how to carry out the solutions they have developed. For example, they might decide to help alleviate homelessness by making a presentation to a county board or volunteering in a homeless shelter.
8. **Wishing.** In the final stage, students reflect on how the project went and what they have learned. They also analyze the impact of their work. For example, if they sent a report to a local legislator, did they get a response?

Assessing Web-Based Lessons

It should not be surprising that alternative educational systems such as distance learning tend to use a variety of nontraditional, alternative assessment strategies. A wealth of information on alternative assessment may be found at http://www.ncrel.org/sdrs/areas/as0cont.htm.

The Miami Museum of Science (http://www.miamisci.org/ph/lpdefine.html) describes four forms of alternative assessment, three of which are commonly used to assess online learning:

- **Authentic project assessment.** Teacher measures the student's ability to perform activities based on tasks and situations.
- **Portfolio assessment.** Students develop a "purposeful" collection of work that helps to define their efforts and achievements in specified area(s).
- **Journal assessment.** Students keep ongoing records of expressions, experiences, and reflections on a given topic. Teachers can require journals to use various modes of reflecting such as writing, drawing, painting, sculpting, and role-playing.

Each of these assessments requires teachers to use a rubric and/or checklist to determine the level of progress and accomplishment for each student. Many such instruments are available, but teachers frequently create their own matched to the task. Some teacher-created examples may be seen in the lessons at the Tom Snyder web site (http://online.tomsnyder.com). A rubric for judging the quality of WebQuests is available at http://edweb.sdsu.edu/webquest/webquestrubric.html. (Also see the Appendix.)

Offering Courses and Programs with Distance Technologies

Types and Examples of Distance Learning Courses and Programs

Web-based courses. Web courses became popular in higher education before they caught on at K–12 levels. However, since 1996, a virtual high school (VHS) movement has been thriving in the United States (Clark, 2001;

Loupe, 2001; Roblyer & Elbaum, 2000; Roblyer & Marshall, 2002). Funded by a federal grant in 1996, the Concord Consortium's Virtual High Schools project began offering courses in 1997 and was the first major VHS initiative with participating schools around the country. Since then, VHSs have emerged in many locations. Some VHS programs are created for use within existing "brick-and-mortar" schools (the Concord VHS schools); some are separate, completely online programs run by school districts or state departments (Florida Virtual High School); others were developed as special university projects; and still others are emerging as entrepreneurial enterprises of companies (Apex Learning).

VHS programs were established based on the belief that they could help close the Digital Divide by providing better educational access to students, regardless of their location or socioeconomic status. However, as with other types of distance learning programs, VHS courses have proven to have comparatively high dropout and failure rates. Also, students who sign up for them are predominantly Caucasian and taking courses for advanced placement or other elective upper level credit. This picture may be changing as schools provide better access to students taking VHS courses and encourage more students to take advantage of them. It has become clear that not all students can succeed in online environments (Roblyer & Marshall, 2002). Successful online students seem to need more than the usual degree of organization and self-motivation, as well as better than average computer skills.

The apparent success of many VHS courses also sparked interest in online courses at middle and even elementary school levels. Schools such as the Odyssey School in Las Vegas offer courses in kindergarten through eighth grades, primarily to students who cannot attend school or who cannot learn in traditional classroom settings. Former Secretary of Education William Bennett is chair of a firm opening an online school called K12. Its initial course offerings are for grades K–2, with plans to expand later to other grade levels (Loupe, 2001).

Web-based degree programs. Degree programs offered exclusively via the Internet also are becoming more common. Most web-based degree programs are offered by universities in higher education and several, such as the University of Phoenix, offer all courses and degrees completely online. A few VHS programs have obtained the state approvals needed to offer high school diplomas (Carr, 1999). The University of Missouri at Columbia High School opened its diploma program in October 1999, and Indiana University High School began its diploma program the following January; at that time it already had a waiting list of 500 students.

Characteristics of Effective Web-Based Courses and Programs

Basic requirements to implement web-based courses and programs. Although many instructional programs have online components, educators agree it is much more difficult to design and implement effective courses and programs that are exclusively web based. Two fundamental characteristics of organizations offer successful online instruction:

- **Trained course designers and instructors.** Putting a course online involves much more than transferring traditional course materials to the Internet, and experience has shown that not all good teachers make good online instructors. Most organizations that offer online courses put teachers through a rigorous training program that includes becoming a student in an online course, looking at effective online course models, and designing and trying out online units.
- **Administrative and technical support system.** Because teachers and students never meet face to face and are completely dependent on their online delivery system, organizations offering successful courses or programs must have extensive support systems in place to offer online registration, course materials, library services, and grade reporting. They also must have technical support staff on hand "24/7" to address problems promptly and efficiently.

Most organizations quickly realized that the administrative and technical support required for successful web-based courses and programs requires a considerable investment in infrastructure. Some, like Temple University, already have opted to limit their online offerings. Others, like the University of Maryland University College, continue to build their infrastructure—investing in the online future of education.

Characteristics of successful online courses. It has become clear during the past few years that effective online courses are not limited by content area, topic, or objective. Effective online courses have been offered in every content area from math to music and from physics to physical education. A review of these courses yields the following three common, essential characteristics:

- **Well-designed and structured courses.** Just as with any course, effective online courses must be well planned and systematically designed to take advantage of the unique capabilities and constraints of the learning environment. Marques, Hamza, and Alhalibi (1999) recommend a 10-step sequence to design effective virtual courses: (1) assess needs and necessary conditions to satisfy them; (2) estimate development cost, effort, and implications; (3) plan the virtual classroom; (4) design the virtual classroom; (5) prepare and distribute contents; (6) enable communication; (7) implement online student assessment methods; (8) implement class management procedures; (9) set up the system; and (10) maintain and update the virtual classroom. Alley and Jansek (2001) list 10 characteristics of a high-quality online learning environment:

1. Knowledge is constructed, not transmitted.
2. Students can take full responsibility for their own learning.

3. Students are motivated to want to learn.
4. The course provides "mental white space" for reflection.
5. Learning activities appropriately match student learning styles.
6. Experiential, active learning augments the web site environment.
7. Solitary and interpersonal learning activities are interspersed.
8. Inaccurate prior learning is identified and corrected.
9. "Spiral learning" provides for revisiting and expanding prior lessons.
10. The master teacher is able to guide the overall learning process.

■ **Engaging, collaborative activities.** Although some students prefer courses to be individual, tutorial-like ones where they work at their own pace through a sequence of tasks, the most enjoyable courses seem to be those in which students are highly engaged in discussion and collaboration. Many online courses encourage this kind of engagement through bulletin boards or conferences. Klemm (1998) described eight ways of achieving more student engagement through online conferences:

1. **Require participation.** Participation in each conference should be a required, graded activity rather than an optional one.
2. **Form learning teams.** If handled properly, collaborative activities can encourage a "team spirit" toward learning.
3. **Make activity interesting.** Appeal to student backgrounds, experiences, interests, and concerns.
4. **Don't settle for opinions.** Student contributions should be based on their readings and research.
5. **Structure the activity.** Have a specific series of tasks and a definite beginning and end to the activity.
6. **Require a deliverable.** The activity should revolve around a product to develop and turn in.
7. **Know what you're aiming for.** Set up expectations for adequate participation and communicate them clearly to students. Instructors should provide consistent, ongoing critiques and feedback to encourage involvement.
8. **Use peer grading.** Ask students to rate each other on their contributions to the conference. (This is the most controversial of Klemm's recommendations. Not all experts agree this is a workable strategy.)

■ **An interactive learning community.** Teachers and students agree that online courses are more motivating if they simulate the community one finds in a good face-to-face course. Solloway and Harris (1999) say that so-called "learning communities" in web-based courses are the result of careful planning and strong support by the instructor and a support team. However, it is becoming apparent that learning communities require more than just well-designed instruction. They also involve strategic, ongoing efforts on the part of the instructor to encourage student-to-student interaction, as well as student-to-instructor interaction, and to have students get to know each other as learners and as people. They are communities in the truest, most culture-based sense of the word.

Effective assessment strategies for online courses and programs. While alternative assessments are popular in online lessons, many online learning course systems also offer traditional assessment options. WebCT, for example, has a test module so instructors can develop objective tests, have students take them online, grade them automatically, and summarize test results across the class. Other systems such as UMUC's Web Tycho have an Assignments area in which students can post files of compositions and other electronic products.

An example of an online course developed on the University of Maryland University College (UMUC) Web Tycho system is shown in Figure 8.7.

Figure 8.7 Example of a Web-Based Course in UMUC's Web Tycho System

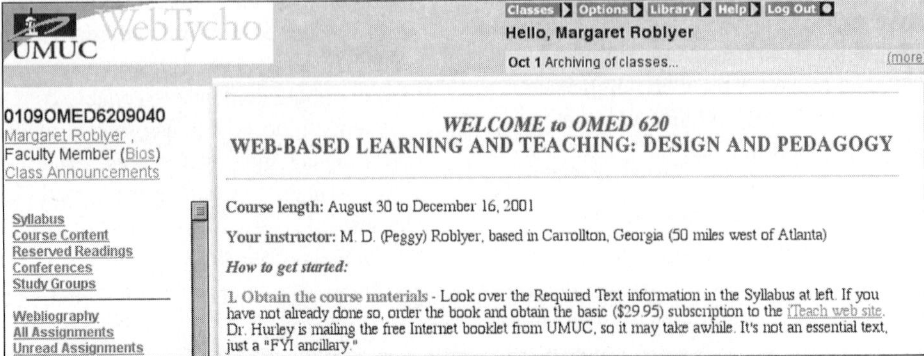

Source: Used by permission of the University of Maryland University College.

Exercises

Record and apply what you have learned.

Chapter 8 Self-Test

To review terms and concepts in this chapter, take the Chapter 8 self-test. Select Chapter 8 from the front page of the Companion Website (located at http://www.prenhall.com/roblyer), then choose the *Multiple Choice* module.

Portfolio Activities

ISTE The following activities address ISTE National Educational Technology Standards for Teachers (NETS-T) and will help you add to your professional portfolio. To complete these activities online and save or submit the materials electronically, select Chapter 8 from the front page of the Companion Website (http://www.prenhall.com/roblyer), then choose the *Portfolio* module.

1. ***An Internet Resource Map (NETS-T Standards: I-B, II-C, V-A)*** Develop a chart, diagram, multimedia presentation, or web page that documents in an easy-to-read format the names and purposes of each of the following Internet resources described in this chapter: web browsers, search engines, gophers, e-mail, listservs, bulletin boards, chat rooms, FTP, images and animation, regular and streaming video/audio, electronic whiteboards, MUDs and MOOs, videoconferencing, web authoring tools, push technologies, site capturing, intranets, Internet-TV, and avatars. Label or present the purpose of each resource. Give URL links to examples of each resource. (*Hint:* You can use the subheadings given in the chapter to group the resources into types. Make a graphic or a hotspot for each type, list or present graphically the resources under each heading, and connect the major types in a chart or multimedia stack.)
2. ***Personal Web Page (NETS-T Standards: V-A, D)*** Look at samples of personal home pages on the Internet. Use storyboards or sticky notes to plan a design for your own home page. If you have access to web page development software, develop your home page from your own design. Review your page and make sure it meets the criteria given in this chapter.

Questions for Thought and Discussion

These questions may be used for small-group or class discussion or may be subjects for individual or group activities. To take part in these discussions online, select Chapter 8 from the front page of the Companion Website (http://www.prenhall.com/roblyer), then choose the *Message Board* module.

1. In a 1998 debate in *Time* magazine, powerful representatives of two sides squared off. The following quotes are in response to this question: *Should schools be connected to the Internet?* Using information in this chapter combined with other readings, how would you respond to each of these statements?

   Vice President Al Gore: "Access to the basic tools of the information society is no longer a luxury for our children. It is a necessity. . . . We must give our children . . . the chance to succeed in the information age, and that means giving them access to the tools that are shaping the world in which they live."

   David Gelernter: "First learn reading, writing, history, and arithmetic. Then play Frisbee, go fishing, or surf the Internet. Lessons first, fun second. . . . If children are turned loose to surf, then Internet in the schools won't be a minor educational improvement, it will be a major disaster."
2. The following is a quote from the 2000 report *Fool's Gold: A Critical Look at Computers and Childhood* by the Alliance for Childhood:

   > Those who place their faith in technology to solve the problems of education should look more deeply into the needs of children. The renewal of education requires personal attention to students from good teachers and active parents, strongly supported by their communities. It requires commitment to developmentally appropriate education and attention to the full range of children's real low-tech needs—physical, emotional, and social, as well as cognitive.

   In light of the increasing importance of the Internet as an information resource and an instrument for students' research, how would you respond to this statement?

Collaborative Activities

The following activities address ISTE National Educational Technology Standards for Teachers (NETS-T) and can be done in small groups. Each group should present the findings to the class in a format they know how to use (word-processed report, presentation software, multimedia product). Completed group products can be copied and shared with the entire class and/or included in each person's personal portfolio:

1. ***Internet Ethical Issues (NETS-T Standards: VI-A through E)*** Select one of the following issues related to Internet use and do an Internet search for recent information and developments on the subject. Develop a web page to summarize the findings and share them with the class:
   - Objectionable materials and/or predators
   - Viruses
   - Copyright
   - Plagiarism
   - Netiquette
   - Student privacy
   - Accuracy of Internet information.
2. ***Web-Based Lesson Design (NETS-T Standards: II-A through E)*** Follow procedures outlined in Chapter 11 of the *Starting Out. . .* booklet to design a lesson that uses Internet resources to carry out one of the following models:
   - Electronic penpals or "keypals"
   - Individual and cooperative group research projects

- Electronic mentoring (telementoring)
- Electronic (or virtual) field trips
- Group development of products
- Collaborative problem solving
- Parallel problem solving
- Real-time data analysis
- Social action projects.

3. ***Web-Based Courses and Programs*** Working in small groups, go to each of the following sites and review the online programs and courses. Identify examples of design and support processes they have put into place to ensure their online instruction is effective. Make a presentation of your findings for the class:

High Schools:
Concord Consortium VHS Project (http://vhs.concord.org)
Florida Online High School (http://www.flhs.net)
Kentucky VHS Project (http://vhs.concord.org)
Maryland VHS (http://www.kvhs.org)
University Online Degree Programs:
University of Maryland University College (http://www.umuc.edu)
Pennsylvania State University World Campus (http://www.worldcampus.psu.edu/pub/index.shtml)
University of Phoenix (http://www.universityofphoenix.com)
Western Governors University (http://www.wgu.edu/wgu/index.html)

Integrating Technology Across the Curriculum Activities

The *Integrating Technology Across the Curriculum* CD-ROM is a set of technology integration ideas and links to online lessons, arranged as a searchable database. The CD comes packaged with this textbook. Complete the following exercise using this CD:

Look at the section of this chapter entitled "Types and Examples of Web-Based Lessons and Projects." Examples from the CD have been identified for most of the strategies described in this section. Locate examples on the CD for the rest of the strategies. Make a chart like the one at right listing the strategies and the integration ideas.

Sample Integration Ideas for Internet Strategies

Internet Integration Strategies	Name of Integration Idea from CD
Electronic mentoring	
Discussion forums	
Peer lounges	
Parallel problem solving	

References

Abilock, D. (1996). Integrating e-mail into the curriculum. *Technology Connection, 3*(5), 23–25.

Adler, S. (2000). The ABCs of PDFs. *Technology & Learning, 21*(3), 41–46.

Alley, L., & Jansek, K. (2001). The ten keys to quality assurance and assessment in online learning. *Journal of Interactive Instructional Development, 13*(3), 3–18.

Bailey, G., & Blythe, M. (1998). Outlining, diagramming, and storyboarding, or how to create great educational web sites. *Learning and Leading with Technology, 25*(8), 6–11.

Bernard, R., & Amundsen, C. (1989). Antecedents to dropout in distance education: Does one model fit all? *The Journal of Distance Education, 4*(2), 25–46.

Biemiller, L., & Young, J. R. (1998, May 15). Spending bill provides $37 million for improving the Internet. *The Chronicle of Higher Education, 44*(36), A31.

Biner, P. (1993). The development of an instrument to measure student attitudes toward televised courses. *The American Journal of Distance Education, 7*(1), 62–73.

Bull, G., Bull, G., & Bull, S. (2000). Java applets. *Learning and Leading with Technology, 27*(8), 42–45.

Bull, G., Bull, G., & Dawson, K. (1999). The universal solvent. *Learning and Leading with Technology, 27*(2), 36–39.

Bull, G., Bull, G., & Lewis, D. (1998). Introducing dynamic HTML. *Learning and Leading with Technology, 26*(2), 43–45.

Bull, G., Bull, G., & Sigmon, T. (1997a). Interactive web pages. *Learning and Leading with Technology, 24*(6), 13–17.

Bull, G., Bull, G., & Sigmon, T. (1997b). Common protocols for shared communities. *Learning and Leading with Technology, 25*(1), 50–53.

Bybee, D. (1996). Congress passes telecommunications act of 1996. *ISTE Update, 8*(5), 1.

Cafolla, R., & Knee, R. (1996). Creating World Wide Web sites. *Learning and Leading with Technology, 24*(3), 6–9.

Cafolla, R., & Knee, R. (1996–1997). Creating World Wide Web sites: Part II—Implementing your site. *Learning and Leading with Technology, 24*(4), 36–39.

Cafolla, R., & Knee, R. (1997). Creating educational web sites: Part III—Refining and maintaining the site. *Learning and Leading with Technology, 24*(5), 13–16.

Carnavale, D., & Young, J. (2001, July 13). Telecourses change channels. *The Chronicle of Higher Education.* Available online: http://chronicle.com/weekly/v47/i44/44a02901.htm.

Carpenter, C. (1996). Online ethics: What's a teacher to do? *Learning and Leading with Technology, 23*(6), 40–41, 60.

Carr, S. (1999, December 10). Two more universities start diploma-granting virtual high schools. *The Chronicle of Higher Education.* Available online: http://chronicle.com.

Carr, S. (2001, July 13). PBS sticks to its strategy for telecourses. Unafraid of competition from the Internet. *The Chronicle of Higher Education.* Available online: http://chronicle.com/weekly/v47/i44/44a03102.htm.

Center for Children and Technology. (1996). Telementoring: Using telecommunications to develop mentoring relationships. *CCT Notes, 4*(1), 1–3.

Cheng, H., Lehman, J., & Armstrong, P. (1991). Comparison of performance and attitude in traditional and computer conferencing classes. *The American Journal of Distance Education, 5*(3), 51–64.

Clark, T. (2001, October). *Virtual schools: Trends and issues.* Report commissioned by the Distance Learning Resource Network, a WestEd Project. Co-sponsored by the Centre for the Application of Information Technologies at Western Illinois University. Available online: http://www.dlrn.org/trends.html

Coulter, B., Feldman, A., & Konold, C. (2000). Rethinking online adventures. *Learning and Leading with Technology, 28*(1), 42–47.

Coussement, S. (1995). *Educational telecommunication: Does it work? An attitude study* (ERIC Document Reproduction No. 391 465).

Cyrs, T. E. (1997). Competence in teaching at a distance. In T. E. Cyrs (Ed.), *Teaching and learning at a distance: What it takes to effectively design, deliver, and evaluate programs.* San Francisco: Jossey-Bass.

D'Ignazio, F. (1996). Think intranet. *Learning and Leading with Technology, 24*(1), 62–63.

Dille, B., & Mezack, M. (1991). Identifying predictors of high risk among community college telecourse students. *The American Journal of Distance Education, 5*(1), 24–35.

Dillon, C., Hengst, H., & Zoller, D. (1991). Instructional strategies and student involvement in distance education: A study of the Oklahoma televised instruction system. *Journal of Distance Education, 6*(1), 28–41.

Dyrli, O. (1994). Riding the Internet schoolbus: Places to go and things to do. *Technology and Learning, 15*(2), 32–40.

Elmer-Dewitt, P. (1995, July). On a screen near you: Cyberporn. *Time Magazine, 146,* 1.

Everhart, N. (1997). Web page evaluation: Views from the field. *Technology Connection, 4*(3), 24–26.

Fabos, B., & Young, M. (1999). Telecommunication in the classroom: Rhetoric versus reality. *Review of Educational Research, 69*(3), 217–259.

Fulford, C., & Zhang, S. (1993). Perceptions of interaction: The critical predictor in distance education. *The American Journal of Distance Education, 7*(3), 8–21.

Furst-Bowie, J. (1997). Comparison of student reactions in traditional and videoconferencing courses in training and development. *International Journal of Instructional Media, 24*(3), 197–205.

Gelernter, D. (1998, May 25). Should schools be wired to the Internet: No: Learn first, surf later. *Time Magazine, 151*(20), 55.

Gibson, C., & Graf, A. (1992). Impact of adults' preferred learning styles and perception of barriers on completion of external baccalaureate degree programs. *Journal of Distance Education, 7*(1), 39–51.

Gore, A. (1998, May 25). Should schools be wired to the Internet:Yes, it's essential to the way kids learn. *Time Magazine, 151*(20), 54.

Gray, T. (1997). No crazy gods. *Learning and Leading with Technology, 25*(1), 43–45.

Gross, P. (1997). Engaging the disengaged: How is it different when using distance education? In *Walking the tightrope: The balance between innovation and leadership. Proceedings of the Annual International Conference of the Chair Academy,* Reno, NV (pp. 56–60) (ERIC Document Reproduction No. 407 008).

Guernsey, L. (1998, March 27). Colleges debate the wisdom of having on-campus students enroll in online classes. *The Chronicle of Higher Education Online.* Available online: http://chronicle.com.

Hardy, D. W., & Boaz, M. H. (1997). Learner development: Beyond the technology. In T. E. Cyrs (Ed.), *Teaching and learning at a distance: What it takes to effectively design, deliver, and evaluate programs.* San Francisco: Jossey-Bass.

Harris, J. (1994). Teaching teachers to use telecomputing tools. *The Computing Teacher, 22*(2), 60–63.

Harris, J. (1997). Content and intent shape function: Designs for web-based educational telecomputing activities. *Learning and Leading with Technology, 24*(5), 17–20.

Harris, J. (1997–1998). Wetware: Why use activity structures? *Learning and Leading with Technology, 25*(4), 13–17.

Harris, J. (1998a). Assistive annotations: The art of recommending web sites. *Learning and Leading with Technology, 25*(6), 58–61.

Harris, J. (1998b). *Virtual architecture: Designing and directing curriculum-based telecomputing.* Eugene, OR: ISTE.

Harris, J. (2000). Taboo topic no longer: Why telecollaborative projects sometimes fail. *Learning and Leading with Technology, 27*(5), 36–41.

Hartley, K. (2000). Online simulations. *Learning and Leading with Technology, 28*(3), 32–35.

Hawkins, J., & Macmillan, K. (1993). So what are teachers doing with this stuff? *Electronic Learning, 13*(2), 26.

Hoffman, D., & Novak, T. (1999, July). *The growing digital divide: Implications for an open research agenda.* Report sponsored by the Markle Foundation. Nashville, TN: Vanderbilt University, Owen Graduate School of Management. Available online: http://www.markle.org/index.stm.

Jerram, P. (1995). Videoconferencing gets in sync. *New Media, 5*(7), 48, 50–55.

Kearsley, G., Hunter, B., & Furlong, M. (1992). *We teach with technology.* Wilsonville, OR: Franklin, Beedle, & Associates, Inc.

Klemm, W. (1998). Eight ways to get students more engaged in online conferences. *T.H.E. Journal, 26*(1), 62–64.

Klesius, J., Homan, S., & Thompson, T. (1997). Distance education compared to traditional instruction: The students' view. *International Journal of Instructional Media, 24*(3), 207–220.

Knee, R., Musgrove, A., and Musgrove, J. (2000). Lights, camera, action: Streaming video on your web site. *Learning and Leading with Technology, 28*(1), 50–53.

Lamb, A., Smith, N., & Johnson, L. (1997). Wondering, wiggling, and weaving: A new model for project- and community-based learning on the Web. *Learning and Leading with Technology, 24*(7), 6–13.

Lim, C. (2001). Computer self-efficacy, academic self-concept, and other predictors of satisfaction and future participation of adult distance learners. *The American Journal of Distance Education, 15*(2), 41–52.

Loupe, D. (2001). Virtual schooling. *eSchool News, 4*(6), 41–47.

Ludlow, B. L. (1994). A comparison of traditional and distance education models. In *Proceedings of the Annual National*

Conference of the American Council on Rural Special Education, Austin, TX (ERIC Document Reproduction No. ED 369 599).

Machtmes, K., & Asher, J. (2000). A meta-analysis of the effectiveness of telecourses in distance education. *The American Journal of Distance Education, 14*(1), 27–46.

Marques, O., Hamza, K., & Alhalibi, B. (1999). How to design a virtual classroom: 10 easy steps to follow. *T.H.E. Journal, 27*(2), 96–98, 100, 102, 104, 106, 108–109.

McClelland, D. (1997, August). Web publishing made easy. *MacWorld, 1*(8), 104–110.

McCullen, C. (2001). Going the distance. . .with technology. *Technology & Learning, 21*(7), 45–47.

McHenry, L., & Bozik, M. (1997). From a distance: Student voices from the interactive video classroom. *TechTrends, 42*(6), 20–24.

McNabb, M. (2001). In search of appropriate usage guidelines. *Learning and Leading with Technology, 29*(2), 50–54.

Mitchell, K., Finkelhor, D., & Wolak, J. (2001). Risk factors for and impact of online sexual solicitation of youth. *Journal of the American Medical Association, 285*(23), 3011–3014.

Molnar, A. (1978). The next great crisis in American education: Computer literacy. *AEDS Journal, 12*(1), 11–20.

Monaghan, P. (1998, June 19). University of Washington professors decry governor's visions for technology. *The Chronicle of Higher Education Online.* Available online: http://chronicle.com.

Moore, M. (1995). The death of distance. *The American Journal of Distance Education, 9*(3), 1–4.

Moore, M. G., & Kearsley, G. (1996). *Distance education: A systems view.* Belmont, CA: Wadsworth Publishing Co.

Moskal, P., Martin, B., & Foshee, N. (1997). Educational technology and distance education in central Florida: An assessment of capabilities. *The American Journal of Distance Education, 11*(1), 6–22.

Munro, K. (1998, March 24). Monitor a child's access. Internet parental filtering utilities. *PC Magazine, 17,* 185–194.

National Center for Education Statistics. (2001). Internet access in U.S. public schools and classrooms. Washington, DC: NCES. Available online: http://nces.ed.gov/pubsearch/pubsinfo.asp?pubid = 2001071.

Odasz, F. (1999–2000). Collaborative Internet tools. *Learning and Leading with Technology, 27*(4), 11–15.

Osborn, V. (2001). Identifying at-risk students in videoconferencing and web-based distance education. *The American Journal of Distance Education, 15*(1), 41–54.

Osiakwan, C., & Wright, D. (2001). Distance training for operating equipment: A cost–benefit and return-on-investment analysis. *The American Journal of Distance Education, 15*(1), 69–79.

Randall, N. (1998, March 24). Defend against invaders. Internet desktop security utilities. *PC Magazine, 17,* 177–182.

Repp, R. (1999). The World Wide Web: Interfaces, databases, and applications to education. *Learning and Leading with Technology, 26*(6), 40–41, 60–61.

Richards, C., and Ridley, D. (1997). Factors affecting college students' persistence in online computer-managed instruction. *College Student Journal, 31,* 490–495.

Riddle, J. (1990). *Measuring affective change: Students in a distance learning class.* Paper presented at the Annual Meeting of the Northern Rocky Mountain Educational Research Association, Greeley, CO (ERIC Document Reproduction No. ED 325 514).

Roblyer, M. (1992). Electronic hands across the ocean: The Florida–England connection. *The Computing Teacher, 19*(5), 16–19.

Roblyer, M. D. (1998). Is distance ever really dead: Comparing the effects of distance learning and face-to-face courses. *Learning and Leading with Technology, 25*(8), 32–34.

Roblyer, M. D. (1999). Is choice important in distance learning? A study of students' motives for taking Internet-based courses at community college and high school levels. *Journal of Research on Computing in Education, 32*(1), 157–171.

Roblyer, M. D. (2000). Digital desperation: Research reports on a growing technology and equity crisis. *Learning and Leading with Technology, 27*(8), 50–53, 61.

Roblyer, M. D., & Ekhaml, L. (2000). How interactive are your distance courses? A rubric for assessing interactivity in distance learning. *Online Journal of Distance Learning Administration, 3*(2). Available online: http://www.westga.edu/~distance/summer32.htm.

Roblyer, M. D., & Elbaum, B. (2000). Virtual learning? Research on the status of virtual high schools. *Learning and Leading with Technology, 27*(4), 58–61.

Roblyer, M. D., & Guarino, T. (1999). Why do students choose distance learning or face-to-face course delivery? *Journal of Research in Education, 9*(1), 84–85.

Roblyer, M. D., & Marshall, J. (2002). Predicting success of virtual high school distance learners: Preliminary results from an educational success prediction instrument. *Journal of Research on Technology in Education* (in press).

Roblyer, M. D., & McKenzie, B. (2000). Distant but not out-of-touch: What makes an effective distance learning instructor? *Learning and Leading with Technology, 27*(6), 50–53.

Roblyer, M. D., and Wiencke, W. (2002, under review). Design and use of a rubric to assess and encourage interactive qualities in distance courses.

Rose, D. (1994). *Minding your cybermanners on the Internet.* Indianapolis, IN: Alpha Books.

Ross, T. W., & Bailey, G. D. (1996). Creating safe Internet access. *Learning and Leading with Technology, 24*(1), 51–53.

Royer, R. (1997). Teaching on the Internet: Creating a collaborative project. *Learning and Leading with Technology, 25*(3), 6–11.

Russell, T. L. (1992). Television's indelible impact on distance education: What we should have learned from comparative research. *Research in Distance Education, 4*(4), 2–4.

Russell, T. L. (1997). *The "no significant difference" phenomenon as reported in research reports, summaries, and papers.* Raleigh: Office of Instructional Telecommunications, North Carolina State University.

Sage, S. (2000). A natural fit: Problem-based learning and technology standards. *Learning and Leading with Technology, 28*(1), 6–12.

Seamon, D. (1999). Expanded description of SGML. *Learning and Leading with Technology, 27*(2), 39.

Shea, V. (1994). *Netiquette.* San Francisco: Albion Books.

Sherritt, C. (1996). *A fundamental problem with distance programs in higher education* (ERIC Document Reproduction No. ED 389 906).

Simonson, M., Smaldino, S., Albright, M., and Zvacek, S. (2000). *Teaching and learning at a distance: Foundations of distance education.* Upper Saddle River, NJ: Merrill/Prentice Hall.

Skipton, C. (1997, May 5). As the worlds turn: VRML authoring and modeling software. *New Media, 7*(6).

Smith, C. K. (1996). Convenience vs. connection: Commuter students' views on distance learning. Paper presented at the Annual Forum of the Association for Institutional Research, Albuquerque, NM (ERIC Document Reproduction No. ED 397 725).

Solloway, S., & Harris, E. (1999). Creating community online. *Educom Review, 34*(2). Available online: http://www.educause.edu/ir/library/html/erm99021.html.

Stephenson, N. (1992). *Snow crash.* New York: Bantam Books.

Thomerson, D., & Smith, C. (1996). Student perceptions of the affective experiences encountered in distance learning courses. *The American Journal of Distance Education, 10*(3), 37–48.

Thompson, G. (1990). How can correspondence-based distance learning be improved? A survey of attitudes of students who are not well disposed toward correspondence study. *Journal of Distance Education, 5*(1), 53–65.

Threlkeld, R., & Brzoska, K. (1994). Research in distance education. In B. Willis (Ed.), *Distance education: Strategies and tools.* Englewood Cliffs, NJ: Educational Technology Publications.

Trend, D. (2001). *Welcome to cyberschool.* Lanham, MD: Rowman and Littlefield.

Van Dusen, G. (1997). *The virtual campus: Technology and reform in higher education.* ERIC Digest. Washington, DC: ERIC Clearinghouse on Higher Education (ERIC Document Reproduction No. ED 412 815).

Wallace, L. (1996). Changes in the demographics and motivations of distance education students. *Journal of Distance Education, 11*(1), 1–31.

Walsh, J., & Reese, B. (1995). Distance learning's growing reach. *T.H.E. Journal, 22*(11), 58–62.

Wang, A., & Newlin, M. (2000). Characteristics of students who enroll and succeed in web-based classes. *Journal of Educational Psychology, 92*(1), 137–143.

Westbrook, T. (1997). Changes in students' attitudes toward graduate business instruction via interactive television. *The American Journal of Distance Education, 11*(1), 55–69.

Wilkes, C., & Burnham, B. (1991). Adult learner motivations and electronic distance education. *The American Journal of Distance Education, 5*(1), 43–51.

Withrow, F. (1992). Distance learning: Star schools. *Metropolitan Universities, 3*(1), 61–65.

Wolcott, L. (1996). Distant, but not distanced. A learner-centered approach to distance education. *TechTrends, 41*(4), 23–27.

Zirkin, B., & Sumler, D. (1995). Interactive or non-interactive: That is the question!!! An annotated bibliography. *Journal of Distance Education, 10*(1), 95–112.

9 CHAPTER

A Link to the Future: Emerging Developments in Technology Integration

William R. Wiencke, University of West Georgia

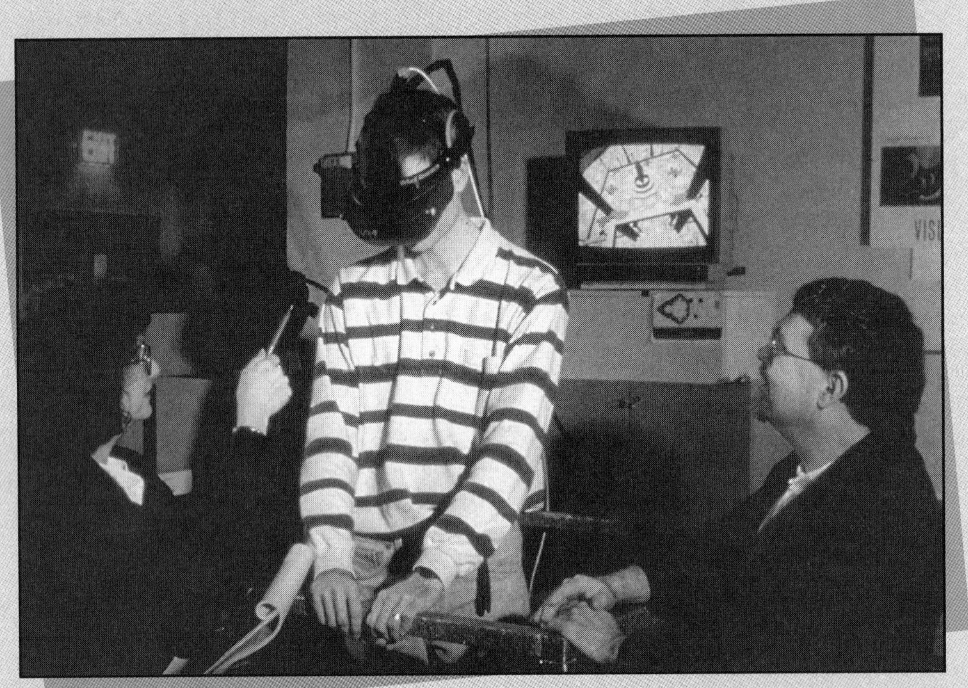

In the evenings on the planet Mars, when the fossil sea is warm and motionless, Mr. K sits in his room, listening to his book. . . .

From *The Martian Chronicles*, a screenplay based on the book by Ray Bradbury

The best way to predict the future is to create it.

Peter F. Drucker

Any sufficiently advanced technology is indistinguishable from magic.

Arthur C. Clark, *The Lost Worlds of 2001*

This chapter covers the following topics:

- Four kinds of technology trends that will shape learning environments in the future
- Capabilities, applications, benefits, and limitations of emerging technologies in four areas

Objectives

1. Identify emerging technologies in each of four areas:
   - Networking
   - Handheld systems (innovative equipment)
   - Visualization
   - Human-to-computer interfaces.
2. Identify applications of these technologies for education.
3. Based on predictions of developments in technical resources, develop a personal vision for the kind of role technology will play in shaping a future education system.
4. Describe professional skills required by educators and students who wish to benefit from, cope with, and help direct emerging technology developments.

Introduction: Classrooms and Other Learning Environments of the Future

A wise observer once remarked that today's science fiction is tomorrow's reality. The "audible texts" that sang to Ray Bradbury's futuristic Martians are now the interactive storybooks our children use at school and the books-on-tape we listen to in our cars. Soon we will listen to our interactive e-books and speak to our electronic librarians. Visions of the future are suffused with images of technologies that may seem magical and far fetched now, just as cellular phones and fax machines seemed only a few decades ago. And, though the technology images we see when we look into the future of education are murky and ill defined, we know that they will mirror current technical trends and the goals and priorities we set today for tomorrow's education.

Peter Drucker's observation has never seemed so relevant as when we consider the potential of technology for education. The "futuristic" developments described in this chapter either already exist or will likely become commonplace in the near future, and they have nearly unlimited potential for altering educational opportunities. As with so many "miraculous" technologies, the question is how we will take advantage of their capabilities to bring about the kind of future education systems our society wants and our economy needs.

The purposes of this chapter are to describe the trends in hardware, software, and applications development that drive societal uses of technology and to present a vision for how these trends could be reflected in a restructured educational system in the near future. Each of the futuristic technologies that are likely to play an important role is described, along with current integration strategies and those that may develop. Because teachers will play a critically important role in shaping this future, we end the chapter by describing some skills and sense of mission teachers must acquire in order to take part in this activity.

Historical Reinvention: A Technology-Infused History Curriculum Unit in the Not-Too-Distant Future

Kay is sitting in the Local Learning Lab (LLL), listening to her e-book. She is reviewing videos of the historical period 1774–1776 that she downloaded from the library as well as summaries she wrote and recorded about these events in her English classes. These activities are preparing Kay for her role in the first of five virtual reality (VR) simulations in a unit called *Historical Reinvention,* a component of her virtual American history class. The VR activities in the unit are described here.

- **Part 1. 1776: Decisions Past, Decisions Possible.** What key decisions were made in 1776? Who helped make them? Why were they made? What impact did they have on subsequent American history? What would have been different if different decisions had been made?
- **Part 2. 1860: Uncivil War.** What impact did the decisions of 1776 have on events of a century later? What would have been different at this time if other decisions had been made in 1776?
- **Part 3. 1900: Industrious America.** What would our country's entry into the Industrial Age have been like if different decisions had been made in 1776?
- **Part 4. 1945: Our World at War.** How would the world be today if different decisions had been made in 1776? Would there have been a world war? If so, would our role in it have been different?
- **Part 5. Current Day: The Past as Prologue.** What would our world have been like today if different decisions had been made in 1776?

In the first VR activity, Kay plays the role of Lyman Hall, one of the signers of the Declaration of Independence. It is her job to represent Hall's opinions and concerns as they would have been at that time and make the decisions for him in the first series of meetings held in 1775–1776 to discuss the controversial topic of American liberty.

Kay is not happy about having to play the part of a man in this simulation, but she already has learned from her research and discussion groups that there were no women in the Philadelphia congress. She knows she can play a female in each of the other four simulations because they take place at various time periods after 1776. She has worked hard to prepare for this VR role-playing activity by reading the materials her teacher has introduced, participating in videoconferencing discussion groups, researching the online history databases, and writing analyses of the decisions made at these historical meetings. At first, it was a little overwhelming, but she is beginning to understand her Lyman Hall character and see how his background and that of his Georgia associates helped shape his decisions in 1776. Since the students have the power to make different decisions from those made by the men in Philadelphia, she has decided to do one thing differently from what Hall actually did. She is determined to vote against allowing slavery in this new country and, through her research, she thinks she has found a way to make a case for Hall taking this position. If everyone agrees with her and slavery is prohibited in the Declaration of Independence, she is interested to see what impact this will have on the subsequent VR simulations.

The LLL is in the community center near her home, and soon Kay is joined there by several classmates and an American history resource teacher. They all don their VR gear, headsets, and arm covers that allow them to join students and teachers in a virtual environment that includes students at two schools and three other LLLs in various locations in the school district. All students in the county high schools are taking this American history course together in what the state calls *distributed learning environments.* These are several "congresses" like hers whose members are connected by high-speed networks to each other. Each meets in the virtual class using the avatars they developed in their art class using graphics toolkits. Kay's art teacher helped her make her avatar look like the pictures she found of Lyman Hall. The VR environment created by computer science classes looks like the room in Philadelphia where the pioneers of American liberty met in 1775. Kay is excited and eager to start the simulation; she is ready to make history.

Issues Shaping the Use of Emerging Technologies

Education's use of "magical" technological developments on the horizon are not without problems and controversies. Several issues will shape the impact of these trends on teaching and learning:

- **Hardware development will continue to outstrip software abilities to take advantage of them.** This has been the case since computer development began its race in the 1970s, and we have seen no tendency to alter this course. Computer processors not only continue to be smaller, faster, and more capable, but operating systems often are behind in their ability to take advantage of these capabilities. In addition, other technologies such as memory and data storage that are required to support the processors are more difficult to develop at the same pace.
- **Education's response to new technologies.** Most of the developments discussed in this chapter come to us by way of military applications and the entertainment industry. Business tends to profit first from these developments, followed much later by education. This trend of the better funded areas of our society driving technology innovation seems unlikely to change. Education typically uses technological methods well past the time that newer, more capable tools become available. Integrating technology into instructional methods has traditionally been a long, slow process—a trend unlikely to change even as society changes around it.
- **Lack of access means lack of educational opportunities.** Now and for some time to come, there will be students whose families and schools cannot afford access to the technologies discussed here. As these resources become more central to education, this lack of access will translate ever more quickly into limited learning opportunities unless special efforts are made to provide them.
- **Developments in brain mapping.** As a result of work on mapping the functions of various areas of the human brain, much has been revealed about human learning and behavior. However, the implications of this new knowledge for guiding educational methods are still very controversial. Although one often hears references to "brain-based" education and "brain-friendly" classroom environments, few guidelines exist for connecting brain research to such strategies and no studies exist to indicate any impact on students' achievement.

Four Trends Driving the Use of Emerging Technologies in Education

Trends in emerging technologies and new developments in older technologies hold promise for making fundamental changes in our society and its education systems. Some of these trends are apparent to us right now; some will become clearer in the next few years.

The trends described here do not focus directly on the Internet, which many agree has had and will continue to have a dramatic influence on education and work. (See Chapter 8.) Denby (2000) predicts that the Internet's successor, called the *Evernet,* will be a system that is available to us anytime and anywhere through wireless connections. The Internet, while an existing technology, will make it possible for us to take advantage of new trends and will help reap the advantages of many of the advanced capabilities discussed in this chapter.

This chapter also does not focus on artificial intelligence (AI), which has been a staple of science fiction's vision of the future. AI has not had the same level of impact on education as it has had on activities such as chess playing and industrial training and problem solving. Some still predict that computers will be smarter than humans in 20 years, but Bringsjord (2001) is among those who doubt that computers ever will have the capability to solve many of the routine problems humans do. He says that computers "have inner lives on a par with rocks. No amount of processing speed will ever surmount that obstacle" (p. 33). Although expert systems have seen use in industry training, education applications such as the ALEKS system, which is used to assess learning of factual knowledge in arithmetic and algebra (Canfield, 2001), are still rare. Some R&D experts in education predict many applications in the future (Mason-Mason & Tessmer, 2000). However, at this writing AI has yet to have the long-awaited impact once predicted for it.

Trend 1: Emerging Developments in Networking

Wireless Networking

Today, it would be difficult to find a school facility that does not have some sort of local-area network (LAN). Networks provide access to both administrative and instructional resources in the classroom, the media center, computer lab, and the administrative office. The addition of an Internet gateway adds the resources of the World Wide Web to all systems connected to the LAN.

Almost all school networks use some sort of fixed-wire configuration to connect the computers or nodes. However, recently a new method of connecting systems using wireless technology has come into greater use. Although wireless technologies have been available for some time, their use had been limited by their higher cost and the lack of standardization. Today, equipment costs are coming down and a new standard from the Institute of Electrical and Electronics Engineers (Yager, 2001) has provided the industry with the guidelines necessary to support the interconnection of a diverse number of wireless devices.

In the past, schools chose to use a wireless infrastructure primarily as a cost-effective means to connect a building's systems when traditional wiring proved too expensive. This was often the case when the design and structural materials in older buildings provided physical impediments to the running of wire (Dominick, 2000). This was usually a solution of last resort at a cost many times greater than if standard wire could have been used.

Today a facility can be totally wireless or use a combination of traditional wire and wireless technologies. Wireless networks require placement of access points at strategic locations where people will be using computers. Typical wireless coverage is a 300-foot radius from the access point. (See Figure 9.1.) However, variables such as building materials and room layout can impact this figure. In addition to access points, each device that will utilize wireless access requires a network interface card (NIC) capable of connecting to the wireless system. Wireless technologies will continue to decrease in cost and increase in speed.

Interoperability

Two other factors impact the growth of these systems, security and interoperability. These two factors are also closely related. Interoperability refers to the capability of wireless devices to communicate with each other as well as the many peripheral devices (e.g., printers and scanners) to which users of traditional LANs have become accustomed. As of 2002, two protocols exist: Bluetooth, developed by a consortium of companies including IBM, 3COM, Ericsson,

Figure 9.1 Apple AirPort Wireless Network Access Point

Source: Used by permission of Apple Computer. Photo © 2002 by Hunter Freeman.

Intel, Agere Systems, Microsoft, Motorola, Nokia, and Toshiba, and Jini from Sun Microsystems (Guerard, 2000). Although these technologies support traditional peripheral devices, they also open up access to an entire range of devices including projection systems, headsets, cell phones, and other handheld devices.

Linking devices provide a foundation that allows portable wireless devices to move from one network community to another and be seamlessly recognized and accepted by the new network. This ease of movement between divergent networks, although simplifying movement, increases problems with the second factor: security. The systems must be able to allow easy access but also secure the network from unwanted intruders. In addition, data that are free from the confines of wires are more likely to be received by others for whom the information is not intended. Wireless security issues are being addressed. However, secure access must be provided before wireless technology can be fully implemented.

Trend 2: Emerging Developments in Visualization

Although the Internet was first established during the 1970s to support research for the Department of Defense, the DoD has allowed free access since the 1980s. Its use, however, did not explode until after 1995 when the World Wide Web became widely available. A primary reason for the popularity of the web was its ability to display images. Prior to this time, the Internet was only text based. Although images could be sent, they had to be downloaded and then opened by a separate program to be viewed. The web provided access and viewing all within the same browser application. Images transformed the Internet into the vast communication and commerce system it is today.

Images will continue to play an important part in our daily lives and to an even larger degree in education. Advancements in digital imaging and video as well as the ability to create and/or explore virtual worlds will impact the way students learn. Information on digital imaging and video can be found in Chapter 7; developments in virtual environments are described here.

VR Systems

Once only dreamed of in science fiction, virtual reality is now available for use in the classroom. The first VR environments were created for the military and aerospace industry. These systems required sophisticated computers with advanced capabilities in generating computer graphics in real time. VR environments can represent real or imaginary worlds in which the user interacts through multiple senses. The primary interface is visual with advanced systems providing three-dimensional representations within a full peripheral range of view. The display would be placed over the user's eyes using goggles or a helmet referred to as a head-mounted display (HMD). (See Figure 9.2.) Other

Figure 9.2 Virtual Reality Equipment

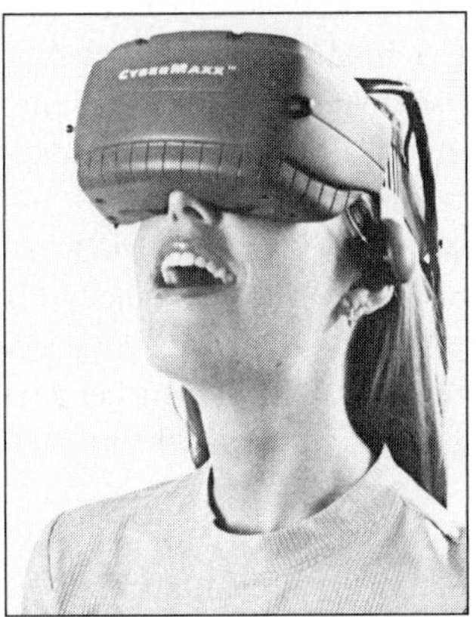

Source: Courtesy of Victor Maxx Technologies, Inc.

configurations use a large curved projection screen to immerse the user into the environment. The main objective in both displays is to replace all "real" world views with those of the virtual one.

Other interfaces include sound and tactile ones. Sound usually is presented to the user through stereo headphones that may or may not be built into the HMD. The user wears a glove or brace-like device that provides tactile feedback when an object in the virtual world is grasped.

The images in such a system are computer generated from a 3D model, which is developed and then shaded or rendered by the system based on predetermined lighting conditions. The views are regenerated each time the user moves within the simulated world, requiring the computer to regenerate the appropriate scene. Complexity of the scene is kept at a minimum to decrease the time required to refresh the view. The faster the scene refreshes, the more realistic the movement through the virtual environment becomes. A negative consequence of this trade-off between speed and accuracy is that the images contain little detail and are of video game quality.

Full immersion virtual environments require expensive hardware to both create and view the simulated world (Comer, 1999). Although advancements in PC-based modeling software have enabled the creation of virtual worlds on microcomputers, realistic environments are still limited to Unix-based workstations from Silicon Graphics or Sun Microsystems as examples. However, alternatives are now available that allow the creation of virtual environments. Although they are not immersive, they can be used on readily available computer systems (Young, 2000).

VRML and Other Development Tools

One such development is Virtual Reality Modeling Language (VRML). Just as Hypertext Mark-up Language (HTML) describes what a *web* page will look like in a browser, VRML describes the geometry and behavior of the *virtual world* or scene. VRML files can be viewed in either *Netscape* or *Internet Explorer* with the necessary plug-in. Creating worlds in VRML also requires building a 3D model of the environment as with the traditional VR models described above. This can be accomplished with modeling software such as *3D Studio* from Discrete, which can then output the VRML code, or you can code the world directly as you would a web page with HTML.

Just as advancements over HTML have been made available through Extensible Mark-up Language (XML), Extendible 3D (X3D) is the next-generation standard for 3D on the web. Announced in August 2001 by the Web3D Consortium, it promises to bring rich and compelling 3D graphics to the web for a wide variety of applications and devices (Web3D Consortium, 2001).

The advantage of using VRML is that the virtual world can be accessed through a web browser. This simplifies the distribution especially since no expensive proprietary software is required. Although the realism of full immersion is not available, the lower cost associated with the technology required to experience the environment makes VRML more suited for education.

Another method available for VR development is QuickTime VR (QTVR) from Apple Computer. QTVR provides the same ease of distribution as VRML using the standard *QuickTime* player available free from Apple Computer (http://www.apple.com/quicktime/download/), but requires much less effort to create the environment. In QTVR, a series of photographs is taken at 360 degrees around a pivotal point. For example, a classroom could record by setting up the camera in the middle of the room on a tripod. A series of 16 photos would be taken at 22.5-degree intervals. The photos are then input into *QuickTime VR Authoring Studio,* which "stitches" them together into a seamless panorama view of the room. In addition, because QTVR worlds use actual photographs to create the panorama, it provides a more realistic representation than the computer-generated systems.

Future trends in VR will include more realistic and complex environments enabled by advancements in graphic programming and more powerful processors. Visual interfaces will provide higher resolution and a wider more realistic peripheral view. There will also be an increase in the number of senses the systems will be able to control.

Trend 3: Emerging Developments in Interfaces

First developed more than 100 years ago with the invention of the typewriter, the keyboard still reigns as the primary interface for interacting with a computer. Though the Macintosh brought the addition of the point-and-click mouse to the traditional keyboard, little has changed about input methods. This is not to say that advancements in interfaces are not currently available, they are just not widely adopted for general use.

Voice Recognition

Voice recognition—speaking to your computer—has been available for a number of years. Plagued by high error rates and long configuration time, these systems were slow to provide the robust features users demanded. Today, however, voice recognition has greatly improved and is a reasonable interface option. Stand-alone products such as IBM's *ViaVoice* and Dragon's *Naturally Speaking* work with a number of existing productivity programs. The newest edition of Microsoft's *Office* suite, XP, has voice recognition built into the programs. However, adoption of the technology has been more visible in phone directory services and automated call centers than as an everyday computer interface.

One of the main reasons for the slow rate of general adoption is also a source of possible impact on classroom instruction. Speaking or dictating your thoughts is a very different skill than writing or keyboarding them. We have all refined our writing skills to flow from our minds to our fingers. To rechannel this flow to our vocal cords requires considerable effort to become as fluent as we are by hand. As with all endeavors, this added effort translates into extra time—time many are not willing to invest when traditional methods currently meet their needs.

In the classroom, time also translates into a change in teaching and learning styles. Traditional instructional methods are difficult to change while a change in students' mode of interaction could have a major effect on current assessment methods. One interesting outcome of the difference between writing and speaking has had a positive impact on a specific group of students. Students with specific learning disabilities who traditionally have difficulties with reading and writing have shown improvement in their writing when using speech recognition systems (MacArthur, 2000). Perhaps the future will see the adoption of a combination of these interfaces to meet the special needs of individual students.

Handwriting and Drawing

Another interface advancement is handwriting recognition. First launched to the general public by Apple Computer for their ill-fated Newton handheld system, it is now used daily by the many users of handheld personal digital assistants (PDAs). The first PDA systems were saddled with microkeyboards that required a stylus to press the keys. The Palm PDA reintroduced handwriting to the handheld market. Other systems from Compaq and Hewlett-Packard have followed. However, in a move to appease users of traditional interfaces, some PDAs can now be plugged into a foldable full-size keyboard. In some instances, these PDA/keyboard combinations are replacing laptop computers.

Although not a replacement for traditional computer interfaces, recognition of individuals for security reasons is becoming more sophisticated. Recent tragic events in schools have highlighted the need for quick identification of students who are authorized to be on campus. Many schools have instituted photo identification cards as one solution. New technologies based on the computerized scanning of fingers (Fingerprint technology, 2001), entire hands, faces (Face-recognition, 2001), and irises (Grotta, 2001) have been installed in some schools. In addition to security, these systems are also used for quick and accurate processing of lunch purchases and book checkout in the library. The advantage of these systems is the accuracy of identification combined with making ID cards unnecessary. These systems are controversial, however. Parents' main concerns center around right-to-privacy issues (N. H. parents, 2001).

Direct Connections to the Brain

An interface with possible implications for the future is currently being investigated by medical researchers working with patients who are completely paralyzed. Unable to use common adaptive devices, subjects communicate with the computer through a direct connection to their brain. One implant that has shown success was located in the area of the brain that controls motor movement. The patient was able to move the mouse pointer by merely thinking about it (Goettling, 1999). It is possible that future interfaces linked directly to the areas of the brain that control speech will enable us to just "think" the text to be inserted into our word-processed documents.

Trend 4: Emerging Developments in Handheld Systems

Advances in handheld computers are making these small devices the hot new technology. Originally developed as a PDA designed primarily to be an electronic appointment/phone/task organizer, they have expanded to include support for many office and education applications. For this reason, the term *handheld* or *pocket PC* is more applicable than PDA.

Currently there are two basic types of handheld computers categorized by their operating system. Palm and Handspring systems use the Palm operating system, while Compaq and Hewlett-Packard run Windows CE or the new Pocket PC 2002 operating system from Microsoft (Orubeondo, 2001). Similar applications are available on both operating systems. One of the main selling points of these systems is their low cost of a few hundred dollars as compared to the expense of a laptop computer. Although not as fully functional as a laptop, they come very close and create the possibility of providing a computer for every student in a classroom.

Data can be entered into a handheld system in a number of ways. The default method is by using a stylus to write on a designated area of the screen that recognizes letters and numbers written in a specific format. This works well for short notation, but is not functional for extensive

Figure 9.3 Handspring's Treo Communicator

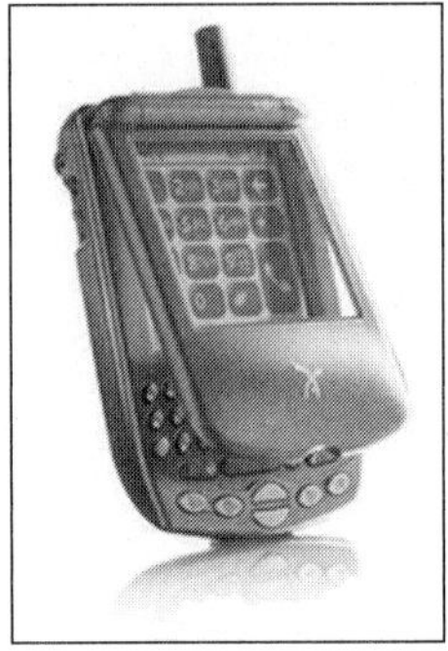

Source: Used by permission of Handspring, Inc. (http://www.Handspring.com)

note taking. Fortunately, full-sized folding keyboards are now available that attach to the handheld, facilitating quick data entry. Many business users are leaving their laptop computers in the office and replacing them in the field with this configuration. The newest interface, enabled by an increase in memory and processing capabilities, is voice recognition.

Uses of Handheld Systems

Handheld systems are used more as an extension of a traditional personal computer. The PC is used in the home, school, or office as a base. The handheld computer then becomes a portable extension that can easily travel with the user. Information or data on the handheld computer is transferred or synchronized with files on the base PC. Data can also be transferred or "beamed" directly between handheld systems via a built-in infrared data port. A handheld computer can also be connected directly to a LAN, since many support the 802.11 wireless networking protocol. If you are away from the range of the network, handheld systems have accessories that enable cell phone connections for both voice and data transfers. The combination of cell phone and handheld technologies has become so popular that cell phones are now being marketed with handheld capabilities (e.g., Ericsson r380), and handheld systems are incorporating cell phones (e.g., Handspring Treo in Figure 9.3).

Students can use their handheld systems in class or in the library to take notes or begin reports, which can then be transferred to their word processor on the base system. Other applications include collecting data in the field for a science experiment and writing progressive stories that are shared and expanded on by beaming directly between systems. In addition to the typical office applications, a growing number of these types of products can be used in education including drill and practice, reference, graphing calculators, and assessment.

The New E-book

Handheld systems are also revitalizing the e-book industry. Originally introduced as a way to carry a number of books within a small portable electronic device, e-books failed to catch on due to the cost of this dedicated appliance. The original e-book device could store and retrieve only the downloaded texts. Although smaller in format than the original e-book appliance, handheld systems support e-book text formats with free downloadable readers from Microsoft and Adobe. Poftak (2001) describes some current "e-book experiments" at schools in Dayton, Chicago, Austin, and Clarksville, Maryland; Shields and Poftak (2002) describe other activities in Michigan schools. Applications range from beaming students homework to reading electronic versions of books found on the web. Such mundane uses are still far from the dream of an altered teaching and learning experience envisioned by Poftak and others.

Wearable Systems

The next step in portability beyond handheld systems is the development of wearable computers. Whereas handheld devices are designed to provide all resources in the palm of your hand, wearable systems aim at creating a transparent association between user and computer. In essence, the computer would become a transparent part of your everyday life.

Wearable systems distribute the components of the computer to different areas of the body. The main processor and storage could be attached to your belt or reside in a pocket (Kay, 1999). The screen could be incorporated into your glasses in a way similar to that of the heads-up display used by fighter pilots. You could see through the glasses as you normally would but for interacting with the computer, the information would be superimposed over your normal view. Input could be accomplished by voice or by a keyboard (Kiser, 2000). Connecting the pieces would be done either wirelessly or using the electrical charge naturally present in your body.

Wearable systems are used by the military and in some manufacturing and distribution industries. Current systems are a bit bulky and have not quite achieved the transparent interface ideal. However, as miniaturization continues, systems will become less noticeable and will be incorporated into our daily routine.

Problems to Overcome

Though it seems from the descriptions here that handheld devices are the answer to many of the lingering problems of getting technology into the hands of all students, they have not been welcomed as readily as one might think. One major problem is that they are often categorized together with cell phones and pagers, which are often banned from school campuses. In addition, some of their unique capabilities, such as sharing information by beaming between systems, is seen as a way students could pass answers during a test or just pass personal notes in class (School boards, 2001).

Impact of the Four Trends for Educational Methods

The four trends described here will combine to have several kinds of impact on educational administration, teaching, and learning. Some of the impact already is being felt, as the examples discussed next show.

Flexibility in Classroom Organization and Configuration

Wireless networking, in combination with laptop and handheld devices, allows teachers the flexibility to group students into learning stations. When students do not have to stay at statically placed computers, instructional options increase dramatically. Students can gather data, form study groups, or do other learning activities outside the traditional boundaries of the classroom (Shields, 2001). Trotter (2001) describes a district in Orland Park, Illinois, that equipped many of its students and teachers with handheld Palm III's for use with its wireless network. With these handhelds, they do activities such as collecting data from temperature probes and creating concept maps of wetland ecosystems. One teacher observed that "the kids who have Palms get more into their homework; they do it on the Palms and beam it to me; you eliminate paper, eliminate notebooks" (p. 8). Soloway et al. (2001) describe some of the innovative uses of handheld devices in schools. One such activity is a "socio-kinesthetic simulation" in which students walk around the classroom with their handhelds and beam each other messages that are either "germ laden" or "germ free." After the initial spread of the "infection," students can view the history of the messages and see the transmission patterns they brought about. This exercise illustrates graphically how disease spreads in a population. Another innovation is "PalmSheets" or interactive exercises customized to students' individual needs and beamed to them from the teacher. After students fill them in, they beam them back to the teacher for analysis.

Access to Computing Power in Remote Sites

Wireless networking and interoperability mean that as widespread access becomes more commonplace, we will move from an information delivery paradigm to a communications model. For example, students on a field trip will carry portable devices that link to the Internet or the school's server. They can look up references related to the field trip and e-mail their reports back to school. Bull, Bull, and Whitaker (2001) refer to information transferred or "clipped" from the Internet to a handheld computer as *web clippings*. With the reduced costs of handheld equipment comes an increased possibility of grants or loaner systems for home use, thus increasing connectivity and access for even the poorest schools and students.

Ease and Flexibility in Home Networking

The availability of home and business systems linked to the Internet increases the communication capabilities among students, parents, and teachers. Advanced learning resources once accessible only at school are now available from anywhere. In addition to better resources for home-schooled students, this capability also allows students enrolled in schools to do more school-related work from their homes. It also means that parents will have better, more timely access to their children's activities and records, as well as to communications with their teachers.

VR-Based Therapies for People with Disabilities

The use of VR to aid in the rehabilitation of people suffering from emotional and psychological disabilities has increased the effectiveness of their rehabilitation and assimilation into the mainstream of school and society (Torpy, 2001).

Interfaces for People with Disabilities

Voice/audio interfaces (the way people communicate with computers) will begin to allow partial or full hands-free interactions with computer applications (Editors, 1998; Morris, 1998). Voice interfaces have been in development for several years, but with the advent of smaller handheld systems, the need for voice processing in lieu of typed input has increased dramatically. Many software application packages now include voice recognition software. Examples include word processors that allow direct dictation into a document; operating systems that accept voice commands for copying and moving files or formatting disks; e-mail systems on which people can leave voice messages; and automobile computers that check e-mail, make phone calls, and give directions.

Constructing Environments and Knowledge

Instead of building one model, students can build and manipulate many models in 3D environments. For example, students could build a house and walk around in it, observing its structure and components, measuring things, taking readings of temperatures and densities, and removing and changing things as they go. Models do not need to represent physical constructions such as a building. They also can be virtual places that the students generate themselves. Patterson (2001) describes desktop VR in use at the Willoway CyberSchool. Students use a 3D technology called *ActiveWorlds* to create virtual spaces on the Internet. They can gather in these spaces to attend classes or work together on projects. Using VRML, students can have their own avatars who "attend" these spaces, allowing the introduction of body language into cyberspace (p. 38). *ActiveWorld's* "face-to-face interaction and anthropomorphic characters . . . add a human level to distance education" (p. 38).

Virtual Field Trips with *QuickTime VR*®

Students already can "travel" to other countries on the Internet. With *QuickTime VR,* their experiences will be even more realistic. They also will be able to travel to other planets or other periods in history to observe and take part in activities there (Comer, 1999). They can go as themselves or as the persona their avatars represent.

Greater Dependence on Visual Learning

The ability to record and edit digital video will increase the number of projects students can produce through this medium. Greater bandwidth will support the transmission of streaming video, allowing visual examples to explain complex learning situations.

Decreased Emphasis on Keyboarding

New kinds of interfaces could have a profound impact on communications and computer uses across society. The differences between dictating text and writing characters on paper require entirely different processing skills. This change in communication techniques could enhance or deter student writing ability. E-mail already is more visual and voice activated, allowing students and teachers to communicate more easily with each other over distances. Systems also are beginning to provide more accurate handwriting recognition and will allow the inputting of both character and graphic data with a stylus.

Future Challenges for Teachers

Visions of Technology's Role in Restructuring Education

Many educators maintain that technology is essential to the curriculum reform and school restructuring needed to improve the educational system (Bruder, Buchsbaum, Hill, & Orlando, 1992; Salisbury, 1996; Wiburg, 1995–1996). The proper role for computers and related technology in education has stimulated continued, often intense debate for some years. Although computers captured the imaginations of educational innovators early in the 1960s, no commonly held vision ever emerged to show how technology would enhance—let alone change—education. Even now, with the growing dissatisfaction with traditional teaching and learning systems and a consensus on the need to change or restructure American education, considerable disagreement persists over the role technology will play in a restructured system.

Replacing teacher functions versus changing teacher roles. In educational technology's early days, when resources were available only through centrally controlled computer systems, some foresaw technology eventually replacing the teacher as the primary instructional delivery system (Norris, 1977). When microcomputers placed the power of technology directly in the hands of teachers, the image of technology shifted from replacing teachers to supplementing and enhancing teacher-based instruction. Criticized as expensive, inefficient, and outdated, technology again is proposed as an alternative to delivering instruction primarily through teachers (Reigeluth & Garfinkle, 1992). This proposal assumes that technology-based delivery systems will achieve better results by standardizing instructional methods and decreasing personnel costs. Some critics advocate technology replacing the traditional roles of both schools and teachers (Perelman, 1993). Others feel that teachers and schools must remain an important part of the instructional process, but that technology tools will empower them to teach better and use their time more productively. As requests for curricular reform increase, far-reaching changes in traditional teacher roles seem an inevitable part of the total restructuring package.

Enhancing existing methods versus changing the nature of education. Even if teachers retain an important role, considerable debate remains over how technology will *change* those roles. Even the new technologies described in this chapter are only mirrors that either can reflect a vision to restructure a school's fundamental operations and educational goals or one that supports existing structures. Soloway et al. (2001) feel that curriculum must change substantially to take advantage of new technologies such as handheld systems.

The role of distance learning. New developments in distance learning technologies promise to alter drastically our traditional concepts of what constitutes education, teaching, and learning. Some innovative course delivery systems made possible by distance technologies already are bringing about a radical restructuring of learning opportunities at all levels (Elbaum, 1998; Owston, 1997). Dede (1996) offers several new forms of expression that may reform traditional methods even further in the future. These include *knowledge webs* for distributed online conferences, links to information and experts, and virtual exhibits to duplicate real-world settings; *virtual communities* to complement face-to-face classroom activities; experiences in *synthetic environments* to "extend learning by doing in real world settings" (p. 25); and *sensory immersion* in virtual reality environments. All of these "futuristic technologies," which the Internet has made more accessible than ever before, give new life and practicality to restructuring efforts.

Summary principles for the future. Literature on technology's role in restructuring yields some common principles. The following recurring themes are central to building a more effective system of education:

- **Teachers will retain a key role.** Although teacher roles will undergo radical changes, few consider replacing teachers with technology-based delivery systems. Even where teachers are not available or are in short supply, such as in rural schools and highly technical subject areas, the technology strategy of choice to optimize the power of available teachers is networking or distance learning. Technology resources also will help teachers shift their emphasis from delivering information to facilitating learning.

■ **Interdisciplinary approaches will flourish.** Curriculum will change from a disjointed collection of isolated skills training to integrated activities that incorporate many disciplines and call for teacher collaboration. The theme-based projects described in the Part IV chapters of this book illustrate how technology resources can both focus and facilitate these cross-disciplinary activities.

■ **Research and problem-solving skills will gain attention.** Pure constructivist principles may prove difficult to implement under current constraints and resource limitations, but educational goals already are undergoing two kinds of shifts. First, an increasing emphasis on general-purpose study and research skills seeks to help learners in any content area. Use of databases, online information services, and hypermedia systems will promote success in this new direction of studies. Second, the emphasis is shifting from learning isolated skills and information within each content area to learning how to solve problems specific to each area. Again, the engaging qualities of technology resources such as videodiscs, multimedia, and distance learning help teachers to focus students on such complex goals that call for underlying basic skills.

■ **Assessment methods will change to reflect the new curriculum.** New calls for "authentic assessment" methods mirror the need to make both instruction and evaluation of progress more relevant to student needs. Assessment of performance is shifting from paper-and-pencil tests to performance-based methods and student portfolios. Technology-based production tasks can help accomplish this kind of assessment goal and help track acquisition of component skills.

■ **Distance learning will play a large role.** The number of educators and organizations in distance learning shows that it has already altered our educational system. Nearly all colleges and universities either offer courses or degrees via distance technologies or plan to do so in the near future. Also, there is a thriving "virtual high school" movement in progress. In this sense, the "death of distance" (Moore, 1995) already has made our educational system a different place than it was a half century ago. The challenge for educators is not just to use technology, but to use it in ways that acknowledge its benefits and limitations. Clearly, 21st-century educators will have to deal with many issues their predecessors could not even have imagined.

Future Skills for the Technology-Savvy Teacher

In addition to the demanding requirements listed in Chapter 1, educators must prepare for a technology-permeated future by keeping up with change. They must learn to adopt effective strategies, such as reading technical and educational publications, attending training sessions, and perusing Internet sites, for keeping as current as possible on the new and anticipated technologies described in this chapter, as well as methods of using them. If technology is to make a real difference in their work, teachers must have a vision of what they are working toward, recognize the kind of infrastructure necessary to bring about their vision, and be active in building what is needed for change and growth.

These activities must become part of the repertoire of the future educator. Teachers must adopt an outlook that their preservice preparation is only a first step in what must be a lifelong exploration of ways to use technology and other resources to improve education. Technology is coming to represent both a constant resource and a continual reminder that educators never can become satisfied with their methods, skill levels, or results.

Exercises

Record and apply what you have learned.

Chapter 9 Self-Test

To review terms and concepts in this chapter, take the Chapter 9 self-test. Select Chapter 9 from the front page of the Companion Website (located at http://www.prenhall.com/roblyer), then choose the *Multiple Choice* module.

Portfolio Activities

ISTE The following activities address ISTE National Educational Technology Standards for Teachers (NETS-T) and will help you add to your professional portfolio. To complete these activities online and save or submit the materials electronically, select Chapter 9 from the front page of the Companion Website (http://www.prenhall.com/roblyer), then choose the *Portfolio* module.

1. ***Technology Impact on Content Areas (NETS-T Standard: I-B)*** Prepare your personal vision of how each of the four areas of development described in this chapter will change education in *your* future. Name at least one technology in each of the areas and give your own description of how it will impact teaching and learning practices in your area.
2. ***In-Depth Impact (NETS-T Standard: I-B)*** Prepare a list of five resources (publications, web sites) or activities (attendance at certain meetings) that will help you keep up with important technology developments in your area of interest.

Questions for Thought and Discussion

These questions may be used for small-group or class discussion or may be subjects for individual or group activities. To take part in these discussions online, select Chapter 9 from the front page of the Companion Website (http://www.prenhall.com/roblyer), then choose the *Message Board* module.

1. In William Clark's 1994 article about the "high-tech classroom of the future," he says that the evolution of the classroom "will be characterized by the steady replacement of traditional basal programs by multiple media programs and collections of supplemental materials. Some of these materials will be classroom resident. Others will flow through various manifestations of the information highway" (p. 38). Do you agree with Clark's predictions? Do you feel the impact of these changes will be beneficial or not?
2. Baines (1997) said that "the frenetic race to acquire and use technology in the schools is often attributed to . . . the demands of corporate leaders who want competent workers. However, when Fortune 500 companies were surveyed about the ideal education for children of the 21st century, [they emphasized] the need for analytical, logical, higher-order, conceptual, and problem solving skills, along with proficiencies in writing, reading, and . . . communication" (p. 495). Do you think these two statements are contradictory? Give examples from this chapter about how one can help bring about the other.

Collaborative Activities

The following activities address ISTE National Educational Technology Standards for Teachers (NETS-T) and can be done in small-groups. Each group should present the findings to the class in a format they know how to use (word-processed report, presentation software, multimedia product). Each summary should have a graphic like the one in Figure 1.5 or a table to help communicate the information. Completed group products can be copied and shared with the entire class and/or included in each person's personal portfolio.

1. ***Scenarios of the future (NETS-T Standards: I-B, II-B)*** Prepare your own scenario of how a future curriculum unit that incorporates "technologies of the future" (similar to *Historical Reinvention*) would be structured and carried out.
2. ***Impact of future technology (NETS-T Standards: I-B, II-B)*** Have the groups exchange curriculum scenarios they have developed. Each group identifies the new technological innovations in the scenario and discusses the impact of each innovation on reshaping education in the future in the way the scenario shows.

Integrating Technology Across the Curriculum Activities

The *Integrating Technology Across the Curriculum* CD-ROM is a set of technology integration ideas and links to online lessons, arranged as a searchable database. The CD comes packaged with this textbook. Complete the following exercise using this CD:

How will some of the developments described in this chapter change the way some of the lessons on the CD will be carried out? For each of the four trends described in this chapter, select a lesson and describe the impact an emerging technology may have for enhancing this activity. For example, locate lessons that require use of "probeware/MBL" technologies. Write a description of how smaller, more portable data-gathering computer equipment will change the way these lessons are done.

References

Baines, L. (1997). Future schlock: Using fabricated data and politically correct platitudes in the name of education reform. *Phi Delta Kappan, 78*(7), 492–498.

Bringsjord, S. (2001). Just imagine: What computers can't do. *The Education Digest, 66*(6), 31–33.

Bruder, I., Buchsbaum, H., Hill, M., & Orlando, L. (1992). School reform: Why you need technology to get there. *Electronic Learning, 11*(8), 22–28.

Bull, G., Bull, G., & Whitaker, S. (2001). Web clippings. *Learning and Leading with Technology, 28*(5), 54–57.

Canfield, W. (2001). ALEKS: A web-based intelligent tutoring system. *Mathematics and Computer Education, 35*(2), 152–159.

Clark, W. (1994, October). The high-tech classroom of the future: What will it be like? *Curriculum Product News, 38,* 62.

Comer, S. (1999). Immersive imaging technology: VR for the web in academia. *Syllabus, 13*(1), 22–26.

Dede, C. (1996). Distance learning-distributed learning: Making the transformation. *Learning and Leading with Technology, 23*(7), 25–30.

Denby, D. (2000, November 27). The speed of light: The high stakes race to build the next Internet. *The New Yorker,* 133–141.

Dominick, J. (2000). Wireless on campus. *Syllabus, 14*(4), 19–22.

Editors. (1998). PC computing 10th anniversary time capsule. *PC Computing, 11*(8), 197–212.

Elbaum, B. (1998, Winter). Is the virtual high school "educational reform"? *Concord.Org: Newsletter of the Concord Consortium.* Concord, MA, pp. 10–11.

Face-recognition tech means kids get lunch for a smile. (2001, September). *eSchool News,* p. 12.

Fingerprint technology speeds school lunch lines. (2001, March). *eSchool News,* p. 8.

Goettling, G. (1999). Harnessing the power of thought. *Georgia Tech Alumni Magazine Online, 76*(1). Available online: http://gtalumni.org/news/magazine/sum99.

Grotta, S. (2001). Bio-keys. *PC Magazine, 20*(11), 162–174.

Guerard, E. (2000). Bluetooth will streamline school connectivity. *eSchool News, 3*(9), 10.

Kay, E. (1999). The next small thing. *Inside Technology Training, 3*(3), 24–26.

Kiser, K. (2000). Wearable training. *Inside Technology Training, 4*(4), 20–29.

MacArthur, C. (2000). New tools for writing: Assistive technology for students with writing difficulties. *Topics in Language Disorders, 20*(4), 85–100.

Mason-Mason, S., & Tessmer, M. (2000). Expert systems as a mindtool to facilitate mental model learning. *ETR&D, 48*(4), 43–62.

Moore, M. G. (1995). The death of distance. *The American Journal of Distance Education, 9*(3), 1–4.

Morris, J. (1998). User interfaces. *PC Magazine, 17*(11), 162–163.

N. H. parents turn thumbs down on hand scanner. (2001, October). *eSchool News, 4*(10), 14.

Norris, W. (1977). Via technology to a new era in education. *Phi Delta Kappan, 58*(6), 451–453.

Orubeondo, A (2001). Handheld OSes continue to evolve. *InfoWorld, 23*(30), 50.

Owston, R. (1997). The World Wide Web: A technology to enhance teaching and learning? *Educational Researcher, 26*(2), 27–33.

Patterson, J. (2001). Distance education: Bridging the gap between student and teacher. *eSchool News, 3*(12), 37–40.

Perelman, L. (1993). *School's out: Hyperlearning, the new technology, and the end of education.* New York: William Morrow.

Poftak, A. (2001). Getting a read on e-books. *Technology & Learning, 21*(9), 22–36.

Reigeluth, C., & Garfinkle, R. (1992). Envisioning a new system of education. *Educational Technology, 22*(11), 17–22.

Salisbury, D. (1996). *Five technologies for educational change.* Englewood Cliffs, NJ: Educational Technology Publications.

School boards weigh ban on student laptops, PDA's. (2001, October). *e-School News, 4*(10), 1, 44.

Shields, J. (2001). Top 10 technology breakthroughs for schools; wireless networking. *Technology & Learning, 22*(4), 18–20.

Shields, J., & Poftak, A. (2002). A report card on handheld computing. *Technology & Learning, 22*(7), 24–34.

Soloway, E., Norris, C., Curtis, M., Jansen, R., Krajcik, J., Marx, R., Fishman, B., & Blumenfield, P. (2001). Making palm-sized computers the PC of choice for K–12. *Learning and Leading with Technology, 28*(7), 32–34, 56–57.

Torpy, B. (2001, September 2). One marine's second chance. *The Atlanta Journal-Constitution,* p. A1.

Trotter, A. (2001). Handheld computing: New best tech tool or just a fad? *Education Week, 21*(4), 8–14. Available online: http://www.edweek.org/ew/newstory.cfm?slug=04palm.h21&keywords=trotter.

Web3D Consortium. (2001, September 17). New-generation X3D open web 3D standard launched with leading browser-company support. Available online: http://www.web3d.org/news/pressreleases/x3dprl.htm.

Wiburg, K. (1995–1996). Changing teaching with technology. *Learning and Leading with Technology, 23*(4), 46–48.

Yager, T. (2001). Wireless networking standard dominance? *InfoWorld, 23*(46), 61–62.

Young, J. (2000, October 6). Virtual reality on a desktop hailed as new tool in distance education. *The Chronicle of Higher Education,* p. A43.

PART IV

Integrating Technology Across the Curriculum

The chapters in this part will help teachers learn:

1. To identify some of the current issues in various subject-area instruction that may impact the selection and use of technology
2. To describe some popular uses for technology in today's curricula
3. To identify exemplary Internet sites for subject-area instruction
4. To create instructional activities that successfully model subject-area integration strategies

Introduction

Part IV addresses the use of technology in various subject areas. In an effort to model subject-area integration, the disciplines have been grouped by chapter as follows:

Chapter 10: Technology in Language Arts and Foreign Language Instruction

English and foreign language technology applications are grouped together in Chapter 10 because they are both language-related topics. Language arts in this chapter includes the communications skills (reading, listening, speaking), addressed primarily in the elementary grades, as well as English topics (writing and literature), which are the focus at secondary levels. Foreign language topics include the learning of foreign languages and English for Speakers of Other Languages (ESOL).

Chapter 11: Technology in Mathematics and Science Instruction

Science and mathematics topics are considered closely related, and curricula for them are often intertwined. This chapter looks at how technology applications help integrate the teaching of these topics and how they address the special curriculum needs of each.

Chapter 12: Technology in Social Studies Instruction

Technology applications covered in Chapter 12 include those for history, social studies, civics, and geography. Social sciences may be one of the subject areas most influenced by recent technological advances.

Chapter 13: Technology in Art and Music Instruction

This chapter focuses on technology applications for the topics in arts instruction to which the majority of K–12 students are exposed: music (appreciation, theory, and performance) and art (drawing, painting, and image production).

Chapter 14: Technology in Physical Education and Health Education

The closely related subjects of physical education and health are generally not allocated the status of the more "academic" subject areas. However, the quality of the teaching of these subjects may play a major role in the future success of our students. Instructional technology provides a number of resources that may maximize the effectiveness of the limited time that typically is given to these subjects.

Chapter 15: Technology in Special Education

Chapter 15 is the only chapter identified by population rather than by topic. Technology applications for students with special needs are addressed in Part IV because the curriculum for them has many unique characteristics. Needs of special students addressed in this chapter include those for learners with mental disabilities and behavioral/emotional disorders as well as those with physical disabilities (e.g., hearing impaired, visually impaired, nonspeaking, wheelchair-bound), and gifted and talented students.

Structure of Each Chapter

Issues and Problems Related to Technology Use in the Content Area

Chapters in this part provide information to support both single-subject and interdisciplinary integration strategies. Each chapter has a brief description of current issues that affect the use of instructional technology in a specific content area. Most teachers do not ask *whether* they should use technology, but *when, how,* and *for what* they should use it. Considering how quickly technologies and their applications develop, answers to these questions are bound to change. However, one of the greatest benefits of the infusion of technology into schools is an increased reflection about teaching and learning strategies; these chapters are designed to promote this reflection.

How Technology Is Integrated into the Content Area

Each chapter suggests integration strategies and technology resources to implement them in the subject area.

Useful Web Sites for Subject-Area Instruction

A selection of exemplary web sites is given for each subject area. The selection usually includes one from a national organization in the field and others that provide either teacher or student resources.

Sample Integration Ideas for Subject-Area Education

Chapters 10 through 15 provide both resources and models for curriculum integration. In the form of technology integration lesson ideas. Teachers are encouraged to use these activities and elaborate on them, customizing them to meet students' needs and to match facility resources. The *Integrating Educational Technology Across the Curriculum* CD-ROM that accompanies this book provides additional integration ideas to illustrate how technology is integrated into each content area.

Chapter Activities to Record and Apply What You Have Learned

Exercises at the end of each chapter give students and instructors a number of options for applying what has been learned. Suggestions are provided for both individual and team projects as well as prompts to stimulate group discussions.

CHAPTER 10

Technology in Language Arts and Foreign Language Instruction

Lynne Anderson-Inman, University of Oregon
Kimberley Ketterer, Eugene (Oregon) School District

The Internet and other new technologies of information and communication are redefining the nature of literacy and literacy instruction.

Leu (2001)

Understanding how literacy may be affected by a shift from printed to digital forms is more than an academic exercise . . . the transformations of literacy that are beginning to become evident are major threads running through the fabric of everyday life.

Reinking (1998)

This chapter covers the following topics:

- Current issues and problems in language arts and foreign language instruction
- How technology is integrated into language arts and foreign language instruction
- Example World Wide Web site resources for language arts and foreign language instruction
- Example activities for a variety of integration strategies in language arts and foreign language instruction.

Objectives

1. Identify and discuss some of the current issues related to the integration of technology into language arts and foreign language instruction. (NETS 6)
2. Describe some effective ways in which technology can be integrated into language arts and foreign language instruction. (NETS 1 and 2)
3. Demonstrate knowledge of ways in which the Internet can be used to support the integration of technology into language arts and foreign language instruction. (NETS 1 and 2)
4. Design and implement instructional activities that model effective ways to integrate technology into language arts and foreign language instruction. (NETS 2 and 3)

TECHNOLOGY INTEGRATION EXAMPLE

English and Foreign Language Instruction

TITLE: Revolutionary Uses of Technology

BASED ON: Skarecki, E., and Insinnia, E. (1999). Revolutions in the classroom. *Learning and Leading with Technology, 26*(7), 23–27.

GRADE LEVEL: 7–8

CONTENT AREA/TOPIC: English literature and French

LENGTH OF TIME: Three weeks

Step 1: What's the Relative Advantage—Why Use Technology in Language Arts and Foreign Language Teaching?

As part of their summer professional development series, teachers in the middle schools of the New Wave School District attended a workshop on how to create and use interdisciplinary curriculum. As they considered ways to create multidiscipline units to enhance the curriculum, Ms. Hansen, an English teacher, and Mr. Milner, the French teacher, agreed they would like to identify and work together on areas that presented special teaching problems for each of them. They realized that a study of Dickens' classic *A Tale of Two Cities* would be a natural link between the two subjects. Ms. Hansen always found it a challenging task to engage her students in the book, and Mr. Milner was always searching for ways to give his students meaningful English-to-French translation projects. They agreed that the many Internet web sites on the French Revolution could help make the events and concepts more vivid and supply a wealth of background on the setting of the book. Mr. Milner also knew of many sources in French that could enrich the book study and pave the way for later meaningful translation work. They decided to have the students work in small groups to report on various parts of the book, then create a web page of their compositions and source links, with both English and French versions.

Step 2: Planning Assessment—What Are Appropriate Assessment Strategies?

The teachers agreed that there would be three major products in the unit: the students' analysis papers on their assigned chapters, the web site development, and the translations. Ms. Hansen also had a short-answer test that covered important features of the book; she decided to use this to compare the approach she used before with this new one to see how much of this information students learned. They decided to adapt an existing writing

Figure 10.0 Woodberry Forest School's Site on the French Revolution

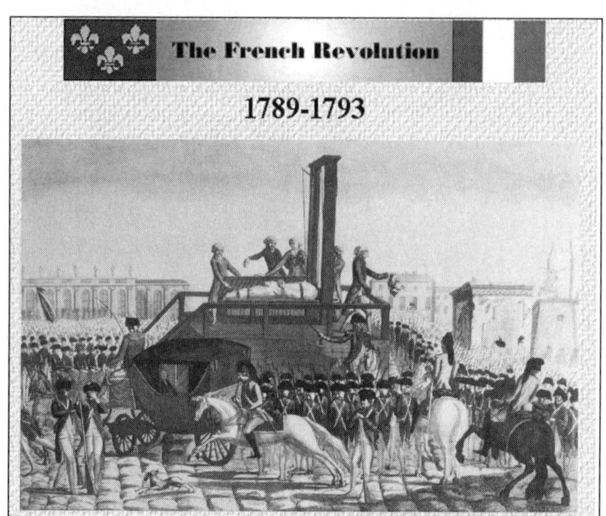

Source: Adapted from the Woodberry Forest School Web page (http://www.woodberry.org). Painting is *Mort de Louis Capet 16th Nom, le 21 Janvier 1793* by Giraudon, from Art Resource, NY.

rubric to assess the written products and a web site checklist they had received from the technology resource teacher to evaluate the web site. Mr. Milner recognized that the students' translation skills might not be up to the level of translating everything for the site, so he decided to grade them primarily on producing translations of certain parts such as titles, photo credits, and special sections such as the famous opening line of the novel: "It was the best of times; it was the worst of times."

Step 3: Planning Instruction—What Are Appropriate Integration Strategies?

The teachers decided on the following sequence of activities for the unit:

- **Week 1:** Ms. Hansen introduces the book and the web site project in her class. She discusses the setting of the story and begins a discussion of the place and time period. She forms small groups and assigns each of them to locate information on the story setting through a series of web sites she has bookmarked for them. They discuss their findings and how the book proceeds through critical events of the French Revolution. The students begin their reading. In Mr. Milner's class, the students begin to look at French texts on the Rev-

TECHNOLOGY INTEGRATION EXAMPLE (*CONTINUED*)

olution and compile key vocabulary such as "scarecrow" and phrases such as "To the guillotine!" He makes sure these words and phrases are in the dictionary of the French version of *Appleworks*. He has the students practice word processing these words and phrases in sentences and brief summaries.

- **Week 2:** Ms. Hansen assigns chapters on which each of the small groups will report. She hands out analysis questions to guide their summaries and has them develop concept maps using the *Inspiration* program. When they are ready to begin their written summaries, Ms. Hansen has the students word process their drafts and locate illustrations for their products on the bookmarked web sites. Mr. Milner works with the students to begin doing the translations. They scan in some of the images from books he has on the subject and web sites the students have located.
- **Week 3:** The students begin work on the English and French versions of the web site. With the help of the technology resource teacher, they plan how the web site will look and navigate. Each group has summaries to do, images to insert and credit, and links to enter. They end the unit with a joint class presentation and an announcement to the school that the web site is up and ready for viewing.

Step 4: Logistics—Preparing the Classroom Environment and Instructional Materials

The week before the unit, Ms. Hansen set up the classroom computers by creating a special bookmark file for the *Tale of Two Cities* unit. Mr. Milner also bookmarks French sites he has located, and obtains texts and images describing and showing events during the French Revolution. They schedule the Computer Lab for the time in the second week during which students will need to do their word-processed summaries, and in the third week which they will need to complete the web site work.

Step 5: Evaluating and Revising Integration Strategies

After they complete the unit, the two teachers reflect on how well it worked, and how they could improve it if they decide to use this approach again. Some of the questions they asked were:

- Did the students become more engaged in the book and the translations than they would have otherwise?
- Did the additional tasks of locating, using, and discussing web sites seem to add to the students' insights on the book study?
- Did the use of web sites make important background research proceed faster than it would have been in the library?
- Did students reflect more insight and knowledge on the post-unit test than had groups in previous years?
- Were the classrooms and lab times organized for efficient work?

After reviewing their findings, they agreed the unit went very well and was well received by students and parents alike. The post-unit test reflected only slightly higher scores than in other years, but it was clear that more of the students were engaged in the study of the book. Mr. Milner observed that, since the translation work was being done for a web site that many would see, students were much more motivated to do the required translations. The teachers decided to include communications with and virtual visits to a sister school in France in the next unit to further increase motivation to communicate in French and to have an even richer source of information on the book and its historical setting.

Introduction

The "language arts" are those language-based processes by which we think, learn and communicate. (See NCTE and IRA Standards for the English/Language Arts in Figure 10.1.) Because the "language arts" exist for any language, whether it is one we know well or one we are just learning, it is appropriate to consider the role of technology in the teaching of language arts simultaneously with its role in the teaching of a foreign language. In the elementary grades, the language arts curriculum focuses primarily on developing the fundamental skills of reading, writing, listening, and speaking. In the later grades, language arts instruction is increasingly embedded in courses that focus on literature, composition, and formal communication (either in a student's native language or a foreign one). Because literacy skills and processes are fundamental to successful performance in most other disciplines, there is also considerable language arts instruction in content-area courses (e.g., the social studies, sciences and mathematics.) This latter is often referred to as "reading and writing in the content area," or is grouped under the label of study skills and strategies.

In this chapter we provide an overview of how technology can be used to enhance language arts instruction in all of the above venues. And, because technology resources and integration strategies are similar, whether used for language arts or foreign language instruction, this chapter discusses them together. This approach is based on the assumption that the same language arts dimensions are visible and required for instruction in all languages, although curriculum emphasis and instructional timing may vary. The ideas shared in this chapter also presuppose a somewhat constructivist approach to learning, where emphasis is on learning that is more student centered than teacher centered, and activities are more authentic than artificial. Many current technology resources can be used to facilitate this approach to learning and our chapter focuses more on these than other technological applications. Hence, we have emphasized ideas and suggestions for integrating technology into language arts and foreign language instruction that are based on the following assumptions:

Figure 10.1 Standards for English/Language Arts

The standards for English/Language Arts were copublished by the National Council for Teachers of English (NCTE) and the International Reading Association (IRA) in 1996. Listed below are summaries of the 12 standards, taken from the NCTE website (http://www.ncte.org/standards).

1. Students read a wide range of print and nonprint texts to build an understanding of texts, of themselves, and of the cultures of the United States and the world; to acquire new information; to respond to the needs and demands of society and the workplace; and for personal fulfillment. Among these texts are fiction and nonfiction, classic and contemporary works.
2. Students read a wide range of literature from many periods in many genres to build an understanding of the many dimensions (e.g., philosophical, ethical, aesthetic) of human experience.
3. Students apply a wide range of strategies to comprehend, interpret, evaluate, and appreciate texts. They draw on their prior experience, their interactions with other readers and writers, their knowledge of word meaning and of other texts, their word identification strategies, and their understanding of textual features (e.g., sound–letter correspondence, sentence structure, context, graphics).
4. Students adjust their use of spoken, written, and visual language (e.g., conventions, style, vocabulary) to communicate effectively with a variety of audiences and for different purposes.
5. Students employ a wide range of strategies as they write and use different writing process elements appropriately to communicate with different audiences for a variety of purposes.
6. Students apply knowledge of language structure, language conventions (e.g., spelling and punctuation), media techniques, figurative language, and genre to create, critique, and discuss print and nonprint texts.
7. Students conduct research on issues and interests by generating ideas and questions, and by posing problems. They gather, evaluate, and synthesize data from a variety of sources (e.g., print and nonprint texts, artifacts, people) to communicate their discoveries in ways that suit their purpose and audience.
8. Students use a variety of technological and information resources (e.g., libraries, databases, computer networks, video) to gather and synthesize information and to create and communicate knowledge.
9. Students develop an understanding of and respect for diversity in language use, patterns, and dialects across cultures, ethnic groups, geographic regions, and social roles.
10. Students whose first language is not English make use of their first language to develop competency in the English language arts and to develop understanding of content across the curriculum.
11. Students participate as knowledgeable, reflective, creative, and critical members of a variety of literacy communities.
12. Students use spoken, written, and visual language to accomplish their own purposes (e.g., for learning, enjoyment, persuasion, and the exchange of information).

- Instruction should be student centered and developmentally appropriate.
- Instruction should focus on integrating multiple language arts skills (reading, writing, speaking, and listening) whenever possible.
- Activities should be interactive and emphasize meaningful (as opposed to rote) learning.
- Language arts instruction should be integrated with content instruction.
- Activities should provide real-life applications.
- Instruction should assist students in achieving established proficiency standards.

Issues and Problems in Language Arts and Foreign Language Instruction

The integration of technology into language arts and foreign language instruction has led to a number of concerns for educators, many of which remain unresolved. In the following sections we provide an overview of a few of these concerns, divided into two sections: those related to all language arts instruction (including foreign language) and those specific to foreign language instruction.

Issues and Problems Related to Technology in Language Arts Instruction

Educators interested in adopting computers and other forms of advanced technology as tools for language arts teaching and learning have had to face a number of issues and overcome a variety of problems, only some of which are specific to the focus of their instruction. Like teachers in all subject areas, they face difficulties in acquiring access to sufficient hardware and software, and struggle with uncertainties over how best to use the technological access they do have. In addition, they have had to deal with issues related specifically to their chosen areas of instruction. The three examples below give the reader a flavor for the type of concerns that language arts educators are currently facing.

Keyboarding instruction. Without question, the most common application of technology in the language arts is for writing. To date, the most common way to write using a computer has required input through a keyboard. This has raised the issue of whether keyboarding instruction should be prerequisite to the use of computers for writing. Those in favor argue that students will learn bad habits if they use the keyboard without proper training, that these bad habits might become permanent, and that failure to learn proper fingering will inhibit fluent and speedy keyboarding. Those against requiring keyboarding instruction as a prerequisite argue that too much student time and computer resources are spent on getting kids trained to type quickly, that students need only basic keyboard familiarization, and that keyboarding instruction will likely be a waste of time unless students have real-world applications in which to use the computer. All too often, teachers complain that the computer labs in their schools are booked entirely for computer literacy and keyboarding instruction. Such scheduling precludes their use by teachers interested in integrating technology into their curricula.

Both arguments are legitimate and most teachers have resolved the issue, at least temporarily, by favoring keyboarding instruction if it is available and needed, but not preventing students from using the computer if they do not yet have good keyboarding skills. Many students arrive in school with years of computer experience. Teachers have rightly seen that it makes little sense to prevent continued access to this powerful tool simply because a student cannot type 30 words a minute using the "correct" fingering. On the other hand, teachers have also rightly seen that students with more refined keyboarding skills are often able to integrate the technology into their academic lives more completely and effectively (Anderson-Inman, Knox-Quinn, & Horney, 1996). Numerous excellent programs are available for teaching keyboarding skills, as well as a variety of low-cost software games for practicing the required finger patterns. In addition, recent advances in speech-to-text software now allow students to speak their ideas into the computer, as opposed to typing them. As voice recognition software becomes increasingly reliable and continues to drop in price, we may well see the end of the keyboarding controversy.

Reading on the computer versus reading from print. Computers were not orginally designed for reading, and it has taken technology a long time to produce text on the screen that is easily readible. Even today with high-resolution text and graphics, reading from a computer monitor is still more awkward than reading from print on paper. This awkwardness, as well as concerns about endangering eyesight, infringing on copyright, and acquiring access to resources, has prevented many language arts teachers from embracing electronic texts as tools for teaching reading or reading to learn. Technology advocates have long predicted the demise of the traditional book, but language arts teachers have generally not agreed with that prediction nor worked to make it come true. Nonetheless, hundreds of thousands of electronic texts are available to teachers and students, many of them freely accessible to anyone with an Internet connection. At issue is why would anyone want to read documents in electronic form (as opposed to printing them out or just buying the book)? What are the advantages of reading electronic text as opposed to traditional print? And if we move to reading electronic text, does that mean death to our traditional reading materials and textbooks?

Anderson-Inman and Horney (1998) have proposed seven features of electronic text that distinguish it from traditional print and make it useful to teachers engaged in literacy instruction. They argue that because electronic text is malleable, it can be modified, enhanced, programmed, and linked in ways that support instruction in reading and promote improved comprehension by students reading independently. Furthermore, because electronic text can be more quickly searched than paper-based text, it can be a tool for studying language patterns or observing change in character and theme over time. Finally, because electronic text can be shared over long distances instantaneously, it lends itself to collaborative endeavors and cross-culture communication. Features such as these make electronic books and documents extremely useful for studying, as opposed to simply reading (Anderson-Inman & Horney, 1999). And it is this distinction that is increasingly capturing the attention of language arts teachers. The questions are no longer "Should I use electronic text for reading instruction?" and "What will happen to students' abilities to read print-based text if I do?" Instead, teachers are asking questions such as "How can I find the electronic texts I need?"and "How can I best integrate them into the curriculum?" The debate over electronic versus paper-based text is being resolved as teachers see advantages to both formats and seek to capitalize on the strengths of each when teaching students to read effectively and meaningfully.

Media literacy as opposed to print literacy. To be able to live and work in a world that increasingly operates in a variety of media formats, students need to be media literate, not just print literate. This often places language arts teachers in a difficult position, in part because their training as professionals gives supremacy to the medium of print, and in part because the need for teaching media literacy places additional pressure on an already full curriculum, in terms of both time and material resources. To be media literate, students need to be able to locate, access, analyze, evaluate, manipulate, and communicate information effectively in a variety of formats. This includes knowing how to find appropriate electronic information sources to be incorporated into their research products and presentations, as well as the ability to access and use information stored in a variety of formats including CD-ROM, still and moving images, text, sound, and print. Understandably, this selection requires critical thinking and informed decision-making skills. By extension, being media literate also requires knowledge of the hardware (e.g., computers, televisions, VCR, scanners, camcorders, digital cameras, etc.) that these materials might be stored on and how to use these devices to create and present multimedia products reflecting success on curriculum objectives. Skill in the use of various media can support the integration of information technology across curricular areas and can give students opportunities to integrate information into meaningful learning experiences, projects, and presentations (Toomey & Ketterer, 1995).

Issues and Problems Related to Technology in Foreign Language Instruction

Foreign language instruction is provided to students in a variety of different ways. In the past, foreign language instruction was not introduced until students were in secondary school, where foreign language teachers focused on the rules of grammar, memorizing vocabulary, or translating text. The National Council of State Supervisors of Foreign Languages (NCSSFL) currently endorses foreign language instruction for all students beginning in the elementary grades, and advocates the use of more interactive and authentic approaches to foreign language learning. They recognize three models for foreign language instruction at the elementary level: FLEX (foreign language experience or exploratory), FLES (foreign language in the elementary school), and immersion. FLEX is designed to provide an introductory but limited foreign language experience to presecondary students. FLES seeks to provide students with sequential language learning experiences that work toward proficiency. Immersion delivers all or part of a student's curriculum in the target foreign language. Embedded in any model of foreign language learning are three issues, each relevant to the ways in which and the extent to which technology is integrated into instruction: (1) direct instruction of discrete language skills versus contextualized learning, (2) the relative difficulty of cognate versus noncognate languages, and (3) content-obligatory instruction versus content-compatible instruction.

Direct versus contextual language instruction. A longstanding debate in foreign language instruction is the extent to which instruction should focus on teaching discrete language skills (grammar, vocabulary, translation) as opposed to providing students with a more contextualized approach to learning the language. Overall, the immersion approach to teaching foreign language translates to less classroom emphasis on direct rules of grammar and more on immersing students in situations that require speaking and listening to the second language, especially within the context of relevant dialogue (Campbell, 1984; Genesee, 1987). The target language is taught as it is used to learn within the curriculum.

The teaching of language through integrated curriculum puts into practice the approach language professionals identify as contextualized language instruction. Language is introduced and taught in context, that is, real situations are used that encompass all aspects of a conversational exchange: the physical setting, the purpose of the exchange, the roles of the participants, the socially accepted norms, in addition to the medium, topic, tone, and register of the exchange (Hymes, 1974). This approach argues that students cannot learn a foreign language simply by listening to input. They must be active conversational participants (Long, 1981). The stance a teacher takes on this debate will determine the approaches to integrating technology. A teacher adopting a more skills-based approach will, for example, be more likely to look for good language tutorials. A teacher adopting an immersion approach, on the other hand, would be more likely to access the web in search of authentic reading materials in the target language.

Cognate versus noncognate languages. Foreign language learning is greatly influenced by characteristics of the language to be learned. If the language is a noncognate language such as Japanese or Chinese, nothing about the language is related to English; this heightens the learning curve for students. By contrast, cognate languages such as Spanish and French are much easier for English speakers to learn because words from both languages are incorporated into their language base. The contrast in difficulty is best demonstrated by the writing systems. Japanese and Chinese are written in kanjis, symbolic representations of the language that have no similarity to English orthography. Spanish and French, on the other hand, use the same letters as the English language, with only a few variants. For English-speaking students, learning to read and write in a noncognate language is much more difficult. The role of technology in foreign language instruction, and the difficulties of adopting technology-based tools, will be influenced by whether the target language is a cognate or noncognate language. However, with the improvement in computer operating systems, keyboards can be adjusted to meet the writing and publishing needs of most languages. Even with the noncognate languages, adjustments can be made in hardware and operating systems to enable students to write using the symbolic character set rather than forcing students to use the English character representation.

Content-obligatory versus content-compatible language. Teaching a foreign language assumes a language base through which teachers and students can describe experiences, express and discuss ideas, communicate with peers, and actively develop extensions for their learning. In a foreign language classroom, there are gaps between the students' levels of cognitive reasoning, receptive language, and expressive language (Curtain & Pesola, 1994). The difficulty for teachers becomes how to teach conceptually at the appropriate receptive language level and provide students activities that engage them at their productive language. The model for such planning was developed by Snow, Met, and Genesee (1989) and illustrates how teachers determine language learning outcomes for the content areas they are teaching in a second language. These outcomes derive from two considerations: (1) the language essential to an understanding of content material (content-obligatory language) and (2) the language that can be taught naturally within the context of a particular subject matter (content-compatible language). For the teacher, this task of distinguishing between content-obligatory language and content-compatible language is part of the process of planning instruction. As such, it also influences how technology will be integrated into the teaching and learning process. For example, software has been designed that teaches content-obligatory language through drill and practice. Simultaneously, educators can focus on content-compatible language by providing students with opportunities to produce multimedia projects using text, speech, and graphics as a way of exploring content-compatible dialogues and interactions.

Strategies for Integrating Technology into Language Arts and Foreign Language Instruction

The following sections explore technology applications to language arts and foreign language instruction under three major topics: (1) writing and publishing, (2) reading and studying, and (3) communication and collaboration.

Technology to Support Writing and Publishing

In the mid-1980s, educators were introduced to a new approach to writing instruction that focused on writing as a process, as opposed to writing as a product. Led by Donald Graves (1984), Lucy Calkins (1986), and others, writing teachers learned to guide students through a process for writing that encouraged an iterative set of activities focused on planning, drafting, revising, editing, and publishing. The process was clearly more than a means to an end; it became recognized as the medium for learning what real writing is all about and for learning how to become writers. Fortunately for writing instructors, the computer was simultaneously finding its way into schools. With the introduction of word processing software, students gained access to electronic tools to support this new approach to writing, one based on reflection and frequent modification. Writing in a word processing environment facilitates both the production and revision of text, thus freeing students to focus on ideas and how to share them. In the following paragraphs we address technology resources available to teachers and students for all stages of the writing process.

Planning. The type of planning that a student does for a writing project will depend largely on the type of writing being produced. If the assignment is to write a poem, students usually need a motivating influence during the planning stage. This can come from seeing samples from other students on the Internet, or from using unusual or experimental forms of poetry for which word processors can facilitate development: dada, sound poems, optophonetic poems, oulipo, snowballing, iceograms, iterative poetry, and transformations (See in Chapter 5, Technology Integration Idea 5.10, Writing Poetry to Develop Literacy.)

If the assignment is to write a fictional story, then the student needs to brainstorm ideas for the story line, setting, and major characters; refine and organize those ideas; and generate a plan for presenting each story element in an intriguing manner. If the assignment is to write a report, then the student needs to gather information on the topic from a variety of sources; synthesize and arrange this information into categories or subtopics; and generate a plan for presenting the information in a logical way. Both types of planning can be facilitated by using information organizing software such as electronic outlining and concept mapping programs. (See Technology Integration Idea 10.1.)

Electronic outliners are now integrated into almost all major word processing programs and so are easily accessible as planning tools. When using an electronic outliner, ideas and information are typed as headings and subheadings, all of which are automatically given prefixes using the standard outline hierarchy of numbers and letters. The advantages to using software designed specifically for outlining are that new headings/subheadings can be easily inserted anywhere in the outline, that headings/subheadings can be shifted around quickly to reflect a student's thinking and planning, and that the prefixes serving as organizational clues are automatically changed to reflect the outline's revised organization (Anderson-Inman, 1995).

Software to support concept mapping or webbing is also being used in schools for planning. One of the most popular programs is *Inspiration,* by Inspiration Software, Inc., a product that has electronic tools for both outlining and diagramming. The diagramming side of the program can be used to create a variety of graphic displays, all of which are useful for students who like to think and plan using visual representations of their ideas. For example, students can easily brainstorm a cluster map of ideas for a story and then rearrange or expand on the ideas for later development. Students can also use the program to generate a hierarchical map of key concepts to be explored for a research paper, and link those concepts with labels that demonstrate their conceptual relationship. Outlining or mapping in an electronic environment (see Figure 10.2) facilitates the planning process because changes can be made easily and quickly, supporting such endeavors as initial brainstorming on a story topic, as well as synthesizing research information gathered from multiple sources (Anderson-Inman & Zeitz, 1994). For students working in a foreign language, the same types of tools are either available in the target language or adaptable from those designed for English speakers.

TECHNOLOGY INTEGRATION IDEA 10.1

Using Concept Mapping in Writing

TITLE: *Inspiration* for Students' Writing

CONTENT AREA/TOPIC: Writing

GRADE LEVEL: High school

NETS FOR STUDENTS: Standards 3, 4

DESCRIPTION: An electronic outliner is a program designed to allow the easy development of hierarchically organized outlines. This can be a valuable activity to motivate students to analyze and write about a variety of topics. One example of this kind of activity is using electronic outlines to enhance the study of a play. Begin by scanning in the text of the play and organizing it by main categories of acts and scenes, with subcategories of stage directions, production notes, and dialogue under each scene. After the text is entered, students can use the electronic outline to study the play's features. For example, if a class is studying characterization, students can reorganize the text in a given scene or act so that each character's lines can be viewed together as a group. This makes it easier for students to see the development of speech patterns or other aspects that help them understand character development. The same outline can be reordered to study plot elements, settings, or production requirements.

Source: Anderson-Inman, L., & Zeitz, L. (1994, May). Beyond notecards: Synthesizing information with electronic study tools. *The Computing Teacher,* 21–25.

Drafting. Drafting is the stage of the writing process when students put ideas and information into words, sentences, and paragraphs. When drafting, the student is engaging in the act of composing text, a creative act leading to words and sentences that might later be revised or refined. The term *drafting* for this stage implies an impermanence to the product (i.e., a draft) and therefore reflects the notion that students will continue to plan, rethink, and reorganize their ideas, even while producing text. Depending on the availability of equipment, students can draft directly on the computer using a word processing program or type in their handwritten draft when they reach some level of completion.

Word processing programs have been adopted widely in schools and include various features that support the process of drafting text. (See Technology Integration Idea 10.2.) Regardless of their complexity, all word processing

Figure 10.2 ***Inspiration* Concept Map for *To Kill a Mockingbird***

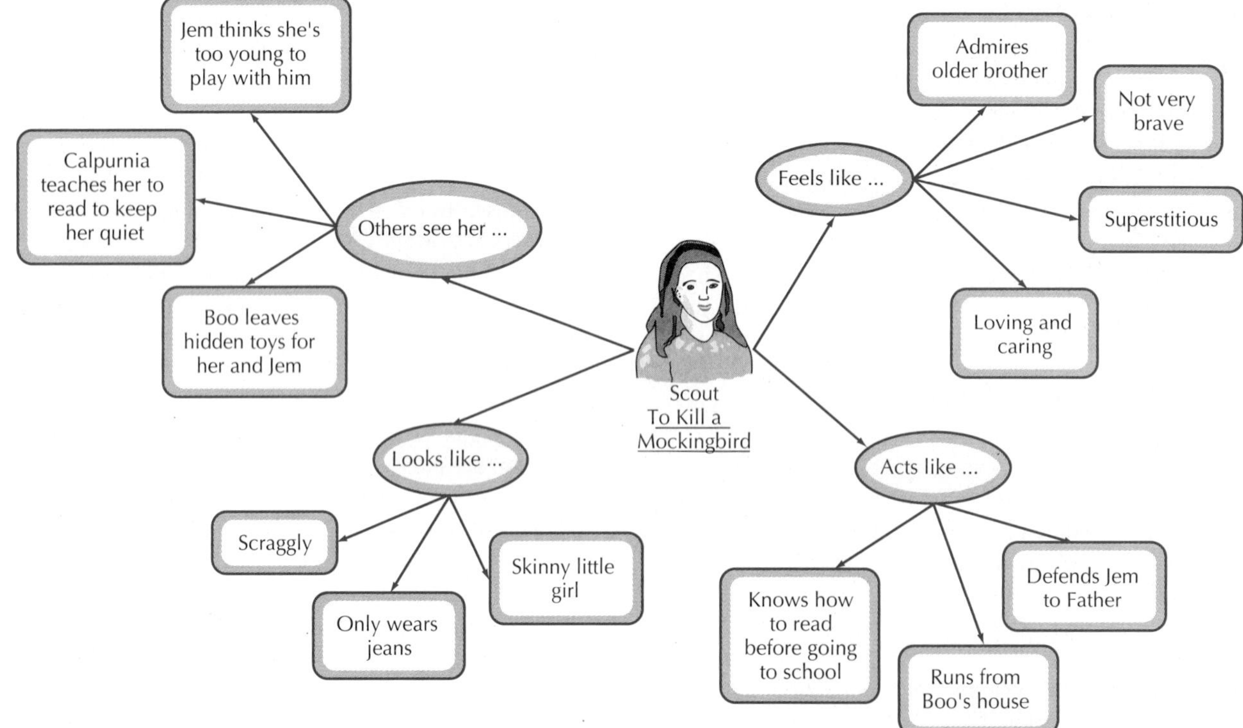

Source: Used by permission of Inspiration Software, Inc.

Technology Integration Idea

Using Word Processing for Writing and Revising

TITLE: Word Processing in Early Foreign Language Learning

CONTENT AREA/TOPIC: Writing, foreign language learning

GRADE LEVEL: 7–8

NETS FOR STUDENTS: Standard 4

DESCRIPTION: Beginning language students need the practice of writing simple compositions in the language they are studying. Yet students who have limited vocabulary and grammar mastery frequently find it difficult and tedious to accomplish this. Word processing lets them make corrections more quickly, and combining their writing with graphics makes the activity more exciting and helps them convey complex thoughts they are not yet able to express. One such activity is student autobiographies: a self-portrait in writing. In an assignment presented to them in French, ask them to incorporate items such as name, age, birthday, family members, grandparents and their nationalities, friends, activities they like to do on weekends, religion, favorite TV programs, foods they like to eat, favorite sports, places they have visited, remarks about their school, and languages they speak.

Source: Lewis, P. (1997). Using productivity software for beginning language learning. *Learning and Leading with Technology, 24*(8), 14–17.

programs enable students to write and revise in electronic text—text that is supportive of drafting because it is easily modified to reflect additions, deletions, revisions, and corrections. Word processing programs include other features depending on the instructional goal and the age of intended users. For example, word processing software designed for early elementary students, such as *Kid Pix* and the *Amazing Writing Machine* by the Learning Company, includes a simplified word processor, drawing tools, easily imported graphics, and simple formatting features. For upper elementary students, programs such as *AppleWorks* by Apple Computer include spelling and grammar checkers, a thesaurus, and language analyzers to support skill building within the writing process. Middle and high school students commonly use full-featured integrated packages such as the *Office* suite by Microsoft, Inc., which contains *Microsoft Word,* a sophisticated word processing program capable of handling the increasingly complex demands of students throughout their learning careers. Word processing software, integrated spell-checking programs, and/or keyboard adaptations exist for all the major languages and can be used by foreign language students for writing projects in the target language.

Revising and editing. Revising is the stage during which students make changes in the paper's content or structure that reflect decisions about how to improve its overall quality. To revise well, students have to move from composing text to analyzing it, looking for what needs to be added, deleted, or rearranged. One of the best ways for teachers to assist in this process is to project a student's typed draft onto a screen, then model the thinking and decision making that goes into analyzing and revising the text. If projecting from a computer, changes can be made to the text as the students watch, facilitated by the fluidity of the electronic writing environment. Teachers often use peer feedback to help identify ways in which a paper can be improved. Although getting student input is a good idea, peers frequently are not sophisticated enough as writers to provide truly useful input. Students need to watch and listen to a mature writer engage in the thought processes that lead to identifying what needs to be changed and deciding what content and structural changes will lead to improvement.

Editing, as opposed to revising, is the process of refining a paper so that it adheres to standard conventions for spelling, syntax, punctuation, and style. Editing is a far more superficial task than revising, but no less important. All word processing programs have features that support the editing process. These include spell checkers and grammar checkers, as well as electronic search capabilities to verify consistent word usage, tone, and tense. Although editing can be done at various times during the writing process (for example, a quick spell check is useful before turning a draft over to teacher or peers for feedback), major attention to editing should be left until after a paper has undergone revision. It makes no sense to struggle over word choice and sentence structure when there are gaps in thinking that might require significant additions or major structural alterations.

Many word processing programs now provide "on-the-fly" synchronous feedback about the accuracy of writers' spelling and grammar as they are drafting their text. It is often a good idea to have students turn this feature off while drafting so they can concentrate on producing a body of text, without worrying about spelling and grammatical accuracy. When editing, this feature can then be turned back on. In addition, some students find it helpful to have the text read out loud when they are editing—feeling it is easier to hear their mistakes than see them. Technology can support this approach to editing if the computer is outfitted with screen reading software, or if the word processing program has a text-to-speech feature. Using this approach, students listen while their words are read out loud, sometimes with simultaneous text highlighting, and then make changes as needed to improve word choice, reduce redundancy, or eliminate trite expressions.

Publishing. Reports, newspaper articles, brochures, slide shows, and web pages are examples of publishable formats available to students for sharing their written work with peers, teachers, and the larger community. (See Technology Integration Idea 10.3.) Publishing provides students with an audience for their writing, often an audience that goes beyond the classroom or school. Two types of publishing can be used by language arts and foreign language teachers: (1) traditional publishing, in which students produce paper products such as reports, books, newspaper articles, brochures, and (2) electronic publishing, in which students share their writing in electronic forms such as web sites, electronic books, multimedia slide shows, and news broadcasts. Both forms of publishing can take advantage of technology tools with specialized features for working with text, graphics, and other forms of media. These tools include word processors, multimedia authoring programs, and HTML editors, all of which can be used by students to organize, manipulate, and display information in a variety of publishable formats.

Desktop publishing programs are designed to facilitate the production of professional looking printed products such as books, newspapers, and magazine articles. In the past, there were significant differences between word processing software and the programs used for desktop publishing. As word processing programs have become increasingly sophisticated, however, most of these distinctions have all but disappeared. Now, both types of software include features that support layout, design, and high-end graphic manipulation. Using these features, students can publish their work in traditional forms such as reports, books, newspapers, and brochures. Foreign language students can also use word processing and desktop publishing software to create the same range of products. Improvements in computer operating systems now enable keyboard adjustments suitable for meeting the publishing demands of most languages. Even with noncognate languages such as Japanese and Chinese, adjustments can be made in hardware and operating systems to enable students to write and publish in the language's symbolic character set rather than *romanji*—a set of English character representations.

An increasingly popular form of publishing in schools leads to one or more forms of "multimedia." The term *multimedia* refers to "interactive, computer-based products that are rich with sound, pictures, and text" (Elin, 2001, p. 6). The product may be designed for presentation to an audience (e.g., an electronic slide show created with software such as *PowerPoint* by Microsoft); pressed to a CD (e.g., a set of electronic reading materials created with *StoryBook Weaver* by Learning Company), or distributed via the Internet (e.g., a web site containing students' *HyperStudio* projects). An alternate term, *hypermedia,* is frequently used when the interactivity is accomplished through "links" embedded in the text, and some or all of those links lead to other forms of media. Multimedia authoring environments can help teachers blend a constructivist, integrated curriculum with a responsiveness to student diversity in learning style. Working in these environments students can use text and other forms of media to share their writing in both linear and nonlinear formats.

Multimedia authoring programs exist for all educational levels and can be used to meet many of the language arts curriculum standards in writing and speaking. In the primary grades, the slide show features of *Kid Pix* by Learning Company and *AppleWorks* by Apple Computer allow students to combine images and text to create interactive presentations appropriate for sharing electronic book reports, papers, and storybooks. *StoryBook Weaver* by Learning Company is a creative writing program appropriate for students in the upper elementary grades and can support student-centered projects constructed to extend theme concepts, knowledge, and skills. By combining an authoring application such as *HyperStudio* by Knowledge Adventure, with different peripherals such as scanners, video, and digital cameras, older students can create interactive

TECHNOLOGY INTEGRATION IDEA 10.3

Using Technology to Publish Student Works

TITLE: New Millenium Newspapers

CONTENT AREA/TOPIC: Writing news stories

GRADE LEVEL: 5–9

NETS FOR STUDENTS: Standards 3, 4, 5

DESCRIPTION: This activity has students creating newspaper-type stories with predictions about the future; these Special Edition newspapers are published in a "web newspaper." Some motivating activities to get students writing include creating a sample entertainment newspaper section circa 2010 or writing time capsule predictions about various areas of society in the future, for example, education, fashion, environment, health, sports, and science.

Source: Reissman, R. (1999). Predicting the future: Students create content for new millennium newspapers. *Learning and Leading with Technology, 27*(2), 18–21.

multimedia presentations that explore a subject in depth while simutaneously demonstrating both their visual literacy and text-based literacy skills.

Multimedia authoring tools are particularly useful for foreign language instruction because they encourage students to interact communicatively with one another in the unfamiliar language in a nonthreatening environment, thus encouraging self-expression. Writing and publishing in a hypermedia or multimedia environment provides concrete, visual, and manipulative practice that aids students' comprehension of concepts and engages them in projects that enhance their motivation, self-confidence, and language proficiency (Schrum & Glisan, 1994). By using text, sounds, and graphics to complete a project or presentation, foreign language students develop concepts and skills necessary to negotiate meaning in the target language. And because multimedia authoring can be highly motivating, students are often challenged to increase their communication skills in order to present, demonstrate, and explain their completed projects to a large audience. Both *Kid Pix* and *StoryBook Weaver* can be used in either an English or Spanish environment.

A specialized tool for hypermedia authoring is an HTML editor, software designed specifically to support the creation of web pages. HTML stands for Hypertext Markup Language, an agreed-on system for formatting and encoding text and other forms of media so that any piece of information in a document can be linked to any other piece of information on any computer connected to the Internet (Alessi & Trollip, 2001). HTML editors eliminate the necessity of having to learn HTML code by enabling students to add HTML tags using a graphical interface. Learning to build web pages using HTML editors in order to share written work with a global audience is quickly becoming commonplace at all school levels. Many schools have their own web sites and regularly use them to publish student work. While most HTML editors (e.g., *DreamWeaver* by MacroMedia and *GO-Live* by Adobe) are appropriate for use by students in the upper grades, web editors specifically designed for the primary grades are beginning to emerge. *SiteCentral* by Knowledge Adventure is a "drag-and-drop" environment that assists young students to create web pages. In addition, some web browsers (e.g., *Netscape Communicator* and the newer versions of *Internet Explorer*) include an HTML editor. Overall, web publishing is a powerful vehicle for encouraging student creativity and making student projects available to a worldwide audience. In the foreign language classroom, web publishing is used for the same purpose, with the added incentive that native speakers worldwide might be attracted to the students' work.

Publishing on the web does not, however, require learning to use an HTML editor. Teachers and students can also submit written work to web sites designed specifically to serve as clearinghouses for student writing, ensuring students their work will reach an interested audience. For example, *KidPub* (http://www.kidpub.org/kidpub) accepts students' stories, sent as e-mail messages, and posts them on the web, along with a brief profile of each student author. *Byte-bookie* (http://ipl.org/youth/Byte-bookie/), sponsored by the Internet Public Library, accepts and posts book reviews written by students. Both web sites are outstanding publishing venues for the written work of students in grades 4 through 8. Another great outlet is *KidNews* (http://www.vsa.cape.com/~powens/Kidnews3.html), which publishes student news stories in a number of different categories. Foreign language students might join the *International Newsday Project* (http://www.gsn.org/project/newsday/index.html), a student-developed news exchange where students construct an electronic newspaper using articles submitted by other students from around the world.

Technology to Support Reading and Studying

Technology can be used to support the development of reading skills and habits in three major ways. Each is described below briefly, with examples from the literature and from commercial programs used as illustration. In addition, technology can be used for notetaking, a study strategy recommended to promote more in-depth understanding of both traditional textbooks, as well as electronic reading materials.

Computer-guided instruction. Technology can be used to provide early readers with computer-guided instruction—tutorials and practice on basic reading skills using examples and passages carefully controlled for reading difficulty. This approach to reading instruction is most frequently found in the elementary grades of schools with Title I programs (federal funds designed to support the academic progress of students from disadvantaged homes). Key to the success of these computer-based reading programs is a diagnostic system that places students in the program at an appropriate level and then monitors their progress through frequent testing. Using student performance as a guide, programs can automatically adjust the difficulty of the reading passages presented and/or the type of reading instruction provided. The students can move at their own speed and often make excellent reading progress. Although generally not tightly integrated with the traditional curriculum, the programs are usually designed to supplement regular classroom instruction in reading, not supplant it.

One popular guided reading program is *Accelerated Reader* (AR) by Advantage Learning Systems. AR presents students with story passages to read, requires them to take a quiz on each passage, keeps track of their scores, and provides reports to teachers. AR has been popular since its introduction in 1986, in part because it provides a broad choice of stories at varying levels, thus making it appropriate for diverse types of students. Another example of this type of program is *Reading Adventures,* a literature-based reading program for grades 1 through 6 published by NCS Learn as part of their *SuccessMaker* series. A key feature is its computer-based assessment component called the Initial Placement Motion, a diagnostic process designed to place students at the appropriate level within the reading material.

Computer-supported comprehension and vocabulary development. Second, technology can be used to provide students with electronic reading materials that have been modified to support vocabulary development and promote reading comprehension. This is accomplished by embedding various types of supportive resources into the text of an electronic reading document, whether on CD-ROM or the web. Anderson-Inman and Horney (1997, 1999) describe this type of reading material as "supported text," or text that has been linked to various resources, each designed to support some aspect of the reading process. For example, in a supported text electronic reading environment, unfamiliar terms can be linked to simple definitions; unfamiliar concepts and processes can be linked to explanations, pictures, or animations; graphic overviews can be used to provide the big picture; contextual information can be provided with summaries or videos to eliminate gaps in prior knowledge; and timelines can be integrated to provide chronological perspective. A supported text document also can include the following:

- Text-to-speech capabilities so passages can be read out loud,
- Instructional annotations to prompt specific types of metacognitive reading skills, or
- Links to other documents to facilitate learning more on a given topic.

When these resources are carefully selected and integrated into electronic versions of students' reading materials, the result can be improved vocabulary development and enhanced comprehension (Horney & Anderson-Inman, 1994), particularly for at-risk students (Horney & Anderson-Inman, 1999).

Basically, two types of digital reading materials are available to teachers and students. The first is comprised of plain digital texts that can be enhanced with supportive resources by the teacher or inserted into commercially available reading systems designed to support the reading process. This type can be created by scanning printed text and using OCR software to turn the print into electronic text. Digital text materials also can be acquired by downloading documents from the web that are in the public domain, that is, no longer under copyright protection. Most of these have little or nothing in the way of features to support reading comprehension, but are freely available to teachers using the web and can be found on almost any topic. Especially rich are the many digital libraries containing literature of all genres and in various languages. For example, see the *Online Literature Library* (http://www.literature.org) for a selection of literature in English and the *Electronic Text Center* at Columbia University (http://www.columbia.edu/cu/lweb/indiv/ets/offsite.language.html) for a list of major online text collections in other languages. These can be used in conjunction with a screen reader (to enable students to hear the text read), a desktop dictionary (to quickly access definitions for unfamiliar words), or inserted into commercially available reading systems equipped with dictionaries, text-to-speech capabilities, and features to support various types of studying. Three such reading systems are *E-Reader* by CAST, Inc., *WYNN,* by Arkenstone, and *Kurzweil 3000,* by Kurzweil, Inc.

A free electronic reading system, the *Microsoft Reader,* is available online from Microsoft, Inc. (http://www.microsoft.com/reader/). A large number of e-books are already compatible with this system available online from commercial publishers or free from the *Electronic Text Center* at the University of Virginia (http://etext.virginia.edu/e-books/). When reading an e-book using *Microsoft Reader* students have instant access to dictionary definitions and annotations, and can highlight text, write notes, and bookmark pages. Digital text is also available on the web for the many small electronic reading machines and handheld personal digital assistants emerging on the market. For example, the University of Virginia's *Electronic Text Center* provides more than 1,600 digital books ready for downloading into Palm Pilots (Palm, Inc.) or pocket PCs (designed by Hewlett-Packard, Casio, and Compaq).

The second type of digital reading material is comprised of electronic documents that have already been enhanced with various types of supportive resources designed to promote reading comprehension. These might be distributed commercially on CD-ROM or accessed by teachers and students on the web. A popular form of reading material on CD-ROM, especially for younger students and students who do not speak English as their native language, is the "talking book." These electronic reading materials have built-in text-to-speech capabilities, usually combined with text highlighting, and sometimes user control over such things as speed, voice, and text segmentation. An excellent literature-based collection of talking books is the *Start to Finish* series by Don Johnston, Inc. Each CD-ROM in the series provides students with one or more pieces of classic literature, rewritten at about the fourth-grade level. The text is supported with helpful illustrations, text-to-speech capabilities, vocabulary definitions, and various supplementary materials for promoting or assessing comprehension. The assumption is that talking books enhance reading fluency and word recognition by supporting the process of "reading while listening" (RWL), a process that purportedly motivates students to read, models the correct pronunciation of unfamiliar or irregular words, shifts attention from individual words to understanding the narrative, and enhances reader confidence (Bergman, 1999). Recent research suggests, however, that these beneficial effects occur only when students have control of the narration rate, so that they can make connections between the graphemes they see and the phonemes they hear (Bergman, 1999).

Supported text materials are also available to teachers and students on the web. For example, researchers at the Center for Electronic Studying, University of Oregon, have been developing a library of digital texts designed specifically to support the vocabulary development, reading comprehension, and electronic literacy skills of at-risk readers. Funded by the U.S. Department of Education, Office of

Special Education Programs, and known as Project INTERSECT, the digital library comprises examples of electronically enhanced expository texts, narrative texts, and primary source documents. Each of the texts has a basic array of supportive resources designed to help readers overcome problems with unfamiliar vocabulary and new concepts. In addition, many of the texts have instructional supports designed to foster effective reading skills or promote use of study features available only in electronic texts (e.g., the search mechanism). Research with supported text materials such as those under development for Project INTERSECT reveals that the electronic reading materials can have a positive effect on students' understanding of content area vocabulary, their comprehension of critical text passages, and their motivation for independent reading (Anderson-Inman & Horney, 1998).

Computer-assisted notetaking. An effective way to learn from content area reading materials is the process of taking and reviewing notes on what is written (Caverly, Orlando, & Mullen, 2000). Teachers have worked for years to teach students some form of outlining or notetaking as a study strategy for learning material contained in content-area textbooks or other reading materials. The widespread use of electronic outliners and the increasing availability of software designed for mapping and webbing has brought this teaching into the 21st century. Students can now take notes using one of these electronic information organizers, a process that has numerous benefits over taking notes on paper (Anderson-Inman, 1995). Two of the most prominent advantages are (1) the ability to easily modify (add to, reorganize, etc.) the notes as learning continues and (2) the ability to use the notes in various creative ways to study for tests or prepare for other forms of accountability. Research on the use of computer-assisted notetaking indicates this approach can have a powerful and positive impact on text comprehension for students from a wide range of reading levels (Adams & Anderson-Inman, 1991; Anderson-Inman, Knox-Quinn, & Horney, 1996; Anderson-Inman, Knox-Quinn & Szymanski, 1999; Anderson-Inman, Redekopp, & Adams, 1992; Tenny, 1988).

Computer-enhanced critical thinking. Each discipline has higher order reading and thinking skills, those practiced by experts of the discipline. Technology can be used to enrich discipline-specific reading and writing by providing access to reading materials and study environments that support the development of these critical thinking skills. By encouraging access to online archives, libraries, and databases, students can be taught to locate, organize, and synthesize information from multiple sources to determine patterns and trends, draw conclusions related to their hypotheses, and make generalizations based on original research. By connecting students to authentic materials and promoting web-based research, teachers can help expand and support content learning, promote the use of critical thinking, and open students' minds to global interactions.

Key to the development of critical thinking skills is access to primary source documents that can be read and interpreted by the student, without prior summary or interpretation by an expert. For this endeavor, the Internet can be used to access materials not available in most school libraries, materials that give students a pool of primary source texts and pictures to be used for authentic historical, literary, and scientific inquiry (Craver, 1999). However, it is important that teachers be given well-researched strategies for promoting these advanced literacy skills in today's classrooms. Toward this goal, the Center for Electronic Studying, University of Oregon, has developed a "web-based study environment" designed specifically to support the teaching of historical inquiry on topics related to Spanish colonialism (http://anza.uoregon.edu). The core of this web site is a series of original diaries (in both Spanish and English) generated on two expeditions led by Juan Bautista de Anza in the years 1774–1776, the last of which led to the founding and settling of San Francisco. Research with teachers led to the development of the *GATHER model* for teaching historical inquiry using web-based study environments such as Web de Anza. The GATHER model is comprised of six specific steps that enable students to conduct research in the same way that historians do, albeit aided by an online archive of primary source documents and computer-based study tools. The six steps in the GATHER method are as follows:

1. **G**et an overview.
2. **A**sk a probing question.
3. **T**riangulate the data.
4. **H**ypothesize a tentative answer.
5. **E**xplore and interpret the data.
6. **R**ecord and support your conclusions.

Technology to Support Communication and Collaboration

In addition to giving students access to enormous repositories of information and resources from around the world, the Internet has also expanded students' opportunities for communication and collaboration. Students, unconstrained by geographic boundaries, are now able to communicate with students and experts worldwide. Providing students with tools for online communication, and supporting projects in which these tools are used for collaborative projects worldwide, opens up a variety of exciting areas for integrating technology into the curriculum.

E-mail and threaded discussion. The ability to communicate via a computer with other students has unexpectedly provided powerful support for the curriculum, especially in the area of language arts activities. Access to e-mail is beginning to have a significant impact on the quantity and quality of student communications with the outside world. Students are frequently more motivated to write well when sharing ideas long distance and in a manner that assumes a speedy response. For example, students were found to communicate more clearly and use better spelling and grammar when they wrote for audiences at other sites (Cohen & Riel, 1989). Authentic uses for electronic communications include gathering information for projects, interviewing experts and mentors, and developing an understanding of another culture through correspondence with peers. Teachers are increasingly designing lessons and projects that promote electronic information exchange between students and outside resources. Foreign language students given e-mail accounts can communicate with students in their target language countries for first-hand research. E-mail also promotes the use of their written skills as they communicate with keypals in foreign countries to practice authentic communication with native speakers.

Threaded discussions are moderated asynchronous electronic discussions on specific topics where students respond to the postings of previous participants. Specially designed software helps to keep track of the order in which students post their comments and provides links among comments that can be navigated easily. When participating in threaded discussions, students can share and learn from the ideas of multiple other students, guest experts, or community leaders anywhere in the world. Because the topics have focus, these electronic discussions can explore issues and ideas in some depth, bringing in opinions and information from beyond the four walls of a traditional classroom.

Networked collaboration and support. Technology can be used to promote collaboration, both online and in the classroom. (See Technology Integration Idea 10.4.) Collaborative online projects are an excellent way for students to experience global learning and practice critical thinking skills. For example, teachers can subscribe to online projects such as *MayaQuest, AustraliaQuest,* and *AmazonQuest* through Classroom Connect (http://quest.classroom.com), all of which are great examples of students learning together online with teachers, students, and experts from around the world. Using the Internet, students follow a team of researchers as they travel to and around a specific location in search of answers to specific questions. The students help direct the team's activities via online surveys. All of the *Quest* journeys are presented in both English and Spanish.

Networks can also be used for in-class communication and collaboration. Knox-Quinn (1995) describes a synchronous writing project conducted in a school computer lab in which joint (and anonymous) contributions to a collaborative narrative led to the development of unique story elements and a student willingness to engage the emerging text in novel (often personal) ways. In another project, Anderson-Inman, Knox-Quinn, and Tromba (1996), describe the use of wireless networked notetaking to support students struggling to comprehend the teacher's presentations and lectures. In this latter case, a notetaker's laptop computer was wirelessly linked to that of a student who was unable to understand the lecture due to a hearing impairment. The notetaker relayed the teacher's lecture through text and the student's in-class comprehension improved. More recently, networked notetaking has been used to support ESL students in general education classrooms, leading to improved grades and a reduction in dropouts (Knox-Quinn & Anderson-Inman, 2001).

Video conferencing and distance education. And finally, with the increasing demand for foreign language instruction, combined with shortages of qualified teachers, technology-supported distance education has become extremely important in the learning of foreign languages. This method provides a way for students to study languages, especially noncognate languages such as Chinese, Japanese, and Russian, even when there is a local scarcity of qualified educators. With the advent of online web courses and videoconferencing systems, this method of instruction has become more cost effective and efficient for all school districts—both urban and rural.

TECHNOLOGY INTEGRATION IDEA 10.4

Learning

TITLE: Cyber Traveling in the Loire Valley

CONTENT AREA/TOPIC: French

GRADE LEVEL: 5–6

NETS FOR STUDENTS: Standards 3, 4, 5

DESCRIPTION: In this activity, students practice their French language skills by taking a virtual trip to the Loire Valley region of France and writing in French about their findings. They are asked to prepare a written report on a chateau of their choice, writing (en Francais) facts about it such as when it was built, who built it, architectural style, its history, its location, and when you can visit it. Students use the French version of *AppleWorks* to prepare their reports. After they are complete, they create web pages to publish and share their work.

Source: Chenuau, J. (2000). Cyber traveling through the Loire Valley. *Learning and Leading with Technology, 28*(2), 22–27.

Useful Web Sites for Language Arts Instruction

International Reading Association

http://www.ira.org

The International Reading Association is an international professional organization concerned with research and professional development related to instruction in reading, writing, and other literacy skills. It publishes a number of professional journals, several of which have regular columns focusing on the integration of technology in reading and language arts.

Reading Online

http://www.readingonline.org

Reading Online is an electronic journal published monthly by the International Reading Association. The journal regularly includes articles and columns on the use of technology for literacy instruction.

National Council of Teachers of English

http://www.ncte.org/

The National Council of Teachers of English is a leading professional organization for improving the teaching of English and language arts at all grade levels. The site presents a wide variety of information valuable to K–12 teachers.

Center for Electronic Studying

http://ces/uoregon.edu

The Center for Electronic Studying at the University of Oregon is a research and outreach center focused on the use of technology for improving students' skills and strategies in the areas of reading, writing, and studying. The center hosts Project INTERSECT (http://intersect.uoregon.edu), a digital library of supported texts, and the Computer-Based Study Strategies web site, which lists professional development materials and instructional modules on the use of computer study tools (http://cbss.uoregon.edu).

Children's Literature Web Guide

http://www.acs.ucalgary.ca/~dkbrown/index.html

The Children's Literature Web Guide provides a gateway site to the growing number of Internet resources related to books for children and young adults. The site includes such features as Best Books, Web Traveler's Toolkit: Essential Kid Lit Websites, and What We're Reading: Commentary on Children's Books.

KidPub

http://www.kidpub.org/kidpub

This site allows students to publish their own writing on the Internet and contains more than 11,000 stories and poems written by young people. In sections labeled KidMud and Keypals, students are able to find and communicate with other students interested in writing.

Useful Web Sites for Foreign Language Instruction

American Council on the Teaching of Foreign Languages

http://www.actfl.org

A national organization dedicated to the improvement and expansion of the teaching and learning of all languages at all levels of instruction. The site includes links to publications, workshops, proficiency testing, conventions and expos, special projects, jobs, and resources for teachers and administrators at the elementary through graduate grade levels.

Language Resources

http://www.itp.berkeley.edu/~thorne/HumanResources.html

This site lists links to language and culture web sites. It attempts to provide quality over quantity in the links the author has chosen as valuable resources. A variety of languages are included in the links, with Middle English, Scandinavian, and South Asian languages, Swahili, Tagalog, and Yiddish among them. Also included is a link to the University of Oregon Font Archive, where different language fonts can be legally downloaded directly from the Internet.

Language Links

http://polyglot.lss.wisc.edu/lss/lang/teach.html

A compilation of ideas for using Internet resources as a language teaching tool. It also offers links to sites that have pedagogical information.

Internet Activities for Foreign Language Classes

http://members.aol.com/maestro12/web/wadir.html

This site includes how-to-write activities for the web, reading strategies for web activities, a web lesson evaluation form, and 480 favorite teacher URLs for Spanish, French, and German. Sample web lessons are included as well for seven different languages.

Language Learning and Technology

http://llt.msu.edu

This is the site for the refereed journal entitled *Language Learning and Technology*. Selected articles from the current issue are online. The journal is intended for second language and foreign language educators. The current issue is published online including a PDF format of each issue.

University of Toledo—The Famous Foreign Language Bookmarks

http://www.forlang.utoledo.edu/BOOKMARK/Bookmark.html

Classical, French/Francophone, German, Japanese, Latin American/Spanish, and Russian bookmarks for web sites are listed.

Exercises

Record and apply what you have learned.

Chapter 10 Self-Test

To review terms and concepts in this chapter, take the Chapter 10 self-test. Select Chapter 10 from the front page of the Companion Website (located at http://www.prenhall.com/roblyer), then choose the *Multiple Choice* module.

Portfolio Activities

ISTE The following activities address ISTE National Educational Technology Standards for Teachers (NETS-T) and will help you add to your professional portfolio. To complete these activities online and save or submit the materials electronically, select Chapter 10 from the front page of the Companion Website (http://www.prenhall.com/roblyer), then choose the *Portfolio* module.

1. ***Integration Skills (NETS-T Standards: II-A, B, C; V-B)*** Learning to communicate in writing is a key skill in both the language arts and foreign language areas. Select one of the integration strategies described in the chapter that use word processing, concept mapping, or the Internet to aid writing instruction. Develop a classroom activity based on this strategy. Be prepared to teach or demonstrate the activity to the class. If possible, use your activity with the targeted age group before you bring it to the class. The lesson and your reflections on the teaching experience should be placed in your portfolio.
2. ***Scenario (NETS-T Standards: II-C, V-B)*** Imagine that you are the language arts or foreign language resource teacher for a small school district. Money for materials and equipment is tight, but you know the district sorely needs upgraded technology resources to support its instructional programs in your area. It is your job to make a good, clear case for purchasing software and other resources that will make demonstrable improvements in the programs. Develop a presentation on a hypermedia software or web page that documents your rationale for why technology must become an integral component of the programs and outline which resources must be obtained. Be prepared to present this case in class. Put an introduction and either printouts or links to your presentation in your professional portfolio.

Questions for Thought and Discussion

These questions may be used for small-group or class discussion or may be subjects for individual or group activities. To take part in these discussions online, select Chapter 10 from the front page of the Companion Website (http://www.prenhall.com/roblyer), then choose the *Message Board* module.

1. Many educators believe that with the growth of media and information technology, media literacy is as important as or even more important than print literacy. Describe your position on the relative importance of these two "literacies." Cite facts from this chapter and from the literature on this topic to support your position.
2. Describe some ways that instructional technology could be used to help a foreign language teacher achieve an immersion approach to foreign language instruction. Are virtual trips to foreign countries and virtual conversations with citizens of those countries as good as actually going there? If not, describe the differences between them and what teachers could (or could not) do to make up for them.

Collaborative Activities

The following activities address ISTE National Educational Technology Standards for Teachers (NETS-T) and can be done in small groups. Each group should present the findings to the class in a format they know how to use (word-processed report, presentation software, multimedia product). Completed group products can be copied and shared with the entire class and/or included in each person's personal portfolio.

1. ***Evaluation (NETS-T Standard: II-C)*** Work with a classmate or small group and evaluate three language arts and three foreign language software products. Use the software evaluation form from Chapter 4. Include a copy of evaluations in your portfolio.
2. ***Interdisciplinary Integration Strategies (NETS-T Standards: I-B; II-A, B, C)*** Work with a classmate or small group to locate and document examples in the literature (e.g., your professional journals) of using technology to support each of the following kinds of teaching strategies:
   - Writing across the curriculum
   - Integrating foreign language instruction with other content areas.

Annotate these with descriptions of how technology enhances the instruction. Include these descriptions in your personal portfolio.

Integrating Technology Across the Curriculum Activities

The *Integrating Technology Across the Curriculum* CD-ROM is a set of technology integration ideas and links to online lessons, arranged as a searchable database. The CD comes packaged with this textbook. Complete the following exercise using this CD:

Review some of the example integration ideas on the CD cited in this chapter for English/language arts and foreign language education. Now make up one of your own matched to an integration strategy described in this chapter. Add it to the CD. Be sure to identify each of the descriptors for it, including the relative advantage.

References

Adams, V., & Anderson-Inman, L. (1991). Electronic outlining: A computer-based study strategy for handicapped students in regular classrooms. In J. Marr & G. Tindall (Eds.), *The Oregon conference monograph 1991.* Eugene, OR: University of Oregon.

Alessi, S. M., & Trollip, S. R. (2001). *Multimedia for learning* (3rd ed.). Boston: Allyn & Bacon.

Anderson-Inman, L. (1995). Computer-assisted outlining: Information organization made easy. *Journal of Adolescent and Adult Literacy, 39*(4), 316–320.

Anderson-Inman, L., & Horney, M. (1997). Electronic books for secondary students. *Journal of Adolescent and Adult Literacy, 40*(6), 486–491.

Anderson-Inman, L., & Horney, M. (1998). Transforming text for at-risk readers. In D. Reinking, M. McKenna, Labbo, L., & Kieffer, R. (Eds.), *Handbook of literacy and technology: Transformations in a post-typographic world* (pp. 15–43). Mahwah, NJ: Lawrence Erlbaum Associates.

Anderson-Inman, L., & Horney, M. (1999). Electronic books: Reading and studying with supportive resources. *Reading Online.* Available online: http://readingonline.org/electronic_archives.

Anderson-Inman, L., Knox-Quinn, C., & Horney, M. (1996). Computer-based study strategies for students with disabilities: Individual differences associated with adoption level. *Journal of Learning Disabilities, 29*(5), 461–484.

Anderson-Inman, L., Knox-Quinn, C., & Szymanski, M. (1999). Computer-supported studying: Stories of successful transition. *Career Development and Exceptional Individuals, 22*(2), 185–212.

Anderson-Inman, L., Knox-Quinn, C., & Tromba, P. (1996). Synchronous writing environments: Real-time interaction in cyberspace. *Journal of Adolescent and Adult Literacy, 40*(2), 134–138.

Anderson-Inman, L., Redekopp, R., & Adams, V. (1992). Electronic studying: Using computer-based outlining programs as study tools. *Reading and Writing Quarterly: Overcoming Learning Difficulties, 8,* 337–358.

Anderson-Inman, L., & Zeitz, L. (1994). Beyond notecards: Synthesizing information with electronic study tools. *The Computing Teacher,* 21–25.

Bergman, O. (1999). Wait for me! Reader control of narration rate in talking books. *Reading Online.* Available online: http://readingonline.org/articles/art_index.asp?HREF=/articles/bergman/index.html.

Calkins, L. (1986). *The art of teaching writing.* Portsmouth, NH: Heinemann.

Campbell, R. N. (1984). *The immersion approach to foreign language teaching. Studies on immersion education: A collection for the United States educators.* Sacramento: California State Department of Education.

Caverly, D. C., Orlando, V. P., & Mullen, J. L. (2000). Textbook study reading. In R. F. Flippo & D. C. Caverly (Eds.), *Handbook of college reading and study strategy research* (pp. 105–147). Mahwah, NJ: Lawrence Erlbaum Associates.

Cohen, M., & Riel, M. (1989). The effect of distant audiences on students' writing. *American Educational Research Journal, 26* (2), 67–72.

Craver, K. W. (1999). *Using Internet primary sources to teach critical thinking skills in history.* Westport, CT: Greenwood Press.

Curtain, H., & Pesola, C. A. B. (1994). *Languages and children: Making the match* (2nd ed.). New York: Longman Publishing Group.

Elin, L. (2001). *Designing and developing multimedia.* Boston: Allyn & Bacon.

Genesee, F. (1987). *Learning through two languages: Studies of immersion and bilingual education.* Cambridge, MA: Newbury House.

Graves, D. H. (1984). *A fresh look at writing.* Portsmouth, NH: Heinemann.

Horney, M. A., & Anderson-Inman, L. (1994). The ElectroText Project: Hypertext reading patterns of middle school students. *Journal of Educational Multimedia and Hypermedia, 3*(1) 71–91.

Horney, M. A., & Anderson-Inman, L. (1999). Supported text in electronic reading environments. *Reading and Writing Quarterly: Overcoming Learning Difficulties, 15*(2), 127–168.

Hymes, D. (1974). *Foundations of sociolinguistics.* Philadelphia: University of Pennsylvania.

Knox-Quinn, C. (1995). Authentic classroom experiences: Anonymity, mystery and improvisation in sychronous writing environments. *Computers, Writing, Rhetoric and Literature.* Available online: http://www.en.utexas.edu/~cwrl/v1n2.html.

Knox-Quinn, C., & Anderson-Inman, L. (2001). Migrant ESL: High school students succeed using networked laptops. *Learning and Leading with Technology, 28*(5), 18–21, 52–53.

Leu, D. (2001). Internet project: Preparing students for new literacies in a global village. *The Reading Teacher, 54*(6), 568–572.

Long, M. H. (1981). Input interaction and second language acquisition. In Winitz, H. (Ed.), *Native language and foreign language acquisition.* Annals of the New York Academy of Sciences No. 379. New York: Academy of the Sciences.

Reinking, D. (1998). Introduction: Synthesizing technological transformations of literacy in a post-typographic world. In D. Reinking, M. McKenna, L. Labbo, & R. Kieffer (Eds.), *Handbook of literacy and technology: Transformations in a post-typographic world.* Mahwah, NJ: Lawrence Erlbaum Associates.

Schrum, J. L., & Glisan, E. W. (1994). *Teacher's handbook: Contextualized language instruction.* Boston, MA: Heinle and Heinle Publishers.

Snow, M. A., Met, M., & Genesee, F. (1989). A conceptual framework for the integration of language and content in second/foreign language instruction. *TESOL Quarterly, 23,* 201–217.

Tenny, J. (1988). *A study of the effectiveness of computer-mediated and rereading study strategies.* Unpublished doctoral dissertation, University of Oregon, 1989, American Doctoral Dissertations, 14197.

Toomey, R., & Ketterer, K. (1995). Using multimedia as a cognitive tool. *Journal of Research on Computing in Education, 27* (4), 472–481.

Resources

Software

Accelerated Reader (AR) (Advantage Learning)
Amazing Writing Machine (Learning Company)
AppleWorks (Apple)
DreamWeaver (MacroMedia)
E-Reader (CAST, Inc.)
GOLive (Adobe)
HyperStudio (Knowledge Adventure)
Inspiration (Inspiration Software, Inc.)
Kid Pix (Learning Company)
Kurzweil 3000 (Kurzweil, Inc.)
Microsoft Office (Microsoft)
Microsoft Reader (Microsoft)
SiteCentral (Knowledge Adventure)
Start to Finish series (Don Johnston, Inc.)
StoryBook Weaver (Learning Company)
SuccessMaker (NCSLearn)
WYNN Reader (Arkenstone)

Devices

Palm Pilots (Palm, Inc.)
Pocket PCs (designed by Hewlett-Packard, Casio, and Compaq)

CHAPTER 11

Technology in Mathematics and Science Instruction

Ed Dickey and Jon Singer, University of South Carolina

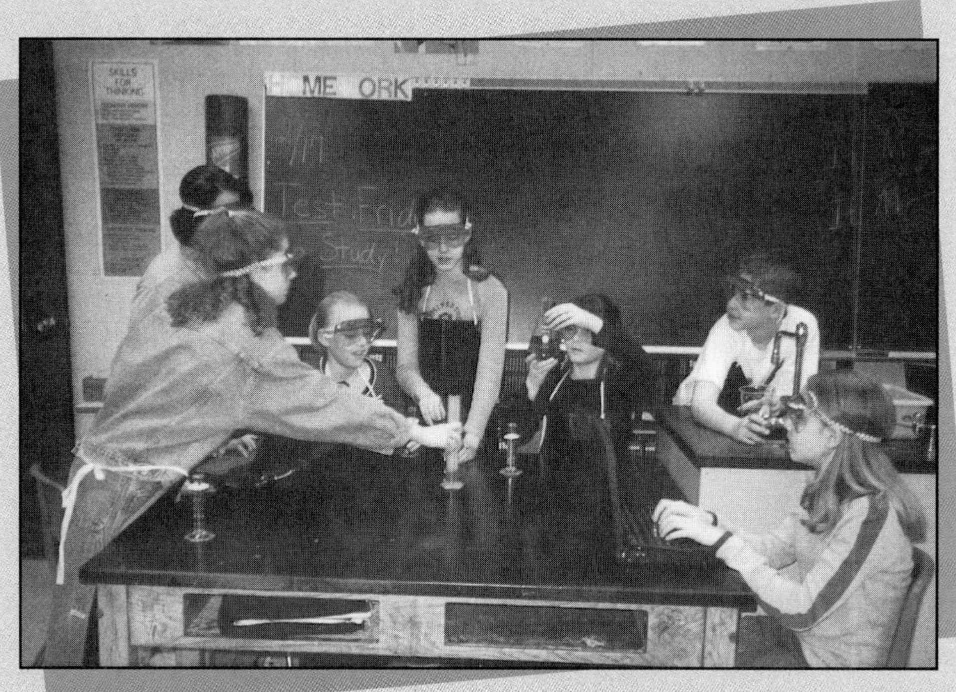

The terms and circumstances of human existence can be expected to change radically during the next human life span. Science, mathematics, and technology will be at the center of that change—causing it, shaping it, responding to it. Therefore, they will be essential to the education of today's children for tomorrow's world.

Benchmarks for Scientific Literacy (American Association for the Advancement of Science, 1993)

The purpose of using technology is not to make the learning of mathematics easier, but richer and better.

Alfinio Flores (1998)

This chapter covers the following topics:

- Current issues and problems in mathematics and science instruction
- How technology is integrated into mathematics and science instruction
- Example World Wide Web resources for mathematics and science instruction
- Integration strategies for using technology in mathematics and science instruction

Objectives

1. Identify some of the current issues in mathematics and science instruction that impact the selection and use of technology.
2. Describe popular uses for technology in mathematics and science curricula.
3. Identify exemplary Internet sites for mathematics and science.
4. Create instructional activities for mathematics and science instruction that model successful integration strategies.

Introduction

Mathematics and science education are of critical importance to the future of our students. Efforts to reform teaching and learning in these two areas have been at the center of the national standards movement. U.S. elementary students perform well compared to students in other nations, but that performance diminishes as our students progress through school (Beaton et al., 1997–1998). Technology provides many opportunities to build students' conceptual knowledge as well as to connect learning to problems found in our world. This chapter highlights current issues and problems in mathematics and science education and describes strategies for integrating technology into the teaching and learning processes for these areas.

Issues and Problems in Mathematics Education

Standards in Mathematics Education

The *Principles and Standards for School Mathematics,* released in 2000 by the National Council of Teachers of Mathematics (NCTM), serves as a primary resource and guide for all who make decisions that affect the mathematics education of students in prekindergarten through grade 12. Building on the previously produced landmark trio of *Curriculum and Evaluation Standards for School Mathematics* (1989), *Professional Standards for Teaching Mathematics* (1991), and *Assessment Standards for School Mathematics* (1995), the *Principles and Standards* document describes a vision of mathematics teaching and learning. Achieving this vision requires "solid mathematics curriculum, competent and knowledgeable teachers who can integrate instruction with assessment, education policies that enhance and support learning, classrooms with ready access to technology, and a commitment to both equity and excellence" (NCTM, 2000b, p. 3). The *Principles and Standards* document calls for a common foundation of mathematics to be learned by all students. Six principles address crucial issues fundamental to all school mathematics programs:

- Equity
- Curriculum
- Teaching
- Learning
- Assessment
- Technology

In the Technology Principle, NCTM stresses that "technology is essential in teaching and learning mathematics" and "it influences the mathematics that is taught and enhances students' learning" (NCTM, 2000b, p. 24). "In the mathematics classroom envisioned in *Principles and Standards,* every student has access to technology to facilitate his or her mathematics learning under the guidance of a skillful teacher" (NCTM, 2000b, p. 25).

There are ten mathematics standards for prekindergarten through grade 12:

Content Standards

- Number and Operations
- Algebra
- Geometry
- Measurement
- Data Analysis and Probability

Process Standards

- Problem Solving
- Reasoning and Proof
- Communication
- Connections
- Representations

Through these principles and standards, NCTM provides guidance on how to prepare students for a society that requires mathematical knowledge for filling crucial economic, political, and scientific roles in a highly technological workplace.

Implementing the *Principles and Standards for School Mathematics*

Helping teachers change their teaching styles to meet the vision described in the NCTM standards is not an easy task. The standards seek a fundamental shift in the way most teachers work (Burrill, 1997). Technology can serve as a catalyst to move teachers toward an instructional style that is more student centered, active, and relevant to the world in which we now live.

Research points to three implications for the selection and use of software related to mathematics education. First, the teachers should consider an appropriate combination of off- and on-computer activities. Second, they should consider technology as a mathematical tool rather than as a pedagogical tool. Third, they should view technology as a tool for developing student thinking. One way to accomplish

TECHNOLOGY INTEGRATION EXAMPLE

Mathematics and Science Instruction

TITLE: Hot and Cold Data

BASED ON: Albrecht, B. (1999). Revolutions in the classroom. *Learning and Leading with Technology, 26*(5), 32–36.

GRADE LEVEL: Middle to high school grades

CONTENT AREA/TOPIC: Physics, graphing, and measurement concepts

LENGTH OF TIME: Three weeks

Step 1: What's the Relative Advantage—Why Use Technology in Mathematics and Science Instruction?

Ms. Belt and Mr. Alter, the physics and mathematics teachers, respectively, at Pinnacle High School, were excited about the new computer-based laboratories (CBLs) that had just arrived. For the past year, the two teachers had been reading about these calculator devices and had attended district training workshops in preparation for using them in their classrooms. As they learned more about how CBLs can "grab" temperature data and display it in graphs and spreadsheets, they realized that activities with CBLs provide a natural link between science and mathematics studies. Having students use CBLs would be an ideal way to give them hands-on insights into the relationship between these two important skill areas. They also agree that having students collect their own data and see it displayed immediately makes data analysis more visual and meaningful. They decided that a unit on heating and cooling experiments would make maximum use of this capability. Students could take temperature measurements with the CBL probes, then use mathematical procedures to graph and analyze the resulting data.

Step 2: Planning Assessment—What Are Appropriate Assessment Strategies?

The teachers decided they would assess students' progress in each of three areas: carrying out scientific experiments, investigating physics principles, and using mathematics to analyze and display data. Because using these CBLs would be the basis of many activities to come, they decided to develop a performance test on CBL procedures that each student would have to pass. The teachers also decided to create a checklist of the steps in each experiment and grade students in small groups on how they carried out the assigned steps, as well as how well they wrote up and presented their findings to the class. They designed a mid-unit test in which students looked at example charts and interpreted the data. Finally, they developed an end-of-unit test on which pairs of students were graded on their ability to replicate data from a CBL experiment and interpret data without assistance.

Step 3: Planning Instruction—What Are Appropriate Integration Strategies?

The teachers decided to team-teach the unit to draw together even more the links between the two content areas. Working together, they designed the following sequence of activities:

- **Week 1: Introduce unit activities and CBLs and provide hands-on practice.** Introduce the unit with a *Consumer Reports*-type scenario. Makers of camp stoves each claim their product (which used three different fuels: white gas, kerosene, and butane) heated water faster than other stoves. The students have to establish which claim is correct and write up their findings for the *CR* magazine. Demonstrate how students can use the CBL to grab data and how it displays temperatures in graph form. Hold discussion about interpreting CBL data. Students carry out

Figure 11.0 A CBL-Generated Graph

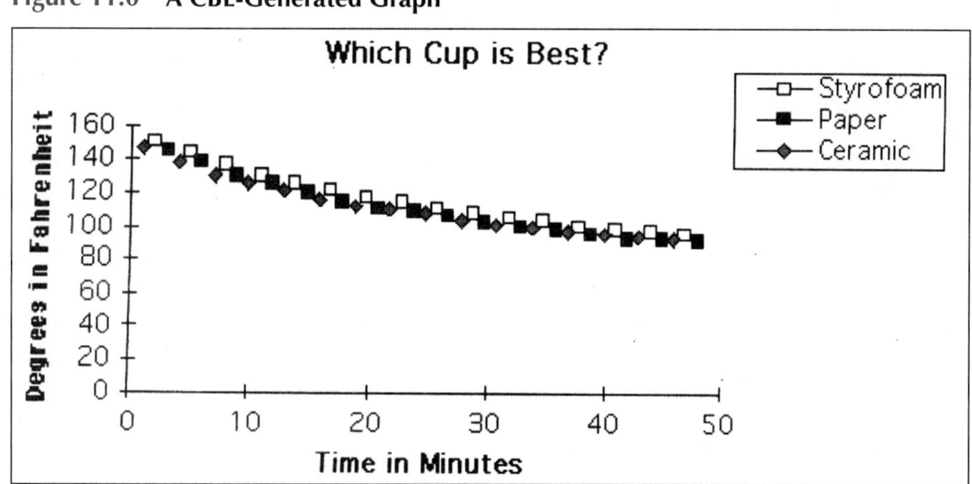

Source: Caniglia, J. (1997). The heat is on! Using the calculator-based laboratory to integrate math, science, and technology. *Learning and Leading with Technology, 25*(1), p. 23.

TECHNOLOGY INTEGRATION EXAMPLE *(CONTINUED)*

the introductory experiment in three large groups. Using camp stoves borrowed from a local sporting goods store, students use the CBLs to heat water to boiling. They go through the step-by-step procedures for hands-on experiments, write up their findings, and present them to the whole class. Hold a whole-class discussion to interpret results and write up a summary for *CR*.

- **Week 2: Carry out heating/cooling experiments and present findings.** As Ms. Belt helps small groups prepare materials for the next set of experiments, Mr. Alter has students do individual performance checks on CBL procedures and provides additional instruction, as needed. Each small group is assigned a heating/cooling experiment, for example, which cup holds heat longest: styrofoam, paper, or ceramic? Which color container holds heat longest: white, black, or metallic? Each group completes its assigned experiment, answers the question, writes up findings, and presents them to the class by inserting spreadsheet and graphed data into a *PowerPoint* presentation.
- **Week 3: Do mathematical analyses and presentations; take final tests.** Each group works with the data to explore linear, quadratic, and exponential functions of graphed data. Finally, students work in pairs to do their replication experiment and answer questions on the meaning of the graphs.

Step 4: Logistics—Preparing the Classroom Environment and Instructional Materials

The teachers get a local sporting goods store to loan them three different camp stoves for the first experiment/demonstration. They test each of the CBLs and calibrate them, as needed. They design and copy each of the performance measures and make copies of lab sheets they will need during the experiments.

Step 5: Evaluating and Revising Integration Strategies

At the end of the unit, the teachers reviewed the students' work and discussed how the unit had worked. Some of the questions they asked were:

- Were most students comfortable with the equipment after the initial demos and example experiment?
- Were student groups able to work together well and be actively engaged in the project work?
- Were students able to work independently to carry out experiments after the initial guided small-group activity?
- Did students do well on the final tests on interpretation of data?

Mr. Alter and Ms. Belt were happy with the overall performance of the class. They were impressed at how engaged students had become in using the CBLs to gather and analyze data. Perhaps most encouraging, two female students seemed especially excited by the work they had done on the scientific experiments; they asked Ms. Belt to give them information on careers in science and mathematics. The teachers concluded that this kind of multidisciplinary unit worked very well. They decided to plan other CBL experiments to be carried out on a longer term basis and at locations outside the classroom.

these goals is to use computer software and applications that can be extended, for long periods of time, across topics, to engage students in meaningful problems and projects, rather than providing a variety of applications with no internal coherence (Clements, 1998).

Arguably, the practice of teaching mathematics has been more traditional than any other curriculum area. The point of view that opposes the call for reform holds that the existing system is adequate, that change is not necessary, and that the standards movement and mathematics reform are passing fads—similar to the "new math" of the 1960s—and will eventually go away. Some community members, including parents and teachers, do not see any reason to change. They argue that the new standards are too complex and that we need only teach the majority of students the "basic skills."

There has also been an ongoing controversy about the use of calculators in mathematics classes. Many teachers and parents feel that students will never learn mathematics skills unless they do these operations themselves and that society is becoming too dependent on technology to do our thinking for us. These views continue to shape the way technology is—and is not—used in classrooms.

How Technology Is Integrated into Mathematics Teaching and Learning

Technology to Support Number and Operations

Software tools can provide great assistance in building students' conceptual understanding of numbers and operations on numbers as well as providing a means of building computational skills. Programs such as *Easy Early Math* (EME Corporation), *NumberSense* (Bradford), or *Unifix* (Didax) can supplement concrete manipulative materials to assist in understanding place value and "carrying" in addition through the use of base-10 blocks. (See Figure 11.1.)

Programs that represent multiplication as a grid or fractions as parts of a whole provide students with concrete and dynamic representations of critical concepts. Using computer animations students can experience the meaning of numerators and denominators in a way that surpasses how a book or even a teacher can explain.

The use of calculators also provides students with an important means of developing number sense. While care must

Figure 11.1 Software Addressing Number and Operations from *Easy Early Math*

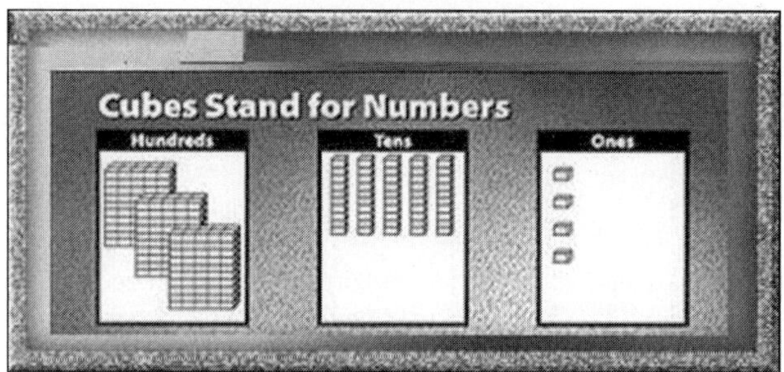

Source: Used by permission of EME Corporation.

Figure 11.2 Spreadsheet for Solving "What-If" Questions

What's in the Bag?							
NAME	RED	YELLOW	GREEN	ORANGE	BROWN	BLUE	TOTAL
Tisha	8	13	7	9	15	1	53
Suzie	7	17	5	7	16	3	55
Ming	11	19	3	7	12	4	56
Juan	9	11	8	5	17	7	57
Tod	12	10	8	4	17	4	55
SAMPLE SIZE	5						
CLASS TOTALS	52	70	31	32	77	19	276
MEAN	9.4	14	6.2	6.4	15.4	3.8	55.2
MEDIAN	9	13	7	7	16	4	55
MODE	NONE	NONE	8	7	17	4	55
PERCENTS	18.8%	25.4%	11.2%	11.6%	27.9%	6.9%	

Source: Used by permission from Drier, H. (2001, January 4). Collecting and numerically analyzing M&M's data. Available online: http://curry.edschool.virginia.edu/teacherlink/math/activities/excel/M&Mnumerical/home.htm.

be given to avoid dependence, one can be certain that as adults, children will regularly use calculators as computational tools. It is critical that the tool be used and studied as part of children's mathematics education (Dessart et al., 1999).

Computer spreadsheets also provide an environment in which children can explore number concepts, operations, and patterns. (See Technology Integration Idea 11.1.) Students can work with the basic operations, explore "what-if" type problems, and build a foundation for algebraic thinking. Activities such as planning a fund-raising activity (Zisow, 2001) or analyzing data gathered about M&M's (Drier, 2001) provide teachers with an important software tool to help build students' number sense. (See Figure 11.2.)

Technology to Support Algebra

As students acquire number sense they can begin to make generalizations that lead them to concepts in algebra. Technology provides students with a means for exploring the critical concept of functions. Through graphing calculators and computer algebra systems, students can graph functions accurately, explore mathematical models of real-life phenomena, and explore the symbolic representations and patterns. CBLs (a.k.a. probeware) provide a means to link either calculators or computers to scientific data gathering instruments such as thermometers or pH meters, hence allowing students to gather and then analyze data. (See Figure 11.3.)

Research has shown that the use of graphing calculators can improve students' understanding of functions and graphs as well as the interconnections between the symbolic, graphical, and numerical representations of problems (Dunham & Dick, 1994). (See Technology Integration Idea 11.2.) Besides calculators many computer-based programs such as *Green Globs* (Sunburst), *Derive* (TI), and *TI Interactive!* provide learning environments across three different mathematical realms.

Technology to Support Geometry

Interactive or dynamic geometry software provides students with an environment in which to make discoveries and conjectures related to geometry concepts and objects. Here abstract ideas can be played out on a computer screen making concepts more real as well as providing a

Technology Integration Idea 11.1

Learning with Spreadsheets

TITLE: What If? Problem Solving with Spreadsheets

CONTENT AREA/TOPIC: Algebra

GRADE LEVEL: 6–9

NETS FOR STUDENTS: Standards 3, 5, 6

DESCRIPTION: Students tend to solve math word problems by using an intuitive "guess and check" strategy. Spreadsheets are a natural tool to support this strategy because they allow students to find patterns, guess and check, and set up tables. Spreadsheet-based strategies are illustrated for several different kinds of algebra word problems, including "How many coins of each kind in a given total?" and "What is a the temperature when Celsius and degrees Fahrenheit are equal?"

Source: Feicht, L. (2000). Guess and check: A viable problem solving strategy. *Learning and Leading with Technology, 27*(5), 50–54.

TECHNOLOGY INTEGRATION IDEA 11.2

Learning with Graphing Calculators

TITLE: Studying Graphs and Functions

CONTENT AREA/TOPIC: Algebra graphs and functions

GRADE LEVEL: 7–11

NETS FOR STUDENTS: Standards 3, 5, 6

DESCRIPTION: In this activity, students use spreadsheets and graphing calculators to graph the pattern in a scenario that describes a morning run taken by a boy named Julio. After each student presents a spreadsheet-generated graph of Julio's run, small groups work together to decide which graph is the best representation of the data in the scenario. This leads to a class investigation on two topics: the best fit function for the data and the families of curves and the effects of parameters on the behavior of the defined function. They use graphing calculators to do these investigations, discussing questions such as "Can a linear function, a quadratic function, a third-degree polynominal, or an equation in exponential form describe the data adequately and accurately?" The activity can be extended by doing the same investigation of other scenarios.

Source: Manoucherhri, A., & Pagnucco, L. (1999–2000). Julio's run: Studying graphs and functions. *Learning and Leading with Technology, 27*(4), 42–45.

TECHNOLOGY INTEGRATION IDEA 11.3

Learning Math with the Internet

TITLE: Taking Shape: Linking Geometry and Technology

CONTENT AREA/TOPIC: Geometry

GRADE LEVEL: 3–5

NETS FOR STUDENTS: Standards 3, 4, 5, 6

DESCRIPTION: Teachers often help students understand geometry concepts by having them make lists and draw items with various shapes in the world around them, for example, basketball hoops for circles and monkey bars for rectangles. This activity expands on that strategy. Students bring in pictures of objects with various geometrical shapes and scan them into files to create a *Geometry in the World* virtual book. By reviewing all the pictures as a whole class, they create categories to account for all of the pictures: cones, angles, horizontals and verticals, multiple shapes, and circles. Each category becomes a chapter for the book. Students work in small groups to do a web page for their chapter. They end with a class presentation of the whole site and a discussion of the geometry concepts they learned.

Source: Renne, C. (2000). Taking shape: Linking geometry and technology. *Learning and Leading with Technology, 27*(7), 58–62.

doorway into mathematical reasoning and proof. As Renne (2000) illustrates, Internet resources also can help students make connections between geometry and the world around them. (See Technology Integration Idea 11.3.)

Instead of memorizing geometric facts or concepts, students can explore and arrive at conclusions on their own. For instance, using a program such as *The Geometer's Sketchpad* (Key Curriculum Press), students can construct and measure the interior angles of a polygon (see Figure 11.4) and determine the formula that relates the measure of the angle to the number of sides.

Software capable of depicting solid or three-dimensional objects on a screen provides learners with a way to visualize objects that are difficult to imagine. *StudyWorks* (MathSoft) and *3D Images* (Bradford) each provide software capable of depicting 3D shapes. (See Figure 11.5.)

Understanding the nature and properties of transformations and symmetry has become increasingly important and can be found in nearly all state mathematics standards. Again, software packages can facilitate learning and instruct students in this area. Web sites are available that teach symmetry (Dorsey et al., 2001), and software such as *KaleidoMania!* (Key Curriculum Press), goes further into using symmetry and geometric transformations to create artistic objects.

Technology to Support Measurement

Measurement using standard instruments (rulers, scales) is critical, but measurement using electronic devices is im-

Figure 11.3 Students Using Graphing Calculators

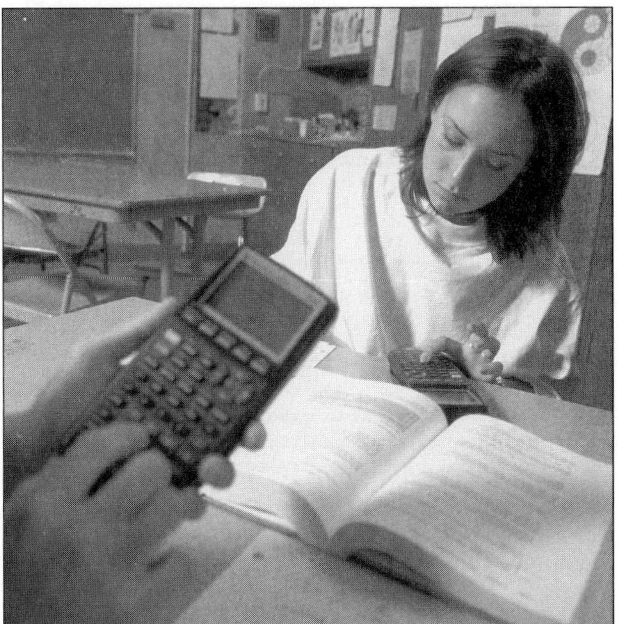

Source: Bonnie Kamin/ PhotoEdit.

Figure 11.4 Example of *The Geometer's Sketchpad* Activity

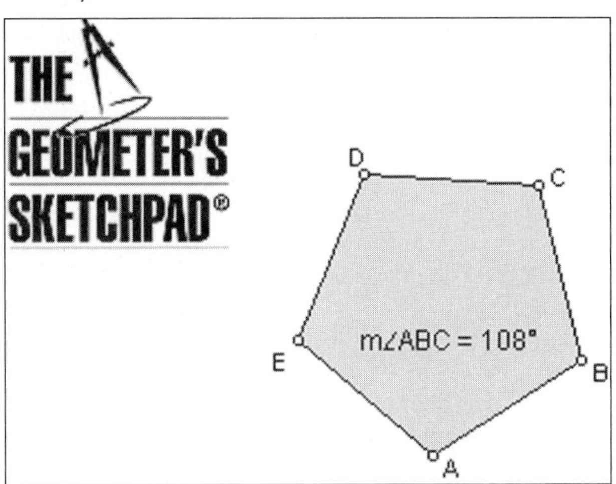

Source: Dynamic Geometry® and *The Geometer's Sketchpad®* are registered trademarks of Key Curriculum Press, 1150 65th St., Emeryville, CA 94608, 1-800-995-MATH. The Resource Center for The Geometer's Sketchpad can be found at: www.keypress.com/sketchpad.

Figure 11.5 Sample Object in *StudyWorks* 3D Software

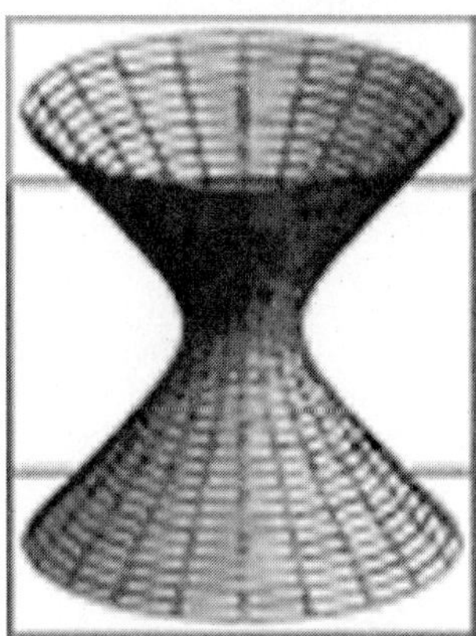

Source: Reprinted by permission of MathSoft, Engineering & Education, Inc. Image created by StudyWorks, a MathSoft product.

portant as well. Global positioning systems (GPS) provide teachers and students with a unique measurement opportunity. Day (1999) suggests several ways to use a GPS to develop measurement skills. (See Figure 11.6.)

Web-based resources such as the *Lady Bug Maze* activity (NCTM, 2000a) provide environments where students can combine measurement as well as number and geometry skills to solve problems in a game-like setting. Morgan and Jernigan (1998–1999) describe how to use spreadsheets to help students explore measurement concepts. (See Technology Integration Idea 11.4.)

Technology to Support Data Analysis and Probability

United States students scored well in the area of data analysis on the Third International Mathematics Science Study (Beaton et al., 1997–1998). The importance of statistical inference and probability has already had an impact in U.S. schools. Technology provides an ideal means of developing student knowledge and skill related to data analysis. Programs such as *Tabletop* and *Tabletop Junior* (Broderbund) allow students to examine data in a spreadsheet format and then represent it graphically, possibly in a Venn diagram or in more traditional graphs. *Fathom* (Key Curriculum Press; see Figure 11.7) is a more comprehensive package designed for schools to analyze and represent statistical data in a wide range of forms.

Data resources from the World Wide Web also provide students with realistic statistics and the opportunity to conduct investigations that are timely and relevant. Examples 5.4 and 5.5 from the NCTM *Principles and Standards of School Mathematics* web site illustrate how data collection and representation might occur (NCTM, 2001). Dixon and Falba (1997) also describe activities for producing graphs using Internet data.

Figure 11.6 Example of a GPS Unit

Source: Courtesy of Garmin Corporation. Copyright © Garmin Corporation.

Figure 11.7 Screen Capture from *Fathom*

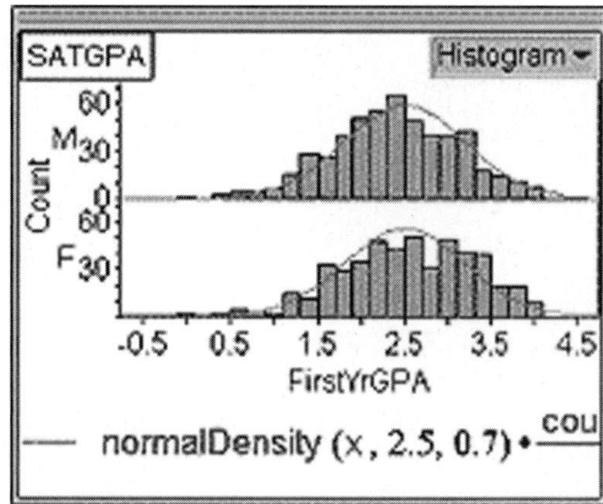

Source: Used by permission of Key Curriculum Press. Guided tour at http://www.keypress.com/catalog/products/software/Prod_Fathom.html

Technology to Support Problem Solving

Much effort has been given to developing students' ability to solve problems using the mathematical skills they have acquired. Computer programming can help develop problem-solving abilities by allowing students to analyze and decompose a problem and use systematic trial and error to find solutions. A modern (and free) language such as *Python* (Van Rossum, 2001) can provide students with a means of learning to write computer code for the purpose of solving problems.

The *Jasper Woodbury Series* videodiscs also serve to develop student problem-solving skills. (See Figure 11.8.) Adhering closely to the situated cognition learning theory, each videodisc contains a 30-minute story leading to a challenge. Students must view and re-view the video to obtain the information necessary to arrive at a solution and document their thinking.

Technology to Support Reasoning and Proof

The mathematical thinking centers on reasoning and ultimately the concept of deductive proof. Technology provides opportunities for students to use inductive reasoning to develop and test conjectures and, through careful instruction, it can form the foundation for developing proof. The *Geometer's Sketchpad* "scripts" each student construction using a format that contains "Givens" and "Reasons" similar to that found in a geometric proof.

Technology to Support Communication

The Internet offers students the opportunity to communicate with each other or even with experts in different fields. Expressing ideas in written form is essential and, therefore, students must convert their mathematical thinking into words. Projects such as the Math Forum's different *Problems of the Week* allow teachers to pose problems that their students must then solve and communicate the solution (http://mathforum.com/pow/). *Ask*

TECHNOLOGY INTEGRATION IDEA 11.4

Learning with Spreadsheets

TITLE: Measuring Up

CONTENT AREA/TOPIC: Measurement—Ratio and Proportions

GRADE LEVEL: 7–10

NETS FOR STUDENTS: Standards 3, 5, 6

DESCRIPTION: Students create a spreadsheet to calculate ratios and proportions, using the measurements of students in the class as a database. They begin by taking measurements of each student in the class and entering these data into a spreadsheet. They use their own data compared to Leonardo da Vinci's calculations based on his 1492 drawing "The Proportions of the Human Figure" to predict "the perfect numbers." After they compare their results, they discuss their conclusions about da Vinci's hypothesized "perfect proportions."

Source: Morgan, B., & Jernigan, J. (1998–1999). A technology update: Leonardo da Vinci and the search for the perfect body. *Learning and Leading with Technology, 26*(4), 22–25.

Figure 11.8 Screen Capture from the *Adventures of Jasper Woodbury Series* from LEArning, Inc.

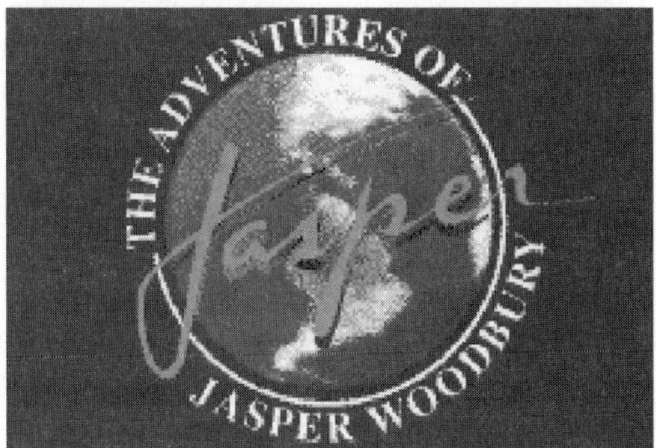

Source: Used by permission of Vanderbilt University. Copyright © Cognition and Technology Group at Vanderbilt.

Dr. Math (the Math Forum at http://mathforum.com/dr.math/) provides contacts to experts who can answer questions.

Using computers and calculators in group settings promotes social interaction and discourse. Teachers often find that grouping students in pairs greatly enhances learning, augmenting teacher-to-student or computer-to-student communication to a richer student-to-student-to-computer type of communication.

Technology to Support Connections

Computer- or calculator-based laboratories allow students to explore realistic models by acquiring and displaying data, then performing analyses. This also links the learning of mathematics to science. The process of discovering a mathematical model helps students understand the phenomenon being examined and provides an implicit relevance to an otherwise abstract subject.

Dynamic manipulation environments, whether in geometry through a program such as *The Geometer's Sketchpad* or in algebra with *Derive,* offer a context where students can solve problems and address challenges by building interactive, manipulable mathematical models (Finzer & Jackiw, 1998).

Technology to Support Representations

By its very design, the computer represents the reality we experience. Computer software accentuates this characteristic by addressing, sometimes separately and sometimes simultaneously, the different ways in which mathematics is perceived. At the elementary level, models for numbers and operations can be displayed on the computer screen in a way that allows students to derive and construct their own meaning for the mathematical concepts being represented. At higher levels, abstract concepts can be made more concrete.

Manipulative devices, often used by elementary teachers to develop conceptual understanding, can also be represented on the computer screen. (See Figure 11.9.) Mankus (2000) describes and provides several examples of how on-

Figure 11.9 Screen Capture from *Virtual Pattern Blocks,* a Virtual Manipulative

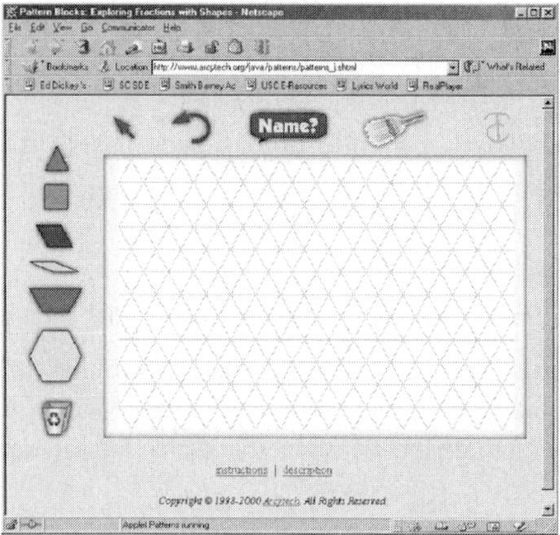

Source: Used by permission of Jacobo Bulaevsky, Arcytech, http://www.arcytech.org.

line interactive manipulatives can be used to develop understanding. Cannon and his colleagues (2001) maintain a library of virtual manipulatives for all grade levels that are tied to each of the standards' content strands.

 Useful Web Sites for Mathematics Instruction

National Council of Teachers of Mathematics

http://www.nctm.org

Home page of the professional organization that developed the first curriculum standards. Wide range of resources including journals, conferences, newsletters, and products. Electronic version of *Principles and Standards* (http://standards.nctm.org).

Math Forum

http://mathforum.com

Resources for students, teachers, and anyone interested in mathematics education. Among the best: *Ask Dr. Math* (to answer questions), *Problem of the Week* (challenges at all levels and math subjects), and *Discussion Groups* (virtual communities interested in math).

Texas Instrument Resources for Educators

http://www.ti.com/calc/docs/resource.htm

As one would expect, this site includes numerous resources for using calculators and computers in the classroom. It also includes ideas for parents to help their children develop an interest in and comfort with mathematics.

Eisenhower National Clearinghouse

http://enc.org/

A collection of effective curriculum resources, high-quality professional development materials, and useful information and products to improve K–12 mathematics and science teaching and learning.

Cynthia Lanius Collection

http://math.rice.edu/~lanius/Lessons/

An outstanding collection of web-based, interactive mathematics lessons.

History of Mathematics

http://www-groups.dcs.st-and.ac.uk:80/~history/

Biographies, historical topics, even "famous curves" can be found at this comprehensive collection illustrating how mathematics has developed as a human endeavor.

PBS Mathline

http://www.pbs.org/teachersource/math.htm

High-quality lessons, activities, and professional development for teachers addressing mathematics concepts and connections.

Issues and Problems in Science Education

Standards in Science Education

The National Research Council (NRC) released the *National Science Education Standards* in 1996. This document along with the *Benchmarks for Scientific Literacy* (AAAS, 1993) still provides direction for teachers and decision makers involved with K–12 science education. Although the two documents do not totally agree on all facets of what should be taught at which grade level and to what extent, they both embody the same fundamental educational vision. This shared vision includes these facets:

Emphasizing inquiry. Inquiry into authentic questions generated from student experiences is the central strategy for teaching science. Teachers focus inquiry predominantly on real phenomena, in classrooms, outdoors, or in laboratory settings, where students are given investigations or guided toward fashioning investigations that are demanding but within their capabilities (NRC, 1996, p. 31).

Scientific literacy. Scientific literacy is the knowledge and understanding of the scientific concepts and processes required for personal decision making, participation in civic and cultural affairs, and economic productivity (NRC, 1996, p. 22).

Focus on understanding, not surface knowledge. Many science educators believe that, if we want students to learn science, mathematics, and technology, we must radically reduce the sheer amount of material now being covered. The overstuffed curriculum places a premium on the ability to commit terms, algorithms, and generalizations to short-term memory and impedes the acquisition of understanding (AAAS, 1993, p. xi).

Implementing the *National Science Education Standards* and *Benchmarks for Scientific Literacy*

Achieving the shared vision described in the two national science education documents can be facilitated by the use of technology. Through the use of computers, electronic media, and the Internet, teachers can move from serving as the sole authority for scientific facts or principles to managers of instructional processes that put their students into active, inquiry roles.

Several groups are conducting curriculum development and research to explore the integrated use of technology to support the major science education goals articulated in the *National Science Education Standards* and the *Benchmarks for Scientific Literacy.* A few examples include the University of Michigan's project-based science curriculum (Singer, Krajcik, Marx, & Clay-Chambers, 2000) and *Kids as Global Scientists* (Songer, 1998), *STAR LEGACY* by the Learning Technology Center at Vanderbilt University (Schwartz, Linn, Brophy, & Bransford, 2000), University of California at Berkeley's *Web-Based Integrated Science Environment—WISE* (Linn, Bell, & Hsi, 1999), and Northwestern University's *Struggle for Survival* (Reiser, Tabak, Sandoval, Smith, Steinmuller, & Leone, 2001) and *Global Warming* (Edelson,1998).

Research focused on engaging students in extended inquiry experiences has identified and offered insights surrounding the challenges faced by teachers (Krajcik, Blumenfeld, Marx, Bass, Fredericks, & Soloway, 1998; Linn, 1992; Roth & Roychoudhury, 1993). Several of these challenges can be addressed through the use of learning technologies (Edelson, 1998; Linn, 1998; Spitulnik, Stratford, Krajcik, & Soloway, 1998).

How Technology Is Integrated into Science Teaching and Learning

Technology to Support Scientific Processes

One key aspect of engaging in a scientific experiment or investigation is the collection and analysis of data. The use of computer or calculator probes is one means to support this endeavor. Probeware is a type of educational software tool consisting of hardware devices (probes) and software that allows for the collection, organization, and analysis of data. (See Technology Integration Idea 11.5.) The use of probes allows students to visualize scientific phenomena and to re-

TECHNOLOGY INTEGRATION IDEA 11.5

Learning with MBL/Probeware

TITLE: Measuring with Precision vs. Accuracy

CONTENT AREA/TOPIC: Scientific methods

GRADE LEVEL: 5–7

NETS FOR STUDENTS: Standards 3, 5, 6

DESCRIPTION: In this activity students learn the difference between precision and accuracy by comparing the reading of a scale of temperature with its physical meaning. Have a container of hot water and one of cold water to use as high and low reference points. Students make two kinds of readings: one from a scale marked by every 10 degrees centigrade, and the other from a scale marked every 1 degree centigrade. Although both are accurate, the second reading reflects greater precision. Have the students work in groups to use the probes to take various readings using each scale. After all groups have completed and recorded their readings, calculate the range for each scale. Half the range is the *precision.* The difference between the reference thermometer and the temperature probe is the *accuracy.* Discuss the difference with the students.

Source: Flick, L. (1989). "Probing" temperature and heat. *The Computing Teacher, 17*(2), 15–19.

ceive immediate graphical representations. Probes allow for "real-time" data collection. "Real-time" implies that students can engage in a scientific activity (rolling carts down a ramp, making pH readings in a river, etc.) and immediately visualize the data in a variety of formats (charts, graphs, digits, etc.). Probes can be utilized both in traditional laboratory settings as well as being used in a variety of field experiences. Probes have been associated with the use of calculators (CBLs) and computers (microcomputer-based labs or MBLs), but handheld technologies such as Palm Pilots or Handspring Visors are also being explored as a means of supporting probes.

Technology to Support a Scientific Inquiry Environment

Technology can be utilized to create environments that provide students with strategies and tools to engage in extended inquiry. The fundamental characteristic of these types of technology is that they provide a framework for supporting the process of conducting an investigation. Inquiry involves several interrelated processes, such as asking and refining questions, collecting data and information, and communicating ideas. In addition to using technology to support these individual scientific processes, technology can also help students to navigate and think through how these processes are related, answering questions such as "Where do I start?" "What do we do next?" and "What does this mean?"

One example of this type of learning environment is the *Web-Based Integrated Science Environment (WISE)* from the University of California at Berkeley. The WISE project provides several strategies to support the inquiry process. "Amanda the Panda" can be used to provide hints and clues. An outline of steps (which can be expanded) helps to guide the students through the investigation. The main portion of the screen displays the current evidence, external page discussion, or anything else needed to conduct the project. Other examples of programs that support the inquiry process include *Symphony* (University of Michigan) and *STAR LEGACY* (Vanderbilt University).

Technology to Support Scientific Literacy

According to the *National Science Education Standards,* a scientifically literate person will be able to "ask, find, or determine answers to questions derived from curiosity about everyday experiences" (NRC, 1996, p. 22). Good science instruction can facilitate this goal through engaging students in extended investigations and grounding the concepts and processes being taught with everyday experiences and personal interests. (See Technology Integration Idea 11.6.) The World Wide Web is a very rich resource that allows students to explore and gather information concerning their personal interests. One major impediment for utilizing the Internet is a lack of organization. The Internet houses countless sites with a plethora of interesting information; however, searching the web may become extremely frustrating to teachers and students. The Internet contains sites that may be inappropriate for children, accuracy of information may be circumspect, and web sites are constantly changing. For example, many middle school science classes conduct astronomy units. If a student or teacher uses a typical search engine (*Lycos, Google,* etc.) and enters "S-A-T-U-R-N," two things are quickly learned. First, the search will yield an unmanageable number of sites, and secondly, more than 99% of them will be dealing with cars not planets.

Digital libraries are collections of web sites and other multimedia collections that have been prescreened for specific learners or populations. An example of this type of technology is the University of Michigan's Middle Years

Digital Library (MYDL) and its associated search interface *Artemis. Artemis* is a search interface that allows students to organize their research questions, share their questions and interesting sites, and provide critiques and feedback to other class members. The *Artemis* search interface searches the digital library first before searching the web using a commercial search engine.

Technology to Support Student Understanding of Science Concepts

In *Benchmarks for Science Literacy,* the phrase "Students should know that. . ." is routinely used when describing specific benchmarks associated with content and processes. In the "Habits of Mind" chapter, the authors clearly define what they mean by this phrase. Key components of "knowing" include the ability to connect one idea to another, apply ideas in new and different contexts, and utilize skills in appropriate situations inside and outside of school. (See Technology Integration Idea 11.7.)

Deep understanding or "knowing" is more likely to develop when students are provided opportunities to actively construct their understanding of a discipline (Krajcik et al., 1998; Roth, 1994). This performance perspective suggests that students construct knowledge by engaging in learning environments that require them "to explain, muster evidence, find examples, generalize, apply concepts, analogize, (and) represent in a new way"(Perkins, 1993, p. 29).

TECHNOLOGY INTEGRATION IDEA 11.6

Learning Science with the Internet

TITLE: Cyber Data

CONTENT AREA/TOPIC: Earth science

GRADE LEVEL: 2–12

NETS FOR STUDENTS: Standards 3, 4, 5, 6

DESCRIPTION: This activity focuses on gathering data to investigate greenhouse gases in the atmosphere and global warming. Students use two Internet sites to obtain data on global temperatures and atmospheric concentrations of carbon dioxide and use the data to answer questions about these topics. Students plot monthly average carbon dioxide concentrations for a given year and observe patterns in increases and decreases. Then they graph the temperature data for a year and compare these data with the carbon dioxide data. They discuss possible links between the biosphere and atmosphere. Finally, they use the Internet to gather other information on global warming and discuss the current trends.

Source: Slattery, W., Hundley, S., Finegan-Stoll, C., & Becker, M. (1998). Collecting science in a net. *Learning and Leading with Technology, 26*(1), 25–30.

TECHNOLOGY INTEGRATION IDEA 11.7

Learning with Multimedia

TITLE: Using Technology to Develop Habits of Mind

CONTENT AREA/TOPIC: Science, ecology

GRADE LEVEL: 4–6

NETS FOR STUDENTS: Standards 4, 5, 6

DESCRIPTION: This project focuses on using multimedia development projects to foster "habits of mind" such as perseverance, problem solving, and cooperation. Emphasis is also placed on developing communications skills and growth in writing ability. The topic for one multimedia project was "biomes around the world," but this approach works well with other topics. Teachers divide students into cooperative groups of two to three. Students are introduced to the topic of biomes and asked to select a biome they wish to study. Each group of students formulates questions about their biome to be answered through research. They look for information on its characteristics, its location on earth, its climate, and threats to its ecosystem. They present their final multimedia stacks at a local city multimedia fair and at an evening presentation for parents.

Source: Bennett, N., and Diener, K. (1997). Habits of mind. *Learning and Leading with Technology, 24*(6), 18–21.

Figure 11.10 Screen Capture from *Decisions, Decisions* Software

Source: Used by permission of Tom Snyder Communications.

Figure 11.11 Screen Capture from *echem* Simulation Software

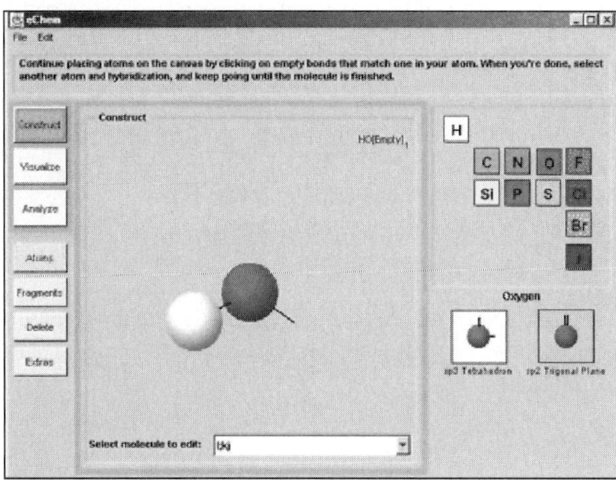

Source: Courtesy of University of Michigan's Highly Interactive Computing in Education Research Group.

In addition to the technology described previously (learning environments, data collection devices, digital libraries, etc.), understanding can also be supported through the use of simulating, visualizing, and modeling software.

Science simulation software can be an extremely effective tool in helping students understand and experience practical applications of scientific thinking. One class of simulations involves creating situations in which students must learn and apply concepts and skills to solve a problem, mystery, or puzzle. Two examples of this type of simulation are *Decisions, Decisions* developed by Tom Snyder Productions and *Struggle for Survival* developed at Northwestern University. (See Figure 11.10.) In *Decisions, Decisions* students take on the role of advisors to a mayor of a fictitious town concerning environmental problems. In *Struggle for Survival* students role-play a group of scientists trying to understand why finches are dying in the Galapagos. In either project students learn to apply scientific thinking, discern between relevant and irrelevant information, filter out erroneous data, and draw conclusions based on incomplete data. Applications like this are often extremely motivating for students.

In addition to creating learning environments that set up problem spaces, simulations can also allow students to engage in scientific phenomena that would otherwise be difficult to visualize. Technology can create simulations of events that may otherwise occur too quickly, too slowly, or be too dangerous, too costly, or too difficult to visualize. This type of simulation includes software that cuts across all four major science disciplines. Biological examples include virtual dissections, and programs like *BioLogica* developed by the Concord Consortium. *BioLogica* allows learners to manipulate biological processes at a variety of related levels. Programs such as *Interactive Physics* or *FutureLab* allow students to study a variety of physic concepts such as optics and motion in a virtual laboratory where traditional confounding factors such as friction and gravity can be eliminated. Earth science concepts can be visualized through programs such as *Worldwatcher* developed at Northwestern University. Concepts associated with chemistry such as the structure and properties of organic molecules can be illustrated by *echem,* which was developed at the University of Michigan. (See Figure 11.11.)

Technology to Support the Building of Scientific Models

The *Benchmarks for Scientific Literacy* articulates several common themes that "pervade science, mathematics, and technology" (AAAS, 1993, p. 261). Two of these themes are systems and models. Technology does exist to help learners visualize and model complex phenomena. One such tool is the qualitative modeling tool *Model-It* developed at the University of Michigan. *Model-It* allows the learner to make qualitative models of cause-and-effect relationships. Using *Model-It,* the user creates objects with which he or she associates measurable, differing quantities called variables and then defines relationships between those variables to show the effects of one variable upon another.

Useful Web Sites for Science Instruction

National Science Teachers Association

http://www.NSTA.org

Home page for the professional organization for science educators. This site includes information regarding conferences, publications, and curriculum for the teaching and learning of science.

American Association for the Advancement of Science

http://www.AAAS.org

AAAS is the parent organization for Project 2061. Project 2061 is a long-term project that focuses on science education reform.

National Science Resource Center

http://www.si.edu/nsrc/default.htm

The NSRC collects and disseminates information about exemplary teaching practices, curriculum, and resources.

The following web sites are Science Education research projects that contain exemplary curriculum projects and technologies:

EduTech Institute

http://www.cc.gatech.edu/edutech/index.html

An education research institute affiliated with Georgia Institute of Technology that focuses on the innovative use of technology to support science, math, and design education.

Learning Research and Development Center

http://www.lrdc.pitt.edu/

LRDC is a large research center based at the University of Pittsburgh and dedicated to improving the learning of children and adults in a variety of settings.

Concord Consortium

http://concord.org/

The Concord Consortium is a nonprofit research and development organization dedicated to a revolution in education through the use of information technologies.

MIT Media Laboratory Research Group

http://www.media.mit.edu/

The home page for the MIT Media Laboratory describes its mission as "enabling technologies for learning and expression by people and machines."

Eisenhower National Clearinghouse

http://www.enc.org

This is the web site of the Eisenhower Foundation, which awards grants to science education projects.

Web-Based Integrated Science Environment (WISE)

http://wise.berkeley.edu/welcome.php

This project, based out of the University of California at Berkeley, focuses on the development of adaptable inquiry-based science curriculum.

Science Controversies On-Line

http://scope.educ.washington.edu/

This project is the next generation of WISE curriculum.

Center for Learning Technology in Urban Schools

http://www.letus.org/

This center is a collaborative enterprise between two major research institutions (University of Michigan and Northwestern University) and two major urban school districts (Chicago Public Schools and Detroit Public Schools). The center is exploring the use of technology to facilitate the learning of science.

Exercises

Record and apply what you have learned.

Chapter 11 Self-Test

To review terms and concepts in this chapter, take the Chapter 11 self-test. Select Chapter 11 from the front page of the Companion Website (located at http://www.prenhall.com/roblyer), then choose the *Multiple Choice* module.

Portfolio Activities

ISTE The following activities address ISTE National Educational Technology Standards for Teachers (NETS-T) and will help you add to your professional portfolio. To complete these activities online and save or submit the materials electronically, select Chapter 11 from the front page of the Companion Website (http://www.prenhall.com/roblyer), then choose the *Portfolio* module.

1. ***Integration Skills (NETS-T Standards: II-A, B, C; V-B)*** Select one of the integration strategies from the chapter and develop a classroom activity for a mathematics or science content area that is modeled after the strategy. Be prepared to teach or demonstrate the activity to the class. If possible, use your activity with the targeted age group before you bring it to the class. The lesson and your reflections on the teaching experience should be placed in your portfolio.
2. ***Web Site Authoring (NETS-T Standards: II-C; V-B, D)*** Develop a web site that summarizes the strategies described in this chapter for integrating technology into mathematics or science. If possible, make the site specific to your "specialty area": a math or science topic or a grade level in which you plan to teach. For example: "Leland's Technology Integration Strategies for 9th Grade Biology." Identify supporting resources and insert links to web sites for each strategy you describe. Include a link to the site or a hardcopy of the pages in your portfolio.

Questions for Thought and Discussion

These questions may be used for small-group or class discussion or may be subjects for individual or group activities. To take part in these discussions online, select Chapter 11 from the front page of the Companion Website (http://www.prenhall.com/roblyer), then choose the *Message Board* module.

1. The following quote offers a rather pessimistic view on reforming mathematics instruction in this country. Will technology be able to expedite the process? Should we try to revamp our mathematics instruction by "teacher proofing" instruction via multimedia and Internet technologies?

   > The national call for the reform in mathematics teaching and learning can seem overwhelming, because it requires a complete redesign of the content of school mathematics and the way it is taught. The basis for reform is the widespread belief that the United States must "restructure the mathematics curriculum—both what is taught and the way it is taught—if our children are to develop the mathematical knowledge (and the confidence to use that knowledge) that they will need to be personally and professionally competent in the twenty-first century. Simply producing new texts and retraining teachers will not be sufficient to address the major changes being recommended.
   >
   > —Mathematical Sciences Education Board, 1991

2. The following quote makes a strong case for developing a high degree of scientific literacy for each citizen. Is this individual skill level really necessary in the age of the Internet? Won't it be possible to easily contact experts or other resources that can compensate for personal lack of scientific knowledge?

   > All of us have a stake, as individuals and as a society, in scientific literacy. An understanding of science makes it possible for everyone to share in the richness and excitement of comprehending the natural world. Scientific literacy enables people to use scientific principles in making personal decisions and to participate in discussions of scientific issues that affect society. A sound grounding in science strengthens many of the skills that people use every day, like solving problems creatively, thinking critically, working cooperatively in teams, using technology effectively, and valuing life-long learning.
   >
   > —National Science Education Standards Overview

Collaborative Activities

The following activities address ISTE National Educational Technology Standards for Teachers (NETS-T) and can be done in small groups. Each group should present the findings to the class in a format they know how to use (word-processed report, presentation software, multimedia product). Completed group products can be copied and shared with the entire class or included in each person's personal portfolio.

1. ***Evaluation (NETS-T Standard: II-C)*** Work with a colleague and evaluate three mathematics and three science software products. Use the software evaluation form in Chapter 4. Include a copy of the evaluations in your portfolio.
2. ***Evaluation (NETS-T Standards: I-B, II-C)*** Work with a colleague and reread the list of the principles/goals for the mathematics and science standards offered in this chapter. Select two each of the mathematics principles and science goals and locate web sites or software products that exemplify the "spirit" of those principles and goals. Write a brief description of the web sites or software products and tell why the sites or products are exemplary. Include the written descriptions in your personal portfolio.

Integrating Technology Across the Curriculum Activities

The *Integrating Technology Across the Curriculum* CD-ROM is a set of technology integration ideas and links to online lessons, arranged as a searchable database. The CD comes packaged with this textbook. Complete the following exercise using this CD:

Review some of the example integration ideas on the CD cited in this chapter for mathematics and science instruction. Now make up one of your own matched to an integration strategy described in this chapter. Add it to the CD. Be sure to identify each of the descriptors for it, including the relative advantage.

References

American Association for the Advancement of Science. (1993). *Benchmarks for science literacy.* New York: Oxford University Press.

American Mathematical Association of Two-Year Colleges (1995). *Crossroads in mathematics: Standards for introductory college mathematics before calculus.* Memphis, TN: Author.

Beaton, A. E., et al. (1997–1998). Mathematics achievement in the middle school years; Mathematics achievement in the primary years; Mathematics achievement in the final year of secondary school. *IEA's third international mathematics and science study.* Chestnut Hill, MA: Boston College.

Bennett, N., and Diener, K. (1997). Habits of mind. *Learning and Leading with Technology, 24*(6), 18–21.

Burrill, G. (1997). The NCTM standards: Eight years later. *School Science and Mathematics, 97*(6), 335–339.

Caniglia, J. (1997). The heat is on: Using the calculator-based laboratory to integrate math, science, and technology. *Learning and Leading with Technology, 25*(1), 22–27.

Cannon, L., et al. (2001, January 5). National library of virtual manipulatives for interactive mathematics. Available online: http://matti.usu.edu/nlvm/index.html.

Clements, D. H. (1998, January 3). From exercises and tasks to problems and projects: Unique contributions of computers to innovative mathematics education. Available online: http://forum.swarthmore.edu/technology/papers/papers/clements/clements.html.

Day, R. (1999, January 4). Find it, track it, map it, time it: Mathematics and applications of a global positioning system (GPS). Available online: http://www.math.ilstu.edu/%7Eday/nctm99/www.html.

Dessart, D. J., et al. (1999, May/June). Research backs calculators. *NCTM's Mathematics Education Dialogues,* p.6. Available online: http://www.nctm.org/dialogues/1999–05.pdf.

Dixon, J. K., and Falba, C. J. (1997). Graphing in the information age: Using data from the World Wide Web. *Mathematics Teaching in the Middle School, 2*(5), 298–304.

Dorsey, M., et al. (2001, January 4). An introduction to symmetry. Available online: http://www.geom.umn.edu/~demo5337/s97a/.

Drier, H. (2001, January 4). Collecting and numerically analyzing M&M's data. Available online: http://curry.edschool.virginia.edu/teacherlink/math/activities/excel/M&Mnumerical/home.html.

Dunham, P. H., & Dick, T. P. (1994). Research on graphing calculators. *Mathematics Teacher, 87,* 440–445.

Edelson, D. C. (1998). Realising authentic science learning through the adaptation of scientific practice. In D. Tobin & B. J. Fraser (Eds.), *International handbook of science education.* Dordrecht, The Netherlands: Kluwer.

Feicht, L. (2000). Guess and check: A viable problem solving strategy. *Learning and Leading with Technology, 27*(5), 50–54.

Finzer, W., and Jackiw, N. (1998, January 5). Dynamic manipulation of mathematical objects. Available online: http://forum.swarthmore.edu/technology/papers/papers/s2k/.

Flick, L. (1989). "Probing" temperature and heat. *The Computing Teacher, 17*(2), 15–19.

Flores, A. (1998, January 30). Electronic technology and NCTM standards. Available online: http://forum.swarthmore.edu/technology/papers/papers/flores.html.

Krajcik, J., Blumenfeld, P., Marx, R. W., Bass, K. M., Fredericks, J., & Soloway, E. (1998). Inquiry in project-based science classrooms: Initial attempts by middle school students. *Journal of the Learning Science, 7*(3&4), 313–350.

Linn, M. C. (1992). The computer as learning partner: Can computer tools teach science? In K. Sheingold, L. G. Roberts, & S. M. Malcom (Eds.), *This year in school science 1991: Technology for teaching and learning* (pp. 31–69). Washington, DC: American Association for the Advancement of Science.

Linn, M. C. (1998). Learning and instruction in science education: Taking advantage of technology. In D. Tobin & B. J. Fraser (Eds.), *International handbook of science education.* Dordrecht, The Netherlands: Kluwer.

Linn, M., Bell, P., & Hsi, S. (1999). Using the Internet to enhance student understanding of science: The knowledge integration environment. *Interactive Learning Environments, 1*(6), 4–38.

Mankus, M. L. (2000). Using virtual manipulatives on the web to develop number sense. Presented at NCTM Annual Meeting, Chicago. Available online: http://mason.gmu.edu/~mmankus/talks/nctmch00.htm.

Manoucherhri, A., & Pagnucco, L. (1999–2000). Julio's run: Studying graphs and functions. *Learning and Leading with Technology, 27*(4), 42–45.

Morgan, B., & Jernigan, J. (1998–1999). A technology update: Leonardo da Vinci and the search for the perfect body. *Learning and Leading with Technology, 26*(4), 22–25.

National Council of Teachers of Mathematics. (1989). *Curriculum and evaluation standards for school mathematics.* Reston, VA: Author.

National Council of Teachers of Mathematics. (1991). *Professional standards for teaching mathematics.* Reston, VA: Author.

National Council of Teachers of Mathematics. (1995). *Assessment standards for school mathematics.* Reston, VA: Author.

National Council of Teachers of Mathematics. (2000a, January 4). Learning geometry and measurement concepts. Available online: http://standards.nctm.org/document/eexamples/chap4/4.3/Part3.htm#applet.

National Council of Teachers of Mathematics. (2000b). *Principles and standards for school mathematics.* Reston, VA: Author.

National Council of Teachers of Mathematics. (2001, January 5). E-Example 5.4: Accessing and investigating data using the World Wide Web; E-Example 5.5: Collecting, representing, and interpreting data. Available online: http://standards.nctm.org/document/eexamples/chap5/5.4/index.htm and http://standards.nctm.org/document/eexamples/chap5/5.5/index.htm.

National Research Council. (1996). *National science education standards.* Washington, DC: National Academy Press.

Niess, M. L. (1997). Using *Geometer's Sketchpad* to construct geometric knowledge. *Learning and Leading with Technology, 24*(4), 27–31.

Perkins, D. (1993, Fall). Teaching for understanding. *American Educator,* pp. 8, 28–35.

Reiser, B. J., Tabak, I., Sandoval, W. A., Smith, B. K., Steinmuller, F., & Leone, A. J. (2001). BGuILE: Strategic and conceptual scaffolds for scientific inquiry in biology classrooms. In S. M. Carver and D. Klahr (Eds.), *Cognition and instruction: Twenty-five years of progress.* Mahwah, NJ: Erlbaum.

Renne, C. (2000). Taking shape: Linking geometry and technology. *Learning and Leading with Technology, 27*(7), 58–62.

Roth, W., & Roychoudhury, A. (1993). The development of science process skills in authentic contexts. *Journal of Research in Science Teaching, 30*(2) 127–152.

Roth, W. M. (1994). Experimenting in a constructivist high school physics laboratory. *Journal of Research in Science Teaching, 31,* 197–223.

Schwartz, D., Linn, M., Brophy, S., & Bransford, J. (2000) Toward the development of flexibly adaptive instructional designs. In C. Reigeluth (Ed.), *Instructional-design theories and models: New paradigms of instructional theory* (pp. 183–214). Mahwah, NJ: Erlbaum.

Singer, J., Krajcik, J., Marx, R., & Clay-Chambers, J. (2000). Constructing extended inquiry projects: Curriculum materials for science education reform. *Educational Psychologist, 35*(3), 165–167.

Slattery, W., Hundley, S., Finegan-Stoll, C., & Becker, M. (1998). Collecting science in a net. *Learning and Leading with Technology, 26*(1), 25–30.

Songer, N. (1998). Can technology bring students closer to science? In D. Tobin and B. J. Fraser (Eds.), *International handbook of science education.* Dordrecht, The Netherlands: Kluwer.

Spitulnik, M. W., Stratford, S., Krajcik, J., & Soloway, E. (1998). Using technology to support students' artefact construction in science. In B. J. Fraser & K. G. Tobin (Eds.), *International handbook of science education* (pp. 363–381). Dordrecht, The Netherlands: Kluwer.

Van Rossum, G. (2001, January 5). Python language website. Available online: http://www.python.org/.

Zisow, M. A. (2001). Fundraising with technology. *Learning and Leading with Technology, 28*(4), 36–41.

Resources

Mathematics Software

Math Keys (MECC)
Easy Early Math (EME Corporation)
Addition/Subtraction (EME Corporation)
Geometer's Sketchpad (Key Curriculum Press)
KaleidoMania! (Key Curriculum Press)
MicroWorlds Math Links (LCSI)
Algebra (Boxer Learning)
Cognitive Tutor: Algebra I (Carnegie Learning)
Graphers (Sunburst)
Unifix Software 2.0 (Didax)
Representing Fractions
The Hidden Treasure of Al-Jabr (Sunburst)
Math Arena (Sunburst)
Shape Up! (Sunburst)
Green Globs and Graphing Equations 2.2 (Sunburst)
Destination Math (Riverdeep Interactive Learning)
Tangible Math (Riverdeep Interactive Learning)
Lady Bug Maze (NCTM)
Mathematica 3.0 (Wolfram Research, Inc.)
Scholar 2.01 (Future Graph, Inc.)
StudyWorks for Math (MathSoft, Inc.)
Star Wars Math (Lucas Learning Ltd.)
MathView (Waterloo Maple, Inc.)
Derive 5.0 (Texas Instruments)
TI Interactive! (Texas Instruments)
Virtual Tiles (William K. Bradford Publishing Co.)
3D Images (Bradford)
NumberSense (Bradford)
Tabletop and *Tabletop Jr.* (Broderbund)

Science Software

Botanical Gardens (Sunburst)
Inventor Labs (Sunburst)
Decisions, Decisions (Tom Snyder Communications)
Science Court (Tom Snyder Communications)
Science Seekers (Tom Snyder Communications)
Struggle for Survival (Northwestern University)
BioLogica (Concord Consortium)
FutureLab (Innovative Education)
Interactive Physics (MSC Working Knowledge)
Math Type 3 (Design Science, Inc.)

Mathematics Videodiscs

The Adventures of Jasper Woodbury (LEArning, Inc.)
The Adventures of Fizz and Martina (Tom Snyder Communications)
The Perfect Pizza Caper (HRM Video)
Windows on Math (Optical Data Corporation)
Math Sleuths (Videodiscovery)
Worldwatcher (Northwestern University)
echem (University of Michigan)
Model-It (University of Michigan)
A.D.A.M. (A.D.A.M Software)
Ultimate 3D Skeleton (DK Interactive Learning)
My First Amazing Science Explorer (DK Interactive Learning)

Space Academy (Science for Kids)
Magic School Bus (Microsoft)
Planetary Taxi (Grolier)
Rainforest Design (Tom Snyder Communications)
DataStudio (PASCO Scientific)
Logal SimLibrary (Riverdeep Interactive Learning)
Logger Pro (Vernier)

Science Videodiscs

KinderVentures (Optical Data Corporation)
Windows on Science (Optical Data Corporation)
The Living Textbook (Optical Data Corporation)
Great Solar System Rescue (Tom Snyder Communications)
Great Ocean Rescue (Tom Snyder Communications)
Anatomy and Physiology (Videodiscovery)
Chemistry at Work (Videodiscovery)
Science Sleuths Elementary (Videodiscovery)
Understanding Earth (Videodiscovery)
Bioethics Forum (Videodiscovery)
Science Discovery (Videodiscovery)
Death Traps (Videodiscovery)
Life Cycles (Videodiscovery)
Atmosphere (Videodiscovery)
Water Planet (Videodiscovery)
Physics at the Indy 500 (Videodiscovery)
Evolution (Videodiscovery)
The Universe (Videodiscovery)
General Biology (Biodiscs)
Genetics (Biodisc)

CHAPTER 12

Technology in Social Studies Instruction

M. D. Roblyer, University of Maryland University College

We shall not cease from exploration
And the end of all our exploring
Will be to arrive where we started
And know the place for the first time.
T. S. Eliot

This chapter covers the following topics:

- Current issues and problems underlying the use of technology in social studies instruction
- A description of how technology is integrated into social studies instruction
- Example World Wide Web site resources for social studies instruction
- Example activities for a variety of integration strategies in social studies instruction.

Objectives

1. Identify some of the current issues in social studies instruction that may impact the selection and use of technology.
2. Describe strategies for integrating technology into social studies curricula that support curricular goals.
3. Identify useful technology resources and Internet sites for social studies.
4. Create instructional activities for social studies instruction that model effective integration strategies.

Introduction

Since the Industrial Revolution, science and technology have shaped the world in fundamental ways. In the 1990s, computer technologies and the emergence of the Internet have accelerated this influence. Better, faster, worldwide communications have made the world at once smaller and more complex. Life was simpler—and less informed—when people did not know so much about themselves and others so quickly. Now, with so much new information at hand, we have much to discover about our world and its people. But it is through this exploration that we make our world more like the place we want it to be.

The National Council for the Social Studies (NCSS) has adopted the following formal definition for the social studies:

> Social studies is the integrated study of the social sciences and humanities to promote civic competence. Within the school program, social studies provides coordinated, systemic study drawing upon such disciplines as anthropology, archaeology, economics, geography, history, law, philosophy, political science, psychology, religion, and sociology, as well as appropriate content from the humanities, mathematics, and the natural sciences. The primary purpose of social studies is to help young people develop the ability to make informed and reasoned decisions for the public good as citizens of a culturally diverse, democratic society in an interdependent world. (NCSS, 1994, p. 3)

As an area that focuses on the interconnections of people and the earth, social studies education has been affected by the impact of technology perhaps more than any other content area. Not only is there more to learn about the world than ever before, the information is changing constantly and dramatically. Fortunately, the same technologies that created this more complex world also can help teach about it.

Issues and Problems in Social Studies Education

Social Studies Instruction Standards

The national social studies standards were released by the NCSS in 1994. Because educational standards were developed for social studies as well as for many of the individual disciplines that make up social studies, it is necessary to point out the distinction. Social studies standards address overall curriculum design and comprehensive student performance expectations. The individual discipline standards for civics, economics, geography, government, and history provide more specific content detail.

The NCSS hopes that curriculum designers will use the social studies standards for creating the overall framework and then fill in the detail using the discipline standards. The 10 themes that form the framework of the social studies standards, along with a brief description of each, are presented next (NCSS, 1994; http://www.ncss.org/standards/toc.html).

Culture. The study of culture prepares students to answer questions such as these: What are the common characteristics of different cultures? How do belief systems, such as religion or political ideals, influence other parts of the culture? This theme typically appears in units and courses dealing with geography, history, sociology, and anthropology as well as multicultural topics across the curriculum.

Time, continuity, and change. Humans seek to understand their historical roots and to locate themselves in time. Knowing how to read and reconstruct the past allows one to develop a historical perspective and to answer questions such as these: Who am I? What happened in the past? How am I connected to those in the past? How has the world changed and how might it change in the future? Why does our personal sense of relatedness to the past change? This theme typically appears in courses in history and others that draw upon historical knowledge and habits.

People, places, and environments. The study of people, places, and human–environment interactions assists as students create their spatial views and geographic perspectives of the world beyond their personal locations. Students need the knowledge, skills, and understanding to answer questions such as these: Where are things located? Why are they located where they are? What do we mean by "region"? How do landforms change? What implications do these changes have for people? This theme typically appears in units and courses dealing with area studies and geography.

Individual development and identity. Personal identity is shaped by culture, groups, and institutional influences. Students should consider such questions as these: How do people learn? Why do people behave as they do? What influences how people learn, perceive, and grow? How do people meet their basic needs in a variety of contexts? How do individuals develop from youth to adulthood? This theme typically appears in units and courses dealing with psychology and anthropology.

Individuals, groups, and institutions. Institutions such as schools, churches, families, government agencies, and

Technology Integration Example

Social Studies Instruction

TITLE: *Studying Our Past, Mapping Our Future*

BASED ON: Parmenter, B., & Burns, M. (2001). GIS in the classroom: Challenges, opportunities, and alternatives. *Learning and Leading with Technology, 28*(7), 10–17.

GRADE LEVEL: 7–8

CONTENT AREA/TOPIC: Geography, civics, and history

LENGTH OF TIME: Six weeks

Step 1: What's the Relative Advantage—Why Use Technology in Social Studies?

Mr. McAlpine, a middle school social studies teacher, taught the state and local studies classes for his school's eighth-grade students. He had always felt that one of his most important tasks as a social studies teacher at this level was to help his students see that *people* shape the history and growth of an area, and that the students themselves could have a major role in shaping the future of areas in which they live. He knew this was important preparation and background for the civics and history courses they would take in high school. However, he also knew how difficult it was to get students to grasp complex, abstract concepts like the relationship between past history, current conditions, and future developments. He decided that this concept would become more meaningful to students if they gathered information from local citizens about the history of their local area and used their findings to hypothesize plans for the area's future.

As he brainstormed activities, he looked for resources that could make historical and geographical concepts more real and compelling to students and would emphasize their ability to shape their future. In a recent district workshop, he had learned that the U.S. Census Bureau provides a geographic information system (GIS) viewer on its web site through which students can see databases of past and current data about any given area overlaid on actual maps. He read about a project where students created "life maps" of people and places on GIS maps of the area during different periods of time (Audet & Ludwig, 2000). He had also experimented with the simulation software that gave students an active role in decision making about social issues. He decided to integrate these and other resources into a 6-week unit around three major activities: identifying events that shaped the history and growth of the area, creating life maps of people from the history of the local area, and developing a "growth scenario" for the future.

Step 2: Planning Assessment—What Are Appropriate Assessment Strategies?

Mr. McAlpine decided that each of the activities in the unit should have a graded, small-group product. The products would be time lines showing local events and population growth; life maps of people, places, and events in the local area; and a map presentation of their growth scenario for the future. For the first two products, he created a checklist of required components and characteristics; he had a rubric to assess the future plan they would create. Because all of these were small-group projects, each assessment included the criterion of working effectively with others in the group.

Step 3: Planning Instruction—What Are Appropriate Integration Strategies?

Mr. McAlpine decided he would use the following sequence to accomplish the goals of the unit:

Figure 12.0 Local Maps Created with GIS Viewer Provided by U.S. Census Bureau

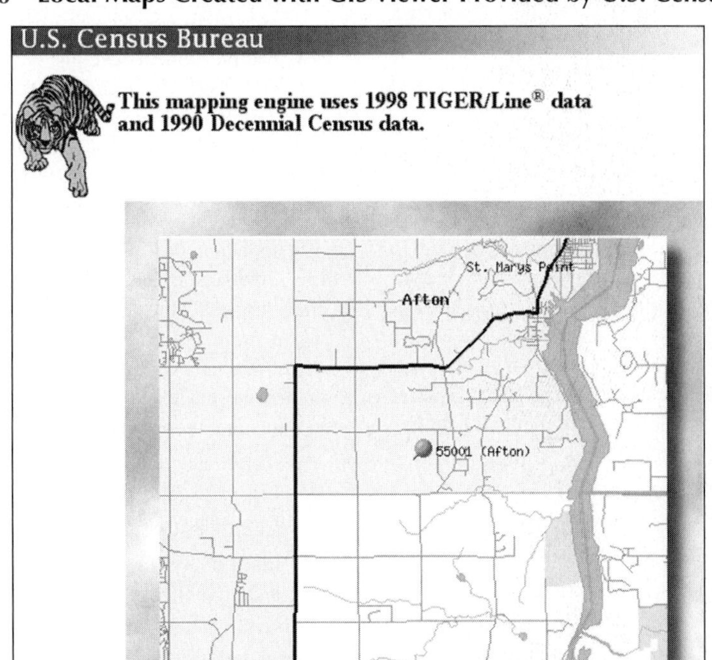

TECHNOLOGY INTEGRATION EXAMPLE *(CONTINUED)*

- **Week 1: Introduce the unit.** Introduce the unit to the class as "Our Area: Past, Present, and Future." Show actual photos of the same local area at different periods of time. Compare the photos and discuss what kinds of things changed and why. Tell them about the products they will create during their study of the evolution of their area. Ask students to "volunteer" parents, grandparents, or great grandparents who would come to school so the class could interview them and gather information about events that shaped the local area. Have the class brainstorm questions to ask during interviews with their "senior authorities." Demonstrate the Tom Snyder *Timeliner* software. Form small groups and assign each small group a time period. Give each some background history materials on the time periods, and have them experiment with creating time lines of events that occurred in the United States and the world during their particular time period.
- **Week 2: Gather information and create time lines.** Have student groups interview the local expert(s) for their assigned time period. After compiling their notes on answers to the questions, have each use the Tom Snyder *Timeliner* software to create a time line of events during their time period. They import pictures to illustrate local events. Each group presents its time line and describes how the people and events they learned about helped shape the local area.
- **Weeks 3–4: Create life maps.** Demonstrate the U.S. Census web site to students. Show how they can select a map of their local area by entering their zip code, and how they can create data overlays of recent population statistics and other data. Form small working groups and have each group experiment with displaying a different kind of data on the same area. Have them present their displays to the whole class. Show an example "life map" created at another school. Each group imports the GIS map into a graphics package and creates a "life map" of the person they interviewed, showing places and events the person discussed and the boundaries of the town at that time. They present their maps to the class.
- **Weeks 5–6: Create future scenarios with GIS data.** Introduce this phase in the unit by having student groups use the Tom Snyder *Decisions, Decisions: Town Government* software to explore citizens' roles in governing the local community. Lead a discussion comparing each of their findings. Then tell students to imagine they are a citizen's action committee tasked with planning a growth scenario for their community for the next decade. Have each group look at a different area of growth (e.g., housing, transportation, recreational areas, services such as waste disposal and water). As a whole class, they download historical census data from the U.S. Census Bureau web site, put it in a spreadsheet, and use it to project population statistics for the area during the next 10 years. In small groups, they discuss the implications of this population growth for their area of concern. Using the map they created for their life maps, they show what would need to be planned for development to keep up with the area's growth. Mr. McAlpine helps them print their maps on transparency sheets. Using an overhead projector, they overlay the maps and "negotiate" to resolve any conflicts they see (e.g., new housing versus a larger city park). As a whole class, they merge the maps into one to reflect on the plan for the future. They end the unit by reflecting on their decisions and the implications they would have for the area.

Step 4: Logistics—Preparing the Classroom Environment and Instructional Materials

In the weeks before the project began, Mr. McAlpine had to organize several kinds of resources. First, he had to obtain historical photos and data on the community. Then he had to identify the resource people who could be used as authorities on each decade from 1950 through 2000 and set up interview times. To have his students see and discuss the U.S. Census Bureau web site and GIS maps as a whole class, Mr. McAlpine needed to schedule the use of a large-screen projection system and obtain permission to print transparencies on the computer lab's laser printer. Finally, he had to make sure the two software packages worked on his classroom computers.

Step 5: Evaluating and Revising Integration Strategies

Mr. McAlpine tried out the lesson and administered the following self-assessment to review how it worked for him:

- Did students' products reflect growth in their thinking about people's roles in shaping their future?
- Did the students become engaged in each of the tasks?
- Did each of the software and web resources and small groups work as smoothly as expected?
- Did most students score well on the checklists and rubric?

Also, he interviewed students about their perceptions of the unit. As expected, they were most positive about the interviews of local people and the hands-on work with the web site. They were less enthusiastic about having to work in small groups. After considering all the outcomes, Mr. McAlpine decided the unit was a success. He resolved to contact the state GIS office for more local data for various time periods that students could use in their work. He also decided to look for strategies to make his students feel more positive about working in groups.

the courts play an integral role in our lives. It is important that students learn how institutions are formed, what controls and influences them, how they influence individuals and culture, and how they are maintained or changed. Students may address questions such as these: What is the role of institutions in this or other societies? How am I influenced by institutions? How do institutions change? What is my role in institutional change? This theme typically appears in units and courses dealing with sociology, anthropology, psychology, political science, and history.

Power, authority, and governance. Understanding the historical development of power, authority, and governance and their evolving functions in contemporary U.S. society and other parts of the world is essential for developing civic competence. In exploring this theme, students confront questions such as these: What is power? What forms does it take? Who holds it? How is it gained, used, and justified? What is legitimate authority? How are governments created, structured, maintained, and changed? How can individual rights be protected within the context of majority rule? This theme typically appears in units and courses dealing with government, politics, political science, history, law, and other social studies.

Production, distribution, and consumption. Because people have wants that often exceed available resources, a variety of ways have evolved to answer these questions: What is to be produced? How is production organized? How are goods and services distributed? What is the most effective allocation of factors of production such as land, labor, capital, and management? This theme typically appears in units and courses dealing with economic concepts and issues.

Science, technology, and society. Modern life would be impossible without technology and the science that supports it. But technology raises many questions: Is new technology always better than old? What can we learn from the past about how new technologies result in broader social change, some of which is unanticipated? How can we cope with the ever-increasing pace of change? How can we preserve our fundamental values and beliefs in the midst of technological change? This theme draws on the natural and physical sciences, social studies, and the humanities and appears in a variety of social studies courses, including history, geography, economics, civics, and government.

Global connections. The realities of global interdependence require an understanding of the increasingly important and diverse global connections among world societies and the frequent tension between national interests and global priorities. Students need to be able to address such international issues as health care, the environment, human rights, economic competition and interdependence, age-old ethnic enmities, and political and military alliances. This theme typically appears in units or courses dealing with geography, culture, and economics, but may also draw on the natural and physical sciences and the humanities.

Civic ideals and practices. An understanding of civic ideals and practices of citizenship is critical to full participation in society and is a central purpose of the social studies. Students confront such questions as these: What is civic participation and how can we be involved? How has the meaning of citizenship evolved? What is the balance between rights and responsibilities? What is the role of the citizen in the community and the nation and as a member of the world community? This theme typically appears in units or courses dealing with history, political science, and cultural anthropology and fields such as global studies, law-related education, and the humanities.

School systems usually address social studies curriculum by teaching topics from these strands in the elementary and middle school levels. In high school, social studies tends to become divided into specific areas such as history and civics. Thus, the term *social studies* is one used more at K–8 levels.

Depth Versus Breadth

Depth versus breadth—and its closely related issue of teaching for understanding—are major issues in social studies instruction, particularly in the history discipline. Standardized testing and many curriculum architectures tend to emphasize broad survey coverage and mastery of facts. Those who stress depth point out that covering historical episodes in a thorough fashion breathes life into the past and is pivotal to the development of understanding. Others counter that the study of changes over a long chronological period remains central to students' understanding of historical context. This issue is complex and not likely to be resolved soon. In fact, a broad consensus may never be reached. It is more likely that individual school districts, principals, school improvement teams, and frontline teachers will ultimately make the choice of how best to educate their students.

Perils of the Information Explosion

Information related to social studies topics and issues is prolific on the Internet; this ready availability of information creates several concerns. First, some believe that Internet information has the potential to alter the traditional relationship between student and teacher since students no longer depend on the teacher as a primary source of facts or opinions. Teachers tell of students bringing printed web pages to school that contradict what the textbook says, or even what the teacher says. In the past, most information that students learned was sifted through some sort of filter; today, those filters often are nonexistent. Students can find sites that profess Nazi and Ku Klux Klan ideology, treat rumor as fact, and promote conspiracy theories that range from UFO landings in Roswell, New Mexico, to the CIA selling drugs in American cities. Even very bright students may be drawn to some of these sites and never question their accuracy.

Many educators believe we need information or media literacy now more than ever. Some believe that rather than shying away from the hate or conspiracy sites, we should be using them as demonstration tools to teach our students how to become critical consumers of information. As Harp (1996) puts it, schools must "mobilize their curriculum leaders into quality management" (p. 38) to monitor and help students become more analytical about the information they receive.

The "History Wars"

Harp (1996) also describes a battle over world and American history standards that has raged during the last several years—a battle that shows just how important Americans view the teaching of history. The controversy centers around whether or not U.S. history curriculum excludes or marginalizes non-European cultures and fails to represent the perspectives of minorities. As Harp notes, the call for a "more inclusive history" resulted in a major project at UCLA to "draw up a new social studies curriculum stressing more multicultural themes and encouraging critical perspectives" (p. 34). However, the history standards released in 1995 by the UCLA project were so controversial that the U.S. Senate voted to disavow the group's work. Subsequently, social studies leaders have been working to develop a more balanced approach to these standards and the views of our history they represent. In the meantime, states such as Vermont have developed their own standards as well as a CD-ROM that they feel will "help teachers begin to make better sense of the myriad influences bombarding their history and social studies classrooms" (Harp, 1996, p. 38).

How Technology Is Integrated into Social Studies Education

Social studies instruction traditionally has been "fact driven." The nature of the subject matter, with its historic dates and geographic names, certainly has contributed to this approach. In addition to organizing and presenting such information quite effectively, technology resources for social studies instruction also support a treatment of social studies content that many educators feel results in more meaningful learning. Integration strategies are suggested here to address each of the 10 strands in the NCSS national social studies standards. The following examples should not be considered exhaustive of all the potential technology resources offered for this important area.

Using Technology to Learn About Culture

An understanding of and appreciation for cultural similarities and differences permeates instruction in history, geography, and state studies at lower grades (K–8), and courses in sociology, anthropology, and civics at higher grades (9–12). Technology resources can support these culture-related goals in many meaningful ways.

Exploring cultures. When students take virtual trips to Internet sites around the world and do WebQuests to gather information about other places and cultures, it provides them with rich opportunities to explore other cultures and compare them with our own.

Working with people of other cultures. Distance projects, such as keypals communications and social action projects with students in other locations, allow students to compare each other's belief systems (e.g., religious or political ideals) as they work together.

Seeing examples of other cultures. Videos, videodiscs, and multimedia encyclopedias provide a rich array of visual examples of the products and traditions of various cultures and serve as the basis for research projects comparing these cultures with our own.

Reflecting cultures in artworks. Especially at lower grade levels, teachers often have students research information about a culture and then prepare art products such as drawings or models to reflect their findings. For these kinds of projects, graphics programs allow even the "artistically challenged" student to create something artistic. (See Technology Integration Idea 12.1.)

Useful Web Sites for Teaching About Cultures

Culture, Diversity, and Multiculturism

http://www.ncbe.gwu.edu/links/langcult/multi.htm

Provides extensive lists of links from the National Clearinghouse for English Language Acquisition & Language Instruction Educational Programs (formerly NCBE) for resources relating to multicultural education and cultural diversity issues worldwide.

Equity & Cultural Diversity

http://eric-web.tc.columbia.edu/equity/

Provides links to conference information, directories, digests, and other resources.

One World, Our World

http://www.onewow.org

Created by those who have served in the Peace Corps, this site is dedicated to the principles of tolerance, leadership, and conflict resolution.

Global Grocery List

http://landmark-project.com/ggl/

This long-standing project generates real, peer-collected data for student computation, analysis, and conclusion building within the context of social studies, science, mathematics, and other disciplines.

Using Technology to Learn About Time, Continuity, and Change

The study of history has evolved from learning facts and dates to focusing on the meaning of events and their impact on the evolution of individual countries and the world. Technology can help teach historical perspective in several ways.

TECHNOLOGY INTEGRATION IDEA 12.1

Learning About Culture

TITLE: *Kid Pix* in Multicultural Education

CONTENT AREA/TOPIC: Multicultural Education

GRADE LEVEL: Elementary

NETS FOR STUDENTS: Standards 1, 3

DESCRIPTION: As students learn about cultures that illustrated their histories with artworks, they can use *Kid Pix* to create their own stories or tell about their own histories or those of their families. Native Americans of the Pacific Northwest carved totem poles to record the histories of the tribes and families. Students can use *Kid Pix* to create their own totem poles that tell about themselves and their families. The people of Ghana would create a special cloth with designs and symbols from their culture as a gift for someone who left for another village. The Ghanians called the fabric *Adrinka* (good-bye) cloth after the dye used to produce the designs. Students can use *Kid Pix* to create unique designs for their own "good-bye cloths." Many cultures create masks to use in rituals, to protect themselves against evil spirits or gods, or to present plays or tell stories. Students can use *Kid Pix* features to design their own masks for use in plays or dramatizations.

Source: Chan, B. (1993). *Kid Pix around the world: A multicultural activity book.* Reading, MA: Addison-Wesley Publishing Company.

Researching events. The Internet has dozens of sites focusing on every period of history. Students can use these web sites in the context of WebQuest projects or simply as additional information resources to gather information for discussion or research papers. These sites are especially useful to show students how different people can have dramatically different perspectives on the same events.

Examining time sequences. Students often have difficulty understanding and remembering sequences of events. Students can use a program such as Tom Snyder's *Timeliner* to develop time lines of events and make them more visual. (See Figure 12.1.)

Examining visual records. Students no longer need just read about history. Videos, videodiscs, and multimedia encyclopedias provide a wealth of actual pictures and film footage of people, events, and places. These provide additional information sources for research projects and make history come alive for students. (See Technology Integration Idea 12.2.)

Useful Web Sites for Teaching History

The History Highway 2000: A Guide to Internet Resources (Trinkle & Merriman, 2000) is a comprehensive listing of Internet resources on history. Some of these include the following:

American Memory

http://lcweb2.loc.gov:8081/ammem/ammemhome.html

Sponsored by the Library of Congress, consists largely of primary source materials. Exhibits are archived and are updated regularly.

Figure 12.1 Example Historical Time Line from *Timeliner*

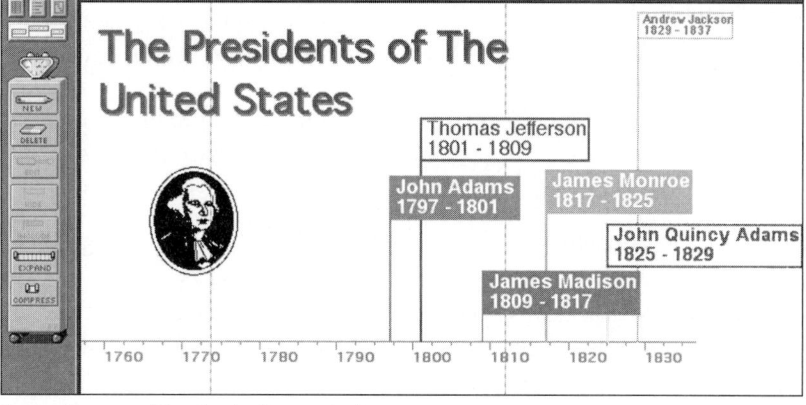

Source: Courtesy of Tom Snyder Communications.

TECHNOLOGY INTEGRATION IDEA 12.2

Learning About Time, Continuity, and Change

TITLE: Student WebQuest on Anne Frank

CONTENT AREA/TOPIC: History

GRADE LEVEL: 7–9

NETS FOR STUDENTS: Standards 3, 4, 5

DESCRIPTION: After a beginning discussion about the Holocaust, students are asked to imagine they have been hired to create a documentary for a major news network about Anne Frank and the children of the Holocaust. They are assigned to small groups to work on various sources of information, for example, literature about the children, art produced by children about the Holocaust, and information from interviews of people who knew Anne Frank. The teacher gives the students a variety of web sites to visit and specific questions to answer and items of information to obtain. After each group obtains its information, they work on combining it to develop a multimedia documentary.

Source: Yoder, M. (1999). The student Web Quest. *Learning and Leading with Technology, 26*(7), 6–9, 52–53.

Creating Online Materials for Teaching United States History

http://etext.lib.virginia.edu/history/

A favorite of many history teachers and professors. Includes historical documents, for example, posters, photos, and political cartoons, which are arranged chronologically. Also has links to teacher-developed lessons.

The History Channel

http://historychannel.com

This site provides additional information on video programs on the History Channel.

History Text Archive

http://historicaltextarchive.com/

Presents an avenue to an abundance of resources for students and teachers on data about U.S. history.

Horus Gateway to Historical Time and Space

http://www.ucr.edu/h-gig/horuslinks.html

An outstanding place for historians to begin. This site is helpful for students of all ages and the topics range from simple historical data to specific topics like Native American history. Nearly 4000 links are organized into multiple categories.

Teaching with Historic Places

http://www.cr.nps.gov/nr/twhp/descript.html

This comprehensive site is sponsored by the National Park Service for both students and teachers. It also serves as a model for students to "do" their own history about their city or community.

University of Oklahoma Law Center

http://www.aw.ou.edu/ushist.html

A chronology of U.S. historical documents. This site offers full-text versions of historic documents ranging from the Magna Carta to the German surrender of WWII to the most current state of the union address.

Using Technology to Learn About People, Places, and Environments

The study of geography and its impact on people and civilizations has been enhanced dramatically with the use of several technologies, some of which have been readily available to schools only within the past few years.

Developing and using maps. No longer do students need to struggle with paper, pencil, and ruler as they draw their own maps. Mapping utilities allow more interactive, hands-on uses of existing maps, as well as creation of new ones. Students can use software such as Tom Snyder's *Neighborhood Map Machine,* or web sites such as *MapBlast* (www.mapblast.com/myblast/index.mb), which allows users to make maps, gather and attach information such as local weather, and download the products to Palm Pilots or other similar devices.

Using location data. Tools such as GISs and global positioning systems (GPSs), once the province of business and government researchers, are now increasingly available to teachers and students. The number of GIS sites on the Internet is continually increasing. Sites such as the one available from the U.S. Census Bureau (http://www.census.gov) have built-in GIS viewers that allow users to overlay data about an area on top of a map. These tools make data more visual and easy to use as students consider questions about the relationship between people and their locations. (See Technology Integration Idea 12.3.) GPS instruments may become a standard part of the geography classroom. For example, students connected via distance learning can use GPSs to locate each other and to study their geographic locations.

Collaborating on projects. Some teachers report having classes in different locations use e-mail and the Internet to collaborate on travel brochures and other products about the region. These collaborations allow exchanges of information and discussions of how life in two places is similar or different because of the characteristics of the regions.

Practicing facts. Some topics in the social studies curriculum still require memorization of facts (e.g., states and capitals). Teachers can use drill-and-practice software, test generators, or web sites (http://www.interactivetest.com) to give students the practice they need.

Useful Web Sites for Teaching About People, Places, and Environments:

Environmental Defense Scorecard

http://www.scorecard.org/

Gives information about environmental conditions and pollution indexes for any area of the United States.

National Geographic Society

http://www.nationalgeographic.com/kids/

The NGS has a number of sites that are useful to schools, teachers, and parents. This one is just for kids and it is full of resources as well as fun.

Population Education

http://www.zpg.org/education/library/

Provides numerous curriculum items and information to kids about how to be responsible citizens of the world.

U.S. Census Bureau

http://www.census.gov

Provides data and information on the U.S. population, along with a GIS viewer for using the data.

Nations of the World Atlas

http://www.lineone.net/discovery/places/nations/

Comprehensive atlas provides up-to-date information and maps for every country in the world. Find out about the geography, climate, economy, politics, and history, plus key facts and national statistics, for any country.

Perry-Castaneda Map Collection

http://mahogany.lib.utexas.edu/Libs/PCL/Map_collection/Map_collection.html

This site provides a comprehensive map collection.

Human Rights Web

http://www.hrweb.org/

Offers a great deal of general information about human rights, including how individuals can get involved in making a difference around the world.

EDSITEment

http://edsitement.neh.gov/

A mega site produced by the National Endowment for the Humanities. This particular link is to the portion that links to sites about every place in the world. The general site is excellent for many disciplines, but this

TECHNOLOGY INTEGRATION IDEA 12.3

Learning About People, Places, and Environments

TITLE: Data Tools for Real-World Learning

CONTENT AREA/TOPIC: Geography

GRADE LEVEL: 11–12

NETS FOR STUDENTS: Standards 5, 6

DESCRIPTION: In this project, students and teachers work with residents and local officials to understand and care for their environment. In one activity, the students conduct a survey of safety hazards in their school neighborhoods. Using a rubric they helped to create, they rated buildings around their school as to how much of a safety hazard each posed. They enter their ratings for each building into a GIS system that already included street addresses for the region. Using color coding for each category of rating, they produce thematic maps to show patterns of unsafe conditions. School and law enforcement officials were able to use these thematic maps to prioritize areas needing immediate safety attention.

Source: Hunter, B., & Xie, Y. (2001). Data tools for real world learning. *Learning and Leading with Technology, 28*(7), 18–24.

portion is a must for those who are teaching about people and places.

EduGreen

http://edugreen.teri.res.in/

Sponsored by the Pan Asian Network, a program initiative of the International Development Research Centre of Canada, which helps researchers and communities in the developing world find solutions to their social, economic, and environmental problems.

Stately Knowledge: Facts About the United States

http://www.ipl.org/youth/stateknow/

Provides links to all 50 states. From there students can find an abundance of information about their part of the country.

Figure 12.2 Example from *Decisions, Decisions: The Constitution*

Source: Courtesy of Tom Snyder Communications.

Using Technology to Learn About Individual Development and Identity

Many of the same technology uses described under the first strand (culture) also can be used here to enhance students' learning of how personal identity is shaped by culture, groups, and institutional influences. In addition, students can use web sites such as the American Memory Collection (http://memory.loc.gov) to see how influences from many lands have helped shape the American experience. Also, multimedia software such as Sunburst's *Multimedia: The Human Body* (described in Chapter 7) can help students see more clearly how our body's physical systems develop, how we become learning organisms, and why we behave the way we do.

Using Technology to Learn About Individuals, Groups, and Institutions and Power, Authority, and Governance

Students can use technology resources to help them learn how institutions of various kinds developed, how they affect us, and how we can help shape them.

Simulated problem solving. To learn how to respond appropriately to institutions that affect their lives, students need to learn through hands-on experience with real-life issues and problems. Software such as Tom Snyder's *Decisions, Decisions: The Constitution* can help provide these opportunities in a feasible time frame. (See Figure 12.2.)

Clarifying abstract concepts about governance. Students often have difficulty understanding concepts such as apportionment and the electoral vote versus the popular vote. Spreadsheet lessons have been used to help clarify these concepts and let students experiment with various "what if?" scenarios with simulated data.

Learning where to go for up-to-date information. Local, state, and federal government agencies increasingly rely on their Internet sites to represent them and to disseminate important information on events and issues of concern to citizens. Students need to know how to find and use the web sites of their local and state agencies, as well as national ones such as these:

Democratic Party: http://www.democrats.org/party/positions

Republican Party: http://www.rnc.org/search

U.S. Congress: http://www.thomas.loc.gov

U.S. House of Representatives: http://www.house.gov

U.S. Senate: http://www.senate.gov

White House: http://www.whitehouse.gov

U.S. Information Agency: http://www.civnet.org

Other Useful Web Sites

Lives: The Biography Resource

http://amillionlives.com/

A wonderful link to a wealth of biographies about people famous and not so famous. Reading biographies assists students in solidifying their own dreams and aspirations.

Multiculturalpedia

http://www.netlaputa.ne.jp/~tokyo3/e/

This is the place to discover the customs and habits of groups of people all over the world. In learning about others, students learn to respect one another.

Using Technology to Learn About Production, Distribution, and Consumption

Several kinds of technology resources can clarify complex economic principles by making them more visual and by showing students their practical applications.

Simulating transactions. Students can use software simulations designed for this purpose to explore fundamentals about the stock market. Teachers have students select some stocks and use a spreadsheet to track their rise and fall. (See Technology Integration Idea 12.4.) A quick version of the same kind of stock market activity is available on the Internet at locations such as http://www.ncsa.uiuc.edu/edu/RSE/RSEyellow/gnb.html. (See Figure 12.3.)

Illustrating economic principles. Spreadsheet activities have become very popular for showing students mathematical concepts such as loan amortization. Internet sites such as the currency converter at http://www.xe.net/ucc/ and train fare information at http://cnnfn.cnn.com/services/travelcenter/cityguide.html also are useful for this purpose. Students can use these kinds of resources to compare prices for goods and services around the world.

Useful Web Sites for Teaching About Production, Distribution, and Consumption:

EcEdWeb

http://www.ecedweb.unomaha.edu

This is the most widely recognized web site for teaching economics.

Econlinks

http://www.ncat.edu/~simkinss/econlinks.html

A portal to a variety of economic and financial information, it is designed primarily for college students, but is very usable for teachers and high school students, especially those in advanced placement classes.

Figure 12.3 Stock Market Simulation

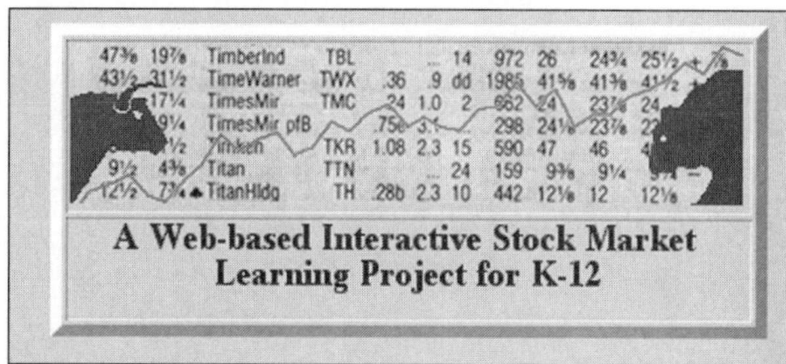

Source: Courtesy of the National Center for Super Computing Applications (NCSA) and the Board of Trustees of the University of Illinois.

CNNfn: The Financial Network

http://www.cnnfn.com/

Provides information on up-to-date stock quotes and exchange rates for any country in the world, among other data.

U.S. Department of the Treasury

http://www.ustreas.gov/

This site is an excellent source of background information.

Using Technology to Teach About Science, Technology, and Society

The implicit connections between this strand and technology make it an ideal area in which to integrate technology-based activities. However, students need to know more than just how to use various technology tools, they also must learn how new tools come about as a result of needs in our society (see Technology Integration Idea 12.5), the impact of technologies on our lives, and our ethical responsibilities as we use these powerful resources.

TECHNOLOGY INTEGRATION IDEA 12.4

Learning About Production, Distribution, and Consumption

TITLE: Buy Low/Sell High: A Study of the Stock Market

CONTENT AREA/TOPIC: Economics and business math

GRADE LEVEL: High school

NETS FOR STUDENTS: Standards 3, 5, 6

DESCRIPTION: Students learn how to invest in corporate stocks by creating simulated investment "portfolios." Each student chooses five companies whose stock they want to "purchase." Everyone in the class starts with $1,500 in seed money to purchase stocks at the current market value. Using a spreadsheet, they track their portfolio's performance over a period of time, from 6 weeks to 3 months. Students visit a web site called "Investing for Kids" or "StockMaster," the stock market site referenced in the Web Links section of *Encarta.* Or they can access a wealth of business news and financial information to track the performance of selected stocks by visiting the web site of Microsoft Investor. At the end of the tracking period, they report on their earnings and losses by displaying their spreadsheets.

Source: Based on a lesson from *Microsoft Productivity in the Classroom* (1997) by the Microsoft Corporation.

TECHNOLOGY INTEGRATION IDEA 12.5

Learning About Science, Technology, and Society

TITLE: Invention Events

CONTENT AREA/TOPIC: Technology education, history

GRADE LEVEL: 5–8

NETS FOR STUDENTS: Standards 3, 5

DESCRIPTION: Students select an invention of interest to them. They peruse a series of web sites to gather information and background on their inventions. After they complete their research, students enter the inventions and the information about them into a database. Fields include items such as invention name, category, date of patent or invention, inventor, and significant effect of invention. After discussion on the inventions selected and researched by the class members, students each create time lines to place their inventions historically. They show events surrounding the introduction of their inventions.

Source: Barrett, J. (2001). Indispensable inventions. *Learning and Leading with Technology, 29*(1), 22–26.

Other Useful Web Sites for Teaching About Science, Technology, and Society

National Geographic Society

http://www.nationalgeographic.com/features/96/inventions/

Provides incredible materials for families, teachers, and schools. This is one of the neatest interactive places on the Internet for kids to learn about inventions, inventors, and the "accidents" that often lead to discovery.

Blacks in Technology: Past and Present

http://www.users.fast.net/~blc/xlhome2.htm

The inventions of several African Americans are explored.

Using Technology to Teach About Global Connections

This is an area with much overlap with the environmental and ecological issues covered in the physical sciences. Science and social science teachers often team up on projects to help students learn about these issues.

Researching global issues. WebQuests and social action projects (see Chapter 8) are popular in this area. These projects have students use web sites to locate background information and up-to-date developments, and allow them a framework in which to work collaboratively on issues of international concern such as pollution and the environment, health care, and human rights. (See Technology Integration Idea 12.6.)

Simulating crisis problem solving. Packages like *SimCity* (MAXIS/Electronic Arts) allow students to study economic and environmental issues in an authentic way. For example, a teacher may decide to simulate a hypothetical environmental crisis in a small city. The students work in teams, each assigned a different role as campaign advisors to the mayor. The advisors are provided with written material that gives them background information and social

TECHNOLOGY INTEGRATION IDEA 12.6

Learning About Global Connections

TITLE: Community Information on the Web

CONTENT AREA/TOPIC: Social studies, environmental science

GRADE LEVEL: 6–8

NETS FOR STUDENTS: Standards 4, 5, 6

DESCRIPTION: To enter a CyberFair held by area schools, students must create a web site about their community. The web site must highlight local environmental concerns or efforts to promote environmental awareness. Each class participating in the development takes one of the issues under the main topic of environmental awareness, for example, preparation for disasters, beach erosion, waste management, and water pollution. Teachers provide examples, discussion questions, and guidelines as starting points. Students are given a variety of web sites and local information that addresses the topic. They supplement these findings by interviews with local citizens. As they work together to create their CyberFair entry, students gain an in-depth understanding about and respect for their community.

Source: Soloman, G., & Andres, Y. (2000). Community information: Sharing it all on the web. *Learning and Leading with Technology, 25*(8), 44–48.

studies content. The team must decide as a unit on a series of decisions the mayor must make to deal with the crisis. The computer guides the teams through the crisis and records their decisions. Like many other simulations of its kind, a program like this enables the student to learn information in a just-in-time fashion, apply it immediately to a problem-solving scenario, examine situations from multiple perspectives, and work with others on a team to make complex decisions.

Useful Web Sites for Teaching About Global Connections

The Global Schoolhouse

http://www.gsh.org/

In addition to linking kids, this site has all sorts of sources for teachers and ideas for exciting shared learning experiences.

Children's Games from Around the World

http://www.rice.edu/projects/topics/edition11/games-section.htm

One of the universals of culture is that all children play games. This is a great source for teachers and students to learn how people in other countries play games.

Greatest Places

http://www.greatestplaces.org/

Sponsored by the Science Museum of Minnesota, the site allows visitors to explore many places in the world, along with interesting phenomena, such as mirages.

The Smithsonian Institution

http://www.si.edu

This site provides a wealth of information on history, technology, and culture.

Water in Africa

http://www.peacecorps.gov/wws/water/africa/

This site is designed to help students learn important knowledge and skills in geography, language arts, and other disciplines by studying the use of water in 24 African countries. This web site, which features online lessons developed by teachers and is built around 600 photos and anecdotes, can be browsed by country, with basic country information and maps provided.

Asia in the Schools: Preparing Young Americans for Today's Interconnected World

http://www.asiaintheschools.org/

This web site addresses the status of teaching about Asia in the school, identifies problems, and proposes some solutions.

Using Technology to Teach About Civic Ideals and Practices

Civics is usually considered the area in which students learn how to participate in society and, as such, it touches on a wide variety of topics. It may include an introduction to citizenship education, where students learn the fundamental rights and responsibilities of citizens, or law-related education, where students learn how to be participating citizens. Many schools include service learning and volunteer requirements under this heading. Character education is another area that appears under the umbrella of civic education because, in most of the states that now require it, good citizenship requires many of the same qualities required for good character, for example, responsibility, respect, perseverance, participation, and honesty.

Voting and survey simulations. Many teachers turn to simulated activities to teach important background concepts about voting. Some lessons have students developing surveys, collecting data, and using databases and spreadsheets to analyze the results. (See Technology Integration Idea 12.7.)

Ethical simulations and problem solving. Simulations of ethics and social issues (e.g., Tom Snyder's *Decisions, Decisions: Lying, Cheating, Stealing* and *Decisions, Decisions: Prejudice*) are becoming increasingly popular for allowing students hands-on practice with addressing ethical issues of concern to the community.

Useful Web Sites for Teaching About Civic Ideals and Character Education

Association of Moral Education

http://www4.wittenberg.edu/ame/

Supports self-reflective educational practices that value the worth and dignity of each individual as a moral agent in a pluralistic society.

Character Education Partnership

http://www.character.org

This is a coalition of organizations dedicated to developing moral character and civic virtue in the nation's youth.

Six Seconds

http://www.6seconds.org/home.html

This nonprofit organization is dedicated to bringing emotional intelligence into practice in schools, families, organizations, and communities.

Civinet

http://www.civnet.org/

This web page is devoted to all who have an interest in teaching and learning about civics. It includes

TECHNOLOGY INTEGRATION IDEA 12.7

Learning About Civic Ideals and Practices

TITLE: Exploring "Hot Button" Community Issues

CONTENT AREA/TOPIC: Social studies, civics

GRADE LEVEL: 7–9

NETS FOR STUDENTS: Standards 3, 5, 6

DESCRIPTION: This simulation activity asks students to work as staffers for a politician. They are assigned to design, administer, and analyze a simple poll on an important community issue; to develop a position statement based on poll results; and to persuasively present the candidate's stand on the issue. The teacher introduces the topic by bringing into class several press reports about proposals by the president, the state's governor, or a local politician on important public issues. Students discuss how they think such proposals are developed and what role public opinion plays. Introduce this simulation activity and the concept of "hot button" issues—topics that voters care passionately about—and craft positions and programs accordingly. They design the poll form, poll their classmates, use a spreadsheet to analyze the data, and develop a briefing paper for "their boss, the politician."

Source: Based on a lesson from *Microsoft Productivity in the Classroom* (1997) by the Microsoft Corporation.

connections to teachers in the emerging democracies for those who might wish to set up communication between their class and a class abroad.

The American Bar Association (ABA)

http://www.abanet.org/publiced/

The ABA has for more than 30 years provided materials for teachers that relate to teaching students about the law. In addition, at this site, there are lesson plans and information about celebrating Law Day.

Constitutional Rights Foundation

http://www.crf-usa.org/

Develops, produces, and distributes programs and materials to teachers, students, and public-minded citizens all across the nation.

The Center for Civic Education (CCE)

http://www.civiced.org/

The CCE has sponsored civic education programs for 30 years. It also oversaw the writing of the civics and government standards and is quite active in more than 50 emerging democracies around the world. It works with the National Conference of State Legislatures to deliver the Project Citizen program to all 50 states, U.S. territories, and countries around the world.

Library of Congress

http://lcweb.loc.gov

This site is the gateway to a wealth of information on all topics.

The National Institute for Citizen Education in the Law (NICEL)

http://www.indiana.edu/~ssdc/nicel.html

NICEL is a nonprofit organization dedicated to strengthening democracy and justice through education about law and democratic values. It is best known for its work on the National Mock Trial.

Street Law

http://www.streetlaw.org/program.html

Provides a combination of lessons and texts that have been used in classrooms for years. The majority of these materials are now available on the web.

Exercises

Record and apply what you have learned.

Chapter 12 Self-Test

To review terms and concepts in this chapter, take the Chapter 12 self-test. Select Chapter 12 from the front page of the Companion Website (located at http://www.prenhall.com/roblyer), then choose the *Multiple Choice* module.

Portfolio Activities

ISTE The following activities address ISTE National Educational Technology Standards for Teachers (NETS-T) and will help you add to your professional portfolio. To complete these activities online and save or submit the materials electronically, select Chapter 12 from the front page of the Companion Website (http://www.prenhall.com/roblyer), then choose the *Portfolio* module.

1. ***Scenario (NETS-T Standards: V-B, VI-A)*** Imagine you have been teaching social studies for 10 years at both the elementary and high school levels. The emergence of the Internet and the World Wide Web has interested you, but you are very concerned about the proliferation of misinformation that has coincided with the growth of the Internet. You would like to do a presentation at the next state social studies conference to help alert your colleagues about the pressing need for information literacy in social studies instruction. Before you go through the process of applying to present a paper, you need to search the web for dramatic examples of erroneous or misleading information. Assume the role of the teacher in the scenario and locate some examples that could be shown at a presentation for social studies teachers. Be prepared to show and narrate your examples to the class. Include a written report of your findings in your personal portfolio.
2. ***Integration Skills (NETS-T Standards: II-A, B, C; V-B)*** Select one of the integration strategies described and illustrated in the chapter for powerful resources such as GIS, GPS, and simulations. Develop a classroom activity for a social studies content area using one or more of these resources. Be prepared to teach or demonstrate the activity to the class. If possible, use your activity with the targeted age group before you bring it to the class. The lesson and your reflections on the teaching experience should be placed in your personal portfolio.

Questions for Thought and Discussion

These questions may be used for small-group or class discussion or may be subjects for individual or group activities. To take part in these discussions online, select Chapter 12 from the front page of the Companion Website (http://www.prenhall.com/roblyer), then choose the *Message Board* module.

1. In his article on character education, Perry Glanzer (2001) makes the following observation. Do you believe, as he says, that we should make a sharp division between political positions and character education? Find and share evidence to support your position:

   > As committed educators, we should resist promoting lists of virtues that serve a political agenda or are justified primarily on political grounds. If educators fail to delve into motivational factors, character education can turn very authoritarian in practice. We must allow children to express ... motivations for moral behavior. Teachers could aid this process by creating a community of inquiry in the classroom that allows the discussion of deeper philosophical and religious issues that relate to ethics. In this way, students may discuss reasons to be virtuous and choose those that are more convincing than political or cultural pressure. (Glanzer, 2001, p. 693)

Collaborative Activities

The following activities address ISTE National Educational Technology Standards for Teachers (NETS-T) and can be done in small groups. Each group should present the findings to the class in a format they know how to use (word-processed report, presentation software, multimedia product). Completed group products can be copied and shared with the entire class and/or included in each person's personal portfolio.

1. ***Hypermedia Project (NETS-T Standards: I-B; II-A, B, C; V-D)*** Select one of the social studies strands and develop a hypermedia product designed to teach a specific social skill in the strand. Use the integration strategies and examples offered in this text as a reference point for your work. Include in your product links to web sites that support your activities. Include a disk copy and a hardcopy of this stack in your personal portfolio.
2. ***Software Review (NETS-T Standard: II-C)*** As a team, evaluate six software titles that relate to one of the social studies content areas. Use the guidelines offered in Chapter 4 for judging the usefulness of the software. Include these evaluations in your personal portfolio.

Integrating Technology Across the Curriculum Activities

The *Integrating Technology Across the Curriculum* CD-ROM is a set of technology integration ideas and links to online lessons, arranged as a searchable database. The CD comes packaged with this textbook. Complete the following exercise using this CD:

Review some of the example integration ideas on the CD cited in this chapter for addressing the social studies strands. Focus on all the lessons that teach concepts about elections (search by the keyword "election"). Young students frequently find voting and elections complex and confusing concepts. They do not understand exactly the process by which a U.S. president is elected. Technology resources can help clarify many of these concepts in visual and engaging ways. Now make up one of your own on an elections-related topic. Match it to an integration strategy described in this chapter. Add it to the CD. Be sure to identify each of the descriptors for it, including the relative advantage.

References

Audet, R., and Ludwig, G. (2000). *GIS in schools.* Redlands, CA: Environmental Systems Research Institute, Inc.

Glanzer, Perry. (2001). Exit interviews: Learning about character education from post-Soviet educators. *Phi Delta Kappan, 82*(9), 691–693.

Harp, L. (1996). The history wars. *Electronic Learning, 16*(2), 32–39.

National Council for Social Studies. (1994). *Expectations of excellence: Curriculum standards for social studies.* Washington, DC: Author.

Trinkle, D. A., & Merriman, S. A. (Eds.) (2000). *The history highway 2000: A guide to Internet resources.* Armonk, NY: M. E. Sharpe.

Additional Reading

Bellan, J. M., & Scheurman, G. (1998). Actual and virtual reality: Making the most of field trips. *Social Education, 62*(1), 35–40.

Brady, R. H. (1994). An overview of computer integration into social studies. *Social Education, 58*(5), 312–314.

Braun, J. A., Jr., & Risinger, C. F. (Eds.). (1999). *Surfing social studies: The Internet book.* Washington, DC: National Council for the Social Studies.

Brooks, D. L. (1994). Technology as basic to history—social studies: It's long overdue. *Educational Technology, 34*(7), 19–20.

Brown, J., Fernlund, P., & White, S. (1998). *Technology tools in the social studies curriculum.* Wilsonville, OR: Franklin, Beedle, & Associates.

Carroll, T. (1995). Carmen Sandiego: Crime can pay when it comes to learning. *Social Education, 59*(3), 165–169.

Eisner, E. W. (1991). Art, music, and literature within social studies. In J. P. Shaver (Ed.), *Handbook of Research on Social Studies Teaching and Learning.* New York: Macmillan.

Etchinson, C. (1996). Native knowledge: Asking questions by e-mail. *Learning and Leading with Technology, 23*(8), 70.

Goldsworthy, R. (1997). Real world field trips. *Learning and Leading with Technology, 24*(7), 26–29.

Johnson, C., & Rector, J. (1997). The Internet ten: Using the Internet to meet social studies curriculum standards. *Social Education, 61*(3), 167–169.

Lombard, R. (1995). Children, technology, and social studies. *Social Studies and the Young Learner, 7*(3), 19–21.

Mollica, D. (1995–1996). Architects of the world. *Learning and Leading with Technology, 23*(4), 56–59.

Parker, W. C. (1994). The standards are coming. *Educational Leadership, 51*(5), 84–85.

Rembelinsky, I. (1998). "Us" and "them" multimedia explorations of prejudice and intolerance in American history. *Learning and Leading with Technology, 25*(4), 42–47.

Risinger, F. C. (1998). Instructional strategies for the World Wide Web. *Social Education, 62*(3), 110–111.

Rose, S. A., & Fernlund, P. M. (1997). Using technology for powerful social studies learning. *Social Education, 61*(3), 160–166.

Rose, S. A., & Winterfeldt, H. F. (1998). Waking the sleeping giant: A learning community in social studies methods and technology. *Social Education, 62*(3), 151–152.

Semrau, P. (1995). Social studies lessons integrating technology. *Social Studies and the Young Learner, 7*(3), 1–4.

Shawhan, J. P. (1998). Civil war online, using the Internet to teach U.S. history. *Learning and Leading with Technology, 25*(8), 22–27.

Singleton, L. R., & Giese, J. R. (1998). American memory: Using Library of Congress online resources to enhance history teaching. *Social Education, 62*(3), 142–144.

Thomas, D. F., Creel, M. M., & Day, J. (1998). Building a useful elementary social studies website. *Social Education, 62*(3), 154–157.

White, C. (1997). Technology and social studies: An introduction. *Social Education, 61*(3), 147–148.

Wilson, E. K., & Marsh, G. E. (1995). Social studies and the Internet revolution. *Social Education, 59*(4), 203–207.

Resources

Software

Decision, Decisions: Lying, Cheating, Stealing (Tom Snyder Communications)

Decision, Decisions: Prejudice (Tom Snyder Communications)

Decisions, Decisions: The Constitution (Tom Snyder Communications)

Decisions, Decision: Town Government (Tom Snyder Communications)

Multimedia: The Human Body (Sunburst)

Neighborhood Map Machine (Tom Snyder Communications)

SimCity (Maxis Software)

Timeliner (Tom Snyder Communications)

CHAPTER 13

Technology in Art and Music Instruction

Daniel Newsom, Berklee School of Music
M. D. Roblyer, University of Maryland University College

. . . Arts instruction provides many unique opportunities for students to hone analytical skills to critically evaluate the flood of messages that fill a technologically saturated environment. The communicative language of the new technologies—sound, animation, music, drama, video, graphics, text, and voice—is also the language of the arts.

R. Robinson and C. Roland, from *Technology in Arts Education* (1994)

This chapter covers the following topics:

- Current issues and problems in art and music instruction
- How technology is integrated into art and music instruction
- Example World Wide Web site resources for art and music instruction
- Example activities for a variety of integration strategies in art and music

Objectives

1. Identify some of the current issues in art and music education that may impact the selection and use of technology.
2. Describe integration strategies for technology in art and music curricula.
3. Identify exemplary Internet sites for art and music.
4. Create instructional activities for art and music instruction that successfully model integration strategies.

Introduction

Many arts educators have resisted pressure to use computers and other instructional technologies, complaining of the contradiction inherent in blending impersonal machines with traditionally humanistic endeavors. In reality, however, technology always has played a part in the arts. Over the centuries, technology has provided tools, materials, and processes that aided artists' creative expression. In more recent times, the phonograph in music and the camera in visual arts have changed people's definitions of *art.* The integration of computers and other forms of electronic technology represents the next logical step in the evolution of the arts.

Issues and Problems Common to Art and Music Education: The Arts in the Information Age

Many educators and members of the community question the need for instructional technology in the arts curriculum. Even some proponents of technology applications in other disciplines balk at investments in technology for the arts. Robinson and Roland (1994) offer four reasons to link the goals of a school arts program with rapidly developing instructional technologies:

1. By integrating new technologies into the arts curriculum, instructors expose students to new and exciting modes of artistic expression. All media have a place in the curriculum if they enable students to achieve desired instructional outcomes. New technologies warrant special attention because they constitute entirely new genres that may alter paradigms about art.
2. The new technological culture requires today's students to develop a whole new set of literacies that go far beyond computer literacy. Arts instruction provides many unique opportunities for students to hone analytical skills to critically evaluate the flood of messages that fill a technologically saturated environment. The communicative language of the new technologies—sound, animation, music, drama, video, graphics, text, and voice—is also the language of the arts. Thus, arts teachers are particularly well positioned to help students develop skills as both critical producers and critical consumers of electronic media.
3. In the workplace of tomorrow, workers often will have to generate creative solutions to problems. An arts program that develops students' potentials for innovation in the areas of music, animation, graphics, multimedia, desktop publishing, and other emerging technologies will enable those students to compete in tomorrow's global business environment.
4. The arts counterbalance the massive infusion of technological change that society is experiencing. Technology can be seductive, and people need to keep in mind unique human abilities. Citizens of tomorrow's world will need coping skills that enable them to keep their aesthetic sensibilities in the face of breathtaking technological advances. Arts education will help develop and maintain these skills.

Another version of this view, which calls for an understanding of "appropriate technologies," is described as follows in the National Standards for Arts Education:

> For the arts, technology thus offers means to accomplish artistic, scholarly, production, and performance goals. But the mere availability of technology cannot ensure a specific artistic result: the pencil in a student's hand ensures neither drawing competency nor a competent drawing. Nor, by itself, will exchanging the pencil for an airbrush or a computer graphics program create a change in the student.

Issues and Problems in Music Education

New Technologies and Established "Traditional" Music Programs: Integration or Accommodation?

The traditional approach to music education at the secondary level focuses almost exclusively on the music and theoretical tenets of the Western European tradition (Labuta & Smith, 1997; Music Educators National Conference Staff, 1994). Musical literacy is its first prerequisite, its performing ensembles are modeled after the wind band and symphony orchestra, and extracurricular status is given to the jazz big band format. Even within many instrumental music programs, string ensembles and wind ensembles operate entirely independently of one another; singers rehearse and perform *a cappella* or with only piano accompaniment; and musicians interested in rock, hip-hop, and other contemporary styles are effectively excluded from all school-sponsored activities. Repertoire is grounded firmly in those pieces regarded as "classics" of the Western European, Broadway, jazz, or concert band canons, with only token attention paid to world and popular musics (Newsom, 1998).

In its publication, *The School Music Program: A New Vision,* the Music Educators National Conference

Technology Integration Example

Art and Music Instruction

TITLE: *The Fine Art of Electronic Portfolios*

BASED ON: Duxbury, D. (1999). Revolutions in the classroom. *Learning and Leading with Technology, 28*(3), 28–31, 41.

GRADE LEVEL: Middle to high school grades

CONTENT AREA/TOPIC: Music and art composition, technology skills

LENGTH OF TIME: Ongoing throughout the school year

Step 1: What's the Relative Advantage—Why Use Technology in Art and Music Instruction?

The music, arts, and technology resource teachers at Eureka High School were discussing the new block scheduling plans in which music, art, and technology credits would share one of the four 90-minute units students would attend each day. The teachers realized that a logical thread among these three curricula would be to have students develop a web-based portfolio of their music, art, and poetry. They felt this would meet several needs. First, it would be a way of working with each student at individual levels of musical and artistic expertise. This was important because students in their classes would range from beginners at musical composition or art skills to advanced musicians or artists who were active in choir, band, orchestra, and/or art studios. Second, it had always been difficult to find an audience for student work; the teachers knew that having others view their work was motivating and provided helpful feedback to students at all levels. A web-based format would make it easier to share the students' works. Third, it would be easy to create projects that linked skills across the disciplines, for example, having students use a Musical Instrument Digital Interface (MIDI) keyboard and music editor to prepare a musical composition that expresses the feeling or mood of a painting. Finally, the teachers realized that an electronic portfolio could serve a valuable, ongoing assessment tool for students' art, music, technology, and language development, and would help students develop skills in using technology to present their work and to communicate and share information with others.

Step 2: Planning Assessment—What Are Appropriate Assessment Strategies?

The teachers decided they each would use a component of the portfolio as the basis of student assessment each grading period. The art and music teachers would assign each student individual benchmarks to achieve in their composition and skill development. Their achievement of these skills would be assessed by rubrics and checklists the teachers would create. The technology teacher would assess students' web-based portfolios according to web production checklists he had been using in his classroom. Students' grades would be a combination of the three assessments, with each content area weighted according to which one was being emphasized during the grading period.

Figure 13.0 Student Using MIDI Synthesizer and Music Notation Software

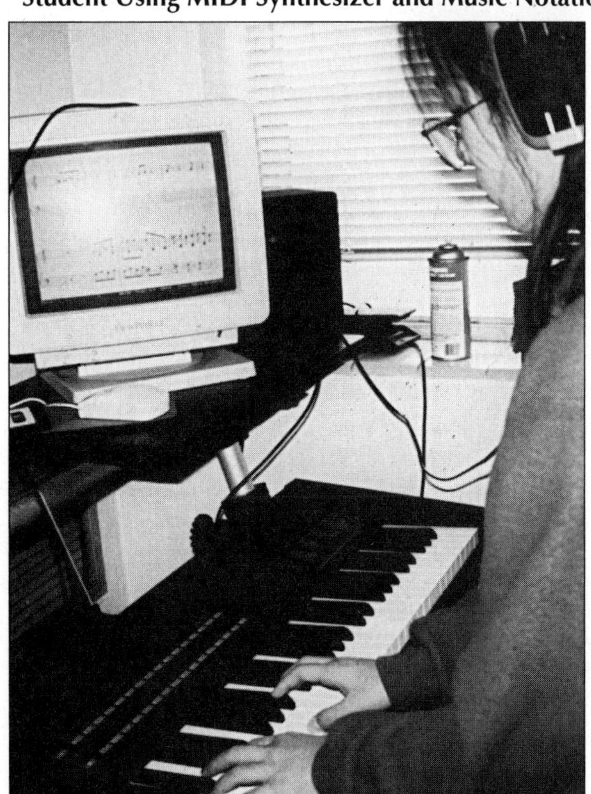

TECHNOLOGY INTEGRATION EXAMPLE *(CONTINUED)*

Step 3: Planning Instruction—What Are Appropriate Integration Strategies?

The teachers decided they would follow the same sequence of activities for each grading period:

- **Review skill levels and set benchmarks.** The art and music teachers meet with each student, review accomplishments to date, and set benchmarks for individual skill development. Some students with lower skill levels are placed in small groups so teachers can spend more time working with them.
- **Review portfolio requirements.** The technology teacher meets with each student, reviews the portfolio, and sets tasks to add to the technical and aesthetic presentation.
- **Decide on projects.** A different project is set for each grading period. For example, for the first project, the teachers decide to have students use their MIDI keyboards and notation software to write a musical composition based on the music of a period they have been studying in their history class. Then the students use image manipulation software to create a collage of colors and images that come to mind as they listen to the music composition they or their fellow students have created. The technology teacher helps them add their sound and graphic creations to their portfolios.
- **Determine group presentations.** Each teacher identifies whole-group presentations that need to be done. For example, the music teacher demonstrates techniques with the MIDI keyboard and music notation software. The art teacher designs a presentation on how to use layering techniques in Adobe *Photoshop* to create a graphic collage. The technology teacher develops demonstrations of video and audio editing techniques. After a group presentation, the teachers work with each student as needed to complete the required products.
- **Arrange reviews and final presentations.** The teachers arrange for various experts in other locations to do online reviews of the students' creations and give them feedback. Students will revise their products as time permits and as they feel appropriate. The teachers arrange for an "Evening at Eureka" show to be given at the end of the grading period, with computers set up in a lab to display each student's work. Parents and friends are to be invited via the school web site and desktop-published invitations created by the art students.

Step 4: Logistics—Preparing the Classroom Environment and Instructional Materials

The technology teacher creates a "main page" for the student portfolios, with links to each student's work. He also creates a link from the school's main page to the portfolios section. The music teacher has a MIDI keyboard classroom, but there aren't enough keyboards for each student to have one for a whole period. The teachers arrange the schedule so that half the class attends band or orchestra practice, works in the art studio, or works on their individual portfolios in the computer lab, while the other half works on composition.

Step 5: Evaluating and Revising Integration Strategies

At the end of each grading period, the teachers review the students' portfolios, assess progress, and discuss ways to make the work go more smoothly. Some of the questions they asked were as follows:

- Did most students meet the individual benchmarks set for them?
- Are students actively engaged in the project work?
- Do the group demonstrations provide adequate initial instruction before students begin individual work?
- Were the classrooms and lab times organized for efficient work?

The teachers are gratified to see that most students seem motivated by the idea of using a multimedia web format to display their work and are making good progress on their benchmarks. However, it is apparent that many students need more individual instruction than the demonstrations can provide. The teachers decide to begin videotaping a series of short demos so that students can view them individually or in small groups, as needed, after the initial presentation. They agree that the scheduling proves a continuing challenge. They decide to request that additional MIDI keyboards and software be obtained to support this work. Also, English and history teachers have approached them about coordinating the portfolio work with students' writing and research projects. The teachers agree to work together to merge these skill areas into students' portfolio assessments.

(MENC) states: "The K–12 music curriculum that was established by the 1930s has evolved only gradually since that time. . . . [T]he curricula that were acceptable in the past will be inadequate to prepare students for the 21st century" (MENC, 1994, p. 3). The pamphlet goes on to designate technology as one of seven areas where the new music curriculum is fundamentally different from the traditional curriculum. (See Figure 13.1.)

An even greater obstacle to an understanding and acceptance of new technologies in music education is the notion that the stated objectives of a traditional music curriculum cannot be achieved when students use computers and electronic instruments to study music theory, history, composition, and performance. Many administrators and teachers view *music technology* as a discrete discipline, separate from the "core" activities such as band, orchestra, chorus, and general music. Instruction in performance, theory, and composition rightfully takes place in the "music room," while the MIDI keyboard lab is where students "do music technology" (Colwell & Goolsby, 1992; Hoffer, 2001; Mark, 1996). Even those who actively endorse the use of music technology consign its curricular integration

Figure 13.1 Music Competencies and Standards

Areas of Competency in Music Technology (TI:ME: http://www.ti-me.org/)	MENC Standards (MENC: http://www.menc.org/)
1. Electronic Music Instruments • Different kinds of MIDI controllers 2. MIDI Sequencing 3. Music Notation Software 4. Computer-Assisted Instruction 5. Multimedia and Digitized Media 6. Internet and Telecommunications • Internet protocols • File sharing between computers and between platforms 7. Information Processing, Computer Systems, and Lab Management • Word processing, database, spreadsheet, graphics • Presentation software • Calendar/scheduling software	1. Singing, alone and with others, a varied repertoire of music 2. Performing on instruments, alone and with others, a varied repertoire of music 3. Improvising melodies, variations, and accompaniments 4. Composing and arranging music within specified guidelines 5. Reading and notating music 6. Listening to, analyzing, and describing music 7. Evaluating music and music performances 8. Understanding relationships between music, the other arts, and disciplines outside the arts 9. Understanding music in relation to history and culture

to a lab or "alternative" learning environment. Having accommodated technology by building a lab or putting a digital piano in the classroom, little effort is made toward seamless and transparent integration in, for example, music theory or performance classes.

The Music Director as Small Business Administrator

A typical secondary school music program involves hundreds of students, rooms full of instruments and other equipment, wardrobes of uniforms and choral robes, libraries of sheet music, methods books and other print resources, and large budgets. Like all teachers, the music director has duties ranging from tracking students' academic progress to coordinating off-campus field trips. It is not unusual for a music director in charge of a large ensemble to submit as many as 25 different forms for *each off-campus performance.* The music director is also in charge of the largest inventory of physical assets outside of the athletic department. In addition, the music director must be his or her own director of development, constantly on the lookout for continuing or increased funding. All of these issues make knowledge of information management software a high priority—if not a stated requirement—for the efficient operation of a successful music program.

How Technology Is Integrated into Music Education

Technology has had profound effects on the evolution of sound production and treatment by such devices as the piano, the violin, the guitar, the concert hall, and the recording studio. Early notation systems, guitar tablature, and the MIDI have all sought to translate the essence of musical sound into written performance instructions for the instrumentalist or computer.

Successful curricular integration of music technology requires an understanding of and competency in the operation of a particular tool combined with an ability to make pedagogically sound decisions concerning its use in a teaching and learning environment. In addition to general-purpose software (e.g., word processing, spreadsheet, web authoring), two categories of computer-based tools can serve the specific needs of music teachers: *instructional software* comprises the many programs developed for particular use in a teaching situation; *music production software* or *tool programs* (Abeles, 1995, p. 259) are those developed by the music instrument industry for professional use in composition, recording, and performance. The field of instructional software continues to grow in variety and sophistication. Most titles in this category now provide several types of instruction (e.g., tutorial, drill and practice, games) in one package. Music production software encompasses sequencing (MIDI and digital audio), digital audio editing (often a component of a sequencing program), and music notation. While these programs offer teachers maximum flexibility in designing curriculum, they require more involvement from the teacher in directing instruction, assessment, training, and technological maintenance.

Even though, as Muro (1994), Rudolph (1996), and Mauricio (2000) have shown, effective music instruction with technology can occur without the computer, the first step in the process of integrating music technology may well be the purchase of an electronic keyboard. For financial reasons, many schools that have to choose between a *computer* or *keyboard* lab choose the latter.

Music learning usually begins with the kinesthetic skills associated with playing an instrument or singing and then, depending on the student, the teacher, and the teaching environment, deepens to address the aesthetic and theoretical issues associated with writing and performing music. Studying music can mean learning how to play an instrument, learning how to create music for others to play, or acquiring an understanding of music through study of music theory, history, and criticism. Modern technologies that support these processes are now almost always software based. Most will provide effective instruction with just a computer; others may require additional hardware (such as a MIDI-compatible piano-type keyboard) in order to access real-time performance features.

Software developers market instructional software to specific age groups or levels of experience. Some of these programs can accommodate beginning through advanced levels of learning in a single package, as is the case with many music theory programs. Those designed for younger children (pre-K through elementary) feature learning activities acted out or directed by animated characters (e.g., *MIDIsaurus* or *Music Ace*). Those designed for secondary school or college would naturally have a less juvenile interface, but still might employ such devices as synthesized applause for correct answers (e.g., *Practica Musica*). We should emphasize that, as is the case with noncomputerized instruction, tactics designed to reach the young do not inherently compromise the quality of instruction. Other software packages have no explicitly pedagogical agenda and are more than likely designed by the music industry for professional use. While these programs offer the teacher more flexibility in lesson design, their curricular integration demands more preparation time.

The ability to make informed decisions about choosing, purchasing, installing, integrating, and maintaining the following technologies must be considered essential for any music teacher working in an environment where technology is fully integrated (Technology Institute for Music Educators, http://www.ti-me.org):

1. Electronic musical instruments [synthesizers, alternative MIDI controllers, electric instruments (guitars, basses, etc.), and sound recording and reinforcement equipment]
2. Computer hardware: computers, MIDI interfaces (where needed), cables (audio, universal serial bus, serial, FireWire), printer(s), scanner(s), CD burner, digital camera, projection systems
3. Other related furniture: workstation desks, keyboard stands, microphone stands, speaker mounts
4. High-speed connection to the Internet and e-mail
5. Age- and experience-appropriate software for the students:
   a. MIDI/audio sequencer
   b. notation program
   c. theory and history software (CD-ROMs)
6. Software for the director/teacher:
   a. all the programs being used by the students
   b. advanced-level MIDI sequencer/digital audio recorder-editor/notation program
   c. productivity or information management software to ensure the efficient running of the music program: word processing, database, spreadsheet, presentation tools, calendar, page layout (for concert programs, flyers, etc.), data backup, operating system, and computer hardware and software troubleshooting and repair
   d. a reference library of other software under consideration for future curricular use.

Technology to Support Music Composition/Production

For the purposes of this chapter, *music production* is understood to mean any activity in which music is created or edited. The two essential tools in this process are sequencers and notation software, and each can play a vital role in teaching both production and performance. Sequencers enable the user to record, edit, and play back digital audio and MIDI information. Notation programs generally have fewer recording and playback options, but offer more flexibility in score and page setup, part extraction, text formatting, and other print-related issues. In other words, a sequencer approaches issues related to making music in the *aural* domain, while notation software addresses issues related to the *visual* representation of music. MIDI data can be accessed by both sequencers and notation programs.

Sequencers are available in both hardware and software form. The hardware sequencer is usually found as an integrated component of a synthesizer workstation—a synthesizer with the capability of recording multiple tracks of MIDI information. Software sequencers run as an application on a computer and therefore require a more complete MIDI workstation (computer, MIDI controller, sound module, and a MIDI interface), but are exponentially more powerful with increased processing speed, storage capacity, and a bigger screen on which to display data.

The more powerful sequencing programs (e.g., *Logic Audio, Digital Performer*) simulate the functions of the recording studio. Music is recorded to tracks and assigned to channels for playback and editing. Software plug-ins are digital equivalents of outboard signal modifiers such as echo chambers and compressors and, depending on the power of the computer being used, provide the composer with a desktop recording studio equipped with virtually unlimited mixing options. Many sequencers offer the ability to record sound directly to the computer's hard drive with the use of a microphone. (See Figure 13.2.) These data, called digital audio, then become available for editing.

With very few exceptions, all sequencers allow both step and real-time recording. Once the notes are entered, the

Figure 13.2 Screen Capture from *MicroLogic Sequencer*

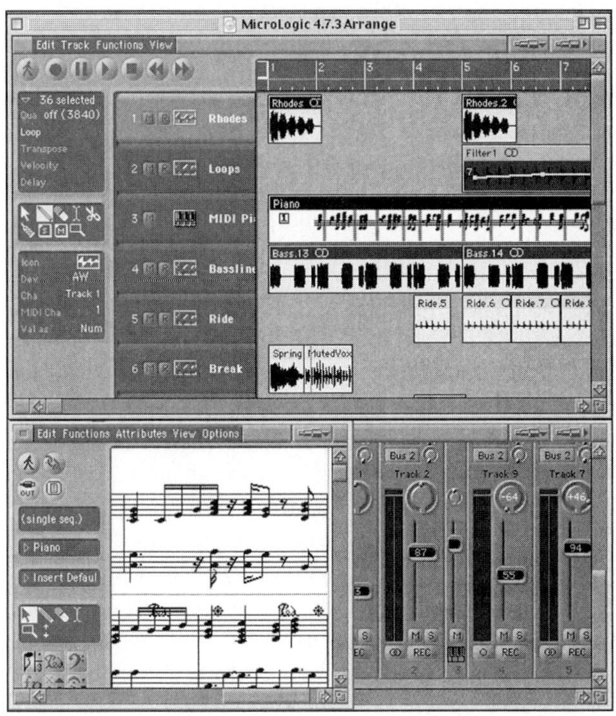

Source: Courtesy of Emagic, Inc.

music can be edited like any other data on the computer: cut, copied, and pasted. All performance parameters can be controlled by the user independently of one another, including pitch, tempo, volume, and dynamics. With a sequencer, the teacher can demonstrate issues related to both performance and composition virtually simultaneously. Some programs designed for young children have sequencing components that enable composition. The "Doodle Pad" component of *Music Ace,* for example, allows the user to drag different shaped happy faces (representing notes of different rhythmic values) on to a staff. In addition, the user can assign each note to one of several different sounds (e.g., piano, violin) as represented by a different color. With proper direction, however, even elementary school students can be taught the basic operations of even the most sophisticated professional software. By middle school, many students possess either the instrumental technique or the computer skills (or both) necessary to take advantage of more complicated processes such as digital audio editing and adding musical expression to their MIDI data (Newsom, 1999; Ohler, 1998). (See Technology Integration Idea 13.1.)

Projects that begin life at a computer workstation in a lab can be used in other situations throughout the music program. Students can create notation files that are then used to facilitate performance in the rehearsal room or at a concert. Students who are especially proficient on an instrument (including voice) can create a sequenced instrumental "bed" over which they can perform.

Technology to Support Music Performance

Notation software offers all of the power and flexibility of word processing applied to sheet music. In a school music program, it expedites all tasks related to ensuring that each student has something to play: rearranging music for alternate instrumentations, recreating lost or missing parts from the score, transposing parts, and simplifying difficult passages. When printed, notation documents are legible and have a professional look, eliminating the confusion that often results from handwritten parts. Finally, as is the case with all computer-generated data, existing documents can be corrected or revised without having to reenter the music from scratch. Notation files are small by comparison to digital audio, video, and graphics files, so entire libraries (hun-

Technology in Music Education

TITLE: Play the Recorder on the Computer

CONTENT AREA/TOPIC: Music composition

GRADE LEVEL: K–5

NETS FOR STUDENTS: Standards 4, 5, 6

DESCRIPTION: Studying the recorder is often used as a way of teaching and reinforcing music composition concepts to students at all levels. In this lesson, students use *Recorder Teacher* software to learn how to play the recorder. The teacher demonstrates the fingering for various notes by showing the software tutorial. As students try playing notes, the program plays them to let students check that they are playing them correctly. Tonguing and blowing concepts also are demonstrated. As students begin to write their own musical compositions, the computer plays them. Finally, students test their skills in two different ways: fingering or note reading. *Recorder Teacher* and other programs like the one used in this lesson are available at http://www.theshops.co.uk/childsplay.

Source: Dillon, R. (1998). In the key of "see and hear": How students can learn to play the recorder by playing musical computers. *Learning and Leading with Technology, 26*(2), 15–17.

dreds of scores, parts, and handouts) can be stored in an insignificant amount of hard disk space.

In addition to all of these advantages, notation software makes possible the creation of theory lessons, quizzes, and other handouts that combine notation with text and other graphics. Screen captures of short passages can be made in the notation document and then inserted into a word processing document. Advanced notation programs allow for maximum flexibility in generating more unusual or irregular layouts.

To clarify the different roles of the sequencer and the notation program in the teaching of performance, it is helpful to consider the hypothetical scenario of an ensemble class. To support sectional or individual practice, the teacher enters the score of a piece into a sequencer. Once the music has been entered, the student or teacher can choose which parts need to be heard. In this way, a clarinet section could rehearse to a sequence consisting of the entire ensemble minus the clarinets. The second clarinet player could practice sectional passages by selecting only the clarinet parts for playback, but muting the second clarinet part. Meanwhile the notation program would be used to create those parts. These techniques have been demonstrated very effectively by Tom Rudolph (1996).

The piano lab has given way to the electronic keyboard lab, where students can develop keyboard skills as well as learn theory and harmony (Mark, 1996). Keyboard labs can now be networked with devices that allow the teacher to communicate with individual students or groups of students by means of a microphone and headphones.

Technology to Support Self-Paced Learning

Many instructional software titles resist classification simply because they offer so many different types of instruction. Furthermore, even when a program has been marketed as one type, an enterprising teacher may choose to use it in another role. Most CD-ROM-based programs can accommodate both self-paced learning or an activity more closely directed and monitored by the teacher. *Practica Musica,* for example, can be used as a tutorial in music fundamentals with little or no input from the teacher. It can also serve as a drill program when a student needs help with a particular topic relating to ear training or music theory. Therefore, teachers must be ready to consider multiple integration strategies when evaluating and using instructional software. While interactivity and multimedia make instructional software a *potentially* more powerful teaching aid than an inert textbook, these programs cannot replace a teacher's careful supervision. In the end, the responsibility for effective teaching—with or without technology—rests with the teacher. (See Figure 13.3.)

Technology to Support Skills Practice

Almost all instructional software programs either have a designated drill component or can be utilized as such. They are probably the easiest programs to install and learn. Many have the capability of maintaining the records of multiple students on the same computer. Companies generally provide online demos of these programs, so teachers can sample them before they buy.

Technology to Support the General Music Curriculum

The term *general music* refers broadly to those courses in which there is no explicit formal performance agenda. Simply stated, the goal of the general music curriculum is to cultivate in students an understanding and appreciation of music. This is accomplished at the elementary level through singing, moving, playing, and creating. These activities can usually serve the needs of all students until instruction on a band or stringed instrument becomes an option, usually around the fourth grade. General music classes at the secondary level seek to engage students who for some reason have not joined a performing ensemble. The questions of what to teach in general music, how to teach it, and what its educational value is relative to the much more conspicuous "product" of an orchestra or chorus are complex and beyond the scope of this chapter (Runfola & Rutkowski, 1992). Nevertheless, technology has a long history of supporting the general music curriculum. It can enhance the experience of music for even the most reluctant, disenfranchised, or inexperienced students.

In the late 19th century, Frances Elliot Clark saw the potential of technology to help foster "music appreciation" among greater numbers of students who had no other access to performances of the classics (Labuta & Smith, 1997). In 1911, the Victor Talking Machine Company formed an education department to support her efforts. Over the course of almost a century, the presence of music playback technology in a music classroom—today's "stereo system"—has become commonplace. More recently, desktop music systems (e.g., the MIDI sequencer) have prompted new definitions of musicianship that recognize intuition and innate musical creativity as well as traditional conservatory-track modes of preparation. As

Figure 13.3 Screen Capture from *Practica Musica,* Music Theory and Ear Training Software

Source: Courtesy of Ars Nova.

suggested above, students with little or no "formal" musical training or (piano) keyboard skills can create and edit compositions using a sequencing program with step entry capability. Students can also perform analyses on music using preexisting MIDI files and/or digital audio imported from a CD. Once the pieces have been imported into a sequencer, students can explore all aspects of musical form, harmony, orchestration, and other parameters. Sequencers and audio editing software offer the student the ability not only to *listen* to prerecorded music but also to *manipulate* it. Students can demonstrate their understanding of musical form by literally separating a piece of recorded music into its structural components. In this way, expositions, recapitulations, second choruses, guitar solos, and so on all become discrete audio events, which can in turn be rearranged—resequenced—into new formal configurations. Students with performance skills can record MIDI data over their favorite audio recordings using different kinds of MIDI controllers. More advanced analysis projects—such as those that might take place in an advanced placement music theory class, can now be undertaken using music software as a presentation tool. Consequently, the general music class can accomplish a great deal more than simply providing those students who are supposed to be unmusical or at least untrained with a passive listening experience.

Although the scenarios just discussed lend themselves best to a situation with multiple computers, even a single computer can provide valuable support for a general music curriculum. Rudolph and Peters (1996) have demonstrated how a computer running sequencing software can support music instruction with Orff instruments.

Of the nine National Standards for Music Education, the only one that refers specifically to music history is the last one: "Understanding music in relation to history and culture." General music teachers have long sought to foster a deeper understanding of a musical work (especially for the musically nonliterate) by situating it in its historical context. This is an excellent way to introduce younger students to the practice of research, while offering older students unlimited opportunities for independent projects. The Internet is rapidly becoming the most powerful research tool available to students and teachers at all levels of education. Students and teachers can access card catalogs, electronic books, online journals, archived and current newspaper articles, audio and MIDI files, video clips, databases of thousands of out-of-print books, and discussion groups on every topic imaginable. Productive educational use of the Internet is limited only by the user and, to some extent, the connection speed and processing power of the computer.

Building a web site is in many ways the perfect culminating activity for a general music class. Students can do much of the planning in groups—even offline, if computer access is limited. Within each group, students can assign areas of the site according to individual strengths and literacies: A student who cannot read music may be proficient with a web page authoring tool; some students can search the Internet for relevant graphics while others look for text or sound. Videos and now DVDs continue to be a source of valuable historical reference material. Many documentaries formerly available on videotape are now available on DVD, which offers the user random access to the entire film. Any of these media can be captured on a computer's hard drive and incorporated into a student- or teacher-authored web page or software presentation. Finished projects can be viewed locally on a single computer, burned to a CD for multiple computers, posted on a school intranet, or uploaded to an Internet site so that parents or other students around the world can see it, link to it, and perhaps even contribute their own material. Finally, a compelling general music class has the potential to be a highly effective recruiting tool. Students who initially feel out of place in their school's music program may find an exciting and challenging alternative role for themselves after taking a general music class. Often, it is access to music technology that attracts these students.

Interdisciplinary Strategies

Beyond the opportunities for interdisciplinary study that will inevitably present themselves in a general music class, student-produced music and research can enhance a variety of other aspects of school life. Multimedia-based research projects in the humanities can easily include music that underscores a presentation or that is itself the object of study. A sequencer can facilitate the work of student composers who want to supply music for dance projects or video footage of athletic events. The close relationship between music and physics calls for projects that examine the science of sound.

Useful Web Sites for Music Education

See the National Standards for Music Education at http://www.music.org/Outreach/InfoEdMusic/ElemSec/Context.html and the following sites:

Berklee College
http://pt3.berklee.edu
This site, hosted by Berklee College of Music, is for preservice teacher training in music technology.

Technology Institute for Music Educators (TI:ME)
http://www.ti-me.org/
This national organization provides the most comprehensive curriculum of inservice teacher training in music technology.

Classical [MIDI] Archives
http://www.prs.net/midi.html
Provides 13,000 MIDI files by almost 1,000 composers. All are in the public domain and all are free.

The Vermont MIDI Project

http://www.vtmidi.org/

This network of more than 60 schools across Vermont is an online music mentoring project where students in grades 1–12 submit their music compositions for sharing and critiquing by professional composers, teachers, and other students.

SmarterKids Education Center

http://www.smarterkids.com/rescenter/glossary.asp

Provides a Teacher Talk glossary of educational terms.

Madison Metropolitan School District

http://www.madison.k12.wi.us/music/tech/techindx.htm

This is Madison, WI, Metropolitan School District's music technology web site.

Whatis.com

http://whatis.techtarget.com/

This is an online encyclopedia of terms related to computing and information technology.

Exploring MIDI

http://nuinfo.nwu.edu/musicschool/links/projects/midi/expmidiindex.html

This web site provides an introduction to MIDI for those who would like to learn more about basic concepts in MIDI and its application in the world of music.

Music Educators National Conference

http://www.menc.org/

Provides information about the Music Educators National Conference and many links to resources on the Internet.

The Academy of Digital Music

http://www.minuet.demon.co.uk/clasical.htm

MIDI files of extended classical works are for sale at this site.

K–12 Resources for Music Educators

http://www.globalclassroom.org/resource.html#music

This is a web site for band, orchestra, vocal, and general music.

MIDI and Music Technology Resources for Teachers

http://www.isd77.k12.mn.us/resources/staffpages/shirk/midi.html

This is a collection of links to resource sites.

Worldwide Internet Music Resources

http://www.music.indiana.edu/music_resources/

Provides links to music resource sites from the Indiana University School of Music.

Rock and Roll Hall of Fame

http://www.rockhall.com/educate/lssnplan/index.html

This web site has a collection of interdisciplinary lesson plans related to rock music and pop culture.

The Media Mashine

http://www.mashine.com/

A useful site for musicians and educators seeking information on making music with Macintosh computers. Member areas contain sample music lab configurations.

Searching the Internet for a Certain MIDI File

http://www.aitech.ac.jp/~ckelly/midi/help/midi-search.html

Structures searches for MIDI files

Grovemusic.com

http://www.grovemusic.com/

Provides information on accessing, subscribing to, and purchasing *Grove's Dictionary of Music and Musicians.*

Music Education and Teaching Links

http://www.geocities.com/terudolph/time/

This page of links for music educators is maintained by master clinician Dr. Thomas E. Rudolph.

Teaching Materials

http://www.stevenestrella.com/mused/webdelivery.html

http://www.emagicusa.com/education/downloads.html

http://www.soundtree.com/edcorner/edindex.html

http://www.lessonplanspage.com/Music.htm

These four sites provide online tutorials, lesson plans, and integration strategies

Issues and Problems in Art Education

Academic Versus Studio

Many visual arts educators advocate redefining the field to give it a larger role in the school reform movement. They want to rethink who receives art education and how it is taught. In many school districts, students receive an hour or so of art instruction per week. The lessons often focus on producing some art products, leaving little time for curriculum that introduces students to other aspects of art, such as art history, aesthetic principles, or criticism. At the end of elementary or middle school, schools direct students with obvious talent toward elective courses that continue the focus on producing art. Critics of this approach argue that it reaches a relatively small number of students, and even then it narrowly defines art education. From a political perspective, this approach gives art educators a weak power base and subjects the discipline to the constant scrutiny of budget cutters.

But how can art instruction give all students strong art backgrounds that go beyond just producing art? Much debate recently has centered on a philosophy of art instruction called discipline based art education (DBAE). Proponents of DBAE want to give students four kinds of broad and rich experiences with works of art:

1. Making art (art production)
2. Responding to and making judgments about properties and qualities in visual forms (art criticism)
3. Acquiring knowledge about the contributions of artists and art to culture and society (art history)
4. Understanding how people justify judgments about art objects (aesthetics).

Art production, art history, art criticism, and aesthetics are the foundation *disciplines* that make up DBAE. Critics of DBAE worry that studio training within art instruction will suffer and that students' creativity will be stifled. Some contend that proponents of DBAE are more interested in producing a population of museum patrons than in developing individual artistic expression. Others believe that DBAE's emphasis on academics will discourage students who may not perform well in the traditional classroom, but find the process of creating art fun and motivating.

DBAE seems to have influenced the development of the visual arts standards. Proponents believe that art will gain acceptance as a mainstream subject only by broadening instruction to include more than just students who draw or paint well. DBAE's supporters believe it offers just such a broad framework.

How Technology Is Integrated into Art Education

Using Technology to Produce and Manipulate Images

The most common type of hardware resource in art instruction is image digitizing equipment. Graphic scanners are computer peripherals that transfer print materials into digital images on a computer. A scanner can transfer any image, photograph, line drawing, or text into a graphics file in a cost-effective and efficient manner. An artist can also capture an image from a video source (camcorder or VCR) using digitizing software. Finally, a digital camera records images directly to disk. This equipment provides the user with an extremely flexible system for developing digital images. Students can then use computer software to manipulate digital images. This is a good example of using technology to foster creativity. Indeed, the ability to digitize still images and video has opened up a whole new genre of art.

A wide variety of software is available to teachers and students who are interested in producing computer art. Simple paint programs are available for very young students; in fact, teachers often use these types of programs when first introducing students to the computer. Integrated software and hypermedia authoring programs always include fairly sophisticated draw or paint tools, which provide good intermediate tools for the developing computer artist. High-level programs suitable to the advanced artist would be used primarily at the high school level. One way a student might use paint or draw software would be to design the layout for a hypermedia project. By using these tools, a student who does not possess a great deal of artistic ability can produce a very attractive design. Using technology in this fashion models the strategy of integration to remedy an identified weakness.

Using Technology to Support Graphic Design

Art educators can choose among a number of software options to let students explore graphic design. A range of animation programs is available, from simple cell-type animation to more advanced programs that offer features like *tweening*. The latter enable the user to change one frame to the next by moving through as many as 64 intermediate positions in between. Other programs are specifically geared toward cartoon production and allow artists to add music and sound. Today's more powerful programs speed up the process by providing two-dimensional animation.

An art studio would not be complete without an image manipulation program like *Adobe Photoshop,* which enables students to edit clip art or digitized photos. High-end programs provide hundreds of options and special effects for altering images. Morphing software enables the user to transform images smoothly from one shape to another. This technique offers tremendous potential for artistic expression and, by demonstrating how easily images can be altered, helps foster the development of visual literacy skills.

Finally, as Quesada (1998) and Steed (2001) describe, students can use 3D and modeling and animation software to communicate ideas visually through computer-generated models, animation, and imagery. One such activity is in an interdisciplinary assignment called "Pocket Lint Project." Students use whatever they can pull out of their purses or pockets as the basis for developing a character. They use 3D and animation software to create a model for their characters and use geometry to "convey a sense of emotion" (Quesada, 1998, p. 54). Other good curriculum uses are described in Technology Integration Idea 13.2.

Using Technology to Support Desktop Publishing with Graphics

Many schools look to their own graphics arts programs to create brochures and newsletters as part of student learning

TECHNOLOGY INTEGRATION IDEA 13.2

Technology in Art Education

TITLE: Visualize It in 3D

CONTENT AREA/TOPIC: Art, astronomy

GRADE LEVEL: 7–12

NETS FOR STUDENTS: Standards 4, 5, 6

DESCRIPTION: Many concepts in school learning are symbolic, rather than concrete, and students spend a great deal of time learning what the symbols mean. A good way to make many symbolic concepts more understandable is by making them more visual through 3D models. One such concept in which a 3D model is useful is for depicting a solar eclipse. After students discuss what a solar eclipse is and view a video or photos of it in class, they create a 3D model of the sun and moon. Then they use animation effects to demonstrate how the eclipse takes place, and store the animation as a *Quicktime* movie. Models of various groups are presented for comparison and discussion. Other activities in which learning can be enhanced through 3D models include cell structures and air flow patterns in science, volume problems in math, choreography in the performing arts, and virtual sculptures in art.

Source: Steed, M. (2001). 3-D visualization: Using 3-D software to represent curricular concepts. *Learning and Leading with Technology, 29*(3), 14–20.

activities. Because students get such good experience creating and producing these publications, the activities can be considered a kind of internship to prepare for actual jobs as graphic artists for newspapers or other companies.

Using Technology to Share Students' Creative Works

Videodiscs and videotapes have many programs that guide users through art experiences using a variety of approaches. Some study specific artists; others simulate journeys through famous museums. The high quality of videodisc images along with the technology's quick access give both students and teachers a powerful and flexible teaching and learning tool. Integrating high-quality, interactive video into instructions often enables the teacher to increase students' motivation to learn.

The Internet offers a number of resources that are helpful to the art student and teacher. Many museums around the world have sites that enable the user to take a virtual tour through the museum. Although clearly this is not the same as viewing the works in person, these sites do offer a way for students to easily explore and expand their knowledge base. Some sites make their server available for students to post their own creations and learn how to create art using a certain medium like paper maché, batik, or origami. Some teachers are using the Internet as a way to develop students' problem-solving abilities and to foster group cooperation skills by having students create their own web sites. Others use these sites as the basis for multicultural "field trips" to gather examples of art and music around the world (Quesada, 1998). It is important to remember when using the Internet for arts instruction that the images are reproductions; students will need to be made aware of the idea of scale and constantly be reminded that they need to keep the limitations of digital imagery in perspective.

Useful Web Sites for Art Education

National Art Education Association (NAEA)

http://www.naea-reston.org/

This general arts education site contains useful information about NAEA programs and also has a long list of contacts in state education departments.

ArtsEdge

http://artsedge.kennedy-center.org/artsedge.html

The Kennedy Center's national arts education dissemination network offers lesson plans, curriculum planning information, and other resources.

ArtsEdNet

http://www.artsednet.getty.edu/

The Getty Center for Education in the Arts provides extensive curriculum, lesson plan, and resource collections, including a library on discipline-based arts education and a catalog of arts education materials for purchase.

Arts World Wide

http://epals.home.minspring.com/ArtsWorldwide/default.htm

This is an EricPals course for grades 10–12 that promotes cultural literacy and creative expression through the visual arts.

The National Gallery of Art's Education Site

http://www.nga.gov/education/education.htm

This site for the National Gallery of Art's education division offers a variety of programs and resources for teachers. There is a complete listing of the museum's free-loan educational materials, programs, educational activities and events at the Gallery, and internship and volunteer opportunities.

Berit's Best Sites for Children

http://db.cochran.com/li_showElems:theoPage:theo:3531:0.db

This site lists and evaluates the best art sites for children and is frequently updated and covers a wide variety of art perspectives.

WebMuseum

http://sunsite.unc.edu/wm/

This excellent site for students to learn about artists and art history contains more than 10 million documents including many images and extensive biographical information on artists.

The Art Teacher Connection

http://www.primenet.com/~arted

This site has links to lesson plans and art resources on the web as well as a student art connection.

Exercises

Record and apply what you have learned.

Chapter 13 Self-Test

To review terms and concepts in this chapter, take the Chapter 13 self-test. Select Chapter 13 from the front page of the Companion Website (located at http://www.prenhall.com/roblyer), then choose the *Multiple Choice* module.

Portfolio Activities

ISTE The following activities address ISTE National Educational Technology Standards for Teachers (NETS-T) and will help you add to your professional portfolio. To complete these activities online and save or submit the materials electronically, select Chapter 13 from the front page of the Companion Website (http://www.prenhall.com/roblyer), then choose the *Portfolio* module.

1. ***Integration Skills (NETS-T Standards: II-A, B, C; V-B)*** Design an integration strategy (or choose one from the chapter) and develop a visual arts and/or music classroom activity. Be prepared to teach the activity to the class. If possible, use your activity with the targeted age group before you bring it to class. The lesson and your reflections on the teaching experience should be placed in your personal portfolio.
2. ***Scenario (NETS-T Standards: II-C, V-B)*** You have accepted a job as a coordinator for a new charter school that will center its curriculum around the study of art and music. Your budget allocation for art and music technology is $75,000. Prepare a spreadsheet that indicates how you plan to spend the funds: categories (e.g., hardware, software, furniture, cabling), quotes from at least two vendors, shipping charges, and applicable taxes (if any). A cover memo to the board of directors will set forth your fiscal and pedagogical rationales for the items you are purchasing. Prioritize your choices so that you are prepared to delete some items in the event the board decreases the funding. In the course of completing this project, you should contact teachers in the field, vendors, and college instructors. In a database, keep a log of contacts and a summary of your conversations. You are encouraged to use the Internet as much as possible for your research. The final budget proposal should be included in your personal portfolio.

Questions for Thought and Discussion

These questions may be used for small-group or class discussion or may be subjects for individual or group activities. To take part in these discussions online, select Chapter 13 from the front page of the Companion Website (http://www.prenhall.com/roblyer), then choose the *Message Board* module.

1. Consider the following quote from *The Electronic Word: Democracy, Technology, and the Arts* by Richard Lanham (1995). Following Lanham's examples of the newspaper, railroad, and musical instrument industries, what "businesses" were music educators in before the advent of the "electronic word," and has this development forced a similar reassessment? Do you see the "business" of teaching music facing redefinition with the emergence, proliferation, and dominance of computerized technologies?

   Many areas of endeavor in America pressured by technological change have already had to decide what business they were really in, and those making the narrow choice have usually not fared well. The railroads had to decide whether they were in the transportation business or the railroad business; they chose the latter and gradual extinction. Newspapers had to decide whether they were in the information business or only the newspaper business; most who chose the newspaper business are no longer in it. A fascinating instance of this choice is now taking place in the piano industry. Steinway used to own the market, and it has decided to stay in the piano business. Yamaha decided it was in the keyboard business—acoustic and electronic—and has, with Roland, Korg, and other manufacturers, redefined the instrument. Time has yet to tell who will win, financially or musically. (p. 64)

2. You are applying for a job as a music teacher. What questions will you ask about the institution's policy toward technology? What integration strategies are in place? If little or no technological infrastructure exists (e.g., Internet access, campus-wide e-mail), what plans are there to install such equipment? How many music teachers are there at this site and what is their proficiency with educational technology? Will an emphasis on using music technology be welcome? How important is it for you to work in an environment where informed attitudes about technology are expected of the faculty and administration? Based on your student teaching experience and site observations, do you see the opportunities for integrating music technology increasing?

Collaborative Activities

The following activities address ISTE National Educational Technology Standards for Teachers (NETS-T) and can be done in small groups. Each group should present the findings to the class in a format they know how to use (word-processed report, presentation software, multimedia product). Completed group products can be copied and shared with the entire class and/or included in each person's personal portfolio.

1. ***Evaluation (NETS-T Standard: II-C)*** Work with a classmate or small group and evaluate three visual arts and three music software products. Use the software evaluation form from Chapter 4. Include a copy of evaluations in your personal portfolio.

2. ***Interdisciplinary Integration Strategies (NETS-T Standards: I-B; II-A, B, C)*** Work with a classmate or small group to locate and document examples in the literature (e.g., your professional journals) of using technology to support each of the following kinds of teaching strategies:

   - Using technology to produce musical composition and artwork in the classroom
   - Integrating arts or music instruction with other content areas.

   Annotate these with descriptions of how technology enhances the instruction. Include these descriptions in your personal portfolio.

Integrating Technology Across the Curriculum Activities

The *Integrating Technology Across the Curriculum* CD-ROM is a set of technology integration ideas and links to online lessons, arranged as a searchable database. The CD comes packaged with this textbook. Complete the following exercise using this CD:

Review some of the example integration ideas on the CD cited in this chapter for music and art instruction. Now make up one of your own matched to an integration strategy described in this chapter for music or art. Add it to the CD. Be sure to identify each of the descriptors for it, including the relative advantage.

References

Abeles, H. (1995). *Foundations of music education* (2nd ed.). New York: Schirmer Books.

Colwell, R.J., and Goolsby, T. (1992). *The teaching of instrumental music* (2nd ed.). Upper Saddle River, NJ: Prentice Hall.

Dillon, R. (1998). In the key of "see and hear": How students can learn to play the recorder by playing musical computers. *Learning and Leading with Technology, 26*(2), 15–17.

Hoffer, C.R. (2001). *Teaching music in secondary schools.* Belmont, CA: Wadsworth/Thomson Learning.

Labuta, J., & Smith, D. (1997). *Music education: Historical contexts and perspectives.* Upper Saddle River, NJ: Prentice Hall.

Lanham, R. (1995). *The electronic word: Democracy, technology, and the arts.* Chicago: University of Chicago Press.

Mark, M. (1996). *Contemporary music education* (3rd ed.). New York: Schirmer Books.

Mauricio, D. (2000). See Music Tech Ensemble information available online: http://hhs.suhsd.k12.ca.us/musictech/index.html.

Muro, D. (1994) *The art of sequencing* [video]. Miami, FL: CPP/Belwin.

Music Educators National Conference Staff. (1994). *The school music program: A new vision.* Reston, VA: MENC.

Newsom, D. (1998). Rock's quarrel with tradition: Popular music's carnival comes to the classroom. *Popular Music and Society, 22*(3), 1–20.

Newsom, D. (1999). Computers and music at Harvard-Westlake School. *The Resource Guide for Music Educators (Korg/Soundtree), 5*(2), 8.

Ohler, J. (1998). The promise of MIDI technology: A reflection on musical intelligence. *Learning and Leading with Technology, 25*(6), 6–15.

Quesada, A. (1998). The arts connection. *Technology and Learning, 19*(2), 52–58.

Robinson, R., & Roland, C. (1994). *Technology and arts education.* Tallahassee, FL: Florida Department of Education.

Rudolph, T. (1996). *Teaching Music with Technology.* Chicago: GIA Publications, Inc.

Rudolph, T., & Peters, K. (1996). *The MIDI sequencer in the music classroom* [video]. Chicago: GIA Publications, Inc.

Runfola, M., & Rutkowski, J. (1992). General music curriculum. In Richard Colwell, (Ed.), *Handbook on research on music teaching and learning.* New York: Schirmer Books.

Steed, M. (2001). 3-D visualization: Using 3-D software to represent curricular concepts. *Learning and Leading with Technology, 29*(3), 14–20.

Resources

Music Production Software

Acid Pro 2.0 (Sonic Foundry)
Band-in-a-Box (PG Music)
Cakewalk Pro Audio (Cakewalk)
Cubase VST (Steinberg)
Digital Performer (Mark of the Unicorn)
Finale 2001d and *Finale Allegro* (Coda Music)
FreeStyle 2.3.1 (Mark of the Unicorn)
iMovie 2 (Apple Computer)
iTunes (Apple Computer)
Logic Audio (Platinum, Silver, Gold) (Emagic)
MicroLogic AV (Emagic)
MusicPrinter Plus (Temporal Acuity)
Overture 2 (Cakewalk)
QuickTime and *QuickTime Pro* (Apple Computer)
Sibelius (Sibelius Software)
Sound Forge 5.0 (Sonic Foundry)
SoundMaker (Micromat)

Instructional Software

Alfred's Essentials of Music Theory (Alfred Publishing Company)
Apple Pie Music CD-ROM (Clearvue/eav)
Children's Songbook (Voyager)
Cool School Interactive (Cool Breeze Systems)
Diatonic Chords (Temporal Acuity)
Inner Hearing/Harmonic Hearing (Musical Hearing)
Instruments of the Symphony Orchestra (Clearvue/eav)
Juilliard Music Adventure (Theatrix)
Make Music and *Making More Music* (Amazon.com)
Melodious Dictator (Temporal Acuity)
MetroGnomes' Music (The Learning Company)
MIDIsaurus, Vols. 1–4 (MusicWare)
Music Ace I and *II* (Harmonic Vision)
Piano Discovery System (Jump! Music)
Practica Musica (Ars Nova)

MIDI Interfaces

Fast Lane (MOTU)
Midisport 2X2 (MIDIman)
MT-4 (Emagic)

14 CHAPTER

Technology in Physical Education and Health Education

Bonnie Mohnsen, Bonnie's Fitware

Schools could do more than perhaps any other single institution in society to help young people, and the adults they will become, to live healthier, longer, more satisfying, and more productive lives.

Carnegie Council on Adolescent Development

This chapter covers the following topics:

- Current issues and problems in physical education and health education
- How technology is integrated into physical education and health education
- Example World Wide Web site resources for physical education and health education
- Example activities for a variety of integration strategies in physical education and health education

Objectives

1. Identify some of the current issues in physical education and health education that may impact the selection and use of technology.
2. Describe some popular uses for technology in physical education and health education.
3. Identify exemplary Internet sites for physical education and health.
4. Create instructional activities for physical education and health education that successfully model the integration of technology.

TECHNOLOGY INTEGRATION EXAMPLE

Physical Education and Health Instruction

TITLE: *Personal Fitness Plans You Can Live With*

BASED ON: Manteno (Illinois) Community Unit No. 5 School District WebQuest at http://www.manteno.k12.il.us/lweedon/webquest.htm

GRADE LEVEL: 9–12

CONTENT AREA/TOPIC: Biology, health, physical education, and technology

LENGTH OF TIME: Six weeks

Step 1: What's the Relative Advantage?—Why Use Technology in Physical Education and Health Instruction?

Mr. Martinez, a high school physical education/health teacher, is concerned that the state no longer requires health or physical education courses for all students, even though there is a national trend toward low exercise levels and poor eating habits among teenagers. He talks to the biology teacher and the technology education (TE) teachers about a project the three of them could do on eating habits and exercise that would meet requirements for courses in physical education/health, biology, and technology. They agree the project would have more impact to current and future students if it could be presented via a web page. That way, it could be more easily presented to many students, allow links to related information, be easily updated as more information is added, and serve as a resource for future classes. Mr. Martinez finds a web site at a school district in Illinois that could be a model for their project: http://www.manteno.k12.il.us/lweedon/webquest.htm.

The teachers decide to write descriptions of various "example teenagers" and have their students work in pairs and small groups to design health and fitness plans appropriate for each example. The plans students develop will relate to human growth and development concepts they are covering in biology, and web site design will address skills required in the technology education class. Mr. Martinez shows several simulations that the teachers agree will help make concepts about the need for fitness more visual and compelling to students. He will demonstrate heart monitors to show students how diet and exercise affect heart rate and other physical characteristics. Then he will show how to document and track this information on a spreadsheet.

Step 2: Planning Assessment—What Are Appropriate Assessment Strategies?

They decide to have three sets of assessments: (1) The TE teacher will assess and grade the web site pages with web evaluation criteria he already uses; he also will assess group work skills. (2) The biology teacher will have a checklist of questions about the human anatomy/physiology, nutrition, and body system functions; she will ask for images and descriptions that address these questions. (3) Mr. Martinez will adapt the grading rubric at the Manteno web site and assess students' plans as to specific and appropriate recommendations for lifestyle changes, exercises, and eating habits.

Figure 14.0 ***Fitness Scores* from Bonnie's Fitware**

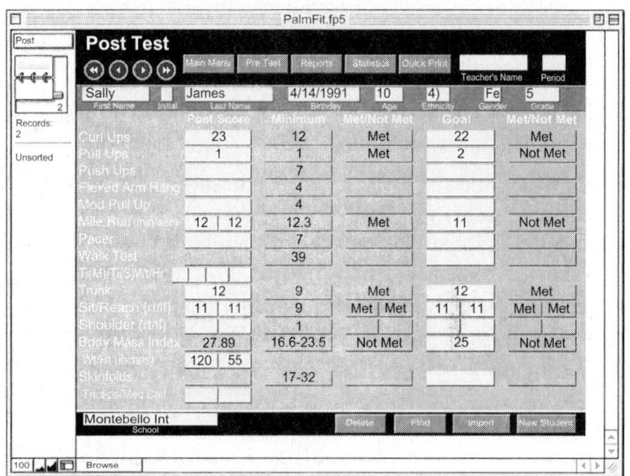

Source: Courtesy of Bonnie Mohnsen.

Step 3: Planning Instruction—What Are Appropriate Integration Strategies?

The three teachers agree on the following sequence of instruction and activities:

- **Week 1: Assigning the project and collecting information.** Describe and discuss in each class the requirements for the project and the learning activities that will take place. **Biology class:** Assign readings and hold class discussions of body systems. To review concepts, use assignments sheets with *ADAM: The Inside Story* (ADAM), *InnerBody Works* (Tom Snyder Communications), and *How Your Body Works* (Mattel). **PE/Health class:** Show video *Personal Fitness: Looking Good/Feeling Good* (Kendall-Hunt). Review concepts about diet and exercise. Analyze the impact of diet with simulations such as *Pyramid Challenge* and *DINE Healthy* (DINE Systems) and prepare fitness plans using *Fitness Scores* (Bonnie's Fitware). **Technology class:** The teacher works with the whole class to design the web site struc≥≥ture and assigns each group to work on a section.

TECHNOLOGY INTEGRATION EXAMPLE *(CONTINUED)*

- **Week 2: Preparing information and materials. Biology class:** The teacher assists as students finish working on their simulation assignments and as they take notes and gather materials to answer the biology questions. **PE/Health:** Students begin their word-processed descriptions of appropriate fitness plans for their "example teenagers." **Technology class:** The small groups begin to storyboard their section of the site.
- **Week 3: Prepare and display web site products.** Students complete design work on their web pages and enter the information into them. Students present their web pages in each class, and teachers use their checklists and rubrics to assess the work.

Step 4: Logistics—Preparing the Classroom Environment and Instructional Materials.

The teachers check out the software and videos from the Media Center and gather the assignment sheets to be used with them. Each teacher prepares copies of the rubrics and checklists. The TE teacher agrees to put these on the web site, so students can look at them online. The biology teacher decides to have students do most computer simulations at the computer lab, so she schedules times for it. Mr. Martinez coordinates which students can work in pairs or small groups and prepares materials to communicate this information to the students.

Step 5: Evaluating and Revising Integration Strategies

After they completed the unit, the three teachers reviewed the web site again, looked at summary data from the checklists and rubrics, and discussed how the activities progressed. They agreed that the project worked well and determined how they might share class time in the future to make the work easier to coordinate. They fine-tuned the checklists and rubrics to better assess individual and group contributions. They agreed that, although students loved the body and nutrition simulations, they were time consuming. They decided to limit the number done inside class time, and allow students to do more on their own time for extra credit.

Introduction

Today, the health of young people—and the adults they will become—is critically linked to the health-related behaviors they choose to adopt. Although strong evidence exists that participation in health and physical education classes can help develop healthy behaviors in children, many schools are like the one in the *Personal Fitness Plans You Can Live With* example at the beginning of this chapter; courses once considered mandatory are no longer required.

However, as the example shows, educational technology offers teachers valuable resources in efforts to inform and empower students to make the right health choices. The most effective methods of instruction are student-centered approaches like the ones in *Personal Fitness Plans You Can Live With:* hands-on, cooperative learning activities, and activities that include problem solving and peer instruction to help students develop skills in decision making, communications, goal setting, resistance to peer pressure, and stress management (Kane, 1993; Seffrin, 1990). This chapter provides more details and examples of technology resources and integration strategies that teachers can use to help prepare students to lead longer and healthier lives.

Issues and Problems in Physical Education and Health Education

Marginalization of Health and Physical Education

As reflected in the *Personal Fitness Plans You Can Live With* example, health education and physical education are not as valued by the educational community as they once were. Schools currently are refocusing their priorities on issues such as meeting standards in content areas and increasing scores on state and national tests. The result is less emphasis on health instruction and physical education. This is unfortunate, since three out of four deaths are due to preventable chronic conditions (U.S. Department of Health and Human Services, 1996). In addition, cognitive functioning is related to proper nutrition and physical activity (Caine & Caine, 1995). Also, children's self-concept and self-esteem (Payne & Issacs, 1995), as well as their prosocial skills (Borba, 1989), are positively affected by their involvement in physical activities.

To achieve desired results, experts recommend the following: 50 hours of health instruction per school year, and 150 minutes of physical education instruction per week for grades K–5 and 225 minutes for grades 6–12. However, the actual amount of time contributed to health and physical education in most schools is far less. One solution may be the kind of technology-enabled curriculum integration shown in the *Personal Fitness Plans You Can Live With* example. Teachers can address several subject areas simultaneously while allowing students to see the connections between what they learn in school and real-life situations. Technology resources improve communications among and productivity of students and teachers; allow more hands-on, visual learning experiences; help motivate students to spend more time on activities; and serve as a platform for students' products.

Need for Informed Selection of Health and Fitness Resources

According to the American Library Association (1989), "To be information literate, a person must be able to recognize when information is needed and have the ability to locate, evaluate, and use effectively the needed information. . . information literate people are those who have learned how to learn." The national health standards speak directly to this issue. Because anyone can post anything on the Internet, students need to become more information literate so they can be good consumers of health and fitness products and information. Specifically, they must be able to differentiate between accurate and inaccurate information in the context of health education.

Lack of Student Motivation

Graham, Holt-Hale, and Parker (1998) point out that today's children are less physically active in part because they spend more of their free time on television and computer games, rather than outside physical play. This society-wide trend affects both the motor development and health of our country's youth. Although technology may be partially responsible for the current decline in physical activity, it also holds the potential for motivating youngsters to increase their levels of physical activity. Several of the computer games available in arcades, such as downhill skier and golf games, require participants to be physically engaged in order to be successful in the game. However, this is a poor substitute for mandatory physical education during school hours.

Need to Address Standards

School physical education has come far from an early emphasis on physical training and calisthenics. It evolved into sports education, then lifetime activities, and became the current focus on health-related fitness, behavioral competencies, and motor skills needed for lifelong engagement in enjoyable physical activity. This current shift is due, in part, to the national physical education standards (see Figure 14.1) introduced in 1995. The national health education standards (see Figure 14.2) were published in the same year. The focus of the health education standards is health literacy—the capacity of individuals to obtain, interpret, and understand basic health information along with the competence to use such information to enhance health.

Figure 14.1 Physical Education Standards

1. Demonstrates competency in many movement forms and proficiency in a few movement forms.
2. Applies movement concepts and principles to the learning and development of motor skills.
3. Exhibits a physically active lifestyle.
4. Achieves and maintains a health-enhancing level of physical fitness.
5. Demonstrates responsible personal and social behavior in physical activity settings.
6. Demonstrates understanding and respect for differences among people in physical activity settings.
7. Understands that physical activity provides opportunities for enjoyment, challenge, self-expression, and social interaction.

Source: National Association for Sport and Physical Education (1995).

Figure 14.2 Health Education Standards

1. Students will comprehend concepts related to health promotion and disease prevention.
2. Students will demonstrate the ability to access valid health information and health-promoting products and services.
3. Students will demonstrate the ability to practice health-enhancing behaviors and reduce health risks.
4. Students will analyze the influence of culture, media, technology, and other factors on health.
5. Students will demonstrate the ability to use interpersonal communication skills to enhance health.
6. Students will demonstrate the ability to use goal-setting and decision-making skills to enhance health.
7. Students will demonstrate the ability to advocate for personal, family, and community health.

Source: Joint Committee on National Health Education Standards (1995).

Drawing on the findings from the School Health Policies and Programs Study (SHIPPS), Pate and Small (1995) state: "Instruction practices in physical education often do not reflect the goals set by either the national health objectives or the National Physical Education Standards" (p. 312). This has not changed much since the introduction of the national standards. Although there has been some movement in certain areas of the country, there is certainly a need for greater implementation of the standards. Technology can play a role by making it easier to post and share key information. As health and physical educators share their successful standards-based curricula on the Internet, this may encourage broader implementation of standards.

How to Handle Controversial Health Issues

Controversial subject matter has proven to be another challenge for health education. Many special interest groups press for the inclusion of their issue into the health education curriculum. But including too many such issues actually can water down a curriculum and make it less effective. One area of particular concern is human sexuality. Many experts believe information and guidance on sexual decisions are essential; others feel students should be taught that abstinence is the only choice and that teaching about a controversial subject tends to legitimize it in the mind of the student. Other controversial topics include date rape, suicide, drugs, violence, and character education. Technology resources such as videos and well-chosen web sites can provide valuable insights on these topics as well as help to facilitate the logistics of instruction when only a subset of the total class is involved.

How Technology Is Integrated into Physical Education and Health Education This section is aligned with the following national physical education (PE) and health education (HE) standards noted in the parentheses below:

1. Technology to Support Improvements in Fitness (PE 3, 4)
2. Technology to Develop and Improve Motor Skill Performance (PE 1, 2)
3. Technology to Improve Students' Beliefs and Interactions Related to Physical Activity (PE 5, 6, 7)
4. Technology to Assess and Enhance Personal Health (HE 3, 6)
5. Technology to Support the Procurement of Valid Health Information (HE 1, 2, 4)
6. Technology to Influence Others' Health Behaviors (HE 5,7)
7. Technology to Support Interdisciplinary Instruction.

See Technology Integration Idea 14.1 to see how the following integration strategies can be implemented.

Technology to Support Improvements in Fitness

Technology devices and software are available to help analyze, monitor, and improve fitness. Exercise equipment, such as treadmills, stair steppers, and stationary bikes, meet the criteria of a technology device designed to improve fitness. Used in combination with monitors, these devices can show students the results of their efforts in terms of heart rate, speed, and power. The Concept II Rowers, for example, show a small boat moving across the screen; the faster the student rows, the faster the boat moves. Connecting two rowers together provides the opportunity for indoor rowing races. Displaying the output of monitoring equipment to the Internet provides for competition between students across the country.

Electronic blood pressure devices, body composition analyzers, pedometers, activity monitors (e.g., Cal Trac), and spirometers are devices that assist with analyzing and monitoring fitness levels. Each device measures a different aspect of student health and fitness, allowing students to use their own bodies for data collection and analysis. The most popular device in this category is the heart monitor (e.g., Polar Vantage). Students wear the heart watches around their wrists while an elastic band holds the transmitters to their chests. The transmitter senses the heartbeat from the heart's electrical impulses and transmits each beat to the wristwatch receiver through radio transmission. Younger children benefit from using the *HeartTalker*, where instead of reading their heart rates on a wrist watch receiver, they receive audio feedback regarding their heart rate and exercise time from headphones attached to the transmitter. Heart monitors are especially effective for providing students with feedback as to whether or not they are in their target heart rate zones and benefiting from the training effect for cardiorespiratory endurance. (See Figure 14.3.)

Students also can be put in charge of their own learning along with the development of fitness goals and plans. *Health Related Fitness Tutorial/Portfolio* (Bonnie's Fitware) guides students through the five areas of health-related fitness: flexibility, muscular strength, muscular endurance, body composition, and cardiorespiratory endurance. The electronic portfolio portion of this software allows students to enter fitness scores, exercises, caloric

TECHNOLOGY INTEGRATION IDEA

Technology-Enabled Physical Education

TITLE: Integrating Technology into Middle School Physical Education

CONTENT AREA/TOPIC: Physical Fitness and Social Skills

GRADE LEVEL: 6–8

NETS FOR STUDENTS: Standards 3, 5, 6

DESCRIPTION: Because schools are limiting time spent on physical education and health courses in grades 6–8, technology-based strategies can help teachers integrate these topics into other content areas to create interdisciplinary lessons. Technology also can help make time spent on PE and health more hands-on and productive. Students can keep personal fitness goals and achievements as part of their electronic portfolios; analyze and graph data from their uses of heart monitors; view videos that demonstrate model performances, various sports, and other motor activities to learn more about how the body works; and use the Internet to research sports and physical activities in other countries and historical periods. Another interdisciplinary physical activity is *orienteering*. This is a combination of walking, running, and hiking while following a map and using a compass. Teachers can introduce the activity with a video such as *Finding Your Way in the Wild* (Quality Video) or the *Orienteering Simulation* (Bonnie's Fitware).

Source: Mohnsen, B. (2000). Vaughn, Nekomi, and Luis: What they were doing in middle school physical education. *Learning and Leading with Technology, 27*(5), 22–27.

Figure 14.3 Student with Heart Monitor

Source: Courtesy of Bonnie Mohnsen, 2001.

Figure 14.4 Student Using Palm Computer to Track Fitness Information

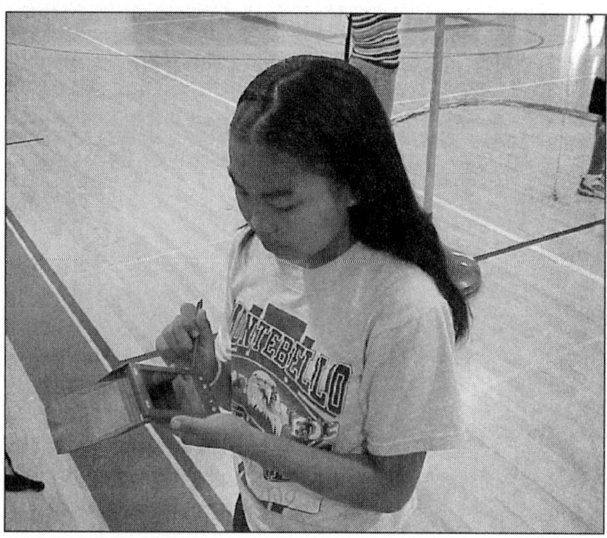

Source: Courtesy of Bonnie Mohnsen, 2001.

input/output, drawings or video clips, journal entries, and fitness plans. Spreadsheet applications can be used to calculate and graph individual nutrition and fitness goals. *Muscle Flash* (Bonnie's Fitware), with grade-specific versions, teaches and quizzes students about the names, locations, functions, and exercises for a variety of muscles through a flash card simulation.

Technology to Develop and Improve Motor Skill Performance

Technology can provide students with information, model performances, and feedback, along with opportunities for self-analysis and monitoring of improvement in the area of motor skill performance. In order for students to develop a new motor skill, they must first understand and observe a model performance. Instructional broadcasts on motor skills provide a model demonstration of the skill to be learned. Software (e.g., Bonnie's Fitware's *Volleyball* and Diamar's *Golf Tips*) also provides learners with model skill performances and a description of not only the how, but also the why. Knowing *why* a skill is performed in a certain manner is beneficial to the learning of new skills and, more significantly, to the transfer of that learning to new movement experiences.

Asking students to set personal goals and then monitoring their progress on motor skill acquisition is motivational to the student, but often a paperwork nightmare for a physical educator responsible for 200 to 600 students. Palm computers help physical educators organize their data collection (e.g., grades, attendance, fitness scores) during the instructional period. Once the data have been transferred to a desktop or notebook computer, they can be analyzed and reported to students and parents in a variety of formats. Electronic portfolios can put students in charge of collecting, recording, and analyzing their motor skill achievement, fitness performance, social interactions, and cognitive learning. (See Figure 14.4.) The electronic portfolios can be accessed using notebook, subnotebook, or even palm computers.

Once students begin to practice motor skills, feedback becomes the significant component for perfecting performance. Digital video cameras record performance and allow for replay and analysis. The use of video is most effective when it is shown to the student immediately after the performance along with external verbal feedback and cues (Darden & Shimon, 2000; Doering, 2000). Video replay is best used with students of at least an advanced beginner skill level. Students need some knowledge of the skill and some viable mental image of it in order to use the information these images provide. For students with advanced skills, replay also is useful for strategy and tactics. Because advanced movement is so fast and sometimes difficult to analyze at normal speed, slow motion replay and freeze-frame capabilities are essential.

To provide for student self-analysis, a digital video camera should be placed at one station in a learning circuit (e.g., for tennis skills). Each phase of the skill is modeled while students work in pairs to identify critical features, patterns, and concepts associated with the skill. (See Figure 14.5.) Then students rotate through the stations in small groups, with one group beginning at the digital camcorder station. One student tosses the tennis balls, the second student executes a forehand stroke, the third student provides feedback, and the fourth person films the skill performance. The student-coach uses the first set of columns on a criteria sheet to provide specific feedback. On the rotation after the filming, the students review the images. The instant replay provides immediate feedback for the performer, who uses the second set of columns on the criteria sheet to self-assess performance.

Student projects can be used to assess and further develop students' understanding and performance of motor

Figure 14.5 Students Monitoring Performance with Video Camera

Source: Courtesy of Bonnie Mohnsen, 2001.

skills. All motor skills fall into a general movement pattern category (i.e., overhand pattern, kicking pattern). Understanding the relationship between skills using the same movement pattern helps when transferring knowledge and experience from one motor skill to another (i.e., overhand throw to volleyball serve). Students working in small groups can investigate one movement pattern and record their findings on video. Next they can visit other classes and film examples of their particular movement pattern. Each group then shares its video with the rest of the class.

The examples so far in this section have targeted standard 1; however, standard 2 also addresses motor skill improvement. Students must analyze their own movement performance using scientific principles of movement and create their own practice plan in order to improve performance. Physical educators often have believed that this learning would occur through the process of osmosis—simply participating in sport would transfer this learning to students. We now understand that for students to see the connection between sports and science or sports and improvement, they must understand some basic cognitive concepts.

Broadcasts, such as *SportsFigures* (ESPN), provide information on the science of sports. Each lesson includes step-by-step explanations of the scientific principles. ESPN recently launched a companion web site (http://www.sportsfigures.espn.com/sportsfigures). The site, designed for teachers, students, and parents, contains interactive components such as educational games, video clips and curriculum information to support student learning.

Software packages, such as *Biomechanics: The Easy Way* (Bonnie's Fitware) and *SimAthlete* (Bonnie's Fitware), provide reference information on the important biomechanical and motor learning concepts (e.g., goal setting, feedback, stability, force production). *Biomechanics: The Easy Way* then quizzes students on their understanding and application of the concepts while *SimAthlete* goes a step farther by asking students to create a practice plan (coach) for different athletes. The better the practice plan, the better the athlete performs during competition. *Measurement in Motion* (Learning in Motion) takes biomechanical analysis to another level by encouraging open-ended exploration. The software uses video clips (supplied by the teacher or captured using student subjects) and allows for measurement and analysis of movement performance (e.g., ball rotation, limb speed).

Technology to Improve Students' Beliefs and Interactions Related to Physical Activity

Standards 5, 6, and 7 address primarily the affective domain. Although software to address this area is very limited, videos and the Internet can provide opportunities to address these areas. Broadcast shows, such as *The Wonder Years, Boston Public,* and after-school specials often focus on social and self-esteem issues related to physical activity. In one of the *Wonder Years* episodes, a segment focused on picking teams in physical education. Physical educators use this clip as a journal writing prompt when asking students how they would feel if they were the last one picked for a team.

The Internet offers an ideal medium for connecting students with different backgrounds and beliefs and providing them with the opportunities for interactions related to physical activity. Many of us had pen pals when we were students. Today, our students have keypals (a.k.a. e-pals). Keypals are students who connect with one another via electronic mail. They can share ideas, concerns, physical education/activity experiences, information, written assignments, and research. And, they learn to accept individuals from other communities and cultures. Sites (http://www.pesoftware.com/epals.html or http://www.epals.com/) are available to help teachers get started with this type of activity. They can visit one of the sites to find other physical educators interested in teaming for this type of project.

Students also can access an array of individuals with knowledge and expertise related to physical education, sports, and fitness. Olympic athletes, professional athletes, biomechanists, medical doctors, exercise physiologists, and motor learning specialists can provide students with insights regarding "real-life" experiences related to physical activity. Bonnie's Fitware sponsors the Olympic Athlete Project (http://www.pesoftware.com/news.html). This project began in 1995, when an Olympic rower was identified to share his trip to the Olympics with students. Steven Segaloff was a potential Olympic coxswain when he began communicating with students across the United States. He sent e-mail messages every other week that dealt with his sport, his training program, the selection process, his relationship with the other rowers (teamwork), and his feelings about training and participating in the Olympics. Students, in turn, e-mailed back asking specific questions of interest to them.

An appreciation for a sport or dance can be enhanced through an understanding of its origins. The Internet and encyclopedias (both online and on CD-ROM) provide students with access to a wealth of information including the history of sports and dances. However, it is important that students are prepared to use this research tool. Students must learn to double check all references, examine author credentials, and cite resources.

Technology to Assess and Enhance Personal Health

When studying health, students are motivated when they can see a connection between what they are studying and their own bodies. When attempting to motivate individuals to change their lifestyles and adopt a wellness approach toward their health, information alone is not enough. Fortunately, software is available to guide students through the process of making changes. These programs help students apply their knowledge to problem-solving situations. Record keeping, visual representation, and data analysis are all components of these programs.

Many nutritional analysis programs are currently available. These programs ask the user for age, weight, height, gender, and amount of physical activity, and then calculate the individual's nutritional needs. The user records the types and amounts of foods eaten daily, and the program creates a report that lists calories ingested, the nutrient values for all foods, and the total of all nutrients ingested. These reports then are used to determine if the student has met the recommended dietary allowances (RDA) and whether the number of calories ingested was excessive. *DINE Healthy* (DINE Systems) exposes poor nutritional and fitness behaviors through its analysis of daily food intake and physical activity. Appropriate menus and exercises are recommended for a healthier lifestyle. The software serves as the student's personal trainer for fitness and nutrition.

Another type of program along these lines is the risk assessment program. These programs ask the user to input data regarding his or her lifestyle. Questions include height, weight, gender, age, cholesterol level, blood pressure, smoking habits, alcohol usage, physical activity habits, family medical history, nutritional information, and use of seat belts. Based on the data received, the program determines the individual's life expectancy, cardiovascular disease risk, and/or cancer risk. Several shareware programs on risk assessment are available, as well as web-based software at sites such as http://www.bodybalance.com/hra.

Technology to Support the Procurement of Valid Health Information

Historically, the health education textbook has been the primary source of information and reading in a health education class. Today, students have access to a wide variety of Internet sites and software. As noted earlier, students need instruction on how to distinguish between accurate and inaccurate information.

KidsHealth (See Figure 14.6) is an example of a health-related site targeted at young students. Popular software includes *What Is a Belly Button?* and *Welcome to Bodyland* (IVI Publishing) for primary students, *My Amazing Human Body* (DK Multimedia) for upper elementary, *ADAM: The Inside Story* (ADAM) for middle school, and *Bodyworks* and *How Your Body Works* (Mattel) for high school students. Children and teenagers can use these and other resources to research health topics, including the side effects of commonly used medicines or symptoms of major medical illnesses.

Technology to Influence Others' Health Behaviors

When dealing with all of the complex issues in health education, a mentoring relationship offers great potential for promoting self-analysis and metacognition on the part of the older student. E-mail and videoconferencing may also be used to set up online projects with other classes around the world. For example, fifth-grade classes in different parts of the world collaborate on studying local safety issues. When they complete their research, they collaborate on developing a web page that promotes environmental health. Students also are able to discuss the differences between various cultures with regard to subjects such as drug use or government-sponsored health care.

Using the WebQuest (http://edweb.sdsu.edu/webquest/webquest.html) strategy, students are given an authentic problem to solve along with web resources on the topic. Students typically work in collaborative teams. Each student explores the linked sites related to a specific role on the team. Students then teach what they have learned to the other team members. Finally, higher level questions guide students toward more challenging thinking and a deeper understanding of the topic being explored. An excellent example of a WebQuest is the "personal trainer."

Figure 14.6 *KidsHealth* Web Site

Source: Courtesy of KidsHealth.org

Video resources also are an efficient way to remove logistical hurdles when teaching health-related issues. Videos allow students to hear similar information and advice from a voice other than the teacher's. They also allow students to see health issues in "real-life" settings. A great site to search for videos is the California Clearinghouse (http://clearinghouse.k12.ca.us).

Some resources let students see the consequences of ill-advised choices, whether it be smoking, drugs, or poor nutrition. These resources include video-based simulations that foster decision-making and critical thinking skills. Simulation programs place students in situations where they have to apply their knowledge to solve medical or health mysteries. A popular simulation videodisc, *Science Sleuths* (Video Discovery), uses humorous mysteries to engage students in the process of problem solving and critical thinking. The mystery episodes are fictitious but introduce important health concepts and processes. Students can access video interviews, conduct science experiments, and examine photos, articles, charts, graphs, and much more. Topics related to health education include "Blood Components and Function," "Human Development and Heredity," and "The Nervous System."

Technology to Support Interdisciplinary Instruction

The popular opinion regarding interdisciplinary instruction for health and physical education is that these subject areas support learning in other subjects. However, the perspective of the health and physical educators is that interdisciplinary instruction requires a symbiotic relationship—where subject areas support each other. Mohnsen (1998) offers an example of an interdisciplinary health-related fitness unit where the physical education teacher focuses on the benefits of physical training and conditioning and the health education teacher focuses on health issues related to diet and physical activity. The science teacher explores how the digestive system works and the mathematics teacher provides word problems on the input and output of calories. See Technology Integration Idea 14.1 earlier in this chapter for an example of an interdisciplinary lesson that integrates physical education, science, and math along with the use of computers. Technology teachers can help with these interdisciplinary units by providing Internet research support and multimedia project development tools that let students demonstrate their learning.

Useful Web Sites for Physical Education and Health Instruction

American School Health Association

http://www.ashaweb.org/

This is the professional organization for health educators.

Centers for Disease Control and Prevention

http://cdc.gov/

This site offers a broad range of current information on health and wellness, and is an excellent source for students and teachers for quality information.

Go Ask Alice

http://www.goaskalice.columbia.edu/

This site lets the student or teacher ask questions about health and wellness issues. Visitors simply send in their questions, which are then answered by a team of experts from the Columbia University Health Question & Answer Service.

Kids Health

http://www.kidshealth.org/

This site helps parents, children, teens, and professionals find answers to commonly asked health questions. Topics include the benefits of different types of vitamins, the food pyramid, healthy children's recipes, how to read food labels, and keeping fit.

Health Teacher

http://www.healthteacher.com/

This site offers a comprehensive, sequential K–12 health education curriculum that consists of almost 300 lesson guides that meet national health education standards and provide skills-based assessment methods.

University of Alberta Health Centre Health Information Page

http://www.ualberta.ca/healthinfo

This site provides access to free interactive software that teaches about various health topics relevant to young adults. Although designed for students in post-secondary educational institutions, most are useful for high school students and some for junior high students.

MedTerms

http://www.MedTerms.com

Provides quick and easy access to an online medical dictionary.

Quackwatch

http://www.quackwatch.com

Provides comprehensive information on health quackery, including general observations, questionable products, inaccurate sources of health advice, consumer protection, questionable advertisements, legal and political activities, consumer education, health promotion strategies, tips for practitioner selection, and ideas for research projects.

Gray's Anatomy Online

http://www.bartleby.com/107/

Contains 1,247 drawings from the classic 1918 publication by the same title along with a subject index with 13,000 entries.

Brain Pop

http://www.brainpop.com

Provides information on a wide variety of health topics and diseases. Video clips on various health topics are also included.

President's Council on Physical Fitness and Sports

http://www.indiana.edu/~preschal/

Covers information on the President's Challenge (one of two popular fitness testing batteries in the United States), activities in which the President's Council is involved, and digests that summarize the most recent research on physical activity and fitness.

The Fitness Files

http://mainetoday.webpoint.com/fitness

This site offers four main areas to navigate: Fitness Fundamentals, Get Active, The Injurenet, and Fuel for Fitness. Within these links, students can learn the basic principles of fitness, how to calculate their target heart rates, which activities can help them stay active, how to stretch properly, and what foods are essential for a healthy diet.

Sport Videos

http://www.sportsid.com

This is the premiere site for video instruction in the area of sport skills. Select the sport you are teaching and then select the skill; a short video clip is provided that describes and illustrates the motor skill or specific technique.

Ancient Olympics

http://www.upenn.edu/museum/Olympics/olympicintro.html

Covers all aspects of the Ancient Olympics.

Science of Sport

http://www.exploratorium.com/sport/index.html

This interactive site addresses the science of sport—specifically baseball, cycling, skateboarding, and hockey.

Orienteering

http://www.astro.uio.no/~kjetikj/compass/

Demonstrates the power of using the Internet for independent study. This one provides a complete tutorial on how to use a compass.

Circus Skills

http://www.juggling.org/help/circus-arts/

Covers directions for ball spinning, diabolo, footbag, frisbee, stilts, unicycling, and many other skills related to circus activities.

California Physical Education Web Site

http://www.stan-co.k12.ca.us/calpe/

Comprehensive physical education site. Links to a wide variety of sports, dance, and gymnastics sites as well as links to other major physical education sites (e.g., PE Central, PE Links 4U) on the Internet.

Country Western Dance

http://www.ibiblio.org/schools/rls/

Provides a comprehensive listing of dance steps and terms related to country western dancing.

Using Technology in Physical Education Newsletter

http://www.pesoftware.com/technews/news.html

Published 10 times per year, this newsletter provides physical educators with the latest information on using technology in physical education.

Exercises

Record and apply what you have learned.

Chapter 14 Self-Test

To review terms and concepts in this chapter, take the Chapter 14 self-test. Select Chapter 14 from the front page of the Companion Website (located at http://www.prenhall.com/roblyer), then choose the *Multiple Choice* module.

Portfolio Activities

ISTE The following activities address ISTE National Educational Technology Standards for Teachers (NETS-T) and will help you add to your professional portfolio. To complete these activities online and save or submit the materials electronically, select Chapter 14 from the front page of the Companion Website (http://www.prenhall.com/roblyer), then choose the *Portfolio* module.

1. ***Collecting Data on Physical Activities (NETS-T Standards: I-B; II-B, E; III-D; V-B, C)*** Create an activity in an elementary, middle school, or high school setting that encourages students to engage in physical activities such as walking around the school campus each day. Include the use of technology devices such as heart monitors to collect

data on physical activity. Develop a spreadsheet template for recording distances and charting progress. Develop an example of computer-generated advertising such as flyers and sign-up sheets for the activity. Place a copy of all products, along with a description of the activity, in your personal portfolio.

2. ***Research (NETS-T Standards: I-B, II-C, V-B)*** Contact a physical education or health education teacher who is interested in having her classes work on interdisciplinary research projects using the Internet that incorporate physical education and health concepts. As a beginning point, offer to share a list of health and PE web sites that are useful for this purpose. Provide the teacher with a disk copy of the bookmarks or a simple hypermedia product that includes buttons to the links.

Questions for Thought and Discussion

These questions may be used for small-group or class discussion or may be subjects for individual or group activities. To take part in these discussions online, select Chapter 14 from the front page of the Companion Website (http://www.prenhall.com/roblyer), then choose the *Message Board* module.

1. What type of support do you think the author is talking about in the quote below? Is instructional technology part of the problem, part of the solution, or neutral? Is the problem likely to get worse or better? With the help of computer technology, more and more people are now working from their homes. Will this trend lead to more or less physical activity?

> Support is greatly needed if physical activity is going to be increased in a society as technologically advanced as ours. Most Americans today are spared the burden of excessive physical labor. Indeed, few occupations today require significant physical activity, and most people use motorized transportation to get to work and to perform routine errands and tasks. (Satcher, 1997, foreword)

2. Is there a way to turn the passive activities discussed in the quote below into ones that require physical activity? Can any of these activities be used to promote physical activity? What role can schools play in changing the amount of leisure time spent on sedentary activities?

> Even leisure time is increasingly filled with sedentary behaviors, such as watching television, surfing the Internet, and playing video games. (Satcher, 1997, foreword)

Collaborative Activities

The following activities address ISTE National Educational Technology Standards for Teachers (NETS-T) and can be done in small groups. Each group should present the findings to the class in a format they know how to use (word-processed report, presentation software, multimedia product). Completed group projects can be copied and shared with the entire class and/or included in each person's Personal Portfolio.

1. ***Web-Based Activity (NETS-T Standards: II-A, III-A)*** Work in a small group to design a web-based learning activity (e.g., WebQuest, Scavenger Hunt) for either a health education or physical education class. Be sure to select one or two standards on which to focus the content for the activity. Include a copy of the activity, along with any relevant web sites needed for completing the learning activity, in your personal portfolio.
2. ***Public Service Announcement (PSA) (NETS-T Standard V-D)*** Work with your team to develop a 60-second public service announcement. The PSA should provide parents with health tips and information on how to engage their children in quality physical fitness activities. Resources may include teachers in the field or on the Internet. Include a copy of the PSA in your personal portfolio.
3. ***Lesson Integration Strategies for Instructional Software (NETS-T Standards: II-A through E; II-C, D; III-B; IV-A, B)*** Using the five-step integration sequence described in the *Personal Fitness Plans You Can Live With* example at the beginning of this chapter, small groups prepare an integration sequence for how to use technology resources to help incorporate PE and health concepts into a real or fictional classroom. (Students should pay special attention to the "justification" description in Step 1.) They present their findings to the class.

Integrating Technology Across the Curriculum Activities

The *Integrating Technology Across the Curriculum* CD-ROM is a set of technology integration ideas and links to online lessons, arranged as a searchable database. The CD comes packaged with this textbook. Complete the following exercise using this CD:

Review some of the example integration ideas on the CD cited in this chapter for physical education and health education. Notice that some of them combine the teaching of these areas with other content areas such as mathematics. Consider these questions: What technology materials and strategy could support teaching physical education and English/language arts together? What technology materials and strategy could support teaching health and science together? Which web sites could support teaching physical education and the social sciences together? Now make up a technology integration idea of your own matched to an integration strategy described in this chapter. Add it to the CD. Be sure to identify each of the descriptors for it, including the relative advantage.

References

American Library Association. (1989). *Report from American Library Association's Presidential Committee on Information Literacy.* Washington DC: Author.

Borba, M. (1989). *Self esteem builders resources.* Torrance, CA: Jalmar Press.

Caine, R. N., & Caine, G. (1995). Reinventing schools through brain-based learning. *Educational Leadership 52*(7), 43–47.

Darden, G., & Shimon, J. (2000). Revisit an "old" technology: Videotape feedback for motor skill learning and performance. *Strategies, 13*(4), 17–21.

Doering, N. (2000). Measuring student understanding with a videotape performance assessment. *Journal of Physical Education, Recreation, and Dance, 71*(7), 47–52.

Graham, G., Holt-Hale, S., & Parker, M. (1998). *Children moving: A reflective approach to teaching physical education.* Mountain View, CA: Mayfield Publishing Co.

Joint Committee on National Health Education Standards. (1995). *National health education standards.* Atlanta, GA: American Cancer Society.

Kane, W. M. (1993). *Step by step to comprehensive school health: The program planning guide.* Santa Cruz, CA: ETR Associates.

Mohnsen, B. (1998). *Concepts of physical education: What every student needs to know.* Reston, VA: National Association for Sport and Physical Education.

Mohnsen, B. (2000). Vaughn, Nekomi, and Luis: What they were doing in middle school physical education. *Learning and Leading with Technology, 27*(5), 22–27.

National Association for Sport and Physical Education. (1995). *Moving into the future: National standards for physical education.* Reston, VA: Author.

Pate, R. R., & Small, M. L. (1995). School physical education. *Journal of School Health, 65*(8), 312–317.

Payne, V. G., & Issacs, L. D. (1995). *Human motor development: A lifespan approach* (3rd ed.). Mountain View, CA: Mayfield Publishing Co.

Satcher, D. (1997). Physical activity and health: A report of the surgeon general. Washington, DC: U.S. Government Printing Office.

Seffrin, J. R. (1990). The comprehensive school health curriculum. *Journal of School Health, 60*(4), 151–156.

U.S. Department of Health and Human Services. (1996) *Physical activity and health: A report of the surgeon general.* Atlanta, GA: U.S. Department of Health and Human Services, Centers for Disease Control and Prevention, National Center for Chronic Disease Prevention and Health Promotion.

Additional Reading

Anderson, A., & Weber, E. (1997). A multiple intelligence approach to healthy active living in high school. *Journal of Physical Education, Recreation, and Dance, 68*(4), 57–68.

Benham-Deal, T., & Deal, L. O. (1995). Heart-to-heart: Using heart rate telemetry to measure physical education outcomes. *Journal of Physical Education, Recreation, and Dance, 66*(3), 30–35.

Dorman, S. (1997). CD-ROM use in health instruction. *Journal of School Health, 67*(10), 444–446.

Dorman, S. (1998). Ten reasons to use technology in the health classroom. *Journal of School Health, 68*(1), 38–39.

Ellery, P. J. (1996). Embracing computer technology in physical education instruction. *The Chronicle of Physical Education in Higher Education, 51*(7), 3–18.

Ellery, P. J. (1997). Using the World Wide Web in physical education. *Strategies, 10*(3), 5–8.

Friesen, R., & Bender, P. (1997). Internet sites for physical educators. *Strategies, 11*(1), 34–36.

Ignico, A. A. (1997). The effects of interactive videotape instruction on knowledge, performance, and assessment of sport skills. *The Physical Educator, 54*(1), 58–63.

Justice, B. (1996). Eating right? Fat chance! Teaching math and nutrition with spreadsheets. *Learning and Leading with Technology, 23*(6), 16–19.

Kirk, M. F. (1997). Using portfolios to enhance student learning and assessment. *Journal of Physical Education, Recreation, and Dance, 68*(7), 29–33.

Mitchell, D. L., & Hunt, D. (1997). Multimedia lesson plans—help for preservice teachers. *Journal of Physical Education, Recreation, and Dance, 68*(2), 17–20.

Mohnsen, B., & Schiemer, S. (1997). Handheld technology—practical application of the Newton messagepad. *Strategies, 11*(2), 12–14.

Poedubicky, V., Brown, L., Hoover, H., & Elias, M. J. (2000). Using technology to promote health. *Learning and Leading with Technology, 28*(4), 18–21, 56.

Ragon, B. M., & Bennett, J. P. (1996). Something more to consider, combining health education and physical education. *Journal of Physical Education, Recreation, and Dance, 67*(1), 14–15.

Strand, B., Mauch, L., & Terbizan, D. (1997). The fitness education pyramid—integrating concepts with the technology. *Journal of Physical Education, Recreation, and Dance, 68*(6), 19–27.

Resources

Videos/Videodiscs

All Fit, Juggling Star, Motor Learning: Secrets to Learning New Sports Skills, Science and Myths of Tennis, SlimGoodbody, The Jump Rope Primer, and *The World of Volleyball* (Human Kinetics)
Golf with Al Geiberger (SyberVision)
Personal Fitness: Looking Good/Feeling Good (Kendall/Hunt Publishing Company)
Science Sleuths (Video Discovery)
SportsFigures (ESPN)
Finding Your Way in the Wild (Quality Video)

Software

ADAM: The Inside Story (ADAM)
Biomechanics: The Easy Way, Health-Related Fitness Tutorial/Portfolio, Muscle Flash, Orienteening Simulation, SimAthlete, and *Volleyball* (Bonnie's Fitware)
Bodyworks and *How Your Body Works* (Mattel)
DINE Healthy and *Pyramid Challenge* (DINE Systems)
Golf Tips (Diamar)
Measurement in Motion (Learning in Motion)
My Amazing Human Body (DK Multimedia)
Resource Network (BARN) (Pyramid Media)
What Is a Bellybutton? and *Welcome to Bodyland* (IVI Publishing)
InnerBody Works (Tom Snyder Communications)

Technology Devices

Beat, Accurex, or Vantage Heart Monitors (Polar)
HeartTalker (New Life Technologies)
Body Composition Analyzer (Futrex)

CHAPTER 15

Technology in Special Education

Dave L. Edyburn, University of Wisconsin–Milwaukee

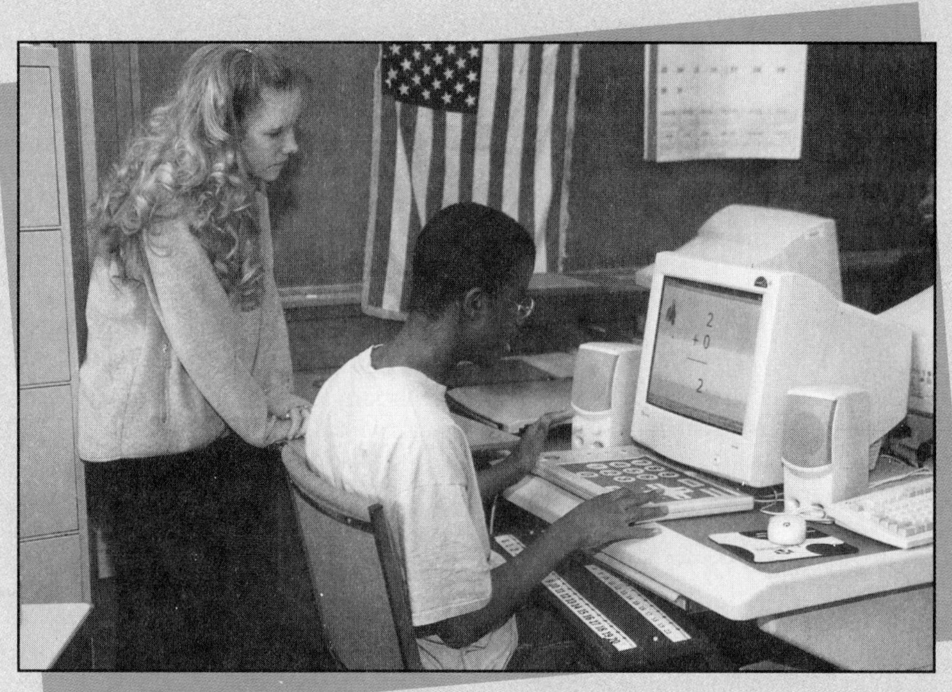

For most of us, technology makes things easier. For a person with a disability, it makes things possible.

Judy Heumann, Assistant Secretary, U.S. Department of Education, Office of Special Education Programs

This chapter covers the following topics:

- Current issues and problems in special education
- How technology is integrated into special education
- Example World Wide Web resources for special education
- Example activities for a variety of integration strategies in special education

Objectives

1. Differentiate among the terms *impairment, disability,* and *handicap.*
2. Compare and contrast assistive technology and instructional technology.
3. Identify current issues affecting the acquisition and use of technology in special education.
4. Explore applications of assistive, instructional, and productivity technologies commonly used by students with disabilities and their teachers.
5. Provide web-based exercises to explore resources, products, and strategies that enhance teaching, learning, and performance for students and special education teachers.

Introduction

Education for students with special needs encompasses strategies for both those with physical and/or mental deficits and those with special gifts or talents. Although technology can be used to enhance education for both populations, this chapter addresses primarily applications for students with disabilities.

While the terms *impairment, disability,* and *handicap* are often used synonymously, differences among these concepts have important implications for the use of technology in classrooms. An *impairment* involves an abnormality or loss of function in a physical, anatomical, or psychological structure. Impairments to human function may be congenital (present at birth) or acquired through accident or disease. It is important not to make assumptions concerning a person's ability or limitations simply because he or she has an impairment.

When an impairment limits an individual from performing an activity in a manner normally expected for human beings (communicating with others, hearing, movement, manipulating objects, etc.), we refer to this as a *disability.* A student who has lost the function of his right arm has an impairment; this condition will have little or no impact on a variety of life functions. However, this student may encounter situations where the inability to use two arms places him at a disadvantage with others (that is, a handicap). A *handicap* arises when an individual is unable to fulfill a role due to an impairment or disability. It is critical to understand that a handicap is not a characteristic of an individual. Rather, a handicap results from the mismatch between one's abilities and the demands of an environment (Cook & Hussey, 1995).

In the United States, federal law recognizes several types of disabilities. Most citizens are likely to know one or more individuals whose life function has been affected by disability in some form: deaf, deaf-blind, hard of hearing, mental retardation, multihandicapped, orthopedically impaired, other health impaired, seriously emotionally disturbed, specific learning disability, speech impaired, or visually handicapped.

The fields of special education and rehabilitation have had a long-standing interest in technology. Historically, the emphasis on technology for individuals with disabilities has been thought of as assistive technology, that is, extending the abilities of an individual in ways that provide physical access (i.e., wheelchairs, braces) and sensory access (i.e., Braille, closed captioning). Indeed, the legal definition of assistive technology is considerably broad:

> §300.5 Assistive technology device.
> As used in this part, Assistive technology device means any item, piece of equipment, or product system, whether acquired commercially off the shelf, modified, or customized, that is used to increase, maintain, or improve the functional capabilities of a child with a disability. (Authority: 20 U.S.C. 1401(1))

More recently, we've come to understand that additional attention must also be given to the use of technology for teaching and learning. In this chapter we use the term *special education technology* to cover both dimensions of assistive technology and instructional technology. Regardless of the specific application of technology, the general goal is always the same: to harness the potential of technology in ways that offer an individual with a disability increased opportunities for learning, productivity, and independence—opportunities that otherwise would not be available. In the next section, we explore several issues involved in capturing the potential of technology for individuals with disabilities.

Issues and Problems in Special Education Technology

A number of topics currently attract the attention and energy of professionals working in the field of special education technology. The following descriptions provide a brief introduction to six contemporary issues.

Legal and Policy Directives

During the past 15 years, a series of federal legislative actions have produced laws and funding initiatives that seek to expand the use of technology by individuals with disabilities and consequently open new opportunities for learning, employment, and independent living. The most notable of these laws include the following:

- The Technology-Related Assistance Act for Individuals with Disabilities (Public Law 100–407), passed in 1988, provides funding for statewide systems and services to provide assistive technology devices and services to individuals with disabilities.
- The Americans with Disabilities Act (ADA) of 1990 (Public Law 101-336) is considered landmark civil

TECHNOLOGY INTEGRATION EXAMPLE

Technology for Students with Special Needs

TITLE: *Helping Students with Disabilities Blend In*

BASED ON: Judd-Wall, J. (1996). Curriculum blending: Computerized surveying activities for everyone. *Learning and Leading with Technology, 23*(8), 61–64.

GRADE LEVEL: All grade levels

CONTENT AREA/TOPIC: Research methods, data analysis, charting, and graphing

LENGTH OF TIME: Three weeks

Step 1: What's the Relative Advantage—Why Use Technology to Help Teach Students with Special Needs?

Three of the students in Ms. Montoya's sixth-grade class had special needs. Dorothy had cerebral palsy and came to class in her motorized wheelchair. Although bright and enthusiastic, she had difficulty with fine-motor skills and could not write or use the computer keyboard and mouse. Ralph was a shy, sweet boy with mild mental deficits. Geraldo had hearing impairments and was reluctant to speak in class. Ms. Montoya made special efforts to involve Dorothy, Ralph, and Geraldo in all class activities and had shown the other students how to welcome them into their work and play. She consulted with the school district's Special Education Resource Office to obtain an alternate keyboard and input software for Dorothy and special speech development software for Geraldo. She tried several resources and strategies to help develop Ralph's reading skills and found that he especially liked working with interactive books. However, she wanted a class project that could involve all students, and show that each one of them could make a valuable contribution to the work despite their varying talents and ability levels. She learned in a district workshop about curriculum blending or curriculum overlapping, the practice of having students at all ability levels (including those with physical or learning disabilities) work on the same activities, but grading them differently. She decided to do a curriculum blending project that involved having the class do a survey of students in the school. Dorothy and Geraldo and others would be put in charge of gathering the data using an alternative input and spoken word processor system recommended by the Special Education Resource Office. The system could voice the questions and students could enter responses directly onto a touch panel on the computer screen. Ralph could work in the group that did initial tasks in the data analysis, and the whole class could learn how to do research and ask different levels of "what if" questions from compiled data. She correlated several required math skills with these activities.

Step 2: Planning Assessment—What Are Appropriate Assessment Strategies?

Ms. Montoya developed assignment sheets for each student which indicated tasks they would be required to do and how they would be graded. The sheets were tailored to the ability and skill levels of each student. Although tasks were different, criteria were similar and included accomplishing all tasks, working with others in the group, and completing a required product.

Step 3: Planning Instruction—What Are Appropriate Integration Strategies?

Ms. Montoya designed the following sequence of activities around a survey on "our favorite fruits."

Figure 15.0 Curriculum Blending Activities

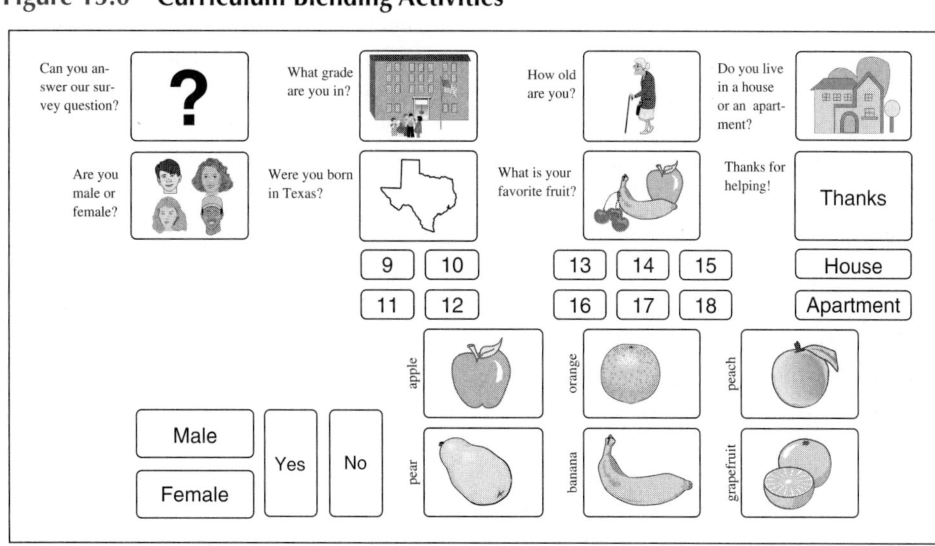

Source: Graphic from Judd-Wall, J. (1996). Curriculum blending: Computerized surveying activities for everyone. *Learning and Leading with Technology, 23*(8), p. 63.

TECHNOLOGY INTEGRATION EXAMPLE (CONTINUED)

- **Week 1: Introduce the survey project and train students.** Give students the assignment sheets and discuss the purposes and uses of survey research. Work with them to design a simple "script" for the survey, enter it into the voice word processor, and show them how the input system works to collect data. Have them discuss methods of getting students to stop and complete the survey (e.g., offer them a sticker that says "I voted!" as some voting places offer on election days). Have students rehearse the sequence in advance, so it will move quickly when they actually begin the survey.
- **Week 2: Do the survey.** Select a location (e.g., near the library) for data collection. Ask Geraldo to be in charge of encouraging students who pass by to participate in the survey. Place Dorothy in charge of demonstrating how the system input works. (Begin the survey script by touching the "Can you answer our survey question?" icon. If the person agrees to participate, the student asks the questions by touching the correct icon, and the computer gives a typed and a voice response.)
- **Week 3: Analyze the results and do summary products.** Have Ralph assist with printing, sorting, and organizing the responses. Have students make the responses into a bar graph and calculate percentages (e.g., What percentage of the eighth grade prefers apples?) and query the data (Do older students prefer different fruits than younger ones?). Have all students help prepare a bulletin board to post their findings for the school to see. Place pictures of students around the bulletin board, identifying the roles they played in the survey.

Step 4: Logistics—Preparing the Classroom Environment and Instructional Materials

Ms. Montoya worked closely with the special education personnel to set up the special computer system and learn how to use it. She had to obtain permission to have the "survey station" in the hall outside the library and asked the main office to publicize it in the morning announcements. She had to spend extra time with Geraldo and Ralph to prepare them for their roles.

Step 5: Evaluating and Revising Integration Strategies

At the end of the unit, Ms. Montoya reviewed the project and reflected on its impact. Some of the questions she asked were as follows:

- Did students at all ability levels accomplish required tasks?
- Did students (including those with special needs) seem engaged in the learning?
- Did students (including those with special needs) seem to acknowledge that all of them had made a valuable contribution to the class?
- Did the activities go smoothly with the alternative computer system?

Ms. Montoya was happy with how involved the students were in the survey. Parents of all three students with special needs came by to see the bulletin board and express their pride in their children's work. Ms. Montoya and the principal agreed they would have to work on locating the computer station so as not to disrupt hall traffic, since the "talking computer" had created quite a crowd. However, the principal also asked her to share her project with other teachers who had students with special needs.

rights legislation since it expands the scope of coverage of employers and agencies mandated to provide accessible transportation systems, buildings and programs, and communication systems for individuals with disabilities.

- Reauthorization of the Individuals with Disabilities Education Act (IDEA) in 1997 (Public Law 105–17) mandates that every individual educational program (IEP) team "consider" assistive technology when planning the educational program of an individual with a disability.

Clearly, the U.S. Congress has been persuaded that technology can offer individuals with disabilities significant benefits. As a result, advocacy for the use of technology has been transformed into a web of legal and policy mandates. This means that teachers, administrators, and special education technology specialists must be well versed in federal and state laws, policies, and procedures. To learn more about the legal and policy foundations of the field of special education technology, consult the following resources: Blackhurst (1997), Blackhurst and Edyburn (2000), U.S. Department of Education (2000), and the web resources listed at the end of the chapter.

Consideration of Assistive Technology

The issue of assistive technology consideration is a rather recent development. Its origin can be traced to the Individuals with Disabilities Education Act Amendments of 1997 (Public Law 105–17), which contained a requirement for IEP teams to consider assistive technology in the development of the IEP: "The IEP Team shall—(v) consider whether the child requires assistive technology devices and services" [Section 614 (d)(3)(B) Consideration of Special Factors].

Whereas some observers believe this language reflects a new federal policy, Golden (1998) argues that it simply formalizes a previous responsibility:

> The IDEA requires schools to provide AT if it is needed for a student to receive a free appropriate public education (FAPE). FAPE can include a variety of services such as special education, related services, supplementary aids and services, program modifications or support for school personnel. AT, just like other components of FAPE, must be provided at no cost to parents. The specific IDEA requirement for schools to provide AT is as follows:
> 300.308 Assistive Technology
> *Each public agency shall ensure that assistive technology devices or assistive technology services or both, as those*

terms are defined in 300.5–300.6 are made available to a child with a disability if required as part of a child's (a) Special education under 300.17; (b) Related services under 300.16; or (c) Supplementary aids and services under 300.550(b)(2). (p. 4)

Golden's analysis highlights a critical issue: free appropriate public education (FAPE). Schools are required to provide assistive technology for students that need such tools, if they are necessary, so the student can participate in and benefit from a free appropriate public education. The historical implications of this requirement are unquestioned in the context of mobility (i.e., a powered wheelchair) and communication (i.e., an augmentative communication system). However, because the requirement covers all disabilities, there is an urgent need for research, development, and policy to inform our understanding of the use of assistive technology to mitigate cognitive impairments—a key characteristic associated with mild disabilities (Edyburn, 2000).

The implications of this mandate are far reaching given the broad definition of assistive technology, the high incidence of mild disabilities, and the lack of decision-making guidelines about how technology contributes to helping students participate in and benefit from FAPE. As a result, there has been a tremendous need in the field for training and resources regarding the requirement to "consider assistive technology." Several noteworthy resources have been developed to ensure that the intent of the legislation does indeed get implemented by including students, parents, teachers, administrators, and technology specialists in the consideration process (Chambers, 1997; Golden, 1998; Zabala, 2000).

Trained Personnel

In recent years, considerable progress has been made to identify the knowledge and skills needed by teachers (Lahm & Nickels, 1999) and specialists (Lahm, 2000) relative to the use of technology in special education. Individuals can use competency statements to document their experience, knowledge, and skills in their own teaching portfolio. University teacher preparation programs and in-service workshop providers can review the competency frameworks and align individual competency statements with specific courses and training events in order to communicate the specific outcomes participants will gain.

Despite the efforts of most universities to improve the preparation of teachers to use technology in the classroom, most teachers begin their career with minimal experience in using technology in ways that (1) enhance their own productivity, (2) enhance the effectiveness of instruction and the success of all students, or (3) enable them to acquire and use assistive technology for students in need of performance support. The common three-credit course, first developed in the 1980s, continues to be the norm for preparing teachers; unfortunately, it is generally inadequate to exploit the power and possibilities technology offers. The problem is even more acute at the graduate level when teachers and therapists seek advanced training or speciality work in special education technology. One survey found only 21 programs in the United States that provide course work leading to a certificate or degree in special education technology (RESNA, 2001). At the present time, most preparation programs are clearly inadequate to provide the quality and depth of training needed by every professional to use products already found in the marketplace.

A third issue regarding the adequacy of personnel trained in special education technology involves the use of interdisciplinary teams for evaluating the need for assistive technology and decision making in the selection of appropriate devices and services. The current assistive technology delivery systems were originally developed to respond to the needs of students with low-incidence disabilities (approximately 1.4 million students in the United States). The sheer size of the high-incidence population requires a rethinking of service delivery systems such that the first step in accessing assistive technology services is not a referral for a comprehensive multidisciplinary evaluation. Currently, many students who have access to assistive technology have obtained that access as a result of advocacy efforts that challenge the system rather than through a systemic process that ensures all students in need of devices have them (Edyburn, 2000).

Inclusive Classrooms

During the 1990s, a major change occurred in how special education services were delivered. Rather than placing students with disabilities in separate classrooms (self-contained special education) and allowing them to participate in selected classes in general education (mainstreaming), efforts were made to include them in the general education classroom (inclusion). This philosophical shift has been controversial (Fuchs & Fuchs, 1991; Kauffman, 1989; Meyen & Skrtic, 1995; Stainback & Stainback, 1984; Wang & Walberg, 1988) and continues today. Nonetheless, students with disabilities now spend the majority of the school day in general education classrooms and receive a variety of support services (U.S. Department of Education, 2000).

Although students with disabilities have gained physical inclusion into general education, access to the general education curriculum is still limited. That is, without appropriate modifications, a student in a wheelchair cannot conduct the same science experiment as other students because he cannot get close enough to the lab bench in his wheelchair to manipulate the chemicals and beakers. Likewise, when the bulk of subject matter content is contained in teacher-made materials and textbooks, a significant portion of the students do not have access to the information they are expected to learn (i.e., students who are blind, students with learning disabilities who cannot read at grade level). Given the expectation that all students will achieve high academic standards, there is an urgent need for assistive technology to help students in the general education classroom succeed.

Universal Design

Principles of universal design have emerged from our understanding of the design of physical environments for individuals with disabilities. Perhaps the best example of the success of universal design principles are curb cuts. Originally designed to improve mobility for people with disabilities within our communities, curb cuts not only accomplish that, but also improve access for people with baby strollers, roller blades, bikes, etc. Readers interested in additional information about the origins of universal design are encouraged to visit the Center for Universal Design at North Carolina State University (http://www.design.ncsu.edu/cud/).

More recently, universal design concepts have been applied to computers. The TRACE Center at the University of Wisconsin, Madison, has spearheaded conversations among the disability community and technology developers concerning initiatives to include disability accessibility software as part of the operating system so that access would be provided as the computer came out of the box (rather than require an individual to track down assistive technology specialists to make specialized modifications). Today, accessibility control panels are available on every computer. To learn more about the design initiatives of the staff at TRACE, visit http://www.trace.wisc.edu/world/.

In the past few years, a concerted effort has been made to apply universal design principles to learning. A leader in the area of universal design for learning has been the Center for Applied Special Technology (CAST). CAST feels universal design is a critical issue if students with disabilities are going to be able to access the general education curriculum. To learn more about universal design and access to the curriculum, visit the Center for Accessing the General Education Curriculum (http://www.cast.org/naec/).

Teachers working with students in inclusion settings face a relentless demand to modify curricular, instructional, and assessment materials. Modifications will always be necessary as a result of technology, media, and materials that are not designed with an understanding of the range of diversity found in every classroom. It is also important to note that modifications are always reactive. This means that students with disabilities often experience a delay in obtaining information that is readily available to their peers without disabilities. Universal design seeks to alter this paradigm by providing a new way of thinking about access that is proactive rather than reactive. For additional information about universal design, consult the following resources: Dolan (2000), Edyburn (2001), Grogan and Ruzic (2000), Orkwis and McLane (1998), Rose (2000), and Rose, Sethuraman, and Meo (2000).

Accountability

Schools have demonstrated a willingness to devote an increasing percentage of their budgets to the purchase of assistive and instructional technology in recent years. Few voices have challenged the general trends in technology acquisition by schools during the late 1990s. It is fortunate that accountability questions have not been asked because little evidence exists to document the impact of these expenditures.

Several recent initiatives suggest a new era of accountability and technology in education as tools are developed to evaluate levels of technology integration and the impact of technology on learning (Anneberg Institute of School Reform, 1999; CEO Forum, 1999; Milken Family Foundation, 1999; SEIR*TEC, 1999). Increasingly, questions such as "What effect have our recent investments in technology had on teaching and learning?" are raised by educators and policy makers.

Questions of effectiveness have also been raised in the context of assistive technology. That is, what types of outcomes should be expected when individuals with disabilities use assistive technology (Fennema-Jansen, 2001; Smith, 2000)? King (1999) describes a model that identifies key factors involving motivation of the AT user to pursue and complete tasks, physical effort, cognitive effort, linquistic effort, and time. Zabala and Korsten (1999) have suggested that a series of changes can be expected when assistive technology is used effectively: changes in quality, quantity, accuracy, rate, frequency, spontaneity, independence, and others. Their work offers an important starting point for creating a useful framework for developing a measurement and decision-making system documenting the effective use of assistive technology. Another promising development in the maturation of the profession comes from the work of the QIAT Consortium (http://www.qiat.org/), which has sought to operationally define quality indicators for assistive technology services (QIAT Consortium, 2001).

How Technology Is Integrated into Special Education

The purpose of this section is to provide information about general approaches to using assistive and instructional technology and to describe specific products that are commonly integrated into curricula for helping students with special needs achieve academic, behavioral, or social goals. The information is organized around foundational concepts, disability-specific applications, subject matter applications, and productivity applications.

Foundations

The assistive technology evaluation process generally seeks to identify solutions on a continuum involving no technology ("no tech"), low technology ("low tech"), and advanced technology ("high tech"). No-tech solutions involve assessing the feasibility of teaching a person to use his or her body in a different manner to minimize the impact of an impairment (i.e., one-handed typing). The obvious advantage to solutions involving no technology is that they are available in any environment at any time. Low-tech solutions are generally considered to be nonelectrical. Personal word lists, highlighting markers, and organizing systems are all examples of low-technology solutions that can provide a person with appropriate levels of support to be successful in specific tasks. These solutions tend to be relatively inexpensive but quite flexible for enhancing individual performance. High-tech solutions are defined as complex electrical or hydraulic systems (i.e., stair lift, powered wheelchair, voice-activated environmental control). Clearly, high-tech solutions tend to be the most costly and have the greatest number of restrictions regarding their use (user skill level, limited portability, etc.).

Professional practice indicates that evaluation of potential solutions begins with no-tech, continues to low-tech, and then to high-tech solutions as the needs dictate. For example, the ability to spell words is most efficient when the words are committed to memory. However, if a person displays persistent difficulty spelling from memory (no-tech solution), low-tech options like personal word lists or portable dictionaries may be helpful. High-tech solutions like electronic spelling checkers should be considered only after other options have proven less satisfactory because of the dependency on batteries, fragileness, and so on.

Two common approaches for technology use by individuals with disabilities involve remediation and compensation (King, 1999). Remediation involves helping an individual learn or improve performance, often the focus of education, training, and therapy. Compensation focuses on using technology to accommodate difficulties performing specific tasks, for example, providing for the use of a calculator in recognition that a child has been unable to learn the multiplication facts. Both approaches can be used when integrating technology into instruction or therapy.

Disability-Specific Applications of Technology

Because some applications of technology in special education are commonly associated with specific disabilities, the following information provides a brief overview of specific examples of technologies as they are used by individuals with disabilities. The discussion is sequenced on a continuum beginning with low-incidence disabilities and ending with high-incidence disabilities.

Technology applications and sensory disabilities. Sensory disabilities involve impairments associated with the loss of hearing or vision. If loss of vision is complete, a person is considered blind. An individual is considered partially sighted if some visual acuity remains. Similarly, if loss of hearing is complete, a person is considered deaf. *Hearing impaired* is the term used to describe an individual with some hearing.

For an individual who is blind, three kinds of technology facilitate independence and access to environments and information. Canes and sensor technology are used to provide the person with mobility and orientation information when navigating various environments. Other essential tools convert printed information into audio so that a person who is blind can gain information by listening rather than reading. This is accomplished through the use of a scanner, optical character recognition (OCR) software, and speech synthesis. It works by placing text material on the scanner, and having the material scanned into the computer. The OCR software then converts the scanned information into text, and then the speech synthesis tools read the material read aloud. *L&H Kurzweil 3000* (Lernout & Hauspie Speech Products) and *Scan and Read Pro* (Premier Programming Solutions) are common text-to-speech systems used by individuals who are blind. Finally, screen readers are another common application for individuals who are blind. Screen readers work as utility software, operating in the background of the computer operating system and reading any text that appears on the screen: menus, text, web pages, and so on. Selected examples of screen readers include *Hal Screen Reader* (Dolphin Computer Access), *Home Page Reader for Windows* (IBM Special Needs Systems), *JAWS for Windows* (Freedom Scientific), and *OutSPOKEN* (ALVA Access Group).

The challenges for a partially sighted individual typically involve the need to have text information enlarged, or the contrast altered, in order to perceive printed information. When information is in printed form (i.e., books, magazines, flyers), a closed-circuit television (CCTV) magnification system can be used. Essentially, these systems are composed of a video camera mounted on a frame with a television monitor. Users place materials on the desktop below the camera, set the desired magnification level, move the materials around as necessary, and then the information appears on the monitor in a size that can be read comfortably by the individual. Similar challenges also arise for partially sighted individuals when using the computer. Many individuals' needs can be met by simply activating the font magnification control panel (see Figure 15.1). This function allows users to select the desired magnification of everything appearing on the screen. Screen magnification is a powerful tool built-into all computers. The proactive nature of this design not only helps people with disabilities but also provides support for the general population as it experiences the failing eyesight associated with aging.

Individuals who are deaf often can use technology without significant modifications. However, one problematic area involves the use of audio feedback (i.e., error messages) and the reliance on sound in multimedia software. When designers provide essential information only in audio form, this information is inaccessible to deaf individuals. As a result, advocacy and design initiatives encourage all information to be available in multiple formats (e.g., error messages that produce an auditory signal as well as a message on the screen; multimedia software that includes closed captioning of audio tracks).

Figure 15.1 Accessibility Control Panel

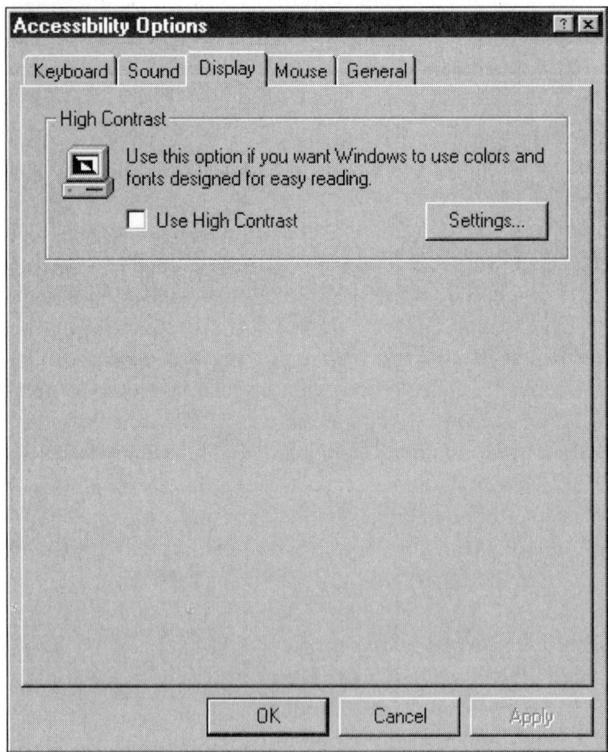

Individuals with hearing impairments need few modifications to be able to use computers. A new technology is finding increasing acceptance in classrooms: FM amplification systems (Easterbrooks, 1999). These systems involve the teacher wearing a wireless microphone and students with hearing impairments and some students with learning disabilities involving auditory processing difficulties wearing receivers that amplify the teacher's voice and serve to focus attention. These devices are also referred to as assistive listening devices and are increasingly found in movie theaters as an accommodation for patrons of all ages.

Technology applications in moderate and severe cognitive disabilities. A variety of conditions may impair an individual's cognitive abilities. Such disabilities are often referred to as cognitive disabilities, developmental disabilities, or mental retardation. For individuals with moderate and severe cognitive disabilities, considerable effort is devoted to ensuring that they acquire daily living skills such as personal hygiene, shopping ability (Wissick, 1999b), and use of public transportation. In addition, functional skills such as money management (Browder & Grasso, 1999) and employability skills (Fisher & Gardner, 1999) must be taught. A promising line of research has focused on the creation of video-based instructional materials to enhance acquisition, maintenance, and transfer of functional and community-based behaviors (Mechling & Langone, 2000; Wissick, 1999a, 1999b; Wissick, Gardner, & Langone, 1999).

Teachers working with students with moderate and severe cognitive disabilities need to be familiar with an array of devices that provide an alternative means for accessing the computer since the typical keyboard may be problematic for many students. To simplify the physical or cognitive demands of interacting with the computer, alternative keyboards like IntelliKeys (IntelliTools) (see Figure 15.2) can be used to create customized keyboards (i.e., enlarging the keys to provide more space for the student to press a key, removing keys that are not relevant for a given software package; programming multistep functions such as save, print, and quit into a single key press). Switches are also commonly used for controlling the computer as well as activating environmental control systems. Companies like AbleNet assist teachers in integrating the assistive technology into instruction.

Technology Applications for Young Children

Early intervention with young children with developmental delays and disabilities has been shown to positively affect later development. As a result, considerable resources have been devoted to screening and intervention programs to help young children and their families. Innovative projects such as TEChPLACEs utilize the web for teachers and parents to share resources and strategies to help young children with disabilities (Hutinger & Clark, 2000).

Unlike the application of technology with school-aged children where instruction tends to be teacher directed, considerable emphasis is placed on child-centered activities in preschool learning environments. As a result, the use of technology with young children tends to emphasis academic readiness skills (i.e., recognizing letters, counting, problem solving) and creative activities (i.e., exploratory play). Early intervention programs are likely to use computers with software products like the Edmark Early Learning series (*Bailey's Book House, Millie's Math House*), *JumpStart* (Preschool and Pre-K, from Knowledge Adventure), *Kid Pix* (Broderbund), and *Stickybear's Early Learning Activities* (Optimum Resources).

Technology Applications and Communication Disorders

Impairments in speech and developmental delays in language are among the most prevalent of all disabilities. Cochran (2000) describes the nature of communication disorders as

> problems with hearing, articulation (producing speech sounds), voice, fluency, or language. Speech disorders involve difficulty producing the actual sounds of a language intelligibly and fluently. In contrast, language disorders may include difficulty comprehending, planning, or producing communication appropriately. (p. 304)

Speech-language clinicians often use technology to create therapy materials and manage client records. In addition, the computer and specialized software (*IBM SpeechViewer III for Windows,* IBM Special Needs Systems) can be used in therapy with children and adults who

Figure 15.2 Student Using IntelliKeys Alternative Keyboard

Source: IntelliKeys, Classic or USB, by IntelliTools, Inc. Used with permission.

have articulation difficulties. When an individual is nonverbal or has speech that is unintelligible, therapists create communication boards with pictures that can be pointed to and sequenced to communicate. Products like *Boardmaker* (Mayer-Johnson) feature extensive collections of words and symbols for use in making communication boards. Specialized electronic communication systems, known as voice output communication aids (VOCA), can store hundreds of picture symbols that users can access individually or as a sequence so that the digitized voice can speak on their behalf. While such systems require sufficient cognitive skills to use, VOCAs provide a powerful communication tool. Examples of common VOCAs include 32 Message Communicator (Enabling Devices), AlphaTalker II (Prentke-Romich), One-Step Communicator 20 (AbleNet), Ultimate 8 (TASH), and the Vantage (Prentke-Romich).

Technology Applications and Mild Disabilities

Mild disabilities are considered the most prevalent type of disability and include learning disabilities, serious emotional disabilities, and mental retardation. Current estimates indicate 3.8 million students, ages 6–21, have a mild disability (U.S. Department of Education, 2000), representing more than 71% of the students receiving special education services. Meese (2001) describes the following characteristics as being associated with mild disabilities: cognitive characteristics (intellectual ability, attentional deficits, memory and thinking skills), academic characteristics (reading, language arts, mathematics), and social-emotional characteristics (pp. 27–35).

Typically, the important issue for these students is not physical access to the technology. Rather, critical issues tend to involve reading, writing, memory, and retention of information. Whereas some learning difficulties are pervasive (inability to read at grade level), many students have difficulty learning in only one aspect of the curriculum. As a result, we now turn our attention to the next section dealing with instructional applications of technology in special education.

Subject Matter Applications of Technology in Special Education

Whereas the historical application of technology in special education has focused on assistive technology, renewed attention is being given to instructional technology in order for students with disabilities to gain access to the general education curriculum. In this section, we explore some specific examples of technology as it used in the teaching and learning of reading, writing, math, and study skills.

Integrating technology into reading. A characteristic associated with many disabilities is difficulty in learning how to read and developing grade-level reading skills (Chard & Bos, 1999; Dannehl & Rodhouse, 1999; Prochaska, 1999; Richards, 1998; Swanson, 1999). As a result, special education teachers tend to devote a great deal of time and energy to the teaching of reading and are likely to use a variety of software products to remediate students' reading abilities.

Software products such as *Bailey's Book House* (Edmark), *FirstWords* (Laureate Learning Systems), *JumpStart Kindergarten Reading* (Knowledge Adventure), *Reader Rabbit* (Learning Company), and *Simon Sounds It Out* (Don Johnston) are commonly used in classrooms where emergent readers are working on acquiring specific skills as well as appreciation of reading.

Increasingly, CD ROM-based multimedia books are available to engage students in reading on the computer and to provide reading support (e.g., text-to-speech to read individual words or a whole page, comprehension checks, prereading activities). Examples of products that have been demonstrated as effective for students struggling in reading include *Arthur's Teacher Trouble,* part of the Living Books series (Learning Company), *Reading Realities* (Teacher Support Software), and *Start-to-Finish Books* (Don Johnston).

In addition to direct instruction on reading, special education teachers must often make decisions about compensatory reading interventions. These types of tools are provided to students in recognition that they may not have the decoding abilities to read grade-level text materials but they can comprehend the material. Specific text-to-speech products that help students with disabilities include *CAST eReader* (CAST), the Quicktionary Reading Pen (WizCom) (see Figure 15.3), and L&H Kurzweil 3000 (Lernout & Hauspie Speech Products).

Integrating technology into writing. The use of technology to enhance writing is a topic previously discussed in this book. Nearly all of the instructional interventions described

Figure 15.3 Quicktionary Reading Pen

Scan a word with the Quicktionary Reading Pen to hear the word and see a definition.

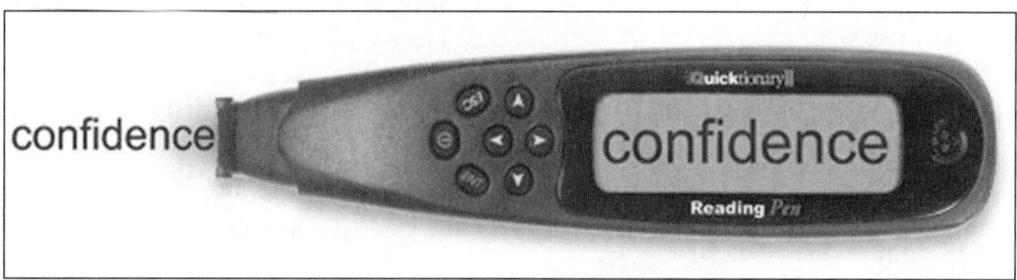

Source: Courtesy of WizCom Technologies.

Figure 15.4 *Co:Writer* Is an Example of a Word Prediction Word Processor

CoWriter

Swimming
My favorite thing to do in summer is to go swimming.

Co:Writer Demo Writer

I know how to s

1: see
2: swim
3: start
4: seem
5: say
6: send
7: stop
8: save

Source: *Co:Writer* is a copyright of Don Johnston Inc. To purchase this product, contact Don Johnston Inc., 1-800-999-4660; www.donjohnston.com.

Figure 15.5 *Write:OutLoud* Talking Word Processor

Write:OutLoud adds speech synthesis to a word processor so that users can listen to what they have written.

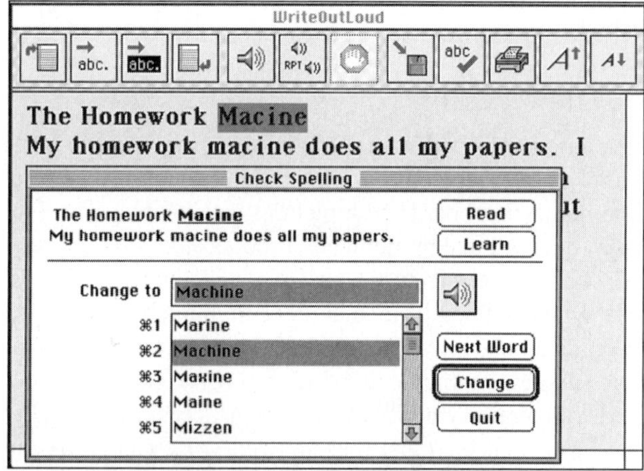

Source: *Write:OutLoud* is a copyright of Don Johnston Inc. To purchase this product, contact Don Johnston Inc., 1-800-999-4660; www.donjohnston.com.

in the previous sections are also applicable to students with disabilities. Indeed, a number of products (i.e., AlphaSmart, *Inspiration*) have extremely high market share in both special and general education.

Many tools have been developed to support students who struggle in various phases of the writing process. For students who are unable to write by hand, who have illegible handwriting, or find handwriting extremely tedious, voice recognition software (examples) may be an option. While the potential of voice recognition software is that users can dictate their written work to the computer rather than having to compose using the keyboard, in practice, many systems are challenging to use. Some students who are slow typists or have difficulty spelling can benefit from word prediction software (*Co:Writer,* Don Johnston) that attempts to complete a word as letters are entered. (See Figure 15.4.) Talking word processors (*Write:OutLoud,* Don Johnston) feature speech synthesis to allow students to hear what they have written. (See Figure 15.5.) WYNN (Freedom Scientific) is a specialized word processor that provides an array of support tools to students with learning disabilities.

Other products have been developed that alter the instructional context for writing. *Language Experience Recorder* (Teacher Support Software) is used by teachers to capture the oral language students use in describing events and stories and then save the information so it can be used as part of reading instruction. The process of writing and illustrating stories effectively engages students in the publishing aspect of writing and often serves to enhance written expression by allowing the students to engage in an extended prewriting activity as they create their picture and then write about it. *EasyBook Deluxe* (Sunburst Communications) and *Storybook Weaver* and *My Own Stories* (Learning Company) are examples of such writing software. *Hollywood High* (Theatrix Interactive) enables older students to write scripts that are acted out by animated characters.

An excellent introduction to the difficulties some students with disabilities experience relative to written expression have been outlined by Cheryl Wissick of the University of South Carolina as part of a *PowerPoint* presentation that has been published on the Internet (http://www.ed.sc.edu/caw/ldwrite/index.htm). This is a powerful and practical example of how *PowerPoint* can be used to change the format of written reports. Smith, Boone, and Higgins (1998) call attention to the power and potential of the web as a publication outlet for student writers.

Integrating technology into math. Technology integration in math seems to have been advanced by the early availability of calculators. Indeed, calculators are an important intervention for students with disabilities. Pellerito (2001) says that many formats are available: handheld, talking, computer based, and specialized. Figure 15.6 illustrates a specialized calculator, the *Coin-U-Lator®* (Programming Concepts, Inc.), that was developed to assist students having difficulty counting coins and making change.

Innovative instructional strategies have also been created to engage students with disabilities in mathematical thinking and problem solving. Anderson and Anderson (1999, 2001) review products like *The Graph Club, AppleWorks, ClarisWorks for Kids,* and *The Cruncher* to highlight specific spreadsheet and graphing functions that help students manipulate and visualize mathematical concepts. Symington and Stanger (2000) describe the development and evaluation of a series of products (*Number Concepts1, Number Concepts2, MathPad, Mathpad Plus: Fractions and Decimals*) specifically designed to make mathematics curricula accessible to students with disabilities. Christle, Hess, and Hasselbring (2001) report on innovative web-based development to enhance the mathematical problem-solving abilities of middle school students.

Figure 15.6 Coin-U-Lator®

The Coin-U-Lator is an example of a specialized calculator that helps students with disabilities when learning about coin values and counting money.

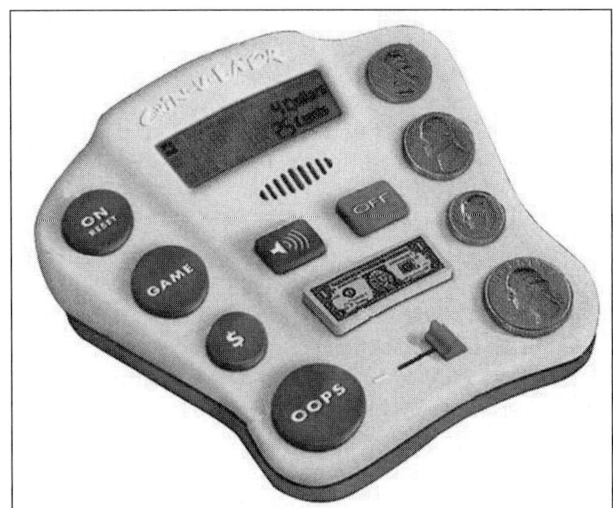

Source: Courtesy of Programming Concepts, Inc.

Enhancing Study Skills with Technology

One of the clearest findings from educational research focuses on the relationship between time on task and learning: Academic achievement is positively correlated with the amount of time students spend engaged in meaningful learning activities. As a result, one promising application of technology in special education involves the use of interactive study tools to assist, support, and engage students in relevant and challenging learning activities. Given that difficulties associated with study skills and homework are common among both students with and without disabilities (Anderson-Inman, Knox-Quinn, & Szymanski, 1999; Epstein, Munk, Bursuck, Polloway, & Jayanthi, 1999; Nelson, Epstein, Bursuck, Jayanthi, & Sawyer, 1998), the strategies and following technologies have widespread application for enhancing the academic achievement of all students.

Personal organizers. Many students experience organizational difficulties that negatively impact their school work. To address this challenge, some schools require all students to maintain a personal planner to track their homework assignments. Many types of personal planning systems are available and illustrate the lifelong importance of using an organizational system that enhances one's personal productivity. *DayRunner* (http://www.dayrunner.com) and *FranklinPlanner* (http://www.franklincovey.com) are but two examples. One of the trendiest applications of personal productivity technology is the Palm Pilot (http://www.palm.com). Palm users can carry this portable handheld device around and enter information with a stylus. At the end of the day, the information can be synchronized with a software version on the computer. When an individual has regular access to a computer, computer-based day planners such as *AnyDay* (http://www.anyday.com) or *My Yahoo!* (http://my.yahoo.com) may also be useful.

Study skill strategies. An important component of helping students improve their academic performance involves instruction on effective study skill strategies. A variety of web sites have been created that offer students access to a comprehensive collection of strategies, tools, and resources for fostering effective study skills. Notable examples include *The Study Strategies Home Page* from the University of Minnesota–Duluth (http://www.d.umn.edu/student/loon/acad/strat/) and *Study Guides and Strategies* from St. Thomas University (http://www.iss.stthomas.edu/studyguides/). Lynne Anderson-Inman has validated a series of computer-based study skill strategies for students with disabilities and made the high-quality materials available at her web site as downloadable resources (http://npip.com/CBSS/sampler.htm).

Study guides. One method that teachers can use to enhance the academic performance of all students is to create study guides that structure and focus students' attention on essential knowledge and skills. Of course, the tool of choice for this type of task is a word processor. However, software products like *BuildAbility* (Don Johnston) and

HyperStudio (http://www.hyperstudio.com) can also be used to create computer-based interactive study guides. Although initially time consuming to create, interactive study guides can be used with all students or just those who need it and these materials can be reused or modified with minimal time and energy.

Practice quizzes. This category of tools is especially promising for supporting inclusion. Teachers can create electronic quizzes that are correlated with a specific textbook reading (i.e., Chapter 8). The address of the quiz can be given to any student in need of the extra support. Quizzes are scored upon completion and teachers have the option of receiving notification of the results via e-mail. Talk about a time saver! Several popular, free, electronic quiz services include *QuizStar* (http://4teachers.org/), *Online Quiz Center* (http://motted.hawaii.edu), and *FunBrain* (http://funbrain.com).

An important process in many learning activities involves consulting reference sources. Naturally, this is where access to the World Wide Web is invaluable. Some popular ready reference sites include *Ask Jeeves for Kids* (http://www.ajkids.com) and *Online Calculators* (http://wwwsci.lib.uci.edu/HSG/RefCalculators.html). One interesting interface design can be found at http://lightspan.com. When users click on the *Study Scout* icon, a separate browser window is opened with icon access to a calculator, dictionary, thesaurus, encyclopedia, maps, and the *CIA World Fact Book.*

Homework help. A variety of web sites have been created especially to help students with their homework. A few personal favorites are listed here: *Yahoo! Reference* (http://dir.yahoo.com/reference/index.html), *StudyWEB* (http://www.studyweb.com/), *John December's List of Essential Resources* (http://www.december.com/cmc/info/), *Information Please* (http://www.infoplease.com/), *High School Hub* (http://www.highschoolhub.org/hub/hub.htm), *The Writer's Center: Resources for Writers and Teachers* (http://www.colostate.edu/depts/WritingCenter/tools.htm), *Alphabet Superhighway* (http://www.ash.udel.edu/ash), *Dave's Math Tables* (http://www.sisweb.com/math/tables.htm), and *Schoolwork.Org* (http://www.schoolwork.org/index.html).

Productivity Applications of Technology

An important strategy for improving educational outcomes focuses on enhancing the tools we provide to teachers. Although individual tools can be very valuable, we really need to be thinking about collections of tools (i.e., toolkits). The challenge of creating a toolkit to support the work of classroom teachers is a powerful technology integration strategy. Indeed, much of what students are able to accomplish, or not, is directly related to the competencies of their teachers. As a result, it is vital to develop technology toolkits that equip teachers with the tools necessary to support the diversity of student abilities found in inclusive classrooms.

When considering individual student needs, accommodations and modifications can be made in each of three areas: curriculum, instruction, and assessment. As a result, general and special education teachers are encouraged to explore how a few tools (i.e., word processor, e-mail, web browser, and presentation software) and specific productivity skills can be used to locate, create, or modify instructional methods or materials. (Also see Technology Integration Ideas 15.1 and 15.2.)

TECHNOLOGY INTEGRATION IDEA 15.1

Using Word Processing and Graphics to Help Meet Students' Special Needs

TITLE: Twenty Ideas for Using Technology to Meet Students' Special Needs

CONTENT AREA/TOPIC: Language arts: reading

GRADE LEVEL: 4–6

NETS FOR STUDENTS: Standards 3, 4

DESCRIPTION: Word processing and graphics can be used to create materials and support a variety of activities to meet the needs of students with limited English proficiency, sensory deficits, learning disabilities, or physical limitations. Twenty such ideas are described here. One is using large print for students with visual limitations. For these students, printing text in large type makes them better able to do activities with charts and signs. Some programs come with large-sized letter stickers for the keyboard to allow these students to use the word processor to support their writing. Other ideas include alphabet books, sentence strips, changed stories, predicting outcomes, rewritten endings, compound words, sequencing events, spoken stories, reading journals, selling stories, bookmarks, puppet faces, mobiles, illustrated stories and idioms, book jackets, cartoon makers, before and after charts, time lines, and story surveys.

Source: Schipper, D. (1991). Practical ideas: Literature, computers, and students with special needs. *The Computing Teacher, 19*(2), 33–37.

TECHNOLOGY INTEGRATION IDEA 15.2

Using Multimedia to Help Meet Students' Special Needs

TITLE: Using Technology to Meet Special Needs

CONTENT AREA/TOPIC: Language arts: reading

GRADE LEVEL: 4–6

NETS FOR STUDENTS: Standards 3, 4, 6

DESCRIPTION: Many adolescents with learning disabilities are highly motivated to get their driver's license, but have difficulty with the written portion. This activity lets students use multimedia development software to create a guide that will help them study for this exam. Not only does the activity help them with language and study skills, it helps them use computers in a way that empowers them, instead of merely drilling or tutoring them. Divide the class into pairs of students, and give each a portion of the total booklet to analyze and present in the product. Students who are nonreaders or who have very low reading levels are paired with those who are better readers. When the entire product is completed, students present it to other classes and use it to study for the driver's examination.

Source: Speziale, M., and La France, L. (1992). Multimedia and students with learning disabilities. *The Computing Teacher, 20*(3), 31–34.

Integrating Technology into Professional Development

A common characteristic of special education technology service delivery involves the use of interdisciplinary teams to evaluate the need for assistive technology. Given the diverse backgrounds, teams seldom have an extensive shared knowledge base. As a result, many technology teams engage in ongoing professional development in order to enhance their collaborative problem-solving abilities.

Products like *The GATE* (Orcca Technology) provide an introduction to the role and function of each member of an interdisciplinary assistive technology team. This CD-ROM product is useful for new and experienced teams to periodically review their working relationships. Teams also have an ongoing need to identify exemplary training materials that can be used with teachers and parents. Interesting examples include *Assistive Technology Viewer,* a visual introduction to assistive technology (http://natri.uky.edu) and the *Family Guide to Assistive Technology,* an online textbook designed for parents (http://www/pluk.org/AT1.html).

Increasingly, teams are finding that distance education provides a flexible means to participate in high-quality professional development. One of the leading providers of assistive technology online courses is the Special Needs Opportunities Windows (SNOW) project from the University of Toronto (http://snow.utoronto.ca).

Technology Applications for Gifted and Talented Students

Heward (2000) says that, according to the Gifted and Talented Children's Act of 1978, gifted and talented students are those "possessing demonstrated or potential abilities that give evidence of high performance capability in such areas as intellectual, creative, specific academic or leadership ability, or in the performing or visual arts, and why by reason thereof require services or activities not ordinarily provided by the school (PL 95;-561, Title IX, Section 902)" (p. 534).

The primary issue surrounding and shaping education for gifted students is how to identify students who merit these special "services or activities not ordinarily provided by the school." Heward gives a comprehensive discussion of these issues and describes criteria schools use to identify students who qualify as gifted and talented.

Heward (2000) also observes that "... the increasingly sophisticated use of technological tools and related methods will provide gifted students with greater connectivity and independence in the future" (p. 572). Citing work by Howell (1994), he finds that technology integration for gifted and talented students should revolve primarily around three strategies (p. 572):

- **Electronic communities.** Communicating with people from distant and differing cultures and languages encourages and provides new avenues for expression.
- **Database research.** Using global resources (e.g., on the Internet) to research topics allows gifted students to explore ideas and events more quickly and in greater depth.
- **Interactive and multimedia presentations.** Developing presentations based on their research allows students to display their discoveries in ways that make them more independent learners.

Finally, when gifted students engage in cooperative group work on products such as web sites and multimedia presentations, they are working in a motivational environment in which they can learn important social skills required for them to be effective and productive in the world of work.

Useful Web Sites for Special Education

General Sites

The American Association on Mental Retardation

http://www.aamr.org/

American Foundation for the Blind

http://www.afb.org/

Autism Resources

http://web.syr.edu/~jmwobus/autism/

The Behavior Home Page

http://www.state.ky.us/agencies/behave/homepage.html

Children and Adults with Attention Deficit Disorder (CHADD)

http://www.chadd.org

Deaf World

http://www.deafworldweb.org/

Gifted Resources Home Page

http://www.eskimo.com/~user/kids.html

LD Online

http://www.ldonline.org

Net Connections for Communication Disorders and Sciences

http://www.mankato.msus.edu/dept/comdis/kuster2/welcome.html

Special Education Resources in Spanish

http://paidos.rediris.es/needirectorio/index.html

Disability Information Web Sites

Disability Resources Monthly (DRM) Guide to Disability Resources on the Internet

http://www.disabilityresources.org/

A huge collection of disability web links is maintained in an easy-to-use format by an authoritative organization, *Disability Resources Monthly.*

Complete Disability Network

http://members.aol.com/disablenet/Main/DisableNet.html

This network is operated by people with disabilities for people with disabilities; more than 1,000 pages and over 5,000 links.

The Cornucopia of Disability Information

http://codi.buffalo.edu/

Provides a comprehensive collection of links to disability web sites.

LD Online

http://www.ldonline.org

An award-winning site concerning learning disabilities; useful for children, parents, and teachers.

Accessibility Web Sites

WebAble!

http://www.webable.com

This is an authoritative site for hundreds of Internet-based resources on accessibility and disability-related resources.

Designing a More Usable World—For All

http://www.trace.wisc.edu/world/

This document outlines a vision for designing environments that are functional, effective, and accessible for everyone.

Microsoft's Accessibility and Disability Home Page

http://www.microsoft.com/enable/

Provides news and information about accessibility as well as Microsoft accessibility products.

Apple Computer's Disability Home Page

http://www.apple.com/education/k12/disability/

Provides information about Macintosh accessibility features as well as links to third-party developers, news, and resources.

Assistive Technology Information Web Sites

Careers in Assistive Technology

http://www.infinitec.org/assistechcareer.html

Provides basic descriptions of several career options for work involving assistive technology and individuals with disabilities.

Closing the Gap

http://www.closingthegap.com/

This organization focuses on computer technology for people with special needs through its bimonthly newspaper, annual international conference, and extensive web site.

National Assistive Technology Advocacy Project

http://www.nls.org/natmain.htm

Provides a variety of resources advocating for the acquisition and use of assistive technology.

RESNA TA Project

http://www.resna.org/taproject/index.html

This is the web site for the technical assistance project supporting the Tech Act projects in each state. Browse the links for the state contacts to locate information on the Tech Act project in your state.

Instructional Technology Materials Web Sites

IntelliTools Activity Exchange

http://www.intellitools.com

Search for ready-to-use teacher-made materials that utilize IntelliTools products; download the files and you are ready to use the materials with your students.

Toolboxes and QuickStarts for Special Education

http://www.ed.sc.edu/caw/toolbox.html

Created and maintained by Cheryl Wissick at the University of South Carolina, this page profiles a variety of technology integration strategies and resources for teachers and students.

EduHound

http://www.eduhound.com

This megasite provides links for teachers who want to use technology to enhance instruction.

Legal Issues and Policies Web Sites

Assistive Technology Resource Manual

http://www.isbe.net/assistive/index.html

This is an easy-to-use and comprehensive electronic publication created by the Illinois State Board of Education concerning assistive technology.

IDEA Practices

http://www.ideapractices.org/

This technical assistance site supports the efforts of teachers and administrators implementing IDEA'97.

Disability Related Issues—A Web Pathfinder for Student Research

http://www.disrights.org/guide/research.html

This site focuses on researching disability-related issues on the World Wide Web and organizes resource links by search strategy and topic.

Sites for Gifted Education

National Association for Gifted Children

http://www.nagc.org

This is the web site of the professional association for teachers of gifted and talented students.

The National Research Center on the Gifted and Talented

http://www.gifted.uconn.edu/

Web site of an organization sponsored by the U.S. Department of Education to support research and development in gifted education.

Exercises

Record and apply what you have learned.

Chapter 15 Self-Test

To review terms and concepts in this chapter, take the Chapter 15 self-test. Select Chapter 15 from the front page of the Companion Website (located at http://www.prenhall.com/roblyer), then choose the *Multiple Choice* module.

Portfolio Activities

ISTE The following activities address ISTE National Educational Technology Standards for Teachers (NETS-T) and will help you add to your professional portfolio. To complete these activities online and save or submit the materials electronically, select Chapter 15 from the front page of the Companion Website (http://www.prenhall.com/roblyer), then choose the *Portfolio* module.

1. ***Information Presentation (NETS-T Standards: I-B; II-B, C; V-B, D; VI-B)*** Select a specific disability and use the web sites named in this chapter to obtain information about its characteristics and how to meet the special learning needs of students who have this disability. Prepare a short *PowerPoint* presentation for parents and teachers to give a summary of your findings. Place it in your personal portfolio.

2. ***Resources for Various Disabilities (NETS-T Standards: II-A, B, C; III-B; V-B, D; VI-B)*** Using the *Closing the Gap Resource Guide* (http://www.closingthegap.com) and *AbleData* (http://www.abledata.com) reference systems, identify assistive technology products that may be potentially useful for one of the students described below. Prepare a word-processed summary or web page summary of these resources. Place the file or URL and web page description in your personal portfolio.

   - Student whose handwriting is not legible
   - Student whose vision prevents him from reading text that is smaller than 48 points
   - Student who needs an alternative to the standard keyboard
   - Student who needs to have the text on the screen read aloud

3. ***Professional Development Plan (NETS-T Standards: I-B, C; V-A)*** A commitment to engage in ongoing professional development is critical for professionals working in the area of special education technology. Access the following web sites given in this chapter and create a word-processed professional development plan that outlines organizations you could join, conferences you could attend, and other possibilities for maintaining a high degree of current awareness

concerning developments in special education technology. Place the plan in your personal portfolio.

- **Council for Exceptional Children (CEC):** http://www. cec.sped.org
- **Technology and Media (TAM) Division of CEC:** http:// www.tam.cec.org
- **Special Education Technology Special Interest Group (SETSIG):** web address pending ISTE assignment
- **Closing the Gap:** http://www.closingthegap.com
- **California State University Northridge:** http://www. csun.edu/cod/
- **Special Education Technology Practice Conference Calendar:** http://www.setp.net/ConfCal.html

Questions for Thought and Discussion

These questions may be used for small-group or class discussion or may be subjects for individual or group activities. To take part in these discussions online, select Chapter 15 from the front page of the Companion Website (http://www.prenhall.com/roblyer), then choose the *Message Board* module.

1. Give your reaction to the comment below. Does much of the software used today actually stunt creativity? How does this statement relate to special education populations?

   > Many teachers stress that with technology, the student will get the right answer, faster. The obsession with getting the right answer and producing high results on quantitative tests could result in severe reduction in the willingness for the student or the teacher to be creative. Creativity calls for a willingness to make mistakes or to produce results that lie outside the estimated norms. While there is software which encourages students to use their imagination, most of it emphasizes there is only one right answer. How can teachers encourage alternative, creative ways to arrive at a solution, when the equipment the students employ will only tolerate the most direct answer? (Vertrees & Beard, 1997, p. 34)

2. The quote below espouses an optimistic view on the influences that assistive technology will have on children with disabilities. What evidence can you cite to support this position? What do you think those on the other side of the issue would say?

   > Although there are many arguments on both sides of the issue, it is apparent that new technologies can provide the tools to bring more children with disabilities into "regular" educational settings. In my opinion, assistive technology will certainly mainstream more and more children in wheelchairs, children who cannot physically speak, see, or hear, and children who need computers to write, organize, think, and function educationally. (Behrmann, 1998, p. 81)

Collaborative Activities

The following activities address ISTE National Educational Technology Standards for Teachers (NETS-T) and can be done in small groups. Each group should present the findings to the class in a format they know how to use (word-processed report, presentation software, multimedia product). Completed group products can be copied and shared with the entire class or included in each person's personal portfolio.

1. ***Develop a Resource Guide for Parents (NETS-T Standards: I-B; II-A; III-B; V-B, D; VI-B)*** Parents with children with special needs often seek the counsel of teachers regarding technology purchases they can make at home to support the education progress of their child. Explore the following resources and compile a word-processed or web page resource guide that you could share with parents to assist them in learning more about assistive technology. Divide the task so that each person in the group prepares a part of the resource guide.

   - Alliance for Technology Access. (2000). *Computer resources for people with disabilities* (3rd ed.). Alameda, CA: Hunter House.
   - Alliance for Technology Access: http://www.ataccess.org
   - DREAMMS for Kids: http://www.dreamms.org
   - Family Village: http://www.familyvillage.wisc.edu/
   - Parents Helping Parents: http://www.php.com/
   - The Sibling Support Project: http://www.chmc.org/departmt/sibsupp/

2. ***Bibliography of Research on Disabilities (NETS-T Standards: I-B; II-B; V-A, B; VI-B)*** Visit the online version of the *Journal of Special Education Technology* (http://jset.unlv.edu). Explore the tables and appendix in the literature synthesis articles in issue 15–1 (1999 in review. . .) or 16–2 (2000 in review. . .). Create a bibliography of articles on a topic or disability and prepare an annotated bibliography on a topic or disability.
3. ***Annotated Listing of Assistive Technology Sites (NETS-T Standards: I-B; II-B; V-A, B; VI-B)*** Visit the *Closing the Gap Essential Bookmark Collection for Assistive Technology Coordinators* site (http://www.closingthegap.com; click on the Bookmarks link). Review the purpose of the project, the categorization system used to store helpful links for assistive technology coordinators, and visit selected sites within three or more categories. Select and describe the most valuable sites you discovered.

 Integrating Technology Across the Curriculum Activities

The *Integrating Technology Across the Curriculum* CD-ROM is a set of technology integration ideas and links to online lessons, arranged as a searchable database. The CD comes packaged with this textbook. Complete the following exercise using this CD:

Review some of the example integration ideas on the CD cited in this chapter for special education. Now make up a technology integration idea of your own matched to an integration strategy described in this chapter. Add it to the CD. Be sure to identify each of the descriptors for it, including the relative advantage.

References

Anderson, C. L., & Anderson, K. M. (1999). Integrating spreadsheets into mathematics for students with disabilities. *Special Education Technology Practice, 1*(4), 37–39.

Anderson, C. L., & Anderson, K. M. (2001). Using software to help visualize mathematical processes. *Special Education Technology Practice, 3*(2), 13–18.

Anderson-Inman, L., Knox-Quinn, C., & Szymanski, M. (1999). Computer-supported studying: Stories of successful transition to postsecondary education. *Career Development for Exceptional Individuals, 22,* 185–212.

Anneberg Institute of School Reform. (1999). *Tools for accountability.* Available online: http://www.aisr.brown.edu/accountability/toolbox/default.html.

Behrmann, M. (1998). Assistive technology for young children in special education. *Association for Supervision and Curriculum Development Yearbook,* 73–93.

Blackhurst, A. E. (1997). Perspectives on technology in special education. *Teaching Exceptional Children, 29*(5), 41–48.

Blackhurst, A. E., & Edyburn, D. L. (2000). A brief history of special education technology. *Special Education Technology Practice, 2*(1), 21–36.

Browder, D. M., & Grasso, E. (1999). Teaching money skills to individuals with mental retardation: A research review with practical applications. *Remedial and Special Education, 20,* 297–308.

CEO Forum. (1999). *CEO Forum STaR chart.* Available online: http://www.ceoforum.org

Chambers, A. C. (1997). *Has technology been considered? A guide for IEP teams.* Reston, VA: CASE/TAM Assistive Technology Policy and Practice Group.

Chard, D. J., & Bos, C. S. (1999). Moving from research to practice: Professional development to promote effective teaching of early reading. *Learning Disabilities Research and Practice, 14,* 189–267.

Christle, C. A., Hess, J. M., & Hasselbring, T. S. (2001). Technology research in practice: Taking a virtual trip to the mall to learn math. *Special Education Technology Practice, 3*(2), 23–31.

Cochran, P. S. (2000). Technology for individuals with speech and language disorders. In J. D. Lindsey (Ed.), *Technology and exceptional individuals* (3rd ed., pp. 303–325). Austin, TX: ProEd.

Cook, A. M., & Hussey, S. M. (1995). *Assistive technologies: Principles and practice.* St. Louis, MO: Mosby.

Dannehl, L., & Rodhouse, A. (1999). Literacy software for children with disabilities. *Closing the Gap, 18*(4), 6–7, 38–39.

Dolan, B. (2000). Universal design for learning. *Journal of Special Education Technology, 15*(4), 44–51.

Easterbrooks, S. (1999). Improving practices for students with hearing impairments. *Exceptional Children, 65,* 537–554.

Edyburn, D. L. (2000). Assistive technology and students with mild disabilities. *Focus on Exceptional Children, 32*(9), 1–24.

Edyburn, D. L. (2001). Technology integration strategies: Universal design and technology integration, finding the connections. *Closing the Gap, 20*(1), 21–22.

Epstein, M. H., Munk, D. D., Bursuck, W. D., Polloway, E. A., & Jayanthi, M. (1999). Strategies for improving home–school communication about homework for students with disabilities. *Journal of Special Education, 33,* 166–176.

Fennema-Jansen, S. (2001). Measuring effectiveness: Technology to support writing. *Special Education Technology Practice, 3*(1), 16–22.

Fisher, S. K., & Gardner, J. E. (1999). Introduction to technology in transition. *Career Development for Exceptional Individuals, 22,* 131–151.

Fuchs, D., & Fuchs, L. (1991). Framing the REI debate: Abolitionists versus conservationalists. In J. W. Lloyd, N. N. Singh, & A. C. Repp (Eds.), *The regular education initiative: Alternative perspectives on concepts, issues, and models* (pp. 241–255). Sycamore, IL: Sycamore Publishing Company.

Golden, D. (1998). *Assistive technology in special education: Policy and practice.* Reston, VA: CASE/TAM Assistive Technology Policy and Practice Group.

Grogan, D., & Ruzic, R. (2000). Walking the walk: Universal design on the web. *Journal of Special Education Technology, 15*(3), 45–49.

Heward, W. (2000). *Exceptional children: An introduction to special education.* (6th ed.) Upper Saddle River, NJ: Prentice Hall.

Howell, R. D. (1994). Technological innovations in the education of gifted and talented students. In J. L. Genschaft, M. Mirely, & C. L Hollinger (Eds.), *Serving gifted and talented students.* Austin, TX: PRO-ED.

Hutinger, P. L., & Clark, L. (2000). TEChPLACEs: An Internet community for young children, their teachers, and their families. *Teaching Exceptional Children, 32*(4), 56–63.

Individuals with Disabilities Education Act, 20 U.S.C., § 1400 *et seq.* (1997).

Kauffman, J. M. (1989). The regular education initiative as Regan–Bush education policy: A trickle-down theory of education for the hard-to-teach. *Journal of Special Education, 23*(3), 256–278.

King, T. W. (1999). *Assistive technology: Essential human factors.* Boston: Allyn & Bacon.

Lahm, E. A. (2000). Special education technology: Defining the specialist. *Special Education Technology Practice, 2*(3), 22–27.

Lahm, E. A., & Nickels, B. L. (1999). What do you know? Assistive technology competencies for special educators. *Teaching Exceptional Children, 32*(1), 56–63.

Mechling, L., & Langone, J. (2000). The effects of computer-based instructional program with video anchors on the use of photographs for prompting augmentative communication. *Education and Training in Mental Retardation and Developmental Disabilities, 35*(1), 90–105.

Meese, R. L. (2001). *Teaching learners with mild disabilities: Integrating research and practice.* Belmont, CA: Wadsworth/Thomson Learning.

Meyen, E. L., & Skrtic, T. M. (1995). *Special education and student disability.* Denver, CO: Love Publishing.

Milken Family Foundation. (1999). *Milken exchange indicators.* Available online: http://www.mff.org/edtech/.

Nelson, J. S., Epstein, M. H., Bursuck, W. D., Jayanthi, M., & Sawyer, V. (1998). The preferences of middle school students for homework adaptations made by general education teachers. *Learning Disabilities Research and Practice, 13*(2), 109–117.

Orkwis, R., & McLane, K. (1998). *A curriculum every student can use: Design principles for student access. OSEP topical brief.* Reston, VA: Council for Exceptional Children. Also available online: http://www.cec.sped.org/osep/udsign.htm.

Pellerito, F. (2001). Go figure: Calculator options for students with special needs. *Special Education Technology Practice, 3*(2), 19–22.

Prochaska, R. (1999). Access to literacy instruction in inclusive settings. *Closing the Gap, 18*(3), 1, 10–11.

QIAT Consortium. (2001). Quality indicators for assistive technology services. *Special Education Technology Practice, 3*(1), 14–15.

RESNA. (2001). Web site about the 21 training programs. Available online: http://www.resna.org.

Richards, R. T. (1998). Linking standards and technology with students who experience reading difficulties. *Reading Improvement, 35*(4), 197–200.

Rose, D. (2000). Universal design for learning. *Journal of Special Education Technology, 15*(1), 67–70.

Rose, D., Sethuraman, S., & Meo, G. J. (2000). Universal design for learning. *Journal of Special Education Technology, 15*(2), 56–60.

SEIR•TEC. (1999). *SEIR•TEC technology integration progress gauge.* Available online: http://www.seirtec.org/publications/guage6_0.doc.

Smith, R. O. (2000). Measuring assistive technology outcomes in education. *Diagnostique, 25*(4), 307–325.

Smith, S., Boone, R., & Higgins, K. (1998). Expanding the writing process to the web. *Teaching Exceptional Children, 30*(5), 22–26.

Stainback, W., & Stainback, S. (1984). A rationale for the merger of special and regular education. *Exceptional Children, 51*(1), 102–111.

Swanson, H. L. (1999). Reading research for students with LD: A meta-analysis of intervention outcomes. *Journal of Learning Disabilities, 32,* 504–532.

Symington, L., & Stanger, C. (2000). Math = Success: New inclusionary math software programs add up to a brighter future. *Teaching Exceptional Children, 32*(4), 28–33.

U.S. Department of Education. (2000). *Twenty-second annual report to Congress on the implementation of the Individuals with Disabilities Eduation Act.* Washington, DC: Author. Available online: httl://www.ed.gov/offices/OSERS/OSEP/OSEP2000AnlRpt/.

Vertrees, D. R., & Beard, L. A. (1997). Special education technology: . . . And then what? *The Florida Technology in Education Quarterly, 9*(2), 26–36.

Wang, M. C., & Walberg, H. J. (1988). Four fallacies of segregationism. *Exceptional Children, 55*(2), 128–137.

Wissick, C. A. (1999a). Quickstarts: Developing functional literacy skills around food. *Special Education Technology Practice, 1*(3), 22–25.

Wissick, C. A. (1999b). Quickstarts: Let's go grocery shopping. *Special Education Technology Practice, 1*(4), 33–36.

Wissick, C. A., Gardner, J. E., & Langone, J. (1999). Video-based simulations: Considerations for teaching students with developmental disabilities. *Career Development for Exceptional Individuals, 22*(2), 233–249.

Zabala, J. S. (2000). *Joy Zabala's resources for assistive technology in education.* Available online: http://sac.uky.edu/~jszaba).JoyZabala.html.

Zabala, J. S., & Korsten, J. E. (1999). *Beyond "try it! you'll like it. . .or maybe you won't?": Making a measurable difference with assistive technology.* Preconference workshop handout. 1999 Closing the Gap Conference, Minneapolis, MN.

Resources

32 Message Communicator (Enabling Devices)
AlphaSmart (AlphaSmart, Inc.)
AlphaTalker II (Prentke-Romich)
AppleWorks (Apple Computer)
Arthur's Teacher Trouble, part of the Living Books series (Learning Company)
Boardmaker (Mayer-Johnson)
BuildAbility (Don Johnston)
CAST eReader (CAST)
ClarisWorks for Kids (Apple Computer)
Coin-U-Lator® (Programming Concepts, Inc.)
Co:Writer 4000 (Don Johnston)
The Cruncher (Knowledge Adventure)
EasyBook Deluxe (Sunburst)
Edmark Early Learning series (Edmark)
FirstWords (Laureate Learning Systems)

The GATE (ORCCA Technology)
The Graph Club (Tom Snyder Communications)
Hal Screen Reader (Dolphin Computer Access)
Hollywood High (Theatrix)
Home Page Reader for Windows (IBM Special Needs Systems)
HyperStudio (Knowledge Adventure)
IBM SpeechViewer III for Windows (IBM Special Needs Systems)
Inspiration (Inspiration Software)
IntelliKeys (IntelliTools)
JAWS for Windows (Freedom Scientific)
JumpStart Kindergarten Reading, Preschool and Pre-K (Knowledge Adventure)
Kid Pix (Broderbund)
Language Experience Recorder (Teacher Support Software)
L&H Kurzweil 3000 (Lernout & Hauspie Speech Products)
MathPad, Mathpad Plus: Fractions and Decimals (IntelliTools)
My Own Stories (Learning Company)
Number Concepts1 (IntelliTools)
Number Concepts2 (IntelliTools)
One-Step Communicator 20 (AbleNet)
OutSPOKEN (Alva Access Group)
Quicktionary Reading Pen (WizCom Technologies)
Reader Rabbit (Learning Co.)
Reading Realities (Teacher Support Software)
Scan and Read Pro (Premier Programming Solutions)
Simon Sounds It Out (Don Johnston)
Start-to-Finish Books (Don Johnston)
Stickybear's Early Learning Activities (Optimum Resources)
Storybook Weaver (Learning Company)
Switches (AbleNet)
Ultimate 8 (TASH)
Vantage (Prentke-Romich)
Write:OutLoud (Don Johnston)
WYNN (Freedom Scientific)

APPENDIX

Technology Assessment Instruments

This Appendix contains rubrics and checklists to help teachers assess their uses of technology in the classroom. Each instrument has been selected as the best and most useful of its kind. The following are included in this Appendix:

Figure A.1 Rubric for Assessing School/District Technology Plans (Kimball & Sibley, 1998)

Criteria	1	2	3	4
Broad-Based Support Contributions (Administration, Teachers, Students, Community, Staff)	A list of contributors is not provided.	A list of contributors is provided but does not describe their constituencies. Equitable representation is not apparent because of a lack of detail.	A comprehensive list of contributors describes their constituencies. Representation is provided by at least three of the objectives' five areas. The principal is included.	A comprehensive list of contributors describes their constituencies. Representation is across all five areas of the objective. The principal is included.
Broad-Based Support Process	No process for equitable representation is described.	The process to ensure equitable representation is briefly mentioned, not emphasized.	[blank in copy]	The process to ensure equitable representation is emphasized and mentioned in detail.
Breadth of Needs Assessment	A needs assessment is not provided.	A needs assessment is referenced but covers only one element of the school environment (equipment or staff development, but not both).	A needs assessment is referenced and more than one element is analyzed, but it does not completely assess staff, student, and community needs.	The needs assessment is comprehensive and consists of detailed information about staff-development needs and competencies, attitudinal surveys, equipment inventories, and school and district context.
Depth of Needs Assessment	Broad generalizations are made about what the school needs but without reference to an assessment.	A needs assessment is referenced, but the instrument is informal, brief, and not specific. For example, a computer count is provided without details on where or how they are used.	A needs assessment is referenced with some level of detail, although the instrument and data are not provided and additional detail may be needed on collection and analysis.	The assessment in any given area is detailed and thorough. The instrument and generalizations about the data are provided. Raw data may be included in an appendix.
Needs Assessment of Equipment	No equipment inventory is provided.	An inventory exists only for computers and without indicating vintage.	The inventory moves beyond computers to include phones and television, but it does not address infrastructure or equipment vintage.	A comprehensive equipment inventory includes computers, infrastructure, access, interactive television, telephones, and other equipment.
Mission and Vision	No clear mission or vision is articulated.	Vision is skill-based only and does not address larger school or district outcomes.	Vision focuses on technology outcomes and avoids presenting a learning outcome.	Vision is comprehensive and deals with large learning outcomes of students, not just technology outcomes. The statement identifies the learning process skills and values.
Goals and Objectives	General learning goals are unclear or absent.	Goals are equipment-based instead of based on learning outcomes. Objectives are unlinked to goals or absent. Objectives or goals are neither measurable nor obtainable.	Goals are broad and comprehensive but not completely clear. They are linked to objectives but are not readily obtainable or measurable. Goals are loosely tied to state or district documents.	Goals are broad and comprehensive, addressing teaching and learning needs, as well as being clear, attainable, and measurable. Objectives are delineated from goals and further define how they will be met.
Action Plans with Timelines. Responsibilities, and Budgets	An action plan exists, but timelines and responsibilities are nonexistent or limited. Assessment is not mentioned. The plan is not curriculum-based.	The action plan is tied specifically to the goals and objectives, although identified task, timeline, responsibility, funding, and assessment are incomplete and several elements are missing.	The action plan is tied specifically to the goals and objectives. Identified task, timeline, responsibility, funding, and assessment components are thorough, although one or more elements are missing.	The action plan is tied specifically to goals and objectives. Each task identifies a task, timeline, responsibility, funding, and assessment.

Figure A.1 Continued

Criteria	1	2	3	4
Program Integration	The document never mentions connections with other efforts.	The TUP mentions other efforts but is not explicit in connecting with them.	The TUP is loosely coupled to other documents and needs, and program changes are integrated much of the time.	The TUP is tightly coupled to the other reform, curriculum, or accountability documents, with the approach fully integrated.
Curriculum Integration	The plan focuses on technology outcomes and skill-based goals, and does not address how it can enhance curriculum.	The plan mentions curriculum integration and enhancement but lacks detail.	The plan specifically identifies how the curriculum can be enhanced by the use of technology with detail. A technology-rich environment is described, but strategies for enhanced teaching are not explored thoroughly.	The plan specifically identifies not only how technology enhances the curriculum, but also what a student using the technology may do in such an environment. The plan addresses strategies of teaching and learning that can be enhanced as a result of technology integration.
Evaluation	No formal evaluation is described.	An evaluation process is described but without detail, comprehensiveness, or reference to learning outcomes.	An evaluation process and instrument are described in detail, but without comprehensiveness. Links to goals and objectives are not apparent.	An evaluation process and instrument are described in detail and are comprehensive in nature. Evaluation is timely and tied to objectives.
Multiyear Planning	A timeline is not mentioned.	The plan covers only one academic year or project.	The plan covers more than one year but is short-term in nature and does not refer to ongoing planning and support.	The plan is multiyear and shows its links to multiyear funding, support, and planning activities.
Standards	The document does not mention equipment or software standards beyond brand names.	Equipment standards are mentioned but not well specified.	Equipment standards are specific but narrow in scope.	Equipment standards are specific and comprehensive, and a process describes how they will be used.
Funding Alternatives	Funding resources are not mentioned.	Funding is mentioned, but it primarily focuses on budgeting or specific site funding without addressing other income needed to implement the plan.	Specific funding sources are described but limited to traditional sources and without specific budget figures.	Specific funding sources are described, including current and future funding sources; it also includes information on reallocation and use of resources and budget figures.
School Pilot Projects (Research and Development)	No R&D projects are mentioned or planned as part of the project.	R&D efforts are mentioned but lack detail. No timelines, assessments, or scalabilities are mentioned.	Specific R&D efforts are described, but scalability is not articulated. Timelines and measurements are mentioned but are not specific.	Specific R&D efforts are described, with implications for future work (scalability) articulated. The R&D efforts have a timeline and measurable instruments in place.
Educational Research	No educational research is mentioned as part of the project.	Educational research is only broadly mentioned.	Specific educational research is mentioned but without connections to school efforts.	Specific educational research is mentioned and connections are made to school efforts.
Model Classroom Configurations	No classroom or school configurations are described.	Classroom configurations are mentioned but lack detail. (e.g., "there will be three computers and a printer in each room").	Classroom configurations are described in detail but may be restrictive as the "only" right way; typically, only one type of configuration is described.	Classroom and school configurations are specifically described with links to teaching and learning outcomes. They are provided as possible solutions to particular problems but are not prescriptive in nature.

Figure A.1 Continued

Criteria	1	2	3	4
Facilities (Electricity, Security, etc.)	Facilities issues are not mentioned.	Facilities issues are mentioned but lack enough detail to build into an action plan.	Facilities issues are identified and articulated, but solutions and suggestions lack detail or clarity.	Specific facility issues are identified, addressed, and include recommended solutions, budgets, and responsibilities.
Maintenance and Support	No maintenance and support are provided.	Support plans are mentioned but without enough detail or clarity to implement.	Support plans are mentioned with clarity and detail but do not consider long-term issues.	Specific support plans are articulated. This included the process for specific support issues and ongoing equipment replacement, staff development, and repair.
Software Agreements (Site Licensing and Policies)	No software agreements or policies are mentioned.	Software agreements and policies are mentioned, but specifics are not articulated in the plan.	Specific software policy is articulated but not tied to site needs.	Specific software policy is articulated and plans are given for accommodating software needs at the site.
Copyright and Acceptable-Use Policy	No copyright or acceptable-use policy is described.	Copyright and acceptable use are mentioned, but the plan does not articulate specific policies.	[blank in copy]	Copyright and acceptable-use policies are articulated in the document, and samples are available.
Gifts and Disposal	No policy is provided for disposing of and receiving gifts of equipment and services.	Policy is provided but is not clear or articulated.	Specific policy is articulated about disposal and gifts, but it is not tied to the standards.	Specific policy is articulated about moving and disposing of equipment. Gift acceptance is tied directly to standards.
Staff Development	The document does not mention staff development.	Staff development is mentioned but not clearly articulated as to its accomplishment or evaluation.	Staff development is articulated but limited to single modalities and is not clearly supported by resources.	Staff development is addressed either in the action plan or in a separate section. It includes multiple strategies, incentives, and resources.

Source: Rubric for Technology Plan Analysis from Kimball, C., & Sibley, P. (1998). Am I on the mark? Technology planning for the E-rate. *Learning and Leading with Technology, 25*(4), pp. 56–57.

Figure A.2 Rubric for Assessing Cooperative Group Work (Truett, 2001)

Cooperative Group Rubric

Student Name ______________________

Date ______________________

	Beginning 1	*Developing 2*	*Focused 3*	*Exemplary 4*
Contribution to group				
Is punctual	Doesn't hand in assignments.	Hands in many assignments late.	Hands in most assignments on time.	Hands in all assignments on time.
Researches information	Does not collect information.	Contributes little information.	Contributes information that mainly relates.	Contributes a good deal of relevant information.
Shares information	Shares no information with group.	Shares some information with the group.	Shares important information with the group.	Communicates and shares all information with the group.
Cooperation within group				
Cooperates with group members	Never cooperates.	Seldom cooperates.	Usually cooperates.	Always cooperates.
Listens to group members	Always talks and never allows others to speak.	Talks much of the time and rarely allows others to speak.	Talks too much at times, but usually is a good listener.	Balances listening and speaking well.
Makes fair decisions	Always wants things his or her way.	Often sides with friends and doesn't consider all viewpoints.	Usually considers all viewpoints.	Total team player.
Responsibility to group members				
Fulfills duties	Does not perform any duties.	Performs very little in the way of duties.	Performs nearly all duties.	Performs all duties.
Shares responsibility	Always relies on others to do work.	Rarely does work—needs constant reminding.	Usually does the work—seldom needs reminding.	Always does assigned work without being reminded.

Source: Rubric for Assessing Cooperative Group Work from Truett, C. (2001). Sherlock Holmes on the Internet. *Learning and Leading with Technology, 29*(2), p. 39.

Figure A.3 Technology Impact Checklist: Is the Activity Working?
Developed by M. D. Roblyer

How Do You Know When You Have Integrated Technology Well?

_____ An outside observer sees the technology activity as a seamless part of the lesson.
Comments:

_____ The reason for using the technology is obvious to you, the students, and others.
Comments:

_____ The students are focusing on learning, not on the technology.
Comments:

_____ You can describe how technology is helping a particular student.
Comments:

_____ You would have difficulty accomplishing lesson objectives if the technology weren't there.
Comments:

_____ You can explain easily and concisely what the technology is supposed to contribute.
Comments:

_____ All students are participating with the technology and benefiting from it.
Comments:

How Do You Know When You Have Not Integrated Technology Well?

_____ You consistently see the technology as more trouble than it is worth.
Comments:

_____ You have trouble justifying cost and preparation time in terms of benefits to your students.
Comments:

_____ Students spend more time trying to make the technology work than on learning the topic.
Comments:

_____ The problem you were trying to address is still there.
Comments:

Source: Based on concepts in Milone, M. (1998). Technology integration master class. *Technology and Learning, 19*(1), 6–10.

Figure A.4 Technology Classroom Impact Rubric
Developed by M. D. Roblyer

Level	Frequency of Use	Source of Direction	Nature of Integration	Purpose of Technology Uses
1—**Minimum infusion**	Used from time to time, but not every day.	Primarily teacher directed.	Technologies are used as add-ons to other learning activities.	Skill learning (e.g., calculators, games, tutorials) and tools to improve efficiency and appearance of products (e.g., word processing, spreadsheets, databases, presentation software).
2—**Intermediate infusion**	Used more routinely, nearly every day.	Primarily teacher directed, but students begin to initiate some uses.	Technologies help structure some learning activities.	Same uses as level 1, but software also used to organize information, support problem-solving/ reasoning skills, and discover concepts and relationships. Internet search engines and CD-ROM encyclopedias used for research.
3—**High infusion**	Used every day for some kinds of activities.	Equally teacher directed and student directed.	Technologies used to change the nature of some learning activities; begins to be used seamlessly as part of many activities.	Same uses as levels 1 and 2, but technology tools used increasingly for organization and analysis of data, creation of presentations to communicate more effectively, and use of e-mail and Internet to communicate with those inside and outside the school.
4—**Maximum infusion**	Used as routine part of many daily activities.	Primarily student directed with teachers providing supportive learning environment and introducing new technology resources as appropriate to the content.	Technologies used seamlessly with all other activities; students and teachers rely on technologies and teaching/learning could not occur without them.	All uses in levels 1–3; in addition, students can select technologies that are appropriate for a variety of other purposes, paralleling the way professionals in the workforce use technology.

Source: Based on concepts in Sun, J. (2000). How do we know it's working? *Learning and Leading with Technology, 27*(7), 32–35, 41, 49.

Figure A.5 Essential Criteria Checklist for Evaluating Instructional Courseware
Developed by M. D. Roblyer

The following is an example checklist based on essential qualities that can be used to discriminate between acceptable and unacceptable courseware material. If courseware does not meet these criteria, it probably should not be considered for purchase. For each item, indicate Y for yes if it meets the criterion, or N for no if it does not.

Title ______________________________ Publisher ______________________

Content Area ______________________________ Hardware Required: ______________

Courseware functions: _____ Drill and practice _____ Instructional game
_____ Tutorial _____ Problem solving
_____ Simulation _____ Other: ______________________

I. Instructional Design and Pedagogical Soundness

_____ Teaching strategy is matched to student needs/levels and is based on accepted methods
_____ Presentation on screen contains nothing that misleads or confuses students
_____ Readability and difficulty are at an appropriate level for students who will use it
_____ Comments to students are not abusive or insulting
_____ Graphics fulfill important purpose (motivation, information) and are not distracting to learners

Criteria specific to drill-and-practice functions:

_____ High degree of control over presentation rate (unless the method is timed review)
_____ Appropriate feedback for correct answers (none, if timed; not elaborate or time consuming)
_____ Feedback is more reinforcing for correct than for incorrect responses

Criteria specific to tutorial functions:

_____ High degree of interactivity (not just reading information)
_____ High degree of user control (forward and backward movement, branching on request)
_____ Comprehensive teaching sequence so instruction is self-contained and stand-alone
_____ Adequate answer-judging capabilities for student-constructed answers to questions

Criteria specific to simulation functions:

_____ Appropriate degree of fidelity (accurate depiction of system being modeled)
_____ Good documentation available on how program works

Criteria specific to instructional game functions:

_____ Low quotient of violence or combat-type activities
_____ Amount of physical dexterity required appropriate to students who will use it

II. Content

_____ No grammar, spelling, or punctuation errors on the screen
_____ All content accurate and up to date
_____ No racial or gender stereotypes; not geared toward only one sex or to certain races
_____ Exhibits a sensitive treatment of moral and social issues (e.g., perspectives on war or capital punishment)
_____ Content matches required curriculum objectives

III. User Flexibility

_____ User normally has some control of movement within the program (e.g., can go from screen to screen at desired rate; can read text at desired rate; can exit program when desired)
_____ Can turn off sound, if desired
_____ Interface is easy to use (e.g., similar format from screen to screen for forward and back movement in program)

IV. Technical Soundness

_____ Program loads consistently, without error
_____ Program does not break, no matter what the student enters
_____ Program does what the screen says it should do
_____ Program works on desired platform
_____ If included, online links work as indicated
_____ If included, animations and videos work as indicated

Decision: _____ Is recommended for purchase and use
_____ Is not recommended

Figure A.6 Rubrics for Self-Assessing Personal/Professional Productivity Skills

MyCompass The Professional Development Portal for Arizona Educators

MyCompass

Main Menu: Rubrics

Rubric Category: Personal/Professional Productivity Skills

Each subcategory has 4 levels of proficiency: Entry, Emergent, Fluent, and Proficient.

Subcategory: Classroom Management Skills

Entry	I am aware of the benefits of classroom management software such as grading software, an automated attendance program, student progress reporting software, and a student information database.
Emergent	I use at least one of the following: grading software, an automated attendance program, student progress reporting software, and/or a student information database.
Fluent	I use two or more of the following: grading software, an automated attendance program, student progress reporting software, and a student information database.
Proficient	I am comfortable teaching others to use classroom management software such as grading software, an automated attendance program, student progress reporting software, and a student information database.
Subcategory:	Word Processing/Publishing Skills
Entry	I know how to select different fonts, resize text, and apply font styles to selected text to create emphasis.
Emergent	I use a spell checker for accuracy before publishing word processing documents. I can use the thesaurus for better meaning in word selection. I am able to change page margins when I need more room for my information. I set tabs and hanging indents to position text precisely, and manipulate text justification to enhance the readability of documents. I adjust the viewing percentage when it helps to see more of the document.
Fluent	I am able to create multiple columns of text, and insert page and/or column breaks where needed. I create multiple sizes of tables for information to be displayed neatly. I use custom headers and footers to increase understanding. I enter footnotes and endnotes to give credit for others' works. I access and modify existing templates to meet my needs, and save in different file formats for sharing with others.
Proficient	I am proficient in using a word processing program to merge database files for minimizing time spent on redundant tasks. I print labels and envelopes from address books, and create my own templates for future use. I have learned how to insert graphics precisely to aid in creating meaning. I insert logically named hyperlinks for accessing pertinent web pages and save in HTML format for posting on the Internet.

Subcategory: Graphics Skills

Entry	I do not use digital graphics in my classroom, but I have begun to see their use for enhancing my classroom instruction.
Emergent	I use basic drawing/painting tools such as a pencil, spray can, paint bucket, eraser, and common shapes tools. I duplicate, move, and modify graphics I have created.
Fluent	I am able to use a scanner or digital camera to acquire graphics for use in a graphics program. I import/export graphics to and from different programs, including images from the Internet for educational fair use.
Proficient	I am comfortable teaching others to use a variety of graphics types in different applications, including word processing, spreadsheet, presentation, web publishing, and database programs.

Subcategory: Spreadsheet Skills

Entry	I can insert words and numbers within the cells of a spreadsheet program, and move the data among specific cells using cut/copy/paste commands. I format the data within cells to change its appearance, and resize rows and columns to accommodate the amount of data within cells. I am able to change page orientation, insert headers and footers to increase understanding, and preview pages before printing.

Figure A.6 Continued

Emergent	I use multiple formulas for automatic calculations of numbers. I am able to insert text boxes to help explain and create charts for visual aids.
Fluent	I can reconfigure options/preferences to meet my spreadsheet needs and save in different spreadsheet formats for sharing with others.
Proficient	I can articulate the difference between absolute and relative references. I am proficient in using spreadsheet software to sort data, filter data, and create lookup tables.
Subcategory: Database Skills	
Entry	I am in the investigative stage of using database software as an educator. I have not had the opportunity to find uses for databases in my classroom instruction.
Emergent	I can manipulate the contents of a field by using cut/copy/paste/clear/duplicate commands. I am able to find/sort/query records. I format text attributes to emphasize different fields. I create various reports to display specific types of data and can modify print layouts as well.
Fluent	I am able to modify database layouts and print multiple types of reports. I am able to import/export records and print/merge a word processing document. In my databases, I create auto-entry and calculation fields and construct complex queries for sorting data.
Proficient	I am proficient in using a database program to create a macro or a script. I create database templates for later use. I know how to design a database that can be manipulated from the Internet.
Subcategory: Presentation Skills	
Entry	I am in the exploration stage of integrating multimedia presentations in my classroom. I have not had opportunity to find uses for them in my classroom instruction.
Emergent	I know how to open and run existing presentations. I can create new slides and format their backgrounds and color schemes. I use different formatting for textual information that I want to emphasize. I create/insert/format graphics and define the transition from slide to slide.
Fluent	I am able to create and modify presentation templates. I try to optimize elements for effective visual display. I understand that good design takes into account the amount of information presented on each slide. I am able to produce speaker's notes, print outs, and screen versions of my presentations.
Proficient	I am proficient in using presentation software to edit document and application preferences. I import/export presentations among different programs, and can group multiple presentations. My presentations include multiple media types such as video and audio clips. I save my presentations in HTML format for publishing to the web.

Source: Used by permission of iAssessment.

Figure A.7 Criteria for Evaluating Commercial Multimedia Software Products
Developed by M. D. Roblyer

_____ **Instructional planning.** Target audience and prerequisite skills are specified.

Comments:

_____ **Support.** Computer hardware and software requirements are specified.

Comments:

_____ **Instructional adequacy.** Instructional objectives are clearly stated. Practice activities are provided that actively involve the learner. Instructional activities needed to complete learning tasks are made explicit.

Comments:

_____ **Information content.** Information is current and accurately represents the topic. Examples, practice exercises, and feedback are meaningful and relevant.

Comments:

_____ **Information reliability.** Information is accurate, i.e., presented in a truthful, valid way.

Comments:

_____ **Clear, concise, and unbiased language.** Courseware content is presented clearly. (Text, pictorial, graphical, auditory, and video information all are presented clearly.)

Comments:

_____ **Interface design and navigation.** Courseware screen elements (titles, text areas, navigation buttons, etc.) are easy to understand. Directions are understandable.

Comments:

_____ **Feedback and interactivity.** If tests are present, they are matched to objectives. Feedback is appropriate to content, learning tasks, learner response, and learning environment.

Comments:

_____ **Evidence of effectiveness.** During student uses of courseware, there was evidence of learning/performance gains. The courseware supplies information to teachers and students on how it measures student learning.

Comments:

Figure A.8 Criteria for Evaluating Multimedia Products
Developed by M. D. Roblyer

Content

_____ All information is the most current, up-to-date available.
_____ All information is factually accurate.
_____ Content is free from typos and misspellings, and from punctuation and grammatical errors.
_____ No ethnic, slang, or rude names are used; content is presented in a professional way.
_____ No questionable vocabulary, slang terms, or curse words are used.
_____ Content sources (including sources of graphics) are properly referenced.

Instructional Design

_____ Instructional objectives are clear; the instructional purpose is aligned with school curriculum, rather than being for entertainment.
_____ All necessary information is provided in the product to make concepts clear; users will be able to understand what is being presented from the information provided.
_____ If tests or other assessments are provided, they are matched directly to objectives.
_____ To add interest and motivation for users, information is presented in an innovative and creative way.

Organization and Navigation

_____ Screens are designed for easy navigation; it is clear how to get to and from various parts of the product.
_____ To aid navigation and use, the product has a consistent look and feel throughout.
_____ Buttons and links all work as indicated.

Appearance

_____ Use of varying fonts and type sizes is controlled, so as not to interfere with readability.
_____ Type is large enough to read when projected.
_____ Color contrasts with background for easy reading.
_____ Bold or plain style is used for main text; no shadow and outline if text is more than a few words. Fancy fonts and type styles are readable.
_____ Only brief main ideas are listed in a single frame, rather than paragraphs of text.

Graphics, Videos, and Sound

_____ Graphics, videos, and sound are included as appropriate to help communicate information on the topic; they are not included just for show.
_____ No obscene or rude graphics or visuals are included.
_____ Use of graphics (e.g., animations, screen changes) is controlled and does not distract from reading.
_____ Pictures and sounds associated with buttons and links are appropriate to the purpose and content of the frames.

Source: Based on concepts from Brunner, C. (1996). Judging student multimedia. *Electronic Learning, 15*(6), 14–15; Clark, J. (1996). Bells and whistles . . . but where are the references: Setting standards for hypermedia projects. *Learning and Leading with Technology, 23*(5), 22–24; and Litchfield, B. (1995). Helping your students plan computer projects. *The Computing Teacher, 22*(7), 37–43.

Figure A.9 Rubric for Assessing Interactive Qualities of Distance Learning Courses
Developed by M. D. Roblyer

RUBRIC DIRECTIONS: The rubric shown below has five (5) separate elements that contribute to a course's level of interaction and interactivity. For each of these four elements, circle a description below it that applies best to your course. After reviewing all elements and circling the appropriate level, add up the points to determine the course's level of interactive qualities (e.g., low, moderate, or high)

Low interactive qualities	1–9 points
Moderate interactive qualities	10–17 points
High interactive qualities	18–25 points

Scale (see points below)	Element #1: Social/Rapport-Building Designs for Interaction	Element #2: Instructional Designs for Interaction	Element #3: Interactivity of Technology Resources	Element #4: Evidence of Learner Engagement	Element #5: Evidence of Instructor Engagement
Low interactive qualities (1 point each)	The instructor does not encourage students to get to know one another on a personal basis. No activities require social interaction or are limited to brief introductions at the beginning of the course.	Instructional activities do not require two-way interaction between instructor and students; they call for one-way delivery of information (e.g., instructor lectures, text delivery) and student products based on the information.	Fax, web pages, or other technology resource allows one-way delivery of information (text and/or graphics).	By end of course, most students (50%–75%) are replying to messages from the instructor, but only when required; messages are short and sometimes unresponsive to topics.	Instructor responds only randomly to student queries; responses usually take more than 48 hours; feedback is brief and provides little analysis of student work or suggestions for improvement.
Minimum interactive qualities (2 points each)	In addition to brief introductions, the instructor requires one other exchange of personal information among students, e.g., written bio of personal background and experiences.	Instructional activities require students to communicate with the instructor on an individual basis only (e.g., asking/ responding to instructor questions).	E-mail, listserv, conference/ bulletin board, or other technology resource allows two-way, asynchronous exchanges of information (text and graphics).	By end of course, most students (50%–75%) are replying to messages from the instructor and other students, both when required and on a voluntary basis; replies are short but usually responsive to topics.	Instructor responds to most student queries; responses usually are within 48 hours; feedback sometimes offers some analysis of student work and suggestions for improvement.
Moderate interactive qualities (3 points each)	In addition to providing for exchanges of personal information among students, the instructor provides at least one other in-class activity designed to increase communication and social rapport among students.	In addition to requiring students to communicate with the instructor, instructional activities require students to communicate with one another (e.g., discussions in pairs or small groups).	In addition to technologies used for two-way asynchronous exchanges of information, chat room or other technology allows synchronous exchanges of primarily written information.	By end of course, all or nearly all students (90%–100%) are replying to messages from the instructor and other students, both when required and voluntarily; replies are detailed and responsive to topics.	Instructor responds to all student queries; responses usually are within 48 hours; feedback usually offers some analysis of student work and suggestions for improvement.

Figure A.9 Continued

Scale (see points below)	Element #1: Social/Rapport-Building Designs for Interaction	Element #2: Instructional Designs for Interaction	Element #3: Interactivity of Technology Resources	Element #4: Evidence of Learner Engagement	Element #5: Evidence of Instructor Engagement
Above average interactive qualities (4 points each)	In addition to providing for exchanges of personal information among students and encouraging communication and social interaction, the instructor also interacts with students on a social/personal basis.	In addition to requiring students to communicate with the instructor, instructional activities require students to develop products by working together cooperatively (e.g., in pairs or small groups) and sharing feedback.	In addition to technologies used for two-way synchronous and asynchronous exchanges of written information, additional technologies (e.g., teleconferencing) allow one-way visual and two-way voice communications between instructor and students.	By end of course, most students (50%–75%) are both replying to and initiating messages when required and voluntarily; most messages are detailed and responsive to topics, but may be wordy or rambling.	Instructor responds to all student queries; responses usually are prompt, i.e., within 24 hours; feedback always offers detailed analysis of student work and suggestions for improvement.
High level of interactive qualities (5 points each)	In addition to providing for exchanges of information and encouraging student–student and instructor–student interaction, the instructor provides ongoing course structures designed to promote social rapport among students and instructor.	In addition to requiring students to communicate with the instructor, instructional activities require students to develop products by working together cooperatively (e.g., in pairs or small groups) and share results and feedback with other groups in the class.	In addition to technologies to allow two-way exchanges of text information, visual technologies such as two-way video or videoconferencing technologies allow synchronous voice and visual communications between instructor and students and among students.	By end of course, all or nearly all students (90%–100%) are both replying to and initiating messages, both when required and voluntarily; most messages are detailed, responsive to topics, and reflect effort to communicate well.	Instructor responds to all student queries; responses are always prompt, i.e., within 24 hours; feedback always offers detailed analysis of student work and suggestions for improvement, along with additional hints and information to supplement learning.
Total each:	_____ pts.	_____ pts.	_____ pts.	_____ pts.	_____ pts.
Total overall:	_____ pts.				

Source: Based on concepts in Roblyer, M. D., & Ekhaml, D. (2000). How interactive are YOUR distance courses? A rubric for assessing interaction in distance learning. *The Online Journal of Distance Learning Administration, 3*(2). Earlier version available online: http://www.westga.edu/~distance/summer32.html.

Figure A.10 Rubric for Assessing Middle School Web Pages (Chenau, 2000)

Rubric for Sixth-Grade Web Page

Excellent:

_____ directions followed
_____ visually pleasing
_____ excellent organization of information
_____ information grammatically sound (French and English)
_____ all words are correctly spelled
_____ font shows accent marks
_____ links and anchors work
_____ special effects enhance, not detract

Very Good:

_____ directions followed
_____ visually pleasing
_____ mostly clear writing
_____ few grammatical and/or spelling mistakes
_____ font shows accent marks
_____ links and anchors work
_____ special effects usually enhance, not detract

Fair:

_____ directions mostly followed
_____ visually distracting
_____ writing occasionally unclear
_____ many grammatical errors and/or misspellings
_____ font does not display accents
_____ not all links and anchors work

Unacceptable:

_____ directions not followed
_____ visually confusing
_____ writing unclear
_____ many grammatical errors and/or misspellings
_____ font does not display accents
_____ links and anchors do not work
_____ special effects distract

Source: Rubric for Assessing Middle School Web Pages from Chenau, J. (2000). Cyber traveling through the Loire Valley. *Learning and Leading with Technology, 28*(2), p. 26.

Figure A.11 Checklist of Criteria for Evaluating Web Sites
Developed by M. D. Roblyer

Check each of the following criteria *before* and *after* designing a page.

Content

_____ All information is accurate; plan to update the page periodically. The "last time updated" date is given.
_____ Information is complete but not excessive or redundant.
_____ Information is well organized and clearly labeled.
_____ Information is interesting, informative, and worthwhile.
_____ Information is not redundant to many other sources; there is a reason to put it on the Web.
_____ All text has correct spelling, grammar, and punctuation.
_____ Level of content and vocabulary is appropriate for intended audience.
_____ Content is free from stereotyping, coarse or vulgar language, or matter that could be offensive to typical users.
_____ Author(s) of the page are clearly identified.
_____ The page gives an e-mail address or other way to contact authors.

Visual and Audio Design

_____ The site has a consistent look.
_____ Graphics, animations, videos, and sounds make an important contribution; each serves a purpose.
_____ Pages have only one or two fonts.
_____ Each page uses a limited number of colors, especially for text.
_____ Colors have been selected to be compatible with the Netscape 216 color palette.
_____ Type colors/styles and text-to-background contrast have been selected for good readability.
_____ Each graphic is designed to fit 640 × 480 pixel screens, allowing for scroll bars/toolbars.
_____ Each page is limited to 2–3 screens; the most important information is at the top.
_____ The pages are simply and attractively designed; they make a user want to read the information.

Navigation

_____ Pages load quickly.
_____ Pages have simple, consistent navigation scheme to let users get to desired places quickly and easily.
_____ The first page indicates clearly how the site is organized and how to get to items of interest.
_____ Links (text and icons) are easy to identify. Graphics and sounds are clearly identified.
_____ Icons clearly represent the information they link to.
_____ Each supporting page has a link back to the home page.

Miscellaneous (for larger sites and pages)

_____ Requests for private information are secured.
_____ Page information is kept short enough so that it can be printed out quickly.
_____ The user can choose to load alternate versions of the page such as text only or smaller images.
_____ The site has its own search engine for locating items within the pages.
_____ Branching is organized so that all content is no more than three clicks away from the home page.

Use the following tips to make your sites and pages easier to design and use:

_____ Organize the site on paper ahead of time before putting it on the computer.
_____ To speed loading, limit graphics to no more than 50K and re-use images whenever possible.
_____ Use GIFs for line art or graphics with limited colors and sharp edges; use JPEGs for photos with many colors and smooth gradients. Avoid PICT and other formats that must be converted by users.
_____ Test out your page with a real browser.
_____ Use a GIF spacer (1 × 1 transparent GIF) to space paragraphs, indents, or alignments on pages.

Source: Based on concepts in Everhart, N. (1997). Web page evaluation: Views from the field. *Technology Connection, 4*(3), 24–26; Gray, T. (1997). No crazy gods. *Learning and Leading with Technology, 25*(1), 43–45; and McClelland, D. (1997, August). Web publishing made easy. *MacWorld, 1*(8), 104–110.

Figure A.12 Web Page Evaluation Rubric

Score	5 or 4	3 or 2	1 or 0
Ideas and Content	• Information is accurate and current • Ideas come mainly from primary sources • Authors show knowledge and insight • Effective use of technology demonstrated • All information relates to the overall purpose	• Information not always clear • Primary source use is not always clear • Content connections not always clear • Does not relate content to larger context • No way to check validity of information • Strong purpose not demonstrated	• Information incomplete or inaccurate • Information not from primary sources • Little or no overall context for information • Value of information is unclear • No way to check validity of information • Lacks sense of purpose or central theme
Score	**5 or 4**	**3 or 2**	**1 or 0**
Organization	• Inviting opening page draws the visitor inside • Details are logical and effective • Layout of pages provides good direction • How to explore an idea is clear • Each page begins with a clear transition • Easy to navigate through the pages	• Inconsistent structure of pages • Sequencing is inconsistent • Some pages incomplete • Some links disjointed; lack purpose • Unclear connections among sections • Sense of being lost or unsure navigating	• No orientation for visitors • Sequencing unclear • Pages lack closure • No focus for links • Pages are inconsistent • Difficult to navigate in an organized way
Score	**5 or 4**	**3 or 2**	**1 or 0**
Language and Conventions	• Organizational structure is clear and coherent • Grammar and usage are correct • Punctuation is accurate • Spelling is generally correct • Site needs little or no editing	• Long or incomplete paragraphs • Minor problems with grammar or usage • Internal punctuation sometimes missing or wrong • Spelling is usually correct • Site needs some editing	• Paragraph structure is missing • Errors in grammar or usage noticeable • Many punctuation mistakes • Frequent spelling errors • Site needs extensive editing
Score	**5 or 4**	**3 or 2**	**1 or 0**
Presentation	• Web site is clearly identified; easy to find • The layout is clear and easy to follow • Backgrounds and text work well together • Graphical elements are used consistently • Multimedia adds to the main purpose • Links are appropriate	• Web site easy to find • Layout of most pages is easy to follow • Backgrounds and text are not effective • Inconsistent or inappropriate graphics • Multimedia sometimes doesn't add to the main purpose • Use of links is unclear	• Web site hard to find • Layout is confusing or inappropriate • Backgrounds and text not effective • Graphics only decorative or are inappropriate • Multimedia unrelated to the topic • Too many unrelated links, or too few links
Score	**5 or 4**	**3 or 2**	**1 or 0**
Technical	• Links work properly • Graphics are optimized • Works in all browsers • Works in text only mode • Multimedia resources work properly	• Not all links work properly • Graphics are generally optimized • Pages don't work in all browsers • Text-only mode could be improved • Multimedia resources work most of the time	• Links don't work properly • Graphic elements not optimized • Specific browsers needed • Text only mode does not work • Resources fail to work

Source: Adapted by Clarence Bakken and Sara Armstrong in conjunction with Challenge 2000, CTAP Region IV Technology Leadership Academy and the Institute for Research on Learning, based on work done by Al Rogers, Global SchoolNet Foundation and CyberFair Contest. From Eastern Illinois University web site, http://www.ux1.eiu.edu/~cfmgb/web.htm.

Figure A.13 WebQuest Rubric (Dodge, 2000)

A Rubric for Evaluating WebQuests

The WebQuest format can be applied to a variety of teaching situations. If you take advantage of all the possibilities inherent in the format, your students will have a rich and powerful experience. This rubric will help you pinpoint the ways in which your WebQuest isn't doing everything it could do. If a page seems to fall between categories, feel free to score it with in-between points.

	Beginning	Developing	Accomplished	Score
Overall Aesthetics (This refers to the WebQuest page itself, not the external resources linked to it.)				
Overall Visual Appeal	0 points There are few or no graphic elements. No variation in layout or typography. OR Color is garish and/or typographic variations are overused and legibility suffers. Background interferes with the readability.	2 points Graphic elements sometimes, but not always, contribute to the understanding of concepts, ideas and relationships. There is some variation in type size, color, and layout.	4 points Appropriate and thematic graphic elements are used to make visual connections that contribute to the understanding of concepts, ideas and relationships. Differences in type size and/or color are used well and consistently.	
Navigation & Flow	0 points Getting through the lesson is confusing and unconventional. Pages can't be found easily and/or the way back isn't clear.	2 points There are a few places where the learner can get lost and not know where to go next.	4 points Navigation is seamless. It is always clear to the learner what all the pieces are and how to get to them.	
Mechanical Aspects	0 points There are more than 5 broken links, misplaced or missing images, badly sized tables, misspellings and/or grammatical errors.	1 point There are a few broken links, misplaced or missing images, badly sized tables, misspellings and/or grammatical errors.	2 points No mechanical problems noted.	
Introduction				
Motivational Effectiveness of Introduction	0 points The introduction is purely factual, with no appeal to relevance or social importance OR The scenario posed is transparently bogus and doesn't respect the media literacy of today's learners.	1 point The introduction relates somewhat to the learner's interests and/or describes a compelling question or problem.	2 points The introduction draws the reader into the lesson by relating to the learner's interests or goals and/or engagingly describing a compelling question or problem.	
Cognitive Effectiveness of the Introduction	0 points The introduction doesn't prepare the reader for what is to come, or build on what the learner already knows.	1 point The introduction makes some reference to learner's prior knowledge and previews to some extent what the lesson is about.	2 points The introduction builds on learner's prior knowledge and effectively prepares the learner by foreshadowing what the lesson is about.	

Figure A.13 **Continued**

	Beginning	Developing	Accomplished	Score
Task (The task is the end result of student efforts . . . not the steps involved in getting there.)				
Connection of Task to Standards	0 points The task is not related to standards.	2 points The task is referenced to standards but is not clearly connected to what students must know and be able to do to achieve proficiency of those standards.	4 points The task is referenced to standards and is clearly connected to what students must know and be able to do to achieve proficiency of those standards.	
Cognitive Level of the Task	0 points Task requires simply comprehending or retelling of information found on web pages and answering factual questions.	3 points Task is doable but is limited in its significance to students' lives. The task requires analysis of information and/or putting together information from several sources.	6 points Task is doable and engaging, and elicits thinking that goes beyond rote comprehension. The task requires synthesis of multiple sources of information, and/or taking a position, and/or going beyond the data given and making a generalization or creative product.	
Process (The process is the step-by-step description of how students will accomplish the task.)				
Clarity of Process	0 points Process is not clearly stated. Students would not know exactly what they were supposed to do just from reading this.	2 points Some directions are given, but there is missing information. Students might be confused.	4 points Every step is clearly stated. Most students would know exactly where they are at each step of the process and know what to do next.	
Scaffolding of Process	0 points The process lacks strategies and organizational tools needed for students to gain the knowledge needed to complete the task. Activities are of little significance to one another and/or to the accomplishment of the task.	3 points Strategies and organizational tools embedded in the process are insufficient to ensure that all students will gain the knowledge needed to complete the task. Some of the activities do not relate specifically to the accomplishment of the task.	6 points The process provides students coming in at different entry levels with strategies and organizational tools to access and gain the knowledge needed to complete the task. Activities are clearly related and designed to take the students from basic knowledge to higher level thinking. Checks for understanding are built in to assess whether students are getting it.	
Richness of Process	0 points Few steps, no separate roles assigned.	1 point Some separate tasks or roles assigned. More complex activities required.	2 points Different roles are assigned to help students understand different perspectives and/or share responsibility in accomplishing the task.	

Figure A.13 Continued

	Beginning	Developing	Accomplished	Score
Resources (Note: you should evaluate all resources linked to the page, even if they are in sections other than the Process block. Also note that books, video and other off-line resources can and should be used where appropriate.)				
Relevance & Quantity of Resources	0 points Resources provided are not sufficient for students to accomplish the task. OR There are too many resources for learners to look at in a reasonable time.	2 points There is some connection between the resources and the information needed for students to accomplish the task. Some resources don't add anything new.	4 points There is a clear and meaningful connection between all the resources and the information needed for students to accomplish the task. Every resource carries its weight.	
Quality of Resources	0 points Links are mundane. They lead to information that could be found in a classroom encyclopedia.	2 points Some links carry information not ordinarily found in a classroom.	4 points Links make excellent use of the web's timeliness and colorfulness. Varied resources provide enough meaningful information for students to think deeply.	
Evaluation				
Clarity of Evaluation Criteria	0 points Criteria for success are not described.	3 points Criteria for success are at least partially described.	6 points Criteria for success are clearly stated in the form of a rubric. Criteria include qualitative as well as quantitative descriptors. The evaluation instrument clearly measures what students must know and be able to do to accomplish the task.	
Total Score				**/50**

Source: From Bernie Dodge web site, http://edweb.sdsu.edu/webquest/webquestrubric.html.

GLOSSARY

action research—According to Gay and Airasian, a process in which teachers collect evidence and make decisions about their own knowledge, performance, beliefs, and effects in order to understand and improve them

algorithm—A step-by-step solution to a problem (e.g., a programming problem)

anchored instruction—Constructivist term for learning environments that focus on meaningful, real-life problems and activities

applet—A program that is written in the Java language and is designed to carry out a useful task on the Internet (e.g., showing a clock to tell the exact time)

applications software—Computer programs written to support tasks that are useful to a computer user (e.g., word processing) in contrast with *systems software*

Archie—A system located on the Internet and designed for finding files through lists of archived files from various locations

artificial intelligence (AI)—Computer programs that try to emulate the decision-making capabilities of the human mind

ASCII (American Standard Code for Information Interchange)—A standardized, commonly accepted format for representing data (e.g., characters and numbers) so that programs and files created with one program and stored in ASCII can be used by another program

assembler—A low-level programming language that uses mnemonic commands that are one step up in complexity from "machine language" (binary numbers)

authoring system—A program designed to help nonprogrammers write computer-based instructional programs (e.g., CAI or multimedia); can be either a high-level programming language or a series of nonprogramming prompts

automaticity—A level of skill that allows a person to respond immediately with the correct answer to a problem

avatar—A graphic representation of a real person in cyberspace; a three-dimensional image that a person can choose to represent him or her in a virtual reality environment

backup copy—A copy of a disk that is made to guard against loss of files if an original disk is lost or destroyed

bar code—A set of lines that represents a number such as a UPC (Universal Product Code)

bar-code reader—A device that reads and interprets bar codes

BASIC (Beginners All-Purpose Symbolic Instruction Code)—A high-level programming language designed for beginning programmers; popular with early microcomputers

baud rate—The speed at which data are transmitted across communication lines between computers measured in bits per second (bps); 1 baud = 1 bps

BBS (See *bulletin boards.*)

binary—A condition of two possible states (e.g., on or off, 1 or 0). For computers, binary refers to the coding system that uses 1s and 0s

bit—A binary digit, either a 1 or a 0; several bits together (usually eight) make up a byte of computer storage that can hold a letter or a character

BitNet—A network used primarily by higher education organizations; replaced by the Internet

bomb—Condition in a computer when a program stops operating due to an error of some kind; also, to stop operating

bookmark—To mark an Internet location so one can remember it and return to it later; or the place so marked

boot/boot up—To start up a computer system; a "cold boot" is turning on the device from a power switch; a "warm boot" is restarting from the keyboard without shutting off power

bps (bits per second)—The speed at which data are transmitted across communication lines between computers

browser—A software package (e.g., *Netscape, Internet Explorer*) that allows one to look at information on the Internet in graphic, rather than just text, format

bug—An error in a computer program caused either by faulty logic or program language syntax (named by early programmer and systems designer Grace Hopper, who found a moth in the machinery of a broken computer)

bulletin boards (BBS)—A computer system set up to allow notices to be posted and viewed by anyone who has access to the network

button—A place on a computer screen, usually within a hypermedia program, that causes some action when the user clicks on it using a mouse; also called a *hot spot* or *link*

byte—A group of binary digits (bits) that represents a character or number in a computer system; designates a unit of computer storage (see also *K, M,* and *G*)

C—A structured programming language originally designed for use on the Unix operating system and widely used on today's microcomputers

CAI (computer-assisted instruction)—Software designed to help teach information and/or skills related to a topic; also known as *courseware*

calculator-based lab (CBL)—Calculator with probes or sensors connected to it to allow gathering of numerical data

card—One frame or screen produced in a hypermedia program such as *HyperStudio* (several cards together make a stack)

CAT (computer-assisted testing)—Using a computer system to administer and score assessment measures; also, computer adaptive testing

CAV (constant angular velocity)—A videodisc format that makes available up to 54,000 images or 30 minutes of full-motion video per side; images can be selected and viewed randomly (see also *CLV*)

CD-I (compact disc interactive)—A type of CD-ROM used on special players with built-in computer and TV capabilities

CD-ROM (compact disc-read only memory)—Removable computer storage medium that can store images and/or up to 250,000 pages of text

central processing unit (CPU)—The circuitry in a computer that processes commands composed of the controller, the arithmetic/logic unit (ALU), and internal memory

CGI (Common Gateway Interface)—A specification on the Internet for how data will be collected at a web site; CGI programs are written in a language such as PERL

chat room—A location on the Internet set up to allow people to converse in real time by typing in messages or allowing their avatars to meet and "talk" to each other

chip—A piece of silicon inside a computer on which electronic circuits have been placed by depositing small paths of a metal such as aluminum; an integrated circuit

client—Programs like browsers and FTP software designed to carry out various activities for people to help them use the Internet

clip art—One or more pieces of professionally prepared art work, stored as files and designed to be inserted into a document such as a newsletter

clone—A computer designed to operate like another brand of computer, but usually not made by the same company as the original

CLV (constant linear velocity)—A videodisc format that can hold up to 60 minutes of full-motion video; designed for playing straight through, users cannot access individual frames as CAV discs allow (see also *CAV*)

CMI (computer-managed instruction)—Computer software systems designed to keep track of student performance data, either as part of CAI programs or by themselves

COBOL (COmmon Business Oriented Language)—A high-level language designed specifically for business applications

code—Lines of commands or instructions to a computer written in a certain language (e.g., BASIC or C); the act of writing such instructions

cold boot (See *boot.*)

command—One instruction to a computer written in a computer language

compiler—A computer program that converts all statements of a source program into machine language before executing any part of the program (in contrast with *interpreter*)

computer—Usually equivalent to *computer system* (see below); sometimes refers to the CPU part of the system

computer-assisted design (CAD)—Software used by architects and others to aid in the design of structures such as houses and cars

computer-assisted instruction (See *CAI.*)

computer-assisted testing (See *CAT.*)

computer language—A communication syntax and vocabulary used to write computer programs

computer literacy—Term coined by Arthur Luehrmann in the 1960s to mean a set of basic abilities everyone should have with computer systems; now has variable meanings

computer-managed instruction (See *CMI.*)

computer system—A set of devices designed to work together to accomplish input, processing, and output functions in order to accomplish tasks desired by a user

conferencing—Communication between people in two or more places made possible by computer systems connected by communication lines

constructivism—Teaching/learning model based on cognitive learning theory; holds that learners should generate their own knowledge through experience-based activities rather than being taught it by teachers (see also *directed instruction*)

control unit (controller)—The part of the computer system housed in the CPU that processes program instructions

cookie—A small piece of text transferred to a web browser through a server for the purpose of tracking the Internet usage habits of the person using the browser

courseware—Instructional software; computer software used to enhance or deliver instruction

CRT (cathode ray tube)—A TV-like screen on which information from a computer system may be displayed; a monitor; a primary output device for a microcomputer system

cursor—A line, block, or underline displayed on the computer screen that shows where information may be inserted

cut and paste—The act of copying text from one location in a document, deleting it, and then inserting it in another location

data—Elements of information (e.g., numbers and words)

database—A collection of information systematized by computer software to allow storage and easy retrieval through keyword searching; the program designed to accomplish these tasks

database management system (DBMS)—Computer software designed to facilitate use and updating of a collection of information in a database

data processing—Organizing and manipulating data for a specific purpose (e.g., to keep track of income and expenses, to maintain student records)

debug—To review a computer program and remove the errors or "bugs"

desktop—The screen that appears first upon starting up a Macintosh computer or an MS-DOS computer with Windows; a graphic user interface (GUI) designed to make it easier for nontechnical people to use a computer

desktop publishing—Term coined in 1984 by the president of the Aldus Corporation to refer to the activity of using software to produce documents with elaborate control of the form and appearance of individual pages

desktop videoconferencing—A computer-to-computer form of live action interactive two-way video/audio; a typical desktop videoconferencing system has a video camera, microphone, and speakers at each workstation

Digital Divide—Term coined by Lloyd Morrisett, former president of the Markle Foundation, to mean a discrepancy in access to technology resources between socioeconomic groups

digitized sound—Audible noises (e.g., music, voices) that are transferred to a computer storage medium by first encoding them as numbers

directed instruction—A teaching and learning model based on behavioral and cognitive theories; students receive information from teachers and do teacher-directed activities (see also *constructivism*)

disc—A CD-ROM or videodisc; refers to optical storage media as opposed to magnetic storage

disk—A computer storage medium on which data and programs are placed through a magnetic process

disk drive—A device in a computer system used to store data on floppy disks or microdisks and retrieve data

diskette (See *disk.*)

distance learning—Using some means, electronic or otherwise, to connect people with instructors and/or resources that can help them acquire knowledge and skills

distributed intelligence (See *shared intelligence.*)

DOS (disk operating system)—The systems software that allows a computer to use applications programs such as word processing software; the operating system on IBM-type computers as opposed to those manufactured by Apple

dot-matrix printer—Output device that produces paper copy by placing patterns of dots on the paper to form letters

download—To bring information to a computer from a network or from a computer to a disk

drill and practice—An instructional software function that presents items for students to work on (usually one at a time) and gives feedback on correctness; designed to help users remember isolated facts or concepts and recall them quickly

DVD (digital versatile disc)—A type of CD-ROM electronic storage medium that holds a minimum of 4.7 gigabytes of information

Dynamic HTML (DHTML)—Programming language that can allow the same URL to display a different page depending on conditions such as the time of day or the previous pages; see also *HTML, URL*

e-book—A flat panel computer display that is designed to resemble a book, but offers interactive graphics and searchable text features not possible in printed books; also an online text

electronic bulletin boards (See *bulletin boards.*)

electronic gradebook—Software designed to maintain and calculate student grades

electronic mail (e-mail)—Messages sent via telecommunications from one person to one or more other people

electronic portfolio—A collection of a person's work designed to demonstrate their skills and levels of proficiency in an area of expertise, presented in an electronic format such as a web site or multimedia product

electronic whiteboard—A device connected to a computer to allow users at different sites to see what the instructor writes or draws during demonstrations; stores demonstrations as computer files

emoticon—A series of characters used together to convey emotion; for example, a sideways smiley face :-) designates a happy mood

Ethernet—Type of local-area network (LAN) in which several data transmissions among network users can be sent at any given time (in contrast with token-passing networks, which allow only one transmission at a time)

Events of Instruction, Gagné's—The nine kinds of activities identified by learning theorist Robert Gagné as being involved in teaching and learning

expert systems—A form of artificial intelligence (AI) that attempts to computerize human expertise

export—To save all or part of a document in a format other than that in which the program created it (e.g., as a text file) so it can be used by another program

external storage—Devices outside the computer's internal circuitry that store information and/or data (in contrast with *internal memory*)

field—The smallest unit of information in a database

file—The product created by a database program; any collection of data stored on a computer medium

file server—In a local-area network (LAN), the computer that houses the software and "serves" it to the attached workstations

File Transfer Protocol (See *FTP.*)

firewall—A system set up to prevent someone from going to certain locations on the Internet; may be done by keyword or by site name

flame—An e-mail or newsgroup message that usually is emotional and often derogatory in nature

flat file database—Database program that creates single files (in contrast with *relational database*)

floppy disk (See *disk.*)

flowchart—A planning method that combines rectangles, diamonds, and other figures joined by arrows to show the steps of a problem solution in graphic form; used by programmers to show a program's logic and operation before it is coded into a computer language

font—A type style used in a document (e.g., Courier, Palatino, or Helvetica)

footer—A line in a document that can be set to repeat automatically at the bottom of each page; usually indicates a title and/or pagination (see also *header*)

format—To prepare a disk to receive files on a computer; to initialize a disk; to design the appearance of a document (e.g., the font, type styles, type size)

FORTRAN (FORmula TRANslater)—One of the earliest high-level computer languages; designed for mathematical and science applications

FTP (File Transfer Protocol)—On the Internet, a way of transferring files from one computer to another using common settings and transmission procedures; also, to transfer files

full justification (also simply *justification*)—In word processing or desktop publishing, a type of text alignment in which text is both flush right on the right margin and flush left on the left margin (in contrast with right or left justified or centered)

fuzzy logic—A logic system in artificial intelligence (AI) designed to parallel the decision-making processes of humans by accounting for subjectivity and uncertainty

G (gigabyte)—Roughly 1 billion bytes of computer storage

game (See *instructional game.*)

geographic information systems (GIS)—A computer system that is able to store in a database a variety of information about geographic locations

GIGO (garbage in/garbage out)—Popular term meaning that if the data that go into a computer are faulty or badly organized, the result will also be inaccurate

gopher—An Internet storage and search system developed at the University of Minnesota and named after the school's mascot; most gopher servers are being converted to web sites, which can be more easily accessed with Internet search engines

GPS (global positioning system)—An instrument that uses a satellite to pinpoint the exact geographic location where the GPS signal originates and cross-references it with mapping software to show the location to a user

gradebook (See *electronic gradebook.*)

gradekeeping software (See *electronic gradebook.*)

grammar checker—The part of the word processing software designed to check text for compliance with grammar and usage rules

graphic user interface (GUI, often pronounced "gooey")—Software that displays options to the user in graphic formats consisting of menus and icons, rather than text formats (e.g., the Macintosh and Windows desktops)

graphics tablet—Type of input device on which pictures are hand-drawn and transferred to the computer as files

graphing calculator—A calculator with advanced functions and a small LED display; allows users to enter equations and shows graphs that result from those equations

hacker—Computer user who demonstrates an unusual, obsessive interest in using the computer; a computer user who engages in unauthorized use of a computer system

handheld computer—A portable computing device; see also *personal digital assistant*

hard copy—A paper printout of a computer file from a printer, plotter, or other output device

hard disk (hard disk drive)—In a computer system, a secondary storage device, usually housed inside the computer, but can be external; holds from 20 megabytes to 1 or more gigabytes of information

hardware—The devices or equipment in a computer system (in contrast with *software* or *computer programs*)

header—A line in a document that can be set to repeat automatically at the top of each page; usually indicates a title and/or pagination (see also *footer*)

heart monitor—Device consisting of a transmitter, which senses the heartbeat from the heart's electrical impulses, and a wrist-watch receiver, which receives and records each beat through radio transmission from the transmitter

high-level language—Computer programming language (e.g., *FORTRAN, BASIC, COBOL*) designed with syntax and vocabulary like a human language so that less technical people can use it to write programs

hot spot (See *button.*)

HTML—Hypertext Markup Language; the primary programming language used to develop web pages

HyperCard—Authoring software designed for Macintosh systems to create products called *stacks* which consist of a series of frames or *cards*

hypermedia—Software that connects elements of a computer system (e.g., text, movies, pictures, and other graphics) through hypertext links

hypertext—Text elements such as keywords that can be cross-referenced with other occurrences of the same word or with related concepts

icon—On a computer screen, a picture that acts as a symbol for an action or item

IEP—Individual educational plan; the educational program required by law to be designed for each student with a disability

ILS (See *integrated learning system.*)

image processing—Process of using a software program such as **Adobe Photoshop** to make changes to a digital image

import—To bring into a document a picture or all or part of another document that has been stored in another format (see also *export*)

information literacy—A set of skills defined by Johnson and Eisenberg as the "Big Six"; includes abilities to look for, evaluate, and use information from various sources; considered to be a subset of technological literacy

information service—A set of communications (e.g., e-mail) and storage/retrieval options made available by a company such as America Online

Information Superhighway—A popular term with various meanings associated with the worldwide linkage of information; sometimes synonymous with the Internet

initialize (See *format.*)

ink-jet printer—Type of output device that produces hard copy by directing a controlled spray of ink onto a page to form characters

input device—Any device in a computer system (e.g., keyboard, mouse) designed to get instructions or data from the user to the processing part of the system

instant messaging (IM)—A communications service that allows users to create a private chat room which only members of a mutually agreed-upon list may enter; the system alerts a user when someone from the IM list is online

instructional game—Type of software function designed to increase motivation by adding game rules to a learning activity

integrated circuit (See *chip.*)

integrated learning system (ILS)—A network that combines instructional and management software and usually offers a variety of instructional resources on several topics

integrated software packages—Software products (e.g., *Microsoft Works* and *ClarisWorks*) that have several applications in a single package (e.g., word processing, database, spreadsheet, and drawing functions)

intelligent CAI—Computer-assisted instruction with software logic based on artificial intelligence (AI) principles

interactive storybook—Software designed to display a story in any sequence selected by the person reading it

interactive video—Videodiscs that allow the user to control the order and speed at which items from the disc are displayed on a screen. (In Level I, control is through a bar code reader or remote control; in Level III, control is through a menu on a computer screen.)

interface—Cables, adaptors, or circuits that connect components of a computer system; the on-screen method a person employs to use a computer (see also *graphical user interface*)

internal memory—Integrated circuits inside a computer system designed to hold information or programs; ROM and RAM (in contrast with *external storage*)

Internet—A worldwide network that connects many smaller networks with a common set of procedures (protocols) for sending and receiving information

Internet Explorer—A popular browser software used to access the Internet

interoperability—The capability of wireless devices to communicate with each other and with many kinds of peripheral devices

interpreter—A computer program that converts program code into machine language and executes one statement of a source program before converting and executing the next (in contrast with *compiler*)

intranet—A subset of the Internet, usually available only to the members of the organization that set it up

I/O (input/output)—The process of getting instructions and/or data into and out of a computer system; devices that perform both functions (e.g., disk drives)

IP (Internet Protocol)—A standard, agreed-upon way of coding and sending data across the Internet

ISDN (Integrated Services Digital Network)—A digital telecommunications system in which all types of data (e.g., video, graphics, text) may be sent over the same lines at very high speeds

ISP (Internet service provider)—A company or other organization (e.g., a university) that provides access to the Internet

Java—Originally called OAK, a high-level programming language developed by Sun Microsystems. An object-oriented language similar to C++ , it has become popular for its ability to do interactive graphic and animation activities on web pages

joystick—Input device, used primarily with games, that moves on-screen figures or a cursor

JPEG (Joint Photographic Experts Group)—A file format for storing and sending graphic images on a network

justification (See *full justification.*)

K (kilobyte)—A unit of computer memory or disk capacity that is roughly equivalent to 1,000 bytes

keyboard—Any of a variety of input devices that have keys imprinted with letters, numbers, and other symbols in order to allow a user to enter information

keyboarding—The act of using a computer keyboard to enter information into a computer system; sometimes used to mean efficient, ten-finger typing as opposed to hunt-and-peck typing

keypals—Electronic penpals; people who correspond via e-mail

LAN (See *local-area network.*)

laptop computer—Small, standalone, portable personal computer system

laserdisc (See *videodisc.*)

laser printer—An output device that produces hard copy by using a controlled laser beam to put characters on a page

LCD (liquid crystal display or diode) panel—A device consisting of light-sensitive material encased between two clear pieces of glass or plastic designed to be placed on an overhead projector; projects images from the computer screen to a large surface

light pen—Input device that allows a user to select items from a screen by sensing light on various points in the display

listserv—On the Internet, a program that stores and maintains mailing lists and allows a message to be sent simultaneously to everyone on the list

local-area network (LAN)—A series of computers connected through cabling or wireless methods to share programs through a central file server computer

Logo—A high-level programming language originally designed as an artificial intelligence (AI) language but later popularized by Seymour Papert as an environment to allow children to learn problem-solving behaviors and skills

Logowriter—A word processing program that incorporates logic and drawing capabilities of the Logo language

low-level language—Programming language such as assembler designed for use by technical personnel on a specific type of computer (see also *high-level language*)

M (megabyte)—A unit of computer memory or disk capacity that is roughly equivalent to 1 million bytes

machine language—A computer language consisting of commands written in 1's and 0's; designed for a specific type of computer

mainframe—Type of computer system that has several peripheral devices connected to a CPU housed in a separate device; has more memory and capacity than a microcomputer

mark sense scanner—Input device that reads data from specially coded sheets marked with pencil

MBL (microcomputer-based laboratory)—A type of instructional software tool consisting of hardware devices (probes) and software (probeware) to allow scientific data to be gathered and processed by a computer

MECC (See *Minnesota Education Computing Corporation.*)

media literacy (See *technological literacy.*)

memory—Circuitry inside a computer or media such as disks or CD-ROMs that allows programs or information to be stored for use by a computer

menu—List of on-screen options available on a specific topic or area of a program or GUI

metropolitan-area network (MAN)—A network whose components are distributed over an area larger that a LAN but smaller than a WAN

microcomputer—Small, stand-alone computer system designed for use by one person at a time

MIDI (musical instrument digital interface)—A device and software that allows a computer to control music-producing devices (e.g., sequencers, synthesizers)

minicomputer—A type of computer system in a range between microcomputers and mainframes. (In practice, minicomputers and mainframes are becoming indistinguishable.)

Minnesota Education Computing Corporation (MECC)—Originally established as the Minnesota Education Computing Consortium, one of the first organizations to develop and distribute instructional software for microcomputers

modem—A device that changes (MOdulates) digital computer signals into analog frequencies that can be sent over a telephone line to another computer and changes back (DEModulates) incoming signals into ones the computer can use

monitor—An output device that produces a visual display of what the computer produces (see also *CRT*)

MOO—MUD object oriented; a specific type of multiuser dungeon (MUD) system developed by Stephen White; see also *MUD*

Mosaic—One of the first browser programs designed to allow Internet resources to be displayed graphically rather than just in text

motherboard—The main circuit board inside a microcomputer that holds all of the integrated circuits, chips, and connection slots for attaching additional circuit boards required to control peripheral devices (e.g., monitor, keyboard, disk drive)

mouse—Input device that a computer user moves around on the table beside the computer in order to control a pointer on a screen, and presses down (clicks) in order to select options from the screen

MPEG (Motion Picture Experts Group)—A file format for storing and sending video sequences on a network

MS-DOS (Microsoft Disk Operating System)—A type of systems software used on IBM and IBM-compatible computers

MUD—Multiuser dungeon (or dimension or domain); a location on the Internet where several users at a time can interact with each other's avatars (graphic representations of each other); see also *MOO*

multimedia—A computer system or computer system product that incorporates text, sound, pictures/graphics, and/or video

netiquette—Etiquette guidelines for posting messages to online services, especially in e-mail

Netscape Communicator—A popular browser software used to access the Internet

network (See *local-area network, metropolitan-area network,* and *wide-area network.*)

neural network—A type of AI program designed to work like a human brain and nervous system

node—One station or site on a computer network

online—Being connected to a computer system in operation

operating system—A type of software that controls system operation and allows the computer to recognize and process instructions from applications software such as word processing programs

optical character recognition (OCR) (See *mark sense scanner.*)

optical disc—Storage medium designed to be read by laser beam (e.g., CD-ROM, videodisc)

optical mark reader (See *mark sense scanner.*)

optical scanner—Input device that converts text and graphics into computer files

output device—Any device in a computer system (e.g., monitor, printer) that displays the products of the processing part of the system

pagination—Automatic page numbering done by a word processing or desktop publishing program

password—A word or number designed to limit access to a system to authorized users only

PDA (See *personal digital assistant.*)

peripherals—Any hardware devices outside the CPU

personal computer (PC) (See *microcomputer.*)

personal digital assistant (PDA)—A handheld computer that can function as a cellular phone, fax machine, and personal organizer; uses a stylus, keyboard, or voice recognition device for input

photo CD—A compact disc format designed by the Eastman Kodak Company to store and display photographs

piracy (See *software piracy.*)

pitch—The number of characters printed per inch, usually 10-pitch or 12-pitch

pixel—The smallest unit of light that can be displayed on a computer screen

PLATO (Programmed Logic for Automatic Teaching Operations)—One of the earliest computer systems (mainframe-based) designed for instructional use; developed by the University of Illinois and Control Data Corporation

plotter—An output device designed to make a paper copy of a drawing or image from a computer screen

plug-in—A program that adds a specific feature or service to a computer system; many types of audio and video messages are played through plug-ins.

point size—A unit designating the height of a typeface character; 72 points = 1 inch

presentation software—Programs designed to allow people to display pictures and text to support their lectures or talks

primary storage (See *internal memory.*)

primitive—A simple command in the Logo programming language that does one operation (e.g., FORWARD)

print graphics—Software designed to produce graphics on paper (e.g., cards, banners)

printer—Output device that produces a paper copy of text and graphics from a computer screen

probeware (See *MBL.*)

problem-solving software—Instructional software function that either teaches specific steps for solving certain problems (e.g., math word problems) or helps the student learn general problem-solving behaviors for a class of problems

program (See *software.*)

prompt—On a computer screen, an indicator that the system is ready to accept input; can be any symbol from a C:\> to a ?

proportional spacing—Displaying text so that each character takes up a different amount of space depending on its width

public domain software—Uncopyrighted programs available for copying and use by the public at no cost

push technologies—A system set up to send out information whether or not anyone requests it. Some push systems are set up specifically to locate and return information with certain characteristics whenever it appears on the Internet.

QuickTime—Program designed by Apple Computer Company to allow short movies or video sequences to be displayed on a computer screen

RAM (random access memory)—Type of internal computer memory that is erased when the power is turned off

record—In a database file, several related fields (e.g., all the information on one person)

relational database—Database program that can link several different files through common keyword fields

relative advantage—Term coined by Everett Rogers to refer to the perception by potential adopters of an innovation of the degree to which the new method or resource has advantages over the old one; major factor in determining whether the innovation is adopted

repurposing—Use of a program to show videodisc images in a different sequence from the one stored on the disc and for a purpose that may be different from what the developer of the disc intended

retrofit—Rewiring a building such as a school to permit networked communications

ROM (read-only memory)—Type of internal computer memory designed to hold programs permanently, even when the power is turned off

rubric—An instrument designed to assess complex behaviors such as writing; consists of a set of elements that define the behavior and ratings that describe levels of performance for each element

sans serif—Typefaces that have no small curves (serifs or "hands and feet") at the ends of the lines that make them up; usually used for short titles rather than the main text of a document

scaffolding—Term associated with learning theorist Vygotsky's belief that teachers can provide good instruction by finding out where each child is in his or her development and building on the child's experiences

search and replace (also *find and replace*)—A function in a program such as a word processing package that looks for all instances of a sequence of characters and/or spaces and replaces them with another desired sequence

search engine—An Internet software (e.g., *Google, Excite*) that helps people locate Internet sites and information related to a given topic

secondary storage (See *external storage.*)

shared intelligence—A way of looking at intellect as residing in several persons, rather than in single individuals

shareware—Uncopyrighted software that anyone may use, but each user is asked to pay a voluntary fee to the designer

simulation—Type of software that models a real or imaginary system in order to teach the principles on which the system is based

snail mail—Regular postal service mail, as opposed to e-mail

software—Programs written in a computer language (in contrast with *hardware*)

software piracy—Illegally copying and using a copyrighted software package without buying it

software suite—Software sold as one package but containing several different, unintegrated programs such as *Microsoft Office* (see also *integrated software package*)

spamming—Any unsolicited e-mail or other messages, usually sent in large numbers to all users of a system; spam is the electronic equivalent of junk mail

speech synthesizer—An output device that produces spoken words through a computer program

spell checker—Part of a software package such as word processing or desktop publishing that looks for misspelled words and offers correct spellings

spreadsheet—Software designed to store data (usually, but not always, numeric) by row–column positions known as *cells;* can also do calculations on the data

sprite—Object in some versions of the Logo programming language that the user can define by color, shape, and other characteristics and then use to do animations on the screen

streaming video/audio—A way of transmitting video or audio on the Internet so that it can be seen or heard as the file downloads

structured query language (SQL)—A type of high-level language used to locate desired information from a relational database

supercomputer—The largest of the mainframe computer systems with the greatest storage space, speed, and power

switches—Equipment to compress data in order for information to be transmitted at higher speeds [e.g., Asynchronous Transfer Mode (ATM) switches]

synthesizer—Any of a series of output devices designed to produce sound, music, or speech through a computer program

SYSOP—The SYStem OPerator in a network; a person responsible for maintaining the software and activities on the network and assisting its users

systems software—Programs designed to manage the basic operations of a computer system (e.g., recognizing input devices, storing applications program commands)

technological literacy—Technical skills required for using information technology in education and the workplace

telecommunications—Communications over a distance made possible by a computer and modem or a distance learning system such as broadcast TV

telecomputing—Term coined by Kearsley to refer specifically to communications involving computers and modems

teleconferencing—People at two or more sites holding a meeting through computers and telephone lines

test generator—Software designed to help teachers prepare and/or administer tests

thesaurus—In word processing and desktop publishing, an optional feature that offers synonyms or antonyms for given words

TICCIT (Time-shared, Interactive, Computer-Controlled Information Television)—An early instructional computing system developed by Brigham Young University and the Mitre Corporation that combined television with computers

touch screen—Type of input device designed to allow users to make selections by touching the monitor

Trojan horse—Type of virus that gets into a computer attached to a legitimate program

turtle—In the Logo programming language, the triangle-shaped object that can be programmed to move and/or draw on the screen

tutorial—Type of instructional software that offers a complete sequence of instruction on a given topic

URL (Uniform Resource Locator)—A series of letters and/or symbols that acts as an address for a site on the Internet

Usenet group—On the Internet, one of a series of news groups that offer bulletin boards of information on a specific topic

variable—In programming languages, a name that stands for a place in computer memory that can hold one value

Veronica—On the Internet, a program that searches for files across gopher servers

video editing—Using a software package such as *iMovie* to make additions and changes to a selection of digital video

videoconferencing—An online "meeting" between two or more participants at different sites using: a computer or network with appropriate software; video cameras, microphone, and speakers; and telephone lines or other cabling to transmit audio and video signals

videodisc (also *laserdisc*)—Storage medium designed for storing pictures, short video sequences, and movies

virtual office—A space set up on a Web site to exchange documents and messages with colleagues working on the same activity

virtual reality—A computer-generated environment designed to provide a lifelike simulation of actual settings; often uses a data glove and/or headgear that covers the eyes

virus—A program written with the purpose of doing harm or mischief to programs, data, and/or hardware components of a computer system

visual literacy—A set of skills defined by Christopherson to include interpreting, understanding, and appreciating the meaning of visual messages; using visual messages to communicate; and using visual thinking to conceptualize solutions to problems; considered to be a subset of technological literacy

voice recognition—The capability provided by a computer and program to respond predictably to speech commands

VRML (Virtual Reality Modeling Language)—A specification for displaying three-dimensional objects on the Internet

warm boot (See *boot.*)

wearable systems—Computer components worn on one's body or clothing; usually accessed through voice recognition or other alternative input device

web site—A location on the World Wide Web identified with a Uniform Resource Locator (URL); web sites are physically located on a server connected to the Internet

whiteboard (See *electronic whiteboard.*)

wide-area network (WAN)—An interconnected group of computers linked by modems and other technologies

window—A box in a graphic user interface that appears when one opens a disk or folder to display its contents

word processing—An applications software activity that uses the computer for typing and preparing documents

word wraparound—In word processing, the feature in which text automatically goes to the next line without the user pressing Return or Enter

worksheet—Another name besides *spreadsheet* for the product of a spreadsheet program

World Wide Web (WWW)—On the Internet, a system that connects sites through hypertext links

worm—A type of virus that eats its way through (destroys) data and programs on a computer system (see also *virus*)

zone of proximal development—Term coined by learning theorist Vygotsky to refer to the difference between two levels of cognitive functioning: adult or expert and child or novice.

Name Index

Subject Index

CD-ROM User Manual

Integrating Technology Across the Curriculum: A Database of Strategies and Lesson Ideas

Items on the CD-ROM

- ***Integrating Technology Across the Curriculum.*** This database of over 500 technology integration lesson ideas and strategies was prepared with the *FileMaker Pro®* database program. The database was stored as a "runtime version" so that the program itself is not needed to use it.
- ***Adobe Acrobat®* Reader Information.** Software is included to allow this User Manual to be printed out so multiple copies of it can be made. Once the entire folder is loaded onto your hard drive, clicking on the User Manual file automatically brings up the file in the *Adobe Acrobat®* reader.

Acknowledgments

Thomas Edison said, "Success is 10% inspiration and 90% perspiration." I must express my thanks to those who contributed some of the 90% on this product. At the top of the list are the fiercely competent professionals at Merrill. Debbie Stollenwerk continues to be my role model, mentor, and friend as well as my editor. Editors Kim Lundy and JoEllen Gohr are studies in professionalism and perseverance. Dan Parker is as affable a person as he is a technical whiz. Finally and, as always, most important, my debt is to my husband, Bill Wiencke, and my daughter, Paige. Not only couldn't I have done it without them, I would never want to try.

Part I: Introduction

What Is the *Integrating Technology Across the Curriculum* Database?

Integrating Technology Across the Curriculum is a collection of over 500 technology integration ideas stored in a computer program called a "database." Database programs let people put information into the computer in such a way that it is easy to get out only those items of information that meet a certain need. For example, a teacher may want lesson ideas that use multimedia/hypermedia at elementary levels. Rather than reading each lesson to find those that meet this particular need, the teacher simply tells the database to list only those lessons that use multimedia with Grades K–5.

Classroom-tested technology integration examples have been published in many formats (e.g., articles, books, on the Web). Lessons were gleaned from several of these sources. They were summarized and placed on a database developed with *FileMaker Pro®* software.

Why Was This Collection Developed?

This collection of lesson ideas was developed to promote and support the integration of technology into teaching in content areas such as mathematics, science, and language arts. These "technology integration strategies," or descriptions of when, where, and how to use technology to help teach school topics, help schools take advantage of technology's power and potential in several ways. They help:

- **Focus teacher training on technology integration strategies,** rather than on how various technologies work
- **Allow teachers to look at good, classroom-tested examples** of integration strategies in many content areas
- **Give preservice/inservice teachers and teacher educators good models** for how to use technology resources (e.g., multimedia, spreadsheets, the Internet)
- **Help teachers find specific technology integration strategies** to meet their classroom needs.

Who Can Use This Product?

Integrating Technology Across the Curriculum is useful for:

- **Classroom teachers** looking for resources and lesson ideas
- **Teacher educators and trainers** showing examples of technology integration in various content areas
- **Inservice/preservice teachers** learning how to use databases.

How Can It Be Used?

This database could supplement and enhance any teacher training course or workshop; or it could be useful to teachers in classrooms. Activities that could be done with it include the following.

- **Locating an idea to meet a certain need.** Teachers can use it to answer questions such as: "Can technology be used to support teaching writing in an interdisciplinary way?" or "What are some good examples of using spreadsheets in mathematics?"
- **Illustrating technology integration strategies for various resources.** Have students ask, "How can word processing be used in areas other than language arts?"
- **Teaching database use and searches.** Show preservice students how to locate all lessons for a given grade level, content area, and/or type (e.g., plans in science at the fifth grade level), or teach them how to add lessons of their own.

What Do You Have to Know to Use It?

This product was designed for non-technical teachers and students. You do not have to know much about databases to use it. That is because this manual gives explanations and examples to help new users, and the database structure itself is very intuitive and easy to use.

New in This Version

In this, the second version of *Integrating Technology Across the Curriculum,* several new and valuable features have been added:

- **Over 250 additional lesson ideas.** Many of the new entries focus on the Internet and online learning and have been drawn from sites recommended by Blue Web 'n, an online collection of prize-winning Internet teaching and learning strategies. Other new entries have been based on articles from 1999–2002 issues of ISTE's *Learning and Leading with Technology.*
- **Relative advantage emphasis.** This new lesson descriptor focuses on the unique or powerful aspects technology resources bring to a lesson, thus allowing teachers to do something they could not do or could not do as well as they could without the resources. *Relative advantage* is a term used by diffusion of innovations expert Everett Rogers to refer to perceptions by those considering the adoption of an innovation of the benefits of the new method or resource over what they currently use. (See the list of the types of Relative Advantage in Figure 1.)

Part II: Contents of the Database

An Overview of the Lessons

The 500+ lesson ideas in this database are drawn from these sources:

- **The International Society for Technology in Education's (ISTE)** ***Learning and Leading with Technology*** **(formerly** ***The Computing Teacher*****).** Many articles from this popular periodical, now in its 30th year of publication by the country's premier educational technology

Figure 1 Lesson Idea Descriptors

Grade Levels:

Grade-free
Pre-K
Kindergarten
Primary
Elementary
Middle School
Secondary
1
2
3
4
5
6
7
8
9
10
11
12

Content Areas:

Interdisciplinary
Art
English
Foreign Languages
Language Arts
Mathematics
Music
Physical Education
Social Studies
Science
Technology
Other

Topics:

Algebra
Anthropology
Archeology
Arithmetic
Art history
Astronomy
Biology
Botany
Business math
Calculus
Charting/graphing
Chemistry
Civics
Computer applications
Cultures
Drawing/painting
Ecology
Economics
Electricity
French
Geography
Geology
Geometry
German
Grammar
Health and nutrition
History
Literature
Math problem solving
Math word problems
Measurement
Multicultural
Musical composition
Music history
Physical education
Physics
Poetry
Political Science
Problem solving (non-math)
Programming
Psychology
Reading
Research methods
Sociology
Spanish
Spelling
Statistics
Study skills
Trigonometry
Vocabulary
Weather
Writing
Other

Technologies:

All
Adaptive/assistive devices
Alternative keyboards
Animation software
Artificial intelligence
Atlases
Audio players
Barcode generators
Brainstorming tools
Calculators
CD-ROM
Charting/graphing
Computer Assisted Design (CAD)
Concept maps
Databases
Desktop publishing
Dictionaries (word atlases)
Distance learning
Drill and practice software
Electronic books
Electronic encyclopedia
E-mail
Fax
Games
GIS
Graphics tools
Groupware
Handheld computer/PDA
Instructional software
Internet
Local Area Network (LAN)
Logo
Map utilities
MIDI interfaces
Movies/videos
Multimedia/hypermedia
Music synthesizers
PDF files
Presentation software
Probeware/MBL
Problem solving software
Programming languages
Robotics
Simulation software
Speech synthesizers
Spreadsheets
Statistical software
Story starters
TDD
Tutorial software
VCR
Video development
Videodisc-Level I
Videodisc-Level III
Virtual reality
Voice recognition
Word prediction software
Word processing

Relative Advantage:

Makes unfamiliar topics more visual, understandable
Makes abstract topics more visual, concrete
Supports manual operations in high level learning
Interaction and immediate feedback support skill practice
Visual presentations help illustrate real-life relevance
Visual presentations aid transfer to real-world problems
Professional, polished looking products motivate students
Format aids collaborative, cooperative group work
Develops technological/information literacy skills
Saves teacher time in grading students' work
Provides self-paced instruction to motivated students
Saves teacher/student time on production tasks
Saves money on consumable materials
Easier, faster access to information sources
Easier, faster updates/corrections to work products

Note: Some of the "Technologies" descriptors have no lesson entries. Users can use the *Add Lesson Idea* feature to add their own lesson entries for these if they like.

organization, are by teachers describing their own successful classroom strategies. Lesson activities selected in this database were based on the best lessons from a dozen years of these articles.

- Internet lesson and project sites recommended by Blue Web 'n, an online collection of prize-winning Internet teaching and learning strategies.
- ***Productivity in the Classroom*** **booklets** (also available at Microsoft's online site) were produced by Microsoft, Inc., in conjunction with Scholastic, Inc. Lessons in this database were based on some of these activities. Visit their site: **http://www.microsoft.com/education** (Look under the K–12 area and select "Instructional Resources.")
- ***Problem Solving Across the Curriculum*** by John Beaver (Copyright © 1994 by ISTE).
- **Lesson plan issues of *The Florida Technology in Education Quarterly.*** Lessons on the database are based on those in the Spring 1991 ESE lesson ideas issue, the Winter 1992 elementary lesson ideas issue, and the Spring 1993 telecommunications issue (all selected by *FTEQ* Editor M. D. Roblyer).

Each lesson in the database is an edited, summarized version based on the original article or lesson plan.

Organization of the Database

The first screen that appears shows the three main activities:

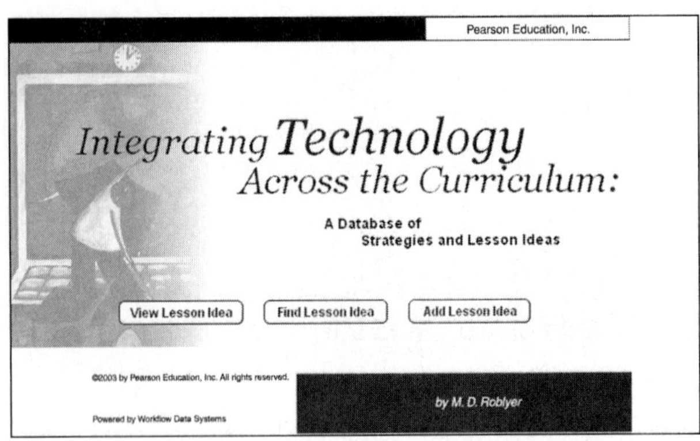

View lesson plan. See a list of the 500 lesson idea titles. Each lesson has five main screens or "pages" (see example, beginning on this page):

- **Page 1** gives lesson objectives.

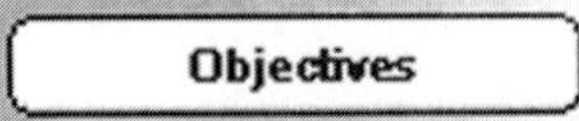

- **Page 2** lists the lesson descriptors (Grade Levels, Content Areas, Topic Areas, Technologies, and Relative Advantage).

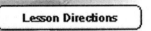

- **Page 3** describes lesson activities and assessments.

- **Page 4** shows images associated with the lesson.

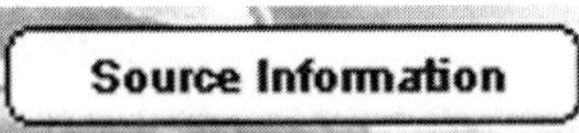

- **Page 5** gives reference information on where the lesson was obtained.

Find lesson plan. Each lesson is stored with a set of "descriptors" or labels that describe the contents and let teachers locate lessons that meet their needs. For example, one descriptor is "Grade Levels" (the grade levels the lesson addresses); another is "Technologies." (See a listing of descriptors in Figure 1.) Teachers also can locate lesson entries by "keywords." For example, type in "butterflies" in the Directions field to see if there are any lessons on butterflies.

Add lesson plan. This option lets teachers enter their own descriptors and lesson activities to describe a new lesson and add it to the collection.

Other options such as printing lessons and duplicating lessons may be selected from later screens. See directions for how to use Find, Add, and Other Options under **Part III** of this manual.

Anatomy of a Typical Lesson

Five screens make up the "skeleton" or underlying structure of the database:

- **Page 1:** Lesson plan objectives and national content area standards the plan addresses.

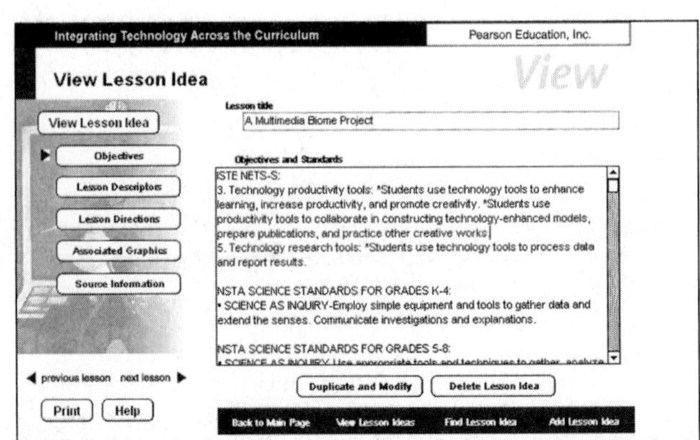

- **Page 2:** Descriptors that define the lesson plan characteristics (see a list of all descriptors in Figure 1).

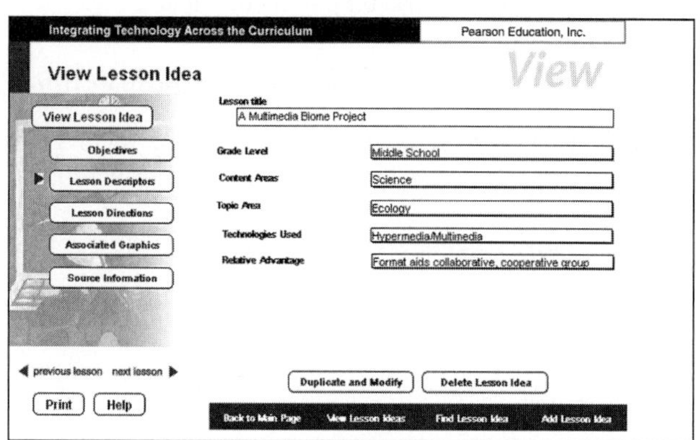

- **Page 3:** Detailed directions for the lesson idea. At the bottom of the lesson directions for all non-Internet lessons is a list of required resources a teacher needs to carry out the lesson activities. Also at the bottom of this field are suggestions for assessments.

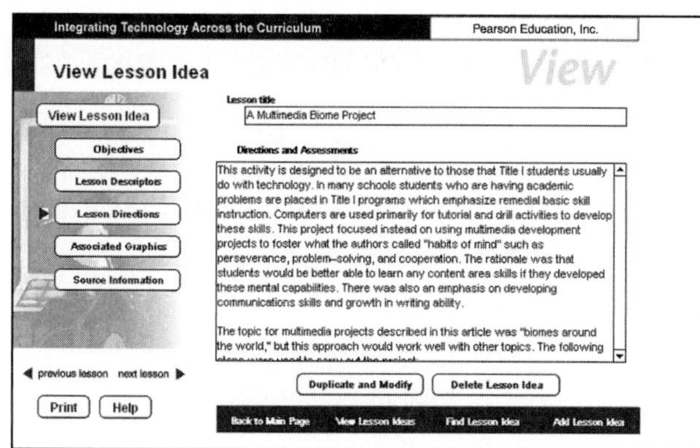

- **Page 4:** Many plans also have associated graphics (e.g., diagrams, photos, or screens of example products).

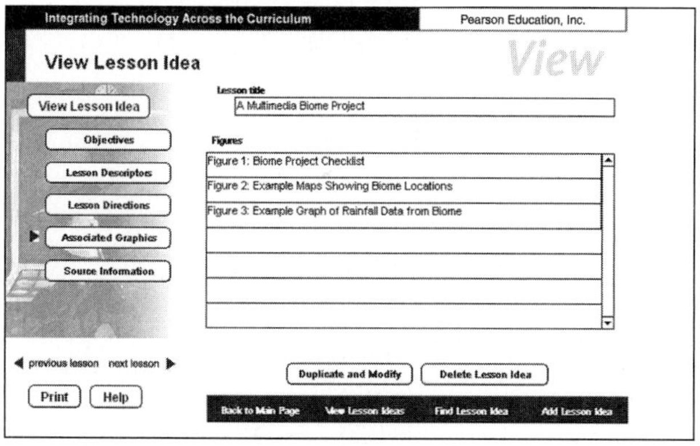

- **Page 4 continued:** Click on one of the graphics in the list; a page with the image appears. Sometimes the size of the computer screen makes these images too small to see clearly on the monitor. In these cases, it is necessary to print the image and look at the paper copy.

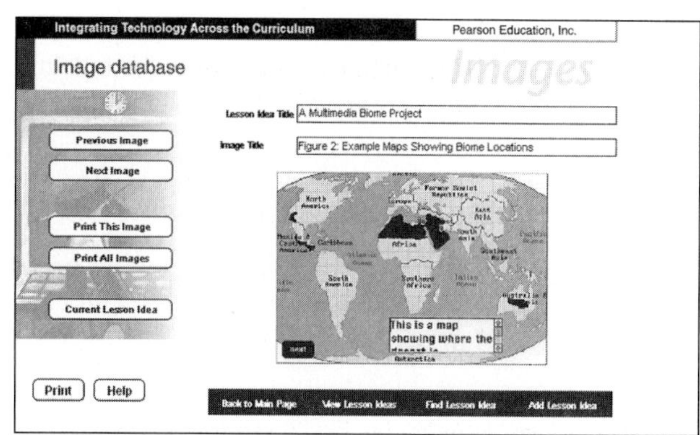

- **Page 5:** Author name(s), bibliographic source, and site of field-tests, if any.

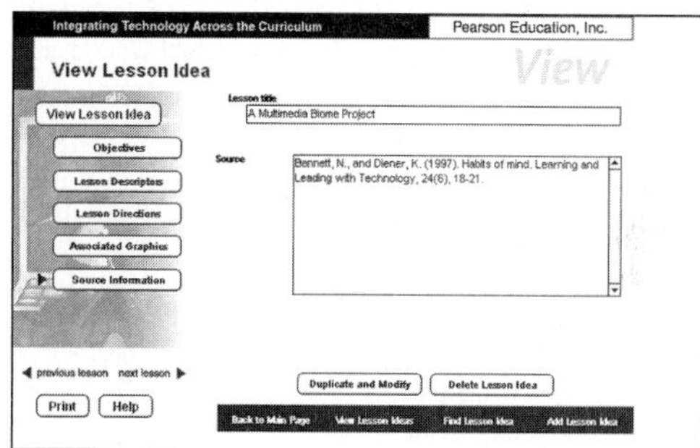

Part III: How to Use the Database

How to Start the Program

The database may be opened and used directly from the CD, or it may be moved to the hard drive first and used from there. Use from the hard drive is required if you want to add to or modify the lessons.

- **To use from the CD in the Macintosh platform:**
  - Insert the CD.
  - Open the Macintosh folder and double-click the Lesson icon to load the database file.
- **To use from the CD in Windows 95, 98, 2000, NT, and XP platforms:**
  - Insert the CD.
  - Double-click "My Computer."
  - Select the CD drive.
  - Open the Windows folder.
  - Double-click the Lesson icon to load the database file.
- **To use on your hard drive:**
  - If you want to modify lessons or add your own lessons, you **must** move the database to your own hard drive. (You cannot store anything on the CD-ROM.)
  - Insert the CD.

– Follow your system procedures for moving the lesson and art files over to your hard drive. (Usually this means dragging the files from the CD to your hard drive window.)

How to Protect the Hard Drive Copy

PLEASE NOTE: To protect the copyright on this product, we have limited the number of times you can copy it on to your hard drive.

Once the database is on your hard drive, it is very easy to change it—even unintentionally. *For example, if you highlight one of the Descriptor fields, the one you highlight will take the place of the ones that came with the database.* However, if the copy on the hard drive becomes damaged, or you change it unintentionally and want to re-install it, you may do so only a limited number of times. That is why it is a good idea to protect the copy on your hard drive and make sure you don't make changes unintentionally by doing the following:

- **Macintosh version:** Once the file is on your hard drive—and before you run the program—click once on the file name to highlight it. Then press Open-Apple-I. The box shown here will appear. To lock the file, click on the option at the bottom left.

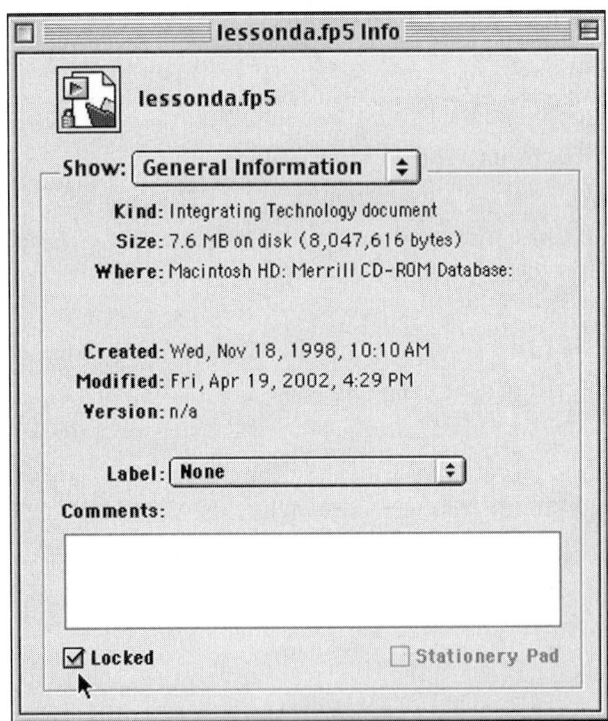

When you want to add or modify lesson ideas, you can bring this box up again and unlock the file by clicking the same option.

- **Windows versions:** Once the file is on your hard drive—and before you run the program—right-click once on the file name, and select the Properties option from the box. Under General options, select "Read only." As with Mac versions, you can unlock the file when you want to add lesson ideas to the database or modify them.

How to Find Lesson Ideas by Browsing through Titles

From the main screen, clicking "View Lesson Idea" gives you a list of lesson titles through which you can scroll.

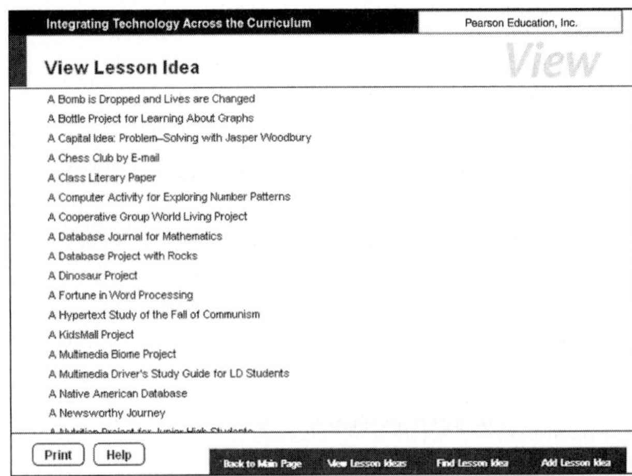

When you want to see more detail on a lesson, click *once* on the title to see its Objectives page. Click on one of the other tabs to see the Lesson descriptors, Lesson directions, Associated graphics, or Source information pages for that lesson.

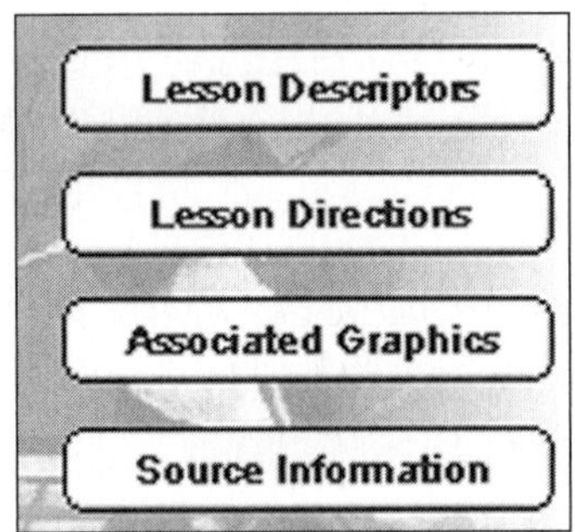

To review a lesson's descriptors, click on Lesson Descriptors, then on one of the descriptor boxes; a pulldown menu will show you all the descriptors. The ones checked are those for the lesson.

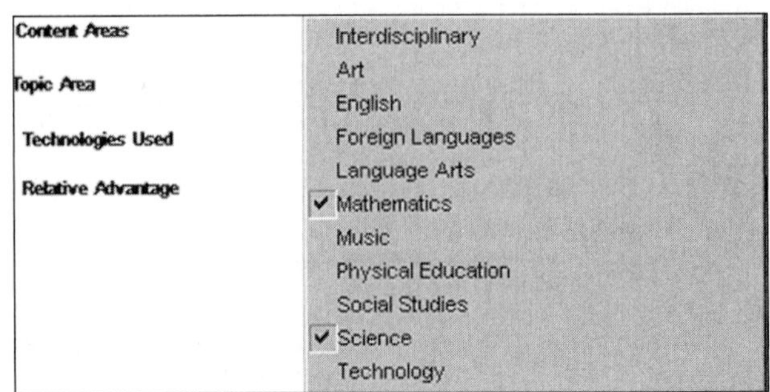

How to Find Lesson Ideas by Using Descriptors

- **Click on** ***Find Lesson Idea*** from the ***View Lesson Idea*** screen or the ***Main Menu*** screen.
- **Click on** ***Find by Criteria.***
- **Select options you want** under each descriptor by clicking on a box, then clicking on the option.

NOTE: If you want more than one option under a descriptor (e.g., Spreadsheets AND Graphics under the Technologies descriptor), hold the Shift key down each time you select an option. Repeat this step until all desired options are checked.

- **After you select all options, click** ***Start Search.*** You will see a list of lessons that meet the criteria.
- **Click on a lesson title to see its contents.** When you are finished looking at a lesson, click the "Previous lesson" or "Next lesson" button to see another lesson in the group from your search.

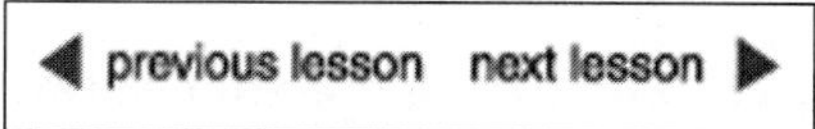

How to Find Lessons by Using Keywords

- **Click on** ***Find Lesson Idea*** from the ***Main Menu*** screen or the ***View Lesson Idea*** screen.
- **Click on** ***Find by Keyword.***
- **Type in words** you want to find under *each field.*
- **Click** ***Start Search.***

How to Find Lessons by Using a Combination of Descriptors and Keywords

You can use a combination of descriptors and keywords to do a search. For example, if you want an Internet lesson idea that addresses the topic of "money," you would select ***Find Lesson Idea,*** then click on ***Find by Keyword*** and enter "money" in the ***Lesson Directions*** field. Then click on ***Find by Criteria*** and select "Internet" from the ***Technologies*** list and click ***Start Search.***

How to Add Your Own Lessons

To add a new lesson idea, first load on to your hard drive all of the files from the CD-ROM. You cannot add lesson ideas to the database on the CD-ROM.

- **Click on** ***Add Lesson Idea*** from the main screen.
- **Fill in information** in all descriptor boxes. Be sure to give the lesson a title so the lesson appears in the list.
- **Fill in information** for all of the related screens: Objectives, Lesson Descriptors, Lesson Directions, and Source Information.

How to Modify Existing Lessons

As you do for adding a new lesson plan, first load on to your hard drive all of the files from the CD-ROM.

- **Select** ***Duplicate and Modify*** from the View screen to make a copy of an existing lesson.
- **Make changes to it** as desired. Remember to change the title; otherwise, the lesson will have the old title with the word "copy" after it. The program will save the new lesson to your hard drive automatically.

Other Options

Additional options are at the bottom of the main pages:

- **Printing.** Print a lesson by selecting ***Print.*** Print graphics by clicking ***Associated Graphics,*** selecting the image from the list of images, then clicking ***Print This Image.*** To print all images associated with a lesson, click the ***Print All Images*** button.
- **Help.** Clicking Help provides you with an explanation and examples of various options and how to use them.
- **Navigation options.** You can return to the main page or choose other options to try.

Saving to Disk

Use the following steps to save a lesson or the entire database to a disk other than the hard drive.

- **Save a single lesson plan** by selecting Import/Export, then select Export from the File menu. Then:
  - **Select the location** (the disk and the folder or directory) where you want to save the lesson plan.
  - **Name the file** when you see the Save As box. If you want to view the lesson plan without having *FileMaker Pro®* on your hard drive, save in a text file or other format.
- **Save the entire database** by selecting **Save a Copy** from the program's **File Menu.** (You will need a Zip disk to hold all the contents.)

Part IV: Classroom Applications

This collection can be used in many ways by several kinds of people. No matter who uses it, it is best to begin by reviewing the following sequence of introductory activities.

- **Get familiar with the database structure.** You either can page through lessons one at a time, or you can search for lessons that have certain words in them or that address certain students, tools, or topics.
- **Examine the parts of an activity.** Look at the information provided with each lesson idea activity.
- **Peruse the lesson ideas.** Page through several lesson ideas to get a feel for the kinds of approaches represented.
- **Do some sample searches.** Try locating lesson ideas that meet your needs.

Example Applications for College Instructors

Teacher educators can use this collection of lesson ideas and activities as model applications of the technology tools and teaching methods they introduce in their classrooms. Some example uses follow.

Example Activity #1: Find a way to teach poetry. With the whole class, do a search on lessons by using "poetry" in the ***Lesson Directions*** field. Divide the class into small groups; have each group analyze one of the lessons in the database, discuss it, and develop a lesson based on that approach. Have each group present its lesson to the class, explaining why the technology resource they used contributed significantly to teaching poetry.

Example Activity #2: How is the Internet being used? With the whole class, do a criteria search on lessons using "Internet" in the ***Technologies*** field. After each student reads the lessons and reviews uses of the Internet, hold a class discussion on the ways the Internet is being used and how it is contributing to learning. Divide the class into small groups; have them develop their own lessons using the Internet and present them to the class.

Example Activity #3: Develop a good lesson. Have the class form small groups and select a technology resource such as word processing or multimedia. Have them search for and review lessons that use this resource and develop a good lesson of their own to add to the database. It must specify all required descriptors and detailed directions. Have groups present their lessons to the class.

Example Applications for Pre K–12 Teachers

Inservice teachers can use this collection as a source of ideas for how to use technology to teach various topics and content area standards. Some example uses follow.

Example Activity #4: Collaborative projects. An area that is seeing great emphasis in recent years is teaching students how to work cooperatively to develop products and solve problems. Teachers can locate examples of how to do this effectively by doing a search for "collaboration" or "collaborate" or "cooperative" in the ***Lesson Directions*** field.

Example Activity #5: Addressing ISTE or national standards. Each lesson in the database lists ISTE NETS-S and national standards addressed for each of several content areas. Teachers can do a search on the ***Objectives*** field to find lessons that address desired standards, e.g., ISTE Standard 1, Civics, Economics, NCTE, NSTA, NCTM, History, Science.

Example Activity #6: Interdisciplinary activities. Teachers can locate good examples of teaching activities that address more than one content area in the same lesson. They can do a search by criteria, and select Interdisciplinary in the ***Content Areas*** field.

Example Applications for Teacher Education Students

As they learn how to integrate various technologies into the classroom, future teachers can see what classroom teachers consider good uses of these resources. Some example uses follow.

Example Activity #7: Find a multicultural activity. Many lessons model how to emphasize multiculturalism in the course of content area learning. Students can find these examples by doing a search by criteria using "Multicultural" or "Cultures" in the ***Topic Areas*** field, or by searching ***Lesson Directions*** using the keyword "cultural."

Example Activity #8: How is technology used in the (*insert your own*) content area? Students can do a search for all lessons in a given content area, browse through all the lessons, and review which technology resources are used and how they are used. This activity will give them a good introduction to and overview of how technology is being integrated into their content areas.

Example Activity #9: What are some whole-class strategies? Many K–12 classrooms have only one computer. By searching on "one computer" in the ***Lesson Directions*** field, teacher education students can see examples of how inservice teachers are making the best use of limited resources. The lessons will model how to structure goals and objectives and carry out activities that can be accomplished with one computer.

Starting Out on the Internet
A Learning Journey for Teachers

Second Edition

M. D. Roblyer
University of Maryland University College

Upper Saddle River, New Jersey
Columbus, Ohio

Vice President and Publisher: Jeffery W. Johnston
Editor: Debra A. Stollenwerk
Development Editor: Kimberly J. Lundy
Editorial Assistant: Mary Morrill
Production Editor: JoEllen Gohr
Production Manager: Pamela D. Bennett
Director of Marketing: Ann Castel Davis
Marketing Manager: Krista Groshong
Marketing Services Manager: Tyra Cooper

Copyright Information:

Adobe® and the Adobe® *Acrobat* logo are registered trademarks of Adobe Systems Incorporated. This book is not endorsed or sponsored by Adobe Systems Incorporated, publisher of Adobe *Acrobat*®, Adobe *PageMaker*®, and Adobe *Photoshop*®.

Apple®, Macintosh®, and the Apple *QuickTime*® logo are all registered trademarks of Apple Computer, Inc., registered in the U.S. and other countries.

HyperStudio® is a registered trademark of Knowledge Adventure, Inc.

Microsoft® and Microsoft.com® are registered trademarks of the Microsoft Corporation in the United States and/or other countries.

Microsoft *Word*® and Microsoft *PowerPoint*® are either trademarks or registered trademarks of the Microsoft Corporation in the United States and/or other countries.

Netscape® and the Netscape N and Ship's Wheel logos are registered trademarks of Netscape® Communications Corporation in the U.S. and other countries.

RealAudio®, *Real Player*®, and the Real Networks® logo are all trademarks of RealNetworks, Inc. All rights reserved.

NOTE: Every effort has been made to provide accurate and current Internet information in this book. However, the Internet and information posted on it are constantly changing; it is inevitable that some of the Internet addresses listed in this textbook will change.

10 9 8 7 6 5 4 3 2 1
ISBN 0-13-110970-7

❦

Table of Contents

Dedication

for Marilyn Comet—
educational technology luminary, great lady, great friend

Preface

Why This Book Was Written

The most enduring metaphor for the Internet is that of a highway, perhaps because it is such an appropriate comparison. Highways, like the Internet, can be paths to adventure and new knowledge, ways to get quickly to destinations already known, and courses to wander casually in search of new discoveries.

However, either the paved roads of a countryside or the electronic pathways of the World Wide Web also can be a confusing collection of perplexing signs and symbols, places to get lost and frustrated, a series of dead ends. The difference between these two experiences is understanding the basics of "travel" and the resources available to help the traveler.

Many educators are beginning to recognize how important it is to "get out on the road" and begin learning a new way for themselves and their students to see the world. This book is designed to be an easy way for them to learn some of the basics required to become a skilled "Internet traveler." An old proverb holds that a journey of a thousand miles begins with but a single step. This booklet has a series of first steps to get educators started on what could be a most enlightening journey.

What You Need to Prepare for the Trip

Before setting out on a journey, some preparation always is in order. However, you needn't learn everything at once. One of the best things about the Internet is that you don't have to be a very technical person to use it, just as you need not be an auto mechanic to drive a car! At first, teachers may want to ask someone to prepare their "vehicle" for them to get them started. Later, they can learn more technical items about Internet use so they don't have to rely as much on others.

But not even the best driver's manual can substitute for driving experience; getting out on the Internet is the best way to learn it. Before you start, though, be sure you have obtained the following **two** items.

❶ **An Internet-ready computer.** Any veteran traveler knows that having a well-equipped vehicle can make all the difference in the quality of a trip, and so it is with the Internet. To make your Internet travel go smoothly, make sure you have a computer:

RAM is the memory that holds programs while they are being used.

☛ *With fast enough speed and enough Random Access Memory (RAM) to do Internet tasks:*

Good: 1.6 GHz speed, 128 Megabytes (MB) RAM
Better: 1.7 GHz speed, 256 MB RAM
Best: 2.0 GHz or better speed, 512 MB or more RAM

Speed at which signals are sent between computers is measured in bits per second, or bps.

☛ *Equipped with a fast enough connection:*

Good: A computer with a 56 thousand bits per second (bps) modem, and connected to a telephone line.

Better: A computer with connection via a satellite system (e.g. DISH® Network or DirectTV®), cable modem (from a cable company), or Digital Subscriber (DSL) line (from the phone company).

Best: A computer on a network (e.g., at a school) that is connected to the Internet with a T1 line or better

☛ *Equipped with browser software:* Browsers are programs that display web pages as pictures so you can look ("browse") through them and do tasks with them. The most common web browsers are:

- *Netscape Communicator®*
- Microsoft's *Internet Explorer®*

However, companies such as America Online have their own browsers. Each of these browsers has versions for Windows PC and Macintosh computers.

In this book, we will show screen examples with *Netscape Communicator®*, although others are similar. Below is an example of the Prentice Hall web site as viewed through the *Netscape Communicator®* browser.

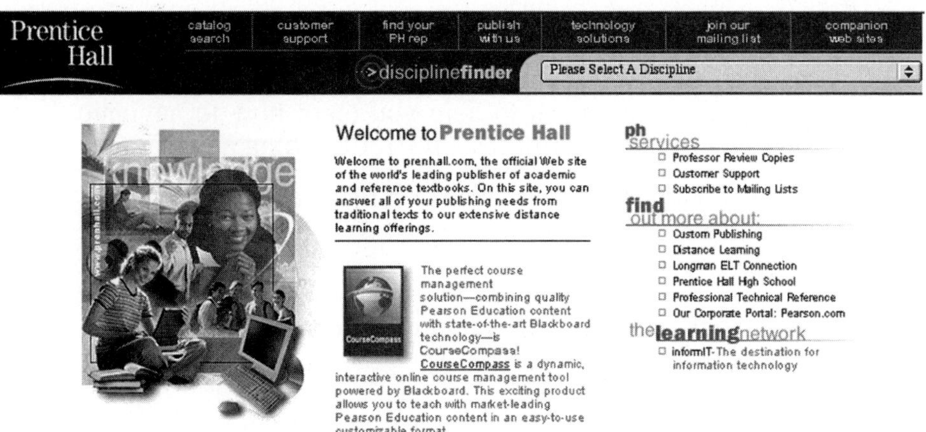

Netscape Browser Displaying the Prentice Hall Web Site

❷ **An Internet connection.** Next, you need to be connected to the Internet. What exactly does it mean to be "connected?" Although there are several different ways, they all mean you are able to use browser software to have your Internet-ready computer send electronic signals over lines and make contact with other Internet-ready computers. But access to the Internet is not free. Even schools or districts that provide it free to their teachers must pay someone for it. If you have no group that provides access for you, shop for the best **Internet Service Provider (ISP)**. Look for three things when you shop for an ISP:

Reliability: Can you get on the Internet whenever you want? Or is the line busy or is the provider's computer "down" a lot of the time?

Good support: Is someone available "24/7" (24 hours a day, seven days a week) to help you if you have problems or questions?

Fair price: Is there a reasonable flat fee, or do they charge by the minute?

If you have an Internet-ready computer and a connection to the Internet, you are ready to begin the steps in this book!

How to Use This Book

Appropriate for use either on an individual computer or in a lab setting, *Starting Out on the Internet: A Learning Journey for Teachers* takes a step-by-step approach to help you learn how to navigate the Internet and use it as a powerful resource for teaching and learning.

Look for the following icons or pictures to help guide you through each of the 11 sections:

This "book" icon at the beginning of each section signals new Internet terms and concepts you will want to learn.

This "light bulb" icon marks "helpful hints" or additional explanation to help you understand the new information.

Look for this image throughout each section and at the end of each section for "Try This!" exercises for you to check your learning at each step. Answers to these exercises can be found in the Appendix of this book.

Also look for the following web site to support your learning activities:

http://www.prenhall.com/startingout

This site has two features that you can use to help develop your Internet knowledge and skills:

- **Section self-tests** – The site has a set of review questions for each section you can answer and receive immediate feedback on correctness.

- **Sample personal web site** – These web pages are used with Section 11 as you learn how to develop your own personal web site.

Enjoy the trip!

Acknowledgments

Many people look upon writing a book as an impossible undertaking. In fact, it is. But what they may not realize is how similar an enterprise it is to what classroom teachers do every day. Both involve accomplishing tasks with too little time, resources, and knowledge. Both require commitment and sacrifice: time taken away from family and friends and long hours without adequate rest or "down time." Both have teaching as their purpose and learning as their ultimate goal. But perhaps most important, both teachers and writers must love their work to make it all worth it.

My thanks go out once more to all the people who make it possible for me to do what I love. For this book, I am obliged especially to recognize my continuing debt to my friend, mentor, and editor Debbie Stollenwerk; other Merrill professionals JoEllen Gohr, Heather Fraser, Kim Lundy, Mary Morrill, and Dan Parker; my family, Bill and Paige Wiencke; and friends such as Sherry Alter and Paul Belt, Marilyn and Herb Comet, Barbara Hansen, Sharon and Jon Marshall, Mary Ann Myers, and Gwen McAlpine and Paul Zimmer.

Thanks, also, to the educators who read this book about the Internet as a way to become even better at what they do. Beginning to integrate technology into an already packed classroom and school agenda may seem impossible to others. But all we teachers know that for those who feel passionate about what they do, the difficult really is no problem, and the impossible just takes a little more time.

M. D. Roblyer

ONE - *Understanding URLs*
How to Use Internet Addresses

New Terms

- *Uniform Resource Locator (URL)*
- *Server*
- *Domain name*
- *Domain designator*
- *Suffix*

Required Parts of a URL

Every home in the United States has an address so people can find it and make deliveries of mail and other items. Each place you "visit" on the Internet also has an address, and for much the same reasons. However, the Internet is less tolerant of mistakes in an address than is the U. S. Post Office! Each address must be entered exactly, with every punctuation mark in place, or it will not work.

Internet addresses are called Uniform Resource Locators, or **URLs**. Look at the example URL shown below in a browser window. The line where the URL is entered is called the address line:

Bring up the browser on your computer screen and enter the above URL in the address line. Then press Return or Enter to "travel" to this address on the Internet.

Every URL has four required parts (although it can have more optional ones that will be described later):

http://www.nasa.gov
❶ ❷ ❸ ❹

❶ Each web page address begins with **http://** which stands for HyperText Transfer Protocol. The "http://" shows it is an Internet address.

❷ Most, but not all, addresses contain **www,** which stands for World Wide Web.

A "server" is a computer that has a site on the Internet.

❸ The next part of the address here is **nasa**, the name of the computer or "server" to which you connect. Every server on the Internet has an assigned label called the "domain name." **nasa** shows that this computer belongs to the National Aeronautic and Space Administration, a government agency that offers educators a wealth of resources on its web site.

Domain designators for public schools usually include the state name.

Examples:
k12.ny.us (New York)

k12.fl.us (Florida)

❹ Finally, another required part of the domain name, called a "domain designator," tells what kind of group owns the server. Some example domain designators are:

org = organization	**com** = business
gov = government agency	**edu** = university
k12.__.us = public schools	**net** = network
mil = military agency	**aus** = Australia

Note that "net" is often used instead of "org" for many schools and other organizations. There are many more designators, and more are being added all the time as the need arises. The U. S. non-profit organization that sets up domain names is the Internet Corporation for Assigned Names and Numbers (ICANN).

You can learn more about ICANN at **http://www.icann.org**

Optional Parts of a URL

If an organization is a large one, it may have more than one server; or it may split up a large computer into sections. Then the domain name will have more parts. For example, the University of Maryland University College (**umuc**) has a server called **tychousa1** used for its distance courses:

http://tychousa1.umuc.edu

Optional parts called "suffixes" can come after a domain designator. Suffixes show locations on the server that are set aside for specific purposes. For example, the UMUC Academic Calendar is shown at a certain location on the UMUC server indicated by the suffix after the slash:

http://www.umuc.edu/calendar

In the spaces below, answer the following questions about the parts of the following URL.

http://www.kidlink.org/english/general/index.html

1. What does **www** stand for?

    ____

2. What is the name of the computer or server that displays this site?

    ____

3. Which part of the URL identifies this as an Internet address?

    ____

4. What is the domain designator in this URL, and what kind of group does it indicate owns this site?

    ____

5. Why are there slashes in this URL?

    ____

Three URL Uses

Three things to learn how to do with URLs are locate them, read them, and "fix" errors in them.

- **Locating URLs.** If you want to visit a site, but you don't know its URL, one way to find it is to make an educated guess. For example, let's say you want to find the website for the National Council of Social Studies. Since you know it will have an "org" designator and organizations usually use their initials in URLs, a good guess would be: **http://www.ncss.org**

Guess a URL for each of the following.
Then go on the Internet and type in the URLs to see if you are correct.

1. **National Council of Teachers of Mathematics**
   Correct answer: ______________________________

2. **The Music Educators National Conference**
   Correct answer: ______________________________

- **Reading URLs.** If someone gives you a URL, very often you can tell what and where it is by reading its parts. Look at an example:

http://www.noaa.gov

If you knew that the URL someone gave you was one on weather, you might guess this is for the National Oceanic and Atmospheric Administration (NOAA), a government agency that offers students and teachers a wealth of up-to-date information on the weather.

Can you read the URL for each of the following?
Type in the URL, and go to the site to see if you are right.

1. For students with vision problems: **http://www.afb.org**
   Whose site is this? ______________________________

2. For a department in the federal government: **http://www.ed.gov**
   Whose site is this? ______________________________

- **Fixing errors in URLs.** Someone may give you a URL with an error in it (or you may write down one incorrectly!) There are five common errors you can look for and correct:

If you have trouble with a URL, try cutting off the suffixes and going to the main page of the site.

Error #1 – Omitting one of the parts. The most common omission is the "http:// (or the "www" if it needs it).

Error #2 – Wrong domain designator. For example, people often substitute "com" for "org."

Error #3 – Punctuation errors. People often confuse forward slashes (/) and back slashes (\), and hyphens (-) with underlines (_). Also, there are no spaces in a URL. Spaces are designated with an underscore (_).

Error #4 – Punctuation omitted. If you leave out a "dot" or a slash, the URL will not work.

Error #5 – Misspellings. Most misspellings in URLs seem to occur in suffixes.

Can you spot errors in each of the following URLs?
Correct each, then enter it in a browser to check..

1. The Eisenhower National Clearinghouse, a site with lesson plans and other resources for teachers:

   What's the error? **http://enc.org** ____________________________

2. The American School Heath Association:

   What's the error? **http://www.ashaweborg** ____________________

TRY THIS!

Section One
Summary Exercises: Understanding URLs

Exercises 1.1 – Review of New Terms and Concepts

__________ 1. Name for the part of the Internet address that tells what kind of group owns the server (e.g., "edu")

__________ 2. The "/roblyer" part of the following URL is an example of one of these: http://www.prenhall.com/roblyer

__________ 3. What the acronym URL stands for

__________ 4. The following URL has this kind of error: http://www.white house.gov

__________ 5. A computer that has a site on the Internet

Exercises 1.2 – Practice Activities to Expand Your Skills

1. **Locate a URL** – You try to locate the web site for the American Educational Research Association, but the URL you thought would work (http://www.aera.org) sent you to a technical association. What other URL might you try? (**HINT:** Try a different domain designator.)

   ____

2. **Read a URL** – Whose web site do you think each of the following is?

   http://www.ira.org/ ______________________________
   http://peabody.vanderbilt.edu ______________________________

3. **Fix a URL** – See if you can find and fix the errors in these URL's:

a) Apple Computer site to download their movie software:
http://apple.edu/quicktime/download/______________________________

b) Organization that publishes information about educational software
http:\\www.spa.org ______________________________

c) A special server on the University of California at Berkeley web site with science exploration environments for K–12 schools
http://wise.berkley.edu/ ______________________________

TWO – *Navigating the Net*
How to Move Around in Web Pages

Five Ways to Go

New Terms

- *Links, hot links, or hot spots*

You can move around from web page to web page on the Internet by using five different options. The first two options are to use two kinds of ***links*** that have been programmed into the web page itself. These are also known as "*hot links*" or "*hot spots*."

These links are programmed to send your browser to another location on the Internet, either within the site or to another site, when you click on them with your mouse. These programmed links can be:

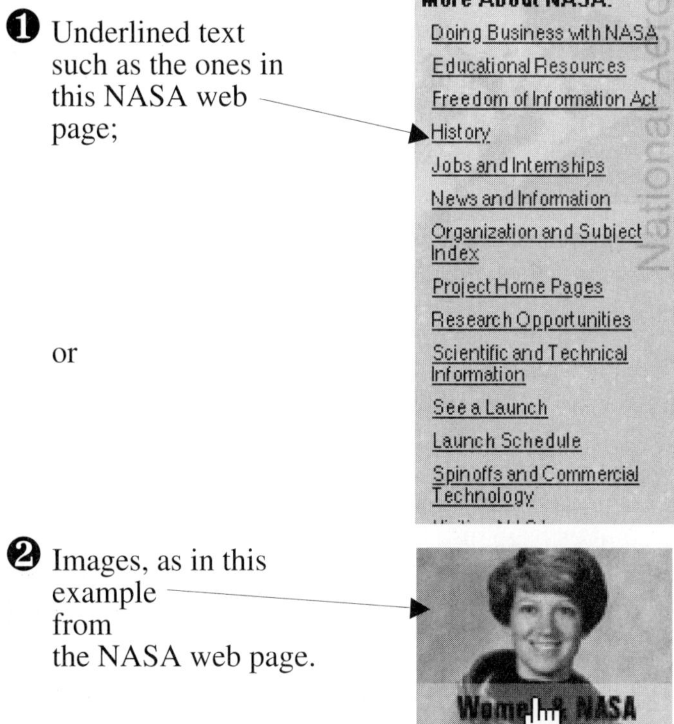

❶ Underlined text such as the ones in this NASA web page;

or

❷ Images, as in this example from the NASA web page.

How do know when images are links? When you pass a mouse pointer over the image (without clicking) and the pointer turns into a "browser hand" such as the one on the "Women & NASA" picture above, you know it is a link. Any part of a web page can be programmed to be a link.

Three other options are available on your browser menu bars. See the NASA web page example below.

❸ **Back button**

❹ **Forward button**

❺ **Go Menu** (in *Internet Explorer*®, use **File Menu**)

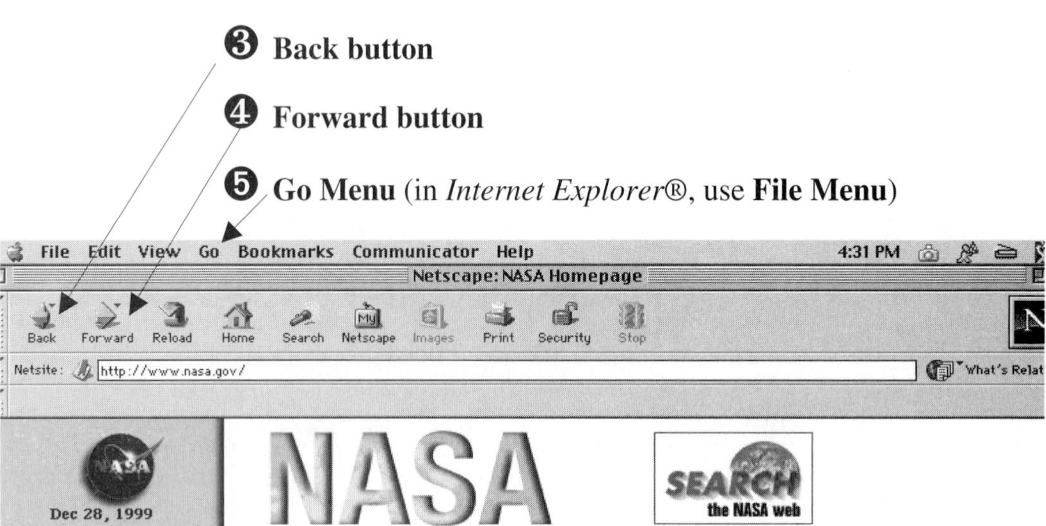

Forward and Back buttons let you go *one step at a time* on a linear path through a chain of web pages you have visited. For example, if you go to the NASA web page and click the "Educational Resources" link, you can click on the **Back button** to take you back to the NASA home page.

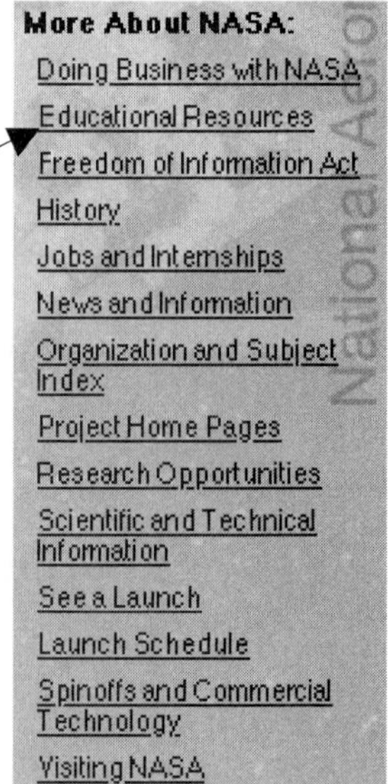

If you want to go back to the Educational Resources page, use the **Forward button**. You can travel back and forth in this way, just as if you were traveling back and forth visiting houses on the same road.

Notice that the **underlined links change color** after you click on them. Colors of visited and unvisited links depend on preferences specified in each browser.

Go to the NASA home page at: ***http://www.nasa.gov***
Do the following:

- Click on the "NASA for Kids" link.
- Pass your mouse pointer over the pictures on this page to locate one of the image links. Click on it.
- Click on the **Back button** twice to go back to the NASA home page.
- Click on the **Forward button** to go back though the pages you visited.

While the **Forward and Back buttons** let you go in a straight line, back and forth to pages you have been, the **Go Menu** lets you "jump around" randomly to web pages you have visited. For example:

The Go Menu is only in Netscape. In Internet Explorer, past links are listed under the File Menu.

From the NASA home page we clicked on these links:

- Educational Resources link
- Listing of Education Programs
- Educational Technology Programs

The result is the **Go Menu** listing you see here. ➔ You can click on the **Go Menu** and scroll down to select and visit any of the pages listed there.

Go Bookmarks Communicator Help
Back ⌘[
Forward ⌘]
Home ⌘home
✓ Programs
A GUIDE TO NASA EDUCATION PROGRAMS
NASA Education Programs
NASA Home Page

Create your own Go Menu listing and try it out!
Go to a URL such as: **http://www.si.edu**
(This is the web site for the Smithsonian Institution.)
Do the following:

Click on some of the underlined and/or image links on this page. After each visit, look at the **Go Menu** and see how it has changed. Now pull down the **Go Menu** and select one of the pages listed there to travel to it.

TRY THIS!

Section Two
Summary Exercises: Navigating the Net

Exercises 2.1 – Review of New Terms and Concepts

__________ 1. Of images and text on a web page, which can be links?

__________ 2. How do you know when an item on a web page is a link?

__________ 3. What does it mean when an underlined link changes color?

__________ 4. If you want to return to a site's home page, but you had visited many of its pages since then, what would be the most efficient way to get back there?

__________ 5. What does it mean when this appears as you pass your mouse over something on a web page? ——▶

Exercises 2.2 – Practice Activities to Expand Your Skills

1. **Navigation Aids** – Many very large, complicated web sites help site vistors by providing an at-a-glance guide called a "site map." (This will be discussed in **Section Five**.) Go to one such site: the University of Maryland University College (UMUC) web site at http://umuc.edu. What other navigation aid do you see on this page? How do you use it?

2. **More Activities with Go Menus** – Listings of pages you have visited will erase in a **Go Menu** and a new list will start when you go "down another road." For example, go the Smithsonian page, then go to other pages in this order:

   1 - The White House: **http://www.whitehouse.gov**
   2 - Library of Congress: **http://lcweb.loc.gov**
   3 - The History Channel: **http://historychannel.com**
   4 - U. S. Census Bureau: **http://www.census.gov**

All these web pages above should be listed under "Go." However, now go back to the Library of Congress and go to *another* web site, let's say, the National Weather Service (http://www.noaa.gov). Check the **Go Menu** now. The History Channel and the U.S. Census Bureau (visits 3 and 4) will not be listed now! **Go Menus** are programmed to act this way, so do not be surprised when pages you have visited are not listed anymore.

THREE – *Starting Up Search Engines*
How to Locate Information on the Internet

What Is a Search Engine?

New Terms

- *Search engine*
- *Keyword search*

In many ways, the Internet is a reflection of our world: a place rich in resources and information. Before the Internet, it was difficult to locate specific resources or items of information. Now there is so much information on the Internet that companies have developed special searching programs to help us locate things.

These searching programs are called *search engines*. According to Search Engine Watch, a site with information on all available search engines (http://www.searchenginewatch.com), there are many kinds of search engines. Two commonly cited types are:

❶ **Major search engine sites.** Some popular ones are:

- **All the Web** http://www.alltheweb.com
- **Alta Vista** http://www.altavista.com
- **Ask Jeeves** http://www.askjeeves.com
- **Lycos** http://www.lycos.com
- **Yahoo!** http://www.yahoo.com

Search engines are sometimes called "web crawlers."

❷ **Metacrawlers.** These programs use more than one search engine at the same time to locate things:

- **Dog Pile** http://www.dogpile.com
- **Mamma** http://www.mamma.com/
- **Metacrawler** http://www.metacrawler.com
- **Search.com** http://www.search.com

Two Ways to Use a Search Engine

Both types of search engines can be used in two ways:

- **Subject index searches.** The search engine site provides a list of topics you can click on.
- **Keywords.** Type in combinations of words that could be found in the URLs of sites or documents you want.

To examine these ways, try these examples. First:

Go to the Yahoo! search engine site at:

http://www.yahoo.com

Example #1: Using subject index searches. Let's say that after reading about distance learning programs, you are wondering how many distance learning programs there are in K–12 schools. If you used "distance learning" keywords, you would get a great many higher education sites. So you might want to begin with a subject search under Education, K–12.

All the underlined text titles you see on Yahoo!'s main page actually are hot links of categories you can click on to locate Internet web sites under that heading.

The listed results of an Internet search are sometimes called "hits."

- Find and click on the link that says "Education." The search engine sends you to yet another listing.
- Find and click on the link for "K–12." It sends you to yet another listing. Click on "Distance learning," and you see a great many links related to distance programs in K–12 schools. Each link is a web page.

Example #2: Using keywords. If you know that certain words would be in the titles of web sites you are looking for, you may want to do a keyword search. Let's say you are intrigued by what you have read about voice recognition and want to locate more information. Try the following search:

- Find the box on the Yahoo! site that looks like the one below and type the words voice AND recognition (joined by the word AND).

[ ] Search

Many sites have their own built-in search engine that lets you use keywords to search the contents of the site. Look for the phrase "Search this site."

- You also can type in whole phrases to do a search. For example, try "voice recognition" using quote marks around the phrase. Either way, you get a listing of companies and organizations that are doing things with this technology.

Search Engine Sites

Different search engines are useful for different purposes and each has its own procedures. The University of Central Florida's Instructional Technology Resource Center (ITRC) has a very useful summary of when and how to use each of the search engines. Look for it at:

http://www.itrc.ucf.edu/conferences/pres/srchtool.html

Examples taken from the ITRC site include:

- **To browse a broad topic:**
  Use Yahoo! or Lycos
- **To search for a narrow topic:**
  Alta Vista, AlltheWeb, or Google
- **To search the largest Internet amount:**
  Metacrawler or Ask Jeeves (meta-search engines)

For other types of sites (e.g., filtered ones for kids, multimedia search engines) and a wealth of information on search methods, check out Search Engine Watch at:

http://searchenginewatch.com

Keyword Search Strategies

Newer search engine sites such as Google and Ask Jeeves have natural language features built into them that make productive searches relatively easy and efficient. However, depending on the topic and the search engine you use, you may get too many hits or some may be on unintended area (e.g., Macintosh apples, rather than Macintosh computers). You can use strategies to combine keywords in ways that focus your search.

Each search engine site has its own "syntax" for joining keywords using Boolean logic operators (and, or, not). A search engine might use AND to connect the keywords:

Example: software AND evaluation

or it may allow either AND or plus signs:

Example: +software +evaluation

Try these examples on Google or Yahoo! (which uses the Google search engine software):

1. You want to see samples of computer lab rules for schools. You try the following:

"computer lab" +rules

However, you get a lot of Lab Rules for college and universities. To narrow the search and eliminate many (but not all) of the Lab Rules that aren't in K-12 schools, do the following:

"computer lab" +rules –college –university

2. Your science students want to find some sites with information on worms. When they type in "worms," they get a lot of information on worm computer viruses. So you tell them to do the following:

worm –virus

3. Your students are looking for information on the history of paper, but entering the terms "history" and "paper" yield thousands of hits on collections of papers of various historical figures. A better way would be to enter this complete phrase (quotes included):

"history of paper"

Section Three
Summary Exercises: Starting Up Search Engines

Exercises 3.1 – Review of New Terms and Concepts

__________ 1. If you wanted to locate a school's web site, and you know the name of the town where the school is located, you might select a search engine you could use in this way, rather than doing a keyword search.

__________ 2. These kinds of search engine sites use more than one search engine at once to do a search.

__________ 3. When you do a search by putting quotes around two or more words together, it makes the search look for this.

__________ 4. If you were on the web site of an educational software company to obtain information about one of its products, what search mechanism would you probably use?

__________ 5. Many search engines use this symbol for the Boolean operator "NOT."

Exercises 3.2 – Practice Activities to Expand Your Skills

Part A – Try these keyword searches:

1. Students in your literature class want more information on the Trojan Horse used by the Greeks to fool the Trojans during the Trojan Wars. When they put in "Trojan Horse," they get a lot of hits on computer viruses. What should they do to narrow the search?

2. You want to see if there are any online journals that you can use to read up on distance education. What series of terms and operators could you use?

3. KidPub (http://www.kidpub.org/kidpub) publishes children's writing and helps kids connect with other young writers. Find other web sites that support young writers.

4. Locate online French-to-English (or other languages) dictionaries. Try the same for other languages like Spanish or German.

Part B – Before doing the following searches, decide:

- *Which search engine might be best for the search?*
- *Which search method would you use: subject or keyword?*

1. **Web Sites to Support Mathematics** – Graphing calculators (or computer-based labs or CBL) are a powerful technology resource in mathematics and science content areas. Locate lesson plans that focus on graphing calculators or CBLs.
2. **Web Sites to Support History** – Locate sites that could give students information on the history of the State of Iowa (or substitute your own state).
3. **Web Sites to Support Art Education** – Locate web sites of five art museums where your students could go on "virtual field trips" to see famous paintings.
4. **Web Sites to Support Literature** – Locate a web site that has examples of Japanese haiku poetry.
5. **Web Sites to Support Writing Instruction** – Locate a web site with a rubric to judge the quality of students' written compositions.
6. **Web Sites to Support Health and Physical Education** – Locate web sites to help teach the topics of drug prevention and physical fitness.
7. **Web Sites to Support Special Education** – Many laws have been passed relating to education of students with special needs. Locate information on recent federal legislation on this topic.
8. **U. S. Department of Education Report** – Locate a report on "Computer and Internet Use Among People with Disabilities" located on the following web site: U. S. DOE website: http://ed.gov/ (**Hint:** Look for the Publications link)
9. **Technology Lesson Plans for Teachers** – Locate online lesson plans that show how to use various technologies in teaching.
10. **Technology Product Assessments** – Locate web sites with rubrics and other instruments that could help assess the quality of students' multimedia and web page products.

FOUR – *Using Bookmarks*
How to Mark Web Pages for Later Use

New Terms

• *Bookmark*

How to Make a Bookmark

You may visit so many sites on the Internet that you can quickly lose track of where you found a valuable site on a certain topic. You could write all of them down, but a quicker way is to use bookmarks.

Bookmarks is a feature in your browser. It lets you mark the address of sites you want to remember. Making a bookmark is very simple. Just travel to the site and when it is on the screen, go to the **Bookmark Menu** and select "**Add Bookmark**." A bookmark title for that site appears at the bottom of the bookmark list. See the example below for adding the Global Schoolhouse site:

In Internet Explorer®, bookmarks are listed under the Favorites Menu.

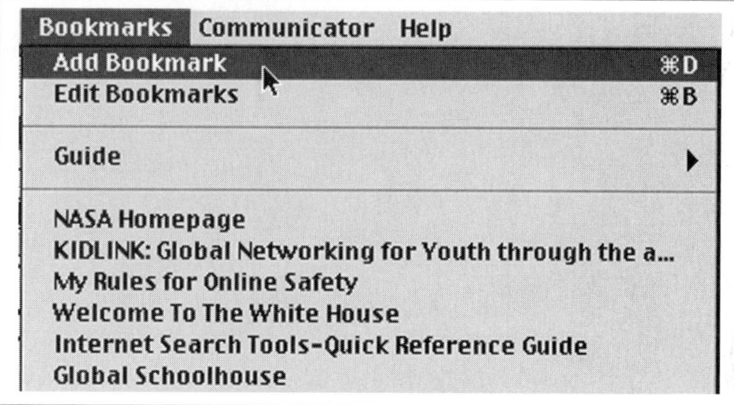

Try making a bookmark.
One site you should remember is the one for the International Society for Technology in Education (ISTE).

http://www.iste.org

Go to the ISTE site on the Internet and create a bookmark for it.

How to Delete Bookmarks

You may want to mark some sites only temporarily, then delete them. On many browser versions, the edit feature is listed on the **Bookmark Menu** (see p. 17). Other browser versions may list it under the **Edit Menu**.

To delete a bookmark, select **Edit Bookmarks**. A window will appear with a list of your current bookmarks. Click on the bookmark you want to delete and select "Cut" or "Clear" from the Edit menu, as shown below:

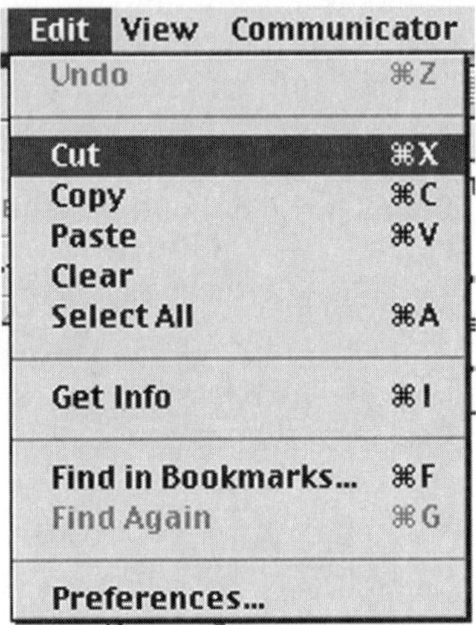

How to Organize Bookmarks

As noted in *Integrating Educational Technology into Teaching*, (Roblyer, 2003, Chapter 8) "well–prepared bookmark files are great resources for teachers and should be shared with others who have similar interests." But what is a "well–prepared bookmark file?"

For a bookmark collection to be most useful to you and others, it should be organized into sections, much like a library or any collection of materials. After you create bookmarks, you can organize them into categories of related items.

For example, let's say you are a middle school language arts teacher and you make bookmarks for the following English and Reading sites you have found:

- **International Reading Association: http://www.ira.org**
- **National Council of Teachers of English:** http://www.ncte.org
- **Teachers and Writers Collaborative:** http://www.twc.org/
- **Rensselaer Writing Center:** http://www.rpi.edu/web/writingcenter/
- **The KidPub Children's PublishingCenter:** http://www.kidpub.com/

Now you want to place these into a section of your bookmarks file and add other bookmarks on this topic later. Here is what you do:

Bring up the **Edit Bookmarks** option in your browser. Create a new folder by selecting "**New**" under the **File Menu:**

Give the folder an appropriate name: for example, "English & Reading sites." Now drag the icons for all five sites, one at a time, into the folder you just created. See below for an example of what this might look like in the Bookmark menu after a folder is created in this way:

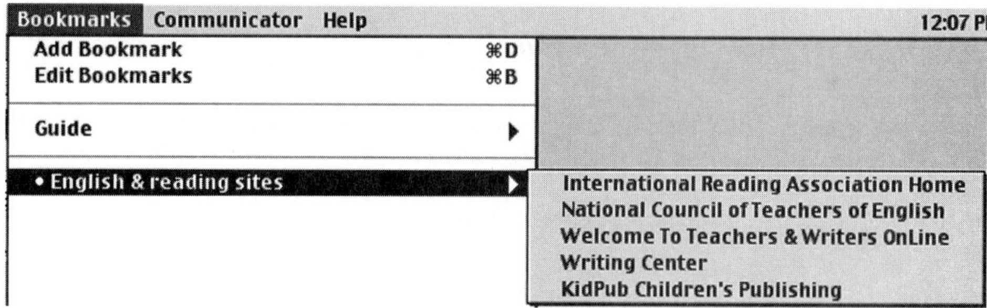

TRY THIS!

Section Four Summary Exercises: Using Bookmarks

Exercises 4.1 – Review of New Terms and Concepts

__________ 1. Term for Bookmarks in *Internet Explorer®*

__________ 2. Menu you would use to get to the Edit Bookmarks option

__________ 3. Menu you use to make a new Folder for Bookmarks

__________ 4. This is what you create to organize Bookmarks under topics

__________ 5. What to do with Bookmark files besides organizing your own work

Exercises 4.2 – Practice Activities to Expand Your Skills

Try creating and organizing your own bookmark files for the following topics. Create a bookmark for each of the sites listed. Then create a folder with an appropriate name for each topic and drag in the bookmarks. (If any bookmarks don't work, try deleting the suffix and locating the information or report on the main site.)

Topic #1: Alternative Assessment Sites

- **Dr. Helen Barrett's Electronic Portfolios**
  http://electronicportfolios.com/

- **Kathy Schrock's Guide for Educators - Assessment Rubrics**
  http://school.discovery.com/schrockguide/assess.html

- **Rubric Creator Site by Rubistar**
  http://rubistar.4teachers.org/index.shtml

Topic #2: Digital Divide and Equity Reports

- **Digital Divide.org: Policy Solutions for the Digital Divide**
  http://www.digitaldivide.org/

- **The Growing Digital Divide (Hoffman and Novak, 2000)**
  http://www.markle.org/news/_news_pressreport_index.stm

- **Losing Ground Bit by Bit: Benton Foundation Report**
  http://www.benton.org/Library/Low-Income/home.html

FIVE – *Evaluating Internet Information*
How to Assess Web Site Quality

Why You Should be Careful

New Terms

- *Web page criteria*
- *Site map*

At a time when everything in the world seems so high-tech and highly-controlled, the Internet is, in some ways, a wild frontier. While there are oversight agencies that set up and monitor general items such domain designators (see p. 2 of this book), no one controls who posts web pages or the quality of their content.

Three kinds of problems arise from this lack of control. One of these, the hazards of offensive or dangerous subject matter or illegal activities, is dealt with in the next section (**SIX – Avoiding Internet Pitfalls**). The other two problems are less perilous but still have serious implications for teachers and students. Web pages can be less than useful for two reasons:

- **Content.** The Internet's vast information storehouse, unfortunately, contains some information that is incomplete, inaccurate, and/or out of date. It even has some sites that are works of complete fiction presenting themselves as fact.

- **Design.** We have learned a great deal in recent years about what makes a web site functional and easy to use. However, some sites are so poorly designed that people may find it difficult or impossible to locate and/or read the information they have to offer.

At the end of this chapter (p. 25), you will find criteria for evaluating web site quality, usefulness, and reliability. These criteria have been gleaned from several sources and are from Chapter 8 of *Integrating Educational Technology into Teaching* (Roblyer, 2003). Two of the categories (content and design) are described in more depth in this section.

Criteria for Evaluating Web Page Content

Students frequently accept as authoritative any information they find on the Internet. However, young people must learn that blind acceptance of any information (on the Internet or elsewhere!) is a risky practice. An essential skill for the Information Age is being able to evaluate information critically and look for the following signs that content is accurate and reliable:

- **Known author.** The web page author is a person or organization with a recognized name and authority. Be wary of those in which the author is not stated, whose credibility would be difficult to ascertain, or who have a known bias.
- **Contact information.** Authors of genuine sites usually give an e-mail address and/or other information one may use to contact them and ask questions about the content.
- **Frequent updates.** The site should list the last time the site was updated on the front page. Information has more credibility if the site is well-maintained.
- **References or links to other sites.** Some sites list documents they used as sources for the information. Others contain links to other sites one may use to verify statements and facts. Any information on a web page should be able to be authenticated by other sources.

You can help your students understand how important it is to confirm web site information by having them look at a site such as the following one and apply criteria for assessing information accuracy:

http://www.lme.mankato.msus.edu/newhartford/newhtfd.html

(HINT:
There is no such place as New Hartford, MN!)

Criteria for Evaluating Web Page Design

Another way to help verify the quality and accuracy of information on a web page is to look at its design. Web pages have more credibility if they are easy to use and have a professional-looking layout. Look for these characteristics to judge design quality:

- **Good structure and organization.** The first page of the site indicates clearly how to get to its various parts. Some sites do this with an option bar that appears at the top, bottom, or side of every page in the site. That way you can get easily to any part. See this example option bar from the U. S. DOE at: http://www.ed.gov/

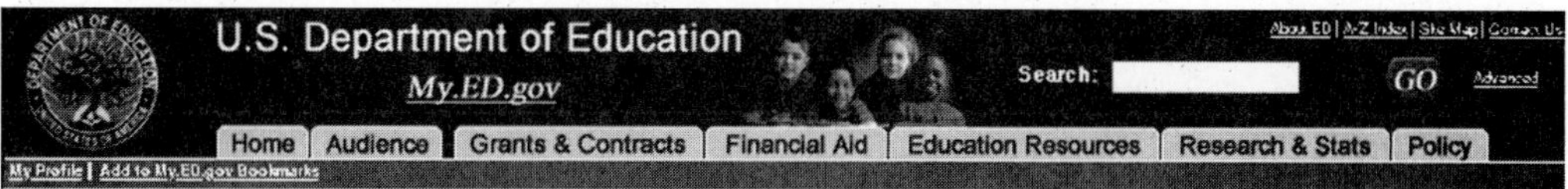

Text or graphic links are clear. Branches are organized so that you can get back to the main page in no more than three clicks.

One device for large sites provides a link to a **site map** or an at-a-glance guide to the contents. (This was discussed briefly in Section 2 Exercises.) See the site map example below from the University of Maryland University College web site: http://umuc.edu

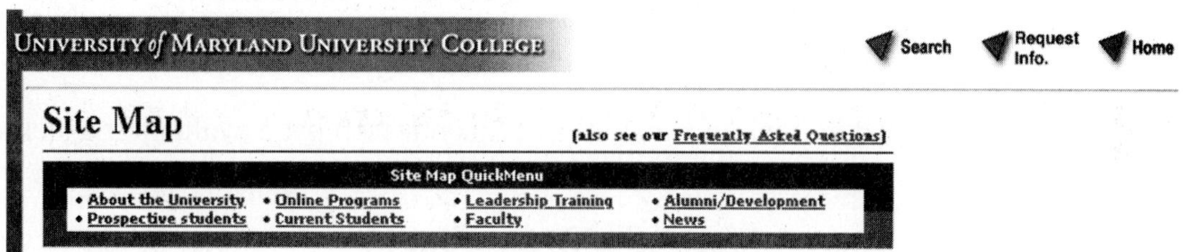

- **Visual design.** Pages are designed for good readability. There are a limited number of colors and fonts; fonts are easy to read, and colors are selected for contrast with the background. Graphics do not distract from reading the content. You can tell from looking at an icon the information you will get when you click it.

- **Easy navigation.** Pages load quickly. It's easy to get around in the site. Links are provided so you can get back to the main page from any part of the site. The most important information is given at the top of the page. All links work as they should. Larger sites have their own built-in search engine. See the example on the next page of the search engine at the U. S. House of Representatives web site at: http://thomas.loc.gov/

THOMAS
Legislative Information on the Internet
In the Spirit of Thomas Jefferson, a service of The Library of Congress
Congress Now: House Floor This Week | House Floor Now | Senate Schedule
Search Bill Text 107th Congress (2001-2002):
Bill Number Word/Phrase Search Clear

- **Miscellaneous.** Pages are short enough that each can be printed quickly. Video, sounds, and graphics help present the information, but pages provide alternate ways of getting the same information for those who lack advanced browser capabilities (e.g., frames).

More Information on Evaluating Web Pages

Additional information and links to web page evaluation checklists and rubrics may be found at the following sites:

Kathy Schrock's Guide for Educators – Collected links to web page evaluation rubrics and other assessment tools:

http://school.discovery.com/schrockguide/assess.html

Web Evaluation for Primary, Middle, and Secondary Grades – Three rubrics K–12 students can use to evaluate the quality of web sites.

http://www.siec.k12.in.us/~west/online/eval.htm

In addition, you can use the criteria checklist on the following page.

Web Page Evaluation Criteria and Tips
(from Chapter 8 of *Integrating Educational Technology into Teaching*, 3rd edition)

1. **Content**

_______ All information is accurate. The "last time updated" date is given.
_______ Information is complete but not excessive or redundant.
_______ Information is well-organized and clearly labeled.
_______ Information is interesting, informative, and worthwhile.
_______ Information is not redundant to other sources; there is a reason to put it on the Web.
_______ All text has correct spelling, grammar, and punctuation.
_______ Level of content and vocabulary are appropriate for intended audience.
_______ Content is free from stereotyping, coarse or vulgar language, or matter that could be offensive to typical users.
_______ Author(s) of the page are clearly identified.
_______ The page gives an e-mail address or other way to contact authors.

2. **Visual and Audio Design**

_______ The site has a consistent, common look and feel across pages.
_______ Graphics, animations, videos, and sounds make an important contribution.
_______ Pages have only one or two fonts.
_______ Each page uses limited numbers of colors, especially for text.
_______ Colors have been selected to be compatible with the *Netscape* 216-color palette.
_______ Type colors/styles and text-to-background contrast were selected for readability.
_______ Each graphic is designed to fit 640 x 480 pixel screens (allowing for scroll bars/toolbars).
_______ Each page is limited to 2 - 3 screens; the most important information is at the top.
_______ The pages are simply and attractively designed and make a user want to read them.

3. **Navigation**

_______ Pages load quickly.
_______ Pages have simple, consistent navigation scheme for quick, easy navigation.
_______ The first page shows clearly how the site is organized and how to get to all items.
_______ Text and icon links are easy to identify. Graphics and sounds are clearly identified.
_______ Icons have been well-chosen to represent the information they link to.
_______ Each supporting page has a link back to the home page.

4. **Miscellaneous (for larger sites and pages)**

_______ Requests for private information are secured.
_______ Page information is kept short enough that it can be printed quickly.
_______ Users can choose to load alternate versions of pages (e.g., text only, smaller images).
_______ The site has its own search engine for locating things within the pages.
_______ Branching is organized so all content is three clicks or fewer from the home page.

Use the following tips to make your sites and pages easier to design and use:

_______ Organize the site on paper ahead of time before inputting it to the computer.
_______ To speed loading, limit graphics to no more than 50K and re-use images whenever possible.
_______ Use GIFs for line art or graphics with limited colors and sharp edges; use JPEGs for photos with many colors and smooth gradients. Avoid PICT and other formats that must be converted by users.
_______ Test out your page in a real browser.
_______ Use a GIF spacer (1x1 transparent GIF) to space paragraphs, indents, or alignments on pages.

TRY THIS!

Section Five
Summary Exercises: Evaluating Internet Information

Exercises 5.1 – Review of New Terms and Concepts

__________ 1. One device on a web page that helps users by giving them an easy-to-read summary table of all links in the site

__________ 2. Larger sites need this built-in feature to help users find items on the site

__________ 3. One way you can tell a web site is accurate and reliable

__________ 4. How a well-designed web page should help users who may have limited browser capabilities (e.g., frames)

__________ 5. Another word for moving around in a web site

Exercises 5.2 – Practice Activities to Expand Your Skills

Try going to the following page of "spurious web sites." Using criteria you have learned from page 22 of this section, identify features about each of the following that allow you to tell they are spurious:

http://www.users.csbsju.edu/%7Eproske/evalwebp.html

- The True but Little–Known Facts About Women with Aids

____

- A press release from Mattel Toys

____

- An article in the *British Medical Journal*

____

- California Crop Report

____

- Psychosocial Parameters of Internet Addiction

____

SIX – *Avoiding Internet Pitfalls*
How to Recognize and Prevent Problems

Types of Problems

New Terms

- *Firewalls*
- *Filtering software*

As has been noted before, the Internet is a reflection of our society. This means that, like the world at large, there are some places on the Internet that pose potential dangers for those who venture on its paths. This does not mean people should avoid taking advantage of the Internet altogether, anymore than we should refrain from traveling because of the potential dangers of accidents or other threats. It does mean that educators and their students should be aware of the kinds of problems that can arise when they use the Internet and take steps to prevent them.

Five kinds of potential problem areas are discussed in this section. Also described are strategies that educators can use to make the Internet a safer, more worry-free place for teaching and learning.

Problem #1: Accessing Sites with Inappropriate Materials

Like a big-city bookstore, the Internet has materials that parents and teachers may not want students to see, either because they are inappropriate for an age level or because they contain information or images considered objectionable. Unfortunately, it is easy to access these sites unintentionally. For example, only three letters (the domain designator) differentiate the web site for our nation's Executive Branch (http://www.whitehouse.gov/) from one with X-rated images and materials.

Since it is so easy to access these sites without meaning to, classroom or lab Internet–usage rules do not safeguard against this problem. Most schools have found that the best way to prevent access to sites with inappropriate materials is to install **firewall** and/or **filtering software** on individual computers or on the school or district network that connects them to the Internet.

- **Filtering software.** An individual or a school can purchase and install these programs on one or more computers to limit user access to prohibited sites either on the basis of keywords, a list of off-limits sites, or a combination of these methods. Although there are many more on the market, review these sample sites:

- *Cyber Patrol* (http://www.cyberpatrol.com)
- *Cyber Sitter* (www.cybersitter.com /)
- *Cybersnoop* (http://www.pearlsw.com)
- *Net Nanny* (http://www.netnanny.com)
- *Surf Watch* (http://www1.surfcontrol.com)
- *WatchDog* (http://www.sarna.net/watchdog)
- *X-Stop* (http://www.xstop.com)

Filtering programs also have other desirable features, such as keeping track of the time students spend on Internet sessions and reports of attempted site accesses. A site that can help teachers, parents, and others identify products to help meet various filtering needs is:

Get Net Wise: http://www.getnetwise.org/tools/

- **Firewall software.** These programs protect a computer from attempts by others to gain unauthorized access to it. Firewall software can be installed on individual computers but usually are part of a school or district network. Although the primary purpose of firewall software is to protect a computer from an outside attack, schools are finding that it also may prevent the user of the computer from *going* to a site. Therefore, it must be tailored to allow desired access.

Problem #2: Safety Issues for Students

Because they lack the experience that helps alert them to dangerous situations, young people are at special risk on the Internet in two different ways:

- **Online predators.** Young people tend to believe what they hear and read. Therefore, in a chatroom they may not consider the possibility that a 12-year-old named "Mary" may actually be a 50-year-old man.

- **Sales pitches aimed at children.** This is a problem similar to that posed by television commercials. Many Internet sites have colorful, compelling images that encourage people to buy. Young people may make commitments they cannot fulfill. Review another very helpful Internet site that addresses these issues. (See site on next page.)

http://www.safekids.com/child_safety.htm

This site has a document called *Safety on the Information Highway*, which was developed for the National Center for Missing and Exploited Children by newspaper columnist Lawrence J. Magid.

Kids' Rules for Online Safety

Magid says, "Teenagers are particularly at risk because they often use the computer unsupervised and because they are more likely than younger children to participate in online discussions regarding companionship, relationships, or sexual activity." He recommends teaching children a set of online rules. See the list of these rules at:

http://www.safekids.com/kidsrules.htm

Think of some ways you could teach these online rules to students.

For example,
you might have students create a multimedia presentation
of the rules listed above, or
you could have them role-play how they would react
if they encountered one of the problems Magid describes.

Problem #3: Fraud on the Internet

Teachers may find that the fastest, easiest way to order computer products and/or teaching materials is to go to a company's web site and order them online. However, most areas of the Internet are not secure. That is, what you do on the Internet can be monitored by others. Some people use this monitoring capability to look for a credit card number or other information they can use fraudulently.

As online consumers, teachers must be sure to purchase products only from well-known, reputable sites that offer a secure server. Secure servers have special programs to prevent outside monitoring of transactions. The URL for a secure server usually begins with "**https**" instead of the usual "**http**."

Problem #4: Computer Viruses

Viruses are programs written for malicious purposes. They come in several varieties and are named according to the way they work, e.g., worms, logic bombs, and Trojan horses. Two ways to get viruses on your computer from the Internet are through:

- **E-mail attachments with viruses.** An increasingly popular way to send files and programs to friends or colleagues is to attach them to e-mail messages. However, if a computer contains a virus that is programmed to attach itself to files, the virus can be sent inadvertently along with the file. When the person receiving the attachment opens it, the virus transfers to his/her computer.

- **Downloaded files and programs with viruses.** Procedures for transferring or downloading programs, documents, and other items from an Internet site to a computer are described in **Section Eight** of this book. As with e-mail attachments, viruses can attach themselves to files and programs and be received along with the item being downloaded.

What can you do to prevent these problems? Four procedures are recommended:

- **Keep virus–protection software up–to–date.** Always maintain, use, and keep updated a copy of a program designed to detect and safeguard against viruses.

- **Download only from reputable sites.** If you have never heard of or dealt with an organization before, downloading files from them can be risky. Shareware programs are a frequent source of attached viruses.

- **Never open e-mail attachments from unknown sources.** Be wary of e-mails from people or organizations you don't know, especially those with an eye-catching name like "Be sure you read this!" Do not open a suspicious e-mail or attachment before you confirm it has been sent for legitimate purposes.

- **Never open e-mail attachments until you confirm their origin.** Some viruses are programmed to send e-mails and attachments automatically through someone's e-mail program and to infect the computers of the recipients that open them. Even if you know the sender, be careful of opening attachments unless you are sure the person sent them intentionally.

Problem #5: Copyright Issues for Educators

The Internet is such a rich and easy-to-access source of documents, images, and other resources, it sometimes is easy to forget that many of these resources are copyrighted and protected by U. S. copyright laws.

To prevent problems, teach your students to look for copyright notices at the sites whose items you want to use. Then do the following:

- **If the site clearly is copyrighted**, contact the owners to request permission to use items.

- **If the site has no copyright statement,** be sure to reference the site by its URL and owner name on any materials you create with the resources.

Section Six
Summary Exercises: Avoiding Internet Pitfalls

Exercises 6.1 – Review of New Terms and Concepts

__________ 1. Software that protects a computer or network from viruses and other malicious attacks

__________ 2. Name for a program written for the specific purpose of doing harm to others' computers

__________ 3. What is said to be on a computer when software is in place to protect it from outside attacks

__________ 4. Key element in most of Magid's rules for children online

__________ 5. Software that is designed to keep users from going to specific sites uses either a list of prohibited URLs or this

Exercises 6.2 – Practice Activities to Expand Your Skills

1. **Update your security software** – Learn about the latest and best firewall and/or filtering software or download some free copies. Go to the following site and enter "Internet security" on its search engine: http://www.zdnet.com

2. **Tools for Families site** – Go to the GetNetWise site (http://www.getnetwise.org/tools) and follow procedures identified there for selecting a software that does the following:

   - Filters violence on a Windows NT computer for instant messaging, chats, e-mail, and the WWW
   - Monitors usage of any technology on a Macintosh computer

3. **Legal-use questions** – Let's say that you find an Internet site with a nice rubric you want to post on your own web site. You want it handy, so you don't want your students going to another URL for it. What procedure should you use in each of the following cases?

   a) The site has no copyright statement ________________________________

   b) The site has a label at the bottom of the first page that says: *Copyright 2003, M. D. Roblyer* ________________________________

SEVEN – *Downloading and Using Images*
How to Obtain and Use Internet Graphics

New Terms

- *Download*
- *Image formats*
- *gif*
- *jpeg*
- *bmp*
- *eps*
- *pdf*
- *pict*
- *tif*

Why Images Are Important

The Internet has been around in text format since 1969. However, it became the society-wide phenomenon we know today only when the first web browser, *Mosaic*, made it possible for the Internet to appear on computer screens as images.

Why do images make such a difference? There may be two reasons. First, pictures are an "information shortcut." The old adage that "a picture is worth a thousand words" means that people grasp many concepts more quickly when they are presented as images rather than as text. Second, people seem able to remember a great deal of information visually.

But it is possible to take advantage of the visual tapestry of the Internet in ways other than receiving information. You can use your browser to "capture" or download any image you see from any web page and store it on your computer. Once you download an image, you can use it in a word–processing or desktop–publishing file, or even to create your own web pages.

How to Download Images

Let's say you wanted to have students use word processing to make an illustrated booklet of the three branches of the U. S. government. You might go to sites for each of these branches and capture images for them to use in their booklets.

Look at the following example. Several images appear on the White House web site for kids located at:

http://www.whitehouse.gov/kids

See a picture of this web site on the following page.

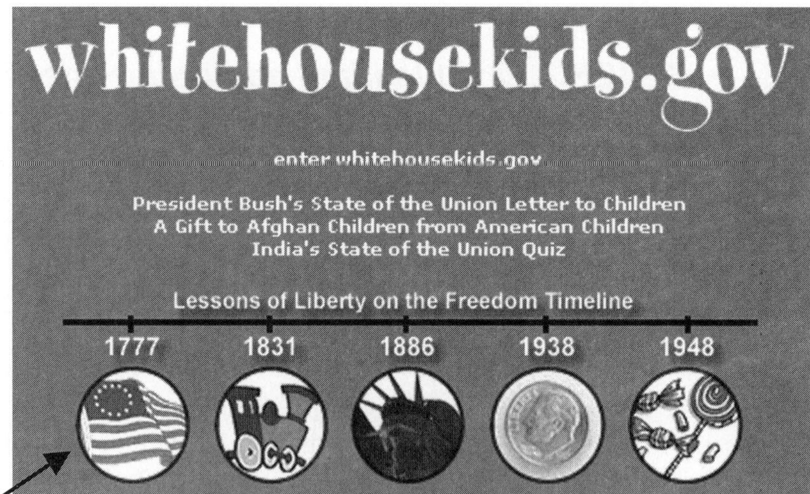

1777 flag

You can capture or download the image of the 1777 flag you see on this page. To "grab" an image from a web page is very simple, but the procedure differs slightly between Macintosh and Windows computers. To download the flag image, do the following:

- **On a Macintosh computer:** Click on the flag image, but instead of letting up the mouse after you click, hold it down until a menu like this one appears:

Back
Forward
Reload

Open this Page in Composer
Send Page...

Page Source
Page Info

Open this Link
Copy this Link Location
Add Bookmark for this Link
New Window with this Link
Save this Link as...

Open this Image
Copy this Image Location
Save this Image as...
Copy this Image
Load this Image

Downloading images in this way is a feature provided in your browser software.

Now drag down and select the "Save this image as…" option to save the image to your computer. See directions for what to do next after the Windows PC step (p. 35).

- **On a Windows PC**. Right-click on the flag image and, instead of letting up the mouse after you click, hold it down until a menu appears:

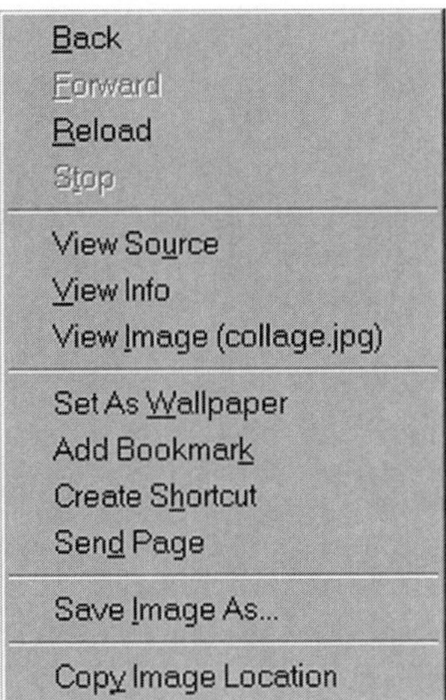

Now drag down and select "Save image as…" to save the image to your computer.

For either computer, after you select the "Save as" option, a box will appear to allow you to save the image on your computer. Depending on whether you have a Macintosh or PC computer, this box will look something like the following:

Save Image as:

1777.gif

The file name that will appear here will always be the name under which it was stored when it was put on the web page. The file name under which this flag image was stored is: 1777.jpg.

However, before you click "Save" to save the file, you can change this name to something you may find easier to remember. For example:

Save Image as:

flag.gif

Images on U. S. government web site are usually considered public domain and may be used without permission for educational purposes.

Downloading an image from the Internet is easy. But remember that many images you find on web pages are copyrighted, and their legal use is determined by copyright law and the owner of the web site. If you are not sure if you can use an image legally, contact the web site owner to request permission.

What to Do with Downloaded Images

After you save an image on your computer, you can insert it in documents or other web pages. However, you may need to change the **image format** from the original file format to another one.

Several image formats have been developed over the years to serve various purposes: either a certain computer or operating system required it, or certain formats deal better with differences among image types (e.g., photos rather than drawn images or clip art).

You can tell the format of an image by its suffix. For example, the flag was a **gif** file format. Images downloaded from web pages will be in one of the following formats:

- **gif** – Stands for "Graphics Interchange Format." Used for drawn images, illustrations, clip art, or animations.

- **jpeg** – Stands for "Joint Photographic Experts Group." Used for photographs.

If you want to use images to do your own web pages (see directions in **Section Eleven** of this booklet), they must be in one of these two formats.

There are several other types of image formats useful on computers. Some of the more common ones are listed below:

- **bmp** – Stands for "bitmapped." A standard format developed originally for use on DOS and Windows-compatible computers.
- **eps** – Stands for "Encapsulated Post Script." Developed to transfer artwork between any software packages that used PostScript printing files.
- **pdf** – Stands for "Portable Document Format." Used to store document pages as images. (See **Section Eight** of this booklet for more information on **pdf** files and software to read them.)
- **pict** – Short for "Picture" format, this was developed originally for use on Macintosh computers.
- **tif** – Stands for "Tagged Image File." Designed to be a flexible format for exchanging files among various software application and computers.

The user manual of each software package tells which image format it can take.

You can use images downloaded from web sites in several kinds of programs in addition to web page development, including:

- **Word processing** (e. g., *Microsoft Word®*),
- **Desktop publishing** (e. g., *Adobe PageMaker®*),
- **Presentation software** (e. g., *PowerPoint®*), and
- **Hypermedia authoring software** (e. g., *HyperStudio®*).

However, if you want to use images from the web in software packages that require formats other than **gif** or **jpg**, you may have to obtain and use an image manipulation software such as *Adobe Photoshop®* to save the image into another format.

Section Seven
Summary Exercises: Downloading Images

Exercises 7.1 – Review of New Terms and Concepts

__________ 1. Image format that animated graphics often are in

__________ 2. The first step in downloading an image from a web site on either a Macintosh or Windows PC platform

__________ 3. Sites from which you probably can use images for educational purposes without requesting permission

__________ 4. This determines the legal use of a copyrighted image

__________ 5. What you need to in order to save a downloaded image in an image format to use in another program

Exercises 7.2 – Practice Activities to Expand Your Skills

1. **Downloading Your Logo** – Say you want to do a *PowerPoint* presentation for your school or district. Go to your school or district web site and download its logo. Insert it on the title page of a *PowerPoint* presentation. Here is how it might look ➔

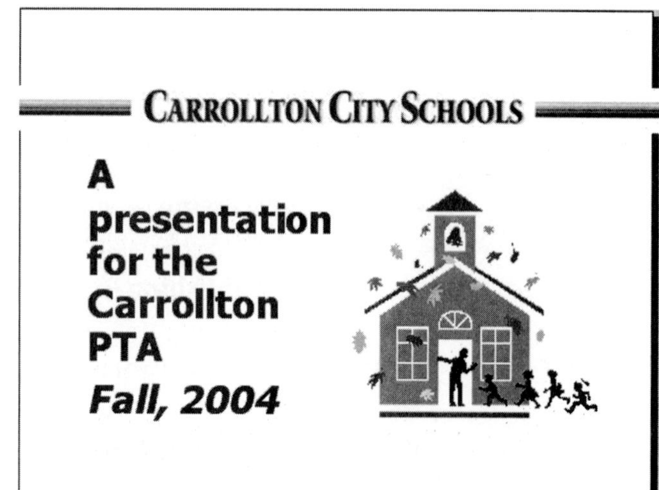

2. **Lesson Images** – Roblyer's *Integrating Educational Technology into Teaching* (2003) describes a lesson called "Selling a Space Mission." Students must do a persuasive *PowerPoint* presentation to gain funding for a hypothetical space mission. Here are web sites from which your students could obtain images for their presentations. Go to these sites and download some images they might find useful:

   - **The NASA web site:** http://www.nasa.gov
   - **The Dreamtime/NASA Partnership:** http://www.dreamtime.com
   - **U.S. Space and Rocket Center:** http://www.spacecamp.com/

EIGHT – *Downloading Programs and Plug-ins*
How to Obtain Needed Web Resources

Kinds of Resources to be Downloaded

New Terms

- *plug-in*
- *pdf format*
- *streaming video*
- *streaming audio*

Web browsers made the Internet visual, but recent developments have given it sound and motion. Special programs called **plug-ins** have been created to allow people to see and hear these multimedia features that make the Internet increasingly life-like.

Although plug-ins tend to change and update rapidly, the Internet has a built-in way of allowing people to take full advantage of the Internet's multimedia features and keep up with advancements required for their use. Instead of buying the programs on disk or CD, Internet users can download many of them directly from the company site. This section describes some of the kinds you will need and procedures for downloading them.

Programs and Plug-ins You Will Need

- **Updated browser versions.** Most new computers come with a browser program stored on the hard drive. However, browsers change versions frequently. It is necessary to keep an up-to-date version in order to see newer Internet features. Download newer versions of browsers from the Netscape and Microsoft web sites:

®

Netscape Communicator® is available at:
http://www.netscape.com/

®

Internet Explorer® is available at:
http://www.microsoft.com/downloads/

- **Adobe *Acrobat*® viewer plug-in.** This program lets you see **pdf** (Portable Document Format) files. These are pages stored as images so they may be printed out with a page appearance identical to the original document. A **pdf** format is particularly important when the original text contains both print and images, or when one wants to see the appearance of the original document. For example, one might photograph and store the pages of the Declaration of Independence so history students could see them. Although the program to create **pdf** files must be purchased, the *Acrobat*® viewer plug-in required to see already-stored **pdf** files is available free from Adobe®, Inc at:

http://www.adobe.com/products/acrobat/readstep.html

- **Streaming video and audio player plug-ins.** A new and exciting Internet capability is seeing action or hearing sounds live on the Internet. Streaming is so–called because it sends or "streams" images and sounds a little at a time so one need not download the files completely before using the contents. However, once these files are seen and stored on a computer, they also may be seen and/or heard later. *Real Player*® and *Real Audio*® are examples of these plug-ins.

Real Player® and *Real Audio*® are available at:

Real Networks.com
http://www.real.com/

- **Movie player plug-in.** Videos that have been digitized and stored as movie files may be viewed through a plug-in. One of the earliest, but still most useful, plug-ins for seeing these videos is the *QuickTime®* player available from the Apple Company. Although originally designed as a movie player, more recent versions of *QuickTime®* can also be used with streaming video and audio.

The *QuickTime®* player is available from:

Apple Computer, Inc.: **http://www.apple.com/**

How to Download Browsers and Other Programs

Downloading a program or plug-in is easy; simply go to the web site and follow the directions! Usually, the site provides very clear steps. Once you supply the information the site requests and click on the button to begin downloading, you will see a box similar to the following:

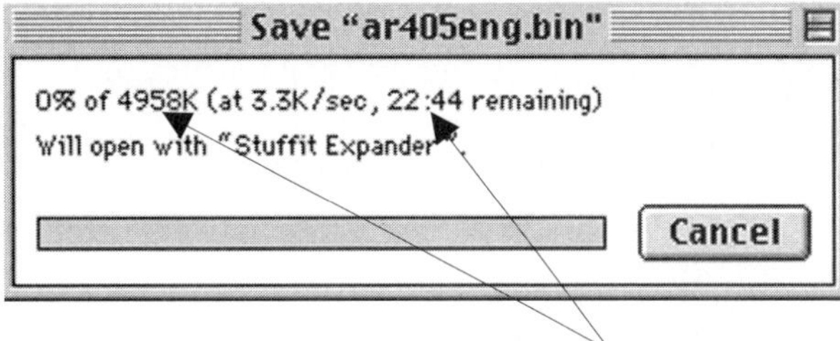

This box shows you how the download is progressing and approximately how much time is left before the download is complete. The downloading process usually places an icon for the program on your desktop. After the plug-in is downloaded, double-click on the icon to install the plug-in in the appropriate folder or directory. The program itself provides directions.

TRY THIS!

Section Eight
Summary Exercises: Downloading Programs and Plug-ins

Exercises 8.1 – Review of New Terms and Concepts

__________ 1. Documents in this format retain their original appearance when downloaded.

__________ 2. *Adobe Acrobat®*, *Real Player®*, and *Real Audio®* are examples of this kind of software.

__________ 3. Popular movie player available from Apple

__________ 4. What **pdf** stands for

__________ 5. *Real Player®* allows users to do this

Exercises 8.2 – Practice Activities to Expand Your Skills

Download the four plug-ins described below to your own computer. Try out each of them with the files indicated.

❶ *Adobe Acrobat®* at: **http://www.adobe.com/products/acrobat/readstep.html**

Now use this plug-in to look at the PDF versions of U. S. DOE reports such as *The Corporate Imperative: A Business Guide for Implementing Strategic Education Partnerships* available at: **http://www.ed.gov/pubs/strategicpartner/**

❷ *Real Player®* and
❸ *Real Audio®* at: **http://www.real.com/**

Now use the *Real Audio®* plug-in to listen to current news stories on National Public Radio at: **http://www.npr.org/**

❹ *QuickTime®*: **http://www.apple.com/**

Now use this plug-in to look at *QuickTime®* movies related to education available from Apple at: **http://ali.apple.com/events/aliqttv/**

NINE – *Internet Troubleshooting*
How to Recognize and Address Common Errors

New Terms

- *Dead link*
- *HTML*
- *Java*
- *Perl*

Three Kinds of Errors

Like most technologies, the Internet presents its share of "head scratchers." The majority of these errors and problems can be corrected easily; others require more complicated "fixes" or adjustments. Three of the most common difficulties for Internet users are:

- **Site connection failures.** After you enter the URL, the site won't come up on the screen.
- **Site features won't work.** The animation, movie, or sound file on the site will not work.
- **Memory errors.** The computer or the browser does not have enough Random Access Memory (RAM) to load a site or use a plug-in.

Problem ❶: A Site Won't Connect

This is the most common problem people encounter, and it may occur for any of several reasons. The error message for each problem indicates the cause.

- **URL syntax errors.** As mentioned in Section One of this book, each dot and letter in a URL has to be correct, or the site won't load. The most common error message for this problem is: ". . . unable to locate the server. Please check the server name and try again." If this message appears, check the URL syntax and make sure you have not done any of the following:
  - Confused the letter "l" with the number "1"
  - Confused the letter "O" with the number "0"
  - Confused the hyphen "-" with the underline "_"
  - Confused forward slash "/" with backward slash "\" in the "http://" or in suffixes
  - Omitted a required punctuation mark
  - Misspelled a part of the URL
  - Used the wrong domain designator (e.g., "edu" instead of "org")

Many URL errors occur in suffixes that follow the domain designator. Try omitting all suffixes beyond the slash and going directly to the main part of the URL. The main page may show the links you want, or the site may have a built-in search engine you can use.

- **Local or domain server down.** If you have checked the URL syntax and are positive it is correct, it may be that the server that hosts the web site is not working temporarily. It may have a technical problem or simply may be down for regular maintenance. In this case, you may get an error message like the one shown previously. Wait for a day or two and try it again.

  A rarer cause of connection failures is that the server handling Internet traffic for the network or for users in the geographic region is not working properly. Error messages say "Failure to resolve domain error. Try this site again later" or "Page has no content."

- **Bad or dead links.** If a URL repeatedly fails to connect and you are sure the syntax is correct, the site may have been taken off the Internet. This is a **bad or dead link**. If this is the case, you may get the same error message given previously or the site may provide a message that says "bad link."

- **Firewalls.** Sometimes a site will not connect because a network's firewall blocks it. (See **Section Six** of this book.) If you think your network's firewall is blocking your access to a site in error, contact your network administrator and request that this be adjusted.

Problem ❷: Internet Features Won't Work

If an Internet site indicates that it has a special feature such as an animation, movie, or sound but it will not work for you, there are three possible causes:

- **Plug-in required.** It may be that your computer does not have the special program or plug-in required to play the movie or sound. Usually, if a special plug-in is needed, the site will have a link to where you can go to download the plug-in and install it on your computer. (See **Section Eight** on Downloading Programs and Plug-ins.)

- **Compatibility errors.** The Internet works because there are agreements in place about how to make various machines and programs "talk" to each other. However, sometimes there are differences between operating systems or versions of software that make them incompatible. Some sites can be seen only with *Netscape*; some only with *Internet Explorer*. The web page usually indicates if it requires a specific browser.

- **Programming errors.** Internet web pages usually are written in a combination of three programming languages: HyperText Markup Language (HTML), Java, and less often, Perl. HTML is the basic language that sets up and formats a page, Java is used for special features like counters or chatrooms, and Perl is used to write "CGI scripts," which are used when the site wants people to enter information into the web page (e.g., a survey).

  If you get a Javascript error message, make sure Java is enabled (select **Preferences** under the **Edit Menu)** and/or download a newer version of Java. (See **Section Eight** on Downloading Programs and Plug-ins.) If you have an enabled, up-to-date version but still get a Javascript error message, it may be that there really is an error in the Java or Perl language of the program or script. In this case, the only thing you can do is to contact the site and alert them to the error.

Problem ❸: Out-of-Memory Error Messages Appear

In addition to the problems described above, you may get errors because your computer or the program lacks the memory required to see the images at the site or to run the plug-in. On a Macintosh, you may get an error message that says you have insufficient memory or the site may keep trying to load indefinitely. If this occurs, try allocating more memory to the browser. On the Macintosh, click once on the program icon for the browser and select "**Get Info**" from the **File Menu**. When the Information box appears, click on **Show: Memory** and enter larger numbers in the boxes.

Section Nine
Summary Exercises: Internet Troubleshooting

Exercises 9.1 – Review of New Terms and Concepts

__________ 1. A URL that has worked in the past fails to connect over a period of days. Error message says it cannot find the site. What is the likely problem?

__________ 2. You enter the your school district URL. An error message says it cannot find the server. What should you do?

__________ 3. The site has an icon labeled "Play movie." You click on it, but nothing happens. What should you do?

__________ 4. You enter a URL for a site and get an error message that says "You are not permitted access to this site." What is the likely problem?

__________ 5. There is an online survey you would like to complete, but the survey will not allow you to enter anything. What is a possible problem?

Exercises 9.2 – Practice Activities to Expand Your Skills

Spot the errors in the following URLs that would result in an error message. Correct them and go to the site to make sure they work:

1. http://www.psuedu ______________________________
2. http//www.iste.org ______________________________
3. http://www.app1e.com ______________________________
4. http://www.animfactory.com/af-animals-bears-page-aa.html
   ____
5. http://www.quotationspage.c0m/ ______________________________

TEN – *Integrating the Internet into Teaching* Strategies, Resources, and Lesson Links

New Terms

- *tele-mentoring*
- *e-pals*
- *keypals*
- *electronic field trip*
- *virtual field trip*
- *social action project*

Powerful Teaching and Learning Strategies

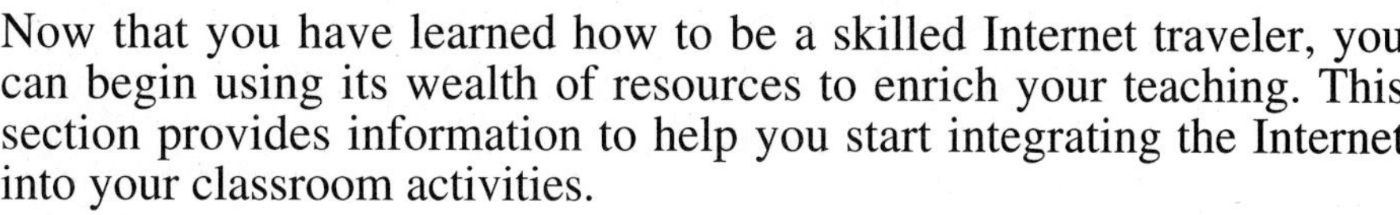

Now that you have learned how to be a skilled Internet traveler, you can begin using its wealth of resources to enrich your teaching. This section provides information to help you start integrating the Internet into your classroom activities.

The following are models of how to integrate the Internet into classroom activities in many content areas. Go to the URL for each lesson and think about how you might adapt the strategy for you own uses. (**Section Eleven** shows you how to design your own web site to support online activities.)

Strategy #1: Electronic Penpals (E-pals or Keypals)

- **How People Live in Europe and the Middle East.** Kids in the U.S. e-mail their contemporaries in other countries to ask questions about the European countries that they will be studying. **http://www.kidlink.org/KIDPROJ/Euro/**

- **Math Penpals.** Students communicate with their "math penpals" on a variety of topics that have mathematical themes, e.g., weather data (daily high/low temperatures, weekly precipitation) will be shared weekly. Monthly events include surveys and comparison pricing.
  http://www.kidlink.org/KIDPROJ/Math/

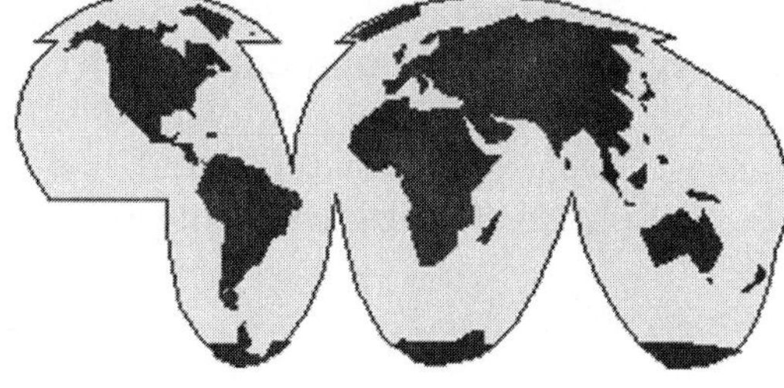

Strategy #2: Individual and Cooperative Research Projects

- **Chewing the Fat and Other Novel Expressions.** Students in paired schools in England and New Zealand research each other's use of slang. **http://www.interlink.org.nz/projects/chewfat/chewfat2.html**

- **Global Wildlife Migration Study.** As students track the journeys of a dozen migratory species each spring, they share their own field observations with classrooms across the hemisphere. **http://www.learner.org/jnorth/**

Migratory bird on the Smithsonian National Zoo Web Site. Photo available at: http://natzoo.si.edu/

- **Tooth Tally Project.** In this project, losing a tooth becomes a teachable moment. As first graders in various locations compare how many teeth they lose, they practice counting skills, collect data, and learn to make and interpret graphs. **http://wilburnes.wcpss.net/tooth01.htm**

Strategy #3: Electronic Mentoring

- **Telementoring Young Women in Science, Engineering, and Computing.** Program funded by the National Science Foundation to provide online communities of support for young women taking technical courses in high school.
  http://www.edc.org/CCT/telementoring/index2.html

National Science Foundation
WHERE DISCOVERIES BEGIN
nsf.gov

- **The History of Spanish Texas.** A 4th grade teacher asks members of a university electronic forum to give her students information on the Spanish explorers.
  http://riceinfo.rice.edu/armadillo/Projects/letters.html

- **Ask an Expert.** This site provides links to people who have volunteered their time to answer questions and web pages that provide information on various topics.
  http://www.askanexpert.com/

Strategy #4: Electronic (Virtual) Field Trips

- **Lots of Bread.** In this field trip about bread baking, students learn about nutrition and do science labs to explore principles at work in bread-making processes.
  http://www.field-guides.com/sci/bake/index.htm

- **Field Trips International.** Many teachers take their students on field trips in their local community. This site allows teachers and students to document their field trip and share it with others around the world.
  http://www.gsn.org/project/fieldtrips/

- **My America Virtual Field Trip.** Students are guided by a set of four questions as they tour selected sites: What does America mean to you? If you are an American citizen, what does it mean to you to be American? What are some of the privileges Americans have which are lacking in other parts of the world? Who were the first people living in the United States?
http://www.field-guides.com/ss/america/index.htm

- **Impressionists**. Students explore impressionism by taking a virtual tour of five impressionist paintings, and exploring techniques (theme, color, and brushwork) artists used to create their masterpieces.
http://www.biography.com/impressionists/

Strategy #5: Group Development of Products

- **Global Warming**. Student teams collaborate to decide whether or not to support a piece of legislation that would decrease the emissions of greenhouse gases by 20% by the year 2005. After online research, they prepare a multimedia position statement.
- **http://students.itec.sfsu.edu/ITEC815/antaramian/**
- **MusicLand Theme Park.** Students become a team of designers assigned to build a new music theme park in their city. It will have different "Lands" for each of several musical genres. Each design team chooses a musical genre to research and decide on a definitive time period and appropriate location for the genre.
http://www.itdc.sbcss.k12.ca.us/curriculum/musicland.html

- **Personal Trainer.** Students become personal trainers employed by a fitness consulting firm that provides individualized diet and exercise portfolios. They are assigned a client and develop a weekly exercise program and menus that will fit into the person's lifestyle.
http://www.itdc.sbcss.k12.ca.us/curriculum/personaltrainer.html

- **The Real Scoop on Tobacco.** Students become experts about tobacco and issues surrounding its use. They create an attention-getting music video, skit, or TV commercial that visually conveys the message that kids shouldn't smoke.
http://www.itdc.sbcss.k12.ca.us/curriculum/tobacco.html

- **Weather Scrapbook.** Students research the weather topics and create a presentation of their findings with *Microsoft PowerPoint* or *FrontPage*. They learn how to put together their own multimedia weather scrapbook.
http://www.educationcentral.org/stormy/main.htm

From the National Oceanographic and Atmospheric Administration (NOAA) at: http://www.noaa.gov/

Strategy #6: Social Action Projects

- **Save the Beaches.** Students pick trash on their local beaches, analyze it, and collaborate online with other sites to develop ways to prevent beach pollution.
http://www.swindsor.k12.ct.us/Schools/tems/beaches/index.html

- **Teen Court.** This volunteer organization was established to give youth offenders a chance to clear their arrest from their permanent record by performing community service and other duties ordered by the court. All teens admit their guilt and agree to accept a sentence given to them by a jury of their peers. (A judge is present.)
http://www.thinkquest.org/library/lib/site_sum_outside.html?tname=2640&url=2640/

For more ideas and information on how to integrate the Internet into curriculum, see: M. D. Roblyer's *Integrating Educational Technology into Teaching* (Prentice Hall, 2003).

TRY THIS!

Section Ten
Summary Exercises: Integrating the Internet into Teaching

Exercises 10.1 – Review of New Terms and Concepts

__________ 1. Another word for providing students with online mentors to guide their learning

__________ 2. An online "journey" students may take to a location to which they would not ordinarily be able to travel

__________ 3. A person with whom one may exchange correspondence by e-mail

__________ 4. Online projects designed to focus students on developing answers for social problems and issues

__________ 5. Organization whose web site is: http://www.kidlink.org

Exercises 10.2 – Practice Activities to Expand Your Skills

The following are three groups of sites with lesson plans and other materials you can use to develop your own Internet-based teaching and learning strategies. Enter some or all of these links into your browser and create bookmarks for each site as you connect to it. Create a folder for each group, or create folders for your own categories of links. (See **Section Four** of this book for help on using bookmarks.) Look for lesson plans, strategies, and resources that will be of particular use to you in teaching your content area.

Internet Lesson Plans and Teaching Resources

- **The Blue Web 'n Library** – A compilation of hundreds of links to prize-winning lesson and resource sites at: **http://www.kn.pacbell.com/wired/bluewebn**

- **High Plains Regional Technology Consortium** – A collection of lessons and teacher resources at: **http://4teachers.org/intech/lessons/**

- **KIDPROJ** – A site that sponsors ongoing technology projects for kids to join at: **http://www.kidlink.org/KIDPROJ/index.html**

- **The Apple Learning Exchange** – Lesson plans available from the Apple Computer, Inc. at: **http://ali.apple.com/**

- **The ThinkQuest Internet Challenge** – School winners of the ThinkQuest competitions to design web-based learning projects at: **http://www.thinkquest.org**

- **The WebQuest Page** – Site of teacher-and-student-designed webquest projects hosted by San Diego State University at: **http://edweb.sdsu.edu/webquest/webquest.html**

- **Virtual Field Trips Site** – Lists of annotated virtual field trips on nature topics with additional teacher's resources for each of the trips. **http://www.field-guides.com**

Content Area Lessons and Other Resources for Teachers

- **Discovery.com** – A searchable bank of lessons plans on all subject areas maintained by the Discovery Channel's web site at: **http://school.discovery.com/lessonplans/**

- **Microsoft Lesson Connection** – A searchable database of lesson plans maintained by Microsoft at: **http://www.k12.msn.com/LessonConnection/Teacher.asp**

- ***The New York Times*** – A searchable bank of lesson ideas maintained by *The New York Times* at: **http://www.nytimes.com/learning/teachers/lessons/archive.html**

- **Smithsonian Institute** – Lesson plans and other teaching resources on a variety of topics maintained by the Smithsonian at: **http://educate.si.edu/**

- **United Nations** – Teaching modules, classroom activities, and on-going events to help teach global issues: Human Rights, Health, Land Mines, Environment, Women, and Poverty at:
http://www.un.org/Pubs/CyberSchoolBus/

- **U. S. DOE** – A searchable bank of lesson activities and other resources maintained by the U.S. DOE at:
http://www.ed.gov/free/subject.html

Sites to Help with Collaboration Among Schools

- **"World's Largest" Keypal Locator service** – This site links up students from all over the world to work together and exchange information on topics of mutual interest.
http://www.epals.com/

- **The Global SchoolNet Foundation** – A site of examples of past collaborative projects and information on how to join current ones at:
http://www.gsn.org/pr/index.html

- **Web–Assistance Site.** University of Minnesota site to help K – 12 educators learn how to set up their own Internet servers, link K – 12 educators and students at various sites, and help them find and use K – 12 web resources. **http://web66.umn.edu/**

ELEVEN – *CREATING YOUR OWN WEB SITE*
How to Create New Pages and Adapt Existing Ones

Why You May Want Your Own Web Site

New Terms

- HTML editor
- *Netscape Composer®*
- upload
- FTP
- table
- index page
- storyboard

The Internet is becoming an increasingly common way for people to communicate. Just as sending e-mails is becoming as commonplace as telephone calls to contact individuals, posting web pages is becoming an accepted strategy for delivering information and/or working with many people at the same time.

In education, teachers are using web pages to:

- **Communicate information to parents, students, and others on a continuing basis** – Web-based newsletters and flyers can take the place of paper ones. Also, some schools are beginning to post (password protected) student progress reports so parents can track this important information.

- **Structure and carry out lessons** – Many of the learning strategies described in **Section Ten** of this book require a web site. A site may serve a variety of purposes, depending on the type of lesson. Sometimes teachers have students create their own web site as part of a learning activity.

What You Need to Create Your Own Web Site

You can use two different strategies to create your own "web presence." These include:

- **Creating pages from scratch** and linking them, or

- **Downloading or "grabbing" existing pages** and modifying them for your own use.

This section will show you how to use each of these methods to develop your own personal web site.

For either of these strategies, you will need **three** different resources in order to create your web site:

You can download and pre-view both free and fee-based FTP and web page development software at: http:// download. cnet.com

FTP is also a verb! You use FTP software to FTP your files to the server.

❶ **Web development software** – Although you can create pages by programming them in HTML code, teachers will find that using an *HTML editor* (i.e., web page development software) is preferable; it is easier, faster, and requires much less technical skill.

As with most tool software, web page development software packages vary considerably as to features and prices. Packages such as Microsoft *FrontPage* and Macromedia *Dreamweaver* are full-featured and must be purchased. However, other more basic software is available free or as a free component of another software package. One of the latter, *Netscape Composer*®, is a built-in web page development software component of the browser *Netscape Communicator*®.

In this book, we use *Netscape Composer*® to illustrate how to develop web pages. If you don't have the software, you can download it free from this site:

http://home.netscape.com/download/

❷ **File Transfer Protocol (FTP) software** – After developing all the pages of your site, you must transfer or upload them to a server. To do this, you need *FTP* software. If your web site will be housed on your school or district server, technical personnel there may provide an FTP package or they may want to upload your pages for you. If your site will be on another server, contact the web administrator to find out required procedures.

❸ **Server to house the web site** – Your web site must have a "home," that is, a computer or server on which it resides. Most teachers choose to have their web site on their school or district server. If so, you may want to find out the procedures that have been established in your school or district for obtaining required permissions and for uploading pages to the server.

A Few Caveats When Creating Web Page Information

Before you begin developing pages, consider these items:

- **Limit sharing of personal information** – Since so many people will have access to your web site, you may wish to limit personal information such as pictures and telephone numbers. Most teachers include only an e-mail address.

- **Limit photos and large graphics** – These take a long time to load and can be frustrating to users (e.g., parents) who wish to see the information on your site.

- **Address web page criteria** – Use the same criteria for your own page that you wish to see in other sites. Review criteria for effective web pages on page 25 of this book. You may want to select other teacher sites you like and follow their structure.

A Suggested Development Sequence: Eight Phases

In *Integrating Educational Technology into Teaching*, Roblyer (2003) recommends a sequence of eight phases to successfully developing a web page or web site:

Inspiration (Inspiration Software, Inc.) is a useful software for creating a plan for the structure of your web site and showing how the pages link together.

Phase 1: Plan and storyboard – Planning and design are the most difficult, important—and most frequently neglected—first steps in developing a web site. Though most people want to get to the fun of development, planning is critical to a well-designed web site. Storyboard (i.e., make a rough sketch of) a plan for the site by using cognitive mapping software or 3" x 5" sticky notes placed on large pieces of poster board to represent the web pages.

Phase 2: Develop pages with text – The next step is to create blank web pages and insert text elements such as titles, paragraphs of description, and any text labels that will later serve as links. There are three kinds of page structures: basic, basic with anchors on the page, and frames. (This section focuses on designing basic pages.)

Phase 3: Insert images and sounds – Pictures, animations, and movies come next. Images and animations must be in GIF or JPEG format; movies and sounds must be in MPEG format. (See **Section Seven** for information on various formats for graphic images.) If movies or audio are to be streamed, the page should inform the user and provide a way to obtain the plug-in needed to see or hear the item (See **Section Eight**.)

Phase 4: Insert links and frames – After all pages are designed, insert links or "hot spots" from text and images to other pages in the site and locations on the Internet.

Phase 5: Insert interactive elements – If desired, make the web page "interactive" by inserting Java applets, CGI scripts, and mail-to commands to gather comments from users who visit your site.

Phase 6: Test in a browser – Many development programs have a built-in preview system, but it is essential to test the site with an actual browser to observe how it will work when it is published on the Web.

Phase 7: Publish (upload) the site – For others to see created web pages, developers must place them on a server. This is called publishing the site. If the user can sit down at the keyboard of the computer acting as the server, the files may be moved over from a disk to the hard drive. For servers that are not nearby, the user may upload the pages to the server as FTP files.

Phase 8: Gather evaluation comments, revise, and maintain the site – The best web sites are those that are updated regularly based on user comments and the continuing insights of the developers. This may be done through CGI programs built into the page (See Phase 5 above) or simply through inviting e-mailed comments.

Next, try an exercise in building your own page. In this exercise, you will be creating a web site like the one at the following URL. Go to this sample site first and see what you will be creating: **http://www.prenhall.com/startingout**

Step 1: Starting the First Page

To obtain a blank *Netscape Composer®* page, load *Netscape Communicator®* and select **New – Blank Page** from the **File Menu.**

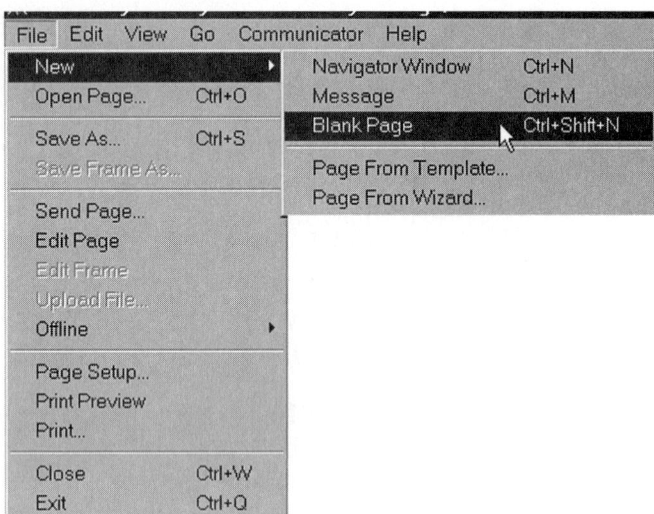

Set a name and background color by selecting **Page Colors and Properties** from the **Format Menu**:

If you want to use a pattern or an image for your background instead of a color, click the Image box instead of the Background box, and choose an image file stored on your hard drive.

- Click the **General Tab**; type “index.html” for the title.

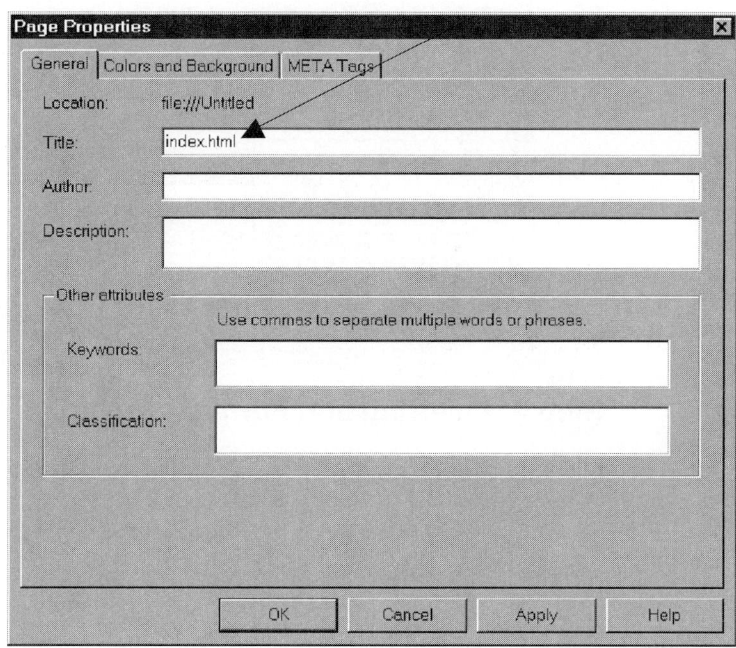

- Click the **Colors and Background** tab (see example, next page); click the **Use custom colors** button; click the **Background** box. Color options will appear; click on white for the background color. Click **OK** to confirm the choices and return to the page. Select **Save As** from the **File Menu** and save the page under the name: **index.html**

  Note that you can select Color, Alignment, Size, and other formatting options from the Format Menu, as well as from the **Format Toolbar**.

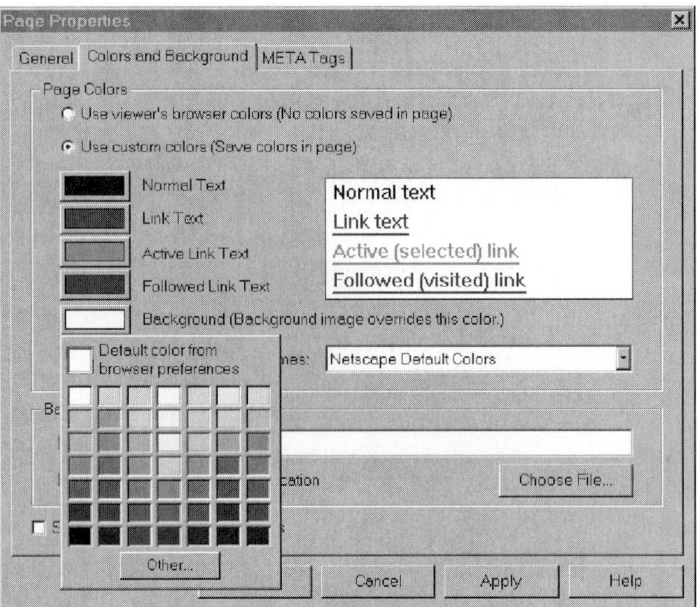

Step 2: Inserting and Formatting Text

Click on the page and type a title and a welcome like the one shown in the example below:

G.L. Branch's Home Page

Welcome to my page!
Click on one of the links below to learn about me.

- After you type the text as shown, format it. First, highlight it by dragging your mouse across it.
- On the **Format Toolbar**, click the arrow beside the **Text Color** box and drag down to select a text color.
- On the **Format Toolbar**, select **Font Size** and enter 18 for the size.
- On the **Format Toolbar**, click the **Alignment** icon and drag down to select **Centered**.

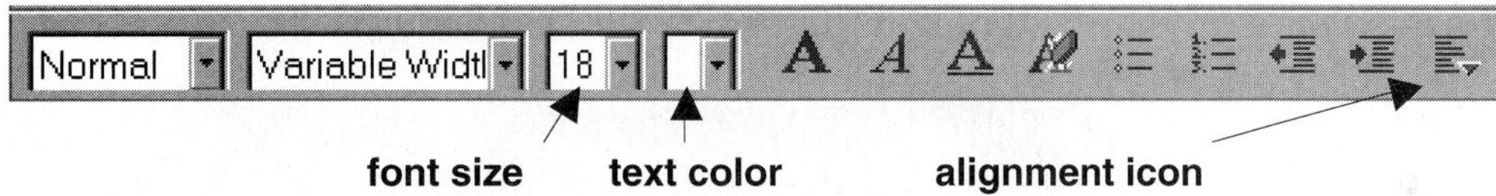

Before you insert any images, all should be saved as gif or jpeg format and placed in the same directory or folder on your hard drive as the pages.

Step 3: Inserting Graphics

Thousands of free and inexpensive graphics are available for your use in your web pages. Here are some sites to peruse in search of just the right image or background:

- **List of links to graphics sites:** http://www.free-graphics.com
- **Microsoft's graphics site:** http://dgl.microsoft.com
- **Graphics, buttons, bullets, rules, and animations:** http://www.belsnwhistles.com
- **Collection of free and for-a-fee animated graphics:** http://www.animfactory.com

If you want to use the tree image shown in the example for this exercise, go to the example web site **(http://www.prenhall.com/startingout)** and download it using the steps described in **Section Seven**.

- When you have an image that you want to insert from your hard drive, first click on the area of the page where you want it to appear. In this example, click just to the left of the "G. L. Branch" title and make a space above the text for the tree image by pressing Enter or Return to bring the text down several lines.

- Select **Image** from the **Insert Menu,** and click on **Choose File.** Select the tree image (or another image you want to insert) from the hard drive; click **OK**.

- Double-click on the tree image OR select **Image Info** from the **Format Menu**. Click on the **Paragraph tab,** select **Center** alignment by clicking on the **Center** radio button, and click **OK**.

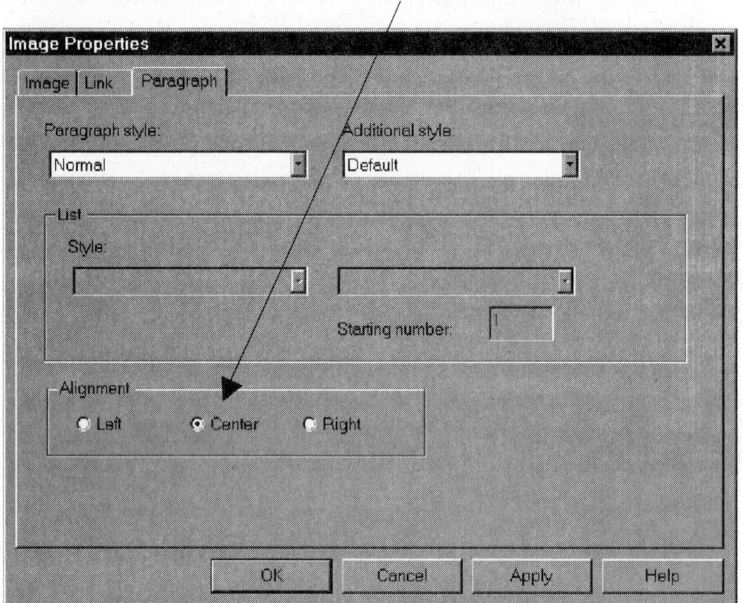

Now the page should look like the example on the next page.

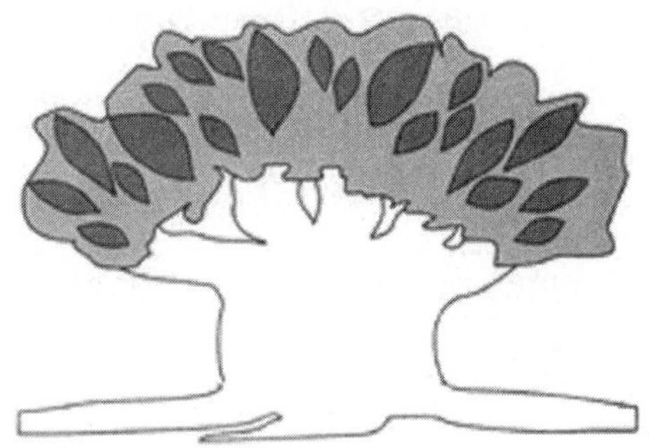

G.L. Branch's Home Page

Welcome to my page!
Click on one of the links below to learn about me.

Step 4: Inserting Tables

In a word processing document, you can use tabs to space text items evenly across a page. In an HTML page, you must insert a *table* and place the text in its cells. To create the set of labels you see in the example below (which will later become links to other pages), do the following:

- Click just below the text you have inserted and select **Table** from the **Insert Menu**.

- Enter “1” for the number of Rows and “4” for the number of columns.

- Click the **Center** radio button for **Alignment**. Click **OK.**

- Click inside each cell in the Table and enter the words shown in the example. **DO NOT** press Enter or Return after typing a word in a cell. Either click inside another cell or click outside the table. The table should look like this:

Personal	Professional	My School

Step 5: Creating Additional Pages

A web site typically consists of several pages. The one in the example we are creating here has three:

- **A home page** (the **index.html** page you just created)
- **A personal page:** See example on page S-65.
- **A professional page:** See example on page S-66.

Web pages can be saved with either the "html" or the "htm" suffix.

Create the text of each page by using the procedures described in Steps 1 through 3. You can either make these pages look like the examples shown here, or you can experiment with your own text and graphics.

Be sure to **Save** each of the pages (in the same folder as the "index.html" page) as: **mypersonalpage.htm** and **myprofpage.htm**. (We will use these names to make links in Step 6.)

On each page, create only the text, not the Table below it. We will insert Tables in Step 6 (page S-67).

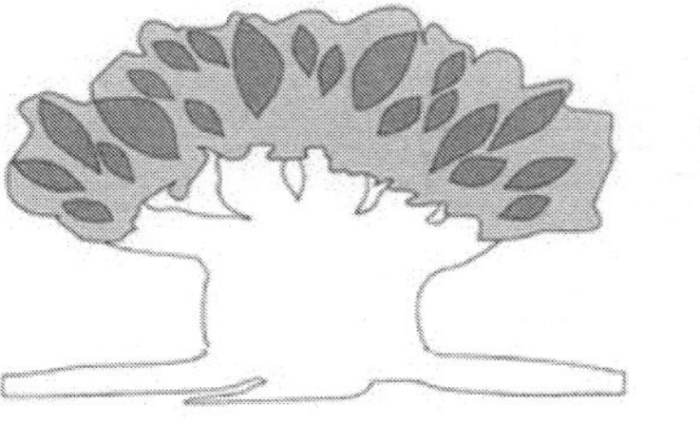

G.L. Branch's Personal Page

My background - I am originally from Cumberland, Maryland. I am married and have two children. I have the following degrees:

- B.A. in English/Secondary Education from the University of Maryland, College Park
- M.Ed. (online) from the University of Maryland University College (UMUC), Adelphi

My interests and hobbies - I enjoy spending time with my family and doing the following activities:

- I work one weekend a month with other volunteers for Habitat for Humanity. This year we built a house for a family in our community.
- I like to travel and take photographs of the places we visit. I always digitize the photographs and make them into an online "album" so I can share them easily with my students and friends.

My work - I am a fifth grade teacher at the Neuwave Elementary School. Learn more about my work by visiting my Professional page (see link below).

HOME	Professional	My School

Click here to e-mail me

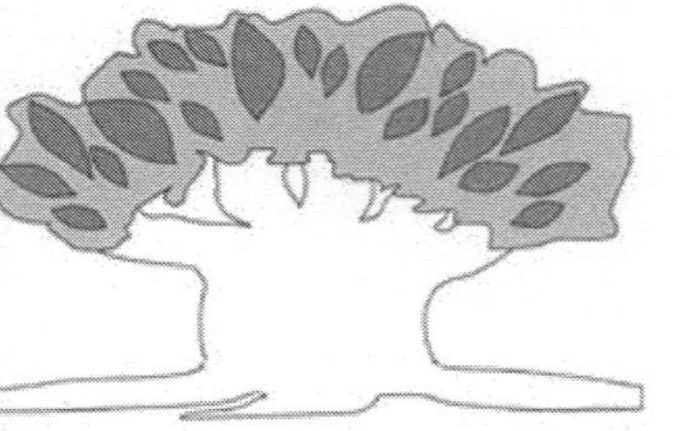

G.L. Branch's Professional Page

Teaching Experience - I have been a Teacher for 14 years and have loved every minute (well, most minutes!) of it. Here is where I have taught:

- The Green Montessori School - Potomac, Maryland
- Excelsior Elementary School - Fresno, California
- Neuwave Elementary School - Albany, New York

Teaching Specialties - I am especially proud of the following recent accomplishments:

- Writing across the curriculum - I have developed some great lessons to encourage my students to write in science, social studies, and other areas. (E-mail me if you want to get a copy.)
- Workshops for teachers - I have developed and given workshops on how to use digital cameras and digitized images in teaching various topics and how to develop your own web site.

Favorite Links - Here are a few of my favorite sites. Click on each one to go there:

- Electronic Portfolios
- Blue Web'n Lesson Plans Site
- M. D. Roblyer Textbook
- ISTE Site

Personal	HOME	My School

Click here to e-mail me

Step 6: Inserting Links Between Pages

To link all your pages together to make a web site, make the labels in the Table into links in the following way:

- Go back to the **index.html** page and highlight the "Personal" label in the first cell of the table.

- Select **Link** from the **Insert Menu**. Under the Link tab, type **mypersonalpage.htm** in the URL line as shown below. Click OK.

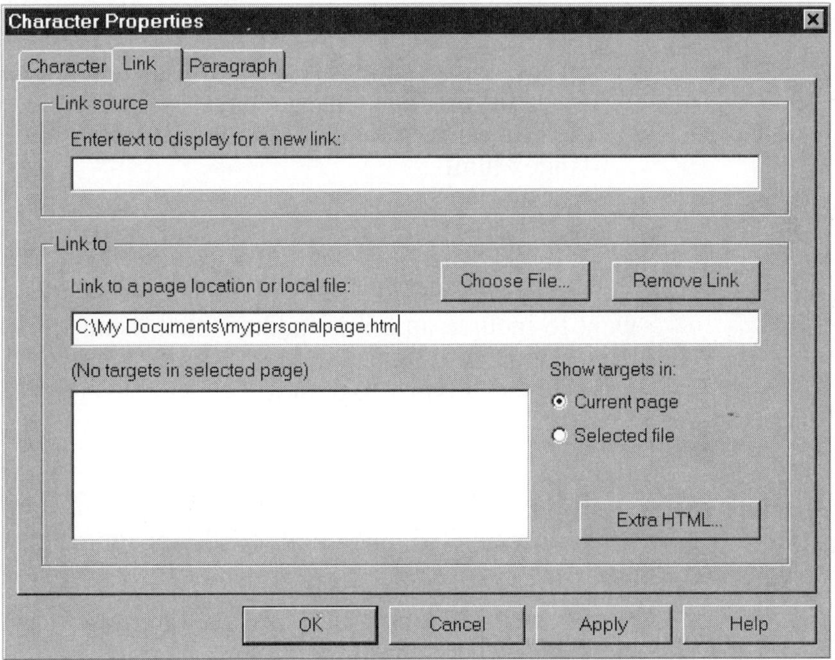

- Now highlight the "Professional" label in the next cell. Again, select **Link** from the **Insert Menu**. Under the Link tab, type **myprofpage.htm** in the URL line as shown below. Click OK.

- Highlight the **My School** label and follow the same procedure. However, for this name, put a URL instead of a page name. You can either put the following URL (the one for the author's university web site) or the URL of your own school: **http://www.umuc.edu**

- Insert this **Table** of links on each of the other two pages in this way. Choose **Select Table** from the **Edit Menu**. Then select **Copy** from the **Edit Menu**. Go to **mypersonalpage.htm**, click below the text on the page and select **Paste** from the **Edit Menu**. The table should appear there.

- However, since the page you are on now *is* the Personal page, you don't need a link to it in the Table of links. Highlight the "Personal" label and change it to read "HOME" instead. Highlight the "HOME" label, select **Link** from the **Insert Menu**, and change the link to "index.html" to link it to the Home page

- Follow the same procedure for inserting and modifying the links on the "myprofpage.htm" page. This time you'll change the "Professional" label to read "HOME" and change the link to "index.html".

Step 7: Inserting Links Within a Page

You may want to have links to other sites in your pages. Also, you will want to include an e-mail address that users can click on to bring up a message page in their e-mail software. Practice inserting both kinds of links on the "myprofpage.htm."

- On the section of Favorite Links, highlight the text that says "M. D. Roblyer Textbook." Select **Link** from the **Insert Menu**. Insert the following URL and click OK: **http://www.prenhall.com/roblyer**

- Follow the same procedure for the other links. Insert the following URL's and then re-save your page:

  – **Electronic Portfolios:** http://electronicportfolios.com/

  – **Blue Web'n Lesson Plans Site:** http://www.kn.pacbell.com/wired/bluewebn/

  – **ISTE Site:** http://www.iste.org

- Insert a line of text below the **Table** of links: "Click here to e-mail me." Highlight it and select **Link** from the **Insert Menu**. Insert the following:

mailto:*YOUR E-MAIL ADDRESS HERE*

Step 8: Previewing Pages in a Browser

Although your pages may look fine in *Netscape Composer*®, always test them in a "live" browser to see how they will look on the Internet. Before you do this step, make sure you have saved each of your pages:

- Be sure you are connected to the Internet and have all three pages open in *Netscape Composer*®. From the **File Menu,** select **Page – Open.** Click the **Navigator** radio button.

- Click "Choose file" and choose from your computer the name of the page you want to preview. Type "index.html" to preview this page. Click on all links to make sure they work. If there are errors, correct them and save the changes.

- To see your changed document, you will need to click "reload" in your browser.

- "Mailto" is an HTML command that indicates an e-mail address follows. When you insert your own e-mail address, it creates a link that brings up your e-mail address in the user's default e-mail program.

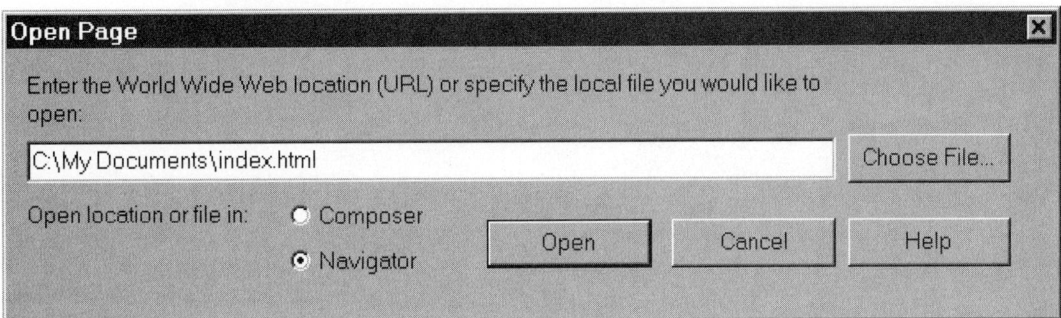

Step 9: Uploading to a Server

The most technical step in developing a web site is to use an FTP software package to transfer (upload) the page files you have created to a server (computer) on which they will reside.

Most schools or districts that have their own server also have their own FTP software and procedures they want you to follow for uploading new files. However, if you are using another site (e.g., one made available to you by your ISP), you will need to contact the web administrator of that server for usernames and passwords required for you to FTP files.

You will need a directory or folder in which all your page files and graphics will be stored. If one does not already exist on the server, the web administrator will need to create one for you. On the next page is an example of one such package: the *WS_FTP* program (Ipswitch, Inc). All FTP programs have the same basic steps: (a) connect with the server, (b) highlight files to be transferred from your disk or hard drive, and (c) click an arrow to transfer them. However, procedures to accomplish these will look slightly different in each software.

Remember that you will not be able to do Steps 9 and 10 here unless you have a server to which you can upload. Also, if you need an FTP software package, you can download a package from the following web site:

http://download.cnet.com

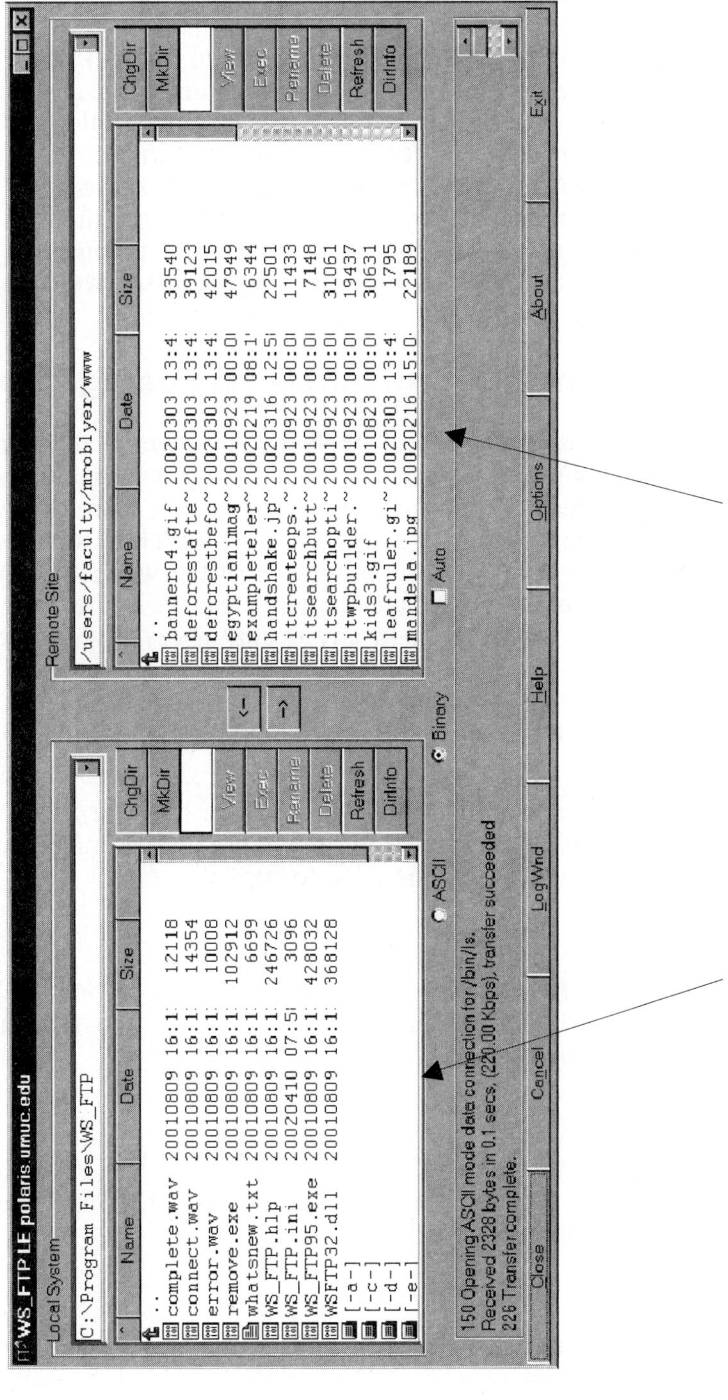

Window showing files to be uploaded

Window showing files on the server

Step 10: Using the URL

After you upload your files, you have an Internet address! The URL for your address consists of the server name and a suffix. (Review the URL on the Prentice Hall server for the example web site we used in this section.) The "index.html" page has links to all the other pages in your site. After you FTP the page files, try out your URL. Pages should look just about as they did when you viewed them in the browser. If you wish to make changes at this point, change the pages on your computer using your web development software and upload them again.

An Alternate Strategy: Modifying Existing Pages

Another way of creating a web site is to "grab" an Internet page design you like and use it as a template for your own. Grabbing pages is easy. However, it is important to remember that many page elements (e.g., designs, logos, graphics) are copyrighted. Their legal use is determined by copyright law and by the owner of the web site. If you are not sure whether you can use page elements legally, contact the web site owner to request permission. In any event, always credit the source site on your page.

Try grabbing pages and modifying them in the following way:

After you "grab" and save a page, be sure to place all the page elements in the same folder and re-insert the images and background.

- **Enter and copy the URL** – In your browser, enter the URL for the example web site (http://www.prenhall.com/startingout) and drag your mouse over the URL to copy it.

- **Open the page in *Netscape Composer*®** – Select **Open Page** from the **File Menu,** paste the URL, and open the page in *Netscape Composer*®.

- **Save the page** – Select **Save As** from the **File Menu.** (You may get a copyright warning at this point.) Save the page on your computer under a desired name.

- **Make desired changes** – Make changes as you like. Save the page and follow procedures for uploading it and its graphic elements to a server (Step 9).

Section Eleven
Summary Exercises: Creating Your Own Web Site

Exercises 11.1 – Review of New Terms and Concepts

__________ 1. The action of transferring new web pages to a server

__________ 2. Software required if you want to transfer page files from your computer to a server connected to the Internet

__________ 3. What you should make sure of before using a page element you have "grabbed" from an existing Internet site

__________ 4. Another name for a web page development software

__________ 5. An HTML command that indicates that an e-mail address follows and, when followed by your own e-mail address as a link from your web site, sends users who click on it to your e-mail address in their e-mail program

Exercises 11.2 – Practice Activities to Expand Your Skills

1. **Insert a rule** – Did you notice an extra graphic feature in the web page example? Bring up the Personal page and click below "G. L. Branch's Personal Page." Select **Horizontal Line** from the **Insert Menu**. Change its width by double-clicking on it and increasing its height.

2. **Add a background** – Add a background image instead of a background color. When you have a page in *Netscape Composer*®, select **Page Colors and Properties** from the **Format Menu**; click the **Colors and Background** tab and the **Use Image** box. Choose an image stored on your computer and click OK. What does it look like?

3. **Add and re-size a graphic** – Each of the free graphics sites has steps you must follow to obtain a graphic. Try one of them. Also try re-sizing the graphic. Double-click on it and change its height and width.

4. **Create your favorite links** – Most teachers list their own set of "favorite links" on their web site. Prepare your own set and insert them on your page as links to the sites.

5. **Preview in both browsers** – Sometimes pages look different in different browsers. Try previewing your page in *Internet Explorer*®. Does it look any different?

APPENDIX: Answers to Exercise Questions

Section One

Page S-3
1. World Wide Web
2. kidlink
3. http://
4. "edu" shows it is owned by a higher education organization
5. slashes in "http://" are required to show it is an Internet address. Other slashes indicate suffixes.

Page S-4
1. http://www.nctm.org
2. http://www.menc.org

Page S-5 – top of page
1. American Federation for the Blind
2. U. S. Department of Education

Page S-5 – bottom of page
1. Slashes are in the wrong direction
2. No dot between server name (ashaweb) and domain designator (org)

Page S-6: Exercises 1.1 – Review of New Terms and Concepts
1. domain designator
2. suffix
3. Uniform Resource Locator
4. spaces in server name
5. server

Page S-6: Exercises 1.2 – Practice Activities to Expand Your Skills
1. http://www.aera.net
2. http://www.ira.org: International Reading Association
3. http://peabody.vanderbilt.edu: Peabody College of Education at Vanderbilt University
   a. "www" is omitted
   b. slashes are backward
   c. server name (Berkeley) is misspelled

Section Two

Page S-10: Exercises 2.1 – Review of New Terms and Concepts

1. Both can be links
2. When you run the mouse over it, the pointer turns into a browser hand
3. The link has been clicked on previously
4. Look for a “Back to Home” link or use the Go Menu
5. It’s a link

Page S-10: Exercises 2.2 – Practice Activities to Expand Your Skills

Like many large sites, it has a pull-down menu of commonly-used links

Section Three

Page S-15: Exercises 3.1 – Review of New Terms and Concepts

1. Subject index search
2. metacrawler
3. complete phrase
4. internal search engine
5. minus sign: “–“

Page S-15: Exercises 3.2 – Practice Activities to Expand Your Skills, Set A

1. Enter “Trojan horse” –virus
2. “distance education” +journal +online
3. search on: writing +children +online
4. search on: “French to English” +dictionary

Page S-15: Exercises 3.2 – Practice Activities to Expand Your Skills, Set B

1. keyword search using any search engine
2. Yahoo! subject index search; keyword search using any search engine
3. Yahoo! or Google subject index search
4. keyword search using any search engine
5. keyword search using any search engine
6. keyword search using any search engine
7. keyword search using any search engine
8. site internal search engine
9. Go to web sites recommended in this book and do site internal search
10. Go to web sites recommended in this book and do site internal search

Section Four

Page S-20: Exercises 4.1 – Review of New Terms and Concepts

1. Favorites
2. Bookmarks Menu
3. File Menu
4. Folder
5. share them with others

Section Five

Page S-26: Exercises 5.1 – Review of New Terms and Concepts

1. site map
2. internal search engine
3. known author, valid contact information, recent update, can be verified by authoritative sources
4. provides alternative ways to view information
5. navigation

Page S-26: Exercises 5.2 – Practice Activities to Expand Your Skills

Sites have unknown authors, no valid contact information, have no indication of updates, and/or no sources or links to use to verify authenticate information

Section Six

Page S-32: Exercises 6.1 – Review of New Terms and Concepts

1. firewall software
2. virus
3. firewall
4. parental involvement
5. filtering software

Page S-32: Exercises 6.2 – Practice Activities to Expand Your Skills

3a. Contact the web site owner or administrator; if no contact information, use the element and credit the source
3b. Contact the web site owner or administrator for permission

Section Seven

Page S-38: Exercises 7.1 – Review of New Terms and Concepts

1. gif
2. click on it
3. images on federal government web sites
4. copyright law and the owner of the web site
5. image manipulation software such as *Adobe PhotoShop*

Section Eight

Page S-42: Exercises 8.1 – Review of New Terms and Concepts

1. pdf
2. plug-in
3. Quicktime®
4. portable document format
5. hear streamed audio files

Section Nine

Page S-46: Exercises 9.1 – Review of New Terms and Concepts

1. bad or dead link (site has been removed or server is not working)
2. wait and try it again later; probably down temporarily
3. download the plug-in required to play it
4. your firewall software is preventing access
5. Javascript problem; make sure Java is enabled in browser or try downloading an updated Java version

Page S-46: Exercises 9.2 – Practice Activities to Expand Your Skills

1. missing dot between "psu" and "edu"
2. missing colon (":") after http
3. apple spelled with a numeral one instead of a letter "l"
4. hyphens ("–") are used instead of underlines ("_")
5. zero in "com" instead of letter "o"

Section Ten

Page S-52: Exercises 10.1 – Review of New Terms and Concepts

1. telementoring
2. electronic or virtual field trip
3. keypal or e-pal
4. social action projects
5. KidLink online activity and lesson plan site

Section Eleven

Page S-70: Exercises 11.1 – Review of New Terms and Concepts

1. uploading
2. FTP software
3. you are permitted to use it
4. HTML editor
5. mailto